HANDBOOK OF MONETARY ECONOMICS

VOLUME I

HANDBOOKS
IN
ECONOMICS

8

Series Editors

KENNETH J. ARROW
MICHAEL D. INTRILIGATOR

NORTH-HOLLAND
AMSTERDAM · NEW YORK · OXFORD · TOKYO

HANDBOOK OF MONETARY ECONOMICS

VOLUME I

Edited by

BENJAMIN M. FRIEDMAN
Harvard University

and

FRANK H. HAHN
Cambridge University

1990

NORTH-HOLLAND
AMSTERDAM · NEW YORK · OXFORD · TOKYO

ELSEVIER SCIENCE PUBLISHERS B.V.
Sara Burgerhartstraat 25
P.O. Box 211, 1000 AE Amsterdam, The Netherlands

Distributors for the United States and Canada:
ELSEVIER SCIENCE PUBLISHING COMPANY INC.
655 Avenue of the Americas
New York, N.Y. 10010, U.S.A.

Library of Congress Cataloging-in-Publication Data

Handbook of monetary economics / edited by Benjamin M. Friedman and
    Frank H. Hahn.
        p.   cm. -- (Handbooks in economics; 8)
    Includes bibliographical references.
    ISBN 0-444-88027-5 (set). -- ISBN 0-444-88025-9 (v. I). -- ISBN
0-444-88026-7 (v. II)
    1. Money. 2. Monetary policy. I. Friedman, Benjamin M.
II. Hahn, Frank. III. Series: Handbooks in economics ; bk. 8.
HG221.H24   1990
332.4--dc20   90-6983
                                                                  CIP

ISBN for this set: 0 444 88027 5
ISBN for this volume: 0-444-88025-9

No responsibility is assumed by the publisher for any injury and/or damage to persons or property
as a matter of products liability, negligence or otherwise, or from any use or operation of any
methods, products instructions or ideas contained in the material herein.

PRINTED IN THE NETHERLANDS

INTRODUCTION TO THE SERIES

The aim of the *Handbooks in Economics* series is to produce Handbooks for various branches of economics, each of which is a definitive source, reference, and teaching supplement for use by professional researchers and advanced graduate students. Each Handbook provides self-contained surveys of the current state of a branch of economics in the form of chapters prepared by leading specialists on various aspects of this branch of economics. These surveys summarize not only received results but also newer developments, from recent journal articles and discussion papers. Some original material is also included, but the main goal is to provide comprehensive and accessible surveys. The Handbooks are intended to provide not only useful reference volumes for professional collections but also possible supplementary readings for advanced courses for graduate students in economics.

KENNETH J. ARROW and MICHAEL D. INTRILIGATOR

CONTENTS OF THE HANDBOOK*

* Detailed contents of this volume (Volume I of the Handbook) may be found on p. xxi.

VOLUME II

PART 6 – MONEY, OTHER ASSETS, AND ECONOMIC ACTIVITY

PART 7 – MONEY, INFLATION, AND WELFARE

PART 8 – MONETARY POLICY

PREFACE TO THE HANDBOOK

Monetary economics has always represented a symbiosis, albeit at times an uncomfortable one, between a priori theorizing and the development and exploitation of empirical evidence. Formal theory describing an economy with money, and perhaps other financial instruments as well, has its clear antecedents in the more general structures of utility maximization and economic equilibrium. Just as clearly, this theory has steered decades of empirical research in the field. In the other direction, quantitative analysis of such fundamentals as the relationship between money and prices (for example, Smith, Tooke, Thornton) antedated anything remotely recognizable as modern economic theory. Indeed, the very existence of money itself is not a missing link for which analysis of formal models has cried out in order to connect otherwise loose conceptual strands, but – quite to the contrary – an institutional datum, the incorporation of which has proved either naggingly untidy or endlessly challenging, depending on one's point of view. The interaction here between theory and evidence has been very much a two-way street.

Yet a further influence that has significantly complicated the development of monetary economics is the direct relevance of so many of the behavioral questions at issue for the conduct of actual public policies. Which policy framework is optimal under any particular set of circumstances, or which policy action is optimal in any specific situation within a given overall framework, not only depends importantly on theoretical presumptions but often turns on comparisons among identifiable quantitative magnitudes. As a result, it is difficult if not impossible to separate either theoretical or empirical work in monetary economics from the evaluation (explicit or otherwise) of actual policies carried out in the past or, correspondingly, judgments about potential future policies.

Because of this fundamental two-way interaction between the theoretical and the empirical aspects of monetary economics, together with the relationship of both to matters of public policy, any organization of material comprehensively spanning the subject is bound to be arbitrary. We have arranged the 23 surveys commissioned for this Handbook in a way that we think reflects some of the most important logical divisions within the field. No single way of organizing this material, however – especially a linear sequencing, as publication in book form requires – can fully encompass interrelationships as rich, and among lines of thinking as diverse, as is the case in monetary economics. Different

Handbook of Monetary Economics, Volume I, Edited by B.M. Friedman and F.H. Hahn
© *Elsevier Science Publishers B.V., 1990*

arrangements are in some ways equally plausible, and we could just as well have chosen any of several potential alternatives.

It is important to recognize at the very outset that monetary theory has to contend with the handicap that it is not easily accommodated within the most complete and general theory of equilibrium which we have. It has been recognized for a long time, and many chapters in this Handbook refer to it, that at the very heart of any satisfactory theory there will have to be an account of transaction costs and of "missing markets". Monetary theory cannot proceed in the elegant manner of Arrow and Debreu, which collapses the future into the present, nor can it ignore the actual process of exchange. These are the facts of the situation, and they have the consequence of launching the monetary economist on journeys where no generally agreed upon axiomatic guideposts are available. This in turn has two further consequences: the assumptions that monetary economists make often attempt to encapsulate empirical regularities rather than axioms, and the subsequent theorizing has not often attained the definiteness one would like.

While a "high" monetary theory is, at best, incomplete at present, it is not obvious that this is widely felt to be a serious matter. Much of monetary theory and econometrics is macroeconomics, and the aim is to build (simple) models which can be estimated. Such models are often based on "the representative agent" who behaves very much as in a microeconomic textbook. This construct often allows one to sidestep problems of multiple equilibria or, for instance, the distribution of money balances. But there clearly is a tension between this manner of proceeding and the recognition that, for instance, money is a means of exchange between agents differently situated, with different preferences and possibly different beliefs. This tension is even more readily apparent if the model is to encompass borrowing and lending, or the trading of debts, neither of which can strictly occur in an economy made up only of "representative" agents. The reader will find some of these tensions reflected, repeatedly, in the present volume.

We decided to start this Handbook with "fundamentals" which are of concern to those who study the transition from an Arrow–Debreu economy to one in which an intrinsically worthless means of exchange has value. The chapters by Ostroy and Starr (Chapter 1) and by Duffie (Chapter 3) study this question. The first of these concerns the transaction role of money and so takes explicit note of transaction costs. It is interesting to realize that what appears so simple, and for so long has been taken as so simple, is not so at all but requires all the wit of a theorist. Duffie, also paying attention to transaction costs, achieves a satisfactory integration of money into general equilibrium theory. It goes beyond the shortcuts of the assumed "money in advance" requirement. There are still assumptions here which one would wish to relax, but the chapter goes a long way toward providing the required understanding.

The other chapter in Part I, by Hahn (Chapter 2), is not so much concerned with foundations of general equilibrium theory with money, but with one consequence of allowing explicitly for transaction costs: the "flexibility" or "liquidity" property of assets. In an economy with transaction costs, which has trading at all dates, uncertainties may be resolved or reduced as time proceeds, and the optimum plan would then allow for the probability that asset composition should be changed.

But of course it may be argued that general equilibrium theory is itself open to sufficient empirical objections as to make it doubtful that modifying it to allow for money is a profitable strategy. For instance, the theory neglects strategic interactions of agents as well as the more familiar possibilities of imperfect competition. Moreover, it is essentially a long-run equilibrium theory. Benassy (Chapter 4) gives an account of what has come to be known as "non-Walrasian equilibrium" theory, to which he has made many contributions. He shows how such a theory may form a foundation for macroeconomics. The reader will note that it is useful to recognize that equilibrium must be defined relatively to the environment in which agents operate, and that it is a mistake to think of the models Benassy discusses as "disequilibrium" models.

Shubik (Chapter 5) gives an account of his research into a game-theoretic approach to monetary theory. For some readers these will be unfamiliar waters. But we have learned in recent years that game theory is a promising route to a theory of institutions, and it is these that will have to be understood before monetary theory has been properly formulated. Shubik's chapter discusses the main lines such theorizing can take.

As we have already noted, the problems of "fundamentals" need to be understood and, one hopes, resolved. They arise whether one is concerned with macroeconomic theory or, indeed, with empirical investigation. Both have a need to "simplify", but in each case it is important that one knows what it is that is being simplified. On the other hand it is possible that investigating how the presence of money and other financial instruments modifies simple models which we already know well may itself be a route along which new insights can be gained.

The contributions in Part III are just of this type. Orphanides and Solow (Chapter 6) undertake a thorough and exhaustive study of canonical growth models modified by the presence of money. They critically examine earlier work in this direction, and they pay particular attention to the investment decision when there is an alternative asset to which savings can be directed. As elsewhere in this Handbook, the reader will find that paying attention to the existence of money in an economy matters.

In recent years the overlapping generations (O.G.) model has come to play a large part in macroeconomic theorizing. Brock (Chapter 7) modifies it to allow for transaction costs. This is a desirable modification, since in many O.G. models money has no recognizable purpose other than being the (often the only) means of transferring consumption from one period to the next. Brock's chapter is thus an advance on what we have, and exactly the right move to bring genuine monetary phenomena into the orbit of the model. Here too the analysis goes deeper than merely postulating a "money in advance" constraint.

It is worth remarking that O.G. models are both more robust and more interesting than is sometimes believed, at least at the abstract level. Of course the postulate of two-period lives is highly unrealistic. On the other hand, it is difficult to think of a *qualitative* conclusion of these models – for example, the existence of many equilibrium paths, or of sunspot paths – that is plausibly at risk from more realistic life times. At first sight one might think this false, since infinitely lived agents who with perfect foresight plan their optimal future must obey a transversality requirement. The latter, it might then be thought, will preclude "disagreeable" paths for the economy. But recent research has shown this not to be the case when agents discount the future sufficiently highly.[1] On the other hand, infinitely lived agents may make a difference to the "indeterminacy" results of standard O.G. models. There may then be a difference in qualitative conclusions as one passes from finitely to infinitely lived agents. It takes, however, a peculiar perception of the world to regard the latter as the more "realistic" approach. In general, economies with finitely lived agents who discount the future are unlikely to be grossly mal-analyzed in O.G. models with two-period lives.

In parallel with such "fundamental" analyses of why money exists and under what circumstances it will be valued, investigation of the empirical and institutional facts of the demand for and supply of money has also made recognizeable advances in recent years. As Goldfeld and Sichel (Chapter 8) show, the main "event" in this regard has been the collapse of previously long-standing empirical regularities relating familiar measures of money to aggregate income and prices over time. Although their chapter documents this phenomenon only for the case of the United States, research along the lines of that which they summarize has amply shown that conventional money demand functions have suffered similarly in other countries as well.[2] As their chapter shows, there is no lack of potential explanations for the breakdown of these prior relationships, and so there is at least room for cautious optimism that, in the future, "normalcy" (if a stable money demand function is that) may be restored. But it is also possible that that may not occur or, if it does, that it may not be for some substantial time. Along the way, investigation of competing hypotheses about just why all this has happened is a potentially rich source of new insights.

[1] See Boldrin and Montruchio (1986).
[2] See, for example, Fair (1987).

The other two chapters in Part IV, by Brunner and Meltzer (Chapter 9) and by Modigliani and Papademos (Chapter 10), lay out these authors' conceptions of how money demand interacts with money supply in a setting that explicitly includes the important institution of a banking system.[3] As a result, the analysis distinguishes "inside" from "outside" money. In addition, both sets of authors further enrich the institutional setting by distinguishing debt (or "credit") from either money or capital. Brunner and Meltzer's analysis provides the basis for the emphasis on the monetary base which has characterized many of their contributions over the years, an emphasis that has by now influenced the practical conduct of monetary policy in many countries. Modigliani and Papademos focus even more directly on the working of the banking system itself and its implications for the money supply process.

Although much of monetary economics not surprisingly concentrates on the role of money per se, it is also important to recognize that actual economies (unlike many O.G. models) have more assets than just money. Willingness to hold money itself therefore represents, in part, a decision not to hold wealth in other forms. At the same time, conditions determined by the interaction of money supply and money demand can also influence the terms on which other assets will be held, terms that in turn potentially affect macroeconomic outcomes in any of a variety of familiar ways. The three chapters in Part V address several important features of the pricing of non-money assets that have also played important roles in monetary economics.

Merton (Chapter 11) systematically lays out in a general form the theory of pricing of speculative assets in a frictionless continuous-time setting, which his own work, along with that of Samuelson and others, has developed.[4] The theory in this form has long been the central workhorse of "finance", as a distinct field of economic inquiry. But an important development in recent years, which is still ongoing, is the erosion of any recognizable barrier between financial economics and monetary economics.[5]

The other two chapters in Part V use more specialized apparatus, based on a discrete-time framework, to focus on specific aspects of asset pricing that have traditionally been important to empirical monetary economics. Intertemporal aspects of asset pricing – what makes the subject interesting, really – are at the heart of both. Singleton (Chapter 12) reviews not only the empirical evidence bearing on asset pricing behavior per se (and presents the results of new tests) but also the connections that the literature in this area has drawn between asset pricing and macroeconomic behavior in explicitly dynamic settings. Shiller's

---

[3] Our friend and colleague Karl Brunner co-authored this chapter with Allan Meltzer, but died before the Handbook went to print. We take this opportunity to express our admiration for Karl's outstanding contribution to monetary economics, and our sorrow at his passing.

[4] Merton's chapter is an expanded and updated version of his contribution to the *Handbook of Mathematical Economics* (1981), edited by Arrow and Intrilligator.

[5] See, for example, the discussion in Fischer and Merton (1984).

chapter (Chapter 13), including McCulloch's data for the United States which we hope will be useful to many researchers in the field, consolidates and interprets the literature of the term structure of interest rates. While this subject may at first seem somewhat specialized, the term structure has long been a central issue in monetary economics because of the need to bridge the gap between asset returns that are at least proximately (and, in most models, in the short run) subject to direct influence by the central bank – primarily short-term interest rates – and the long-term asset prices and yields that are typically more important in theories of how what happens in financial asset markets influences non-financial economic activity.

But how *do* the prices and yields determined in the asset markets affect the nonfinancial economy? This question, which moves monetary economics to the center of macroeconomics, is the focus of all four chapters in Part VI. Abel (Chapter 14) adopts a partial equilibrium approach, reviewing the literature of consumption and investment, and surveying both theoretical developments and empirical results. Blanchard (Chapter 15) assumes a general equilibrium perspective, and therefore frames the issue as the specific question of whether changes in the quantity of money or its growth rate affect real output (Is money non-neutral?) and, if so, why. Both Abel's chapter and Blanchard's leave the reader with a strong sense of the ultimately empirical nature of monetary economics as a field of study. While it is straightforward to state, in the abstract, hypotheses about what determines consumption and/or investment, and likewise to advance theories about whether money is neutral and why, these chapters show that comparative evaluation of competing theories in this area is also, in the end, largely an empirical matter.

Although it is often merely implicit, an aspect of economic behavior that underlies much of what monetary economics has to say about how money affects spending and output is that credit markets are imperfect. For example, Abel's review of the modern consumption literature makes clear the importance of any constraints that arise from consumers' not being able to borrow at the same interest rate at which they can lend – in some cases, being unable to borrow at all – and hence having to base consumption spending in part on the flow of current income. The same phenomenon is also relevant to investment behavior (as well as in the field of "corporate finance").[6] Jaffee and Stiglitz (Chapter 16) show how "credit rationing" can arise, not just temporarily when lending rates adjust slowly, but as a consequence of profit-maximizing lenders' equilibrium response to adverse selection and incentive effects due to information imperfections and asymmetries. It is worth pointing out explicitly that, here again, a phenomenon that has played an important part in monetary economics but would be difficult if not impossible to rationalize in a world

---

[6]See, for example, the "pecking order" hypothesis advanced by Myers and Majluf (1984).

populated only by "representative agents", is fully consistent with standard norms of economic theorizing in a more general setting. Jaffee and Stiglitz also review the empirical evidence bearing on effects of credit rationing on spending and output.

Whether or not credit markets are perfect also bears importantly on questions of fiscal policy. Haliassos and Tobin (Chapter 17) review the issues that have dominated the discussion of fiscal effects on non-financial economic activity. Along with the Barro–Ricardo "debt neutrality" hypothesis, according to which debt-for-taxes substitutions do not affect spending, Haliossos and Tobin also address whether money is "superneutral" in the sense that real variables in the steady state are invariant with respect to the growth rate of money, and whether debt-for-money substitutions ("open market operations") affect real behavior. In each case they first show the conditions under which the kind of policy action in question would leave all real variables unchanged, and then evaluate the theoretical and empirical plausibility of these conditions.

Regardless of whether money does or does not affect output in either the short or the long run, money and monetary policy are still of prime interest to economists on account of their consequences for prices – a subject about which, at least at the qualitative level, disagreement like that surrounding the effect of money on output is strikingly absent. The three contributions in Part VII focus on the relationship between money and inflation, importantly including implications for economic welfare. McCallum's chapter (Chapter 18) is a broad survey of theoretical models and empirical evidence on this subject, encompassing both steady-state relationships and the co-movements of money and prices (and output) over the business cycle. McCallum also reviews the growing literature that provides a different perspective on inflation via a positive analysis of the behavior of monetary policy.

For many macroeconomic theories, the cost of inflation is the induced economizing in money balances and hence the induced increase in transaction costs. On the face of it, however, this (except perhaps in hyperinflation) seems too small a cost to explain the belief that inflation is ever enemy number one. Driffil, Mizon and Ulph (Chapter 19) consider, both theoretically and empirically, this and other possible costs – most importantly, the possibility that higher inflation necessarily implies greater uncertainty about inflation and/or greater variability of relative prices, and hence an erosion of the price system's ability to allocate resources efficiently. Like so much else in economics, it will be found that the subject requires more sophisticated treatment than it usually receives from politicians and bankers.

The subject of inflation is also related to what, since Milton Friedman, has been called the theory of the optimum quantity of money. Woodford (Chapter 20) provides a very detailed and sophisticated analysis of this problem. For instance, it has been held that rising price levels, by leading agents to hold less money in their portfolios, would lead in steady states to a higher capital–labor ratio than would otherwise be the case. Hence, it was argued, the rise in output per capita would have to be taken into account in a judgment of the welfare effects of inflation. Woodford shows this view to be mistaken. Indeed, his chapter's range is so wide and his arguments so meticulous that it is likely that his will become the standard account of this matter.

As we have been at some pains to emphasize, in monetary economics the connections between research on economic behavior and implications for economic policy are sufficiently pervasive that most of the chapters in this Handbook bear on matters of monetary policy, either implicitly or directly, despite the fact that their principal focus lies elsewhere. Even so, no collection of essays attempting to survey the field could be complete without a straightforward examination of some of the major issues surrounding the conduct of actual monetary policy. The Handbook therefore concludes with three contributions that do just that.

The chapters by Fischer (Chapter 21) and by Friedman (Chapter 22) mostly take up aspects of monetary policy that arise in the context of monetary policy for a single (closed) economy. Although Fischer discusses the gold standard, his interest in it here is not as a means of regulating exchange rates among countries' currencies but as a way of resolving, for any one country, the age-old dilemma of rules versus discretion (which, of course, also pervades many other aspects of decision-making, both public and private). As he shows, recent advances, based in part on game-theoretic concepts, have done much to clarify long-standing views as well as to open new roads for analysis. Friedman takes the discussion closer to the actual practice of monetary policy by addressing the nuts-and-bolts question of how the central bank operates: How should it evaluate the merits of alternative policy instruments? And should it use any target(s) intermediate between its policy instrument and the intended macroeconomic outcomes? As is so often the case, while the way of framing these questions is fundamentally shaped by underlying theoretical constructs, the answers, for any given country at any given time, turn on magnitudes that can only be determined empirically.

Finally, Dornbusch and Giovannini (Chapter 23) broaden the discussion by introducing the entire range of considerations that become relevant when the economy whose monetary policy is in question is interacting, in non-trivial ways, with others. At the most basic level, placing the economy in an explicitly international setting relaxes one constraint (its spending must equal its output) and introduces one extra variable to be determined (the price of its money in terms of foreign currency). But the immediate implication of a gap between aggregate spending and output (for any one economy) is a capital inflow or outflow, which over time accumulates into a stock of assets or liabilities with further consequences for behavior in both financial and real markets. At this stage, as Dornbusch and Giovannini aptly show both theoretically and empirically, the economics of monetary policy becomes inseparable from open-economy macroeconomics – a fitting place for this Handbook to conclude.

BENJAMIN M. FRIEDMAN
Harvard University

FRANK H. HAHN
Cambridge University

References

Boldrin, M. and L. Montrucchio (1986) 'On the indeterminacy of capital accumulation paths', *Journal of Economic Theory*, 40: 26–39.

Fair, R.C. (1987) 'International evidence on the demand for money', *Review of Economics and Statistics*, 69: 473–480.

Fischer, S. and R.C. Merton (1984) 'Macroeconomics and finance: The role of the stock market', *Carnegie-Rochester Conference Series on Public Policy*, 21: 57–108.

Myers, S.C. and N.S. Majluf (1984) 'Corporate financing and investment decisions when firms have information that investors do not have', *Journal of Financial Economics*, 13: 187–221.

CONTENTS OF VOLUME I

Chapter 7

Overlapping Generations Models with Money and Transactions Costs

W.A. BROCK 263

PART 1

MONEY IN THE WALRASIAN ECONOMY

Chapter 1

THE TRANSACTIONS ROLE OF MONEY*

JOSEPH M. OSTROY

University of California, Los Angeles

ROSS M. STARR

University of California, San Diego

Contents

*We are indebted to Eduardo Siandra for research assistance.

Handbook of Monetary Economics, Volume I, Edited by B.M. Friedman and F.H. Hahn
© *Elsevier Science Publishers B.V., 1990*

1. Introduction

Of the three commonly acknowledged roles that money plays – unit of account, store of value and medium of exchange – it is in the last role as a facilitator of transactions, or essential lubricant to the mechanism of exchange, that money first comes to our attention.

   The transactions role of money cannot be separated from its function as a store of value. If after the sale of one commodity for money, but before the purchase of another commodity with it, money perished, it could hardly serve as a medium separating purchase from sale. Though a medium of exchange must necessarily be a store of value, stores of value are not necessarily money. What distinguishes money from other stores of value is its liquidity, and what underlies the liquidity of money is the fact that it is the common medium through which other commodities are exchanged. We shall not define "liquidity" here (see Chapter 2 by Hahn in this Handbook); but the essential points are that liquidity is the ready convertibility through trade to other commodities and that it is a property not of the commodity itself but something that is established through the trading arrangement.

   The transactions role of money can be readily separated from its usage as a unit of account by observing that the unit of account might be pounds of salt or a more stable foreign currency without being a medium of exchange. There are certainly good reasons why the medium of exchange should also serve as a unit of account, although this matter has not received much attention. Nevertheless, and despite the widespread observation that the unit of account is almost always the medium of exchange, there is widespread agreement that the unit of account is the least significant of money's three roles.

   These commonplace observations would seem to confirm the conclusion that among money's three roles, the transactions one is at the top of the hierarchy. However, as measured by the attention paid to it in monetary theory, the transactions role is a distant second to the store of value. Perhaps this is as it should be. After all, some of the more important propositions in the history of monetary theory concern the "veil of money" or the "neutrality of money", phrases suggesting that although we could not do without the lubricating functions of a medium of exchange, they may be taken for granted to get onto more important matters. Simply because a property is unique does not imply that it is worthy of special attention. The fact that money is always the medium of exchange, just as it is almost always the unit of account, does not necessarily mean that in this it is economically more significant than in its role as a store of value, even though it shares that property with other durable goods.

   But the dominance of the store of value over the medium of exchange function in monetary theory is not the conclusion of a openly contested debate. The game was rigged from the start in the sense that the prevailing theory, especially general equilibrium theory, could accommodate the store of value function more readily than it could the medium of exchange. In this chapter we shall report on recent developments to make general equilibrium theory a more hospitable setting for the transactions role of money. In the remainder of this introduction we shall cast a quick backward glance at the historical tradition, point out some critiques of this tradition that have helped to shake its grip, and then go on to summarize, with the aid of some informal stories, where we shall be heading.

A *caveat*: We shall confine ourselves to general equilibrium rather than partial equilibrium approaches to our subject. Thus, even though the phrase "transactions role of money" has in the past been virtually synonymous with the work of Baumol (1952) and Tobin (1956), that literature will not be discussed below.

1.1. The Walras–Hicks–Patinkin tradition: Integrating money into value theory

Walras (1900) not only gave us the first systematic account of general equilibrium theory, he was also conscientious in his efforts to incorporate money into it. Above all, he sought to incorporate money in a way that would be consistent with the rest of his scheme. Walras accomplished this by making a distinction between the stock of money, an object without any utility of its own, and the "services of availability" of the stock, which does enter into household utility functions and firm production functions. Thus, money is put in a similar footing with other (capital) goods and an equation of the offer and demand for money can be derived from the utility-maximizing hypothesis.

Walras' suggestion, coming as it did in an advanced theoretical treatise when marginal analysis was still a novelty, was ahead of its time. By the 1930s, Hicks (1935), who had certainly absorbed the lessons of Walras, could see the logic of Walras' approach. For Hicks, "marginal utility analysis is nothing other than a general theory of choice" and since money holdings can readily be regarded as choice variables, the obvious methodological conclusion was that monetary theory can and should be incorporated into a suitably generalized version of value theory.

Patinkin's treatise (1965) represents the culmination of this tradition. Here was a comprehensive statement of many of the key ideas in modern monetary theory and macoeconomics carefully constructed along value-theoretic lines.

The unstated presumption of the Walras–Hicks–Patinkin tradition was that without being firmly embedded in the more rigorous choice-theoretic general equilibrium principles of value theory, monetary theory would be weak and undisciplined. What this tradition did not question was the capacity of the existing value theory to accommodate the challenge of monetary exchange. The goal was the integration of monetary and value theory but it was understood that this would be achieved by integrating monetary theory *into* the structure of existing value theory.

1.2. Critiques of the tradition

The clarity and comprehensiveness of Patinkin's presentation helped to make it the standard general equilibrium account of monetary theory. Unavoidably, it became an object of closer scrutiny. Of the many commentaries on Patinkin's work, we point to two that were influential in stimulating a fresh look at the transactions role of money.

Hahn (1965) posed a basic existence problem: Does a model of a monetary economy have an equilibrium? In addition, what guarantees that all of the equilibria to such an economy are monetary rather than barter, i.e. ones in which the price of money is zero?

With the individual's demand for money arising from the presence of real money balances in the utility function, what happens when the individual's real money balances are zero? Real money balances may be zero for two very different reasons. First, the price of commodities in terms of money may be positive, but the individual's nominal balances are zero. Second, the individual's nominal balances may be positive, but the price of commodities in terms of money may be infinite. According to one reasonable scenario, in the second case where money is worthless there would be no demand for it. Hahn points out this leads to the conclusion that there exists a non-trivial, non-monetary equilibrium. It is only under the more dubious assumption that when money is worthless there is a positive demand for nominal balances, that Hahn is able to show the existence of an equilibrium with a postive price for money.

This is the lesson that Hahn drew from his thought experiment.

> All this suggests that while Patinkin has rendered signal services he has failed to provide a model which can serve as an adequate foundation for monetary theory. Such a model, it seems to me, must have two essential features beside price uncertainty. It must distinguish between abstract exchange opportunities at some notionally called prices and actual transactions opportunities.

In an exchange economy, putting money, even real money balances, into the utility function is an unreliable choice-theoretic short cut for modelling the transactions role of money. Suppose that the utility function is $u(x, m/P)$, where x is a vector of non-money commodities and m/P is nominal money balances divided by some index of the price of non-money commodities. These tastes are given independently of w the initial endowments of non-money commodities. At prices p for the non-money commodities, suppose that the utility-maximizing demands are $x(p)$ and $m(p)$. Now, change the initial endowment so that $w = x(p)$, i.e. at the prices p the individual does not want to trade. Note that the utility function and the marginal rate of substitution between real money balances and other commodities remains the same whether or not the individual plans to trade. In other words, the transactions role of money is not well approximated by simply putting money into the utility function.

Clower (1967) continued the attack. He focused directly on the description of the household budget constraint. In a money economy, "money buys goods, goods buy money, but goods do not buy goods". The last injunction about goods not directly buying goods is not implied by the standard general equilibrium budget constraint used by Patinkin. This constraint is simply the accounting identity that the total value of all purchases must equal the total value of all sales.

There are conditions under which the accounting constraint would be consistent with the monetary exchange injunction. If individuals supplied labor services to firms for which they received money and purchased commodities with that money from firms, then for every dollar of sales of labor services there would be a dollar with which to buy commodities. Feenstra (1986) uses such conditions to establish a kind of equivalence between the money-in-the-utility function and money for transactions purposes approaches. But even if such restrictions were imposed – certainly not in an exchange economy – it seems appropriate to allow the restriction to appear explicitly through the budget constraint rather than implicitly through the utility function.

Clower's critique led to a position similar to Hahn's:

> The natural point of departure for a theory of monetary phenomena is a precise distinction between money and nonmoney commodities. In this connection it is important to observe that such a distinction is possible only if we assign a special role to certain commodities as means of payment.

The lesson, according to Clower, is that exchange is a relation among commodities and monetary exchange is evidence that the relation is asymmetric. To capture this asymmetry, he proposed what has come to be known as the *cash-in-advance* constraint. Dividing commodities into those that are non-money and the money commodity, let $z = (z_i)$ be the vector of net trades of non-money commodities and let $z_m = M - M_0$ be the net trade in money, the difference between final holdings $M \geq 0$ and the initial money balances held at the start of the period M_0. To the standard budget constraint,

$$p \cdot z + z_m = 0 \,,$$

Clower proposed the addition of

$$p \cdot [z]^+ \le M_0$$

to capture the idea that purchases, $[z_i]^+ = \max\{z_i, 0\}$, must be financed by money on hand rather than by sales of other commodities as the standard budget constraint allows.

   This proposal is not without its difficulties, and one might be tempted to say that it is as arbitrary as the earlier practice it was designed to replace of putting money in the utility function. One difficulty is that the proposal originates from a rather synthetic position – that exchange is a relation among commodities. A closer look at the rationale for a common medium of exchange reveals a more satisfying starting point: exchange is a relation among individuals. It is from the problematics of this relation among individuals that we can understand the function of an asymmetric relation among commodities involving a medium of exchange. Another difficulty is that as an added constraint, it cuts down on the exchange opportunities available with the standard budget constraint. Is this restriction gratuitous or is it symptomatic of the features of a money economy that does not operate according to the frictionless barter ideal? Whatever questions it raises, the proposal does provide an indisputable transactions role for money, something that is lacking in the Walras–Hicks–Patinkin tradition.

1.3. Some parables of monetary exchange

In this subsection we relate some simple stories of exchange relations among individuals. They are designed as introductions to the more formal models, described in Sections 2–5. Their purpose is to illustrate among a variety of possible transactions scenarios the common denominator for monetary exchange. That common denominator is the problem, taken for granted in traditional theory, of enforcing budget constraints.

1.3.1. A pair of Robinson Crusoes

Two elderly, largely self-sufficient gentlemen live on an island. Having only the most anemic impulses to truck and barter, their sole contact is the irregular exchange of dinners. Since both agree that meal preparation is onerous, they take turns. However, because dinners are exchanged so infrequently and because their memories are not what they used to be, these Robinson Crusoes cannot always agree on who gave the last dinner. On several occasions both have claimed to have provided the last meal. Each gentleman recognizes that this is a self-serving claim since this is what each would like to remember, but neither is sufficiently confident of his recollection to be sure of the truth. These disagreements have produced so much tension and ill-will that dinners are now exchanged even less frequently.

To attenuate this problem, the one who is coming to dinner next picks up a stone and paints it an artificially colored green to distinguish it from other stones and brings it to his host. At the next planning session for a dinner, the most recent host will be reminded by the presence of the green stone that it is his turn to be invited, and he will be expected to bring the stone with him when he arrives. Indeed, without receiving the stone the host may feel justified in turning away his guest as not having the required evidence of an invitation.

This quite rudimentary story reveals an essential feature of monetary exchange. Money is a commonly acknowledged record-keeping device. Here the only information about the past which has to be recorded is who gave the last dinner. Each gentleman "pays" for his dinner by transferring the record of this fact to the other.

1.3.2. Record-keeping at a central clearing-house

Let us separate into two parts the problem of equilibrium in exchange. First, there is the problem of finding market-clearing prices for which we invoke the mythical auctioneer. The second problem has to do with the actual execution of these trades. If the auctioneer had knowledge of every individual's excess demands and supplies, there is a centralized solution. The auctioneer could simply feed this information into a transportation-type computer algorithm and upon receipt of an answer instruct each individual to transfer specified quantities of commodities to certain other individuals. But this is more information than the auctioneer is typically presumed to have. In searching for equilibrium prices, it is only aggregate excess demand (or supply) for each commodity that is required for the auctioneer to find equilibrium prices, not its detailed distribution across individuals.

Consider the execution problem for a clearing-house with no inventories and only the information that aggregate excess demands are zero. We shall also impose the logistical limitation that individuals cannot trade with the clearing-house all at once. This will mean that at least the first few traders who come to drop off excess supplies will not be able to take away all of their excess demands. Again there is a record-keeping problem.

An obvious record-keeping device is for the clearing-house to issue blue chips to each person in the amount of the excess of the value of the goods supplied compared to those received. Because prices are fixed at market-clearing values, each person can silently spend his chips on the available supplies when he returns to the auctioneer, knowing that all supplies will eventually be claimed by those who have a demand for them.

1.3.3. Exchange without a clearing-house

After finding and announcing prices at which excess demand for each commodity is zero, suppose the auctioneer retires from the scene. It is up to the individuals themselves to fulfill their own excess demands. Trade takes place not at a central depot but in a decentralized setting in which opportunities for exchange are presented as a sequence of meetings between pairs of individuals. Suppose, further, that each person wishes to minimize the numbers of trades, i.e. periods, to fulfill his excess demands.

If each person knew the entire configuration of everyone's excess demands as well as the order of pairwise meetings, the minimization problem would again admit a somewhat more complicated but nevertheless similarly centralized solutions as in the previous auctioneer parable. Here the solution would require individuals to trade not only on their own account but to act as intermediaries, taking goods to be passed on to others. This minimum time and trade algorithm of barter exchange would often contradict the rule of quid pro quo – the stipulation that the value of each pairwise net trade evaluated at Walrasian market-clearing prices is zero. Even though each person aims to execute an overall net trade with zero market value, the most efficient way to accomplish this in a sequence of pairwise trades is not to constrain each bilateral commodity transfer to be zero.

When individual excess demands are not single-valued at equilibrium prices, there is a further problem. Markets may clear at certain prices for a specified vector in the aggregate excess demand correspondence; however, when individuals come to execute their trades they need not pick the ones consistent with market clearance. It is tempting to dismiss this as a minor qualification and certainly we shall not dwell on it. Nevertheless, it is symptomatic of an issue that cannot be dismissed: the amount of information that is compatible with equilibrium when the problem of executing trades is ignored – in this case, just prices – can be much too coarse to accommodate what has to be known to execute trades. See Townsend and Wallace (1987) and Benveniste (1987).

It may be objected that once an individual moves away from his Walrasian "budget-line" by making a non-zero-valued net trade, there is no reason why there should be an eventual return. For example, once a positive-valued net trade is made so that an individual's wealth has been augmented, why should he then agree to a wealth-reducing trade later on? While this doubt will be recognized below, it need not apply here because we are operating under the hypothesis of complete information – everyone knows all excess demands. In this setting undetected cheating is impossible. An individual who takes more than he gives at some pairwise meeting is simply executing a part of the overall plan to which the members of the economy have submitted themselves. It is as though the participants are agents in a firm carrying out their assigned tasks in front of each other. The lesson we draw is that in a world of complete information the requirements for enforcing overall budget balance are met, so quid pro quo is an avoidable constraint on the transactions process.

The thought experiment demonstrates by contradiction the importance of *incomplete information* as a key determinant of "the inconveniences of barter" underlying monetary exchange. Assume to the contrary that individuals know only their own excess demands. Even if one knows the order of the names of one's future trading partners, one does not know very much about them. This has two important consequences. First, there are the hazards of indirect trade. It is no longer possible to know that you can take goods to pass onto others. Second, the quid pro quo constraint comes into its own. Technologically, there may still be advantages to violating the quid pro quo even if individuals eschew indirect barter and trade only on their own account. But there is an incentive to cheat because it is impossible to distinguish between a person who is honestly trying to fulfill his excess demands and someone who is only pretending.

Trader A: I want a candybar. I just gave two bottles of wine to someone and I deserve a candybar as part of my compensation.
Trader B: Why did you give up two bottles of wine?
Trader A: The person I gave it to said he had previously given up a bushel of wheat.

How does monetary exchange resolve this problem? Not by removing any technological transaction costs, but by changing the relative rewards associated with various strategies. The problem is how to enforce the overall budget constraint underlying market-clearing excess demands while also permitting individuals temporarily to violate these constraints in the course of fulfilling those excess demands. Again, what is called for is a record-keeping device. One commodity with utility like any other could serve that function as a kind of physical record provided each person had sufficiently plentiful supplies of it. The willingness of an individual to part with it in payment for an excess of the value of commodities received over those given up is evidence that he is willing to bear the cost of his purchase. Of course a commodity record-keeping device is a relatively crude instrument. The same function could be abstracted by a system of electronic fund transfers provided that accounts were monitored by an agency with sufficient police powers to punish "overissuers".

The previous examples have introduced money as a device for implementing exchange without entering essentially into the determination of the equilibrium allocation. The trades predicted by the frictionless barter theory could then be implemented once money is introduced to deal with the frictions. If that were always the case, money would indeed be a veil. Such a conclusion is not warranted: monetary equilibrium can be quite distinct from barter with or without frictions. This is the purpose of the next example.

1.3.4. A chicken–egg economy

Each of a large number of individuals has his own chicken which has a 50—50 chance of laying an egg each day. The chickens have no value when sold because they lay eggs only for their original owners. There may be trade in eggs but not in chickens.

Ideally, the large numbers of individuals should permit the members of this economy to take advantage of the law of large numbers, namely each would exchange the 50–50 probability of an egg each day for the virtual certainty of one-half of an egg (eggs are divisible). Assuming risk aversion on the part of the owners, this would be an efficient allocation. But here again we must deal with the consequences of the technological transactions costs of incomplete information, especially private information. The chicken's owner is the only one who knows whether it has laid an egg. Thus, the proposed ideal trade to take advantage of the law of large number is unenforceable. What is to prevent someone whose chicken has had an average run of eggs from pretending that it is below average, or someone with an above average run pretending that it is only average, and pocketing the difference between actual and stated egg production.

It is clear that for trades to be enforceable they must be dependent on one's actual trading history and not on ex ante expected values while for trades to be efficient the reverse must be true. In this parable, there is no record-keeping/monitoring device that will resolve the problem of executing efficient trades.

What kind of trading arrangements are possible? Consider the following alternative. When you buy an egg you write a check in favor of the seller who deposits it to the credit of his account and which is automatically debited from the buyer's account so cumulative records of each person's trading history are kept by an outside authority (not by the person himself). So far, this is just information-gathering. The teeth of such a device is contained in the restriction that one cannot have a cumulative balance below a certain number of (negative) eggs. Once that level is reached, consumption must be curtailed until one's balance rises above this level. Now there is no such thing as cheating. One may consume at any rate provided this does not conflict with one's minimum egg balance. This means that one is forced to perceive the costs of additional consumption today in terms of the increased probability of having to curtail future consumption.

1.4. *Introducing general equilibrium theory to monetary exchange*

In each of the stories discussed above we found that the transactions role of money calls into question the modelling of trade via a single budget constraint. Repeatedly, we found on closer examination of the problem of implementing trades, the single budget constraint must be replaced by a sequence of budget constraints. This was the role of the green stone in the story of the two Robinson Crusoes. The exchange of dinner for the stone brought the accounts into balance period by period so that the sometime dinner companions did not have to rely on their memories. The introduction of blue chips in the story of the central clearing-house or the parable about the auctioneer who retired from the scene after equilibrium prices were announced led to a similar conclusion – the need for a tracking device to monitor departures from the overall balance during the interim trading periods so as to ensure that individuals would stick to a trading plan the overall net value of which is zero. In the chicken–egg economy, the issue is once again that a single idealized intertemporal budget constraint is unworkable and is replaced by what is effectively a sequence of overdraft constraints.

The stories vary in the extent of which the responsibility for trade is left to an outside authority and is therefore centralized or is left to the individuals themselves and is therefore more decentralized. The greatest contrast is between the clearing-house and the story about the auctioneer who retires from the scene to leave the individuals to trade on their own in pairs. The latter is the only one in which the purely logistical problems of exchange are present. Even in the chicken–egg economy, there is no difficulty in bringing buyers and sellers together to exchange.

Despite the variation in the levels of *logistical* decentralization in these stories, there is a common element of *informational* decentralization, and it is this element that is directly responsible for the change from a single budget constraint to the imposition of a sequence of budget constraints. The common element is the private information each individual has about his own circumstances. Even in the most logistically centralized story, the clearing-house does not know individual excess demands.

Informational decentralization does not by itself lead to the imposition of the sequence of budget constraints but the causal connection is rather immediate. It is the presence of private information that leads to an obvious *moral hazard* problem when individuals face only a single intertemporal budget constraint in the course of executing intertemporal trades. The lack of enforceability of this single constraint leads to the necessity of a temporal sequence of constraints.

In the following sections we describe some of the contributions that have aimed at elaborating the transactions role of money in a theory of exchange. We begin in Section 2 with the program of modern general equilibrium theory to meet the challenge of finding an internally consistent role for money. In Section 3 we consider models that do not precisely fit the modern general equilibrium mold but ones that focus on the logistics of bilateral exchange. These models serve as a vehicle for displaying the disadvantages of barter commonly believed to be fertile ground for uncovering the transactions role of money. Also, in Section 3 we consider the related problem of how one or more commodities might emerge as media of exchange. In Section 4 we look more closely at the implications for the allocation of resources when the budget enforcement problem cannot be taken for granted. In Section 5 we focus on the development and application of one model of a sequence of binding monetary constraints, the *cash-in-advance* constraint proposed by Clower. Concluding comments are contained in Section 6, and Section 7 provides a brief guide to some related work not specifically referenced in the text.

2. The modern general equilibrium transactions costs approach

At about the same time that Patinkin's *Money, Interest and Prices* appeared, advances were being made in general equilibrium theory. Of particular importance for our purposes were the conscious efforts to include time-dated and event-contingent commodities. This work, associated with the names of Arrow and Debreu, culminated in the publication Debreu's *Theory of Value* (1959). In this section we report on efforts to understand the transactions role of money via models directly inspired by these post-Walrasian contributions. This meant that the problem was viewed from the perspective of "an Arrow–Debreu economy", i.e. the inability to accommodate monetary exchange was attributed to the presence of certain theoretical devices used in the model and described below. Out of this frictionless framework, the response was to model frictions as the transactions costs of making certain kinds of exchanges, from which a role for money could be deduced.

We describe first the frictionless non-monetary economy. Goods are defined by their characteristics, location, and date of delivery. This formal structure corresponds to a fully articulated system of futures markets.[1] A household's

---

[1]Uncertainty can be treated in the model by augmenting the description of a commodity to include the state of the world in which it is deliverable. A contract is then characterized by what it promises, when, where, and under what realization of uncertain events. This formal model of the full set of Arrow–Debreu contingent contracts requires active markets in a variety of distinct instruments, many more than are generally available and actively traded in actual economies. A partial reduction in the large number of contracts needed can be achieved by the use of Arrow securities (Arrow insurance contracts) [Arrow (1964)], which specify a credit to the holder in numeraire on realization of a specified event.

endowment consists of goods (presumably including labor) available at a variety of dates. Its budget is simply the value of this endowment plus the present discounted value of the streams of future profits of the share of business it owns. This budget is in the nature of a lifetime budget constraint. The presence of the futures markets eliminates the distinction between income and wealth. Given this lifetime budget constraint, the household allocates its wealth to the purchase of present and future consumption. It acquires a portfolio of present goods and of contracts for future delivery of its desired consumption plan sufficient to exhaust its budget constraint. Firms buy contracts for present and future inputs, and sell contracts for present and future output to maximize the present discounted value of profits.

Once these contracts are fully arranged, the balance of economic activity consists of their fulfillment. The intertemporal allocation process in the Arrow–Debreu model can be described in the following way: there is a single date of active trade where trade takes place in current goods and in futures contracts for future delivery of goods. There is no need for markets to reopen in the future – all desirable trades have already been arranged. But absent reopening of markets, there is no function for money. Hence, the Arrow–Debreu theory establishes sufficient conditions for money to be useless and positively denies it any intertemporal allocative function.

Though striking, this conclusion is unsurprising; money has no job to perform here because its job is being done by futures markets. The Arrow–Debreu futures markets are designed to perform all intertemporal allocative functions. These are essentially two: price and output determination at each point in time and intertemporal reallocation of purchasing power. The first function can of course be performed by spot markets (with intertemporal perfect foresight). The second is a capital market function. The futures markets allow sales of current output to finance future acquisitions, and they allow sales of future output to finance current purchases. The result is that money and debt instruments, devices for the intertemporal transfer of purchasing power, are otiose. The equilibrium allocation is Pareto efficient. Any technically possible reallocation giving an intertemporal consumption plan preferable for some households would necessarily degrade the well-being of others.

Conversely, if the conditions that allow the futures markets so fully to exercise their function are absent, we may expect a role for money and for futures markets in money (debt instruments). In fact, futures markets for most goods are generally inactive (loosely speaking, do not exist). The reason for this is the structure of transactions costs, which favors spot over futures transactions. In the presence of differential transactions costs on spot and future transactions, the Arrow–Debreu model becomes inapplicable and we are led to a sequence economy model [Hahn (1971)].

The basic idea of a sequence economy is that markets reopen over time.

There is a single essential revision of the Arrow–Debreu model that creates a role for money: require that budget balance be fulfilled at each trading date rather than only in the lifetime budget constraint. In the sequence economy, budget constraints apply at each date. At each date, the value of goods and contracts for future delivery that an agent sells to the market must be at least as large as the value of goods and contracts he accepts from the market. The rationale for this constraint is strategic: this is how the lifetime budget constraint is reliably enforced in an intertemporal setting.

Differential transaction costs on spot and futures markets (in particular, higher costs on futures) imply that markets may reopen over time and agents will face a budget constraint at each date. For a given agent, the time pattern of the value of his planned consumption may differ from that of his endowment. In order to implement such plans consistent with the sequence of budget constraints, futures markets may be used or real assets held intertemporally as stores of value. Transaction costs are not a source of inefficiency in themselves. Part of economic activity is the reallocation of goods and resources. If the reallocation process is a resource-using activity, then resources devoted to it are engaged productively. Any durable good, ownership claim, or futures contract can perform the function of shifting purchasing power forward or back in time, but transaction and storage costs associated with some instruments may be wasteful. These are real resource costs incurred only for the fulfillment of sequential budget constraints and technically unnecessary to implement the allocation. These costs, and any reallocation of consumption plans undertaken to avoid them, represent an efficiency loss. Introduction of fiat money – assumed to be transaction costless – results in an allocation that is closer to Pareto efficient. Households may transfer purchasing power over time by accumulating and depleting their money balances and by the use of money futures contracts (loans). If the desired timing of purchase and of sale transactions do not coincide, money acts as a carrier of purchasing power between the two transaction dates. Money restores allocative efficiency by allowing both fulfillment of the sequential budget constraints and the use of only spot goods transactions, without distortion of the lifetime consumption plan.

Transaction costs, like prices, are correctly computed as present discounted values. Hence, one reason that transaction costs may be higher on futures markets than on spot markets is the timing with which the costs are actually incurred. Costs are incurred at the transaction date and at the delivery date. The present discounted value of the transaction cost for a spot transaction planned now for execution in the distant future will be small. In contrast, the transaction cost on a futures transaction conducted in the present, but with the same distant delivery date, may be substantial. Hence, time discounting notably strengthens the argument for reliance on spot rather than futures markets. Under uncertainty, the argument for spot markets as a low-cost device is again strengthened by considering Arrow–Debreu contingent commodity futures or Arrow securities markets as the alternatives. Because of the multiplicity of contingencies, many contingent futures contracts will be written that will not be executed by delivery. Furthermore, contracts contingent on the occurrence of specified events are necessarily costly to write and enforce. Subject to a different, possibly Pareto inefficient, allocation of risk-bearing, a reduction in the number and complexity of transactions and a corresponding reduction in transaction costs is achieved by reliance on spot rather than futures markets.

2.1. *Pareto inefficient equilibrium in a non-monetary economy: An example*

Let there be two households, A and B. There is one good available at two dates: 1 and 2. Both households have the same utility function,

$$u(c(1), c(2)) = [c(1)]^{1/2}[c(2)]^{1/2} ,$$

and the same transaction technology,

$$z_1(1) = \tfrac{1}{2}x_2(1) + \tfrac{1}{2}y_2(1) ,$$

$$z_2(2) = 0 ,$$

where $c(t)$, $t = 1, 2$, is the consumption at date t; $z_\tau(t)$ is the transaction cost incurred at date τ from transactions conducted on the market at date t, $x_\tau(t)$ and $y_\tau(t)$ are the purchases and sales, respectively, on the market at t for delivery at τ. That is, spot transactions are costless in both periods, futures purchases and sales are costly. The households differ in endowment:

$$\omega^A(1) = 2 , \qquad \omega^A(2) = 0 ,$$

$$\omega^B(1) = 0 , \qquad \omega^B(2) = 2 ,$$

where $\omega^i(t)$ is i's endowment of spot goods at t.

Plainly, since spot transactions are costless and futures are costly, an efficient allocation will use spot markets only. But in order to fulfill the budget constraint in each period, A must buy any period 2 consumption he requires on the futures market thereby incurring the cost in current goods $\tfrac{1}{2} \cdot x_2^A(1)$ per unit for his futures purchase. Similarly, B must sell future endowment on the period 1 market to finance current consumption and current transaction costs. The transaction costs put a wedge between buying and selling (shadow) prices:

$$MRS_{1,2}^{A} = \frac{p_1(1)}{p_2(1) + (1/2)p_1(1)} \, ,$$

$$MRS_{1,2}^{B} = \frac{p_1(1) + (1/2)p_1(1)}{p_2(1)} \, ,$$

where $p_\tau(t)$ is the price on the market at date t for the good delivered at τ.

The difference in MRSs facing A and B is indicative but not conclusive of an allocative inefficiency. If the transaction costs faced by A and B in trade were necessary to achieve a reallocation, then the spread in their MRSs would represent an unfortunate necessity. But given the transaction technology available, such costs are not inevitable. Spot transactions have no costs. The spread in MRSs comes from the use of futures markets with their attendant higher transaction cost. Any allocation that uses futures markets here is necessarily inefficient. Only the sequential budget constraint mandates the use of futures markets and represents the source of Pareto inefficiency. Efficient allocations in the example are characterized by the use of spot trade only and $MRS_{1,2}^{A} = MRS_{1,2}^{B} = 1$.

2.2. Intertemporal transactions cost models: Sequence economy

We now present a formal pure exchange sequence economy model with transactions costs [Hahn (1973), Kurz (1974a, b), Heller and Starr (1976)]. First the non-monetary version will be presented, then it will be extended to include money.

We are interested in four principal results here:

(I) Under suitable sufficient conditions involving continuity, convexity, and non-emptiness of demand functions, there exist market-clearing prices and an equilibrium allocation in the non-monetary economy.

(II) Contrary to the First Fundamental Theorem of Welfare Economics, in the model with transactions costs the allocation associated with the general equilibrium in (I) is not generally Pareto efficient. This is the result of applying the time sequence of budget constraints as opposed to the lifetime budget constraint of an Arrow–Debreu model.

(III) In the monetary economy additional assumptions assure non-triviality of the monetary equilibrium (a finite determinate monetary price level).

(IV) Even the non-trivial monetary equilibrium allocation of (III) is not quite sufficient to assure Pareto efficiency. The allocation will be Pareto efficient if there is perfect capital market. That is, the allocation is Pareto efficient if the transaction costs of money are nil and either a non-negative money holding condition is not a binding constraint or the transaction costs of notes (money futures) are also nil.

Commodity i for delivery at date τ may be bought spot at date τ or futures at any date t, $1 \leq t < \tau$. The complete system of spot and futures markets is available at each date (although some markets may be inactive). The time horizon is date K; each of H households participates in the market at time 1 and cares nothing about consumption after K. There are n commodities deliverable at each date. At each date and for each commodity, the household has available the current spot market, and futures markets for deliveries at all future dates. Spot and futures markets will also be available at dates in the future and prices on the markets taking place in the future are currently known. Thus, in making his purchase and sale decisions, the household considers without price uncertainty whether to transact on current markets or to postpone transactions to markets available at future dates. There is a sequence of budget constraints, one for the market at each date. That is, for every date the household faces a budget constraint on the spot and futures transactions taking place at that date, equation (4) below. The value of its sales to the market at each date (including delivery of money) must balance its purchases at that date.

In addition to a budget constraint the agent's actions are restricted by a transactions technology. This technology specifies for each complex of purchases and sales at date t, what resources will be consumed by the process of transaction. It is because transaction costs may differ between spot and futures markets for the same good that we consider the reopening of markets allowed by the sequence economy model. Specific provision for transactions cost is introduced to allow an endogenous determination of the activity or inactivity of markets. In the special case where all transaction costs are nil, the model is unnecessarily complex; there is no need for the reopening of markets, and the equilibrium allocations are identical to those of the Arrow–Debreu model. Conversely, in the case where some futures markets are prohibitively costly to operate and others are costless, then there is an incomplete array of active spot and futures markets.

All of the n-dimensional vectors below are restricted to be non-negative:

$x_\tau^h(t)$ = vector of purchases for any purpose at date t by household h for delivery at date τ.

$y_\tau^h(t)$ = vector of sales analogously defined.

$z_\tau^h(t)$ = vector of inputs necessary to transactions undertaken at time t; the index τ again refers to date at which these inputs are actually delivered.

$\omega^h(t)$ = vector of endowments at t for household h.

$s^h(t)$ = vector of goods coming out of storage at date t.

$r^h(t)$ = vector of goods put into storage at date t.
$p_\tau(t)$ = prices vector on market at date t for goods deliverable at date τ.

With this notation, $p_{it}(t)$ is the spot price of good i at date t, and $p_{i\tau}(t)$ for $\tau > t$ is the futures price (for delivery at τ) of good i at date t.

The (non-negative) consumption vector for household h is:

$$c^h(t) = \omega^h(t) + \sum_{j=1}^{t} (x_t^h(j) - z_t^h(j)) + s^h(t) - r^h(t) \geq 0 \quad (t = 1, \ldots, K).$$

$$\tag{1}$$

That is, consumption at date t is the sum of endowments plus all purchases past and present with delivery date t minus all sales for delivery at t minus transactions inputs with date t (including those previously committed) plus what comes out of storage at t minus what goes into storage. We suppose that households care only about consumption and not about which market consumption comes from. Thus, households maximize $U^h(c^h)$, where c^h is a vector of the $c^h(t)$'s, subject to constraint.

The household is constrained by its transactions technology, T^h, which specifies, for example, how much leisure time and shoe-leather must be used to carry out any transaction. Let $x^h(t)$ denote the vector of $x_\tau^h(t)$'s [and similarly for $y^h(t)$ and $z^h(t)$].

A household's plan should be consistent with transaction technology,

$$(x^h(t), y^h(t), z^h(t)) \in T^h(t) \quad (t = 1, \ldots, K). \tag{2}$$

Naturally, storage input and output vectors must be feasible, so

$$(r^h(t), s^h(t + 1)) \in S^h(t) \quad (t = 1, \ldots, K - 1). \tag{3}$$

The budget constraints for household h are then:

$$p(t) \cdot x^h(t) \leq p(t) \cdot y^h(t) \quad (t = 1, \ldots, K). \tag{4}$$

Households may transfer purchasing power forward in time by using futures markets and by storage of goods that will be valuable in the future. Purchasing power may be carried backward by using futures markets.

Let $a^h(t) \equiv (x^h(t), y^h(t), z^h(t), r^h(t), s^h(t))$, the vector of h's actions on the market at date t. Let a^h be a vector of the $a^h(t)$'s h's K-period trading plan. Define x^h, y^h, z^h, r^h and s^h similarly. Define $B^h(p)$ as the set of a^h's which satisfy constraints (1)–(4). The household maximizes $U^h(c^h)$ over $B^h(p)$. $U^h(\cdot)$ is assumed to be continuous, concave, and monotone. Denote the demand correspondence (i.e. the set of maximizing a^h's) by $\gamma^h(p)$.

The correspondences $\gamma^h(p)$ are always homogeneous of degree zero in $p(t)$, as is seen from the definition of $B^h(p)$. We can therefore restrict the price space to the simplex. Let S^t denote the unit simplex of dimensionality, $n(K - t + 1)$. Let $P = \times_{t=1}^K S^t$.

An *equilibrium* of the economy is a price vector $p^* \in P$ and an allocation a^{*h}, for each h, so that $a^{*h} \in \gamma^h(p^*)$ for all h and

$$\sum_{h=1}^H x^{*h} \leq \sum_{h=1}^H y^{*h}$$

(the inequality holds coordinate-wise), where for any good i, t, τ such that the strict inequality above holds, it follows that $p_{it}^*(\tau) = 0$.

To ensure the existence of equilibrium, in addition to the usual conditions on preferences and endowments (convexity, continuity, positivity of income, etc.) we will need some structure on the transactions and storage technologies. These are just the sort of assumptions the general equilibrium model ordinarily requires of production technologies. The transactions and storage technologies should be closed convex sets including the origin, admitting free disposal, positive income net of transactions costs, and implying bounded levels of purchase and sale (no wash sales).

We have then

Theorem (Existence of equilibrium for the closed convex non-monetary economy). *In the non-monetary economy, under assumptions assuring non-emptiness, closure and boundedness of budget sets, there is a price vector $p^* \in P$ and an allocation $\langle a^{*h} \rangle_h$ such that*

$$a^{*h} \in \gamma^h(p^*),$$

$$\sum_{h=1}^H x^{*h} \leq \sum_{h=1}^H y^{*h},$$

with $p_{it}^*(\tau) = 0$ for i, t, τ such that the strict inequality holds.

If the sequence economy model were fully analogous to the Arrow–Debreu model we could then demonstrate that the allocation resulting from the equilibrium was Pareto efficient. The analogy is incomplete, however, and the result fails. Equilibrium allocations in the model may not be Pareto efficient. Money and a monetary equilibrium are required to overcome inefficiencies arising from the sequential structure of budget constraints (4). The illustration of this point is the previous example.

2.3. A monetary economy

The demand for goods in the sequence economy model is overdetermined: goods are desired as objects of consumption and as carriers of value between trading opportunities. The second demand may interfere with the first. When it does so, the introduction of a fiduciary or fiat money with negligible transactions and storage costs can change the equilibrium allocation to one that is Pareto efficient. It is important here that the private and social opportunity cost of holding money in inventory be negligible. If not, then an unnecessary wedge remains between buyers' and sellers' intertemporal MRSs, and first-order conditions for Pareto efficiency will fail. Since the opportunity cost of holding real goods in inventory will generally be non-negligible, there is an efficiency gain through the use of fiduciary (bank) or fiat money in place of commodity money.

The model may now be trivially modified to incorporate fiat money and bonds by introducing money as a zeroth commodity for which the household has no direct utility. The non-trivial modification is to ensure the existence of equilibrium with a positive price of money in each period. A futures contract for delivery of money is a bond (discounted note). Let $x_{0t}^h(t)$ [the zeroth component of $x_t^h(t)$] denote the total amount of spot money acquired by household h in the market at date t. Similarly, let $y_{0t}^h(t)$ be the disbursement of spot money at t. Now if $\tau > t$, then $y_{0\tau}^h(t)$ is a commitment made at time t to deliver $y_{0\tau}^h(t)$ units of money at date τ. Suppose that by convention each bond (discounted note) promises one unit of money. Then $y_{0\tau}^h(t)$ is the number of bonds with maturity date τ sold by h. Similarly, $x_{0\tau}^h(t)$ is the number of bonds purchased by household h with maturity date τ.

Spot money trades at a price of $p_{0t}(t)$ at date t [and $p_{0\tau}(t) = 0$ is thereby a possibility]. The equilibrium of a monetary economy is said to be *non-trivial* (that is, the economy is really monetary) if $p_{0t}^*(t) \neq 0$ for all t. The price of a bond maturing at τ is denoted $p_{0\tau}^*(t)$. With this convention we may write the budget constraints on the household as in (4), except that $p(t)$, $x(t)$, and $y(t)$ all contain an added group of zeroth components, one for each delivery date.

The interpretation is that spot money on the market at t can be acquired by spot and futures sales of goods and bond sales. Similarly, spot and futures purchases of goods and bond purchases can be paid for in cash, goods, bonds or goods futures.

What is to prevent a household from disbursing an unlimited amount of money $y_{0t}^h(t)$? The answer is to be found in constraint (1) for the zeroth component: "consumption" of money is a non-negative number. It is possible to disburse money for considerably more than one's current money holding without violating (1), but there must be corresponding receipts of money to balance out the discrepancy.

The volume of monetary trade planned in period t is simply the gross volume of planned spot money disbursements, $\sum_h y_{0t}^h(t)$, or receipts, $\sum_h x_{0t}^h(t)$. These will be equal in equilibrium. The demand for money (as a stock) at p is $\sum_h r_{0t}^h(t)$ where $r_{0t}^h(t)$ is an element of $a^h \in \gamma^h(p)$.

Money is held in this model as a low-cost means of intertemporal transfer of purchasing power. If bonds have a positive nominal interest yield, then non-interest-bearing money will be held to avoid the transaction costs of buying and liquidating bonds. In the convex cost case treated here money will then be held only for short periods where a bond's interest yield (over the short interval) would not compensate for the transaction costs of purchase and sale. In a non-convex transaction cost model [Heller and Starr (1976)], there is a tendency to concentrate transactions so that large intertemporal wealth transfers take place through bonds while small ones use money.

Since we are dealing with fiat (rather than commodity) money, utility maximization will always imply zero consumption of money. We shall assume that there is a positive endowment of spot money, at least at the beginning, and that at no time is there any input of cash being used up by the transaction process. Therefore, by (1),

$$r_0^h(t) - s_0^h(t) = \omega_0^h(t) + \sum_{j=1}^{t} [x_{0t}^h(j) - y_{0t}^h(j)] .$$

Thus, net additions to storage of cash at t equals endowment plus total net acquisitions from the market, where the total is taken over all previous transaction dates. Hence, a household needs to deliver cash only to the extent that his promises to others exceed the promises of others to him.

Transactions and storage technologies will also include money and bonds, since both of these may be costly to exchange. There is a further constraint that the household must satisfy: the terminal condition that holdings of money at the end of time should be at least equal to the money endowment. Without this artificial requirement, no one would want to hold a positive money stock at the end. This would drive money's terminal price to zero. But then no one would hold money at $K - 1$, and so forth. The problem arises because of the use of a finite horizon. This restriction is characterized as

$$\sum_{\tau=1}^{K} [x_{0K}^h(\tau) - y_{0K}^h(\tau)] + s_0^h(K) \leq \sum_{\tau=1}^{K} \omega_0^h(\tau) \equiv M^h . \tag{5}$$

The constraint (5) says that the household is required to have at the economy's terminal date holdings of nominal money equal to its endowment thereof. One interpretation of this is that the money's issuer lends money at periods up to K and calls back its loan at the end of K.

As before, $\gamma^h(p)$ is the demand correspondence of household h, constrained to fulfill (1)–(5) (with the additional zeroth components corresponding to money and bonds). The correspondences $\gamma_t^h(p)$ are again homogeneous to degree zero in $p(t)$. Let S^t denote t the unit simplex of dimensionality $(n+1)(K-t+1)$. Let S_α^K denote the unit simplex of dimensionality $n+1$ with the restriction that $p(T) \in S_\alpha^K$ implies $p_{0K}(K) = \alpha$, where $0 < \alpha < 1$. Define

$$P^\alpha = \{(p(1), p(2), \ldots, p(K)) \mid p(t) \in S^t, p(K) \in S_\alpha^K\} \, .$$

By the same reasoning as before, γ_p^h is convex, compact and upper semicontinuous. Use of P^α as the price space amounts to assuming that the terminal price of money is exogenously set at $\alpha > 0$. A more elaborate economic rationale could be based on expectations [Grandmont (1977)] or terminal period taxation [Starr (1974)]. The use of infinite horizon models is more complex. Anchoring the terminal value of money at $\alpha > 0$ and assuming sufficient substitutability in consumption and transactions between periods results in a downward-sloping demand condition on money – if its value in preterminal periods goes down, nominal demand goes up.

We can now establish the existence of an equilibrium with a positive price of money for the monetary economy.

Theorem (Existence of non-trivial equilibrium for the monetary economy). *Under assumptions assuring non-emptiness, closure, and boundedness of budget sets, and assuring downward-sloping demand for money for any α, $0 < \alpha < 1$, there is a price vector $p^* \in P^\alpha$ and an allocation $\langle a^{*h} \rangle_h$ such that*

$$a^{*h} \in \gamma^h(p^*) \, ,$$

$$\sum_{h=1}^{H} x^{*h} \leq \sum_{h=1}^{H} y^{*h} \, ,$$

with $p_{it}^*(\tau) = 0$ for i, t, τ such that the strict inequality holds, and $p_{0t}^*(t) \neq 0$ for all t.

The conditions so far developed are not quite sufficient to guarantee the Pareto efficiency of the allocation arising in a non-trivial monetary equilibrium. The reason is that (1), the non-negativity requirement applied to spot money, may be a binding constraint on some households in equilibrium. This can arise since there may be non-zero transaction costs in the money futures (bond) market generating a capital market imperfection. This difficulty need not necessarily arise. It will not if money holdings, r_{0t}^h, of all agents h at each date t, happen to be strictly positive in equilibrium. An alternative sufficient condition is that transaction costs on the money futures (bond) market be nil.

The source of Pareto inefficiency in equilibrium is a capital market imperfection deriving from the multiplicity of sequential budget constraints (4). When the cost of intertemporal transfer of purchasing power is not a binding constraint the resulting allocation is Pareto efficient. Intertemporal allocative efficiency will be achieved in three principal circumstances: (i) by simple good luck in the timing of endowments so that there is no need to use the capital market (an "inessential" sequence economy); (ii) when spot money stocks are strictly positive in equilibrium at all dates for all households; and (iii) when the transaction costs for spot and futures money are nil. Under any of these conditions, in equilibrium with a positive price of money in each period, the household demand problem subject to (4), the sequential budget constraint, is equivalent to the problem with a lifetime budget constraint. Then the First Fundamental Theorem of Welfare Economics from the Arrow–Debreu model applies. Hence, we are led to:

Theorem. *For any $0 < \alpha < 1$, let $p^* \in P^\alpha$ with $p^*_{0t}(t) > 0$ for $t = 1, \ldots, K$, be a non-trivial equilibrium price vector for the monetary economy fulfilling with equilibrium allocation $\langle a^{*h} \rangle_h$ and consumption plan $\langle c^{*h} \rangle_h$. Let money futures be transaction costless, or let $r^h_{0t}(t) > 0$ for all h, all $t = 1, \ldots, K$. Then $\langle a^{*h} \rangle_h$ is a Pareto-efficient allocation.*

The proof of the theorem consists of demonstrating that for each household, under the nil transaction cost conditions posited, the sequence of budget constraints (4) collapses to a simple lifetime budget constraint. Then the First Fundamental Theorem of Welfare Economics (a Walrasian equilibrium allocation is Pareto efficient) applies, and the theorem is proved.

The role of money in the sequence economy model is to provide the means of achieving an allocation consistent with a single lifetime budget constraint. The inefficiencies that occur in the non-monetary version of the model are those of an imperfect capital market: discrepancies across agents in their intertemporal marginal rates of substitution of consumption. Conversely, in an equilibrium of the fully monetized model, intertemporal MRSs are equated across all households.

The institutional distortion that plagues sequence economy models is the sequence of budget constraints – one for each period – facing agents as they trade. In order to pay for purchases, agents who wish to buy goods in one period must sell goods in the same period and vice versa. The resolution of the inefficiency is to sever the temporal link between commodity buying and selling transactions while continuing to fulfill the sequential budget constraint. The introduction of "money" is designed to achieve this. Money is defined as a commodity of positive price and zero transaction cost that does not directly enter in production or consumption. Rather than engage in costly futures trades to achieve budget balance at each trading date, traders use trade in money to bridge the gap in timing between desired sales and purchases. The assumption of zero money transaction cost is of course extreme but it captures the essential point: a major cost reduction relative to commodity trade. Money as a store of value with nil transaction costs spot and futures (a perfect capital market) allows undistorted intertemporal reallocation despite the sequential budget constraint.

3. The logistics of decentralized barter exchange

The starting point for this section is an issue that Walras had (wisely, for his purposes) glided over in his theory of multilateral exchange: the problem of exchange without a clearing-house described in Subsection 1.3.3. This problem is suggested by the idea that money eliminates the oft-quoted "disadvantages of barter"; and the efforts here are devoted to modelling the disadvantages of barter as a way of confirming and perhaps enlarging our intuition about the transactions role of money.

Despite the different starting points and matters of detail and emphasis, the conclusions reached both in this section and the previous one can be summarized in largely similar terms. The reasons differ, but each approach describes the overall gains from trade as occurring via a sequence of exchanges; and both point to the need for trades to be "balanced" (satisfy the quid pro quo) at each exchange, a need that conflicts with the potential for exploiting all the gains from trade. The role of money is to attenuate this conflict.

3.1. Dwelling on the disadvantages of barter

Jevons (1893) focused on the problems of coordinating trade among agents as the essential rationale for the use of a medium of exchange. He argued that without a medium of exchange, trade was necessarily limited to exchange of reciprocally desired goods, e.g. the trade between the hungry tailor and the ill-clad baker. Jevons called the situation where the supplier of good A is a demander of good B and vice versa a "double coincidence" of wants. A priori it appears that such double coincidences are rare even in the presence of market-clearing equilibrium prices that assure that for every buyer there is somewhere a willing seller.

> The earliest form of exchange must have consisted in giving what was not wanted directly for that which was wanted. This simple traffic we call barter . . . and distinguish it from sale and purchase in which one of the articles exchanged is intended to be held only for a short time, until it is parted with in a second act of exchange. The object which thus temporarily

intervenes in sale and purchase is money. At first sight it might seem that the use of money only doubles the trouble, by making two exchanges necessary where one was sufficient; but a slight analysis of the difficulties inherent in simple barter shows that the balance of trouble lies quite in the opposite direction . . . the first difficulty in barter is to find two persons whose disposable possessions mutually suit each other's wants. There may be many people wanting, and many possessing those things wanted; but to allow of an act of barter there must be a double coincidence, which will rarely happen.

The more likely event (i.e. absence of double coincidence of wants) is that for two traders, one of whom is the supplier of a good (good 1), the other demands, the latter's excess supplies – though of sufficient value at market prices to purchase the demand – are of a good (good 2) which the former does not require. Jevons argues that it is to overcome the absence of double coincidence of wants that monetary trade is introduced. The supplier of good 1, though apparently reluctant to accept good 2 in trade, will accept money. The supplier has less use for money than he had for good 2, but by common consent money can be traded directly for what the supplier of good 1 demands. Menger (1892) notes:

It is obvious . . . that a commodity should be given up by its owner in exchange for another more useful to him. But that every economic un- it . . . should be willing to exchange his goods for little metal disks apparently useless as such, or for documents representing the latter, is a procedure so opposed to the ordinary course of things, that . . . [it is] downright "mys- terious".

It takes an economy of at least three goods and at least three agents to generate a need for a medium of exchange. Three goods are needed since in a two-good economy, an individual's demand for one good implies, by budget balance, an equivalent supply of the other. Hence, in a two-good economy, the double coincidence condition is fulfilled and no need for a medium of exchange can arise. Three agents are required since, in a two-agent economy, market clearing implies the double coincidence condition and, hence again, there is no need for a medium of exchange. This simplicity is lost in a three-trader, three-good economy and a use for a medium of exchange arises. As Menger notes:

Even in the relatively simple . . . case, where an economic unit, A, requires a commodity possessed by B, and B requires one possessed by C, while C wants one that is owned by A – even here, under a rule of mere barter, the exchange of the goods in question would as a rule be of necessity left undone.

Formalizing this example, let the households be A, B, and C. Let the price vector, $p = (1, 1, 1)$. Let the household desired purchases be denoted x^A, x^B, and x^C and sales y^A, y^B, and y^C:

$$x^A = (1, 0, 0), \qquad x^B = (0, 1, 0), \qquad x^C = (0, 0, 1),$$

$$y^A = (0, 1, 0), \qquad y^B = (0, 0, 1), \qquad y^C = (1, 0, 0).$$

Note that this array constitutes a general equilibrium trading plan. For each demander there is a willing supplier. However, double coincidence of wants is not fulfilled. For every pair of agents there is no trade so that each agent can receive a good he demands in exchange for one he wishes to supply.

Suppose a zeroth good, money, also with a price of 1, is introduced and that the convention is adopted that money can be given in trade even when there is no excess supply and can be accepted though there is no excess demand. Then let any pair, e.g. A and B, meet to trade. Good 2 goes from A to B and a payment in money goes from B to A. This gives the new array:

$$x^A = (0, 1, 0, 0), \qquad x^B = (1, 0, 0, 0), \qquad x^C = (0, 0, 0, 1),$$

$$y^A = (1, 0, 0, 0), \qquad y^B = (0, 0, 0, 1), \qquad y^C = (0, 1, 0, 0).$$

Then let another pair trade, B and C for example. This gives the array:

$$x^A = (0, 1, 0, 0), \qquad x^B = (0, 0, 0, 0), \qquad x^C = (1, 0, 0, 0),$$

$$y^A = (1, 0, 0, 0), \qquad y^B = (0, 0, 0, 0), \qquad y^C = (0, 1, 0, 0).$$

Finally, C and A trade and all excess supplies and demands are reduced to nil.

The role for money as a medium of exchange derives from an over-determinacy in the demand for goods in the trading process. When two agents trade, a supplier of one good is paid by delivery of goods of equal value from the buyer, quid pro quo. Goods are required as objects of consumption and as carriers of value to fulfill the quid pro quo. The second demand for goods derives from two conditions: the pairwiseness (or small group structure) of trade and the strategic requirement of the quid pro quo. Absent a medium of exchange, the overdeterminacy then implies that an equilibrium allocation cannot generally be implemented in a relatively short trading time using a pairwise decentralized trading process. It will require lengthy trade or signifi-cantly more complex organization. The alternative is to introduce a monetary commodity, providing an extra degree of freedom for the system to alleviate the overdeterminacy. The provision of money can allow revision of the trading process to permit implementation of the equilibrium allocation by decentralized pairwise trade in relatively short trading time.

The examples above treat a pure exchange economy with specialized endowments. In an economy with production, the counterpart of these examples is a tradition, going back to Adam Smith (1776), relating the role of money as a medium of exchange to the degree of specialization in production. An agent's output may be specialized, but his desired consumption is diverse, and is acquired through trade. If exchange were difficult, that difficulty would discourage specialization, by making it costly to implement in equilibrium; "division of labor is limited by the extent of the market [ease of trade]". A suitably acceptable, durable, and divisible good, that is a money, is required to even out transactions between agents whose desired trades with one another are non-synchronous or unequal in value.

> When the division of labour has been once thoroughly established, it is but a very small part of a man's wants, which the produce of his own labour can supply. He supplies the far greater part of them by exchanging that surplus part of the produce of his own labour, which is over and above his own consumption, for such parts of the produce of other men's labour as he has occasion for. Every man thus lives by exchanging. But when the division of labour first began to take place, this power of exchanging must frequently have been very much clogged and embarrassed in its operations . . . Every prudent man in every period of society after the first establishment of the division of labour, must naturally have endeavored to manage his affairs in such a manner, as to have at all times by him, besides the peculiar produce of his own industry, a certain quantity of some one commodity or other, such as he imagined few people would be likely to refuse in exchange for the produce of their industry.

Among the forms of specialization we expect to see in a low transaction cost economy is specialization in the transaction process itself. Specialists in trade include merchants, retailers, wholesalers, and financial intermediaries. Consistent with Smith's viewpoint, the distinct function of intermediary agents can be explained by scale economies in transaction costs. The use of intermediaries implies an increase in the gross volume of trade, since each commodity or security is traded several times. If scale economies on transaction costs are present, the savings associated with the concentration of transactions compensates for the added volume. A formal model of these views would use the transaction cost structure of Section 2 while characterizing transactions service firms with a non-convex technology. To model specialization in production activities, a fully articulated production sector with indivisibility in inputs (e.g. specialized labor) or other non-convexity would be appropriate. A general formal treatment of the Smithian view of the interaction of money and specialization is still absent from the literature.

3.2. A model of bilateral trade

First consider a static pure exchange economy (i.e. without production). The principal issues on the structure of bilateral trade can be posed in this model.

Let there be a fixed finite number of households H, with preferences represented by utility functions $U^h(c^h)$, $h = 1, \ldots, H$. Let

b^h = household h's endowment vector, $b^h \in R^N_+$,

c^h = household h's planned consumption vector, $c^h \in R^N_+$,

x^h = planned vector of net purchases by household h, $x^h \in R^N_+$,　　　(6)

y^h = planned vector of net sales by household h, $y^h \in R^N_+$,

p = vector of market prices, $p \in R^N_+$.

Prices are announced by an abstract market mechanism, sometimes personified as the Walrasian auctioneer, and are treated parametrically by households. Household h chooses c^h to

$$\max U^h(c^h)$$
(7)

subject to

$$p \cdot c^h = p \cdot b^h .$$
(8)

Then $x^h = [c^h - b^h]^+$ and $y^h = [b^h - c^h]^+$, where the $[\cdot]^+$ indicates the vector of non-negative elements of the argument. Prices, p, are said to be equilibrium prices when choosing c^h as in (7) above gives $\sum_h c^h = \sum_h b^h$, or equivalently:

$$\sum_h x^h = \sum_h y^h .$$
(9)

Note that

$$y^h \leq b^h$$
(10)

coordinate-wise, and

$$p \cdot x^h = p \cdot y^h .\tag{11}$$

An array $(p, \langle x^h \rangle_h, \langle y^h \rangle_h, \langle b^h \rangle_h)$, fulfilling (6)–(11), can be called a general equilibrium trading plan. Our task now is to discover how the plan can be implemented.

There is a single essential revision of the general equilibrium model that ensures a role for a medium of exchange: replace the single budget constraint, (8) or (11), by a multiplicity of budget balance requirements, one for each bilateral trade. (8) and (11) require only that the total value of a household's purchases be paid for by the total proceeds of sales. (8) and (11) impose no restriction on individual transactions. The requirement that generates a demand for a medium of exchange is to require that sales pay for purchases *at each transaction*.

We denote this restriction as the quid pro quo constraint. Under bilateral trade, implementing an agent's trading plan, x^h and y^h, will involve many individual transactions, in most of which a planned purchase (a positive element of x^h) will not coincide with a planned sale (a positive element of y^h) of equal value. Fulfillment of the quid pro quo constraint will then require that the deficiency be satisfied by delivery of some good, either an ordinary commodity, or a specifically designated money.

The origins of the quid pro quo constraint are strategic [Ostroy (1973)]. The restriction is needed in a bilateral trade setting to ensure individual fulfillment of the budget constraint (8) or (11). Without the quid pro quo restriction applied to individual transactions there might be no effective means to prevent violation of budget constraint and a resultant shortage of some good at the completion of trade.

We will take the trading period to be divided into a large countable number of instants suitable for trade. At each instant each trader can trade with at most one other trader, pairwise. Denote an arbitrary finite schedule in which each trader meets each other trader precisely once (disjoint pairs meeting simultaneously) as a *round*.

Let the number of trading instants in a round be K. K must be at least as large as the number of agents minus one. Trading instants are denoted $k = 1, \ldots, K$. At the start of the kth instant trader i's deliverable supplies will be represented by w_i^k. $w_i^1 = b_i$. The change in i's holdings between k and $k + 1$, $a_i^k = w_i^{k+1} - \omega_i^k$, is the trade i performs in instant k. Trader i's hitherto unsatisfied excess demands on entering k are $v_i^k = v_i^1 - \sum_{\kappa=1}^{\kappa=k-1} a_i^\kappa$. $v_i^1 \equiv x^i - y^i$.

Consider the meeting and trade between i and j at instant k. Each brings his holdings w_i^k and w_j^k, to the pair. Positive entries in the vector a_i^k indicate goods going from j to i and negative entries, goods going from i to j. After trading, i's holdings will be $w_i^{k+1} = w_i^k + a_i^k$ and j's will be $w_j^{k+1} = w_j^k + a_j^k$. We place the following three restrictions on a_i^k, a_j^k:

(A.1) $w_i^k + a_i^k \geq 0$, $w_i^k + a_i^k \geq 0$ (non-negativity of holdings),

(A.2) $a_i^k = -a_j^k$ (pairwise trade),

(A.3) $p \cdot a_i^k = 0 = p \cdot a_j^k$ (the quid pro quo).

Should trades fulfill (A) for all $i, j \in I$ and $k = 1, \ldots, K$, we shall say that the sequence of trades is admissible.

The non-negativity requirement, (A.1), says that a trader can at no time have a negative holding of any commodity. A trader cannot deliver in trade more of a commodity than he currently holds. This may be interpreted as a prohibition on the issue of I.O.U.s.

The pairwiseness condition, (A.2), says that in the process of trade, goods delivered are received, and vice versa. To the extent that goods are lost in storage or used up in transactions costs, this occurs in a separate process.

The quid pro quo condition, (A.3), requires that in the trade between i and j, each delivers to the other goods of equal value. Full payment is made for value received where goods are evaluated at equilibrium prices.

Conditions (A.1) and (A.2) are feasibility restrictions defining bilateral exchange. The origins of (A.3) are strategic; it is needed to enforce the budget constraint (8) or (11).

Given prices, an order of meetings for the pairs of traders, and an admissible sequence of trades, the outcome can be described as the resulting allocation of goods among traders. At the end of one round the outcome for trader i is $\sum_{k=1}^{K} a_i^k$. We will say that full execution of excess demands has been achieved in one round if

(E) $\displaystyle\sum_{k=1}^{k=K} a_i^k = x^i - y^i$, $\forall i$.

Should time run out ($k = K$) before all demands are fulfilled and supplies delivered, (E) will not be satisfied.

Will (E) be fulfilled without violating (A)? To answer this question we need a model of how trading decisions are made. We will characterize the trading decision of pair i, j, the trading rule, as a function of i, j's current holdings w_i^k, w_j^k, and other information, $L_{i,j}^k$. The current holdings define the set of trades possible consistent with (A). Other information allows them to choose among the possibilities.

Define a trading rule as a function $\rho(w_i^k, w_j^k \mid L_{i,j}^k) = (a_i^k, a_j^k)$, where $L_{i,j}^k$ is the set of information, beyond their current holdings, available to the pair at instant k. An economic arrangement is generally described as decentralized if it involves individual agents making decisions to further their individual aims based on a fairly small body of universally communicated information (e.g. prices) and on information which the agents themselves may be supposed to possess (e.g. individual tastes and endowments).

Hence, we say a trading rule is *decentralized* if

(D.1) $L_{i,j}^k = \{(v_i^k, v_j^k), p\}$,

or

(D.2) $L_{i,j}^k = \{(v_i^k, v_j^k), (i, j), p\}$.

Conversely, a non-decentralized trading procedure may be characterized by

(C) $L_{i,j}^k = \{(v_1^k, v_2^k, \ldots, v_H^k), (i, j), p\}$.

(D.1) describes as decentralized a rule that formulates a pair's trade by using prices, the pair's current excess demands and supplies. (D.1) is anonymous; (D.2) allows the rule to use the names of the agents as well. (C) represents as non-decentralized a procedure that requires information on all agents' excess demands in order to formulate the trade for any pair of agents. The informational requirements of (C) are thought to be sufficiently great as to imply centralization in the collection and dissemination of the information, and in implementation of the rule. A rule that actually makes full use of (C) would require traders to make trades based on the excess demands of other traders with whom they may have no remaining opportunity to trade in the balance of the round.

Two weaker concepts of full execution are useful. In particular, we wish to consider a trading process that requires more than one round of meetings between pairs of traders to arrange for contracting and payment of obligations. Another approaches full execution as a limit after a multiplicity of repeated trading opportunities. These alternatives will allow us to discuss the trade-off between trading time and trading organization. Hence, we say that full execution is achieved in three rounds if, for each i:

(E.3) $\displaystyle\sum_{k=1}^{k=3K} a_i^k = x^i - y^i$.

We now seek to describe convergence to full execution as the limit of a trading process. Let ψ^ν be a sequence of reals, $1 \geq \psi^\nu \geq 0$, with $\psi^\nu \to 0$. Then we say that full execution is approached as ψ^ν if

$$(E.\psi^\nu) \qquad \sum_i p \cdot [v^{1+\nu k}]_+ \leq \psi^\nu \sum_i p \cdot x^i .$$

That is, we measure execution by the proportion of the value of demands that is fulfilled. By the end of the νth round, suppose at least the proportion $1 - \psi^\nu$ of the original value of excess demand has been fulfilled. Then we say that trade converges to full execution as ψ^ν.

In actual trading processes, certain commodities and agents enter with distinct asymmetric functions differing from those of other goods or agents. We will find it useful to distinguish money as a special commodity. Among traders we will distinguish one that acts as a bank.

The distinctive element of actual monetary economies is that almost all transactions have as one side a financial instrument thought of as "money". In order for successful monetary trade to take place without violating (A.1), non-negativity, agents must have, at each trading instant, sufficient money to finance their current purchases. The money will come from endowment or the proceeds of past sales. We are interested then in characterizing economies with sufficient endowment of money so that illiquidity due to exhaustion of money holdings in the course of trade need not be a problem. In actual economies, this is ensured partly through purposeful timing of transactions (one goes to the bank for cash before buying lunch), but direct treatment of the timing decision would introduce greater complexity than we wish to treat in this model. Hence, we will characterize, at least at first, a monetary economy as one endowed with a sufficient stock of a monetary commodity to be used as medium of exchange. It must be distributed sufficiently broadly in sufficiently great quantity (in value terms) among the holders that all agents find that they can finance all desired purchases from endowment of the money commodity. This is obviously too strong a requirement to be taken seriously as a primitive description of an actual economy. Rather, it reflects the array of holdings that agents may arrange at the start of the trading process, to facilitate the subsequent process of trade. The alternative, developed later below is to describe a bank as an institution that creates monetary credit instruments, hence overcoming shortage of monetary commodity. Both of these approaches ignore – under the assumption that it is too complex to model – explicit timing decisions of individual agents designed to assure continuous liquidity as needed. This requirement enters essentially, however, in the analysis of sequence economies with transactions costs.

Definition (Monetary economy). The economy is said to be monetary if there is a good, 0, so that for all households h,

$$p_0 \cdot b_0^h \geq p \cdot x^h .$$

A monetary economy is hence described here by the property that there is a zeroth good universally held in a quantity sufficient to finance all purchases. In the trading rule used to demonstrate the superiority (decentralizability) of monetary trade, the zeroth good enters (like money) essentially asymmetrically in the exchange process.

Definition (Bank credit economy). The economy is said to be a bank credit economy, if there are goods d (debt), and c (banknotes), for which the non-negativity requirement (A.1) is waived for trades between households and the bank.

A bank is defined here as a trader that can buy household debt and issue its own debt instruments. Debt necessarily involves negative holdings of the debt instrument by its issuer. Hence, the definition describes a limited violation of (A.1). This means that the bank is allowed to extend credit (contrary to the idea of informational decentralization) in a way that other traders are forbidden.

The role of money as a medium of exchange consists in allowing full execution to be achieved expeditiously (in one round) by a decentralized rule, whereas in the absence of money, full execution requires more time, ample goods inventories to act as trading stocks, or sufficient information to support a non-decentralized rule. These results are embodied in the following theorems.

Theorem 1. *Let* $(p, \langle x^h \rangle_h, \langle y^h \rangle_h, \langle b^h \rangle_h)$ *be a general equilibrium trading plan. Then there is a trading rule satisfying* (A), (C) *and* (E).

Theorem 2. *There is no trading rule that, for all general equilibrium trading plans* $(p, \langle x^h \rangle_h, \langle y^h \rangle_h, \langle b^h \rangle_h)$, *fulfills* (A), (E), *and* (D.2) *[or* (D.1)*]*.

Theorem 3. *Let* $(p, \langle x^h \rangle_h, \langle y^h \rangle_h, \langle b^h \rangle_h)$ *be a general equilibrium trading plan of a monetary economy. Then there is a trading rule fulfilling* (A), (E), *and* (D.1).

Theorem 4. *Let* $(p, \langle x^h \rangle_h, \langle y^h \rangle_h, \langle b^h \rangle_h)$ *be a general equilibrium trading plan of a bank credit economy. Then there is a trading rule fulfilling* (A), (E.3), *and* (D.2).

Theorem 5. *Let* $(p, \langle x^h \rangle_h, \langle y^h \rangle_h, \langle b^h \rangle_h)$ *be a general equilibrium trading plan. Then there is a trading rule fulfilling* (A), (E.$(\frac{1}{2})^\nu$), *and* (D.1).

Theorem 6. *Let* $(p, \langle x^h \rangle_h, \langle y^h \rangle_h, \langle b^h \rangle_h)$ *be a general equilibrium trading plan. For some agent* h^*, *let* $b^{h^*} \geq \sum_{h \neq h^*} x^h$ *(the inequality holds co-ordinate-wise). Then there is a trading rule fulfilling* (A), (E), *and* (D.2).

Theorems 1 and 2 demonstrate the trade-off between full execution and limited information. Together, they say that although there exists a rule that makes (A) and (E) compatible for every general equilibrium, that rule must be centralized. Theorem 3 says that if there is a commodity such that the value of each trader's holdings of it is at least equal to the value of his planned purchases of all other commodities, then decentralized trading is compatible with full execution. In particular, the commodity 0 in Theorem 3 is regarded as money, and it behaves as money in the trading rule used to prove that theorem.

Theorem 4 applies to an economy with a bank. If the bank provides sufficient credit instruments, then the decentralized trade suggested in Theorem 3 can occur with the credit instruments acting as money, though additional time for financial transactions may be required. Theorem 5 says that, absent the money or credit of Theorems 3 and 4, decentralized trade can converge to full execution over many trading rounds. It will converge geometrically over time, but there is apparently no guarantee of achieving full execution in finite time. Theorem 6 says that the presence of a trader with sufficient trading stocks to act as a clearing-house allows full execution to be achieved in one round of decentralized trade.

To summarize, in a bilateral trading model we have the following results:

(i) It is not generally possible to implement a general equilibrium trading plan in one round in a decentralized fashion without money, bank credit, or large trading inventories (Theorem 2).

(ii) Implementation is possible without money or credit using non-decentralized trading procedures (Theorem 1), in a decentralized fashion requiring much more than one round (Theorem 5), or in one round of decentralized trade if there are ample trading inventories (Theorem 6).

(iii) Monetary trade using money or credit instruments allows decentralized implementation of the allocation in one round. In the case of the bank credit model some extra trading time may be needed to arrange and repay credit (Theorems 3 and 4).

Points (i) and (ii) summarize the inconvenience of barter. Point (iii) says that money allows rapid decentralized implementation of a general equilibrium trading plan.

3.3. Discussion of proofs of Theorems 1–6

The proof of Theorem 1, existence of a centralized procedure, is by construction and comes in two parts. First it is shown that the complex of excess demands and supplies can always be decomposed into a finite number of elementary configurations (chains) so that each agent in the chain has an excess demand for one good, excess supply of another and, for each good, supply equals demand across the chain. A chain can be represented as shown in Figure 1.1. This is read: "A has an excess supply of 1 for which B has an excess

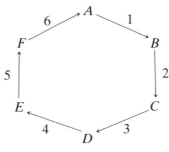

Figure 1.1

demand; B has an excess supply of 2 for which C has an excess demand; ... 6 for which A has an excess demand". A centralized trading procedure is developed for trades in chains. The centralized procedure for the economy then is for each pair of traders, when they meet to trade, to perform the sum of the trades appropriate to the chains they have in common.

We wish to show that each chain can have its demands fulfilled in a single sequence of trades. The trading procedure that achieves this is simple to state but requires sufficient information and coordination to allocate traders to chains and to let them know what chains they have in common. Hence, it does not qualify as decentralized. When two traders meet, if they are members of a common chain they exchange excess supplies corresponding to the chain. This breaks the chain into two smaller disjoint chains. The process continues until all chains are of unit length, i.e. excess demands are fulfilled. This can be illustrated diagrammatically. Suppose A and C are the first elements of the chain to meet. They exchange excess supplies. The resulting array is Figure 1.2, i.e. two smaller disjoint chains. The process is repeated for each chain separately until each excess demand is fulfilled.

This complexity is unavoidable. Theorem 2 says that it is not generally possible to find a decentralized trading rule that moves in limited time to the equilibrium allocation. The proof consists of presenting two different economies with some traders identical in each. The example is set up so that

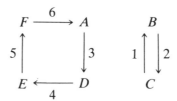

Figure 1.2

the trades these traders must make in one economy to achieve equilibrium consistent with other traders' demands would preclude achievement of equilibrium in the other. Under a decentralized rule, however, the traders cannot distinguish between the two for purposes of deciding on their trades, since the difference is not in their own excess demands but in others'. Hence, full execution is not generally decentralizable.

In the proof of Theorem 3, commodity 0 acts as the medium of exchange. When two traders meet, commodities of which one has an excess supply and the other has an excess demand go from the supplier to the demander until the supply or the demand is exhausted. Failure of the quid pro quo is made up by trade in 0. The procedure is decentralized since each pair needs only information on its own excess demands and supplies in order to make an intelligent trading decision. By definition of a monetary economy, there is sufficient stock of good 0 so that the procedure may be followed without violating (A.1), non-negativity.

The proof of Theorem 4 simply requires that credit arrangements be made with the bank in the first round so that each agent has banknotes at the beginning of the second round sufficient to finance all of his planned purchases in the round. Theorem 3 is then applied to the resulting array. In the third round the only activity is repayment of bank credit.

In the proof of Theorem 5 all goods act indiscriminately as a means of payment in a trading rule that otherwise follows the rule in Theorem 3. It can be shown that by the end of one round, at least half the initial demands are satisfied. Unfortunately, goods acting as a means of payment may end the first round in the hands of those who do not demand them. The procedure is repeated in the second round, so that outstanding demands are reduced to a fourth of their initial level, and so forth.

In the proof of Theorem 6, agent h^* acts as a clearing-house. His large endowment allows him successfully to fulfill this function.

What do we conclude from the analysis of this section? Essentially, that implementing a general equilibrium allocation by bilateral trade is a tricky proposition, one made significantly easier by the introduction of a single medium of exchange, in ample quantity, entering asymmetrically in the trading process. The trade-offs presented in this problem are among trading time, informational decentralization, and inventories. Sufficient slack in any one of these three variables can make up for stringency in the other two. When all three are at the minimal levels consistent with a general equilibrium plan, it is not generally possible to organize pairwise trade to the equilibrium allocation.

Pairwiseness is associated with three restrictions on the structure of trade:

(1) The quid pro quo; a multiplicity of pairwise budget constraints.

(2) Non-negativity; traders in bilateral transactions can deliver only goods they have.

(3) Informational decentralization; the information or coordination needed to implement trades must be available pairwise.

These conditions are familiar; they are fulfilled by the individual's single trade with the market in the Arrow–Debreu model. But here they are applied to each pairwise trade. The multiplicity of bilateral trades – and their inter-dependence – implies, however, that extending these conditions to the bilateral trading model is not innocuous. It so overdetermines the system that – in contrast to the Arrow–Debreu general equilibrium model – expeditious trade to equilibrum is not generally possible. This represents the inconveniences of barter. The introduction of money as a medium of exchange, in sufficient quantity to avoid the non-negativity constraint binding, restores sufficient flexibility to allow all three conditions to be fulfilled and to allow trade to proceed to equilibrium. Hence, the superiority of monetary trade.

3.4. The spontaneous emergence of media of exchange

It is useful to divide the elementary issues concerning monetary exchange into two separate questions:
- What is the function of a common medium of exchange?
- Why have certain commodities become media of exchange?

With regard to the first question, we have seen that in both the bilateral trade model above and in the transactions costs variant of the multilateral Arrow–Debreu model of the previous section, the function of a common medium of exchange is to enforce the accounting identity budget constraint in a sequential trading environment. With regard to the second question, it is common to provide a checklist of desirable characteristics such as portability, divisibility, and durability. In this chapter we omit any discussion of the characteristics of a money commodity while implicitly assuming that it has all of the properties necessary to fulfill its role as a medium of exchange. There is, however, a related question

- How have certain commodities come to be used as media of exchange?

Jones (1976) addressed this question from a point of view first stressed by Menger. Menger (1892) claimed that money need not be a creature of the state, but could arise spontaneously through the market behavior of in-dividuals.

The setting is again one of barter through bilateral exchange. Each individual has an excess demand vector of the form:

$$(0, \ldots, -1, \ldots, 1, \ldots),$$

i.e. there is one commodity to be purchased and one to be sold. The aggregate pattern of excess demands among the population is such that at the one-for-one exchange rate aggregate excess demands for each commodity is zero.

The quid pro quo is taken for granted. The question is: How will it be imposed? Will it be through direct barter where individuals accept as payment for goods sold only what they wish ultimately to consume, or will it be through indirect barter? And if through indirect barter, is there a pattern in which one (or a few) goods emerge as the unique medium of indirect trade? Note that the monetary pattern of exchange amounts to a replacement of the traditional double coincidence of wants by an indirect double-coincidence that individuals spontaneously recognize as less costly to achieve.

Subadditivity in transactions costs

If indirect exchange is to be less costly than direct, the cost of exchanging commodity i for j will have to be greater than the cost of exchanging i for k and for exchanging k for j. Suppose c_{ij} and c_{ik} are the costs of exchanging i for j and i for k, respectively. If these costs are additive in the sense that they can be additively decomposed into

$$c_{ij} = c_i^s + c_j^b,$$

where c_i^s is the selling cost of i and c_j^b is the buying cost of j, then

$$c_{ij} < c_{ik} + c_{kj} = c_i^s + c_k^b + c_k^s + c_j^b.$$

The immediate conclusion is the opposite of what we are seeking: direct barter is less costly than any indirect barter. Because arguments based on the physical characteristics of commodities or on transport costs typically have this additive form, they will have a limited role in explaining the function of a medium of exchange as well as its spontaneous emergence. As in the model of the previous section, we therefore ignore variations in the physical properties of commodities and assume that they are all indistinguishable.

It is in the search or time costs of exchange that Jones finds the subadditivity essential to an explanation of indirect trade. Let p_i be the probability that a trader will wish to buy or sell commodity i. There is no correlation between the commodity a trader wishes to buy and the one he wishes to sell. Thus, $p_i p_j$ represents the probability that a trader will wish to exchange i for j.

In this market with random pairwise meeting among traders, a trader wishing to exchange i for j who refuses to make any indirect exchanges must expect that the number of meetings required to make such an exchange will be

$$\frac{1}{p_i p_j}.$$

Adopting a two-stage strategy of trading i for k and then k for j, the expected number of meetings will be

$$\frac{1}{p_i p_k} + \frac{1}{p_k p_j}.$$

Therefore, if $p_k > p_i + p_j$, there is subadditivity in the time costs of exchange since

$$\frac{1}{p_i p_j} > \frac{1}{p_i p_k} + \frac{1}{p_k p_j}.$$

The logic of this argument implies that if indirect trade is advantageous, the most desirable course of action is to use a commodity n for which $p_n = \max\{p_k\}$, a commodity that is most frequently bought and sold.

Jones confined his attention to *unconditional* trading strategies in which a plan to trade i for k and then k for j is maintained even if the trader happens to meet someone willing to trade i for j directly before he meets someone willing to trade i for k. Recently, Oh (1989) has provided a revised version with more flexible and rational *conditional* trading strategies. With these strategies, Oh demonstrates that the optimal strategy for any individual is to exchange the good he has either for the good he ultimately wants or for any other with a higher probability of being traded. It follows from this observation that if $p_n > p_i$ for $i \neq n$, all the individuals not endowed with good n will use it as a generally acceptable medium of exchange; and, provided that the gains from making a chain of indirect trades is undertaken only if it promises more than some sufficiently small expected gain, most of the indirect trade is confined to the good n. Thus, a good that is commonly known to be more frequently traded becomes the essentially unique medium of indirect exchange.

4. The consequences of budget enforcement for the allocation of resources

The term "dichotomy" is used in monetary theory to indicate the separation between the real and the monetary sectors of the economy. It refers to the dichotomous manner in which relative and nominal prices are determined;

relative prices are determined in the real sector of the economy and nominal
prices are determined in the monetary sector. (See Subsection 5.1 for a
definition of the *classical dichotomy*.) The models of the transactions role of
money described so far recapitulate the dichotomy tradition.

For example, in the models of the previous section the timing element was
limited to the issue of how rapidly full execution of what was more or less a
given static equilibrium could be achieved. The role of money as a record-
keeping device or as a medium of indirect exchange was confined to demon-
strations of the minimality of the time to execute those trades subject to the
constraints of sequential bilateral exchange and the quid pro quo. We might
conclude that after demonstrating the rationale of monetary trade as an aid in
executing exchange, we are free to regard the execution problem as solved and
return to the frictionless theory of value for the determinants of real allocations.

A similar lesson can also be drawn from the contents of Section 2. Although
it was certainly necessary to introduce transactions costs in the Arrow–Debreu
theory, the role that money played encourages a dichotomous treatment of the
model. First, recognize that money functions to undo the sequence of budget
constraints that would otherwise restrict equilibrium allocations. Then point
out that once money is introduced the model can be solved by looking only at
its "real" features, which may include transactions costs.

For the remainder of this chapter instead of concentrating on the transactions role of money without any special consideration as to how this affects the
allocation of resources, we change our focus to admit some of the consequences for "real" theory of the budget enforcement problem. In Subsection
4.1 we study a simple model due to Townsend (1980) in which the enforcement
problem has at least a marginal impact unless some rather idealized government intervention is pursued. In Subsection 4.2 we analyze a stochastic variant
of the model of Subsection 4.1 due to Green (1987) in which the enforcement
problem fundamentally alters the allocation of resources.

4.1. Another version of the "Pair of Robinson Crusoes"

In our story of the two Robinson Crusoes exchanging dinners, the nature of the
exchange precluded double coincidence at any trading date. Let us consider a
related problem analyzed by Townsend (1980).

There are two *types* of individuals, type A and type B. Their endowments,
w_t^A and w_t^B, in period t alternate according to the following simple scheme:

$$w_t^A = \begin{cases} 0, & t \text{ even}, \\ 1, & t \text{ odd}; \end{cases}$$

$$w_t^B = \begin{cases} 1, & t \text{ even}, \\ 0, & t \text{ odd}. \end{cases}$$

Each type evaluates the intertemporal consumption stream $c = (c_0, c_1, \ldots, c_t, \ldots)$ according to the same utility function:

$$U(c) = \sum_{t \in T} \beta^t u(c_t),$$

where $T = \{0, 1, \ldots, t, \ldots\}$. The single period utility function $u(\cdot)$ is strictly concave, differentiable and increasing on R_+.

The gains from trade arise from the smoothing of consumptions over time compared to the "feast or famine" pattern of initial endowments. Commodities are assumed to be perishable. This smoothing is made possible by assuming that an individual of type A always meets an individual of type B in every period so that there is always an opportunity to "exchange". Suppose that an A and B, once paired, never meet again. Then the obligation to give when you have a positive endowment might be regarded as part of a social contract between each individual and the rest of society, rather than an exchange between a pair of individuals. Indeed, such a contract might be enforceable, since it would meet the necessary if not sufficient condition that there is common knowledge between any pair when one of them does not live up to the social agreement. Alternatively, such an agreement could be described in terms of the sequence economy model of Section 2 as one in which there are forward markets for the sale and delivery of future commodities: sell today while simultaneously buying forward for tomorrow. To forestall these possibilities, assume that once the individuals begin to trade they are on their own without recourse to a higher authority, or alternatively that the costs of making forward transactions are prohibitive.

With the myopic perspective of spot trading only without any enforcement mechanism, the complete absence of a double coincidence of wants at each date leads to the conclusion that there will be no trading. Into this impasse, Townsend introduces a transferable asset, without any utility of its own, called "money" to encourage exchange. Is it serving the same role as the money described in the previous models of exchange? Certainly, it helps to facilitate transactions; but, more specifically, it does this through the familiar device of undoing the inhibitions on trade caused by the sequence-of-budget-constraints problem.

In several respects this model can be regarded as a special case of the more general sequence economy of Section 2. However, it does go beyond the finite end-point assumption of the sequence economy model (and the bilateral exchange models of Section 3) by introducing an infinitely receding time horizon. Following Townsend, we examine the implications for the allocation of resources of this elementary model with a money budget constraint.

With money, the budget constraint in each period becomes:

$$m_{t+1} = p_t(w_t - c_t) + m_t \geq 0, \quad t \in T,$$

where m_{t+1} is the money carried over from period t and p_t is the price of the commodity at date t in terms of money. In addition, of course, $m_0 \geq 0$.

The fact that an individual's money balances must always be non-negative means that the value of his current excess demands $\max\{p_t(c_t - w_t), 0\}$ cannot exceed his money balances at the start of the period m_t. With a single commodity, current purchases will be positive only when sales are zero, so the money budget constraint is effectively a cash-in-advance constraint, i.e. $p_t(w_t - c_t) < 0$ implies $w_t = 0$, and therefore since $m_{t+1} \geq 0$ we must have:

$$m_t \geq p_t c_t .$$

Maximizing the intertemporal utility function U given above subject to the money budget constraints yields the following first-order conditions for a maximum:

$$-\beta^{t-1} \frac{u'(c_{t-1})}{p_{t-1}} + \beta^t \frac{u'(c^t)}{p_t} + \theta_t = 0 ,$$

where θ_t is the Lagrange multiplier associated with the tth budget constraint.

To interpret this condition, if an extra dollar is transferred from consumption on c_{t-1} to c_t the individual will have to give up c_{t-1}/p_{t-1} units of consumption at $t-1$ to obtain c_t/p_t units of consumption at t, which at the margin leads to a loss of utility of

$$\beta^{t-1} \frac{u'(c_{t-1})}{p_{t-1}}$$

compared to the gain of

$$\beta^t \frac{u'(c_t)}{p_t} .$$

If $\theta_t = 0$, the loss balances the gain and

$$\frac{u'(c_{t-1})}{\beta u'(c_t)} = \frac{p_{t-1}}{p_t} .$$

This is the condition that would prevail in an intertemporal optimization problem with the single intertemporal budget constraint of the form:

$$(*) \qquad \sum_{t \in T} p_t(w_t - c_t) = 0 .$$

It is also the necessary condition for a Pareto-optimal allocation in this economy where an individual of type A always meets an individual of type B. However, as long as $\theta_t > 0$, the first-order conditions from the single budget constraint problem and the Pareto-efficient allocation are necessarily violated.

Because θ_t is the Lagrange multiplier for the tth constraint, we have:

$$\theta_t \cdot m_t = 0 ,$$

i.e. the tth constraint is only binding when $m_t = 0$. Is there a monetary equilibrium in which the money budget constraint is never binding, i.e. a monetary equilibrium in which money is a veil allowing the frictionless Pareto-efficient barter allocation to be realized?

This question is similar to that of the optimal quantity of money treated elsewhere in this Handbook. It is readily concluded that for efficiency, prices must be decreasing over time at the rate $1 - \beta$ and Townsend shows that if the monetary budget constraint is to be non-binding this will require at least one of the individuals to be accumulating money balances over time in contradiction to the maximizing hypothesis of equilibrium. With lump-sum taxes on money balances, it is possible to construct a monetary equilibrium with effectively non-binding budget constraints through a government engineered deflation. However, such an equilibrium requires specific information about which individual to tax in each period and therefore violates the anonymity that would presumably underlie a decentralized description of equilibrium. Townsend also shows that there do exist monetary equilibria without any lump-sum taxes. They are Pareto superior to autarchy but not Pareto optimal.

4.2. Record-keeping in the chicken–egg economy

From the model of the previous subsection we could conclude that despite the absence of forward markets, the introduction of money could, under certain government policies, be a "veil" for the frictionless barter economy in the sense that the budget enforcement problem could be resolved without any loss in efficiency. Here we describe a model in which money, or any other mechanism for coping with the budget enforcement problem, is never a veil.

Amend the description of the sequence of endowments in the model of

Subsection 4.1 so that in each period an individual has a 50–50 chance of having an endowment of 0 to 1. (In the parable of Subsection 1.3, the endowment refers to whether or not one's chicken laid an egg.) Let $c = (c_1, \ldots, c_t, \ldots)$ be a consumption sequence, where $c_t \in R$ is modified to include the possibility of negative consumption! (This is to eliminate the complications that would follow from boundary conditions on consumption.)

Without the benefit of trade the utility of an individual's initial endowment, the random sequence ω, is:

$$EU(\omega) = \sum_{t=0}^{t=\infty} \frac{\beta^t[u(0) + u(1)]}{2} = \frac{[u(0) + u(1)]}{2(1 - \beta)} .$$

In this model the gains from trade are due entirely to risk-pooling. With a large number of individuals, literally a continuum, the per capita endowment would be 1/2 with probability one. This would permit each individual to exchange his random variable ω for the perfectly certain consumption stream $c^* = (1/2, 1/2, 1/2, \ldots)$. Assuming as we shall that $u: R \rightarrow R$ is concave (to reflect risk aversion) and increasing, then

$$EU(\omega) < EU(c^*) = \sum_{t \in T} \beta^t u(1/2) = \frac{u(1/2)}{(1 - \beta)} .$$

It is evident that if each individual were to receive the consumption stream c^*, this would be a Pareto-efficient allocation for the economy as a whole. [Of course, this would not be the only Pareto-efficient allocation. Let the set of individuals be I and λ a population measure on I with $\lambda(I) = 1$. Then any allocation $c(i) = (\alpha(i), \alpha(i), \alpha(i), \ldots)$ in which each individual receives a constant stream of consumption and

$$\int \alpha(i) \, d\lambda(i) = 1/2$$

would also be Pareto efficient.]

The stream c^* can be singled out as the symmetric or equal treatment allocation for the individuals who are in fact ex ante identical. It is the obvious candidate for equilibrium among the Pareto-efficient allocations. If information about the realizations of individual endowments were public, then c^* could be achieved as a competitive equilibrium through the use of forward/contingent contracts [Arrow (1964) and Debreu (1959)].

To describe this equilibrium, let $s^t = (s_0, s_1, \ldots, s_t) \in \{0, 1\}^{t+1}$ be a realization of an individual's random endowment – called an event – up to and including date t. Thus, $\omega_t(s^t) = s_t$ is the individual's endowment at t in the event s^t. For each event s^t there is an event-contingent price $p_t(s^t)$ for commodities.

(A full description of an event should include the realization of endowments for all individuals, but that can conveniently be ignored here.)

Once commodities and prices are refined to be event contingent, we can construct the all-important budget constraint as:

$$(**) \qquad \sum_{t \in T} \sum_{s^t \in \{0,1\}^{t+1}} p_t(s^t)[c_t(s^t) - \omega_t(s^t)] = 0 \,,$$

where $c_t(s^t)$ is the consumption choice at t contingent on s^t and $z_t(s^t)$ is the net trade at s^t. The budget constraint $(**)$ is the state-contingent analog of $(*)$ in Subsection 4.1. Of course, this does not imply *for any particular realization of the individual's endowment* that realized purchases will equal realized sales.

It readily follows that setting $p_t(s^t) = \beta^t$, $t \in T$, the expected value of the individual's lifetime endowment is $[2(1 - \beta)]^{-1}$. If the individual were to set $c_t(s^t) = 1/2$, all s^t and all $t \in T$, then $(**)$ would be satisfied. At these prices, such a trading plan would maximize expected utility $EU(c)$ subject to the budget constraint and, with a continuum of individuals, markets would clear with probability 1.

The analysis is rather different when information about the realization of an individual's endowment is private. Radner (1968) was one of the first to call attention to the difficulties for contingent commodity analysis when information about events is not common knowledge. With different information among individuals about an event, it would be difficult to write enforceable event-contingent contracts. The equilibrium trading arrangement under common information *could* be carried out under private information. Each time an individual's chicken does not lay, the individual could request 1/2 an egg and each time it does, the individual could offer 1/2 an egg. But without an omniscient enforcement mechanism, narrow self-interest would argue the outcome would be otherwise. (Recall the similar problem in the model of bilateral exchange in Subsection 3.1.)

Radner's solution was to limit event-contingent exchanges to those that were common knowledge. If we followed this prescription while assuming that information was private, i.e. each individual was the only one who knew whether his chicken had laid an egg, there would be no trade since no event would be common to more than one individual. Since Radner's work, there has been considerable progress in the analysis of moral hazard problems and in the literature on incentives as a whole. Green (1987) has made a contribution to this field, and one particularly relevant for monetary theory, by posing and then answering the question: What is an efficient incentive-compatible trading arrangement for this economy?

With private information it is evident that incentive compatibility will preclude the achievement of a trading arrangement yielding expected utility $EU(c^*)$. In the equilibrium trading plan $z^* = (z_t^*(s^t))$, net trades at t are independent of the history of the event before t, i.e.

$$z_t^*(s_0, s_1, \ldots, s_{t-1}, s_t) = z_t^*(s_0', s_1', \ldots, s_{t-1}', s_t) \, .$$

Indeed, this is the key to providing complete risk-pooling. However, any incentive-compatible trading arrangement with private information must necessarily be *dependent* on the realization of one's endowment. Since any such dependency is incompatible with full efficiency, *the conditions for incentive compatibility and full efficiency are therefore disjoint* [see Taub (1988)].

   This conclusion goes beyond the model of Subsection 4.1 where it was shown that with certain policies there was an optimum quantity of money that would overcome the obstacles posed by the sequence of money budget constraints so that the economy could reach an allocation which overcame the budget enforcement problem. Here the first-best allocations under common information about events are simply unachievable as an equilibrium under any trading arrangement when there is private information. We do not point to this as an instance of "market failure" in the sense that there are potentially corrective actions by the government that would lead to a fully efficient allocation. Rather, we see this as an illustration of one of the essential differences between frictionless barter model and a more decentralized environment in which the record-keeping function of a trading arrangement has an essential role to play: in a decentralized economy the record-keeping function of money imposes a binding constraint on trade.

   With private information, how would trade take place? Green (1987) provides an idealized description. Imagine competition among "banks" to operate a trading arrangement for the economy. The winner will be the bank offering the best arrangement in the sense of providing the highest expected utility to individuals subject to the condition that the bank does not lose money, a condition necessarily including a proviso that the arrangement be incentive compatible.

   The arrangement, or contract, is a sequence of functions:

$$z_t : \{0, 1\}^{t+1} \to R \, , \quad t = 0, 1, 2, \ldots \, .$$

The quantity $z_t(s^t)$ gives the net purchase at t to which an individual whose endowment history is s^t is entitled. (If $z_t < 0$, the individual is called upon to supply that many units of the commodity.) These functions must be chosen to encourage individuals always to tell the truth.

   Let $r^t : \{0, 1\}^{t+1} \to \{0, 1\}^{t+1}$, $t \in T$, be a sequence of functions describing the reported endowment histories for an individual as a function of the actual endowment histories, or events. The fact that all endowment histories are private information means that the bank must rely on reports rather than events.

The consequence for an individual who adopts $r = \{r'\}$ when the bank offers the contract $z = \{z_t(r')\}$ is the expected utility

$$EU(z \mid r) = \sum_{t \in T} \beta^t E_{s^t}[u(\omega_t(s^t) + z_t(r^t(s^t)))] .$$

For the contract z to be incentive compatible, it must encourage individuals always to report the events, i.e. for all reporting strategies r'_0

$$EU(z \mid s) \geq EU(z \mid r) .$$

The arrangement must also be feasible for the economy as a whole. Here Green takes a certain liberty by allowing the bank itself to face a single budget constraint over time rather than a sequence of constraints, one at each date. The bank can take β units of consumption at t and transform it into one unit of consumption at $t + 1$, and vice versa. The conjunction of the feasibility and incentive-compatibility conditions define the optimal contract $z = (z_t(s'))$.

To emphasize the distinctions between the trading arrangement z^* with public information and forward/contingent contracts and the optimal incentive contract z when information is private, it is useful to recall the framework of Section 2. There we focused on the modifications in modern general equilibrium theory that would prevent individuals from carrying out all their trading plans at the initial date so that markets would reopen over time. Clearly, z^* is a trading arrangement in which markets will not reopen. Of course, trade occurs throughout $t \in T$, but these trades represent the execution of clauses of the grand contract made at the initial date.

A cause for markets reopening was the hypothesis that forward trading was more costly than spot. In the chicken–egg model the assumption of private information establishes this hypothesis by making the kind of forward trading described by z^* "impossible", or at least not strategically viable.

Sequential trading brings with it a new problem: it is necessary to keep track of each individual's trading history to enforce budget constraints. In the model of Section 2 this could be done in a rather simple way. Because it was common knowledge that the time horizon was fixed and finite, it sufficed to impose a single lifetime constraint that the sum of the values of all net trades must equal zero by the end of the trading horizon. Such a constraint is not possible in the chicken–egg model. [Furthermore, in a finite horizon version of the model, where it would be possible, it is not desirable; see Townsend (1982).]

The budget constraint underlying the optimal contract z must persuade each individual at each date that no matter what his previous history, the rewards from truthful reporting outweigh those from misrepresentation. This is achieved by keeping track of the individual's previous net contributions and allowing the individual to consume an annuitized amount based on this quantity. Green exhibits the similarities between the consumption function underlying the contract z and the permanent income hypothesis of Friedman (1957). Foley and Hellwig (1975) also draw this parallel in their study of the behavior of a single individual facing a similar problem.

Taking the chicken–egg model as representative of the budget enforcement problems with sequential trading, there is a clear-cut difference between such models and ones for which there is a single lifetime constraint. To help clarify the difference, let us distinguish between *prospective* wealth and *transactions* or *recorded* wealth. Prospective wealth is the expected discounted value of one's future endowment stream evaluated according to expected prices. Transactions wealth is the cumulated value of one's previous net trades.

In the forward/contingent contracts version of the chicken–egg model with a single lifetime budget constraint, transactions wealth is *not* a determinant of the optimal contract, z^*. However, in the private information version in which the enforcement problem is necessarily an integral feature of the trading arrangement, transactions wealth *is* a determinant of the optimal z. Indeed, one way to highlight the transactions role of money in comparison to the emphasis on its store of value function in the Walras–Hicks–Patinkin tradition is to call attention to the relative weights assigned to transactions and prospective wealth as determinants of behavior. In the Walras–Hicks–Patinkin tradition, the weight assigned to transactions wealth is nil.

5. The cash-in-advance constraint

Among recent approaches in monetary theory, the cash-in-advance model has been virtually the only one to focus on the transactions role of money. In this section we discuss two general equilibrium extensions of the cash-in-advance idea due to Grandmont and Younes (1972) and Lucas (1980) and applications of this model of the transactions role of money to changes in the money supply.

Compared to the complete symmetry with which all commodities enter the budget constraint in standard theory, the cash-in-advance condition singles out the money commodity by stipulating that sales of it *and no other commodity* can be used to finance current purchases. The background conditions underlying this restriction are that the timing of purchases and sales do not coincide and money obtained from current sales is not available until the next "period". On the face of it, the constraint would seem to be a rough approximation to a money economy without credit markets. However, once credit markets are introduced one could simply borrow money against current sales, for example through the use of credit cards, to relax the budget constraint to the point where it was, except for a small interest charge, of the usual form in which current sales of *all* commodities can be used to finance current purchases. In other words, with credit markets the standard form of the budget constraint would rather closely approximate the description of the choice set for an individual in a money economy.

Kohn, a forceful advocate of the cash-in-advance constraint [Kohn (1984)], has addressed this criticism in Kohn (1981). Acknowledging its validity as applied to the individual, he points out the fallacy of composition when applied to the economy as a whole. Since borrowing and lending net to zero, the money borrowed by one person to evade the cash constraint represents a corresponding tightening of the constraint for the lender. As a description of the exchange opportunities of the representative trader, the cash-in-advance constraint is applicable to an economy with credit markets. Similarly, objections to the highly stylized timing of payments in the model are also shown by Kohn to survive modifications. Modifications in the payments arrangement, however, cannot, and should not, be too drastic. There does have to be a limit of the speed of transactions. "If a model is to express money's role as medium of exchange, it cannot allow expenditure to be financed by contemporaneous income" [Kohn (1981, p. 192)].

5.1. Existence and quantity-theoretic properties of equilibrium

Grandmont and Younes (1972) responded to Hahn's critique of Patinkin using the suggestion proposed by Clower (see Subsection 1.2). Individuals have the lifetime intertemporal utility functions for the consumption stream $c = (c_0, c_1, \ldots, c_t, \ldots)$ used in Subsections 4.1 and 4.2. Each individual receives an endowment of perishable commodities w in each period so that an individual's lifetime endowment is

$$\omega = (w, w, \ldots) .$$

There are no forward markets but individuals do have expectations at each t about all prices $(p_{t+1}, p_{t+2}, \ldots)$ in the future which depend on prices at t and prices in the previous k periods. An individual's price expectations at t are given by the single-valued mapping $\psi(p_t, \ldots, p_{t-k}) = (p_{t+1}, p_{t+2}, \ldots)$. Price expectations are stationary in the sense that ψ does not depend explicitly on t. In addition, if prices have been constant in the past, it is assumed that they are expected to be constant in the future, $\psi(p, \ldots, p) = (p, p, \ldots)$.

The central feature of the model is the budget constraint. Letting c_t and m_{t+1} be the final allocations of goods and money while w and m_t are the initial allocations of goods and money at the start of period t, we have the accounting identity,

$$m_{t+1} = m_t + p_t \cdot (c_t - w) ,$$

as well as the modified cash-in-advance constraint,

$$p_t[c_t - w]^+ \leq m_t + kp_t \cdot [c_t - w]^- ,$$

where $k \in [0, 1]$ measures the "viscosity" of the payments arrangement. At one extreme is Clower's description of the cash-in-advance constraint where $k = 0$, and at the other is the traditional budget constraint where $k = 1$. In between, some but not all of current sales may be used to finance current purchases.

Standard quantity-theoretic propositions familiar from the Walras–Hicks–Patinkin tradition also apply here. For example, let $x_t = (c_t, m_t) = \xi(p, \ldots, p, m_{t-1})$ be the utility-maximizing demands of an individual when money balances available for purchases at t are m_{t-1} and prices at t and for the previous k periods have been equal to p. A *stationary state* satisfies the additional condition $m_t = m_{t-1}$, denoted by $x = (c, m) = \xi^*(p)$. Then $(c, \alpha m) = \xi^*(\alpha p)$, all $\alpha > 0$. Thus a doubling of prices and money balances leaves equilibrium real quantities c unchanged in long-run stationary equilibrium.

On the existence of a specifically monetary equilibrium where the individuals wish to hold the stock of money on hand, the authors show that there will exist such a stationary long-run equilibrium provided that at the equilibrium prices there is some trade, that $k < 1$, and that traders do not discount the future too much (β is not too small). The first two qualifications are precisely those necessary to give money a transactions function to perform. The third is required to give individuals sufficient concern for the future so that they care about making further trades.

The *classical dichotomy* between the monetary and the real sectors of the economy asserts that one can in effect solve for the equilibrium in a monetary economy first by finding equilibrium relative prices in the "barter" version of the model and then determining nominal prices by appealing to the quantity of money. The barter version of the model is, of course, the frictionless ideal. In such a scenario money is clearly an inessential veil covering the real allocation. The classical dichotomy is closely related to the optimal money supply mentioned in Subsection 4.1 and elsewhere in this Handbook.

When money is *not* needed for transactions, i.e. $k = 1$, the stationary long-run equilibrium is certainly Pareto optimal, and when $k < 1$, the stationary long-run equilibrium will typically be Pareto inferior, i.e. Pareto inferior to some other reallocation of resources that obeys only the overall aggregate constraints on resources but not necessarily any monetary exchange constraints. These remarks suffice to show that the classical dichotomy is not valid in the cash-in-advance model when money has a transactions role; or, the transactions role of money imposes a binding constraint on the allocation of resources compared to the frictionless barter ideal. (Compare Section 4 above.) However, if individuals discount the future very little, their willingness to hold money to finance future purchases increases and in the limit as the discount becomes nil (β approaches unity) Grandmont and Younes show that the stationary long-run equilibria of the model converges to an optimal barter allocation. In this limiting case the classical dichotomy does hold. [See Grandmont and Younes (1973) for other means to achieve this same conclusion.]

5.2. A cash-in-advance version of the chicken–egg model

In Subsection 4.2 we presented Green's version of the chicken–egg model, the primary purpose of which was to emphasize the similarity between the budget enforcement problems leading to monetary exchange and the necessary properties of incentive-compatible intertemporal trade when there is private information. In this subsection we describe Lucas's (1980) version of the chicken–egg model. The evident similarities to be brought out between the two should make the Lucas version with its institutionally imposed cash-in-advance constraint appear to be less arbitrary than it might otherwise seem.

Suppose, instead of random variations in endowments, each person's chicken always lays one egg each day but a person's current tastes for eggs are random. For example, on any day t one could have, with equal probability, a relatively strong desire ($s_t = 1$) or weak desire ($s_t = 0$) for eggs and these random variations are independent and identically distributed throughout $t \in T$. Letting $c = (c_1, c_2, \ldots, c_t, \ldots)$ be a sequence of quantities of eggs consumed in each period, where c_t may depend on the realization of $s^t = (s_0, \ldots, s_t)$, the expected discounted utility of c is given by

$$EU(c) = \sum_{t \in T} \beta^t E[u_{s_t}(c_t(s^t), s_t)] \, .$$

Assuming that random variations in tastes are common knowledge, we could create forward/contingent markets. With a continuum of individuals, the equilibrium trading arrangement might be as follows: when $s_t = 1$ set $c_t = 3/2$ and when $s_t = 0$ set $c_t = 1/2$. In comparison to the previous version of the chicken–egg model when the gains from trade came from the smoothing of consumption over time, here the gains come from being able to vary consumption with random changes in one's tastes. Note, however, that in terms of net trades, Green's version of the idea forward/contingent contracts model and Lucas's would be identical.

Lucas did not ask what the optimal incentive compatible intertemporal contract is. Instead, he proposed an institutional arrangement for trade that clearly is incentive compatible. Recall the distinction between prospective wealth and transactions wealth made in Subsection 4.2. Lucas's trading arrangement resolves the enforcement problem by adopting a budget constraint that effectively eliminates prospective wealth in favor of a constraint based entirely on transactions wealth.

Starting with a given non-negative amount of money, the individual is proscribed in his purchases precisely by a cash-in-advance constraint. The difference between one's money balances at date t and date $t + k$ represents the sum of the values of net trades between those two dates, or the change in the individual's transactions wealth. Of course, an individual is permitted to be a reckless spender if he has the money balances; however, since money holdings are non-negative and current purchases are constrained by current money holdings, the future costs of current spending can be perceived today.

Suppose initial money balances at t to be m_t and prices to be always unity. An individual receiving an endowment of one unit of a perishable commodity each period who has received the taste shock s_t will divide his transactions wealth and current income, m_t and 1, respectively, into current consumption c_t and money with which to start the next period m_{t+1} so as to solve the following:

$$V(m_t, s_t) = \max_{c_t, m_{t+1} \geq 0} \left\{ u(c_t, s_t) + \beta \int V(m_{t+1}, s_{t+1}) \, dF(s_{t+1}) \right\}$$

subject to

$$m_{t+1} = m_t + 1 - c_t$$

and the cash-in-advance constraint

$$c_t \leq m_t .$$

Here V is the value function for the intertemporal maximization problem and F is the cumulative distribution function on the taste shock in each period. Since the optimal solution does not depend explicitly on t, we may describe the optimal choices by the policy functions $c_t = c(m_t, s_t)$ and $m_t = m(m_t, s_t)$.

The main contribution of Lucas's paper is the demonstration of a stationary stochastic equilibrium, i.e. a distribution of the population based on their money balances that is invariant from period to period. This equilibrium parallels the optimal contract in Green. Superficially, the "mechanism" associated with this equilibrium seems to be decentralized, whereas Green's mechanism does not. The latter specifies current consumption for the individual for every sequence of reported endowment histories, whereas the former allows the individual to make his own decisions as a function of his current money balances and taste shock. However, once the maximizing operation is performed, the Lucas equilibrium becomes a mechanism in which current consumption is a function of the history of past taste shocks (including the current one).

The recursive structure of c_t and m_t, above, imply that $c_t = m(m_t, s_t)$ can be written as $F_t(s_0, s_1, \ldots, s_t; m_0)$. Thus, a mechanism description of a net trade in the Lucus scheme is $z'_t(s_0, s_1, \ldots, s_t; m_0) = F_t - 1$. The difference between the two mechanisms is not so much decentralization as it is decentralization via prices. Lucas's scheme z' may not have the optimality properties of Green's optimal enforcement mechanism z, but it does represent an enforcement mechanism permitting decentralized decision-making through prices.

5.3. Responses to changes in the money supply

Consider the model of Subsection 5.1 in stationary long-run equilibrium. Suppose there is a one-time change in the money supply. With expectations function ξ arbitrarily given, it is difficult to say what the short-run response to this change will be. However, if expectations are "rational" and distributional effects can be ignored, there is an obvious prediction: the change in the money supply will not only have no long-run real consequences, it will also have no short-run consequences as well. For example, if the money supply doubles, and everyone now holds double their previous amounts of money, and the expectation is that current and future prices will double, there is an equilibrium in which the real allocation remains unchanged. The work discussed below aims to show that modifications in the cash-in-advance model do lead to short-run real consequences despite the imposition of correct expectations.

Distributional effects would cause a monetary injection to disturb prices in the short-run unless the injection were neutralized by distributing it on a pro-rata basis. Grossman and Weiss (1983) and Rotemberg (1984) move away from the "helicopter drops" method in exploring the short-run consequences of the distributional impacts of monetary injections. The monetary payments scheme itself is the source of the distributional impacts. They hypothesize a staggered payments scheme in which individuals hold money balances to make purchases for two periods at a time, rather than one. Inventory arguments of the Baumol–Tobin type are invoked to rationalize the advantages of making withdrawals only every other period. Also, to create a circular flow of money among households, half the population withdraws money for purchases at each date.

Grossman and Weiss analyze the consequences of an open-market purchase of bonds for money, say at date 1. That half of the population away from the bank at date 1, call them the B's, receives none of the extra money. The increase in money balances will have to be held by the half of the population that is at the bank, the A's. For the A's to hold the whole of the increased supply, their share of nominal spending must rise, e.g. if in a steady state A's share of spending was one-half, it will have to be greater than one-half in the first period after the open-market operation. But this will occur only if nominal and real interest rates decline. In a particular representation of this idea in a model with fixed output, they show that open market operations also lead to delayed price increases. In the long run the distribution effects work themselves out, but in the meantime there are systematic disturbances.

Rotemberg also developed a similar staggered system of money withdrawals with variable capital and output possibilities. Analyzing the effects of a one-time purchase of capital for money by the government, the distributional consequences of the monetary scheme leads not only to price increases but also to short-run increases in capital and output before returning to the steady-state equilibrium.

6. Concluding remarks

The transactions role of money is one of the most palpable of economic phenomena and would therefore seem to offer one of the first challenges for the theory of exchange. We know, of course, that the theory of exchange developed as a response to other challenges, notably as a theory of relative price determination and allocation of resources, topics for which it was appropriate to abstract from the frictions required to make room for money. In addition, the frictions required for monetary exchange, such as differential costs of spot and forward transactions and the strategic issues of incomplete information and incentive compatibility, are recent developments. This may explain the slow growth of the transactions role of money as a branch of the theory of exchange.

By now, however, the branch has clearly emerged and judged by the quantity of recent research it is undergoing a growth spurt. In this survey we have attempted to describe *some* of the contributions that have made it more visible. In this section, we provide a synopsis of key points.

The transactions role of money challenges the implicit logistical and informational assumptions of the theory of exchange. To begin, it is vital that trade be sequential, which involves more than the time-indexing of commodities. There are various sources of "sequentiality". One is the costs of making forward contracts in an otherwise highly organized market setting, which creates a need for markets to reopen over time. Another is the simple fact that in most instances individuals trade with each other one at a time.

The sequential nature of trade makes informational demands that go beyond the knowledge of prices that suffices in the traditional theory of exchange.

These informational elements underlie the disadvantages of barter. Most importantly, private information about one's own situation – present in un-organized as well as organized markets – introduces strategic problems of budget enforcement. There are many ways to cope with this problem. Whether through the comparatively primitive use of commodity money or the more sophisticated electronic funds transfer, money is a device to record and make public one's trading history.

A useful analogy can be made between the role of money as a record-keeping device and the theory of signalling [Spence (1974)]. Both originate from moral hazard. In signalling, divided knowledge makes it difficult to identify differences in economically relevant characteristics such as worker productivity. Compared to education which may be an observable proxy for productivity, money is quite a noisy signal. It says nothing about the personal characteristics of the bearer or the previous transactions that caused the individual to have these "credits". And, of course, it is this property of money th?t it only signals the lowest common denominator of personal characteristics that makes it a transferable signalling device.

Is the transactions role of money important? One way of measuring its importance is by the consequences of the budget enforcement problem for the allocation of resources. The natural yardstick for measurement is the departure from the no-enforcement-problem Walrasian ideal. A model in which the budget enforcement problem can be completely resolved through the (costless!) introduction of money so as to duplicate the allocation of resources in frictionless barter world can be regarded as a modern interpretation of the classical dichotomy. In such an economy, money, once present, is of no further consequence. The models of Section 2 and Subsection 3.2 fit this description.

While it seems reasonable and even desirable to examine the rationale behind the transactions role of money in a model exhibiting this dichotomy, if that were all there was, this would place a rather definite upper bound on the importance of the transactions role. Such models would serve as solutions to the intellectual puzzle: "Why money?" But there is no reason to believe that this dichotomy is valid, either in theory or in practice. Budget enforcement problems do have real consequences as the models of Sections 4 and 5 illustrate. There is even reason to believe that exploring the properties of models in which budget enforcement problems are always a binding constraint on behavior may illuminate our understanding of macroeconomics.

7. Bibliographic note

Section 2: Classical economists recognized money's role as an intertemporal asset. Formalization of the model with a sequence of budget constraints is, however, relatively recent. The fully explicit non-monetary general equilibrium model developed by Arrow and Debreu is fully expounded in Debreu (1959). The fully detailed sequence economy model with transaction costs, Hahn (1971), was presented as the Walras–Bowley lecture at the North American meeting of the Econometric Society in New York, 1969.

An antecedent of this model, without explicit monetary structure, was Radner (1972). Foley (1970) developed independently the transaction cost structure without the temporal sequence of markets. Work on efficiency includes Hahn (1973) and, most importantly, Starrett (1973), where the role of money and examples of inefficient equilibrium allocation in its absence are developed. Additional work on existence of equilibrium is due to Kurz (1974a, 1974b) and Heller (1974) and, in the case of non-convex transaction costs, to Heller and Starr (1976). The importance of the sequential structure of budgets is noted in exposition in Hahn (1982) and Gale (1982).

Alternative models emphasizing the reopening of markets include the over-lapping generations model (treated elsewhere in this Handbook) and the temporary equilibrium model. The latter is discussed in Hicks (1939) and Arrow and Hahn (1971). The role of money as a portfolio asset there is due to Grandmont (1974), and Grandmont and Younes (1972, 1973); the field is surveyed in Grandmont (1977). Also notable in this regard are Bewley (1980, 1983), and Foley and Hellwig (1975).

Section 3: The classical economists, Smith (1775), Jevons (1893), and Menger (1892), clearly recognized the coordination problem in pairwise trade and money's function in alleviating it. Modern formal studies along this line include Niehans (1969, 1971), Ostroy (1973), Ostroy and Starr (1974), Starr (1972, 1976, 1986), Sontheimer (1970), Veendorp (1970), Eckalbar (1984, 1986), Norman (1987), Madden (1975, 1976), Graham, Jennergen, Peterson and Weintraub (1976), Feldman (1973), and Goldman and Starr (1982). Shubik (1973) is explicit that money facilitates coordination of separate, but necessarily interdependent, trading decisions.

Further contributions to the "Menger problem" are found in Kiyotaki and Wright (1989) and Iwai (1988). See O'Driscoll (1986) for the history.

King and Plosser (1986) develop a model of the informational advantages of money based on their physical properties. Modern antecedents of this tradition are Brunner and Meltzer (1971) and Alchian (1977).

Section 4: Gale (1980, 1982) and Townsend (1983, 1987) are two con-tributors who have emphasized the incentive issues underlying monetary exchange.

Section 5: An incomplete list of other work on the cash-in-advance approach is: Clower and Howitt (1978), Fried (1973), Jovanic (1982), Lucas and Stokey (1987), Stockman (1981), and Svensson (1985). Lucas (1988) contains a further study of the short-run consequences of changes in the money supply. Akerlof (1979, 1982) and Akerlof and Milbourne (1980) also study the short-run consequences of money shocks, but through an inventory policy framework rather than a cash-in-advance model. Scheinkman and Weiss (1986) exhibit the consequences for cyclical behavior when borrowing constraints are binding.

References

Akerlof, G.A. (1979) 'Irving Fisher on his head: The consequence of constant threshold-target monitoring of money holdings', *Quarterly Journal of Economics*, 93: 169–187.

Akerlof, G.A. (1982) 'The short-run demand for money: A new look at an old problem', *American Economic Review*, 72: 35–39.

Akerlof, G.A. and R.D. Milbourne (1980) 'Irving Fisher on his head II: The consequence of the timing of payments for the demand for money', *Quarterly Journal of Economics*, 94: 145–157.

Alchian, A. (1977) 'Why money?', *Journal of Money, Credit and Banking*, 9: 131–140.

Arrow, K.J. (1964) 'The role of securities in the optimal allocation of risk-bearing', *Review of Economic Studies*, 31: 91–96.

Arrow, K.J. and F.H. Hahn (1971) *General competitive analysis*. San Francisco: Holden-Day.

Baumol, W.J. (1952) 'The transactions demand for cash: An inventory theoretic approach', *Quarterly Journal of Economics* 66: 545–556.

Benveniste, L.J. (1987) 'Incomplete market participation and the optimal exchange of credit', in: E.C. Prescott and N. Wallace, eds., *Contractual arrangements for intertemporal trade*. Minneapolis: University of Minnesota Press.

Bewley, T. (1980) 'The optimum quantity of money', in: J.H. Kareken and N. Wallace, eds., *Models of monetary economies*. Minneapolis: Federal Reserve Bank of Minneapolis.

Bewley, T. (1983) 'A difficulty with the optimum quantity of money', *Econometrica*, 51: 1485–1504.

Brunner, K. and A. Meltzer (1971) 'The use of money: Money in the theory of an exchange economy', *American Economic Review*, 61: 784–805.

Clower, R.W. (1967) 'A reconsideration of the microfoundations of monetary theory', *Western Economic Journal*, 6: 1–8.

Clower, R. and P. Howitt (1978) 'The transactions theory of the demand for money: A reconsideration', *Journal of Political Economy*, 86: 449–466.

Debreu, G. (1959) *Theory of value*. New York: Wiley.

Eckalbar, J.C. (1984) 'Money, barter, and convergence to the competitive allocation: Menger's problem', *Journal of Economic Theory*, 32: 201–211.

Eckalbar, J.C. (1986) 'Bilateral trade in a monetized pure exchange economy', *Economic Modelling*, 3: 135–139.

Feenstra, R.C. (1986) 'Functional equivalence between liquidity costs and the utility of money', *Journal of Monetary Economics*, 17: 271–291.

Feldman, A.M. (1973) 'Bilateral trading processes, pairwise optimality and Pareto optimality', *Review of Economic Studies*, 40(4): 463–474.

Foley, D.J. (1970) 'Equilibrium with costly marketing', *Journal of Economic Theory*, 2: 276–291.

Foley, D.K. and M. Hellwig (1975) 'Asset management with trading uncertainty', *Review of Economic Studies*, 42: 327–346.

Fried, J. (1973) 'Money, exchange and growth', *Western Economic Journal*, 11: 285–301.

Friedman, M. (1957) *A theory of the consumption function*. New York: National Bureau of Economic Research.

Gale, D. (1978) 'The core of a monetary economy without trust', *Journal of Economic Theory*, 18: 456–491.

Gale, D. (1980) 'Money, information and equilibrium in large economies', *Journal of Economic Theory*, 23: 28–65.

Gale, D. (1982) *Money: In equilibrium*. New York: Cambridge University Press.

Goldman, S.M. and R.M. Starr (1982) 'Pairwise, *t*-wise, and Pareto optimalities', *Econometrica*, 50: 593–606.

Graham, D.A., L.P. Jennergen, D.W. Peterson and E.R. Weintraub (1976) 'Trader–commodity parity theorems', *Journal of Economic Theory*, 12: 443–454.

Grandmont, J.M. (1974) 'On the short run equilibrium in a monetary economy', in: J.H. Dreze, ed., *Allocation under certainty: Equilibrium and optimality*. U.K.: Macmillan; New York: Halsted Press–John Wiley & Sons, 213–228.

Grandmont, J.M. (1977) 'Temporary general equilibrium theory', *Econometrica*, 45: 535–572.

Grandmont, J.M. and Y. Younes (1972) 'On the role of the money and the existence of a monetary equilibrium', *Review of Economic Studies*, 39: 355–372.

Grandmont, J.M. and Y. Younes (1973) 'On the efficiency of a monetary equilibrium', *Review of Economic Studies*, 40: 149–165.

Green, E. (1987) 'Lending and the smoothing of uninsurable income', in E.C. Prescott and N. Wallace, eds., *Contractual arangements for intertemporal trade*. Minneapolis: University of Minnesota Press.

Grossman, S. and L. Weiss (1983) 'A transactions-based model of the monetary transmission mechanism', *American Economic Review*, 73: 871–880.

Hahn, F.H. (1965) 'On some problems of proving the existence of an equilibrium in a monetary economy', in: F.H. Hahn and F.P.R. Brechling, eds., *The Theory of Interest Rates*. London: Macmillan, 126–135.

Hahn, F.H. (1971) 'Equilibrium with transaction costs', *Econometrica*, 39: 417–439.

Hahn, F.H. (1973) 'On transaction costs, inessential sequence economies and money', *Review of Economic Studies*, 40: 449–461.

Harris, M. (1979) 'Expectations and money in a dynamic exchange model', *Econometrica*, 47: 1403–1419.

Heller, W.P. (1974) 'The holding of money balances in general equilibrium', *Journal of Economic Theory*, 7: 93–108.

Heller, W.P. and R.M. Starr (1976) 'Equilibrium with non-convex transactions costs: Monetary and non-monetary economies', *Review of Economic Studies*, 42(2): 195–215.

Hicks, J.R. (1935) A suggestion for simplifying the theory of money', *Economica* II, No. 5: 1–19. Reprinted in: J.R. Hicks, *Critical Essays in monetary theory*. Oxford: Oxford University Press, 1967.

Hicks, J.R. (1939) *Value and capital*. Oxford: Oxford University Press.

Iwai, K. (1988) 'The evolution of money – A search-theoretic foundation of monetary economics', CARESS Working Paper 88-03, University of Pennsylvania.

Jevons, W.S. (1893) *Money and mechanism of exchange*. New York: D. Appleton.

Jones, R.A. (1976) 'The origin and development of media of exchange', *Journal of Political Economy*, 84: 757–775.

Jovanovic, B. (1982) 'Inflation and welfare in the steady state', *Journal of Political Economy*, 90: 561–577.

Kareken, J.H. and N. Wallace, eds. (1980) *Models of monetary economies*. Minneapolis: Federal Reserve Bank of Minneapolis.

King, R.G. and C. Plosser (1986) 'Money as the mechanism of exchange', *Journal of Monetary Economics*, 17: 93–115.

Kiyotaki, N. and R. Wright (1989) 'On money as a medium of exchange', *Journal of Political Economy*, 97: 927–954.

Kohn, M. (1981) 'In defense of the finance constraint', *Economic Inquiry*, 19: 177–195.

Kohn, M. (1984) 'The finance (cash-in-advance) constraint come of age: A survey of some recent developments in the theory of money', Working Paper Series, Dartmouth College.

Kurz, M. (1974a) 'Equilibrium with transaction cost and money in a single market exchange economy', *Journal of Economic Theory*, 7: 418–452.

Kurz, M. (1974b) 'Equilibrium in a finite sequence of markets with transactions cost', *Econometrica*, 42: 1–20.

Lucas, R.E., Jr. (1980) 'Equilibrium in a pure currency economy', in: J.H. Kareken and N. Wallace, eds., *Models of monetary economies*. Minneapolis: Federal Reserve Bank of Minneapolis.

Lucas, R.E. (1988) 'Liquidity and interest rates', Unpublished manuscript, University of Chicago.

Lucas, R.E. and N. Stokey (1987) 'Money and interest in a cash-in-advance economy', *Econometrica*, 55: 491–513.

Madden, P.J. (1975) 'Efficient sequences of non-monetary exchange', *Review of Economic Studies*, 42: 581–596.

Madden, P.J. (1976) 'Theorem on decentralized exchange', *Econometrica*, 44: 787–791.

Menger, K. (1892) 'On the origin of money', *Economic Journal*, 2: 239–255.

Niehans, J. (1969) 'Money in a static theory of optimal payment arrangements', *Journal of Money, Credit and Banking*, 1: 706–726.

Niehans, J. (1971) 'Money and barter in general equilibrium with transactions costs', *American Economic Review*, 61: 773–783.

Norman, A.L. (1987) 'A theory of monetary exchange', *Review of Economic Studies*, 54: 499–517.

O'Driscoll, G.P. (1986) 'Money – Menger evolutionary – theory', *History of Political Economy*, 18: 601–616.

Oh, S. (1989) 'A theory of a generally acceptable medium of exchange and barter', *Journal of Monetary Economics*, 23: 101–119.

Ostroy, J.M. (1973) 'The informational efficiency of monetary exchange', *American Economic Review*, 63: 597–610.

Ostroy, J.M. and R.M. Starr (1974) 'Money and the decentralization of exchange', *Econometrica*, 42: 1093–1113.

Patinkin, D. (1965) *Money, interest and prices*. New York: Harper and Row.

Radner, R. (1968) 'Competitive equilibrium under uncertainty', *Econometrica*, 36: 31–58.

Radner, R. (1972) 'Existence of equilibrium of plans, prices and price expectations in a sequence of markets', *Econometrica*, 40: 279–296.

Rotemberg, J. (1984) 'A monetary equilibrium model with transactions costs', *Journal of Political Economy*, 92: 40–58.

Scheinkman, J.A. and L. Weiss (1986) 'Borrowing constraints and aggregate economic activity', *Econometrica*, 54: 23–45.

Shubik, M. (1973) 'Commodity money, oligopoly, credit and bankruptcy in a general equilibrium model', *Western Economic Journal*, 4: 24–38.

Smith, A. (1775) *An inquiry into the nature and causes of the wealth of Nations*. Modern Library, New York: Random House.

Sontheimer, K. (1972) 'On the determination of money prices', *Journal of Money, Credit and Banking*, 4: 489–508.

Spence, M. (1974) *Market signaling: Information transfer in hiring and related processes*. Cambridge, Mass.: Harvard University Press.

Starr, R.M. (1972) 'The structure of exchange in barter and monetary economies', *Quarterly Journal of Economics*, 86: 290–302.

Starr, R.M. (1974) 'The price of money in a pure exchange monetary economy with taxation', *Econometrica*, 42: 45–54.

Starr, R. M. (1976) 'Decentralized non-monetary trade', *Econometrica*, 44: 1087–1089.

Starr, R.M. (1986) 'Decentralized trade in a credit economy', in: W.P. Heller, R. Starr and D. Starrett, eds., *Equilibrium analysis: Essays in honor of Kenneth J. Arrow*, vol. II. New York: Cambridge University Press.

Starr, R.M. ed. (1989) *General equilibrium models of monetary economies: Studies in the static foundations of monetary theory*. San Diego: Academic Press.

Starrett, D. (1973) 'Inefficiency and the demand for money in a sequence economy', *Review of Economic Studies*, 40: 289–303.

Stockman, A. (1981) 'Anticipated inflation and the capital stock in a cash-in-advance economy', *Journal of Monetary Economics*, 8: 387–393.

Svensson, L.E. (1985) 'Money and asset prices in a cash-in advance economy', *Journal of Political Economy*, 93: 919–944.

Taub, B. (1988) 'Efficiency in a pure credit economy', Virginia Tech. Working Paper.

Tobin, J. (1956) 'The interest-elasticity of transactions demand for cash', *Review of Economics and Statistics*, 38: 241–247.

Townsend, R.M. (1980) 'Models of money with spatially separated agents', in: J.H. Kareken and N. Wallace, eds., *Models of monetary economies*. Minneapolis: Federal Reserve Bank of Minneapolis.

Townsend, R.M. (1982) 'Optimal multiperiod contracts and the gain from enduring relationships under private information', *Journal of Political Economy*, 90: 1166–1186.

Townsend, R.M. (1983) 'Financial structure and economic activity', *American Economic Review*, 73: 895–911.

Townsend, R.M. (1987) 'Economic organization with limited communication', *American Economic Review*, 77: 954–971.

Townsend, R.M. and N. Wallace (1987) 'Circulating private debt: An example with a coordination problem', in: E.C. Prescott and N. Wallace, eds., *Contractual arrangements for intertemporal trade*. Minneapolis: University of Minnesota Press.

Ulph, A.M. and D.T. Ulph (1975) 'Transaction costs in general equilibrium theory – a survey', *Economica*, 42: 355–372.

Veendorp, E.C.H. (1970) "General equilibrium theory for a barter economy', *Western Economic Journal*, 8: 1–23.

Walras L. (1900) *Elements of pure economics*. Translated and edited by W. Jaffe. Homewood, Illinois: Irwin.

Chapter 2

LIQUIDITY

FRANK HAHN

University of Cambridge

Contents

Handbook of Monetary Economics, Volume I, Edited by B.M. Friedman and F.H. Hahn
© Elsevier Science Publishers B.V., 1990

1. Introduction

Liquidity, and the closely related notion of flexibility, are intuitively understood by economists and others. One has in mind the ease of conversion of an
asset at a particular date into something else by means of a market transaction.
It is connected with the idea that liquidity increases the set of choices at some
date so that the liquidity of, for instance, a portfolio depends on the date
specified for conversion. The rewards of liquidity are also pretty obvious: it
enables agents to respond at less cost to new information [e.g. Hicks (1974)]. It
seems clear that this reward will go up with the value of new information and
with the costs of switching [e.g. Jones and Ostroy (1984)]. For instance, if an
agent comes to hold the view that some future event (signal) will resolve a
great deal of uncertainty, then, ceteris paribus, it seems plausible that he will
wish to increase his liquidity. This makes interesting grist for the macroeconomic mill. The ease of conversion of an asset into something else suggests
the importance of transaction costs. These, in turn, may be formulated in terms
of search theory [Lippman and McCall (1986)] and be closely related to the
extent of the market. For instance, "thin" markets make for illiquidity because
buyers and sellers must search for each other. This then suggests an important
externality first brought to our attention by Diamond (1986). Agents, ignoring
the gain to the liquidity of existing market participants which would result from
their entry, are deterred from entering because of the market's illiquidity.
Hence, a thin market may never grow fat although it would be Pareto
improving were it to do so.

All these and many other ideas are at an informal level quite obvious. Some
of them have been around for a long time. Certainly Keynes (1930) in the
Treatise understood many, although not all, of them, and Marshak seems to
have seen almost all aspects quite clearly [Marshak (1938, 1949), Makower and
Marshak (1938)]. Nonetheless, the ideas were too vague and slippery to find a
comfortable place in what has come to be regarded as good theorising. In
recent years many attempts have been made to rectify this [e.g. Goldman
(1974) and Hirschleifer (1972)].

Many of these have yielded valuable sharpness, but often at a fairly high
price. For instance, it is customary to deal with very partial and, often, very
special models. It is customary, for instance, to consider only the composition
of a given sum devoted to assets. That means that the savings and portfolio
decisions are separated, which is valid in only special circumstances. It may
also deprive us of some insights. More unfortunate is the frequent abstraction
from risk aversion by (implicitly) assuming that utility functions are linear. This
leads Lippman and McCall (1986), for instance, to claim that they have found

"an operational measure of liquidity", i.e. one that is independent of the agent. But perhaps this is unsurprising in an analysis that abstracts from the characteristics of agents. It may also not be useful. It is also not clear how a purely search-theoretic approach, which leads to a liquidity ordering of assets by considering differences in the expected time to sell an asset under an optimum search policy, is to be integrated into present equilibrium theories of an economy. While no doubt there has been a gain of clarity, there is a distinct impression that the search for complete ordering of assets by liquidity has been misdirected. After all, we have long ago given up the attempt to find an ordering by riskiness except for special cases [Rothschild and Stiglitz (1970)].

What is of greatest interest is that any study of liquidity soon leads to the conclusion that if it is an important element in an economy's analysis, then many of our theories of the economy are in need of change. For instance, the recognition of the importance of transaction costs leads us to conclude that agents will maximise, subject to a number of, rather than a single, budget constraints [Hahn (1971, 1973)]. This has serious consequences for General Equilibrium Theory. Indeed, liquidity considerations may be used to account for "missing markets" which we now know to have more serious consequences for received theory than we once thought [Geanakoplos and Mas-Collel (1985)]. Search theory suggests imperfect markets (or no markets in the traditional sense) and so has considerable implications for competitive theory. Ideally, it should be combined with a theory of bargaining [Rubinstein and Wolinsky (1986), Gale (1986)] which, in turn, leads to a modification of search theory itself. Lastly, present theories of asset pricing pay no attention to the liquidity characteristics of assets.

Clearly, there are problems here for many research endeavours and it will not occasion surprise that these matters will not be resolved in what follows. My plan is modest. I shall build on the literature rather than survey it. However, at appropriate points note will be taken of how it relates to what is being presented. I shall also make an elementary attempt to point to some of the macro-economic implications of the analysis. At the end, I shall once again highlight our large areas of ignorance.

2. Portfolio choice with transaction costs

In this section I am concerned with an economy in which, for every state and date, all assets have well-defined prices. I call this a perfect market economy to distinguish it from economies in which exchange is accompanied by search and/or bargaining. Agents are assumed to know prices as functions of the state and date. However, transactions are costly. Transaction costs may be subjective, for instance because agents value time spent transacting, and/or they may arise from the need to employ middlemen (brokers, estate agents, etc.). It is these middlemen who obviate the need for search or for bargaining. For the present I shall concentrate on these latter costs.

Let $a \in R^m$ be a vector of assets held by an agent and let b be another asset vector. Then define $k(b, a, s)$ as the transaction cost of moving from a to b in state s where b is attainable. The mth component of a represents money. If a' differs from a only in the mth component, then $k(a', a, s) = 0$ all s.

I shall consider an agent with a three-period horizon: $t = 1, 2, 3$. Uncertainty is to be thought of as an event tree. The agent knows at $t = 1$ that he is at node σ_1. From this node there are n branches terminating in n nodes σ_2. From the latter there are again n branches terminating in nodes σ_3. I define $s_1 = \sigma_1$, $s_2 = \sigma_1 \sigma_2$ (where S_2 is the n-dimensional set of s_2) and $s_3 = \sigma_1 \sigma_2 \sigma_3$ (where S_3 is the n^2-dimensional set of s_3). At $t = 1$ the agent has a probability distribution on S_2 and a conditional distribution on S_3. I write $Ex(s_2)$ as the expected value of x at $t = 2$ and $E_{s_2} x(s_3)$ as its expected value at $t = 3$ conditional on the realisation s_2.

I now define $a(s_t)$ as the agent's asset vector at t in state s_t. A unit of asset k at t yields a money return $r_k(s_{t+1})$ in the following period in state s_{t+1}. It is postulated that $r_m(s_{t+1}) = 0$ for all s_{t+1}. To economise on notation, let $R(a(s_t), s_t)$ be the total money return at s_t on the asset vector $a(s_{t-1})$. In obvious notation, $R_k(a(s_{t+1}), s_t) = r_k(s_t)$. The price vector of assets at s_t is written $q(s_t) \in R_+^m$. One takes $q_m(s_t) = 1$ all s_t. There are l consumption goods and $c(s_t) \in R_+^l$ is the agent's consumption vector at s_t and $p(s_t)$ is the money price vector. The agent receives money income $y(s_t)$ at s_t. Let $\alpha(s_t) = (c(s_t), a(s_t))$ and assume that the agent starts with zero assets. The budget sets are:

$$B(s_1 0) = \{\alpha(s_1) \mid p(s_1)c(s_1) + q(s_1)a(s_1) + k(a(s_1), 0, s_1) \leq y(s_1)\} ; \quad (2.1)$$

$$B(s_2, a(s_1)) = \{\alpha(s_2) \mid p(s_2)c(s_2) + q(s_2)a(s_2) + k(a(s_2), a(s_1), s_2) \leq y(s_2)$$
$$+ R(a(s_1), s_2) + q(s_2)a(s_1)\} ,$$

$$B(s_3, a(s_2)) = \{\alpha(s_3) \mid p(s_3)c(s_3) + k(a(s_3), a(s_2), s_3) \leq y(s_3) + R(a(s_2), s_3)$$
$$+ q(s_3)a(s_2)\} . \quad (2.2)$$

In defining $B(s_3, a(s_2))$ we can put $a(s_3) = 0$ since $t = 3$ is the end of the agent's horizon. I write $B^*(s_t, a(s_{t+1})) = B(s_t, a(s_{t-1})) \cap \{a(s_t) \mid a(s_t) \geq 0\}$ when short sales are not possible.

Now assume that the agent has a well-behaved separable von Neuman utility function with discount factor δ, $(0 < \delta < 1)$. He makes his choices by solving the following programme:

$$V(y(s_1), s_1) = \max_{B^*(s_1, 0)} [u(c(s_1)) + \delta EV(a(s_1)s_2)] , \quad (2.3)$$

where

$$V(a(s_1)s_2) = \max_{B^*(s_2, a(s_1))} [u(c(s_2)) + \delta E_{s_2} V(a(s_2), s_3)], \tag{2.4}$$

$$V(a(s_2), s_3) = \max_{B^*(s_3, a(s_2))} u(c(s_3)). \tag{2.5}$$

We now consider the optimum asset choice, i.e. the first-order conditions that need to be satisfied.

To simplify, I shall assume that $k(a(s_t), a(s_{t-1}), s_t)$ is linear. I return to this below. In Figure 2.1 the function is drawn in the (k_j, a_j) plane. Let $k_{1j}(s_t), k_{2j}(s_t)$ be the partial differential coefficients (where necessary, different for left-hand and right-hand) with respect to $a_j(s_t)$ and $a_j(s_{t-1})$, respectively. Evidently one has $k_{1j}(s_t) = -k_{2j}(s_t)$. Also $k_{1j}(s_t) > 0$ for $a_j(s_t) > a_j(s_{t-1})$ or for $\Delta a_j(s_t) > 0$ when $a_j(s_t) = a_j(s_{t-1})$. Similarly, $k_{1j}(s_t) < 0$ for $a_j(s_t) < a_j(s_{t-1})$ or for $\Delta a_j(s_t) < 0$ when $a_j(s_t) = a_j(s_{t-1})$. To simplify once again, I assume that both branches in Figure 2.1 have the same absolute slope and write

$$|k_{1j}(s_t)| = \tau_j(s_t).$$

Lastly, let $S_{2j}^- \subset S_2$ be defined by

$$S_{2j}^- = \{s_2 \mid \bar{a}_j(s_t) \le \bar{a}_j(s_{t-1})\},$$

where $\bar{a}_j(s_t)$ and $\bar{a}_j(s_{t-1})$ are optimum asset choices.

Using (2.4) one finds the first-order conditions for $a_j(s_1) > 0$ to be:

$$\zeta(s_1)(q_j(s_1)\tau_j(s_2)) = \delta E \zeta(s_2)(r_j(s_2) + q_j(s_2 + \tau_j(s_2))) - 2\delta E_{S_{2j}^-} \zeta(s_2)\tau_j(s_2), \tag{2.6}$$

where $\zeta(s_t)$ is the shadow price of income at s_t. The first term on the r.h.s. is the expected utility gain on the marginal unit of asset j if that marginal unit were to be held until $t = 3$. It includes $q_j(s_2) + \tau_j(s_2)$ because that is what is saved in s_2 by buying the marginal unit in s_1 (rather than in s_2). The last term represents deductions that have to be made because the marginal unit is not to be held until $t = 3$.

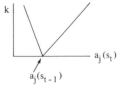

Figure 2.1

It will be helpful to rewrite (2.6) as

$$\zeta(s_1)q_j(s_1) = \delta E(\zeta(s_2)r_j(s_2) + q_j(s_2)) + \delta E_{s_{2j}^+}\zeta(s_2)\tau_j(s_2)$$

$$- \delta E_{s_{2j}^-}\zeta(s_2)\tau_j(s_2) - \zeta(s_1)\tau_j(s_1), \qquad (2.7)$$

where $S_{2j}^+ = \{s_2 \mid a_j(s_2) > a_j(s_1)\}$. This makes it clear that the presence of transactions costs does not necessarily imply that money will command a "liquidity premium". The sign of the sum of the last three terms is ambiguous. Suppose, for instance, that $S_{2j}^- = \emptyset$. Then the agent plans to buy more of the asset at $t = 2$ whatever the state. One must now take account of the intertemporal substitution of transaction costs. By buying one more unit at $t = 1$ an amount $E_{s_{2j}^+}\zeta(s_2)\tau_j(s_2)$ is saved from $t = 2$ which must be compared to the cost $\zeta(s_1)\tau_j(s_1)$. So the term $E_{s_{2j}^-}\zeta(s_2)\tau_j(s_2)$ must be large enough before money commands a "liquidity premium". This simple argument suggests that it will not be easy to relate some agent-independent definition of liquidity to the agent's choice – in particular, it is unlikely that, except in special cases, simple comparative statics will be available.

Where of course (2.7) differs from the usual first-order conditions is in explicitly making first-period choice depend on the optimum second-period choice. Of course, in a three-period model this would generally be true even without transaction costs since $\zeta(s_2)$ is determined by the whole optimum plan. But when there are no transaction costs, as (2.7) shows, the agent can be taken as maximising the expected (derived) utility of wealth. With transaction costs wealth is not unambiguously defined and indeed depends on future plans. In many traditional theories of asset choice this, by no means negligible, fact is ignored.

The first-order conditions for the optimum choice of $a_j(s_2)$ are:

$$\zeta(s_2)q_j(s_2 + \tau_j(s_2)) = \delta E_{s_2}\zeta(s_3)(r_j(s_3) + q_j(s_3) - \tau_j(s_3)),$$

when $\bar{a}_j(s_2) > \bar{a}_j(s_1)$,

$$\zeta(s_2)(q_j(s_2) - \tau_j(s_2)) = \Psi_j(s_2) + \delta E_{s_2}\zeta(s_3)(r_j(s_3) + q_j(s_3) - \tau_j(s_3)),$$

when $\bar{a}_j(s_2) < \bar{a}_j(s_1)$, and where $\Psi_j(s_2)$ is the shadow price of the "no short sales" constraint. And when $\bar{a}_j(s_2) = \bar{a}_j(s_1)$,

$$\zeta(s_2)(q_j(s_2) - \tau_j(s_2)) \leqq \delta E_{s_2}\zeta(s_3)(r_j(s_3) + q_j(s_3) - \tau_j(s_3))$$

$$\leqq \zeta(s_2)(q_j(s_2) + \tau_j(s_2)).$$

(Note that at $t = 3$ all assets are sold.)

These expressions can be substituted into (2.7) to obtain:

$$\zeta(s_1)q_j(s_1) \leqq \delta E[\zeta(s_2)r_j(s_2) + \delta E_{s_2}\zeta(r_j(s_3) + q_j(s_3) - \tau_j(s_3))] - \tau_j(s_1)\zeta(s_1) \, . \tag{2.8}$$

It will be seen that second-period (marginal) transaction costs do not enter directly into (2.8). This is because the value, gross of transaction costs, at which an asset is reckoned at $t = 2$ is equal to its expected utility value at $t = 3$ (plus possibly the shadow price of not being able to sell short). The tangent discontinuity of the transaction cost function at the point of zero transactions and the "no short sales constraint" explains the possibility of an inequality in (2.8). That is, at $t = 2$ the marginal gain from a sale falls short of, and the marginal cost of a purchase exceeds, third-period expected marginal benefit.

The assumption that the transaction cost function is linear and that both branches have the same absolute slope simplifies the algebra but does not affect our understanding of the equilibrium conditions. This is also true of the neglect of possible fixed elements in transaction costs (which lead to discontinuities in the transaction cost function). If we include them, then the algebra becomes more complicated but no essentially new element is introduced. Clearly, inequalities will be more prominent.

3. Liquidity and comparative statics

While the derivation of first-order conditions gives some insights, these conditions are not very informative when it comes to comparative statics. This is particularly true in the present instance when one is interested in showing that intuitively plausible propositions are consistent with rational choice. Unfortunately, it seems that no one has succeeded in doing this, and one might argue that the really interesting theoretical conclusion is that it cannot in general be done. That is, that our intuition in these matters is not supported by the usual paradigm.

The procedure which has been adopted is to define a ranking by liquidity of assets which is independent of the characteristics of the agent. One such (partial) ranking, proposed by Jones and Ostroy (1984), is as follows. They define $K(a, s, \alpha) = \{b \mid k(b, a, s) \leqq \alpha\}$ and say that portfolio a is no less liquid (flexible) than portfolio a' if $K(a, s, \alpha) \supset K(a', s, \alpha)$ for all s and α. It is clear that this definition provides only a partial ordering.

They are now interested in the proposition, most recently suggested by Hicks (1974), that when an agent expects more uncertainty to be resolved in the second period (than he did with earlier beliefs), then he will also choose a more liquid portfolio. That is so because the agent knows that there is a higher likelihood that he will wish to change any portfolio which he had chosen in the first period. Hence, were he to stick to his original portfolio (before his beliefs were different), he would incur higher transaction costs.

Jones and Ostroy formalize beliefs as follows. (I adapt their analysis to the construction of the previous section.) Let $\Pi \in R^n_+$ be a probability vector on S_2 giving prior beliefs. Let $\beta(s_2) \in R^n_+$ be the probability vector on S_3 conditioned by the realisation of s_2. Let $(\beta(s_2))$ be the matrix of these vectors and consider two belief structures: $B(\Pi, (\beta(s_2)))$ and $B' = (n', \beta'(s_2))$ with $\sum \Pi\beta(s_2) = \sum \Pi'\beta'(s_2)$. Then [following Blackwell (1951)] one says that belief structure B is more variable than belief structure B' if for any convex function $\theta(\cdot)$ one has

$$\sum \Pi\theta(\beta(s_2)) > \sum \Pi'\theta(\beta'(s_2)) .$$

When the belief structure is more variable, then the agent expects more uncertainty to be resolved in the second period.

Using this notation let

$$\max_{B^*(s_2, a(s_1))}\left[u(c(s_2)) + \delta \sum_{s_3} \beta(s_2)V(a(s_2), s_3)\right] \equiv a(a(s_1), \beta(s_2))$$

It is easily seen that $a(\cdot)$ is a convex function of $\beta(s_2)$. Let $a(s_1)$ be the portfolio chosen with beliefs B and $a'(s_1)$ the portfolio chosen with beliefs B'. Then a central proposition of Jones and Ostroy is the following:

Proposition (Jones and Ostroy). *If $a(s_1)$ is not less flexible than $a'(s_1)$ according to the definition given above, implies that*

$$a(a(s_1), \beta(s_2)) - a(a'(s_2), \beta(s_2))$$

is convex on s_2, then the ordering of beliefs by variability induces an order: $a(s_1)$ not less flexible than $a'(s_1)$.

This proposition then confirms our intuition at a cost. The convexity of the difference is not itself intuitively acceptable. Jones and Ostroy give a number of other propositions designed to make it so under various special assumptions concerning the transaction cost function. They are not implausible, but our original intuition did not seem to depend on such special functions. Moreover, their construction already has a number of special features, e.g. it seems to have linear utility functions in the background and it abstracts from the savings decision. Theirs is undoubtedly a worthwhile contribution, but it leaves it unclear why our intuition does not work in general. The answer is likely to be found in the attempt to obtain a flexibility or liquidity ranking which is independent of the agent. On the face of it, this must be as restrictive as attempting to formulate a ranking of the riskiness of portfolios which is independent of the agent.

Somehow one would like the idea of liquidity to be related to the cost of reversing a decision taken earlier. In the present context this suggests that the cost of selling an asset in the second period which was bought in the first should play a role in our understanding. Here is a sketch of a more subjective procedure. Suppose then that we ask the following question: How much purchasing power can we take away from the agent in $t = 1$ when we reduce selling costs to zero to make him as well off as he is when these costs are positive?

Let $q(s_2) + \tau(s_2) = \hat{q}(s_2)$ be the price vector of assets including transaction costs of purchasing. If κ is a vector let κ^+ denote the vector with components $\max(0, \kappa_i)$. Then the budget constraint sets of an agent who has had T taken away at $t = 1$ but incurs no selling costs at $t = 2$ are:

$$\hat{B}(s_1, -T) = \{\alpha(s_1) \mid p(s_1)c(s_1) + q(s_1)a(s_1) + k(a(s_1), 0, s_1)$$
$$\leq y(s_1) - T\},$$

$$\hat{B}(s_2, a(s_1)) = \{\alpha(s_2) \mid p(s_2)c(s_2) + q(s_2)(a(s_2) - a(s_1))^+ \leq y(s_2)$$
$$+ R(a(s_1), s_2) + q(s_2)(a(s_1) - a(s_2))^+\}.$$

We can now write this agent's programme as we did in (2.3) and (2.4). Let

$$W(y(s_1 - T, s_1)) = \max\{u(c(s_1)) + \delta E W(a(s_1), s_2)\}. \tag{3.1}$$

Then T is to be defined implicitly by

$$W(y(s_1) - T, s_1) = V(y(s_1), s_1). \tag{3.2}$$

Let $\hat{a}(s_1)$ be the solution to the problem (3.1). Call $\hat{a}(s_1)$ *perfectly liquid*. This is justified by the fact that there are no costs associated with reversing in the second period a decision to buy in the first. Of course the agent still incurs the uncertainty of the asset's gross return. One can now think of T as an index of the illiquidity of the portfolio $a(s_1)$ which is the portfolio which is actually chosen. It measures the maximum an agent would be prepared to pay to escape reversal costs. This measure is not objective, i.e. it depends essentially on the characteristics of the agent.

But it can be used to confirm our intuition. Jones and Ostroy note that $v(y(s_1), s_1)$ is increasing with the variability of beliefs. That is because more informative processes are valued. On the other hand, $W(y(s_1) - T, s)$ is independent of the variability of beliefs since in that programme the agent cannot do better than to maximise the expected (derived) utility of wealth (calculated at the selling price) at the beginning of the second period (at least when first-period consumption is given). Hence, from the definition, T will be smaller when the variability of beliefs is higher and that, on the definition here proposed, means that the portfolio chosen will be less illiquid. This is what intuition suggests should be the case.

The "objective" ranking proposed by Jones and Ostroy cannot deliver this result because an agent is interested in the costs of a change in asset position only for states at which he will find it optimal to change. Hence, the agent may regard a chosen a as more flexible than another without satisfying the Jones–Ostroy criterion.

As already noted in the Introduction, the position taken here is at variance with that adopted by Lippman and McCall (1986) who have proposed an "operational" measure of liquidity, i.e. one that is largely indepedent of the agent. It will be recalled that it is the expected time taken to sell an asset under an optimum search rule. This definition can be adapted to measure the liquidity of a whole portfolio. As I have also already remarked, the "operational" characterisation is bought at the price of making very special assumptions concerning preferences (they are linear in payoffs) and so hardly surprising. In addition they themselves find that, even so, the discount factor of an agent affects the measure of liquidity (by affecting the optimum search rule). They remark that, nonetheless, the ranking of assets by their measure of liquidity will be similar for all agents because they face similar costs of search and distribution of offers. This seems empirically dubious and is also only defensible on a somewhat mechanistic view of search costs.

Nonetheless, they show that their measure leads to some definite comparative statics conclusions including (in a different form) the one we have already discussed. I consider these now.

They show that a higher discount factor, by lowering the critical acceptance price in search, will lower the expected delay in selling and so lead to higher "liquidity". This result should cause one to pause, since it does not easily fit in with our intuition. A higher discount factor in models without search may bring the date of planned sale nearer, but it also reduces the present value of transaction costs. It also, of course, may (will) affect savings. The ambiguity of how a higher discount factor will affect our proposed measure, T, is a reflection of contrary forces being at work. Indeed, if risk aversion is allowed for, even the purely search-theoretic comparative statics definition would be at risk. Certainly one would expect intertemporal marginal rates of substitution to be different for different discount factors.

The next proposition is indeed intuitively acceptable. It is that an increase in the thickness of the market (measured by the frequency of offers) induces an increase in liquidity ("if the interest rate is near zero or the frequency of offers is very high"). The proviso arises from the simple algebra of search theory and can be explained by the fact that a lower expected time between offers causes a reduction in the discount factor which would raise the expected time of sale unless interest rates were close to zero. In the measure of liquidity proposed here we would interpret a thicker market as one with lower transaction costs and come to the same comparative statics conclusion: any given portfolio will be more liquid than before. Moreover, for well-behaved utility functions the chosen portfolio will be more liquid.

There is of course a connection here between the search-theoretic and straightforward transaction cost approach. Ordinary economic theory suggests that when there is inducement to search there will also arise middlemen who can profitably reduce search costs. Ordinarily agents then do not search but pay a middleman, which is the transaction cost of the theory. Middlemen, in turn, will charge more in markets where the frequency of offers and bids is low. As I have already noted, such a story is not only required by ordinary observation of the world but also by economic theory which supposes that profitable niches do not remain unoccupied.

Keynes (1936) suggested that the ranking of assets by liquidity should be based on which is "more certainly realisable at short notice without loss". Lippman and McCall have no difficulty in incorporating this into their definition. Related is the idea that liquidity should be measured by the discount on its "true" value which would occur if the asset has to be sold within one period. Lippman and McCall show that this measure of an asset's liquidity varies with search costs in the same way that their measure does. Neither definition, however, leads to plausible comparative statics. Thus, while trivially higher search costs make an asset more liquid on the Lippman and McCall definition it is quite unclear how this affects the liquidity of the assets which will be chosen. After all, a lower average search time will be associated with accepting a lower price for the asset. It is the virtue of the work of Jones and Ostroy that they show their awareness of the simple injunction not to invent definitions which cannot be shown to be useful and usable.

4. Money

The first-order conditions derived in Section 2 show that money will command a liquidity premium over any asset which, with positive probability, will be reduced in the second period. This statement is to be interpreted as follows. Given this premiss, the expected return in utility on the purchase price of an asset, including transaction costs, must exceed one if that asset is to be bought in the first period. On the assumption that the probability of selling (some of) any asset in the second period is never zero, one can speak of a liquidity preference for money. From equation (2.6) we can say that the rate of return of any asset j which is to be bought in the first period cannot be less than, say,

p_j, where

$$p_j = 2\delta \, \mathrm{E}_{s_{2j}^-} \zeta(s_2)\tau_j(s_2)/q_j(s_1) + \tau_j(s_1) \, . \tag{4.1}$$

If then $\bar{p} = \min_j p_j$ it will be positive on our assumptions. This procedure formalizes the Keynesian claim that liquidity preference sets a lower bound on the rate of return of any asset which is to be bought in the first period.

One could now consider yet another ordering of assets by liquidity. This is achieved by utilizing the premium p_j an asset must earn over money if that asset is to be bought in an optimum plan. An asset j with p_j less than p_k of another asset k would then be ranked as more liquid than asset k. This, of course, is again a non-objective characterisation. It does not lead to any definite comparative statics propositions without special assumptions. For instance, more variable beliefs, which we have seen to increase the liquidity of portfolios according to a certain criterion, need not increase $\bar{p}$, that is, the more liquid portfolio need not contain more money relative to other assets. That is because there is no simple way in which variability of beliefs can be related to the sets S_{2j}^-.

This difficulty does not arise if there is only one other asset besides money – the case most frequently found in the literature [e.g. Baumol (1952)]. Then, since an increased variability of beliefs reduces our measure, T, it must be that the new portfolio contains relatively more money since that is the only way in which T can be lower. This can then be interpreted as due to a rise in $\bar{p}$ at the old portfolio. While simplification in theorising is essential, the two-asset simplification must strike one as altogether too drastic.

It should now be noted how the analysis so far ties up with the transactions demand for money. It will not have escaped the reader's notice that for certain states s_2 an asset bought at $t = 1$ may be (partially or wholly) sold not because s_2 is informative – it may not convey any information – but because incomes in that state are lower than required for consumption. As we have noted earlier, transaction costs are thought of as arising when an asset is exchanged against money (or vice versa) while we have ignored transaction costs which may be involved in going from money into consumption goods. The income uncertainty makes for an uncertain transaction requirement for money at $t = 2$ and so for an expectation of incurring transaction costs on the sale of assets bought at $t = 1$. (If we had included the state in the utility function there would have been a further source of uncertainty – the optimum consumption at $t = 2$ even if incomes and prices had been certain.)

But even this does not do full justice to the generality of the approach. Suppose incomes at $t = 2$ were certain to be zero, while at $t = 3$ they were again $y(s_3)$. Then the agent whose optimum consumption at $t = 2$ is non-zero would know that some assets of $t = 1$ will need to be converted into consumption goods via money. It is easy to see how transaction costs can then lead the agent to demand money at $t = 1$. Except for the absence of a fixed element in transaction costs, the arguments are to be found in Tobin (1958) and Baumol (1952). If one abandons the artificial three-period setting and supposes that incomes are zero in every odd period and positive (and possibly stochastic) in even periods, one readily sees how what is known as the transaction motive for liquidity can be encompassed by the analysis. However, to ensure a strictly positive demand for money one of course needs to have the premium sufficiently high relative to the return on other assets. It is here that a plausible fixed cost element in transaction costs must be invoked. But that is familiar territory.

5. Sensitivity to new information

Although I have been critical of the so-called "operational" measure of liquidity derived from search theory, search may be important when considering liquidity. Many assets do not have a quoted resale price partly because they are too specialised and partly because first ownership renders them idiosyncratic ["named" goods, Hahn (1971)]. For instance, there may be a large market in second-hand cars but one's own second-hand car is not a perfect substitute for someone else's, even of the same make and vintage. These considerations apply to most physical assets which, however, may well be sold in a perfect market when new (and homogeneous).

The optimum search rule in the general setting that has here been used to study the agent's asset choice is a good deal more complicated than the familiar ones. (Of course one must now extend the horizon beyond three periods.) The decision to search (attempt to sell) is of course endogenous. Since agents may be updating beliefs through time and know that they will be doing so, a search begun at one date and state may be broken off at another date and state without a sale. A serious analysis would be highly desirable but cannot be undertaken here.

There is, however, one element in this account that should be discussed, even if only sketchily. Liquidity is connected to the *speed of response* to new information. A related idea is that the elasticity of substitution between assets should be smaller the less liquid the portfolio. Let us for a moment return to the transaction cost scenario. Suppose that the realisation of s_2, by providing new information, leads to a change in the expected relative returns of assets calculated on the price per unit, including transaction costs of buying them new. An agent who could sell assets at the same gross price as that which they can be bought, would rearrange his portfolio in the obvious manner. But if transaction costs make the selling price less than the gross purchase price he will do less in the way of rearranging his portfolio. In other words, the relative expected returns of two assets must change by more than would otherwise be the case, for one to be substituted for another. The measure of illiquidity, T, that has been discussed is really a measure of the expected losses in expected utility due to reduced substitutability.

If one now thinks of a longer horizon, it is easy to see that transaction costs may make it optimal to retain an asset longer than would be the case if the portfolio were perfectly liquid. Search considerations reinforce that conclusion. As already noted earlier, in a well-functioning market economy it is not the optimum search rule of the agent that is of sole interest (except perhaps in labour markets because of the obvious moral hazard), but the optimum search of a middleman to whom the agent can sell (e.g. second-hand car dealers). As a first approximation, one can thus collapse the costs of search onto present transaction costs. Search is a good basis for understanding transaction costs.

All of this leads to the conclusion that the responsiveness of a portfolio to new information will be lower the higher is our measure of illiquidity. For physical assets that have returns for only a finite time this means that it will take longer before they are replaced by other assets. The agent of course knows that reduced profitability of responding to new information is entailed in the choices of certain assets, and this will affect the demand for them when new. Therefore our earlier conclusion that more variable beliefs, i.e. the belief that the future will resolve more uncertainty, lead to a more liquid portfolio choice may be particularly relevant to investment decisions in physical assets simply because of their (implicit) high transaction costs.

Some of these remarks can, at a cost, be formalised, but not on this occasion. After all, these ideas are not very new. For instance, it is commonly observed that equity markets allow agents to invest in productive assets without risking the large costs of disinvestment that may be made desirable by certain events either directly or indirectly through the information that they convey. Yet, although this is a commonplace, it is frequently forgotten as, for instance, in the literature that considers managers as agents of equity holders. The same is true of the theory of investment. Arrow (1968) has taken account of the possible irreversibility of investment, but as far as I know there are no studies of the effects on investment of an expectation that a future event (e.g. an election) will resolve some uncertainty. In particular, it is not likely that investors can ever make investment decisions myopically since they must scan future possible events sufficiently to reach a belief as to the probability that they will incur the costs of disinvestment. The possible avenues these considerations open up for macro-economic theorising are sufficiently obvious.

6. Liquidity and welfare

It is by now a familiar proposition that the quantity of non-interest-bearing money held by agents may be too small [Friedman (1967)]. The proposition itself is by no means as secure as it is often taken to be. This is due to at least two flaws. First, an economy with money and transaction costs is not the economy of traditional Welfare Economics that is used to deduce the proposition. Secondly, the proposition takes no account of the intrinsic constraints on allocations that arise from "missing markets". Thus, while a correct "optimum quantity of money" theorem can be stated [e.g. Grandmont (1983); see also Woodford, Chapter 20 in this Handbook], it relates to a very special economy. As we have already argued, the main theoretical issues of liquidity are closely connected with the lack of insurance possibilities which, in turn, are closely related to transaction costs and information.

In any case, our earlier analysis suggests that current theories of the optimum quantity of money over-estimate the opportunity cost of holding money. That is, they do not take account of the liquidity premium money commands even if there were no "shoe-leather" costs. That premium, as we have seen, is due to the possibility that an asset bought at one date and state is optimally sold at a future date and state and so incurs the cost of selling. This certainly, for instance, means that the expected instantaneous rate of return on a non-money asset is not the true cost of holding money.

In the literature, transaction costs are often modelled by a "money in advance constraint" [Clower (1967), Lucas and Stokey (1987), and Grandmont and Younes (1973)]. As long as that constraint has a positive shadow price, it is argued, a Pareto improvement is possible since it is costless to society to reduce that shadow price to zero. However, when account is taken of other assets, of the costs of moving between assets and the motive for liquidity that arises from the possibility of learning, matters are no longer so straightforward and at present the question in such a setting has not been thoroughly studied.

Indeed, liquidity and flexibility pose some hard problems for welfare analysis, particularly conceptual ones. To take just one example: consider the financing of an innovation, perhaps, in the form of a new firm. When all the estimates of likely returns have been made an individual agent must still consider those private events the occurrence of which could lead him to prefer some other form of asset. That is, the tradability of the investment becomes significant. If the market is expected to be thin, tradability costs may be high. The innovation may never be financed. But it is clear that the outcome is not clearly related to any social criterion of the desirability of the innovation. The individual agent is concerned with the costs involved in a transfer of ownership which, as such, is not self-evidently of social concern. In particular, it would seem that a device whereby agents can insure the cost of transacting "at the beginning", somewhat on the lines of our construction of the illiquidity measure T, should be Pareto improving.

Questions such as these require serious theoretical attention. They are closely related to the welfare economics of missing markets when the number of markets is taken as endogenous and when, as a first approach, transaction costs are proxies for search in thin markets. Some quite obvious points will then gain significance. For instance, the transaction costs of different markets may be related. Thus, the market for some asset may be thin (and have high transaction costs) while it would not be so costly to trade in if some complementary asset were traded as well. [See Grossman and Hart (1979) for a related point.] But there are also more straightforward-looking questions. For instance, what is the welfare effect of a tax on transactions such as registration fees and stamp duties? One would expect agents to choose asset portfolios for which the likelihood of wishing to sell is lower than before the tax. But whether this can be shown to be Pareto better or worse is an open question.

7. Concluding remarks

There are two topics that have not been discussed, largely because such literature as there is concerning them opens up too much territory for this chapter.

The first of these concerns work on the idea that agents may have a "preference for flexibility" [Koopmans (1964), Kreps (1979)]. Kreps, following on from Koopmans, has axiomatised the notion and characterised a representation of such preferences. Essentially, the idea is that there is a (partial) ordering over opportunity sets. Jones and Ostroy, proceeding from a different perspective, have, as we have seen, used a similar idea in characterising the flexibility of a portfolio. It is not at all clear at present whether a new theory of preference for flexibility is required since, as we have seen, a quite traditional approach reveals such a preference. That is, agents can be taken to be learning from events and to know that they will learn and how they will learn. This may be asking a good deal especially if preferences are uncertain (i.e. s appears as an argument in the utility function). A preference for flexibility may become important if the traditional Savage and Bayesian apparatus is found to be insufficiently descriptive and/or because of problems occasioned by events that initially were assigned zero probability. Indeed, the idea that most agents know that there are possible events that they have not either described or thought of is an appealing one, and it is in such a context that preference for flexibility may be found most useful. But these are matters more fundamental than liquidity, and it would not be appropriate to speculate about them here.

The second matter is, of course, the macro-economic implications of liquidity considerations. Here it is clear that much will depend on the model of the economy in which they are embedded. For instance, if an increase in the variability of beliefs leads to a higher demand for money and close money substitutes at the expense of productive assets, and if prices are not "perfectly flexible", there will be "real" macro consequences. Clearly, one could construct both a classical and a Keynesian story. The policy conclusions would of course be quite different. For instance, in the Keynesian case one may conclude that the higher demand for liquidity should be accommodated by an elastic supply of money and money substitutes. However, the Keynesian case also requires a departure from the postulates that all expectations that matter are price expectations.

There are also simpler matters that arise. It is a familiar notion that rational individuals who are ("as if") infinitely lived will ensure the neutrality of open market operations [Barro (1974)]. This conclusion is derived by considering the correctly calculated real wealth effect of such operations which is zero. However, changes in the tax obligations associated with the operation will mean changes in the frequency and amount of transactions necessitated by the payment of tax. It will then depend on the exact nature of transaction costs and the manner in which taxes are collected whether the neutrality proposition remains valid.

It so happens that so far macro-economic theory has not come to serious grips with the phenomenon of liquidity preference in its widest sense. In particular, it has not allowed for transaction costs and uncertainties that arise for assets, especially real assets, other than money. That this is so is well illustrated by the popularity of the "representative" agent. This device abstracts from transactions that are the result of the heterogeneity of agents. Many propositions of macro-economics are seriously at risk from this neglect. However, I have neither the ability nor space to make an attempt at a remedy.

References

Arrow, K.J. (1968) 'Optimal capital policy with irreversible investment', in: J.N. Wolfe, ed., *Value capital and growth*. Oxford University Press.

Barro, R.J. (1974) 'Are government bonds net wealth?', *Journal of Political Economy*, 82: 1095–1117.

Baumol, W.J. (1952) 'The transaction demand for cash: An inventory-theoretic approach, *Quarterly Journal of Economics*, 66: 545–566.

Blackwell, D. (1951) 'The composition of experiments', in: *Proceedings of the Second Berkeley Symposium of Mathematical Statistics and Probability*. University of California Press.

Clower, R.W. (1967) 'A recommendation of the microfoundations of monetary theory', *Western Economic Journal*, 6: 1–9.

Diamond, P. (1986) 'Money in search equilibrium', *Econometrica*, 52: 1–21.

Friedman, M. (1967) *The optimum quantity of money*. London: Macmillan.

Gale, D. (1982) *Money in equilibrium*. Nisbet and Cambridge University Press.

Gale, D. (1986) 'Bargaining and competition', *Econometrica*, 56: 785–818.

Geanakoplos, J. and A. Mas-Collel (1985) 'Real indeterminacy with financial assets'. mimeo.

Goldman, S. (1974) 'Flexibility and the demand for money', *Journal of Economic Theory*, 9: 203–222.

Grandmont, J.M. (1983) *Money and value*. Cambridge University Press.

Grandmont, J.M. and Y. Younes (1973) 'On the efficiency of monetary equilibrium', *Review of Economic Studies*, 40: 149–165.

Grossman, A. and O.D. Hart (1979) 'A theory of competitive equilibrium in stock market economics', *Econometrica*, 47: 293–330.

Hahn, F.H. (1971) 'Equilibrium with transaction costs', *Econometrica*, 39: 417–439.

Hahn, F.H. (1973) 'On transaction costs, inessential sequence economies and money', *Review of Economic Studies*, 40: 449–461.

Hicks, J.R. (1974) *The crisis in Keynesian economics*. New York: Basic Books.

Hirschleifer, J. (1972) 'Liquidity, uncertainty and the accumulation of information', in: F. Carter and S.L. Ford, eds., *Uncertainty and expectations in economics*. Oxford: Basil Blackwell.

Jones, R.A. and Ostroy, J.M. (1984) 'Flexibility and uncertainty', *Review of Economic Studies*, 164: 13–32.

Keynes, J.M. (1930) *A treatise on money*. London: Macmillan.

Keynes, J.M. (1936) *The general theory of interest, employment and money*. London: Macmillan.

Koopman, T. (1964) 'On flexibility of future preference', in: M.W. Shell and G.L. Bryan, eds., *Human judgement and optimality*. New York: Wiley.

Kreps, D. (1979) 'A representation theory for preference for flexibility', *Econometrica*, 47: 565–577.

Lippman, S.A. and J.D. McCall (1986) 'An operational measure of liquidity', *American Economic Review*, 76: 43–55.

Lucas, R.E. and N.L. Stokey (1987) 'Money and interest in a cash in advance economy', *Econometrica*, 55: 491–514.

Makower, H. and J. Marshak (1938) 'Assets, prices and monetary theory', *Economica*, 55: 261–288.

Marshak, J. (1938) 'Money and the theory of assets', *Econometrica*, 6: 311–325.

Marshak, J. (1949) 'Role of liquidity under complete information', *American Economic Review, Papers and Proceedings*, 39: 182–195.

Rothschild, M. and J.E. Stiglitz (1970) 'Increasing risk: I and II', *Journal of Economic Theory*, 2: 225–243 and 3: 66–84.

Rubinstein, A. and A. Wolinsky (1986) 'Decentralised trading, strategic behaviour and the Walrasian outcome'. Hebrew University, Jerusalem, mimeo.

Tobin, J. (1958) 'Liquidity preference as behaviour towards risk', *Review of Economic Studies*, 25: 65–86.

Woodford, M. (1990) 'The optimum quantity of money', in: B.M. Friedman and F.H. Hahn, eds., *Handbook of monetary economics, Volume 2*. Amsterdam: North-Holland.

Chapter 3

MONEY IN GENERAL EQUILIBRIUM THEORY

DARRELL DUFFIE*

Stanford University

Contents

* The author is in debt to Frank Hahn, Kenneth Arrow, Jean-Michel Grandmont, David Levine, and John Roberts for useful conversations. The author is personally responsible for errors. This chapter was written in November 1986.

Handbook of Monetary Economics, Volume I, Edited by B.M. Friedman and F.H. Hahn

1. Introduction

This chapter provides conditions for the existence of general monetary equilibrium in a simple setting, and discusses the role of money in general equilibrium theory. The phrase *general monetary equilibrium* evokes widely divergent images and interests. This chapter is sharply disciplined in focus, concentrating on the problems of pure outside fiat money in the setting of Arrow and Debreu (1954). The principal contribution of general equilibrium theory has been its axiomatic validation of our benchmark model of price taking, individual rationality, and market clearing. Equilibria exist, albeit under strong conditions. While monetary theorists continue to draw insights from this benchmark model, it has been difficult to find conditions implying any role for money in general equilibrium. As Hahn (1965) points out, the basic role of money as a medium of exchange is lost unless it also fills its role as a numeraire. If the value of money in relation to goods is zero, it cannot serve its purpose at all. This is worrisome in a finite horizon model. Since terminal money lays no apparent claim to goods or services, the terminal value of money would seem to be zero. This implies, by the same reasoning, that the value of money is zero in the penultimate period, and so on. Since we have yet to reach a terminal period in our real economy, devices used in the literature to induce a terminal value of money by forcing agents to return strictly positive amounts of money to the exchange authority after terminal trading seem innocuous in studying the properties of monetary equilibria, since these devices have smaller and smaller effects as the time horizon goes to infinity.

Nevertheless, and understandably, the unraveling value of money in finite horizon economies is such a stark and simple story that recent efforts to find monetary equilibria have concentrated on infinite horizon settings. Among these efforts, the results of Bewley (1980) and of Gale and Hellwig (1984) are seminal. In Bewley's infinite horizon model, uncertainty generates a precautionary demand for money. Since there are no other stores of value, agents hold money as insurance against shortfalls in endowment value. Driven by convexity of preferences, this effect is also present with purely deterministic fluctuations, and is the essence of the demand for money in the overlapping generations monetary models such as Black (1974) and Balasko and Shell (1980, 1981a, 1981b). As a store of value, money has difficulty in competing with interest-bearing assets, and the value of money may be driven out unless transactions costs give some advantage to money in relation to other assets. We see this transactions cost advantage modeled indirectly by adding cash-in-advance constraints [Clower (1967)], utility for holding money [Brock (1974)], credit verification costs [Woodford (1986)], or legal restrictions [Bryant and

Wallace (1983)]. Gale and Hellwig (1984) address this problem head on, showing existence of monetary equilibria. In their model of an infinite number of identical infinitely lived agents, money competes as a store of value against investment in firms controlled individually by agents. Because payments of dividends by an agent's firm to the agent require a transactions cost, money can survive as a store of value. This follows the spirit of the early inventory models of demand for money of Baumol (1952), Miller and Orr (1956), and Tobin (1956). While the structure of the Gale–Hellwig model is special indeed, there are no known limits on its ultimate extensions.

To reopen the finite horizon discussion, however, one can find grounds for an extremely general and tractable class of models by re-examining the question of a terminal value for money. If monetary markets are operated by an authority set up for the common good, it is natural to suppose that the authority would be willing to collect money left at the market after terminal trading and to dispose of it. (This implies potential moral harzard on the part of agents employed by the authority to dispose of money, but most central banks manage to dispose of worn currency without much difficulty.) A mere accounting identity would then force the total value of purchases to exceed the total value of sales. In monetary markets, however, buying and selling are distinct activities and are commonly given distinct prices, and a value for money can indeed be accommodated in the bid–ask spread. In any case, this story leads precisely to the definition of an equilibrium given first by Foley (1970) (without money) and Hahn (1971) (without and then with money):

> buying prices, selling prices, and optimal trades by agents given these prices, such that the total amount of each commodity (or money) bought is no greater than the total amount of each commodity (or money) sold.

Others, such as Starrett (1973), Kurz (1974a, 1974b, 1974c), Okuno (1973), and Hayashi (1974) have worked with this definition. The next section shows that this formulation is flexible enough to admit general monetary equilibrium in a static setting under standard regularity conditions, under the assumption: *not trading at all is Pareto inefficient.* After all, if money derives its value as a medium of exchange, equilibrium requires at least this latent demand for exchange. Existence with outside money based on this assumption resolves a dichotomy pointed out by Hayashi (1974), and extends naturally to the stochastic setting of Radner (1972), with security trading and incomplete markets. After showing existence of monetary equilibria in Section 2, we turn to an analysis of efficiency, indeterminacy, non-convexities, and incomplete markets in Section 3.

2. A simple model of monetary equilibrium

2.1. Preamble

The following simple model promotes the view that there is a natural setting admitting existence of monetary equilibria. Yamazaki (1989) has extended the results to a richer setting with non-convexities. The two main aspects of this work that differ from earlier work are:

(i) (*A place for money.*) A non-zero bid–ask spread at any non-zero of volume of trade is maintained throughout the existence proof. Any trade then implies a value for money.

(ii) (*A demand for money.*) An assumption that *Pareto-optimal allocations require trade* generates a demand for monetary transactions services. Since "pure money" has value only as an efficient medium of exchange, one needs a demand for exchange in order to give positive value to money.

If, in the last period of a finite horizon economy, there is a non-zero price for money, then money has a non-zero price in preceding periods by virtue of its facility also as a store of value, as shown by Heller (1974) among others. Thus, in order to convince the reader that monetary equilibria exist in finite horizon economies, the onus is essentially to demonstrate monetary equilibria in a static model, with the *pure outside fiat money* features:

(i) no "utility" for, or "real backing" of, money,

(ii) strictly positive money endowments, and

(iii) no cash-in-advance constraints or requirements to "return money to authorities" after trade.

A lengthier discussion of the implications and motivation of our model follows the formal results.

2.2. The model

Our point of departure is the model of Foley (1970) and Hahn (1971). We take a static complete markets setting, leaving the extension to a stochastic incomplete markets economy for later work. As discussed, the essential technical difficulties rest with the static economy induced at the terminal date.

A set of m agents is characterized, for each $i \in \{1, \ldots, m\}$, by a preference relation $\geq_i \subset \mathbb{R}^l_+ \times \mathbb{R}^l_+$ over bundles of l commodities, an endowment bundle $\omega_i \in \mathbb{R}^l_+$, an endowment $M_i \in [0, \infty)$ of money, and a transactions technology set $T_i \subset \mathbb{R}^l_+ \times \mathbb{R}^l_+ \times \mathbb{R}^l_+$, where $(b, s, z) \in T_i$ means that purchasing the bundle b and selling the bundle s can be accomplished at the cost of a bundle $z \in \mathbb{R}^l_+$. We write $x \geq_i y$ for $(x, y) \in \geq_i$ (meaning x is preferred to y), and $x >_i y$ if

$x \geq_i y$ and not $y \geq_i x$ (meaning x is strictly preferred to y). We always take it that $\geq_i$ is complete (meaning either $x \geq_i y$ or $y >_i x$ for any x and y in $\mathbb{R}^l_+$) and transitive, meaning $x \geq_i y$ and $y \geq_i z$ imply that $x \geq_i z$. A choice $(b, s, z) \in T_i$ by agent i leaves the consumption bundle $x_i = \omega_i + b - s - z$, and is *budget feasible* for i at buying prices $p^B \in \mathbb{R}^l$ and selling prices $p^S \in \mathbb{R}^l$ provided $x_i \geq 0$ and

$$p^B \cdot b - p^S \cdot s \leq M_i .$$

The actual transaction procedure would be to receive $p^S \cdot s$ in money, the unit of account, and spend at most the total amount of money $M_i + p^S \cdot s$ in purchasing b. As did Foley (1970) and Hahn (1971), we view buying goods and selling goods as separate activities, at distinct exchange prices. At prices (p^B, p^S), a budget feasible choice (b, s, z) is *optimal* for i provided $\omega_i + b - s - z \geq_i \omega_i + b' - s' - z'$ for any budget feasible choice (b', s', z'). A *monetary equilibrium* for $(\geq_i, \omega_i, M_i, T_i)$ is a collection

$$((b_1, s_1, z_1), \ldots, (b_m, s_m, z_m), (p^B, p^S)) \in (\mathbb{R}^{3l})^m \times \mathbb{R}^{2l}$$

such that, given prices (p^B, p^S), the choice $(b_i, s_i, z_i) \in T_i$ is optimal for each $i \in \{1, \ldots, m\}$, and the allocation $\{(b_i, s_i, z_i)\}$ is *feasible*: $\Sigma_i b_i \leq \Sigma_i s_i$. This is the definition of Foley (1970) and Hahn (1971), except that transactions costs here are borne individually as in Heller (1974), rather than brokered by firms. Hahn (1971) has the added generality of a sequence of time periods.

2.3. Efficiency

As usual, feasible choices $\{(b_i, s_i, z_i)\}$ are *efficient* if there are no feasible choices $\{(b'_i, s'_i, z'_i)\}$ such that $\omega_i + b'_i - s'_i - z'_i \geq_i \omega_i + b_i - s_i - z_i$ for all i, with strict preference for some i. The following efficiency result will later be useful in proving existence, and will also reappear in the general discussion of efficiency in Section 3. The preference relation $\geq_i$ is *semi-strictly convex* if

$$x >_i y \Rightarrow [\alpha x + (1 - \alpha)y] >_i y$$

for all $\alpha \in (0, 1)$, and *non-satiated* at a choice $(b, s, z) \in T_i$ if there exists a choice $(b', s', z') \in T_i$ such that $\omega_i + b' - s' - z' >_i \omega_i + b_i - s_i - z_i$.

Proposition 1. *Suppose* $(((b_1, s_1, z_1), \ldots, (b_m, s_m, z_m))(p^B, p^S))$ *is a monetary equilibrium with* $p^B = p^S$. *If, for all i, T_i is convex and $\geq_i$ is semi-strictly convex and non-satiated at feasible choices, then the allocation $\{(b_i, s_i, z_i)\}$ is efficient.*

Proof. Suppose $\{(b'_i, s'_i, z'_i)\}$ Pareto dominates $\{(b_i, s_i, z_i)\}$. For any i, let $(b, s, z) \in T_i$ be such that $\omega_i + b - s - z >_i \omega_i + b_i - s_i - z_i$. By semi-strict convexity,

$$\omega_i + \alpha(b - s - z) + (1 - \alpha)(b'_i - s'_i - z'_i) >_i \omega_i + b_i - s_i - z_i.$$

for all $\alpha \in (0, 1)$, implying that $p^B \cdot [\alpha b + (1 - \alpha)b'_i] - p^S \cdot [\alpha s + (1 - \alpha)s'_i] > M_i$ for all $\alpha \in (0, 1)$, implying that $p^B \cdot b'_i - p^S \cdot s'_i \geq M_i$ for all i since $p^B \cdot b_i - p^S \cdot s_i \leq M_i$. For some i, $p^B \cdot b'_i - p^S \cdot s'_i > M_i$. Thus $p^B \cdot \sum_i b'_i - p^S \cdot \sum_i s'_i > 0$, which contradicts $p^B = p^S$ and $\sum_i b_i \leq \sum_i s_i$. $\square$

2.4. Assumptions

Turning to existence, we note that if money has value only as a medium of exchange and is in strictly positive supply, then monetary equilibrium must imply some demand for exchange, yielding our first assumption: the inefficiency of not trading.

(A.1) The allocation $0 \in \mathbb{R}^{3lm}$ is not efficient.

Of course, if the total supply of money $M = \sum_{i=1}^{m} M_i$ is zero, then (A.1) can be dispensed with, so we offer an alternative:

(A.1') $M = 0$.

Our next three assumptions are typical, although convexity of the transactions technology is objectionable. Remedies for non-convexities are discussed in Section 3.

(A.2) For all i, T_i is closed, convex, and includes 0.

(A.3) (Free disposal). For all i, if $(b, s, z) \in T_i$ and $(b', s') \in [0, b] \times [0, s]$, then $z' \geq z \Rightarrow (b', s', z') \in T_i$.

(A.4) (Costly transactions). For all i, if $(b, s, z) \in T_i$ and $(b, s) \neq 0$, then $z \neq 0$.

We add an assumption that transactions costs are not so large as to make all strictly positive sales infeasible. By strictly positive sales s, we mean $s \in \text{int}(R^l_+)$, denoted $s \gg 0$.

(A.5) For all i, there exists $(b, s, z) \in T_i$ such that $s \gg 0$.

We make strong assumptions on agents' preferences and endowments; these can be weakened along a traditional route by more complicated transactions assumptions, as in Kurz (1974a). The relation $\geq_i$ is *strictly monotone* if $[x \geq y \geq 0, \ x \neq y] \Rightarrow x >_i y$ and *continuous* if $\{x: x \geq_i y\}$ and $\{x: y \geq_i x\}$ are closed for all y in $\mathbb{R}^l_+$.

(A6) For all i, $\geq_i$ is continuous, strictly monotone, semi-strictly convex, and non-satiated at feasible choices.

Assumption (A.6) is satisfied, for example, by preference relations represented by increasing strictly concave utility functions.

(A.7) For all i, $\omega_i \gg 0$.

2.5. Existence of monetary equilibria

Theorem 1. *Under condition* (A.1) *or* (A.1') *and* (A.2)–(A.7), *there exist monetary equilibria for the economy* $(\geq_i, \omega_i, M_i, T_i)$.

Proof. Let $\bar{\Lambda}$ be any diagonal $l \times l$ matrix with diagonal elements in $(0, 1)$, let I denote the $l \times l$ identity matrix, and let $\omega = \sum_{i=1}^m \omega_i$. For any $v \in [0, m\omega]$, let

$$\Lambda(v) = \frac{\|v\|}{\|m\omega\|} \bar{\Lambda} + \frac{\|m\omega\| - \|v\|}{\|m\omega\|} I .$$

Let Δ denote the unit simplex for $\mathbb{R}^l$. For purposes of this proof only, we normalize buying prices to this simplex, and express selling prices and the value p^M of money relative to buying prices. We define the *volume of trade*, a useful technical concept, as the maximum $v \in \mathbb{R}^l$ (element-by-element) of the vectors $\bar{b} = \sum_i b_i$ and $\bar{s} = \sum_i s_i$ defining total purchases and sales. At buying prices $p \in \Delta$ and total volume of trade $v \in [0, m\omega]$, we set selling prices at $\Lambda(v)p$. We can then establish $\bar{p}^M = m[(I - \bar{\Lambda})\mathbf{1}] \cdot \omega/M$, where $\mathbf{1} = (1, 1, \ldots, 1)$, as an upper bound on the price of money relative to the buying prices of goods.

We have the constrained budget and demand correspondence as follows. For any $(v, p, p^M) \in [0, m\omega] \times \Delta \times [0, \bar{p}^M]$, let

$$\beta_i(v, p, p^M) = \{(b, s, z) \in T_i \cap [0, \omega]^3: p \cdot b - [\Lambda(v)p] \cdot s \leq p^M M_i, \ \omega_i + b$$
$$- s - z \geq 0\} ,$$

$$\varphi_i(v, p, p^M) = \{(b, s, z) \in B_i(v, p, p^M): \omega_i + b - s$$
$$- z \geq_i \omega_i + b' - s' - z', \forall (b', s', z') \in B_i(v, p, p^M)\},$$

$$\varphi(v, p, p^M) = \sum_{i=1}^{m} \varphi_i(v, p, p^M).$$

For any $(\bar{b}, \bar{s}) \in [0, m\omega]^2$, let $\tau(\bar{b}, \bar{s}) = \{\max(\bar{b}, \bar{s})\}$, where $\max(\cdot, \cdot)$ denotes the element-by-element maximum function. This defines a *volume-of-trade correspondence*. For any $(\bar{b}, \bar{s}, v) \in [0, m\omega]^3$, let

$$\mu(\bar{b}, \bar{s}, v) = \arg\max_{p \in \Delta} p \cdot (\bar{b} - v) + [\Lambda(v)p] \cdot (v - \bar{s}).$$

For any $(p, v) \in \Delta \times [0, m\omega]$, if $M = 0$, let $\nu(p, v) = \{\bar{p}^M\}$; and if $M > 0$, let

$$\nu(p, v) = \{[p - \Lambda(v)p] \cdot v/M\} \subset [0, \bar{p}^M].$$

Finally, for any $[p, p^M, (\bar{b}, \bar{s}, \bar{z}), v] \in \Delta \times [0, \bar{p}^M] \times [0, m\omega]^3 \times [0, m\omega]$, let

$$\psi[p, p^M, (\bar{b}, \bar{s}, \bar{z}), v] = \mu(\bar{b}, \bar{s}, v) \times \nu(p, v) \times \varphi(v, p, p^M) \times \tau(\bar{b}, \bar{s}).$$

We may think of μ setting commodity prices to maximize the market value of excess demand; ν setting the relative price p^M of money so as to clear the market for money; φ as the total demand function for purchases, sales, and transactions inputs at relative prices $(p, \Lambda(v)p, p^M)$ for buying, selling, and money; and τ supplying a sufficient level of transactions services in both the purchases and sales markets.

By the continuity of Λ and the usual arguments, μ has non-empty convex values and is upper semicontinuous. These conditions also apply obviously to the singleton-valued continuous correspondences ν and τ. As for φ, one must show that φ is upper semicontinuous; the other properties are quickly verified. For upper semicontinuity of φ_i, the only delicate point to check is lower semicontinuity of β_i. This follows from the usual argument. That is, given $(v_n, p_n, p_n^M) \to (v, p, p^M)$ and $(b, s, z) \in B_i(v, p, p^M)$, let (b', s', z') be chosen so that $\omega_i + b' - s' - z' \gg 0$ and so that $p \cdot b' - [\Lambda(v)p] \cdot s' < p^M M_i$. [This can be done by (A.2), (A.3), (A.5), and (A.7).] For n sufficiently large, (b', s', z') satisfies these same strict inequalities relative to (v_n, p_n, p_n^M). For each n sufficiently large, let $\alpha_n \in (0, 1)$ be chosen so that

$$(b_n, s_n, z_n) \equiv \alpha_n(b', s', z') + (1 - \alpha_n)(b, s, z) \in B_i(v_n, p_n, p_n^M).$$

Since we can allow $\alpha_n \to 0$ with this property, β_i is lower semicontinuous, and φ_i is therefore upper semicontinuous. This implies that φ is upper semicontinuous.

Since μ, ν, φ, and τ are non-empty valued, convex valued, and upper semicontinuous, ψ inherits these properties, and has a fixed point $[p, p^M, (\bar{b}, \bar{s}, \bar{z}), v]$ by Kakutani's Fixed Point Theorem. Since $(b_i, s_i, z_i) \in \varphi_i(v, p, p^M) \Rightarrow p \cdot b_i - [\Lambda(v)p] \cdot s_i \leq p^M M_i$ for all i, and since $[p - \Lambda(v)p] \cdot v = p^M M$ for $M > 0$, we know that our fixed point has the property: $p \cdot (b - v) + [\Lambda(v)p] \cdot (v - \bar{s}) \leq 0$. Suppose, for some $k \in \{1, \ldots, l\}$, that $v_k > \bar{s}_k$. Let $q \in \Delta$ have $q_k = 1$. Then, since $\bar{b}_k = v_k$ by definition of τ, we have $q \cdot (\bar{b} - v) + [\Lambda(v)q] \cdot (v - \bar{s}) = (v_k - \bar{s}_k) > 0$, a contradiction of the definition of μ. Thus, $v \leq \bar{s}$, and therefore $\bar{b} \leq \bar{s}$, and there exist $(b_i, s_i, z_i) \in \varphi_i(v, p, p^M)$ for $i \in \{1, \ldots, m\}$ such that $\sum_{i=1}^{m} b_i \leq \sum_{i=1}^{m} s_i$. If $p^M \neq 0$, it follows that

$$((b_1, s_1, z_1), \ldots, (b_m, s_m, z_m), p/p^M, \Lambda(v)p/p^M)$$

is a monetary equilibrium, since the restriction of (b_i, s_i, z_i) to $[0, \omega]^3$ is not a binding constraint, given that $s_i \leq \omega_i$ and the inoptimality of buying and selling the same commodity at prices $p^S \leq p^B$ under (A.4).

Suppose $p^M = 0$. If $v = 0$, then $\Lambda(v) = I$, and $((0,0,0), \ldots, (0,0,0,), p, p)$ is a monetary equilibrium for the economy $(\geq_i, \omega_i, 0, T_i)$, $i \in \{1, \ldots, m\}$ (with zero money endowments). This, however, contradicts the inefficiency of no trade assumption (A.1) and Proposition 1. If $v \neq 0$, then $\bar{s}_k > 0$ for some $k \in \{1, \ldots, l\}$. But strict monotonicity (A.6) then implies that $p_k > 0$, implying that $p_k v_k > 0$, yielding the contradiction $p^M > 0$. Thus, $p^M > 0$, and the proof is complete. □

For the existence of equilibrium without free disposal of commodities, somewhat stronger conditions on the transactions technology sets will suffice, as shown by Kurz (1974a). One requires that the equilibrium buying price of any commodity is not zero, which follows, for example, if one can always be made strictly better off by buying some of a commodity for free and incurring the transactions costs. Our discussion of the efficiency and determinacy of monetary equilibria in Section 3 will hinge partly on the above method of proof, which implies existence of a class of equilibria with interesting properties.

2.6. Example

We display a simple example of monetary equilibria for two agents and two commodities. Let $\geq_1$ and $\geq_2$ be represented by the same utility function

$u: \mathbb{R}_+^2 \to \bar{\mathbb{R}}$ defined by $u(x) = \log(x_1) + \log(x_2)$ for $x \gg 0$ and $u(x) = -\infty$ otherwise. Let $T_1 = T_2 \subset \mathbb{R}_+^6$ be defined by $(b, s, z) \in T_i \Leftrightarrow z_k \geq 0.1(b_k + s_k)$ for $k \in \{1, 2\}$, or a 10 percent transactions loss. Let $\omega_1 = (8.1, 12.1)$ and $\omega_2 = (\frac{119.9}{9}, \frac{80.1}{11})$. Let $M_1 = 0$ and $M_2 = 2$. We claim that the prices $p^B = (10, 11)$ and $p^S = (9, 10)$; the trades $b_1 = (1, 0)$, $s_1 = (0, 1)$ and $b_2 = (0, 1)$, $s_2 = (1, 0)$; and the transactions costs $z_1 = z_2 = (0.1, 0.1)$ determine a monetary equilibrium. The resulting allocation is $x_1 = (9, 11)$ and $x_2 = (11/0.9, 9/1.1)$. Budget feasibility follows easily. The first-order conditions for agent 1 at (b_1, s_1, z_1) are satisfied, since

$$\frac{(p_1^B, p_2^S)}{100} = \left[(1 - \tau) \cdot \frac{\partial u(x_1)}{\partial x_{11}}, (1 + \tau) \cdot \frac{\partial u(x_1)}{\partial x_{12}} \right] = \left(\frac{1 - \tau}{x_{11}}, \frac{1 + \tau}{x_{12}} \right)$$

and

$$\frac{p_1^S}{100} < \frac{1 + \tau}{x_{11}}, \quad \frac{p_2^B}{100} > \frac{1 - \tau}{x_{12}},$$

where $\tau = 0.10$ is the minimal transactions loss. Similarly, the first-order conditions for agent 2 are satisfied, and we have a monetary equilibrium. We note that this economy satisfies all of the conditions (A.1)–(A.7) of our existence theorem. In particular, not trading is inefficient. This ends the example.

2.7. Discussion

Although many scenarios present themselves in support of our formulation, we might imagine the following one.

A monetary authority operates markets of exchange of l commodities for money at each time t in $\{0, 1, \ldots, T\}$ at commodity spot purchase prices $p_t^B \in \mathbb{R}^l$ and spot sales prices $p_t^S \in \mathbb{R}^l$. (These prices and other quantities may be random.) We may have $p_t^B \neq p_t^S$ in equilibrium, since transactions costs may be severe enough to prevent arbitrage over the bid–ask spread: $p_t^B - p_t^S$. If the total volume of trade in period t is $v_t \in \mathbb{R}^l$, then the amount of money added to the economy in period t is $\Delta M_t = (p_t^S - p_t^B) \cdot v_t$, an accounting identity. The monetary authority has no preferences, does not consume, and is able to costlessly dispose of commodities and money left at the market after trade. We are thinking of money as currency, rather than its creditory forms, and thus require non-negative balances of money by agents. One could also add credit or securities such as futures, bonds, or deposits to the model. In fact, there may also be a barter sector at different exchange prices p_t. For simplicity, we have implicitly assumed that the barter transactions technology is dominated by the monetary exchange technology, as did Hahn (1971) and Heller (1974). More generally, an equilibrium would involve a mixture of barter and monetary transactions [Kurz (1974c)], but the spirit of our analysis covers this case, and a generalization to a mixed-exchange model is easy. Since mixed equilibrium allocations at $p_t^B = p_t^S$ are Pareto optimal by the same "adding up" argument of Arrow (1951) and Debreu (1954) used in the proof of Lemma 1, one must only make regularity condition (A.1) apply to trades in the monetary sector. One would also expect to find a mixture of brokered and individualistic transactions technologies. Many have assumed a purely brokered technology run by firms. We follow Heller's (1974) purely individualistic transactions technology for simplicity, making for a pure exchange model. Our results will hold up under the purely brokered convention, or under a mixture of individualistic and brokered transactions.

Now, in a particular state of the world, after payment of dividends of all securities at the last period T, we are left with an economy $(\geq_i, \omega_i, M_i, T_i)$, as in our formulation. If a monetary equilibrium for the economy exists, then a natural demand for money as a store of value exists at time $T-1$, at least in those states of the world for which $(\geq_i, \omega_i, M_i, T_i)$ emerges at time T with positive conditional probability. There is thus a natural source of value for money at time $T-1$. Of course, given positive time preference or time fluctuations in consumption, bonds may also act as a store of value with a rate of return that dominates the return on money. Without transactions costs, this would drive out any value for money. Given transactions costs, selling money and buying bonds at $T-1$, and then selling at time T bonds for consumption (which may be very cumbersome) or bonds for money, can be more costly than holding money between $T-1$ and T at a lower (gross) return. One can easily imagine that agents generally choose to hold money between successive periods of sufficiently short duration, rather than incurring the costs of converting deposits or securities for every transaction.

This story is well understood and can be found, for example, in Heller (1974). The object of our formal model is to provide a foundation for the missing link: a terminal value for money. The fact that agents do not end up holding money after exchange at time T is hardly surprising, and not contradictory of any natural aspects of our economy. If a terminal period were really "announced", one should be confident that agents will indeed sell all money, so long as converting money itself is not a costly transaction. (Incidentally, adding a transactions cost to exchange of money will not overturn our existence result.) Furthermore, the exchange authority can induce agents to acquire money in an initial period, rather than directly endowing agents with money, by offering a negative bid–ask spread at time zero. The same device used in our proof applies in this case. In particular, one need not use an infinite horizon model to study monetary equilibria, although an infinite horizon model may allow convenient time-independent representations of equilibria.

In our simple model, money is neutral, in the sense that an equilibrium allocation is still an equilibrium allocation for any strictly positive scaling of commodity prices and money endowments. Money is not *inessential*, a distinction of Hahn (1973a), in the sense that the presence of money, in particular its distribution among agents, has real allocational effects. Transactions costs do not pay an important role in the proof of Theorem 1. One may conjecture that existence also obtains without transactions costs. The underlying natural model that includes a barter sector, however, would call for distinctions in the relative transactional efficiency of the monetary sector. This is in line with the view of Hicks (1935): that we will not make convincing progress in understanding the role of money in markets until we come to grips with transactional frictions.

3. Inefficiency, indeterminacy, non-convexities, and incomplete markets

3.1. General discussion

Many readers know that the topics *inefficiency*, *indeterminacy*, and *non-convexity* are closely related, particularly in the context of monetary equilibria. We briefly review these issues. For simplicity of exposition, we often use differentiable notions, some of which extend by the use of convex analysis.

There are at least three sources of inefficiency in both monetary and non-monetary economies.

(i) In a model with a sequence of markets under uncertainty, an absence of complete forward markets can prevent agents from equating their marginal rates of substitution among bundles of goods that are not available through markets. Thus, certain technologically feasible transfers of goods by other than market feasible transactions can Pareto improve an equilibrium allocation.

(ii) With distinct markets for buying and selling, such as one would find in a monetary economy, it can happen that buying prices differ from selling prices, and agents' marginal rates of substitution can therefore differ even among marketed bundles of goods, another potential source of inefficiency.

(iii) Typical convexity assumptions are often unrealistic, especially for transactions technologies, which are thought to demonstrate increasing returns to scale. With non-convexities (in either preferences or production technologies), equating marginal rates of substitution among agents to marginal costs of firms is necessary but not sufficient for Pareto optimality. Value-maximizing firms with increasing returns to scale, moreover, will not necessarily produce so as to equate prices with marginal costs.

We have not even mentioned asymmetric information, also a potential source of inefficiency, as it has yet to be dealt with satisfactorily even in non-monetary general equilibrium theory. As commented by Hahn (1980), various sources of inefficiency are so endemic that a discussion of Pareto optimality in the context of monetary theory may be placing undue stress on the role of money in inefficiencies. To the contrary, money may mitigate each of these problems. In any case, one typically comes face to face with these sources of inefficiency only when modeling an economy in a setting that is sufficiently rich to encompass money in a non-trivial way.

One notes that incompleteness of markets (i) is merely evidence of non-convexities in the transactions technology (iii). With lump-sum costs for setting up markets, a non-convexity, entrepreneurs or governmental authorities will naturally neglect to set up every possible market. Indeed, market completeness may be evidence of inefficiency, in that too many resources may have been allocated to setting up markets. Furthermore, numerous markets imply a low level of activity on each, and further welfare losses can result from overly thin markets. Of course, given non-convexities, the particular structure of incomplete markets that endogenously arises will generally be inefficient. For an exception, see Duffie and Jackson (1989); for an example of an equilibrium allocation that Pareto dominates another equilibrium allocation generated by the addition of a market, see Hart (1975). We have more to add shortly concerning inefficiency and indeterminacy in the context of a smooth model of financial market incompleteness. As for production non-convexities in general equilibrium, there is a large and growing theory on existence and inefficiencies. Readers may consult Guesnerie (1984) for a survey, and Bonnisseau and Cornet (1986a, 1986b), Cornet (1986), as well as Dehez and Drèze (1986) for recent contributions. One contemplates a model in which, due to non-convexities in the technology of setting up and maintaining markets, a central authority might step in to operate markets (maximizing an objective function that eludes this author). Bonnisseau and Cornet, for example, show the existence of equilibria with a large class of objectives for the firm (here, the exchange authority), provided the firm can allocate costs or profits by some scheme such as profit shares, taxes, or subsidies. As far as existence is concerned, one can alternatively exploit the effects of a large number of small agents in convexifying the excess demand correspondence. For two applications of this idea to the existence of monetary equilibrium, see Heller and Starr (1976), who obtain approximate equilibria for a large finite number of agents using the Shapley–Folkman theorem, and Gale and Hellwig (1984), who follow Hildenbrand (1974) in exploiting the convexifying effects of a non-atomic measure space of agents. [See Yamazaki (1989).]

Inefficiencies caused by variation in buying and selling prices (ii) can be ameliorated in two ways. First, brokerage firms can undertake to provide certain transactions services. If the technology is convex, value-maximizing firms (in complete markets) will produce and allocate transactions services in a Pareto-optimal manner. In a completely brokered transactions model, the bid–ask spread is then merely replaced by the price of transactions services, and the usual assumptions and arguments imply efficiency. Completely brokered and completely individualistic transactions models are at opposite ends of a spectrum that seems to have been hiding from the eyes of theorists. Second, the notion of efficiency used in the simple model of Section 2 already accounts for the fact that transactions technologies are individualistic. Relative to this constraint, we may still have inefficiencies caused by the value of money itself. In our proof of existence, the relative size of the bid–ask spread can be made arbitrarily small by choosing the matrix $\bar{A}$ arbitrarily close to the identity matrix, meaning an arbitrarily small value of money relative to goods. As the relative value of money shrinks to zero, buying prices converge to selling prices, and price distortions caused by endowments of money can be made arbitrarily small. Thus, relative to the transactions technology, we may have large or arbitrarily small inefficiencies. This is also a source of real indeterminacy in equilibrium allocations, it seems.

3.2. *Incomplete markets with inside money: Indeterminacy and inoptimality*

Although many of the above comments are speculative, we do have a specific model of existence, inoptimality, and indeterminacy of equilibrium in incomplete markets with money. Although we limit ourselves to the case of inside money so as to apply currently available results, there should be little doubt that the following conclusions extend in a natural way to outside money and the equilibrium notion used in the simple model of Section 2.

   We take two periods of trade, with uncertainty in the form of a random state $s \in \{1, \ldots, S\}$ to be revealed in the second period. With l commodities, the consumption space is thus $\mathbb{R}^L$, with $L = l(S + 1)$. The initial period component of a typical bundle $x \in \mathbb{R}^L$ is denoted $x_1 \in \mathbb{R}^l$; the final period component in state s is denoted $x_2(s) \in \mathbb{R}^l$, for each $s \in \{1, \ldots, S\}$. Similarly, spot commodity prices are represented by a price vector $p \in \mathbb{R}^L$ of the form $(p_1, p_2(1), p_2(2), \ldots, p_2(S))$. Securities, N in number and represented by an $S \times N$ dividend matrix d, are available for trade in the initial period. The (s, n)-element of d is the number of units of account paid to a holder of one unit of the nth security in state s of the final period, just as in the original model of Arrow (1953). The initial prices of the N securities are given by a vector $q \in \mathbb{R}^N$. We always take it that the first security is money, meaning that $d_{s1} = 1$ for all $s \in \{1, \ldots, S\}$ and that $q_1 = 1$. Agents are not endowed with securities; they are held in zero net supply. In particular, we are dealing with inside money, which may be borrowed (held negatively, as a credit instrument).

Leaving transactions costs out of the picture, the m agents are represented by a preference relation $\geq_i \subset \mathbb{R}_+^L \times \mathbb{R}_+^L$ and an endowment $\omega^i \in \mathbb{R}_+^L$, for each $i \in \{1, \ldots, m\}$. Each agent chooses a consumption plan $x \in \mathbb{R}_+^L$ and a security portfolio $\theta \in \mathbb{R}^N$. Given prices (p, q) for commodities and securities, a plan $(x, \theta) \in \mathbb{R}_+^L \times \mathbb{R}^N$ is *budget feasible* for agent i if initially budget feasible:

$$p_1 \cdot (x_1 - \omega_1^i) + q \cdot \theta \leq 0,$$

and if budget feasible in each terminal state $s \in \{1, \ldots, S\}$:

$$p_2(s) \cdot [x_2(s) - \omega_2^i(s)] \leq d_s \theta,$$

where d_s is the sth row of d. If $N = 1$, or money is the only security, this is a pure consumption–loan model, such as that faced by one generation of an overlapping generations model. If $N < S$, markets are incomplete; there are some consumption plans that cannot be financed by any portfolio of securities. A budget feasible plan (x, θ) for agent i is *optimal* for i if there is no budget feasible plan (x', θ') for i such that $x' >_i x$. An *equilibrium* is a collection

$$[(x^1, \theta^1), \ldots, (x^m, \theta^m), p, q] \in (\mathbb{R}_+^L \times \mathbb{R}^n)^m \times \mathbb{R}^L \times \mathbb{R}^N$$

such that, for each agent $i \in \{1, \ldots, m\}$, the plan (x^i, θ^i) is optimal for i given prices (p, q) for consumption and securities, and such that markets clear: $\sum_i x^i - \omega^i = 0$ and $\sum_i \theta^i = 0$. Existence of equilibria in this model was first shown by Werner (1985) and Cass (1984). The following result is from Duffie (1987), which gives much weaker conditions than (A.6) and (A.7).

Theorem 2. *Under assumption (A.6) and (A.7), there exist equilibria for the incomplete markets model* $[(\geq_i, \omega_i), d]$*. Moreover, for any* $\lambda \in \mathbb{R}_{++}^S$ *with* $\sum_s \lambda_s = 1$*, there exists an equilibrium*

$$[(x^{\lambda 1}, \theta^{\lambda 1}), \ldots, (x^{\lambda m}, \theta^{\lambda m}), p^\lambda, q^\lambda]$$

with $q^\lambda = d^\top \lambda$.

The second part of the theorem states that for any *state price vector* λ [an interior element of the $(S-1)$-dimensional unit simplex], there exists an equilibrium in which the market value of any security is merely the value of its state-contingent future dividends, discounted at the given state prices λ. Normalizing state prices to the unit simplex guarantees that money retains its role as a numeraire. The indeterminacy in security valuation shown in Theorem 2 suggests the potential for indeterminacy in the real allocation,

which has indeed been shown by Geanakoplos and Mas-Colell (1985), Balasko
and Cass (1989), and Werner (1986). To illustrate this indeterminacy, and to
contrast with the results of Debreu (1972), who showed that complete markets
equilibrium allocations are locally unique, we record the following version of
Debreu's *smooth preference* assumptions.

(A.6′) For each agent i, the preference relation $\succeq_i$ is represented by a
continuous utility function $u_i: \mathbb{R}^L_+ \to \mathbb{R}$ with the following properties at each
$x \in \mathbb{R}^L_{++}$:

    (i) u_i is three times continuously differentiable (smooth),

    (ii) the first partial derivative $Du_i(x)$ is in $\mathbb{R}^L_{++}$ (strictly monotone),

    (iii) $h^\top D^2 u_i(x) h < 0$ for all non-zero $h \in \mathbb{R}^L$ such that $Du_i(x)h = 0$ (differen-
tiably strictly convex preferences), and

    (iv) the closure of $\{y \in \mathbb{R}^L_+ : u_i(y) \geq u_i(x)\}$ is contained by $\mathbb{R}^L_{++}$.

The boundary condition (iv) states roughly that a bundle with some of every
good is better than any bundle with nothing of some good. Assumption (A.6′)
is satisfied, for example, by Cobb–Douglas utility functions.

    Theorem 2 allows for $S - 1$ degrees of freedom in security valuation. Is there
a similar degree of freedom in the equilibrium allocation $(x^{\wedge 1}, \ldots, x^{\wedge m})$ as the
state price vector λ varies in the $(S - 1)$-dimensional simplex? The answer is
essentially "Yes, for most economies", as shown by Geanakoplos and Mas-
Colell (1985) and Cass (1985). Specifically, we say *the dimension of real
allocational indeterminancy of* $((\succeq_i, \omega_i), d)$ *is* n if the set of equilibrium
allocations for the economy contains a subset diffeomorphic to the interior of
the n-dimensional unit simplex. We parameterize an economy by its endow-
ment vector $\omega = (\omega^1, \ldots, \omega^m) \in \mathbb{R}^{mL}_+$, and say that a condition holds *generically* if it holds for all endowments ω except those in a closed subset of $\mathbb{R}^{mL}_+$ of
Lebesgue measure zero. We add the following regularity conditions on the
dividend matrix d.

(A.8) $1 \leq N < m$.

An $S \times N$ matrix with $N \leq S$ is in *general position* if every $N \times N$ sub-matrix
formed by deleting rows is non-singular.

(A.9) d is in general position.

Theorem 3 (Geanakoplos and Mas–Colell). *Suppose* $N < S$ *(incomplete markets). Under conditions* (A.6′), (A.8), *and* (A.9), *generically the dimension of
real allocational indeterminacy is* $S - 1$.

Our interpretation, parameterizing the indeterminacy by the state price vector λ, is given in the method of proof of Werner (1986). While some have claimed that a useful model of monetary equilibria should exhibit determinacy of the allocation, one cannot simply wish away the allocational degrees of freedom apparent in this result. Presumably aspects of the economy that are yet to be modeled, perhaps calling for a non-Walrasian model, also play a role in determining the equilibrium allocation. It has been apparent for some time in the overlapping generations genre of models that money plays a role in the indeterminacy of allocations. [Santos and Bona (1986) may represent the state of this art.] An examination of the source of Theorem 3 shows that the indeterminacy does not depend on one of the securities being money. Furthermore, if there are no securities ($N = 0$) or no uncertainty ($S = 1$), the indeterminacy disappears.

For incomplete markets, Geanakoplos and Polemarchakis (1986) define a notion of constrained sub-optimality of the following sort. Given prices (p, q), a budget feasible plan (x, θ) for agent i is *spot optimal for* i if there is no consumption plan x' such that (x', θ) is budget feasible and $x' >_i x$. A *fixed portfolio equilibirum* is a collection

$$[(x^1, \theta^1), \ldots, (x^m, \theta^m), p, q] \in (\mathbb{R}_+^L \times \mathbb{R}^N)^m \times \mathbb{R}^L \times \mathbb{R}^N$$

such that, given prices (p, q), for each agent i the plan (x^i, θ^i) is spot optimal, and markets clear. In particular, an equilibrium is a fixed portfolio equilibrium. An equilibrium allocation $a = ((x^1, \theta^1), \ldots, (x^m, \theta^m))$ for the incomplete markets economy $((\geq_i, \omega_i), d)$ is *constrained sub-optimal* if, for any $\epsilon > 0$, there exists a fixed portfolio equilibrium allocation $\bar{a} = ((\bar{x}^1, \bar{\theta}^1), \ldots, (\bar{x}^m, \bar{\theta}^m))$ with $\|a - \bar{a}\| \leq \epsilon$ such that $(\bar{x}^1, \ldots, \bar{x}^m)$ Pareto dominates $(x^1, \ldots, x^m)$. Under the same preference assumptions (A.6), and with a slightly different model, Geanakoplos and Polemarchakis give additional regularity conditions under which incomplete markets equilibria are generically constrained sub-optimal. (Here, the result is generic with respect to both endowments and preferences.) In other words, at equilibrium, a central planner could make a slight change in portfolios so as to improve the resulting market-clearing consumption allocation.

4. Concluding remark

To repeat, the aims of this chapter are extremely narrow relative to those of the modern literature on monetary equilibrium theory. Grandmont (1983), on the other hand, is an excellent synthesis of classical and neoclassical theories of monetary equilibria.

References

Arrow, K. (1951) 'An extension of the basic theorems of classical welfare economics', in: J. Neyman, ed., *Proceedings of the Second Berkeley Symposium on Mathematical Statistics and Probability*. Berkeley: University of California Press.

Arrow, K. (1953) 'Le rôle des valeurs boursières pour la répartition la meillure des risques', *Econometrie*, pp. 41–47; discussion, pp. 47–48, Colloq. Internat. Centre National de la Recherche Scientifique, no. 40 (Paris, 1952) C.N.R.S. Paris, 1953; translated in *Review of Economic Studies*, 31 (1964): 91–96.

Arrow, K. and G. Debreu (1954) 'Existence of an equilibrium for a competitive economy' *Econometrica*, 22: 265–290.

Balasko, Y and D. Cass (1989) 'The structure of financial equilibrium with exogenous yields: The case of incomplete markets', *Econometrica*, 57: 135–162.

Balasko, Y. and K. Shell (1980) 'The overlapping-generations model, Part I', *Journal of Economic Theory*, 23: 281–306.

Balasko, Y. and K. Shell (1981a) 'The overlapping-generations model, Part II', *Journal of Economic Theory*, 24: 112–142.

Balasko, Y. and K. Shell (1981b) 'The overlapping-generations model, Part III', *Journal of Economic Theory*, 24: 143–152.

Baumol, W. (1952) 'The transactions demand for cash: An inventory theoretic approach', *Quarterly Journal of Economics*, 66: 545–556.

Bewley, T. (1980) 'The optimum quantity of money', in: J. Kareken and N. Wallace, eds., *Models of monetary economics*. Minneapolis: Federal Reserve Bank of Minneapolis.

Bewley, T. (1984) 'Fiscal and monetary policy in a general equilibrium model', Working Paper 690, Cowles Foundation for Research in Economics at Yale University.

Black, F. (1974) 'Uniqueness of price level in monetary growth models with rational expectations', *Journal of Economic Theory*, 7: 53–65.

Bonnisseau, J.-M. and B. Cornet (1986a) 'Existence of equilibria when firms follow bounded losses pricing rules', Research Paper 8607, CORE, Louvain-La-Neuve, Belgium.

Bonnisseau, J.-M. and B. Cornet (1986b) 'Existence of marginal cost pricing equilibria in an economy with several non convex firms', Unpublished, CERMSEM, Université Paris I.

Brock W. (1974) 'Money and growth: The case of long-run perfect foresight', *International Economic Review*, 15: 750–777.

Bryant, J. and N. Wallace (1983) 'A suggestion for further simplifying the theory of money', Research Paper 62, Federal Reserve Bank of Minneapolis, Research Department.

Cass, D. (1984) 'Competitive equilibrium with incomplete financial markets', CARESS Working Paper 84-09, University of Pennsylvania.

Cass, D. (1985) 'On the "Number" of equilibrium allocations with incomplete financial markets', CARESS Working Paper 85–16, University of Pennsylvania.

Cass, D., M. Okuno and I. Zilcha (1979) 'The role of money in supporting the Pareto optimality of competitive equilibrium in consumption loan type models', *Journal of Economic Theory*, 20: 41–80.

Clower, R. (1967) 'A reconsideration of the microfoundations of monetary theory', *Western Economic Journal*, 6: 1–9.

Cornet, B. (1986) 'The second welfare theorem in nonconvex economies', Unpublished, Université Paris I, Panthéon–Sorbonne, and CORE, Université Catholique de Louvain, Belgium.

G. Debreu (1954) 'Valuation equilibrium and Pareto optimum', *Proceedings of the National Academy of Sciences*, 40: 588–592.

G. Debreu (1970) 'Economies with a finite set of equilibria', *Econometrica*, 38: 387–392.

G. Debreu (1972) 'Smooth preferences', *Econometrica*, 40: 603–615.

G. Debreu (1976) 'Smooth preferences: A corrigendum', *Econometrica*, 44: 831–832.

Dehez, P. and J. Drèze (1986) 'Competitive equilibria with increasing returns', Research Paper 8623, CORE, Louvain-la-Neuve, Belgium.

Duffie, D. (1987) 'Stochastic equilibria with incomplete financial markets', *Journal of Economic Theory*, 41: 405–416; Corrigendum, 49: 384.

Duffie, D. and M. Jackson (1989) 'Optimal innovation of futures contracts', *Review of Financial Studies*, 2: 275–296.

Foley, D. (1970) 'Economic equilibrium with costly marketing', *Journal of Economic Theory*, 2: 276–291.

Friedman, M. (1969) *The optimum quantity of money*. Chicago: Aldine.

Gale, D. (1982) *Money: In equilibrium*. Cambridge University Press.

Gale, D. and M. Hellwig (1984) 'A general-equilibrium model of the transactions demand for money', CARESS Working Paper 85–07, University of Pennsylvania.

Geanakoplos, J. and A. Mas–Colell (1985) 'Real indeterminacy with financial assets', Unpublished, Cowles Foundation, Yale University.

Geanakoplos, J. and H. Polemarchakis (1986) 'Existence, regularity, and constrained suboptimality of competitive portfolio allocations when the asset market is incomplete', in: W.P. Heller and D.A. Starrett, eds., *Uncertainty information and communication. Essays in honor of Kenneth J. Arrow*, Vol. III. Cambridge University Press.

Grandmont, J.-M. (1983) *Money and value: A reconsideration of classical and neoclassical theories*. Cambridge University Press.

Green, J. and E. Sheshinski (1975) 'Competitive inefficiencies in the presence of constrained transactions', *Journal of economic Theory*, 10: 343–357.

Guesnerie, R. (1984) 'First best allocation of resources with non convexities in production', Unpublished, Ecole des Hautes Etudes en Sciences Sociales, Paris.

Hahn, F. (1965) 'On some problems of proving the existence of an equilibrium in a monetary economy', In: F. Hahn and F. Brechling, eds., *The theory of interest rates*. London: Macmillan.

Hahn, F. (1971) 'Equilibrium with transaction costs', *Econometrica*, 39: 417–439.

Hahn, F. (1973a) 'On the foundations of monetary theory', in: M. Parkin and A. Nobay, eds., *Essays in Modern Economics*. Longman Group.

Hahn, F. (1973b) 'On transaction costs, inessential sequence economies, and money', *Review of Economic Studies*, 40: 449–461.

Hahn, F. (1980) 'Discussion', in: J. Kareken and N. Wallace, eds., *Models of monetary Economies*. Minneapolis: Federal Reserve Bank of Minneapolis.

Hahn, F. (1983) *Money and inflation*. Cambridge, Mass.: MIT Press.

Hart, O. (1975) 'On the optimality of equilibrium when the market structure is incomplete', *Journal of Economic Theory*, 9: 53–83.

Hayashi, T. (1974) 'The non-Pareto efficiency of initial allocation of commodities and monetary equilibrium: An inside money economy', *Journal of Economic Theory*, 7: 173–187.

Heller, W. (1972) 'Transactions with set-up costs', *Journal of Economic Theory*, 4: 465–478.

Heller, W. (1974) 'The holding of money balances in general equilibrium', *Journal of economic Theory*, 7: 93–108.

Heller, W. and R. Starr (1976) 'Equilibrium with non-convex transactions costs: Monetary and non-monetary economies', *Review of Economic Studies*, 43: 195–215.

Hicks, J. (1935) 'A suggestion for simplifying the theory of money', *Economica*, 2: 1–19.

Hildenbrand, W. (1974) *Core and equilibria of a large economy*. Princeton University Press.

Honkapohja, S. (1978) 'On the efficiency of a competitive monetary equilibrium with transaction costs', *Review of Economic Studies*, 45: 405–415.

Kurz, M. (1974a) 'Arrow–Debreu equilibrium of an exchange economy with transaction cost', *International Economic Review*, 15: 699–717.

Kurz, M. (1974b) 'equilibrium in a finite sequence of markets with transaction cost', *Econometrica*, 42: 1–20.

Kurz, M. (1974c) 'Equilibrium with transaction cost and money in a single market exchange economy', *Journal of Economic Theory*, 7: 418–452.

Levine, D. (1985a) 'Efficiency and the value of money', Unpublished, University of California, Los Angeles.

Levine, D. (1985b) 'Liquidity with random market closure', Research Paper 85, University of Cambridge, Economic theory Discussion Paper.

Miller, M. and D. Orr (1956) 'A model of the demand for money by firms', *Quarterly Journal of Economics*, 80: 413–435.

Okuno, M. (1973) 'Essays on monetary equilibrium in a sequence of markets', Technical Report 120, Institute for Mathematical Studies in the Social Sciences.

Ostroy, J. and R. Starr (1974) 'Money and the decentralization of exchange', *Econometrica*, 42: 1093–1113.

Radner, R. (1972) 'Existence of equilibrium of plans prices and price expectations in a sequence of markets', *Econometrica*, 40: 1135–1191.

Santos, M. and J. Bona (1986) 'On the structure of the equilibrium price set of overlapping-generations economies', Unpublished, Department of Mathematics, University of Chicago.

Sontheimer, K. (1972) 'On the determination of money prices', *Journal of Money, Credit and Banking*, 4: 489–508.

Starr, R. (1972) 'The structure of exchange in barter and monetary economies', *Quarterly Journal of Economics*, 86: 290–302.

Starr, R. (1974) 'The price of money in a pure exchange monetary economy with taxation', *Econometrica*, 42: 45–54.

Starrett, D. (1973) 'Inefficiency and the demand for "money" in a sequence economy', *Review of Economic Studies*, 40: 437–448.

Tobin, J. (1956) 'The interest elasticity of transactions demand for cash', *Review of Economics and Statistics*, 38: 241–247.

Werner, J. (1985) 'Equilibrium in economies with incomplete financial markets', *Journal of Economic Theory*, 36: 110–119.

Werner, J. (1986) 'Asset prices and real indeterminacy in equilibrium with financial markets', Unpublished, University of Bonn.

Woodford, M. (1986) 'Asset bubbles and fiat money', Unpublished, University of Chicago and New York University.

Yamazaki, A. (1989) 'Monetary equilibria in a continuum economy with general transaction economies', RUEE Working Paper 89-39, Department of Economics, Hitotsubashi University, Tokyo, Japan.

PART 2

MONEY IN NON-WALRASIAN SETTINGS

Chapter 4

NON-WALRASIAN EQUILIBRIA, MONEY, AND MACROECONOMICS

JEAN-PASCAL BENASSY

CEPREMAP, Paris

Contents

Handbook of Monetary Economics, Volume I, Edited by B.M. Friedman and F.H. Hahn
© *Elsevier Science Publishers B.V., 1990*

1. Introduction

This chapter is concerned with non-Walrasian equilibria, money and macro-economics. We shall thus naturally begin this Introduction with a brief description of the salient characteristics of non-Walrasian equilibria, give a few motivations why such equilibria should be considered, and show what role money has in such a theory. A summary of subsequent sections will end the Introduction.

1.1. Non-Walrasian equilibria

Non-Walrasian equilibria, also often called equilibria with rationing, are a wide class of equilibrium concepts that generalize the traditional notion of Walrasian equilibrium by allowing markets not to clear (i.e. aggregate demand to differ from aggregate supply) and therefore quantity rationing to be experienced. Their scope is best described by first examining Walrasian equilibrium as a reference.

In a Walrasian equilibrium by definition all markets clear, that is, total demand equals total supply for each good. This consistency of the actions of all agents is achieved by price movements solely in the following manner: all private agents receive a price signal (i.e. a price for every market) and assume that they will be able to exchange whatever they want at that price system. They express Walrasian demands and supplies that are functions of this price signal only. A Walrasian equilibrium price system is a set of prices for which total demand and total supply are equal on all markets. Transactions are equal to the demands and supplies at this price system. No rationing is experienced by any agent since demand and supply match on all markets.

Two characteristics of the Walrasian model deserve to be stressed: all private agents receive price signals and make rational quantity decisions with respect to them. But no agent makes any use of the quantity signals sent to the market. Also, no agent actually sets prices, the determination of which is left to the "invisible hand" or to the implicit Walrasian auctioneer. Of course there are some real world markets for which the equality between demand and supply is ensured institutionally, for example the stock market, which inspired Walras. But for other markets, where no auctioneer is present, there is, as Arrow (1959) noted, "... a logical gap in the usual formulations of the theory of the perfectly competitive economy, namely, that there is no place for a rational decision with respect to prices as there is with respect to quantities", and, more specifically, "each individual participant in the economy is supposed to take prices as given and determine his choice as to purchases and sales accordingly; there is no one left over whose job is to make a decision on price".

Non-Walrasian theory takes this strong logical objection quite seriously, and its purpose is to build a consistent theory of the functioning of decentralized economies when market clearing is not axiomatically assumed. An almost immediate corollary is that rationing may appear, and that quantity signals will have to be introduced together with price signals. Using this enlarged set of signals allows us to generalize the concept of Walrasian equilibrium in the following directions:

- More general price formation schemes can be considered, ranging from full rigidity to full flexibility, with intermediate forms of imperfect competition. Moreover, each market may have its own price determination scheme.
- Demand and supply theory must be substantially modified to take into account these quantity signals. One thus obtains a theory of effective demand, generalizing Walrasian demand which only takes price signals into account.
- Price theory must also be amended in a way that integrates the possibility of non-clearing markets, the presence of quantity signals, and makes agents themselves responsible for price making
- Equilibrium in the short run is achieved by quantity adjustments as well as by price adjustments.
- Finally, expectations, which in market-clearing models are concerned with price signals only, must now include quantity signals expectations as well.

1.2. Why study non-Walrasian equilibria?

The set of equilibria just outlined is clearly more general than the concept of Walrasian equilibrium. But this does not imply per se that they should be more relevant. There are, however, a number of reasons that make the use of non-Walrasian equilibria relevant in various institutional contexts.

The most obvious one is that there are in the world a number of planned (or partially planned) economies where the determination of prices is not left to "market forces", but where prices are fixed for some length of time by a central planning authority. In such economies non-Walrasian theory is clearly a relevant tool of analysis.

But we shall now argue that this theory is also quite relevant for free market economies. First, and from an institutional point of view, we have already noted that, except for a very limited number of markets, there is no real world auctioneer to carry out the "Walrasian tatonnement". Prices are determined by the interaction of decentralized agents in the various markets. Clearly, the modelling of price and quantity determination is such markets must involve a different representation than the "autioneer" one. Notably the quantity signals sent by the traders, which only the Walrasian auctioneer used in Walrasian theory, must play a role in such representations. We shall actually see a few examples below.

Secondly, some recent theoretical developments in industrial economics, labor economics or the study of some financial markets such as credit markets all point out the possibility of non-market-clearing situations, due either to the game-theoretic nature of the price-making process, or to various informational imperfections. We thus need a theory that can accommodate in a general equilibrium setting the possibility of these non-market-clearing situations.

Thirdly, and though a significant body of macroeconomic literature has developed recently to show that employment fluctuations could be made consistent with market-clearing models, many real world phenomena such as the massive unemployment or the idleness of productive capacities observed in the recent years may seem difficult to reconcile with a general market-clearing view of the world. In the absence of conclusive empirical tests, it is preferable to stick to a more general level of analysis.

1.3. The role of money

Having explained the nature of non-Walrasian equilibria, we now have to say a few things about the role of money in the theory. As it turns out, and will appear below, almost all formalizations of non-Walrasian equilibria have been made in the framework of *monetary* economies, where money plays its three traditional roles of numeraire, medium of exchange and reserve of value. Besides its convenience in formalization, the use of a monetary framework is not entirely fortuitous. Non-Walrasian theory aims at representing the functioning of market economies. Actual market economies are characterized in general by the famous problem of "absence of double coincidence of wants", and in such a case it is well known that in the absence of a medium of exchange, the coordination of trading poses immense, and usually insoluble, coordination problems. It is thus natural that a theory that aims at describing decentralized economies be set in the framework of a monetary economy.[1] We may note that the issue of the absence of double coincidence of wants will appear in some applications below.

A final specific feature of money should be stressed: money can be interpreted as commodity money (such as gold). But the recent evolution of money tends to privilege the interpretation of money as fiat money, i.e. an (almost)

---

[1] Of course this does not mean that equilibria with rationing cannot be modelled in non-monetary economies. See, for example, Benassy (1975b).

costlessly produced legal medium of exchange. In this last case money (or rather the quantity of money) becomes a policy variable. We shall also scrutinize money in this respect, and notably try to link our results with the traditional debates on the "neutrality" of monetary policy.

Of course the monetary nature of the economies studied explains that there exists a most natural link with macroeconomics, which also studies monetary economies. This link will be particularly explored in the last two sections of this chapter.

1.4. Historical antecedents

Equilibria with rationing have a double ancestry. On the one hand, Walras (1874) developed a model of general equilibrium with interdependent markets where adjustment was made through prices. On the other hand, Keynes (1936) built, at the macroeconomic level, a concept of equilibrium where adjustment was made by quantities (the level of national income) as well as by prices. The Keynesian model was chiefly used under the form of the IS–LM model, as developed by Hicks (1937). The Walrasian model was elaborated into a very rigorous and beautiful construction, notably in Hicks (1939), Arrow and Debreu (1954), Debreu (1959), and Arrow and Hahn (1971), and it became the basic concept in microeconomics. As a result of these evolutions, a growing gap developed between microeconomics and macroeconomics.

A few isolated contributions in the postwar period made some steps towards modern non-Walrasian theories. Samuelson (1947) and Tobin and Houthakker (1950) studied the theory of demand under conditions of rationing. Hansen (1951) introduced the ideas of active demand, close in spirit to that of effective demand, and of quasi-equilibrium where persistent excess demand created steady inflation. Patinkin (1956, ch. 13) considered the situation where firms might not be able to sell all their "notional" output. Hahn and Negishi (1962) studied non-tatonnement processes where trade could take place before a general equilibrium price system was reached. Hicks (1965) discussed the "fixprice" method as opposed to the flexprice method.

A main impetus came from the stimulating works of Clower (1965) and Leijonhufvud (1968). Both were concerned with the microeconomic foundations of Keynesian theory. Clower showed that the Keynesian consumption function made no sense unless reinterpreted as the response of a rational consumer to a rationing of his sales on the labor markets. He introduced the "dual-decision" hypothesis, a precursor of modern effective demand theory, showing how the consumption function could have two different functional forms, depending on whether the consumer was rationed on the labor market or not. Leijonhufvud (1968) insisted on the importance of short-run quantity adjustments to explain the establishment of an equilibrium with involuntary unemployment. These contributions were followed by the macroeconomic model of Barro and Grossman (1971, 1976), integrating the "Clower" consumption function and the "Patinkin" employment function in the first non-Walrasian macroeconomic model.

The main subsequent development was the construction of rigorous microeconomic concepts of non-Walrasian equilibria. These truly bridged the gap between traditional microeconomics and macroeconomics. On the one hand, they generalized the Walrasian general equilibrium concept in the multiple ways we described in Subsection 1.1 above. One the other hand, they allowed macro models to be derived that synthesized and generalized hitherto disjoint macro theories within a general unified framework. These concepts of non-Walrasian equilibria, and a few macroeconomic applications, will be our main concern in this chapter.

1.5. Scope and outline of the chapter

In order to have a homogeneous framework we shall be concerned here exclusively with non-Walrasian models that have been developed at the *general equilibrium* level. This means that we shall not cover some recent theories of price determination[2] which, though non-Walrasian, have been only developed so far in partial equilibrium contexts. Subject to this limitation, we shall try to give a fairly broad outline of the available microeconomic concepts and their properties.

Section 2 deals with the functioning of non-clearing markets in a monetary economy and the formation of quantity signals, obviously a fundamental element for all that follows. Section 3 exposes the main concepts of equilibrium in the case polar to that of Walrasian equilibrium, that with fixed prices. This gives a very broad class of equilibria, and Section 4 studies their optimality (or rather suboptimality) properties. Section 5 introduces endogenous price making by agents in a framework akin to that of imperfect competition; two concepts, with objective and subjective demand curves, are presented. Section 6 introduces expectations into the non-Walrasian framework. The last two sections are devoted to simple macroeconomic applications of the microeconomic concepts: Section 7 gives a simple exposition of the famous three-goods–three-regimes fixprice macroeconomic model. Finally, Section 8 presents a micro–macro model of imperfect competition and unemployment. These models allow us to apply all the concepts seen previously in a framework

---

[2] Examples are the theory of contracts, efficiency wages, theories of trade unions, bargaining, and many others.

that allows to deal with such macroeconomic problems as unemployment and the effectiveness of government policy.

At the end of every section a short subsection indicates the origins of the material in that section, and gives some brief notes on supplementary references.

2. Markets, money and quantity signals

2.1. *A monetary economy*

As we indicated above, we shall describe the various concepts of non-Walrasian economics in the framework of a monetary economy. One good, called money, serves as numeraire, medium of exchange and reserve of value. Assume that there are l active markets in the period considered. On each of these markets one of the l non-monetary goods, indexed by $h = 1, \ldots, l$, is exchanged against money at the price p_h. Call p the l-dimensional vector of these prices (money being the numeraire, its price is of course equal to one).

To simplify the exposition, we shall consider in the following sections a pure exchange economy. The agents in this economy are indexed by $i = 1, \ldots, n$. At the beginning of the period agent i has a quantity of money $\bar{m}_i \geq 0$ and holdings of non-monetary goods represented by a vector ω_i, with components $\omega_{ih} \geq 0$ for each good.

Consider an agent i in market h. He may make a purchase $d_{ih} > 0$, for which he pays $p_h d_{ih}$ units of money, or a sale $s_{ih} > 0$, for which he receives $p_h s_{ih}$ units of money. Define $z_{ih} = d_{ih} - s_{ih}$ as his net purchase of good h and z_i the l-dimensional vector of these net purchases. Agent i's final holdings of non-monetary goods and money, x_i and m_i, are, respectively,

$$x_i = \omega_i + z_i$$

and

$$m_i = \bar{m}_i - pz_i .$$

Note that the last equation, which describes the evolution of money holdings, is simply the conventional budget constraint. At this stage we may also note that the use of a monetary structure of exchange tremendously simplifies the formalization. Indeed, if we considered for example a barter structure of exchange between the l non-monetary goods, there would be $l(l-1)/2$ markets, one for each pair of goods, a number quite greater than l for an economy with many goods. Furthermore, having a monetary structure allows us to speak unambiguously of *the* demand or supply for good h, the implicit counterpart of such demands and supplies being always money. In a barter economy such demands and supplies would not be meaningful, since each good would be traded on $l - 1$ markets against $l - 1$ different counterparts.

2.2. Walrasian equilibrium

Having described the basic institutional structure of the economy, we now describe its Walrasian equilibrium in order to contrast it with the non-Walrasian equilibrium concepts that will follow. We must still describe the preferences of the agents, and we shall thus assume that agent i has a utility function $U_i(x_i, m_i) = U_i(\omega_i + z_i, m_i)$, which we shall assume throughout strictly concave in its arguments. Note that money appears in the utility function in a way that will be made clearer below (Section 6).

As indicated above, each agent is assumed to be able to exchange as much as he wants on each market. He thus transmits demands and supplies that maximize his utility subject to the budget constraint; the Walrasian net demand function $z_i(p)$ is the solution in z_i of the following program:

$$\max U_i(\omega_i + z_i, m_i)$$

s.t.

$$pz_i + m_i = \bar{m}_i .$$

This yields a vector of Walrasian net demands $z_i(p)$. Note that there is no "demand for money" since there is no such thing as a market for money. A Walrasian equilibrium price vector p^* is defined by the condition that all markets clear, i.e.

$$\sum_{i=1}^{n} z_i(p^*) = 0 .$$

The vector of transactions realized by agent i is equal to $z_i(p^*)$.

Walrasian equilibrium allocations possess a number of good properties. By construction they are consistent both at the individual and market levels. Furthermore, they are Pareto optimal, i.e. it is impossible to find an allocation that would be at least as good for all agents, and strictly better for at least one. We shall later contrast this with the suboptimality properties of non-Walrasian equilibria.

2.3. Demands, transactions and rationing schemes

Since we shall be dealing with non-clearing markets, we must now make an important distinction, i.e. between demands and supplies on the one hand, and the resulting transactions on the other. Demands and supplies, denoted $\tilde{d}_{ih}$ and $\tilde{s}_{ih}$, are signals transmitted by each agent to the market (i.e. the other agents) before exchange takes place. They represent as a first approximation the exchanges agents wish to make on each market, and thus do not necessarily match on a specific market. Transactions, i.e. purchases or sales of goods, denoted respectively as d_{ih}^* or s_{ih}^*, are exchanges actually made, and must thus identically balance on each market:

$$\sum_{i=1}^{n} d_{ih}^* = \sum_{i=1}^{n} s_{ih}^* , \quad \forall h .$$

The exchange process must generate consistent transactions from any set of possibly inconsistent demands and supplies. Some rationing will necessarily occur, which may take various forms, such as uniform rationing, queueing, priority systems, or proportional rationing, depending on the particular organization of each market. We shall call a rationing scheme the mathematical representation of each specific organization. To be more precise, define:

$$\tilde{z}_{ih} = \tilde{d}_{ih} - \tilde{s}_{ih} , \qquad z_{ih}^* = d_{ih}^* - s_{ih}^* .$$

A rationing scheme in a market h is described by a set of n functions:

$$z_{ih}^* = F_{ih}(\tilde{z}_{1h}, \ldots, \tilde{z}_{nh}) , \quad i = 1, \ldots, n , \tag{1}$$

such that

$$\sum_{i=1}^{n} F_{ih}(\tilde{z}_{1h}, \ldots, \tilde{z}_{nh}) = 0 , \quad \text{for all } \tilde{z}_{1h}, \ldots, \tilde{z}_{nh} .$$

We shall generally assume that F_{ih} is continuous, non-decreasing in $\tilde{z}_{ih}$ and non-increasing in the other arguments. Before examining further the possible properties of these rationing schemes, we give an example, that of a queue (or priority system).

In a queueing system the demanders (or the suppliers) are ranked in a predetermined order, and are served according to that order. Let there be $n - 1$ demanders, ranked in the order $i = 1, \ldots, n - 1$, each having a demand $\tilde{d}_{ih}$, and a supplier indexed by n who supplies $\tilde{s}_{nh}$. When the turn of demander i comes, the maximum quantity he can obtain is what demanders before him, i.e. agents $j < i$, have not taken, i.e.

$$\tilde{s}_{nh} - \sum_{j<i} d^*_{jh} = \max\left(0, \tilde{s}_{nh} - \sum_{j<i} \tilde{d}_{jh}\right).$$

The level of his purchase is simply the minimum of this quantity and his demand, i.e.

$$d^*_{ih} = \min\left[\tilde{d}_{ih}, \max\left(0, \tilde{s}_{nh} - \sum_{j<i} \tilde{d}_{jh}\right)\right].$$

As for the supplier, he sells the minimum of his supply and of total demand:

$$s^*_{nh} = \min\left(\tilde{s}_{nh}, \sum_{j=1}^{n-1} \tilde{d}_{jh}\right).$$

It is clear that total purchases equal total sales on the market h, whatever demand and supply.

2.4. Properties of rationing schemes

We now study three possible and important properties that a rationing scheme may satisfy: voluntary exchange, market efficiency and non-manipulability.

There is *voluntary exchange* in market h if no agent can be forced to purchase more than he demands, or to sell more than he supplies, which is expressed by

$$d^*_{ih} \le \tilde{d}_{ih}, \qquad s^*_{ih} \le \tilde{s}_{ih}, \qquad \text{for all } i,$$

or equivalently in algebraic terms:

$$|z^*_{ih}| \le |\tilde{z}_{ih}|, \qquad z^*_{ih} \cdot \tilde{z}_{ih} \ge 0, \qquad \text{for all } i.$$

In reality most markets meet this condition (except perhaps some labor markets) and we shall henceforth assume that it always holds. This allows us to classify agents in two categories: unrationed agents, for which $z^*_{ih} = \tilde{z}_{ih}$, and rationed agents who trade less than they wanted.

The second property we shall study here is that of market efficiency, or absence of friction, which corresponds to the idea of exhaustion of all mutually advantageous exchanges. A rationing scheme is efficient, or frictionless, if one cannot find simultaneously a rationed demander and a rationed supplier in the corresponding market. The intuitive idea behind it is that in an efficiently organized market a rationed buyer and a rationed seller should be able to meet, and would exchange until one of the two is not rationed. Together with the voluntary exchange assumption, this implies the "short-side" rule, according to which agents on the short side of the market can realize their desired transactions:

$$\left(\sum_{j=1}^{n} \tilde{z}_{jh}\right) \cdot \tilde{z}_{ih} \leq 0 \Rightarrow z_{ih}^{*} = \tilde{z}_{ih} \, .$$

This rule also implies that the global level of transactions on a market settles at the minimum of aggregate demand and supply. We may note that this market efficiency assumption is quite acceptable if one considers a small decentralized market where each demander meets each supplier (like the queue described above). It becomes less acceptable if one considers a fairly wide and decentralized market, because some buyers and sellers might not meet. We may note in particular that the market efficiency property is usually lost by aggregation of submarkets (whereas on the contrary the voluntary exchange property remains intact in this aggregation process). As a result, the global level of transactions may be smaller than either total demand or supply. Figure 4.1 actually depicts how the aggregation of two frictionless submarkets yields an inefficient aggregate market, at least in some price range. The market efficiency assumption is very useful for constructing simple macroeconomic models, but we must keep in mind that it may not always hold. Fortunately, this hypothesis is not necessary for the microeconomic concepts presented in the next sections.

We now consider a third important property of rationing schemes, that of non-manipulability. A rationing scheme is non-manipulable if an agent, once rationed, cannot increase the level of his transactions by increasing his demand or supply, as shown in Figure 4.2. A non-manipulable scheme can be written in the form:

$$d_{ih}^{*} = \min(\tilde{d}_{ih}, \bar{d}_{ih}) \, ,$$
$$s_{ih}^{*} = \min(\tilde{s}_{ih}, \bar{s}_{ih}) \, ,$$

where the bounds $\bar{d}_{ih}$ and $\bar{s}_{ih}$ depend only on the net demands of the other agents (and are thus independent of $\tilde{z}_{ih}$). Otherwise the scheme is manipulable. For example, the queueing system described above is non-manipulable, and can be written in the above form, with

$$\bar{d}_{ih} = \max\left(0, \tilde{s}_{nh} - \sum_{j<i} \tilde{d}_{jh}\right), \quad 1 \leq i \leq n-1 \, ,$$
$$\bar{s}_{nh} = \sum_{j=1}^{n-1} \tilde{d}_{jh} \, .$$

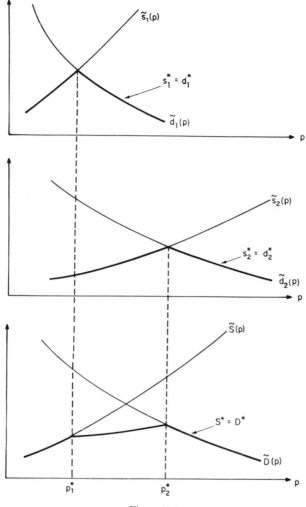

Figure 4.1

On the contrary, a proportional rationing scheme, for example, is manipulable. To characterize the non-manipulability property more formally, it is convenient to separate $\tilde{z}_{ih}$ from the other net demands, and thus to write a rationing scheme in the form:

$$z_{ih}^* = F_{ih}(\tilde{z}_{ih}, \tilde{z}_{-ih}), \quad i = 1, \ldots, n,$$

with

$$\tilde{z}_{-ih} = \{\tilde{z}_{jh} \mid j \neq i\},$$

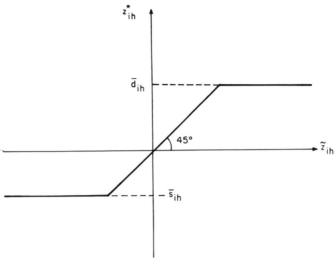

Figure 4.2

where $\tilde{z}_{-ih}$ is the set of net demands on market h, except for agent i's demand. The rationing scheme on market h is non-manipulable if it can be written in the form:

$$F_{ih}(\tilde{z}_{ih}, \tilde{z}_{-ih}) = \begin{cases} \min[\tilde{z}_{ih}, G_{ih}^{d}(\tilde{z}_{-ih})], & \text{if } \tilde{z}_{ih} \geq 0, \\ \max[\tilde{z}_{ih}, -G_{ih}^{s}(\tilde{z}_{-ih})], & \text{if } \tilde{z}_{ih} \leq 0, \end{cases}$$

with

$$G_{ih}^{d}(\tilde{z}_{-ih}) \geq 0, \qquad G_{ih}^{s}(\tilde{z}_{-ih}) \geq 0$$

2.5. Price and quantity signals

We just saw how transactions would occur in a non-clearing market. In such a market each agent receives, in addition to the traditional price signal, some quantity signals. In what follows we shall concentrate on markets that satisfy the properties of voluntary exchange and non-manipulability.[3] These may be represented as

$$z_{ih}^{*} = \begin{cases} \min(\tilde{z}_{ih}, \bar{d}_{ih}), & \tilde{z}_{ih} \geq 0, \\ \max(\tilde{z}_{ih}, -\bar{s}_{ih}), & \tilde{z}_{ih} \leq 0, \end{cases}$$

[3] Manipulable schemes lead to a perverse phenomenon of "overbidding" which prevents the establishment of an equilibrium [cf. Benassy (1977b, 1982)].

or more compactly by

$$z_{ih}^* = \min\{\bar{d}_{ih}, \max(\tilde{z}_{ih}, -\bar{s}_{ih})\} ,$$

with

$$\bar{d}_{ih} = G_{ih}^d(\tilde{z}_{-ih}) , \qquad \bar{s}_{ih} = G_{ih}^s(\tilde{z}_{-ih}) . \tag{2}$$

The quantities $\bar{d}_{ih}$ and $\bar{s}_{ih}$, which henceforth we shall call the perceived constraints, are the quantity signals that agent i receives in market h in addition to the price p_h.

To make notation more compact, we can represent the rationing functions and perceived constraints concerning an agent i [equations (1) and (2)] as vector functions:

$$z_i^* = F_i(\tilde{z}_i, \tilde{z}_{-i}) , \tag{3}$$

$$\bar{d}_i = G_i^d(\tilde{z}_{-i}) , \qquad \bar{s}_i = G_i^s(\tilde{z}_{-i}) , \tag{4}$$

where $\tilde{z}_i$ is the vector of demands expressed by agent i and $\tilde{z}_{-i}$ is the set of all such vectors for all agents, except agent i.

We will see in the following sections that the introduction of quantity signals plays a fundamental role in both demand and price theory, and that their consideration allows us to enlarge the set of possible equilibria in a very substantial manner.

2.6. Notes and references

The distinction between monetary and barter economies is of course a traditional one. A recent restatement is in Clower (1967). The informational problems encountered in non-monetary economies are stressed in Ostroy (1973), Ostroy and Starr (1974) and Veendorp (1970).

The representation of rationing schemes and quantity signals in this section are taken from Benassy (1975a, 1977b, 1982). An alternative approach to rationing and quantity signals is that of Drèze (1975), which will be seen in the next section.

The voluntary exchange and market efficiency properties have been also discussed under various forms in Clower (1960, 1965), Hahn and Negishi (1962), Barro and Grossman (1971), Grossman (1971) and Howitt (1974). The problem of manipulability was studied in Benassy (1977b).

3. Fixprice equilibria

We now start with a first concept of a non-Walrasian equilibrium, that of a fixprice equilibrium. This concept is of interest for several reasons. First, it will give us a very general structure of non-Walrasian equilibria, since we shall find that under some very mild conditions fixprice equilibria exist for every positive price system and every set of rationing schemes. Secondly, as we shall see in Section 5, they are a very useful building block in constructing other non-Walrasian equilibrium concepts with flexible prices. Third, the study of their optimality (or rather suboptimality) properties will also be useful for the subsequent concepts.

We thus assume that the price system p is given. As we indicated, we assume that the rationing schemes on all markets are non-manipulable. Accordingly, transactions and quantity signals are generated on all markets according to the formulas seen above [equations (3) and (4)]:

$$z_i^* = F_i(\tilde{z}_i, \tilde{z}_{-i}), \tag{3}$$

$$\bar{d}_i = G_i^d(\tilde{z}_{-i}), \qquad \bar{s}_i = G_i^s(\tilde{z}_{-i}). \tag{4}$$

We immediately see that all that remains in order to obtain a fixprice equilibrium concept is to determine how demands themselves are formed, a task to which we now turn.

3.1. Effective demand and supply

Demands and supplies are signals that agents send to the "market" (i.e. to the other agents) in order to obtain the best transactions. As we saw above, the Walrasian demands and supplies are the best responses to a price signal under the assumption (which is actually verified ex post in a Walrasian equilibrium) that each agent can buy or sell as much as he demands or supplies. We shall now consider an agent i faced with a price vector p and vectors of perceived constraints $\bar{d}_i$ and $\bar{s}_i$, and we shall see how he can choose a vector of effective demands $\tilde{z}_i$ that leads him to the best possible transaction.

Let us first start with the determination of this optimal transaction. Agent i knows that on market h his transactions are limited to the interval given by the perceived constraints:

$$-\bar{s}_{ih} \le z_{ih} \le \bar{d}_{ih},$$

so that his best transaction is the solution in z_i of the following program:

$$\max U_i(\omega_i + z_i, m_i)$$

s.t.

$$pz_i + m_i = \bar{m}_i,$$

$$-\bar{s}_{ih} \le z_{ih} \le \bar{d}_{ih}, \quad h = 1, \ldots, l.$$

Since the function U_i is strictly concave, the solution is unique and we denote it as $\xi_i^*(p, \bar{d}_i, \bar{s}_i)$. However, in our system an agent does not announce directly a vector of transactions, but sends a vector $\tilde{z}_i$ of effective demands and supplies in order to obtain this optimal transaction. If agent i sends a demand $\tilde{z}_{ih}$ on market h, he will obtain a transaction equal to

$$\min[\bar{d}_{ih}, \max(\tilde{z}_{ih}, -\bar{s}_{ih})],$$

so that a demand leading to the optimal transaction must be a solution in $\tilde{z}_{ih}$ of

$$\min[\bar{d}_{ih}, \max(\tilde{z}_{ih}, -\bar{s}_{ih})] = \zeta_{ih}^*(p, \bar{d}_i, \bar{s}_i).$$

This equation has actually an infinity of solutions if ξ_{ih}^* is equal to any of the bounds $\bar{d}_{ih}$ or $-\bar{s}_{ih}$. In order to work with demand functions and not correspondences, in what follows we shall make a selection in the above set of solutions, and define the effective demand of agent i on market h, denoted as $\tilde{\xi}_{ih}(p, \bar{d}_i, \bar{s}_i)$, as the solution in z_{ih} of the following program:

$$\max U_i(\omega_i + z_i, m_i)$$

s.t.

$$pz_i + m_i = \bar{m}_i,$$

$$-\bar{s}_{ik} \le z_{ik} \le \bar{d}_{ik}, \quad k \ne h.$$

In words, the effective demand on a market h corresponds to the exchange that maximizes utility, taking into account the constraints on the *other* markets. Because of the strict concavity, we obtain a function. Repeating this program for all markets h, we obtain a vector function of effective demands, $\tilde{\xi}_i(p, \bar{d}_i, \bar{s}_i)$. This vector of effective demands, has a double property. First, as is easy to check, it leads to the best transaction vector $\xi_i^*(p, \bar{d}_i, \bar{s}_i)$ [see, for example, Benassy (1977b, 1982)]. Secondly, whenever a constraint is binding on a market h, the corresponding demand (or supply) is greater than the constraint or the transaction, which thus "signals" to the market that the agent trades less than he would want.

We shall immediately give an illustrative example of this definition, due to Patinkin (1956) and Barro and Grossman (1971), namely that of the employment function of the firm. Consider, indeed, a firm with a production function $y = F(l)$ exhibiting diminishing returns, and faced with a price p on the output market and a wage w on the labor market. The Walrasian demand for labor, which results from the maximization of profit $py - wl$ subject to the production function $y = F(l)$, is equal to $F'^{-1}(w/p)$. Assume now that the firm faces a constraint $\bar{y}$ on its sales of output. According to the above definition the effective demand for labor, $\tilde{l}^d$, is the solution in l of the following program:

$$\max py - wl$$

s.t.

$$y = F(l) ,$$
$$y \le \bar{y} ,$$

which yields an effective demand for labor:

$$\tilde{l}^d = \min\{F'^{-1}(w/p), F^{-1}(\bar{y})\} .$$

We see that the effective demand for labor may have two forms: the Walrasian demand just seen above if the sales constraint is not binding, or, if this constraint is binding, a more "Keynesian" form equal to the quantity of labor just necessary to produce the output demand. We see immediately on this example that effective demand may have various functional forms, which intuitively explains why non-Walrasian models generally have multiple regimes (see, for example, the three-goods, three-regimes model in Section 7 below).

3.2. Fixprice equilibrium

With the above definition of effective demand, we are now ready to give the definition of a fixprice equilibrium, found in Benassy (1975a, 1982), which we shall call a K-equilibrium for short:

Definition 1. A K-equilibrium associated with a price system p and rationing schemes represented by functions F_i, $i = 1, \ldots, n$, is a set of effective demands $\tilde{z}_i$, transactions z_i^* and perceived constraints $\bar{d}_i$ and $\bar{s}_i$ such that:

(a) $\tilde{z}_i = \tilde{\zeta}_i(p, \bar{d}_i, \bar{s}_i) , \quad i = 1, \ldots, n ,$

(b) $z_i^* = F_i(\tilde{z}_i, \tilde{z}_{-i})$, $i = 1, \ldots, n$,

(c) $\bar{d}_i = G_i^d(\tilde{z}_{-i})$, $i = 1, \ldots, n$,

$\bar{s}_i = G_i^s(\tilde{z}_{-i})$, $i = 1, \ldots, n$.

We see that in a fixprice K-equilibrium the quantity constraints $\bar{d}_i$ and $\bar{s}_i$ from which the agents construct their effective demands [equation (a)] are the ones that will be generated by the exchange process [equation (c)]. At equilibrium the agents thus have a correct perception of these quantity constraints.

Equilibria defined by these equations exist for all positive prices and rationing schemes satisfying voluntary exchange and non-manipulability [Benassy (1975a, 1982)]. The "exogenous" data consist of the price system and the rationing schemes in all markets F_i, $i = 1, \ldots, n$. One may wonder whether for given such exogenous data the equilibrium is likely to be unique. A positive answer has been given by Schulz (1983) who showed that the equilibrium is unique, provided the spillover effects[4] from one market to the other are less than 100 percent in value terms. For example, in the simplest traditional Keynesian model, this would amount to assuming a propensity to consume smaller than one.

We shall denote by $\tilde{Z}_i(p)$, $Z_i^*(p)$, $\bar{D}_i(p)$ and $\bar{S}_i(p)$, the values of $\tilde{z}_i$, z_i^*, $\bar{d}_i$ and $\bar{s}_i$ at a fixprice equilibrium.

As a simple example of a fixprice equilibrium, consider the traditional Edgeworth box example (Figure 4.3), which represents a single market where agents A and B exchange a good (measured horizontally) against money (measured vertically). Point O corresponds to initial endowments, DC is the budget line of the two agents at price p, points A and B are the tangency points of the indifference curves with this budget line.

Measuring the level of exchanges along the line OC, we see that A demands a quantity OA, B supplies a quantity OB. They exchange the minimum of these two quantities, i.e. OA, and agent B is rationed. Perceived constraints are respectively OA for agent B and OB for agent A. Agent B is constrained on his supply, while A is not constrained.

We may now say a few words about the properties of the allocations at a fixprice K-equilibrium. First, considering a particular market h, the transactions of the various agents are, by construction, mutually consistent, since they result from rationing schemes:

$$\sum_{i=1}^{n} z_{ih}^* = 0, \quad \forall h.$$

---

[4] There is a spillover effect when a (binding) constraint in one market modifies the effective demand in another market.

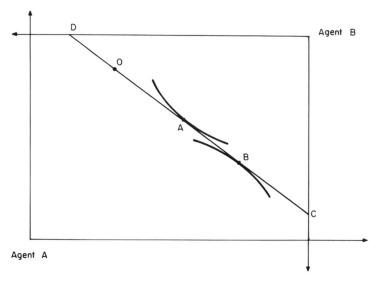

Figure 4.3

Demands and supplies need not balance, however, and in a particular market one may have three different categories of agents:

(a) unrationed agents such that $z_{ih}^* = \tilde{z}_{ih}$,

(b) rationed demanders such that $\tilde{z}_{ih} > z_{ih}^* = \bar{d}_{ih}$, and

(c) rationed suppliers such that $\tilde{z}_{ih} < z_{ih}^* = -\bar{s}_{ih}$.

Note that since our concept permits inefficient rationing schemes, one may have both rationed demanders and rationed suppliers on the same market. If, however, the rationing scheme on the market considered is frictionless, at most one side of the market is rationed.

If we now consider a particular agent i, we see that his transactions vector z_i^* is the best, taking account of the perceived constraints on all markets, because effective demand has been constructed so as to yield precisely this optimal trade. Mathematically z_i^* is the solution in z_i of the following program, already seen above:

$$\max U_i(\omega_i + z_i, m_i)$$

s.t.

$$pz_i + m_i = \bar{m}_i,$$

$$-\bar{s}_{ih} \leq z_{ih} \leq \bar{d}_{ih}, \quad h = 1, \ldots, l.$$

3.3. An alternative concept

We now present an alternative concept of a fixprice equilibrium, due to Drèze (1975),[5] which we shall recast using our notations. That concept deals directly with the vectors of transactions z_i^* and quantity constraints $\bar{d}_i$ and $\bar{s}_i$. The original concept by Drèze actually dealt with uniform rationing, so that the vectors $\bar{d}_i$ and $\bar{s}_i$ were the same for all agents.

Definition 2. A fixprice D-equilibrium for a given set of prices p is defined as a set of vectors of transactions z_i^* and quantity constraints $\bar{d}_i$ and $\bar{s}_i$ such that:

(a) $\sum_{i=1}^{n} z_{ih}^* = 0$, $\forall h$.

(b) The vector z_i^* is a solution in z_i of

$$\max U_i(\omega_i + z_i, m_i)$$

s.t.

$$pz_i + m_i = \bar{m}_i,$$

$$-\bar{s}_{ih} \le z_{ih} \le \bar{d}_{ih}, \quad h = 1, \dots, l.$$

(c) $\forall h$, $z_{ih}^* = \bar{d}_{ih}$ for some i implies $z_{jh}^* > -\bar{s}_{jh}$, $\forall j$,
$\qquad z_{ih}^* = -\bar{s}_{ih}$ for some i implies $z_{jh}^* < \bar{d}_{jh}$, $\forall j$.

Let us now interpret these conditions. Condition (a) is the natural requirement that transactions should balance on each market. Condition (b) says that transactions must be individually rational, i.e. they must maximize utility subject to the budget constraint and the quantity constraints on all markets. In the notations of the preceding subsection, $z_i^* = \xi_i^*(p, \bar{d}_i, \bar{s}_i)$. We should note at this stage that using quantity constraints under the form of maximum upper bounds and lower bounds on trades implicitly assumes rationing schemes that exhibit voluntary exchange and non-manipulability, as we saw in Section 2.

Condition (c) basically says that rationing may affect either supply or demand, but not both simultaneously.[6] We recognize here with a different formalization the condition of market efficiency that is thus built in this definition of equilibrium, whereas it was not in the previous definition.

---

[5] The original concept of Drèze actually deals with the more general case of prices variable between given limits.

[6] The original paper also stipulated that one good should not be rationed at all, a condition aimed at suppressing trivial equilibria such as that where all agents would be constrained to trade nothing. Identifying this unrationed good as the medium of exchange allows for a more symmetric presentation.

Drèze (1975) proved that an equilibrium according to Definition 2 exists for all positive price systems and for uniform rationing schemes under the traditional concavity assumptions for the utility functions. The concept is easily extended to some non-uniform bounds [Grandmont and Laroque (1976) and Greenberg and Müller (1979)], but in this last case it is not specified in the concept how shortages are allocated among rationed demanders or rationed suppliers. Because of this usually there will be an infinity of fixprice equilibria corresponding to a given price, as soon as there are two rationed agents on one side of a market.

As we noted in the preceding subsections the two concepts are, implicitly or explicitly, based on a representation of markets under the form of rationing schemes satisfying voluntary exchange and non-manipulability. This suggests that if, in the first definition, we further assume that all rationing schemes are efficient, the two definitions should yield similar sets of equilibrium allocations for a given price system. This was indeed proved by Silvestre (1982, 1983) for both exchange and production economies.

3.4. Notes and references

The two concepts of fixprice equilibrium described in this chapter have been developed in Benassy (1975a, 1977b, 1982) and Drèze (1975), respectively. An alternative concept, which does not use quantity signals, is due to Younes (1975). An early model of equilibrium with a non-clearing labor market is due to Glustoff (1968). The relations between various concepts have been explored by Silvestre (1982, 1983) and D'Autume (1985). Fixprice equilibrium has been modelled as a Nash equilibrium in Böhm and Levine (1979) and Heller and Starr (1979). However, this approach yields a large number of unwanted equilibria (including the no-trade one) for reasons described in Benassy (1982).

Various extensions of these concepts have been studied. Drèze (1975) constructed equilibria where some prices are subject to exogenous bounds, or indexed on each other, an issue pursued in Dehez and Drèze (1984). The problems of manipulable rationing schemes were studied in Benassy (1977b, 1982). Fixprice equilibrium in a barter economy was modelled in Benassy (1975b). Section 5 below describes endogenous price making in various frameworks of monopolistic competition.

The issue of uniqueness of a fixprice equilibrium has been studied by Schulz (1983) who gives sufficient conditions for global uniqueness in the Benassy model. We indicated that the Drèze equilibrium is usually not unique, but uniqueness results can be obtained in some specific cases [Laroque (1981)].

4. Optimality

One of the great virtues of a Walrasian equilibrium is the property of Pareto optimality. So it is quite natural to inquire whether the large class of fixprice equilibria possesses either the Pareto-optimality property, or even a weaker optimality property taking into account the fact that agents trade at given prices. As we shall see, these two questions are usually answered in the negative. Before going on to each of these criteria, we first characterize our equilibria in a differential way.

4.1. Characterization of equilibria

As we saw above, transactions at a fixprice equilibrium are the solutions in z_i to the following program:

$$\max U_i(\omega_i + z_i, m_i)$$

s.t.

$$pz_i + m_i = \bar{m}_i \,,$$

$$-\bar{s}_{ih} \le z_{ih} \le \bar{d}_{ih} \,, \quad \forall h \,.$$

Call λ_i and δ_{ih} the Kuhn–Tucker multipliers of the above constraints. The Kuhn–Tucker conditions for this program can be written, assuming an interior maximum, as

$$\frac{\partial U_i}{\partial m_i} = \lambda_i \,,$$

$$\frac{\partial U_i}{\partial z_{ih}} = \lambda_i p_h + \delta_{ih} \,.$$

The multiplier λ_i can be interpreted as the marginal utility of income. δ_{ih} is an index of rationing for agent i on market h:

$\delta_{ih} = 0 \,,$ if i is unconstrained on market $h(z_{ih}^* = \tilde{z}_{ih})$,

$\delta_{ih} > 0 \,,$ if i is constrained in his demand for good $h(0 \le z_{ih}^* < \tilde{z}_{ih})$,

$\delta_{ih} < 0 \,,$ if i is constrained in his supply of good $h(0 \ge z_{ih}^* > \tilde{z}_{ih})$.

Let us call the "shadow price" of good h the ratio $(\partial U_i / \partial z_{ih})/(\partial U_i / \partial m_i)$. The above relations allow us to compute the shadow price of good h for agent i as

$$\frac{\partial U_i / \partial z_{ih}}{\partial U_i / \partial m_i} = p_h + \frac{\delta_{ih}}{\lambda_i} . \tag{5}$$

We may thus note that the shadow price of good h is greater than, equal to, or smaller than p_h depending on whether i is constrained on his demand, unconstrained, or supply constrained, in market h.

We shall use the above results to study the optimality properties of fixprice equilibria. Before starting we must make one further remark and assumption. It is clear that it would be too easy to show that fixprice equilibria are inefficient if some markets were functioning inefficiently themselves. We thus assume in what follows that all markets are frictionless. This immediately implies that the numbers δ_{ih} will be zero for at least all agents on the short side of every market h.

4.2. Pareto optimality

We now inquire whether fixprice allocations have the property of Pareto optimality. From a heuristic point of view, we should first note that the constraint of trading at fixed prices does not necessarily rule out Pareto optimality, as Figure 4.4 shows. Indeed, there is a point on the budget line,

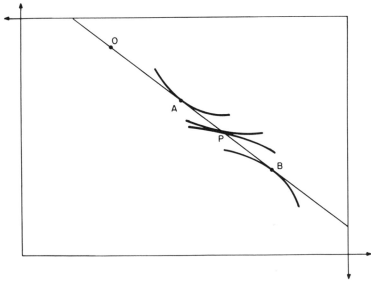

Figure 4.4

point P, which is a Pareto optimum. But it clearly differs from the fixprice equilibrium A. Continuing with the Edgeworth box example, it is easy to see that this situation is fairly general. Indeed, the set of Pareto optima is the contract curve, whereas the set of fixprice equilibria, when we vary the price, is the lentil shaped curve (Figure 4.5). We see that these two curves intersect only at the Walrasian equilibrium point.

An interesting way to look at this problem is to note (cf. Figure 4.4) that at point P trader A would exchange more than he wants at that price. This leads to the intuition that efficiency would require forced trading, or that voluntary trading would generally imply inefficiency. This has been studied and made rigorous in Silvestre (1985) who showed that Pareto optimality and voluntary exchange were satisfied together only at the Walrasian allocation.

We can also see in a direct manner why fixprice equilibria generally are not Pareto optima. For that let us first recall the differential characterization of a Pareto optimum. Such an optimum can be obtained by maximizing a weighted sum of agents' utilities, subject to the material "adding up" constraints:

$$\max \sum_{i=1}^{n} v_i U_i(\omega_i + z_i, m_i)$$

s.t.

$$\sum_{i=1}^{n} z_{ih} = 0, \quad h = 1, \dots, l,$$

$$\sum_{i=1}^{n} m_i = \sum_{i=1}^{n} \bar{m}_i.$$

The Kuhn–Tucker conditions for such a program can be rewritten in the traditional form:

$$\frac{\partial U_i / \partial z_{ih}}{\partial U_i / \partial m_i} = p_h, \quad i = 1, \dots, n,$$

that is, the "shadow price" of every good h must be the same for all agents.

Now we can see why fixprice equilibria usually are not Pareto optimal: in a market h there are always some agents who are unconstrained (namely those on the short side). For these agents, in view of the above characterizations [equation (5)], the shadow price of good h is equal to p_h. If the allocation is a Pareto optimum the shadow price must be the same for all agents, and thus equal to p_h for all agents, which implies

$$\delta_{ih} = 0, \quad \forall i, \forall h.$$

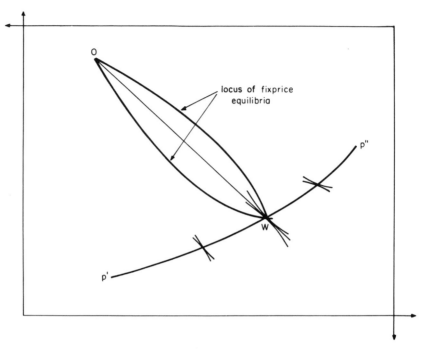

Figure 4.5

This means that all agents are unconstrained on all markets, i.e. that we are in a Walrasian equilibrium.

4.3. Constrained Pareto optimality

We now investigate a less demanding notion of optimality, which takes into account the fact that trades take place at a given price system. We shall thus say that an allocation is a constrained Pareto optimum if there is no allocation which (a) satisfies the physical feasibility conditions, (b) satisfies the budget constraints for the given price vector p, and (c) Pareto dominates the allocation considered. In the one-market Edgeworth box example of Figure 4.4, we see that the set of constrained Pareto optima is the segment AB, and the fixprice equilibrium A is one of them. We shall see, however, that this property does not generally extend to the multimarket case.

Indeed, coming back to the general framework, we see that a constrained-Pareto-optimal allocation can be obtained as a solution of the following program:

$$\max \sum_{i=1}^{n} v_i U_i(\omega_i + z_i, m_i)$$

s.t.

$$\sum_{i=1}^{n} z_{ih} = 0, \quad \forall h ,$$

$$pz_i + m_i = \bar{m}_i , \quad \forall i .$$

Note that we do not need to write the feasibility constraint for money, which follows from the other equalities.

The Kuhn–Tucker conditions for this program can be written:

$$\frac{\partial U_i/\partial z_{ih}}{\partial U_i/\partial m_i} = p_h + \mu_i \delta_h , \tag{6}$$

where μ_i is positive, and represents somehow the degree to which agent i is constrained, as compared to the others. The numbers δ_h can have any sign. For example, in the case of the Edgeworth box of Figure 4.4, which displays excess supply for the single good, the δ_h will be negative. In general the numbers μ_i and δ_h will depend in a more complex manner both on the price system p and on the weights v_i chosen for each agent.

If we now compare the shadow prices at a constrained Pareto optimum [equation (6)] with those in a fixprice equilibrium [equation (5)], we see that a constrained Pareto optimum will obtain only under very special circumstances. Indeed formula (6) above shows that an agent i should be either constrained in all markets where δ_h is different from zero (if $\mu_i \neq 0$) or constrained in none (if $\mu_i = 0$). A particular case where this occurs in the situation of classical unemployment in the three-goods model (Section 7 below), but this type of situation will occur infrequently if many markets do not clear.

Indeed, there are other cases where constrained optimality structurally cannot hold. Consider, for example, a situation of generalized excess supply where typically each agent is constrained on the goods he sells ($\delta_{ih} < 0$) and unconstrained for the goods he purchases ($\delta_{ih} = 0$). In such a case there is no way the shadow prices at a fixprice equilibrium can be written in the form given in equation (6), and the corresponding equilibrium will be suboptimal, even taking into account the constraint that trades must me made at given prices. A symmetric situation occurs with generalized excess demand. Particularly striking examples of this suboptimality will be given in Sections 7 and 8.

More generally, we may expect suboptimality to occur when there are several markets with excess demands of the same sign [a situation that also leads to multiplier effects; see Benassy (1975a, 1982) for a study of the relation between the two]. As a typical example, consider the case, traditional in

Keynesian theory, of an excess supply in several markets, and consider two markets h and k in excess supply. Consider two agents i and j, i being a rationed supplier in k and an unrationed demander in h, j being a rationed supplier in h and an unrationed demander in k. Then the conditions seen above immediately lead to:

$$\frac{1}{p_h}\frac{\partial U_i}{\partial z_{ih}} = \frac{\partial U_i}{\partial m_i} > \frac{1}{p_k}\frac{\partial U_i}{\partial z_{ik}},$$

$$\frac{1}{p_k}\frac{\partial U_j}{\partial z_{jk}} = \frac{\partial U_j}{\partial m_j} > \frac{1}{p_h}\frac{\partial U_j}{\partial z_{jh}}.$$

One thus sees that i and j would both be interested in exchanging goods h and k directly against each other at the prices p_h and p_k, which suggests a simple Pareto-improving trade. Of course, in general, in the absence of double coincidence of wants, such Pareto-improving trades will be more complex, making them quite difficult to achieve by decentralized agents. The existence of unrealized exchange possibilities at the economy level therefore suggests that in such cases government intervention may improve the situation of the private sector. Whether this actually holds will be investigated in the examples of Sections 7 and 8.

4.4. Notes and references

The suboptimality properties of non-Walrasian equilibria have been particularly studied in Benassy (1973, 1975a, 1975b, 1982), Drèze and Muller (1980), Silvestre (1985) and Younes (1975).

The problem of the Pareto optimality of non-Walrasian allocations has been notably scrutinized in Silvestre (1985).

The notion of constrained Pareto optimality used in this section is due to Uzawa (1962). Another quite interesting form of constrained optimality, based on pairwise exchanges, is due to Arrow and Hahn (1971). Whether fixprice allocations are constrained Pareto optimal has been investigated in Benassy (1973, 1975a, 1982) and Younes (1975). The treatment in this section follows the former. Drèze and Muller (1980) have shown that constrained optimality may be obtained through "coupons rationing".

The inefficiency of multiplier states had been discussed in Clower (1965) and Leijonhufvud (1968). This was developed formally in Benassy (1973, 1975a, 1977a, 1982). The role of expectations is discussed in Benassy (1982, 1986) and Persson and Svensson (1983). The properties of monetary and barter economies are compared in Benassy (1975b, 1982).

5. Price making and equilibrium

At this stage, the theory is still in need of a description of decentralized price making by agents internal to the system. We shall describe in this section a few concepts dealing with that problem, and we shall see that, just as in demand and supply theory, quantity signals play a prominent role. It is actually quite intuitive that quantity signals must be a fundamental part of the competitive process in a truly decentralized economy. Indeed, it is the inability to sell as much as they want that leads suppliers to propose, or to accept from other agents, a lower price, and conversely it is the inability to buy as much as they want that leads demanders to propose, or accept, a higher price. Various modes of price making integrating these aspects can be envisioned. We shall deal here with a particular organization of the pricing process where agents on one side of the market (most often the suppliers) quote prices and agents on the other side act as price takers. The general idea relating the concepts in this section to those of the previous ones is that price makers change their prices so as to "manipulate" the quantity constraints they face (that is, so as to increase or decrease their possible sales or purchases). As we shall see, this model of price making is quite reminiscent of the imperfect competition line [Chamberlin (1933), Robinson (1933), Triffin (1940), Bushaw and Clower (1957) and Arrow (1959)] and more particularly of the theories of general equilibrium with monopolistic competition, as developed notably by Negishi (1961, 1972).

5.1. The general framework

We thus now assume that each agent i controls the prices of a (possibly empty) subset H_i of the goods. Goods are distinguished both by their physical characteristics and by the agent who sets their price (we thus consider two goods sold by different sellers as different goods, a fairly usual assumption in microeconomic theory since these goods differ at least by location, quality, etc.), so that

$$H_i \cap H_j = \{\emptyset\} , \quad i \neq j .$$

Each price maker is thus alone on his side of the market. We can further subdivide H_i into H_i^d (goods demanded by i) and H_i^s (goods supplied by i). Agent i appears, at least formally, as a monopolist on markets $h \in H_i^s$, as a monopsonist on markets $h \in H_i^d$.

We denote by p_i the set of prices controlled by agent i and by p_{-i} the set of prices controlled by the other agents (i.e. the rest of prices):

$$p_i = \{ p_h \mid h \in H_i \} ,$$
$$p_{-i} = \{ p_j \mid j \neq i \} .$$

Each agent will choose a price vector p_i taking the other prices p_{-i} as given; the equilibrium structure is thus that of a Nash-equilibrium in prices corresponding to an idea of monopolistic competition. The basic idea behind the modelling of price making itself in such models is, as we indicated above, that each price maker uses the prices he controls to "manipulate" the quantity constraints he faces. In particular, because the price makers are alone on their side of the markets they control, their quantity constraints on these markets have the simple form:

$$\bar{s}_{ih} = \sum_{j \neq i} \tilde{d}_{jh} , \quad h \in H_i^s ,$$

$$\bar{d}_{ih} = \sum_{j \neq i} \tilde{s}_{jh} , \quad h \in H_i^d ,$$

i.e. the maximum quantity that price setter i can sell is the total demand of the others, and conversely if he is a buyer.

In order to be able to pose the problem of the choice of prices by price makers as a standard decision problem, all we now need to know is how the constraints faced by an agent on all markets vary as a function of the prices he sets.

We now describe two approaches and equilibrium concepts dealing with that problem: one based on objective demand curves, the other on subjective demand curves.

5.2. Objective demand curves

The implicit idea behind the objective demand curve approach is that each price maker knows well enough the economy to be able to compute under all circumstances the actual quantity constraints he would face. Since we are considering a Nash equilibrium, he must be able to perform this computation for any set p_{-i} of prices set by the other agents, and any prices p_i set by himself, i.e. he must be able to compute his constraints for any vector of prices once all feedback effects have been accounted for.

On the other hand, we know, from Section 3 above, that for a given organization of the economy (i.e. in particular rationing schemes) and for a given set of prices p a fixprice equilibrium is characterized by net demands $\tilde{Z}_i(p)$, transactions $Z_i^*(p)$ and perceived constraints $\bar{D}_i(p)$ and $\bar{S}_i(p)$. If the agent has full knowledge of the parameters of the economy (a strong assumption of course, but one that is embedded in the notion of an objective demand curve), then he knows this and the "objective demand curve" will be given by the two vector functions $\bar{D}_i(p)$ and $\bar{S}_i(p)$.

Accordingly, the price p_i maximizing the utility of agent i is the solution in p_i of the following program:

$$\max U_i(\omega_i + z_i, m_i)$$

s.t.

$$pz_i + m_i = \bar{m}_i,$$

$$-\bar{S}_i(p) \le z_i \le \bar{D}_i(p),$$

which yields the optimum price of agent i as a function of the prices of the other agents:

$$p_i = \psi_i(p_{-i}).$$

We can now give the definition of an equilibrium:

Definition 3. An equilibrium with price makers is characterized by a set of p_i^*, $\tilde{z}_i$, z_i^*, $\bar{d}_i$, $\bar{s}_i$, $i = 1, \ldots, n$, such that
  (a) $p_i^* = \psi_i(p_{-i}^*)$, $\forall i$, and
  (b) $\tilde{z}_i$, z_i^*, $\bar{d}_i$ and $\bar{s}_i$ form a fixprice equilibrium for the price vector p^*, i.e. they are equal respectively to $\tilde{Z}_i(p^*)$, $Z_i^*(p^*)$, $\bar{D}_i(p^*)$ and $\bar{S}_i(p^*)$, for all i.

Further description and conditions for existence can be found in Benassy (1988). We shall see in Section 8 below a macroeconomic application of this concept. Before that let us give a simple example in the Edgeworth box already considered above (Figure 4.6).

Assume now that agent B (the seller) sets the price. The "objective demand curve" is then agent A's demand, and thus corresponds to the locus of tangency points between various budget lines and A's indifference curves. This is depicted as the curved line OMW in Figure 4.6, where W is the Walrasian point. The equilibrium point is then simply point M, the tangency point of this curve with B's indifference curve, which yields agent B the highest possible utility, given A's objective demand behavior.

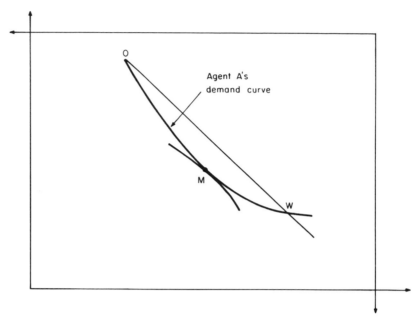

Figure 4.6

5.3. Subjective demand curves

Of course assuming every agent knows the "true" objective demand curve as defined above is a very strong assumption in view of all the parameters involved. Another approach, the subjective demand curve approach, consists in having each price maker estimate the demand and supply curves. These estimated curves are called the subjective, or perceived demand or supply curves.

   Formally the perceived demand curve links the maximum quantity a price maker i can sell on a market $h \in H_i^s$ he controls, i.e. $\bar{s}_{ih}$, to the prices p_i he sets. It will be denoted as

$$\bar{S}_{ih}(p_i, \theta_i),$$

where θ_i is a vector of parameters (for example, the position or elasticity of the perceived demand curve), themselves estimated on the basis of price–quantity signals, as we shall see below. We assume that $\bar{S}_{ih}$ is non-increasing in p_h. Symmetrically, the perceived supply curve, which indicates the maximum quantity a price maker i can purchase on a market $h \in H_i^d$ he controls, will be denoted as

$$\bar{D}_{ih}(p_i, \theta_i),$$

and we shall assume it is non-decreasing in p_h.

Now the parameters θ_i are not arbitrary but must be estimated so as to fit the price–quantity observations. We thus assume that the estimated parameter is a function of current signals (and, of course, but this is left implicit, of all past signals):

$$\theta_i = \theta_i(\bar{p}, \bar{d}_i, \bar{s}_i).$$

Because we are going to consider an equilibrium concept for the current period, this estimation procedure must be such that perceived demand and supply curves "go through" the observed point [Bushaw and Clower (1957)], i.e.

$$\bar{D}_{ih}[p_i, \theta_i(\bar{p}, \bar{d}_i, \bar{s}_i)] = \bar{d}_{ih}, \quad \text{for } p_i = \bar{p}_i,$$
$$\bar{S}_{ih}[p_i, \theta_i(\bar{p}, \bar{d}_i, \bar{s}_i)] = \bar{s}_{ih}, \quad \text{for } p_i = \bar{p}_i.$$

As an example, imagine agent i is a price setter for a good h he sells, and the perceived demand curve has the form:

$$\theta_{ih} p_h^{-\varepsilon},$$

where the elasticity ε may have been estimated from earlier observations. Then the above consistency equation yields:

$$\theta_{ih} p_h^{-\varepsilon} = \bar{s}_{ih},$$
$$\theta_{ih} = p_h^{\varepsilon} \cdot \bar{s}_{ih}.$$

We can now make explicit the procedure of price formation. Agent i, facing a price p_h and constraints $\bar{d}_{ih}$ and $\bar{s}_{ih}$ on markets $h \notin H_i$, will choose his prices so as to maximize his utility, i.e. the solution in p_i to the program:

$$\max U_i(\omega_i + z_i, m_i)$$

s.t.

$$pz_i + m_i = \bar{m}_i,$$
$$-\bar{s}_{ih} \le z_{ih} \le \bar{d}_{ih}, \qquad\qquad h \notin H_i,$$
$$-\bar{S}_{ih}(p_i, \theta_i) \le z_{ih} \le \bar{D}_{ih}(p_i, \theta_i), \quad h \in H_i,$$

which yields a function $p_i = \mathcal{P}_i(p, \bar{d}_i, \bar{s}_i)$ since the parameters θ_i are themselves functions of the signals p, $\bar{d}_i$ and $\bar{s}_i$. We can now define an equilibrium as a situation where quantities are optimal given prices and no price maker has interest in changing his price, i.e.

Definition 4. An equilibrium with price makers consists of a set of prices p_i^*, demands $\tilde{z}_i$, transactions z_i^* and quantity signals $\bar{d}_i$ and $\bar{s}_i$ such that
  (a) $p_i^* = \mathcal{P}_i(p^*, \bar{d}_i, \bar{s}_i)$, $\forall i$, and
  (b) The quantities $\tilde{z}_i$, z_i^*, $\bar{d}_i$ and $\bar{s}_i$ form a fixprice equilibrium for p^*.

A further description of this concept and its properties, as well as existence proofs, can be found in Benassy (1976b, 1982). We may now make a few remarks, notably comparing the two concepts with subjective and objective demand curves.

The first and obvious one is that the two cateteries of objective and subjective demand curves are not antagonistic: the objective demand curve would arise as a particular case of the subjective demand curve approach if the family of subjective demand curves happens to contain the objective one. In fact, the most natural and fruitful way to interpret subjective demand curves is as a temporary state in an ongoing learning process. Indeed, the theory developed here gives a natural way of "learning" about the demand curve: each realization p, $\bar{d}_i$ and $\bar{s}_i$ in a period is a point on the "true" curve of that period. Using the sequence of these observations, plus any extra information available, the price makers can use statistical techniques to yield an estimation of the "objective" demand curve. Thus, the parameters of the family of subjective demand curves in one period correspond to whatever has been learned up to that period. Whether such learning would lead to the "true" demand curve is still an unresolved problem.

5.4. Notes and references

The two concepts described in this section are taken from Benassy (1988) for the objective demand curve approach, and Benassy (1976b, 1982) for the subjective demand curve approach. The studies in general equilibrium with subjective demand curves originate in the seminal work of Negishi (1961, 1972). The "consistency condition" for subjective demand curves had been given by Bushaw and Clower (1957). The theory of a general equilibrium with objective demand curves was first developed in the Cournotian "quantity setting" framework by Gabszewicz and Vial (1972), then in some specific models with price makers by Marschak and Selten (1974) and Nikaido (1975). The general treatment in this section follows Benassy (1988).

We should note that we have described the two "extremes" in terms of consistency with the data: the "objective" demand curve, on the one hand, is *the* correct one, and is determined uniquely by the data of the economy. On the other hand, subjective demand curves are much more numerous as they are only required to satisfy the minimal consistency requirement of "going through" the observed point on the "true" curve. One may think of various less demanding requirements in between the two extremes. For example, one may assume that the price makers know, maybe by local experiments, the slope of the "true" demand curve at the point considered [Silvestre (1977)].

We should also note that we have maintained throughout the assumption of a Nash equilibrium in prices, investigating the consistency of the quantity responses to these prices. Another direction of research is to abandon the "monopolistic competition" assumption and to go to a more oligopolistic framework where agents should conjecture the price responses of competitors to their own actions [Hahn (1978), Marschak and Selten (1974)].

6. Expectations

6.1. The problem

Up to now we have dealt with an equilibrium structure in the period considered, implicitly a short-run one, but of course the economy extends further in the future, as we are reminded at least by the presence of money as a store of value. More generally the presence of stocks (inventories, capital goods, financial assets) makes it necessary to form expectations.

We now show that expectations are actually present in the theory, and how they can be integrated explicitly. This integration of expectations goes through an evaluation of the utility of stocks, which are the physical link between present and future. The construction of such indirect utilities allows us to convert expectations on future exchanges into effective demands and supplies for current goods.

The general method can be sketched as follows. Each agent actually plans for the current and future periods. Expectations for future periods take the form of prices and quantity constraints (for price takers) or expected demand curves (for price makers). These may be deterministic or stochastic. These expectations are formed via expectations schemes that link future price–quantity expectations to all price–quantity signals received in past and current periods. This formulation is thus quite general and covers any expectations scheme, "rational" or not, based on actually available information.

By a standard dynamic programming technique [Bellman (1957)] we can reduce the multiperiod problem to a single period one, where the valuation of all stocks (and notably money) depends upon future expectations, and thus, via the expectations schemes, upon the current and past price–quantity signals. We are thus formally back to the one-period formulation used in Section 3, with the only difference that current and past price–quantity signals must be added in the valuation functions.

6.2. The indirect utility of money

We now show how to derive the indirect utility of money from expectations in a framework similar to that seen in Section 3. However, instead of assuming that agent i has a one-period utility function $U_i(x_i, m_i)$ we assume that he plans for two periods, current and future (the method would extend without difficulty to any finite number of periods). Variables relative to the future period are denoted by a superscript e, for expected. Agent i has a utility function for current and future consumptions,

$$V_i(x_i, x_i^e) \, ,$$

assumed strictly concave, where

$$x_i = \omega_i + z_i \, ,$$

$$x_i^e = \omega_i^e + z_i^e \, .$$

At the beginning of the current period, the agent holds an initial quantity of money $\bar{m}_i$. He transfers to the second period a quantity m_i equal to

$$m_i = \bar{m}_i - pz_i \geq 0 \, .$$

The expected transactions in the second period must satisfy:

$$p^e z_i^e \leq m_i \, .$$

Each agent must furthermore form expectations about the price and quantity constraints he will face in the future period. We denote these as

$$\sigma_i^e = \{ p^e, \bar{d}_i^e, \bar{s}_i^e \} \, .$$

Assume that agent i has consumed $x_i = \omega_i + z_i$ in the first period, and transfers a quantity of money m_i to the second period. Given some expectations $\sigma_i^e = \{ p^e, \bar{d}_i^e, \bar{s}_i^e \}$, his expected second-period transactions are those that maximize his utility under the budget constraint, and taking all quantity signals into account. Thus, z_i^e is the solution of the following program:

$$\max V_i(\omega_i + z_i, \omega_i^e + z_i^e)$$

s.t.

$$p^e z_i^e \leq m_i \, ,$$

$$-\bar{s}_i^e \leq z_i^e \leq \bar{d}_i^e \, .$$

We denote functionally the vector z_i^e solution of this program as

$$Z_i^e(z_i, m_i, p^e, \bar{d}_i^e, \bar{s}_i^e) = Z_i^e(z_i, m_i, \sigma_i^e) \, .$$

We can then write the level of utility expected in the first period as

$$U_i^e(\omega_i + z_i, m_i, \sigma_i^e) = V_i[\omega_i + z_i, \omega_i^e + Z_i^e(z_i, m_i, \sigma_i^e)] \, .$$

Under this form the indirect utility function depends explicitly on expectations of future signals σ_i^e. We see that we have a utility function having $\omega_i + z_i$ and m_i as arguments, but "parameterized" by the expectations σ_i^e. We may note at this stage that this utility function has the natural property of homogeneity of degree zero with respect to m_i and p^e.

If the expectations were given, the analysis would actually stop here. But of course in general the expectations will depend upon all information available up to the current period. We can, in particular, make these expectations explicitly dependent upon current period signals, which we will write, if expectations are deterministic, as

$$\sigma_i^e = \phi_i(\sigma_i) \, ,$$

and the utility function will then be

$$U_i(\omega_i + z_i, m_i, \sigma_i) = U_i^e[\omega_i + z_i, m_i, \phi_i(\sigma_i)] \, .$$

If expectations are stochastic, and described by a cumulative probability distribution $\psi_i(\sigma_i^e \mid \sigma_i)$, then the indirect utility will be

$$U_i(x_i, m_i, \sigma_i) = \int U_i^e(x_i, m_i, \sigma_i^e) \, d\psi_i(\sigma_i^e \mid \sigma_i) \, .$$

With these indirect utility functions we can proceed to the same equilibrium analysis as that performed in Section 3 or 5.

Note also that for price makers what should be forecasted is expected demand curves, not price and quantity signals.

6.3. An example

Let us consider an agent living two periods, working l and l^e, and consuming c and c^e in these two periods. We assume this agent has a utility function:

$$V(c, l, c^e, l^e) ,$$

which we shall assume, for the simplicity of exposition, separable in its arguments.

The second-period plan of this agent, given c and l, will be given by the following maximization problem:

$$\max V(c, l, c^e, l^e)$$

s.t.

$$p^e c^e \leq m + w^e l^e ,$$

$$c^e \leq \bar{c}^e ,$$

$$l^e \leq \bar{l}^e .$$

Consider first the case where the agent is unconstrained in the second period. Then we obtain the second-period Walrasian levels of consumption and employment:

$$c^{ew}(m, w^e, p^e) , \quad l^{ew}(m, w^e, p^e) ,$$

where these two functions are homogeneous of degree zero in m, w^e and p^e. The indirect utility is written:

$$V[c, l, c^{ew}(m, p^e, w^e) , l^{ew}(m, p^e, w^e)] ,$$

which depends only on expected price signals, p^e and w^e, just as in Walrasian theory.

Consider now the case where the agent expects to be labor constrained in the second period, and thus $l^e = \bar{l}^e$. Then clearly his second-period consumption will be equal to

$$c^e = \frac{m + w^e \bar{l}^e}{p^e} .$$

and the indirect utility function is

$$V\left[c, l, \frac{m + w^e \bar{l}^e}{p^e}, \bar{l}^e\right].$$

We first remark that an expected quantity signal $\bar{l}^e$ now enters the indirect utility function together with the expected price signals. Secondly, as the marginal utility of future consumption c^e decreases with its level, the marginal utility of money will be increasing as $\bar{l}^e$ decreases, i.e. as employment perspectives become dimmer, which highlights the role of money as precautionary savings against an expected inability to sell labor.

Finally, consider now the case where the agent does not expect to be constrained in his labor supply in the second period, but in his consumption purchases, so that $c^e = \bar{c}^e$. Then it is logical for him to supply just that quantity of labor necessary to pay for the consumption, i.e.

$$l^e = \max\left\{0, \frac{p^e \bar{c}^e - m}{w^e}\right\},$$

so that in that case the utility function is

$$V\left[c, l, \bar{c}^e, \max\left\{0, \frac{p^e \bar{c}^e - m}{w^e}\right\}\right].$$

Here again an expected quantity signal $\bar{c}^e$ enters the utility function;

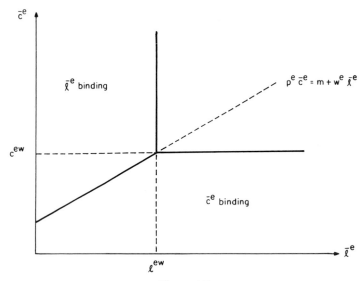

Figure 4.7

furthermore, the marginal utility of money will decrease as $\bar{c}^e$ decreases, even becoming zero if $m \geq p^e \bar{c}^e$. We see this time that an expected inability to purchase goods may induce some kind of "flight from money".

Which of the three utility functions will be relevant is easily seen from Figure 4.7. We may note that in all three cases the indirect utility function is homogeneous of degree zero in m, p^e and w^e, even though expected quantity signals have been added.

6.4. Notes and references

A treatment of expected quantity signals in a macroeconomic setting appears in Grossman (1972) which formalizes the investment accelerator.

The integration of quantity expectations into the theory of non-Walrasian equilibria was made in Benassy (1973, 1975a).

Subsequent applications in micro- or macroeconomic frameworks are found in Grandmont and Laroque (1976), Hildenbrand and Hildenbrand (1978), Muellbauer and Portes (1978), Benassy (1982, 1986), Neary and Stiglitz (1983) and Persson and Svensson (1983). The particular utility function example of this section is borrowed from Benassy (1976c) and Muellbauer and Portes (1978).

We should note that non-Walrasian concepts are fully consistent with perfect foresight [Neary and Stiglitz (1983)]. In that case the structure of the model is formally identical to that of a one-period model.

7. A macroeconomic model

We now describe a simple version of the well-known fixprice macro model of Barro and Grossman (1971, 1976). This will allow us to see that non-Walrasian models may have a variety of "subregimes" and, moreover, that the same policy variable (which we shall take here to be government spending or a simple form of monetary policy) may have completely different effects on activity, employment and welfare depending on the particular regime the economy is in.

7.1. The model

We consider here a simple aggregate monetary economy with three goods, money, output and labor, and three agents, an aggregate firm, an aggregate household and the government. Accordingly, there are two markets where output and labor are exchanged against money, respectively at the price p and wage w. These are assumed rigid in the period considered. Each market is assumed to function without frictions so that the transaction on each is equal to the minimum of supply and demand. The transactions on output and labor will be denoted by y and l.

The firm has a production function $F(l)$ which we assume strictly concave. The firm does not hold any inventories, maximizes current profits $py - wl$, which it fully redistributes to the household.

The household has an initial endowment of labor l_0 and of money $\bar{m}$. It consumes c, works l and its budget constraint is

$$pc + m = wl + \pi + \mu\bar{m} \ .$$

The variable μ is one of the policy parameters of the government, who can multiply the initial quantity of money by μ. This particular, but popular, policy variable has been chosen because, as we shall see below, it is neutral in Walrasian equilibrium. The household's utility function will be taken to be of the general form:

$$U(c, l_0 - l, m/p^e)$$

which, as we saw in the preceding section, can be derived from an intertemporal utility maximization problem. In order to make the exposition more compact, in what follows we use the particular logarithmic specification:

$$U = \alpha_c \log c + \alpha_l \log(l_0 - l) + \alpha_m \log(m/p^e) \ ,$$

with

$$\alpha_c + \alpha_l + \alpha_m = 1 \ .$$

Note that, because of this particular form, in what follows we will not need to specify how p^e is determined, which will simplify the exposition.

Finally, the government can choose, besides the parameter μ, its level of output purchases g, which it pays by monetary creation (taxation could also be added without difficulty, but is omitted for the sake of expositional simplicity). As a result of the different government policies, the final quantity of money in the economy will be $\mu\bar{m} + pg$.

7.2. Walrasian equilibrium

Before studying its non-Walrasian regimes, we briefly describe the Walrasian equilibrium of this economy.

The Walrasian demands and supplies of the firm are obtained by maximizing profit $py - wl$ subject to the production function $y = F(l)$. This immediately yields:

$$y^s = F[F'^{-1}(w/p)], \qquad l^d = F'^{-1}(w/p).$$

The household maximizes utility subject to its budget constraint:

$$pc + m = \mu\bar{m} + \pi + wl,$$

which yields:

$$c^d = \alpha_c \left(\frac{\mu\bar{m} + \pi + wl_0}{p} \right),$$

$$l^s = l_0 - \alpha_l \left(\frac{\mu\bar{m} + \pi + wl_0}{w} \right).$$

The Walrasian equilibrium is obtained by solving the equations:

$$l^* = l^s = l^d, \qquad y^* = y^s = c^d + g,$$

with, in addition, $\pi = py^* - wl^*$.

It is easy to check that in this Walrasian equilibrium money is neutral, i.e. that, other things equal, the equilibrium price and wage are proportional to μ, whereas quantities traded are independent of μ. Changes in g, however, are obviously non-neutral. More precisely, an increase in g leads to a reduction in w/p, an increase in employment and production, but a reduction in private consumption. There is thus a crowding out effect of g, though of less than 100 percent, due to the fact that the labor supply is elastic.

7.3. The regimes

We now assume that p and w are given and derive the level of transactions for the various subregimes. Anticipating what follows, we see that there are three possible regimes in this model:
- Keynesian unemployment with excess supply for both output and labor;
- classical unemployment with excess supply of labor and excess demand for goods;
- repressed inflation with excess demand for labor and output.

7.4. Keynesian unemployment

This regime is characterized by excess supply on both markets. In particular the household faces a (binding) constraint $\bar{l}^s$ on the labor market. Its effective demand for consumption $\tilde{c}$ is thus the solution in c of the program:

$$\max \alpha_c \log c + \alpha_l \log(l_0 - l) + \alpha_m \log(m/p^e)$$

s.t.

$$pc + m = \mu\bar{m} + \pi + wl \,,$$

$$l \leq \bar{l}^s \,,$$

where the last constraint is binding. The solution is

$$\tilde{c} = \frac{\alpha_c}{\alpha_c + \alpha_m} \left[\frac{\mu\bar{m} + \pi + wl^{\bar{s}}}{p} \right],$$

a traditional Keynesian consumption function, with $\alpha_c/(\alpha_c + \alpha_m)$ as the marginal propensity to consume out of income. Because $\bar{l}^s$ is binding, it is equal to the household's transaction on labor l^*, so that, given the definition of π, $\tilde{c}$ can be written in the even more familiar Keynesian form:

$$\tilde{c} = \frac{\alpha_c}{\alpha_c + \alpha_m} \left[\frac{\mu\bar{m}}{p} + y \right].$$

Because of the excess supply of goods, transactions on the goods market are demand determined, so that y is equal to total output demand, i.e. $\tilde{c}$ plus government demand for output $\tilde{g}$:

$$y = \tilde{c} + \tilde{g} = \frac{\alpha_c}{\alpha_c + \alpha_m} \left[\frac{\mu\bar{m}}{p} + y \right] + \tilde{g} \,,$$

yielding:

$$y^* = \frac{\alpha_c}{\alpha_m} \cdot \frac{\mu\bar{m}}{p} + \frac{(\alpha_c + \alpha_m)}{\alpha_m} \tilde{g} = y_k \,. \tag{7}$$

We recognize here a traditional Keynesian multiplier, with $(\alpha_c + \alpha_m)/\alpha_m$ being the multiplier.

Labor transactions l^* are equal to the firm's demand for labor which, since the firm is constrained in its output sales, is equal to the quantity just necessary to produce y_k, i.e.

$$l^* = F^{-1}(y_k) = l_k .$$ (8)

We may also compute private consumption $c^* = y^* - \tilde{g}$:

$$c^* = \frac{\alpha_c}{\alpha_m} \left(\frac{\mu \bar{m}}{p} + \tilde{g} \right) .$$

We can now make a few observations. The first is that money is no longer neutral, but that an increase in μ will increase production, employment and private consumption. These will also be increased by increases in government spending. The traditional results of Keynesian "multiplier" analysis are thus valid in this regime.

Maybe the most striking fact is that an increase in government spending will increase not only production and employment, but also private consumption. There is thus no crowding out, quite the contrary, since even though the government collects real output from the private sector, more of it is available for private consumption, a quite remarkable by-product of the inefficiency of the Keynesian multiplier state.

7.5. Classical unemployment

In this case there is excess supply of labor and excess demand for goods. The firm, being on the "short" side in both markets, is able to carry out its Walrasian plan, so that

$$l^* = F'^{-1}(w/p) = l_c ,$$ (9)

$$y^* = F[F'^{-1}(w/p)] = y_c .$$ (10)

We immediately see that "Keynesian" policies have no impact on employment and production. In fact, it is easy to check that their main effect is to aggravate excess demand on the goods market. If we further assume that the government has priority in the goods market, then the actual consumption is equal to

$$c^* = y^* - \tilde{g} = y_c - \tilde{g} .$$

There is a 100 percent crowding out effect of government expenditures, which thus appears as an undesirable policy instrument. Note that this time crowding out does not occur through prices, but by a direct rationing mechanism.

The only thing that affects the level of employment and production is the level of real wages, thus validating the "classical" presumption that there is unemployment because "real wages are too high".

7.6. Repressed inflation

In this regime there is excess demand in both markets. In particular the consumer is faced with a binding constraint $\bar{c}$ (actually equal to his purchases c^*) in the goods market. His supply of labor $\tilde{l}^s$ is given by the solution in l to the following program:

$$\max \alpha_c \log c + \alpha_l \log(l_0 - l) + \alpha_m \log(m/p^e)$$

s.t.

$$pc + m = \mu\bar{m} + wl + \pi \,,$$

$$c \le \bar{c} \,,$$

where the last constraint is binding. The solution to this program is

$$\tilde{l}^s = l_0 - \frac{\alpha_l}{\alpha_l + \alpha_m} \left[\frac{\mu\bar{m} + \pi + wl_0 - p\bar{c}}{w} \right].$$

We see from this formula that rationing in the goods market leads the household to reduce its supply of labor. Because there is excess demand of labor, the actual transaction l^* is equal to this supply $\tilde{l}^s$. Now let us again assume that the government has priority on the goods market. Then

$$\bar{c} = c^* = y^* - \tilde{g}$$

and, again using the definition of profits π, the above equation is rewritten:

$$l^* = l_0 - \frac{\alpha_l}{\alpha_l + \alpha_m} \left[\frac{\mu\bar{m} + wl_0 - wl^* + p\tilde{g}}{w} \right],$$

yielding:

$$l^* = l_0 - \frac{\alpha_l}{\alpha_m} \left(\frac{\mu\bar{m} + p\tilde{g}}{w} \right) = l_r \,. \tag{11}$$

Output transactions y^* are equal to supply which, because the firm is constrained in its labor purchases, is equal to the maximum quantity producible with l_r, i.e.

$$y^* = F(l_r) = y_r .$$ (12)

We now may note that the economic policy variables have an effect completely opposite to that in the Keynesian regime. In particular, increases in the quantity of money or in government spending diminish employment and production. Furthermore, private consumption, again assuming government priority, is

$$c^* = y^* - \tilde{g} = y_r - \tilde{g} .$$

Since an increase in $\tilde{g}$ reduces y_r, there is a more than 100 percent crowding out effect. An increase in $\tilde{g}$ reduces c^* by an even greater quantity! The mechanism at work in this regime is some kind of "supply multiplier" [Barro and Grossman (1974)] by which a reduction in the amount of goods available for consumption reduces the supply of labor, which itself reduces further the amount of goods produced, etc.

7.7. The general picture

As we have seen above, the three regimes of our model display strikingly different properties concerning the determination of employment and activity and the response to policy variables. It is therefore important to know for which values of the "exogenous" parameters μ, $\bar{m}$, p, w and $\tilde{g}$ each of the three regimes obtains. As the reader may easily check, both the employment level and the nature of the regime are determined by finding out the lowest of the three possible employment levels computed above [cf. equations (7)–(12)], i.e.

$$l^* = \min(l_k, l_c, l_r) ,$$

$$y^* = \min(y_k, y_c, y_r) .$$

It is convenient to depict the three regimes in the space $(\mu \bar{m}/p, w/p)$, $\tilde{g}$ being parametric. Figure 4.8 has been drawn for $\tilde{g}$ equal to zero. As $\tilde{g}$ increases, point W will move southwest. The triangles are iso-employment or iso-output lines. The highest level of employment and production occurs at W, the Walrasian equilibrium point.

On this diagram we see particularly well that the spillover effects from the goods market to the labor market matter a lot: even if the real wage is "right"

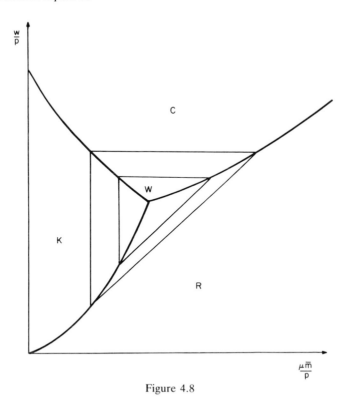

Figure 4.8

(i.e. equal to its Walrasian equilibrium level, which corresponds to the horizontal line going through W), we may have inefficiently low values of employment due to insufficient (or excessive) demand in the output market.

7.8. Efficiency properties

We want now to highlight in this particular macroeconomic example the inefficiencies that we described in the more general model of Section 4. We noted particularly that in cases of generalized excess demand or supply, which lead to the existence of multiplier effects, there were most likely potential Pareto-improving trades at the given price system. We now verify this in the two regimes concerned, those of Keynesian unemployment and repressed inflation. Since all mutual gains from trade have been exhausted in trades of money versus output or labor, we investigate direct trades of labor against output.

Let us start with the interior of the Keynesian regime. Because $l_k < l_c$, we have:

$$F'(l) < \frac{w}{p},$$

so that the firm would increase its real profit by directly purchasing labor for output. Consider now the household. Since it is unconstrained in the goods market and constrained on the labor market, we have:

$$\frac{1}{p}\frac{\partial U}{\partial c} = \frac{\partial U}{\partial m} > \frac{1}{w}\frac{\partial U}{\partial(l_0 - l)},$$

so that the household would also gain in selling directly labor for output.

Symmetrically in the interior of the repressed inflation regime we have:

$$F'(l) < \frac{w}{p},$$

$$\frac{1}{p}\frac{\partial U}{\partial c} > \frac{\partial U}{\partial m} = \frac{\partial U}{\partial(l_0 - l)},$$

so that again the firm and household could profitably directly exchange output for labor.

We should at this point make a caveat: The above inefficiency results might suggest that the monetary nature of exchange is the problem, and that allowing barter trades to be carried out between households and firms would allow us to alleviate the market failure. This would be missing the fundamental issue, which is that both the market failure and monetary exchange are caused by the lack of double coincidence of wants. Such an issue cannot be discussed adequately in this very aggregated model, but will be tackled in the more disaggregated model of the next section.

7.9. Notes and references

The model of this section was originally developed by Barro and Grossman (1971, 1974, 1976). Elements of it can be found in Solow and Stiglitz (1968) and Younes (1970). The particular adaptation in this section is taken from Benassy (1976a, 1977a). Subsequent adaptations can be found in Malinvaud (1977), Hildenbrand and Hildenbrand (1978) and Muellbauer and Portes (1978). The Classical–Keynesian unemployment terminology appears in Malinvaud (1977).

Various extensions of this basic macroeconomic model have been considered: introduction of a bonds market [Barro and Grossman (1976), Hool (1980), Benassy (1983)]; consideration of foreign trade [Dixit (1978), Neary (1980), Cuddington, Johansson and Lofgren (1984)]; capital accumulation [Ito (1980), Picard (1983)]; fluctuations [Benassy (1984)], etc. A number of macroeconomic applications with varying assumptions on price rigidities are found in Benassy (1986). These concepts have also been applied to socialist economies [cf. notably Portes (1981), or see also Kornai (1980, 1982) for an alternative formulation]. Finally, a number of applied econometric models have been developed. See, for example, the surveys in Quandt (1982) and Sneessens (1981).

8. A model with imperfect competition and unemployment

We now use the developments of the preceding sections to construct a simple "micro–macro" model of imperfect competition adapted from Benassy (1987), displaying endogenous price making resulting from explicit utility or profit maximization by agents. Within this framework we study such problems as the efficiency properties of the equilibrium, the existence of unemployment or the effectiveness of simple governmental monetary policies. Notably we try to emphasize the similarities (or dissimilarities) of this model with the Walrasian one, which is the main general equilibrium alternative with flexible prices.

8.1. The model

We consider a monetary economy with three types of goods: money; different types of labor, indexed by $i = 1, \ldots, n$; and consumption goods, indexed by $j = 1, \ldots, m$. There are three types of agents: households, indexed by $i = 1, \ldots, n$; firms, indexed by $j = 1, \ldots, m$; and government. Consumer i is the only one to be endowed with labor of type i, and firm j is the only one to produce good j. We call w_i the money wage for type i labor, p_j the price of good j, and w and p the corresponding vectors:

$$p = \{p_j \,|\, j = 1, \ldots, m\}, \qquad w = \{w_i \,|\, i = 1, \ldots, n\}.$$

Firm j produces a quantity of output y_j according to a production function:

$$y_j = F_j(l_j), \qquad l_j = (l_{ij} \,|\, i = 1, \ldots, n\},$$

where l_{ij} is the quantity of labor i used by firm j (and thus purchased from household i). We assume F_j strictly concave in its arguments. Firm j maximizes its profits π_j:

$$\pi_j = p_j y_j - w l_j = p_j y_j - \sum_{i=1}^{n} w_i l_{ij} \,.$$

Household i has initial endowments l_{i0} of type i labor, and $\bar{m}_i$ of money. It consumes a vector:

$$c_i = \{c_{ij} \mid j = 1, \dots, m\} \,.$$

Its budget constraint, in the absence of government intervention, is

$$pc_i + m_i = w_i l_i + \bar{m}_i + \sum_{j=1}^{m} \theta_{ij} \pi_j \,,$$

where m_i is the final quantity of money and θ_{ij} the share of firm j owned by household i. The quantity of labor l_i is equal to

$$l_i = \sum_{j=1}^{m} l_{ij} \le l_{i0} \,.$$

We assume, as in the preceding section, that the government can manipulate by policy action the initial money holdings, increasing them proportionately by a factor μ, so the initial holdings of household i become $\mu \bar{m}_i$ and the budget constraint becomes:

$$pc_i + m_i = w_i l_i + \mu \bar{m}_i + \sum_{j=1}^{m} \theta_{ij} \pi_j \,.$$

This particular policy has again been chosen because it is known to be "neutral" in Walrasian equilibrium,[7] which will allow an easy comparison.

Household i maximizes a utility function of the form:

$$U_i(c_i, l_i, m_i, \mu) \,,$$

which is assumed to be strictly quasi-concave in c_i, $-l_i$ and m_i, and separable in the three first arguments. The presence of the first two arguments is obvious. The arguments m_i and μ represent the indirect utility of money, and we assume that U_i is homogeneous of degree zero in m_i and μ. As we saw in the preceding section, the indirect utility of money should be homogeneous of degree zero in money and expected prices. The implicit idea behind our assumption is thus that, other things equal, future prices are expected to move proportionately to

---

[7] See, for example, Grandmont (1983) for a thorough discussion of this issue in Walrasian models.

μ. As we shall see in Subsection 8.6 below, this proportionality of prices to μ is indeed consistent with the working of the model.

This model has a particular market structure where each good (labor or consumer good) is sold by a single agent to a multitude of other agents: labor of type i is sold by household i to all firms $j = 1, \ldots, m$. Output j is sold by firm j to all households $i = 1, \ldots, n$. We assume, as is traditional in such models, that the price is decided upon by the single seller, who thus appears formally as a "monopolist". So firm j sets price p_j, household i sets wage w_i, taking all other prices and wages as given. We assume that they do so using objective demand curves, as described in Section 5 above. The equilibrium is thus a Nash equilibrium in prices and wages, conditional on these objective demand curves.

8.2. Objective demand curves

Each seller sells only one good and, as we shall see below, sets its price high enough so as to be willing to satisfy all demand for that good. In equilibrium each agent will thus be constrained only on his sales, and we shall somehow have a situation of "general excess supply". We now compute the objective demand curves in this zone of general excess supply. These objective demand curves will be functions of the vectors p and w, and of the policy parameter μ. So, for given p, w and μ we must find out which demands for goods and labor types will arise once all feedback effects have been taken into account. As indicated in Section 5, this boils down to finding total demand for goods i and j at a fixprice K-equilibrium corresponding to p, w and μ.

For given (p, w, μ) firm j is constrained on its sales of output j. It thus solves the following program in l_j:

$$\max p_j y_j - w l_j$$

s.t.

$$y_j \leq F_j(l_j) \, ,$$

where y_j is a binding constraint exogenous to the firm. The solution is a set of labor demands $L_{ij}(y_j, w)$, and a cost function $\chi_j(y_j, w)$.

Similarly, consider a household i which solves the following program:

$$\max U_i(c_i, l_i, m_i, \mu)$$

s.t.

$$pc_i + m_i = \mu \bar{m}_i + w_i l_i + \sum_{j=1}^{m} \theta_{ij} \pi_j \, ,$$

where p, w, μ, l_i and the profits π_j are given. The solution is a set of consumption demands:

$$C_{ij}\left(\mu \bar{m}_i + w_i l_i + \sum_{j=1}^{m} \theta_{ij} \pi_j, \, p, \, \mu \right).$$

Consider now the following mapping:

$$y_j \rightarrow \sum_{i=1}^{n} C_{ij}\left(\mu \bar{m}_i + w_i l_i + \sum_{j=1}^{m} \theta_{ij} \pi_j, \, p, \, \mu \right),$$

$$l_i \rightarrow \sum_{j=1}^{m} L_{ij}(y_j, \, w),$$

$$\pi_j \rightarrow p_j y_j - \chi_j(y_j, \, w).$$

Assuming a unique fixed point, this yields functions $Y_j(p, w, \mu)$, $L_i(p, w, \mu)$ and $\Pi_j(p, w, \mu)$ which represent, respectively, the objective demand for good j, for labor i, and the associated profits of firm j.

Secondly, let us note that the functions L_{ij} are homogeneous of degree zero in w, the functions C_{ij} are homogeneous of degree zero in μ, w_i, p, and π_j, and profits themselves are homogeneous of degree one in p_j and w. From that we deduce Y_j and L_i are homogeneous of degree zero, and Π_j homogeneous of degree one in the arguments p, w and μ.

8.3. Equilibrium: Definition and characterization

Following Section 5, we describe the equilibrium as a Nash equilibrium in prices and wages, conditional on the objective demand curves. The quantities are those corresponding to a fixprice equilibrium associated with the prices and wages. We now derive the optimal price and wage responses of the agents.

Consider first firm j; it will solve the following profit maximization program A_j in p_j, y_j and l_j:

$$\max p_j y_j - w l_j$$

s.t.

$$y_j \leq F_j(l_j),$$

$$y_j \leq Y_j(p, w, \mu).$$

$$(A_j)$$

We assume this program has a unique solution, which thus yields optimal price p_j as a function of the other prices and wages:

$$p_j = \psi_j(p_{-j}, w, \mu),$$

where $p_{-j} = \{p_k \mid k \neq j\}$.

In order to characterize the equilibrium quantities simply, we also need to characterize the optimal production plan of the firm (y_j, l_j) as a function of the same variables, so that we write this optimal plan functionally as

$$(y_j, l_j) = \varphi_j(p_{-j}, w, \mu).$$

Consider now household i. It chooses the wage w_i, labor sales l_i and consumption vector c_i so as to maximize utility according to the following program A_i in w_i, l_i and c_i:

$$\max U_i(c_i, l_i, m_i, \mu)$$

s.t.

$$pc_i + m_i = \mu \bar{m}_i + w_i l_i + \sum_{j=1}^{m} \theta_{ij} \Pi_j(p, w, \mu), \qquad (A_i)$$

$$l_i \leq L_i(p, w, \mu),$$

$$l_i \leq l_{i0},$$

which yields the functions:

$$w_i = \psi_i(w_{-i}, p, \mu),$$

$$(l_i, c_i) = \varphi_i(w_{-i}, p, \mu),$$

where $w_{-i} = \{w_k \mid k \neq i\}$.

We assume in all that follows that the disutility of labor becomes high enough near l_{i0}, so that the last constraint in the above program A_i is never binding, and we shall accordingly ignore it henceforth.

We can now define our equilibrium with imperfect competition as a Nash equilibrium as follows:

(a) $w_i^* = \psi_i(w_{-i}^*, p^*, \mu),$ $\forall i$,
(b) $p_j^* = \psi_j(p_{-j}^*, w^*, \mu),$ $\forall j$,
(c) $(l_i^*, c_i^*) = \varphi_i(w_{-i}^*, p^*, \mu),$ $\forall i$,
(d) $(y_j^*, l_j^*) = \varphi_j(p_{-j}^*, w^*, \mu),$ $\forall j$.

The first two sets of equalities express the Nash property in prices and wages, and determine p^* and w^*. The last two sets of equations give the optimal production, work and consumption plans of the agents, which correspond to their transactions on all markets. Note that because of the definition of the objective demand curves, which is based on a fixprice equilibrium notion, the consistency of transactions is automatically ensured, so that we do not need to add the traditional equations stating the equality between purchases and sales on every market.

Of course the equilibrium will change as μ changes. In what follows we assume that to a given government policy is associated a unique equilibrium. In order to study its various properties, we now characterize it by deriving a number of relevant partial derivatives.

Consider first firm j, and recall the program yielding its optimal actions:

$$\max p_j y_j - w l_j$$

s.t.

$$y_j = F_j(l_j) , \tag{A_j}$$
$$y_j \leq Y_j(p, w, \mu) .$$

Let us assume an interior solution, so that in particular all components of l_j are strictly positive. Then the Kuhn–Tucker conditions associated to this program yield immediately:

$$\frac{\partial F_j}{\partial l_{ij}} = \frac{w_i}{p_j} \frac{1}{(1 - 1/\varepsilon_j)} , \tag{13}$$

where $\varepsilon_j = -(p_j/y_j)\partial Y_j/\partial p_j$ is the absolute value of the own price elasticity of objective demand. At an equilibrium, ε_j is greater than 1.

These conditions can also be rewritten, using the cost function $\chi_j(y_j, w)$ of firm j:

$$\frac{\partial \chi_j}{\partial y_j} = p_j\left(1 - \frac{1}{\varepsilon_j}\right) , \tag{14}$$

which is the traditional "marginal cost equals marginal revenue" equation. Let us turn now to the optimal program of household i:

$$\max U_i(c_i, l_i, m_i, \mu)$$

s.t.

$$pc_i + m_i = \mu \bar{m}_i + w_i l_i + \sum_{j=1}^{m} \theta_{ij} \Pi_j(p, w, \mu) \tag{A_i}$$
$$l_i \leq L_i(p, w, \mu) .$$

We assume an interior solution so that in particular all consumptions are positive. Call λ_i the "marginal utility" of wealth, i.e. the Kuhn–Tucker multiplier of the budget constraint. We obtain the following conditions:[8]

$$\frac{\partial U_i}{\partial m_i} = \lambda_i , \qquad \frac{\partial U_i}{\partial c_{ij}} = \lambda_i p_j , \tag{15}$$

$$\frac{\partial U_i}{\partial l_i} = -\lambda_i w_i \left(1 - \frac{1}{\varepsilon_i}\right) , \tag{16}$$

where $\varepsilon_i = -(w_i/l_i)\partial L_i/\partial w_i$. Again, at equilibrium, $\varepsilon_i > 1$.

With the help of these differential characterizations, we can now describe some salient properties of our equilibrium.

8.4. Underemployment, underproduction and inefficiency

We now show that, even though prices are fully flexible and rationally decided upon by agents, the equilibrium allocation has properties that strongly differentiate it from those of a Walrasian equilibrium.

First we see that at equilibrium there is both underemployment and underproduction. Indeed, equation (14) shows that at the going price and wage firm j would be happy to produce and sell more, if the demand was forthcoming, thus displaying underproduction. Symmetrically, equation (16) shows that household i would like to sell more of its labor if the demand was present, thus displaying underemployment.

We further show that employment and production throughout the economy are inefficiently low in the following strong sense: it is possible to find increases in production and employment that would increase all firms' profits and all households' utilities at the equilibrium prices and wages.

Consider indeed at the given price and wage system p^* and w^* some small arbitrary increases $dl_{ij} > 0$. These yield extra amounts of employment and production:

$$dl_i = \sum_{j=1}^m dl_{ij} > 0 ,$$

$$dy_j = \sum_{i=1}^n \frac{\partial F_j}{\partial l_{ij}} dl_{ij} > 0 .$$

---

[8] We actually assume to simplify that the influence of w_i on household i's profit income is negligible, which will be the case if there are many households, and each owns negligibles shares of each firm.

Consider first the profit variation for firm j:

$$d\pi_j = p_j \, dy_j - \sum_{i=1}^{n} w_i \, dl_{ij} \,.$$

In view of equations (13), this is easily found equal to

$$d\pi_j = \frac{p_j \, dy_j}{\varepsilon_j} > 0 \,. \tag{17}$$

We now assume that the extra production in the economy is redistributed to households in such a way that the value of the extra consumptions for each household sums up to the value of its extra labor and profit incomes, which is written for household i as

$$\sum_{j=1}^{m} p_j \, dc_{ij} = w_i \, dl_i + \sum_{j=1}^{m} \theta_{ij} \, d\pi_j \,. \tag{18}$$

The increment in utility, since m_i and μ do not change, is

$$dU_i = \sum_{j=1}^{m} \frac{\partial U_i}{\partial c_{ij}} \, dc_{ij} + \frac{\partial U_i}{\partial l_i} \, dl_i$$

which, using equations (15), (16), (17) and (18), becomes:

$$dU_i = \lambda_i \left[\frac{w_i \, dl_i}{\varepsilon_i} + \sum_{j=1}^{m} \frac{\theta_{ij} p_j \, dy_j}{\varepsilon_j} \right] > 0 \,. \tag{19}$$

Equations (17) and (19) clearly show that the incremental employment and production will increase all agents' utilities or profits. We may note that this inefficiency result is stronger than Pareto inefficiency since we have constrained the incremental trades to be consistent with the equilibrium price–wage system, whereas such a constraint is not required to prove Pareto inefficiency. We should also note that these inefficiencies are quite similar to those observed in "Keynesian type" general excess supply states [see, for example, Benassy (1977a, 1982)].

We now investigate in the following subsections whether these inefficiencies can be alleviated, either in a decentralized manner or by governmental policy.

8.5. Decentralized trading and the problem of double coincidence of wants

We first investigate whether the inefficiencies observed in our equilibrium can be overcome in a decentralized manner, and we shall see that the problem of double coincidence of wants is crucial in that respect. Though we did not say anything explicit on that topic, we implicitly assumed some kind of double coincidence of wants by assuming interior solutions in the maximization programs (A_i) and (A_j) above. Indeed, this was equivalent to assuming that at equilibrium

$$l_{ij}^* > 0, \qquad c_{ij}^* > 0, \quad \forall i, j,$$

which means that each firm employs every household and each household consumes some of every good. It is easy to see that under such circumstances agents themselves could undertake the Pareto-improving trades mentioned in the preceding section by making simple propositions to their usual trading partners.

Consider, for example, firm j. It can decide to employ extra quantities of labor $dl_{ij} > 0$, $i = 1, \ldots, n$, producing an extra output $dy_j > 0$. Assume now that firm j distributes (in kind) to each household i the supplementary quantity of good j:

$$\frac{w_i \, dl_{ij}}{p_j} + \frac{\theta_{ij} \, d\pi_j}{p_j} = dc_{ij} ,$$

where $d\pi_j$ is equal to

$$d\pi_j = p_j \, dy_j - \sum_{i=1}^{n} w_i \, dl_{ij} .$$

It is easy to check that these quantities are summing to dy_j, and that every household is better off both as a worker–consumer [because of equations (15) and (16)] and as a shareholder [because of equations (13) and (14)].

We can further note that such Pareto-improving trades can be made by only pairs of trading partners. Consider indeed any pair formed of a household i and a firm j, and the following trade proposition: the household i works more for firm j by dl_{ij}, thus allowing an extra production of [by formula (13)]

$$dy_j = \frac{\partial F_j}{\partial l_{ij}} \, dl_{ij} = \frac{\varepsilon_j}{\varepsilon_j - 1} \frac{w_i}{p_j} \, dl_{ij} .$$

The firm pays in kind (i.e. with output j) the equivalent of its wage to household i, i.e. the quantity $dc_{ij} = w_i \, dl_{ij}/p_j$ of output j, so that the increment of utility to household i is (not counting possible profit receipts as a shareholder)

$$dU_i = \frac{\partial U_i}{\partial c_{ij}} dc_{ij} + \frac{\partial U_i}{\partial l_i} dl_{ij}$$

$$= \frac{\lambda_i w_i \, dl_{ij}}{\varepsilon_i} > 0 \; .$$

The firm thus retains as a surplus a positive quantity, equal to

$$dy_j - dc_{ij} = \frac{1}{\varepsilon_j - 1} \frac{w_i}{p_j} dl_{ij} \; ,$$

which it can distribute to its shareholders, making all of them better off.

We see that under our implicit assumptions the equilibrium could be fairly easily upset by simple decentralized trade propositions, as the workers and the firms' shareholders would unanimously want to carry the above production and exchange plans.

We now see that such will not be the case if we have *absence of double coincidence of wants*. This last condition means that no consumer purchases the goods from the firm he works for, and no firm employs households to which it sells goods, i.e.

$$l_{ij}^* \cdot c_{ij}^* = 0 \; , \quad \forall i, j \; . \tag{20}$$

This could happen, for example, if we had the following condition:

$$\left(\frac{\partial F_j}{\partial l_{ij}} \right) \left(\frac{\partial U_i}{\partial c_{ij}} \right) = 0 \; , \quad \forall i, j \; ,$$

i.e. either household i has no utility for output j, or it is not productive for firm j [of course, less stringent conditions could also lead to condition (20)].

In such a case of absence of double coincidence of wants, the solutions to programs (A_i) and (A_j) are not interior, and the marginal conditions must be rewritten. In particular, conditions (13) and (15) are rewritten as:

$$\frac{\partial F_j}{\partial l_{ij}} \le \frac{w_i}{p_j} \frac{1}{1 - 1/\varepsilon_j} \; , \quad \text{with equality if } l_{ij}^* > 0 \; , \tag{21}$$

$$\frac{\partial U_i}{\partial c_{ij}} \le \lambda_i p_j \; , \qquad \text{with equality if } c_{ij}^* > 0 \; . \tag{22}$$

Then generally an exchange between a household i and a firm j, such as we described above, will not be Pareto improving, either because the household is not productive enough for firm j [condition (21) with strict inequality] or because the household does not derive enough utility from good j [condition (22) with strict inequality].

We thus see that in the case of absence of double coincidence of wants propositions of trade involving usual trading partners will not usually lead to Pareto improvements. The Pareto-improving trades of Subsection 8.4 still exist (we shall exhibit an example in Subsection 8.7 below), but they are typically quite complex, since workers must be allocated only to firms where they are productive, and goods only to consumers who actually enjoy them. These trades will normally involve groups of agents, some of which are not usual trading partners. Finding such Pareto-improving chains of trades may thus involve some very complex calculations, quite beyond the computing capacities of private agents. On the other hand, this task cannot be delegated to a central authority, since it is difficult to envision in a free market economy that such an authority could dictate private agents' incremental production activities and trades, even if they would turn up to be Pareto improving, and anyway there is no reason to believe that this central authority would have enough information on the private sector to find these Pareto-improving trades. So such improvements have rather been sought via more impersonal policy actions, in particular "demand" policies. In the next subsection we investigate one such policy, monetary policy.

8.6. Neutrality of monetary policy

We have seen in the preceding subsections that our imperfect competition equilibrium displayed some inefficiency properties very akin to traditional Keynesian excess supply states, but that, because of the absence of double coincidence of wants, these inefficiencies could not be expected to be remedied by the actions of private agents. We thus now investigate a traditional "Keynesian" policy to cure such inefficiencies, a monetary policy, and we now see that, in spite of its "Keynesian" characteristics, the system described above reacts to monetary policy in a more "Walrasian" than "Keynesian" manner. Namely, monetary policies taking the form of proportional increases in initial money holdings (i.e. $\mu > 1$) are ineffective, or "neutral", just as in Walrasian models. As a response to such a policy, production, employment and utilities do not change. Prices, wages and profits are multiplied by μ.

The proof of that result is actually quite trivial in view of the homogeneity properties of our system. Let us look at the programs (A_j) and (A_i) yielding the optimal actions of agents; from program (A_j) it is clear that

$$\psi_j(\mu p_{-j}, \mu w, \mu) = \mu \psi_j(p_{-j}, w, 1),$$

$$\varphi_j(\mu p_{-j}, \mu w, \mu) = \varphi_j(p_{-j}, w, 1).$$

And, similarly, program (A_i) yields:

$$\psi_i(\mu w_{-i}, \mu p, \mu) = \mu \psi_i(w_{-i}, p, 1),$$

$$\varphi_i(\mu w_{-i}, \mu p, \mu) = \varphi_i(w_{-i}, p, 1).$$

In view of these homogeneity properties, y_j^*, l_j^*, l_i^* and c_i^* are homogeneous of degree 0 in μ, whereas p^* and w^* are homogeneous of degree one in μ.

8.7. The possibility of effective policies

We saw above that our system reacted to monetary stimulus like a Walrasian system, i.e. by a proportional increase in prices and wages with no impact on quantities, in spite of the inefficiencies. One should, however, not jump to the conclusion that our system will react similarly to a Walrasian one for any choice of policy, even including monetary policy, and we now prove this by considering a different policy, namely a price–wage freeze coupled with a small monetary expansion $d\mu > 0$. To carry out the exercise we make the further assumption of "stabilized" money holdings", i.e. that at the equilibrium considered $m_i^* = \bar{m}_i$. Such will be the case if the economy is in a state of long-run equilibrium to start with. This also contains as a particular case the situation, most often considered in the literature, where the model is symmetrical.

Consider, then, at fixed prices and wages, an increase $d\mu$ in money holdings. The basic intuition is that multiplier effects will provoke increases in the levels of employment and production, and this will increase profits and utilities.

To make this intuition rigorous, let us first note that in view of equations (14) and (16), the firms will be willing to make small expansions of production and the households will willingly increase their labor sales if the demand is forthcoming. Let us now compute the profit and utility increments associated with new trades; again using equations (14) and (15) we find:

$$d\pi_j = \frac{p_j \, dy_j}{\varepsilon_j}. \tag{23}$$

Turning now to households we find:

$$dU_i = \sum_{j=1}^{m} \frac{\partial U_i}{\partial c_{ij}} \, dc_{ij} + \frac{\partial U_i}{\partial l_i} \, dl_i + \frac{\partial U_i}{\partial m_i} \, dm_i + \frac{\partial U_i}{\partial \mu} \, d\mu \, .$$

Homogeneity of degree zero in m_i and μ implies (remember we start from μ equal to one):

$$\frac{\partial U_i}{\partial \mu} = -\frac{m_i^*}{\mu}\frac{\partial U_i}{\partial m_i} = -m_i^* \frac{\partial U_i}{\partial m_i}.$$

Using equations (16) and (17) the above utility increment is rewritten:

$$dU_i = \lambda_i\left[\sum_{j=1}^m p_j\, dc_{ij} + dm_i - w_i\left(1 - \frac{1}{\varepsilon_i}\right)dl_i - m_i^*\, d\mu\right].$$

Let us differentiate the budget constraint,

$$\sum_{j=1}^m p_j\, dc_{ij} + dm_i = \bar{m}_i\, d\mu + w_i\, dl_i + \sum_{j=1}^m \theta_{ij}\, d\pi_j,$$

and combine with the preceding equation so that

$$dU_i = \lambda_i\left[\frac{w_i\, dl_i}{\varepsilon_i} + \sum_{j=1}^m \theta_{ij}\, d\pi_j + (\bar{m}_i - m_i^*)\, d\mu\right].$$

In view of the assumption of stabilized money balances, the last term disappears[9] and finally, using (23):

$$dU_i = \lambda_i\left\{\frac{w_i\, dl_i}{\varepsilon_i} + \sum_{j=1}^m \theta_{ij}\frac{p_j\, dy_j}{\varepsilon_j}\right\}. \tag{24}$$

Note that formulas (23) and (24) look very much like what we found in Subsection 8.3, but now the increases dy_j and dl_i are not arbitrary but must result from voluntary trading. The appendix shows that such increases can actually be engineered at fixed wages and prices via the monetary increase $d\mu$ through traditional multiplier effects, yielding increases of the form:

$$p_j\, dy_j = k_j\, d\mu, \quad k_j > 0,$$
$$w_i\, dl_i = k_i\, d\mu, \quad k_i > 0.$$

Feeding these into equations (23) and (24), we find:

$$d\pi_j = \frac{k_j}{\varepsilon_j}\, d\mu > 0,$$

$$dU_i = \lambda_i\left[\frac{k_i}{\varepsilon_i} + \sum_{j=1}^m \theta_{ij}\frac{k_j}{\varepsilon_j}\right]d\mu > 0.$$

[9] Note that alternatively additional balanced money transfers $(m_i^* - \bar{m}_i)\, d\mu$ would also eliminate the last term and take care of these distributional problems.

The policy considered thus leads to strict increases in all firms' profits and all households' utilities. We should now emphasize that the reaction of the economy to that particular policy is very different from the reaction of the same economy starting from Walrasian equilibrium, where there would be no additional employment and production following a price–wage freeze and a monetary expansion, since in particular firms would not want to produce more, being already at their Walrasian employment-production plan.

Now we should of course end this section with a strong caveat on how its results should, and should not, be interpreted. The main purpose was to show that, although monetary policy has the same neutrality properties as those found in Walrasian models, other policies may yield substantially different results in the two settings. The particular policy studied here was chosen for convenience of the demonstration, and *not* as an advice to block all prices and wages and reflate to cure unemployment. Indeed, it is clear that in this model the ultimate cause of inefficiency lies in the fact that partial market power allows agents to set prices and wages "too high". The Nash structure and resulting spillovers create the inefficiencies. A more constructive approach would be to investigate how to reduce the "monopoly power" of the agents on their respective markets, an investigation that is beyond the scope of this chapter, but should be the subject of future research.

8.8. Notes and references

The model in this section is based on Benassy (1987). Earlier models linking imperfect competition and non-Walrasian equilibria are found in Benassy (1976b, 1977a, 1982), Negishi (1977, 1979), Hahn (1978), Hart (1982), Snower (1983), and Weitzman (1985).

Appendix

In this appendix we briefly show how to compute the multipliers in the zone of general excess supply. Let us recall the equations determining quantities in this region (cf. Subsection 8.2):

$$y_j = \sum_{i=1}^{n} C_{ij}\left(\mu \bar{m}_i + w_i l_i + \sum_{j=1}^{m} \theta_{ij} \pi_j, \, p, \, \mu \right), \tag{25}$$

$$l_i = \sum_{j=1}^{m} L_{ij}(y_j, \, w), \tag{26}$$

$$\pi_j = p_j y_j - \chi_j(y_j, \, w), \tag{27}$$

Differentiating the consumption functions, the labor demand functions and equation (27), we obtain, in value terms:

$$p_j \, dc_{ij} = \alpha_{ij} \left(w_i \, dl_i + \sum_{j=1}^{m} \theta_{ij} \, d\pi_j \right) + \gamma_{ij} \, d\mu , \tag{28}$$

$$w_i \, dl_{ij} = \beta_{ij} p_j \, dy_j , \tag{29}$$

$$d\pi_j = \beta_{0j} p_j \, dy_j . \tag{30}$$

We assume that all goods, including money, are "normal" in production and consumption, so that

$$\alpha_{ij} \geq 0 , \qquad \beta_{ij} \geq 0 , \qquad \gamma_{ij} \geq 0 , \tag{31}$$

and

$$\sum_{j=1}^{m} \alpha_{ij} < 1 , \tag{32}$$

and, by definition,

$$\sum_{i=1}^{n} \beta_{ij} + \beta_{0j} = 1 . \tag{33}$$

Note that $\beta_{0j} = 1/\varepsilon_j$ at the equilibrium point, and is positive in the excess supply zone.

Combining equations (28)–(30) with the equalities

$$dy_j = \sum_{i=1}^{n} dc_{ij} \quad \text{and} \quad dl_i = \sum_{j=1}^{m} dl_{ij} ,$$

we obtain the following equation in output variations:

$$p_k \, dy_k = \sum_{j=1}^{m} \rho_{kj} p_j \, dy_j + \nu_k \, d\mu , \tag{34}$$

where

$$\rho_{kj} = \sum_{i=1}^{n} \alpha_{ik} (\beta_{ij} + \theta_{ij} \beta_{0j}) ,$$

$$\nu_k = \sum_{i=1}^{n} \gamma_{ik} .$$

Call ρ the square matrix with elements ρ_{kj}. Straightforward manipulation using properties (31)–(33) shows that:

$$\sum_{k=1}^{m} \rho_{kj} < 1 \, .$$

The matrix $I - \rho$ thus has a dominant diagonal with positive on-diagonal terms and negative off-diagonal terms. Call η the inverse matrix. It has only positive terms. From (34) we find:

$$p_j \, \mathrm{d}y_j = \sum_{k=1}^{m} \eta_{jk} v_k \, \mathrm{d}\mu = k_j \, \mathrm{d}\mu \, . \tag{35}$$

We assume that each good is consumed by at least one household, so that all v_k are strictly positive, and thus $k_j > 0$ for all j.

Inserting (35) into equation (29) and summing over j we find:

$$w_i \, \mathrm{d}l_i = \sum_{j=1} \beta_{ij} p_j \, \mathrm{d}y_j$$

$$= \left(\sum_{j=1}^{m} \beta_{ij} k_j \right) \mathrm{d}\mu = k_i \, \mathrm{d}\mu \, . \tag{36}$$

If each household i's work type is demanded by at least one firm, $\beta_{ij} > 0$ for at least one j, and so all k_i are strictly positive.

References

Arrow, K.J. (1959) 'Towards a theory of price adjustment', in: M. Abramowitz, ed., *The allocation of economic resources*. Stanford: Stanford University Press.

Arrow, K.J. and G. Debreu (1954) 'Existence of an equilibrium for a competitive economy', *Econometrica*, 22: 265–290.

Arrow, K.J. and F.H. Hahn (1971) *General competitive analysis*. San Francisco: Holden–Day.

Balasko, Y. (1979) 'Budget-constrained Pareto-efficient allocations', *Journal of Economic Theory*, 21: 359–379.

Barro, R.J. and H.I. Grossman (1971) 'A general disequilibrium model of income and employment', *American Economic Review*, 61: 82–93.

Barro, R.J. and H.I. Grossman (1974) 'Suppressed inflation and the supply multiplier', *Review of Economic Studies*, 41: 87–104.

Barro, R.J. and H.I. Grossman (1976) *Money, employment and inflation*. Cambridge: Cambridge University Press.

Bellman, R. (1957) *Dynamic programming*. Princeton: Princeton University Press.

Benassy, J.P. (1973) 'Disequilibrium theory', Ph.D. Dissertation and Working Paper, University of California, Berkeley. Hungarian translation in *Szygma* (1974).

Benassy, J.P. (1975a) 'Neo-Keynesian disequilibrium theory in a monetary economy', *Review of Economic Studies*, 42: 503–523.

Benassy, J.P. (1975b) 'Disequilibrium exchange in barter and monetary economies' *Economic Inquiry*, 13: 131–156.

Benassy, J.P. (1976a) 'Théorie néokeynésienne du déséquilibre dans une économie monétaire', *Cahiers du Séminaire d'Econométrie*, 17: 81–113.

Benassy, J.P. (1976b) 'The disequilibrium approach to monopolistic price setting and general monopolistic equilibrium', *Review of Economic Studies*, 43: 69–81.

Benassy, J.P. (1976c) 'Théorie du déséquilibre et fondements microéconomiques de la macroéconomie', *Revue Economique*, 27: 755–804.

Benassy, J.P. (1977a) 'A neoKeynesian model of price and quantity determination in disequilibrium', in: G. Schwödiauer, ed., *Equilibrium and disequilibrium in economic theory*. Boston: D. Reidel Publishing Company.

Benassy, J.P. (1977b) 'On quantity signals and the foundations of effective demand theory', *The Scandinavian Journal of Economics*, 79: 147–168.

Benassy, J.P. (1978) 'Cost and demand inflation revisited: A neo-Keynesian approach', *Economie Appliquée*, 31: 147–168.

Benassy, J.P. (1982) *The economics of market disequilibrium*. New York: Academic Press.

Benassy, J.P. (1983) 'The three regimes of the IS–LM model: A non-Walrasian analysis', *European Economic Review*, 23: 1–17.

Benassy, J.P. (1984) 'A non-Walrasian model of the business cycle', *Journal of Economic Behavior and Organization*, 5: 77–89.

Benassy, J.P. (1986) *Macroeconomics: An introduction to the non-Walrasian approach*. New York: Academic Press.

Benassy, J.P. (1987) 'Imperfect competition, unemployment and policy', *European Economic Review*, 31: 417–426.

Benassy, J.P. (1988) 'The objective demand curve in general equilibrium with price makers', *Economic Journal Supplement*, 98: 37–49.

Böhm, V., and P. Levine (1979) 'Temporary equilibria with quantity rationing', *Review of Economic Studies*, 46: 361–377.

Bushaw, D.W. and R. Clower (1957) *Introduction to mathematical economics*. Homewood, Illinois: Richard D. Irwin.

Chamberlin, E.H. (1933) *The theory of monopolistic competition*. Cambridge, Mass.: Harvard University Press.

Clower, R.W. (1960) 'Keynes and the classics: A dynamical perspective', *Quarterly Journal of Economics*, 74: 318–323.

Clower, R.W. (1965) 'The Keynesian counterrevolution: A theoretical appraisal', in: F.H. Hahn and F.P.R. Brechling, eds., *The theory of interest rates*. London: Macmillan.

Clower, R.W. (1967) 'A reconsideration of the microfoundations of monetary theory', *Western Economic Journal*, 6: 1–9.

Cuddington, J.T., P.O. Johansson and K.G. Lofgren (1984) *Disequilibrium macroeconomics in open economies*. Oxford: Basil Blackwell.

D'autume, A. (1985) *Monnaie, croissance et déséquilibre*. Paris: Economica.

Debreu, G. (1959) *Theory of value*. New York: Wiley.

Dehez, P. and J.H. Drèze (1984) 'On supply constrained equilibria', *Journal of Economic Theory*, 33: 172–182.

Dixit, A. (1978) 'The balance of trade in a model of temporary equilibrium with rationing', *Review of Economic Studies*, 45: 393–404.

Drèze, J.H. (1975) 'Existence of an exchange equilibrium under price rigidities', *International Economic Review*, 16: 301–320.

Drèze, J.H. and H. Muller (1980) 'Optimality properties of rationing schemes', *Journal of Economic Theory*, 23: 131–149.

Fitoussi, J.P. (1983) 'Modern macroeconomic theory: An overview', in: J.P. Fitoussi, ed., *Modern macroeconomic theory*. Oxford: Basil Blackwell.

Gabszewicz, J.J. and J.P. Vial (1972) 'Oligopoly "à la Cournot" in a general equilibrium analysis', *Journal of Economic Theory*, 4: 381–400.

Gary-Bobo, R. (1987) 'Locally consistent oligopolistic equilibria are Cournot–Walras equilibria', *Economic Letters*, 23: 217–221.

Glustoff, E. (1968) 'On the existence of a Keynesian equilibrium', *Review of Economic Studies*, 35: 327–334.

Grandmont, J.M. (1983) *Money and value*. Cambridge: Cambridge University Press.

Grandmont, J.M. and G. Laroque (1976) 'On Keynesian temporary equilibria', *Review of Economic Studies*, 43: 53–67.

Greenberg, J. and H. Muller (1979) 'Equilibria under price rigidities and externalities', in: O. Moeschlin and D. Pallaschke, eds., *Game theory and related topics*. Amsterdam: North-Holland.

Grossman, H.I. (1971) 'Money, interest and prices in market disequilibrium', *Journal of Political Economy*, 79: 943–961.

Grossman, H.I. (1972) 'A choice-theoretic model of an income investment accelerator', *American Economic Review*, 62: 630–641.

Hahn, F.H. (1978) 'On non-Walrasian equilibria', *Review of Economic Studies*, 45: 1–17.

Hahn, F.H. and T. Negishi (1962) 'A theorem on non tatonnement stability', *Econometrica*, 30: 463–469.

Hansen, B. (1951) *A study in the theory of inflation*. London: Allen & Unwin.

Hart, O. (1982) 'A model of imperfect competition with Keynesian features', *Quarterly Journal of Economics*, 97: 109–138.

Heller, W.P. and R.M. Starr (1979) 'Unemployment equilibrium with myopic complete information', *Review of Economic Studies*, 46: 339–259.

Henin, P.Y. and P. Michel, eds. (1982), *Croissance et accumulation en déséquilibre*. Paris: Economica.

Hicks, J.R. (1937), 'Mr. Keynes and the classics: A suggested interpretation', *Econometrica*, 5: 147–159.

Hicks, J.R. (1939) *Value and capital*. Oxford: Clarendon Press. 2nd edition, 1946.

Hicks, J.R. (1965) *Capital and growth*. London: Oxford University Press.

Hildenbrand, K. and W. Hildenbrand (1978) 'On Keynesian equilibria with unemployment and quantity rationing', *Journal of Economic Theory*, 18: 255–277.

Honkapohja, S. (1979) 'On the dynamics of disequilibria in a macro model with flexible wages and prices', in: M. Aoki and A. Marzollo, eds., *New trends in dynamic system theory and economics*. New York: Academic Press.

Hool, B. (1980) 'Monetary and fiscal policies in short-run equilibria with rationing', *International Economic Review*, 21: 301–316.

Howitt, P.W. (1974) 'Stability and the quantity theory', *Journal of Political Economy*, 82: 133–151.

Ito, T. (1980) 'Disequilibrium growth theory', *Journal of Economic Theory*, 23: 380–409.

Iwai, K. (1974) 'The firm in uncertain markets and its price, wage and employment adjustments', *Review of Economic Studies*, 41: 257–276.

Keynes, J.M. (1936) *The general theory of money, interest and employment*. New York: Harcourt Brace.

Keynes, J.M. (1937) 'Alternative theories of the rate of interest', *Economic Journal*, 47: 241–252.

Kornai, J. (1980) *Economics of shortage*. Amsterdam: North-Holland.

Kornai, J. (1982) *Growth, shortage and efficiency*. Oxford: Basil Blackwell.

Laroque, G. (1981) 'On the local uniqueness of the fixed price equilibria', *Review of Economic Studies*, 48: 113–129.

Leijonhufvud, A. (1968) *On Keynesian economics and the economics of Keynes*. Oxford: Oxford University Press.

Malinvaud, E. (1977) *The theory of unemployment reconsidered*. Oxford: Basil Blackwell.

Marschak, T., and R. Selten (1974) *General equilibrium with price making firms*. Berlin: Springer-Verlag.

Muellbauer, J. and R. Portes (1978) 'Macroeconomic models with quantity rationing', *Economic Journal*, 88: 788–821.

Neary, J.P. (1980) 'Nontraded goods and the balance of trade in a neo-Keynesian temporary equilibrium', *Quarterly Journal of Economics*, 95: 403–430.

Neary, J.P. and J.E. Stiglitz (1983) 'Towards a reconstruction of Keynesian economics: Expectations and constrained equilibria', *Quarterly Journal of Economics*, 98, Supplement: 196–201.

Negishi, T. (1961) 'Monopolistic competition and general equilibrium', *Review of Economic Studies*, 28: 199–228.

Negishi, T. (1972) *General equilibrium theory and international trade*. Amsterdam: North-Holland.

Negishi, T. (1977) 'Existence of an under employment equilibrium', in: G. Schwödiauer, ed., *Equilibrium and disequilibrium in economic theory*. Boston: D. Reidel Publishing Company.

Negishi, T. (1979) *Microeconomic foundations of Keynesian macroeconomics*, Amsterdam: North-Holland.

Nikaido, H. (1975) *Monopolistic competition and effective demand*. Princeton: Princeton University Press.

Ostroy, J. (1973) 'The informational efficiency of monetary exchange', *American Economic Review*, 63: 597–610.

Ostroy, J. and R. Starr (1974) 'Money and the decentralization of exchange', *Econometrica*, 42: 1093–1114.

Patinkin, D. (1956) *Money, interest and prices*. Row, Peterson and Company. 2nd edition, Harper and Row, New York, 1965.

Persson, T. and L.E.O. Svensson (1983) 'Is optimism good in a Keynesian economy?', *Economica*, 50: 291–300.

Picard, P. (1983) 'Inflation and growth in a disequilibrium macroeconomic model', *Journal of Economic Theory*, 30: 266–295.

Picard, P. (1985) *Théorie du déséquilibre et politique économique*. Paris: Economica.

Portes, R. (1981) 'Macroeconomic equilibrium and disequilibrium in centrally planned economies', *Economic Inquiry*, 19: 559–578.

Quandt, R.E. (1982) 'Econometric disequilibrium models', *Econometric Review* 1: 1–63.

Robinson, J. (1933) *The economics of imperfect competition*. London: Macmillan.

Samuelson, P.A. (1947) *Foundations of economic analysis*. Cambridge, Mass.: Harvard University Press.

Schulz, N. (1983) 'On the global uniqueness of fixprice equilibria', *Econometrica*, 51: 47–68.

Silvestre, J. (1977) 'A model of general equilibrium with monopolistic behavior', *Journal of Economic Theory*, 16: 425–442.

Silvestre, J. (1982) 'Fixprice analysis of exchange economies', *Journal of Economic Theory*, 26: 28–58.

Silvestre, J. (1983) 'Fixprice analysis in productive economies', *Journal of Economic Theory*, 30: 401–409.

Silvestre, J. (1985) 'Voluntary and efficient allocations are Walrasian', *Econometrica*, 53: 807–816.

Silvestre, J. (1988) 'Undominated prices in the three goods model', *European Economic Review*, 32: 161–178.

Sneessens, H. (1981) *Theory and estimation of macroeconomic rationing models*. New York: Springer-Verlag.

Snower, D.J. (1983) 'Imperfect competition, underemployment and crowding out', *Oxford Economic Papers*, 35: 569–584.

Solow, R.M. and J. Stiglitz (1968) 'Output, employment and wages in the short run', *Quarterly Journal of Economics*, 82: 537–560.

Tobin, J. (1952) 'A survey of the theory of rationing', *Econometrica*, 20: 521–553.

Tobin, J. and H.S. Houthakker (1950) 'The effects of rationing on demand elasticities', *Review of Economic Studies*, 18: 140–153.

Triffin, R. (1940) *Monopolistic competition and general equilibrium theory*. Cambridge, Mass.: Harvard University Press.

Uzawa, H. (1962) 'On the stability of Edgeworth's barter process', *International Economic Review*, 3: 218–232.

Veendorp, E.C.H. (1970) 'General equilibrium theory for a barter economy', *Western Economic Journal*, 8: 1–23.

Walras, L. (1874) *Eléments d'économie politique pure*. Lausanne: Corbaz. Definitive edition translated by W. Jaffé, *Elements of pure economics*. Allen and Unwin, London, 1954.

Weitzman, M.L. (1985) 'The simple macroeconomics of profit sharing', *American Economic Review*, 75: 937–953.

Younes, Y. (1970) 'Sur les notions d'équilibre et de déséquilibre utilisées dans les modèles décrivant l'évolution d'une économie capitaliste'. Paris: CEPREMAP.

Younes, Y. (1975) 'On the role of money in the process of exchange and the existence of a non-Walrasian equilibrium', *Review of Economic Studies*, 42: 489–501.

Chapter 5

A GAME THEORETIC APPROACH TO THE THEORY OF MONEY AND FINANCIAL INSTITUTIONS

MARTIN SHUBIK

Yale University

Contents

*The research is partially supported by a grant from the Office of Naval Research under Contract Authority NR 047–006. Revisions were supported in part by NSF No. SES 8812051.

Handbook of Monetary Economics, Volume I, Edited by B.M. Friedman and F.H. Hahn
© *Elsevier Science Publishers B.V., 1990*

1. Process or equilibrium?

This is a sketch of a game theoretic and gaming approach to the development of an appropriate microeconomic theory of money and financial institutions.

The phrase "money and financial institutions" is used to stress that a theory of money alone cannot be fruitfully constructed in an institutional vacuum. The monetary and financial system of an economy are part of the socio-politico-economic control mechanism used by every state to connect the economy with the polity and society. This neural network provides the administrative means to collect taxes, direct investment, provide public goods, finance wars and facilitate international and intertemporal trade.

The money measures provide a crude but serviceable basis for the accounting system which, in turn, along with the codification of commercial law and financial regulation, are the basis for economic evaluation and the measurement of trust and fiduciary responsibility among the economic agents.

A central feature of a control mechanism is that it is designed to influence process. Dynamics is its natural domain. Equilibrium is not the prime concern, the ability to control the direction of motion is what counts.

Bagehot (1962) noted that a financial instrument originally designed for one purpose may take on a life of its own and serve a different purpose. In particular, most of the instruments may have been invented to facilitate trade but they provided a means for control. Money and financial institutions provide the command and control system of a modern society. The study of the mechanisms, how they are formed, how they are controlled and manipulated and how their influence is measured in terms of social, political and economic purpose pose questions not in pure economies, not even in a narrow political economy, but in the broad compass of a political economy set in the context of society.

A basic purpose of the approach adopted here is to show the minimal conditions which require that financial institutions and instruments emerge as necessary carriers of process. The thrust is for the development of a mathematical institutional economics.

2. One theme, many problems

The macroeconomist deals with here and now. Keynes (1973, p. 296) noted that: "Economics is a science of thinking in terms of models joined to the art of choosing models which are relevant to the contemporary world." The very nature of economic advice is such that it has to be based, at its best, upon a blend of perceptive ad hoc assumptions combined together to provide a sufficient socio-political context for the economic argument presented to justify the advice. The niceties of tight logical checks, completeness and consistency analyses and broad sensitivity analysis can only be afforded as they are called forth in the hurried battle of the adversarial process in which economic advice and policy advocacy is embedded.

There are many microeconomic theorists who use their skills to address problems of policy in the small, such as pricing of utilities, regulation of banks or evaluation of special subsidies. Yet the development and study of the microeconomic foundations of the price system, other means of exchange [see Shubik (1970)] and the politico-economic institutions of economic guidance calls for a level of detachment, scope and abstraction that are all difficult to justify when any form of direct economic advice is being given.

Often apparently complex and ill-defined problems are genuinely complicated. The historian is well aware that there may be thousands of interacting factors which at one time or another come to the front center of the stage for a brief moment in the limelight and are then replaced by other factors. Thus, historians of the American Civil War can still debate the relative importance of the northern railway and logistic system in contrast with the death of Stonewall Jackson prior to Gettysburg. Whole theories may be based on the economic value of slaves; the importance of central land masses; the strategic value of control of the seas; the linkage between tyranny and the control of irrigation systems; freedom and mountain valleys and so forth.

In a lesser, but fortunately more precise, way, the economist concerned with the understanding of economic institutions faces a complex multivariate system. But hopefully there is enough special structure and stability of structure that he can break up his general investigations into more specialized and well-defined segments prior to assembling a general theory.

It is argued here that there are several basic subtopics which can be investigated separately, yet which are needed jointly in the eventual construction of an underlying theory of money and financial institutions. Before we begin to discuss the different, but necessary, partial approaches, several general assertions concerning the construction of any satisfactory theory of money and financial institutions are made.

2.1. Some assertions

Assertion 1

An adequate theory of money and financial institutions must be able to account for segments of the economic system where the economic agents are few in number and large.

Comment. Virtually all of the efficient market price system and information conditions results depend upon there being a continuum of small agents. Yet the evidence is that this is not so for the major tax authorities, banks of issue and other government agencies; this is also a poor approximation for banking, insurance, investment banking, utilities and major manufacturing in general.

Assertion 2

The existence of money and financial institutions would be needed in a world with no exogenous uncertainty whatsoever. The presence of transactions costs caused by the technology of exchange is sufficient to cause aggregation and hence uncertainty.

Comment. Decisions and contracts, even in a world without exogenous uncertainty, utilize time and other economic resources. Lawyers, accountants, bookkeepers and other administrative workers in the information, communication and control structure of the economy of any society organized as a state are not and never have been free goods, even as a first approximation for those interested in answering most of the basic questions in political economy.

Assertion 3

The counterfactural assumption of complete markets (often defended as an adequate first approximation for some problems) may obviate the need for money, contracts and other financial institutions in a world with time and perfect trust. However, the need to write the rules of the game to enforce contracts in a world with less than perfect trust is sufficient to call for financial instruments and institutions even with zero transactions technology costs.

Comment. Transactions costs, whether generated by technology or by strategic considerations of trust and enforcement, are more central to the presence of money and financial institutions than is the presence of exogenous uncertainty. The presence of transactions costs creates many new problems when exogenous uncertainty is present, but without any costs to a transactions technology or any cost to trust, the presence of complete markets wipes out the problems of exogenous uncertainty.

Assertion 4

The theory of the general equilibrium system provides a highly useful benchmark and starting point from the development of a theory of money and financial institutions. But the next steps involve recognizing that game theoretic modeling and methods are more general. The basic results of general equilibrium theory may be reinterpreted as results obtained from a class of strategic market games with a continuum of economic agents with no agent of significant size, or, in some instances, from games with a finite number of players.

Assertion 5

Although game theoretic methods are advocated here as appropriate to helping to reconcile micro- and macroeconomics, two warnings are called for. Many of the basic difficulties involve the modeling of carriers of process. The techniques of cooperative game theory appear to be of only limited worth [but see Gale (1982)]. In particular, for problems involving economic dynamics, the core and value solutions do not seem to be fruitful.

Although the extensive and strategic forms for representing games appear to be of considerable value in modeling,[1] there are many difficulties with the noncooperative equilibrium solution concept which is most frequently used. We do not have a universally accepted prescription or description for how rational economic agents should or do behave in a multiperson game of strategy. The macroeconomists have "solved" their problem in an ad hoc manner by making behavioral assumptions and claiming that their approximations, such as a propensity to consume or save, are "good enough". The microeconomic model of individualistic rational, maximizing man does not extend to provide a unique prescription for behavior. Although noncooperative solution concepts such as *perfect equilibrium* are frequently utilized, the justification for doing so is by no means always compelling.

2.2. A division of tasks

The four major factors which must be considered are (1) topics, (2) models, (3) solution concepts and (4) numbers.

The complexity of the monetary and financial system of our societies considered as a whole must be divided into bite-sized pieces so that we can isolate and analyze the many different phenomena to avoid being overwhelmed by their interactions.

A natural starting point is one period models without exogenous uncertainty. Figure 5.1 suggests a structure for a sequence of problems starting with the

---

[1]For some problems such as the study of random pairing in a barter market the extensive and strategic forms may offer *too much* structure. The coalitional form may be regarded as more flexible.

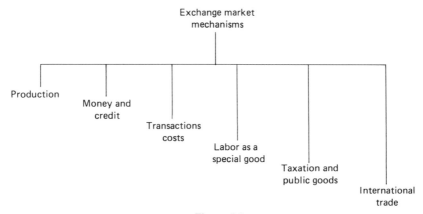

Figure 5.1

simplest; that being of an exchange economy. Complications may then be added individually or jointly. At the top of Figure 5.1 is an exchange market technology with no frills. We may then add, one at a time or in combinations, production, money and credit, transactions costs; the treatment of labor as a special commodity or set of commodities; the addition of mechanisms for the collection of taxes and the distribution of public goods; and international trade.

Associated with every one of these topics there are four classes of treatment which must be considered. They are:

(1) utility and preference assumptions;
(2) exogenous uncertainty and information conditions;
(3) multistage models and full dynamics; and
(4) number of participants: few, many, countable, other.

Prior to discussing the specific work and its relevance, we turn to comments on general equilibrium and macroeconomics.

3. The debt to general equilibrium

The theory of general equilibrium has provided an elegant tight mathematical description for the existence of an efficient price system. In order to be able to produce a precise and analyzable mathematical structure for the intermixture of the insightful, verbal, but loosely mathematical description of Walras (1954), Arrow and Debreu (1954), McKenzie (1959), Debreu (1959) and others refined and presented a sparse noninstitutional set of conditions on preferences and production technology for the existence of a price system.[2]

[2]Koopmans (1977, p. 264) has referred to the work on the static price system as "preinstitutional".

Paradoxically the quest for precision provides the key to the understanding of the importance of institutional detail. By starting with the simplest most stripped-down noninstitutional description of production and exchange it becomes easy to start to construct mechanisms and add minimal institutional factors one at a time. The simplicity provides clarity. In particular, the ease with which it is possible to see both what the general equilibrium model does and does not do contributes to its usefulness.

The general equilibrium theory has provided a basis for understanding the efficiency properties of a price system. But up to and including the Debreu version it did not establish any distinction between a competitive or a centralized price system. The existence theorems are independent of the number of agents. The concept of complete markets is made clear. No matter how "unrealistic" we may find a time dated contingent commodity, it is well defined and complete markets provide a meaningful economic upper bound. But implicit, if not explicit, in the mathematics is that time, chance and trust do not matter when markets are complete. Implicit, but not explicit in the first vigorous mathematical treatments of general equilibrium, is that somehow either information, perception and understanding are perfect or the differentials among individuals do not matter.

Clearly abstracted away are transactions costs, government, public goods, oligopolistic segments, the need for money, or any special role for labor. Implicit in the many time period model is the meaning of a real rate of interest and the need for highly restrictive assumptions before this scalar index can be regarded as more than a crude approximation for the generally uneven change in the growth of resources.

The clear mathematical formulation of general equilibrium answered some important questions concerning the existence of an efficient price system; but its abstract unreality provided a sound basis for posing in a precise manner many more questions than it has answered. The attempts to define and answer these new questions amount to the construction of a mathematical institutional economics where the emphasis is upon the description and analysis of mechanisms which are the carriers of process. But the carriers of process are implicit in the rules of the game when the economy is viewed as a game of strategy. Thus, features of the economy such as money and financial institutions should emerge as any attempt is made to enlarge a static mathematical description into a process oriented description. Even the work on computation and algorithms for the calculation of general equilibrium prices of Scarf with Hansen (1973) and Smale (1976), or the more recent work of Scarf (1986) on prices with indivisibilities, can be given a process or institutional interpretation. Who is meant to be producing the prices (the Gosplan, or are they meant to emerge from markets?)? How much information is required by whom?

In Section 5 it is argued that the most promising way to go forward from the basis provided by general equilibrium theory is by means of game theoretic methods, in particular strategic market games. But enormous simplifications are available when it is possible to make the assumption that individuals are all price-takers because they are individually of a size that is insignificant with respect to the markets as a whole. This assumption can be made rigorous by considering a continuum of economic agents and was first done formally by Aumann (1964) for cooperative games, and Dubey and Shapley (1977), Schmeidler (1980) and Jaynes, Okuno and Schmeidler (1978) for games in strategic form. These provide a linkage in the reinterpretation of models with price-taking as a special class of the broader game theoretic models.

4. From general equilibrium to macroeconomics: The challenge

The hope to unify through a theory of money the insights and advocacy of a Keynes with the general equilibrium theory is somewhat misplaced. The assumptions made about economic institutions, politico-economic power and socio-economic behavior, whether of entrepreneurs, investors, consumers or government agencies, are necessary to the socio-politico-economic applied orientation of virtually all of macroeconomic theory. These assumptions and observations are highly specific to the socio-political and institutional structure of the society being examined.

A full general theory of macroeconimic dynamics does not lie solely within the domain of economics. The monetary and financial structure of the society provides a command and control system through which the socio-political forces exert guidance and control on the economy. But a control system is not the control.

A theory of money and financial institutions at the level of abstraction of general equilibrium theory is a theory of mechanisms and how they might work given the combination of economic forces and more or less exogenous socio-political forces.

At best the microeconomic theorist, for some time to come, cannot bridge the gap between the parsimonious description of rational economic man and the socio-political behavioral actors of the macroeconomic advisors.

A view adopted here is that staying with the parsimonious and counter-factual model of economic man, an extensive and strategic form game theoretic view of the structure of financial control enables us to go beyond general equilibrium. This can be done at a level of abstraction at which the logic of economic process enables us to examine the nature and need for minimal financial instruments and institutions. Thus, the questions which must be asked and answered are, for example: What are the essential properties of money and credit? What are the essences of the commercial, merchant and central banking functions? What are the essential functions of insurance? At what level of economic complexity will bankruptcy laws, seniority conditions, futures contracts, bonds or other instruments come into existence? Is there a natural structure and upper bound to the number of essentially different financial instruments? I suggest that there is [Shubik (1975)].

But even with an exploration of minimal financial institutions and functions, the micro foundations of macroeconomics will have only begun to have been erected. The institutions and instruments appear as a logical necessity in any attempt to well define the rules of a strategic market game. Yet the dynamics of process models depend delicately upon the behavioral assumptions concerning the actors and it is here that the gap between the viewpoints of the microeconomic theorists and macroeconomists is large.

5. Strategic market games

5.1. Game theory models and playable games

Good modeling requires a judicious balance between detail and abstraction, between "realism and relevance", and simplification and tractability. Models should not only be sufficiently well defined to be mathematically analyzable but they should be playable as games (and possibly used as experimental games). This additional gaming criterion provides a "debugging device" and serves as a check on the complexity and ease or difficulty with which the mechanism is run. The need for clarity concerning details of the rules of the game is such that clearing houses, small change, warehouse receipts or bills of lading appear as necessities. An instrument may have many institutionally different forms but its function will be necessary to all systems. Thus, clearing houses and bankruptcy laws have many manifestations in different societies but are necessary whenever mass credit operations exist.

The actual playing of a game also calls attention to the limitations caused by transactions costs and time to many mechanisms. Thus, for example, there is nothing logically wrong in giving one's stockbroker a continuous function expressing one's demand for IBM shares as a function of the prices of wheat and gold; but any attempt to play this as a game will suggest the use of simpler messages.

In our attempt to stress mechanisms and to find the minimal conditions which require the invention of financial instruments and institutions, the risk is run that one set of critics will feel that the simplifications are gross distortions of "the real world", while the mathematically oriented theorist may feel that the models are too cluttered up with unnecessary detail. It is possibly helpful to look at the models as playable games which can be analyzed rather than stress immediate realism.

5.2. Market mechanisms

How is price formed? There are undoubtedly many ways. We can imagine pairs meeting randomly and contracting or recontracting; or an auctioneer calling price or individuals haggling, matching with partners elsewhere and returning to bargain if not satisfied. More prevalent in a mass retail economy is where one walks into a store and accepts the posted price or walks out without buying that item, although other purchases may be made. In a stock exchange a double auction mechanism may be used. Retail price formation is often different from wholesale sales to the trade and these may differ from intrafirm producer sales. The facts of inventory costs, transportation and delivery time lags modify the price-setting process. In complicated deals price may appear fixed to the untutored eye, but the lawyers are adjusting price via conditions on the deal. In socialist economies there may be a feedback system involving market, political and bureaucratic pressure; in capitalist economies oligopolistic power plays a role in some sectors.

Short of performing detailed ad hoc industrial studies, "realism" is not that easy to achieve in describing price mechanisms. Rather than propose realism as the criterion, the gaming test is used – mechanisms that are simple and easy to use are constructed. Gale (1986a, 1986b), Rubinstein and Wolinsky (1984), Binmore and Herrero (1984) and others have considered random pairing mechanisms. These are discussed elsewhere. Here the emphasis is on one-move mechanisms. An eventual program is to classify classes of mechanisms by axiomatic properties. Dubey, Mas-Colell and Shubik (1980) present five axioms which can be stated nontechnically and intuitively as follows:

(i) *Convexity*: traders have available a convex set of strategies.
(ii) *Anonymity*: in the market only the message sent by the trader matters.
(iii) *Continuity*: the outcomes vary continuously with the strategies.
(iv) *Aggregation*: the trading opportunities for any player are influenced by all others only through the mean of the messages of all others.
(v) *Nondegeneracy*: it must be possible for individual players to influence to a substantial extent their trading possibilities in the market.

With these five axioms they established inefficiency of all interior boundary noncooperative equilibria (N.E.) with a finite number of traders and efficiency of interior N.E. with a continuum of traders.

Axiom (iii) rules out the Bertrand–Edgeworth class of models.

An interesting distinction between the games satisfying the Dubey, Mas-Colell and Shubik axioms and the Bertrand–Edgeworth model is that in the former there is continuity in the variation of payoffs to variation in an individual's strategy, but the efficiency of equilibria requires a continuum of players, while in the latter there is a discontinuity in the variation of payoffs as strategies are varied but the efficiency of equilibrium can be achieved with a finite number of traders. [See Benassy (1986) for further analysis, and Dubey, Sahi and Shubik (1989) for axioms covering both Cournot and price mechanisms.]

The concept of strategic market game is formally related to Hurwicz's (1960, 1973) approach to the design of resource allocation methods.

Shubik (1973), Shapley (1976), Shapley and Shubik (1977), Dubey and Shubik (1978a, 1980b), Okuno and Schmeidler (1986) and Dubey (1982) constructed and established the noncooperative equilibrium properties of three models which can be described as a one-sided Cournot type of model, a two-sided Cournot and a double auction or two-sided Bertrand–Edgeworth model.

Consider an exchange economy with n players and $m + 1$ commodities where the $m + 1$st commodity is used as a money and there are m markets. Let the utility function of individual i be $\varphi_i(x_1^i, x_2^i, \ldots, x_m^i, x_{m+1}^i)$, where x_j^i is individual i's final holding (in R_+^{m+1}) of good j ($j = 1, \ldots, m + 1$). Let the initial endowment of individual i be $(a_1^i, a_2^i, \ldots, a_{m+1}^i)$.

In model 1 (the sell-all model) all individuals are required to put up for sale all their resources except their money. They use the money to buy resources and after trade are paid for what they have sold. A strategy for individual i is a set of m numbers $(b_1^i, b_2^i, \ldots, b_m^i)$, where $b_j^i \geq 0$ and $\sum_{j=1}^m b_j^i \leq a_{m+1}^i$:

$$p_{m+1} = 1, \qquad p_j = \sum_{i=1}^n b_j^i \Big/ \sum_{i=1}^n a_j^i, \qquad x_j^i = b_j^i/p_j, \quad \text{for } j = 1, \ldots, m,$$

(1)

and

$$x_{m+1}^i = a_{m+1}^i - \sum_{j=1}^m b_j^i + \sum_{j=1}^m a_j^i p_j,$$

(2)

where p_j = the price of good j.

This model is exposited in detail in Shapley and Shubik (1977). It should be noted that a strategy is a physical act not a bid or a verbal statement. The strategy of an individual has the "unrealistic" feature that an individual must sell all of his goods rather than consume directly from his resources, buying only for consumption above his initial endowment. The second or two-sided Cournot model corrects for this.

The strategy of an individual i is a set of $2m$ numbers $(b_1^i, q_1^i; b_2^i, q_2^i; \ldots; b_m^i, q_m^i)$, where $0 \leq b_j^i$ and $\sum_{j=1}^m b_j^i \leq a_{m+1}^i$ and $0 \leq q_j^i \leq a_j^i$, for $j = 1, \ldots, m$. Here $p_{m+1} = 1$ and

$$p_j = \sum_{i=1}^{n} b^i_j \Big/ \sum_{j=1}^{n} q^i_j , \quad \text{if } \sum_{i=1}^{n} q^i_j > 0 ,$$

$$= 0 , \qquad\qquad \text{if } \sum_{i=1}^{n} q^i_j = 0 , \tag{3}$$

$$x^i_j = a^i_j - q^i_j + b^i_j/p_j , \quad \text{for } j = 1, \ldots , n , \tag{4}$$

and

$$x^i_{m+1} = a^i_{m+1} + \sum_{j=1}^{m} q^i_j p_j - \sum_{j=1}^{m} b^i_j . \tag{5}$$

As individuals can buy and sell simultaneously in the same market the possibility for "wash sales" appears[3] and for finite numbers of players a continuum of equilibria may be encountered. An example of this possibility is given by Shubik (1984a, pp. 434–438). The proof of convergence of N.E. to the competitive equilibria (C.E.) as the players are replicated is given in Dubey and Shubik (1978a).[4]

The third model is in the style of Bertrand–Edgeworth in the sense that price rather than quantity is the prime strategic variable. A strategy is no longer a physical act of sending goods to the market but a contingent statement of size $4m$ of the form $(p^i_1, q^i_1, \tilde{p}^i_1, \tilde{q}^i_1; \ldots ; p^i_m, q^i_m, \tilde{p}^i_m, \tilde{q}^i_m)$, where p^i_j and q^i_j are the price and amount of good j an individual i is willing to buy, and $\tilde{p}^i_j$ and $\tilde{q}^i_j$ are the price and amount an individual i is willing to sell of good j. Theoretically we would like to be able to enforce:

$$\sum_{j=1}^{m} p^i_j q^i_j \le a^i_{m+1} . \tag{6}$$

This states that an individual's buying commitment can never be larger than his cash on hand. But ex ante there is no way to enforce this unless an inspection

---

[3]A wash sale occurs when an individual both buys and sells simultaneously in the same market thereby thickening it. For example if an individual has 100 units of a commodity and wants 100 more he could buy 100 or combine the sale of 100 with the purchase of 200. This would create a wash sale of 100. The wash sale provides a useful enlargement of strategies to establish the existence of N.E. with active trade [see Shapley (1976), Peck and Shell (1985, 1986) and Yao (1987)].

[4]Okuno and Schmeidler (1986) construct a strategic market game where the players use as strategies linear excess demand functions. They obtain approximate efficiency of the N.E. They observe that their main motivation "is to eliminate myopic assumptions inherent in the Walrasian model on the one hand and in the Shubik or Cournot type models on the other". I have no argument with their logic, but I suggest that playability is an important criterion.

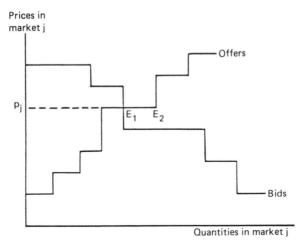

Figure 5.2

procedure is instituted. The condition (6) when p^i_j and q^i_j are bids can be extremely strong as the probability that one can purchase everything may be low.

In this market mechanism a bid and an offer histogram is constructed for each market. Bids are displayed as summed in descending order and offers in ascending order. Market price is established at the intersection of the two histograms. This is shown in Figure 5.2. There are several details concerning market price information and residual excess supply or demand (in Figure 5.2 the amount E_1E_2 is excess offers at the market price p_j) and these, together with the study of the N.E. and the relation to the C.E. are given in Dubey (1982) and Dubey and Shubik (1980b). An important distinction between the previous models and this is that there are noncooperative equilibria (N.E.) which are competitive equilibria (C.E) with as few as two individuals active on each side of a market.

5.2.1. On the number of simple mechanisms

One can envision a special language for trade involving only names of goods, quantities, bids, offers and prices. A move by a trader is a message concerning bids and offers for quantities of goods at various prices. The mass market is a device which aggregates the messages of traders and determines final market prices and trades. It is suggested elsewhere [Shubik (1979)] that if each trader has only a single move and if the market mechanism is limited in complexity, there are only a few simple market mechanisms.

5.2.2. *Enough money*

All three games described above have one move per player and all moves are made simultaneously; thus the velocity of money is at most one. In order for it to be feasible to achieve a C.E. of the exchange economy as an N.E. of the strategic market game, for the sell-all model it is required that at equilibrium:

$$\sum_j p_j x_j^i \le a_{m+1}^i . \tag{7}$$

As all nonmonetary assets are sold and all purchases paid for in money, the amount of money needed is at least the market value of all assets other than money.

For the two models, where the individual can consume directly from his assets the cash requirements are smaller, they are:

$$\sum_j p_j \max[(x_j^i - a_j^i), 0] \le a_{m+1}^i . \tag{8}$$

Given the condition that all transactions must involve the use of a specific commodity and given the transactions technology as fixed, the feasible set of trades for any trader will be constrained by his holding of cash. The worst case is where he must buy everything. This is shown in (7), the best case is shown in (8). If the exchange economy associated with a strategic market game (i.e. with the same preferences and endowments) has one or more C.E. such that the cash requirements at some C.E. cannot be met, this C.E. will not be a feasible outcome of the strategic market game, but a boundary N.E. will exist where the relative price of the commodity money will reflect not only its value in consumption, but also its shadow price as a capacity constraint on trade.

Even with a continuum of traders a N.E. of a strategic market game cannot approach a C.E. unless that outcome is feasible, but this requires enough cash. Without enough cash N.E. exist but are not efficient.

It is possible that the inequalities may not be satisfied by selecting good $m + 1$ as the means of payment, but by changing to good j they could be satisfied. A discussion of alternative choices of a means of payment is given by Shubik (1986b).

Suppose that there were not enough money, in the sense that there were no money that could satisfy the inequalities. A natural question to ask is: If we can change the game (and the exchange economy) by increasing the monetary endowments of the players, can we guarantee that we can eventually satisfy the enough money conditions at a C.E. of the new exchange economy?

As the amount of money[5] is varied the number of C.E. can change and the

---

[5]The word "money" is used often as a broad phrase covering an item used for the means of payment, but also having properties such as a store of value, serving as numeraire and possibly having other features. Here possibly "means of payment" is more precise and restrictive than "money", but this should be clear enough from the context.

relative prices can change radically. In particular, the marginal relative worth of the money could drop with increasing quantities so that the enough money condition is never satisfied. A sufficient condition to eventually achieve enough money is that:

$$\frac{\partial \varphi_i / \partial x^i_{m+1}}{\partial \varphi_i / \partial x^i_j} \geq \Delta, \quad \text{for all } j, \text{ for all endowments.} \tag{9}$$

Intuitively this says that there will always be some lower bound to the purchasing power of money for any commodity. Dubey and Shapley (1977c) discuss this further.

If we assume that utility functions are of the form:

$$F(\varphi_i(x^i_1, \ldots, x^i_m) + x^i_{m+1}), \tag{10}$$

or more simply:

$$\varphi_i(x^i_1, x^i_2, \ldots, x^i_m) + f_i(x^i_{m+1}), \quad \text{with } f' > 0, f'' < 0, \tag{11}$$

then all exchange economies associated with the class of games $\Gamma(n, k)$, defined by having n traders with preferences as in (10) and (11) and initial endowments of the form $(a^i_1, a^i_2, \ldots, a^i_m, a^i_{m+1} + k)$, will all have the same number of C.E. In particular, if the game $\Gamma(n, 0)$ has no interior C.E. it becomes meaningful to consider the minimum amount of money required to be able to achieve one C.E. as a N.E., and the amount required to attain all C.E.[6]

For this class of games it is meaningful to identify the C.E. which require the minimal and maximal amounts of money to finance trade. An immediate objection which can be raised against this observation is that condition (10) is unreasonable as it implies a no income effect. This is, to some extent, a difficult empirical question; as a first-order approximation it may be reasonable to assume that as individuals become richer the income effect of prices becomes weaker. Thus, for example, it might be that as a first approximation we have:

$$\phi_i(x^i_1, \ldots, x^i_{m+1}) = \varphi_i(x^i_1, \ldots, x^i_{m+1}), \qquad \text{for } x^i_{m+1} \leq k_1,$$
$$= \varphi_i(x^i_1, \ldots, x^i_m, k_1) + f_i(x^i_{m+1} - k_1), \quad \text{for } k_1 \leq x^i_{m+1}. \tag{12}$$

For the extremely rich it might even be reasonable to assume that beyond some k_2 the marginal utility of further wealth becomes approximately constant.

---

[6] Although with continuum of agents it may be somewhat evident to establish that with enough money any C.E. is a N.E., the establishing of strict equivalence is more problematical.

5.3. *Complete markets and enough money*

We may adopt the definition of commodity money as a commodity which has intrinsic value to a consumer (i.e. it appears as an argument of the utility function) and has complete markets, or is directly exchangeable into every other good. Figure 5.3 illustrates this. There are four commodities represented by the numbered points. Each line connecting two points signifies a simple market, i.e. a market (with some unspecified mechanism) where i can be exchanged directly for j. In Figure 5.3(a) there is no money; in 5.3(b) good 1 is a money; in 5.3(c) goods 1 and 3 are monies; and in 5.3(d) all goods are monies.

With complete markets all goods are money; there is always enough money to finance every individual's trade without credit. Using an extension of the Dubey–Shubik (1978a) model a strategy of an individual trader becomes of dimension $m(m-1)$ if there are m goods; as each can be directly exchanged for any other there are $m(m-1)/2$ markets, but in any market (say apples for oranges) an individual can be on either side (or both simultaneously). Amir, Sahi, Shubik and Yao (1987) have been able to prove the existence of pure strategy N.E.[7]

A natural question to ask is: Are there N.E. in the game with complete markets which are not C.E.? The answer is yes and is established by the example below where there are four types of traders, a continuum of each type and three commodities.

Let the utility functions be given:

$$u_0(x_1, x_2, x_3) = x_1^{1/3} x_2^{1/3} x_3^{1/3} \, ,$$

$$u_1(y_1, y_2, y_3) = y_1^{1/3} y_2^{2/3} \, ,$$

$$u_2(z_1, z_2, z_3) = z_2^{1/3} z_3^{2/3} \, ,$$

$$u_3(w_1, w_2, w_3) = w_1^{2/3} w_3^{1/3} \, .$$

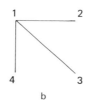

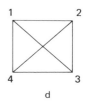

Figure 5.3

[7]A somewhat different model proposed by Shapley is that after all bids and offers are received they are all aggregated in a central agency which calculates and announces the clearing prices. Sahi and Yao (1987) have analyzed this model and proved existence.

The initial endowments are:

$$(a_1^0, a_2^0, a_3^0) = (1, 1, 1),$$
$$(a_1^1, a_2^1, a_3^1) = (0, 3, 0),$$
$$(a_1^2, a_2^2, a_3^2) = (0, 0, 3),$$
$$(a_1^3, a_2^3, a_3^3) = (3, 0, 0).$$

The final N.E. allocations are:

$$(x_1, x_2, x_3) = (2, 2, 2),$$
$$(y_1^1, y_2^1, y_3^1) = (1, 1, 1),$$
$$(z_1^2, z_2^2, z_3^2) = (0, 1, 1),$$
$$(w_1^3, w_2^3, w_3^3) = (1, 0, 1),$$

with prices

$$p_{12} = 2 = p_{23} = p_{21}$$

and

$$p_{12} p_{23} p_{31} = 8.$$

However, the unique C.E. is easily seen to consist of the price vector $(1, 1, 1)$ and gives rise to the following final allocations:

$$(1, 1, 1), \quad (2, 1, 0), \quad (0, 2, 1) \quad \text{and} \quad (1, 0, 2).$$

This N.E. violates the no-arbitrage condition that $p_{ij} p_{jk} p_{ki} = 1$. It would be destroyed as a N.E. if credit were available. It depends upon there being only one round of trade so that no individual can take advantage of the full arbitrage circuit for $p_{ij} p_{jk} p_{ki} > 1$.

This model cannot be generalized to many periods without specifically introducing instruments for futures trading. Although logically we can imagine the trade of today's eggs for wheat to be delivered six years from now, if they are traded at all, commodities for lengthy future delivery are traded via futures contracts which are paper instruments which take on a life of their own until they are extinguished when the contract is filled.

When there are only a finite number of traders the N.E. are not efficient. The approach to efficiency depends on the thickness of markets. But two phenomena influence the thickness of markets when numbers are finite. They are the number of markets used (the more, the thinner the markets for the same volume of trade) and the absence or presence of wash sales (as already noted).

The presence of transactions costs[8] combined with the thinness of markets both contrive to provide reasons for some markets to fail to materialize.

Remark on the selection of a numeraire

When there is only a single money and m markets it is easy and natural to select money as a numeraire and set $p_{m+1} = 1$ without any reference to equilibrium conditions. The game only determines m prices, thus prices emerge in terms of the money. With complete markets prior to the emergence of equilibrium $m(m-1)/2$, prices must be determined and the numeraire cannot be neutrally meaningfully selected without imposing a no-arbitrage requirement.

5.4. Not enough money and the need for credit

When there is a restriction to one money and markets exist only between it and all other goods three cases must be considered. Both the absolute quantity and the distribution of the monetary good count, thus three possibilities are that:
    (1) there is enough money well distributed;
    (2) there is enough money but badly distributed; and
    (3) there is not enough money.
There are four basic ways in which a money shortage or maldistribution can be overcome, they are by:
    (1) introducing more markets;
    (2) producing more money and distributing it appropriately;
    (3) increasing velocity of circulation; or
    (4) introducing credit.
As transactions costs decrease, communications improve and population increases, new markets may appear, but even to casual empiricists there are futures contracts which are not available and risks which cannot be hedged efficiently.

In the description of macroeconomic disequilibrium and inflation, stories abound about governments resorting to the printing press, to debasing coinage or to plundering gold and silver mines elsewhere. Even with the entry of new gold, it is necessary to specify how the gold is introduced to the economy. Does the government sell it in return for labor (pay the army, for instance) or other resources? Does it enter via gold miners selling the extra resources? Purely

---

[8]See Chapter 1 by Ostroy and Starr in this Handbook for a detailed discussion of transactions costs.

formally it is straightforward to regard the supply of a commodity as parametrically given and study the variations. One can also model the production of gold, but unless the production and preference conditions are appropriate even with production there is no guarantee of enough money. A more prevalent way in which the lack of money is ameliorated is by the invention of credit instruments.

Before turning to credit, some comments on the velocity of money are in order. There are technological bounds on many timing aspects of economic life. The quickening or slowing of payments strategically without resorting to credit instruments has only limited possibilities. Individuals can change the frequency of their purchases of some inventories and modify or select faster production processes. However, although changes in the velocity of money may be an important problem in economic policy and control, except for adding considerable complication to the description of a strategic market game to provide strategic choice over timing, no central conceptual problems in a theory of money appear to depend on the changes in velocity. For this reason it is suggested that in spite of Tobin's criticism [see Karaken and Wallace (1980, p. 90)] fixed move models probably provide a useful simplification in the development of a theory of money. Variation in velocity is an important applied problem but a red herring in the basic understanding of money and financial institutions.

The most essential way in which a monetary economy copes with shortage of money is with credit and other financial instruments.

6. Strategic market games with credit

In an attempt to construct games with credit arrangements the following factors must be taken into account, and how they are dealt with must be specified within the model:
- (a) the nature of the credit instrument;
- (b) the nature of the issuer and borrower;
- (c) default conditions on the borrower;
- (d) default conditions on the lender;
- (e) a one-period or multiperiod model;
- (f) the presence or absence of exogenous uncertainty; and
- (g) intergenerational transfer of assets and liabilities.

6.1. Instruments and issuers

There are three divisions of economic agents as issuers and borrowers which merit consideration. They are (1) individuals, (2) private institutions and (3) public institutions. The fundamental distinctions among them are reflected, in general, in large differences in economic size, life and special rules differentiating and delimiting their strategic possibilities. These differences will be manifested in the construction of a game with distinguished classes of players.

In a world with only private individuals there are two sorts of loan arrangements we may consider. The first is where there is bilateral personal credit, as is often found among friends, and the second is where an anonymous money market exists in which all I.O.U. notes are accepted and treated as fungible. These are discussed further in Subsection 6.5.

Although both large merchants and manufacturers have provided and often do provide banking and insurance functions, we consider just the bank and its issue of banknotes and checks.[9] The models are noted in Subsection 6.8.

Possibly one of the more important ways the money supply has been supplemented has been by the bill of exchange involving originally merchants and bill specialists and now usually involving two merchants and two banks. No attempt has been made yet to build a formal model isolating the factors which contribute to giving it an independent life.

The last special agent is the government or government agencies. At a level of some detail there are important distinctions. In the United States much government agency financing is done with the "the full faith and credit" of the U.S. government, but the level of guarantee may vary with the agency involved. At the level of abstraction and aggregation employed here "the government" is considered as a single financial agency. As a modeling choice we may wish to consider it outside of the private economy – as the referee or controller of the game. Alternatively, it may be considered as within the game in which case as it is such a specialized player, a careful specification of its motivation and payoff function is required. The government may issue coin, banknotes and checks. This is discussed further in Subsection 7.6.

6.2. Default conditions, single- and multiperiod models

As soon as credit is introduced into a game, unless it is limited so that even under the worst scenario the debtor can pay back fully, it becomes necessary to add default conditions as part of the rules of the game. In all modern enterprise economies there is a body of law dealing with insolvency, bankruptcy, corporate liquidation and reorganization, the garnishing of income and other factors which come into play when there is a failure to repay debt at the appointed time.

---

[9]It is of interest to ask at what level of detail in modeling and game design one would expect the need for coin as contrasted with banknotes to appear – most probably where there is a need for low value, and high velocity, and high durability – an easy natural source for a central government to provide a public service and take a seignorage profit.

Insolvency may involve only a timing problem. A debt is not met at a due date, but available assets are more than adequate to cover it (and any accrual) given enough time for orderly liquidation. In a bankruptcy the firm or individual, even fully liquidated, may not be able to cover the debt outstanding. At the level of abstraction here rather than use the legal language with its many special meanings, perhaps a more neutral terminology such as "repayment failure rules" are called for. Shubik and Wilson (1977) and Dubey and Shubik (1979) unfortunately did not follow this advice.

When the rules are needed to take care of a settlement after default, a considerable difference emerges between the single-period and multiperiod game. In the single-period game the settlement takes place at the end of play. When there is more than one period a decision must be made whether to settle during the game or roll over the loan hoping to recoup before the end of play. When a settlement is made, the procedure has to reflect the purposes of the design of the rule. These may include deterrence to discourage debtors from failure, rehabilitation to improve their chances of being economically valuable to the society, restitution to help optimize the return to creditors, and administrative speed and low cost. But in making restitution, if borrowing and lending have involved aggregations of individuals we must specify seniority conditions. There is also the danger that a single failure may set off a chain of failures. The question of "what are the optimum repayment failure rules" is complex and has not yet been fully answered. This is also true of the role of limited liability.

6.3. A digression on the cashless society, transactions costs and Pareto optimality

Implicit in much of the discussion on exchange and exchange and production is the proposition that the technology of exchange is costless. Pesek (1976) has noted that much of the discussion on banking is as though it is a costless occupation, yet an examination of the actual costs involved indicates that it is not unlike the telephone companies or manufacturing.

Even a casual examination of transactions costs suggests many operational reasons for different financial instruments which, from some point of view, would be regarded as the same. Thus, for some sets of questions there are no interesting differences among economies run with coins, fiat paper, banknotes, checks or a computerized accounting credit system. Given the technological breakthrough in the last few decades in communication and computation, it might appear that transactions costs are falling so precipitously that the cashless society where only accounting money exists is becoming a real possibility [see Black (1970) and Fama (1980)]. As a start in theorizing about the properties of the means of payment it is possibly worth not making any distinction. But there are indications that the transactions costs, accounting and anonymity features are such that coins and paper fiat money are here to stay while the use of checks may be eroded by accounting transfers. Mayer (1974, p. 168) in a popular book on banking suggests that the cost of processing a check might have been around $0.20 in the early 1970s. In a second book [Mayer (1984, pp. 71–74)] the estimates appear to be higher. The conceptual and accounting difficulties in attributing individual cost to this joint production operation are at least as bad as in evaluating the cost of the individual telephone call, but the rough message is that the total expense of the payments system of the banks has a nontrivial average transactions cost. Paper money, in contrast, may last for a few years[10] and at the cost of a few cents for the note, serves for many anonymous transactions. Coins may last for several decades,[11] each costs a fraction of the face value of the coin and serves for even more transactions than notes. There are different ways in which we might try to attach significance to these difficulties, such as weighting the different instruments by both the dollar size and frequency of use of the instrument. There are conceptual difficulties, the empirical information is shaky, but it is suggested here that the prospects for the cashless society are not high.

Once the importance of transactions costs are acknowledged the concept of Pareto optimality of competitive exchange needs adjustment. As noted by Arrow (1981) the feasible set of outcomes with transactions costs depends on the initial distribution of resources. Rogawski and Shubik (1986) have studied a strategic market game with transactions costs and shown the existence of pure strategy N.E. and for large numbers their approach to efficiency in the transactions cost constrained set. But although results may be obtained with production technologies represented by cones or convex sets, many of the more interesting problems with transactions costs involve set-up costs, indivisibilities and complicated joint production, none of which has yet been treated game theoretically in the context of a theory of money and financial institutions.[12]

6.4. A digression on two types of anonymity

For the major purposes of the economics of payment, the check, credit card or accounting entry are as anonymous as cash. From the point of view of Mrs.

---

[10]The average life of a Federal Reserve Note (from an estimate of the Department of the Treasury, Bureau of Engraving and Printing in 1986, personal correspondence, 19 September 1986) is 18 months for the $1 bill; 2 years for $5; 3 years for $10; 5 years for $20; 9 years for $50; and 23 years for $100. The cost of production is $26 per 1000 notes regardless of denomination.

[11]The U.S. Mint produces the coinage. A casual estimate based on sampling pocket change is that a quarter may remain in circulation for more than 25 years.

[12]But see Gale and Hellwig (1984) for a treatment of nonconvex transactions costs.

Jones who tells her husband that she had to stay late in the office while she had a night on the town, there is a considerable difference. The anonymity of the clearinghouse dealing with records is not the anonymity of cash. The presence of vast quantities of $100 bills used by the underground economy and others attests to the differences between cash payment and a system of clearance that leaves a paper trail for the tax man, suspicious spouse or other control group.

The difference between the two types of anonymity is sufficient to provide a reason strong enough by itself to be a barrier to the introduction of a cashless society.

6.5. The money market

Everyone a banker

A popular thought in the casual discussion of competitive finance is that anyone should be able to become a banker. A way to try to operationalize this as a playable game is as follows.

There are n individuals and m goods, and for simplicity in minimizing the need to discuss the need for future markets, we limit the game to one period. Each individual i has a utility function of the form:

$$\varphi_i(x^i_1, \ldots, x^i_m) + \mu^i \min\left[0, \sum_{j=1}^m p_j(x^i_j - a^i_j)\right],$$

where $(a^i_1, \ldots, a^i_m)$ is the initial endowment of i and the p_j are the prices formed. We must specify how prices are formed and justify the structure of the extra term on the utility function.

If every individual is able to issue I.O.U. notes which are accepted as a means of payment by all others, then we may use the same sort of market mechanism as was shown for the two-sided Cournot market with the following changes. here, as in that market, a bid by an individual is of the form $(b^i_1, q^i_1, b^i_2, q^i_2, \ldots, b^i_m, q^i_m)$, but the sum $\sum_{j=1}^m b^i_j$ is no longer bounded by a quantity of commodity money a^i_{m+1}; each b^i_j is a personal I.O.U. note sent to the market denominated in a unit of account, say dollars.

In order for this game to become playable we have to have rules concerning the redemption of I.O.U. notes and what happens if there is a failure to redeem. If there were no punishment for default, the incentive to issue I.O.U. notes would be unbounded and would destroy any proposed active equilibrium. By introducing a bankruptcy penalty which can be extraeconomic, such as going to prison or losing a hand, where the severity of the penalty increases with the level of debt, we bound the level of borrowing of any individual who is maximizing his payoff given the actions of all others. Without loss of generality the specific functional form suggested in (13) serves as well as the form:

$$\varphi_i(x_1^i, x_2^i, \ldots, x_m^i; x_{m+1}^i) \tag{14}$$

defined on $R_m^+ \times R$, where $x_{m+1}^i = \sum_{j=1}^m p_j(x_j^i - a_j^i)$. This is illustrated in Figure 5.4 where the key controlling feature of the severity of the penalty as a deterrent to failing to redeem I.O.U. notes is the slope of the contours as they proceed into the negative orthant. As long as the penalty for issuing one dollar of unredeemed debt is greater than the worth of an extra dollar of income, the penalty is sufficiently severe to discourage strategic default. If there is no strategic default at equilibrium, the specifics of the severity of the penalty for varying levels of final debt will not matter. "Harsh enough" can be operationalized. This is not so with incomplete markets and exogenous uncertainty where an optimal bankruptcy penalty may involve a number of bankruptcies.

In Figure 5.4 the basic distinction between a utility function of forms (13) and (14) is that (13) gives an indifference curve of the form $A'CE'$ which implies that in this one-shot game left over ownership of I.O.U. notes are of no value, but negative amounts are of negative value. The curve ACE arising from (14) looks like a more conventional indifference curve, somewhat transposed, so that part appears in the negative orthant. This indicates that the creditor has

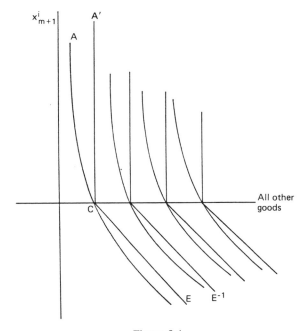

Figure 5.4

value for outstanding debt, a situation which is usually true if the game continues and there is some hope of repayment.

For a continuum of traders all of the C.E. of the associated exchange economy will be N.E., but in each instance the default penalty establishes only a lower bound on price. Beyond that lower bound the multiplication of all prices by $k > 1$ gives an equilibrium associated in its real good distribution with the equilibrium for $k = 1$.

After all players have selected their strategies and the m prices are formed by adding together all goods, the goods are shipped and the net balances of each trader are reported from each market to a clearinghouse. The balances bear only the name of the individuals. The clearinghouse sets up accounts for all individuals and cancels debits and credits to achieve a net balance. In this one-period model, as final positive balances are worthless no one wishes to end with positive balances. Those with negative balances suffer the penalty. In the one-period game there is no need to consider seniority or credit failure domino effects. Implicit in this formulation is an avoidance of having to deal with others than those who fail to redeem their paper at an outside bank.

Mathematically this model can be regarded as identical with there being a shadow bank clearinghouse which exchanges personal I.O.U. notes for bank notes. As long as there is only one trading period and a nonzero default penalty, with a continuum of traders the coincidence of the exchange economy's C.E. with N.E. of the strategic market game can be established. One can make the default penalty infinite [see Schmeidler (1980)] but there is no need to. The harsher the penalty, the lower the bound on equilibrium prices.[13]

There is no particular logical or technological reason to rule out letting all individuals directly monetize their I.O.U.s. A playable one-period game has been described. Even at this level of simplicity a clearinghouse is needed as well as a device or referee to report failure to redeem and to enforce a penalty on defaulters. In general, individual I.O.U.s are not accepted as money because of lack of information and trust. Even in a highly computerized world the cost of a universal trustworthy credit evaluation system is sufficiently substantial to rule out "everyone a bank" as a viable arrangement.

6.6. The money market, gold and liquidity

Above it has been suggested that although there is nothing logically wrong with all individuals using their own I.O.U.s as money, for reasons of trust,

---

[13]As the penalty is increased the disutility of going bankrupt for a dollar increases. Any price level where the disutility of going bankrupt exceeds the marginal value of extra purchase can be supported. With a high penalty the lower bound on the price level approaches zero. The distribution of real resources is not influenced.

administration and identification this is not a good approximation of the way things are or even will be. A closer approximation is that there is an identifiable trusted known institution which serves as an intermediary. This institution evaluates and judges creditworthiness. It may accept the debt of otherwise unknown individuals and exchange this unknown debt for its known debt which is accepted in payment by all. In doing this the institution either becomes a specialized differentiated player in the game or should be regarded as a controller out of the game. In the next two sections this institution is considered in the form of public or private banks.

Before considering banks, an economy is examined which already has gold as a commodity money, but might nevertheless benefit from the existence of a market in which the gold can be borrowed.

In examining an exchange economy which uses a commodity money for exchange there are three possibilities concerning the amount of money available and the needs of trade. They are:

(a) All have enough to finance efficient trade:

$$\sum_{j=1}^{m} p_j \max[(x_j^i - a_j^i), 0] \le a_{m+1}^i, \quad \forall i \in N, \tag{15}$$

where p_j are prices at a C.E.[14]

(b) There is enough money in the economy as a whole to finance efficient trade, but it is badly distributed:

$$\sum_{j=1}^{m} \sum_{i=1}^{n} p_j \max[(x_j^i - a_j^i), 0] \le \sum_{i-1}^{n} a_{m+1}^i, \tag{16}$$

but for some i $\sum_{j=1}^{m} p_j \max[(x_j^i, a_j^i), 0] > a_{m+1}^i$.

(c) There is not enough money for efficient trade:

$$\sum_{j=1}^{m} \sum_{i=1}^{n} p_j \max[(x_j^i - a_j^i), 0] > \sum_{i=1}^{n} a_{m+1}^i. \tag{17}$$

These observations are for a one-period (or normalized form) model. New problems appear when a multiperiod model is considered and futures markets, short sales and other trades involving timing are considered.

In the first of the three cases, as there is both enough money and it is well distributed, no credit or money market facilities are needed. In the third case (relative to the C.E. under consideration) there is not enough money in the system to finance liquidity. In the second case, by introducing a money market

---

[14]We have discussed the possibility that there may only be enough money to attain one C.E. and not the others, in Subsection 5.2.

it is possible to correct the maldistribution of money and achieve the C.E. trade in the associated strategic market game. The money market is a simple quantity mechanism in which those who wish to lend money offer it to the market and those who wish to borrow bid I.O.U. notes. Figure 5.5 shows the two-stage game. The amount an individual i offers to lend is z^i. The amount that an individual j offers to pay for his loan at the end of play is u^j. Hence, an endogenous rate of interest ρ emerges as:

$$1 + \rho = \sum_{j=1}^{n} u^j \bigg/ \sum_{k=1}^{n} z^k$$

$$= 1, \quad \text{if either sum is zero}. \tag{18}$$

After the money market has cleared, exchange takes place with the conditions that:

$$\sum_{j=1}^{m} b_j^i \le a_{m+1}^i - z^i + u^i/(1 + \rho). \tag{19}$$

The final payoff is given by:

$$\varphi_i(x_1^i, \ldots, x_m^i)$$

$$+ \mu_i \min\left[0, \left(a_{m+1}^i - \sum_{j=1}^{m} b_j^i + \sum_{j=1}^{m} p_j q_j^i - \rho u^i/(1 + \rho) + \rho z^i\right)\right], \tag{20}$$

where $x_j^i = a_j^i - q_j^i + b_j^i/p_j$, for $j = 1, \ldots, m$. For a sufficiently strong default penalty there will be a pure strategy N.E. with $\rho > 0$ for finite numbers[15] and $\rho = 0$ for a continuum of traders.

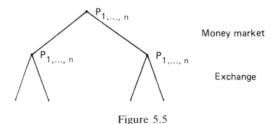

Figure 5.5

[15]As this is a multistage game, as soon as we consider a finite number of players we need extra conditions (such as perfect equilibrium) to cut down on the possible proliferation of equilibria. The justification of the extra conditions is not obvious.

Gold and liquidity

The consideration of borrowing and lending over more than one period poses new problems concerning default penalties and the meaning of a commodity money and how it enters the utility function. It also poses problems concerning the need for short sales or futures markets in order to achieve efficiency.

A fully satisfactory model of period-by-period default penalties and reorganization has not yet been achieved. For a finite horizon the problem can be avoided by refinancing interim defaults until the end.

The cost of liquidity is modeled as follows. Consider a game which is played for k periods. In each period there are m nondurable commodities and a durable commodity money, say gold. Each individual i wishes to maximize

$$\sum_{t=1}^{k} \beta^{t-1} \varphi_i(x_{1t}^i, \ldots, x_{mt}^i, x_{m+1,t}^i), \tag{21}$$

where the component $x_{m+1,t}^i$ which enters the utility function is to be interpreted as the consumption value of gold as a consumer good, say as jewelry. We may consider a game with three moves in each period. At the start of the period each individual divides the gold he possesses into two piles, one for jewelry and one for money. For simplicity, the production processes which take gold money to jewelry and vice versa are regarded as costless and immediate. There is no wear and tear on the gold. Each individual i starts with an amount of gold $a_{m+1,1}^i$. At each period t he divides it so that:

$$a_{m+1,t}^i = y_t^i + w_{m+1,t}^i, \tag{22}$$

where y_t^i is the amount of monetary gold at the start of period t and $w_{m+1,t}^i$ is the amount of jewelry. Jewelry can be sold for money but yields no consumption value[16] if sold and the money is not available until the end of the period. Without production costs and time, rather than define jewelry separately we could just give consumption value to untraded gold.

The amount of monetary gold at the start of $t+1$ is:

$$a_{m+1,t+1}^i = y_t^i - \sum_{j=1}^{m+1} b_{jt}^i + \sum_{j=1}^{m+1} p_{jt} q_{jt}^i - \rho_t u_t^i/(1+\rho) + \rho_t z_t^i + x_{m+1,t}^i, \tag{23}$$

where the u_t^i and z_t^i are interpreted as in (18), i.e. the net returns from

[16]The modeling here is somewhat arbitrary; we could split the consumption value of jewelry between buyer and seller in any proportion.

borrowing and lending gold. The $x^i_{t,m+1}$ is the ending amount of jewelry:

$$x^i_{m+1,t} = w^i_{m+1,t} - q^i_{m+1,t} + b^i_{m+1,t}/p_{m+1,t} \, . \tag{24}$$

The existence of active pure strategy N.E. has been proved by Shubik and Yao (1989). The cost or value of liquidity is the consumer value foregone by utilizing a unit of gold for money.

As long as payments are actually made in gold a real cost is paid for liquidity and hence if trade is required at a C.E. outcome this cannot be attained as a N.E. of the market game.

Even with separable utilities intertemporal trade may be required for optimality if endowments vary sufficiently from period to period. A trivial one-nondurable commodity, three-period trading model is useful to focus attention on the modeling and definitional problems concerning credit, futures markets and short sales.

Consider two types of traders with utility functions for three perishable goods:

$$U_1 = 5x_1 + 5x_2 + x_3 \quad \text{and} \quad U_2 = y_1 + y_2 + y_3 \, , \tag{25}$$

with endowments of $(0,0,4)$ and $(1,3,0)$, respectively. By inspection a (boundary) C.E. solution is $p_1 = p_2 = p_3 = 1$, final endowments are $(1,3,0)$ and $(0,0,4)$. The general equilibrium model gives no information about the payment sequence. All that is required is that $\Sigma^3_{j=1} \, p_j(x^i_j - a^i_j) = 0$, for $i = 1, 2$. But for a game to be able to achieve the equilibrium outcome the trading markets must be specified. If there are m new goods each period and they are durable over all k periods, then there will be in total mk time-dated goods by the last period or, in total, for all periods:

$$A = \sum^k_{t=1} mt = mk(mk-1)/2 \quad \text{goods} \, . \tag{26}$$

Thus, complete markets call for $A(A-1)/2$ markets.

If no goods are durable, then the number of markets for a m goods per period is:

$$mk(mk-1)/2 \, . \tag{27}$$

The number of spot markets in (27) is $km(m-1)/2$. Thus, in the simple example with $m = 1$ and $k = 3$ we have three futures markets and no spot markets.

In a complete market model we may ask what is meant precisely by a futures market. Is an exchange of beans now for carrots in six years time a futures trade? Does such an exchange require legal documents and are these documents negotiable and fungible with documents with the same delivery conditions?

It is not useful to be trapped in institutional detail and terminological niceties, but some operational distinctions must be made when there are strategic differences in the market structure.

When we think of trying to play a multiperiod complete market model we are forced to invent financial paper. In the price formation mechanism of (3), where individuals submit quantities, these are physical acts. But you cannot bid now with carrots to be grown six years from now. Carrots are represented by a paper promise to deliver. Furthermore, as soon as a future promise becomes a part of strategy its fulfillment must be guaranteed. But there may be a stage of the game where this is not feasible. A failure to deliver penalty must be specified. As soon as an individual is permitted to sell any item he is not *absolutely* guaranteed to own when delivery is due, a penalty is required.

The distinction between naked and covered futures contracts and short sales can be made on the basis of feasibility. In the exchange model an individual, who by the rules will own 100 tons of wheat in two years time, can sell two-year contracts now and one-year contracts next year to sum to 100 tons, but no more, if it is not certain that he can buy more before the delivery date.

A short sale is a current sale of shares for money together with a promise to deliver the shares at a future, possibly unspecified date. A naked short involves selling shares that are not currently owned. A covered short sale is a sale where the seller already owns the shares to be delivered. The feasibility conditions were aptly phrased by Daniel Drew to whom the following verse is attributed:

He who sells what isn't his'n
Must pay up or go to prison.

If an individual is permitted to sell shares he does not own, he has to either have made a contract to borrow them for current delivery from a third party or the system is permitted to violate conservation. More shares can be sold than exist. If the short contract has an open date, then the calling of the short for delivery becomes part of the lender's strategy set.

The existence of active pure strategy N.E. in a k-period exchange model with complete futures markets (where a future is an exchange of a good now for a contract to deliver a good in the future) follows formally from Amir, Sahi, Shubik and Yao (1987). Existence where there are full futures traded in money follows from Dubey and Shubik (1978b). The more interesting open problem is to be able to characterize the relationship between the amount of a commodity money or credit needed for optimal financing and the configuration and number of futures markets. In business life comments are made about "minimizing or conserving the use of cash". The challenge is to give a precise operational meaning to this statement in the context of a multiperiod strategic market game.

6.7. An outside or central bank

In this and the next section the discussion is once more restricted to the single-period game. A way of running an exchange economy efficiently is by the use of fiat or outside money. Heuristically we may believe that in a mass economy the government's I.O.U. notes can be more generally acceptable than those of a stranger.

Three questions arise. How is the money introduced into the economy? How does it get out? What are the goals and role of the government?

We dispense with the last question first. The government may be regarded as an outside player or referee. Its purpose is to supply money to enable the traders to achieve optimal trade in the markets. If the government actually earns spending power through supplying money, then a convention for spending or disposing of this money must be given and in some sense justified. For example, it might wish to control the direction of growth in the economy.

Two models are noted and motivated. The first can be regarded as apparently nothing more than a reinterpretation of the same mathematical model discussed in Subsection 5.3 for every man his own banker. But the actual play of the game would be different.

6.7.1. The unlimited credit model

The government acts as referee, the single banker, clearinghouse and credit evaluator. Each trader is given a checkbook with bank checks. They can bid any amount they want, but at the end of the game must repay to the government any debt outstanding.[17] Failure to repay triggers a penalty.

In this model there is no limit to the volume of government credit that is issued. There is no charge for the government credit. But we can think of a slightly more complicated game where exogenously the government fixes a money rate of interest and policy as to how it will use its profits.

The game is as follows. The referee fixes $\rho, \mu^1, \mu^2, \ldots, \mu^n$ and

---

[17]To play this as a game it is possibly easiest to computerize the credit system and clearinghouse. An individual enters his name and amounts bid in each market. The system calculates prices and informs all players of their final balances. The government enforces the penalty. The fundamental modeling distinction between this and every man his own banker involves the concept of trust. But the intuitive idea that we trust the government paper more than individual paper is not modeled at this level of simplicity.

$p_1^*, p_2^*, \ldots, p_n^*$. ρ is the rate of interest charged, μ^i is the penalty for a unit of unpaid debt levied against trader i, and p_j^* is the price the referee is willing to pay any player for goods he wishes to give to the referee as payment of debt. A player i attempts to maximize

$$\varphi_i(x_1^i, x_2^i, \ldots, x_m^i) + \mu^i \min\left[0, -(1+\rho) \sum_{j=1}^m b_j^i + \sum_{j=1}^m p_j q_j^i + \sum_{j=1}^m p_j^* s_j^i\right].$$
(28)

A strategy by a trader is as in the two-sided Cournot market model. It is of the form $(b_1^i, q_1^i, \ldots, b_m^i, q_m^i)$, where $0 \le q_j^i \le a_j^i$ for $j = 1, \ldots, m$ and $0 \le b_j^i$, but as he has an open checkbook there is no bound on the sum of b_j^i. After the market prices have been formed and trade has taken place, the remaining part of the strategy of each individual i is that he decides upon a set of goods $(s_1^i, s_2^i, \ldots, s_m^i)$ to sell to the referee. Dubey and Shubik (1983) establish that for $\mu^i > 0$, for n types of traders, it is possible to select ρ and $p^* = (p_1^*, \ldots, p_m^*)$ to point the vector of leftover resources in any direction.

The interpretation of this model is that the referee can use its power to supply the means of payment, as a tax by charging a money rate of interest. The proceeds of the tax can be utilized to remove real resources at the end of the game. Thus, here the rate of interest and disposal prices are exogenous, and are used to control the direction of growth.

6.7.2. The fixed credit or fiat money model

A two-stage model with the government supplying a fixed amount of fiat money or credit has been given by Shubik and Wilson (1977) and Dubey and Shubik (1979). The distinction between this game and the previous one is that the relationship between the specific amount of money M in the economy and the severity of the default penalty $\mu^1, \mu^2, \ldots, \mu^n$ is critical in determining the possibility that some players may elect to go bankrupt for strategic reasons. The limit in the quantity of money places a bound on prices, but the bankruptcy penalty connects the shortfall in money to disutility, hence the strategic choice between the utility of an increased purchase versus the disutility of the penalty must be considered.

Figures 5.6(a) and 5.6(b) show the two-stage process. A player i first bids an amount of I.O.U. notes u^i in order to obtain his share of the fiat money M. For the game with a finite number of players one can consider a strategy where as information about the others is available after each player i has bid u^i the bids in the second stage $(b_1^i, \ldots, b_m^i)$ are all functions of the moves in the first stage. A simpler version is where a strategy by i is a vector $(u^i; b_1^i, \ldots, b_m^i)$, where it is assumed that i is uninformed of the actions of others, as Figure

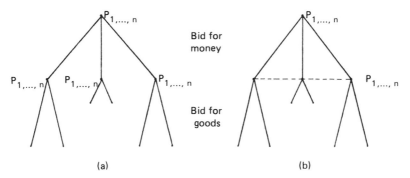

Figure 5.6

5.6(b), but he can bid fractions so that:

$$\sum_{j=1}^{m} b^i_j = s^i = \frac{u^i M}{\sum_{k=1}^{n} u^k} . \tag{29}$$

For simplicity it is assumed that all goods are put up for sale; thus, if the initial endowment of i is $(a^i_1, \ldots, a^i_m)$, then the jth market has $\sum_{i=1}^{n} a^i_j$. The Dubey–Shubik analysis is carried out in terms of a continuum of traders and it is shown that any C.E. can be obtained as a N.E. with an appropriate selection of the M and the default penalty. But if the default penalty is too low for some trader types, they will elect strategic bankruptcy and the money rate of interest, which is defined (in the continuum model) as

$$1 + \rho = \int u/M , \tag{30}$$

will be positive.

6.8. Inside banks

A common way to obtain credit is via a privately owned banking system, but the existence of a private banking system raises a host of new features. A partial list is suggested.
  (1) Who owns the banks?
  (2) If the banks have shares how are they paid for?
  (3) How many banks are needed for efficiency?
  (4) What is the goal of the bank?

(5) What determines the lending limit, if any?

(6) What is the strategy set of the bank?

The two fairly natural answers to Who owns the banks? are that either they are individually owned, as was the case with many merchant banks and banking families, or that they are owned by private stockholders. With the former one can argue for utility maximization by a special player. With the latter profit maximization for the stockholders needs to be justified as a goal.

If we adopt the view (confirmed even by casual empiricism) that the important and prevalent manifestation of bank ownership is via shares, then we need to introduce shares into the model and explain how they are distributed.

An underlying theme in banking and the extension of credit is the minimization of the need for individual trust. To a great extent a commodity money such as gold is a hostage which can be held as a substitute for trust. In a society with not enough gold to be an efficient commodity money we can economize on its use by creating a bank whose capital must be paid up in gold (or in fiat money if it exists and is trusted). If the individuals of the society are willing to abide by the rules and if the failure penalties are sufficiently harsh, then the money supply can be expanded by permitting a bank to lend some multiple $(k > 1)$ of its capital. This can be stated as a formal rule, but the justification of such a rule appears to lie in some form of risk assessment concerning the trust of banking.

The question of how many banks are needed for sufficient competition is linked to the nature of the strategic variables of the banks and the solution concept considered. It is argued here that the two main candidates for a model of bank strategy are the Cournot model, where the banks use the quantity of credit offered as the strategic variable, or the Bertrand–Edgeworth model, where the rate of interest is the strategic variable. For the first to attain efficiency necessarily requires a large number of banks; for the second it requires only two for an efficient noncooperative equilibrium solution.

With only two banks, even though a noncooperative equilibrium solution might include the competitive equilibria, it is possible that there might be a temptation to communicate directly and to collude.

Shubik (1976) somewhat nonrigorously has considered both the Cournot and Bertrand–Edgeworth models of banking. Figure 5.7 shows a Cournot model for the sale of shares and an interest rate setting model for bank competition. $P_{1,2,c}$ stands for both banks and a continuum of traders moving simultaneously. P_c and $P_{1,2}$ indicate the traders and the banks moving alone, respectively.

Consider an economy where a representative trader of type i has an initial endowment of $(a_1^i, a_2^i, \ldots, a_{m+1}^i)$, where the $m + 1$st commodity is gold which serves as a commodity money which is in short supply. Both banks put up all of their shares for sale. These can both be normalized to one. There are at least

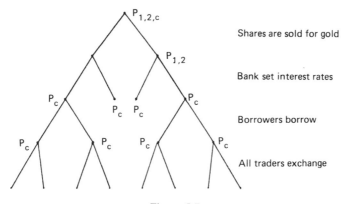

Figure 5.7

two individuals with gold. The referee or government has set two parameters k, the capital to lending ratio or reserve requirements. If capital is u, a bank can lend up to ku. The other parameter is μ, the failure to repay penalty; this could be made individual, $\mu^1, \mu^2, \ldots, \mu^n$, but this refinement does not appear to be needed for the one-stage game. (Although it does influence the range of the price system in equilibrium.) Furthermore, individual penalties, like purely individual taxes, appear to be administratively unwieldy. Historically there has been a split in the bankruptcy law into two sets: personal and corporate. In the model here neither dividends nor bank failure pose a problem as earnings (positive or negative) are flowed through to the stockholders without limited liability.

Let u_k^i be the amount of gold bid by a representative trader of type i for the shares of bank k, where $k = 1, 2$. Thus, traders of type i will obtain:[18]

$$w_k^i = u_k^i \Big/ \sum_{j=1}^{n} u_k^j .\tag{31}$$

The banks select rates of interest ρ_1 and ρ_2 at which they are prepared to lend up to ku_1 and ku_2, where u_j is the total capital of bank j.

The second move of a trader i is to ask for a loan of size g^i with the servicing rule that his bid goes to the bank with the lowest rate. If banks have the same rate the bid is split. If bank j has a higher rate than k, its demand is a decreasing function of $\rho_j - \rho_k$.

---

[18]The notation given is for a finite number of traders n which shows the structure. This can be replaced by n finite types with a continuum of traders.

Loan demand for bank j is:

$$\sum_{i=1}^{n} g^i, \qquad\qquad\qquad \text{for } \rho_j < \rho_k,$$

$$\sum_{i=1}^{n} g^i/2, \qquad\qquad\qquad \text{for } \rho_j = \rho_k, \qquad\qquad (32)$$

$$\max\left\{0, f\left[\left(\sum_{i=1}^{n} g^i - ku_k\right), (\rho_j - \rho_k)\right]\right\}, \quad \text{for } \rho_j > \rho_k.$$

There are many rationing mechanisms for oligopolistic demand [see Shubik (1959)], but the key driving force in obtaining a pure strategy equilibrium is the requirement that if there are t banks (here there are two), then at equilibrium:

$$k \sum_{\substack{i=1 \\ i \neq j}}^{t} u_i \geq \sum_{k=1}^{n} g^k, \quad \text{for } j = 1, \dots, t.$$

This states that the loan capacity for any $t-1$ banks is enough to satisfy all demand.

An individual i obtains the amount of money:

$$v^i = a^i_{m+1} - \sum_{j=1}^{2} u^i_j + g^i, \quad \text{if (33) holds}. \qquad\qquad (34)$$

In the third move of all traders they each bid and offer in all markets. Trader i bids $(b^i_1, q^i_1, \dots, b^i_m, q^i_m)$, where

$$\sum_{j=1}^{m} b^i_j \leq v^i \quad \text{and} \quad b^i_j \geq 0. \qquad\qquad (35)$$

At the end of the game all accounts are settled. If there is no bankruptcy, then the banks will liquidate, pay out profits and return capital to the investors. If the bank reserve money were fiat, that is enough to construct a game with a large enough reserve rate k to have any C.E. attainable as a N.E. If the reserve money is a commodity which enters the utility function, then one can approach efficiency as k becomes large, but not quite attain it. This has not yet been proved rigorously. The heuristic argument is if the reserve money has consumption value (say as jewelry, for example), then there is a utility loss while it is sterilized as bank reserves. This is the cost of liquidity as discussed in Subsection 6.6 in the model with monetary gold and jewelry.

6.8.1. *Comment on the uses of a central bank with private banks*

In the one-period model it is easy to build either an inside or outside banking system to finance trade with a zero money rate of interest. At the level of abstraction of general equilibrium theory there is no need to discuss the finer distinctions among the existence of markets, short sales, futures contracts, fiat money or bank money. In a multistage economy with differentiated strategic players a government will use its central bank for at least two purposes: control of the economy and to aid the efficient financing of trade. In general, even with control there will be a need to vary the money supply. This can be done by a central planning agency or via a set of private banks controlled by a few special weapons in control of the central bank. Two natural candidates are a reserve ratio and a reserve money rate of interest.

6.8.2. *Comment on the costs of banking*

An economic reason for having private banking is that the administrative, informational and other costs are such that the private system is more efficient than the central agency. Political and bureaucratic reasons concern the dilution of power.

The role of the nature of the actual costs of banking is central to these considerations. Part of conventional wisdom might argue for considerable increasing returns to scale in banking, like in a telephone network. Another temptation is to assume, as was done implicitly above, that banking is virtually costless. It has already been noted that the literature and annual reports indicate otherwise.[19]

7. Further directions

The discussion above has concentrated on the game theoretic and gaming applications applied primarily to the one-period exchange economy with and without the need for credit. This is only a start in the investigation of financial instruments and institutions designed to deal with long- and short-term lending, futures, insurance and other factors depending explicitly on the length of production, incomplete markets, transactions costs and exogenous uncertainty.

---

[19]See, for example, the proceedings of the annual conference on Bank Structure and Competition of the Federal Reserve Bank of Chicago started in 1963. Also see the annual reports of any major bank for a cost breakdown.

There are only a few papers on game theoretic applications of strategic market games to these broader problems. A brief commentary, together with some observations on some open problems, closes this survey.

7.1. Production

Dubey and Shubik (1978b) have constructed a strategic market game with a finite number of traders and firms with three stages: trade by all, production, and then trade by all. The existence of the N.E. is proved together with the convergence of the type symmetric noncooperative equilibria to the C.E. Problems with financing are avoided, shares are not actively traded, and it is assumed that firms maximize profits. In a separate paper Dubey and Shubik (1980a) examine the conditions required to have managers maximize profits as a sequence of finite economies approach that with a continuum. Intuitively a manager who owns a substantial part of a firm and uses its product could have three influences on his payoffs if he has market power, they are the substitution effect, the consumer income effect and the owner income effect. All three must attenuate.

In spite of these formal results and especially for the development of a theory of money and financial institutions there are two gaps of importance. There is no satisfactory model of stock voting and stock trading. Unless there is adequate stockholders protection [Shubik (1984a, pp. 574–577)] with voting stock there may easily be no equilibrium price system.[20] The premium paid for control in a takeover, leveraged buyout or tender offer may appear as disequilibrium behavior [see Herman and Lowenstein (1986)] but may be premia in a market where, because of inadequate rules, no pure strategy price equilibrium exists.

As was even indicated in Boehm-Bawerk (1923) and Wicksell (1935) in the development of a theory of capital, the length of production is of considerable importance. It is the length of production which causes much of the need for long-term finance and the length of the time of trade or exchange that causes much of the need for short-term finance. Given a structure of production through time one may wish to ask the analogous question: What is enough money to finance exchange in the one-period, one-stage model? That is, what constitutes enough money to finance multistage, multiperiod exchange and production? This question is also linked to concepts of liquidity and is not yet defined in a satisfactory manner.

---

[20]This can be seen by trying to model the cooperative game and showing that it has no core, unless the appropriate minority protection exists.

7.2. Transactions costs

7.2.1. A comment on exogenous and endogenous uncertainty

It is suggested that if there were absolutely no transactions costs, then there could be complete markets costlessly constructed; hence, exogenous uncertainty could be wiped out by completing markets in contingent trades. If, on the other hand, there is no exogenous uncertainty present but there are transactions costs, if the costs are high enough we may expect aggregate mechanisms to appear and markets to be endogenously incomplete. The uncertainty will be created. This suggests that even without exogenous uncertainty a theory of money and financial institutions is called for to account for the influence of strategic behavior and transactions costs.

An open question is how to characterize conditions where limited markets are superior to complete markets when transactions costs are present. A possible approach is to start with complete markets [Amir, Sahi, Shubik and Yao (1987)], add transactions costs [Rogawski and Shubik (1986)] and then attempt to examine the class of alternative incomplete market games.

7.2.2. On bankers

One simple manifestation of transactions costs is the emergence of brokers and other middlemen. These can be modeled directly. Nti and Shubik (1984) have considered exchange where the exchange must be carried through broker–dealers. A dealer is an individual who buys to resell, a broker is not a principal agent. He acts as agent or middleman serving both buyer and seller for a fee or share of the sale. The existence of equilibria and the convergence to zero profit of competitive dealers is established.

A natural extension of this model, which has not yet been carried out, is indicated as in Figure 5.8. Here the buyers and sellers have the option of

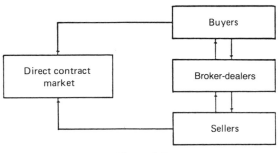

Figure 5.8

trading via brokers and dealers and electing a search mechanism [like that of Gale (1986a, 1986b), for instance], where, however, each encounter has a cost.

7.3. Bankruptcy and insolvency: Complete and incomplete markets

There are four major problems in the modeling of bankruptcy. They can be characterized by (1) the bankruptcy rule for a single-period game with a money and no exogenous uncertainty; (2) the rule for a single-period game with exogenous uncertainty; (3) the rule for bankruptcy, reorganization and insolvency in finite multiperiod game; and (4) the modeling of bankruptcy in infinite horizon models.

The first instance which arises from the need to bound strategic behavior enables us to define an optimal penalty as one which is sufficient to act as a disincentive to strategic default. It does not pay to elect to default. The discussion and analysis in Shubik and Wilson (1977) and Dubey and Shubik (1979) covers this.

When there is exogenous uncertainty without a market for every contingency new problems appear, when there is a random element to the payoffs an extremely harsh penalty may be sufficient to stop all borrowing, and a low enough penalty might stop all lending. A contemplation of inventory theory suggests that under virtually any criterion without infinite penalties an optimal policy should have a positive number of expected bankruptcies much of the time, and a game with an intermediate penalty should have equilibria which dominate the equilibria in games with extreme penalties. Dubey, Geanakoplos and Shubik (1989) have been able to establish this.

The multistage model introduces completely new considerations. At this point the economic welfare of the creditors as well as the fate of the debtors becomes relevant. In an ongoing economy an insolvent debtor may be given time to liquidate enough assets to pay his debts. A bankrupt may be reorganized or totally liquidated. An individual may have assets seized or his income garnished. In modeling these phenomena there is a temptation to become lost in detail, or alternatively to oversimplify by devices such as having simple extremely harsh penalties. No satisfactory treatment of this appears to have been given.

Another open problem is the treatment of bankruptcy in the infinite horizon model. The lack of a specific end together with the possibility for the rollover of loans opens up the opportunities for Ponzi games[21] and attempts to cover up inability to repay by increased borrowing.

---

[21]Named in honor of a great Boston swindler, Mr. Ponzi, who specialized in borrowing from B to pay A.

7.4. Incomplete markets and information

Dubey and Shubik (1977a, 1977b) considered games with an exogenous random move by Nature. Before all individuals move Nature selects one of k states. The traders may have any structure of information concerning the state selected by Nature.

If there are m commodities (other than money) and k states of Nature, then there may be as few as m or as many as mk trading posts depending upon the availability of contingent good markets.

A strategy by a trader consists of a set of moves (one in each market) contingent upon the information he has available prior to having to move.

It is proved that an active N.E. always exists for this game. Furthermore, if all are uninformed and all mk markets exist, then for many traders the C.E. of the Arrow–Debreu market with uncertainty will be approached by N.E.[22]

Regardless of the information conditions a price system always exists which reflects the lack of symmetry of information in the markets. It is also shown by example that more refined futures markets are not necessarily beneficial to all when traders have different information. There are instances where those who are less well informed prefer crude futures markets as it becomes more difficult to sell them worthless paper when there are more markets.

The strategic market game approach to nonsymmetric information is related to the work of Radner (1968, 1979).

A particularly difficult problem to consider is the sale of information and the meaning of the sale of information. A key difficulty in constructing market models for the sale of information comes in the description of the ownership and reproducibility of information viewed as an item of commerce. Shubik (1984b) has constructed a game where one set of players can sell refinements of information sets to others. Equilibrium may be destroyed by the possible sale of information. All may buy or none may buy. An example shows that the results depend on costs. Two problems emerge. The first concerns the rules of dissemination and appropriation and these are dealt with. The second is more fundamental: Is it information or interpretation and analysis that is sold? This has not been dealt with.

Dubey, Geanakoplos and Shubik (1987) have reconsidered the concept of rational expectations in the context of a strategic market game. The type of paradox suggested by Grossman and Stiglitz (1980) is not encountered. There are three basic problems which are encountered with the concept of rational expectations which can be misleading. (1) The idea that the uninformed can figure out what the price will be before they have moved. (2) The idea that the

---

[22]A key element is that all individuals must move simultaneously before price is formed as it is their moves which form price.

informed cannot profit from their information. And (3) the implicit assumption that there are enough participants that the informed will be unable to conceal usefully their knowledge.

It is the actions of individuals which form price; hence, in a simultaneous move game the price which ex post reveals to the uninformed what the informed know is *not* known ex ante. As soon as price formation is modeled as a well-defined mechanism of the game, no paradoxes appear. When there is a continuum of traders ex post the uninformed may now be informed but it is too late, the informed have made their profit. If there are situations where the continuum of agents hypothesis is unreasonable (such as assuming a continuum of central banks, commercial banks and insurance companies), then it is shown by example with the presence of large players their behavior at a N.E. need not reveal their information.

Strategic market games have also been employed by Peck and Shell (1985, 1986) [see also Cass and Shell (1983)] to investigate "sunspot equilibria" where it can be established that an event essentially exogenous to the economy can be used as a correlating device for a set of N.E. strategies.

An aside on insurance and competition

An important open problem in the study of risk, competition and insurance which is naturally formulated as a strategic market game is the tradeoff between the law of large numbers helpful in the providing of insurance and the number of insurance companies where the larger the number of firms, the more likely there will be competition. There is a tradeoff between the law of large numbers and the oligopoly effect which should produce an optimum number of insurance firms. This leaves aside the cooperative possibilities of reinsurance.

7.5. Dynamics

The general attitude adopted here is that except for one-person nonconstant sum games and two-person antagonistic games played repeatedly, the selection of the solution concept and the interpretation of the solution to a dynamic game should be regarded with great circumspection. Even when the markets are thick (modeled by a continuum of agents) the extreme simplicity of the models calls for care in the interpretation of results.

Shubik and Thompson (1959) in a dynamic one-person model have analyzed a *game of economic survival* which illustrates the potential differences in motivation which can arise when a firm must trade off the possibilities of bankruptcy against its ability to pay dividends in an uncertain environment. In essence the firm is regarded as having two accounts; a corporate account, which if depleted it is forced into bankruptcy, and a bank account paid to the owner. The latter represents the accrual of dividends. The maximization of the discounted expected value of the stream of dividends can be contrasted with the minimization of the probability of being ruined in a specified time. There is a close relationship between the policy for the maximization of expected discounted income and the avoidance of bankruptcy and an optimal inventory policy avoiding stockout penalties.[23]

An attempt to extend the analysis to two firms immediately runs into conceptual difficulties concerning the role of threat. When there are only few large players neither normative nor behavioral criteria currently suggested appear to be totally satisfying.

Shubik and Whitt (1973) have examined the simplest of strategic market games with an infinite horizon. Suppose that two individuals initially have $1 - \alpha - \gamma$ and $\alpha + \gamma$ units of paper money. Each period one unit of the (sole) consumer good is put up for sale. In period t the individuals bid x_t and y_t, respectively, and obtain $x_t/(x_t + y_t)$ and $y_t/(x_t + y_t)$, or zero if $x_t = y_t = 0$.

The ownership claims of the players to the income received by the market are $1 - \alpha$ and α, respectively, where $0 < \alpha < 1$, thus:

$$w_{t+1} = w_t - x_t + (1 - \alpha)(x_t + y_t) , \quad \text{where } w_1 = 1 - \alpha - \gamma , \tag{36}$$

and $0 \leq x_t \leq w_t$.

Each player i wishes to maximize

$$U_i = \sum_{t=1}^{\infty} \beta_i^{t-1} u_{it} , \quad \text{where } u_{1t} = x_t/(x_t + y_t) . \tag{37}$$

It is shown that for $\beta_1 = \beta_2 < 1$ a stationary state[24] is eventually reached with $u_1 = 1 - \alpha$ and $u_2 = \alpha$.

Define

$$c = \frac{1 - \alpha - \gamma}{1 - \alpha} .$$

Let $V_n(x, \gamma)$ represent the excess utility obtained by an individual starting with γ more money than his real good income in a game lasting n periods. It

---

[23]Further work on games of economic survival has been done by Miyasawa (1962) and Borch (1966). More recently Radner and Duffie have considered related problems and were able to extend the limited model of Shubik and Thompson considering continuous time.

[24]With $\beta_1 > \beta_2$ one may lose uniqueness [see Shubik and Whitt (1973)].

was shown that if $\beta_1 = 1$, then

$$V_n(p, \gamma) = n(1 - p)(1 - c^{1/n})$$

and

$$\lim V_n(x, \alpha) = -(1 - \alpha) \log\left(1 - \frac{\gamma}{1 - \alpha}\right).$$

The equilibrium analysis immediately extends to concave utility functions φ_i and to a continuum of traders. In this instance the money advantage ends after one period as all immediately spend all.

In his Ph.D. thesis, Housman (1983) has extended this model to include inside borrowing and lending in a money market. An endogenous rate of interest is obtained. There is an open credit market before bids are made. The market is the same type as the commodity market. I.O.U. notes are traded for money. In the Shubik–Whitt model with a finite number of players, hoarding could take place. With a continuum the advantage of extra money is cashed in immediately. With a loan market it is converted into an income stream via a rate of interest.

A major challenge is to extend these models to include not merely borrowing and lending, but also exogenous uncertainty. An important conceptual problem emerges concerning the relationship among the uses of markets and fiat money, banks and insurance companies.

One can ask specifically: How close a substitute for insurance is the use of fiat money and markets? Then, how much closer is lending for a specific number of periods? These problems are related to the work of Bewley (1980) and Friedman (1969). In a recent paper Shubik (1986a) has formulated this problem as a set of stochastic parallel dynamic programs, generalizing the Shubik–Whitt model. The basic model and observations are as follows. Suppose that there are many individuals who every period will have a claim to some of the goods being sold in the market. The claim of each individual is determined by the draw from an independent random variable. Each individual begins with an amount of fiat money and bids before he knows his income. Price is determined as in (1) and each obtains his income. The adding together of all of the goods offered for sale enables the market on the supply side to take advantage of the law of large numbers. No protection, however, is offered for the variability in the individual's income. Because the game is repeated, if there were no banking the individuals could achieve an extra level of self-insurance by utilizing the opportunities for a serial law of large numbers on their income. It is conjectured that as the number of individuals becomes large, each will be able to follow a stationary policy described by the solution to a set of one-person dynamic programs. Much of the money will be in hoard providing insurance. A distribution of wealth which over time maps into itself is expected.

Insurance would immediately supply the use of the cross-sectional law of large numbers for income and would be more efficient than hoarding. This assumes that insurance is a mechanism for public service and not a monopoly.

The introduction of bank loans poses several basic problems in modeling. A well-defined but not totally satisfactory model is that there is a single bank mechanism which accepts deposits and lends. It has an upper bound on debt to any individual and once that level is reached it garnishes all future income until fully paid back. The ability of the bank to provide insurance via deposits and loans can then be studied as a function of two parameters: ρ, the money rate of interest, and D, the upper bound on the amount of debt any individual can attain.

8. On minimal financial institutions

It is suggested here that as money and financial institutions serve both to facilitate trade and provide a control mechanism over the economy, a game theoretic approach is natural to many of the basic problems.

Much of microeconomic theory, including general equilibrium theory, is essentially oriented towards the study of short-term conscious optimization. Macroeconomics and development theory are aimed at a lower horizon and with a viewpoint that is more behavioral rather than strict optimization.

Money and financial institutions provide an important part of the mechanisms and carriers of process which tie in and help embed the economy, with its everyday short-term optimizing forces, into the polity with its concerns for control and the society which provides considerable special structure through custom, law and habit which delineates and constrains economic behavior.

As much as policymakers might like an all encompassing theory of economic dynamics, we do not have one. Furthermore [including structures such as that of Keynes (1936)] no grand theory of economic dynamics that has validity for more than a few years exists, or is likely to exist. Any theory of dynamics which purports to cover more than a few years is socio-economic and politico-economic. It depends heavily on its cultural and political environment. There is, however, a middle ground between the preinstitutional statics of general equilibrium and the grand dynamics of a Marx or Keynes. That middle ground involves the study of the logical and technological properties of the mechanisms required to connect economic life into its political and social environment. Because I believe that it is extremely important to avoid being prematurely trapped in institutional detail, the stress here is upon "unrealistic games", where the mechanisms for price formation, lending, borrowing, banking, insurance, brokering and dealing are minimal.

The advantages of simple playable games are even more than previously stated. There are at least four. The playability criterion provides a simple check for completeness and consistency and comprehensibility. The fact that the game is playable provides an opportunity for experimentation. The stress on simplicity maximizes the chances for analysis. Last, but definitely not least, is the feature that the simplicity of the mechanisms and the games is such that they are not easily mistaken for institutional reality. They avoid the air of apparent relevance to policy of the day.

The economic theorist qua theorist is not a policy advisor. His role is to further basic understanding and to be able to sort out the essence of economic problems and institutions from the relatively ephemeral trappings of current economic problems in a particular polity in a particular society. It is for this reason that the approach to the development of the theory of money and financial institutions is regarded as an exercise in mathematical institutional economics. Furthermore, the role of game theory is suggested as the natural tool to stress the strategic structure of any financial control system. Finally, strategic market games appear to offer the appropriate modeling methods for the development and the exploration of minimal financial institutions using some of the results of general equilibrium analysis as a reference point and a base from which one advances to a more structured understanding of process.

References

Amir, R., S. Sahi, M. Shubik and S. Yao (1987) 'A strategic market game with complete markets', Cowles Foundation Discussion Paper No. 813R, New Haven, CT. Forthcoming in *Journal of Economic Theory*.

Arrow, K.J. (1981) 'Pareto efficiency with costly transfers', in: J. Los et al., eds., *Studies in economic theory and practice*. Amsterdam: North-Holland.

Arrow, K.J. and G. Debreu (1954) 'Existence of an equilibrium for a competitive economy', *Econometrica*, 22: 265–290.

Aumann, R.J. (1964) 'Markets with a continuum of traders', *Econometrica*, 32: 39–50.

Bagehot, W. (1962, 1873) *Lombard Street*. Homewood, Illinois.

Benassy, J.P. (1986) 'On competitive market mechanisms', *Econometrica*, 54: 95–108.

Bewley, T. (1980) 'The optimum quantity of money', in: J.H. Kareken and N. Wallace, eds., *Models of monetary economies*. Minneapolis: Federal Reserve Bank, pp. 169–210.

Binmore, K. and M. Herrero (1984) 'Frictionless non-Walrasian markets', ICERD DP 84/103.

Black, F. (1970) 'A world without money', *Journal of Bank Research*, pp. 9–20.

Boehm-Bawerk, E. von (1923, Germ. 1891) *Positive theory of capital*. New York: G.E. Stechert and Co.

Borch, K. (1966) 'Control of a portfolio of insurance contracts', *The Astin Bulletin*, IV: 59–71.

Cass, D. and K. Shell (1983) 'Do sunspots matter?', *Journal of Political Economy*, 91: 193–227.

Debreu, G. (1959) *The theory of value*. New York: Wiley.

Dubey, P. (1982) 'Price quality strategic market games', *Econometrica*, 50: 111–126.

Dubey, P. and L.S. Shapley (1977) 'Noncooperative exchange with a continuum of traders', Discussion Paper 447, Cowles Foundation, Yale University.

Dubey, P. and M. Shubik (1977a) 'Trade and prices in a closed economy with exogenous uncertainty, different levels of information, money and compound futures markets', *Econometrica*, 45: 1657–1680.

Dubey, P. and M. Shubik (1977b) 'A closed economy with exogenous uncertainty, different levels of information, futures and spot markets', *International Journal of Game Theory*, 6: 231–248.

Dubey, P. and M. Shubik (1978a) 'The noncooperative equilibria of a closed trading economy with market supply and bidding strategies', *Journal of Economic Theory*, 17: 1–20.

Dubey, P. and M. Shubik (1978b) 'Production: a closed economic system with production and exchange modeled as a game of strategy', *Journal of Mathematical Economics*, 4: 253–287.

Dubey, P. and M. Shubik (1979) 'Bankruptcy and optimality in a closed trading mass economy modelled as a noncooperative game', *Journal of Mathematical Economics*, 6: 115–134.

Dubey, P. and M. Shubik (1980a) 'The profit maximizing firm: Managers and stockholders', *Economies et Societes* (Cahiers de l'Institute de Sciences Mathematiques et Economiques Appliquees, Serie EM No. 6, Laboratoire Associe au C.N.R.S.), 14: 1369–1388.

Dubey, P. and M. Shubik (1980b) 'A strategic market gme with price and quantity strategies', *Zeitschrift fur Nationalokonomie*, 40: 25–34.

Dubey, P. and M. Shubik (1983) 'The money rate of interest, capital stock and the financing of trade', Cowles Foundation Preliminary Paper 819518, Yale University, New Haven, CT.

Dubey, P., J. Geanakoplos and M. Shubik (1987) 'The revelation of information in strategic market games: A critique of rational expectations equilibrium', *Journal of Mathematical Economics*, 16: 105–138.

Dubey, P., J. Geanakoplos and M. Shubik (1989) 'Default and efficiency in a general equilibrium model with incomplete markets', Cowles Foundation Discussion Paper No. 879, New Haven, CT.

Dubey, P., A. Mas-Colell and M. Shubik (1980) 'Efficiency properties of strategic market games: An axiomatic approach', *Journal of Economic Theory*, 22: 339–362.

Dubey, P., S. Sahi and M. Shubik (1989) 'Repeated trade and the velocity of money', Cowles Foundation Discussion Paper No. 895, New Haven, CT.

Fama, E.F. (1980) 'Banking in the theory of finance', *Journal of Monetary Economics*, 6: 39–57.

Friedman, M. (1969) *The optimum quantity of money and other essays*. Chicago: Aldine.

Gale, D. (1982) *Money: In equilibrium*. Cambridge: Cambridge University Press.

Gale, D. (1986a) 'Bargaining and competition, Part I: Characterization', *Econometrica*, 54: 785–806.

Gale, D. (1986b) 'Bargaining and competition, Part II: Existence', *Econometrica*, 54: 807–818.

Gale, D. and M. Hellwig (1984) 'A general equilibrium model of the transactions demand for money', ICERD DP 84/100, London School of Economics.

Grossman, S.J. and J.E. Stiglitz (1980) 'On the impossibility of informationally efficient markets', *American Economic Review*, 70: 393–408.

Herman, E.S. and L. Lowenstein (1986) 'The efficiency effects of hostile takeovers: An empirical study', to appear in: *Proceedings of 1985 Takeover Conference*, Columbia University.

Housman, D.L. (1983) '*Some noncooperative game models of exchange*', Ph.D. Thesis Cornell University, Ithica, NY.

Hurwicz, L. (1960) 'Optimality and informational efficiency in resource allocation processes', in: K.J. Arrow, S. Karlin and P. Suppes, eds., *Mathematical methods in the social sciences*. Stanford: Stanford University Press, pp. 17–47.

Hurwicz, L. (1973) 'The design of mechanisms for resource allocation', *American Economic Review*, 63: 1–30.

Jaynes, G., M. Okuno and D. Schmeidler (1978) 'Efficiency in atomless economy with fiat money', *International Economic Review*, 19: 149:157.

Karaken, J.H. and N. Wallace, eds. (1980) *Models of monetary economies*. Minneapolis: Federal Reserve Bank.

Keynes, J.M. (1936) *The general theory of employment, interest and money*. London: Macmillan.

Keynes, J.M. (1973) *Collected works*, Vol. IV. London: Macmillan.

Koopmans, T.C. (1977) 'Concepts of optimality and their uses', *American Economic Review*, 67: 261–274.

Mayer, M. (1974) *The bankers*. New York: Random House.

Mayer, M. (1984) *The money bazaars*. New York: Mentor.

McKenzie, L.W. (1959) 'On the existence of general equilibrium for a competitive market', *Econometrica*, 27: 54–71.

Miyasawa, K. (1962) 'An economic survival game', *Journal of the Operations Research Society of Japan*, 2: 95–113.

Nti, K. and M. Shubik (1984) 'Noncooperative exchange using money and broker-dealers', *International Journal of Mathematical Social Science*, 7: 59–82.

Okuno, M. and D. Schmeidler (1986) 'Allocation rule using linear excess demand functions', in: W. Hildenbrand and A. Mas-Colell, eds., *Contributions to mathematical economics, in honor of Gerard Debreu*. Amsterdam: North-Holland, pp. 361–385.

Peck, J. and K. Shell (1985) 'Market uncertainty: Sunspot equilibria in imperfectly competitive economies', CARESS Working paper 85-22, University of Pennsylvania.

Peck, J. and K. Shell (1986) 'Market uncertainty: Correlated equilibrium and sunspot equilibrium in market games', European University Institute, Florence, EUI 86/244.

Pesek, B.P. (1976) 'Monetary theory in the post-Robinson "Alice-in-Wonderland" Era', *Journal of Economic Literature*, 14: 856–884.

Radner, R. (1986) 'Competitive equilibrium under uncertainty', *Econometrica*, 36: 31–58.

Radner, R. (1979) 'Rational expectations equilibrium: Generic existence and the information revealed by prices', *Econometrica*, 47: 655–678.

Rogawski, J. and M. Shubik (1986) 'A strategic market game with transactions costs,' *Mathematical Social Sciences*, 13: 139–160.

Rubinstein, A. and A. Wolinsky (1984) 'Equilibrium in a market with sequential bargaining', ICERD DP 83/91, London School of Economics.

Sahi, S. and S. Yao (1987) 'The noncooperative equilibria of a trading economy with complete markets and consistent prices', Cowles Foundation Discussion Paper No. 850R, New Haven, CT. Forthcoming in *Journal of Mathematical Economics*.

Scarf, H.S. (1986) 'Neighborhood systems for production sets with indivisibilities', *Econometrica*, 54: 507–532.

Scarf, H.S. with T. Hansen (1973) *The computation of economic equilibrium*. New Haven: Yale Univeristy Press.

Schmeidler, D. (1980) 'Walrasian analysis via strategic outcome functions', *Econometrica*, 48: 1585–1593 (earlier version 1973).

Shapley, L.S. (1976) 'Noncooperative general exchange', in: Lin, ed., *Theory of measurement of economic externalities*. New York: Academic Press, pp. 155–175.

Shapley, L.S. and M. Shubik (1977) 'Trade using one commodity as a means of payment', *The Journal of Political Economy*, 85: 937–968.

Shubik, M. (1959) *Strategy and market structure*. New York: Wiley.

Shubik, M. (1970) 'On different methods for allocating resources', *Kylos*, 23: 332–337.

Shubik, M. (1973) 'Commodity money, oligopoly, credit and bankruptcy in a general equilibrium model', *Western Economic Journal*, 10: 24–38.

Shubik, M. (1975) 'On the eight basic units of a dynamic economy controlled by financial institutions', *The Review of Income and Wealth*, Series 21: 183–201.

Shubik, M. (1976) 'A noncooperative model of a closed economy with many traders and two bankers', *Zeitschrift fur Nationalokonomie*, 36: 10–18.

Shubik, M. (1979) 'On the number of types of markets with trade in money: Theory and possible experimentation', in: V.L. Smith, ed., *Research in experimental economics*. Greenwich: Jai Press.

Shubik, M. (1982) *Game theory in the social sciences*, Cambridge, Mass.: M.I.T. Press.

Shubik, M. (1984a) *A game theoretic approach to political economy*. Cambridge, Mass.: MIT Press.

Shubik, M. (1984b) 'On the value of market information and rational expectations', in: H. Hauptmann, W. Krelle and K.C. Mosler, eds., *Operations research and economic theory*. New York: Springer-Verlag, pp. 119–134.

Shubik, M. (1986a) 'Strategic market games: A dynamic programming application to money banking and insurance', *Mathematical Social Sciences*, 12: 265–278.

Shubik, M. (1986b) 'A note on enough money in a strategic market game with complete or fewer markets', *Economic Letters*, 19: 231–235.

Shubik, M. and G.L. Thompson (1959) 'Games of economic survival', *Naval Logistics Research Quarterly*, 6: 111–123.

Shubik, M. and W. Whitt (1973) 'Fiat money in an economy with one nondurable good and no credit', in: A. Blaquiere, ed., *Topics on differential games*. Amsterdam: North-Holland, pp. 401–448.

Shubik, M. and C. Wilson (1977) 'The optimal bankruptcy rule in a trading economy using fiat money', *Zeitschrift fur Nationalokonomie*, 37: 337–354.

Shubik, M. and S. Yao (1989) 'Gold, liquidity and secured loans in a multistage economy, Part 1: Gold as money', Cowles Foundation Discussion Paper No. 871R, New Haven, CT.

Smale, S. (1976) 'A convergent process of price adjustment and global Newton methods', *Journal of Mathematical Economics*, 3: 1–14.

Walras, L. (1954, Fr. 1874) *Elements of pure economics*. London: Allen & Unwin.

Wicksell, K. (1935) *Lectures on political economy*. Vol. 2: Money. London: Routledge & Kegan Paul.

Yao, S. (1987) 'On Strategic Market Games', PhD. Dissertation, University of California, Los Angeles.

PART 3

MONEY IN DYNAMIC SYSTEMS

Chapter 6

MONEY, INFLATION AND GROWTH

ATHANASIOS ORPHANIDES and ROBERT M. SOLOW*

Massachusetts Institute of Technology

Contents

*We thank Frank Hahn and Michael Woodford for helpful comments.

Handbook of Monetary Economics, Volume I, Edited by B.M. Friedman and F.H. Hahn

0. Introduction

"My main conclusion is that equally plausible models yield fundamentally different results", wrote Jerome Stein in the introduction of his 1970 survey of monetary growth theory. Two decades later all we have is more reasons for reaching the same conclusion.

Is it possible to affect capital accumulation and output by actions that merely change the rate of growth of the stock of nominal money? If there are such effects, will they be permanent, affecting steady-state outcomes, or merely transitory during the transition to the same (real) steady state? The question regarding the superneutrality[1] of money is concerned with the effects of money growth on any real variables in the economy but the possible effects on capital, output and welfare are of greatest interest.

The modern literature really begins with Tobin, who asked the question that has mainly preoccupied the literature ever since 1965. Different long-run rates of growth of the money supply will certainly be reflected eventually in different rates of inflation; but will there be any *real* effects in the long run? Tobin studied this ("superneutrality") question in a simple "descriptive" model with aggregate saving depending only on current income, and seigniorage distributed in such a way as to preclude any distributional effects. He found that faster money growth is associated with higher capital stock and output per person in the steady state. Faster inflation leads savers to shift their portfolios in favor of real capital.

Sidrauski soon embedded the same problem in a model of an immortal consumer maximizing an additive discounted lifetime utility. Then, the steady-state real interest rate can be the utility-based discount rate. If the marginal product of capital depends only on the capital–labor ratio, then capital per person is tied down asymptotically, independently of money growth or inflation. In the Sidrauski model superneutrality prevails.

The later literature is mostly variations on this theme. If the production function is such that the marginal product of capital depends on other things besides the capital intensity of production, then superneutrality can fail. If agents differ in essential ways (including date of birth), constancy of consumption per head is not the same thing as constant consumption during a lifetime; again superneutrality may fail. For the same reason, the distribution of

---

[1]A model is said to exhibit money neutrality if a change in the *level* of nominal money does not affect real variables. Superneutrality applies the same concept to changes in the *rate of growth* of nominal money. In this survey we are only concerned with the superneutrality of money and, as a result, we follow much of the literature in dropping the prefix "super" from references to the word superneutral.

seigniorage proceeds can disturb superneutrality: the aggregate saving rate depends on the stage of the life cycle in which (anticipated) benefits from seigniorage are received.

The main lessons were thus already implicit in the work of Tobin and Sidrauski. For those who can bring themselves to accept the single-consumer, infinite-horizon, maximization model as a reasonable approximation to economic life, superneutrality is a defensible presumption. All others have to be ready for a different outcome.

This is the basic message we attempt to convey in the review of the monetary growth theory that follows. In Section 1 we develop the neoclassical Tobin model and the parallel non-optimizing, non-neoclassical theory that was developed and became known as the Keynes–Wicksell model. In Section 2 we examine the Sidrauski model illustrating the central neutrality result and then show some of its variations in which neutrality with respect to output fails even though the real interest rate is not affected by inflation (in the long run, of course). The Fisher relation is closely examined in Section 3 which concentrates on deviations from the one infinitely lived family models of Section 2. The exact function of money and the sensitivity of the long-run inflation–growth relation to different assumptions about the reasons why money is held are examined in Section 4.

Before embarking on the main theme, we close the introduction by briefly going over some themes that provide a background for what follows.

0.1. Prior beliefs about inflation

Is inflation "good" or "bad"? All three possibilities serve as reasonable priors:

(a) Inflation has no effect on any real variables. How could little green (or other colored) pieces of paper make a real difference anyway?

(b) Tobin's portfolio shift effect: non-interest-bearing money *is* held as an asset, so if we can induce people to hold less of it they will keep their savings in more productive forms. Hence, some inflation increases capital per man and therefore output per man along the growth path (though not the rate of real growth, of course).

(c) Inflation is bad, period. Whatever the function of money is, it becomes harder to sastisfy in the presence of inflation, especially rapid inflation. This is an interesting prior since it is the one held by virtually every policy-maker. Furthermore, the reasons this view is held have nothing to do with the money and growth literature. We know of no study of hyperinflations that mentions the Tobin effect! If the money and growth literature is relevant to anything, this must be where it fits in. (Of course, there never was any implication that the Tobin effect would outweigh the disorganizing consequences of very rapid inflation.)

0.2. Related questions

To the extent that money growth may affect some real variables, is there an optimal rate of growth of money (and therefore inflation) that maximizes welfare? Indeed, whether inflation is positively or negatively related to output in the long run is beside the point if our objective is to maximize not output but something else. The chapter by Woodford on the optimum quantity of money in this Handbook (Chapter 20) deals with this issues in more detail, but for our purposes it should be noted that if money is not superneutral and an optimal rate of growth does exist, the optimal rate may not be the one maximizing output. Thus, the money and growth question is intimately connected with the optimal rate of inflation question.

Does the Fisher relation hold? An answer to this is a byproduct of the money and growth models since the main mechanism for non-neutrality is the effect of inflation on the real rate of interest. As we make clear in Sections 2 and 3, it is also useful to distinguish between mechanisms that exhibit non-neutrality while not invalidating the Fisher relation from those that invalidate the Fisher relation as a means of obtaining non-neutrality.

The money and growth literature is primarily concerned with the question of whether money is neutral across steady states, but it is important to consider the other questions as well in order to understand the development of the literature. Unlike current practice, the same models were sometimes used to examine the short-run employment effects of money as well as the long-run output effects (the catchword is "Keynes–Wicksell models"). Currently, the short-run effects of money are usually analyzed within models that either ignore the long-run neutrality question or assume it to begin with. Other chapters in this Handbook deal explicitly with such short-run models.

0.3. Evidence

Monetary events seem to have effects in the short run. That much seems to be well established. The Phillips curve – to the extent that it is still considered a useful device – is exactly about the relation between output and inflation in the short run. Recently a series of VAR models have been used to illustrate empirically just this short-run relation. Evidence on the long-run relationships is by far more difficult to find. Using long time series data for the United

States, Geweke (1986) finds evidence in support of the superneutrality of money on output. Restricting attention to post war U.S. data, Jun (1988) finds a strong negative correlation between money and output growth. Fischer (1983), in a cross-section time-series regression for 53 countries, reports a negative relationship between inflation and growth. Both the Jun and Fischer results imply anti-Tobin failure of superneutrality conditional on the identifying assumption of the money growth being exogenous in the long run. As Jun makes clear, however, his results may simply be due to a monetary policy rule which is negatively related to output. Since neither study accounts for supply side/productivity shocks and the low growth post-oil shock period of coincides with worldwide high inflation, the results may indeed reflect monetary accommodation of these shocks.

Evidence on whether the Fisher relation is satisfied in the long run also provides information about the long-run neutrality of money. Empirical results for the United States indicate that the hypothesis that the Fisher relation is satisfied in the long run is not rejected. Yet, there is little power against the alternative that inflation has a small effect on the real interest rate [Gali (1988)].

0.4. The role of money in the real economy

In order to make sense out of any theory attempting to examine the possible effects of changing the level/rate of growth of money on real variables, one must first explain the very existence of money in the economy. Why are people willing to hold money and what is its function? Depending on the choice of first principles given and the exact way in which the underlying relationship between money and real variables is postulated, we should expect to and do get different conclusions regarding the effect of money on real variables. Various assumptions are encountered in the models we examine here. The following checklist is intended only as a reminder; the fundamental nature of money is not our business.

- Money is an asset and can be used as a store of wealth. It is held as part of an individual's portfolio because of its rate of return characteristics.
- Money is an asset that facilitates intergenerational transfers. It is held simply because it is known that others will be willing to hold it in the future.
- Money is necessary for transactions. Money must be held for some period of time before a purchase takes place. Either the time it must be held is kept fixed (the one-period cash-in-advance constraint) or it is an endogenous decision within a Baumol–Tobin model of money demand.
- Money facilitates transactions. It is a substitute for leisure or real output in the available "transactions technology".

- Money is a factor of production in much the same way that labor and capital are. It is an inventory.
- Money is an argument in utility: people derive utility from holding money in much the same way as they derive utility from consuming real goods.

It is clear that the last three are shortcuts for the deeper reasons that are given in the first three arguments and unfortunately the results of monetary growth models are quite sensitive to them. This problem was recognized quite early in the literature. Dornbusch and Frenkel (1973), for instance, state, "[C]onflicting or ambiguous results derived from alternative theories are primarily the reflection of different hypotheses about the functions of money" (p. 141).

0.5. The origins of the money and growth literature

The basic mechanism used to link money and growth is through the effects of money on the real interest rate and thereby on capital accumulation. Metzler (1951) points out that the central bank can affect the real interest rate through money market operations and concludes:

> [B]y purchasing securities, the central bank can reduce the real value of private wealth, thereby increasing the propensity to save and causing the system to attain a new equilibrium at a permanently lower interest rate and a permanently higher rate of capital accumulation (p. 112).

Thus, Metzler, in his attempt to explain why the real interest rates is a *monetary* variable, offers the first concrete model in which money can affect output in the long run. Note, however, that Metzler's monetary effect is severely limited by the securities that can ultimately be bought by the central bank through open market operations and is incomplete because he does not examine the effects of inflation on the interest rate (and does not even distinguish between a real and a nominal rate). In fact growth-theoretic concepts are ignored: a "higher rate of capital accumulation" means higher current real investment, not a higher sustainable growth rate.

Mundell (1963) was the first to propose a connection between anticipated inflation and the real interest rate. His argument basically concerns the *impact* effect of an unanticipated permanent increase in the inflation rate. The impact effect is a reduction in the real wealth of individuals which increases their real savings thereby increasing capital and reducing the real interest rate. This, however, is a short-run effect that cannot be expected to affect the steady-state rate of interest.

1. The Tobin effect

It was not until Tobin's (1965) exposition that the portfolio mechanism connecting money growth and capital formation became clear.[2,3] His model is based on the one-sector neoclassical growth model of Solow (1956) and Swan (1956). Output is produced with a linear homogeneous production function so that real net per capita output, y, is:[4]

$$y = f(k) . \tag{1.1}$$

In the non-monetary model, capital, k, is the only form of wealth. In the simplest monetary growth model real per capita money balances, m, are introduced as an alternative form of wealth. Thus, real wealth kept in the form of financial assets, a, is:

$$a = k + m . \tag{1.2}$$

Tobin's basic intuition that became the central issue of all the subsequent literature can be simply stated as follows. Given a level of real wealth, the capital intensity of the economy depends on the composition of wealth among capital and money. If the return of holding money as a financial asset is reduced, the relative composition of assets will shift towards capital, thereby increasing output. The opportunity cost of holding money instead of capital is $r + \pi$, the real rate of return on capital[5] plus inflation,[6] which is the rate of depreciation of the real value of money holdings. Therefore, by increasing the rate of inflation the central bank can shift the composition of financial holdings towards capital.

Clearly, then, if asset holdings remains constant, an increase in the rate of inflation would increase equilibrium capital and output. The level of wealth is, however, an endogenous variable dependent on the saving behavior of the individual and bound to change with inflation. If saving behavior is such that, in equilibrium, wealth is decreased by exactly the same amount that real

---

[2]Some of the analysis, however, follows directly from his earlier papers [Tobin (1955, 1961)].

[3]Other early treatments along the same lines include Johnson (1966, 1967a, 1967b), Sidrauski (1967b) and Tobin (1968). Stein (1966, 1968) also obtained the Tobin effect, but not in a neoclassical framework.

[4]Net output equals gross output minus the linear depreciation of capital. The usual convention of employing lower-case letters as the per capita counterparts of their aggregate counterparts is employed.

[5]In equilibrium r is the marginal product of capital, $f'(k)$.

[6]We assume perfect foresight and we will therefore make no distinction between expected and actual inflation. We will return to this assumption when discussing the dynamics of these models.

money holdings are reduced due to the portfolio selection behavior, then inflation will have no effect on capital intensity; in other words, neutrality will hold. Therefore, it is the interaction of the portfolio composition effect and saving behavior that determines the extent of the effect of inflation on capital.

1.1. The neoclassical model

Following the original non-monetary growth model, Tobin assumed that real private savings are a fixed proportion of real disposable income.[7] Real disposable income is defined to be real output plus the increase in real cash balances (which in turn is the sum of the real value of seignorage – transferred by the government to the private sector – and real capital gains on initial money holdings). Real investment is then the part of real savings that it not absorbed by increases in real cash balances. Thus

$$\dot{K} = s\left(Y + \left(\frac{\dot{M}}{P}\right)\right) - \left(\frac{\dot{M}}{P}\right),\tag{1.3}$$

where P is the price level. Letting θ and n denote the rate of growth of nominal money and the rate of growth of labor, (1.3) can be written in per capita terms as

$$\dot{k} = sy - (1 - s)(\theta - \pi)m - nk .\tag{1.4}$$

Since m is real per capita money balances ($m = M/PN$), it evolves through time according to

$$\dot{m} = m \cdot (\theta - \pi - n) .\tag{1.5}$$

In the steady state,[8] $\pi = \theta - n$ and the steady-state relation between real money balances and capital that is implied by the savings behavior is:

$$0 = sf(k) - (1 - s)nm - nk .\tag{1.6}$$

It is immediately clear from (1.6) that in this case anything that reduces equilibrium real money balances in the steady state will result in a higher level of capital.[9] The model described by (1.3) and (1.4) does not indicate the

---

[7]Hadjimichalakis (1971b) examines several variations of the Tobin model that share the assumption of savings as a fixed proportion of income.

[8]Dynamics and stability issues are briefly discussed later.

[9]Provided that the usual non-monetary stability condition holds, that is $s \cdot f'(k) - n < 0$.

preferences of owners of wealth regarding the form in which they wish to hold their wealth. The model can be closed by specifying a money demand equation[10] capturing the portfolio decision, for instance:

$$m = \phi(r + \pi) \cdot k , \quad \phi' < 0 , \tag{1.7}$$

and the steady-state equilibrium level of capital in terms of the rate of money growth is given by

$$0 = s \cdot f(k) - (1 - s) \cdot n \cdot \phi(f'(k) + \theta - n) \cdot k - n \cdot k , \tag{1.8}$$

so that $dk/d\theta$ is positive.

The assumption that savings is proportional to income results in the most unambiguous statement of the Tobin effect. The portfolio equation (1.7), for example, could be replaced with a quantity theory (or transactions) demand for money of the form:

$$m = \phi(r + \pi) \cdot y \tag{1.9}$$

or

$$m = \phi(r + \pi) \cdot c ,$$

without changing the result since y is a monotone function of k and in equilibrium c increases with y.

The Tobin effect continues to prevail when the fixed savings rate assumption is replaced with a lifecycle based consumption function which makes consumption a function of wealth:

$$c = c(a) , \quad c' > 0 . \tag{1.10}$$

Since, in the steady-state, equilibrium consumption equals net output, if assets are given by (1.2) and the demand for money by (1.7), then the steady-state relation between the rate of money growth and output is given by

$$f(k) = c([1 + \phi(f'(k) + \theta - n)] \cdot k) , \tag{1.11}$$

and again $dk/d\theta > 0$, at any stable steady state.[11]

---

[10] The implication of (1.7) is that the capital market clears instantaneously, with the price level adjusting to equate the demand for money with the supply. The alternative would be to hypothesize slow adjustment of the price level in response to a gap between the right- and left-hand sides of (1.7). Obviously, this would make no difference in steady states.

[11] See Dornbusch and Frenkel (1973) for details on this example.

The Tobin effect, however, is not robust to other seemingly minor modifications of the model. Even under the original assumption of a fixed savings rate out of income, differences in the definition of disposable income – to allow for the services of money balances, for example – could qualitatively change the result.[12] More importantly, however, the effect may be reversed if the assumption of the constancy of the savings rate is relaxed. While for the growth models that simply attempt to relate the rate of savings to growth this assumption may be appropriate, it is totally inappropriate when the interaction between portfolio choice and savings is important.[13] If, for example, savings is discouraged by inflation, the result may be reversed. Levhari and Patinkin (1968) specify the savings rate as a function of the rates of return of the two assets:

$$s = s(r, -\pi), \quad s_1 > 0, s_2 > 0, \tag{1.12}$$

and show that the Tobin effect becomes ambiguous. In the same spirit, Dornbusch and Frenkel specify:

$$c = c(a, \pi), \quad c_1 > 0, \tag{1.13}$$

and show that if inflation has a strong positive effect on consumption demand the Tobin result is reversed.

The most far-reaching criticism, however, was with regard to the exact function of money in the model. Levhari and Patinkin observed that the role of money in Tobin's model is not sufficiently explained. To the extent that Tobin's mechanism was based on portfolio selection and money is an asset that can be dominated, the model should say why money is held in the first place. In Tobin's original formulation the highest level of steady-state capital is achieved when money balances are actually driven to zero. In that case (1.6) collapses to

$$0 = s \cdot f(k) - n \cdot k, \tag{1.14}$$

which is the non-monetary growth model condition of Solow (1956). Levhari and Patinkin suggested treating money as either a consumption good or a production good and showed that, in each case, the Tobin effect does not obtain unambiguously. They justified their treatment by referring to the

---

[12] The starting point was the exchange between Johnson, (1966, 1967a, 1967b) and Tobin (1967). See also Bailey's (1968) and Marty's (1968) comments on Tobin (1968). More recently the issue has been examined by Hayakawa (1979), Bandyopadhyay (1982) and Drabicki and Takayama (1982).

[13] Johnson (1966) first raised this criticism.

optimizing behavior of firms and consumers, but without giving any detailed account of decisions. In Section 2 we turn to models that address this objection and examine the inflation and growth connection in an explicitly optimizing framework in which money is assumed to provide consumption or production services. But first we turn to a brief discussion of the stability properties of the neoclassical model – an issue which haunted the early literature – and examine a parallel literature which examines the monetary growth issue in the absence of the neoclassical assumption of instantaneously clearing markets.

1.2. On stability and uniqueness

The primary objective of this paper is to examine the effects of anticipated inflation on capital accumulation in the stationary state of the economy. We do not attempt to analyze the dynamic implications of the models we discuss, even though they are of at least as great importance. The issue of stability of the stationary equilibrium, however, cannot be avoided since instability would render the stationary state analysis irrelevant. Simply, a change in inflation would not move the economy to the new stationary state, even in the long run.

As was pointed out by Nagatani (1970), Tobin's model exhibits saddlepoint instabily under the assumption of perfect myopic foresight. At the time this was considered to be a fatal flaw of the model since it implied that an economy subject to a perturbation from the steady state – due to an increase in the rate of money growth, for example – would not reach the new steady state if it followed the dynamic path that originated at the old equilibrium. As a result, several modifications of the model were suggested that led to global stability. Most notably, it was pointed out by Sidrauski (1976b) that if expectations are formed adaptively and at a sufficiently slow rate, then the model is globally stable. This, however, did not solve the problem under the presently more popular assumption of perfect foresight. The active versus passive money debate [Olivera (1971), Black (1972)] showed that global stability could be achieved if money is assumed to be passive, with the strange implication that if money is actively used as a policy instrument the economy is unstable, whereas if it is not, then the economy is stable. Most other attempts to achieve global stability, while retaining the perfect foresight assumption, proved fruitless.[14]

Sargent and Wallace (1973) provided an alternative way of approaching the stability issue. They showed that under the perfect foresight assumption the model should exhibit saddlepoint stability if there is to be a unique path to the

---

[14]The exceptions are Hadjimichalakis (1971a, 1971b), Hadjimichalakis and Okuguchi (1979), Burmeister and Dobell (1970) and Drabicki and Takayama (1984), in which global stability is achieved by introducing other elements to the model.

steady state. In a model with a unique steady state, like the Tobin model, an unanticipated perturbation from the steady state should be followed by an instantaneous "jump" to a path that leads to the new steady state. Unless the model exhibits saddlepath stability, the "jump" to the new equilibrium path cannot be uniquely determined. The difference from the earlier interpretation arises from the fact that perfect foresight is assumed to be global and not myopic. As a result the saddlepoint stability of the Tobin model is no longer considered a liability. Note, however, that the attractiveness of the Sargent–Wallace interpretation is due to the resulting uniqueness of the equilibrium path. Yet, Black (1974), Brock (1974) and Calvo (1979) show that steady states could have multiple perfect foresight paths in some models. Calvo presents examples of cases in which no perfect foresight path is locally unique. The resolution of the dynamics in those cases has not yet been worked out to everyone's satisfaction. It involves larger issues than those discussed here.

1.3. The Keynes–Wicksell model

An alternative to the neoclassical monetary models was developed by Rose (1966) and Stein (1966).[15] These models, inspired by the work of Hahn (1960, 1961), constitute an attempt to reconcile the short-run disequilibrium dynamics of the economy with long-run growth. In the Keynesian tradition the economy is not assumed always to be in equilibrium; thus, the models can accommodate variable employment and underutilization of capital. Two key characteristics distinguish these models from the neoclassical model:

(a) there are independent investment and savings function[16] – whereas in the neoclassical market-clearing model investment is identically equal to planned savings, and

(b) prices are changing if and only if there is market disequilibrium – whereas in the neoclassical model markets are always in equilibrium regardless of the level of inflation.

The effect of inflation on steady-state capital in these models turns out to depend on the particular assumptions that are needed in addition to the ones specified above in order to close the model. Stein (1971) builds a model in which the effect depends on whether there is forced saving or saving plans are realized in the steady state. This is partly due to the assumption, shared by most K–W models, that inflation is proportional to excess demand. Excess aggregate demand equals planned consumption plus planned investment less

[15]Other examples include Rose (1969), Stein (1969, 1970, 1971), Nagatani (1969), Tsiang (1969), Hahn (1969) and Fischer (1972).
[16]The "Keynes" part of the model. Other Keynesian features are also incorporated by some authors.

output, $c + i - y$. Since planned savings equals $y - c$, the price dynamics are given by

$$\pi = \lambda \cdot (i - s) . \tag{1.15}$$

The unpleasant implication of this specification is that inflation, even in the steady state, requires unfulfilled demand. Output must be rationed between investment and consumption and the choice of rationing scheme turns out to be one of the determining factors of the steady-state characteristics of the model. A more reasonable alternative, due to Stein (1971) and Fishcher (1972), takes the view that only unexpected inflation is due to market disequilibrium:

$$\pi = \pi^* + \lambda \cdot (i - s) . \tag{1.16}$$

In the long run, $\pi = \pi^*$ and there is no discrepancy between planned and actual savings nor between planned and actual consumption. With perfect foresight, however, π is always equal to π^* and (1.16) implies that the market is always in equilibrium, which effectively transforms the model to a market-clearing one. Reconciliation of short-run disequilibrium and long-run equilibrium is possible if expectations are formed in alternative ways, for example adaptively:

$$\dot{\pi}^* = \beta \cdot (\pi - \pi^*) . \tag{1.17}$$

Following Fischer (1972) we can specify the investment demand function as a stock adjustment demand:

$$i = nk + \phi(k^{\mathrm{d}} - k) , \quad \phi' > 0 , \tag{1.18}$$

where the desired capital stock, k^{d}, is assumed to depend positively on the difference between the expected nominal return on capital, $f'(k) + \pi^*$, and the nominal interest rate, ρ:[17]

$$k^{\mathrm{d}} = k(f'(k) + \pi^* - \rho) , \quad k' > 0 . \tag{1.19}$$

The nominal interest rate, ρ, is determined by equilibrium in the bond market, where the demand for bonds is:

$$b^{\mathrm{d}} = b(f(k) + \pi^*, \rho, k + m) , \quad b_1 < 0, b_2 > 0, b_3 > 0 , \tag{1.20}$$

---

[17]This is the "Wicksell" feature of the model.

and the supply of bonds, b^s, is exogenously given ($b^s = 0$, for example, if we want to examine an economy without bonds).

The implications of this model are examined in Fischer (1972) who shows that despite the alternative characterization of the short-run dynamics, the effect of inflation on steady-state capital accumulation is positive, as in the neoclassical model. So long as market disequilibrium is limited to the short-run dynamics of K–W models, the steady-state effect of inflation on capital seems not to be significantly different from the neoclassical model.[18,19]

2. Money in the utility and production function

2.1. The Sidrauski model

The first formulation of a monetary growth model in an explicitly optimizing framework is due to Sidrauski (1967a). His formulation is based on Ramsey's classic (1928) paper on optimal savings behavior and as a result it resolves the objection to non-optimizing models. An infinitely-lived growing family maximizes the utility of its members by solving an intertemporal maximization problem. Money is introduced by assuming that in addition to consumption, utility is derived from the flow of services derived from real money holdings. The utility functional to be maximized is then:

$$W = \int_0^\infty u(c_t, m_t) \cdot e^{-\delta t} \, dt \,, \tag{2.1}$$

where δ is the rate of time preference of the family.[20] At each point in time real non-human wealth, a, is allocated between capital and real cash balances as in (1.2) which is rewritten here for convenience:

$$a = k + m \,. \tag{2.2}$$

Real per capita assets accumulate according to

$$\dot{a} = f(k) + x - c - n \cdot a - \pi \cdot m \,, \tag{2.3}$$

[18]There are, however, exceptions to this statement. See, for example, the models in Stein (1971).
[19]See also Hayakawa (1986) who reaches a similar conclusion in an optimizing model with disequilibrium dynamics.
[20]Unless otherwise specified the notation is the same as in the previous section. In particular, lower-case letters denote per capita quantities. As before, most time subscripts are suppressed.

where x denotes government transfers.[21,22] The objective, then, is to maximize the welfare functional (2.1) subject to the stock constraint (2.2) and the flow constraint (2.3). To solve the problem we write the present value Hamiltonian:

$$\mathcal{H} = u(c, m) + q \cdot (f(k) + x - \pi \cdot m - c - a \cdot n) + \lambda \cdot (a - k - m) , \quad (2.4)$$

where q is the costate variable associated with the flow constraint (2.3) and λ is the Lagrangian multiplier associated with the stock constraint. Necessary conditions for an internal solution are:

$$\dot{q} = (\delta + n) \cdot q - \lambda , \quad (2.5)$$

$$q \cdot f_k - \lambda = 0 , \quad (2.6)$$

$$u_m - q \cdot \pi - \lambda = 0 , \quad (2.7)$$

$$u_c - q = 0 . \quad (2.8)$$

Substitution of (2.6) into (2.5) gives:

$$\dot{q} = (\delta + n - f_k) \cdot q , \quad (2.9)$$

which determines the steady-state rate of interest:

$$f_k = \delta + n . \quad (2.10)$$

Sidrauski's startling result was that in this simple optimizing monetary growth model the real rate of interest is independent of inflation and the rate of money growth.[23] Furthermore, since, in this model, there is a unique mapping from the marginal product of capital to the level of capital intensity, capital is also independent of inflation. Thus, money is superneutral[24] and the Tobin effect is invalidated.

---

[21] In equation (2.3) assets accumulate due to the return of holding capital, $f(k)$, and government transfers, x. They decumulate due to consumption, c, and the (negative) return on real money holdings, $\pi \cdot m$. The remaining term, $n \cdot a$, simply reflects the required asset accumulation that is necessary to retain a per capita level of assets in the presence of population growth.

[22] It is straightforward to set up the model as a decentralized competitive economy. We set up a command economy here for simplicity. The two problems have the same solution.

[23] Although, as shown by Fischer (1979), this holds only in the steady state. We return to this result in the next section.

[24] Inflation, however, does affect the demand for real balances, m, and affects welfare since money is an argument in the utility function. These issues are discussed in more detail elsewhere in the Handbook.

There are several ways to identify the cause of the difference in the Sidrauski and Tobin results. To make the argument comparable to the discussion of the previous section we will identify the differences in terms of the portfolio decision and savings behavior. In the Sidrauski model the portfolio decision and the savings behavior are derived simultaneously from the necessary conditions for the solution of the problem. Elimination of q and λ from these conditions results in:

$$u_c \cdot (f_k + \pi) - u_m = 0 , \tag{2.11}$$

$$-u_c \cdot (\delta + \pi + n) + u_m + u_{cc}\dot{c} + u_{cm}\dot{m} = 0 . \tag{2.12}$$

Equation (2.11) can be interpreted as the portfolio decision corresponding to equations (1.8) or (1.9) of the Tobin model. To make this more transparent we can examine the special case of the logarithmic utility function:

$$u(c, m) = \log(c) + \log(m) . \tag{2.13}$$

Now, (2.11) becomes:

$$m = (r + \pi)^{-1}c , \tag{2.14}$$

which corresponds exactly to one of the money demand equations in (1.9). It is therefore clear that the difference between the two models lies in the specification of the savings behavior. Equation (2.12) does not quite correspond to the reduced form consumption function. In the steady state and using the utility function (2.13), however, the equation simplifies to:

$$c = (\delta + \pi + n) \cdot m . \tag{2.15}$$

This can be compared to the consumption function specification in (1.13). As was mentioned in the previous section, if, for a given level of assets, inflation has a positive effect on consumption, then the Tobin effect can be neutralized or be overturned.

The superneutrality of money is not, however, a general result within the optimizing framework. In fact it seems to be obtained only as a special case. There are two classes of models that originated from the Sidrauski model and result in non-neutralities. One class, in tune with the original Tobin model, shows that the Fisher relation does not necessarily hold, even in optimizing models that retain most of Sidrauski's assumptions. The other consists of cases in which the Fisher relation continues to hold but the one-to-one mapping from the real interest rate to capital intensity breaks down. For Sidrauski's own model, equation (2.10) says that the real rate of interest is invariant to the rate of inflation so the Fisher relation holds across steady states.

We consider the second class of models first. To break down the correspondence between the interest rate and capital, another variable input of production must be introduced whose optimal level changes with inflation. This introduces an additional margin in the maximization problem which equates the marginal product of capital to the marginal benefit from varying the other input.

2.2. Variations of the Sidrauski model

One such case is that of money in the production function. Suppose, for example, that money is held by firms to facilitate production and can therefore be considered as a complementary factor to capital:

$$y = f(k, m) , \quad f_k, f_m > 0 . \tag{2.16}$$

Money may still be an argument in the utility function, but for simplicity we will assume it no longer is. The utility functional is now:

$$W = \int_0^\infty u(c_t) \cdot e^{-\delta t} \, dt , \tag{2.17}$$

and is being maximized subject to the same constraints as before (with the additional argument in the production function). The new Hamiltonian is:

$$\mathcal{H} = u(c) + q \cdot (f(k, m) + x - \pi \cdot m - c - a \cdot n) + \lambda \cdot (a - k - m) . \tag{2.18}$$

The necessary conditions are (2.5), (2.6), (2.8) and

$$q \cdot f_m - q \cdot \pi - \lambda = 0 , \tag{2.19}$$

which replaces (2.7). As before, the necessary conditions imply that in the steady state (2.10) holds so the marginal product of capital is independent of the growth rate of money. Equation (2.19), however, implies an additional condition that must be met by the marginal product of capital, that is

$$f_k = f_m - \pi . \tag{2.20}$$

As a result, the effect of an increase in inflation on capital accumulation is ambiguous and depends on the partial derivatives of the production function:[25]

$$\frac{dk}{d\theta} = -\frac{f_{km}}{f_{mm}f_{kk} - (f_{km})^2} \,.$$

(2.21)

If the production function is concave, and $f_{km} > 0$, then inflation is negatively related to capital holdings. We will return to the ambiguity of this particular case in Section 4.

Even if money does not appear in the production function, however, non-neutrality is obtained by simply treating labor input as another decision variable.[26] When leisure is an argument in the utility function, labor supply is not inelastic. Then capital per capita is not equivalent to capital per labor unit. Since the interest rate equals the marginal product of capital normalized by labor units, even if the real interest rate is invariant to inflation, capital per capita will not be invariant due to the effect of inflation on labor supply. Let l be an index of leisure varying between 0 and 1. The production function can be written:

$$y = f(k, l) = f(k/(1 - l)) \,.$$

(2.22)

The utility functional is now:

$$W = \int_0^\infty u(c_t, m_t, l_t) \cdot e^{-\delta t} \, dt \,.$$

(2.23)

The new Hamiltonian is:

$$\mathcal{H} = u(c, m, l) + q \cdot (f(k, l) + x - \pi \cdot m - c - a \cdot n) + \lambda \cdot (a - k - m) \,.$$

(2.24)

Necessary conditions are, as in the original problem, (2.5)–(2.8), but there is now an additional margin:

$$u_l - q \cdot f_l = 0 \,,$$

(2.25)

which implies the following relationship that must be satisfied by the marginal product of capital in addition to (2.10):

$$f_k = \frac{u_c}{u_l \cdot (1 - l)} \,.$$

(2.26)

---

[25]This ambiguity was pointed out by Marty (1968). A detailed derivation appears in Fischer (1983).

[26]Leisure was first introduced into the model by Brock (1974).

As a result, money is no longer neutral but the direction of the effect on capital is not obvious. In particular, the direction of the result depends on whether a change in money affects the marginal utility of leisure more or less than the marginal utility of consumption.[27]

The major methodological problem with this type of model is exactly the fact that the direction of the non-neutralities obtained depends on quantities for which no strong prior can possibly exist. The introduction of money into the utility and production functions is, indeed, a useful device which allows for simultaneous examination of optimal savings and money demand. This, as we saw earlier, is necessary for answering the question at hand. It is also reasonable to accept a priori the positive sign of the partial derivatives of money in the two functions. But no more. Unfortunately, the answer turns out to depend on the cross derivatives of money with other arguments in utility or production which makes these models unsuitable for settling the debate as a "practical matter".[28]

Models in which the Fisher relation is violated provide a more promising use of the money-in-the-utility-or-production-function approach for examining non-neutralities. We now turn to those models.

3. The Tobin effect and the Fisher relation

The optimizing models we examined in the previous section share the characteristic of considering a world that consists of a fixed number of large infinitely lived families. Each family makes a decision about how much to consume and save taking into account the welfare of all future generations. As a result the steady-state real interest rate is set according to a modified golden rule and depends only on the rates of time preference and population growth and not on any monetary variables. Thus, the real interest rate is independent of inflation – the Fisher relation. On the other hand, if the optimization problem does not involve maximizing the welfare of all future members of the family, the steady-state real interest rate is not determined by a relation like the modified golden rule and therefore may depend on monetary variables. Then, an increase in the inflation rate could result in a less than one-to-one increase of the nominal interest rate – a decrease of the real rate – and the Tobin effect would apply. The intuition, due to Diamond (1965), was developed in a different context showing how government deficits can affect capital accumulation. To the extent that individuals, for some reason, hold money, the

---

[27]This is shown in Danthine (1985).

[28]It is a separate question whether infinite-horizon optimization models are a suitable vehicle in the first place for discussing any "practical" matter. One could easily have grave doubts.

seigniorage collected by the government represents an alternative form of changing government indebtedness and Diamond's results become relevant for the money and growth literature as well.

To examine the implications of this disconnectedness with the future we must turn to lifecycle models with overlapping generations (OLG). Since OLG models with money are covered in detail elsewhere in this Handbook, the analysis here will be brief. We will examine only steady-state results and we will bypass the important issues of the possible multiplicity of equilibria, stability of equilibria, and equilibria outside the steady state.

3.1. The two-period OLG model with money

In the typical finite life models individuals follow a lifecycle pattern of consumption and savings. They accumulate wealth in the form of capital and money when young, in order to consume it when they retire. At each point in time several generations coexist. In the simplest model, due to Samuelson (1958), individuals live for just two periods. Wealth continuously changes hands as the old exchange their savings (kept in the form of money and capital) for goods produced by the young. In Samuelson's pure consumption-loans model, money is assumed not to provide any services that enter either the production or utility function and is held only as a means of intergenerational trade. As a result, money is not held when it is dominated in rate of return by another asset and the model is unsuitable for examination of the link between inflation and capital accumulation.[29] In this section we examine the implications of assuming, as with the Sidrauski model, that money enters the utility function directly. This type of model has been introduced in the money and growth literature by Stein (1970) and more recently examined by Carmichael (1982), Drazen (1981), Gale (1983), and Weiss (1980). When young, individuals maximize a utility function of the form:

$$W = W(c_1, c_2, m_1, m_2), \tag{3.1}$$

where c_i and m_i $(i = 1, 2)$ denote consumption and real money holdings in the two periods of life.[30] A portion of first-period income is saved either in the

---

[29]For a more detailed examination of OLG models with fiat money, see the volume edited by Kareken and Wallace (1980) and the chapters on the OLG model and optimum quantity of money in this Handbook.

[30]We will abstract from time subscripts whenever possible since we will only deal with steady states. In more detail we should have written $W_t = W(c_{1,t}, c_{2,t+1}, m_{1,t}, m_{2,t+1})$, where W_t denotes the utility of an individual who is young at time t; the first subscript denotes the age of the individual and the second subscript denotes the time.

form of capital or in the form of money. In the second period of his life the individual consumes his income plus whatever he has accumulated from his first-period savings. Despite the similarities with the Sidrauski model several variations of this model exist. They are due to choices that were meaningless in the one family Sidrauski model but are important here. In the OLG model one must specify: (i) whether the individual works in both periods of his life or just when he is young and in the first case, whether the wage is the same for young and old; (ii) whether utility is derived from holding money just in the first period, or in both periods (if in both periods then one must explain what happens to second-period money holdings when the individual dies); and (iii) how seigniorage is being allocated – whether the government give it to the young or to the old or to both. The importance of these assumptions is that they affect the pattern of the lifecycle savings of an individual and, as a result, the aggregate level of wealth in the economy and therefore aggregate capital. To examine this in more detail consider the following example. The individual needs to hold money when he is young to derive utility and he maximizes

$$W = U(c_1) + \frac{1}{(1+\delta)} \cdot U(c_2) + L(m) , \tag{3.2}$$

where m is money holdings per young person. Only the young work, receive a wage, w, and save some of their income in money, m, and capital, k. Only the young hold money and capital. As soon as an individual becomes old he exchanges his money and capital for the consumption good. In addition only the old receive transfers, x, from the government. In equilibrium, the real value of the transfers, x, is such that real total seigniorage equals total real transfers but, as in the Sidrauski model, we assume that the individuals consider it to be unrelated to their actions. Consumption in the first and second periods is:

$$c_1 = w - k - m , \tag{3.3}$$

$$c_2 = k(1 + r) + m/(1 + \pi) + x . \tag{3.4}$$

Solving the problem faced by the young results in the following conditions:

$$U'(c_1) = U'(c_2) \cdot \frac{(1+r)}{(1+\delta)} , \tag{3.5}$$

$$L'(m) = U'(c_1) \cdot \left(1 - \frac{1}{(1+\pi) \cdot (1+r)}\right) . \tag{3.6}$$

Condition (3.6) simply states that the marginal utility of first-period consumption is equated to the marginal utility of (first-period) money holdings appropriately discounted and is the discrete time equivalent of condition (2.11) which obtained in the Sidrauski model.[31]

Condition (3.5) is the equivalent of the dynamic condition of the Sidrauski problem (2.9) or (2.12). In the steady state (2.9) simplified to the modified golden rule condition that the real interest rate equals the rate of time preference plus the rate at which the family grows. Here, however, this would only be true if consumption of an individual were the same in both periods of his life. In that case (3.5) would imply that r is equal to δ, which exactly corresponds to the modified golden rule since there is no "family" growth here. There is no reason, however, for consumption to be the same in the two periods of life. The lifetime consumption pattern is determined together with the savings decision and portfolio choice when the young solve their optimization problem. In equilibrium the real interest rate is therefore determined as a function of the consumption pattern.

Unlike the Sidrauski model, the savings pattern of an individual in the steady state matters in the determination of the aggregate capital level. In other words, it is not only the value of the lifetime consumption of an individual that matters, but the actual allocation of his lifetime consumption between the first and second periods of his life. When viewed from the aggregate level it is this additional margin that invalidates the superneutrality result. Inflation, therefore, has an effect on capital accumulation in this model by changing the slope of the individual consumption path. An alternative interpretation corresponds more closely to Tobin's original mechanism. Inflation increases the relative attractiveness of investing in the form of capital. This has a negative effect on the return to capital thereby causing an increase in first-period consumption.

To examine the effect of inflation further, we close the model assuming constant returns to scale production and competitive markets as in the Sidrauski model. In equilibrium, the interest rate and wage are determined from:

$$r = f'(k) , \tag{3.7}$$

$$w = f(k) - kf'(k) , \tag{3.8}$$

where $f(k)$ is output per young (since only the young work).

Assuming, for simplicity, that there is no population growth, the number of young equals the number of old. Then inflation, π, equals the growth rate of money, θ, and seigniorage per young person, θm, equals the transfer per old

---

[31] Note that when r and π are close to zero, the expression in the parentheses is approximately equal to $r + \pi$, which is what appears in condition (2.11).

person, x. In equilibrium, the steady-state consumption path is:

$$c_1 = f(k) - k \cdot (l + f'(k)) - m , \tag{3.9}$$

$$c_2 = k \cdot (1 + f'(k)) + m , \tag{3.10}$$

and the first-order conditions, (3.5) and (3.6), imply:

$$U'(c_1) = U'(c_2) \cdot \frac{(1 + f'(k))}{(1 + \delta)} , \tag{3.11}$$

$$L'(m) = U'(c_1) \cdot \left(1 - \frac{1}{(1 + \theta) \cdot (1 + f'(k))} \right) . \tag{3.12}$$

Straightforward comparative statics on (3.9)–(3.12) shows that as long as the stability condition for the model is satisfied, $dk/d\theta > 0$, and in the steady state an increase in inflation unambiguously increases steady-state capital.

This precise result, however, does not hold for all variants of the two-period OLG model. Variation, whenever present, comes from the allocation of seigniorage. In the model we just described, the sign of the effect of inflation on capital is invariant to the allocation of seigniorage, but the size of the effect is not. If all seigniorage is given to the young instead of the old, equations (3.9) and (3.10) become:

$$c_1 = f(k) - k \cdot (1 + f'(k)) - (l - \theta) \cdot m , \tag{3.13}$$

$$c_2 = k \cdot (l + f'(k)) + \frac{m}{(1 + \theta)} , \tag{3.14}$$

and the comparative statics showing the effect of inflation on steady-state capital are now determined by (3.11)–(3.14). Capital holdings become smaller and the consumption path flatter, but the steady-state effect of inflation on capital holdings is positive, nonetheless.

In Drazen's model, money provides utility in both periods of life, and is therefore held by both the yound and the old. He shows that, as with the model outlined above, if transfer payments are fixed, then an increase in inflation increases the demand for capital by the young. But an increase in the rate of inflation also increases the seigniorage collected by the government. If that seigniorage is given to the old, it represents an increase in second-period income which has the effect of reducing first-period savings. This transfer mechanism has the same effect as the introduction of government debt in the Diamond model and tends to reduce the demand for capital. In the model outlined above this effect is not strong enough to overturn the positive effect of inflation on capital. We chose to illustrate the extreme case in which all seigniorage is given to the old and saw that even in that case the Tobin effect prevails. In Drazen's model, however, the seigniorage transfer effect is so large that in equilibrium the relationship between inflation and capital is reversed. If the young receive the seigniorage from holding money, capital increases with inflation, while if the old are given the seigniorage the demand for capital decreases with inflation.

In general, the two-period life OLG models do provide a formal justification of the Tobin effect in an explicitly optimizing framework. It is disappointing that the effect can be reversed in some versions by the mere redistribution of seigniorage from one group of individuals to another, an effect whose importance would not a priori seem relevant. This problem may be due to the unnatural time scale of the two-period OLG models. A priori, it is at least as reasonable to assume that money is held during both periods of life as it is to assume that it is held only in the first. The problem, however, is that one period is supposed to represent many decades. The debate as to whether these models are appropriate for studying monetary phenomena at all is still unsettled and its resolution is outside our scope.[32]

3.2. Family disconnectedness with infinite horizons

An alternative model not subject to the criticisms of the two-period OLG model emphasizes not the finiteness of each individual's horizon but the disconnectedness of infinitely lived individuals born in different times. It is much more similar to the Sidrauski model, and as a result better illustrates why superneutrality fails when dissimilarities among individuals are present. The model is based on the Blanchard (1985) formulation of Yaari's (1965) infinite horizon–uncertain lifetime model. The variant discussed below follows Weil (1986) and Whitesell (1988).

In this model, in every instant, a new generation of infinitely lived individuals/families is born which is completely disconnected from past generations. Like the OLG model there is no family growth comparable to the Sidrauski model. Population growth is completely due to the birth of new families. Families differ in the time of their birth much in the same way the old differ from the young in the OLG model. The family maximization problem is exactly the same as in Sidrauski and the interest rate and wage are assumed determined in competitive markets as in the Sidrauski and OLG models. A

---

[32]See, in particular, the criticism in Tobin (1980) which relates the issue to the money and growth issue.

family born at time s faces the following optimization problem at time $t > s$: maximize the welfare function

$$W_{s,t} = \int_t^\infty u(c_{s,v}, m_{s,v}) \cdot e^{-\delta(v-t)} \, dv \tag{3.15}$$

subject to the portfolio selection constraint,

$$a_{s,v} = k_{s,v} + m_{s,v}, \quad \forall v > t, \tag{3.16}$$

and the asset accumulation constraint,

$$\dot{a}_{s,v} = r_v \cdot k_{s,v} + w_v + x_v - \pi_v \cdot m_{s,v} - c_{s,v}, \quad \forall v > t. \tag{3.17}$$

Here, the first subscript indicates the time of birth of the family and all quantities represents the real per capita values of the variables for individual members of any family born at time s. Variables without the first subscript are variables that have the same value for individuals of all families. Here it is assumed that, regardless of age, all individuals supply one unit of labor and receive the same wage, w, and the same government transfer, x.[33]

To keep the model tractable later on, we will assume that the instantaneous utility function is of the logarithmic form:

$$u(c_{s,v}, m_{s,v}) = \log(c_{s,v}) + \log(m_{s,v}). \tag{3.18}$$

The individual's problem is exactly the same as in the Sidrauski model. As we have seen in Section 2, the first-order conditions implied by the maximization are:

$$\dot{q}_{s,v} = (\delta - r_v) \cdot q_{s,v}, \tag{3.19}$$

$$c_{s,v} = (\pi_v + r_v) \cdot m_{s,v}, \tag{3.20}$$

$$1/c_{s,v} = q_{s,v}, \tag{3.21}$$

where $q_{s,v}$ is the costate variable corresponding to the asset accumulation equation of a representative individual born at time s. In the Sidrauski model, in the steady state all individuals have the same level of consumption which

---

[33]The convention we follow is that variables with an age subscript, $z_{s,v}$, represent per capita values for members of one generation, while variables without an age subscript, z_v, represent per capita values for the whole population. As before, variables without any subscripts represent the steady-state per capita values for the whole population.

must therefore be fixed at a constant level. If that were true here, then $c_{s,v}$ would equal $c_{s-\tau,v}$, $\forall \tau$, and $q_{s,v}$ would be a constant. In that case equation (3.19) would collapse to the Sidrauski steady-state superneutrality. Here, however, steady state simply requires that $c_{s,v} = c_{s+\tau,v+\tau}$, $\forall \tau > 0$. The consumption of individuals of different generations may be different, as in the OLG model. But since in the steady state the cross-section of the consumption of individuals of different ages at a given instant corresponds to the time path of consumption for a given individual, it follows that individual consumption is not necessarily a constant. This highlights the key difference with the Sidrauski model. Individual consumption patterns are not required to be completely flat in the steady state. Inflation can affect capital accumulation by changing the relative price of consumption between any two instants thereby changing the pattern of individual consumption. Forward integration of (3.19) and substitution of (3.21) gives the path of individual consumption:

$$c_{s,v} = c_{s,t} \cdot \exp\left(-\int_t^v (r_\mu - \delta) \cdot d\mu\right). \tag{3.22}$$

Let us define human capital, h, as the present value of future non-interest income:[34]

$$h_t \equiv \int_t^\infty (x_v + w_v) \cdot \exp\left(-\int_t^v r_\mu \cdot d\mu\right) dv. \tag{3.23}$$

Then, the individual's total real wealth, b, at time t is:

$$b_{s,t} \equiv k_{s,t} + m_{s,t} + h_t, \tag{3.24}$$

and his lifetime budget constraint, which equates total wealth with the cost of total future purchases of consumption and money services, can be written as:[35]

$$b_{s,t} = \int_t^\infty c_{s,v} \cdot \exp\left(-\int_t^v r_\mu \cdot d\mu\right) dv$$

$$+ \int_t^\infty (\pi_v + r_v) \cdot m_{s,v} \cdot \exp\left(-\int_t^v r_\mu \cdot d\mu\right) dv. \tag{3.25}$$

Substituting the first-order condition (3.20) and solving using equation (3.22)

---

[34]Notice that human wealth is the same for all individuals regardless of their date of birth since it does not depend on current asset wealth – the only distinguishing characteristic between generations.
[35]Formally, (3.25) can be derived by forward integration of the asset accumulation equation (3.17) and a transversality condition.

gives us money holdings and consumption as a function of wealth:

$$c_{s,t} = \delta \cdot b_{s,t}/2 , \tag{3.26}$$

$$m_{s,t} = \delta \cdot b_{s,t}/(2 \cdot (\pi_t + r_t)) . \tag{3.27}$$

In order to examine the behavior of the economy we must transform the relationships describing generation specific variables to economy-wide aggregates. Assuming that the number of families increases at rate n, the economy-wide per capita average for a variable z is obtained by integration:

$$z_t = e^{-n \cdot t} \cdot \int_{-\infty}^{t} z_{s,t} \cdot n \cdot e^{n \cdot s} \, ds . \tag{3.28}$$

Aggregation using equation (3.28) implies that equations (3.20), (3.24) and (3.26) hold unchanged for the economy-wide aggregates as they do for the individuals. These, together with the dynamic equations

$$\dot{m}_t/m_t = \theta - n - \pi_t , \tag{3.29}$$

$$\dot{k}_t = f(k_t) - n \cdot k_t - c_t , \tag{3.30}$$

$$\dot{h}_t = -(w_t + \theta \cdot m_t) + r_t \cdot h_t , \tag{3.31}$$

completely describe the dynamic behavior of the economy.[36] Equation (3.31) is obtained by differentiating (3.23) and setting transfers, x_t, equal to per capita seigniorage, $\theta \cdot m_t$.

When population growth is zero, the model is identical to the Sidrauski model with no population growth. The two models diverge when population growth is positive as the Sidrauski model assumes growth occurs within the (fixed number of) existing families, whereas this model assumes growth occurs by the creation of new families (of fixed size).[37] As a result, although the national income and real money growth identities, (3.29) and (3.30), are identical in both models the consumption function (3.26) is not.

Elimination of all other variables from the steady-state system results in the following equation for steady-state capital:

$$f(k) - n \cdot k = \frac{\delta}{2 \cdot f'(k)} \left[2 \cdot f(k) - n \cdot k + \frac{n \cdot (f(k) - n \cdot k)}{f'(k) + \theta - n} \right] . \tag{3.32}$$

---

[36] In equilibrium, the interest rate and wage are, of course, set as described in equations (3.7) and (3.8).
[37] The assumption of no intra-family growth can be relaxed.

As expected, when $n = 0$ (3.32) simplifies to the modified golden rule $f'(k) = \delta$ and the superneutrality result prevails. On the other hand, it is clear that when $n \neq 0$, then the rate of growth of money, θ, affects the steady-state level of capital. In fact, an increase in the rate of growth of money unambiguously implies a higher level of steady state capital.[38]

The Tobin effect has been shown to arise naturally in models in which money enters the utility function when there is individual heterogeneity in the steady state. The key characteristic of models that attain non-neutrality and the simultaneous invalidation of the Fisher relation seems to be the relaxation of the requirement that steady-state consumption be the same always and for all. The superneutrality result in the Sidrauski model is achieved from a single first-order condition of the individual maximization problem,

$$\frac{\partial U_t}{\partial c_t} = \frac{\partial U_{t+1}}{\partial c_{t+1}} \cdot \frac{(1 + f'(k))}{(1 + \delta)} \ , \tag{3.33}$$

when the model requires that in steady state,

$$\partial U_t / \partial c_t = \partial U_{t+1} / \partial c_{t+1} \ . \tag{3.34}$$

Introducing some slope to individual consumption paths allows Tobin's portfolio mechanism to have a real effect even though other effects at work, such as the distribution of seignorage, may make the Tobin effect ambiguous.

It is clear from (3.34) that individual heterogeneity is not needed for the non-neutrality result. Michener (1979) shows that if the time separability of the utility function is relaxed in the Sidrauski model neutrality fails. According to Carmichael (1982), one of the necessary conditions for the neutrality result is that "the individual's utility function [be] separable with a constant discount rate". Fischer (1979) shows that neutrality does not hold in the Sidrauski model during the transition to the steady state [see also Asako (1983)]. Again, what is at work is the fact that outside of the steady state (3.34) does not hold. Inflation changes the slope of the consumption path during the transition. Danthine, Donaldson and Smith (1987) build a stochastic version of the model by introducing stochastic shocks to productivity. (3.34) does not hold even after the economy achieves stationarity (the stochastic equivalent of a steady state). As a result neutrality fails in the sense that the stationary distribution of the real interest rate and capital depends on the rate of growth of money. Furthermore, they use numerical simulations to show that when the utility function has a constant positive elasticity of substitution the Tobin effect holds – an increase of the rate of growth of money lowers the real interest rate and increases capital, on average.

[38]This is shown in Whitesell (1988).

4. Cash in advance and transactions demand

In Sections 2 and 3 we illustrated several models in which inflation positively affects capital and we attempted to explain why this result does not always obtain. The indeterminacy was shown to be due, sometimes, to a simplifying assumption shared in all of those models, namely that money is held simply because it provides services that directly yield utility or increase the productivity of capital. Even though these models overcome one of the two key criticisms of the original Tobin model – that individual behavior must be consistent with the optimization problems faced by individuals – they fail to provide an adequate explanation of why money is held, and thus do not address the second key criticism of the Tobin model. In particular, the transactions role of money is not adequately detailed even though in the absence of a transactions demand for money there would be no reason for money to be held at all.

This omission is dealt with in a number of models which give greater emphasis to the exact specification of the transactions demand for money. These models are the focus of this section.

4.1. A "shopping costs" model

We start by examining a model which is directly comparable to the models in Section 2. An infinitely lived family maximizes a welfare function subject to a neoclassical production function. The services of money do not appear directly in either the production or utility function – rather it is assumed that the presence of money facilitates the transactions that are necessary for the delivery and/or consumption of output.

A function of real money holdings, $v(m)$, represents the fraction of real resources that are necessary for the task of facilitating transactions. Real money holdings provide "shopping services" in the sense that the more money is held the more real resources are freed from the transactions task, thus $v'(m) < 0$. The specification allows for the explicit recognition that there are decreasing returns to the services that can be provided by holding money. Each additional unit of real money held frees a smaller fraction of resources than the unit preceding it, thus $v''(m) > 0$.

A question of importance in this model is whether the type of transactions that can be facilitated by money holdings is necessary in order simply to consume output or in order to produce it at all.

We will first consider the first alternative: only consumers find the services of money useful.

The optimization problem faced by the individual/family is to maximize the welfare function,

$$V = \int_0^\infty u(c_t) \cdot e^{-\delta t} \, dt \,, \tag{4.1}$$

subject to the portfolio decision constraint,

$$a = m + k \,, \tag{4.2}$$

and the asset accumulation equation,

$$\dot{a} = f(k) + x - c \cdot (1 + v(m)) - n \cdot a - \pi \cdot m \,. \tag{4.3}$$

Notice that (4.1)–(4.3) correspond to equations (2.1)–(2.3) of the Sidrauski model and in fact the necessary conditions (2.5) and (2.6) obtain here as well. But those were exactly the conditions determining that the rate of interest is independent of inflation in the steady state. Thus, Sidrauski's neutrality result obtains here in a model in which the transactions role of money is explicitly modelled and the need to introduce money in either the utility or production function does not arise.

The alternative specification is to assume that money facilitates transactions necessary to produce output and not just consume it.[39] The problem becomes one of maximizing the welfare function (4.1) subject to (4.2) and the asset accumulation equation:

$$\dot{a} = f(k) \cdot [1 - v(m)] + x - c - n \cdot a - \pi \cdot m \,. \tag{4.4}$$

This model is operationally identical to the model of money in the production function that we examined in Section 2. We simply have to make the transformation:

$$f(k, m) = f(k) \cdot (1 - v(m)) \,. \tag{4.5}$$

In Section 2 we have seen that the effect of inflation on capital is ambiguous and depends on the derivatives of the production function. But here we can give an interpretation to those derivatives. In the steady state the analogues of conditions (2.10) and (2.20) are now:

$$\delta = f' \cdot (1 - v) \,, \tag{4.6}$$

$$f' \cdot (1 - v) = -f \cdot v' - \pi \,, \tag{4.7}$$

[39] This specification is due to Dornbusch and Frenkel (1973).

which imply:

$$\frac{dk}{d\theta} = -\frac{-v' \cdot f'}{-(1-v) \cdot f'' \cdot v'' \cdot f - (f' \cdot v')^2}. \tag{4.8}$$

Since the numerator of this expression is positive, the sign of the effect of inflation on capital is determined by the sign of the denominator in (4.8):

$$dk/d\theta \gtreqless 0, \quad \text{as } (1-v) \cdot f'' \cdot v'' \cdot f + (f' \cdot v')^2 \gtreqless 0.$$

If there are no decreasing returns to saving shopping costs by holding money ($v'' = 0$), then higher inflation results in higher steady-state capital. If the economy is close to being fully liquid – in the sense that additional real money holdings provide only minimal resource savings – then v' is small and increases in inflation reduce steady-state capital. In general, however, the effect is obviously ambiguous.

To see the advantages of explicitly modelling the role of money and the pitfalls of not doing so we can compare directly (4.8) with (2.21):

$$\frac{dk}{d\theta} = -\frac{f_{km}}{f_{mm}f_{kk} - (f_{km})^2}. \tag{2.21}$$

When money is simply considered as an additional input in production it seems natural to require convexity which determines the sign of the denominator in (2.21). Then the ambiguity of the effect of inflation is due to the sign of f_{km}.[40] Observing (4.7) we note that when the transactions role of money is explicitly modelled, f_{km} is actually unambiguously positive and the ambiguity results exactly from the fact that we cannot simply *require* the convexity of a production function when money is assumed to be one of the inputs. Whatever the interpretation, however, the primary conclusion we reach is that the effect of inflation on steady-state capital remains ambiguous.

We have thus shown that when the role of money as a facilitator of transactions is specified explicitly, the conclusions regarding the effect of inflation on steady-state capital accumulation remain unchanged.[41] Doubts

---

[40]Fischer (1974) examines in detail models of money demand which would result in the firm behaving as if money entered its production function and studies the restrictions thus placed on the resulting implicit production function.

[41]This is not true of all variables, however. The effects of inflation on money demand are not identical in the two models. Furthermore, the welfare implications are quite distinct. Inflation is detrimental to steady-state welfare in the Sidrauski model because the reduced money balances lower the utility derived by real good consumption even if the level of consumption is not affected by inflation. In the models examined here, only real goods affect utility, thus inflation has no welfare implications in the steady state other than the ones due to the induced real consumption changes.

about the validity of the Tobin effect remain while, at the same time, we observe that the superneutrality result is a non-result.

What is the exact way in which money facilitates transactions? Admittedly, this question was not addressed by the models just exmained and was rather hidden behind the cryptic specification of the function $v(m)$. Unfortunately, the effect of inflation on capital turned out to depend on the properties of the function in one of the models examined. The criticism regarding the ambiguity due to the admission of money in the utility and production functions carries over to the specification of the function $v(m)$. A possible response to this criticism is provided by the models we examine next.

4.2. Cash in advance for consumption and investment purchases

In cash-in-advance (CIA) models the role of money as facilitator of transactions is identified by the simple rule that no transaction can take place unless the money needed for the transaction is held for some time in advance. The methodological problem presented by these models is that in the absence of costs of transferring wealth to and from assets providing higher yields, money would only be held for infinitesimal time intervals and would be of no economic significance. A simple solution to this problem is to assume that money must be held for a fixed period of time before a transaction takes place.[42] Here we briefly examine models of this form, concentrating in particular on any additional intuition that can be gained from them for the money and growth question.

The simplest model parallels the discrete-time formulation of the Sidrauski model and was introduced to the money and growth literature by Stockman (1981).[43] The CIA constraint is that the amount of nominal money that is required for a transaction in one period must be held for at least one period in advance. An infinitely lived individual maximizes the welfare function,

$$\sum_{t=0}^{\infty} (1+\delta)^{-t} u(c_t) ,\qquad\qquad(4.9)$$

subject to a dynamic budget constraint,

$$k_{t+1} - k_t + m_t^{\mathrm{d}} - m_{t-1} \cdot P_{t-1}/P_t = f(k_t) + x_t - c_t ,\qquad\qquad(4.10)$$

where m_t^{d} represents the amount of real money held at the end of period t and

---

[42]The undesirable implications of this ad hoc assumption will be briefly discussed later.

[43]OLG models with cash-in-advance constraints are covered in Chapter 7 of this Handbook.

$m \equiv m_{t-1} \cdot P_{t-1}/P_t + x_t$ equals post-transfer real money holdings at the beginning of period t. Equation (4.10) corresponds to the asset accumulation equation and asset selection constraint of the models we examined earlier. As is, the problem has a simple solution for money demand, i.e. no money is ever held. With positive inflation, money is strictly dominated by capital as an asset and as before we assume that the individual takes the transfer payment as independent of his saving and portfolio decisions. Next we must specify the liquidity constraint. A key assumption in this model, as in the models examined earlier, is whether the liquidity–cash-in-advance constraint pertains to the purchases of consumption goods or all goods, including investment. Under the first alternative the liquidity constraint is simply:

$$m_t \geq c_t, \tag{4.11}$$

whereas under the second alternative it is:

$$m_t \geq c_t + k_{t+1} - k_t. \tag{4.12}$$

The similarities with the "shopping costs" model discussed above are quite obvious. Not surprisingly, the two models provide similar results. When only consumption is subject to the liquidity constraint, (4.11), then the steady-state real rate of interest and capital are independent of inflation. On the other hand, if investment goods as well as consumption goods are subject to the liquidity constraint, (4.12), then the steady-state real interest rate is:[44]

$$r = \delta \cdot (1 + \delta) \cdot (1 + \theta). \tag{4.13}$$

Thus, higher inflation is unambiguously associated with higher steady-state real interest rates and lower capital stock. This strong result is the only basic difference between the CIA and "shopping costs" models. The reason for the difference is that in the shopping costs model it is possible to economize on real money balances and still enjoy the same net level of output by substituting real resources for money in the transactions process. Here, this is ruled out by assumption, and this makes the difference in the result less important.

It is, perhaps, of greater importance to gain further intuition as to why, whenever money is directly connected to production (in addition to or in place of consumption), there develops a negative effect of inflation on capital accumulation. The link seems to be the complementarity of money and capital that appears in these models. This is most direct in the money in the production function model and in the shopping costs model where f_{km} is

[44]The derivation is in Stockman (1981).

presumed positive. In the CIA model the complementarity is indirect but equally clear. Investment of an additional unit of capital in period $t+1$ requires an additional unit of money holdings in period t. Higher inflation increases the cost of the additional unit of investment by increasing the cost of holding the money necessary for the investment. Thus, it reduces the (net of money holding costs) return on a unit of investment. As a result, the demand for capital is reduced and less money is held.

The complementarity of money and capital, whenever present, creates a negative effect of inflation on capital.

4.3. A digression to inside money

Until now, we have examined models in which all money is assumed to be of the outside form, representing non-interest-bearing government debt. In reality a large part of money supply is of the inside form – bank deposits – representing claims to the private sector. The distinction is important because aggregated over the private sector, outside money is part of net wealth of the private sector, whereas inside money is not. Corresponding to at least part of inside money are loans used to finance the purchase of capital goods. Therefore, unlike outside money, inside money is not an alternative to holding capital.

We chose to discuss the implications of this distinction here because inside money can be thought of as being complementary to capital and its presence has the same effect on the economy as the models discussed in the preceding paragraphs. An increase in inside money may well represent an increase in claims to capital holdings.

The importance of the distinction between inside and outside money has been recognized early in the monetary growth literature in papers by Johnson (1969) and Marty (1969). Gale (1983) illustrates the importance of the distinction most clearly in a model similar to the OLG model described by equations (3.2)–(3.4). We have shown in Section 3 that when all money in the economy is of the outside variety, Tobin's portfolio effect holds unambiguously in that model. Gale considers the same model with the alternative assumption that all money is of the inside variety. Consumers hold money (non-interest-bearing bank deposits) and there are always investors willing to invest (even though in equilibrium they make zero profits). As usual, inflation decreases the demand for real money balances.[45] This implies a reduction of real inside money which reduces the supply of funds available for investment. Thus, Tobin's effect is unambiguously reversed when all money is of the inside variety.

---

[45] Inflation is possible because the government can regulate the bank supply of deposits.

4.4. The Tobin effect in a CIA model without capital

The major methodological problem with the rigid CIA model described earlier is that it requires that cash be held for a *fixed* time interval before a transaction takes place. This assumes away the most basic form of economizing cash balances, that of reducing the average time money is held before it is spent – increasing the velocity of money.

Romer (1986) develops a model in which the money-holding period is an endogenous decision. The model is based on the Baumol–Tobin model of money demand. The individual faces a fixed real cost of making cash withdrawals from the bank and must pay for his consumption purchases with cash. Bank deposits offer a positive rate of return, ρ, whereas money has a negative real return due to inflation.

Capital is not explicitly introduced in the model for tractability. As a result there is no production in the model and no income is received from productive activity. Rather, it is assumed that the individual receives income in fixed intervals. Then the effect of inflation on capital accumulation is implicitly represented by the average bank account balance of the individual. That is, "capital" is whatever wealth is not held in the form of money. Higher inflation induces the individual to make trips to the bank more often and make smaller withdrawals. The net effect is that inflation tends to increase "capital" holdings, thus the Tobin effect seems to hold. Romer observes, however, that the effect he finds is "insignificant" for any reasonable values of the parameters in the model and discounts the importance of the Tobin effect he is able to generate.

Once again, we observe that seemingly small variations in a model change the conclusions regarding the effect of inflation on capital accumulation.

5. Concluding remarks

We end where Stein ended 20 years ago. Tobin's 1965 paper succeeded in framing the question that has dominated the literature since: Does the rate of monetary growth have any long-run effect on the real rate of interest, capital-intensity, output and welfare? He also established the framework within which the question would be debated: portfolio choice, where fiat money is one of several competing assets. It has turned out to be difficult to assess the "practical" relevance of the Tobin effect precisely because equally plausible models of portfolio balance can yield quite different answers. (We specify "practical" relevance to emphasize that steady-state arguments, here as elsewhere, must not be taken too literally. If money-growth affects real output for decades at a time but not in the steady state limit, the Tobin effect has won the ball-game that matters.)

The fundamental difficulty is that we do not yet have any clearly preferred way to introduce money into models of the real economy, especially those that feature durable productive assets as well. Models of a monetary economy without real capital cannot be taken seriously as vehicles for the study of money-and-growth. Their implications may not survive the introduction of productive assets; in that case they serve only to mislead. That may well be the case with extant OLG models.

There are undoubtedly bits and pieces of intuition about the long-run role of money-growth and inflation to be had from many of the models that have been proposed. None so far is able to provide a comprehensive understanding of all the likely effects; and thus none provides a method for sorting out the relative significance of opposing effects.

How might the situation be improved? The literature so far has concentrated on the transactions role of money. The precautionary motive for holding money has been neglected. Correspondingly, deterministic models have pre-dominated. The effects of permanent uncertainty have not been studied in this context. To the extent, for instance, that inflation makes the return on real capital more uncertain (in addition to reducing the real return on money holdings) it would induce risk-averse agents to save more. Presumably some of the additional saving could flow towards real assets; the demand for capital could rise, despite the increased riskiness. No doubt further research would turn up other effects as well. The point is that uncertainty could be an important determinant of the longer-lasting effects.

A second line of questioning is suggested by the observation that the money-and-growth literature generally neglects issues that are taken seriously in studies of hyperinflation. To the extent, for example, that inflation damages the efficiency of the transactions technology, the net productivity of real capital will be lower and so will the demand for capital. It seems unsatisfactory to treat such questions by simple dichotomy: to say that they matter at "high" rates of inflation and not at all at "low" rates of inflation. A more unified treatment would have implications for monetary growth theory.

Finally, we call attention to a gap that exists in all growth theory, not merely its money-and-growth branch. Short-run macroeconomics and long-run growth theory have never been properly integrated. It is only a slight caricature to say that once upon a time the long run was treated casually as a forward extension of the short run, whereas nowadays the tendency is to treat the short run casually as a backward extension of the long run. The recent revival of (sort of) "Keynesian" models based on a microeconomics adequate to the study of short-run dynamics may offer an opportunity for the integration of demand-based and supply-based dynamics. The result would probably cast light on the long-run role of monetary phenomena.

References

Asako, K. (1983) 'The utility function and the superneutrality of money on the transition path', *Econometrica*, 51: 1593–1596.
Bailey, M.J. (1968) 'Comment: The optimal growth rate of money', *Journal of Political Economy*, 76: 874–876.
Bandyopadhyay, T. (1982) 'The role of money demand functions in one-sector growth models', *Journal of Macroeconomics*, 4: 225–231.
Black, F. (1972) 'Active and passive monetary policy in a neoclassical model', *Journal of Finance*, 27: 801–814.
Black, F. (1974) 'Uniqueness of the price level in monetary growth models with rational expectations', *Journal of Economic Theory*, 7: 53–65.
Blanchard, O. (1985) 'Debt, deficits, and finite horizons', *Journal of Political Economy*, 93: 223–247.
Brock, W.A. (1974) 'Money and growth: The case of long run perfect foresight', *International Economic Review*, 15: 750.
Burmeister, E. and R. Dobell (1970) *Mathematical theories of economic growth*. New York: Macmillan.
Calvo, G.A. (1979) 'On models of money and perfect foresight', *International Economic Review*, 20: 83–103.
Carmichael, J. (1982) 'Money and growth: Some old theorems from a new perspective', *Economic Record*, 58: 386–394.
Danthine, J.-P. (1985) 'Inflation and growth in utility-maximizing models', University of Lausanne Working Paper, No. 8511.
Danthine, J.-P., J.B. Donaldson and L. Smith (1987) 'On the superneutrality of money in a stochastic dynamic macroeconomic model', *Journal of Monetary Economics*, 20: 475–499.
Diamond, P.A. (1965) 'National debt in a neoclassical growth model', *American Economic Review*, 55: 1126–1150.
Dornbusch, R. and J.A. Frenkel (1973) 'Inflation and growth', *Journal of Money, Credit and Banking*, 5: 141–156.
Drabicki, J.A. and A. Takayama (1982) 'The symmetry of real purchasing power and the neoclassical monetary growth model', *Journal of Macroeconomics*, 4: 215–223.
Drabicki, J.Z. and A. Takayama (1984) 'The stability of a neoclassical monetary growth model', *Economic Studies Quarterly*, 35: 262–268.
Drazen, A. (1981) 'Inflation and capital accumulation under a finite horizon', *Journal of Monetary Economics*, 8: 247–260.
Fischer, S. (1972) 'Keynes–Wicksell and neoclassical models of money and growth', *American Economic Review*, 62: 880–890.
Fischer, S. (1979) 'Capital accumulation on the transition path in a monetary optimizing model', *Econometrica*, 47: 1433–1439.
Fischer, S. (1983) 'Inflation and growth,' NBER Working Paper, No. 1235.
Gale, D. (1983) *Money in disequilibrium*. Cambridge: Cambridge University Press.
Gali, J. (1988) 'Cointegration and the Fisher effect: A note', M.I.T., mimeo.
Geweke, J. (1986) 'The superneutrality of money in the United States: An interpretation of the evidence', *Econometrica*, 54: 1–21.
Hadjimichalakis, M.G. (1971a) 'Money, expectations, and dynamics – an alternative view', *International Economic Review*, 12: 381–402.

Hadjimichalakis, M.G. (1971b) 'Equilibrium and disequilibrium growth with money: The Tobin models', *Review of Economic Studies*, 38: 457–479.

Hadjimichalakis, M.G. and K. Okuguchi (1979) 'The stability of a generalized Tobin model', *Review of Economic Studies*, 46: 175–178.

Hahn, F. (1960) 'The stability of growth equilibrium', *Quarterly Journal of Economics*, 74: 206–226.

Hahn, F. (1961) 'Money, dynamic stability and growth', *Metroeconomica*, 12: 57–76.

Hahn, F. (1969) 'On money and growth', *Journal of Money, Credit and Banking*, 1: 172–187.

Hayakawa, H. 'Real purchasing power in the neoclassical monetary growth model', *Journal of Macroeconomics*, 1: 19–31.

Hayakawa, H. (1986) 'Intertemporal optimization and neutrality of money in growth models', *Journal of Monetary Economics*, 18: 323–328.

Johnson, H.G. (1966) 'The neoclassical one-sector growth model: A geometrical exposition and extension to a monetary economy', *Economica*, 33: 265–287.

Johnson, H.G. (1967a) 'Money in a neoclassical one-sector growth model', in: *Essays in monetary economics*. Cambridge, Mass.: Harvard University Press (Second edition 1969).

Johnson, H.G. (1967b) 'The neutrality of money in growth models: A reply', *Economica*, 34: 73–74.

Johnson, H.G. (1969) 'Inside money, outside money, income, wealth and welfare in monetary theory', *Journal of Money, Credit and Banking*, 1: 30–45.

Jun, S.-I. (1988) 'The long-run neutrality of money: In levels and in growth rates', M.I.T., mimeo.

Kareken, J.H. and N. Wallace, eds. (1980) *Models of monetary economies*. Minneapolis: Federal Reserve Bank of Minneapolis.

Levhari, D. and D. Patinkin (1968) 'The role of money in a simple growth model', *American Economic Review*, 58: 713–753.

Marty, A.L. (1968) 'The optimal rate of growth of money', *Journal of Political Economy*, 76: 860–873.

Marty, A.L. (1969) 'Inside money, outside money, and the wealth effect: A review essay', *Journal of Money, Credit and Banking*, 1: 101–111.

Metzler, L. (1951) 'Wealth, saving, and the rate of interest', *Journal of Political Economy*, 59: 93–116.

Michener, R.W. (1979) 'Two essays in capital theory', unpublished doctoral dissertation, University of Chicago.

Mundell, R. (1963) 'Inflation and real interest', *Journal of Political Economy*, 71: 280–283.

Nagatani, K. (1969) 'A monetary growth model with variable employment', *Journal of Money, Credit and Banking*, 1: 188–206.

Nagatani, K. (1970) ' A note on Professor Tobin's money and economic growth', *Econometrica*, 38: 171–175.

Olivera, H.H.G. (1971) 'A note on passive money, inflation, and economic growth', *Journal of Money, Credit and Banking*, 3: 137–144.

Ramsey, F.P. (1928) 'A mathematical theory of saving', *Economic Journal*, 38: 543–559.

Romer, D. (1986) 'A simple general equilibrium version of the Baumol–Tobin model', *Quarterly Journal of Economics*, 101: 663–685.

Rose, H. (1966) 'Unemployment in a theory of growth', *International Economic Review*, 7: 260–282.

Rose, H. (1969) 'Real and monetary factors in the business cycle', *Journal of Credit, Money and Banking*, 1: 138–152.

Samuelson, P.A. (1958) 'An exact consumption–loan model with or without the social contrivance of money', *Journal of Political Economy*, 66: 467–482.

Sargent, T.J. and N. Wallace (1973) 'The stability of models of money and growth with perfect foresight', *Econometrica*, 41: 1043–1048.

Sidrauski, M. (1967a) 'Rational choice and patterns of growth in a monetary economy', *American Economic Review Papers and Proceedings*, 57: 534–544.

Sidrauski, M. (1967b) 'Inflation and economic growth', *Journal of Political Economy*, 75: 796–810.

Solow, R.M. (1956) 'A contribution to the theory of economic growth', *Quarterly Journal of Economics*, 70: 65–94.

Stein, J.L. (1966) 'Money and capacity growth', *Journal of Political Economy*, 74: 74.

Stein, J.L. (1968) 'Rational choice and the patterns of growth in a monetary economy: Comment', *American Economic Review*, 58: 944–950.

Stein, J.L. (1969) 'Neoclassical and Keynes–Wicksell monetary growth models', *Journal of Money, Credit and Banking*, 1: 153–171.

Stein, J.L. (1970) 'Monetary growth theory in perspective', *American Ecomonic Review*, 60: 85–106.

Stein, J.L. (1971) *Money and capacity growth*. New York: Columbia University Press.

Stockman, A.C. (1981) 'Anticipated inflation and the capital stock in a cash-in-advance economy', *Journal of Monetary Economics*, 8: 387–393.

Swan, T.W. (1956) 'Economic growth and capital accumulation', *Economic Record*, 32: 334–361.

Tobin, J. (1955) 'A dynamic aggregative model', *Journal of Political Economy*, 63: 103–115.

Tobin, J. (1961) 'Money, capital, and other stores of value', *American Economic Review, Papers and Proceedings*, 51: 26–37.

Tobin, J. (1965) 'Money and economic growth', *Econometrica*, 33: 671–684.

Tobin, J. (1967) 'The neutrality of money in growth models: A comment', *Economica*, 34: 69–72.

Tobin, J. (1968) 'Notes on optimal monetary growth', *Journal of Political Economy*, 76: 833–859.

Tobin, J. (1980) 'The overlapping generations model of fiat money: Discussion', in: J.H. Kareken and N. Wallace, eds., *Models of monetary economies*. Minneapolis: Federal Reserve Bank of Minneapolis.

Tsiang, S.C. (1969) 'A critical note on the optimal supply of money', *Journal of Money, Credit and Banking*, 1: 266–280.

Weil, P. (1986) 'Monetary policy and budget deficits with overlapping families of infinitely-lived agents,' Harvard University, mimeo.

Weiss, L. (1980) 'The effects of money supply on economic welfare in the steady state', *Econometrica*, 48: 565–576.

Whitesell, W. (1988) 'Age heterogeneity and the Tobin effect with infinite horizons', Finance and Economics Discussion Series, Federal Reserve Board.

Yaari, M.E. (1965) 'Uncertain lifetime, life insurance, and the theory of the consumer', *Review of Economic Studies*, 32: 137–150.

Chapter 7

OVERLAPPING GENERATIONS MODELS WITH MONEY AND TRANSACTIONS COSTS

W.A. BROCK*

University of Wisconsin at Madison

Contents

*I wish to thank F. Hahn, B. McCallum, S. Williamson, M. Woodford, and R. Wright for very helpful comments on this chapter. I especially thank M. Woodford for a long, constructively critical letter. This work was supported by the University of Wisconsin Alumni Research Fund (WARF), and the NSF under Grant SES-8420872. None of the above is responsible for views, errors, or shortcomings of this paper.

Handbook of Monetary Economics, Volume I, Edited by B.M. Friedman and F.H. Hahn
© *Elsevier Science Publishers B.V., 1990*

1. Introduction

This chapter has the assignment of treating overlapping generations models with money and transactions costs. For brevity I will abbreviate "overlapping generations" as "OG". Before we get into this topic there is the question of boundaries.

The first question we must settle is how wide the definition "OG model" is. Let us begin by saying what it is not. The class "OG model" does not include (a) models where all of the old "care" about the young in the precise sense that the utility of the offspring appears in the utility function of the young [Barro (1974)]; (b) general equilibrium models of the type analyzed by Hahn (1971); and (c) infinite commodity space general equilibrium models of the type analyzed by Bewley (1972). We will, however, use models with an infinite number of goods and an infinite number of agents, as treated by Wilson (1981) for example. We will consider the same good at a different date as a different good. This is standard in general equilibrium theory. This class includes Samuelson's consumption loans model – the basic workhorse of OG macro-economics – as a special case.

In this class the theorem that competitive equilibria are Pareto optimal has to be modified in a fundamental way [Wilson (1981)] and competitive equilibria may be robustly indeterminate [Gale (1973), Woodford (1984)].

The second question we must settle is: What is to be included in the category of "transactions costs"? For the purposes of this chapter the category "transactions costs" includes; (a) cash-in-advance (Clower) constraints; (b) general transactions cost functions derived from first principles; and (c) real balances placed into utility functions or production functions, and tradeoff functions between barter (underground) transactions and monetary transactions [Scheinkman (1980), Singleton (1986)]. We include money-in-the-utility function (MIUF) models so long as this is interpreted as indirect utility say from, for example, a household production approach. Papers that derive real balances in an "as if" utility function or production function are Feenstra (1986), Gray (1984), and Woodford (1986a).

The third issue we must deal with is the usefulness of OG models for monetary theory and what the addition of transactions costs has to add to this raison d'être. Writers in the Kareken–Wallace volume, such as Wallace (1980) and Cass and Shell (1980), argue that Samuelson's (1958) OG model gives the best available model of fiat money. Wallace supports the OG because it integrates the valuation of an intrinsically useless piece of paper that is inconvertible into real goods with the rest of value theory [Wallace (1980)]. The Cass and Shell position is similar except that they stress the fundamental treatment of time in the model as well as its disaggregative character. We take these positions as typical for those who argue for use of OG models in monetary theory, especially against alternatives such as reduced-form macro models.

Several conclusions stem from Wallace's insistence that any model of fiat money confront the intrinsic uselessness of the pieces of paper called fiat money and their postulated inconvertibility. They are:

(a) tenuousness – a continuum of monetary equilibria;

(b) equilibria exist where fiat money has no value and equilibria exist where fiat money has value;

(c) welfare may be higher at equilibria where fiat money has value, but not necessarily [Cass, Okuno and Zilcha (1980)];

(d) a "Modigliani–Miller theorem of open market operations" obtains, i.e. the portfolio of the monetary authority does not matter even for the value of fiat money [Wallace (1981), Chamley and Polemarchakis (1984)]; and

(e) a laissez-faire international monetary system with several valued national fiat monies makes no sense because of rate of return dominance unless there are legal restrictions [Wallace (1980, section 6)].

McCallum (1983, 1984) boils down the main monetary implications of a class [typically used by such macroeconomic writers such as Wallace (1980)] of pure OG models as follows:

> First if the authorities cause the stock of money to grow at a rate even slightly in excess of the rate of output growth, money will be valueless and the price level infinite. Second, stationary equilibriums in which the price level is finite will be Pareto optimal if and only if the growth rate of the money stock is not positive. Third, open-market changes in the stock of money have no effect on the price level.

He argues that all three of these distinctive implications disappear once the medium-of-exchange function rather than the pure store-of-value function of money is taken into account.

The quantity of work on OG models with money is vast. Here we shall content ourselves with attempting to list the principal conclusions of this approach for both normative and positive monetary theory and try to evaluate what happens to these conclusions when various types of transactions costs are introduced into the model.

We shall also, at the end of this chapter, suggest a category of open problems that appear to be important in evaluating the robustness of the normative and positive conclusions for monetary economics to the introduction of transactions costs into the leading OG models used in monetary theory that focus exclusively on the "store-of-value" function of money.

This chapter is organized as follows. In Section 2 we take up normative theory. In particular we review work on welfare analysis of OG models and try to show what impact introducing transactions costs has on this welfare analysis. We will focus exclusively on Pareto optimality in the treatment of welfare. Obviously this has limitations because it is not hard to think up examples of Pareto-optimal equilibria that would strike most observers as undesirable. We focus on Pareto optimality here in order to avoid knotty issues of construction of "welfare functions" and to keep this chapter to a manageable size. Some of our remarks will have to be conjectures since some of these issues are not yet settled. In Section 3 positive analysis is treated. Because of the difficulty in drawing sharp boundaries between "positive" and "normative" topics, some "positive" economics spills over into Section 2. Sections 4 and 5 attempt to grapple with comparison of OG conclusions with conclusions adduced by other leading monetary models. Finally, Section 6 suggests open problems that conclude the chapter.

2. Normative theory

2.1. Tenuousness, indeterminacy, cycles, and sunspots

I will include the well-known tenuousness and indeterminacy of monetary equilibria in the normative category because of the emphasis in the literature on the welfare economics of these equilibria. The first example of these equilibria in the OG model is, to my knowledge, the example of Gale (1973). In Gale's model there is one type of young who live two periods with endowment w_y in the first period of life and endowment w_o in the second period of life. For expository purposes, assume that there is only one young person and one old person alive at each point of time. There is one old person alive at date 1 who holds the existing stock M of fiat money.

2.1.1. Offer curve depiction of Gale equilibria

Equilibria in this model are easy to depict. Draw, at each date t, the offer curve of the young born at date t. That is consider the problem:

$$\text{maximize } U(c_y(t), c_o(t+1)) \tag{1}$$

subject to

$$p(t)c_y(t) + p(t+1)c_o(t+1) = p(t)w_y + p(t+1)w_o .$$

Here $p(t)$, $p(t+1)$, $c_y(t)$, and $c_o(t+1)$ denote price of goods at date t, price of goods at date $t+1$, consumption while young, and consumption while old, respectively. The offer curve O is the locus of solutions to (1) as $p(t)$ and $p(t+1)$ vary. The old person at date 1 faces the constraint:

$$p(1)c_o(1) = p(1)w_o + M . \tag{2}$$

Now draw the Ricardian production possibility frontier $R = \{(c_y, c_o) \mid c_y + c_o = w_y + w_o\}$. We shall, like the bulk of the literature, including Gale (1973), use the concept of perfect foresight or rational expectations equilibrium. Such equilibria are described by the set, $\{(p(t), p(t+1); c_y(t), c_o(t+1))\}$, where $(c_y(t), c_o(t+1))$ solves (1) facing $(p(t), p(t+1))$, $t = 1, 2, \ldots$; $c_y(t) + c_o(t) = w_y + w_o$, $t = 1, 2, \ldots$; and $p(1)$, $c_o(1)$ satisfy (2).

In order to get a set of equilibria where money has value in Gale's model and to show the tenuousness of monetary equilibria, draw an offer curve O through the endowment point (w_y, w_o) in 2-space such that O cuts R but with slope less than one in absolute value. Notice the positive steady state L in Figure 7.1, below. This is a steady-state equilibrium where fiat money has positive value. Notice the sequence $(c_y(t), c_o(t+1))$ that converges to autarchy (w_y, w_o). This is a monetary equilibrium where fiat money loses its value asymptotically. This is the situation depicted on page 24 of Gale (1973) in his analysis of his "Samuelson" case.

This useful diagram and method of analysis, due to Gale (1973) and Cass, Okuno and Zilcha (1980), illustrates several features of the class of OG models most commonly exploited by macroeconomists. First, if there is a steady-state equilibrium where money has value, then there is a continuum of equilibria where money has value. This is sometimes called "indeterminacy". Second, there are steady-state competitive equilibria where money has value, L, and steady-state equilibria (autarchy in our case) where money does not have

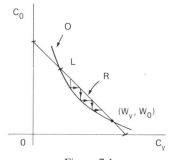

Figure 7.1

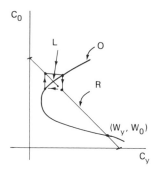

Figure 7.2

value. Third, the presence of money moves the economy to Pareto optimality at the steady state with valued fiat money in this setup. This leads to the general presumption that the presence of valued fiat money in an equilibrium is associated with Pareto optimality. This is not true in all OG setups [Cass, Okuno and Zilcha (1980)].

It is obvious that arbitrarily small policy perturbations such as convertibility of each unit of fiat money to e units of real goods, no matter how small e is, will get rid of the "hyperinflationary" equilibria that converge to autarchy. Figure 7.2 depicts equilibria that cannot be disposed of so easily. The work of Azariadis and Guesnerie (1986) shows that there are sunspot equilibria (to be discussed below) whenever cycles like those in Figure 7.2 are present. Hence "tenuousness" of this type appears difficult to get rid of by minor modifications of the OG model.

2.1.2. Difference equation depiction of Gale equilibria

The Gale equilibria can be depicted alternatively by a difference equation analysis. This is handy for welfare analysis of constant growth rate monetary policies, random growth of the nominal money supply, and comparison with alternative models such as money-in-the-utility-function (MIUF) models and Clower constraint models [Brock and Scheinkman (1980), Scheinkman (1980)].

Put $x(t) = M(t)/p(t)$, where $M(t)$ is nominal money supply at date t. Observe that along any candidate equilibrium path of real balances, $\{x(t)\}$, we must have by the first-order condition for optimality of the young [Brock and Scheinkman (1980)]:

$$U_o(w_y - x(t), w_o + x(t+1))x(t) = U_o(w_y - x(t), w_o + x(t+1))x(t+1) .$$

$$(3)$$

Equation (3) follows from the first-order necessary conditions for an optimum choice of $M_y(t)$ facing the pair of price levels, $p(t)$ and $p(t+1)$, parametrically. Multiply both the first-order necessary condition of optimality for $M_y(t)$ by $M_y(t)$ and evaluate at $M_y(t) = M(t)$ to obtain (3). Call the L.H.S. of (3) $A(\cdot)$ and the R.H.S. $B(\cdot)$. When U is separable $(U(c_y, c_o) = u(c_y) + v(c_o))$ in consumption today and consumption tomorrow, then (3) can be written as a difference equation in the form:

$$A(x(t)) = B(x(t+1)) . \tag{4}$$

Solutions of this difference equation that can be continued forever are equilibria. Note that $B = 0$ at $x = 0$ when $w_o > 0$. As in the offer curve analysis, one may locate the conditions for a positive steady state to exist. Since A and B intersect at O when $w_o > 0$, the condition needed for a positive steady state to exist is that A cuts B from below. This is equivalent to Gale's condition in his "Samuelson" case that the offer curve of the young cuts the PPF from below. We turn now to the impact of transactions costs on this simple story.

To keep things easy, impose a Clower constraint on the old but not on the young. That is, add the constraint,

$$p(t+1)c_o(t+1) \le M_y(t) ,$$

to the old person's budget constraint, where $M_y(t)$ denotes nominal balances formed while young and carried forth into old age. The Clower constraint models the idea that the old person's consumption is constrained by the amount of cash balances, $M_y(t)$, he has on hand even though his endowment is $w_o > 0$. To put it another way, all consumption must be financed out of cash balances, including consumption from his own endowment. This can be viewed as a convenient analytical way of capturing the idea that one's old endowment is not desired. We continue to restrict ourselves to the case where the utility is additively separable.

Then the Clower constraint induces an indirect utility, $v(x(t))$, for the old person which has marginal utility of real balances infinite at zero under natural conditions on the original utility. This is because, if real balances are zero, the old person cannot consume anything while old $[c_o(t+1) \le x(t+1)$ by the Clower constraint]. Now notice that the condition, liminf $B(x) =$ liminf $v'(x)x > 0$, at $x = 0$, implies that all paths that solve $A(x(t)) = B(x(t+1))$ that converge to 0 from the right cannot be continued. Here "liminf" denotes limit inferior (the smallest cluster point). The liminf is taken as $x \to 0$. Hence, hyperinflationary tenuousness cannot occur. Note that this does not rule out that zero real balance equilibrium where no trade between generations takes place, the price level is infinite, and the price of money is zero. We sum this up as

Proposition.   *Transactions   costs   tend   to   eliminate   hyperinflationary   indeterminacy.*

The logic of the proposition is clear by hindsight. Thinking of A as the marginal cost of money and B as the marginal benefit of money, anything that causes a positive marginal benefit of money at a zero level of real balances eliminates hyperinflationary equilibria. To explore this a little more, let $u_o(\cdot)$ be the utility while old. If $w_o = 0$ and $\liminf u_o'(x)x > 0$ as $x \to 0$, then $\liminf B > 0$ as $x \to 0$ and hyperinflationary equilibria are eliminated. Note, however, that this does not eliminate the $x = 0$ equilibrium. So transactions costs are not necessary to mitigate hyperinflationary indeterminacy. Since the hyperinflationary equilibria are inefficient, anything that mitigates them tends to promote efficiency as well.

Transactions costs such as Clower constraints or money in the utility function (MIUF) give money "something to do" each period whose usefulness does not depend entirely upon the "bootstrapping" needed to back up the store or value function of fiat money in OG models. "Bootstrapping" refers to the fact that if the price of money is zero tomorrow it will be zero today in many monetary models. Therefore money must be expected to have positive value tomorrow if it is to have positive value today. Contrast this with a real asset whose ex dividend value is expected to be zero tomorrow. Such an asset can have positive value today even though its ex dividend value is zero tomorrow.

Pure fiat money does not pay positive real dividends. For example, in the MIUF models of Brock (1974), Calvo (1979), and Gray (1984), money can have value, in equilibrium, even if the agents all die at a finite horizon T with probability one so that money is worthless after T. That is to say, real balances generate "dividends" in the form of real services in such models. Of course the amount of work that the money does in generating utility depends on the price level which in turn depends on bootstrapping in MIUF and Clower constraint models. This raises issues about what it is that real balances are doing in the indirect or direct utility function. Feenstra (1986) has discussed the interpretation of real balances in the utility function in terms of liquidity costs. We turn now to "commodity" money or real assets.

2.1.3. Commodity money, stock market assets, and productive land

We introduce real assets into the model along the lines of Lucas (1978) by replacing the budget constraints of the young and old in Gale's model with:

$$c_y(t) + q(t)z(t) = w_y ,$$
$$c_o(t + 1) = w_o + (q(t + 1) + y)z(t) ,$$

where $q(t)$ denotes the price of the asset that pays constant real earnings y at date t, and $z(t)$ denotes the quantity of the asset demanded by the young at date t. There is one perfectly divisible share of the asset outstanding at each point of time. A perfect foresight equilibrium is defined as above in the Gale case except that $z(t) = 1$ at each t (demand for the asset-supply of the asset). Sticking with the separable case, the first-order necessary conditions for a perfect foresight equilibrium are:

$$U_y(w_y + q(t))q(t) = U_o(w_o + q(t+1) + y)(q(t+1) + y). \tag{5}$$

In the same manner as above, paths $\{q(t)\}$ are equilibria provided they can be continued indefinitely. However, a new twist now appears. Think of changing y from zero to a positive value in Gale's model. Then the set of hyperinflationary equilibria that converge to a real balance level of zero moves to a set of equilibria that converge to a negative steady state q_n. It is easiest to see this is the separable case by writing (5) in the form $A(q(t)) = B(q(t+1))$. Increase y from zero to a positive value. Notice that the zero steady state goes to a negative steady state when you do this. This brings us to:

Proposition. *Free disposal of the asset, i.e. limited liability, tends to eliminate welfare-reducing equilibria.*

Let us explore the logic of this proposition. If free disposal of the asset obtains, then any path where $q(t) < 0$ at some finite t cannot be equilibrium. This is so because once the asset goes negative in value the owner can harvest his y and throw the asset away. This is not true however, if the asset is like a nuclear plant that yields earnings of y each period that is perfectly safe yet a chain of self-fulfilling beliefs in a world of unlimited liability can get started where the value of shares in the nuke goes negative and welfare goes down. Here is an example of how limited liability assures Pareto optimality.

2.1.4. A payment of epsilon real earnings of fiat money is efficient

Scheinkman (1977, 1978) and McCallum (1987) have shown how the introduction of a market for claims to an earnings stream of $y > 0$ each period, no matter how small y may be, eliminates the inefficient equilibria in Samuelson (1958) and Gale (1973) OG models. The reason for the Scheinkman/McCallum results is intuitive, by hindsight. The inefficient equilibria are over-accumulative equilibria in that the interest rate is negative enough of the time to fail the Cass (1972)–Benveniste–Gale (1975) efficiency criterion. The appropriate form of this criterion for our case of an overlapping generations economy in the Balasko–Shell (1980) form as used by Sargent (1987, p. 269).

Pareto optimality holds if and only if

$$\sum \left\{ \prod [(1 + r(s))] \right\} = \infty, \tag{6}$$

where the product, $\prod$, runs from $s = 1, \ldots, t$ as the sum, $\sum$, runs from $t = 1, 2, \ldots$ Hence, in the separable case, $1 + r(t) = u'(c_y(t))/v'(c_o(t+1))$. This generalizes to the non-separable case.

But the introduction of a market for claims to $y > 0$, under limited liability, forces the interest rate to be positive enough of the time to force efficiency by the Balasko–Shell criterion.

This finding allows us to state

Proposition. *A payment of $y > 0$ of earnings on fiat money, no matter how small, forces efficiency of all equilibria in OG models provided that free disposal or limited liability obtains.*

Tirole (1985) probes the robustness of Scheinkman's efficiency conclusions to the introduction of population growth and technical change. There exist combinations of exponential population growth and exponential technical change that vitiate Scheinkman's conclusion [Tirole (1985)]. But Dechert and Yamamoto (1985) have shown that if there is no technical progress and if population is eventually bounded, Scheinkman's conclusion holds. Since $y > 0$ can be arbitrarily small in the above proposition this type of inefficiency in OG models can be perturbed away by an arbitrarily small policy intervention. This type of argument has been used by some to argue that we should not take the hyperinflationary equilibria very seriously [see Obstfeld and Rogoff (1983) and their references]. Such writers could use a similar argument to dispose of the inefficiency issue as well. Also see McCallum (1987) on this issue. Note that this argument does not apply to the inefficiency caused by sunspot equilibria [Azariadis (1981), Shell (1977), Cass and Shell (1983)].

2.1.5. The offer curve diagram for an asset market

It is worth pointing out that the offer curve apparatus can be easily amended to depict equilibria when $y > 0$. Just draw the offer curve of the young through the same endowment point (w_y, w_o) as before, but replace the PPF, R, with $R^y = \{(c_y, c_o) | c_y + c_o = w_y + w_o + y\}$. Figure 7.3(a) depicts the steady-state equilibrium, L, and a sequence of equilibria that converge to the lower steady state, L^n, where the value of the asset is negative. Recall that free disposal eliminates these and that they are the analogues of Gale's hyperinflationary equilibria when $y = 0$. Also recall that the case $y = 0$ is the case of pure fiat

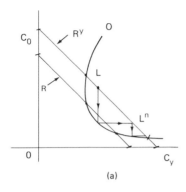

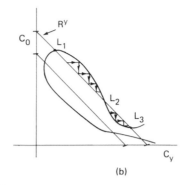

(a)   (b)

Figure 7.3

money. Figure 7.3(b) depicts three positive steady-state equilibria and a continuum of positive equilibria. This shows that $y > 0$ will not get rid of the possibility of a continuum of equilibria. These equilibria are robust in the sense that they cannot be perturbed away by a small perturbation of tastes and endowments.

2.1.6. Uncertainty

The presence of uncertainty, both instrinsic and extrinsic, creates new issues that must be dealt with. First, there is the broad issue of Pareto optimality of equilibria. Does the presence of a stock market force efficiency in a world of uncertainty?

One may introduce a stock market along the lines of Brock (1982) into a one-good heterogeneous agent OG model, but then one faces the well-known issue of what the objective of the "value maximizing firm" is to be in a world where different people want risks and returns packaged differently and there is a paucity of Arrow–Debreu markets available in which to force equality of marginal rates of substitution across different states of the world. Suppose sufficient market completeness [e.g. Krouse (1986, ch. 8)] conditions hold for unanimous security holder agreement on firm value maximization. One can get by with less than a full set of Arrow securities but assume a full set of Arrow securities for simplicity [cf. Krouse (1986)]. In this case there is a common objective for the firm. Each security holder discounts the future net cash flow of the firm using the same discount factors. The presence of a value-maximizing firm will force production efficiency. That is there is no alternative path of aggregate consumption and investment such that aggregate consumption is bigger along a set of non-trivial probability. The reason for this result is that the presence of an aggregative value-maximizing firm provides a numerical ranking for aggregate consumption and capital accumulation paths.

Such a result is of limited usefulness since there may be Pareto improving moves available by reallocating risks even though there are no intertemporal increases in aggregate consumption available. Furthermore, the problem of common agreement on the firm's objective is serious. But little has been done, to my knowledge, in exploring whether the idea of Kihlstrom and Laffont (1982) of introducing "clientele entrepreneurs" who package firms to satisfy homogeneous groups or "clienteles" would restore efficiency. This appears to be an open research area.

2.1.7. Sunspot equilibria, incomplete markets, heterogeneity, and efficiency

It is easy to modify the technique of Azariadis (1981) and Azariadis and Guesnerie (1986) to find examples of OG models where sunspot equilibria exist even if there is a market for claims to an asset that pays $y > 0$ per period. That is to say, there can be equilibria that are random even though preferences and endowments are deterministic. See Shell (1977), Azariadis (1981), and Cass and Shell (1983) for discussions of such equilibria. A method of constructing stationary sunspot equilibria is to construct an offer curve that displays a cycle around L, as in Figure 7.2. Then use the connection between cycles and sunspots developed by Azariadis and Guesnerie. Also see Woodford's (1984) survey. The bottom line is that it is hard to get rid of sunspot indeterminacy in these models.

Sunspots are linked to the presence of incomplete markets. Hence, Azariadis's (1981) suggestion that opening an Arrow–Debreu market for the extrinsic uncertainty source driving the sunspot will nullify the real effects of the sunspot may be relevant for positive economics. To put it another way, macroeconomists and monetary theorists of a practical bent are going to question the quantitative importance of sunspots. This brings up the following question: Under what conditions does the presence of Arrow securities on the sunspot variable nullify the real effects of the sunspot? And, can we find a class of models whose parameter values are consistent with existing empirical studies and whose market institutions reflect the multitude of securities marketed in modern financial capitals such that combinations of Arrow securities that look like modern securities, such as options, do not nullify the real effect of sunspots that are present?

In Azariadis's case young and old agents are allowed to insure against the sunspot state (before it is revealed) on the contingent claims market. If this is interpreted as allowing the young to insure against the sunspot that they are born in before they are born, then this device for getting rid of sunspots is not very realistic. The relationship between the quantitative welfare importance of sunspot equilibria and the magnitude of potential profits to market entrepreneurs creating imaginative securities that nullify the real effects of sunspots is, to my knowledge, an unexplored topic. The discussion in Woodford (1986c, 1987) is useful to researchers working this topic. McManus (1986) attacks a related question in a general equilibrium model with options. He shows that, in a general equilibrium setting, generically the presence of options delivers existence, Pareto optimality, regularity, and finiteness of the number of equilibria. To my knowledge the relationship between sunspot equilibria and options is unexplored.

There is another problem in getting macro-econometricians and other "practical" people to take seriously extrinsic uncertainty and its potential welfare losses, and its case for government intervention.

The theory may have no testable implications. To put it another way, it may be impossible to observationally distinguish the presence of extrinsic uncertainty equilibria from "news" or the implications of information-based equilibrium models [Hamilton and Whiteman (1985), Singleton (1986)]. Merely pointing out wild responses of stock prices to the mutterings of Wall Street "gurus" does not prove that extrinsic uncertainty is present since the gurus may receive information that affects fundamentals that the rest of the market does not have. Similarly, the apparent "over reaction" of the stock market to events such as the assassination of President Kennedy may reflect an impact of an increase of policy uncertainty upon fundamentals which gets partially resolved when a smooth transition of power takes place.

More convincing evidence could be that events like cosmetic accounting changes have no influence on stock prices. In this case, it seems clear that there was no effect on fundamentals yet it seems possible that an event like this may play the role of "extrinsic uncertainty". Some evidence in finance suggests that they do not. See the discussion of event studies in finance in Fama's book (1976), especially the work of Ball on page 377. Other evidence in finance suggests that they do. See DeLong et al. (1987) and references.

Woodford (1986c) develops a setup that may be viewed as an abstraction of earlier writings of Keynes and Kalecki on the role of financial constraints in generating aggregate fluctuations put into a modern equilibrium framework. Sunspot equilibria are generated from a setup with two types of infinitely lived agents ("capitalists" and "workers") facing borrowing constraints. Woodford (1986c) shows that if a deterministic steady state is present such that the equilibrium difference equation is locally stable at that steady state, then there is a continuum of non-stationary deterministic equilibria converging to that steady state. Under these conditions he shows that there is also a stochastic process of sunspot equilibria that behaves like actual business cycle data under plausible parameterizations of preferences and borrowing constraints.

In any event, the long-run concern of the bulk of the economics profession about whether indeterminacy of equilibria and sunspots and the welfare losses that they cause in a case for government intervention, is probably going to turn on the empirical issues.

After all, indeterminacy of equilibria is a phenomenon that has been known for a long time in monetary perfect foresight models. It has also been known for a long time that some means of keeping the economy at a particular equilibrium would increase welfare. See Gray (1984), Obstfeld and Rogoff (1983, 1986), and Laussel and Soubeyran (1987) for discussion, correction, and clarification of earlier literature in this area.

It is not clear that such equilibria have had much influence on policy to date. The extra piece of bad news that sunspot equilibria can exist, as well as a continuum of deterministic equilibria, may have little influence on policy discussions for the same reasons that the discovery of a continuum of de-terministic equilibria has had little influence. This situation may be changing, however.

There has been some apparent influence of such equilibria on policy discussions. See Sargent's (1987, p. 282) discussion of the "slippery side of the Laffer curve". This is the proposition that there are typically two equilibria (two rates of inflation) that will raise the same real revenue from the inflation tax. One of them (the lower inflation rate equilibrium) dominates the other. There is typically a continuum of equilibria converging to the high inflation rate equilibrium just like there is a continuum of equilibria converging to the autarkic equilibrium in Gale's case. The policy comments of Dornbusch (1985) could be interpreted as having been influenced by the possibility of a con-tinuum of equilibria. The possibility of two equilibria raises the question of stability.

Marcet and Sargent (1987) have shown that if an equilibrium exists under least squares learning, the inflation rate converges to the stationary rational expectations equilibrium with a low inflation rate. This equilibrium has "classi-cal" comparative statics in the sense that an increase in the permanent government deficit leads to an increase in the stationary inflation rate. The other equilibrium has reverse comparative statics. It can be argued that least squares learning is an attractive way to model learning dynamics. Lucas (1986) also studies a class of adjustment processes under which the "classical" equilibrium is stable. See the earlier discussion of policy influence of indeter-minacy of equilibria.

One reason for the potential lack of influence of these equilibria on policy may be the "nirvana" fallacy discussed below. Another reason, which is related to the nirvana fallacy, is that the actual implementation of stabilization policy based upon indeterminacy of equilibria such as sunspots may generate more policy noise than the original extrinsic uncertainty. After all, policy determined in a political environment of constantly shifting winning coalitions of special interests may be harder for the economic system to cope with than the indeterminacy of equilibrium that the policy is supposed to fix. To put it another way, for policies designed to cope with market noise caused by indeterminacy of equilibria and/or sunspot equilibria, policy noise may be worse than market noise.

A theoretical issue that was touched upon above that may play role in determining the long-run impact of the indeterminacy of equilibria/sunspot notion on monetary theory and macroeconomics in the question of comparative statics and dynamics. For example, in Gale's (1973) OG model, how is one to investigate the impact on equilibria of a comparative dynamics experiment such as, say, an increase in an old person's endowment at some date $t_o = 2$? Since no other endowments change, the deterministic steady state at dates $t \geq 2$ does not change. It is easy to see from the $A = B$ difference equation discussed above that deterministic steady-state real balances fall at date 1 because B falls at date 2. In the separable case discussed above this causes a drop in the value of money at the steady state for date 1. Such a result seems intuitive. After all, the urge of the young at date 1 to carry wealth into their old age has now dropped at date 1.

Doing such comparative statics or dynamics exercises seems straightforward provided that we stick to the analogue of the positive-valued monetary steady state. In many cases this equilibrium is stable under Marcet–Sargent (1987) dynamics. But how are we to do comparative statics or dynamics for all the other possible equilibria, including the sunspot equilibria? This seems to be an unresolved problem.

One might think that a stability analysis with respect to reasonable learning processes would get rid of "unnatural equilibria" such as sunspots and cycles. But Woodford (1986b) constructs examples of learning processes that converge to a stationary sunspot equilibrium. Grandmont (1985) shows how learning processes can converge to cycles. We do not know of examples of sunspots or cycles that are stable under Marcet–Sargent learning dynamics, but we suspect that such examples can be constructed.

2.1.8. Are sunspots and indeterminacy an OG problem?

Owing to the focus of the literature on sunspots and indeterminacy on OG models, the casual reader may be lulled into thinking that this problem is special to OG models. This is not so. The early paper of Brock (1974) displays a continuum of equilibria in MIUF perfect foresight models. These equilibria satisfy the transversality condition at infinity. They can be Pareto ranked. Subsequent papers, for example Obstfeld and Rogoff (1983, 1986), Gray (1984), and Laussel and Soubeyran (1987), develop and clarify the theme of multiple equilibria in this type of rational expectations model as well as the conditions for uniqueness of equilibrium. The diagrams on page 99 of Gray (1984) and page 680 of Obstfeld and Rogoff (1983) are especially useful in understanding the possibilities that can appear in this model. Scheinkman (1980) displays a continuum of equilibria in a transactions cost Clower constraint model with infinitely lived agents. Hence, no one can argue that these equilibria are due to "myopia" or are caused by looking at "reduced-form" models. Furthermore, Brock (1974) indicates how multiple steady-state equilibria can arise when the utility function is not separable in consumption and real balances. Calvo (1979) shows that indeterminacy can arise in models with real balances in the production function.

It was pointed out by Brock (1974) that the indeterminacy problem was caused by the appearance of the price level in the utility function or the transactions technology that generates the indirect utility function. This creates a non-pecuniary external effect in the sense that the actions of the rest of the agents in the economy change the utility *function* of each agent in the economy. This is so because the price level itself appears in the utility function. The utility function as a function of *real* balances is not changed, however.

There seems to be a loose relationship between the inherent incompleteness of markets when non-pecuniary externalities are present, the inherent incompleteness of markets in OG setups, and the problem of indeterminacy of equilibria. It should be possible to construct complicated equilibria, possibly even chatoic equilibria [Grandmont (1985)], as well as sunspot equilibria, in the examples of Brock (1974), Calvo (1979), and Scheinkman (1980) type models, but I have not seen it done.

Presumably the technique of Boldrin and Montruccio (1986) could be adapted to produce chaotic equilibria in these types of models, but I have not seen it done. Woodford (1985b) shows that stationary sunspot equilibria are possible in the closely related Wilson (1979) and Lucas–Stokey (1984) CIA models. In conclusion, indeterminacy is not unique to OG models.

2.1.9. Robustness of conclusions to many goods

One may view Wilson's paper (1981) as showing that the efficiency conclusions adduced above of the introduction of land, commodity money, or markets for claims to $y > 0$ per period, or certain kinds of transactions costs, are robust to the inclusion of many goods and many agents. The basic idea of Wilson (1981) is that if the value of the aggregate endowment is finite at the equilibrium price, then the equilibrium is Pareto optimal. Hence, any institution like a market for claims to "land" that pays $y > 0$ per period will force the interest rate sequence to satisfy the Balasko–Shell efficiency criterion (6) above. This is closely related to finite valuation of the aggregate endowment. Hence, Wilson's condition will be satisfied in many cases. See Wright (1986) for more on this. Robustness of the results on indeterminacy is another story.

Kehoe and Levine (1985) have examined to what extent the results of Gale (1973) generalize to an n-good economy. Quoting Woodford's (1984) survey:

> They show that the one-good case is very special: in that case one never has local non-uniqueness of non-monetary equilibrium, and a non-monetary

steady state is indeterminate if and only if it is inefficient. But for $n > 1$, it is possible to have a continuum of non-monetary equilibria converging to a non-monetary steady state, whether it is efficient or not. In particular, when $n > 1$, it is possible to have a Pareto optimal non-monetary steady state that is nonetheless indeterminate.

It is interesting that a non-monetary steady state can be efficient even though intergenerational trading through money is not possible.

In conclusion, it seems to be an open area of research to investigate how macroeconomic conclusions such as the Ricardian theorem [Barro (1974)], open market operations analysis [Wallace (1981)], efficiency analysis of interest bearing national debt [Bryant and Wallace (1979)], possible Pareto optimality of a "real-bills" regime [Sargent and Wallace (1982)], etc. stand up to the introduction of many goods.

It seems plausible that you can probably get anything you want if you introduce incomplete markets, agent heterogeneity, and scatter Clower constraints around some of the agents' budget constraints some of the time. There are enough "free parameters" around in these setups that a version of Debreu's (1974) treatment of the Sonnenschein–Mantel–Debreu theorem on the arbitrariness of excess demand will probably exist.

Such a "logical-possibility-school" approach to macroeconomics may not be very persuasive but it is not asking too much that the results survive the introduction of many goods before we are asked to take them seriously. More persuasive than the simple production of a logical possibility would be the production of the same logical possibility in a model context where the choice of the model's parameters is disciplined by empirical studies. The work of Woodford, for example Woodford (1987), is an attempt to get around the charge that theorists come "bearing free parameters undisciplined by empirical studies".

2.2. Modification of the basic OG model for legal restrictions

A prominent development in the use of OG models to attack questions in monetary theory is the literature [Sargent (1987) and references] on the use of legal restrictions to inhibit the intermediation of government bonds by a price-discriminating monopolistic issuer of unbacked paper (such as the U.S. government). In OG models like those of Gale (1973) or Wallace (1980), where fiat money is the only way to carry purchasing power from youth to old age, another store of value that pays interest will drive out money.

In a world with two types of unbacked government paper, like fiat money and government bonds, the issue of rate of return dominance arises. That is to say, government bonds will drive money out of the model since they pay interest and money does not. Indeed, this problem arises in OG models whenever another store of value such as land appears. Returning to the problem of explaining the coexistence of government bonds and fiat money in OG equilibrium, Bryant and Wallace (1984), Sargent and Wallace (1982) and Wallace (1983) rely on legal restrictions. Legal restrictions may be looked upon as a form of institutionally imposed transactions costs.

3. Positive economics

Positive economics may be divided into two broad categories for the purpose of this chapter. The first is whether OG models capture what it is about money that makes it money. The second is the explanation and organization of the cross-sectional and time-series relationships between money and other economic variables that are actually observed.

3.1. Is the stuff in OG models "money"?

Defining "money" is a knotty issue, and is beyond the scope of this chapter. For example, Osborne (1984, 1985), after reviewing discussions by Jevons, Harry Johnson, L. Yeager, G.L.S. Shackle, Wicksell, etc., settles on the following criteria for something to be called money: (a) it must circulate routinely as a medium of exchange, and (b) its holders all must be able to spend it at the same time if they wish (simultaneity of payments). He argues that only the monetary base which is defined to be the sum of currency outstanding and depository institutions' reserve balances at the central bank satisfies these criteria in the United States today. It is not clear that "medium of exchange" has a satisfactory definition.

    Tobin (1980) lists several reasons why he does not think that the OG model is the way to explain money in its customary meaning (assuming we *can* define it). First, money is a universal phenomenon, "surely not observed solely in societies or eras in which the net marginal product of capital has not exceeded the growth rate". Second, "if a nonreproducible asset has been needed for intergenerational transfers of wealth, land has always been available. Quantitatively it has been a much more important store of value than money." Third, to get valued fiat money in the OG model you need saving followed by dissaving. But the dominant pattern has been the reverse, yet money has been observed. Fourth, the constructive immortality of Barro (1974) has shown that agents in an OG may act "as if" immortal provided that they have the *utility* of their descendents in their utility functions. Money may disappear in such a model and Tobin thinks that the particular treatment of bequests is a fragile basis upon which to erect monetary theory. Fifth, he says: "isn't it slightly ridiculous to identify as money the asset that the typical agent of the model would hold for an average of 25 years, say from age 40 to age 65? The average holding period of a dollar of demand deposits is about 2 days." Sixth, social security schemes were widely adopted by societies where fiat money was already present to play the role that M plays in the OG.

He sums up by saying that the OG captures one feature of money: its value to me today depends on its value to you tomorrow which in turn depends on its value to someone else the day after... But it misses money's use as a transactions medium and unit of account – "The traditional explanation of money is the division of labor, the daily recurring need to exchange specialized endowments or products for diversified consumption goods and services." Tobin also mentions the use of money as a common accounting and record-keeping system that all members of society agree upon is analogous to a national language. Thus, the existence of such a device increases the productivity of the economy but it has a basic public good character that is going to be hard to derive endogenously from Arrow–Debreu like setups.

On could argue that Tobin is interpreting a useful metaphor too literally, such as the fifth objection. But other objections, such as the third, are harder to bypass. When you put a realistic time scale in the model so that "generation" becomes a typical pay period, you need enough people who want to save now to consume in the future (to play the role of the "young") and you need people on the other side of the market who want to consume now (to play the role of the "old").

Furthermore, a condition on tastes and endowments of these two groups is needed to insure that the equilibrium value of money is positive. The simple Gale (1973) model tells us that a condition on tastes and endowments is needed to get positively valued fiat money in equilibrium. To put it another way, if the offer curve of the young cuts the production possibility frontier from above, then there is no equilibrium with positively valued fiat money.

Aiyagari (1987) has found conditions for positively valued fiat money in an OG model with a realistic time scale. He examines a sequence of OG models were agents live T periods and takes T to infinity. For T big enough he shows that if the subjective rate of time preference is greater than the rate of growth of population in the economy, no monetary steady state exists, and if the subjective rate of time preference is less than the rate of growth, then a monetary steady state exists. This result holds for a wide class of endowment variations and heterogeneous agents but all are required to discount future utility at the same rate to avoid the problem of the low discount fellow getting all the assets in the long run. Aiyagari's result reflects the tendency of the relation between the rate of time preference and the rate of growth to determine long-run behavior. For the longer the agents live, the more periods they have to indulge in consumption smoothing, and the more time the economic forces behind the permanent income hypothesis have to work. As T gets large the long-run behavior looks like that of Bewley's (1982) general equilibrium turnpike model.

Aiyagari's results are enough to make one nervous about insisting that the OG model with no role for money except the store of value role is the *only* sensible model for monetary theory.

3.2. Open market operations

Perhaps one of the most striking propositions to emerge from the OG approach to monetary theory is the "Modigliani–Miller" theorem on open market operations [Wallace (1981)]. We follow Sargent (1987, ch. 8). Propositions of this genre study the equivalence class of alternative government policies in which particular subsets of variables in equilibrium assume the same values. The idea is to assume an economy in which government and private securities exist and are valued in an initial equilibrium with a given specification of government policy strategies. One solves the equilibrium conditions for the class of government policies that support the old consumption allocation. Irrelevance theorems correspond to movements within the equivalence class of government policies associated with the initial equilibrium. See Sargent (1987, ch. 8) for a nice discussion of this type of proposition.

For example, this type of proposition isolates conditions such that a purchase of government bonds with newly printed money has no effect on the price level. Contrast this with the usual result [Barro (1974, p. 384)] that the price level increases in the same proportion as the increase in the quantity of money. McCallum (1983, p. 33) points out that if real money balances provide a transactions service, then the invariance result is false. The issue turns on the relative usefulness of money and bonds. If money is useful and bonds are not and we are in a Ricardian world where agents capitalize future tax liabilities, then the real quantity of money remains unchanged after the open market purchase. Hence, the price level moves up with the increase in the quantity of money.

3.3. Monetary growth in an OG model with storage available

Another striking result of Wallace (1980) is that when a costless storage technology is available where $1/(1 + d)$ units of goods are left at $t + 1$ for each unit placed into storage at date t, then monetary growth forever at factor $s > d$

leads to valueless fiat money. McCallum (1983), for example, argues that this kind of result would disappear if a medium-of-exchange function for money were appended to the model. Some care has to be taken, however, with this kind of result. It depends on how "essential" the medium of exchange function is [Scheinkman (1980)]. McCallum points out that if one took this result seriously and inserted realistic values for population growth and depreciation rates, Wallace's result would imply that a rate of growth greater than 10 percent per annum of the monetary base would drive the value of the U.S. dollar to zero and the U.S. price level to infinity. Of course, it may be unfair to take a useful metaphor that seriously. But the criticism may be a fair rebuttal to those who argue that the *only* sensible model for monetary theory is an OG model with *only* a store of value role allowed for money and insertion of legal restrictions to save money from being driven out by bonds. See Sargent's (1987) book for a complete discussion of bonds and money in OG models.

4. Modifications of the OG model

Perhaps in reaction to the feeling that the OG model is a useful metaphor but that the store-of-value role assigned to money in the model is too narrow, theorists have been revising and supplementing the OG model.

Bewley (1984) has formulated a heterogeneous agent OG model where (i) agents live many periods; (ii) consumers face individual, but uninsurable risks; there is a continuum of individuals and the individual risks are mutually independent; (iii) there is uncertainty at the aggregate level generated by a random variable which everyone observes; (iv) there is a Clower constraint on payments; and (v) people cannot borrow against future wage income. In this model he proves existence of valued fiat money equilibria as well as analogues of the first and second welfare theorems. He also shows how business cycles or trade fluctuations arise in the model.

Some economists object that the Clower constraint is an ad hoc way to "force" positivity of fiat money in equilibrium. The work of Gale and Hellwig (1984) looks at a transactions cost based model that gets rid of some of the objections to the "adhockery" of the Clower constraint. They formulate a model with infinitely lived individuals facing Baumol–Tobin type inventory problems of moving in and out of cash to transact for goods. Although their model is a general equilibrium model it is not an OG model unless, perhaps, one interpreted their agents as a "caring" family in Barro's (1974) precise sense. In any event they prove the existence of a monetary equilibrium in which the value of money is bounded and bounded away from zero. This eliminates equilibria that converge to non-monetary equilibria – unlike the case in OG models, as illustrated by the Gale model (1973) discussed above, or in the Kehoe–Levine models discussed in the Woodford (1984) survey.

Some economists argue that the OG analytical gambit of modelling "M" as a pure value store in a two-period-lived OG model is a stark and misleading view of money and a stark and misleading way to model the restraints on borrowing and lending that motivate the emergence of money. But Bewley (1986) shows that borrowing restraints on infinitely lived heterogeneous agent models where the agents have asymmetric endowments can lead to analytic behavior much like that of OG models. Hence, OG models may give us insights into the behavior of more attractive models with borrowing restraints.

Recursive cash-in-advance models of money and interest

There has been active recent research on infinite horizon models with cash-in-advance constraints. Example are Danthine, Donaldson and Smith (1985), Lucas and Stokey (1984), Woodford (1985b) and Stockman (1981).

These models may be viewed as OG models with Barro (1974) preferences and with transactions motives for holding money added in addition to the usual store of value motive. In this way money still has value in equilibrium even though its rate of return is dominated by other assets. This is so because of the transactions services that money provides.

Danthine et al. (1985) basically extend money-in-the-utility function models to the case of uncertainty in production and integrate these models with modern asset pricing theory with the objective of explaining correlations between monetary aggregates, financial aggregates, interest rates, and indices of production and consumption. Their main results show that the long-run neutrality of money disappears. This holds for much the same reason that the long-run steady state depends upon parameters of utility such as risk aversion in the stochastic growth model – in contrast to the deterministic growth model where the subjective rate of time preference alone determines the long-run steady-state capital stock [cf. Brock and Mirma (1972)].

5. Comparison and contrast between OG models and transactions-cost-based extensions

Here I will borrow from Sargent (1987). Sargent, in some of his chapters, compares and contrasts the implications of OG models with various other models for monetary theory.

5.1. Goals for these models

Sargent (1987) states six things that we want these types of models to help us to understand. They overlap some with issues that we have already raised. It should be clear by now that the boundary lines between OG models and cash-in-advance (CIA) and MIUF models are hard to draw. Hence, some of the points below will apply to CIA and MIUF models as well. In any event they are:

(1) *Money–price correlations.* Here the issue is what categories of evidence of indebtedness should one include in the aggregate called "money" in order to understand price level–money correlations. This is closely related to aggregation theoretic issues in defining "money" in such a way to get stable demand functions. Similar issues arise in defining monetary aggregrates whose control serves goals such as price level stability.

OG models where money plays no other role than a store of value, led to a view that price level–money aggregate correlations should be strongest for wide aggregates of currency and inside indebtedness. Such models tend to lead one to advocate legal restrictions to stop private government currency-substitutes producers from entering the money business if the goal is price level stability. The CIA and MIUF models tend to shut off such insights at the model-building stage. This remark does not apply to Scheinkman's (1980) adaptation of the CIA model where an alternative technology is available if the opportunity cost of holding government currency is large enough.

(2) *Free banking versus government regulation of banks.* As pointed out in the discussion of (1) above, OG models can lead to quite different views on the government regulation of banks than the CIA and MIUF models. See the literature discussed in Sargent (1987).

(3) *Rate of return dominance.* Here OG models force one to search for legal restrictions or analagous obstructions in order to explain the simultaneous holding of short-term government bonds that pay interest and "barren" currency. The CIA and MIUF models motivate search for "medium of exchange", "liquidity" services, or "precautionary" motives to put into the Clower constraint or the indirect utility or production function in order to explain the rate-of-return dominance paradox.

(4) *International exchange rate determination.* OG models stress the indeterminacy of exchange rates unless there are legal restrictions present. This mode of thinking leads one to examine governments' incentives to place legal restrictions on different kinds of monies in order to gain monetary autonomy and to prevent the formation of a self-destructive inflation commune.

(5) *Effects of open market operations.* As discussed before, OG models lead to a view that open market operations do not change the aggregate price level.

It is as if the government conducted operations substituting one-dollar bills for five-dollar bills.

(6) *Coordination of monetary and fiscal policies.* Both types of models generate strong irrelevance results which stress the interaction of fiscal and monetary policies. This is especially true in the international arena. The OG models teach us that the world is a monetary commune unless there are some kind of legal restrictions. The CIA and MIUF models tend to shut down this view at the point of formulation of the model.

I do not want to leave the reader with the impression that I am hostile to the CIA and MIUF models. After all, the OG models have "implicit theorizing" and arbitrary throttling of other insights built into them by their arbitrary shutting out of other functions of money besides store of value – as Tobin (1980) and others have pointed out. See Sargent's (1987) book for more discussion of these issues.

5.2. Irrelevance theorems

OG models like Gale's (1973) and Wallace's (1980), where money does nothing but play the role of a value store, generate a rich collection of "irrelevance results". As Sargent (1987) points out in his chapter, "Credit and Currency with Overlapping Generations", the main generating mechanism of such results is the fact that equilibria exist in which unbacked currency is valued and coexists with private loans. In such equilibria neither asset dominates the other in rate of return. From this property flows a stream of theorems: the "Modigliani–Miller" theorem of Wallace (1981); the exchange rate indeterminacy proposition of Kareken and Wallace (1981); the "rehabilitation" of the real bills doctrine of Sargent and Wallace (1982); and more.

5.3. Comparison with pure cash-in-advance models

Much recent research has been done investigating versions of Lucas's exchange economy asset pricing model (1978) with a Clower constraint grafted on. The main motivation for this is to generate a "dichotomy" where the real part of the economy can be studied independently of the monetary part. This gambit makes the analytics of rational expectations equilibrium easier.

Since cash-in-advance (CIA) models allow "barren" fiat money to coexist with securities paying a higher return, there are therefore incentives for private firms to market the "stuff" that relaxes Clower constraints. Since, if entry into the money business were free and if the money producers produced perfect substitutes for government money, implicit legal restrictions or some other obstruction must be assumed so that government currency is not driven out. Similar incentives for private money producers are present for MIUF models.

A major result of this work on CIA models is the irrelevance of government financial policy. Given a fixed sequence $\{g(t)\}$ of government expenditures, a large class of financial policies will finance $\{g(t)\}$ with no real effects on real interest rates, consumption, production, etc. Even indexed bonds are irrelevent in wide classes of cases. See Sargent (1987) for a discussion of such results.

A remarkable paper by Wilson (1979) contains a careful discussion of government policies in CIA models. It also contains major irrelevance results. Furthermore, he treats seriously the problem of specifying budget constraints for infinite-lived agents that prevent them from indulging in Ponzi games. Not only that, he takes care of the problem of assuring well-defined intertemporal demand functions for agents who can create "large" budget sets by borrowing and lending. There is much in his paper that has not yet been harvested for macroeconomics.

6. Open problems

The modification of OG models to introduce other functions of money, heterogeneity of agents, uncertainty, different treatments of bequests, etc. is a currently very intensively active area of research. It may be that the list of "open" problems below have been "closed" or have been shown to be unimportant.

6.1. Synthesis of Gale (1973) and Barro (1974)

Here I have in mind replacing Gale's utility function, $U(c_y, c_o)$, with $W = U(c_y, c_o, W') = $, for example $v + BW'$, where W is this generation's utility, v is the utility from own consumption in youth and old age, $B = 1/(1 + b)$, b is the discount rate on descendent's utility, and W' is next generation's utility. Allow the old to pass a bequest of cash balances to their young.

This kind of model has been used by Barro (1974) to analyze wealth effects of government bonds and social security schemes. Aiyagari (1987) has formulated an OG model whose limit could be viewed as Barro's model. Let T be the lifetime of each agent when born. Aiyagari shows that a monetary steady state does not exist as $T \to \infty$ if the growth rate, g, of population is less than b. Vice versa he shows that $g > b$ implies eventual existence and optimality of steady-state valued fiat money. Here is what I think is unknown. Insert Clower constraints into this type of model so that we can preserve valued fiat money when $b > g$. (i) What is the impact upon hyperinflationary tenuousness as well as other kinds of tenuousness? (ii) What is the impact on Wallace's "Modigliani–Miller" theorem of open market operations? (iii) What is the impact on the optimal management of the money supply – the optimum quantity of money? To put it another way, what is the impact of making $b > g$ in OG models, where $b = g$. Alternatively, how does inserting bequests *directly* into the utility function change results relevant to monetary theory from inserting *utility* of the descendents into the parents' utility function.

It seems clear that there is more than one way of inserting Clower constraints into these type of models. For example, Stockman (1981) shows that if you require cash-in-advance to finance consumption only in an infinite horizon [Barro (1974)] model, then the long-run equilibrium steady state of capital is not changed by monetary growth (i.e. money is neutral). But, if cash-in-advance is needed to finance both consumption and investment, then the long-run equilibrium steady state is changed and money is therefore not neutral.

Since models with infinitely lived agents are closely related to OG models with a Barro-type specification of bequests and since there are many studies of monetary theory in the former class of models, it may seem that my open questions listed above have already been treated. But there are two main directions of possible extension that I have not seen. One is a careful introduction of transactions costs such as various kinds of Clower constraints into "Gale-Barro" models where each generation has more than one period of own consumption. What is the economically most reasonable way to insert such constraints into the model?

Second, and closely related to the first, is the impact on the optimal quantity of money when heterogeneous agents are introduced into Gale–Barro models with transactions costs. It seems that a useful formulation of this question would involve a Pareto notion of the optimum quantity of money. To be more specific, confine oneself to constant rate of money growth policies at rate s. Let the proceeeds of money creation be distributed in fraction a_h to household h in a lump-sum manner. Consider the case of h households each with a degree of caring about their descendents,

$$b_1 < b_2 < \cdots < b_H .$$

Since there are transactions costs present the low b fellow, b_1, does not necessarily end up with all of the assets [in contrast to Becker (1980)]. It is important to realize that one household does not necessarily end up with all the wealth in the steady state if b_n is made a function of future utility, W_h', i.e. $b_h = b_h(w_h')$. See Epstein and Hynes (1983) for this treatment.

It is especially easy to see that a Pareto notion of the optimum quantity of money is needed if you conduct this exercise by introducing heterogeneous agents into the MIUF perfect foresight model of Brock (1974). The transactions services of real balances in the indirect utility function take up the "slack" in the first-order necessary conditions for steady-state equilibrium that squeezes wealth out of the high b people in the steady state. The steady-state Pareto problem is to choose a rate of monetary growth that is not Pareto dominated by any other rate of monetary growth across steady states. Of course there are a multitude of Pareto problems that one could formulate. For example, the distribution fractions, a_h, could be subject to policy choice and non-steady-state Pareto problems could be formulated.

The point is that I have not seen a careful study of the optimum quantity of money in a heterogeneous agent, "Gale–Barro", OG model with transactions costs and a careful treatment of the impact of different modelling of bequests.

6.2. Endogenous market structure and financial intermediaries in OG models

We have said very little about what happens to the propositions discussed above when endogenous market structure and financial intermediaries are taken into account. That is because very little has been done in this area. Williamson (1984) starts the task of integrating OG analysis in monetary theory with industrial organization theory. He shows that most of the results discussed above are not robust to the introduction of intermediaries when there are costs to setting up an intermediary firm and, thus, the number of intermediaries is endogenous and is changed by monetary policy.

Bernanke and Gertler (1987) introduce banks into OG models, review recent papers in this area, and present their own analysis of the effects of the introduction of endogenous intermediation on the proposition of OG monetary theory discussed above.

This type of research is very new. I classify this area as open because of the paucity of work in the area and the necessity of removing artificial rigidities in existing OG models due to the lack of integration with industrial organization theory – especially industrial organization theory with a more Austrian flavor. Indeed, a common criticism made by industrial organization economists of Arrow–Debreu and OG based modelling is that it neglects the inherent dynamism of the economic system and induces tunnel vision that misses quantitatively important effects. Phenomena such as Schumpeter's creative gales of destruction are hard to harness to the Arrow–Debreu framework.

After all, we could look very embarrassed as monetary theorists if Schumpeter's creative gales of destruction totally changed the form of money and eliminated "money" as we now know it. See Hester (1985) for a discussion of how monetary rules and prescriptions change when financial innovations are possible.

The conclusion is that it is an important problem to include dynamic phenomena such as financial innovations into our analytic frameworks before their policy prescriptions can be taken seriously. This is a point that is not unique to OG work in monetary theory.

6.3. Integration of policy analysis in OG models with neoclassical political economy to avoid the "nirvana" fallacy

It goes without saying that one of the main motivations for recent OG work in monetary theory is not to organize and explain data, but to have a framework to analyze government policy that is not tainted by "implicit theorizing" [Kareken and Wallace (1980)]. Much of the work is directed toward designing better institutional frameworks in which to conduct policy. But worse than such implicit theorizing as putting real balances into agent's utility functions is the implicit theorizing involved when the behavior of economic agents in manipulating institutions is ignored.

After all, rational firms equate returns to (i) lowering their cost functions, (ii) increasing quality, and (iii) locating new markets (we call this "invisible hand" activity) to returns (i) from getting protection from competition by use of the state, from (ii) lobbying to skew the distributive effects of state interventions such as monetary policy towards the firm and its workers. We call this latter kind of activity "invisible foot activity" [Brock and Magee in Colander (1984)] because competition in this dimension typically burns up resources and causes distortions which lead to welfare losses – in contrast to invisible hand activity.

An example of a policy that might look desirable, ignoring invisible foot activity, would be rifle shot injections of newly printed fiat money into industries currently experiencing distress where moral hazard or diversification problems prevent the emergence of Arrow–Debreu markets to hedge such risks [Scheinkman and Weiss (1986)]. Under plausible conditions such a policy may be ex ante expected utility Pareto improving – especially if the subsidies were lump sum. But if one allows an industry to invest in lobbying activities to convince authorities that their sector was particularly "distressed", one can imagine the distortions that would emerge as concentrated groups gained an advantage over diffuse groups in "documenting" that their group was particularly distressed, as well as the resources wasted in such "documentary" efforts.

See Magee's survey in Colander (1984) of rent-seeking theory in trade to see how the traditional policy conclusions of trade theory are overturned when rent-seeking or invisible foot activity is taken into account. Magee's article reviews work on building an analytical apparatus in which rent-seeking activities can be explicitly modelled and welfare analysis done. The same kind of exploration must be done in monetary economics before we can take the policy prescriptions seriously. Neglecting this kind of institutional analysis of the welfare conclusions of abstract models is sometimes called the "nirvana fallacy" in less formal areas of economic science. The above concerns with innovations and the nirvana fallacy may seem tangential to the focus of this chapter. But not spending a few paragraphs on these concerns may lull the reader into forgetting that they are present.

References

Aiyagari, R. (1987) 'Optimality and monetary equilibria in stationary overlapping generations models with long lived agents: Growth versus discounting', *Journal of Economic Theory*, 43: 292–313.

Aiyagari, R. and M. Gertier (1983) 'The backing of government bonds, debt management policy, and monetarism', Department of Economics, The University of Wisconsin at Madison.

Azariadis, C. (1981) 'Self fulfilling prophesies', *Journal of Economic Theory*, 25: 380–396.

Azariadis, C. and R. Guesnerie (1986) 'Sunspots and cycles', *Review of Economic Studies*, 53: 725–736.

Balasko, Y. (1983) 'Extrinsic uncertainty revisited', *Journal of Economic Theory*, 31: 203–210.

Balasko, Y. and K. Shell (1980) 'The overlapping generations model, 1: The case of pure exchange without money', *Journal of Economic Theory*, 23: 281–306.

Balasko Y. and K. Shell (1981) 'The overlapping-generations model, 2: The case of pure exchange with money', *Journal of Economic Theory*, 24: 112–142.

Balask, Y., D. Cass and K. Shell (1980) 'Existence of competitive equilibrium in a general overlapping-generations model', *Journal of Economic Theory*, 23: 307–322.

Barro, R. (1974) 'Are government bonds net wealth?', *Journal of Political Economy*, 82: 1095–1117.

Becker, R. (1980) 'On the long-run steady state in a simple dynamic model of equilibrium with heterogeneous households', *Quarterly Journal of Economics*, 95: 375–382.

Benveniste, L. and D. Gale (1975) 'An extension of Cass' characterisation of infinite efficient production programs', *Journal of Economic Theory*, 10: 229–238.

Bernanke, B. and M. Gertler (1987) 'Banking in general equilibrium', in: W. Barnett and K. Singleton, eds., *New approaches to monetary economics*. New York: Cambridge University Press, pp. 89–114.

Bewley, T. (1972) 'Existence of equilibria in economics with infinitely many commodities', *Journal of Economic Theory*, 4: 514–540.

Bewley, T. (1982) 'An integration of equilibrium theory and turnpike theory', *Journal of Mathematical Economics*, 10: 233–267.

Bewley, T. (1984) 'Fiscal and monetary policy in a general equilibrium model', Cowles Foundation Working Paper, Yale University.

Bewley, T. (1986) 'Dynamic implications of the form of the budget constraint', in: H. Sonnenschein, ed., *Models of economic dynamics*, 264. New York: Springer-Verlag, pp. 117–123.

Boldrin, M. and L. Montrucchio (1986) 'On the indeterminacy of capital accumulation paths,' *Journal of Economic Theory*, 40: 26–39.

Brock, W. (1974) 'Money and growth: The case of long run perfect foresight', *International Economic Review*, 15: 750–777.

Brock, W. (1982) 'Asset prices in a production economy', in: J. McCall, ed., *The economics of information and uncertainty*. Chicago: The University of Chicago Press, pp. 1–46.

Brock, W. and L. Mirman (1972) 'Optimal economic growth under uncertainty', *Journal of Economic Theory*, 4: 479–513.

Brock, W. and J. Scheinkman (1980) 'Some remarks on monetary policy in an overlapping generations model', in: J. Kareken and N. Wallace, eds., *Models of monetary economies*. Federal Reserve Bank of Minneapolis.

Bryant, J. and N. Wallace (1979) 'The inefficiency of interest-bearing debt', *Journal of Political Economy*, 87: 365–381.

Bryant, J. and N. Wallace (1984) 'A price discrimination analysis of monetary policy', *Review of Economic Studies*, 51: 279–288.

Calvo, G. (1979) 'On models of money and perfect foresight', *International Economic Review*, 20: 83–103.

Cass, D. (1972) 'On capital overaccumulation in the aggregative, neoclassical model of economic growth: A complete characterization', *Journal of Economic Theory*, 4: 200–223.

Cass, D. and K. Shell (1980) 'In defense of a basic approach', in: J. Kareken and N. Wallace, eds., *Models of monetary economies*. Federal Reserve Bank of Minneapolis, pp. 251–260.

Cass, D. and K. Shell (1983) 'Do sunspots matter?', *Journal of Political Economy*, 91: 193–227.

Cass, D., M. Okuno and I. Zilcha (1980) 'The role of money in supporting the Pareto optimality of competitive equilibrium in consumption loan models,' in: J. Kareken and N. Wallace, eds., *Models of monetary economies*. Federal Reserve Bank of Minneapolis.

Chae, S. (1984) 'Liquidity constraints in a monetary economy with incomplete financial markets', CARESS Working Paper 84-O1R, Center for Analytic Research in Economics and the Social Sciences, The University of Pennsylvania.

Chamley, C. and H. Polemarchakis (1984) 'Assets, general equilibrium, and the neutrality of money', *Review of Economic Studies*, 51: 129–138.

Clower, R. (1967) 'A reconsideration of the microfoundations of monetary theory', *Western Economic Journal*, 6: 1–9.

Colander, D., ed. (1984) *Neoclassical political economy: The analysis of rent-seeking and DUP activities*. Cambridge, Mass.: Ballinger.

Danthine, J. (1985) 'Inflation and growth in utility-maximizing models', Department of Economics, Universite de Lausanne.

Danthine, J., J. Donaldson and L. Smith (1985) 'On the superneutrality of money in a stochastic dynamic macroeconomic model', Department of Economics, Universite de Lausanne.

Debreu, G. (1970) 'Economies with a finite set of equilibria', *Econometrica*, 38: 387–392.

Debreu, G. (1974) 'Excess demand functions', *Journal of Mathematical Economics*, 1: 15–21.

Dechert, W. and K. Yamamoto (1985) 'Asset trading in an overlapping generations model with production shocks', Department of Economics, State University of New York at Buffalo.

DeLong, J., A. Shleifer, L. Summers and R. Waldmann (1987) 'The economic consequences of noise traders', Boston University, University of Chicago, and Harvard University.

Dornbusch, R. (1985) 'Comments, Brazil', in: J. Williamson, ed., *Inflation and indexation*. Cambridge, Mass.: M.I.T. Press, pp. 45–55.

Epstein, L. and A. Hynes (1983) 'The rate of time preference and dynamic economic analysis', *Journal of Political Economy*, 91: 611–635.

Fama, E. (1976) *Foundations of finance*. New York: Basic Books.

Farmer, E. (1984) 'Cash, contracts, and Clower constraints', CARESS Working Paper 84-16, Center for Analytic Research in Economics and the Social Sciences, University of Pennsylvania.

Farmer, R. and M. Woodford (1984) 'Self-fulfilling prophecies and the business cycle', CARESS Working Paper 84-12, Center for Analytic Research in Economics and the Social Sciences, The University of Pennsylvania.

Feenstra, R. (1986) 'Functional equivalence between liquidity costs and the utility of money', *Journal of Monetary Economics*, 17: 271–291.

Freeman, S. (1985) 'Transactions costs and the optimal quantity of money', *Journal of Political Economy*, 93: 146–157.

Gale, D. (1973) 'Pure exchange equilibrium of dynamic economic models', *Journal of Economic Theory*, 6: 12–36.

Gale, D. (1983) *Money: In disequilibrium*, Cambridge Economic Handbooks. Cambridge: Cambridge University Press, and Welwyn: J. Nisbet.

Gale, D. (1985) 'The strategic analysis of bequest behavior: A critique of the Ricardian equivalence theorem', CARESS Working Paper 85-31, Center for Analytic Research in Economics and the Social Sciences, The University of Pennsylvania.

Gale, D. and M. Hellwig (1984) 'A general-equilibrium model of the transactions demand for money', CARESS Working Paper 85-07, Center for Analytic Research in Economics and the Social Sciences, The University of Pennsylvania.

Grandmont, J. (1983) *Money and value*. Cambridge: Cambridge University Press.

Grandmont, J. (1985) 'On endogenous competitive business cycles', *Econometrica*, 53: 995–1045.

Grandmont, J. and G. Laroque (1973) 'Money in the pure consumption loan model', *Journal of Economic Theory*, 6: 382–395.

Gray, J. (1984) 'Dynamic instability in rational expectations models: An attempt to clarify', *International Economic Review*, 25: 93–122.

Hahn, F. (1965) 'On some problems of proving the existence of an equilibrium in a monetary economy', in: F. Hahn and F. Brechling, eds., *The theory of interest rates*. London: Macmillan, pp. 126–135.

Hahn, F. (1971) 'Equilibrium with transaction costs' *Econometrica*, 39: 417–439.

Hahn, F. (1973) 'On transaction costs, inessential sequence economies and money', *Review of Economic Studies*, 40: 449–461.

Hahn, F. (1982) *Money and inflation*. Oxford: Basil Blackwell.

Hamilton, J. and C. Whiteman (1985) 'The observable implications of self-fulfilling expectations', *Journal of Monetary Economics*, 16: 353–374.

Heller, W. (1974) 'The holding of money balances in general equilibrium', *Journal of Economic Theory*, 7: 93–108.

Heller, W. and R. Starr (1976) 'Equilibrium with non-convex transactions costs: Monetary and non-monetary economies', *Review of Economic Studies*, 43: 195–215.

Hester, D. (1985) 'Monetary policy in an evolutionary disequilibrium', Department of Economics, The University of Wisconsin, Madison.

Holl, B. (1976) 'Money, expectations, and the existence of a temporary equilibrium'. *Review of Economic Studies*, 43: 439–445.

Kareken, J. and N. Wallace, eds. (1980) *Models of monetary economies*. Federal Reverve Bank of Minneapolis.

Kareken, J. and N. Wallace (1981) 'On the indeterminacy of equilibrium exchange rates', *Quarterly Journal of Economics*, 96: 207–222.

Kihlstrom, R. and J. Laffont (1982) 'A competitive entrepreneurial model of a stock market', in: J. McCall, ed., *The economics of information and uncertainty*. Chicago: The University of Chicago Press, pp. 141–202.

Kehoe, T. and D. Levine (1985) 'Comparative statics and perfect foresight in infinite horizon economies', *Econometrica*, 53: 445–453.

Kehoe, T. and D. Levine (1987) 'The economics of indeterminacy in overlapping generations models', Cambridge University and UCLA.

Krouse, C. (1986) *Capital markets and prices*. New York: North-Holland.

Laussel, D. and A. Soubeyran (1987) 'Speculative bubbles in monetary optimizing models: Towards a synthesis', Southern European Economics Discussion Series, D.P. 58.

Lucas, R. (1978) 'Asset prices in an exchange economy', *Econometrica*, 46: 1426–1445.

Lucas, R. (1986) 'Adaptive behavior and economic theory', *The Journal of Business*, 59: 217–242.

Lucas, R. and N. Stokey (1984) 'Money and prices in a cash-in-advance economy', Center for Mathematical Studies in Economics and Management Science, Working Paper 628, Northwestern University.

Marcet, A. and T. Sargent (1987) 'Least squares learning and the dynamics of hyperinflation', Carnegie Mellon University and Hoover Institution.

McCallum, B. (1987) 'The optimal inflation rate in an overlapping-generations economy with land', in: W. Barnett and K. Singleton, eds., *New approaches to monetary economics*. New York: Cambridge University Press, pp. 325–339.

McCallum, B. (1983) 'The role of overlapping-generations models in monetary economics', *Carnegie-Rochester Conference Series on Public Policy*, 18: New York: North-Holland.

McCallum, B. (1984) 'Macroeconomic effects of monetary policy', *NBER Reporter*, Winter.

McManus, D. (1986) 'Regular options equilibria', CARESS Working Paper 86-13, University of Pennsylvania.

Michener, R. (1981) 'Money, growth and the theory of interest', Ph.D. dissertation, University of Chicago.

Obstfeld, M. and K. Rogoff (1983) 'Speculative hyperinflations in maximizing models: Can we rule them out?', *Journal of Political Economy*, 91: 675–705.

Obstfeld, M. and K. Rogoff (1986) 'Ruling out divergent speculative bubbles', *Journal of Monetary Economics*, 17: 349–362.

Osborne, D. (1984) 'Ten approaches to the definition of money', *Economic Review*, March, Federal Reserve Bank of Dallas.

Osborne, D. (1985) 'What is money today?', *Economic Review*, January: 1-16, Federal Reserve Bank of Dallas.

Patinkin, D. (1983) 'Paul Samuelson's contribution to monetary economics', in: E. Brown and R. Solow, eds., *Paul Samuelson and modern economic theory*. New York: McGraw-Hill, pp. 157–168.

Samuelson, P. (1958) 'An exact consumption–loan model of interest with or without the social contrivance of money', *Journal of Political Economy*, 66: 467–482.

Sargent, T. (1987) *Dynamic macroeconomic theory*. Cambridge, Mass.: Harvard University Press.

Sargent, T. and N. Wallace (1982) 'The real-bills doctrine versus the quantity theory: A reconsideration', *Journal of Political Economy*, 90: 1212–1236.

Scheinkman, J. (1977) 'Notes on asset prices', Department of Economics, The University of Chicago.

Scheinkman, J. (1978) 'Notes on asset trading in an overlapping generations model', Department of Economics, The University of Chicago.

Scheinkman, J. (1980) 'Discussion,' in: J. Kareken and N. Wallace, eds., *Models of monetary economies*. Minneapolis Federal Reserve Bank.

Scheinkman, J. and L. Weiss (1986) 'Borrowing constraints and aggregate economic activity', *Econometrica*, 54: 23–46.

Shell, K. (1971) 'Notes on the economics of infinity', *Journal of Political Economy*, 79: 1002–1012.

Shell, K. (1977) 'Monnaie et allocation intertemporelle', CNRS Paris.

Singleton, K. (1986) 'Speculation and the volatility of foreign currency exchange rates', Graduate School of Industrial Administration, Carnegie-Mellon University.

Stockman, A. (1981) 'Anticipated inflation and the capital stock in a cash-in-advance economy', *Journal of Monetary Economics*, 8: 387–393.

Tirole, J. (1985) 'Asset bubbles and overlapping generations', *Econometrica*, 53: 1499–1528.

Tobin, J. (1980) 'Discussion', in: J. Kareken and N. Wallace, eds., *Models of monetary economies*. Federal Reserve Bank of Minneapolis, pp. 83–90.

Turnovsky, S. and W. Brock (1980) 'Time consistency and optimal government policies in perfect foresight equilibrium', *Journal of Public Economics*, 13: 183–212.

Wallace, N. (1980) 'The overlapping generations model of fiat money', in: J. Kareken and N. Wallace, eds., *Models of monetary economies*. Federal Reserve Bank of Minneapolis.

Wallace, N. (1981) 'A Modigliani–Miller theory for open-market operations', *American Economic Review*, 71: 267–274.

Wallace, N. (1983) 'A legal restrictions theory of the demand for "money" and the role of monetary policy', *Federal Reserve Bank of Minneapolis Quarterly Review*, Winter: 1–7.

Weiss, L. (1980) 'The effects of money supply on economic welfare in the steady state', *Econometrica*, 48: 565–576.

Williamson, S. (1984) 'Four essays on financial intermediation', Ph.D Thesis, Department of Economics, The University of Wisconsin at Madison.

Wilson, C. (1979) 'An infinite horizon model with money', in: J. Scheinkman and J. Green, eds., *General equilibrium, growth, and trade: Essays in honor of Lionel McKenzie*. New York: Academic Press.

Wilson, C. (1981) 'Equilibrium in dynamic models with an infinity of agents', *Journal of Economic Theory*, 24: 95–111.

Woodford, M. (1984) 'Indeterminacy of equilibrium in the overlapping generations model: A survey', Department of Economics, Columbia University.

Woodford, M. (1985a) 'Interest and prices in a cash-in-advance economy', Department of Economics, Columbia University.

Woodford, M. (1985b) 'Keynes after Lucas: Expectations, finance constraints, and the instability of investment', Department of Economics, Columbia University.

Woodford, M. (1986a) 'Asset bubbles and fiat money', Graduate School of Business, The University of Chicago.

Woodford, M. (1986b) 'Learning to believe in sunspots', Columbia University Department of Economics, New York City.

Woodford, M. (1986c) 'Expectations, finance, and aggregate instability', in: M. Kohn and S. Tsiang, eds., *Finance constraints, expectations, and macroeconomics*. New York: Oxford University Press.

Woodford, M. (1987) 'Equilibrium models of endogenous flucatuations: Cycles, chaos, indeterminacy, and sunspots', University of Chicago.

Wright, R. (1986) 'The observational implications of labor contracts in a dynamic general equilibrium model', Department of Economics, Cornell University.

Wright, R. (1987) 'Market structure and competitive equilibrium in dynamic economic models', *Journal of Economic Theory*, 41: 189–201.

PART 4

MONEY DEMAND AND MONEY SUPPLY

Chapter 8

THE DEMAND FOR MONEY

STEPHEN M. GOLDFELD

Princeton University

DANIEL E. SICHEL*

Board of Governors of the Federal Reserve System

Contents

* We thank Benjamin Friedman for his comments. The opinions expressed are those of the authors; they do not necessarily reflect the views of the Board of Governors of the Federal Reserve System.

Handbook of Monetary Economics, Volume I, Edited by B.M. Friedman and F.H. Hahn

1. Introduction

The relation between the demand for money balances and its determinants is a fundamental building block in most theories of macroeconomic behavior. Indeed, most macroeconomic models, whether theoretical or econometric, generally ignore the rich institutional detail of the financial sector and attempt to capture financial factors via the demand and supply of money. Furthermore, the demand for money is a critical component in the formulation of monetary policy and a stable demand function for money has long been perceived as a prerequisite for the use of monetary aggregates in the conduct of policy. Not surprisingly, then, the demand for money in many countries has been subjected to extensive empirical scrutiny. The evidence that emerged, at least prior to the mid-1970s, suggested that a few variables (essentially income and interest rates, with appropriate allowance for lags) were capable of providing a plausible and stable explanation of money demand.

As has been widely documented, especially for the United States but elsewhere as well, matters have been considerably less satisfactory since the mid-1970s. First, there was the episode of the "missing money" when conventional money demand equations systematically overpredicted actual money balances. Moreover, attempts to fit conventional demand functions to a sample that included the missing money period invariably produced parameter estimates with some quite unreasonable properties. Second, in the 1980s, U.S. money demand functions, whether or not fixed up to explain the 1970s, generally exhibited extended periods of underprediction as observed velocity fell markedly.

To be sure, the period since the mid-1970s has been marked by unusual economic conditions in many countries including supply shocks, severe bouts of high and variable inflation, record-high interest rates, and deep recessions. The period also coincided with the widespread adoption of floating exchange rates and, in a number of major industrial countries, with substantial institutional changes brought about by financial innovation and financial deregulation. Where institutional change was particularly marked, it also led to a change in what we think of as "money". The period since 1974 thus provided a very severe test of empirical money demand relationships and it is perhaps not so surprising that this period succeeded in exposing a number of shortcomings in existing specifications of money demand functions.[1]

---

[1] It is perhaps ironic that the emergence of these shortcomings roughly coincided with the adoption by a number of central banks of policies aimed at targeting monetary aggregates. Some have argued that this association is more than mere coincidence. In any event, given the vested interest of policymakers in the existence of a reliably stable money demand function, it is hardly surprising that employees of central banks were among the most active contributors to the most recent literature on money demand.

The repeated breakdown of existing empirical models in the face of newly emerging data has fostered a vast industry devoted to examining and improving the demand for money function. This process has been aided by a growing arsenal of econometric techniques that has permitted more sophisticated examinations of dynamics, functional forms, and expectations. These techniques have also provided researchers with a wide variety of diagnostic tests to evaluate the adequacy of particular specifications. Initially, at least in the United States, this led to two strands of research. The first was what Judd and Scadding (1982a) called "reopening the pre-1973 agenda". As a practical matter this amounted to re-exploring variables (e.g. measures of transactions), functional forms, or dynamics that seemed to be unnecessary in a more tranquil period. A second strand of research was devoted to modifying existing specifications to account for changes brought about by financial innovation and deregulation.

While these various strands of research have yielded considerable insight, matters are still in a state of flux. Part of the reason is that, perhaps not surprisingly, the modeling of financial innovation and deregulation proved to be a quite difficult task. Some have even gone further, suggesting that instabilities in money demand are to be expected, reflecting structural change in the economic and financial environment. Spindt (1987) has characterized the unsettled flavor of the literature by noting that researchers either seem to conclude that no explanation is adequate to explain some recent money demand "puzzle" or that "the author's own, (usually many years old), specification still works just fine, so there isn't really any puzzle at all" [Spindt (1987, p. 1)]. Spindt goes on to suggest that we may need an alternative paradigm, a call that seems to be echoed in other recent reviews of empirical money demand [Judd and Scadding (1982a), Gordon (1984), Roley (1985)].

The outline of the chapter is as follows. Section 2 documents the nature of the difficulties with conventional demand functions, both in the United States and elsewhere. For the remainder of the chapter, however, when empirical results are presented the focus will be exclusively on the United States. Section 3 begins with a brief review of some underlying theoretical models and uses these as a vehicle to re-examine measurement and specification issues such as the definition of money and the appropriate scale and opportunity cost variables. Section 4 considers econometric issues starting with estimation issues in the partial adjustment model and then analyzes criticisms and modifications of the partial adjustment model. This section also discusses the estimation of money demand imposing assumed or estimated long-run relationships and considers questions of simultaneity and the so-called buffer-stock approach. The final section considers the recent behavior of money demand functions and summarizes the current state of affairs.

2. Overview of empirical difficulties

As noted above, prior to the mid-1970s relatively simple specifications appeared to yield a stable demand function for money with plausible long-run parameter values. The subsequent misbehavior of the money demand function, both in the United States and elsewhere, has been widely documented [Goldfeld (1976), Judd and Scadding (1982a), Roley (1985), Fair (1987)]. As a consequence, we will be brief and somewhat selective in summarizing the evidence.

Our present focus will be on postwar quarterly data for which a partial adjustment model of the following form was once deemed to be quite serviceable:

$$\ln m_t = b_0 + b_1 \ln y_t + b_2 \ln r_t + b_3 \ln m_{t-1} + b_4 \pi_t + u_t , \qquad (2.1)$$

where m_t is real money balances, r_t represents one (or more) interest rates, y_t is a transactions variable, and $\pi_t = \ln(P_t/P_{t-1})$ is the rate of inflation associated with the price index, P_t. The inclusion of π_t in (2.1) is meant to encompass the so-called real partial adjustment model ($b_4 = 0$) or the nominal partial adjustment model ($b_4 = -b_3$).[2]

While not fully appropriate, (2.1) is commonly estimated by single equation methods, which, however, do correct for the first-order serial correlation typically found in the residuals of (2.1). The Cochrane–Orcutt procedure is frequently used for this purpose although some variant of nonlinear least squares or maximum likelihood is generally more appropriate.[3]

2.1. U.S. money demand

Results of estimating a version of (2.1) with U.S. data are reported in Table 8.1 for several sample periods. The data pertain to M_1, currency plus checkable deposits, and are measured as seasonally adjusted quarterly averages, while y is measured by real GNP, P by the implicit GNP price deflator, and r is represented by two rates, RCP, the commercial paper rate, and $RCBP$, the commercial bank passbook rate. The data reflect the February 1987 revision of the money stock and the major 1985 revision of the national income accounts. The results reported in Table 8.1 were obtained by Cochrane–Orcutt although the results with full maximum likelihood taking account of the first observation were, for all practical purposes, the same.

---

[2]See Section 4 below for a derivation of (2.1) and a discussion of the two types of adjustment models.

[3]Section 4 below.

Table 8.1
A conventional money demand model

Variable	1952:3–1974:1	1952:3–1979:3	1952:3–1986:4	1974:2–1986:4
Intercept	0.381	−0.313	−0.340	−0.451
	$(1.7)^a$	(2.6)	(4.3)	(2.6)
y	0.131	0.039	0.047	0.044
	(5.0)	(5.0)	(7.1)	(1.3)
RCP	−0.016	−0.013	−0.013	−0.018
	(5.9)	(5.0)	(5.2)	(2.6)
$RCBP$	−0.030	−0.002	−0.003	0.100
	(3.3)	(0.4)	(0.9)	(1.0)
m_{t-1}	0.788	1.007	1.002	0.997
	(12.4)	(47.9)	(67.1)	(32.6)
P_t/P_{t-1}	−0.711	−0.889	−1.033	−0.823
	(6.9)	(9.5)	(10.0)	(2.6)
ρ	0.452	0.367	0.166	0.000
SEE	0.0038	0.0042	0.0061	0.0084

^{a}*t*-statistics in parentheses.

The first column of Table 8.1 gives the results for the relatively tranquil period ending in 1974:1. The results are generally sensible with significant income and interest effects and plausible long-run elasticities. Moreover, the specification appears stable over the period 1952:3 to 1974:1. This is revealed by formal tests of stability, conditional on an assumed sample split (not reported), or by the informal observation that the same specification estimated through the end of 1962 and simulated until 1974:1 does a good job of tracking the actual data. The static and dynamic simulation paths are portrayed in Figure 8.1 along with actual path of real balances. Some root mean square

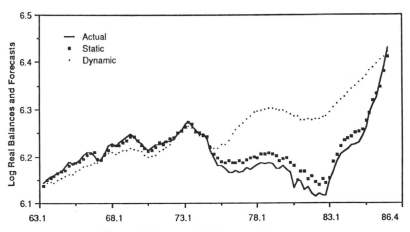

Figure 8.1. Log real balances and forecasts.

Table 8.2
Simulation root mean squared errors[a]

Period	Static	Dynamic
1963–66	0.0053	0.0126
1967–70	0.0051	0.0130
1971–74	0.0044	0.0066
1975–76	0.0180	0.0510
1977–78	0.0199	0.0723
1979–80	0.0226	0.0830
1981–82	0.0285	0.0100
1983–84	0.0202	0.0765
1985–86	0.0114	0.0453

[a]Errors are for the specification of Table 8.1, estimated through 1962:4 and simulated forward as pictured in Figure 8.1.

errors for subsamples of the forecast period for these simulations are given in Table 8.2. The same underlying simulations are summarized in a different way in Figure 8.2 which plots actual and simulated velocity.

Table 8.2 and Figures 8.1 and 8.2 reveal that the behavior of a conventional specification sharply deteriorates after 1974. This poor forecasting performance suggests that the money demand equation underwent some sort of structural change after 1974, at least relative to the specification used in Table 8.1. This is borne out in the last three columns of Table 8.1 and in the formal stability tests reported in Table 8.3. The key shortcoming of the results in Table 8.1 is the fact that the coefficient of the lagged dependent variable is essentially unity, suggesting that we have a misspecified partial adjustment mechanism. This result obtains, even if we restrict the estimation to the post-1974 period.

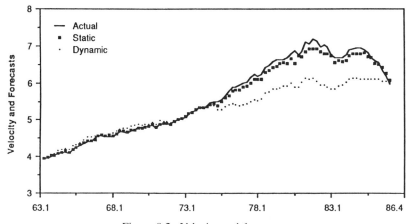

Figure 8.2. Velocity and forecasts.

Table 8.3
Parameter constancy tests

Sample period	Split point	Significance level for F-test
1952:3–1979:3[a]	1974:1	0.0004
1952:3–1986:4[a]	1974:1	0.0364
1952:3–1986:4[b]	1979:3	0.0011

[a]Specification of Table 8.1.
[b]Specification of first column of Table 8.4.

Moreover, a closer examination of the results suggests that the post-1974 period itself may not readily lend itself to finding a single stable specification. This speculation is perhaps more plausible when seen in view of the change in the Federal Reserve operating procedure that was introduced in October 1979, and of the substantial degree of financial deregulation after 1980.

While we discuss more fully below the reasons for the empirical shortcomings we observe that, briefly put, the immediate post-1974 period of the missing money has been largely attributed to the effects of financial innovation. While the specification of the money demand function can be altered to reflect this in various ways described below, one can also "repair" the money demand function by the use of dummy variables. Indeed, Hafer and Hein (1982) have suggested that one could restore stability of the conventional specification over the period 1952–1978 by use of an intercept dummy, D, which takes the value of zero up to 1974:1 and unity thereafter. A re-examination of this issue suggested that this simple device was not quite adequate to restore stability but that slope dummies for y and RCP along with the intercept dummy were sufficient.[4] The results for this specification are given in Table 8.4 for the sample period 1952:3 to 1979:3. While this fix-up of the money demand equation is uninformative as to underlying causes, it does permit an examination of whether the most recent behavior of money demand is consistent with the specification given in Table 8.4. The formal stability test reported in the last row of Table 8.3 suggests that the post-1979 behavior is statistically different.

While the conventional specification does well prior to 1974, the recent revision of the GNP data released in 1985 has cast some doubt about the adequacy of this specification, even in the pre-1974 period. The issue is homogeneity with respect to the price level. Homogeneity of money demand, at least in the long run, is generally presumed to be a feature of any well-specified money demand function. Consequently, rejection of homogeneity is typically taken to be evidence of misspecification. Tests for homogeneity are

---

[4]The set of dummies needed to restore stability is somewhat sensitive to the precise sample period, the presumed point of split, and the exact nature of the stability test.

Table 8.4
Variants of a conventional money demand model

Variable	1952:3–1979:3	1952:3–1979:3	1952:3–1974:1
Intercept	0.198	0.191	0.296
	(1.0)[a]	(1.0)	(1.2)
y	0.110	0.168	0.178
	(4.5)	(4.8)	(4.7)
RCP	−0.016	−0.016	−0.016
	(5.8)	(6.3)	(6.1)
$RCBP$	−0.023	−0.33	−0.037
	(2.8)	(3.6)	(3.5)
m_{t-1}	0.842	0.768	0.740
	(14.5)	(11.7)	(9.7)
P_t/P_{t-1}	−0.768	−0.674	−0.639
	(8.1)	(6.8)	(5.9)
Dy	−0.065	−0.070	–
	(1.6)	(1.8)	
$DRCP$	0.016	0.018	–
	(2.5)	(2.8)	
D	0.466	0.507	–
	(1.5)	(1.7)	
P	–	−0.034	−0.033
		(2.5)	(2.2)
ρ	0.377	0.360	0.425
	(3.5)	(3.3)	(3.6)
SEE	0.0039	0.0038	0.0037

[a]t-statistics in parentheses.

typically accomplished by including ln P_t in an equation like (2.1) and doing a
t-test to see if the coefficient is significantly different from zero. Generally
speaking, at least for sample periods that avoid the missing money, such tests
have accepted homogeneity [see Goldfeld (1973) and Spencer (1985)]. Table
8.4 reports the results of including the variable ln P_t in the conventional
specification through 1974:1 and in the conventional specification augmented
with dummies for the period to 1979:3. The significance of this variable further
serves to call into doubt the adequacy of the partial adjustment model.

Taken as a whole, the evidence for the United States unmistakably suggests
the need to rethink the conventional specification. Before turning to this we
briefly consider results for other countries.

2.2. Money demand: International evidence

Fair (1987) contains a good summary of the empirical evidence on the demand
for money in 27 countries. To facilitate comparisons across countries, Fair uses

a common specification in which the dependent variable is real balances per capita and the explanatory variables are the lagged dependent variable, per capita real GNP, and a short-term interest rate. Table 8.5 contains a selection of Fair's results for OECD countries.[5]

The results in Table 8.5 indicate some considerable similarity in money demand functions across OECD countries. Moreover, the "average" long-run income and interest elasticities are similar to those reported for the United States. With the exception of Germany, these OECD countries also share with the United States a penchant for instability in money demand. Indeed, Fair found such instability present in 13 of the 17 countries tested.[6]

Table 8.5
International money demand; dependent variable: $(m/pop)_t^{a,b}$

Country	Sample	Y/pop	R	π	$(m/pop)_{t-1}$	SEE	STAB[d]
Canada	1962:1–1985:4	0.071	−0.004	−1.66	0.94	0.028	19.1*
		(2.9)[c]	(2.4)	(3.3)			
Japan	1966:1–1985:4	0.084	−0.005	−0.29	0.90	0.023	59.4*
		(1.3)	(3.3)	(0.6)			
France	1964:1–1985:4	0.094	−0.002	−0.49	0.25	0.022	45.3*
		(3.5)	(1.7)	(1.1)			
Germany	1969:1–1985:4	0.343	−0.005	−0.74	0.71	0.013	5.8
		(4.8)	(6.0)	(2.4)			
Italy	1971:1–1985:3	0.130	−0.004	−0.79	0.86	0.019	
		(1.8)	(2.6)	(2.4)			
U.K.	1958:1–1986:1	0.118	−0.005	−0.69	0.44	0.022	17.0*
		(7.0)	(4.9)	(4.2)			
Average		0.140	−0.004	0.78	0.68	0.021	

[a]All variables are in log form except for R, which is in levels.
[b]All estimates are obtained with 2SLS. Only the estimates for the United Kingdom required serial correlation correction. The first-order serial correlation coefficient for the United Kingdom is −0.377 with a t-statistic of 4.3.
[c]t-statistics in parentheses.
[d]The value of the chi-squared statistic for rejecting parameter constancy with sample split following 1972:4. For Germany, the sample split is 1975:4.
*Significant at the 5 percent level.

[5]The results presented are a reparameterization of Fair's to make them comparable with the U.S. specification. In particular, if τ_1 and τ_2 are the coefficients on real and nominal balances in Fair's table 1, these can be reparameterized so that $(\tau_1 + \tau_2)$ and τ_2 are the coefficients on real balances and inflation, respectively. Unfortunately, given the information presented by Fair, it is not possible to obtain standard errors for lagged money under this reparameterization.
[6]For a similar set of findings, see Boughton (1981). Curiously enough, using flow of funds data Fair reports a stable demand function for the United States. In attempting to replicate Fair's results for the United States, we discovered that his stability finding depends somewhat on the exclusion of a rate such as RCBP and on the choice of the sample period. Furthermore, it should be noted that the extra noise in the flow of funds data tends to make it harder to reject parameter constancy.

3. Re-examining the basic specification

As should be apparent from the previous section, conventional specifications of money demand have exhibited substantial shortcomings over the last 15 years. As we shall see, attempts to repair these specifications have led to a re-examination of a wide variety of issues. Some of these issues can best be motivated with reference to the underlying theoretical models so it is to a brief review of these that we now turn.

3.1. A brief theoretical overview

One early approach to the demand for money is the quantity theory of money. An example of this starts with the identity:

$$MV \equiv PT ,\tag{3.1}$$

where M is the quantity of money, V is the velocity of circulation, P is the price level, and T is the volume of transactions. The assumption that V, being determined by technological and/or institutional factors, is relatively constant allows one to recast (3.1) as a demand function for money. Keynes modified this simple story and, in so doing, distinguished among three motives for holding money – transactions, precautionary, and speculative. Overall, the main empirical legacy of Keynes in this area was the introduction of the interest rate into the demand for money, primarily via the speculative motive.

3.1.1. Transactions demand

Most subsequent developments amplified on the Keynesian motives in various ways. Baumol (1952) and Tobin (1956) both applied inventory-theoretic considerations to the transactions motive. In the simplest of these models, individuals are paid (in bonds) an amount Y at the beginning of a period and spend this amount uniformly over the period. This leads to the so-called square-root law with average money holdings given by

$$M = (2bY/r)^{1/2} ,\tag{3.2}$$

where r is the interest rate on bonds and b is the brokerage charge or fixed transactions cost for converting bonds into cash. While the simplicity of (3.2) has appealed to many empirical researchers, it should be noted that the precise form of (3.2) is highly dependent on the assumed payments mechanism. More particularly, under alternative assumptions proportional brokerage charges may be relevant and there may be nonconstant interest and income elasticities.

Yet another application of inventory theory to the transactions demand for money is the work of Miller and Orr (1966), which can also be interpreted as a model of the precautionary motive for money holding since there is a minimum allowable money holding below which a penalty must be paid. As in the Baumol–Tobin (B–T) framework, Miller and Orr (M–O) consider two assets and transactions costs which are fixed per transaction. The key difference is that M–O take cash flows to be stochastic. In the simplest version of their model, cash flows follow a random walk without drift in which in a given time interval (say $1/t$ of a day), there is an equal probability of a positive or negative cash flow of m dollars.

Given a lower bound below which money balances cannot drop (normalized to zero), the optimal policy consists of an upper bound, h, and a return level, z. Whenever money balances reach the lower bound, z dollars of bonds are converted to cash; whenever the upper bound is reached, $h - z$ dollars of cash are converted to bonds. Minimizing the sum of expected per-day transactions and opportunity costs yields the optimal return level:

$$z^* = [(3b/4r)\sigma^2]^{1/3} , \tag{3.3}$$

where σ^2 is the daily variance of changes in cash balances ($\sigma^2 = m^2 t$).

In addition, M–O show that $h^* = 3z^*$ and that the optimal size of average cash balances is given by $M^* = 4z^*/3$. Thus, like the B–T approach, the M–O model yields a constant interest elasticity, although the value is $1/3$ rather than $1/2$. The income or transactions elasticity is a bit more ambiguous since the only "scale" variable is σ^2 which is the product of m^2 and t. If one thinks in terms of m, the size of each cash flow, then the scale elasticity is $2/3$; however, if one thinks in terms of t, the rate of transactions, then the scale elasticity is $1/3$. This ambiguity concerning the scale variable has meant that the M–O model is rarely estimated directly. Nevertheless, as we shall see, the M–O model is extremely useful for analyzing the consequences of innovation in cash management techniques.

3.1.2. Portfolio demand

Along with the transactions and precautionary motives, Keynes' speculative motive has also been reformulated – largely in terms of portfolio theory [Tobin (1958)]. In the two-asset version of this approach, the individual wealth-holder allocates his portfolio between money, treated as a riskless asset, and an asset with an uncertain rate of return. Under the assumption of expected utility maximization, the optimal portfolio mix can be shown to depend on wealth and on the properties of the utility function and the distribution function for the return on the risky asset. Of particular relevance are the degree of risk aversion and the mean and variance of the return on the risky asset. In the general multi-asset case, the demand functions for each asset in the portfolio, including money, depend on all the expected returns and on the variances and covariances of these returns.

From a theoretical point of view, with the usual caveat about income effects, the analysis yields a negative interest elasticity for the demand for money, providing another rationalization of Keynes' liquidity preference hypothesis. From an empirical point of view, however, matters are less satisfactory. To be sure, given specific utility and distribution functions, one can derive estimable asset demand functions.[7] However, given the menu of assets available in most countries, the portfolio approach actually undermines the speculative demand for money. The reason is that if money pays a zero return and if there is a riskless asset paying a positive rate of return (e.g. a savings deposit), then money is a dominated asset and will not be held.[8] In such a setting, to resurrect an asset demand for money one needs to combine the portfolio approach with transaction costs.

Friedman's (1956) restatement of the quantity theory parallels Tobin's portfolio approach in regarding the primary role of money as a form of wealth. Friedman dispenses with the separate motives posited by Keynes, and treats money as an asset yielding a flow of services to the holder. Wealth, both human and nonhuman, is thus one of the major determinants of money demand. However, to circumvent the empirical difficulties with nonhuman wealth, Friedman, reasoning from the fact that wealth is capitalized income, motivates the use of permanent income in a money demand function. Furthermore, as in the Keynesian analysis of the speculative motive, Friedman posits that one aspect of the opportunity cost of holding money is the expected return on bonds. However, since there exist assets other than money and bonds that individuals may hold (e.g. equities or physical goods), Friedman considers the rates of return on these assets as part of the opportunity cost as well. Since the expected rate of return on physical goods can be measured by the expected rate of inflation, this variable also plays a role in Friedman's theoretical analysis.

3.1.3. Combining transactions and portfolio demand

While suggestive, Friedman's approach sidesteps the explicit role of money in the transactions process and also ignores problems of uncertainty. More recent

---

[7]The absence of data on variances and covariances is a potential stumbling block, especially in a world where these change over time. See Subsection 3.2.3.

[8]Obviously the result holds when money pays a positive return as long as the alternative asset has a higher yield. Also, in the presence of inflation, both money and the saving deposit will be risky assets but money will still be dominated.

work has, in fact, emphasized one or both of these aspects, although a fully general treatment of uncertainty in the presence of transactions costs has yet to be developed.[9] The work of Ando and Shell (1975) represents one partial attempt. They consider a world with three assets, one risky and two, money and savings deposits, with certain nominal returns, r_s and r_m. They also treat the price level as uncertain and view individuals as maximizing expected utility where utility is given by $U(C_1, C_2)$ and C_i is the consumption in the ith period. The role of money in the transactions process is captured in a real transactions cost function, $T(M, C_1)$, where holding higher money balances reduces transaction costs and thus, other things equal, raises C_2. Ando and Shell then assume that C_1 is determined independently of portfolio choice and show that the appropriate marginal condition for maximizing expected utility is given by

$$r_s - r_m = T_m(M, C_1). \tag{3.4}$$

Equation (3.4) can be inverted to give money demand as a function of C_1, $(r_s - r_m)$, and the parameters of T. More particularly, the demand for money is seen to be independent of the rate of return on the risky asset and of the expected price level and of wealth as well. To the extent they are robust, these results obviously dramatically simplify empirical work. One possible lack of generality stems from the assumption that C_1 is determined independently of the portfolio decision. The role of this assumption can be seen in the work of McCallum and Goodfriend (1987) who also deal in a three-asset world consisting of money, bonds, and capital.

McCallum and Goodfriend first consider the case of certainty, and start with an intertemporal household utility function of the form:

$$U(C_t, L_t) + \beta U(C_{t+1}, L_{t+1}) + \beta^2 U(C_{t+2}, L_{t+2}) + \cdots,$$

where C_t and L_t are consumption and leisure. The household has a production technology as well as initial real stocks of money (m_{t-1}), bonds (b_{t-1}), and capital (k_{t-1}). Somewhat analogous to the Ando–Shell setup, the role of money is captured by a "shopping time" function $S_t = \psi(C_t, m_t)$, where shopping time, S_t, subtracts from leisure. As McCallum and Goodfriend show, maximizing utility results in a demand for money which can be written as

$$m_t = f(m_{t-1}, k_{t-1}, b_{t-1}, R_t, R_{t+1}\ldots, \pi_t, \pi_{t+1}\ldots), \tag{3.5}$$

[9]See Buiter and Armstrong (1978).

where R_t and π_t are the nominal interest rate and the inflation rate, respectively, and where variables dated after t are anticipated values.[10]

Equation (3.5) is hardly a conventional-looking money demand function but the model does imply such a representation. Indeed, after some manipulation, McCallum and Goodfriend show that (3.5) can be transformed to

$$m_t = g(C_t, R_t) . \qquad (3.6)$$

The rather conventional-looking equation (3.6) results from the fact that the structure of the McCallum–Goodfriend model is such that the use of the choice variable, C_t, in (3.6) allows one to eliminate everything but R_t from (3.5). Of particular interest is the role of initial wealth, which appears in (3.5) via m_{t-1}, b_{t-1}, and k_{t-1} but which has no role in (3.6).

As (3.6) and (3.4) are very close in spirit, the remaining issue is the robustness of (3.6) to alternative assumptions. As McCallum and Goodfriend indicate, on this score there is good news and bad news. First, if we allow for the fact that future variables (e.g. R_{t+1}, π_{t+1}) are not known with certainty, then it is quite likely that no closed form solution analogous to (3.5) will exist. However, as McCallum and Goodfriend show after some further manipulation, (3.6) will continue to be valid. Where the validity of (3.6) is lost is if the intertemporal utility function is not time-separable. While this provides some comfort, the absence of a general portfolio/transactions model is particularly unfortunate, given that financial innovation and deregulation in the United States have increasingly offered to consumers a menu of financial assets that combine portfolio and transactions features.

While we make no pretense at having provided a comprehensive theoretical overview, it nevertheless appears that the bulk of empirical work on money demand has been motivated by one or more of the simple theories we have sketched. Taken as a group, the various theories we have discussed suggest many possible modifications to the conventional specification. For example, both the quantity theory and portfolio approaches suggest the use of a considerably broader range of opportunity cost variables as well as of a measure of wealth. Portfolio theory also suggests the use of measures of uncertainty for the opportunity cost variabes. The transactions approach raises the issue of how the volume of transactions is to be measured and leads one to question the appropriateness of the implicit assumption of a constant real transaction cost embodied in the conventional specification. This latter assumption is particularly suspect in the light of the numerous innovations in financial markets and in the face of the substantial deregulation that evolved, at least in

---

[10] Equation (3.5) follows the simplifying assumption in McCallum and Goodfriend that labor is inelastically supplied. Otherwise, the wage rate would appear in (3.5).

the United States. These issues, however, are best discussed as part of a more systematic review of the specification of money demand.

3.2. A variable-by-variable review

In re-evaluating the performance of the conventional specification, it is useful to consider the measurement and specification issues on a variable-by-variable basis. We begin with the dependent variable, money.

3.2.1. Definition of money

Rather obviously, a first issue in the empirical estimation of money demand is the selection of an explicit measure of money. This choice is typically guided by some particular theoretical framework, but even so such choices are often less than clear-cut. Moreover, what passes for money can be readily altered by changing financial institutions. In the United States, at least, such changes, prompted by private financial innovation and deregulation, have had major implications for the definition of money.

In general, theories based on a transactions approach provide the most guidance and lead to a narrow definition of money that includes currency and checkable deposits. In some institutional settings a plausible measure of checkable deposits is readily apparent. In other settings there may well be a spectrum of checkable assets without any clear-cut dividing line. For example, a deposit account may limit the number of checks per month or may have a minimum check size. Other accounts may permit third-party transfers only if regular periodic payments are involved or may permit check-writing only with substantial service charges. When such deposit accounts should be included in a transactions-based definition of money is not obvious.

Once one moves away from a transactions view of the world, the appropriate empirical definition of money is even less clear. A theory that simply posits that money yields some unspecified flow of services must confront the fact that many assets may yield these services in varying degrees. Such theories have typically relied on a relatively broad definition of money but the definitions utilized are inevitably somewhat arbitrary. To make these issues more concrete, we focus on measures of the money stock for the United States.

3.2.1.1. Traditional aggregates. Table 8.6 reports various official measures and key components. The official narrow definition of money, M1, presently includes currency, traveler's checks, demand deposits at commercial banks, and other checkable deposits (OCDs). OCDs primarily consist of negotiable order of withdrawal (NOW) account. NOWs provide an insured interest-

Table 8.6
Various U.S. money stock measures and components[a]
(December 1986)

Aggregate and component	Amount
M1	$ 730.5
Currency	183.5
Traveler's checks	6.4
Demand deposits	308.3
Other checkable deposits	232.3
M2	2,799.7
M1	730.5
Overnight RPs plus overnight Eurodollars	77.3
Money market mutual fund balances[b]	207.6
Money market deposit accounts[b]	571.3
Savings deposits	366.2
Small-denomination time deposits	853.2
M3	3,488.8
M2	2,799.7
Large time deposits	447.0
Term RPs and term Eurodollars[b]	165.2
Institutional money market mutual funds	84.1

[a]Data are in billions and seasonally adjusted, except as noted.
[b]Not seasonally adjusted. Due to the use of unadjusted data the components of M2 and M3 do not precisely sum to the seasonally adjusted value of M2 and M3.

bearing transactions account and are available at several types of depository institutions (commercial banks, savings banks, and savings and loan associations).[11] Both of these features are a departure from the earlier definition of M1 which, aside from currency, only counted zero-yielding demand deposits available at a single depository institution, commercial banks.

As suggested earlier, even with a transactions-based measure where to draw the line is not always evident. More particularly, it can be argued that one or more of the following components of M2, which are excluded from M1, belong in a transactions measure.

(i) Money market deposit accounts (MMDAs) – insured interest-bearing accounts at depository institutions that permit unlimited transfers to other accounts but only a small number of checks per month.

(ii) Money market mutual funds (MMMFs) – uninsured interest-bearing

[11]NOW accounts were, in fact, introduced by an innovative savings bank in Massachusetts in 1972 but only became available nationally in 1981. During the transition period the old definition of M1 became increasingly outmoded, a problem that has been repeated other times with other financial innovations. While it may be possible to sort these issues out after the fact, as they are occurring they may present thorny problems for the monetary authorities.

accounts that currently can generally function as a checkable account although there were previous restrictions on use (e.g. a minimum check size).

(iii) Repurchase agreements (RPs) – a security sale with an agreement to repurchase it at a specified time and price.

MMMFs rose in the mid-1970s, about the same time as NOWs, and for the same reason: high interest rates stimulated financial institutions to introduce and promote substitutes for demand deposits. MMDAs were a regulatory creation designed to enable depository institutions to compete more easily with MMMFs.

While the MMDAs and MMMFs clearly can be used to make transactions, their exclusion from M1 rests on the view that their features make them less appropriate for such purposes. Indeed, this is borne out by the pattern of use of these accounts which have lower rates of turnover as compared with instruments included in M1. Since the rationale for including RPs in M1 is at first blush unclear, a word of elaboration is called for, especially since a number of authors have argued that redefining narrow money to include RPs could solve the missing money puzzle of the 1970s.

In the 1970s RPs emerged as a popular device for corporate cash management, especially via overnight RPs, which provided, via the differential between sale and purchase prices, a way of converting a zero yielding demand deposit into an earning asset.[12] This suggested to some that RPs and demand deposits were essentially perfect substitutes and that M1 should be redefined to include some types of RPs. Moreover, rough attempts to do this appeared to lead to dramatic improvements in the forecasting of money demand for 1974–76. Subsequent evidence, however, has cast doubt on these findings.[13] For one, transactions costs on RPs appear high enough to question the perfect substitutability assumption. Viewed in this light, RPs become just one of the numerous instruments used by corporate cash managers. Moreover, other institutional features of the market suggest there are substantial limits on using RPs to reduce demand deposits. Finally, even including RPs in M1 does not work all that well after 1976.

As should be evident, defining money may involve some hard choices. Determining what constitutes checkable deposits, for example, involves deciding where one draws the line in a spectrum of transactions-type assets that are substitutable in varying degrees. As to the choice between narrow and broad definitions, given the continued empirical difficulties with narrow definitions and the blurred lines between transactions and portfolio considerations, it is

---

[12]Moreover there were no reserve requirements on RPs. We should also note that even without RPs the prohibition of the payment of explicit interest on demand deposits, of course, did not prohibit the implicit payment of interest on such deposits via the provision of "free" services.

[13]For a discussion of the issues and some empirical results, see Judd and Scadding (1982a).

not surprising that some researchers have advocated the use of a concept like M2 for estimation purposes.

3.2.1.2. Alternative aggregation approaches. In addition to problems of determining which components belong in which aggregate, conventional broad monetary measures obtained by simply adding together quantities of different assets have been criticized for improper aggregation of assets with differing degrees of "liquidity" or as, it is sometimes put, which offer differing degrees of monetary services. Weighting the various components of money by the degree of "moneyness" is an idea that has been advocated over the years, but has experienced a resurgence at the hands of Barnett (1980) and Spindt (1985).

The work of Barnett and Spindt relies on index number and aggregation theory to develop aggregate money indices. For the United States a variety of these indices are now constructed and reported monthly by the Federal Reserve. The aggregates are calculated by the Fisher ideal index number formula given by

$$
\frac{M_t}{M_{t-1}} = \left[\frac{\sum m_{it} a_{it}}{\sum m_{it-1} a_{it}} \frac{\sum m_{it} a_{it-1}}{\sum m_{it-1} a_{it-1}} \right]^{1/2} ,
\tag{3.7}
$$

where m_{it} is the component quantity of the ith asset and the a_{it} is the associated weight. Barnett and Spindt differ in their choice of the a_{it}. Barnett's work aggregates the components of money according to their characteristics as assets in a portfolio, while Spindt aggregate these components according to their characteristics as a transactions medium.

In Barnett's original approach, following Friedman (1956), monetary assets are viewed as durable goods rendering a flow of monetary services. In this framework, the a_{it}'s measure the opportunity or "user" cost for asset i, which is the interest forgone by holding asset i as opposed to an alternative higher-yielding nonmonetary asset. One immediate problem is how these user costs are to be calculated. A first issue concerns the own rate where there are obvious measurement difficulties created by the payment of implicit interest via the provision of services and the existence of explicit service charges. The lack of data make it hard to evaluate the seriousness of these difficulties. More is known, however, as to the consequences of the benchmark yield on the nonmonetary asset.

Current practice is to use a corporate bond rate as the benchmark rate, except when one of the own rates on some m_{it} is higher, and this rate is then used as the benchmark rate. This means that the user cost of this highly liquid asset is zero and the implied monetary services are therefore unreasonably regarded as nil. Even in less extreme situations, the evidence suggests that interest rate movements can produce anomalous variations in user costs. Put another way, the resulting monetary service indices are sensitive to the choice of the benchmark yield. Furthermore, at least as now constructed, the monetary service indices appear to behave somewhat oddly in various parts of the 1980s [see Lindsey and Spindt (1986)]. This has turned interest to an alternative approach to monetary aggregates due to Spindt (1985).

In contrast to aggregation by asset characteristics used by Barnett, Spindt has developed a money stock index based on transaction-theoretic considerations in which the component assets are viewed as differing in the volume of transactions financed per dollar of asset. In terms of the equation of exchange we have:

$$\sum m_i v_i = PQ \, ,$$

where v_i is the net turnover rate or velocity of the ith asset. It is then the v_i that are used as the weights in (3.7). One implementation of this approach is embodied in the series MQ published by the Federal Reserve. MQ includes those assets in M1 plus money market deposit accounts and money market mutual funds.[14]

As with the case of the monetary services index, there are some nasty measurement problems here as well. In the first instance, gross turnover rates are not available for some assets (currency, money market mutual funds). Furthermore, even where available, gross turnover rates reflect a large volume of payments for transactions not reflected in GNP such as financial transactions and payments for intermediate goods. To go from gross turnover to net turnover therefore requires many assumptions. Nevertheless, there is some evidence that the growth rate of MQ "appears fairly robust to variations of most of these assumptions within plausible ranges" [Lindsey and Spindt (1986, p. C-4)].

While the problems in constructing MQ thus appear to be surmountable, when the finished product, MQ, is used in a money demand function, it appears to suffer several disruptions in the 1980s.[15] Nevertheless, the proponents of MQ regard the results as sufficiently promising that two refinements are being pursued. The first is to relax the not realistic assumption that all holders of a given asset necessarily have the same turnover rate (e.g. contrast business and household use of demand deposits). A second refinement is to define velocities in (3.7) with reference to a broader measure of transactions

---

[14]Despite the apparent circularity in using velocity to define the aggregate, MQ will not change if the components m_i remain the same and the v_i change. This can readily be seen by examining (3.7).

[15]Data on MQ are currently only available beginning in 1970 so they cannot easily be used to shed light on the "missing money" period.

than real GNP. The first step here is to define such a measure and some progress on this has been reported in Corrado and Spindt (1986). Of course, as is discussed below, such a measure of transactions could be used with any measure of money. Overall, it would thus appear that the jury is still out on the virtues of applying index theory to yield measures of money.[16]

3.2.1.3. Disaggregation. While "proper" aggregation is one approach to modeling the demands for heterogeneous monetary assets, an equally time-honored tactic is to use a disaggregated approach. For example, even in a world in which the definition of checkable deposits is relatively unambiguous, it is not clear that currency and checkable deposits should be regarded as perfect substitutes, a view that is implicit in simply adding them together to produce a measure of money. Currency and checkable deposits may differ in transactions costs, risk of loss, and ease of concealment of illegal or tax-evading activities. It may thus be preferable to estimate separate demand functions for currency and checkable deposits.

Once we recognize that checkable deposits may consist of heterogeneous subcomponents we have further grounds for disaggregation. An additional basis for disaggregation, alluded to above, is that a given monetary asset may be held by behaviorally diverse groups. What this suggests is that disaggregation offers a way to sidestep the definitional issues at the same time that it permits the use of econometric techniques that take account of the interrelated nature of demand functions. Disaggregation has yielded some promising empirical results but, as with proper aggregation, disaggregation hardly resolves the key empirical difficulties.

3.2.2. Scale variables

Until relatively recently scale variables typically came from among GNP, permanent income, or wealth, all measured in real terms. GNP was used in transactions-oriented models, while permanent income, most frequently measured as an exponentially weighted average of current and past values of GNP, was used by modern quantity theorists. Since permanent income is often viewed as a proxy for wealth; direct measures of wealth (invariably only nonhuman wealth) have also been used. Given that financial transactions can generate a demand for money, the use of wealth is also consistent with a transactions view.

As an empirical matter, given the high correlation of GNP and permanent income, both tended to "work" reasonably well prior to the missing money

---

[16]Should it turn out that such measures yielded sensible and stable money demand functions, considerable thought would still be needed as to how these measures would best be incorporated into the monetary policy process.

episode, while the role of wealth was somewhat more ambiguous, especially if included with an income variable. At a formal level, many early studies viewed the matter as a contest between these three variables, the winner often depending on the sample period, the definition of M, and the econometric details.

When the transactions-oriented models began misbehaving, it was natural to examine whether permanent income or wealth might improve matters. There is a hint that wealth may be part of the story in B. Friedman (1978) but, on balance, as Judd and Scadding (1982a, p. 1008) have noted, "the solution probably does not reside in this area". In more recent years, research on scale variables has focused on the following two aspects of the transactions measure: (i) the construction of more comprehensive measures of transactions; and (ii) the disaggregation of transactions into various components, reflecting the notion that not all transactions are equally "money intensive". We discuss each of these in turn.

The construction of more comprehensive measures of transactions is motivated by the the fact that despite the appearance of "gross" in GNP it is much less inclusive than a general measure of transactions. In particular, it excludes all sales of intermediate goods, transfers, purchases of existing goods, and financial transactions, all of which may contribute to the demand for money. At the same time, focus on the product side ignores the fact that the income side also generates payments needs. Finally, in one sense GNP may overstate transactions because it includes imputed items. While these shortcomings of GNP have long been recognized, thorny data problems have discouraged the construction of more general transactions measures. As a proxy for such a measure, some researchers have used data on gross debits to demand deposit accounts. While in some instances substituting debits for GNP improves things, the effect is small and not terribly robust [see Judd and Scadding (1982a)]. Part of the problem may be that the behavior of debits is rather dramatically affected by financial transactions. Also of importance is the fact that increasing sophistication in cash management that reduces average holdings of money given the level of transactions, may be brought about by an increase in debits.

In recent years, however, there have been some noticeable advances in constructing general measures of transactions, particularly by Cramer (1986) and Corrado and Spindt (1986). Since only limited data are presently available, it is too early to tell if these new data will improve the performance of money demand functions.[17]

---

[17]Corrado and Spindt (1986) make a major attempt to adjust the flow of payments for timing differentials stemming from purchases made on credit. Like Cramer, however, they generally ignore transactions associated with exchanges of real or financial assets. A bit of evidence in Wenninger and Radecki (1986) suggests the latter omission may not be serious. Of course, if a general transactions measure proved useful, we would need to develop an adequate theory for its behavior.

Whatever measure of transactions is chosen, there remains the question of whether it might usefully be disaggregated into several scale variables. Thus, for instance, if real GNP is the basic scale variable, one might separately enter various compents of GNP on the grounds that these components are likely to generate different payments needs. For example, one might posit that consumption is more money intensive than other components of GNP, a hypothesis that is supported by some evidence.[18] In a similar vein, aggregate GNP is unlikely to capture the role of inventory investment since inventory liquidation is reflected negatively in GNP but sales from stocks do generate monetary transactions. As a final illustration, it is likely that domestically produced-domestically consumed goods (DP), exports (X), and imports (IM) are sufficiently different in the nature of their production and distribution processes so as to generate different needs for dollar-denominated transactions balances. The disaggregation of a scale variable to reflect appropriately the nature of international transactions is likely to be particularly important for an economy with a substantial degree of openness, but there is evidence that the distinction is of relevance for the United States as well [Radecki and Wenninger (1985)]. On the whole, while there are some promising indications, there is no firm evidence that disaggregation of GNP yields a dramatic improvement in the behavior of aggregate money demand. The case for disaggregation, however, appears a bit stronger when coupled with the disaggregation of money into type of holder (e.g. consumer vs. business) and type of deposit.[19]

3.2.3. Opportunity costs

Measuring the opportunity cost of money, relative to a given definition of money, involves two ingredients: the own rate on money and the rate of return on assets alternative to money. To keep matters simple we focus on the narrow definition of money: currency plus checkable deposits.

When checkable deposits consisted solely of demand deposits with an explicit yield of zero, most empirical researchers treated the own rate as zero. Strictly speaking, this is not correct since deposit holders may earn an implicit rate of return, either because they receive gifts or services or because transactions fees may be forgone as the level of deposits rises. However, measuring

---

[18]See Mankiw and Summers (1986). A somewhat different argument in favor of consumption is that it serves as a good proxy for permanent income.

[19]For some early evidence on this see Goldfeld (1973, 1976). It should also be noted that formal testing of differential effects of subcomponents of GNP is a bit awkward in a logarithmic specification since the components of GNP are linearly related. Mankiw and Summers get around this by introducing a variable $\alpha[\lambda \log Y + (1 - \lambda) \log C]$ and examining λ with $\lambda = 1$ the conventional model. Swamy, Kennickell and von zur Muehlen (1986) handle the international variables by noting that $GNP = DP(1 + X/DP)(1 - IM/(DP + X))$ and then include each term separately. If the coefficients are the same one can aggregate to log GNP.

this implicit return is no easy matter and it is, perhaps, not surprising that this issue was largely ignored.[20] This luxury is not available when even narrow money pays an explicit return, a situation that began in a small way in the United States in the early 1970s and become increasingly widespread in the 1980 deregulation. Matters are somewhat complicated when only some components of money bear explicit interest and when several components may bear different nonzero rates of return. Both of these situations pertain to the United States at present. The aggregate own rate of return is then a complex function of the interest rates, shares, and elasticities of each of the components. These complexities have generally been ignored. For example, Roley (1985), following Cagan (1984), defines the own rate as the then-prevailing ceiling rate adjusted by the fraction of interest-bearing deposits in M1 and reports only limited success with this variable. More promising, perhaps, is the use of such a variable in a disaggregated analysis that separates out other checkable deposits (OCDs) and demand deposits [see Porter, Spindt and Lindsey (1987)]. Unfortunately, the sample period available for estimating the OCD equation is quite short.

As to the rate of return on assets alternative to money, those researchers adopting a transactions view typically use one or more short-term rates such as the yield on government securities, the yield on commercial paper, or the yield on savings deposits.[21] Those researchers adopting a less narrow view of the demand for money have used a correspondingly broader set of alternatives including proxies for the return on equities and long-term bond rates, either government or corporate. Hamburger (1977) has been one of the most ardent advocates of using long-term bond and equity returns, going so far as to suggest that the use of such variables solved the puzzle of the missing money. However, as a number of writers have observed, Hamburger's model contains a number of constraints (e.g. a unitary income elasticity) that are not warranted by the data [Roley (1985)]. A few studies have used proxies for the entire term structure of interest rates [Heller and Khan (1979)] and while it has been claimed that this specification also repaired the missing money episode, this also has not stood up to closer scrutiny [see Judd and Scadding (1982a)]. Finally, some have emphasized the importance of foreign interest rates and/or exchange rates. While this has been of particular importance outside the United States, there is some evidence that these might be of use for the United States as well. Nevertheless, these do not seem to cure the missing money period [Arango and Nadiri (1981)].

---

[20]For exceptions, see Klein (1974) and Startz (1979).

[21]Even here, there are potential problems. For example, it matters whether interest earned on savings deposits is paid quarterly, monthly, or daily. For the United States, at least, at various points of time all three modes have existed. One might well see a "shift" in a simple money demand function as institutional practice changed.

As noted earlier, some writers have also emphasized the role of expected inflation. This has been variously measured by a distributed lag of actual inflation, by expectational proxies from surveys, and by using predictions of expected inflation generated from some sort of autoregressive process. While no clear-cut consensus appears to have emerged on the use of expected inflation, it should be noted that the nominal partial adjustment model with inflation excluded still embodies a permanent effect of inflation on the demand for real balances.[22]

Those who use a rich variety of interest rates sometimes appeal to the portfolio approach, although, as noted above, there are some problems with this rationale. The portfolio approach also emphasizes the role of variances and covariances of the underlying expected returns. While these are not directly observable, a number of studies have used ex post measures of volatility in interest rates or inflation rates as proxies. While some have found support for such variables, others have concluded that there is little evidence that interest rate volatility affects the demand for M1.[23] One major source of this discrepancy is that there is an embarrassing number of ways in which volatility can be measured and the results appear sensitive to these and, of course, to the remaining aspects of the specification.

A final issue concerning interest rates is the effect of deregulation on the interest elasticity of the demand for money. Deregulation has meant the availability of money substitutes paying competitive rates of return and the availability of increasingly competitive rates of return on transactions balances. Some have argued that these events will lower the elasticity of M1 with respect to market interest rates while others have argued that the elasticity could increase.[24] Not surprisingly, the empirical results are inconclusive with Keeley and Zimmerman (1986) offering evidence of increased elasticities, while Roley (1985) suggests unchanged elasticities. At the very least, however, the possibility of a changed interest elasticity in response to deregulation suggests that a double logarithmic specification, which constrains the elasticity to be constant over the sample period, may be inappropriate.[25]

---

[22] See Goldfeld and Sichel (1987a) and Section 4 below.

[23] Baba, Hendry and Starr (1985) offer evidence in favor of volatility measures, while Garner (1986) provides negative evidence. Garner also contains a substantial number of references to earlier work. Walsh (1984) provides a formal model in which the interest elasticity of the demand for money is explicitly related to interest rate volatility.

[24] Keeley and Zimmerman (1986) consider the latter case while the former view is given in Judd and Scadding (1982b) and Santomero and Siegel (1986). At issue is the extent to which depository institutions had formerly circumvented interest rate ceilings through nonprice competition. Also relevant, at least from a portfolio perspective, is what happens to the variability of interest rates in a deregulated environment. See Roley (1985).

[25] As Freedman (1983) has noted, high interest rates may be needed to sort out the functional form, but episodes of high rates may coincide with shifts in the underlying specification, making these issues difficult to sort out.

3.2.4. Technological variables

The specification used in Section 2 omitted any measure characterizing the transactions technology. Put in the context of the Baumol–Tobin model, this implicitly assumes that (real) transactions costs are constant.[26] In the Miller–Orr variant, we are assuming no changes in the underlying uncertainty of receipts and expenditures. With the advent of the missing money period, these assumptions were immediately called into question, especially since even casual inspection revealed marked improvements in business cash management techniques. Examples of financial innovation in cash management techniques include such arcane-sounding devices as lockboxes, cash concentration accounts, and controlled disbursement accounts. Taken as a group these serve to speed up the collection process, provide firms with better information on cash balances, and reduce the uncertainty of cash flows. In addition to this reduction in uncertainty, the reduction in wire transfer fees which has also taken place, has served to reduce transactions costs. These developments have clearly altered the nature of the transactions process and permitted firms to economize on the need for cash balances.[27]

While some of the innovations in cash management reflected exogenous technological improvements in computers and telecommunications, the introduction of these innovations also reflected endogenous choices by firms. More particularly, the existence and expected continuation of high opportunity costs of holding cash balances directly induced firms to invest in new transactions technologies.[28] While the potential importance of allowing for financial innovation in the specification of money demand is clear, econometric modeling of financial innovation has proved extremely difficult. One basic problem is that there are no reliable direct data on transactions costs. Indeed, we are aware of only one attempt [Porter and Offenbacher (1982)] to include an estimated transactions cost variable in a money demand equation and, while this produced sensible results, given data difficulties even the authors seem cautious in pushing this approach.[29]

[26]Inspection of (3.2) reveals that dividing both sides by the price level makes the demand for real balances a function of the real volume of transactions and the real transactions costs. This, of course, makes the additional implicit assumption that the price index for b is identical to the general price index. Brainard (1976) has suggested that the appropriate brokerage deflator has risen less than the general price index and that ignoring this constitutes a specification error. Brainard further suggests that this misspecification could explain the appearance of money illusion (nonhomogeneity).

[27]See Simpson and Porter (1980) for a detailed description of cash management techniques.

[28]See Simpson and Porter (1980) for a model that embodies an endogenous choice of a transactions technology in a Miller–Orr setup.

[29]One issue is what is meant to be captured by b. For some purposes it is an explicit charge related to wire transfers while for others it is "shoe leather" cost or the value of time in making trips to the bank. Real wages are sometimes used as proxy for the latter effect but this is clearly only part of the story.

As a consequence, most of the evidence on the effects of financial innovation is rather indirect, using time trends to capture exogenous technological change or some function of previous peak interest rates as a proxy for endogenous reductions in transactions costs. The idea behind the latter variable is that high interest rates create an incentive to incur the fixed costs necessary to introduce a new technology but that once interest rates decline the technology remains in place. The use of a previous peak variable is meant to capture this irreversibility and researchers using such a variable have found that it improves the fit of money demand functions. Unfortunately, however, the resulting estimates do not appear very robust, either to small changes in specification or to the use of additional data.[30] Yet another indirect approach is taken by Dotsey (1985) who uses the number of electronic fund transfers over the Fed wire as a proxy for cash management innovations. This variable does appear to repair a specification which exhibits the missing money phenomenon. However, the data are annual from 1920 to 1979 and this, in conjunction with a rather different specification, makes it difficult to know if the quarterly specification considered above would also improve with this proxy.

Overall, Porter and Offenbacher have accurately characterized the situation when they note that while none of the work has led to a fully successful respecification, nevertheless there seems ample reason to presume that the major source of the shift in the 1970s is technological in nature. As a consequence, many empirical researchers remain quite uneasy with their inability to capture adequately relevant changes in transactions costs since it raises the possibility of a continuing source of specification error.

4. Econometric issues

The empirical difficulties described above, as well as prompting a search for an improved specification of the long-run demand for money, have led to a re-evaluation of econometric issues in the treatment of short-run dynamics. We next review these issues focusing first on the partial adjustment model and its shortcomings and then considering improvements and alternatives to this model. More specifically, Subsection 4.1 discusses the derivation and estimation of the partial adjustment model, while Subsection 4.2 reviews criticisms of and alternatives to the partial adjustment model. Subsection 4.3 focuses on general time-series models and on recent efforts to estimate short-run money demand equations which are consistent with imposed long-run relationships. Finally, Subsection 4.4 discusses issues of identification and simultaneity, and considers recent work advocating "buffer stock" money.

---

[30]For a discussion of alternative ways of implementing the previous-peak variable see Simpson and Porter (1980). Also see Judd and Scadding (1982a) and Roley (1985).

4.1. Money demand and the partial adjustment mechanism

"Equilibrium" theories of money demand generate implications about long-run demand for money balances. Estimation requires a short-run dynamic specification, and as noted above, the partial adjustment model has been widely used for this purpose.

4.1.1. Derivation of the partial adjustment model

Partial adjustment is typically motivated by cost-minimizing behavior wherein the costs of disequilibrium are balanced against adjustment costs. Following Hwang (1985), consider a quadratic cost function of the form:

$$C = \alpha_1 [\ln M_t^* - \ln M_t]^2 + \alpha_2 [(\ln M_t - \ln M_{t-1}) + \delta(\ln P_t - \ln P_{t-1})]^2 ,$$

(4.1)

where $M_t = m_t P_t$, $M_t^* = m_t^* P_t$, m_t^* is the "desired" stock of real balances, and P_t is the price level. The first and second terms of (4.1) correspond to the disequilibrium and adjustment costs, respectively.[31] For $\delta = 0$, (4.1) posits that the adjustment term is solely a function of nominal magnitudes, while for $\delta = 1$ the second term in (4.1) takes the form $\alpha_2 (\ln m_t - \ln m_{t-1})^2$. Intermediate values of δ correspond to hybrid models.

Minimizing costs with respect to M_t yields:

$$\ln M_t - \ln M_{t-1} = \mu(\ln M_t^* - \ln M_{t-1}) + \tau(\ln P_t - \ln P_{t-1}) ,$$

(4.2)

where $\mu = \alpha_1/(\alpha_1 + \alpha_2)$ and $\tau = \delta\alpha_2/(\alpha_1 + \alpha_2) = \delta(1 - \mu)$. Thus, when $\delta = 1$, (4.2) reduces to the so-called real partial adjustment model (RPAM) in which real balances are adjusted. Alternatively, when $\delta = 0$, (4.2) reduces to the nominal partial adjustment model (NPAM) in which nominal balances are adjusted.

To complete the story, a standard specification for m_t^* is given by

$$\ln m_t^* = \phi_0 + \phi_1 \ln y_t + \phi_2 \ln r_t + \phi_3 \pi_t ,$$

(4.3)

where y_t is a transactions variable such as real GNP, r_t represents one (or more) interest rates, and π_t is the rate of inflation measured by $\pi_t = \ln(P_t/P_{t-1})$. Combining (4.2) and (4.3) and rearranging terms yields:

$$\ln m_t = \mu\phi_0 + \mu\phi_1 \ln y_t + \mu\phi_2 \ln r_t + (1 - \mu)\ln m_{t-1} + \beta \ln(P_t/P_{t-1}) ,$$

(4.4)

---

[31]A somewhat richer adjustment model would result if money were considered as part of a portfolio. For a good discussion of such a generalized adjustment model, see B. Friedman (1977).

where

$$\beta = \mu\phi_3 + (1 - \mu)(\delta - 1) \,. \tag{4.5}$$

From (4.5) we see that it is impossible to identify simultaneously δ and ϕ_3. If it were known a priori that $\phi_3 = 0$, then an estimate of δ could be inferred from estimates of β and μ. In this case, $\delta = 0$ would yield the NPAM and $\delta = 1$ would yield the RPAM. Similarly, if the value of δ were known a priori, then an estimate of ϕ_3 could be inferred. However, without prior knowledge about δ or ϕ_3, it is impossible to determine simultaneously whether the real or nominal adjustment mechanism is appropriate (value of δ) and to determine whether inflation has an independent effect on the demand for desired real balances (value of ϕ_3).[32] In spite of the identification problem, equation (4.4) provides a useful reduced form.

4.1.2. Estimation of the partial adjustment model

Estimation of equation (4.4), which corresponds to equation (2.1), or more specifically the estimation of the RPAM or NPAM, is typically carried out using the Cochrane–Orcutt procedure on a single equation to allow for first-order serial correlation of residuals. This, of course, ignores questions of simultaneity which are taken up below. Furthermore, as Betancourt and Kelejian (1981) point out, it is possible that the Cochrane–Orcutt procedure is inconsistent in the presence of a lagged dependent variable. To circumvent this difficulty, one may use the two-stage method of Hatanaka (1974), nonlinear least squares, or maximum likelihood.[33]

Despite the conceptual shortcoming of Cochrane–Orcutt, parameter esti-

---

[32] If β is nonzero, inflation certainly affects real balances independently of the Fisher effect operating through nominal interest rates. The identification problem just indicates that it is not possible to determine whether this effect is via m_t^* or via the adjustment mechanism. For a more detailed discussion of the identification problem, see Goldfeld and Sichel (1987a).

[33] Maximum likelihood estimation of a model such as

$$m_t = \alpha m_{t-1} + \beta x_t + u_t \,,$$

$$u_t = \rho u_{t-1} + e_t \,,$$

with a sample size of T, can be obtained by minimizing $\sigma_e^2/(1 - \rho^2)^{1/T}$, where

$$(T - 1)\sigma_e^2 = \sum_{t=3}^{T} [(m_t - \rho m_{t-1}) - \beta(x_t - \rho x_{t-1}) - \alpha(m_{t-1} - \rho m_{t-2})]^2$$
$$+ (1 - \rho^2)(m_2 - \beta x_2 - \alpha m_1)^2 \,.$$

Nonlinear least squares estimation ignores the last term which is the correction for the first observation.

Table 8.7
Maximum likelihood and Cochrane–Orcutt estimates of a standard model

Variable	1952:3–1974:1		1952:3–1979:3	
	ML	CORC	ML	CORC
Intercept	0.399	0.381	−0.309	−0.313
	(1.4)	(1.7)	(2.4)	(2.6)
y	0.135	0.131	0.041	0.039
	(4.2)	(5.0)	(4.8)	(5.0)
RCP	−0.016	−0.016	−0.013	−0.013
	(5.5)	(5.9)	(4.8)	(5.0)
$RCBP$	−0.033	−0.030	−0.003	−0.002
	(3.0)	(3.3)	(0.7)	(0.4)
m_{t-1}	0.780	0.788	1.004	1.007
	(9.7)	(12.4)	(42.6)	(47.9)
P_t/P_{t-1}	−0.711	−0.711	−0.888	−0.889
	(6.8)	(6.9)	(9.5)	(9.5)
ρ	0.488	0.452	0.402	0.367
SEE	0.0038	0.0038	0.0042	0.0042

mates for (4.4) with serially correlated errors obtained by Cochrane–Orcutt generally correspond quite closely to the maximum likelihood estimates. This is illustrated in Table 8.7 for two different sample periods. As a practical matter, despite claims to the contrary, the shortcomings of the conventional specification can hardly be attributed to the Cochrane–Orcutt procedure.

Are first differences the answer? Several researchers have suggested that estimating equation (4.4) in first differences – rather than levels with a serial correlation correction – solves some of the problems of standard money demand equations. To be sure if ρ were essentially unity it would be appropriate to estimate (4.4) in first differences. Even though estimates of ρ are significantly different from unity, some writers have argued that the first difference specification performs better than the levels specification according to two criteria. First, Fackler and McMillan (1983), Gordon (1984), Hafer and Hein (1980), and Roley (1985) observe that a first difference out-of-sample root mean squared error (RMSE) is substantially smaller than a levels RMSE and conclude that the first difference specification is preferred. Second, these researchers also note that a first difference specification satisfies parameter constancy tests over the period of "missing money" in the mid-1970s while a levels specification with a serial correlation correction does not. This is taken as further evidence supporting the first difference specification.

These results, however, are puzzling since levels and first difference specifications for money demand typically have similar parameter estimates. In fact, Plosser, Schwert and White (1982) propose a formal specification test based on a comparison of the levels and first difference parameter estimates. If the levels specification is correct, the levels and first difference estimates should be similar using a suitably defined metric. If the estimates differ significantly, then there is a problem with the levels specification. In any case, this specification test does not have a specific alternative hypothesis. If the levels specification is rejected, no indication is provided as to the correct specification. In the context of money demand, Roley (1985) informally compared levels and first difference parameter estimates. In many of his equations, these estimates are similar.

Given this puzzle, it is not surprising that there are problems with using RMSEs and parameter constancy tests to compare levels and first difference specifications. For the RMSE comparison, the problem is a fundamental noncomparability between the levels and first difference RMSE which is similar to that arising in comparisons of R^2's from models with variously transformed dependent variables [e.g. y vs. $\log(y)$]. When used as an informal specification test, the RMSE comparison has an implicit null hypothesis that the two specifications have the same RMSE. The alternative is that one of the RMSEs is smaller, and that therefore that specification is preferred. However, even when the coefficients are known exactly, the expected RMSEs for the levels and first difference specifications are different. Therefore, it is not appropriate to test these specifications by directly comparing their RMSEs. As shown in Goldfeld and Sichel (1987b), it is possible to calculate an RMSE for the levels specification which can be compared to the first difference RMSE. This is done by using the estimated levels parameters to forecast first differences. For the standard model in equation (4.4), estimated over the sample 1952:3–1973:4 and used to forecast for twenty quarters beyond the end of the sample, the actual first difference RMSE is 0.0052 and the comparable levels RMSE is 0.0049. This suggests that correctly compared RMSEs do not provide evidence in favor of the first difference specification.

For the parameter constancy test comparison, the problem is that for certain parameter shifts the power of an F-test for parameter constancy is much lower in the first difference specification that in the levels specification. Therefore, the fact that first difference specifications satisfy parameter constancy tests may just reflect the inability of these tests to detect certain types of parameter nonconstancy. To demonstrate this we have carried out some Monte Carlo experiments to answer the following question: If the shift in money demand were generated by an intercept shift in the levels specification, how effective would an F-test of parameter constancy be in detecting this shift in a levels with serial correlation correction and a first difference specification?

To pin down the power of the F-test, we estimated equation (4.4) in levels with a serial correlation correction from 1952:3 to 1974:1. We then used these parameters, initial conditions for the money stock and the actual values of the independent variables to generate pseudo data from 1953:1 to 1979:3. Each observation of the generated data included a random normal error, with variance equal to the residual variance of the estimated equation, and also used the preceding observation of pseudo data as the lagged money stock. To parameterize the mid-1970s shift in money demand, we added to each replication of pseudo data the term $\tau D74$, where τ is a parameter indicating the size of the shift and D74 is a dummy variable which is zero from 1952:3 to 1974:1 and unity thereafter. This parameterization is consistent with the work of Hafer and Hein (1980) who argue that the mid-1970s shift in money demand can be represented by an intercept shift. For the levels with serial correlation correction specification, the F-test is calculated directly on each replication of pseudo data. For the first difference specification, the pseudo data is first differenced and then the F-test is calculated.

For different values of τ, we calculated the power of the F-test for parameter constancy splitting the sample after 1974:1 for each specification. These are shown in Table 8.8.[34]

Hafer and Hein estimate the size of the intercept shift to be 0.013. In this range, the F-test for parameter constancy has high power for detecting this nonconstancy in the levels specification. In the first difference specification, however, the F-test has very low power in this range. The reason for this is that an intercept shift in levels appears as a shift in only the period of change in the first difference specification.

Overall, then, the parameter constancy evidence cited by researchers favoring the first difference specification may just reflect the inability of parameter

Table 8.8
Power for 5 percent nominal size F-test of parameter constancy[a]

τ	Levels[b]	First differences
0.000	0.095	0.028
0.005	0.355	0.032
0.010	0.865	0.060
0.015	0.990	0.122
0.030	c	0.452
0.050	c	0.860
0.060	c	0.926

[a]For the levels and first difference specifications, 200 and 500 replications of pseudo data are used, respectively.
[b]Levels with serial correlation correction, using nonlinear least squares.
[c]Not calculated since power $= 0.99$ for $\tau = 0.015$.

[34]Note that the actual sizes of the tests (power at $\tau = 0$) are different from the nominal size of 5 percent. This results from the presence of a lagged dependent variable which affects the small sample properties of the F-test and from the nonlinearity caused by the serial correlation correction.

constancy tests to detect shifts in the first difference specification. The more general point is that, viewed as tests of specification, RMSE comparisons and parameter constancy tests can only reject a specification; they do not indicate that the specification at hand is a good one. Another way to make the same point is to note that satisfying these types of tests of specification is a necessary – but not sufficient – condition for a model to be acceptable. This is just the same as with the more formal Plosser, Schwert and White specification test in which a rejection of the levels specification does not provide evidence in favor of the first difference specification. Therefore, it seems that the RMSE and parameter constancy evidence cited in favor of a first difference specification is rather tenuous.

4.1.3. Temporal aggregation

As just noted, the PAM is typically estimated allowing for serially correlated errors. There is, however, some evidence that the importance of this serial correlation is exaggerated by the temporal aggregation implicit in averaging daily M1 figures to obtain standard quarterly M1 data.[35] As an alternative, last day of quarter Flow of Funds data for M1 can be used instead of the quarterly averaged M1 data. The tradeoff, here, is that there are questions about the quality of the Flow of Funds data.[36]

For comparison with the standard results in Table 8.1, Table 8.9 presents Cochrane–Orcutt estimates of equation (2.1) with serially correlated errors using the alternate last day of quarter data for M1.[37] For the sample period ending in 1974:1, averaged data yielded a statistically significant serial correlation coefficient of 0.452, as compared with a negative and marginally significant value from Table 8.9 of -0.230. Thus, it is apparent that temporal aggregation pushes up the coefficient of serial correlation, a finding consistent with results obtained by Roley (1985).

On the other hand, a further comparison of the results in Tables 8.1 and 8.9 indicates that temporal aggregation, or time-averaging in Table 8.1, reduces

---

[35] In a similar vein, Goodfriend (1985) argues that measurement error in interest rates and income can induce the significance of the lagged dependent variable. Although logically correct, Goodfriend's argument is based on rather rigid and specific assumptions. For an early discussion of the effects of measurement error and temporal aggregation, see Black (1973).

[36] The Federal Reserve also reports a weekly money series but this is only available from the mid-1970s. Roley (1985) analyzes these data, although in a quarterly regression. An alternative way to get at problems of temporal aggregation would be to use all the weekly data.

[37] Last day of quarter data were constructed from Flow of Funds data by cumulating seasonally adjusted quarterly flows using the levels outstanding for 1952:1 as a base. Although last day of quarter interest rates should be used, we used the same measures of interest rates in Tables 8.1 and 8.9 to isolate the effect of just changing the monetary aggregate. Informal experimentation indicated that the use of quarterly average or end of quarter interest rates does not affect the results.

Table 8.9
Conventional money model with flow of funds – M1 data

Variable	1952:3–1974:1	1952:3–1979:3
Intercept	0.042	−0.331
	(0.2)	(3.2)
y	0.107	0.036
	(3.3)	(4.1)
RCP	−0.017	−0.013
	(5.9)	(4.8)
RCBP	−0.019	0.001
	(1.8)	(0.2)
m_{t-1}	0.872	1.013
	(13.4)	(52.3)
P_t/P_{t-1}	−0.720	−0.976
	(4.0)	(6.4)
ρ	−0.230	−0.298
	(1.9)	(3.0)
SEE	0.0067	0.0076

the coefficient on the lagged dependent variable. Thus, the use of temporally aggregated data makes partial adjustment appear to be a more reasonable rationalization of equation (2.1) than it may in fact be. This result is not consistent with Roley who finds that temporal aggregation increases the coefficient on the lagged dependent variable.[38] However, an attempt to replicate Roley's results suggests that his shorter sample period (1959:3–1973:4) and inclusion of real equities as an explanatory variable are responsible for both the size of the effect he finds for the serial correlation coefficient and the *direction* of the effect he finds for the lagged dependent variable coefficient.

These results for the effect of temporal aggregation on the serial correlation and lagged dependent variable coefficients suggest that Roley may have overstated the quantitative importance of temporal aggregation since his results are not robust to alternative sample periods and specifications. However, the general point – that the dynamic structure of money demand is sensitive to temporal aggregation – is correct. Nevertheless, the use of Flow of Funds data does not prevent the problems that beset the standard equation in 1974. The second column of Table 8.9 indicates that the coefficient on the lagged dependent variable is approximately unity with Flow of Funds data. Furthermore, just as with temporally aggregated data, a formal test rejects parameter constancy at 5 percent for the specification in Table 8.9 if the longer sample period is split at 1974:1.

---

[38]Like Roley (1985), Christiano and Eichembaum (1986) also find evidence that temporal aggregation biases upward the coefficient on the lagged dependent variable in a stock adjustment model for inventories.

4.1.4. Functional form

In considering estimation issues in the context of the partial adjustment model we have thus far restricted attention to the double logarithmic or constant elasticity specification. As noted earlier, it has been suggested that a constant elasticity specification, at least with respect to interest rates, may be inappropriate in the face of the financial deregulation of the 1980s. The issue of functional form for the interest rate has, of course, a much longer history in the money demand literature, stemming from debates about the existence of a liquidity trap. The most recent papers on this subject have utilized the generalized Box–Cox transformation, which permits one to estimate a general functional form that has the linear or logarithmic forms as special cases.[39] Given the poor performance of the conventional double logarithmic specification after 1974, it seems natural to question whether the choice of functional form might be at fault.

The generalized Box–Cox transformation can be illustrated with reference to the following equation:

$$\frac{M^{\lambda_0} - 1}{\lambda_0} = \beta_0 + \beta_1 \left(\frac{M^{\lambda_1} - 1}{\lambda_1} \right) + \beta_2 \left(\frac{r^{\lambda_2} - 1}{\lambda_2} \right) + u .\tag{4.6}$$

When all of the λ's are restricted to unity, equation (4.6) reduces to a linear functional form; when the λ's are all zero, (4.6) becomes a logarithmic specification.[40] Alternative values of the λ's correspond to more complex functional forms. Equations like (4.6) can be readily estimated by maximum likelihood methods. In the present case, since (4.4) exhibits first-order serial correlation, we need to estimate (4.6) allowing for this but this is a straightforward matter.[41] Given the estimates, we can gauge the appropriateness of the logarithmic specification by testing the hypothesis $\lambda_0 = \lambda_1 = \lambda_2 = 0$. In the present context, this is most conveniently done by a likelihood ratio test,

---

[39] The basic idea is spelled out in Box and Cox (1964) while the application to money demand was pioneered by Zarembka (1968) and subsequently applied by Spitzer (1976) and Boyes (1978) among others.

[40] L'Hospital's rule implies that

$$\lim_{\lambda \to 0} \frac{x^{\lambda} - 1}{\lambda} = \ln x .$$

[41] The log likelihood function for this is

$$L = \frac{T}{2} \ln(2\pi) + \ln(1 - \rho^2)^{1/2} - (T/2) \ln \sigma^2 - 1/2(U'R'RU/\sigma^2) + (\lambda_0 - 1) \sum \ln M_t ,$$

where T is the sample size, U is the vector of u's, and R is the matrix given by $RU = \varepsilon$, where ε is the "clean" error vector.

Table 8.10
Significance tests for functional form

Specification	End point of sample[a]	Likelihood value	χ^2 (significance level)
Equation (4.4)	1974:1	−164.04	−
Box–Cox (4.4), 6λ's	1974:1	−161.04	5.90 (0.435)
Box–Cox (4.4), 1λ[b]	1974:1	−162.06	3.96 (0.047)
Equation (4.4) + shift dummies[c]	1979:3	−207.66	−
Box–Cox (4.4) + shift dummies, 6λ's	1979:3	−205.64	4.04 (0.672)

[a]All estimation begins in 1952:3.
[b]All λ's are constrained to zero except for P_t/P_{t-1}.
[c]Shift dummies as in Table 8.4.

comparing the likelihood values with and without the restriction on the λ's. Table 8.10 reports the likelihood values and the relevant χ^2 statistics for estimating a generalized Box–Cox version of equation (4.4) for two different sample periods. For the period ending in 1974:1, one cannot reject the hypothesis of a double logarithmic specification. Examination of the asymptotic *t*-statistics of the individual λ's (not shown) suggests that only the coefficient of P_t/P_{t-1} appears to be significantly different from zero. The role of this variable is further examined in row 3 of Table 8.10 where, save for this variable, all of the λ's are constrained to zero. As the results indicate, the logarithmic form can be improved on for P_t/P_{t-1}, but evidence is not particularly dramatic.[42]

For the sample period ending in 1979:3, as in Table 8.4, it is necessary to use dummy variables to yield a specification which passes a stability test. Conditional on the use of these variables, the last two rows of Table 8.10 indicate that one cannot reject the double logarithmic specification.[43] Overall then, at least for the period before 1980, given the use of the partial adjustment model there seems little reason to quarrel with the double logarithmic functional form. There are, of course, reasons to question the partial adjustment model itself.

4.2. Criticisms and modifications of the partial adjustment model

As indicated, equation (4.4) above encompasses the real and nominal partial adjustment models, and corresponds to equation (2.1). As Section 2 made

[42]The asymptotic *t*-static for the λ associated with P_t/P_{t-1} is 2.1, which tells the same qualitative story. It should also be recalled that one cannot reject the restriction in (4.4) that $\beta = \mu - 1$. If this restriction is imposed, there are no significant departures from the double logarithmic specification.

[43]In the estimation which lies behind Table 8.10, we did not do a generalized Box–Cox transformation on the dummy variables. Thus, for example, the shift variable for GNP was entered as $D (\ln y)$.

clear, this equation did not perform well after the tranquil period ending in 1974. This led many researchers to question the appropriateness of the partial adjustment model and this subsection will describe a variety of criticisms and attempted improvements.

4.2.1. Lag structure of independent variables

The partial adjustment model in (2.1) or (4.4) can be rewritten as

$$\ln m_t = b_3 \sum_{i=0}^{\infty} (1 - b_3)^i [b_0 + b_1 \ln y_{t-i} + b_2 \ln r_{t-i} + b_4 \pi_{t-i} + u_{t-i}]. \quad (4.7)$$

As is evident, this model makes the implicit assumption that the independent variables have geometric lags which decay at the same rate. Chant (1976) and Gordon (1984), among others, have noted this criticism.

Chant (1976) considers the adjustment of aggregate money balances in a world of identical agents with Baumol–Tobin money demand functions. He compares the rate and duration of aggregate adjustment to an increase in optimal balances induced either by an interest rate or an income shock. In response to either shock, each household will not adjust to its new higher level until its current stock of money is depleted. With an interest rate shock, this rate of depletion is the same before and after the shock. However, since income is the transactions measure, a positive income shock increases the rate of transactions per fixed period of time. This means that each household will deplete its current stocks of money more rapidly than in response to an interest rate shock, and therefore aggregate adjustment will be completed more rapidly.[44] Chant also analyzes the Miller–Orr model which yields qualitatively similar results except that there is an asymmetric response with respect to positive and negative shocks.[45] In this same spirit, Milbourne, Buckholtz and Wasan (1983) use the Miller–Orr framework and derive an explicit theoretical specification for the level (not logs) of nominal money balances in which the adjustment parameter is a nonlinear function of income and interest rates.

Virtually all empirical work has ignored the complication of the dependence of the speed of adjustment on economic variables as well as the possibility of

---

[44]Chant also shows that alternative assumptions about the distribution of income affect the rate of adjustment of money balances to income and interest rate shocks.

[45]In the Miller–Orr model, a shock leading to a higher desired level of balances increases the upper bound of the band within which money balances are allowed to fluctuate. Aggregate firm balances will adjust smoothly upward as each firm eventually hits the upper or lower bound and adjusts to the new higher return level. On the other hand, however, a shock leading to a lower desired level of balances will decrease this upper bound and return level. Firms that had cash balances just below the old upper bound will now immediately respond by adjusting cash balances to the new return level. Therefore, unlike the response to a positive shock, there will be an immediate discrete decrease in aggregate firm balances.

asymmetric responses to shocks.[46] Rather, through the use of general distributed lag models, researchers have focused on allowing for different adjustment
patterns for each variable. Before considering some of these results, we first
consider an alternative justification for a distributed lag specification.

4.2.2. The role of expectations in providing dynamic structure

Feige (1967) proposed a rationalization for including lags in the short-run
money demand specification which is different than partial adjustment. He
posits that the correct formulation of the long-run demand for money in
equation (4.3) should include expectations of income and interest rates rather
than the actual levels,[47] i.e. rewrite (4.3) as:

$$\ln m_t^* = \phi_0 + \phi_1 \ln y_t^e + \phi_2 \ln r_t^e . \tag{4.8}$$

If expectations are adaptive, then

$$\ln y_t^e - \ln y_{t-1}^e = \sigma(\ln y_t - \ln y_{t-1}^e) , \tag{4.9}$$

$$\ln r_t^e - \ln r_{t-1}^e = \mu(\ln r_t - \ln r_{t-1}^e) . \tag{4.10}$$

Substituting (4.9) and (4.10) into (4.8), and rearranging yields:

$$\begin{aligned}
\ln m = {} & \phi_0[1 - (1 - \sigma)][1 - (1 - \mu)] + (2 - \sigma - \mu) \ln m_{t-1} \\
& + (1 - \sigma)(1 - \mu) \ln m_{t-2} + \phi_1 \sigma \ln y_t - \phi_1 \sigma(1 - \mu) \ln y_{t-1} \\
& + \phi_2 \mu \ln r_t - \phi_2 \mu(1 - \sigma) \ln r_{t-1} .
\end{aligned} \tag{4.11}$$

Note that the presence of lags of m_t as explanatory variables depends on the
adaptive expectations parameters, σ and μ, rather than partial adjustment.
This model can be made more complicated by combining adaptive expectations
with the partial adjustment mechanism which would add the third lag of money
to equation (4.11). With this model, it is possible to test whether the source of
the lag is from partial adjustment, adaptive expectations, or both.

Feige did this using annual data from 1915 to 1963 and found that complete
adjustment occurred within a year and that the appearance of lagged money as

---

[46] Some recent theoretical work by Fusselman and Grossman (1986) suggests there may be a big
payoff to trying to specify correctly the short-run dynamics. Unfortunately, as their paper makes
clear, this is no easy matter.

[47] We should note that π_t is excluded from (4.8). Subsequent research, of course, became
increasingly concerned with inflationary expectations and it is a simple matter to apply Feige's
approach to this variable as well.

an explanatory variable depended solely on adaptive expectations for income. Thornton (1982), using quarterly data from 1952:2 to 1972:4 and a maximum likelihood procedure, found that the partial adjustment mechanism was operative, i.e. full adjustment did not occur within one quarter. In fact, he found that adjustment speeds were implausibly slow, but that inclusion of adaptive expectations for income and interest rates did increase the speed of adjustment.

A rational expectations assumption can also be used to justify the inclusion of lags in a money demand specification. For example, under restrictive assumptions we may posit that agents forecast income and interest rates with low order autoregressions, i.e.

$$\ln y_t^e = \sum_{i=1}^N \sigma_i \ln y_{t-i} \, ,$$

$$\ln r_t^e = \sum_{i-1}^N \mu_i \ln r_{t-i} \, .$$

Substituting these equations into (4.8) includes lags of y_t and r_t as explanatory variables with nonlinear restrictions on the distributed lag parameters. More complicated rational expectations models are also possible. For example, Dutkowsky and Foote (1987) begin with a representative agent maximizing lifetime expected utility over consumption and money subject to a period-by-period budget constraint. Their derived money demand specification looks quite similar to that obtained from the simple rational expectations model above, but with a lagged dependent variable and additional parameter restrictions resulting from the optimization. Dutkowsky and Foote estimate their model with monthly data from 1975 to 1985 and while it seems to "work", their restricted sample period limits the inferences that can be drawn.

4.2.3. General distributed lag models

As indicated above, general distributed lag models have been increasingly used for estimation of money demand. For example, an autoregressive distributed lag model for real balances is of the form:

$$\ln m_t = a + \sum_{i=1}^{n_1} b_i \ln m_{t-i} + \sum_{j=0}^{n_2} [c_j \ln y_{t-j} + d_j \ln r_{t-j} + f_j \pi_{t-j}] \, . \qquad (4.12)$$

As noted above, equation (4.12) is a natural generalization of the partial adjustment model since it allows the adjustment pattern to vary for each independent variable, and the PAM in equation (2.1) with serially correlated errors yields an equation similar to (4.12). More specifically, if $u_t = \rho u_{t-1} + e_t$, then equation (2.1) takes the form:

$$\ln m_t = b_0(1 - \rho) + (b_3 + \rho) \ln m_{t-1} - b_3 \rho \ln m_{t-2}$$
$$+ b_1 \ln y_t - b_1 \rho \ln y_{t-1} + b_2 \ln r_t$$
$$- b_2 \rho \ln r_{t-1} + b_4 \pi_t - b_4 \rho \pi_{t-1} + e_t. \tag{4.13}$$

A comparison of equations (4.12) and (4.13) indicates that imposing appropriate restrictions on (4.12) yields (4.13). Given this relationship between these equations, a natural way to evaluate the PAM is with an encompassing test of these restrictions.

Using (4.12) as an encompasser and including just enough lags to nest (2.1) with serially correlated errors (i.e. $n_1 = 2$ and $n_2 = 1$), the values for the encompassing χ^2 test are shown in Table 8.11 for the sample periods 1953:2–1974:1 and 1953:2–1979:3. The first row of Table 8.11 tests the restrictions that would just reduce the encompasser to (4.13) and we see that these restrictions are not rejected.

Equations (2.1) and (4.12) include π_t in an unrestricted fashion; it is also possible to perform the encompassing tests for the nominal and real PAMs by imposing an additional restriction on the coefficient of π_t in (4.13). These results are also reported in Table 8.11 and show that the RPAM is rejected while the NPAM is not rejected.[48] Similarly, using Canadian data from 1957:1 to 1978:4, Keil and Richardson (1986) find, much to their surprise, that they are unable to reject the nominal PAM.

The above discussion indicates that the nominal PAM passes an encompassing test. However, we should not be too quick to accept this specification. First, as widely documented and discussed above, the equation falls apart in

Table 8.11
Encompassing χ^2 test for PAMs with AR1 errors[a]

Model	1953:2–1974:1	1953:2–1979:3
Equation (4.13)	5.88 (4)[b]	7.52 (4)
Nominal PAM	6.10 (5)	8.47 (5)
Real PAM	44.37* (5)	74.12* (5)

[a]Encompasser is equation (4.12) with $n_1 = 2$ and $n_2 = 1$.
[b]Degrees of freedom in parentheses.
*Significant at 5%.

[48]In the present context the NPAM is defined by setting $b_4 = -b_3$ in (4.13) while the RPAM sets $b_4 = 0$. Using the same setup, Webster (1981) argues that for the period 1960:1–1973:4, an encompassing test rejects the real PAM as above, and also rejects the nominal PAM. However, using the most recent data available, we were unable to replicate Webster's results.

the mid-1970s. Second, as discussed above, equation (2.1) with serially correlated errors does not satisfy homogeneity with respect to the price level in the periods 1952:3–1974:1 and 1952:3–1979:3. It therefore seems reasonable to consider general distributed lag models in their own right as extensions of the PAM to see if they can resolve the missing money and nonhomogeneity problems of the PAM.

Goldfeld and Sichel (1987a) examine both of these issues. Using $n_1 = n_2 = 4$, they show that the general distributed lag model in (4.12) does not exhibit parameter constancy over the period 1953:1–1978:4. On a positive note, it is shown that equation (4.12) does satisfy long-run homogeneity with respect to the price level over these periods.[49] This is tested by replacing the π_t terms in (4.12) with the price level, P_t, and testing the restriction that the coefficients on the P_t's sum to zero. Since this restriction is not rejected we can work with (4.12) which imposes homogeneity.

Equation (4.12) has another advantage over the PAM – it can be used explicitly to test for short- and long-run inflation effects. To use (4.12) to assess whether there is any short-run effect of inflation on real balances, we can test the restriction $f_j = 0$, for all j, in (4.12). A second less restrictive hypothesis is that there is a short-run effect of inflation on real balances, but that there is no long-run effect. In terms of (4.12), this hypothesis is $\sum_{j=0}^{4} f_j = 0$. For the sample periods 1953:1–1973:4 and 1953:1–1978:4, Goldfeld and Sichel (1987a) demonstrate that the hypothesis $f_j = 0$, for all j, is overwhelmingly rejected and that the hypothesis $\sum_{j=0}^{4} f_i = 0$ is also rejected at conventional significance levels. Therefore, there is a short-run and long-run inflation effect during this sample period.

The bottom line of this discussion of general distributed lag models is that they do have some advantages over PAMs, but still suffer from the mid-1970s breakdown. Furthermore, these models are not parsimonious, and since they often lack a structural interpretation their application to policy analysis may be tenuous.

4.3. Dynamic models that impose long-run relationships

An alternative application of general distributed lag models is as the starting point for developing models which impose long-run relationships. Except for early attempts to estimate long-run relationships directly, all of the work

---

[49]For the homogeneity test and for the inflation effects test described in the next paragraph, the model for the longer sample period includes interactive dummy variables at every lag for the commercial paper rate and real GNP.

described above attempts to identify the correct short-run money demand specification from which long-run properties can be inferred. Recently, two related efforts have been made to estimate short-run money demand models in which long-run relationships are imposed. The first utilizes error correction models that assume and impose a constant long-run income elasticity of money. The second effort is described in the cointegration literature in which long-run parameters are *estimated* – rather than assumed and then imposed on a short-run specification.

4.3.1. Models imposing assumed long-run relationships

Hendry (1980) applied the error correction mechanism to money demand in the United Kingdom. To illustrate the derivation of this model from an autoregressive distributed lag model similar to (4.12), we consider a specification with only one lag of each variable as in

$$\ln m_t = b_1 \ln m_{t-1} + c_0 \ln y_t + c_1 \ln y_{t-1} + d_0 \ln r_t + d_1 \ln r_{t-1}. \qquad (4.14)$$

Note that the long-run income elasticity of money demand in this model is $(c_0 + c_1)/(1 - b_1)$. A convenient way to impose a prior value for the elasticity is to rewrite (4.14) as

$$\ln m_t - \ln m_{t-1} = c_0(\ln y_t - \ln y_{t-1}) - (1 - b_1)(\ln m_{t-1} - \theta \ln y_{t-1})$$
$$+ d_0 \ln r_t + d_1 \ln r_{t-1}, \qquad (4.15)$$

where $\theta = (c_0 + c_1)/(1 - b_1)$. To estimate the error correction model one would impose a value for θ, with $\theta = 1$ and $\theta = 1/2$ being commonly used values. Equation (4.15) is called an error correction model because the term $(\ln m_{t-1} - \theta \ln y_{t-1})$ represents last period's error or deviation of money from its long-run relationship with income. The interpretation of equation (4.15) is that agents adjust money balances in response to the change in income, last period's long-run error in money, and to a distributed lag of interest rates.

These models are typically obtained using a general-to-specific modeling methodology. This entails imposing an assumed long-run elasticity on a general distributed lag model such as (4.12), and then sequentially and selectively testing alternative reductions in the lag structure until a parsimonious model is obtained. As mentioned above, Hendry (1980) used this procedure for U.K. money demand. Rose (1985) estimated an error correction model for U.S. money demand. An interesting characteristic of Rose's model is that it does not exhibit the structural shift in the mid-1970s that characterized partial adjustment models, although it does become unstable after 1978.[50] In a later paper, Baba, Hendry and Starr (1985) estimated an error correction model with U.S. data which exhibited structural stability from 1960 to 1984. However, their equation uses several difficult-to-measure concepts such as interest rate volatility, learning-adjusted maximum yields, and after-tax interest rates. Unfortunately, the structural stability is not robust to minor changes in any aspect of what is a rather complicated specification. Nevertheless, these error correction models demonstrate that dynamic specifications imposing long-run relationships are quite able to capture salient elements of money demand.

4.3.2. Models imposing estimated long-run relationships[51]

Following Engle and Granger (1987) we can characterize a long-run relationship between money and income as

$$0 = \ln m_t - \theta \ln y_t . \tag{4.16}$$

It is not, of course, expected that this relationship will be satisfied every period, but if (4.16) describes an equilibrium relationship, then fluctuations around this equilibrium should be stationary, i.e.

$$z_t = \ln m_t - \theta \ln y_t , \tag{4.17}$$

with z_t as a stationary variable. It is also, of course, not expected that m_t and y_t are themselves necessarily stationary. To be more precise, suppose that m_t and y_t are integrated of order d, i.e. they are stationary after differencing d times. This will be denoted as I(d). In general, linear combinations of m_t and y_t, such as z_t, will also be I(d). However, suppose that z_t is integrated of an order less than d, e.g. z_t is I($d - b$), $b > 0$. If this occurs, then m_t and y_t are said to be cointegrated of order (d, b) – denoted CI(d, b) – and m_t and y_t are then said to satisfy a long-run relationship such as (4.16). If m_t and y_t are not cointegrated (a linear combination is not stationary), then they do not satisfy a long-run relationship.

As an economic example, suppose that m_t and y_t are I(1), i.e. the variables are stationary after first differencing ($d = 1$). Suppose, furthermore, that a

---

[50]Although appealing, Rose's stability results require further investigation. First, Rose imposes a unit income elasticity – a restriction rejected by the data. This could affect parameter constancy tests. Second, a general distributed lag model such as (4.12), which is the starting point of the general-to-specific reduction process used by Rose, in unstable over the mid-1970s. This raises further questions about the interpretation of Rose's parameter constancy results.

[51]The discussion of cointegration closely follows Engle and Granger (1987).

linear combination of m_t and y_t is stationary, i.e. the linear combination is integrated of order $d - b$, where $d = 1$ and $b = 1$. Then, m_t and y_t are cointegrated of order $(1, 1)$, and there is a long-run relation between m_t and y_t. This long-run equilibrium entails a constant income elasticity, θ.

Engle and Granger suggest a variety of procedures for testing for the presence of cointegration, i.e. testing for the existence of a long-run relationship. They also demonstrate that cointegrated processes have an error correction representation of the form of equation (4.15) above. Finally, they provide a consistent two-stage procedure for estimating the long- and short-run parameters in (4.15) and (4.17). This entails estimating (4.17) with ordinary least squares and using the residuals (z_t) as the error correction term in (4.15). With the estimated z_{t-1} substituted into (4.15) for $(\ln m_{t-1} - \theta \ln y_{t-1})$, equation (4.15) can be estimated consistently with ordinary least squares.[52]

The cointegration approach seems promising, but there are still some uncertainties as to its implications for money demand. Early applications of this approach often constrained θ to be unity with the hypothesis of cointegration being rejected for some monetary aggregates but not others. One should, of course, test this restriction. Moreover, it might be the case that some other combination of money, income, interest rates, and prices are cointegrated yielding a long-run relationship. As yet there has been little work on detecting multivariate cointegration and then imposing these *estimated* equilibrium relationships on error correction models although a nice example pertaining to Argentina is contained in Melnick (1989). While it is, therefore, difficult to judge if this approach will have a big payoff for money demand estimation, nevertheless cointegration is appealing in that it provides a rigorous time-series framework for applying long-run economic theory.[53]

4.4. Simultaneity, exogeneity, and the nature of the adjustment process

As noted above, the money demand function is often analyzed in isolation and typically estimated by single equation techniques, thus begging the questions of identification and simultaneous equations bias. When this is done, one is

---

[52]In a somewhat different context, Wickens and Breusch (1987) demonstrate that similar procedures yield consistent estimates of long- and short-run parameters if the original variables (say m_t and y_t) are stationary after removal of a linear trend rather than after first differencing. So, whether one believes that the world is characterized by difference stationarity or trend stationarity, it is possible to estimate short-run money demand specifications in which consistently *estimated* long-run relationships have been imposed.

[53]Another application of estimating and imposing long-run relationships appears in Porter, Spindt and Lindsey (1987). They use cointegration to look at the equilibrium relationship between long and short interest rates to obtain a model of rate-setting behavior.

making implicit assumptions about exogeneity and the nature of the money supply process. This subsection examines these assumptions and then analyzes the so-called buffer stock model of money demand which, as we shall see, derives from a particular view of exogeneity.

4.4.1. Identification and estimation

The aggregate money demand function is clearly but one ingredient in a complete macro model and whether the money demand function is identified depends on the structure of the complete model. As a practical matter, the most critical component is the description of the behavior of the monetary authorities. As Cooley and Leroy (1981), Hetzel (1984), and Gordon (1984) have emphasized, the assumption of identification is hardly a trivial one. Loosely speaking, one needs money supply variables that vary independently of the money demand variables and the money demand disturbances. To determine whether this holds, a precise characterization of the money supply process is required. One "story" that lies behind the simple traditional approach to the money demand function is that the Federal Reserve exogenously sets the interest rate and that income and prices are predetermined within the period of the analysis. This set of assumptions also assures the appropriateness of single-equation estimating methods.

Identification can, of course, be achieved with less stringent assumptions.[54] However, even if a model is identified one must examine the issue of estimation. There are, for example, a broad range of specifications of the money supply process that would permit identification of money demand parameters but would yield biased estimates with single equation techniques. In essence, any behavior of the monetary authorities that induces a correlation between the interest rate and the disturbance in the money demand equation would lead to biased estimates.[55] While these biases may be small, researchers have perhaps too often relied on this hope without sufficient checking of the facts.

Proper treatment of the identification and estimation problems in the context of money demand is not a simple problem. Progress requires a complete characterization of the money supply process, including the temporal aspects. For example, if policy rules operate in a weekly or bi-weekly time frame, then

---

[54] For a good discussion of the relevant technical issues in identification, see Engle, Hendry and Richard (1983). They introduce the concept of "weak" exogeneity for identification and contrast it with the notion of strict exogeneity necessary to assure consistency of parameter estimates. Whether estimated parameters correspond to the parameters of interest is where weak exogeneity comes in.

[55] For a good example of this, which also permits an explicit calculation of the size of the bias, see Roley (1985). Also see Rasche (1987).

temporal aggregation issues will arise with quarterly data. Similarly, if there are changes in the operating procedures governing monetary policy, these can affect identifiability and estimation. While there has been only limited progress on these issues to date, there has been considerable attention to one aspect of the problem. In particular, suppose for the moment we assume that the money stock is exogenously set by the monetary authorities. In such circumstances it seems a bit strange to posit a partial adjustment model in which the demand for money adjusts towards some desired level. Put more crudely, how do we reconcile the fact that M is exogenous with the appearance of money on the left-hand side of the conventional equation? To be sure, the variable on the left-hand side is the real stock of money but, given the exogeneity of M, this seems to suggest that we have a price equation and not a money equation. This, in fact, is precisely the tack taken by those who advocate the buffer stock approach to the demand for money.

4.4.2. Inverted money equations and the buffer stock approach

One of the first writers to question the interpretation of the partial adjustment model of short-run money demand was Walters (1967). Noting that the money stock should be regarded as an exogenous variable, and ignoring the niceties of the distinction between real and nominal magnitudes, Walters proposed that the money equation might be more properly regarded as an inverted income equation. While Walters' point was purely analytical, subsequent writers attempted to implement the idea empirically. Of course, once one decides that money is exogenous and that the money demand equation is really another equation in disguise, there is something of an embarrassment of possibilities. Indeed, it has been variously proposed that the money demand equation is an inverted equation for income, the interest rate, or the price level. In recent years, the price level interpretation seems to have become most favored, so we will concentrate on this.[56]

As a starting point, the price interpretation typically begins by noting that the inverted conventional money demand equation is not quite right as a price equation. The precise nature of the defect depends on whether we are dealing with the nominal PAM or the real PAM. We can see this if, denoting the desired stock of money balances as m_t^* and the speed of adjustment as μ, we renormalize the real PAM as:

$$\ln P_t = -\mu \ln m_t^* - (1 - \mu) \ln m_{t-1} + \ln M_t + u_t, \qquad (4.18)$$

---

[56]For a typology of the adjustment assumptions made by various researchers, see Judd and Scadding (1982c). Of course, the mere fact that the writers have inverted the function in various ways should raise some cautions about this approach.

and the nominal PAM as:

$$\ln P_t = -\ln m_t^* - \left(\frac{1-\mu}{\mu}\right) \ln M_{t-1} + \frac{1}{\mu} \ln M_t + u_t .$$ (4.19)

Equation (4.18) has the interpretation that the price level adjusts fully without lag to changes in M, a proposition that is hard to accept empirically. The nominal PAM is even more extreme since with $0 < \mu < 1$, P overadjusts in the short run to changes in M.[57] To remedy this, a partial adjustment model for the price level can be posited directly as in

$$\ln P_t - \ln P_{t-1} = \mu(\ln P_t^* - \ln P_{t-1}) + v_t ,$$ (4.20)

where P_t^* is regarded as the "equilibrium" value of the price level. Money enters equation (4.20) by noting that long-run equilibrium in the money market requires $M_t/P_t^* = m_t^*$. Substituting this into (4.20) yields:

$$\ln P_t = \mu(\ln M_t - \ln m_t^*) + (1 - \mu) \ln P_{t-1} + v_t .$$ (4.21)

Equation (4.21), which has the property that the price level reacts to money shocks with a lag, can be rewritten as:

$$\ln(M_t/P_t) = \mu \ln m_t^* + (1 - \mu) \ln(M_t/P_{t-1}) + v_t .$$ (4.22)

This renormalization gives (4.22) the superficial appearance of a "money demand" equation and has led some writers to estimate (4.22) and to compare its fit and out-of-sample forecasting errors with those of the nominal PAM or the real PAM [e.g. see Coats (1982) or Judd and Scadding (1982c)]. However, this procedure is clearly invalid since OLS estimates of equations (4.21) and (4.22) must yield identical residual errors. In other words, despite its appearance, (4.22) is a "price" equation and the resulting residual variance stems from the stochastic properties of P_t, which cannot be meaningfully compared to the residual variances from the nominal or real PAMs. Looked at another way, (4.22) amounts to regressing $\ln P_t$ on $\ln P_{t-1}$, whereas the lagged price variable is omitted from (4.19) and appears in (4.18) only in constrained form.[58] Another feature of (4.22), the appearance of M_t on both sides of the

---

[57] These interpretations assume M is exogenous. They also ignore the possibility that other components of m_t^* (e.g. the interest rate) can adjust.

[58] The noncomparability of (4.22) with (4.18) and (4.19) has also been observed by Thornton (1985). It should also be noted that one of the key ingredients in (4.22), namely the appearance of P_t^* in m_t^* [see Friedman (1959)], can be utilized in a conventional approach if we specify the determinants of P_t^*. See Goldfeld (1976) or Rasche (1987).

equation, has raised econometric questions that we address in the context of the Carr and Darby (1981) variant of (4.22).

Carr and Darby, starting from the the view that money is subject to exogenous shocks, argue that money balances serve as a shock absorber or buffer stock while money holders choose their new portfolios. They implement this idea by starting with the real partial adjustment model and modifying it with the *unanticipated* component of the money supply as in

$$\ln m_t = (1 - \mu) \ln m_{t-1} + \mu \ln m_t^* + \phi(\ln M_t - \ln_{t-1} M_t) + u_t, \qquad (4.23)$$

where $_{t-1}M_t$ is the nominal money stock anticipated at time $(t-1)$.[59] To see the connection with the price interpretation we can rewrite (4.23) as:

$$\ln P_t = -\mu \ln m_t^* - (1 - \mu) \ln m_{t-1} + (1 - \phi)(\ln M_t - \ln_{t-1} M_t)$$
$$+ \ln_{t-1} M_t - u_t . \qquad (4.24)$$

From (4.24) we see that prices adjust fully and immediately to changes in anticipated money but that unanticipated money has only a partial effect on the price level with the remainder of the effect felt in short-run real money holdings.[60]

To estimate (4.23), Carr and Darby use an autoregression (i.e. $\ln M_t$ regressed on lagged M's) to generate $_{t-1}M_t$. They then substitute this into (4.23) and estimate for the period 1957:1–1976:4 finding that ϕ is significantly positive, which they take as evidence in favor of their model. Although this sample period includes the missing money episode, they do not examine this issue.

Both the estimation procedure of Carr–Darby and their conclusions have come in for extensive criticism. For one, the use of only lagged values of the money supply to generate anticipations is overly restrictive. Second, the use of a "two-step" procedure whereby expectations are generated by one equation and substituted into another requires corrections to generate proper standard errors [Pagan (1984)]. Third, MacKinnon and Milbourne (1984) argue that the error term in (4.23) will be correlated with the unexpected money term, thus

---

[59]Despite our notational inelegance, it is the expectation of $\ln M_t$ that is used in the empirical work. Carr and Darby (1981) also argue that permanent income is the appropriate concept for the long-run demand for money and that transitory income will temporarily be kept as money until adjustment can occur. Thus, transitory income also enters their adjustment equation. This is suppressed in what follows because it is not central to the discussion.

[60]Equation (4.24) tells a rather different story about income shocks. In the standard partial adjustment model, a positive income shock is essentially an outward shift of the IS curve which leads to higher real money demand and higher nominal money demand in the presence of sticky prices. In contrast, in (4.24) a positive income shock must be interpreted as an aggregate supply shock. That is, since an income shock raises m_t^*, it leads to a decrease in the price level.

rendering inconsistent the Carr–Darby estimates. Responding to this last criticism, Carr, Darby and Thornton (1985) argue that money is "exogenous" and so cannot be correlated with the error term. In fact, as Cuthbertson and Taylor (1986) point out, money must be exogenous for the Carr–Darby model to make sense. If money were not exogenous and adjusted in response to other variables in equation (4.23), then an autoregression in M_t is the wrong model for expectations formulation, i.e. if money is not "exogenous" in the Carr–Darby model, agents are irrational.

Indeed, Cuthbertson and Taylor (1986) take the argument one step further by noting that rationality implies testable cross-equation parameter restrictions between (4.23) and the forecasting equation which we can write as:

$$\ln M_t = \gamma Z_{t-1} + v_t \,, \tag{4.25}$$

where Z_{t-1} is the vector of variables used by agents in forecasting nominal money. We can develop the testable cross-equation restrictions by rewriting (4.23) somewhat more generally as:

$$\ln m_t = \beta x_t + \phi(\ln M_t - \ln_{t-1} M_t) + \delta(\ln_{t-1} M_t) + u_t \,, \tag{4.26}$$

where x_t is the vector of variables including m_{t-1} and those in m_t^*. As the Carr–Darby model implies anticipated money should have no role in (4.26), this hypothesis of neutrality can be examined by testing $\delta = 0$.

If we substitute for $\ln_{t-1} M_t$ a general linear function of the forecasting variables in (4.25), $\gamma^* Z_{t-1}$, we can rewrite (4.26) as:

$$\ln m_t = \beta x_t + \phi(\ln M_t - \gamma^* Z_{t-1}) + \delta \gamma^* Z_{t-1} + u_t \,. \tag{4.27}$$

Equations (4.25) and (4.27) form a system of two equations in the two variables, M_t and P_t, and rationality implies that $\gamma^* = \gamma$.

Cuthbertson and Taylor (1986) specify Z_{t-1} to include lags of money and interest rates and estimate the model with quarterly data for the United Kingdom using an iterative nonlinear least squares technique due to Mishkin (1983). They strongly reject the hypothesis of rationality, whether or not neutrality is imposed. They also report that conditional on rationality, neutrality can be rejected at the 5 percent but not the 1 percent level of significance.

In Table 8.12 we report a corresponding set of estimates for the United States obtained via maximum likelihood techniques. These are based on imposing the constraints $\gamma = \gamma^*$ and $\delta = 0$ and on a forecasting equation using two lags of M and of RCP.[61] The same model was estimated without imposing

---

[61]With the exception of the serial correlation parameter, which proved unnecessary, the specification used in Table 8.12 is as in the real PAM used above.

Table 8.12
Maximum likelihood estimates of the Carr–Darby buffer-stock model
under rationality and neutrality[a]

Variable	1952:3–1974:1	1952:3–1980:4
RCP	−0.014	−0.011
	(6.0)	(5.1)
RCBP	−0.016	0.003
	(4.3)	(1.3)
y	0.080	0.013
	(7.4)	(2.1)
m_{t-1}	0.845	0.963
	(36.9)	(80.8)
$(M_t - {}_{t-1}M_t)$	0.804	0.978
	(8.7)	(14.2)
M_{t-1}	1.190	1.084
	(40.7)	(42.1)
M_{t-2}	−0.163	−0.065
	(5.4)	(2.5)
RCP_{t-1}	−0.012	−0.011
	(3.7)	(3.5)
RCP_{t-2}	0.006	0.006
	(2.1)	(2.3)

[a]Estimates of intercepts are not reported. Asymptotic *t*-statistics are
in parentheses.

the restrictions ($\gamma = \gamma^*$, $\delta = 0$) and with the imposition of the constraints one
at a time (not shown in Table 8.12). This allowed the calculation of various
likelihood ratio tests pertaining to rationality and neutrality. For the shorter
sample period the results are as follows: (i) the joint hypothesis of neutrality
and rationality was strongly rejected with a $\chi^2(5) = 22.0$; (ii) the hypothesis of
rationality also is strongly rejected without the imposition of neutrality with a
$\chi^2(4) = 21.3$; and (iii) the hypothesis of neutrality cannot be rejected at the 5
percent level, whether or not rationality is imposed. Although the numbers are
slightly different, the same qualitative conclusions hold for the sample period
through 1980. Furthermore, for this sample period a test of stability with a
presumed break at 1974:1, the period of the missing money, suggests that the
buffer stock model is not stable over the longer period.[62]

Taken with the work of Cuthbertson and Taylor, these results suggest that
the Carr–Darby buffer stock model has some serious problems. Moreover,
even though Cuthbertson and Taylor formulate the Carr–Darby model to
immunize it from the criticisms of MacKinnon and Milbourne (1984), there still
seem to be some loose ends. For one, the Carr–Darby approach does not work

[62]We performed a likelihood ratio test by estimating the Carr–Darby model for the two
subsamples and comparing the individual likelihood values with the complete sample value. This
yielded a $\chi^2(11) = 39.1$, whereas the 1 percent critical value is 24.7.

if the nominal PAM is the underlying money model. One can see this by writing a nominal version of the Carr–Darby model (4.23) as:

$$\ln M_t - \ln P_t = (1 - \mu)(\ln M_{t-1} - \ln P_t) + \mu \ln m_t^*$$
$$+ \phi(\ln M_t - \ln {}_{t-1}M_t) + u_t. \qquad (4.28)$$

Substituting (4.25) into (4.28) and separating out the M_{t-1} component of Z_{t-1}, we can rewrite (4.28) as:

$$\ln M_t - \ln P_t = (1 - \mu)(\ln M_{t-1} - \ln P_t) + \phi(\ln M_t - \gamma_1 \ln M_{t-1}) + W_t, \qquad (4.29)$$

where W_t represents the missing terms in m_t^* and ${}_{t-1}M_t$. Quite evidently, if we choose $\mu = 0$, $\phi = \gamma_1 = 1$, and the remaining parameters so that $W_t = 0$, we will reduce (4.29) to $\ln M_t = \ln M_t$. Put another way, the nominal PAM augmented by the buffer-stock term will always provide a perfect fit.

A somewhat different problem stems from the Cuthbertson and Taylor argument that the Carr–Darby model only makes sense if we interpret equation (4.26) as a price equation. This, in turn, only makes sense if (4.26) is a reasonable equation for the short-run determination of the price level. However, since (4.27) began its life as a real partial adjustment model for money demand, it would be rather surprising if it turned out to be a fully defensible price equation. It certainly appears to omit a variety of factors that show up in conventional "price" equations [e.g. see Gordon (1981)]. Moreover, as MacKinnon and Milbourne (1987) indicate, it also appears to fail a few plausibility tests as a price equation.

Where this seems to leave us is that, at least as modelled to date, the buffer-stock story has some questionable features and doubtful support. At a more philosophical level, it should be noted that models such as Carr and Darby's are often said to include "shock absorber" or "buffer-stock" money. To a certain extent, the "buffer-stock" label used by Carr and Darby is a misnomer since it suggests that these models utilize disequilibrium in a manner different from the standard partial adjustment in money models. In fact, these "buffer-stock" models only differ from the standard models in their exogeneity assumptions since the standard model is also a disequilibrium model. In any case, as noted by one of the proponents of the buffer-stock view, the assumption of an exogenous money supply which underlies (4.25) is a rather extreme one, unlikely to be met in the real world. What this suggests is that the buffer-stock approach needs to be interpreted as a more general proposition about the transmission mechanism of monetary policy and tested in the context of a complete model of the economy, something that has yet to be done in a fully satisfactory way.[63]

5. Concluding remarks

As previously noted, research on money demand has often been motivated by the perceived needs of monetary policy. In the 1970s in the United States, monetary policy had to confront financial innovation and technological change which were reflected, at least in part, in the "missing money" episode of the mid-1970s. In the 1980s, monetary policy has been conducted amidst elimination of interest rate restrictions, explicit legal creation of new financial instruments, and continued financial innovation which have blurred institutional boundaries. As in the 1970s, these developments were reflected in further instabilities in money demand equations.

Some evidence of this recent instability was provided in Section 2, at least for the partial adjustment model. However, since the PAM has been the object of some criticism, it is worth noting that more agnostic models also exhibit parameter nonconstancy in this period. To demonstrate this, we utilized a two-lag GDL with the variables in Table 8.1 and with contemporaneous dummy variables beginning in 1974:2 for the intercept, *RCP*, and *XGNP* Estimating this equation from 1953:1 to 1984:4 with a sample split after 1979:3, parameter constancy could be rejected at the 1 percent significance level. Unfortunately, however, the problems do not end here. We "fixed" this specification by adding enough post-1979:3 dummy variables to make the equation stable through 1984:4 and then tested for parameter constancy through 1986:4 with a sample split following 1984:4.[64] Using the Chow prediction test, parameter constancy is again rejected at less than the 1 percent significance level. This is perhaps hardly surprising when one notes that in 1985 and 1986, M1 grew at 12.1 and 15.3 percent, respectively, rates far exceeding typical ones, either absolutely or relative to the rate of change in real GNP.

While hardly definitive, these results are certainly suggestive of recurring bouts of instability in money demand. These continuing difficulties obviously present problems for monetary policy. Indeed, it was in the face of the unusual

---

[63]See Laidler (1984) for a detailed presentation of this viewpoint and a bibliography of relevant empirical efforts.

[64]The required modifications for the post 1979:3 "fix" provided further evidence of the dramatic shift in the behavior of real balances. We found that parameter constancy for the real balances equation obtained after adding an intercept dummy and interactive dummies for the zero lag of *XGNP*, the first of *RCP*, the first lag of *RCBP*, the zero and second lag of *DPGNP*, and for both lags of real balances.

decline in velocity in 1985–86 that the Federal Reserve chose not to establish a specific target range for M1 in 1987. This action is loosely consistent with Poole's (1970) well-known framework in which additional instability in money demand should lead policy-makers away from a policy of targeting monetary aggregates.[65] Poole's set up, of course, requires stability in the coefficients of the underlying IS and LM curves. In principle uncertainty in these coefficients can be allowed for in choosing an optimal policy.[66] As a practical matter, however, the behavior of the money demand function has badly clouded the choice of an appropriate policy.

Given this, it is hardly surprising that some have sought to divorce the conduct of monetary policy from the existence of a stable money demand specification. Gordon (1984), for example, has suggested that the short-run money demand function is an unnecessary concept, while Poole (1987) adopts a spiritually similar tack. Poole, while suggesting that the underlying demand for money is undoubtedly not as badly behaved as it appears, views the estimation of money demand functions as a futile exercise fraught with econometric difficulties. His main message is that a simple bivariate relationship between velocity and the long-term rate of interest, if estimated in first differences over an appropriate sample period, yields an interest elasticity that is large enough to explain the large velocity decline of the 1980s. Poole concludes that policy rules focusing on the growth of money may still be reasonable in an environment of low and steady inflation. To some, this conclusion may appear to be a leap of faith, especially given the casualness of the empirical evidence offered. Moreover, the monetary authorities are unlikely to target a quantity whose short- and intermediate-run behavior they do not understand.

Rasche (1987), also attempting to circumvent difficulties with money demand equations, estimates first difference velocity specifications with richer specifications and more econometric detail.[67] He concludes that velocity equations are stable over the 1970s and can be made stable over the 1980s with a simple shift. We believe, however, that Rasche's stability findings are less persuasive than they at first seem. The point is that, as discussed more generally in Subsection 4.1.2, failure to reject stability of a first difference specification does not indicate that the specification is better than a comparable

---

[65] In such circumstances the Poole analysis suggests using an interest rate policy or perhaps some sort of "combination" policy. Of course, once one introduces the distinction between real and nominal interest rates and allows for multiple measures of money, the relevant policy punch line is rather less clear.

[66] Brainard (1967) provides an analysis of the case where there is parameter uncertainty. Stability of a sort is important in this framework too since the joint distribution of all the parameters must remain constant for the analysis to go through.

[67] Rasche, however, restricts his attention to postwar data whereas Poole argues that longer period data are needed.

unstable levels specification. In the case of velocity, there is an added complication since the velocity equation needs to be unscrambled to obtain its implications for real balances. Not surprisingly, our empirical work taking account of these problems indicates that a first difference velocity specification does not resolve the missing money problem.[68]

Overall, then, there does not seem to be any clear message for the conduct of monetary policy to be taken from the current state of the money demand literature. A clearer message does, however, run the other way in that the needs of monetary policy justify a continued effort to improve our understanding of money demand. If this effort is to be successful, it is important for academic researchers to keep in mind the needs of policy-makers. One example in which academic research has not done this is in the application and interpretation of parameter constancy tests. More specifically, researchers have often declared victory when a specification satisfies a parameter constancy test. As we have seen, this has been achieved by using first differences, by estimating velocity equations, or by using point-in-time data as opposed to time-averaged data. However, this research often stops before considering the predictive power of the "parameter constant" specifications. It therefore seems to fall short of satisfying the substantive needs of those in the trenches of monetary policy formulation.

This methodological point aside, there remains a continuing need for improvement in the specification of money demand equations. We have previously covered many possible directions for future research and conclude here with a brief summary of what we see as the most promising.

First, there are definitional and measurement issues. What is the appropriate monetary aggregate for money demand? How is the appropriateness of this concept affected by changes in transactions technology? The work of Spindt (1985) and Barnett (1980) is a beginning in this direction. A further question is how to measure transactions costs. This variable is usually omitted from econometric specifications due to the difficulty of measuring it. Obtaining a reliable measure would, however, be important for even such basic aspects of money demand as correctly implementing the Baumol–Tobin transactions

---

[68]To illustrate that a stable first difference velocity specification does not solve the missing money problem, we estimated a standard specification from 1953:1 to 1974:1 with a serial correlation correction [equation (2.1)] and a velocity specification in which the first difference of velocity is regressed on a constant. This velocity equation is stable over the period 1953:1–1979:3 with sample split after 1974:1 with a marginal significance level of 0.183. Using the parameter estimates from 1953:1 to 1974:1 to forecast, both the standard specification and the velocity specification overpredict the log of real balances in every quarter from 1974:2 to 1979:3. The velocity equation, however, overpredicts by a larger amount in each quarter. More specifically, over this forecast period the mean error in log real balances from the standard specification is -0.0143 while from the velocity specification it is -0.0401. What this says is that "stability" per se is not an impressive credential.

approach. Additionally, there are issues of measurement of the own rate on money. This issue is complicated by changes in the legality of paying interest on money and by payment of interest in nonmonetary forms (e.g. reduction of service charges). There are, of course, further complications in the measurement of the own rate on money if a nontraditional aggregate is utilized as, for example, by Spindt and Barnett.

Second, it is important to pay attention to changes in the motivations for holding different types of money. This is particularly relevant since there has been a blurring of the distinction between transactions and other balances. The issues here are two-fold. First, there are some unresolved theoretical issues in the reconciliation of the transactions and portfolio motivations for holding money. Second, there are questions of how to implement empirically these theories since it is difficult to measure the various concepts of uncertainty required by the portfolio approach. Furthermore, there are ever present aggregation issues, i.e. what are the implications of alternative micro based motivations for holding money for the behavior of monetary aggregates. Chant (1976) provides a good discussion of this issue of aggregating Baumol–Tobin or Miller–Orr individual behavior, but it has not been implemented empirically. Chant's framework can also be applied to help understand how quickly adjustment to macro shocks is likely to occur. This is particularly important since problems with the "speed of adjustment" are among the most serious plaguing the PAM.

Applicable to all of these are questions of the appropriate data to use, and in particular whether post-war quarterly data are adequate. Some researchers, such as Poole (1987), have suggested that long-term annual data would be appropriate. Unlike other issues in macroeconomics, very little cross-section work has been done. However, a repeated cross-section data set assembled by the Federal Reserve (1987) might be useful for investigating aggregation and various micro issues.

Fourth, there are some possible changes in the transactions measure for the conventional specification that seem promising. Suggested modifications of real GNP as the transactions measure have often taken two forms. The first argues that real GNP is not the correct measure. Wenninger and Radecki (1986), for example, control for the rapid increase in financial transactions. The second approach argues that different components of real GNP require different quantities of money to finance them. Among others, for example, Mankiw and Summers (1986) have considered the separate impact of taxes, and Radecki and Wenninger (1985) have considered the separate impact of trade.

Fifth, there are a variety of issues arising from shifting central bank operating procedures. What is the interpretation of "money demand" and "money supply" in a world in which monetary aggregates are targeted and controlled by the central bank? Roley (1985), and Gordon (1984) and the various discussions of the buffer-stock approach touch on these issues but more work is needed on this as well as on the issue of how changes in policy regimes and the underlying exogeneity structure should be handled econometrically.

Finally, there are specification questions opened up by the deregulation of interest rates and the consequent need to model rate-setting behavior in conjunction with demand behavior.[69] As should be readily apparent, despite the voluminous literature on the demand for money, there remains considerable scope for further work.

[69]For a recent and promising start on this problem see Moore, Porter and Small (1988).

References

Ando, A. and K. Shell (1975) 'Demand for money in a general portfolio model", in: *The Brookings model: Perspective and recent developments*. Amsterdam: North-Holland.

Arango, S. and M.I. Nadiri (1981) 'The demand for money in open economies", *Journal of Monetary Economics*, 7: 69–84.

Baba, Y., D. Hendry and R. Starr (1985) 'U.S. money demand, 1960–1984', mineo.

Barnett, W.A. (1980) 'Economic monetary aggregates: An application of index number and aggregation theory', *Journal of Econometrics*, 14: 11–48.

Baumol, W.J. (1952) 'The transactions demand for cash: An inventory theoretic approach', *Quarterly Journal of Economics*, 66: 545–556.

Betancourt, R. and H. Kelejian (1981) 'Lagged endogenous variables and the Cochrane–Orcutt procedure', *Econometrica*, 49: 1073–1078.

Black, S.W. (1973) 'Aggregation over time, the supply and demand for money, and monetary policy', *Special Studies Paper*, 35, Federal Reserve Board of Governors.

Boughton, J.M. (1981) 'Recent instability of the demand for money: An international perspective', *Southern Economic Journal*, 47: 579–591.

Box, G.E.P. and D.R. Cox (1964) 'An analysis of transformations', *Journal of the Royal Statistical Society*, Ser. B, 26: 211–243.

Boyes, W.J. (1978) 'An application of specification error tests – the liquidity trap', *The Manchester School*, 2: 139–151.

Brainard, W. (1967) 'Uncertainty and the effectiveness of policy', *AEA Papers and Proceedings*, LVII: 411–425.

Brainard, W. (1976) 'Discussion', *Brookings Papers on Economic Activity*, 3: 732–736.

Buiter, W.H. and C.A. Armstrong (1978) 'A didactic note on the transactions demand for money and behavior towards risk', *Journal of Money, Credit and Banking*, 10: 529–538.

Cagan, P. (1984) 'Monetary policy and subduing inflation', in: *Essays in contemporary economic problems: Disinflation*. Washington: American Enterprise Institute.

Carr, J.L. and M.R. Darby (1981) 'The role of money supply shocks in the short-run demand for money', *Journal of Monetary Economics*, 8: 183–199.

Carr, J., M.R. Darby and D. Thornton (1985) 'Monetary anticipation and the demand for money: Reply to MacKinnon and Milbourne', *Journal of Monetary Economics*, 16: 251–257.

Chant, J.F. (1976) 'Dynamic adjustments in simple models of the transactions demand for money', *Journal of Monetary Economics*, 2: 351–366.

Christiano, L.J. and M. Eichenbaum (1986) 'Temporal aggregation and structural inference in macroeconomics', NBER Technical Working Paper 60.

Coats, W.L. (1982) 'Modeling the short-run demand for money with exogenous supply', *Economic Inquiry*, XX: 222–239.

Cooley, T.F. and S.F. LeRoy (1981) 'Identification and estimation of money demand', *American Economic Review*, 71: 825–844.

Corrado, C. and P. Spindt (1986) '*T* vs. *Q*: The measurement and analysis of monetary transactions', mimeo.

Cramer, J.A. (1986) 'The volume of transactions and the circulation of money in the United States, 1950–1979', *Journal of Business and Economic Statistics*, 4: 225–232.

Cuthbertson, K. and M.P. Taylor (1986) 'Monetary anticipation and the demand for money in the U.K.: Testing rationality in the shock-absorber hypothesis', *Journal of Applied Econometrics*, 1: 355–365.

Dotsey, M. (1985) 'The use of electronic funds transfers to capture the effects of cash management practices on the demand for demand deposits: A note', *Journal of Finance*, 40: 1493–1504.

Dutkowsky, D.H. and W.G. Foote (1987) 'The demand for money: A rational expectations approach', Syracuse University, mimeo.

Engle, R.F. and C.W.J. Granger (1987) 'Co-integration and error correction: Representation, estimation and testing', *Econometrica*, 55: 251–276.

Engle, R.F., D.F. Hendry and J.-F. Richard (1983) 'Exogeneity', *Econometrica*, 51: 277–304.

Fackler, J. and W. McMillan (1983) 'Specification and stability of the Goldfeld money demand function', *Journal of Macroeconomics*, 5: 437–459.

Fair, R.C. (1987) 'International evidence on the demand for money', *Review of Economics and Statistics*, LXIX: 473–480.

Federal Reserve, Board of Governors (1987) 'Changes in the use of transactions accounts and cash from 1984 to 1986', *Bulletin*, 73: 179–196.

Feige, E.L. (1967) 'Expectations and adjustments in the monetary sector', *American Economic Review, Papers and Proceedings*, 57: 462–473.

Freedman, C. (1983) 'Financial innovation in Canada: Causes and consequences', *American Economic Review, Papers and Proceedings*, 73: 101–106.

Friedman, B.M. (1977) 'Financial flow variables and the short-run determination of long-term interest rates', *Journal of Political Economy*, 85: 661–689.

Friedman, B.M. (1978) 'Crowding out or crowding in? Economic consequences of financing government deficits', *Brookings Papers on Economic Activity*, 3: 593–641.

Friedman, M. (1956) 'The quantity theory of money: A restatement', in: M. Friedman, ed., *Studies in the quantity theory of money*. Chicago: Chicago University Press.

Friedman, M. (1959) 'The demand for money: Some theoretical and empirical results', *Journal of Political Economy*, 67: 327–351.

Fusselman, J. and Grossman, S. (1986) 'Monetary dynamics with fixed transaction costs', Department of Economics, University of Chicago, mimeo.

Garner, C.A. (1986) 'Does interest rate volatility affect money demand?', *Economic Review*, Federal Reserve Bank of Kansas City, 71: 25–37.

Goldfeld, S.M. (1973) 'The demand for money revisited', *Brookings Papers on Economic Activity*, 3: 577–638.

Goldfeld, S.M. (1976) 'The case of the missing money', *Brookings Papers on Economic Activity*, 3: 683–730.

Goldfeld, S. and D. Sichel (1987a) 'Money demand: The effects of inflation and alternative adjustment mechanisms', *Review of Economics and Statistics*, 69: 511–515.

Goldfeld, S. and D. Sichel (1987b) 'On the misuse of forecast errors to distinguish between level and first difference specifications', *Economics Letters*, 23: 173–176.

Goodfriend, M. (1985) 'Reinterpreting money demand regressions', in: K. Brunner and A.H. Meltzer, eds., *Understanding monetary regimes*, Carnegie-Rochester Conference Series on Public Policy, Vol. 22. Amsterdam: North-Holland.

Gordon, R.J. (1981) 'Output fluctuations and gradual price adjustment', *Journal of Economic Literature*, 19: 493–530.

Gordon, R.J. (1984) 'The short-run demand for money: A reconsideration', *Journal of Money, Credit and Banking*, 16: 403–434.

Hafer, R.W. and S.E. Hein (1980) 'The dynamics and estimation of short-run money demand', *Federal Reserve Bank of St. Louis Review*, 62: 26–35.

Hafer, R.W. and S.E. Hein (1982) 'The shift in money demand: What really hapened?', *Federal Reserve Bank of St. Louis Review*, 64: 11–16.

Hamburger, M.J. (1977) 'Behavior of the money stock: Is there a puzzle?', *Journal of Monetary Economics*, 3: 265–288.

Hatanaka, M. (1974) 'An efficient two-step estimator for the dynamic adjustment model with autoregressive errors', *Journal of Econometrics*, 2: 199–220.

Heller, H.R. and M.S. Khan (1979) 'The demand for money and the term structure of interest rates', *Journal of Political Economy*, 87: 109–129.

Hendry, D.F. (1980) 'Predictive failure and econometric modelling in macroeconomics: The transactions demand for money', in: *Economic modeling*. London: Heinemann Education Books.

Hetzel, R.L. (1984) 'Estimating money demand functions', *Journal of Money, Credit and Banking*, 16: 185–193.

Hwang, H. (1985) 'Test of the adjustment process and linear homogeneity in a stock adjustment model of money demand', *The Review of Economics and Statistics*, LXVII: 689–692.

Judd, J.P. and J.L. Scadding (1982a) 'The search for a stable money demand function: A survey of the post-1973 literature', *Journal of Economic Literature*, 20: 993–1023.

Judd, P. and J.L. Scadding (1982b) 'Financial change and monetary targeting in the U.S.', in: *Interest rate deregulation and monetary policy*. Federal Reserve Bank of San Francisco, pp. 78–106.

Judd, J.P. and J.L. Scadding (1982c) 'Dynamic adjustment in the demand for money: Tests of alternative hypotheses', *Economic Review*, Federal Reserve Bank of San Francisco, Fall: 19–30.

Keeley, M.C. and G.C. Zimmerman (1986) 'Deposit rate deregulation and the demand for transactions media', *Economic Review*, Federal Reserve Bank of San Francisco, Summer: 47–62.

Keil, M. and W. Richardson (1986) 'The demand for money in Canada: Some empirical tests of lag structures', mimeo.

Klein, B. (1974) 'Competitive interest payments on bank deposits and the long-run demand for money', *American Economic Review*, 64: 931–949.

Laidler, D.E.W. (1984) 'The buffer stock notion in monetary economics', *Economic Journal*, 94, *Supplement*: 17–33.

Laidler, D.E.W. (1985) *The demand for money: Theories and evidence*, 3rd edn. New York: Dun-Donnelley.

Lindsey, D.E. and P.A. Spindt (1986) 'An evaluation of monetary indexes', *Special Studies Papers*, 195, Federal Reserve Board.

MacKinnon, J.G. and R.D. Milbourne (1984) 'Monetary anticipations and the demand for money', *Journal of Monetary Economics*, 13: 263–274.

MacKinnon, J.G and R.D. Milbourne (1987) 'Are price equations really money demand equations on their heads?', mimeo.

Mankiw, N.G. and L.H. Summers (1986) 'Money demand and the effects of fiscal policies', *Journal of Money, Credit and Banking*, 18: 415–429.

McCallum, B.T. and M.S. Goodfriend (1987) 'Money: Theoretical analysis of the demand for money', NBER Working Paper 2157.

Melnick, R. (1989) 'The demand for money in Argentina 1978–1987', mimeo.

Milbourne, R., P. Buckholtz and M.T. Wasan (1983) 'A theoretical derivation of the functional form of short-run money holdings', *Review of Economic Studies*, 50: 531–542.

Miller, M.H. and Daniel Orr (1966) 'A model of the demand for money by firms', *Quarterly Journal of Economics*, LXXX: 413–435.

Mishkin, F.S. (1983) *A rational expectations approach to macroeconomics*. Chicago: University Press, for NBER.

Moore, G.R., R.D. Porter and D.H. Small (1988) 'Modeling the disaggregated demands for M2 and M1 in the 1980's: The U.S. experience', mimeo.

Pagan, A.R. (1984) 'Econometric issues in the analysis of regressions with generated regressors', *International Economic Review*, 25: 221–247.

Plosser, C.I., G.W. Schwert and H. White (1982) 'Differencing as a test of specification', *International Economic Review*, 23: 535–552.

Poole, W. (1970) 'Optimal choice of monetary policy instruments in a simple stochastic macro model', *Quarterly Journal of Economics*, LXXIV: 197–216.

Poole, W. (1987) 'Monetary policy lessons of recent inflation and disinflation', Working Paper 0010, National Bureau of Economic Research.

Porter, R.D. and E.K. Offenbacher (1982) 'Financial innovations and the measurement of the money supply', Conference on Financial Innovations, Federal Reserve Bank of St. Louis.

Porter, R.D., P.A. Spindt and D.E. Lindsey (1987) 'Econometric modeling of the demands for the U.S. monetary aggregates: Conventional and experimental approaches', *Special Studies Paper* 217, Federal Reserve Board of Governors.

Radecki, L.J. and J. Wenninger (1985) 'Recent instability in M1s velocity', *Federal Reserve Bank of New York Quarterly Review*, 10: 16–22.

Rasche, R.H. (1987) 'M1-velocity and money demand functions: Do stable relationships exist?', *Carnegie-Rochester Conference Series on Public Policy*.

Roley, V. (1985) 'Money demand predictability', *Journal of Money, Credit and Banking*, 17: 611–641.

Rose, A. (1985) 'An alternative approach to the American demand for money', *Journal of Money, Credit and Banking*, 17: 439–455.

Santomero, A.M. and J.J. Siegel (1986) 'Deposit deregulation and monetary policy', *Carnegie-Rochester Conference Series on Public Policy*, pp. 179–224.

Simpson, T.D. and R.D. Porter (1980) 'Some issues involving the definition and interpretation of the monetary aggregates', *Federal Reserve Bank of Boston Conference Series*, 23: 161–234.

Spencer, D.E. (1985) 'Money demand and the price level', *Review of Economics and Statistics*, 67: 490–495.

Spindt, P.A. (1985) 'Money is what money does: Monetary aggregation and the equation of exchange', *Journal of Political Economy*, 93: 175–204.

Spindt, P.A. (1987) 'On the supply of the demand for money', *Special Studies Paper*, 215, Federal Reserve Board of Governors.

Spitzer, J.J. (1976) 'The demand for money, the liquidity trap, and functional forms', *International Economic Review*, 17: 220–227.

Startz, R. (1979) 'Implicit interest on demand deposits', *Journal of Monetary Economics*, 5: 515–525.

Swamy, P.A.V.B., A.B. Kennickell and P. von zur Muehlen (1986) 'Forecasting money demand with econometric models', *Special Studies Paper*, 196, Federal Reserve Board.

Thornton, D.L. (1982) 'Maximum likelihood estimates of a partial adjustment-adaptive expectations model of the demand for money', *Review of Economics and Statistics*, LXIV: 325–329.

Thornton, D.L. (1985) 'Money demand dynamics: Some new evidence', *Federal Reserve Bank of St. Louis Review*, 67: 14–23.

Tobin, J. (1956) 'The interest elasticity of transactions demand for cash', *Review of Economics and Statistics*, 38: 241–247.

Tobin, J. (1958) 'Liquidity preference as behavior towards risk', *Review of Economic Studies*, 25: 65–86.

Walsh, C. (1984) 'Interest rate volatility and monetary policy', *Journal of Money, Credit and Banking*, 16: 133–150.

Walters, A.A. (1967) 'The demand for money – the dynamic properties of the multiplier', *Journal of Political Economy*, 75: 293–298.

Webster, C. (1981) 'The demand for money in quarterly models', in: *Proceedings of a Conference: Empirical Studies on Money Demand*. Center for the Study of American Business.

Wenninger, J. and L.J. Radecki (1986) 'Financial transactions and the demand for M1', *Federal Reserve Bank of New York Quarterly Review*, 11: 24–29.

Wickens, M. and T.S. Breusch (1987) 'Dynamic specification, the long-run and the estimation of transformed regression models', CREP Discussion Paper 154.

Zarembka, P. (1968) 'Functional form in the demand for money', *Journal of the American Statistical Association*, 63: 502–511.

Chapter 9

MONEY SUPPLY

KARL BRUNNER

University of Rochester

ALLAN H. MELTZER*

Carnegie-Melon University and American Enterprise Institute

Contents

*We are indebted to Benjamin Friedman for helpful comments on an earlier draft.

Handbook of Monetary Economics, Volume I, Edited by B.M. Friedman and F.H. Hahn

1. Introduction

Conjectures about aggregate effects of intermediation, debt, financial regulation and deregulation are common in economists' discussions. Standard macroeconomic models provide no basis for these discussions. Models in the IS–LM tradition do not distinguish between inside and outside money or, more relevantly for present purposes, money produced by governments and central banks and money produced by intermediaries. These models also fail to recognize the role of credit and the interaction between the credit market and the money market closely associated with the intermediation process. Recent work in the rational expectations tradition typically treats the production of money as a stochastic process; the money stock changes randomly, and the stochastic process is not affected by the institutional structure or by economic processes. Textbooks continue to present the traditional multiple expansion of deposits as an activity separate from macroeconomic analysis; money changes in a deterministic way that is independent of market forces.

Strong assertions about the role of money and the controllability of the money stock contrast with the weak or non-existent analysis. Some claim that money cannot be reliably defined. Others, most recently real business cycle theorists, claim that money has no systematic relation to any real variable at any time. Still others claim that, while money can be defined, efforts to control money encourage substitution of other assets to a degree that renders monetary control impractical. This view, a version of the banking school claims of the nineteenth century, was revived in the Radcliffe report on British monetary policy in the 1960s and continues to influence discussions of monetary policy and monetary control in the United States and, even more, in Britain.[1] An extreme version of this position is taken by Kaldor (1982) who argues that money is simply a residual in the economic process and is without causal significance. If this assertion is to be taken seriously and appraised, a theory of money supply is required for the appraisal.

Money supply theory addresses these assertions, and others, found in discussions of monetary theory and policy. In addition, money supply theory provides a means of including the behavior of intermediaries and intermedia-

---

[1]A recent example is "Goodhart's law". This law claims that there will be a shift in the demand for any monetary aggregate chosen as a target of monetary policy. Versions of this proposition were common in the United States following the introduction of credit cards and a wider range of substitutes for money in the 1970s. A common claim was that the demand for conventional money – currency and demand deposits – would go to zero and monetary velocity would approach infinity. Shortly after these predictions, monetary velocity declined.

tion as part of a macroeconomic analysis of interest rates, asset prices, output and the price level. Such analysis is a prerequisite for analyzing short- and long-term macroeconomic effects of the regulation of deposit interest rates, portfolio restrictions, reserve requirement ratios, credit ceilings, secondary reserve requirements and other institutional restrictions.

A related set of issues arises in the literature on monetary control. Models in which money is restricted to currency issued by a central bank, or is determined exogenously, or is a residual, or is produced stochastically, cannot clarify issues about monetary control. Money supply theory can and does clarify these issues and permits economists to compare control procedures based on interest rates and monetary aggregates both when there is, and when there is not, a rich array of financial intermediaries and a developed system of financial markets.

An often contentious issue about monetary control concerns the central banks' use of an interest rate or a monetary aggregate as a target or control variable. Conclusions often depend on analysis of restricted cases and do not hold generally. For example, in a model with one interest rate and with debt and real capital perfect substitutes in portfolios, the financing of deficits by issuing debt has no effect on the economy if the interest rate is controlled. In a model with multiple interest rates or with interest rates and asset prices, this is not so. Asset prices change leading to a reallocation of portfolios and effects on output and commodity prices.

A main reason given for interest rate control or interest rate targets is to insulate the economy from shocks to the demand for money. Insulation is achieved in a model with a single rate of interest and a single asset that serves as the only alternative means of holding wealth. Analysis of the money supply process introduces a broader set of assets, so pegging a single rate of interest by supplying bank reserves does not prevent changes in relative prices of assets, with further repercussions on output and the price level. Once these additional assets have a distinct role in portfolios, an interest rate target does not insulate the economy from changes in the demand for money. The reason is that control of a single interest rate, by supplying or withdrawing reserves or money, does not prevent substitution between money and other assets. Money supply theory provides an explanation for the observed differences in the movement of output and prices resulting from substitution with an unchanged interest target fixed by the central bank.

Standard IS–LM analysis treats government debt as a perfect substitute for private capital. The array of assets is characterized by money, usually outside money or currency, and a mix of debt and capital. Changes in the latter mix have no effect on interest rates, asset prices or other aggregates. More recent analysis, following Barro (1974), shows that the value of the debt is just equal to the present value of taxes required to pay interest on the debt, so debt does not change net wealth or asset prices. There are many reasons for treating this conclusion with skepticism. One reason, which has been explored within the framework provided by Barro's model, is that the model ignores redistribution of income and wealth, the major activity of most governments. Once the effects on intergenerational redistribution are included in Barro's model, debt is valued and part of net wealth.[2] Debt issues crowd out real capital. In general, debt does not fully replace capital in portfolios, however. Interest rates and wage rates change, so there are macroeconomic effects of financing deficits by issuing debt. Money supply theory that incorporates asset market decisions considers money, debt and real capital as distinct assets and analyzes the effects of crowding out of capital and the response of interest rates to debt.

Although models that neglect money supply theory are useful for some purposes, the neglect of money supply theory often leads to erroneous conclusions. An example is the comparison of the relative responses to monetary and fiscal policy. In IS–LM models, the relative importance of monetary and fiscal policies depends on the magnitude of the interest elasticity of the demand for money. The introduction of a market for debt or bank credit as part of money supply analysis alters this standard conclusion. The responses to fiscal and monetary policy involve a wider range of substitutes, so analysis of the responses to fiscal and monetary policy must include the effect of changes in prices of the larger set of assets. The absolute size of the interest elasticity of the demand for money no longer plays a critical role. In particular, the monetary effect on output does not vanish with convergence of the interest elasticity of the demand for money to (minus) infinity. This follows from the interdependence of the interest elasticities on the money and credit markets due to the wealth constraint.

There are several alternative approaches to the analysis of money supply and intermediation. Three have been used most extensively in recent work. One approach, illustrated by the work of Benjamin Friedman, considers a wide range of financial assets. Friedman seeks to estimate structural equations representing demand and supply functions for particular assets and liabilities [see Friedman (1977)]. A second approach, used in many large-scale econometric models, remains within the IS–LM paradigm. Disaggregation of asset markets achieves a more complete statement of many details of the money market without altering the structure of the model. Typically the entire system of asset market equations can be reduced to a single money market equilibrium condition, the LM curve, and a single interest rate for analytic purposes. A third approach extends the range of assets and the number of

---

[2]Cukierman and Meltzer (1989) obtain this result in a model similar to Barro (1974). The differences arise because individuals have different ability and productivity, different wealth and different desired bequests; some desired bequests are negative. A present value preserving change in taxes and debt affects intergenerational allocation, wages and interest rates.

relative prices that affect aggregate demand. Exmples of the latter are Brunner (1971, 1973), Brunner and Meltzer (1968, 1972, 1976), Fratianni (1976), Heremans et al. (1976), Korteweg and van Loo (1977), and Neumann (1974). This approach is developed here.[3]

Recent methodological arguments reject the approach taken here and in other studies of financial markets. The reason is that behavior patterns are not derived from first principles expressed by tastes and technology but often reflect institutional arrangements or are expressed in demand or supply functions. We understand the effort initiated by Robert Lucas (and pursued by the Minnesota group under the leadership of Thomas Sargent and Neil Wallace) to generalize Marschak's argument about structure and to achieve structures that are invariant to changes in policy. While such efforts may be useful up to a point, they are ultimately futile in economics. There exists no level of ultimate invariance, whatever the depth of the "analytic excavation". Complete invariance is a denial of the probing, searching, experimenting activities of human beings, emphasized particularly by Hayek, in a world where information is scarce and uncertainty about future states of the world is omnipresent. These broader issues aside, there is, at present, no theory of intermediation capable of generating the broad and complex structure of modern financial arrangements from tastes and technology.

The analysis of institutional arrangements such as the monetary system or structure of financial markets is in its infancy. The history of science shows that scientific progress begins with the successful statement of empirical regularities. Further exploration may eventually express these regularities as implications of relatively complex theories. Insistence on developing first principles first impoverishes science.

Our approach is guided by the empirical regularities of the money supply process. We formulate a market model relating existing institutional arrangements, the behavior of the banks and of the non-bank public and explore the consequences for money, credit, interest rates and asset prices. The framework can be expanded to develop interactions with prices and output, as in Brunner and Meltzer (1976), and to analyze the relation between financial markets and macroeconomic variables.

Section 2 presents a model of money, debt and real capital in an economy without intermediaries. Section 3 extends the model to include banks and shows how the model can be extended to include other intermediaries without altering the basic structure. Sections 4 through 6 discuss applications including interest rate targeting, monetary variability and uncertainty, and monetary control. These applications are followed by a brief conclusion.

---

[3]Some extensions to an open economy with interrelated credit markets are in Brunner (1976b), Korteweg and van Loo (1977) and in Brunner and Meltzer (1974). We do not distinguish between domestic and foreign assets or consider an open economy in this chapter.

2. The markets for money and bonds

In the economy we consider initially, non-human wealth consists of money, debt and real capital. There are no banks or intermediaries. Real capital, K, is productive, earns a real return, and sells at a price, P, so the nominal value of the capital stock is PK. There is a government that finances its spending by issuing base money (currency), B, and bonds, S. Debt is valued at the current rate of interest; vS is the market value of outstanding debt. Since much of the government's spending is for redistribution between and within generations, changes in debt change interest rates and asset prices and, thus, have macro-economic effects.[4]

Figure 9.1 shows the balance sheets of the government and the private sector. Wealth, W, is the market value of the public's assets, net of its liabilities. In this simple model, the public as a whole has no liabilities.

The consolidated balance sheet of the central bank and government shows one asset, Au, consisting of gold, foreign exchange and special drawing rights. Since we do not consider extensions to an open economy, we do not go beyond recognizing that in an open economy with fixed exchange rates, Au is the main source of base money.[5] On the liability side, the stocks of base money and debt expand and contract with budget deficits or surpluses and with open market operations. In many countries, central bank direct purchases of government debt are restricted. The central bank acquires government debt by purchases in the open market, i.e. by exchanging base money for government securities. The sum of base money and government debt minus Au is the cumulated sum of fiscal deficits and surpluses.

With given market value of wealth, there are two independent asset demand equations. Our interest in financial markets, and more accurate measurement,

			Central Bank and Government	
Public				
B			Au	B
vS				vS
PK	W			

Figure 9.1

---

[4]The reason is discussed in footnote 2 above and in Cukierman and Meltzer (1989).

[5]Other assets may appear on the consolidated balance sheet including buildings, military equipment and land, but these are irrelevant for current purposes. Central banks in many countries carry out fiscal functions, for example by buying commodities to support their price. These operations could be reflected by including commodity inventories on the consolidated balance sheet of the central bank and government.

determines the choice of B and S (or vS).[6] The demand functions for base money and debt are shown as equations (1) and (2), and the market value of wealth is shown as equation (3).

$$B = \lambda(\underset{-}{i}, \underset{+}{P}, \underset{+}{p}, \underset{-}{ap}, \underset{+}{W}, \underset{+}{H}, \underset{-}{e}),\tag{1}$$

$$S = \beta(\underset{+}{i - \pi}, \underset{+}{P}, \underset{-}{p}, \underset{-}{ap}, \underset{+}{W}, \underset{+}{H}, \underset{-}{e}),\tag{2}$$

$$W = PK + vS + B.\tag{3}$$

The plus and minus signs below the variables show the responses to the principal arguments of the asset demand functions. The anticipated rate of inflation, π, and the anticipated return to real capital per unit of capital, e, are two of the channels by which anticipations affect the asset markets. Anticipated prices, ap, the anticipated rate of inflation, π, and the nominal rate of interest, i, are the main channels for the effects of anticipated prices on current portfolios.[7] H is human capital. We use equations (1) and (2) and the wealth equation (3) to solve for the equilibrium values of i and P and the stocks of base money, bonds and real capital. Note that the response of β to P is positive. The reason is that an increase in P with the real return, e, constant lowers the real rate of return on real assets, inducing substitution to securities.

The MM curve of Figure 9.2 shows the combinations of interest rates and asset prices at which a constant amount of base money is willingly held. The curve is positively sloped to reflect the fact that higher interest rates offset the effect of higher asset prices on the demand for base money. The CM curve shows the combinations of interest rates and asset prices at which the outstanding stock of government debt is willingly held. The curve is negatively sloped to show that interest rates must fall as asset prices rise to induce the public to hold a given stock of government securities.

The asset markets are in equilibrium at i_0 and P_0. At these prices, with given anticipations, the stocks of base money, government debt and capital are willingly held. Changes in base money and debt change i and P by shifting the CM and MM curves; changes in ap, p, e, W, H and π induced by policy and other changes shift CM and MM simultaneously.

---

[6]Measurement of the aggregate capital stock presents conceptual and operational difficulties that are much greater than measurement of money and debt. The common complaint about the difficulties of accurately measuring money does not apply to the monetary base. The base can be read from the central banks' balance sheet.

[7]The difference between ap and π is the difference between a one-time change in the price level, producing a transitory change in the rate of price change, and a change in anticipated inflation – a persistent change in the rate of price change.

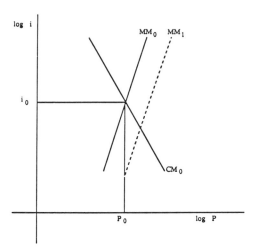

Figure 9.2

2.1. Solutions for i and P

The solutions for i and P from the asset market equations are obtained from equations (1) and (2) holding human wealth, the price level and anticipations constant. Differentiating the bond market (CM) and the money market (MM) equations and using subscripts to denote partial derivatives, we have the slopes of the MM and CM curves expressed as derivatives:

$$MM: \frac{\mathrm{d}i}{\mathrm{d}P} = -\frac{\lambda_P + \lambda_W K}{\lambda_i + \lambda_W v_i S} > 0,$$

$$CM: \frac{\mathrm{d}i}{\mathrm{d}P} = -\frac{\beta_P + \beta_W K}{\beta_i + \beta_W v_i S} < 0.$$

To facilitate comparison of orders of magnitude, we rewrite the derivatives as equivalent elasticities:

$$\text{slope of } MM: \ \varepsilon(i, P \mid MM) = -\frac{\varepsilon(MM, P)}{\varepsilon(MM, i)} > 0,$$

$$\text{slope of } CM: \ \varepsilon(i, P \mid CM) = -\frac{\varepsilon(CM, P)}{\varepsilon(CM, i)} < 0,$$

where $\varepsilon(MM, i) = -[\varepsilon(\lambda, i) + \varepsilon(\lambda, W)\varepsilon(v, i)vS/W]$ and $\varepsilon(MM\ P) = -[\varepsilon(\lambda, P) + \varepsilon(\lambda, W)PK/W]$ and similarly for $\varepsilon(CM, i)$ and $\varepsilon(CM, P)$.

$\varepsilon(MM, i)$ and $\varepsilon(MM, P)$ are the interest elasticity and the asset price elasticity of the excess supply of money. Similarly, $\varepsilon(CM, i)$ and $\varepsilon(CM, P)$ are the interest rate and asset price elasticities of the excess supply of bonds. When intermediation is introduced, the CM elasticities become the interest and asset price elasticities of the excess supply of bank (or intermediary) credit, as noted below. The signs of these elasticities are determined by the signs of the components, the derivatives or partial elasticities of the λ and β functions. These signs are:

$$\varepsilon(MM, i), \; \varepsilon(CM, i), \; \varepsilon(CM, P) > 0 \; ;$$

$$\varepsilon(MM, P) < 0 \, .$$

Similar expressions can be used to describe the vertical shifts of MM and CM induced by changes in variables other than i and P. Expressed in geometric terms (as mixtures of shifts and slopes) and converted to elasticities, these expressions are:

$$\varepsilon(i, B \mid AM) = \frac{\text{slope}(CM) \cdot \text{shift}(MM)}{\text{slope}(MM) - \text{slope}(CM)} \, ,$$

$$\varepsilon(P, B \mid AM) = \frac{-\text{shift}(MM)}{\text{slope}(MM) - \text{slope}(CM)} \, ,$$

where, for a change in the base,

$$\text{shift}(MM) = \frac{1}{\varepsilon(MM, i)} \, .$$

The conditioning expression AM indicates that the elasticity is a total elasticity of the asset market system, holding the output market constant.

We now use these formulas to show the responses of i and P to several of the variables that shift the MM and CM curves of Figure 9.2. The next three subsections discuss these shifts.

2.2. Responses to B, S and open market operations

The positions of the MM and CM curves in Figure 9.2, and the solution values for i and P, depend on B and S and on all variables, other than i and P, that enter as arguments of the λ and β functions. An increase in B shifts the MM curve to the right, lowering interest rates and raising asset prices. The effect of an increase in B is shown in Figure 9.2 by the broken line MM_1. Formally, the responses of log i and log P to a change in log B are

$$\varepsilon(i, B \mid AM) = \frac{\varepsilon(CM, P)}{\Delta} < 0,$$

(4)

$$\varepsilon(P, B \mid AM) = -\frac{\varepsilon(MM, i)}{\Delta} > 0,$$

where $\Delta = \varepsilon(CM, i) \cdot \varepsilon(MM, P) - \varepsilon(MM, i) \cdot \varepsilon(CM, P) < 0$.

The three-asset system, with separate markets for money and debt, introduces a broader range of substitution than the IS–LM framework. Changes in base money (and other variables) affect aggregate demand and output by changing relative prices and wealth. Some familiar propositions of IS–LM analysis no longer hold. The response of the interest rate to the base, $\varepsilon(i, B \mid AM)$, is neither necessary nor sufficient for a positive response of aggregate demand or output to monetary policy. Furthermore, in the IS–LM framework, convergence of the interest elasticity of the demand for money to minus infinity implies that the responses to money converge to zero. In the money-credit market framework, this is not so. The reason is that we cannot assume that $\varepsilon(MM, i)$ converges to infinity without imposing a similar convergence on $\varepsilon(CM, i)$. It follows that as $\varepsilon(i, B \mid AM)$ converges to zero, $\varepsilon(P, B \mid AM)$ remains constant at a positive level.

The interaction of the asset markets prevents the emergence of a liquidity trap. Large interest elasticities weaken the transmission of monetary policy via interest rates on financial assets, but the transmission via asset prices remains fully operative. A liquidity trap requires that $\varepsilon(MM, i)$ converges to infinity more rapidly than $\varepsilon(CM, i)$. This condition is excluded by Walras' law and the postulated substitution [see Brunner and Meltzer (1968)]. The proposition follows from the responses of $\varepsilon(i, B \mid AM)$ and $\varepsilon(P, B \mid AM)$ in equations (4). A uniform convergence of $\varepsilon(CM, i)$ and of $\varepsilon(MM, i)$ to (plus) infinity produces convergence of $\varepsilon(i, B \mid AM)$ to zero but $\varepsilon(P, B \mid AM)$ remains bounded.

Changes in debt affect the asset market equilibrium by changing both i and P. These changes, in turn, change aggregate spending and output, and, thus, change the price level. Consequently, the analysis of fiscal policy differs from the IS–LM analysis. The effects of financing deficits or surpluses are in addition to any effects of taxes and government spending on aggregate demand, and the effects of issuing or withdrawing debt on i and P continue even if the budget deficit or surplus remains unchanged.

The responses to a change in debt are obtained by differentiating the money and debt market equations with respect to S and expressing the results in terms of the partial elasticities that are components of $\varepsilon(i, S \mid AM)$ and $\varepsilon(P, S \mid AM)$:

$$\varepsilon(i, S \mid AM) = \frac{\varepsilon(MM, P)}{\Delta} > 0,$$

$$\varepsilon(P, S \mid AM) = - \frac{\varepsilon(CM, i)}{\Delta} > 0.$$

(5)

In geometric terms:

$$\varepsilon(i, S \mid AM) = \frac{-\text{slope}(MM) \cdot \text{shift}(CM)}{\text{slope}(MM) - \text{slope}(CM)},$$

$$\varepsilon(P, S \mid AM) = \frac{\text{shift}(CM)}{\text{slope}(MM) - \text{slope}(CM)}.$$

Equations (5) show that debt issues raise interest rates and asset prices on real capital, so the response of aggregate demand depends on the relative magnitudes of $\varepsilon(CM, i)$ and $\varepsilon(MM, P)$ and on the relative size of the response of aggregate demand to i and P. Many empirical studies of the effect of debt on interest rates suggest that the effect is hard to detect in the data. Findings of this kind do not imply that the size of the debt is irrelevant once we extend the model beyond the standard IS–LM framework; the effect may be larger or more reliable if money, debt and capital are treated as distinct assets in the empirical studies. Or, the effect of the induced change in asset prices may offset the effect of interest rates wholly or in part.

An open market operation is an exchange of money for debt. Open market purchases increase the base creating an excess supply of money. The MM curve shifts to the right. The reduction of the stock of securities in the public's portfolio shifts the CM curve to the left. A new position of equilibrium following the purchases is shown at the intersection of MM_1 and CM_1 in Figure 9.3. Interest rates fall. Asset prices rise provided the interest elasticity of CM exceeds the interest elasticity of MM. We assume, throughout, that this condition is met.[8]

Open market sales have the reverse effect. The monetary base declines and the stock of securities held by the public increases. In Figure 9.3 an open market sale raises the market interest rate from i_1 to i_0 and lowers the asset price from P_1 to P_0. Both changes reduce aggregate demand and thus lower output and the price level.

---

[8]Tests of this restriction by Korteweg and van Loo (1977, p. 66) for the Netherlands and by Brunner and Meltzer (1968) for the United States support the restriction.

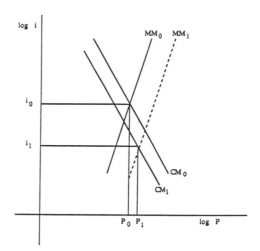

Figure 9.3

2.3. *The Gibson paradox*

In his *Treatise on Money*, Keynes described as a paradox the observed positive relation between interest rates and the price level of current output. He named the paradox for A.H. Gibson who had noted the relation earlier. A large literature has grown up that attempts to explain the Gibson paradox.

In the money–debt–capital model, the paradox disappears. A rising trend in the price level due to inflationary finance produces a positive correlation between the price level and nominal interest rates in two ways. First, the expected relation between market prices and market interest rates is positive, reflecting the effect of the price level on the demands for debt and money weighted by the asset price elasticities of the excess supply functions for credit and money. Second, prices and interest rise with the gradual adjustment of inflationary expectations. Higher expected inflation raises both p and i.

The responses of the interest rate and asset price level to p are:

$$\varepsilon(i, p \mid AM) = - \frac{\varepsilon(CM, p) \cdot \varepsilon(MM, P) - \varepsilon(MM, p) \cdot \varepsilon(CM, P)}{\Delta} > 0 \,,$$

$$\varepsilon(P, p \mid AM) = - \frac{\varepsilon(CM, i) \cdot \varepsilon(MM, p) - \varepsilon(MM i) \cdot \varepsilon(CM, p)}{\Delta} \,,$$

where $\varepsilon(CM, p) = \varepsilon(\beta, p) < 0$ and $\varepsilon(MM, p) = -\varepsilon(\lambda, p) < 0$. The size of $\varepsilon(P, p \mid AM)$ is ambiguous; $|\varepsilon(MM, p)| > |\varepsilon(CM, p)|$ is sufficient to assure that the sign is negative. To assure a positive sign, $|\varepsilon(CM, p)|$ must be large enough to compensate for the relatively low weight, $\varepsilon(MM, i) < \varepsilon(CM, i)$, with which it appears. The implication of this analysis is that an increase in the price level probably lowers asset prices, including prices of traded shares, with the expected rate of inflation unchanged. This effect supplements the effects of non-indexed taxes and depreciation on asset prices.

2.4. Responses to supply shocks

Supply shocks affect i and P by changing the expected return to capital, e, and the two measures of wealth, H and W. The distribution of the responses depends on the type of shock. A shock to labor productivity mainly affects H. A shock to oil prices affects the value of existing capital, included in W, and the expected return, e. A change in tax rates on capital also affects e and W directly. A reduction in taxes on new and existing capital raises the expected after-tax return and the value of existing capital.

Increases in e raise asset prices, and reductions in e lower asset prices. Productivity shocks that increase the expected return to capital also increase the value of existing capital, since existing capital is a close substitute for new capital. The effect of e on the market rate of interest depends on the relative responses of the demands for bonds and money to the change in expected return:

$$\varepsilon(i, e \mid AM) = - \frac{\varepsilon(CM, e) \cdot \varepsilon(MM, P) - \varepsilon(MM, e) \cdot \varepsilon(CM, P)}{\Delta},$$

$$\varepsilon(P, e \mid AM) = - \frac{\varepsilon(CM, i) \cdot \varepsilon(MM, e) - \varepsilon(MM, i) \cdot \varepsilon(CM, e)}{\Delta} > 0.$$

If the reduction in the demand for bonds is relatively large, $|\varepsilon(CM, e)|$ is large, so interest rates rise with e. Conversely, a relatively large $\varepsilon(MM, e)$ implies that market rates decline as the expected return rises.

2.5. Output market responses

This chapter discusses asset market responses and the determination of equilibrium stocks and asset values when money, bonds and capital are distinct assets competing for a place in portfolios. Output and the price level remain fixed throughout. To bring out some of the differences between this analysis and the IS–LM model, this subsection briefly shows the way in which the asset and output markets are joined.

In a closed economy, equilibrium on the output market requires that real output, y, equals real private spending, d, plus real government spending, g:

$$y = d + g .$$

$$d = d(\underset{-}{i - \pi}, \underset{+}{p}, \underset{+}{ap}, \underset{+}{P}, \underset{+}{e}, \underset{+}{W}, \underset{+}{H}) .$$

To study the interaction of asset and output markets, including the effect of monetary or fiscal policy on spending and output, substitute the solutions for i and P obtained from the asset market equilibrium into the spending function. The responses to B, S, and policy changes other than g have the form:

$$\varepsilon(y, x) = c_1 \varepsilon(i, x \mid AM) + c_2 \varepsilon(P, x \mid AM) + \cdots ,$$

where

$$c_1 = \frac{\varepsilon(d, i)}{\Delta} , \qquad c_2 = \frac{\varepsilon(d, P)}{\Delta} ,$$

and

$$\Delta = 1 - \varepsilon(d, i)\varepsilon(i, y \mid AM) + \varepsilon(d, P)\varepsilon(P, y \mid AM) + \varepsilon(d, p)\varepsilon(p, y)$$
$$+ \varepsilon(d, H)\varepsilon(H, y) .$$

   In the model with money, bonds and capital, a change in B or S by open market operations or to finance current government deficits or surpluses affects the output market even if government spending and tax rates are unchanged. These effects are the output market responses to the relative price changes on the asset markets. They are distinct from any real wealth or real balance effects.

   Friedman (1978) and Tobin and Buiter (1976) also introduce a third asset into their models. They then reduce their models with three assets and output to two equations and draw diagrams that look like the standard IS–LM diagram. The analogous procedure in our model would be to draw the output market and asset market relations as two curves in the i, y plane, using the implicit dependence between e and H and y. After substituting the solution for P from the credit market into the output market and the remaining asset market equation the output market relation could be called IS and the asset market relation could be called LM.

   The meaning of the diagram and the two equations is not the same as in the two-asset IS–LM model, however. In the two-asset IS–LM model with only money and capital or money and bonds (or where bonds are treated as a perfect substitute for money or capital), the IS and LM relations are independent equilibrium relations. In models with three assets and two relative prices, the two relations are interdependent. Any change in the stocks of assets or in the demands for assets necessarily shifts both the output (or IS) and the asset market (or LM) relation. Open market operations, deficit finance, changes in productivity or in expectations can no longer be analyzed as a shift in IS along LM or as a shift in LM along IS. Both curves shift in response to these and other changes. A change in the base, for example, changes the positions of the IS and LM curves directly and by changing the asset price level P. If P is replaced by its determinants, the base (and other determinants) affect the positions of IS and LM through the effect of the base on P and of P on the demands for output and assets.

3. Intermediation

The distinction between credit and money was at the center of the banking and currency controversy in the nineteenth century [see Viner (1965) and Thornton (1965)]. Aspects of a modern treatment of many of the same issues can be found in the discussions of intermediation by Gurley and Shaw (1960), Tobin (1963), and Pesek and Saving (1967). This section extends the model of money, bonds and capital to incorporate banks and other financial institutions as part of a theory of intermediation. A main conclusion is that the extension introduces many details that are useful for analyzing the operations of a modern financial system without altering the main implications of the model of money, bonds and capital. Intermediaries provide opportunities for people to increase utility by offering types of assets and liabilities that the public prefers. Intermediaries increase wealth by lowering costs of transacting. Since we abstract from transaction costs, the contribution of intermediaries to wealth is not explored.

Figure 9.4 introduces the balance sheets of banks and non-bank inter-

Public		Banks		Non-bank intermediary		Monetary account of the government		Fiscal account of the government	
C_p	L_b	R	D_p	C_{nb}	T_{nb}	Au			S_T
D_p	L_{nb}		D_{nb}	D_{nb}		A	C_p		
T_b		L_b	T_b	vS_{nb}		AGA	C_{np} $\Big\}$ SB		
T_{nb}		vS_b	A	L_{nb}	W_{nb}	S_{cb}	R		
vS_p	W		W_b				oac		
PK									
W_b									
W_{nb}									

Figure 9.4

mediaries. The development of intermediaries permits the public to hold a wider range of financial assets including demand and commercial bank time deposits, D_p and T_b, and non-bank time deposits, T_{nb}. The public can change its risk position, anticipate future consumption, or exploit opportunities by borrowing from banks (L_b) or non-bank (L_{nb}) financial institutions and by acquiring real assets.

The central bank can acquire securities in the open market, as before, and it can also lend to financial institutions. The remaining symbols on the balance sheets are: R, the volume of bank reserves; A, the amount of borrowing by financial institutions from the central bank; C_p the stock of currency held by the public; D_{nb} the deposits of non-banks at commercial banks; W_b and W_{nb} the values of equity in financial institutions; AGA, advances by the central bank to government agencies; S_{cb}, government securities held by the central bank; and oac, other accounts at the central bank.

Intermediaries hold demand deposits at banks (D_{nb}) and a small amount of currency (C_{nb}) in their tills. Most of their reserves are held as government debt, vS_{nb}. The wealth or net worth of banks and intermediaries is the market value of their charters. Since governments typically do not permit free entry into the industry, there are some potential monopoly profits accruing to banks and financial institutions [see Pesek and Saving (1967)]. W_b and W_{nb} are the capitalized values of these profits.[9]

The underlying structure of the economy remains as in Figure 9.1. After consolidation, the wealth of the public is the same as before. The stock of base money is now divided between currency outstanding and reserves. The source base, SB, is

$$C_p + C_{nb} + R = SB , \tag{6}$$

and the total outstanding stock of government debt, S_T, is

$$S_p + S_b + S_{nb} = S_T - S_{cb} = S , \tag{7}$$

where S is the stock of debt held by the banks and the public. The structure of claims and debts is built on these financial assets.

---

[9]Changes in reserve requirement ratios, changes in regulations affecting interest rates paid on deposits or received on assets, and changes in merger, entry and branching restrictions affect W_b, W_{nb} and W. In many countries, banks are required to lend on favorable terms but can borrow from the central bank on favorable terms also. The net tax or subsidy falls on W_b and W_{nb}. To simplify the analysis, non-deposit liabilities are combined with net worth in the wealth variable. Such liabilities exhibited substantial variation during the past twenty years.

3.1. The government sector

We begin with the monetary authority, the consolidation of all accounts of government agencies that issue money. The agencies differ across countries and over time. Two accounts currently matter in the United States: the consolidated account of the Federal Reserve System and the Treasury's monetary account. Consolidating these accounts provides the framework for the definition, measurement and explanation of the monetary base. The source base, in the terminology developed by the Federal Reserve Bank of St. Louis, is defined as the sum of monetary liabilities of the government's consolidated monetary accounts that are held as assets by banks, other financial institutions and the public.

The consolidated statement implies the relation between the source base and its counterparts – the other components of the consolidated monetary account of the government shown in Figure 9.4. The statement is presented in a relatively general way to suggest opportunities for flexible adjustment of the counterparts to the source base – the net assets acquired by the monetary authority – under different institutional arrangements:

$SB = Au$ (gold + foreign exchange + special drawing rights) + A
(loans to banks under various titles and conditions) + AGA
(loans under various titles and conditions to government agencies) + S_{cb} (government securities) – oac (Treasury deposits + deposits of foreign governments and their agencies – other items, including float).[10]

$$(8)$$

"Other items" consists of "other assets", "other liabilities" and net worth. A, AGA and S_{cb} usually dominate the movement of the source base.

An empirical examination of the money supply process requires investigation of the supply conditions of the major components on the right-hand side of equation (8). These conditions differ between countries reflecting the variety of institutional arrangements for conducting policy operations. Despite these differences, the arrangements can be analyzed in terms of the effect on the base.

One interesting arrangement was considered by the Banco d'Espagna in the 1970s. The Spanish money market was undeveloped, so open market operations could not be conducted in the usual way. To control the base, the Bank proposed to let the commercial banks bid for the right to supply loans. The

---

[10]An excellent description of these accounts and the consolidation is given in Shaw (1950).

bidding process was designed to set the equivalent of the discount rate and, of course, affect interest rates on loans and securities.

Since the middle of the 1970s, the Swiss National Bank has set a target for the growth rate of the monetary base. There is no market for Treasury bills in Switzerland, and the National Bank is prohibited from holding long-term bonds, so open market operations in government securities are not an available option. By far the largest asset on the Bank's balance sheet is the portfolio of gold and foreign exchange. To control the base, the Bank conducts open market operations in the foreign exchange market.

The Deutsches Bundesbank also holds relatively few government securities. The principal assets on its balance sheet are various types of loans to private borrowers that have been sold or discounted by the commercial banks. The Bundesbank also has set a target for the monetary base, or central bank money in the Bundesbank's parlance. The Bundesbank sets interest rates on the assets that it buys, and it changes these rates to control the size of its portfolio and the growth of the monetary base.

The Banca d'Italia's portfolio of government securities was regulated for many years by an arrangement making the Central Bank the residual buyer of new issues of Treasury securities. The prevailing deficit, the choice of coupon rate and of the issue price, in the context of given market conditions, determined the portion of new issues which the central bank was legally obliged to buy. Under these conditions, the Italian Parliament and Treasury controlled the source base. Advances to government agencies, AGA, the third component in the monetary account of the government shown in Figure 9.4, also contributed to the source base in Italy, in contrast to the United States where this item has played no role.

The U.S. base is dominated by S_{cb} and decisions about S_{cb} remain with the central bank. Its choice of strategy determines the conditions under which S_{cb}, and the source base, increase or decrease. A strategy of rigid interest control would reproduce the Italian experience. The United States closely approximated the postwar Italian system during the 1940s, under the interest pegging regime and large, wartime budget deficits. An agreement between the Treasury and the Federal Reserve in March 1951, known as the Accord, permitted the Federal Reserve to let interest rates change at all maturities. Following the Accord, the Federal Reserve conducted monetary policy by various means designed to stabilize short-term interest rates including, at different times, Treasury bill rates, control of the rate on one-day loans of reserves (the Federal funds rate), or member bank borrowing. Under these procedures, the monetary base responds to the excess demand on the markets for credit or debt. As a consequence, the stocks of base money and money often have moved procyclically, reinforcing inflation and recession. The reason is that the Federal Reserve's procedures held short-term rates fixed and supplied base money when the public supplied assets to the banks and withdrew base money when the public's supply of assets to banks declined.

In the 1950s and 1960s, the Bank of Japan held the market rate below the rate of inflation by supplying base money to banks through the discount window at a subsidized borrowing rate. "Window guidance", a form of direct control on borrowing, inhibited the banks from raising rates, and the relatively low rates charged by banks discouraged the development of money market instruments [Suzuki (1980)]. This policy ended after the government increased the stock of debt. After a market for debt developed, the Bank of Japan relied more on open market operations and less on window guidance.

The examples of diverse supply conditions governing the source base bring out that differences in monetary regimes are associated with differences in supply conditions of the source base. Comparison of monetary regimes involves a comparison of these supply conditions and their consequences. Any major change in supply conditions is a change in the monetary regime. Both short-run monetary and long-run price uncertainty can be influenced by the choice of monetary regime. Some arrangements lower the size of unexpected monetary shocks or prevent misinterpretation of the effects of such shocks on output and employment. The choice of supply conditions for the base can lower long-run price uncertainty and the resource cost of uncertainty. A rational choice of policy regime requires an understanding of this link between supply conditions and the excess burden imposed by some types of monetary regime.

The monetary base is obtained from the source base by adding the reserve adjustment magnitude, RAM, to the source base:[11]

$$B = SB + RAM .\qquad(9)$$

RAM is a measure of all changes in required reserves due to changes in reserve requirements ratios. An increase in a reserve requirement ratio is equivalent to a decline in the source base induced by an open market sale, and a decline in a reserve requirement ratio is equivalent to the increase in the source base induced by an open market purchase. The change in RAM is defined as follows:

$$\Delta RAM_t = \Delta r_t^d D_t^P - \Delta r_t^t T_{bt} ,\qquad(10)$$

where r^d is the average reserve requirement on transaction accounts D_t^P, and r^t

---

[11] The source base differs from the amount of outside money by the amount of base money issued against loans to the private sector. This amount is relatively large in many countries. The distinction between outside and inside money, while useful for assessing the monetary sector's contribution to wealth, is not useful for analysis of the money supply.

is the average reserve requirement on non-transaction accounts, T_b. Both r^d and r^t are expressed as decimals. The change in RAM measures the reserves liberated from required reserves, or the reserves impounded into required reserves, by lowering or raising a reserve requirement ratio. The existing level of RAM is the cumulated sum of all past changes.

The monetary base summarizes the actions, other than discount rate changes, taken by the monetary authorities. The monetary multiplier, to be introduced presently, reflects the public's and the banks' behavior. This decomposition of the money stock into multiplier and base offers an opportunity to separate the influence of the monetary authority on money and credit from the influence of the banks and the public. Furthermore, the framework offers an opportunity to examine the consequences of institutional constraints imposed on banks, to assess the strategies and tactical procedures chosen by the central banks and to evaluate the institutional choices available to the monetary authorities.

The expanded model of the money-credit process differs in four principal ways from the model in equations (1)–(3). First, the monetary base consists of currency and reserves. Shifts between the two components alter the stocks of money held by the public and the stock of outstanding credit in different degrees. Second, banks offer types of deposits that differ in maturity, turnover and the rate of interest paid to holders. Shifts from one type of deposit to another, for example from bank time deposits to demand deposits, change the stocks of money – defined as currency and demand deposits – and bank credit in opposite directions. Third, partly as a consequence of the regulation of interest rates paid on different types of deposits, changes in the level of interest rates affect credit and money in different ways. Fourth, differences in reserve requirement ratios and regulations prohibiting payment of interest on required reserves encourage substitution between types of deposits. Banks and other financial institutions are encouraged to develop substitutes for demand (or time) deposits that have many of the properties of these deposits but are subject to lower reserve requirements.

For the present we ignore non-bank institutions and concentrate on a system with banks, government and the public. From the balance sheet of the consolidated banking system, we can define bank credit or earning assets as

$$L_b + vS_b = D_p + T_b - (R - A) + W_b . \tag{11}$$

Money is defined as

$$M = C_p + D_p . \tag{12}$$

Demand deposits include all types of transaction account; time deposits include all non-transaction accounts. Since the source base, SB, in the absence of non-bank intermediaries, is $C_p + R - A$,

$$L_b + vS_b = M + T_b - SB .\tag{13}$$

Neglecting the small amount of banks' net worth, equation (13) shows that, from the definitions of credit and money, we obtain the implication that growth of time deposits (intermediation) increases credit relative to money.

3.2. The U.S. monetary system

The details of each monetary system differ. This subsection develops a framework for the United States' monetary system that encompasses the public, the banks and the monetary authority. The reader who wishes to avoid these details can go to the next subsection where the results are summarized as part of the equilibrium conditions for the stocks of money and credit.

Historically, banks' holding of reserves under the Federal Reserve Act depended on the distribution of deposits between type and size of deposits, location of the bank, and status of membership in the Federal Reserve System. The Monetary Control Act of 1980 extended reserve requirements to other financial institutions, including mutual savings banks, saving and loan associations, credit unions, agencies and branches of foreign banks, and Edge Act corporations. Required reserve ratios for accounts subject to check now vary with the size of the account. For time deposits, required reserve ratios vary with the term to maturity and the type of account. The total required reserve is a weighted average with weights dependent on these characteristics. Let r^d and r^t be the weighted average reserve requrement ratios for demand and time deposits, respectively. Banks satisfy these requirements, by holding deposits at Federal Reserve Banks and by holding currency. (Non-member banks and non-banks hold currency also. Some of these details are neglected.)

Required reserves, R^r, are defined by

$$R^r = r^d D_p + r^t T_b = r^*(D_p + T_b) .$$

The banks' desired net average reserve ratio, $(R - A)/(D_p + T_b)$, depends on the discount rate, $disc$, the market rate, i, the structure of reserve requirements, and the variance of interest rates and reserves, $v(i)$ and $v(R)$. Inclusion of the last term reflects the experience of the U.S. monetary system in the 1930s when the increased variability of the supply of reserves increased uncertainty about reserve supply and encouraged banks to hold relatively large excess reserves. Interest rate variability, $v(i)$, affects the desired reserve position. A well-organized money market, with relatively small transaction costs, lowers $v(i)$ and the desired reserve position. The desired ratio of reserves to total deposits is given by (14) with the signs of derivatives written below the variables:

$$r = \frac{R - A}{D_p + T_b} = r(\underset{+}{r^*}, \underset{-}{i}, \underset{+}{disc}, \underset{+}{v(i)}, \underset{+}{v(R)}) . \tag{14}$$

Changes in reserve requirements ratios affect both the RAM component and the desired ratio of reserves to total deposits. To combine these two sources of change in a single parameter, we define the adjusted reserve ratio, $\bar{r}$:

$$\bar{r} = r + \frac{RAM}{D_p + T_b} .$$

The adjusted reserve ratio is invariant with respect to changes in the reserve requirement ratios. The entire effect of changes in the ratios can be analyzed as a change in the monetary base.

In addition to the allocation between reserves and earning assets, banks allocate between borrowed and non-borrowed reserves. The desired ratio of borrowing to total deposits, b, is:

$$b = b(\underset{-}{disc}, \underset{+}{i}, \dots) , \tag{15a}$$

where $disc$ is the discount rate charged on loans or advances from Federal Reserve banks and the omitted items in the b function include institutional restrictions, occasional rationing by the Federal Reserve and other administrative arrangements. The ratio b is defined by

$$A = b(\cdot)(D_p + T_b) . \tag{15b}$$

Specification of the credit market requires one additional allocation parameter. The banks' wealth (and non-deposit liabilities) satisfies the relation:

$$W_b = n(i^n, i \dots)[1 + t(\ )]D_p ,$$

where n depends on the market rate, i, and the yield i^n offered by banks on W_b. The parameter n assures consistency of the balance sheet items and the market value of bank wealth, W_b.

For many years the Federal Reserve used the level of free reserves as an indicator of the policy stance. Free reserves is the difference between member bank excess reserves and member bank borrowing. At other times, excess reserves fluctuated around a very low level; the Federal Reserve ignored excess reserves and concentrated on member bank borrowing [Meigs (1962), Brunner and Meltzer (1964)]. The level of free reserves is $R - R^r - A$. For a given reserve requirement ratio, the reserve ratio and the ratio of free reserves to total deposits fluctuate together. For a given required reserve ratio and relatively small and unchanging excess reserves, the ratio of borrowing to total deposits dominates movements of the free reserve ratio. Hence the relation of free reserves or member bank borrowing to money, bank credit, interest rates and asset prices can be studied within the framework presented here.

The allocation of the public's financial assets between currency and deposits and the allocation of deposits between demand and time (or saving) accounts affects the stocks of money and credit and, therefore, affects interest rates and asset prices. The ratio of currency to demand (transaction) balances, k, depends on the user cost of currency and deposits and on their respective holding costs. The user costs and holding costs explain major movements in the k ratio. An increase in the frequency of theft raises the holding cost of currency and lowers desired balances. In countries like Japan, where crime rates are low, currency is used for a large share of the public's transactions. The rapid spread of banking facilities lowers the user cost and the holding cost of deposits. Increased uncertainty about bank failures, as in the thirties, raises the holding costs of deposits, while increased geographic mobility, as in wartime, raises the user cost of deposits. Both types of change increase the k ratio.

Financial commentators and some economists have speculated that the spread of credit cards, debit cards, automated tellers and other innovations in banking will reduce desired money balances to zero. Automated transfers are predicted to reduce desired demand deposits toward zero. Credit cards and other innovations are predicted to eliminate the use of currency in transactions. These conjectures are implausible. The marginal productivity of currency as a transaction medium is not likely to approach zero. Currency is used to evade taxes, for illegal transactions and for convenience in small transactions [Cagan (1958), Hess (1971)]. It is instructive to note that during the past fifteen years, the currency ratio in the United States has exceeded the level observed in 1929 by more than 100 percent. This suggests that currency continues to be used in optimal payment arrangements.

Banks offer many different types of time and saving deposits. Johanes and Rasche (1987) find it useful to distinguish between small saving and time deposits and large deposits, mainly negotiable certificates of deposit, to represent current U.S. arrangements. We compress the detail into a single ratio, the ratio of non-transaction, T_b, to transaction accounts, D_p. The latter include all checkable deposits. The allocation between transaction and non-transaction accounts depends on the interest rates paid on each type, i^d on transaction accounts and i^t on time or non-transaction accounts. In addition, the allocation depends on the market interest rate, asset price level and on human and non-human wealth. Signs of partial derivatives appear below the arguments of equation (16). These signs indicate the effect of substitution and wealth on the time deposit ratio. An increase in open market interest rates, holding time deposit rates fixed, encourages direct holding of securities, so intermediary deposits – particularly time deposits – decline. Increases in asset prices lower the return on assets; intermediation increases:

$$t = T_b/D_P = t(\underset{-}{i^d}, \underset{+}{i^t}, \underset{-}{i}, \underset{+}{P}, \underset{+}{W}, \underset{+}{H}) \,. \tag{16}$$

Banks supply deposit and non-deposit liabilities of various kinds by setting prices or interest rates at which deposit may be taken. For some deposits, interest rates have been controlled by government rulings. The ceiling rate for checkable deposits remained at zero for several decades, but banks offered non-pecuniary returns to deposit holders. We summarize the supply conditions in the price-setting functions shown in (17):

$$i^d = f_1(i, \ldots) \,,$$

$$i^t = f_2(i, \ldots) \,, \tag{17}$$

$$i^n = f_3(i, \ldots) \,,$$

where the omitted variables represent institutional restrictions that condition the degree of competition. The difference between the two deposit interest rates reflects market evaluations of the comparative risk and convenience associated with the different bank liabilities. The various rates are tied together in the market place.

The framework can be expanded to take account of the many different types of deposit accounts that banks hold. Treasury or government agency deposits may be less sensitive to interest rates. Foreign deposits may be more dependent on relative rates of interest at domestic and foreign banks. Each of these different types of deposits could be expressed as a ratio to total deposits with the ratio depending on the relevant variables. These liabilities would then be incorporated explicitly into the money and credit market framework, and the effects of changes in these liabilities could be analyzed.

The stocks of money and bank earning assets, or credit, can be expressed as the product of the monetary base and a multiplier. For the condensed framework with one type of demand or checkable deposits and one type of time (or non-transaction) account, we obtain the money, m, and bank credit, a, multipliers starting with equation (6). Denote the monetary base net of borrowing as B^a. Substituting (14) and the currency ratio, k, and using (16), we solve for demand deposits and money:

$$D_{\mathrm{P}} = \frac{1}{(\bar{r} - b)(1 + t) + k} B^a ,$$

$$M = \frac{1 + k}{(\bar{r} - b)(1 + t) + k} B^a ,$$

(18)

where

$$m = \frac{1 + k}{(\bar{r} - b)(1 + t) + k}$$

(19)

and the components of m depend on the factors discussed. Similarly, using (13), we solve for the bank credit multiplier:

$$a = \frac{(1 + n + b - r)(1 + t)}{(\bar{r} - b)(1 + t) + k} .$$

(20)

The allocation ratio n in the numerator of the asset multiplier assures consistency between the values on the balance sheet and market value of wealth, W_b.

If non-bank intermediaries hold currency and deposits at banks, their holdings can be included by letting

$$C_{nb} = k_2 D_{nb} \quad \text{and} \quad D_{nb} = k_3 T_{nb} .$$

The ratios k_2 and k_3 depend on market rates and costs of transacting. The rates paid by non-bank intermediaries affect their share of deposits, so

$$T_{nb} / T_b = t_2$$

depends on the rate paid by intermediaries. These adjustments change the precise form of the m and a multipliers without changing the general framework.

The detail incorporated in the multipliers extends the analysis of the money–credit process, described in equations (1) and (2), by including many of the institutional arrangements that characterize the U.S. financial system. The equations determine the amount of money supplied by banks and the amount of earning assets demanded by banks given the monetary base, the public's demand for money and supply of earning assets to banks. We can now bring these elements together to solve for interest rates and asset prices and the equilibrium stocks of money and bank credit.

3.3. Money and credit

In the expanded system that includes banks and other intermediaries, the demand for money, M^d, is juxtaposed to the supply of money offered by banks. The demand for money is:

$$M^d = \lambda(\underset{-}{i}, \underset{+}{P}, \underset{+}{p}, ap, \underset{+}{W}, \underset{+}{H}, \underset{-}{e}) , \tag{21}$$

where the functional λ is retained for convenience. The equilibrium condition for the money market is:

$$\lambda(\underset{-}{i}, \underset{+}{P}, \underset{+}{p}, \ldots) = m(\underset{+}{i}, \underset{-}{P}, \ldots ; \underset{-}{i^t})B.^{12} \tag{22}$$

The missing items in the demand function are shown in equation (21); the missing items in the supply function are variables representing institutional arrangements and arguments of the functions determining the ratios such as k, t, etc. that are components of the money and credit multipliers.

The credit market replaces the market for government debt, equation (2) in the system without intermediaries. On the credit market, interaction of the public and financial intermediaries distributes the stock of debt among asset portfolios. For the public, buying government securities is an alternative to repaying loans, and selling securities is an alternative to borrowing from intermediaries. The choice depends on the relative costs and returns. We define the public's supply of earning assets as:

$$\sigma = L_b + S - S_p . \tag{23}$$

Equilibrium on the bank credit market requires:

$$\sigma(\underset{-}{i} - \pi, \underset{-}{P}, \underset{+}{p}, ap, \underset{+}{W}, \underset{+}{H}, e, S) = a(\underset{+}{i}, \underset{+}{P}, \ldots ; \underset{+}{i^t})B . \tag{24}$$

Equations (22), (24) and (17) determine the market interest rate, the asset price level and the rate paid by banks on their deposit liabilities, given the monetary base, the stock of securities and the stock of capital. The missing signs under W and H suggest that the responses of σ to human and non-human wealth are ambiguous as a result of the offsetting responses of L_P and $-S_p$.

---

[12] The negative responses of m to P and i^t reflect primarily the effects on the deposit ratio.

3.4. Solutions for i and P in the expanded system

We differentiate the money and credit market equilibrium conditions, form partial elasticities, and express the results as interest rate and asset price elasticities of the excess supplies of money (MM) and bank credit (CM). The signs of these elasticities are identical to the signs of the corresponding elasticities of the system without intermediaries. Their components differ, reflecting the additional information in the expanded system. Equations (25) are the excess supply elasticities:

$$\varepsilon(CM, i) = \varepsilon(a, i) - \varepsilon(\sigma, i) > 0,$$

$$\varepsilon(MM, i) = \varepsilon(m, i) - \varepsilon(\lambda, i) > 0,$$

$$\varepsilon(CM, P) = \varepsilon(a, P) - \varepsilon(\sigma, P) > 0,$$

$$\varepsilon(MM, P) = \varepsilon(m, P) - \varepsilon(\lambda, P) < 0.$$

(25)

The responses of i and P to the policy variables, B and S, for given wealth, output, prices and anticipations follow immediatley. These responses, expressed as elasticities, summarize the interaction on the asset market and specify the magnitude of the responses transmitted to the output market.[13] Equation (26) is the analogue in the system with intermediaries of the responses in equations (4) and (5) earlier. The denominators, denoted Δ, contain the same terms as in the system without intermediaries, although the components of these terms have been modified to encompass intermediary responses as shown in equation (25):

$$\varepsilon(i, B \mid AM) = \frac{\varepsilon(CM, P) - \varepsilon(MM, P)}{\Delta} < 0,$$

$$\varepsilon(P, B \mid AM) = \frac{\varepsilon(MM, i) - \varepsilon(CM, i)}{\Delta} > 0,$$

$$\varepsilon(i, S \mid AM) = \frac{\varepsilon(MM, P)\varepsilon(\sigma, S)}{\Delta} > 0,$$

$$\varepsilon(P, S \mid AM) = -\frac{\varepsilon(MM, i)\varepsilon(\sigma, S)}{\Delta} > 0.$$

(26)

---

[13]The output market responses can be represented as a linear combination of the asset market responses with coefficients that are ratios of output elasticities on the output and asset markets. See Brunner and Meltzer (1976) and Subsection 2.5 above.

Since $\varepsilon(CM, i)$ and $\varepsilon(MM, i)$ are both positive, the sign of $\varepsilon(P, B)$ requires an assumption about relative orders of magnitude. A basic feature of our analysis is that the responses to interest rates on the credit market are much larger than the corresponding responses on the money market. This reflects the hypothesis that interest rates are proximately determined on the credit market and asset prices are proximately determined on the money market. Empirical work by Brunner and Meltzer (1968) and Korteweg and van Loo (1977) supports the hypothesis. Consequently, we assume:

$$\varepsilon(CM, i) > \varepsilon(MM, i) .$$

If the two elasticities are equal, the extended range of substitution induced by changes in the base is restricted to the narrower range considered in the IS–LM framework. In general, however, the range of substitution is larger. Monetary impulses are transmitted from the asset markets to the output market by means of asset prices, interest rates and wealth.

The monetary base affects output by changing i and P. These effects are reinforcing. An increase in the base lowers i and raises P; both changes are expansive. The corresponding responses of output to government debt are offsetting; an increase in S raises both i and P, and a reduction in S lowers i and P. The positively correlated changes in i and P reduce the effect of debt-financed fiscal policy on aggregate demand and output. Debt-induced crowding out of new investment is small and hard to detect if the two effects are approximately equal.

Figure 9.5 combines the MM and CM relations with the price-setting function for i^t, shown as equation (17). The slope of the CM relation is:

$$-\frac{\varepsilon(CM, P)}{\varepsilon(CM, i)} < 0 ,$$

and the slope of MM is:

$$-\frac{\varepsilon(MM, P)}{\varepsilon(MM, i)} > 0 ,$$

as in the earlier discussion. The slope of the i^t relation is unity (up to the level at which interest rates are controlled). If the analysis is extended to include other intermediaries, an additional price-setting function must be added for each intermediary.

The solid lines, MM_0 and CM_0, show an initial position of the money and credit-market equilibrium. The position depends on B and S and on all of the other variables and institutional arrangements summarized in equations (22)

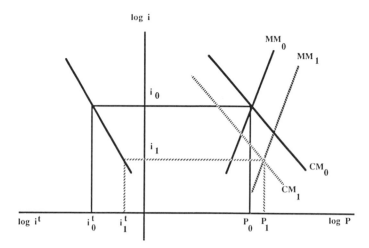

Figure 9.5

and (24). The positions of the *CM* and *MM* relations determine i_0 and P_0, the equilibrium values of the interest rate and asset price level. The banking system sets the rate i_0^t to correspond to the rate earned on its portfolio, summarized by i_0. At the equilibrium position shown in Figure 9.5, the rate i_0^t makes wealth owners indifferent between owning securities directly and holding time deposits at banks (or financial institutions). Interest rate i_0 and asset price P_0 sustain the allocation of assets between money, debt and capital and the allocation of wealth between assets and liabilities. Whenever the open market rate of interest is above the associated rate paid on time deposits, owners of time deposits seek higher yields. They reduce time deposits and purchase debt for their portfolios. Banks (or other financial institutions) lose time deposits and, as the public acquires a larger share of the stock of outstanding securities, the banks' holdings of securities decline. In the terminology that has become common, there is disintermediation. Disintermediation continues as long as the rate paid on time deposits, i^t, is held below the level consistent with the market rate, i.

The analysis shows why efforts to regulate deposit rates in the inflationary conditions of the 1960s and 1970s produced large reductions in time deposits whenever market rates rose above the maximum rate on time deposits. The public bought government securities directly, and new, unregulated intermediaries arose to offer the public assets with attributes very similar to time deposits with regulated rates. The new intermediaries, mainly money market funds, purchased securities directly or purchased unregulated large denomination time deposits, called negotiable certificates of deposit, from banks. Banks indirectly repurchased their deposits by paying rates on the certificates of deposit consistent with the market rate. In this way, with some excess burden, equilibrium was restored between i^t and i.

3.5. Response to the base

Figure 9.5 shows the responses to an increase in the stock of base money by the central bank. The increase is shown by the shifts of MM to the right and CM to the left, to the positions shown by the broken lines MM_1 and CM_1. The shift in MM is given by

$$\frac{-1}{\varepsilon(MM, i)} < 0 ,$$

and the shift in CM by

$$\frac{-1}{\varepsilon(CM, i)} < 0 .$$

At the new equilibrium, interest rates are lower and, under the constraint $\varepsilon(CM, i) > \varepsilon(MM, i)$, asset prices are higher. These initial or impact effects on the asset markets are followed (or accompanied) by changes in output and prices, in the market value of human and non-human wealth, in the expected return to capital and in anticipated prices. The response of these variables to the base and to the reduction in interest rates and the rise in asset prices induced by the increase in base money modifies the initial effects on interest rates and asset prices. Each of the subsequent effects can be analyzed within the framework using the partial elasticities $\varepsilon(i, p \mid AM)$, $\varepsilon(P, p \mid AM)$, $\varepsilon(i, e \mid AM)$, etc. developed in the previous section and in the general equilibrium analysis of Brunner and Meltzer (1976) and Brunner (1976a).

The initial decline in market interest rates, shown in Figure 9.5, reduces the market rate relative to the banks' posted rate on time deposits, i_0^t. At the prevailing rates, the public acquires time deposits and sells securities on the open market. Intermediaries acquire a larger share of the outstanding stock of securities. They respond by reducing the posted rate on time deposits toward i_1^t. At i_1^t the rate paid by banks on time deposits has adjusted to the equilibrium on the asset markets, so the degree of intermediation remains at its new level.

Reductions in the base have opposite effects. The movement from $P_1 i_1$ to $P_0 i_0$ in Figure 9.5 shows the initial effect of a reduction in the base. If interest rates on time deposits had been fully adjusted to i_1, time deposit rates are low relative to i_0. The public acquires securities in the open market and reduces time deposits.

Zero rates of interest on demand deposits induce the public to hold less than the optimal amount of demand deposits. The long-run effect of ceilings on interest rates is expansion of alternatives that avoid the restrictions and the relative decline in the size of institutions that are prohibited from offering substitutes.

3.6. Solutions for money

The response of the money stock to the base and the stock of securities can be written using either the demand or supply equations for money and credit. The two solutions are logically equivalent but not identical. The responses to the base are

$$\varepsilon(M, B \mid AM) = \varepsilon(m, i)\varepsilon(i, B \mid AM) + \varepsilon(m, P)\varepsilon(P, B \mid AM) + 1 < 1,$$
(27a)

$$\varepsilon(M, B \mid AM) = \varepsilon(\lambda, i)\varepsilon(i, B \mid AM) + \varepsilon(\lambda, P)\varepsilon(P, B \mid AM).$$
(27b)

The two expressions are not equally useful for judging orders of magnitude or for forecasting. We have much more reliable information about some of the elasticities than about others. In the case at hand, the knowledge that $\varepsilon(M, B \mid AM)$ is close to unity restricts the values of the elasticities in (27a) and facilitates forecasting the response of the money stock to changes in the base.

The responses of the money stock to S are given in equations (28):

$$\varepsilon(M, S \mid AM) = \varepsilon(\underset{+}{m}, i)\varepsilon(\underset{+}{i}, S \mid AM) + \varepsilon(\underset{-}{m}, P)\varepsilon(\underset{+}{P} S \mid AM),$$
(28a)

$$\varepsilon(M, S \mid AM) = \varepsilon(\underset{-}{\lambda}, i)\varepsilon(\underset{+}{i}, S \mid AM) + \varepsilon(\underset{+}{\lambda}, P)\varepsilon(\underset{+}{P}, S \mid AM).$$
(28b)

Offsetting components and small multiplier elasticities suggest that the effect of S on M, with B unchanged, is relatively small. Changes in S induce some substitution between direct ownership of securities and ownership of time deposits – intermediation and disintermediation – but, if deposit interest rates are not controlled, banks respond by changing interest rates paid on their liabilities and quantitative effects on money are small.

The response of the money and credit multipliers to interest rates depends on the response of the multipliers to the time deposit ratio, since the time deposit ratio is a main channel for effects of interest rates on the banks and the money stock. Interest rate ceilings lower t and reduce the responses of money and credit, mainly by reducing the size of the multipliers' elasticities. Differentiating (19) and expressing the result as an elasticity, we have:

$$\frac{\partial m}{\partial t} \cdot \frac{t}{m} = \varepsilon(m, t) = \frac{-(\bar{r} - b)t}{(\bar{r} - b)(1 + t) + k} < 0,$$

which falls in absolute value as t falls. The effect of t on the credit multiplier is positive; at a lower t the multiplier is smaller, and the elasticity with respect to t is smaller.

The difference between the elasticities of asset and monetary multiplier with respect to the time deposit ratio explains much of the difference in behavior between the money stock and bank credit–bank earning assets. Let E be the stock of earning assets, loans and securities, held by banks. The response of E can be represented, analogously to equations (27) and (28), from the banks' or the public's accounts:

$$\varepsilon(E, B \mid AM) = \varepsilon(a, i)\varepsilon(i, B \mid AM) + \varepsilon(a, P)\varepsilon(P, B \mid AM) + 1$$
$$= \varepsilon(\sigma, i)\varepsilon(i, B \mid AM) + \varepsilon(\sigma, P)\varepsilon(P, B \mid AM),$$

and correspondingly:

$$\varepsilon(E, S) = \varepsilon(a, i)\varepsilon(i, S \mid AM) + \varepsilon(a, P)\varepsilon(P, S \mid AM)$$
$$= \varepsilon(\sigma, i)\varepsilon(i, S \mid AM) + \varepsilon(\sigma, P)\varepsilon(P, S \mid AM).$$

More generally, the different response patterns of E and M reflect all the relevant multiplier elasticities. We can express this as follows. Let x refer to any event modifying financial allocations:

$$\varepsilon(E, x) - \varepsilon(M, x) = [\varepsilon(a, k) - \varepsilon(m, k)]\varepsilon(k, x) + [\varepsilon(a, t) - \varepsilon(m, t)]\varepsilon(t, x)$$
$$+ [\varepsilon(a, r) - \varepsilon(m, r)]\varepsilon(r, x)$$
$$+ [\varepsilon(a, b) - \varepsilon(m, b)]\varepsilon(b, x) + \varepsilon(a, n)\varepsilon(n, x).$$

The following patterns can be shown to hold:

$$\varepsilon(a, k) < \varepsilon(m, k) < 0; \qquad \varepsilon(a, t) > 0 > \varepsilon(m, t); \qquad \varepsilon(a, t) > |\varepsilon(m, t)|;$$

$$\varepsilon(a, r) < \varepsilon(m, r) < 0; \qquad \varepsilon(a, b) > \varepsilon(m, b) > 0.$$

The non-deposit liability ratio, n, which occurs in the asset multiplier plays no role in the monetary multiplier. All five components (k, t, r, b, n) produce a larger numerical response of the asset multiplier than of the monetary multiplier. The responses of E and M differ. Money and credit do not behave as two sides of a coin.

The responses of the money stock to B and S are shown in Figure 9.6. As before, increases in the base shift the MM line to the right and the CM line to the left, lowering i and raising P. The left-hand panel shows the effects on the demand and supply for money. The slope of λ depends on the interest elasticity of the demand for money, and the slope of mB depends on the interest elasticity of the money multiplier. The latter reflects the responses of time deposits, borrowing from the central bank and excess reserve holding of banks. The positions of mB and λ depend on P. An increase in the base moves mB to the left by an amount

$$[1 + \varepsilon(m, P) \cdot \varepsilon(P, B | AM)] \frac{\mathrm{d}B}{B} .$$

The new intersection at λ_1 and mB_1 occurs at the interest rate that clears the money and credit markets, shown at the intersection of MM_1 and CM_1. The movement from the initial equilibrium at λ_0, mB_0, to the new equilibrium at λ_1, mB_1, can be described using the responses summarized in equations (27a) and (27b). Similarly, the responses of mB and λ to a change in S are summarized by the elasticities in equations (28).

An open market operation, $\mathrm{d}B = -\mathrm{d}S$, has effects on i, P and M given in

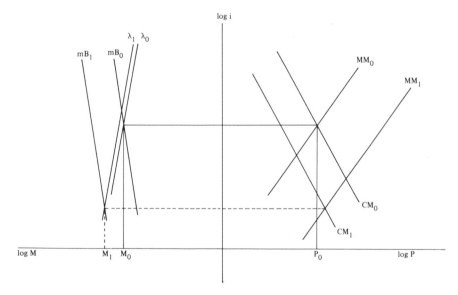

Figure 9.6

equation (29):

$$\frac{di}{i} = \left[\varepsilon(i, B \mid AM) - \varepsilon(i, S \mid AM) \frac{B}{S} \right] \frac{dB}{B},$$

$$\frac{dP}{P} = \left[\varepsilon(P, B \mid AM) - \varepsilon(P, S \mid AM) \frac{B}{S} \right] \frac{dB}{B},$$ (29)

$$\frac{dM}{M} = \left[\varepsilon(M, B \mid AM) - \varepsilon(M, S \mid AM) \frac{B}{S} \right] \frac{dB}{B}.$$

An implication of (29) is that the magnitude of the responses of i and P to changes in the base are not the same for a pure change in the base and an open market operation. When the base changes as part of an open market operation, the response of interest rates to S strengthens the effect on i of a pure change in the base. The effect on P is weaker, since $\varepsilon(P, S) > 0$. The effects of open market operations and base changes on the money stock are approximately the same, given the small value of $\varepsilon(M, S)$ and the weight B/S which is less than $\frac{1}{4}$ in the United States.

4. Interest targets, the "engine of inflation" and reverse causation

The monetary authorities in the United States and many other countries adopt interest rate control as a tactical procedure for implementing policy. Interest rate control requires the central bank to adjust the monetary base to offset changes in interest rates. In a formal sense the base replaces the interest rate as an endogenous variable. In the context of the IS–LM framework, interest rate targeting implies that financial shocks can be fully neutralized by passive adjustment of the money stock. This implication is invalid once we introduce a credit market and consider its interaction with the money market.

Let u be a shock positively affecting σ, and v a shock positively affecting λ. The responses of P and B to these shocks, under a policy of maintaining the interest rate at a given target level, are given in (30) and (31):

$$\varepsilon(P, u) = \frac{\varepsilon(\sigma, u)}{\varepsilon(CM, P) - \varepsilon(MM, P)} > 0,$$

$$\varepsilon(P, v) = \frac{-\varepsilon(\lambda, v)}{\varepsilon(CM, P) - \varepsilon(MM, P)} < 0;$$ (30)

$$\varepsilon(B, u) = \frac{-\varepsilon(\sigma, u) \cdot \varepsilon(MM, P)}{\varepsilon(CM, P) - \varepsilon(MM, P)} > 0,$$

$$\varepsilon(B, v) = \frac{\varepsilon(\lambda, v) \cdot \varepsilon(CM, P)}{\varepsilon(CM, P) - \varepsilon(MM\ P)} > 0.$$ (31)

Positive shocks to σ and λ have opposite effects on P; an increased demand for money reduces P while an increased demand for credit raises P. Under quite general conditions, interest rate targeting does not offset the effects of financial shocks.

Under interest rate control policies, positive shocks to σ and λ increase the stock of base money to offset the movement of interest rates. The response of the base to a unit credit market shock exceeds the response to a unit money market shock if $|\varepsilon(MM, P)| > \varepsilon(CM, P)$. This condition implies that the movements of the base under an interest target procedure are dominated by shifts in the demand for credit and not, as usually described by central bankers, by shifts in the demand for money. The usual conclusion reflects the IS–LM framework in which all financial shocks are analyzed as shocks to the demand for money. A particular example, discussed in Brunner and Meltzer (1966), concerns the interest pegging period. During this period Federal Reserve policy was described frequently as "an engine of inflation". Our analysis suggests that the IS–LM analysis, on which this conclusion was based, was seriously flawed.

4.1. Engine of inflation

During the years 1941–51 the Federal Reserve held the rate on Treasury bills fixed. The outstanding stock of government securities rose during the first four years of the period under the wartime policy of relying heavily on bond-financed deficits. Equation (30) implies that P should rise under these policies. Fisher and Lorie (1977, pp. 25–26) report that one index of P, the time-weighted rate of return on common stocks, rose at a compound annual rate of 51.5 percent in the four years ending December 1945. The base expanded and consumer prices rose at an annual rate of 5 percent, despite price controls during the period.[14] The interest control policy was properly labelled "an engine of inflation" for this period.

After the war, the situation changed. The interest control policy continued, but budget deficits declined, and there were budget surpluses in fiscal year 1947–49 and 1951. The surplus for fiscal 1948 was nearly 20 percent of federal government receipts and more than 24 percent of federal government outlays. Our analysis implies that the large surplus induced a decline in the monetary base under the interest targeting policy and a decline in asset prices. The time-weighted rate of return on common stocks fell to a compound annual rate of 5.7 percent for 1946–49. This is only 11 percent of the return earned under the wartime policies. Consumer prices remained unchanged on average from

---

[14]The annual rate of increase rose to 11 percent in the two years 1945–57 which include the removal of price controls in 1946.

1948 to 1950. The "engine of inflation" did not function. Instead, the decline in the monetary base contributed to the first postwar recession.

The experience under the interest rate control policy gives a clear message: once monetary policy is committed to an interest target, movements of money are dominated by the principal shocks affecting the credit market. During the period 1947–50 the shift from wartime budget deficits to relatively large surpluses was a major factor affecting the credit market. The shift from deficits to surpluses dominated the movement of the monetary base, the money stock and the prices of assets and output. The failure of the interest pegging policy to produce inflation after 1946–47 is largely the result of the evolution of fiscal policy.

4.2. Reverse causation

The relation between money and aggregate demand is often attributed to "reverse causation" – the effect of income on money. In the absence of a theory of money supply, analysis of reverse causation is limited to empirical studies, most recently so-called tests of "causality" using vector autoregression. Money supply theory offers an opportunity to go behind the frequently uninformative patterns of correlation to consider the mechanisms responsible for reverse causation.

If the base is controlled, the principal means by which output can affect money is by changing the multiplier. Cyclical changes in the shocks u and v produce corresponding changes in the interest rate. The resulting responses of the time-deposit ratio and the reserve ratio induce changes in the money (and asset) multipliers. The currency ratio is also affected by cyclical changes in the costs of holding and using currency and checkable deposits. In most periods, the movements of the multipliers induced by the changes in these ratios are too small to explain the observed positive correlation between money and output as the consequence of reverse causation.[15]

There are some apparent exceptions. One is the period 1931–33. During these years the failure of the Federal Reserve to serve as lender of last resort substantially changed the perceived costs of holding currency and bank deposits. A series of bank failures induced a flight to currency and a collapse of the money multiplier. The money stock fell, inducing a further decline in aggregate income and prices and additional flight to currency. This period provides evidence on the high cost of an interest target policy and the failure of the Federal Reserve to function as lender of last resort. It provides little

---

[15]Using Kalman filters to compute unanticipated changes, Meltzer (1985, 1986) finds little evidence of reverse causation in Britain, Canada, Germany, Japan and the United States under fixed or fluctuating exchange rates.

information about the determinants of the money stock under less extreme conditions.

The 1870s furnish a second example often used as evidence of reverse causation. Banking facilities expanded rapidly, lowering the cost of using and holding transaction accounts, thereby changing the money multiplier [see Friedman and Schwartz (1963)]. This experience does not fit the pattern described as reverse causation. Movements of the multiplier were not the result of movements of income. Common underlying forces simultaneously increased real income and the multiplier.

Substantial and persistent reverse causation occurs most often when central banks, under fixed exchange rates or interest rate control policies, supply base money or demand. A very elastic supply of loans by the central bank to banks or private groups at comparatively rigid interest rates is a related example. In the absence of such supply conditions governing the monetary base, reverse effects of output or income on money are negligible.

The dependence of reverse causation on institutional conditions offers an opportunity to assess the alternative explanations of the correlation between money and income. If the correlation is the result of reverse causation, the correlation should vanish in some periods and reappear in others. The money–income correlation is not closely or reliably associated with changes in institutional arrangements. It persists under a wide variety of arrangements. This suggests that the correlation is dominated by the effect of money on income.

5. Monetary variability and uncertainty

In 1979 the Federal Reserve announced that greater emphasis would be given to monetary aggregates in the conduct of monetary policy. Market interest rates were permitted to increase to levels not experienced for a century. Control procedures were changed to give increased emphasis to member bank borrowing. Short-term interest rates were allowed to vary over a wider range.

The Federal Reserve did not adopt procedures capable of achieving reliable control of the monetary base. Two features of the institutional arrangements were particularly troublesome. Banks' required reserves were computed based on deposits held two weeks earlier (known as lagged reserve accounting), and the discount rate paid by banks was kept substantially below prevailing market interest rates. Lagged reserve accounting fixed the amount of reserves banks in the aggregate were required to hold. When the Federal Reserve attempted to reduce money growth, reserves declined relative to the amount banks were required to hold to meet reserve requirements. Banks borrowed from the Federal Reserve, at a subsidized rate, thereby increasing money. The Federal Reserve had the options of refusing to supply the additional borrowing or raising the cost of borrowing, but they did not use these options.

One result of this flawed procedure for controlling money was an increase in the variability of money growth and interest rates. Mascaro and Meltzer (1983, p. 494) show that measures of the variability of money growth and short-term interest rates are three times greater when the nine quarters following the change in procedure are compared to the nine quarters preceding the change. The variability of interest rates on long-term debt increased also.

The effects of increased variability of money on interest rates and asset prices can be analyzed if we let the public's demand for money and short-term securities increase with variability and uncertainty. Our hypothesis is that variability and uncertainty reduce the demand for long-term capital, thereby increasing demand for other portfolio assets. With the change to include V, the variability of unanticipated changes in the stock of money, the money and credit market equilibrium conditions are:

$$m(\underset{+}{i} \ldots)B = \lambda(\underset{-}{i}, \underset{+}{P}, \underset{+}{V}, \ldots),$$

$$a(\underset{+}{i} \ldots)B = \sigma(\underset{+}{i}, \underset{+}{P}, \underset{-}{V}, \ldots).$$

As before, the money market proximately determines the asset price level, and the credit-market equation proximately determines the interest rate on short-term loans and securities. The responses of interest rates and asset prices to V are:

$$\varepsilon(i, V) = -\frac{\varepsilon(\lambda, V)\varepsilon(CM, P) - \varepsilon(\sigma, V)\varepsilon(MM, P)}{\Delta} > 0,$$

$$\varepsilon(P, V) = \frac{\varepsilon(\lambda, V)\varepsilon(CM, i) - \varepsilon(\sigma, V)\varepsilon(MM, i)}{\Delta} < 0.$$

Market interest rates increase with variability and uncertainty, and the asset price level falls.

The analysis again suggests the importance of monetary control procedures and other institutional arrangements. By increasing the variability of shocks and, thus, the demand for money and securities, Federal Reserve procedures raised interest rates, lowered asset prices, and imposed an excess burden on the economy during the period. The relatively high level of interest and the lengthy recession brought an end to the attempt to control money growth in the fall of 1982.

6. Monetary control

An ancient theme in monetary economics concerns the inability of the central bank to control money when there are close substitutes for the particular measure of money the central bank chooses to control. This theme reappeared with heightened emphasis following the deregulation of financial markets. A popular argument is that substitution between types of financial assets weakens monetary control.

James Johannes and Robert Rasche have made semi-annual forecasts of the money multiplier based on the approach discussed in this chapter. These forecasts can be combined with any given path of the monetary base, resulting from the decisions of the central bank, to provide forecasts of the money stock and its rate of growth. Their book [Johannes and Rasche (1987)] summarizes their forecasts and their procedures.

Johannes and Rasche separate the determinants of the money stock into a multiplier and the monetary base, $M = mB$. They interpret the multiplier as a solution reflecting the interaction of asset markets, and they develop an expression for the money multiplier that differs from equation (19) principally by distinguishing between large and small time deposits. Johannes and Rasche estimate a time-series model for each of the components of the money multiplier separately and obtain a forecast of each component. Combining the separate forecasts, using an equation like (19), yields a forecast of the money multiplier. Each month or quarter forecasts are extended and revised using new information.

Monthly forecast errors have been computed for the entire sample, nearly seven years, and for several subperiods. Forecast errors are unbiased and serially uncorrelated. There is no evidence that forecast errors increased during the recent period of financial deregulation and rapid innovation in financial market instruments and practices.[16]

Table 9.1 shows the forecast errors for forecasts made beyond the sample period used in the estimation. Forecasts were made for periods up to twelve months ahead.

Table 9.1
Multiplier forecast errors and standard deviations

Number of observations	Forecast period	Mean absolute percentage error	Standard deviation of percentage error
82	one month	0.0405	0.745
74	three-month moving average (overlapping)	0.0300	0.439
62	six-month moving average (overlapping)	0.0335	0.266
43	twelve-month moving average (overlapping)	0.0453	0.145

[16]An exception is the period during spring 1980 when President Carter imposed credit controls. After the period ended, forecast error variances returned to their previous range.

The mean absolute percentage forecast error is negligible for periods up to twelve months ahead. The standard deviation declines as the period lengthens. These data suggest that effective monetary control, within ±1 percent of the announced target, is feasible and the case for monetary control much stronger than the case against.[17] One reason is that reported results include periods of substantial variability in money and major changes in financial arrangements. The relatively small forecast errors and variability of errors suggest that even under conditions of substantial innovation, the multiplier is predictable and the money stock controllable if the central bank adopts procedures to control the monetary base.

7. Conclusion

Analysis of the money supply process should provide a framework to guide systematic examination of the implications of alternative institutional arrangements and policy decisions. This chapter presents a framework containing many features of modern financial systems. The system can be extended to include many additional features and a wide variety of financial arrangements.

The framework moves beyond standard analyses like IS–LM where bonds and capital are perfect substitutes and where there is only a single interest rate. In such models, control of the single rate permits the central bank to control intertemporal substitution by setting the interest rate at the appropriate level. When there is more than one asset price or interest rate, this is not so. Changes in the stocks of money and debt, to finance the government or to carry out open market operations set off substitution between money, bonds and capital even if a market rate of interest is controlled.

Money supply theory, as presented here, analyzes intermediation and money creation and reduction when money, bonds and capital are less than perfect substitutes in portfolios. The analysis shows the central role of the credit market and its interaction with the money market. A number of applications bring out the differences between the extended model and standard models such as IS–LM. By moving beyond IS–LM, the analysis changes, in a major way, propositions concerning the transmission of monetary impulses and the

---

[17]Lindsey et al. (1984) objected to the findings presented by Johannes and Rasche. They emphasize the possible occurrence of a bias in the variance estimation due to the endogeneity of the monetary base produced by an interest target policy. The argument is flawed, however. First, the argument is, at best, suggestive of possible bias. Possibility does not establish relevance. Second, Johannes and Rasche (1987) demonstrate that an endogenous base does not necessarily imply an underestimate of the error variance. Third, the illustrative cases offered by Lindsay et al. involve essentially simultaneous adjustments of multiplier and base in response to various shocks. The estimation techniques based on univariate Arima processes eliminate simultaneous, mutual adjustments.

interpretation of shocks to the demand for money. Furthermore, the framework can be exploited to analyze a wide range of institutional issues encountered in policy discussions. Some examples are given in the chapter.

The chapter analyzes the financial markets on the assumption of given income and price level and given anticipations. Analysis is restricted to a closed economy. These limitations facilitate the discussion of monetary control, the variability of money growth, interest rate targets and other issues used to illustrate the analysis. These limitations can be removed. Interaction with the output market [Brunner and Meltzer (1976)] and the rest of the world [Brunner (1973), Brunner and Meltzer (1974)] does not modify the general emphasis of this chapter.

References

Barro, R.J. (1974) 'Are government bonds net wealth?' *Journal of Political Economy*, 82: 1095–1117.

Brunner, K. (1971) 'A survey of selected issues in monetary theory', *Schweizerische Zeitschrift fur Volkswirtschaft und Statistik*, 107: 2–146.

Brunner, K. (1973) 'A diagrammatic exposition of the money supply process', *Schweizerische Zeitschrift fur Volkswirtschaft und Statistik*, 109: 481–533.

Brunner, K. (1976a) 'Inflation, money and the role of fiscal arrangements: An analytic framework for the inflation problem', in: M. Monti, ed., *The new inflation and monetary policy*. London: Macmillan, pp. 25–89.

Brunner, K. (1976b) 'The money supply process in open economies with interdependent securities markets: The case of imperfect substitutability', in: M. Fratianni and K. Tavernier, eds., *Bank credit, money and inflation in open economies*, *Kredit und Kapital*, 3: 19–76.

Brunner, K. and A.H. Meltzer (1964) *The Federal Reserve's attachment to the free reserve concept*, Subcommittee on Domestic Finance of the House Committee on Banking and Currency, 88th Congress, 2nd Session.

Brunner, K. and A.H. Meltzer (1966) 'A credit market theory of the money supply and an explanation of two puzzles in U.S. monetary policy', in: T. Bagiotti, ed., *Essays in honour of Marco Fanno*, Vol. II. Padua, pp. 151–176.

Brunner, K. and A.H. Meltzer (1968) 'Liquidity traps for money, bank credit and interest rates', *Journal of Political Economy*, 76: 1–37.

Brunner, K. and A.H. Meltzer (1972) 'A monetarist framework for aggregative analysis', in: K. Brunner, ed., *Proceedings of the First Konstanzer Seminar on Monetary Theory and Monetary Policy*, *Kredit und Kapital*, 1: 31–88.

Brunner, K. and A.H. Meltzer (1974) 'Monetary and fiscal policy in open, interdependent economies with fixed exchange rates', in: E. Claassen and P. Salin, eds., *Recent issues in international monetary economics*. Amsterdam: North-Holland.

Brunner, K. and A.H. Meltzer (1976) 'An aggregative theory for a closed economy', in: J.L. Stein, ed., *Monetarism*. Amsterdam: North-Holland, pp. 69–103.

Cagan, P. (1958) 'The demand for currency relative to the total money supply', *Journal of Political Economy*, 66: 303–328.

Cukierman, A. and A.H. Meltzer (1989) 'A political theory of government debt, and deficits in a neo-ricardian framework', *American Economic Review*, 79: 713–732.

Fisher, L. and J. Lorie (1977) *A half century of returns on stocks and bonds*, Chicago: Graduate School of Business.

Fratianni, M. (1976) 'Domestic bank credit, money and the open economy', in: M. Fratianni and

K. Tavernier, eds., *Bank credit, money and inflation in open economies*, Kredit und Kapital, 3: 77–142.

Friedman, B.M. (1977) 'Financial flow variables and the short-run determination of long-term interest rates', *Journal of Political Economy*, 85: 661–689.

Friedman, B.M. (1978) 'Crowding out or crowding in? Economic consequences of financing government deficits', *Brookings Papers on Economic Activity*, 3: 593–641.

Friedman M. and A.J. Schwartz (1963) *A monetary history of the United States, 1867–1960*. Princeton: Princeton University Press for the National Bureau of Economic Research.

Gurley, J. and E. Shaw (1960) *Money in a theory of finance*. Washington: Brookings Institution.

Heremans, D., A. Sommariva and A. Verheirstraeten (1976) 'A money and bank credit model for Belgium', in: M. Fratianni and K. Tavernier, eds., *Bank credit, money and inflation in open economies*, Kredit und Kapital, 3: 155–208.

Hess, A.C. (1971) 'An explanation of short-run fluctuations in the ratio of currency to demand deposits', *Journal of money, Credit and Banking*, 3: 666–679.

Johannes, J. and R. Rasche (1987) *Controlling the growth of monetary aggregates*. Kluwer-Nijhoff.

Kaldor, N. (1982) *The scourge of monetarism*. Oxford.

Korteweg, P. and P. van Loo (1977) *The market for money and the market for credit*. Leiden: Martinus Nijhoff.

Lindsey, D.E., H.T. Farr, G.P. Gillum, K.J. Kopecky and R.D. Porter (1984) 'Short-run monetary control: Evidence under a non-borrowed reserve operating procedure', *Journal of Monetary Economics*, 13: 87–111.

Mascaro, A. and A.H. Meltzer (1983) 'Long- and short-term interest rates in a risky world', *Journal of Monetary Economics*, 12: 485–518.

Meigs, A.J. (1962) *Free reserves and the money supply*. Chicago: University of Chicago Press.

Meltzer, A.H. (1985) 'Variability of prices, output and money under fixed and fluctuating exchange rates: An empirical study of monetary regimes in Japan and the United States', *Bank of Japan, Monetary and Economic Studies*, 3: 1–46.

Meltzer, A.H. (1986) 'Size, persistence and interrelation of nominal and real shocks: Some evidence from four countries', *Journal of Monetary Economics*, 17: 161–194.

Neumann, M.J.M. (1974) ' A theoretical and empirical analysis of the German money supply process, 1958–1972', *Diskussionsbeitrage 6*. Berlin.

Pesek, B. and Saving, T. (1967) *Money, wealth and economic theory*. New York: Macmillan.

Shaw, E.S. (1950) *Money, income and monetary policy*. Chicago: R.D. Irwin.

Suzuki, Y. (1980) *Money and banking in contemporary Japan*. New Haven: Yale.

Thornton, H. (1965) *An enquiry into the nature and effects of the paper credit of Great Britain (1802)*. New York: Kelley.

Tobin, J. (1963) 'Commercial Banks as Creators of Money', in: G. Horwich, ed., *Banking and monetary studies*. Homewood: Irwin, pp. 408–419.

Tobin, J. and W. Buiter (1976) 'Long-run effects of fiscal and monetary policy on aggregate demand,' in: J. Stein, ed., *Monetarism*. Amsterdam: North-Holland, pp. 273–309.

Viner, J. (1965) *Studies in the theory of international trade (1937)*. New York: Kelley.

Chapter 10

THE SUPPLY OF MONEY AND THE CONTROL OF NOMINAL INCOME

LUCAS PAPADEMOS

Bank of Greece and University of Athens

FRANCO MODIGLIANI

Massachusetts Institute of Technology

Contents

Handbook of Monetary Economics, Volume I, Edited by B.M. Friedman and F.H. Hahn
© Elsevier Science Publishers B.V., 1990

1. Introduction

This chapter reviews the nature of the relation between the supply of money and nominal income and its implications for the conduct of monetary policy. This relation, which is fundamental for monetary analysis and policy, has a number of dimensions. On the assumption that money is a quantity which can be uniquely defined, measured and effectively managed by the monetary authorities, the central question is how changes in the exogenously determined stock of money affect nominal income and its components, aggregate real output and the price level. The answer to this question relates to the so-called "monetary transmission mechanism" which defines the channels and mechanisms through which money may influence real and nominal magnitudes. These channels are described by a variety of paradigms including simple models, such as the equation of exchange or the simple quantity theory, as well as more complex and sophisticated models which take into account the effects of money on real income and prices through the rates of return on assets, wealth, capital accumulation, price and wage setting, and expectations. The theoretical models, which describe the monetary transmission mechanism, and the empirical models, which attempt to capture the quantitative significance and dynamic properties of the analytical paradigms, are at the core of traditional monetary analysis.

However, the relation of the quantity of money to nominal income has two additional dimensions whose importance has become progressively apparent in recent years as a result of fundamental changes and innovations in financial markets, and which constitute the principal concern of this chapter. First, in economies characterized by a variety of financial intermediaries and a large spectrum of financial assets, the identification of "money", the mechanism of money creation and the ability of the central bank to control the supply of money become important issues for policy. Second, in such economies a fundamental question for monetary policy emerges, namely whether the monetary authorities should aim at controlling nominal income by controlling the supply of money, as conventionally defined, or whether they may achieve the final policy targets more effectively via the control of the stocks of other financial assets or by determining the levels of interest rates or exchange rates of domestic money for foreign moneys. If the latter strategies are pursued, the stock of money is determined endogenously by the target value of nominal income and the values of other variables, including those controlled by the central bank. This chapter addresses these issues and examines how the mechanism of money creation and alternative methods of monetary control affect the nature and stability of the relationship between the money supply and nominal income and the controllability of the latter by monetary policy.

A general conclusion which emerges from the analysis is that the most efficient means of monetary control of nominal income depends on behavioral and institutional characteristics of the economy as well as upon the stochastic nature of the environment. Control of nominal income via the control of the supply of money is not always the most effective means of conducting policy. Theoretical analysis can help to point out the basic conditions and factors (behavioral, institutional, stochastic) which determine the relative efficiency of alternative forms of monetary control. The empirical evidence and the practice of policy in various countries confirm the desirability of implementing policy flexibly without adherence to a single approach which focuses exclusively on money supply control to achieve the final policy objectives.

The chapter is organized as follows. In Section 2 we present a review of four basic stochastic models relating the quantity of money to nominal income. These include classical, Keynesian and monetarist models, and a representative post-Keynesian aggregate demand and supply paradigm incorporating the effects of expectations and price dynamics. For each of these models we derive the implied stochastic "velocity" relations between nominal income and the quantity of money. We then examine the role and implications of alternative hypotheses on market behavior and the determinants of expectations for the nature and dynamics of the money–income relation and for the effects of disturbances on nominal income.

Section 3 focuses on the money supply mechanism, recognizing that in a modern financial system, the central bank cannot control the money supply directly but only indirectly by influencing the behavior of financial intermediation (notably banks). We first review the money supply mechanism when financial intermediaries operate under conditions which imply the existence of a simple deterministic "multiplier" relation between the supply of money and the monetary base, and other variables such as reserve requirements which are directly controllable by the central bank. Under such conditions the money stock, although "endogenously" determined by the banking system, is effectively controllable by the central bank. Traditional models of bank asset management are then presented, followed by models of liability management and general equilibrium models of the banking firm. The implications of these models for the creation and control of the money supply are examined, with special emphasis on the effects of deregulation and financial innovations.

In Section 4 we first present macroeconomic models of nominal income determination which incorporate financial intermediaries and specify in some detail the determinants of equilibrium in the markets for bank and non-bank credit. Implicit in one of the models are characteristic elements of the economy's tax structure which influence the demand for credit by corporate firms. We then examine the feasibility and effectiveness of monetary control of nominal income when the monetary authorities employ as intermediate targets, or policy indicators, financial aggregates other than the conventionally defined stock of money. It is shown that real and nominal income can be controlled through alternative monetary and credit aggregates other than $M1$ and that, when the central bank controls a broad monetary or bank credit aggregate, the monetary mechanism involves a different adjustment process and it is best understood by focusing on the interaction of the credit and goods markets. It is demonstrated that, under conditions of uncertainty, the relative effectiveness of alternative monetary and credit aggregates in stabilizing nominal income depends upon the origin and relative magnitude of shocks, the economy's financial structure, behavioral and market characteristics and, in the case of certain disturbances, on an assessment of the welfare costs associated with output and price instability.

The final section summarizes the main theoretical and policy implications of the paper and outlines a number of related topics which deserve further analysis.

2. Simple models of money and nominal income, and the role of monetary policy

2.1. Basic hypotheses and implications

In this section we review a number of basic theories concerning the relationship between the supply of money and nominal income. We then examine the implications of these theories for the nature of the income velocity of money and the conduct of monetary policy. In all models considered in this section, it is assumed the quantity of money is well defined and that it can be directly controlled by the monetary authority up to a random component. The notion of money incorporated in these theories is explicitly or implicitly taken to be the "narrow" one. Money is the financial asset primarily used for transactions purposes, and it has a rate or return which is exogenously fixed in *nominal* terms (usually, though not necessarily, set equal to zero). The role of the banking system in determining the stock of money is either explicitly or implicitly ignored. Banks may create "inside" money but they operate according to the simple, mechanistic rules discussed in Subsection 3.2 below; consequently, the total quantity of money created is not influenced by variations in interest rates or income and it is controllable by the central bank, except for unanticipated shocks affecting the base or the money-base multiplier.

Other simplifying assumptions common to all theories reviewed below are the following: first, all financial and real assets other than money are viewed as perfect (or very close) substitutes so that their real rates of return are equal or differ by constant spreads which are invariant to changes in the quantity of money, income or the average rate of interest. The real interest rate may or may not be influenced by changes in the stock of money, depending upon certain characteristics of market behavior. Second, the theories abstract from the effects of wealth and capital accumulation on the demand for and the supply of the final goods produced and of financial assets. A justification is that the period of analysis is sufficiently short so that the effects of changes in the real value of wealth and changes in the stock of capital can be ignored as a first approximation. One should, however, be aware of the limitations of this approximation, since the *value* of wealth may change quickly as a result of capital gains or losses. Third, for simplicity and in order to focus on the role of monetary policy, the analysis abstracts from the effects of fiscal variables and, within the relatively short period considered, it also ignores the implications of the government budget constraint for the dynamic behavior of the system.

The fundamental differences between the basic theories of nominal income and money supply relate instead to alternative hypotheses concerning three other features of market behavior: first, the mechanism of market clearing in the goods and labor markets and, in particular, the degree of wage and price flexibility in the presence of imbalances in these "real" markets; second, the role of expectations, especially about inflation, in market behavior and differences in hypotheses concerning the determinants of such expectations; and third, the magnitude of the effects of the rate of return on the demands for money and aggregate output. These three sources of differences have important implications for the relationship of nominal income to the money stock. In particular, they determine (i) the extent to which changes in the money supply affect nominal income by affecting primarily the price level or real aggregate output which, in turn, has implications also for the magnitude of the effect, (ii) the dynamic response of nominal income to past and/or anticipated future behavior of money supply, and (iii) the effects on nominal output of alternative real and financial disturbances, for a given money supply. Moreover, they are of critical importance for assessing the desirability, feasibility and effectiveness of stabilization policy and the relative effectiveness of alternative instruments of monetary policy.

We focus on four theories of nominal income, starting with the simplest one, the classical quantity theory, and concluding with what may be referred to as a general contemporary formulation of a macroeconomic model incorporating a specification of the demand for and supply of aggregate output and alternative hypotheses on expectations and the dynamics of price adjustment. The models are summarized in Table 10.1. For each model, we first present the structural–behavioral relations and the specific assumptions made, and then show the implied relationship between nominal income, or its two components (real output and the price level), the money supply and other exogenous deterministic or stochastic variables.

Table 10.1
Simple stochastic models of nominal income

1. *The classical model and the quantity theory*
   (a) *The Fisherian approach*

$$p + y = m + v \,, \tag{1}$$

$$y = \bar{y} + \varepsilon_y \,, \qquad v = \bar{v} + \varepsilon_v \,. \tag{2}$$

$$p = m + \bar{v} - \bar{y} + \varepsilon_p \,, \qquad \varepsilon_p = \varepsilon_v - \varepsilon_y \,. \tag{I}$$

   (b) *The Cambridge approach*

$$m^{\mathrm{d}} = p + k + y \,, \qquad k = \bar{k} + \varepsilon_k \,, \tag{3}$$

$$m^{\mathrm{s}} = m \,, \tag{4}$$

$$m^{\mathrm{d}} = m^{\mathrm{s}} \,, \tag{5}$$

$$y = \bar{y} + \varepsilon_y \,. \tag{6}$$

$$p = m - \bar{k} - \bar{y} + \varepsilon_p \,, \qquad \varepsilon_p = -\varepsilon_k - \varepsilon_y \,. \tag{I'}$$

2. *Liquidity preference with price flexibility*

$$m^{\mathrm{d}} = p + \bar{k} + ki + by + u_{\mathrm{md}} \,, \qquad \bar{k} > 0, k \le 0, b > 0 \,, \tag{7}$$

$$m^{\mathrm{s}} = m + u_{\mathrm{ms}} \,, \tag{8}$$

$$m^{\mathrm{d}} = m^{\mathrm{s}} \,, \tag{9}$$

$$i = r + \hat{\pi} \,, \qquad \hat{\pi} = \hat{p}_{+1} - p \,, \tag{10}$$

$$y = \bar{y} + \varepsilon_y \,, \qquad r = \bar{r} + \varepsilon_r \,, \tag{11}$$

$$p + k(\hat{p}_{+1} - p) = m + \bar{v}(\bar{r}, \bar{y}) - \bar{y} + \varepsilon_p \,, \tag{II}$$

$$\bar{v}(\bar{r}, \bar{y}) = -\bar{k} - k\bar{r} + (1 - b)\bar{y} \,, \qquad \varepsilon_p = -u_{\mathrm{m}} - k\varepsilon_r - b\varepsilon_y, u_{\mathrm{m}} = u_{\mathrm{md}} - u_{\mathrm{ms}} \,.$$

3. *The Keynesian aggregate demand model with price rigidity*

$$m = p + \bar{k} + ki + by + u_{\mathrm{m}} \,, \qquad \bar{k} > 0, k \le 0, b > 0 \,, \tag{12}$$

$$y^{\mathrm{d}} = \bar{y} + c(y - \bar{y}) + d(r - \bar{r}) + u_{\mathrm{d}} \,, \qquad 0 < c < 1, d < 0 \,, \tag{13}$$

$$i = r + \hat{\pi} \,, \qquad \hat{\pi} = \hat{p}_{+1} - p \,, \tag{14}$$

$$p = \bar{p} \,, \qquad \hat{\pi} = 0 \,, \qquad y = y^{\mathrm{d}} + u_{\mathrm{s}} \,. \tag{15}$$

$$y = \bar{y} + \mu(m - \bar{p}) + \mu(\bar{v} - \bar{y}) + \varepsilon_{\mathrm{d}} = \bar{y} + \mu(m - \bar{m}) + \varepsilon_{\mathrm{d}} \,, \tag{III}$$

$$\mu = a(ab + k)^{-1} > 0 \,, \qquad a = d(1 - c)^{-1} < 0 \,,$$

$$\bar{v} = -\bar{k} - k\bar{r} + (1 - b)\bar{y} \,, \qquad \bar{m} = \bar{p} + \bar{y} - \bar{v} \,,$$

$$\varepsilon_{\mathrm{d}} = \mu(ku_y/a - u_{\mathrm{m}}) \,, \qquad u_y = u_{\mathrm{d}} + u_{\mathrm{s}} \,, \qquad u_{\mathrm{m}} = u_{\mathrm{md}} - u_{\mathrm{ms}} \,.$$

Table 1 (cont.)

4. *Aggregate demand, supply, and expectations*

IS: $y^d = \bar{y} + c(y - \bar{y}) + d(r - \bar{r}) + u_d$, $\quad 0 < c < 1, d < 0$, $\qquad$ (16)

LM: $m = p + \bar{k} + ki + by + u_m$, $\quad \bar{k} > 0, k \leq 0, b > 0$, $\qquad$ (17)

F: $i = r + \hat{\pi}$, $\quad \hat{\pi} = \hat{p}_{+1} - p$, $\qquad$ (18)

PC: $(p - p_{-1}) = \alpha(y - \bar{y}) + (\hat{p} - p_{-1}) + u_p$, $\quad \alpha > 0$, $\qquad$ (19)

AS: $y - \bar{y} = \alpha^{-1}(p - \hat{p}) + \varepsilon_s$, $\quad \varepsilon_s = -u_p/\alpha$. $\qquad$ (19')

EX: Adaptive: $\hat{\pi} - \hat{\pi}_{-1} = \gamma(\pi_{-1} - \hat{\pi}_{-1})$, $\quad 0 < \gamma \leq 1$, $\qquad$ (20)

$\qquad$ Rational: $\hat{\pi} = E(\pi \mid I)$. $\qquad$ (21)

$p = \beta[\alpha\mu(m + \bar{v} - \bar{y}) + \hat{p} - \alpha\mu k\hat{p}_{+1} + \alpha(\varepsilon_d - \varepsilon_s)]$, $\qquad$ (IV)

$y = \bar{y} + \beta\mu[(m + \bar{v} - \bar{y}) - \hat{p} - k(\hat{p}_{+1} - \hat{p})] + \beta\varepsilon_d + (1 - \beta)\varepsilon_s$,

$\beta = [1 + \alpha\mu(1 - k)]^{-1}$, $\quad 0 \leq \beta \leq 1$; $\qquad \mu = a(ab + k)^{-1} > 0$, $\qquad a = d(1 - c)^{-1} < 0$,

$\varepsilon_d = \mu(ku_d/d - u_m)$.

(real output and the price level), the money supply and other exogenous deterministic or stochastic variables.

2.2. The classical equilibrium model and the quantity theory of money

The role of money in classical economics is a simple one, and so is the effect of a change in the quantity of money on aggregate nominal income. According to classical theory all markets for goods, including the market for labour services, clear continuously, with relative prices adjusting flexibly to ensure the attainment of equilibrium. Resources are fully utilized and thus aggregate employment and output are always at the "full-employment" or "natural" levels determined by tastes, productive technology and endowments, except for transitory deviations due to real disturbances.

In such an economy, money serves as the numeraire in terms of which the prices of all other commodities are expressed; and it also serves to facilitate the exchange of goods (medium of exchange), but it does not influence the determination of relative prices, real interest rates, the equilibrium quantities of commodities, and thus aggregate real income. Money is "neutral", a "veil" with no consequences for real economic magnitudes; furthermore, its role as a store of value is perceived as limited under the classical assumptions of perfect information and negligible transaction costs.

The relation of nominal income to the quantity of money in the classical equilibrium model is established in two alternative, though fundamentally equivalent, ways. The first approach, associated with Fisher (1911), is based on the equation of exchange, $MV_T = P_T T$, which relates the quantity of money in circulation M to the volume of transactions T in a given period and the price level of the articles traded, P_T. The proportionality factor V_T is the "transactions velocity of circulation", which measures the average number of times a unit of money is employed in performing transactions during that period. A variant of this identity relates the quantity of money to nominal income: $MV = PY$, where P is the price level, Y is the level of real income, assumed proportional to P_T and T, respectively, and V is the "income velocity of circulation". Equation (1) in Table 10.1 restates this identity in logarithms, where a lower-case symbol denotes the logarithm of the corresponding upper-case variable.

The simple quantity theory of money follows from this identity and two propositions concerning the determinants of real income and velocity. The first proposition, implied by the classical view of market equilibrium outlined above, is that money is "neutral" and thus it does not affect aggregate real income ($dy/dm = 0$). The second proposition states that velocity is fundamentally determined by institutional and technological factors – it is a real variable and like other real variables it is independent of the quantity of money ($dv/dm = 0$). Consequently, in any time period both y and v are determined by non-monetary factors, deterministic as well as random, as shown by equation (2). Note that $\bar{y}$ is the equilibrium, "full-employment" or "natural" level of real income, while the deterministic component of velocity $\bar{v}$ is assumed to reflect characteristics of the financial system (such as the degree of synchronization of receipts and expenditures, the frequency of receipts and disbursements, etc.) which change very slowly over time, and in any event are not a function of m. These two propositions embodied in (2) and identity (1) imply the simplest form of the quantity theory: the price level is proportional to the quantity of money, or, equivalently, the price level has a unit elasticity with respect to the stock of money as shown by equation (I).

The alternative approach to the quantity theory, associated with the Cambridge economists Marshall (1923) and Pigou (1917) but with a longer tradition going back to Locke, Cantillon and Adam Smith,[1] emphasizes the role and

[1]See J.M. Keynes (1930), *A Treatise on Money*, vol. 1, p. 229. Keynes' own "real-balance" quantity equation employed in his *Tract on Monetary Reform* and in his *Treatise* is descended from the approach of the Cambridge school.

importance of the demand for money in determining the effect of the supply of money on the price level. The demand for money balances is assumed to be proportional to aggregate nominal income, $M^d = KPY$. This simple formulation of money demand is given by (3) in Table 10.1 expressed in logarithms and also allowing for the influence of a disturbance (ε_k) affecting the proportion of income held in the form of money. Assuming that the supply of money is exogenously fixed as shown by (4), equilibrium in the money market (5) under the classical hypothesis (6) that aggregate real income is at the equilibrium level except for the effects of real shocks, requires that aggregate money demand adjusts through the price level to match the existing supply of money according to (I'). Comparison of this alternative statement of the quantity theory with the Fisherian equation (I) shows the simple relationships between the deterministic and stochastic components of velocity and the Cambridge k: $\bar{v} = -\bar{k}$ (i.e. the velocity is the reciprocal of K) and $\varepsilon_v = -\varepsilon_k$.

The Cambridge formulation of the quantity theory provides a more satisfactory description of monetary equilibrium within the classical model by focusing on the public's demand for money, especially the demand for *real* money balances, as the key factor determining the equilibrium price level consistent with a given quantity of money. Nevertheless, the simple assumptions made about the nature of money demand, in particular the assumed insensitivity to the interest rate and the unit elasticity with respect to real income, together with the acceptance of the classical notion of market equilibrium in the goods markets imply a price level–money relation which, from a practical and policy point of view, is indistinguishable from the Fisherian velocity relation.

2.3. Keynesian theories: Systematic variations in the income velocity of money

Two propositions in Keynes' *General Theory* (1936) have fundamental implications for the role of money in the economy and for the role of monetary policy in controlling nominal income: the first concerns the determinants of money demand and the second the process of wage adjustment and equilibrium in the labor market. "Liquidity preference", the existence of a systematic effect of (nominal) interest rates on money demand, and "wage rigidity", the apparent failure of wages to adjust downward promptly and sufficiently in the presence of unemployment so as to achieve full employment, imply that a change in the quantity of money will, in general, lead to a change in both real and nominal output, and that the magnitudes of the real and nominal effects of money depend upon the interest sensitivity of money demand and the degree of wage and price rigidity.

The usual textbook exposition of the effects of money on income under the

Keynesian assumptions focuses on the case of absolute price rigidity and examines how, in this case, the impact effect of monetary policy on real output depends on the interest elasticity of money demand. It is instructive, however, to examine first the implications of the Keynesian hypothesis of liquidity preference for the money–income relationship under the classical assumption of wage and price flexibility. This will highlight the important implications of that hypothesis – whose quantitative significance is well supported by the empirical evidence – for the dynamic behavior of the price level and relate it to certain monetarist theories of the fifties and sixties and to propositions associated with the neoclassical or "rational expectations" school of the seventies.

2.3.1. Liquidity preference, price flexibility, and expectations

In the *General Theory*, Keynes (1936) discusses in detail various motives for holding money and the reasons that money balances held for "precautionary" and "speculative" purposes are responsive to variations in interest rates. The influence of interest rates on money demand had been examined earlier by Keynes in his *Treatise on Money* (1930) and also by Hicks (1935) in an influential article.[2] In discussing the nature of the interest rate effect, Keynes (1936) emphasizes the role of *uncertainty* about the future market value of alternative assets and of *expectations* about the "maintenable" or "normal" yield of such assets compared to the prevailing interest rate. Hicks (1935) stresses that the theory of money demand should be developed within a framework analogous to that of traditional value theory, i.e. that money demand is the outcome of a problem of choice among alternative assets subject to a balance sheet (wealth) constraint and, consequently, it is influenced mainly by anticipations of yields and risks as well as by transaction costs. The ideas of Keynes and Hicks on the nature and determinants of "liquidity preference" have been developed extensively in numerous studies employing either a portfolio, wealth framework or pursuing a transactions or inventory-theoretic approach.[3] These studies provide rigorous theoretical arguments in support of the hypothesized interest rate effect on money demand.

A stylized specification of the demand for money, consistent with the above

---

[2]Marshall and other Cambridge economists, in discussing the determinants of desired money balances, the proportionality factor k, had mentioned the possible influence of the rate of return on alternative assets but they did not stress its importance or explore its implications. See, for example, Marshall (1923, ch. 4), and statements quoted by Keynes (1930, p. 230).

[3]The most influential contributions are those of Friedman (1956), Tobin (1956, 1958), Allais (1947) and Baumol (1952). See Johnson (1962), Modigliani (1968) and Goldfeld and Sichel (Chapter 8 in this Handbook) for more detailed descriptions of theories of the demand for money. Friedman emphasizes the role of a broad measure of wealth as the key determinant of money demand and presents a "restatement" of the quantity theory.

analyses and adequate for the purposes of our discussion, is given by equation (7) of Table 10.1. In this log-linear specification, k is the semielasticity of money demand with respect to the *nominal* interest rate, i, and b, the elasticity with respect to real income, which may, in general, be different from unity according to some theories of the transactions demand for money.[4] In order to examine the implications of this specification within the classical equilibrium framework, we introduce Fisher's relation, given by equation (10), which states that, given the real interest rate, the nominal interest rate adjusts fully to the expected rate of inflation. The stricter Fisherian hypothesis that the real interest rate is invariant to inflation also holds in this simple classical model.[5] The supply of money is again assumed to be exogenously determined but we now allow for a random component (u_{ms}) reflecting the imperfection of monetary controls. Equilibrium in the money market, given the classical assumptions (11) on the independence of real income and the real interest rate of the quantity of money, implies that the price level must satisfy the "velocity" relation (II). In general, the equilibrium price level in a given period depends not only on the existing average quantity of money in this period but also on the expected price level in the next period. Thus, to obtain the equilibrium price level, it is necessary to specify the determinants of anticipated inflation, which affects the equilibrium price level by influencing the demand for real money balances through its effect on the opportunity cost of holding money or, equivalently, its effect on the own real rate of return on money. The magnitude of this effect depends on the quantitative significance of "liquidity preference", i.e. the semielasticity of money demand with respect to the nominal interest rate.

The nature of the price level–money relation can be illustrated under three alternative hypotheses about the determinants of expected inflation. The simplest hypothesis is that the public anticipates zero inflation (or a given constant rate), which is consistent with an environment where variations in the money stock are once-and-for-all changes (a random walk) around a constant

---

[4]In principle, the determinants of money demand should include the rates of return on all assets, real and financial, which are alternatives to money as well as the own rate of return, which is assumed fixed and equal to i_m. Under the assumption of perfect substitutability among all assets other than money, there are two rates (i_m, i), where i is the nominal rate of return on all non-money assets. Expected inflation, $\hat{\pi}$, affects the demand for money through its effect on the nominal rates of return, including the return on real goods. On the reasonable hypothesis that money demand is homogeneous of zero degree in all rates of return, money demand can be expressed as a function of real rates or $(-\hat{\pi}, r)$ since the own nominal rate, i_m, is taken as given and thus invariant to inflation over the time horizon considered. In economies in which the nominal rate on non-money assets (i) can not adjust freely to reflect anticipated inflation, inflation will affect money demand also through its effect on the real rate, r.

[5]This need not be the case, in general, even with price flexibility as shown in Mundell (1964) and Tobin (1965).

non-inflationary rate of money growth; these changes in the stock of money affect the equilibrium value of the price level but not the anticipated inflation trend. This hypothesis was explicitly or implicitly made in early discussions of liquidity preference under price flexibility, partly under the influence of the non-inflationary conditions prevailing until the early sixties. In this case equation (II) reduces to:

$$p = m + \bar{v}(\bar{r}, \bar{y}) - \bar{y} + \varepsilon_p .\tag{22}$$

The proportionality of the price level to the contemporaneous quantity of money, characteristic of the simple quantity theory, holds in this case with the important qualification that the velocity term, $\bar{v}$, fluctuates in response to variations in the equilibrium levels of real income and the real interest rate and not just as a result of changes in the institutional factors influencing velocity, stressed by the classical economists. A rise in the "natural" real rate will increase the trend velocity (since $k < 0$), while the effect of a change in the equilibrium level of real income on velocity depends on the income elasticity of money demand, with velocity increasing as real income increases if the income elasticity of money demand is less than one. Similarly, the stochastic component of the price level–money relation is affected not only by the disturbances directly affecting the money market but also by any shocks affecting the real rate and real output. The implication for a monetary policy which aims at maintaining price stability is that it should try to adjust the quantity of money so as to offset predictable shifts in velocity, v, due to changes in $\bar{y}$ and $\bar{r}$.

An alternative hypothesis on inflationary expectations is that they are based on the history of inflation. A specific formulation of "backward-looking" expectations, employed extensively since the mid-fifties [e.g. Cagan (1956), Friedman (1956)], is the hypothesis of adaptive expectations stated by equation (20). This hypothesis and equation (II) imply that the price level adjusts gradually to changes in the quantity of money and that the process of adjustment from an initial rate of monetary growth to a new one may involve oscillations of the price level around the new "steady-state" inflation, so that during the period of adjustment to a new equilibrium the price level may rise at a faster rate than the increase in the rate of monetary growth. A simple illustration of the implications of this hypothesis, which is instructive for a comparison with the alternative hypothesis discussed below, is provided for the special case when the speed of adjustment of expectations is relatively prompt ($\gamma = 1$), so that the anticipated inflation is equal to the inflation rate in the previous period. In this case the price level is related to the quantity of money by

$$p = k(1 + k)^{-1}p_{-1} + (1 + k)^{-1}(m + \bar{v} - \bar{y} + \varepsilon_p) ,\tag{23}$$

which implies that

$$p = (1 + k)^{-1} \sum_{t=0}^{\infty} \lambda'[m_{-t} + (\bar{v} - \bar{y} + \varepsilon_p)_{-t}], \tag{24}$$

where $\lambda = k(1 + k)^{-1}$.

The price level in the current period is determined by a weighted average of the quantities of money in previous periods with the weights declining geometrically over time in absolute value if $|k(1 + k)^{-1}| < 1$. This condition, which is necessary for stability, holds since the (long run) total interest elasticity of money demand is typically of the order of -0.2 [see, for example, Goldfeld (1976) and Judd and Scadding (1982)]. Note that since $k < 0$, changes in the money stock in previous periods will have a positive or negative effect on the current price level, depending upon the time interval involved. If the quantity of money is kept constant indefinitely, then the equilibrium value of p is equal to m plus a weighted average of past values of $\bar{v}$, $\bar{y}$ and of random disturbances.

The other common hypothesis of inflationary expectations, which has become popular since the middle seventies, is that they are formed "rationally". The hypothesis implies that expectations are based on all relevant information which includes knowledge about the process determining the price level as summarized by the model considered, in this case relation (II). It follows that the *expected* price level is given by

$$\hat{p} = -k(1 - k)^{-1}\hat{p}_{+1} + (1 - k)^{-1}(\hat{m} + \hat{v} - \hat{y}), \tag{25}$$

which, solved in the "forward direction", defines the expected price level in terms of a weighted average of the expected stock of money, the trend velocity and equilibrium real income in all future periods:

$$\hat{p} = (1 - k)^{-1} \sum_{t=0}^{\infty} \theta'[\hat{m}_{+t} + (\hat{v}_{+t} - \hat{y}_{+t})], \tag{26}$$

where $\theta = -k(1 - k)^{-1}$ and provided that $\lim_{t \to \infty} \theta'\hat{p}_{+t} = 0$. The price level is then given by

$$p = \hat{p} + (1 - k)^{-1}[(m - \hat{m}) + \varepsilon_p], \tag{27}$$

that is, it is equal to the "rationally" anticipated price level, adjusted for the effects of disturbances including any unanticipated transient variations in the quantity of money.

2.3.2. The Keynesian aggregate demand model with price rigidity

The fundamental implication of the second Keynesian hypothesis relating to inflexibility of wages in the presence of persistent unemployment is that it leads to a rejection of the classical proposition that money is neutral. The failure of the average wage rate to adjust promptly when the aggregate demand for labor falls short of the "full-employment" level implies that aggregate employment and output will deviate from their equilibrium values over a potentially long period depending upon the degree of flexibility of wages. In the limiting case of absolute downward wage rigidity, a state of persistent disequilibrium or an "unemployment equilibrium" may result. This limiting case, however, should be viewed as one which is not likely to persist indefinitely since the resulting unemployment will eventually result in wage adjustments and a reabsorption of unemployment; consequently, the underemployment equilibrium may be characterized as pertaining to the "short-run" as compared to the classical full-employment equilibrium $\bar{y}$ toward which the economy may gradually gravitate.

The Keynesian theory of income and money does not rest only on the two propositions of wage inflexibility and liquidity preference but also on another Keynesian concept, that of the "aggregate demand for output", which describes the mechanism through which a quantity of money insufficient to finance a full employment output results in an unemployment equilibrium. That mechanism is based on the consumption–saving decisions of the public and the investment decisions of firms. Formal models of this Keynesian theory have been at the core of macroeconomic analysis in the fifties and sixties, and they still are a central component of the more general aggregative framework developed since the early seventies, discussed below. The first formalizations of the Keynesian theory in terms of a "system of equations", which include the models of Hicks (1937), Lange (1938) and Modigliani (1944), were extended in the fifties and sixties on the basis of theoretical analyses and empirical investigations focusing on the determinants of consumption and investment as well of money demand.[6] These extensions pointed to the important role of other variables, in addition to those emphasized by Keynes, in influencing aggregate demand (such as wealth or permanent income) and the significance of the lagged or gradual adjustment of aggregate demand to changes in the value of its determinants. For present purposes, however, a simple specifica-

---

[6]Among the numerous contributions we note the studies of Friedman (1957), Modigliani and Brumberg (1954), Ando and Modigliani (1963) and Duesenberry (1949), on the determinants of consumption, and the studies of Jorgensen (1963, 1971) and Eisner (1978) on the determinants of investment. Analyses of the mechanism of wage and price adjustments were comparatively limited in number in the fifties and sixties, with notable exceptions, the empirical study of Phillips (1958) and the theoretical models reported in Phelps et al. (1970).

tion of the Keynesian aggregate demand is sufficient for illustrating the impact effect of a change in the quantity of money on real income for the limiting case of perfect price rigidity. The objective of this exercise is to clarify the relative significance of the three propositions – liquidity preference, price inflexibility, and aggregate demand – on the income–money relation through a comparison with the flexible price model outlined in Subsection 2.3.1 above and the more general framework which follows.

A stylized specification of the Keynesian model is given by equations (12)–(15). The first equation, (12), is the condition for equilibrium in the money market, the Hicksian LM relation, which is identical to the one implied by equations (7)–(9) in the previous model examined. Note that u_m is the *net* disturbance in the money market, reflecting both demand and supply shocks. Aggregate demand, expressed in deviations from the full-employment equilibrium, is given by the log-linear specification (13) as a function of (the logarithm of) real income and the real interest rate. The real disturbance u_d incorporates the *net* effect of fiscal variables affecting aggregate demand.[7] Finally, equations (15) state that over the time interval under consideration the average wage rate and thus the average price level is given; consequently, anticipated inflation is zero, and aggregate output adjusts to the level demanded at the given price level. The last equation in (15) together with (13) define the condition for equilibrium in the goods market.

The relationship between the equilibrium level of real output and the quantity of money implied by the Keynesian model is given by the two alternative but equivalent expressions stated in (III). The first expression presents the relation in the familiar Keynesian format: the deviation of real output from its long-run equilibrium level is proportional to the *real* quantity of money. The proportionality factor μ is the elasticity of the (short-run) equilibrium level of real output with respect to the quantity of money, given the price level; it is a generalized Keynesian "money multiplier", expressed as an elasticity. The last term of the first expression in (III) has been stated as a multiple of the difference between the *trend* velocity, as already defined in the liquidity preference model, and the "natural level" of real income. The second expression in (III) states that the percentage deviation of the temporary equilibrium level of output from its full-employment equilibrium value is proportional to the percentage deviation of the quantity of money from the level $\bar{m}$, which is the level consistent with the "natural", full-employment levels

---

[7]Equation (13) can be derived from a more general specification of aggregate demand, with consumption depending upon a general measure of disposable income which includes the effects of inflation on the real value of government debt, provided the government balances its budget, and with investment depending upon the market value of firms' capital relative to the replacement cost of capital or Tobin's q, a quantity also stressed by Keynes as a major determinant of investment. See Papademos and Modigliani (1983).

of real income and real interest rate ($\bar{y}$ and $\bar{r}$) and the prevailing price level, as defined below equation (III).

The "multiplier-elasticity" μ exhibits the usual Keynesian properties: (1) for given values of the interest semielasticity of aggregate demand, a, and the income elasticity of money demand, b, it attains a maximum value, equal to $1/b$, when money demand is interest inelastic (the classical case), and it reduces to zero as the interest elasticity of money demand approaches infinity (the Keynesian case of "liquidity trap"); (2) for finite values of the income and interest elasticities of money demand, the magnitude of the impact effect of money on real income is less than unity, the value implied by the quantity theory, at least as long as b is less than unity, and declines monotonically with the degree of responsiveness of aggregate demand to the real interest rate. Thus the Keynesian proposition of price inflexibility implies that a change in the quantity of money, both nominal and real, is not neutral, in general; and that the effectiveness of monetary policy in influencing real output decreases as the interest elasticity of money demand increases, that is, when the other Keynesian hypothesis of liquidity preference becomes quantitatively relatively important, and also as the interest elasticity of aggregate demand decreases. In the limiting case of the liquidity trap and/or zero interest elasticity of aggregate demand, monetary policy becomes powerless and only fiscal policy (impounded in u_d in our system) can affect output.

2.4. A general model of aggregate output, prices and money

The relation between the stock of money and nominal income is more complex than the one implied by either of the previous models which rest on limiting assumptions about wage and price flexibility and the nature of the market-clearing mechanism. In general, changes in the money stock will affect *both* real output and the price level in the short run and, under certain conditions, in the long run as well. Moreover, the nature of the dynamic response of nominal income to changes in the money stock is complicated and may involve considerable lags and oscillations while, to the extent that expectations affect economic behavior, anticipated future changes in the money supply may also have an impact on nominal income at present. To capture these effects, it is necessary to allow for a more general formulation of the mechanism which describes the interaction of output fluctuations and changes in wages and prices, induced by monetary or real disturbances.

Theoretical and empirical analyses of the output–inflation trade-off have been a central topic of macroeconomics since the observation by Phillips (1958) of an empirical relation between the rate of change of wages and unemployment. These analyses can be grouped as belonging to three phases. Empirical research in the late fifties and in the sixties aimed at generalizing the nature of the Phillips relationship and establishing its validity for various countries and over different time periods. A notable empirical generalization related to the apparent dependence of wage changes on past inflation [e.g. Lipsey (1960), Samuelson and Solow (1960), Perry (1966)] which implied a distinction between the short-run and long-run nature of the Phillips curve. This distinction has important implications for the dynamics of the inflationary process and for the speed with which income responds to macroeconomic policies. It does not alter, however, a fundamental implication of the early analyses of the Phillips curve, namely the existence of a continuum of equilibrium output levels associated with different inflation rates both in the short run and in the long run. This result is contrary to the classical notion of money neutrality which implies a full-employment equilibrium totally independent of the money supply, at least in the long run. This notion was also accepted in principle by Keynes who focused on the existence of temporary equilibria below the full-employment level. Indeed, the early formulations of the output–inflation trade-off were also inconsistent with the Keynesian case of wage rigidity, since they implied that at a maintained unemployment rate higher than the rate consistent with price stability, wages and prices would continue to fall steadily. Unemployment could be permanently reduced only at the cost of a permanently higher rate of inflation requiring a higher rate of money growth.

The non-neutrality of monetary policy in the long run, implied by the Phillips curve relation, was challenged in the late sixties and early seventies. At a theoretical level Friedman (1968) and Phelps (1968) argued that the Phillips statistical relations could not be permanently stable, for they resulted from actions of economic agents induced by unanticipated price fluctuations under conditions of imperfect information. Expectational errors could persist, resulting in transitory output fluctuations, but, in the long run actual and expected price changes could not deviate systematically. Consequently, in the steady state there is a unique "natural" full-employment output level which is invariant to permanent inflation. However, in the short run a change in money growth which causes unanticipated but persisting price changes will result in output and price fluctuations.

At an empirical level, the demonstration that money growth is neutral in the long run focused on tests concerning the impact of anticipated inflation (as inferred from past inflation) on actual inflation in an "expectations-augmented Phillips curve". Empirical evidence that this effect was unitary was consistent with the absence of a permanent trade-off. Anticipations of inflation were mostly assumed to be formed adaptively on the basis of past inflation, thus implying a specific decaying effect of past on current inflation. The proposition that the inflation–unemployment trade-off is vertical in the long run – i.e. that inflation would rise (or fall) indefinitely if unemployment stayed below (or above) some critical level – or that it is effectively vertical for unemployment rates below some critical level which might be labeled the "non-inflationary rate of unemployment or NIRU [see Modigliani and Papademos (1975) and Baily and Tobin (1977)] has been found consistent with the empirical evidence in many countries.

The neutrality of money in the long run, however, is not the most critical issue from a policy point of view. More relevant and important questions are the nature and magnitude of the effect of money on output in the short run and the speed with which changes in the money stock affect output and prices over time. The analyses of the output–price–money interactions developed since the mid-seventies offer answers to these questions based on two basic ideas: (i) an alternative hypothesis on the nature of expectations and (ii) an alternative interpretation of the dependendce of wages on past inflation, which relies on behavioral and institutional factors rather than on expectational effects. The first idea involved the application of the rational expectations hypothesis to macroeconomics by Lucas (1972a, 1972b), Sargent (1976) and Sargent and Wallace (1975). Incorporating the rational expectations hypothesis in the models of employment and output supply of the type constructed by Friedman (1968) and Lucas (1972a, 1972b) yields the rather striking conclusion that changes in the money supply cannot affect output systematically over *any* time horizon. Monetary policy actions are neutral not only in the long run but also in the short run, unless they are unanticipated, in which case they cause errors in price expectations, yielding transitory, *random* output fluctuations. Antici-pated changes in the money stock affect, however, both anticipated and actual inflation, the latter up to a random error.

Fully anticipated monetary policy, however, can influence aggregate output in the short run when agents have rational expectations if price adjustments and the supply of output are constrained by the existence of overlapping (staggered) explicit or implicit wage and price contracts [see Fischer (1977), Phelps and Taylor (1977) and Taylor (1980)]. These contracts imply that markets cannot clear continuously in response to changes in the money stock and that the inertia of inflation can be traced to institutional characteristics and not necessarily to the sluggish adaptation of expectations. Empirically the effect of past inflation on current inflation, estimated by autoregressive terms in the usual augmented Phillips curve specifications, may be interpreted as capturing in part these influences rather than the effects of backward-looking expectations.

For present purposes, the major implications of the above theories for the velocity relation between nominal income and the money stock can be ex-amined by first incorporating, in the traditional aggregate demand model summarized by equations (16)–(18), a stylized specification of the determinants of price adjustments, given by equation (19), or alternatively a specification of the determinants of the supply of aggregate output in the short run, as shown by (19′). Both equations are reduced forms of more complete structural representations of wage–price interactions which, however, abstract from the effects of other factors that may influence the trade-off, that such as permanent or cyclical changes in productivity growth and, more importantly, ignore the existence of rigidities such as may result from long-term contracts. These two aggregate specifications of the trade-off are obviously equivalent, but they are derived from alternative microeconomic theories. Equation (19) can be related to a neo-Keynesian framework of the market-clearing mechanism, where excess demand affects wage adjustments and, according to an oligopolistic pricing model, also price adjustments. Equation (19′) can be derived from the Friedman–Lucas classical model of competitive markets, where erroneous price expectations are responsible for transitory output fluctuations.

It is instructive to examine the implications of the aggregate supply specification (19) on the income–money velocity relation independently of the effects introduced by alternative hypotheses on the nature of inflationary expectations. To this end we obtain first, from equations (16)–(18), what may be called an "aggregate demand" relation between real output and the money supply:

$$y = \bar{y} + \mu(m - \bar{m}) - \mu(p - \bar{p}) - \mu k(\hat{p}_{+1} - p) + \varepsilon_{\mathrm{d}}, \tag{28}$$

where $\varepsilon_{\mathrm{d}} = \mu(k u_{\mathrm{d}}/d - u_{\mathrm{m}})$, and μ is defined below equation (III) in Table 10.1. This expression determines the quantity of aggregate output demanded for a given stock of money which is consistent with equilibrium in the money and final goods markets.

Simultaneous solution of equations (28) and (19) yields the relations (IV) in Table 10.1 between the price level, real output, and the supply of money. These relations are also stated below for convenience:

$$p = \beta[\alpha\mu(m + \bar{v} - \bar{y}) + \hat{p} - \alpha\mu k\hat{p}_{+1} + \alpha(\varepsilon_{\mathrm{d}} - \varepsilon_{\mathrm{s}})], \tag{IV.1}$$

$$y = \bar{y} + \beta\mu[(m + \bar{v} - \bar{y}) - \hat{p} - k(\hat{p}_{+1} - \hat{p})] + \beta\varepsilon_{\mathrm{d}} + (1 - \beta)\varepsilon_{\mathrm{s}}, \tag{IV.2}$$

where

$$\beta = [1 + \alpha\mu(1 - k)]^{-1}, \quad 0 \le \beta \le 1, \quad \alpha \ge 0,$$

$$\mu = a(ab + k)^{-1} > 0, \quad a = d(1 - c)^{-1} < 0,$$

$$\varepsilon_{\mathrm{d}} = \mu(k u_{\mathrm{d}}/d - u_{\mathrm{m}}).$$

The price level and the deviations of real output from the full-employment level depend upon the stock of money adjusted for the effects of the trend velocity and full-employment output $(m + \bar{v} - \bar{y})$, the anticipated price level in the current and next periods $(\hat{p}, \hat{p}_{+1})$, and the aggregate demand and supply disturbances $(\varepsilon_d, \varepsilon_s)$. The proportionality factor, β, which varies between zero and one, reflects the effects of all aggregate demand and supply parameters, in particular the generalized Keynesian multiplier, μ, and the slope of the Phillips curve relation, α. The interest elasticity of money demand, k, affects in a critical way the reduced form parameters μ and β and the dynamics of the system, since it determines the extent to which the anticipated price level in the next period affects the current price level and output. The general expressions for (p, y), as given by (IV), reduce to the relations implied by the classical and Keynesian models, (II) and (III) in Table 10.1, for the limiting cases of perfect price flexibility and downward price rigidity. When the price level adjusts fully within each period $(a \rightarrow \infty)$, then $\beta = 0$, $\alpha\beta = [\mu(1 - k)]^{-1}$, $y = \bar{y}$ and the price level is determined according to the relation (II) in Table 10.1. When the price level is rigid $(\alpha = 0)$ and expectations are consistent with this fact, then $\beta = 1$, $p = \hat{p} = \bar{p}$, and y is determined according to (III) in Table 10.1.

To obtain the final "reduced-form" relations between the price level, real output and the money supply, it is necessary to adopt a hypothesis on the nature of expectations. If expectations are "rational" in the sense of Muth, as specified by equation (21), the anticipated price level is given, as can be inferred from (IV.1), by

$$\hat{p} = \alpha\beta\mu(1 - \beta)^{-1}(\hat{m} + \bar{v} - \bar{y}) - \alpha\beta\mu k(1 - \beta)^{-1}\hat{p}_{+1}, \tag{29}$$

assuming that full-employment output and trend velocity are known. It can be readily shown, employing the definition of β, that $\alpha\beta\mu(1 - \beta)^{-1} = (1 - k)^{-1}$. Therefore, equation (29) is identical to equation (25), which implies that the anticipated price level is given by (26), the expression which holds in the simple classical world of liquidity preference with "rational" expectations. Consequently, when expectations are "rational", the relation between the expected price level and the money supply implied by the general model, which incorporates specifications for a Keynesian aggregate effective demand and a Phillips–Lucas aggregate supply, is the same as the one implied by the simple liquidity preference model. Furthermore, the "rationality" of expectations and the nature of the aggregate supply function, which abstracts from any intertemporal constraints on price dynamics, implies the short-run neutrality of anticipated changes in the money supply in the general model. This known result can be readily demonstrated by substituting (29) into (IV.2) which yields:

$$y = \bar{y} + \beta\mu(m - \hat{m}) + \beta\varepsilon_d + (1 - \beta)\varepsilon_s, \tag{30}$$

and, consequently, $\hat{y} = \bar{y}$. The neutrality of anticipated monetary policy, even in the short run, is of course the implication of the unrealistic joint hypotheses that all price adjustments are instantaneous and that all economic agents know the model's structure (and they believe that price adjustments are instantaneous). In this case, it also follows, from equations (IV.1) and (29), that the price level differs from its anticipated value only by a random term, which partly reflects unanticipated fluctuations in the money supply:

$$p = \hat{p} + \alpha\beta[\mu(m - \hat{m}) + (\varepsilon_d - \varepsilon_s)] . \tag{31}$$

If expectations are formed adaptively, according to equation (20), both aggregate output and the price level in a given period are affected by the money supply in that period and in previous ones. Thus, a change in the stock of money is not neutral but it induces fluctuations of real output which persist in subsequent periods and exhibit oscillations. These oscillations are likely to be damped, so that in the long run real output approaches its full-employment level, $\bar{y}$. The price level also displays oscillations in response to a change in the money supply and, in general, it gradually approaches a new equilibrium level consistent with the new stock of money. To illustrate these general propositions more precisely, we consider the special case when expectations of inflation adapt fully to the error between actual and expected inflation in the previous period ($\gamma = 1$). In this case, $\hat{\pi} = \pi_{-1}$ and $\hat{p} = 2p_{-1} - p_{-2}$, and equation (IV.1) becomes:

$$p_t - \varphi(2 + \alpha\mu k)p_{t-1} + \varphi p_{t-2} = \varphi z_t , \tag{32}$$

where

$$\varphi = [1 + \alpha\mu(1 + k)]^{-1} ,$$

$$z_t = \alpha\mu(m_t + \bar{v} - \bar{y}) + \alpha(\varepsilon_{dt} - \varepsilon_{st}) .$$

The general solution to this second-order difference equation is:

$$p_t = \lambda_1\varphi(\lambda_1 - \lambda_2)^{-1} \sum_{i=0}^{\infty} \lambda_1^i z_{t-i} - \lambda_2\varphi(\lambda_1 - \lambda_2)^{-1} \sum_{i=0}^{\infty} \lambda_2^i z_{t-i} \tag{33}$$

$$+ c_1\lambda_1^t + c_2\lambda_2^t , \quad \lambda_2 \neq \lambda_1 , \quad \lambda_1 \neq 1 ,$$

where λ_1 and λ_2 are the roots of the characteristic equation:

$$s^2 - \varphi(2 + \alpha\mu k)s + \varphi = 0 . \tag{34}$$

The roots are given by

$$\lambda_i = [\varphi(2 + \alpha\mu k) \pm \sqrt{\varphi^2(2 + \alpha\mu k)^2 - 4\varphi}]/2 . \tag{35}$$

The distributed lag weights of (33) will oscillate if λ_1 and λ_2 are complex, that is if $\varphi^2(2 + \alpha\mu k)^2 < 4\varphi$. For finite values of α, φ is positive since $\alpha \geq 0$, $\mu > 0$ and k is nonpositive but small in absolute value. In this case, the roots will be complex if

$$\alpha\mu k^2 < 1 . \tag{36}$$

The above condition is likely to hold. It is obviously satisfied if the demand for money is inelastic with respect to the interest rate ($k = 0$). Note that if the price level adjusts very fast ($\alpha \to \infty$), equation (32) reduces to the first-order difference equation (23). For the case when m_t is constant over time and $\varepsilon_s = \varepsilon_d = 0$, the oscillations of the price level will be damped if $\varphi < 1$, which is satisfied if k is less than unity in absolute value. The dynamic adjustment of the price level and real output to changes in the money supply is examined more fully in Papademos (1987).

3. The money supply mechanism

3.1. Forms and measures of fiat money

The monetary theory underlying the macroeconomic models of nominal income examined in the previous section is a theory of money demand. The role of the money creation process is either ignored or de-emphasized on the assumption that the supply of money is essentially exogenously determined – in particular that it is directly and effectively controlled by the central bank. This assumption is at least approximately valid for economies in which all money is commodity money or is fiat money in the form of currency or checkable deposits issued either by a single monetary authority or by private "deposit" banks operating under a system of "100 percent reserve requirement". In such a system all banks are required to hold against all checkable deposits reserves of 100 percent in the form of vault cash or deposits at the central bank. Clearly, these monetary systems are not representative of those presently existing.

In this section we examine the determinants of the money supply for the type of monetary system prevailing today, and the mechanism and instruments through which the central bank can control the quantity of money and, possibly, the overall size of assets and liabilities of the banking system.

The present monetary system is one of fiat money, while until the First World War the prevailing means of payment was commodity money or paper money convertible into a specified quantity of a commodity (usually gold). Fiat money is the liability (IOU) created by banks, both the central bank and private banks, in payment for the acquisition of government and private financial debt.[8] Fiat money, unlike commodity money, has no intrinsic value and it is produced and maintained at virtually no cost.[9]

The central bank cannot control directly the supply of fiat money which is determined endogenously as a result of the interaction of the behavior of the public, the behavior of private banks as well as of the actions of the central bank. The latter can exercise control over the quantity of money by directly controlling the total of its liabilities (except possibly for bank borrowing – see below) and by using other instruments such as interest rates and reserve requirements. The analysis of the effectiveness and precision of the control procedures and their implications for the functioning of the financial markets and the economy is a main objective of this and the following section. To this end, we first focus on how the behavior of private banks contributes to the determination of the supply of money, given the existing regulatory structure in the United States and other Western economies. In Subsection 3.6 we examine the implications of alternative regulatory environments for the determinacy of the quantity of money.

The examination of the supply mechanism will first concentrate on the determinants of the narrow measure of money, denoted by $M1$, which consists of all customary means of payment, i.e. the currency held by the public (H_p) and the demand deposits held by the public (D), which are taken to include all checkable deposits at all banks and non-bank depository institutions.[10] Money, as narrowly defined, denotes a nominally fixed financial asset which is fundamentally distinguished from other assets by its function as a medium of exchange; it is the concept of "money" employed in most theoretical analyses of money demand and it is the relevant measure for the aggregative models examined in the previous section.

Broader measures of "money" include as components financial assets which are less liquid than $M1$ in the sense that they cannot be used directly for transactions although they are convertible promptly into $M1$ at a relatively low

[8]In certain cases governments have issued paper money to finance the purchase of goods and services. Initially, private banks issued gold receipts, which were used as paper money, in exchange for deposits of gold by their customers; however, this paper money was not fiat money since it was redeemable for gold. Gradually, the fractional reserve system came into existence.

[9]Paper money has low cost of production and maintenance, but the maintenance of demand deposits requires real resources, which could be employed to produce non-monetary goods.

[10]The precise definition of $M1$ by the Federal Reserve is the sum of the currency held by the public, travelers' checks, net demand deposits at commercial banks, other checkable deposits at banks and non-bank depository institutions (*Federal Reserve Bulletin*, January 1987).

cost. We may refer to all deposits which cannot be directly employed in transactions (such as time and savings deposits, certificates of deposit, etc.) as either "time" or "non-transaction" deposits. The distinction, however, between "demand" and "non-transaction" deposits is gradually becoming blurred, as certain types of "non-transaction" deposits can be easily and inexpensively converted into demand deposits as a result of recent technological innovations that allow instantaneous transfers of funds between accounts of various types. The analysis in this and the following section examines the implications of the degree of substitutability between demand and other deposits for the effectiveness of monetary controls. The broader concept of money which includes *all* non-transactions bank deposits will be denoted by *M*2, although this symbol is frequently employed to represent a narrower concept which includes only savings deposits.[11]

3.2. Simple models of the money supply: The money multiplier approach

The salient characteristic of these models is the key role of certain fixed ratios, describing the portfolio behavior of the banks and the public, in determining the relation between the quantity of money and the monetary base or other reserve aggregates controllable by the central bank.[12] A basic feature of deposit banking, which can be traced to the early deposit services offered by goldsmiths, is that banks need to keep only a fraction of the (demand) deposits of the public in the form of "cash" or of liquid assets readily convertible into cash. Under normal conditions and when there is confidence in the banking system, it is expected that the public's demand for currency is a fairly stable fraction of total money balances (or, equivalently, of demand deposits), so that although some portion of deposits is continuously being withdrawn in exchange for currency, this flow tends to be offset by the inflow of currency to be credited to deposits. The proportion of deposits, z, held by banks in the form of cash or very liquid assets is determined by the need to satisfy the depositor's demand for cash, in the face of stochastic inflows and outflows and costs of investment in and liquidation of other assets. The dependence of z on

---

[11]Definitions of money appearing in various official statistics denote by *M*3 or *M*4 the quantity of broad money we consider. Definitions and symbols differ from country to country and they have changed over time in response to financial innovations which have altered the degree of liquidity and other characteristics of certain categories of bank deposits. The symbols used are, of course, unimportant as long as the meaning of the quantity represented is clearly specified.

[12]Multiplier models of the money supply process are presented by Phillips (1920), Meade (1934), Friedman and Schwartz (1963, appendix B), Brunner and Meltzer (1964, 1968), Fand (1967), Burger (1971), and Rasche and Johannes (1987). The multiplier approach to money stock determination is employed in most macroeconomics and money and banking texts [e.g. Dornbusch and Fischer (1987), Havrilesky and Boorman (1978)].

behavioral and institutional factors discussed below. In addition, in most banking systems the monetary authorities require banks to maintain minimum cash reserves in proportion to their deposits.

3.2.1. A simple model with currency and demand deposits

The simplest model of the money supply mechanism assumes that banks are the only financial institutions accepting deposits and that they issue only demand deposits, D. The analysis is based on two main hypotheses: (1) banks maintain cash reserves, R, equal to a fixed proportion, z, of deposits reflecting either regulatory requirements or internally determined liquidity needs, and (2) the public's demand for currency, H_p, is a constant fraction, h, of bank deposits. Banks have no sources of funds other than deposits; they hold their reserves in the form of cash or as deposits at the central bank, and the remainder of their liabilities are utilized for making loans and purchasing debt instruments. The central bank can directly control the size of its total liabilities, currency held by the public and banks' reserves. This quantity is often called the monetary base or high-powered money, and is denoted by H:

$$H = H_p + R . \tag{37}$$

The quantity of money is given as usual by

$$M1 = H_p + D . \tag{38}$$

Equilibrium in the market for high-powered money requires that

$$H^d = H_p^d + R^d = hD + zD = H . \tag{39}$$

It readily follows from this market-clearing condition and the definition (38) that the supply of money is equal to a multiple of the monetary base:

$$M1 = \mu_1 H , \qquad \mu_1 = \left[\frac{1+h}{h+z}\right] \geq 1 . \tag{40}$$

The money-base multiplier, μ_1, which is clearly greater than or equal to one since $0 \leq z \leq 1$, reduces to the reciprocal of the required reserve-deposit ratio in the limiting case when money consists only of bank deposits. Note that as long as there is a stable and non-negligible demand for currency by the public ($h > 0$) and the monetary base is finite, the quantity of money is finite even if banks are not required and do not choose to hold reserves so that z is zero.

The multiplier relation (40) may be usefully derived by an alternative approach, namely focusing on the sequential response of banks and the public to an injection of reserves, ΔH, and showing that it leads to an increment in $M1$ consistent with (40). When the central bank injects new reserves in the banking system, ΔH, for example through the purchase of government securities from banks, initially bank reserves rise by ΔH, all of which represents excess reserves since deposits are unchanged. Consequently, banks use their excess reserves by acquiring earning assets, whether new loans or securities, bidding down interest rates in the process. As banks expand their earning assets by the amount of "excess reserves", they create new deposits equal to the quantity of new assets less the cash balances that the public wants to hold, to maintain the desired ratio h between currency and deposits. Thus, $\Delta D = \Delta H - \Delta H_p = \Delta H - h\,\Delta D$, implying $\Delta D = (1+h)^{-1}\,\Delta H$, and required reserves must increase by $z(1+h)^{-1}\,\Delta H$. Hence, the banking system still has idle reserves which can be used to expand its loans further by an amount $(1-z)(1+h)^{-1}\,\Delta H$. The process of expanding loans, deposits and cash continues with the total amount of deposits created at the end of this process, as a result of an initial increase in reserves by ΔH, given by $(1+h)^{-1}[1+(1-z)/(1+h)+(1-z)^2/(1+h)^2+\ldots]\,\Delta H = (h+z)^{-1}\,\Delta H$. Consequently, the money supply increase tends to $(1+h)(h+z)^{-1}\,\Delta H$, which agrees with equation (40).

3.2.2. A generalization with time deposits, borrowed and excess reserves

The above simple model of the money supply process can be readily extended to allow for the effects of a wider spectrum of bank assets and liabilities, at least as long as one is prepared to assume that different assets and liabilities are held in fixed proportions. These generalizations allow for the derivation of a number of "money multipliers" associated with alternative definitions of the money stock. Moreover, they allow for an examination of the effects on the money supply of banks' borrowing and holding reserves in excess of the required amount. We consider here the implications of one generalization which is useful for the analysis of the alternative approach to the money supply process described in the next section. The financial structure of the economy considered is summarized in Table 10.2, which exhibits the financial assets ($+$) and liabilities ($-$) held by the four sectors listed in the top row.

Banks issue two categories of deposits: demand deposits, D, and time deposits, T. A broad measure of money is then defined by

$$M2 = M1 + T . \tag{41}$$

The category of time deposits is taken to include all non-checkable deposits, i.e. savings and time deposits, as well as other interest-bearing short-term financial instruments such as certificates of deposit issued by banks. Ignoring the possible effects of interest rates on asset demands, it is again assumed that the demands for currency and time deposits can be expressed as constant proportions of demand deposits:

$$H_p^d = hD , \qquad T^d = tD , \quad h, t > 0 . \tag{42}$$

Table 10.2

Financial instruments	Sectors			
	Private non-bank (p)	Banks (b)	Central bank (c)	Government (g)
1. Currency in circulation (H_p)	H_p		$-H_p$	
2. Demand deposits (D)	D	$-D$		
3. Time and savings deposits (T)	T	$-T$		
4. Bank loans (L)	$-L$	L		
5. Reserves (R)		R	$-R$	
6. Bank borrowing (RB)		$-RB$	RB	
7. Bonds and bills (B)	B_p	B_b	B_c	$-B_g$
8. Capital $(P_K K)$ and bank equity (E_b)	$P_k K_p + E_b$	$P_k K_b - E_b$		

Notes:
(i) The private non-bank sector includes households and firms which are alternatively referred to as the non-bank public.
(ii) Bonds and bills include government and private non-bank marketable securities which are assumed to be very close substitutes. The table abstracts from holdings of currency and bank deposits by the government and foreign assets and liabilities. Time and savings deposits are defined to include certificates of deposit and all marketable bank liabilities other than equity. Since total bank borrowing in the interbank market must be zero, bank borrowing represents borrowed reserves from the central bank.
(iii) The net worth of each sector is given by the sum of the entries in each column.

Banks are required to hold reserves in proportion to their deposits, and, in general, the required reserve ratios associated with the two types of deposits may differ. Thus, required reserves, RR, are given by

$$RR = z_D D + z_T T . \qquad (43)$$

In the present generalization we also allow for the possibility that the actual level of reserves may deviate from the required amount for a given bank. In the presence of uncertainty on withdrawals, loan repayments or fluctuations in the yields of assets, some banks may find it prudent and profitable to hold on the average reserves in excess of legal requirements. Consequently, the total reserves, R, of the banking system consist of required reserves, RR, plus the excess reserves, RE, maintained by certain banks:

$$R = RR + RE . \qquad (44)$$

On the other hand, other banks may find that, as a result of unanticipated flows of funds, or because it is profitable, reserves are below the required level and thus they have to borrow reserves from other banks or the central bank. Thus, total reserves can be decomposed into non-borrowed reserves, RU, and borrowed reserves net of interbank lending, RB, which also equal the net amount lent by the central bank:

$$R = RU + RB .$$ (45)

The central bank can, in principle, limit the monetary base, currency in circulation plus total reserves, by controlling its assets, i.e. its holdings of securities and its lending to banks. However, the central bank cannot, in general, fix unilaterally the volume of bank borrowing; it can only endeavor to influence it indirectly through the interest rates it charges, while total reserves also reflect the banks' demand for excess reserves. Thus, the only variable the central bank can directly control (through open market operations) is the size of its portfolio of government securities (B_c). As can be seen from Table 10.2, this is equal to the monetary base less bank borrowing — a quantity commonly referred to as the *non-borrowed* monetary base and which we denote by $M0$. Therefore:

$$M0 = H_p + R - RB = H_p + RU .$$ (46)

It is operationally more useful to derive the multiplier relations of $M1$ or $M2$ to the unborrowed base $M0$ than the total monetary base, because $M0$ is more directly controllable by the central bank. To this end, we first note that the definitional equations (44) and (45) imply that non-borrowed reserves is related to required reserves by

$$RU = RR + RE - RB = RR + RF ,$$ (47)

where RF is the difference between excess and borrowed reserves, often labelled as the free reserves of the banking system.

The determinants of the level of excess and free reserves will be discussed in some detail in the next section. For present purposes, however, and in the spirit of this class of models which approximate behavioral relations in terms of fixed ratios, it is conveniently assumed that the demands for aggregate excess and borrowed, and thus for free reserves, are proportional to the level of demand deposits. Thus,

$$RF^d = fD , \qquad f > 0 .$$ (48)

It immediately follows from equations (42)–(43) and (46)–(48) that the demand for the non-borrowed monetary base can be expressed as a fixed proportion of demand deposits:

$$M0^d = [h + z_D + tz_T + f]D .$$ (49)

The relations between the narrow and broad measures of the money supply and the non-borrowed monetary base are readily derived from the definitions (38), (41), equations (42) and (49), and the condition for equilibrium in the market for base money:

$$M1 = n_1 M0, \qquad n_1 = (1 + h)\theta, \tag{50a}$$

$$M2 = n_2 M0, \qquad n_2 = (1 + h + t)\theta, \tag{50b}$$

where

$$\theta = [h + z_D + tz_T + f]^{-1}.$$

These relations clearly show the implications of the two generalizations introduced in the model, a more complex structure of bank deposits and the possibility of borrowing or holding excess reserves, for the relationships between the money stocks and $M0$ – the so-called money multipliers. The magnitude of the multiplier for either $M1$ or $M2$ is reduced as a result of factors which cause a systematic absorption of central bank reserves in the process of credit-deposit creation generated by an increase in the monetary base such as an increase in the currency-deposit ratio or in the proportion of demand deposits held as free reserves, etc. The coefficient θ in (50), which is common to both multipliers, captures the total effect of these factors on the expansion of demand deposits, while the terms $(1 + h)$ and $(1 + h + t)$ convert this effect into the total quantities of $M1$ and $M2$.

The above monetary base multipliers can be further generalized in a straightforward way to allow for a more complex structure of bank assets and liabilities and for the effects of non-bank financial intermediaries on the money supply process. Suppose that banks issue N categories of deposits or financial instruments denoted by $(D_1, D_2, \ldots, D_N)$, where D_1 represents demand deposits. Let $z = (z_1, z_2, \ldots, z_N)$ be the vector of the required reserve ratios associated with the respective types of deposits, and $d = (d_1, d_2, \ldots, d_N) = (1, D_2/D_1, D_3/D_1, \ldots, D_N/D_1)$. The money multiplier for the Jth monetary aggregate $MJ = H_p + D_1 + D_2 + \cdots + D_J$, is given by

$$\mu_J = \left(h + \sum_{i=1}^{J} d_i \right) \left(h + \sum_{i=1}^{J} d_i z_i + f \right)^{-1}. \tag{51}$$

As long as the additional financial assets incorporated into the model are assumed to be held in fixed proportions to demand deposits, or some other financial aggregate, the essential features of the money supply mechanism presented above are not altered.[13]

These features can be summarized as follows. (1) The supply of money (narrow or broad measure) is a well-defined multiple of a financial aggregate controllable by the central bank, the non-borrowed monetary base. (2) The

[13]All money multipliers in this section have been determined by expressing all financial aggregates relative to demand deposits. Alternatively, the monetary multipliers can be expressed in terms of the ratios of the various financial aggregates to total deposits. The choice of the normalization variable is of course unimportant on the assumption that the quantities of financial aggregates are held in fixed proportions.

size of the multiplier is fundamentally determined by the fact that reserves maintained by banks are a fraction of their deposits, which leads them to respond to an increase in reserves created by the central bank by creating additional deposits equal to a multiple of that increase. Note from (50) that the term $(z_D + tz_T + f)$ of the parameter θ is an overall effective reserve-deposit ratio, and that in a 100 percent reserve banking system the monetary base multiplier is one. (3) These conclusions, however, rely on the assumption that the asset preferences of banks and the public, which affect the process of deposit expansion, are invariant to changes in the values of financial or real variables (such as interest rates or income), at least to a very good approximation. On this assumption, the money supply process is not influenced by economic variables but only by institutional and technical factors or random changes in behavioral patterns, and the supply of money can be taken as a quantity determined "exogenously" by the banking system, up to a stochastic component.

3.3. Interest rates, income and the money multipliers

Public and bank portfolio preferences cannot be taken to be invariant to changes in the rates of return and other economic variables, except as a first approximation. This proposition has been sometimes recognized by the proponents of the multiplier approach who have occasionally allowed for such effects on the basis of plausible behavioral assumptions, but without detailed theoretical analysis of the underlying adjustment process.[14]

The basic implications of "endogenizing" the monetary multipliers by incorporating interest rate effects can be laid out using the general model of the previous section. The financial structure of the economy considered implies that, in principle, the portfolio choices of the public and banks may be influenced by six rates of return: "the" market interest rate on government securities, i; the interest rate on bank loans, i_L; the interest rates on demand and time deposits, i_D and i_T, respectively; the average rate of return on banks' reserves, i_R; and the effective interest rate on banks' borrowing from the central bank (e.g. the discount rate), i_{CB}. Some of these rates will move together depending upon the characteristics of financial markets and institutions. For simplicity, it is assumed here that bank loans and market financial instruments are considered very close substitutes by the borrowers and, consequently, their rates of return differ only by a constant spread, c_L or $i_L = i + c_L$. The interest rates on bank liabilities are either administratively set or market determined. In the latter case, changes in i_D and i_T are associated with fluctuations in the bank loan rate. The precise nature of these relations depends on the degree of competition in the banking sector, the costs of

[14]See, for example, Brunner and Meltzer (1964) and Rasche and Johannes (1987).

providing financial services and on the regulatory structure, as will be shown in Subsection 3.5.

The interest rate effects on the currency ratio and the time deposit ratio can be established by conventionally assuming that the real demands for currency and bank liabilities by the public depend upon the rates of return on these and other competing assets, and are functions of real income, Y, and real wealth, W/P, that is $A^d/P = F_A(i_D, i_T, i, Y, W/P)$, where $A = H_p, D, T$. If it is further assumed that these assets are gross substitutes and that the demands are homogeneous of first degree in real wealth and income, then the ratios of currency and time deposits to demand deposits, h and t, respectively, can be written as follows:[15]

$$h = h(i_D, i_T, i, PY/W),\qquad(52)$$

$$t = t(i_D, i_T, i, PY/W),\qquad(53)$$

where

$$\partial h/\partial i_D < 0,\quad \partial h/\partial i_T \gtrless 0,\quad \partial h/\partial i \gtrless 0,$$

$$\partial h/\partial Y = -\partial h/\partial(W/P) = \eta_{HY} - \eta_{DY} < 0,$$

$$\partial t/\partial i_D < 0,\quad \partial t/\partial i_T > 0,\quad \partial t/\partial i < 0,$$

$$\partial t/\partial Y = -\partial t/\partial(W/P) = \eta_{TY} - \eta_{DY} \gtrless 0.$$

The effect of the demand deposit rate on the currency ratio follows directly from the assumption of gross substitutability. An increase in the interest rate on time deposits or in the market rate of interest, which tends to reduce the demands for both currency and demand deposits, can be expected to result in an increase in the currency ratio on the ground that demand deposits are closer substitutes for time deposits and other financial assets than is currency. The empirical evidence, however, is rather ambiguous and it is reasonable to assume that these interest rate effects, though probably positive, are small.[16] An increase in real income has been found empirically to have a negative effect on the currency ratio, a result consistent with the income elasticity of the demand for currency (η_{HY}) being smaller than the income elasticity of the demand for sight deposits (η_{DY}).[17]

---

[15] The relative demands for currency and bank liabilities also depend on other factors such as the degree of confidence in the banking system, relative transactions costs influenced by institutional and technological developments, etc. The effects of such factors are not considered in this section, but they are incorporated in the autonomous and stochastic terms of the associated (log-linear) equations presented in Subsection 3.6.

[16] See Teigen (1969), Hess (1971) and Becker (1975).

[17] See Cagan (1958) and Kaufman (1966). The results of Goldfeld (1966) and Hosek (1970) suggest a positive effect of the level of income on the currency ratio, while Hess (1971) argues that the response of h to Y depends on the business cycle reflecting the cyclical response of consumption to income.

The effects on the time deposit ratio of the interest rates on demand and time deposits follow unambiguously from their effects on the respective asset demands. The response of the time deposit ratio to an increase in the market rate i can be expected to be negative on the grounds that time deposits are closer substitutes for non-bank financial assets than are demand deposits, so that $\partial F_T/\partial i < \partial F_D/\partial i < 0$. An increase in real income would be expected to also have a negative effect on the time deposit ratio since demand deposits are more directly related to transactions and thus income than time deposits, an aggregate taken to include all "non-transaction" deposits (implying $\eta_{TY} < \eta_{DY}$). Some empirical evidence, however, appears to indicate the existence of a positive relation between the time deposit ratio and income, a result that has been interpreted as reflecting the fact that time deposits have the characteristics of a "luxury" good.[18] Accordingly, it is assumed here that the effect of income on the time deposit ratio is ambiguous.

The banks' portfolio choices influence the money multiplier through their net effect on free reserves relative to demand deposits. Profit maximization by banks implies that the desired level of excess reserves is negatively affected by the rate of return on banks' earning assets, i (i.e. the opportunity cost of holding reserves), and positively affected by the rate of return on such reserves), i_R, and by the effective cost of borrowing from the central bank, i_{CB}. An increase in the cost of borrowing from the central bank induces banks to increase their excess reserves in order to reduce the potential cost of borrowing in the case of unanticipated withdrawals of funds. On the other hand, the demand for borrowing increases with the market rate reflecting an increased demand for credit by the public, but tends to decline in response to a rise in i_{CB}. Consequently, the desired level of free reserves relative to demand deposits is postulated to depend on three interest rates:[19]

$$f = f(i, i_R, i_{CB}),\tag{54}$$

where

$$\partial f/\partial i < 0, \qquad \partial f/\partial i_R > 0, \qquad \partial f/\partial i_{CB} > 0.$$

[18]See Friedman (1959), Teigen (1969), Hosek (1970), Goldfeld (1976), and Moosa (1977). The higher income elasticity of time deposits relative to demand deposits obtained in certain studies is probably due to misspecification bias since the estimated relations do not include the effects of real wealth which should have a significant impact on the demand for "non-transaction" deposits, an impact which empirically may be captured by income. Estimates of the income elasticity of the demand for time deposits in the presence of a wealth variable are small and often statistically insignificant [e.g. Modigliani (1972), Offenbacher and Porter (1982)].

[19]Empirical analyses of the demands for excess, borrowed and free reserves are presented in Andersen and Burger (1969), Hendershott and De Leeuw (1970), Modigliani, Rasche and Cooper (1970) and Frost (1971).

A more detailed discussion of the determinants of the demand for free reserves taking uncertainty into account is provided in the next section.

Substitution of equations (52)–(54) into (50) yields expressions for the supplies of money ($M1$ and $M2$) as functions of interest rates and income:

$$MJ = \mu_J(i, i_D, i_T, i_R, i_{CB}; Y; z_D, z_T)M0, \quad J = 1, 2.$$ (55)

The unborrowed monetary base, $M0$, the required reserve ratios, z_D and z_T, and the interest rates on banks' excess and borrowed reserves, i_R and i_{CB}, can be set by the central bank exogenously. The other three interest rates (i, i_D, i_T) may or may not be determined exogenously, depending upon the regulatory environment and the operating procedures of the central bank. Traditionally, i_D has been considered as administratively fixed or subject to a maximum ceiling. Thus, the money supply function employed in most analyses depends fundamentally on three endogenous variables: i, i_T and Y. The endogeneity of the market interest rate rests on the presumption that the central bank employs $M0$ as its policy instrument. The *total* effect of the market interest rate on the multipliers depends on the relationships between the market rate and the rates of return on bank liabilities, unless the latter are set administratively. Thus, the sign of the total interest rate effect cannot be established a priori at present since it depends on the precise nature of these relationships which are examined in Subsection 3.5.

The partial effects of the five interest rates influencing the money multipliers are summarised in Table 10.3. Briefly, the partial effect of an increase in the market rate on $M1$ is positive, provided the elasticity of the currency-deposit ratio with respect to the market rate is sufficiently small, as argued above. This positive response reflects the reduction in the levels of free reserves and time deposits, relative to demand deposits, resulting from the increase in the market rate. On the other hand, the effect of i on the $M2$ multiplier cannot be determined unambiguously.

Finally, an increase in the level of real income will have a positive effect on μ_1 if its effects on both the currency and time deposit ratios are negative, as

Table 10.3
Interest elasticities of the money multipliers

Interest rate on	Narrow measure $M1$	Broad measure $M2$
Bonds and bank loans, i (market rate)	+	?
Demand deposits, i_D	+	?
Time deposits, i_T	−	+
Excess reserves, i_R	−	−
Borrowed reserves, i_{CB}	−	−

could normally be expected. However, in view of the conflicting empirical evidence cited above on the dependence of h and t on income, the effects of Y on both μ_1 and μ_2 cannot be ascertained a priori unambiguously.

3.4. Bank asset management and a structural model of money stock determination

The alternative approach to the determination of the supply of money relies on an explicit specification of a structural model of bank behavior which describes the determinants of the supply of deposits by banks as well as their demands for earning assets and (free) reserves. The model of bank behavior is then combined with equations describing the determinants of the demands for currency, bank deposits and bank loans by the public to obtain a complete model of the money market determining the stock of money and one or more interest rates.

At the theoretical level, the main advantage of this alternative approach is that it explicitly specifies the mechanism through which the interaction of the public's demands for assets, the banks' behavior and the central bank's actions determine the stock of money. The multiplier approach, even when it allows for interest rate effects, leads to a money supply specification which is a hybrid of "public demands" and "bank behavior" elements, a kind of semi-reduced form rather than a money supply specification. It does not provide a theoretical analysis of the process through which banks' behavior influences the supply of bank deposits. Similarly, the description of the non-bank public's portfolio in terms of ad hoc specifications of financial ratios may impede an accurate analysis of the public's response to an increase in high-powered money. Since the creation of money (bank deposits) is the result of interacting portfolio adjustments by the public and the banks which, in general, are not invariant to the policy actions of the monetary authorities, the structural approach to the money supply mechanism provides a more useful framework for analysing policy-induced behavioral changes, especially for explaining the money supply process under more general institutional settings and in the presence of financial innovations.[20] At the empirical level, estimation of multiplier-type

---

[20]The structural approach, which focuses explicitly on the role of demands for and supplies of "money" and non-monetary assets and on the importance of portfolio and adjustments in the money creation process, has been referred to as the "new view". An important proposition associated with the "new view" is that the traditional analysis of money creation overemphasizes the distinctions between "money" and other financial assets and between banks and other financial intermediaries. Moreover, it is argued that the differences between banks and other financial intermediaries are not related to the monetary nature of bank deposits but rather to restrictions imposed by regulation on bank reserves and deposit rates. The implications of these restrictions for the money supply mechanism are discussed in Subsection 3.5 below. See Gurley and Shaw (1960) and Tobin (1963).

money supply specifications may be subject to considerable identification bias precisely when the analysis fails to take into account that the money supply is not independent of fluctuations in money demand.[21]

In this subsection we present one such structural model of the money creation process which incorporates a fairly detailed analysis of the determinants of banks' demand for earning assets and supply of demand deposits. The money supply mechanism is fundamentally that presented in Modigliani, Rasche and Cooper (1970) with two general modifications.[22] We abstract from certain institutional details and dynamic refinements which are not relevant for present purposes and we extend the formulation to allow for the determination of the stock of time as well as demand deposits and for the use of the unborrowed monetary base, rather than unborrowed reserves, as an instrument of policy. In this model the supply of demand deposits reflects the bank's demand for earning assets. The analysis deals with a relatively short time horizon within which it is reasonable to assume that for an individual bank the quantities of commercial loans and deposits are demand determined. The individual bank's decision reflects the uncertainty and the associated anticipations on the levels of deposits and bank loans that prevail over the decision period. From the balance sheet constraint of banks set out in Table 10.2, and the identities (45) and (47), applied to a specific bank j, we infer that

$$FR_j = (1 - z_D)D_j + (1 - z_T)T_j - L_j - B_j + V_j, \tag{56}$$

where for notational simplicity we let $V_j = E_{bj} - P_k K_{bj}$ and $B_j = B_{bj}$. The bank regards D_j, T_j and L_j as random variables subject to a known (subjective) probability distribution. The only variable the bank directly controls is the investment portfolio, B_j. In the short run, the *net* capital account, V_j, can reasonably be regarded as given. To a given choice of B_j there corresponds an uncertain level of free reserves, depending on the realizations of the three random variables D_j, T_j and L_j. Letting $\hat{D}_j$, $\hat{T}_j$ and $\hat{L}_j$ denote the subjective mathematical expectations of the three random variables and defining by $(x_D, x_T, x_L)_j$ the deviations of the realization of these random variables from

---

[21] See Lombra and Kaufman (1984) for a discussion of the problems associated with the identification and estimation of money supply functions.

[22] The model presented in this subsection analyses the determination of the stock of demand deposits by focusing on the role and determinants of banks' demands for investments and reserves in the presence of uncertainty. The effects of uncertainty for the management of bank assets and reserves were first explored by Edgeworth (1888). More recently, Orr and Mellon (1961), Poole (1968) and Frost (1971) have also examined the implications of uncertainty for banks' reserve management and deposit creation. The analysis of the supply of deposits included in the empirical studies of Meigs (1962), Teigen (1964), De Leeuw (1965), Goldfeld (1966), Goldfeld and Kane (1966), and Hester and Pierce (1968) differ from the one presented here in that they focus on banks' demands for excess and borrowed reserves rather than on their demand for earning assets.

the respective expectations, the relation between free reserves and the bank's investment can be expressed as:

$$FR_j = \widehat{FR}_j(B_j) + x_j \,, \tag{57}$$

where

$$\widehat{FR}_j(B_j) = (1 - z_D)\hat{D}_j + (1 - z_T)\hat{T}_j - \hat{L}_j - B_j + V_j \tag{57a}$$

and

$$x_j = (1 - z_D)x_{Dj} + (1 - z_T)x_{Tj} - x_{Lj} \,. \tag{57b}$$

The probability distribution for D_j, T_j and L_j implies a probability distribution for x_j. The cumulative distribution of x_j is denoted by $\Phi_j(x_j)$.

At each decision point, a bank aims at choosing its investment portfolio so as to maximize its profits. As can be seen from (57a) the choice of B_j determines the expectation of free reserves. Since a bank will not normally plan simultaneously to borrow and hold excess reserves, positive free reserves may be identified with excess reserves, earning a return i_R, while negative free reserves may be identified with borrowed reserves at a cost i_B. Denoting by i_L and i the rates of return on bank loans and the investment portfolio, respectively, the expected profits $\hat{\Pi}_j$ to be maximized can be written as

$$\hat{\Pi}_j = C_{bj} + i_L L_j + iB_j + i_B \int_{-\infty}^{-\widehat{FR}_j} [\widehat{FR}_j(B_j) + x_j] \, d\Phi_j(x_j)$$

$$+ i_R \int_{-\widehat{FR}_j}^{\infty} [\widehat{FR}_j(B_j) + x_j] \, d\Phi_j(x_j) \,, \tag{58}$$

where C_{bj} denotes the cumulative effect of variables affecting profits which are independent of portfolio composition, such as interest paid on deposits, operating costs, etc.

Maximization of (58) with respect to B_j, taking into account (57a), requires that the following first-order condition is satisfied:

$$i - i_R = (i_B - i_R)\Phi_j[-\widehat{FR}_j(B_j)] = 0 \,, \tag{59}$$

where $\Phi_j[-\widehat{FR}_j(B_j)]$ is the probability that x will not exceed $-\widehat{FR}$, or the probability that free reserves are negative. This condition implies that the profit-maximizing value of expected free reserves for the jth bank is given by

$$\widehat{FR}_j^* = -\Phi_j^{-1}[(i - i_R)/(i_B - i_R)] \,, \tag{59'}$$

where Φ_j^{-1}, the inverse of the cumulative distribution Φ_j, is a monotonically non-decreasing function of its argument. The profit-maximizing value of the investment of the jth bank, B_j^*, is obtained by substitution of (59') into (57a) and solving for B_j. The aggregate (optimum) demand for investment by the banking system is determined by summing up the resulting expressions over all banks, assuming they face the same interest rates and are subject to the same reserve requirements. Thus,

$$B_b^d = \sum_j B_j^* = (1 - z_D)\hat{D} + (1 - z_T)\hat{T} - \hat{L} + V_b - FR^d \,, \tag{60}$$

$$FR^d = \sum_j \widehat{FR}_j^* = -\Psi[(i - i_R)/(i_B - i_R)] \,, \tag{61}$$

where $V_b = \sum_j V_j = E_b - P_k K_b$ and $\hat{D}$, $\hat{T}$ and $\hat{L}$ are the aggregate expectations of demand deposits, time deposits and loans, respectively. The function Ψ which is the sum of Φ_j^{-1} exhibits the same properties. The existence of a finite profit-maximizing solution requires that market forces or institutional constraints ensure that $(i_B - i_R) > (i - i_R) > 0$. If this condition is satisfied, then

$$\partial B_b / \partial i = -\partial FR^d / \partial i > 0 \,, \qquad \partial B_b / \partial i_B = -\partial FR^d / \partial i_B < 0 \,, \tag{62}$$

which is consistent with the discussion in the previous subsection.

The aggregate demands for investments and free reserves by the banking system depend upon banks' anticipations of deposits and loans (at the beginning of each period) and the speed with which banks adjust their portfolios to achieve the optimum free reserve target. Both for analytical and for estimation purposes it is important to understand the implications of alternative hypotheses concerning the formation of banks' expectations in terms of observable quantities and the dynamics of portfolio adjustment. Nevertheless, to develop the basic features of an aggregative structural model of the money supply process we focus on the limiting case in which banks are able to forecast perfectly or to adjust fully to any forecast error.[23] Under this hypothesis, the expected values $\hat{D}$, $\hat{T}$ and $\hat{L}$ in (60) are replaced by the actual levels of the respective variables.

To derive a relation between the implied quantity of demand deposits and the unborrowed monetary base, the quantity controlled by the central bank, we first use (60) to substitute for V_b in the balance sheet identity of the banking system implied by Table 10.2 and solve for D to obtain:

$$D = (RU - z_T T - FR^d)/z_D \,. \tag{63}$$

[23]A more general formulation allowing for partial adjustment of portfolios to errors of anticipations and imperfect forecasts based partly on past observations is presented in Modigliani, Rasche and Cooper (1970).

The above supply function for demand deposits is a generalization of the textbook equilibrium relation, $D = RU/z_D$, and accounts for the effects of reserve requirements against time deposits and of the desired level of free reserves. When expectations are imperfect and adjustments to forecast errors are gradual, the supply of demand deposits also depends on unanticipated changes in loans drawn by the public as well as on lagged values of all financial variables.

The optimum level of free reserves, given by (61), depends on the market rate, i, the rate at which banks can borrow, i_B, and the rate they can earn on excess reserves, i_R. In the absence of an interbank market for reserves, i_B would have to coincide with the central bank lending rate, i_{CB}, and i_R with the interest, if any, paid on excess reserves by the central bank. But with an interbank market, such as the Federal Funds market in the United States, i_B and i_R must be thought of as interbank rates and $i_B - i_R$ must be in the nature of a transaction cost and hence small and approximately constant. Thus, (61) can be approximated by

$$FR^d = -\Psi[(i - i_R)/(i_B - i_R)] \simeq \Psi_0(i - i_B), \quad \Psi_0' < 0. \tag{61'}$$

The relation of i_B to i_{CB} depends on the central bank's discount rate policy. If the discount window were wide open, then arbitrage considerations suggest that these two rates would tend to be the same, at least as long as there was any borrowing outstanding. In reality, the use of the window is limited in various ways and involves non-cash costs. Hence, i_{CB} is usually smaller than i_B, at least under the Federal Reserve style of operations. An analysis of the interbank market, which must be omitted here, leads to the conclusion that i_B is related to i_{CB} by

$$i_B = \chi(i_{CB}, FR), \quad \partial\chi/\partial i_{CB} \geq 0, \quad \partial\chi/\partial FR \leq 0, \tag{64}$$

where $\partial\chi/\partial i_{CB}$ is close to and probably less than unity.

Substituting (64) into (61') we find that, when the interbank market is in equilibrium with banks adjusting promptly their portfolios to meet their optimum level of free reserves, so that $FR^d = FR$, the desired (and actual) level of free reserves is given by

$$FR^d = F(i, i_{CB}), \quad \partial F/\partial i < 0, \quad \partial F/\partial i_{CB} \geq 0. \tag{65}$$

Expressions (61) and (64)–(65) have been derived for a given price level. More generally, the above analysis can be restated to determine the relation between the optimum level of real free reserves and interest rates:

$$FR^d = PF_R(i, i_{CB}). \tag{65'}$$

Note that the optimum level of free reserves, as given by (65) or (65'), does not appear to depend on the scale of the banking system. This is not the case, however, as the demand for free reserves by the individual bank is given by the inverse of the cumulative distribution, Φ_j, which reflects the average scale of the individual bank. The aggregate demand for free reserves given by (61) will depend on the average scale of the banking system along the lines implied by the law of large numbers.

Substituting (65') and (46) into (63), and expressing the quantities of currency and time deposits held by the public in terms of their determining factors, that is $H_p^d = PF_H(i_D, i_T, i, Y)$ and $T^d = PF_T(i_D, i_T, i, Y)$, we derive an expression for the supply of demand deposits in terms of $M0$ and other policy-controlled variables:

$$D^s = [M0 - PF_H(i_D, i_T, i, Y) - z_T PF_T(i_D, i_T, i, Y) - PF_R(i, i_{CB})]/z_D . \tag{66}$$

In this subsection it is assumed that the deposit rates, i_D and i_T, are policy determined.

The supply of demand deposits is again seen to be a multiple of the unborrowed base, adjusted for currency demand as well as other factors absorbing reserves, namely time deposits and free reserves. These adjustments depend on the market rate, real income, the price level and policy parameters. While P and Y can be taken as given in the short run in which the money market reaches equilibrium, the interest rate cannot as it responds to the demand for various types of deposits. This can be seen by taking into account the market-clearing condition $D^d = D^s$, or equating the right-hand side of (66) to $D^d = PF_D(i_D, i_T, i, Y)$. By rearranging terms and conveniently omitting the exogenously determined variables, i_D and i_T, the resulting equation can be rewritten as

$$PF_H(i, Y) + z_D PF_D(i, Y) + z_T PF_T(i, Y) + PF_R(i, i_{CB}) = M0 . \tag{67}$$

The above equation represents the equilibrium condition in the market for (non-borrowed) high-powered money. It can be used to solve for the equilibrium market rate:

$$i^* = i^*(M0/P, i_{CB}, i_D, i_T, z_D, z_T, Y) , \tag{67'}$$

and it can be readily established that $\partial i^*/\partial M0 < 0$. Equations (67) or (67') can also be thought of as a generalization of the Hicksian LM curve, except that the policy given monetary quantity is the unborrowed base, and that the relation between i, Y and P is recognized to depend on various policy-controlled variables besides $M0$.

By replacing the solution i^* for i in the supply of demand deposits [equation (66)] or in the demand equation D^d, one obtains a "reduced" form for the stock of deposits which depends on Y, $M0$ and other policy parameters. The stock of $M1$ is then given by the sum of demand deposits described above and the demand-determined stock of currency, given i^*. The stock of $M2$ is obtained by simply adding the demand-determined stock of time deposits to the stock of $M1$. Both currency and time deposits affect $M1$ and $M2$ indirectly by draining reserves, but this is already taken into account in the stock of demand deposits.

This analysis illustrates the central role in the money-creation process of asset preferences of the public and of those of banks, expressed in the demand for free reserves. When these preferences are influenced by asset yields, the quantity of money ($M1$ and $M2$) is determined endogenously *and* simultaneously with the market interest rate, given nominal income. The positive effect of an increase in $M0$ on $M1$ and $M2$ is easily seen to be the consequence of two effects: the increase in $M0$ reduces the market rate, and this reduction in turn increases the demand for $M1$ and $M2$. Similarly, an increase in the central bank rate tends to increase free reserves leading to a fall in the quantities of bank assets and demand deposits and to a rise in the market rate. On the other hand, the effect of a rise in Y on $M1$ is ambiguous, as the increase in T and H_p it induces tends to reduce the reserves available for demand deposits, but the rise in the demand for demand deposits tends to raise i which in turn tends to raise D through a fall in free reserves, T and H_p.

The determination of the equilibrium quantities of narrow and broad monetary aggregates and, more generally, the nature of money market equilibrium in the presence of a banking system can be examined more precisely and related to the aggregative models of Section 2 by employing log-linear specifications of asset demands and allowing for the effects of stochastic elements. Let the public's demand for currency and bank liabilities be given by

$$\ln (A^{d}/P) = a_A + k_A i + b_A y + u_A , \tag{68}$$

where $A = H_p, D, T$; y is the (natural) logarithm of aggregate real income; i is the nominal market interest rate; and u_A, $(A = H, D, T)$ are serially uncorrelated random variables. Suppose, furthermore, that the banks' demand for real free reserves is given by

$$\ln (FR^{d}/P) = f_0 + f_i i + f_{CB} i_{CB} + u_F , \quad f_i < 0, f_{CB} > 0 . \tag{69}$$

Restating the equilibrium condition (67) in deviations from the full employment equilibrium $(\bar{Y}, \bar{r})$ and from given initial levels, $\overline{M0}$, and $\bar{P}$, employing the approximation $x/\bar{x} - 1 = \ln x - \ln \bar{x}$, and regrouping terms, we obtain the following condition for money market equilibrium:

$$mo - \overline{mo} = p - \bar{p} + b_y(y - \bar{y}) + k_i(i - \bar{i}) + s_F f_{CB}(i_{CB} - \bar{i}_{CB}) + u_M , \tag{70}$$

where

$$b_y = s_H b_H + s_D b_D + s_T b_T ,$$
(70a)

$$k_i = s_H k_H + s_D k_D + s_T k_T + s_F f_i$$
(70b)

$$u_M = s_H u_H + s_D u_D + s_T u_T + s_F u_F ,$$
(70c)

$$s_H = \bar{H}_p / \overline{M0} , \qquad s_D = z_D \bar{D} / \overline{M0} , \qquad s_T = z_T \bar{T} / \overline{M0} , \qquad s_F = \overline{FR} / \overline{M0} ,$$
(70d)

and p and mo are the natural logarithms of P and $M0$, respectively.

The above condition clearly shows the interacting behavioral and structural factors influencing the determination of equilibrium in the money markets, when the central bank controls the quantity of non-borrowed high powered money. The income elasticity, the interest semielasticity, and thus the slope of this generalized LM relation (70), are weighted averages of the corresponding asset demand elasticities, weighted by the shares of currency and the various components of reserves (required and free) in $\overline{M0}$. Similarly, the stochastic component of the money market equilibrium condition is a composite of the underlying uncertain factors influencing the behavior of the public (u_H, u_D, u_T) and banks (u_F). Both the slope and the stability of the LM relation depend upon the economy's financial structure, as summarized by the shares in (70d), and policy-determined variables (z_D, z_T, i_{CB}). Clearly, the sources of instability impinging on the money market equilibrium are more complex than usually assumed, when they are identified exclusively with the instability of the demand for transactions balances ($M1$).

Condition (70) should replace equation (17) in Table 10.1 as the relevant condition for money market equilibrium if the central bank employs $M0$ both as an instrument and a monetary target. If, however, the monetary authorities endeavor to achieve the final policy targets by controlling the stocks of monetary aggregates broader than $M0$, such as $M1$ or $M2$, and they are in a position to do so effectively, then the relevant money market equilibrium conditions would be of the general form of (17) in Table 10.1, while the quantity of $M0$ is in this case determined endogenously so as to achieve the desired levels of the intermediate monetary targets.

3.5. Liability management and general equilibrium models of the banking firm

The structural model of money stock determination presented above focuses on the role of bank reserve and asset management as the key, bank-related, behavioral force in the money creation process. The emphasis on bank asset management, which is typical of most money supply models and of textbook expositions, prevailed until the early 1970s as a result of the regulatory and financial environment characteristic of many Western economies from the end of the Second World War until the mid-1970s. During this period, the structure of financial markets and of the banking system remained fairly stable in these economies, notably in the United States, and interest paid on bank liabilities was frequently regulated.

Since the mid-1970s, however, economic and technological changes interacting with growing deregulation of the banking system have allowed banks greater flexibility in managing both their assets and liabilities. Inflation, which was gradually rising since the late 1960s and accelerated after the first energy crisis, and administratively set ceilings on bank deposit rates, which failed to adjust fully to the inflationary environment in order to help institutions that had lent long while borrowing short, induced a shift of funds by the public from deposits to other financial assets. This process of disintermediation imposed burdens on banks which were unable to compete effectively by offering a return on their liabilities comparable to those obtained on marketable securities or on assets provided by other financial intermediaries (e.g. money market funds) and these burdens pushed central banks in the direction of deregulation.[24] Banks' attempts to bypass the regulatory constraints and resist the outflow of funds were facilitated by advances in information and computing technology which reduced the cost of transferring funds between different types of bank liabilities. Technological progress fostered financial innovations allowing banks to offer transactions services out of other forms of bank liabilities. Restrictions on the setting of deposit rates were gradually lifted and since the early 1980s banks have been allowed to compete more or less freely with other financial institutions in pricing their services and attracting funds.[25]

The process of disintermediation, financial innovation and deregulation created serious problems for the interpretation and control of monetary aggregates by monetary authorities. These developments increased the uncertainty associated with the definition and measurement of "money", and had important implications for the functioning of banks, the process of money creation and the effectiveness of monetary controls. Over a number of years, and especially during the transition to a more deregulated banking system, the stochastic stability and predictability of the velocity relations between nominal

---

[24]It should be noted that although in the United States banks were able to borrow considerable amounts of money since the mid 1960s by issuing negotiable certificates of deposit (CDs) at competitive interest rates, Regulation Q frequently imposed ceilings on the rates of negotiable CDs until 1973.

[25]Akhtar (1983), Cagan (1979), Davis (1981), Goodhart (1982) and Wilson (1986) review recent changes in the structure of financial markets and discuss their implications for monetary policy.

income and "money" or, more generally, alternative monetary aggregates, was seriously impaired. So was the ability of central banks to employ monetary aggregates as intermediate targets or guides for policy. Moreover, the modus operandi of banks in the new deregulated environment has affected the relationship between the stock of money and the instruments of monetary policy.

As the preceding analysis in Subsection 3.4 has demonstrated, the stock of money adjusts endogenously and simultaneously with the market interest rate in response to changes in the non-borrowed base or other policy-controlled variables, with the nature of the response reflecting both the public's and banks' asset preferences. In a deregulated environment, banks play a more central role in the adjustment process and in shaping the nature of money market equilibrium, and they may be in a position to offset in part the quantitative impact of monetary policy actions. When deposit rates are administratively fixed, a restrictive policy action aiming at a reduction of the money supply induces a rise in the market interest rate which is accompanied by a rise in the differentials between market and deposit rates, a shift of funds out of the banking system and a decline in the stocks of narrow and broad money. On the other hand, when banks are able to increase deposit rates in line with the market rate, they are able to partly offset, and may possibly frustrate, the authorities' attempts to control the stocks of monetary aggregates. Although interest rates rise and the stock of *base* money initially declines, the effective supply of money and the size of bank liabilities may remain virtually unchanged, especially if currency holdings comprise a very small part of the economy's liquid assets.

These considerations strongly suggest that an analysis of the process of money creation and of the effectiveness of monetary controls in a deregulated environment must place greater emphasis on the behavior of banks and on their role in the money supply mechanism. In recent years there has been a considerable amount of theoretical research on the behavior of "the banking firm". Baltensperger (1980) and Santomero (1984) provide fairly comprehensive surveys of the new theoretical approaches to the modelling of the banking firm. For present purposes, we concentrate on aspects of these analyses which bear directly on the money supply process, emphasizing, in particular, the role of liability management. In the next subsection we present a simple aggregative model of money stock determination, which incorporates stylized relations describing banks' behavior consistent with the microeconomic analysis, and we discuss the model's implications for monetary controls and the determination of nominal income.

Formal models of liability management deal with two basic choices: (i) the deposit-structure decision, concerning the quantity of different types of deposits given the bank's equity capital, and (ii) the capital-deposit decision.

These decisions can be examined either in a partial equilibrium framework by taking as given the level and structure of bank assets, or by considering them jointly with liquidity and asset management problems as part of a more general analysis which determines simultaneously the composition of bank assets and liabilities. The second approach is obviously more general and relevant for the present analysis. Nevertheless, before proceeding with the presentation of general equilibrium models of a banking firm, it is helpful to outline a few of the key features in the modelling of liability management which have appeared in the literature.

The essential factors affecting a bank's management of liabilities are: (1) market structure, in particular the degree of monopoly power enjoyed by a bank; (2) operating or "real resource" costs associated with the provision of deposit and transactions services; and (3) insolvency costs resulting from default losses on bank loans. Analyses of liquidity management have emphasized the role of one or more of the above factors in the determination of the structure of bank liabilities.

The models of Klein (1971) and Monti (1972) provide frameworks for analysing both asset and liability choices by relying on the assumption of monopoly power. On the liability side, it is assumed that deposit rates are not set by regulators; instead, the bank faces the public's demands for deposits and chooses the rates on various deposits. Thus, the quantities of demand and time deposits outstanding are functions of the deposit rates. The bank sets the deposit rates so as to maximize net revenues or the expected rate of return on its equity.[26] The individual bank also faces a demand for loans which is a decreasing function of the loan rate, and it can behave as a monopolistic price-setter. But the market for government securities is perfectly competitive so that government securities are in a perfectly elastic supply at the market rate of return, i. The necessary conditions for profit maximization require that the marginal cost of obtaining funds from demand and time deposits must be equal to the marginal expected revenue on bank assets, which in turn should equal the expected interest rate in the perfectly competitive market for government securities, adjusted for the expected marginal loss from the bank's reserve management. Thus, the rates offered by banks on their deposits depend on the "exogenous" market rate and the parameters of the public's demand functions for the two categories of deposits. If the time deposit function facing the bank is more interest elastic than the demand deposit function, partly because other financial instruments are relatively more substitutable for time deposits, the rate of return on demand deposits will be less than the time deposit rate. The structure of deposit rates is also affected by differential reserve requirements on the two types of deposits, as shown by Miller (1975).

---

[26]Monti examines the implications of alternative bank objectives on bank behavior. Both Klein and Monti assume that bank equity is exogenously fixed.

In Klein's initial formulation, the bank's optimal liability choice is independent of its optimal asset choice. This separability is the result of certain special assumptions about the relation between the loan rate and the composition of earning assets. It also fails to hold if the probability distribution of the reserve flow is not assumed independent of the composition of deposits or if deposits are subject to reserve requirements.[27] The monopolistic models of bank behavior have been criticized because they lead to extreme choices (corner solutions) when the markets for deposits and loans become competitive. The basic reason is that they rely only on demand characteristics, reflecting the preferences of the public and do not take into account the "supply-side", i.e. the production process describing the supply of financial services by banks.

In general, the setting of deposit rates and the resulting structure of deposits should be influenced by the real resource costs incurred in the provision of different types of deposit and loan services. Yet, the role of operating costs and of the associated production technology for financial services has been neglected in most analyses of bank behavior but has been receiving growing attention. It has been examined in a number of studies, including Kareken (1967), Pesek (1970), Stillson (1974), Towey (1974), Saving (1977, 1979), Sealey and Lindley (1977), Niehans (1978), Baltensperger (1980) and Fischer (1983). The analyses presented by these authors differ in their formalization of the production aspects of banks and the assumed regulatory environment.[28] With the exception of Niehans and Baltensperger, they focus on the operational aspects ignoring possible interactions of resource costs with the stochastic factors influencing a bank's portfolio behavior.

A bank can be viewed, in general, as a firm which provides two types of services, "transactions services" and "portfolio management services" (e.g. diversification, intermediation). Each category of deposits offers a combination of services to the depositors which are produced by the bank by combining inputs through a transformation process described by a production function. The services associated with the acquisition of earning assets (such as the extension of loans) are also viewed as the output of a production process. The services provided to depositors can also be related to the acquisition of

---

[27]See Miller (1975) and Baltensperger (1980).

[28]For example, Saving (1979) assumes a production function for the number of demand deposit transactions which depends on a factor input and the average nominal or real transaction size; he also employs a demand function for the resources required for the optimal management of the bank's loan portfolio, and he takes the stock of base money as determined independent of market forces by the central bank. Niehans (1978) employs a production function relating implicitly the volumes of loans and deposits and the required inputs of capital and labor. Fischer (1983) specifies a production function for transactions services which depends on the amounts of labor and capital used and the real quantity of high-powered money held by the bank. Both Fischer and Niehans consider an unregulated environment, where banks are not required to hold reserves and they do so only in order to provide transactions services efficiently. Sealey and Lindley (1977) examine the definition of appropriate concepts of outputs and inputs of the banking firm and develop a model of the technical aspects of production.

financial inputs, that is they may be regarded as intermediate outputs employed by the bank to acquire loans and other assets. The costs incurred in attracting deposits consist of the "resource costs" of the quantities of labor and capital used in producing the services offered by these accounts, plus interest payments on such deposits for their use as loanable funds. For the sake of illustration, we may rely on the simplifying assumption that the production of services associated with different categories of deposits and bank assets are independent of each other and that the quantity of services is related to the respective real quantities of deposits and loans, that is

$$D/P = F^D(K_b^D, N_b^D), \quad T/P = F^T(K_b^T, N_b^T), \quad L/P = F^L(K_b^L, N_b^L), \quad (71)$$

where K_b^J and N_b^J are the quantities of capital and labor employed by the bank in the production of the services associated with liability or asset J ($J = D, T, L$). The quantity of real reserves can also be considered an input in the production of deposit services, as done by Fischer (1983), since without holding cash reserves a bank cannot satisfy the demand for currency. Abstracting initially from the costs and revenues associated with liquidity management (examined in Subsection 3.4) and expected bankruptcy costs (to be discussed below), *real* bank profits are given by

$$\Pi_b/P = r_L L/P + rB_b/P - r_D D/P - r_T T/P - \pi R/P - wN_b, \quad (72)$$

where $N_b = N_b^D + N_b^T + N_b^L$, $\pi R/P$ is the real capital loss on reserves due to inflation, and w is the real wage rate. Banks maximize real profits subject to the production functions (71) and the balance sheet constraint:

$$D + T + E_b = RU + L + B_b + P_k K_b, \quad (73)$$

where RU is given by (47) and (43).

Under competitive conditions, the optimal quantities of deposits, loans and real capital and labor can, in principle, be determined for the individual bank in terms of market interest rates and prices from the first-order conditions for an optimum, if the technical production functions exhibit decreasing returns to scale and to each factor in the relevant range. These efficiency conditions are given below for an alternative approach employing cost functions.

If returns to scale are constant, the size of the representative bank is indeterminate. Both the supply of its deposits and the volume of its loans are determined by demand. Under competitive conditions and free entry, the maximum normal profits for the representative bank are zero, implying market-determined equilibrium relationships between the rates of return on bank deposits and assets, which involve factor costs.

The implications of real resource costs for the determination of the equilibrium size and the structure of bank deposits and assets can, alternatively, be examined by employing a cost function obtained by expressing the cost-minimizing combination of factors in terms of the real quantities of financial assets and liabilities. Assuming initially that reserves consist only of non-interest-bearing required reserves, as determined by (43), and that bank equity is fixed, *real* profits are then given by

$$\Pi_b/P = r_L L/P + r B_b/P - r_D D/P - r_T T/P - \pi R/P - c(L/P, D/P, T/P).$$
(74)

The individual bank determines the optimal quantities of loans and deposits so as to maximize (74) subject to (73). Assuming perfect competition, profit maximization requires that:

$$r_L = r + c_L,$$
$$r_D = (1 - z_D)r - \pi z_D - c_D,$$
(75)
$$r_T = (1 - z_T)r - \pi z_T - c_T,$$

where z_D and z_T are the required reserve ratios on demand and time deposits respectively, c_L, c_D and c_T are the partial derivatives of the cost function with respect to L/P, D/P and T/P, which in general are functions of the volumes of loans and deposits. Provided that the second-order conditions are also satisfied, equations (75) can be considered as specifying the optimum structure of deposits, the supply of bank loans and, given bank equity, the overall size of the individual bank as functions of the market-determined rates of return.

The interpretation of (75) is straightforward. A bank should extend loans until the real return on such loans, net of the real resource costs of providing loans at the margin, is equal to the real market interest rate. Similarly, a bank is willing to supply deposits until the total marginal cost, including the real resource cost of providing deposits, is equal to the marginal revenue on bank's earning assets, net of the real cost of holding reserves. Note that the optimal liability structure for an individual bank is such that the interest rate differential between the two types of deposits reflects differential operating costs and reserve requirements, $r_T - r_D = (c_D - c_T) + (z_D - z_T)(r + \pi)$; the interest rate differential depends upon the *nominal* market interest rate if the required reserve ratios differ. Whether the management of liabilities is independent of the decision concerning the optimal supply of loans depends on the technological processes underlying the cost function $c(L/P, D/P, T/P)$.

With constant returns to scale, the cost function is linear and homogeneous, and the respective marginal costs of producing a unit of transaction and intermediation services depend only on the ratios of the arguments of $c(\cdot)$ in

(74). Accordingly, the scale of the individual bank and the structure of the liabilities cannot be determined from (75). A possible shortcoming of this analysis is that it assumes perfect competition in the markets for deposits and loans. This is equivalent to saying that the individual bank takes interest rates as given, and assumes that at these rates it can supply all the deposits and loans it wants. In general, it would be more appropriate to recognize that the bank faces negatively sloped demand curves for both deposits and loans, as discussed above. Nevertheless, the assumption of perfect competition should provide a reasonable first approximation of market conditions.

The analysis has assumed so far that bank equity is given exogenously and consequently has no influence on the portfolio decisions or the management of liabilities. Analyses of the bank capital decision have followed different approaches emphasizing alternative aspects of a bank's activities and making different assumptions concerning market structure and regulatory requirements. The determination of an optimal capital structure depends on the existence of market imperfections.[29] In fact, the existence of banks and other financial intermediaries is fundamentally related to market imperfections which can be exploited. We first critically review a number of representative contributions to the analysis of the deposit–equity decision of banks and then integrate the effects of equity determination into our analysis.

One of the first, though relatively recent, theoretical studies on the bank capital decision based on optimizing behavior is that of Pringle (1974). He examines the problem employing the Capital Asset Pricing Model, but assuming that various market imperfections cause (fixed) deviations from the equilibrium relationships implied by the model. These deviations, which result in excess returns and costs, are exploited by the individual bank whose objective is to maximize the net value of equity of its shareholders. The bank's balance sheet structure is similar to the one considered here. There are two assets, risky loans and riskless government securities, and three categories of liabilities, deposits which are subject to stochastic fluctuations, borrowing and capital. The bank determines the optimal quantities of loans and equity, while its net liquidity position, the difference between its holdings of securities and borrowing, is determined implicitly by the above decisions and the exogenously determined quantity of deposits. It is also assumed that the bank has a degree of monopoly in the market for bank loans so that the "excess" expected return on bank loans, relative to the risk-free rate of interest, declines with the level of loans, while the net cost of deposits is exogenously determined.

Pringle's analysis demonstrates how the optimal level of loans depends on whether the equity is fixed or it is considered a policy variable controlled by the management. In the latter case the optimal policy is to extend loans up to the point where the excess expected marginal loan revenue is equal to the excess

---

[29]Modigliani and Miller (1958).

marginal cost of equity, which is taken as exogenously given. The certainty-equivalent cost of equity capital is higher than the risk-free interest rate by a constant amount which reflects flotation costs and servicing costs associated with dividend payments, communication with shareholders, etc.[30] Since by assumption the bank pursues a passive policy regarding deposits, the desired level of bank lending is financed with equity capital. The optimal level of loans and the optimal bank size depend *only* on the degree of imperfection in the loan and equity markets, and are independent of the probability distribution of deposits, the risk–return preferences of the public, or the cost of borrowing. By contrast, when equity is constrained to a given level, the optimal quantity of loans depends on all these factors. However, in the single-period analysis and when deposits and the return on the market portfolio are uncorrelated, the existence of a positive optimal equity level presupposes that the net cost of bank borrowing is greater than the net, certainty-equivalent cost of equity funds. This points to a first limitation of this analysis: the equity–deposit choice critically depends on the assumption that equity is less costly than borrowing and does not reflect the fundamental role of equity, distinguishing it from other bank liabilities, in bearing risk and as a means of protecting depositors against losses. A second limitation is that it also critically depends on the assumption of some monopoly power in the market of bank loans. Under competitive conditions in the loan market, implying an exogenously determined rate of return, the individual bank will not be able to adopt a well-defined debt–equity policy or it will be led towards extreme equity choices.

The implications of bank capital adequacy regulations and of deposit insurance, an alternative means of protecting depositors, on the bank liability structure and portfolio allocation have also been examined by, among others, Kahane (1977) and Koehn and Santomero (1980). These studies employ general portfolio-leverage models, introduced to the analysis of the financial firm by Pyle (1971) and Hart and Jaffee (1974), to determine a portfolio and a debt–equity ratio which maximize the rate of return on equity, abstracting from the effects of production, liquidity and bankruptcy costs.[31]

Another approach to the determination of the bank's deposit–equity structure focuses on the role of default losses on loans and the associated costs of bankruptcy. Niehans (1978) formulates this by postulating that the individual bank maximizes expected profits subject to a constraint that the expected cost of bankruptcy, which depends upon the probability distribution of default

---

[30]The excess marginal cost of capital considered by Pringle reflects factors other than those discussed by Brennan (1971) and others and which relate to the excess return on risky securities.

[31]Orgler and Taggart (1983), on the other hand, examine the dependence of the bank's capital structure on the cost of transaction services provided by the bank and on the interacting effects of personal and corporate taxes. Merton (1977) and Sharpe (1978) analyse the determinants of the cost of deposit insurance and its effects of the bank's capital structure by employing the option pricing theory.

losses on loans and the quantities of loans and equity, does not exceed a given minimum level. However, the determination of this minimum acceptable level is not explained or related to a more general formulation of a bank's risk–return preferences.

The effects on the structure of liabilities of the uncertainty of portfolio income and related default risk can be analysed alternatively by considering the impact on expected profits of the expected cost of insolvency. Consider first a bank with a given initial size A of total assets and a given asset structure. Following Baltensperger (1980), the bank's net income from these assets inclusive of capital gains and losses, Y_A, is viewed as a random variable because of potential default losses and consequent uncertainty about the end-of-period value of its investments. It is subject to a known probability distribution function, $G_A(Y_A)$, which depends on both the level of assets and the composition of the bank's portfolio. The bank will be insolvent if, at the end of the period, its deposit liabilities are greater than the value of its assets, $D(1 + i_D) + T(1 + i_T) > A + Y_A - C(D, T)$, that is if its asset income is smaller than a critical value, $\bar{Y}_A$:

$$Y_A < \bar{Y}_A = D(1 + i_D) + T(1 + i_T) + C(D, T) - A , \tag{76}$$

where the cost function $C(D, T)$ represents the resource costs associated with the provision of deposit services and is assumed to depend on the levels of the two types of deposits.

The costs of insolvency, which include costs due to the suspension of dividends, loss of public confidence and possible license suspension by the supervisory authorities, may reasonably be assumed to be proportional to the magnitude of the capital deficiency $(\bar{Y}_A - Y_A)$. The expected cost of insolvency is then given by

$$C_I = C_I(D, T, A) = \int_{-\infty}^{\bar{Y}_A} c_I(\bar{Y}_A - Y_A)\, dG_A(Y_A) , \tag{77}$$

and expected nominal bank profits by

$$\hat{\Pi}_b = E(Y_A) - i_D D - i_T T - i_E E_b - C(D, T) - C_I(D, T, A) , \tag{78}$$

where i_E is the (required) rate of return on equity (the opportunity cost of increasing equity by a dollar). The structure of liabilities which maximizes (78) subject to (77) and the balance sheet constraint, $D + T + E_b = A$, must satisfy the conditions:

$$i_E = i_D + C_D + C_{ID} ,$$
$$i_E = i_T + C_T + C_{IT} , \tag{79}$$

where

$$C_{IJ} = \partial C_I / \partial J = c_I \int_{-\infty}^{\bar{Y}_A} (1 + i_J + C_J)\, dG_A(Y_A)$$

$$= c_I(1 + i_J + C_J)G_A(\bar{Y}_A), \quad J = D, T, \tag{80}$$

and $C_J = \partial C / \partial J$. Thus, the bank's optimal structure of deposits and demand for equity should be such as to equalize the expected total marginal costs of financing from all sources of funds. Since, in general, the marginal operating costs and the expected costs of insolvency may vary with the volume of deposits, these necessary conditions for optimality yield the optimal deposit structure as a function of the rates of return (i_D, i_T, i_E) and, of course, depend upon the probability distribution $G_A(Y_A)$.

We next consider the more general problem of joint determination of the structure of liabilities and the scale of the banking firm taking into account the expected cost of bankruptcy and the costs incurred in the provision of financial services. Since in this case the size of total assets and the asset structure are not taken as given, the management of liabilities, in general, interacts with the bank's choices of its assets. In analysing this problem it is again assumed, for simplicity, that bank reserves consist of non-interest-bearing required reserves, given by (43), and that the real capital held by the bank is fixed at the beginning-of-period level $(K_b = \bar{K}_b)$. Accordingly, the balance sheet constraint becomes:

$$(1 - z_D)D + (1 - z_T)T + E_b = L + B_b + P_k \bar{K}_b, \tag{81}$$

where P_k is the market value of a unit of the bank's real capital.

Let X_L denote the losses on loans in default at the end of the period which is a random variable with an estimated cumulative probability distribution, $G(X_L)$. Default losses on the beginning-of-period quantity of loans L is assumed to be the only source of uncertainty affecting the bank's income, thus ignoring any uncertainty about the value of the bond portfolio. The bank faces bankruptcy if, at the end of the period, the deposit liabilities exceed the value of its assets (which includes the net income earned during the period), that is if $(1 + i_D)D + (1 + i_T)T > (1 + i_D)z_D D + (1 + i_T)z_T T + (1 + i_L)(L - X_L) + (1 + i)B_b + (1 + \pi)P_k \bar{K}_b - C(D, T, L, B_b)$. This will occur if default losses on loans are greater than a critical level, $\bar{X}_L$, given by

$$\bar{X}_L = L + [(1 + i)B_b + (1 + \pi)P_k \bar{K}_b - NTD - C(D, T, L, B_b)](1 + i_L)^{-1}, \tag{82}$$

where $NTD = (1 + i_D)(1 - z_D)D + (1 + i_T)(1 - z_T)T$.

Note that NTD is the end-of-period total quantity of deposits net of reserves required against them. The larger NTD is, the smaller is the critical level $\bar{X}_L$ and the larger the probability that the bank will face insolvency. Suppose that the expected losses from bankruptcy, Q, are proportional to the size of the default losses, with k denoting the proportionality factor:

$$Q = Q(D, T, L, B_b) = \int_{\bar{X}_L}^{L} c_X(X_L - \bar{X}_L)\, dG(X_L). \tag{83}$$

The bank maximizes expected profits:

$$\hat{\Pi}_b = i_L L + iB_b - i_D D - i_T T - i_E E_b - C(D, T, L, B_b) - Q + \pi P_k \bar{K}_b \tag{84}$$

subject to the constraints (81)–(83). If all financial markets are competitive, so that the individual bank perceives the rates of return as given at the beginning of the period, profit maximization with respect to the quantities of financial assets requires that the following first-order conditions are satisfied:

$$i_L - C_L - Q_L = i - C_B - Q_B, \tag{85}$$

$$(1 - z_D)^{-1}(i_D + C_D + Q_D) = i_E = (1 - z_T)^{-1}(i_T + C_T + Q_T), \tag{86}$$

$$i - C_B - Q_B = i_E, \tag{87}$$

where C_J and Q_J are the partial derivatives of the cost function and of (83) with respect to $J = D, T, L$ and B_b. The first condition requires that the net return on loans, net of resource and bankruptcy costs, must equal the net return on bonds. The next two conditions (86) state that the total marginal cost of attracting deposits of type J, including the operating costs of providing deposit services, the marginal contribution of additional deposits to the expected cost of bankruptcy and the costs of maintaining reserves, should equal the marginal cost of attracting equity funds. Consequently, the optimal structure of deposits is such that the total marginal costs of providing demand and time deposits are equal. The last condition (87) states that the net marginal revenue on bonds should equal the rate of return on bank equity. Conditions (86)–(87) yield the optimum relations between the deposit rates and the market rate, which are seen to be generalizations of equations (75) derived above:

$$i_D = (1 - z_D)(i - C_B - Q_B) - C_D - Q_D,$$
$$i_T = (1 - z_T)(i - C_B - Q_B) - C_T - Q_T. \tag{88}$$

Note that these efficiency conditions are achieved through adjustments in the quantities of assets and liabilities by the individual bank given the market-determined interest rates.

The effects of changes in the liability structure and in the bank portfolio on the expected cost of bankruptcy are given by

$$Q_L = c_X[(1 + i_L)^{-1}C_L - 1][1 - G(\bar{X}_L)], \tag{89}$$

$$Q_B = -c_X(1 + i_L)^{-1}[(1 + i) - C_B][1 - G(\bar{X}_L)], \tag{90}$$

$$Q_J = c_X(1 + i_L)^{-1}[(1 + i_J)(1 - z_J) - C_J][1 - G(\bar{X}_L)], \quad J = D, T. \tag{91}$$

The above expressions are functions of (D, T, L, B_b) which affect the critical level, $\bar{X}_L$, even when the marginal resource costs, C_D, C_T, C_L and C_B, are constant. On the assumption that the second-order conditions for a maximum are satisfied, (85) and (88)–(91) can be solved to determine the optimal structure of assets and liabilities for the individual bank in terms of the interest rates (i, i_L, i_D, i_T). According to this model, the demand for earning assets and the supply of liabilities by the bank reflect the nature of the operating costs of providing financial services $C(D, T, L, B_b)$ and the cumulative probability distribution of default losses on loans $G(X_L)$. In the aggregate, the deposit rates, the bank loan rate and the rate on marketable instruments will be determined simultaneously as a result of the interaction of the public's demand for financial assets and bank credit and the banks' competitive offering of financial services.

The model of the banking firm presented above can be readily extended to take into account the role of imperfectly competitive markets for bank deposits and loans and of the effects of the scale of the firm on the probability distribution of default losses on loans. Under imperfect competition, the bank can affect profits by exploiting its market power. Since in this case the deposit rates and the loan rate cannot be taken as given but depend on the respective quantities of deposits and loans, the elasticities of the demand by the public for bank assets and liabilities will affect the profit-maximizing structure of assets and liabilities and the deposit rates. In addition, the law of large numbers implies that as the size of the banking firm and the quantity of credit increase, the probability of default losses per dollar declines. Thus, the bank exhibits stochastic economies of scale, which may be incorporated in the analysis by expressing the variance of the distribution $G(X_L)$ as a function of L. Under perfect competition, these economies of scale, which reduce the expected losses from bankruptcy, must be more than offset at the margin by increasing operating costs at the optimal level of assets and liabilities.[32]

3.6. The money supply process

In this section we present a simple structural model of money stock determination in a deregulated banking system in which interest rates on bank deposits, both demand and time deposits, are not set administratively but are market-

---

[32] Greenbaum (1967), Benston (1972), Baltensperger (1972a, 1972b), and Longbrake and Haslem (1975) have examined the economies of scale in banking operations.

determined. We suppose that the public's demand for financial assets are given by the following log-linear specifications:

$$\ln(A^d/P) = a_A + k_{AD}i_D + k_{AT}i_T + k_{AX}i + b_A y + u_A , \tag{92}$$

where $A = H_p$, D, T, X and $X = B_p + E_b + E_p = B_p + E_b + (P_k K_p - L)$. The financial asset, denoted X, is an aggregate including all the non-bank financial assets in the economy (see Table 10.2). The average rate of return on X is the market interest rate i. The rates of return on the components of X are assumed to differ by constant spreads. Since the sum of the demands for the four assets must equal total private wealth, which is taken as given, that is $H^d + D^d + T^d + X^d = W$, one of the equations in (92) is redundant. Moreover, the wealth constraint implies that the sum of the marginal effects on all assets of a change in a rate of return or in income must be zero.[33] Thus, the semielasticities k_{IJ} of the asset demands (92) with respect to the three interest rates must satisfy the following constraints:

$$i_D: w_H k_{HD} + w_D k_{DD} + w_T k_{TD} + w_X k_{XD} = 0 ,$$

$$i_T: w_H k_{HT} + w_D k_{DT} + w_T k_{TT} + w_X k_{XT} = 0 , \tag{93}$$

$$i: \quad w_H k_{HX} + w_D k_{DX} + w_T k_{TX} + w_X k_{XX} = 0 ,$$

where $w_J = J/W$ is the share of the Jth asset ($J = H_p$, D, T, X) in total wealth. It is assumed that the four assets are gross substitutes, that is $k_{IJ} > 0$ if $I = J$ and $k_{IJ} \leq 0$ if $I \neq J$.

According to the analysis of the previous section the interest rates on bank deposits can be expressed in terms of the market interest rate by

$$i_J = (1 - z_J)i - q_J , \tag{94}$$

where $q_J = (1 - z_J)(C_B + Q_B) + C_J + Q_J$, $J = D, T$. In general, the variables q_J depend on the structure of bank assets and liabilities which affect the marginal resource costs, C_J, and the marginal expected costs of bankuptcy, Q_J, as shown by (89)–(91). For simplicity and in order to focus on the main implications for the money supply process of relaxing the assumption of exogenously fixed deposit rates, it is assumed that q_J are invariant to changes in the quantities of bank assets and liabilities, although they may be subject to serially uncorrelated random disturbances (q_J'). Substitution of (94) into (92) yields the demands for currency and bank deposits as functions of the market rate:

$$\ln(A^d/P) = a_A' + k_A' i + b_A y + u_A' , \tag{95}$$

[33] If the analysis is carried out in discrete time, the sum of the marginal effects on asset demands of a change in an interest rate or income must equal their corresponding marginal effects on saving.

where

$$k'_A = (1 - z_D)k_{AD} + (1 - z_T)k_{AT} + k_{AX} , \tag{95a}$$

$$u'_A = u_A - k_{AD}q'_D - k_{AT}q'_T , \quad A = H, D, T . \tag{95b}$$

The parameter k'_A denotes the total interest semielasticity of the demand for asset A. When i_D and i_T are set exogenously, the interest semielasticities of the asset demands are given by the last term in (95a) so that the parameters k_A in (68) correspond to k_{AX} in (95a), $A = H_p, D, T$.

The equilibrium condition in the market for (non-borrowed) base money is given by (67). Stating this equilibrium condition in deviations from the full employment equilibrium $(\bar{Y}, \bar{r})$, a given stock of base money $\overline{M0}$ and the corresponding equilibrium price level $\bar{P}$, and employing the approximation $x/\bar{x} - 1 = \ln x - \ln \bar{x}$, we obtain:

$$(mo - \overline{mo}) - (p - \bar{p}) = s_H(\ln F_H - \ln \bar{F}_H) + s_D(\ln F_D - \ln \bar{F}_D)$$

$$+ s_T(\ln F_T - \ln \bar{F}_T) + s_F(\ln F_R - \ln \bar{F}_R) , \tag{96}$$

where

$$s_H = \bar{H}_p/\overline{M0} , \quad s_D = z_D\bar{D}/\overline{M0} , \quad s_T = z_T\bar{T}/\overline{M0} , \quad s_F = \overline{FR}/\overline{M0} .$$

The variables F_A, $A = H_p, D, T, R$, denote the real demands for currency, demand and time deposits and free reserves; mo and p are the natural logarithms of $M0$ and P, respectively.

Substituting (95) and (69) into (96) and rearranging terms yields the following condition for equilibrium in the market for base money ($LM0$):

$$(mo - \overline{mo}) - (p - \bar{p}) = b_0(y - \bar{y}) + k'_0(i - \bar{i}) + k_{CB}(i_{CB} - \bar{i}_{CB}) + u'_{M0} , \tag{97}$$

where

$$b_0 = s_H b_H + s_D b_D + s_T b_T , \tag{97a}$$

$$k'_0 = k_0 + \delta_0 , \tag{97b}$$

$$k_0 = s_H k_{HX} + s_D k_{DX} + s_T k_{TX} + s_F f_i , \quad k_{CB} = s_F f_{CB} , \tag{97c}$$

$$\delta_0 = (1 - z_D)\gamma_D + (1 - z_T)\gamma_T , \tag{97d}$$

$$\gamma_D = s_H k_{HD} + s_D k_{DD} + s_T k_{TD} , \quad \gamma_T = s_H k_{HT} + s_D k_{DT} + s_T k_{TT} , \tag{97e}$$

$$u'_{M0} = u_{M0} - \gamma_D q'_D - \gamma_T q'_T , \tag{97f}$$

$$u_{M0} = s_H u_H + s_D u_D + s_T u_T + s_F u_F . \tag{97g}$$

This equilibrium condition differs from the one derived in Subsection 3.4, for the case of fixed deposit rates, in two respects: the dependence on the market interest rate and the stochastic component. The effect of a change in the nominal (and real) quantity of base money on the market interest rate, for a given level of real income, is given by $1/k_0'$, where k_0' is related to the economy's financial structure as shown by (97b). An interesting issue is whether, in a regime of competitively determined deposit rates, an increase in the quantity of base money induces a smaller or larger change in the market rate than in a financial system in which deposit rates are not affected by variations in the market rate. This can be established by first noting that the term k_0 in (97b), which is defined by (97c), is precisely the interest semielasticity of $M0$ when the deposit rates are exogenously fixed [see (70b)]. The second term, δ_0, in (97b) depends on the reserve ratios, z_D and z_T, and the semielasticities of the demands for currency and bank deposits with respect to the two deposit rates, as shown by (97d) and (97e). The role of the required reserve ratios in determining the sign of δ_0 can be seen by considering first the limiting cases of zero and 100 percent reserve requirements.

In the case of zero required reserves, the demand for $M0$ is simply the demand for currency and any free reserves. In this case the *spreads* between the deposit rates and the market rate are not influenced by the level of the market rate, at least not to a large extent.[34] Recalling that $s_D = z_D \bar{D}/\overline{M0}$ and $s_T = z_T \bar{T}/\overline{M0}$, it readily follows from (97c) and (97d) that $\delta_0 = s_H(k_{HD} + k_{HT}) < 0$, $k_0 = s_H k_{HX} + s_F f_i \leq 0$ and thus $|k_0'| > |k_0|$. Thus, when $z_D = z_T = 0$ and deposit rates are competitively determined, an increase in the quantity of base money requires a smaller reduction in the market rate for restoring equilibrium in the $M0$ market than would be necessary with fixed deposit rates. This smaller reduction in the market rate is sufficient to induce the public to substitute for currency market instruments as well as bank deposits, whose own rates also decline. Indeed, since k_{HD} and k_{HT} are likely to be larger than k_{HX}, the required interest rate adjustment is likely to be appreciably smaller. In the other limiting case of 100 percent reserve requirements, the interest rate adjustment required for equilibrium in the $M0$ market is identical to the one required when the deposit rates are fixed. For when $z_D = z_T = 1$, the bank cannot extend any loans and thus the deposit rates are not related to the market rate but represent the service charges imposed by banks on their deposits, $i_D = -q_D$ and $i_T = -q_T$.

Consider next the more general case when $0 < z_D, z_T < 1$ and, for simplicity, suppose that $z_D = z_T = z$. To examine the sign of $\delta_0 = k_0' - k_0$, we use the consistency restrictions (93) implied by the wealth constraint and obtain:

$$\delta_0 = (1 - z)[s_H(k_{HD} + k_{HT}) + s_D(k_{DD} + k_{DT}) + s_T(k_{TD} + k_{TT})]$$
$$= (1 - z)\overline{M0}^{-1}[(1 - z)\bar{H}(k_{HD} + k_{HT}) - z\bar{X}(k_{XD} + k_{XT})] . \tag{98}$$

---

[34]When $z_D = z_T = 0$, the quantity of free reserves held by banks is likely to be higher than in the case of positive required reserves and this will influence the interest rate spreads.

The above expression captures the net effect on the demand for (un-borrowed) base money of the increase in the deposit rates induced by a rise in the market interest rate. The factor $(1 - z)$ simply shows the extent by which i_D and i_T change in response to a change in i, and the terms in square brackets give the effects of the change in deposit rates on the demand for $M0$. An increase in the deposit rates induces the public to substitute D and T for currency (H_p) and non-bank financial assets (X). The first term in the square brackets is the *net* effect on the demand for $M0$ resulting from the substitution of deposits for currency and it is clearly negative if $z < 1$. This term captures the reduction in the demand for the currency component of $M0$ and the increase in the demand for reserves by an amount $z\bar{H}(k_{HD} + k_{HT})$. The second term represents the positive effect on the demand for bank reserves due to a shift from market instruments into bank deposits. Whether the total effect (the sum of the two terms) is positive or negative depends on the magnitudes of the interest semielasticities and of z. Since, however, the value of z is small, typically not greater than 0.1, and on the reasonable assumption that the interest semielasticities of H_p^d and X^d with respect to deposit rates are of the same order of magnitude, we can conclude that δ_0 is likely to be negative when $z < 1$. Thus, the $LM0$ equilibrium relation is likely to be less steep in the i–y plane if deposit rates are competitively determined by banks.

We next examine the nature and stochastic stability of the equilibrium conditions in the money markets ($M1$ and $M2$) in a deregulated banking system with market-determined deposit rates. Following a procedure analogous to the one for the $M0$ market, we find that the condition for equilibrium in the money ($M1$) market can be written as follows:

$$LM1: \quad (m1 - \overline{m1}) - (p - \bar{p}) = b_1(y - \bar{y}) + k_1'(i - \bar{i}) + u_{M0}', \tag{99}$$

where

$$b_1 = a_H b_H + a_D b_D, \qquad a_H = \bar{H}_p/\overline{M1}, \qquad a_D = \bar{D}/\overline{M1} = 1 - a_H, \tag{99a}$$

$$k_1' = k_1 + \delta_1, \tag{99b}$$

$$k_1 = a_H k_{HX} + a_D k_{DX} \le 0, \tag{99c}$$

$$\delta_1 = (1 - z_D)\theta_D + (1 - z_T)\theta_T, \tag{99d}$$

$$\theta_D = a_H k_{HD} + a_D k_{DD}, \qquad \theta_T = a_H k_{HT} + a_D k_{DT}, \tag{99e}$$

$$u_{M1}' = u_{M1} - \theta_D q_D' - \theta_T q_T', \tag{99f}$$

$$u_{M1} = a_H u_{H} + a_D u_D. \tag{99g}$$

The above equilibrium condition in the money ($M1$) market differs from the conventional one because of its responsiveness to interest rate fluctuations and of its stochastic term. The interest semielasticity of (99), k_1', can be decomposed into two components. The first component, k_1, captures the direct effect of a change in the market rate on the demand for $M1$ and it is clearly non-positive. The second component, δ_1, given by (99d), captures the indirect effect on the demand for $M1$ of a change in the market rate through its influence on the market-determined deposit rates; in general, it may be positive or negative since $k_{DD} > 0$. It is likely to be negative, however, since an increase in both deposit rates reduces the demand for currency but it has offsetting effects on demand deposits, the other component of $M1$. Hence, the responsiveness of the market rate to a change in $M1$ is likely to be larger with market-determined than with fixed deposit rates. The total effect depends on the relative importance of cash in providing transactions services, measured by a_H in (99a).

One interesting implication of (99) is that when the central bank raises the required reserve ratios, z_D and z_T, in order to restrict the supply of bank deposits, given $M0$, it also affects the interest sensitivity of the $LM1$ equilibrium condition (it causes a rotation of the $LM1$ schedule in the $i-y$ plane). Another implication of (99) is that its stochastic term, u_{M1}', depends not only on the random elements of the public's demand for currency and demand deposits captured by (99g), but also on fluctuations in the interest rate spreads (q_D', q_T') due to other factors, as can be inferred from (94).

The equilibrium condition in the broad money market ($M2$) is given by:

$$LM2: \quad (m2 - \overline{m2}) - (p - \bar{p}) = b_2(y - \bar{y}) + k_2'(i - \bar{i}) + u_{M2}', \tag{100}$$

where

$$b_2 = c_H b_H + c_D b_D + c_T b_T, c_H = \bar{H}_p / \overline{M2}, \qquad c_D = \bar{D}/\overline{M2}, \qquad c_T = \bar{T}/\overline{M2}, \tag{100a}$$

$$k_2' = k_2 + \delta_2, \tag{100b}$$

$$k_2 = c_H k_{HX} + c_D k_{DX} + c_T k_{TX} \leq 0, \tag{100c}$$

$$\delta_2 = (1 - z_D)\phi_D + (1 - z_T)\phi_T, \tag{100d}$$

$$\phi_D = c_H k_{HD} + c_D k_{DD} + c_T k_{TD}, \qquad \phi_T = c_H k_{HT} + c_D k_{DT} + c_T k_{TT}, \tag{100e}$$

$$u_{M2}' = u_{M2} - \phi_D q_D' - \phi_T q_T', \tag{100f}$$

$$u_{M2} = c_H u_H + c_D u_D + c_T u_T. \tag{100g}$$

The interest semielasticity of the $LM2$ equilibrium condition, k_2', has also been expressed as the sum of two terms. The first one, k_2, represents the direct effect of a change in the market rate on the demand for broad money ($M2$), given the rates of return on bank deposits. This direct effect is non-positive and it is greater in absolute terms than the corresponding interest semielasticity of the demand for narrow money $(M1)$, that is $|k_2| > |k_1|$. The second term, δ_2, represents the indirect effect on the demand for $M2$ of a change in the market rate through its effects on the two deposit rates. Although the sign of the indirect effect appears to be ambiguous, the consistency conditions (93) imply that both ϕ_D and ϕ_T are non-negative and, more specifically, that the indirect effect can be expressed as:

$$\delta_2 = -(\bar{X}/\overline{M2})[(1 - z_D)k_{XD} + (1 - z_T)k_{XT}] \geq 0. \tag{101}$$

Thus, $|k_2'| \leq |k_2|$, that is the total interest semielasticity of the demand for $M2$ when the deposit rates are market determined is smaller in absolute terms than the corresponding elasticity when deposit rates are administratively fixed. The stochastic component of the $LM2$ equilibrium condition is seen to be the sum of a weighted average of the random elements of the public demands for currency and bank liabilities, given the level of interest rates, and of the stochastic variations in the demand for $M2$ induced by random changes in the spreads between deposit and market rates.

The general conclusion which emerges from the above analysis is that the conditions for equilibrium in the money markets with market-determined deposit rates differ from the corresponding conditions with administered deposit rates in two respects, which have implications for the conduct of monetary policy. First, the interest elasticity of the money market equilibrium conditions under the two interest rate regimes differs in ways which depend upon the composition of the market and the aggregate subject to control. The equilibrium condition in the market for base money implies that the demand for $M0$ is likely to be more interest elastic under liability management than under pure asset management. But the demand for broad money $(M2)$ is less interest elastic when deposit rates are set competitively than when they are fixed. Second, the stochastic stability of the money markets is altered in ways which depend on the structure of the markets, the portfolio preferences of the public and the behavior of banks.

The focus of the foregoing discussion on the interest elasticities and the stochastic stability of the money markets is due to their critical role in determining the relative effectiveness of alternative intermediate targets and instruments of monetary policy. As demonstrated by Poole (1970), the choice between the interest rate and the money stock as a policy instrument depends critically on the interest sensitivity and the stability of money demand. Moreover, Modigliani and Papademos (1980, 1987) have shown that the relative effectiveness of alternative monetary aggregates in stabilizing output and price fluctuations hinges, ceteris paribus, on the interest elasticity and stability of the public's demand for the respective monetary aggregates.

The analysis of this subsection also allows the determination of the "multiplier relations" between the narrow and broad measures of money and the monetary base and an examination of the effects of liability management on these relations. From (97), (99) and (100) it follows that the monetary aggregates are related by the following relations, expressed linearly in the logarithms of the respective variables:

$$mJ = \mu_J + mo , \quad J = 1, 2 , \tag{102}$$

$$\mu_J = (b_J - b_0)y + (k'_J - k'_0)i - k_{CB}i_{CB} + (u'_{MJ} - u'_{M0}) ,$$

where the parameters b_J, k_J and the stochastic terms u'_{MJ}, $J = 0, 1, 2$, are defined below equation (97), (99) and (100). The above expressions lead to the following general remarks.

First, the (logarithms of the) money base multipliers for $M1$ and $M2$ depend on the market interest rate and real income as well as upon policy-controlled variables such as the central bank rate and reserve requirements, which affect the interest elasticities, k'_J.

Second, the interest elasticities and the stochastic components of the multipliers depend on the portfolio preferences of the public, the structure of the banking system and, especially under liability management, the various factors determining the spreads between deposit and lending rates. The effects of liability management on the deterministic component of the multiplier relations can be analyzed in a straightforward fashion by comparing the expressions $(k'_J - k'_0)$ and $(k_J - k_0)$, that is $(\delta_J - \delta_0)$, for $J = 1, 2$, which are defined below equations (97), (99) and (100). Similarly, the implications of liability management for the stochastic stability of μ_J follow from a comparison of the random variables $(u'_{MJ} - u'_{M0})$ and $(u_{MJ} - u_{M0})$.

Third, the multiplier relations (102) cannot and should not be interpreted as supply functions determining the quantities of narrow and broad money supplied by the banking system, given the quantity of the non-borrowed monetary base controlled by the central bank. These relations determine the quantities of $M1$ and $M2$, which are consistent with the preferences of the non-bank public and banks, regulatory constraints and other features of financial markets (e.g. technology) as functions of the market interest rate and real income, given $M0$. The quantities of the narrow and broad measures of money can be determined only endogenously and simultaneously with the market rate and real income. For example, the stock of money narrowly defined can be obtained as a function of the policy-controlled variables ($M0$, i_{CB}, z_D, z_T) and the price level by solving simultaneously the $LM0$ and $LM1$ equilibrium conditions, (97) and (99), and the IS equilibrium condition [e.g. equation (16) of Table 10.1]. Alternatively, the multiplier relation (102) for $J = 1$ could be employed together with the $LM1$ and IS equilibrium conditions to obtain the same result, but this is simply an alternative means of taking into account the necessary equilibrium conditions in the money and product markets. In the event that the central bank considers it desirable to achieve (a more or less) precise control of the stock of money ($M1$), then the system of equations defined by $LM0$, $LM1$ and IS can be employed to determine the *required* supply of base money consistent with the target quantity of money ($M1$).

4. Financial structure, the monetary mechanism and the control of nominal income

4.1. Financial structure and the monetary mechanism

In economies with financial intermediaries and a large spectrum of financial assets, monetary authorities may endeavor to achieve effective control over nominal income by controlling the quantity of financial aggregates other than money, narrowly defined by its function as a medium of exchange. Indeed, with the adoption of monetary aggregates as principal targets of monetary policy in the late 1970s, the monetary authorities in various countries have pursued a variety of monetary targets ranging from narrow measures, such as the monetary base or central bank money, to broad measures which include all deposit liabilities of all financial intermediaries. Moreover, a number of central banks have aimed at controlling and monitoring broader financial aggregates, which include non-bank marketable liquid assets, or have focused on the control of credit aggregates, narrowly or broadly defined.[35] The control of credit aggregates has been an important policy objective in a number of European countries (Belgium, Greece, Italy, Sweden) and also in many developing countries. Moreover, the International Monetary Fund has emphasized in its stabilization programmes the importance of controlling total domestic credit.

The wide variety of monetary and credit aggregates pursued as intermediate targets by central banks presumably reflects their differing assessments concerning the stability and predictability of the relation between various financial aggregates and the ultimate policy objective, i.e. aggregate nominal income. These different assessments partly reflect different judgments as to the "degree

---

[35]For example, in recent years the Bank of England has employed as an objective $M0$ (mainly currency in circulation) after having pursued a broad monetary aggregate (sterling $M3$); the Bundesbank targeted central bank money (currency in circulation plus minimum reserve requirements on banks' domestic liabilities) until 1987 and then switched to a broad money target, $M3$; the Banque de France has aimed at controlling $M2$, and in some years $M3$; in Spain the target has been the quantity of liquid assets held by the public and in Portugal the total liquidity held by non-financial residents, which includes Treasury bills; Greece and Italy have adopted a dual objective, a broad measure of money and domestic credit to the private sector.

of moneyness" of different monetary aggregates and partly different views concerning the nature of the monetary mechanism in various countries. The choice of targets, however, has been based primarily on empirical evidence concerning the stochastic stability and dynamic properties of velocity-type relations between nominal income and alternative financial aggregates.

At the conceptual level, it can be argued that the specific structure of financial markets and institutions in a given country (including the extent of integration of domestic and international financial markets) and certain behavioral characteristics of market participants imply that controlling the quantities of certain financial aggregates *other* than money ($M1$) can be expected to influence in a more systematic and effective way the actions of lenders and borrowers and the consequent spending behavior of households and firms.

At the empirical level, research in many countries has demonstrated that the conventional view that the money measure ($M1$) is the most appropriate target and/or policy indicator is not supported unequivocally by the facts. For example, in the United States the evidence presented by B. Friedman (1980, 1983), Cagan (1982), Kopcke (1983), and Kaufman (1979) shows that broad financial and credit aggregates may serve as efficient targets or guides of policy on the basis of the statistical stability of their relation to nominal income or the advance information they provide on income fluctuations. Other empirical evidence, however, suggests that it is impossible to identify a unique aggregate whose relationship to GNP is uniformly superior over different sample periods relative to other aggregates [e.g. Berkman (1980)]. In addition, more recent empirical work reported by B. Friedman (1986, 1988) has shown that the stability of previously established statistical regularities between nominal income and certain monetary and credit aggregates has been impaired when the analysis takes into account data from the 1980s. To summarize, the empirical evidence suggests that control of the money supply ($M1$) is not always the most effective means of controlling nominal income, that a number of broad financial aggregates appear to have at times exhibited a more statistically stable relation to GDP, but that no single financial aggregate can be deemed to be uniformly superior, over all periods and in all countries, as an intermediate target of monetary policy.

These empirical results should not be considered surprising for a number of reasons. First, the fundamental structural changes and innovations in domestic and international financial markets that have taken place in recent years have blurred the distinctions between the set of instruments traditionally labelled as "money" and other financial assets and have led to the creation of numerous easily substitutable financial instruments. These developments have resulted in perturbations in the historical relations between nominal income and the monetary and credit aggregates under potential control of central banks. A second reason is that the observed historical stability of these "velocity" relationships is not independent of the actual policies pursued by the monetary authorities over the sample period. Indeed, it can be argued that a policy that aims at stabilizing the rate of growth of a particular aggregate can be expected to tend to undermine the stability of its velocity relation to nominal income. Consequently, the observed stability of these empirical regularities cannot be expected to persist under alternative monetary strategies.

4.2. Macroeconomic models with a financial structure

A better understanding of the monetary transmission mechanism and of the fundamental behavioral and institutional factors that determine the relative effectiveness of alternative monetary controls requires the development of a theoretical framework which goes beyond conventional monetary theory, with its focus on the role of money narrowly defined as the major determinant of nominal income. This broader framework must allow for a wider spectrum of monetary and credit aggregates as potential targets and indicators of policy and take explicitly into account the role of the structure of financial markets in the monetary mechanism.

The importance of financial markets and institutions in transmitting the effects of monetary policy has been emphasized in a number of extensions of the traditional macroeconomic paradigms. These include the pioneering study of Gurley and Shaw (1960); the critique of Patinkin (1961); the portfolio-balance models of Tobin, Brainard, Brunner and Meltzer [Tobin (1963, 1969), Tobin and Brainard (1963), Brainard (1967), Brunner and Meltzer (1972, 1976)]; the theoretical and empirical analysis associated with the MPS econometric model [Ando (1974), Ando and Modigliani (1975)]; and analyses of the effects of bank deregulation [e.g. Santomoro and Siegel (1981)]. However, monetary analysis in these extended frameworks has focused primarily on the effects of policies which take the form of controlling the money supply and/or interest rates. It has been concerned in part with the way changes in the stock of money ($M1$) are transmitted to nominal income through financial markets and in part with the way in which financial markets may thwart the achievement of the authorities' targets as a result of changes reflecting autonomous developments or in response to the authorities' policy actions.

In a series of papers, Modigliani and Papademos have studied the more general issue of the feasibility and desirability of endeavoring to control nominal income by relying on the control of financial aggregates other than the money supply; and they have demonstrated how the economy's financial structure, behavioral characteristics and stochastic environment determine the effectiveness of alternative forms of monetary and credit control.[36] This

---

[36]See Modigliani and Papademos (1980, 1987), Papademos and Modigliani (1983), and Papademos and Rozwadowski (1983).

analysis has required the development of a theoretical framework which links aggregate nominal output to alternative intermediate targets and instruments of monetary policy on the basis of an appropriate specification of the economy's financial structure.

Financial structure is specified in general by (1) the sources and instruments available to firms and households for financing the acquisition of tangible assets; (2) the menu of financial assets available to households and firms; and (3) the structure and characteristics of financial markets, as defined by the degree of competition (quantity versus price rationing) and the nature and extent of regulation. The models we have developed emphasize the role of credit markets and the economy's financial system in the determination of macroeconomic equilibrium. They incorporate the institutional aspects necessary for establishing the links between nominal and real income and various monetary and credit aggregates. More specifically, these models extend the conventional macroeconomic model (as represented by Model 4 of Table 10.1) in two respects. First, they take explicitly into account the role and behavior of two additional sectors by introducing the banking sector and by disaggregating the non-bank private sector into two separate sectors which reflect, respectively, the behavior of economic agents which are primarily net lenders or net borrowers. These two groups of agents may be identified to a first approximation with households and (corporate) firms. Second, the models allow for a wider array of financial instruments and markets and describe explicitly the determinants of equilibrium in the credit markets. This is essential because, when monetary authorities aim at controlling nominal income by relying on the control of bank credit, the behavioral and stochastic factors which influence the demand for credit can be expected to play an important role in the determination of the macroeconomic equilibrium and its stability, and to influence the effectiveness of credit controls.

Since disaggregation with respect to both sectors and financial markets and specification of certain basic institutional features are required for the study of the effects of alternative monetary controls on nominal income, the analysis is necessarily more complex than that based on the conventional macroeconomic model. For this reason, it is helpful to explore the implications of extensions of the standard macroeconomic model by making use of a series of "successive approximations". This requires analyzing a sequence of models which incorporate alternative hypotheses or formalizations concerning the economy's financial structure, the mechanism of price adjustment, the nature of expectations, the degree of openness of the economy, etc. The functioning of the monetary mechanism is also affected by the fiscal structure of the economy through its effects on the corporate credit market, especially in an inflationary environment; these effects are also taken into account in our analysis. On the basis of these models, the efficiency of alternative monetary and credit aggregates as control devices can be evaluated employing two criteria: (1) their effectiveness in minimizing fluctuations of output and of the price level from targeted values in the presence of random disturbances, and (2) their implications for the dynamic stability of the economy.

4.2.1. A macroeconomic model with a simple financial structure

A basic macroeconomic model incorporating the simplest financial structure necessary for analyzing the feasibility and effectiveness of alternative monetary and credit aggregates is presented in Modigliani and Papademos (1980). This model abstracts from the roles of government, corporate firms and foreign sector and confines the analysis to the Keynesian short run with a pre-determined price level. The economy is divided into two sectors: a private non-bank sector and a bank sector. The banking system issues two types of deposits and holds only one type of earning assets, bank loans, L. In this limiting financial structure there are no marketable debt instruments and, consequently, the only type of credit available to the non-bank public consists of bank loans. The public can hold three assets: physical capital, K, money, $M1$, and savings and time deposits, T. There are three (real) interest rates: the rate on bank loans, r, the rate on demand deposits, r_D, and the rate on savings and time deposits, r_T. The agents in the non-bank private sector are classified into two groups, namely the "deficit" and the "surplus" units, which are defined in terms of the stocks of real capital and money ($M1$) they hold relative to their wealth. Equilibrium in the credit market reflects the behavior of these "deficit" and "surplus" units.

The equations of the model, presented in Table 10.4, can be usefully divided into two parts. Part A describes the determinants of aggregate saving and investment, the demand for money and the conditions for equilibrium in the product and money markets in the short run for a given "received" price level. This part is the same as the standard Keynesian model with price level rigidity, except that investment and money demand have been allowed to be affected, in principle, by other interest rates. The supply of money may be fixed exogenously by the monetary authorities or be demand-determined in the case the central bank controls the supply of other financial assets or fixes the level of interest rates.

Part B of the model describes the economy's financial structure, other than the money market, by specifying (i) the determinants of the demand for borrowing and for bank liabilities, which are identified with the broad measure of money ($M2$), (ii) the budget constraints of the non-bank and bank sectors, (iii) equilibrium conditions in the markets for bank loans and bank liabilities, and (iv) the determinants of the two deposit rates. It is conventionally assumed that the rate on demand deposits is fixed by the central bank and that

Table 10.4
A macroeconomic model with a simple financial structure

A. *The standard Keynesian model*
(T1) Aggregate saving	$S = S(Y)$
(T2) Aggregate investment	$I = I(r, r_T)$
(T3) Commodity market equilibrium	$I = S$
(T4) Demand for money ($M1$)	$M1^d = PL1(r, r_D, r_T, Y)$
(T5) Supply of money	$M1^s = M1$
(T6) Money market equilibrium	$M1^d = M1^s$
(T7) Aggregate supply function	$P = \bar{P}$

B. *Financial structure*
(T8) Demand for borrowing (bank loans)	$\Delta L^d = PB(r, r_D, Y)$
(T9) Demand for bank liabilities	$\Delta M2^d = PL2(r, r_D, r_T, Y)$
(T10) Budget constraint of non-bank sector	$PS + \Delta L^d = PI + \Delta M2^d$
(T11) Budget constraint of bank sector	$\Delta M2 = \Delta L$
(T12) Loan market equilibrium	$\Delta L^d = \Delta L$
(T13) Bank liabilities market equilibrium	$\Delta M2^d = \Delta M2$
(T14) Interest rate determination	(a) $r_D = \bar{r}_D$
	(b) $r_T = f(r)$

Definitions of symbols:
Y = aggregate real output
P = aggregate price level
$\bar{P}$ = "received" price level
S = aggregate real saving
I = aggregate real investment
$M1^d$ = demand for money
$M1^s$ = supply of money
$M2^d$ = demand for bank liabilities
$M2$ = supply of bank liabilities
L^d = demand for bank loans
L = supply of bank loans
r = interest rate on bank loans
r_D = interest rate on demand deposits
r_T = interest rate on savings and time deposits

competition among banks implies a stable spread between the time deposit rate and the lending rate.

The demand for bank loans reflects the behavior of deficit units which borrow to finance their holdings of real capital and money. Surplus units have no debt and have non-negative holdings of savings and time deposits. The flow demand for (net) borrowing or credit during a period, which is given by equation (T8) of Table 10.4, can then be thought of as representing the difference between the investment and saving plus the change in the holdings of real money balances of the set of all units which end up as deficit units at the end of the period. Thus the (net) demand for borrowing can be expressed as:

$$\Delta L^d = PB(r, Y) = P[I_d(r) - S_d(Y) + \Delta L1_d(r, Y)], \tag{103}$$

where $\partial B/\partial r < 0$ and $\partial B/\partial Y \lessgtr 0$ if $\mathrm{d}S_\mathrm{d}/\mathrm{d}Y \gtrless \partial \Delta L1_\mathrm{d}/\partial Y$, and the subscript d is used to denote deficit units.[37] It is given as a function of the borrowing rate only by relying on equations (T14); it is a decreasing function of the interest rate as a rise in this rate leads to an unambiguous decrease in borrowing as both investment and the demand for money by deficit units decline. An increase in income gives rise to two opposing effects: it increases saving and hence the capacity of self-financing which reduces borrowing, but it increases the demand for real money balances which raises the demand for borrowing. The relative magnitudes of the two income effects cannot be settled a priori. It cannot be excluded that the income effect on borrowing may be negative.

Having specified the determinants of credit demand by defict units and the aggregate demands for investment and saving, the budget constraint of the non-bank sector, equation (T10), implicitly yields the (flow) demand for the total liabilities of the banking system, $\Delta M2^\mathrm{d}$, which is displayed as equation (T9) in Table 10.4. It represents the excess of saving over investment of surplus units plus the change in the money balances of deficit units, that is:

$$\Delta M2^\mathrm{d} = PL2(r, r_T, Y) = P[S_\mathrm{s}(Y) - I_\mathrm{s}(r_T) + \Delta L1_\mathrm{d}(r, Y)], \tag{104}$$

where $\partial L2/\partial Y > 0$ and $\partial L2/\partial r \gtrless 0$ if $|\mathrm{d}I_\mathrm{s}/\mathrm{d}r| \gtrless |\partial \Delta L1_\mathrm{d}/\partial r|$ and the subscripts s and d denote surplus and deficit units, respectively. The demand for investment by surplus units is a function of the time deposit rate, r_T, which may be taken as measuring the opportunity cost of investment in physical assets for surplus units. This rate is expressed in terms of the borrowing rate, r, employing (T14). The demand for total bank liabilities is unambiguously an increasing function of income but, it may be an increasing or decreasing function of the interest rate. However, since the interest sensitivity of investment by the surplus units is likely to be greater than the interest sensitivity of the demand for money by the deficit units, an increase in the interest rate would probably increase the total demand for bank liabilities.

This model can be employed to first demonstrate a fundamental proposition, namely that nominal income *can* be controlled not only through $M1$ but also by controlling the supply of total bank credit or a broad monetary aggregate. This can be shown as follows. The enlarged model of Table 10.4, excluding the "policy equation" (T5), contains 14 equations in 13 unknowns since we have

[37] The flow demand for borrowing (and the flow demand for the broad measure of money defined below) correspond to end-of-period stock demands, given the actual stocks held at the beginning of the period. The stock demand for debt by deficit units is assumed to be given by $L^\mathrm{d} = PK_\mathrm{d}^\mathrm{d} + M1_\mathrm{d}^\mathrm{d} - PW_\mathrm{d}$, where K_d and W_d are the end-of-period stocks of real capital and net wealth demanded by deficit units, respectively. Thus, the flow demand for borrowing is given by $\Delta L^\mathrm{d} = P[\Delta K_\mathrm{d}^\mathrm{d} + \Delta(M1^\mathrm{d}/P)_\mathrm{d} - \Delta W_\mathrm{d}^\mathrm{d}] + \Delta P(L/P)_{-1}$. In the Keynesian short run, $P = \bar{P}$ and $\Delta P = 0$ and $\Delta L^\mathrm{d} = P[I_\mathrm{d} + \Delta(M1^\mathrm{d}/P)_\mathrm{d} - S_\mathrm{d}]$. In our earlier exposition of this model it was assumed for simplicity that $\bar{P} = 1$.

added eight equations and six unknowns (ΔL^d, ΔL, $\Delta M2^d$, $\Delta M2$, r_D, r_T) to the original six equations [excluding equation (T5)] in seven unknowns. But two equations are redundant. Walras' Law implies the redundancy of one of the market-clearing equations, and the budget constraint of the non-bank sector implicitly determines the demand for $M2$ given the demands for investment, saving and borrowing. One more equation is thus needed to close the system. In the standard monetarist–Keynesian paradigm, the additional equation is of course equation (T5), by setting $M1^s = \overline{M1}$, and the monetary mechanism can thus be described by the equations of Part A alone.

It should be readily apparent, however, that condition (T5) – exogenously fixing the money supply – is by no means the only way of closing the system. Indeed, from a formal point of view, all that is required is an equation of the form $A = \bar{A}$, where A could by any financial aggregate of the system, and in particular any of the nominal financial variables, as long as it is controlled by the monetary authority. In our illustrative system, for example, eligible variables would include money, $M1$, total bank liabilities, $M2$, and bank loans, L. Once such a variable (or linear combination of variables) has been fixed, all other financial variables will be endogenously determined. In particular, the money supply will be given by (T4) and hence will be demand determined – and yet nominal income will be uniquely determined. It is also possible to show that if we drop the assumption of price rigidity and go to the limiting case of perfect price flexibility, then barring money or inflation illusion, the quantity of money theory of the price level can be replaced by the more general proposition that the price level is proportional to the value of any appropriately chosen nominal stock of a financial aggregate. It follows that, contrary to a long and widely accepted view, in order to control nominal income, it is not necessary to control the money supply but merely to control some financial aggregate, or a linear combination of such aggregates.

The model also brings out the fact that the mechanism at work when the central bank controls a broad monetary or credit aggregate involves different adjustment processes and dynamics from the conventional one and calls for different paradigms, which focus on the interaction of the credit market with the goods markets. This can be illustrated by considering the case when the monetary authorities endeavor to control nominal income by controlling the supply of total bank credit through reserve requirements against bank loans. On the usual assumption that the yield on bank reserves is lower than the loan rate and abstracting from the effects of uncertainty on reserve management, profit maximization by banks implies that the quantity of bank credit is given by $L = R/z$, where R is the supply of bank reserves controlled by the central bank and z is the reserve ratio against bank credit. Thus, the system in Table 10.4 is closed by replacing ΔL on the right-hand side of the equilibrium condition (T12) by $\overline{\Delta L} = \overline{\Delta R}/z$. Substituting equation (T8) or (103) in (T12), and maintaining the Keynesian assumption that the price level is constant at the level $\bar{P}$, yields the condition for equilibrium in the bank credit market:

$$B(r, Y) = \bar{B} = \overline{\Delta L}/\bar{P}, \tag{105}$$

shown in Figure 10.1 as the *BB* curve. It represents the combinations of interest rate and income levels such that the real demand for credit equals the available supply of bank lending. Simultaneous solution of equation (105) and the IS equilibrium condition, obtained from (T1)–(T3), yields the values of real income and the interest rate (Y^*, r^*) – the coordinates of the point of intersection of the two schedules – consistent with simultaneous equilibrium in the goods and credit markets. The equilibrium values of all other variables of the system in Table 10.4, including the money supply, are then obtained as functions of (Y^*, r^*). Clearly, in this case the equilibrium quantity of money is demand-determined.

The slope of the *BB* curve may be either negative or positive depending upon the relative magnitudes of the marginal propensity to save and the marginal effect of income on money demand by deficit units. Figure 10.1 illustrates the case when the *BB* curve has a negative slope, but it is less steep – i.e. is algebraically larger – than the *IS* curve. This is the expected relation between the curves and it ensures the stability of equilibrium.

The functioning of the monetary mechanism when the monetary authorities allow banks to increase lending can be described as follows. In order to expand loans, banks must induce an expansion of investment and credit demand by lowering the lending rate. That is, the increased supply shifts the *BB* curve

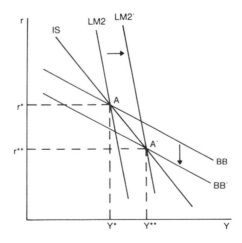

Figure 10.1

downward, to BB', since at each level of income a lower r is required to induce a rise in borrowing. The associated expansion of investment results in higher income and saving to match the increased investment. The new equilibrium is at the point A' with coordinates r^{**} and Y^{**}, where the BB' curve intersects the IS. According to this paradigm, the monetary authorities induce a change in real income by changing the supply of bank credit, with the money market playing only an indirect role through its influence on the demand for credit of deficit units; at the new equilibrium, the supply of money is determined by the quantity demanded, given r^{**} and Y^{**}.

For the simple financial structure of this model, when the central bank controls the quantity of bank credit, it implicitly imposes a limit on the supply of broad money ($M2$), as can be seen from the budget constraint of the bank sector (T11). This implies that the equilibrium must also satisfy the constraint:

$$L2(r, Y) = \overline{\Delta M2}/\bar{P} = \overline{\Delta L}/\bar{P} , \tag{106}$$

which is exhibited in Figure 10.1 as the $LM2$ curve. The slope of this curve may also be either positive or negative, as can be seen from (104). If the $LM2$ has a negative slope, the equilibrium is stable provided that the $LM2$ curve is steeper than the IS, as is the case in Figure 10.1. The budget constraint of the non-bank sector (T10) implies that the equilibrium values of income and the interest rate which clear the markets for goods and bank credit will also clear the market for total bank liabilities. So the $LM2$ intersects the IS and BB curves at the initial and final equilibrium points A and A'. In other words, an increase in the supply of bank credit shifts simultaneously the BB curve down the $LM2$ curve to the right generating the new equilibrium at point A', characterized by a lower interest rate and a higher investment and income.

However, when the central bank endeavors to control income by setting a limit on the quantity of broad money, we find that the functioning of the monetary mechanism cannot be explained in a satisfactory way by focusing on the (broad) money market. According to the conventional paradigm, a policy-induced increase in the supply of bank liabilities (say through a decline in reserve requirements) would lead banks to try to induce the public to hold the increased quantity of $M2$; this could be done by raising the time deposit rate, r_T, and thus r, but this would tend to reduce investment and credit demand and would not help establish an equilibrium consistent with the larger supply of $M2$. Furthermore, this response would not even help to expand $M2$ because in the simple economy considered, $M2$ can only increase if banks expand the acquisition of assets. Note also that the public has no choice but to hold the increased deposits generated by banks' investments.

The paradigm which describes the determination of nominal income when the monetary authorities impose a limit on the total amount of bank liabilities is best understood by examining the adjustment in the bank credit market, since in this economy bank liabilities can be created or destroyed only at the initiative of banks in the process of expanding or contracting loans. Thus, to expand *M*2, banks must induce the public to expand its borrowing (its sale of assets to banks) by lowering their lending rate and inducing an expansion of investment and thus income and saving. It is the rise in income and saving which increases the demand for *M*2 by more than the decrease generated by the fall in the lending and time deposit rates that restores equilibrium in the market for total bank liabilities. Thus, the monetary mechanism corresponding to the control of broad money can be understood more adequately through the bank credit paradigm.

This proposition is of interest for it brings into question a common view that an increase in broad money is expansionary, because it somehow increases the "liquidity" of the economy or because the non-*M*1 part of the broad measure of money is also endowed with "moneyness properties", and thus *M*2 may be a better measure of money than *M*1. Our analysis instead brings to light the fact that an increase in the stock of broad money is expansionary because it is the unavoidable accompaniment of the process of credit expansion. It is the credit expansion, and the resulting rise in investment, that is expansionary and causes the positive association between the stock of broad money and nominal income.

The model has also been used to examine the effects on investment and real income of credit controls when interest rates on non-monetary deposits liabilities (time deposits) are not market-determined but are subject to an effective ceiling. It is found that interest rate ceilings as well as credit rationing reduce the effectiveness of credit policy in the sense of making investment less responsive, through increased disintermediation, to a change in bank credit imposed by the monetary authority. By the same token, the elimination of ceilings or credit rationing may be expected to have a contractionary effect. These results are contrary to those reported for the case in which money (*M*1) is the target variable of the central bank.

The relative effectiveness of bank credit, broad money and narrow money in minimizing the fluctuations of real output around a target level under uncertainty has also been studied on the basis of a linearized version of this simple model incorporating additive stochastic disturbances. The answer is found to depend on the relative variance of the stochastic components of the major behavior equations of the model. Specifically, a bank credit or broad money target is superior to a money (*M*1) target in stabilizing income if the variance of the saving function is smaller than a multiple of a weighted average of the variances of investment and money demand functions. The multiplying factor, which determines the effectiveness of alternative monetary controls given the stochastic environment, depends upon behavioral characteristics of the economy but also upon certain elements of its financial structure, such as the proportion of investment which is financed by borrowing (rather than equity) and the proportion of credit employed in financing investment (rather than in acquiring other assets). The relative effectiveness of alternative monetary controls under uncertainty is further discussed below on the basis of a broader framework incorporating a more complex financial structure and more general hypotheses on the mechanism of price adjustments and expectations.

4.2.2. A model with a more general financial structure and price adjustment mechanism

The analysis presented above was based on a highly stylized model which abstracted from the roles of government and corporate sectors and was confined to the Keynesian short run with a predetermined price level and static expectations. In order to examine more fully the implications of financial structure for the monetary mechanism and the effectiveness of alternative monetary controls, we have developed a broader macroeconomic framework with the following basic features:[38] (1) a fairly comprehensive representation of the economy's financial structure incorporating up to seven financial instruments and markets; (2) disaggregation of the non-financial private sector into two sectors, households and corporate firms, and explicit modelling of the corporate sector's investment and financial decisions, taking into account the effects of inflation, of fiscal structure and their interaction; (3) specification of characteristic elements of the economy's tax structure which may cause inflation to be non-neutral, even when anticipated, and may impinge on the effectiveness of alternative monetary targets; and (4) an expectations-adjusted Phillips curve specification consistent with alternative theories concerning the dynamic behavior of wages and prices and alternative hypotheses on the nature of expectations. This framework is fairly complex, being designed to examine the effects of various policy actions, both monetary and fiscal, on the economy and, in particular, to analyze the effectiveness of alternative monetary controls on the stochastic and dynamic stability of nominal income. For present purposes, we will focus on certain key features of this model which relate to the determinants of the demand for indebtedness, the supply of bank credit and the effects of inflation on credit markets. Then, relying on certain assumptions concerning financial market behavior, the government's budgetary policy and the nature of expectations, we derive a simpler log-linear stochastic version of the general model which is employed to examine the implications of controlling output and inflation via the control of the supply of narrow and broad measures of money and the supply of some components of aggregate debt.

The economy consists of nine aggregate markets and it is divided into four

---

[38]See Papademos and Modigliani (1983) and Modigliani and Papademos (1987) for a full description of this framework.

sectors. There are two "real" markets for final goods and labor services and seven financial markets for currency and bank reserves, demand deposits, time and savings deposits, corporate equity, bank loans, and marketable debt instruments. The latter include government bonds and may include corporate bonds. The four sectors considered are households, corporate firms, banks and the government, which includes the monetary authority. Thus, the financial structure of the economy corresponds broadly to that of Table 10.2. The fiscal structure allows for both corporate and personal taxes and incorporates two features characteristic of many tax systems: nominal interest payments on debt are deductible for tax purposes from corporate profits and nominal income, and nominal capital gains on corporate equity are taxed at a lower rate than the personal tax rate on labor, dividend and nominal interest income.

In this model, all physical assets are treated as held exclusively by the corporate sector which is responsible for all investment activity. Households own real capital indirectly by acquiring corporate equity. It is argued that firms aim at maintaining their total debt, L_f, equal to a fraction l of the replacement cost of the capital stock, that is

$$L_f^d = lPK ,$$ (107)

which implies that the demand for borrowing by corporate firms is given by

$$\Delta L_f^d = lPI + l[(1 + \pi)(1 - \delta) - 1]P_{-1}K_{-1} ,$$ (107')

where $\pi = P/P_{-1} - 1$ is the inflation rate and δ is the (constant) depreciation rate of the existing capital stock.[39] The debt-to-capital ratio l is taken to be largely invariant to changes in the real rates of return and to depend on tax parameters and the average anticipated inflation rate. This proposition is justified by considering the effects of debt on the market value of corporate firms in economies where the tax structure creates a preferred status for debt financing.

Consider first an economy in which there are no corporate and personal taxes or, at any rate, the tax structure is such that no reduction in tax liability is gained by changing capital structure, and in which capital markets are perfect, implying that firms and households can borrow at a common rate. Then, according to the Modigliani–Miller theorem, the market value of the firm is not affected by its financial structure, at least within the range of corporate leverage where expected bankruptcy costs are negligible. Under such conditions, the firm's demand for debt cannot be explained as resulting from the

---

[39] The total demand for debt by corporate firms may be specified more generally as proportional to the sum of the replacement cost of capital and the quantity of liquid assets (money balances) held by firms: $L_f = l[PK + M1_f]$. This specification is adopted in Modigliani and Papademos (1987).

maximization of the market value of the firm, and it may be regarded as economically indeterminate.

However, the Modigliani–Miller assumptions may fail to hold. This may reflect the existence of "market imperfections", taxes, non-negligible bankruptcy costs and other factors. In particular, the fiscal structure in most countries implies that debt financing is preferable because of the deductibility, for tax purposes, of interest payments on debt from corporate profits. This implies that a "levered" firm may have greater market value than a firm with the same real capital and no debt. The (marginal) effect of debt on the firm's market value also depends, in general, on the rate of inflation, if the relevant tax provisions are formulated in nominal terms. In the model we have developed, the market value of a firm, relative to the replacement cost of its capital, q, can be shown to increase linearly with the debt–capital ratio, l. However, the positive effect of increased debt on market value is offset by other factors. As the debt-to-capital ratio rises and interest payments reduce the ratio of profits to earnings before interest and taxes, there is a rising probability of bankruptcy and agency costs, and of insufficient profits for taking advantage of the tax benefits provided by debt. The existence of other tax shields, such as investment credit, further increases the latter probability. Thus, the effects of leverage on the firm's market value can be expressed, more generally, by

$$q(l) = q(0) + \lambda l - \chi(l) , \quad \chi' > 0, \quad \chi'' > 0 , \tag{108}$$

where the debt–capital ratio, l, measures leverage, $q(0)$ is the market value of unlevered firms relative to replacement cost, λ is the value of leverage, which depends on all relevant tax rates (corporate, personal, capital gains), on pretax interest rates and average expected inflation, and the function $\chi(l)$ captures the unfavorable effects of debt on market value.[40] The optimum debt–capital ratio, which maximizes $q(l)$, must be such that $\chi'(l^*) = \lambda$ and it is an increasing

---

[40] The value of leverage can be shown to be related to the relevant parameters by

$$\lambda = \frac{\tau_c r'_T + (\tau_c + \tau_g - \tau_p) \bar{\pi}}{\rho' + \tau_g \bar{\pi}} = \frac{\tau_c i'_T + (\tau_p - \tau_g) \bar{\pi}}{\rho' + \tau_g \bar{\pi}}$$

where r'_T is the after-tax rate on time deposits which in this model is the rate received by households for their indirect ownership of corporate debt via the banks, ρ' is the after-tax rate of return on an unlevered firm, so that $(\rho' - r'_T)$ is the risk premium net of taxes required by households for holding corporate equity, $\bar{\pi}$ is the expected average inflation rate, and τ_p, τ_g, τ_c are tax rates on personal income, capital gains and corporate profits, respectively. The above expression shows that even in the absence of inflation, the tax-related value of leverage is positive since $\tau_c > 0$; moreover, if the risk premium is relatively invariant to changes in interest rates and the after-tax real rate r'_T is unaffected by inflation, the value of leverage increases with permanent inflation since $\tau_c > \tau_p - \tau_g$. See Modigliani (1982) and Papademos and Modigliani (1983, section 2.3).

function of permanent inflation since $\partial l^* / \partial \bar{\pi} = (\mathrm{d} l^* / \mathrm{d}\lambda)(\partial \lambda / \partial \bar{\pi}) > 0$. Thus, the total supply of corporate debt depends on tax parameters and inflation but it does not depend significantly on real interest rates. However, it is influenced indirectly through the effects of real rates on investment and the demand for real capital.

Firms may borrow either directly from households or indirectly through banks. Their demand for bank credit and their supply of corporate bonds in the market depends on the relative cost of these two forms of borrowing and can be expressed as:

$$L_b^d = \phi(i_L - i_B)L_f ,$$

$$B_f^s = [1 - \phi(i_L - i_B)]L_f ,$$

(109)

where $0 < \phi \leqslant 1$ and $\phi' < 0$, L_f is the total supply of corporate debt and i_L and i_B are the interest rates on bank loans and marketable debt instruments (bonds), respectively. The non-bank credit, however, may be interpreted as either direct financing or as indirect financing arranged by unregulated non-bank intermediaries. An objective of our analysis is to determine how the relative effectiveness of controls on bank credit depends on the substitutability between the two forms of credit, especially from the borrower's point of view, which in turn may reflect not only preferences but institutional constraints.

The household supply of credit is determined by its demand for financial assets (in view of the assumption of no direct household holding of physical assets). From standard portfolio theory, we expect that the household's demand for individual financial assets is proportional to the price level and depend upon a vector of relevant after-tax nominal rates of return, initial real wealth, and a measure of income. It can be expected to be homogeneous of zero degree with respect to all nominal rates of return. The vector of nominal rates corresponding to the menu of assets available to households (that is, currency, demand deposits, time deposits, government debt, firm debt and equity) is thus $i = (i_D, i_T, i_G, i_B, i_E)$, it being assumed that currency has a zero nominal return.[41] The vector of corresponding real rates, denoted by r, is given by $r = (i - \hat{\pi}_{+1})(1 + \hat{\pi}_{+1})^{-1}$, where $\hat{\pi}_{+1}$ is the anticipated inflation rate over the coming period. For analytical convenience, we simplify the structure (determination) of interest rates by assuming (1) that the interest rate on demand deposits can be taken as a constant over the period of analysis, (2) that the interest rate on government bonds differs from that on corporate bonds by a constant spread reflecting differential risk, that is $i_G = i_B - s_B$, and (3) that the

---

[41] The relevant rates affecting household decisions are the after-tax rates and, consequently, the nominal and real rates in this section should be interpreted as such. Since in this paper we do not examine in detail the effects of the tax structure on the economy, it is not necessary to introduce additional notation for after-tax rates as in Papademos and Modigliani (1983).

real rate of return on equity can be written as:

$$r_E = \rho + [l/(q - l)]\zeta = r_T + [q/(q - l)]\zeta , \quad \rho = r_T + \zeta , \tag{110}$$

where ρ is the real rate of return on the equity of "unlevered" firms, ζ is a risk premium expressed relative to the real rate on time deposits r_T, and $l/(q - l)$ is the debt–equity ratio. Deviations of the risk premium from its equilibrium value are assumed to be independent of the rates of return or real output.[42] These assumptions imply that the portfolio decisions of the household sector can be accounted for in terms of two independently determined rates, the interest rate on time deposits, i_T, and that on marketable corporate debt, i_B.

The banking system consists of a large number of institutions operating under competitive conditions and constant returns to scale. Banks hold three types of assets: reserves with the central bank, H_b, government bonds, B_{gb}, and bank loans, L_b. For the purposes of this analysis, bank equity can be ignored, so that bank liabilities consist of the two broad categories of deposits, demand and time deposits. Thus, the balance sheet constraint of the bank sector is $H_b^d + B_{gb}^d + L_b^s = D + T$, where the superscript d denotes banks' demand for the respective asset. In the case of loans, we may think of L_b^s as the quantity of loans supplied. Banks are required to hold non-interest-bearing reserves against their liabilities or assets, with the structure of reserve requirements depending upon the financial aggregate chosen by the central bank as its target. Assuming for simplicity that banks hold no excess reserves with the central bank, satisfying their demand for liquid, riskless assets by acquiring short-term government bonds, their demand for other earning assets (their supply of bank loans) can be expressed as:

$$L_b^s = \psi(i_L, i_B)[(1 - z_D)D + (1 - z_T)T] , \quad 0 < \psi \le 1,$$
$$\partial\psi/\partial i_L > 0, \quad \partial\psi/\partial i_B < 0 . \tag{111}$$

The term in square brackets represents banks' unrestricted sources of funds which are allocated among loans and bonds. If the monetary authorities aim at controlling $M2$ or total bank credit, the two required reserve ratios would presumably be set equal, while if they endeavor to control $M1$, z_T would be set equal to zero. Finally, it can be shown, employing the analysis of Section 3, that profit maximization and equilibrium in the market for time and savings deposits imply the following relationship between the rates on time deposits, bank loans and corporate bonds:

$$i_T = (1 - z_T)[\psi i_L + (1 - \psi)i_B] - q_T$$
$$= (1 - z_T)i_L - (1 - z_T)(1 - \psi)s_L - q_T, s_L = i_L - i_B , \tag{112}$$

[42] The risk premium may alternatively be expressed relative to the average real rate on firms' debt, which is defined by $r_F = \phi r_L + (1 - \phi)r_B$.

where $q_T = (1 - z_T)(1 - \psi)s_B + c_B$, s_B is the spread between the rates on corporate and government bonds and c_B represents the costs of intermediation per real dollar of deposits. Note that the spread, s_L, between the loan and bond rates is determined endogenously in general, while s_B is assumed to be a random variable with an expected value which is independent of the level of interest rates.

Equilibrium in the financial markets can then be summarized by the following subsystem of equations:

$$\psi(i_L - i_B)[(1 - z_D)D + (1 - z_T)T] = \phi(i_L - i_B)l(\tau, \bar{\pi})PK , \tag{113}$$

$$H_b = z_D D + z_T T , \tag{114}$$

$$H_p = PF_H(i_T, i_B, Y, W_{-1}) , \tag{115}$$

$$D = PF_D(i_T, i_B, Y, W_{-1}) , \tag{116}$$

$$T = PF_T(i_T, i_B, \hat{Y}^D, W_{-1}) , \tag{117}$$

$$i_T = (1 - z_T)[\psi i_L + (1 - \psi)i_B] - q_T , \tag{118}$$

$$M0 = H_p + H_b , \qquad M1 = H_p + D , \qquad M2 = M1 + T ,$$
$$LB = B_c + B_{gb} + L_b . \tag{119}$$

The first equation states the condition for equilibrium in the market for bank loans obtained from (107), (109) and (111). Equation (114) defines required bank reserves, while the next three equations, (115)–(117), are the equilibrium conditions in the markets for currency and bank liabilities. The right-hand side of each of the equations (115)–(117) defines the demand for the respective financial asset which must equal the available quantity which appears on the left-hand side. The real demands for transactions assets are taken to depend on total real income, while the real demand for time and savings deposits depends on anticipated disposable income, $\hat{Y}^D$. The quantities H_p, D and T are not directly controllable by a monetary authority endeavoring to control the quantity of one of the financial aggregates defined by the four equations in (119): the monetary base ($M0$), the narrow and broad measures of money ($M1$ and $M2$) and total domestic bank credit (LB). This latter quantity is identically equal to the broad measure of the money stock, as can be verified from the balance sheet constraints of the central bank $B_c = H_p + H_b = M0$ and of the other banks $H_b + B_{gb} + L_b = D + T$. Finally, equation (118) restates, for completeness, the relation (112) between the rates on time deposits, bank loans and corporate bonds.

If we exclude the fourth equation in (119), defining LB which equals $M2$, the above subsystem consists of nine equations involving ten "financial" variables, namely $(H_b, H_p, D, T, M0, M1, M2, i_L, i_B$ and $i_T)$. Thus, one more equation is needed to close this subsystem, namely the policy equation specifying that the monetary authority will enforce some stated level of money *or* of any of the financial aggregates defined in (119). The subsystem can be solved for the ten financial variables, and in particular the three rates, i_L, i_B, and i_T, in terms of the real endogenous variables $(K, Y, \hat{Y}^D)$, the price level and anticipated inflation $(P, \hat{\pi})$, initial real wealth W_{-1}, and of course policy controlled parameters (z_D, z_T, τ). In order to evaluate the stochastic performance of alternative policy targets, one requires a complete solution for all the variables in terms of the financial aggregate controlled by the central bank, behavioral and policy parameters, and stochastic disturbances. To this end, we must add, to the financial subsystem, a set of relations describing the behavior of the real variables, the government's budgetary policy and hypotheses concerning the nature of expectations. This is done in the following subsection, where we examine the relative effectiveness of alternative monetary targets under conditions of uncertainty.

4.3. The effectiveness of alternative monetary controls under uncertainty

It should be apparent from the previous analysis that under conditions of certainty the monetary authorities can, in principle, control nominal and real income by controlling the supply of alternative financial aggregates other than the conventional narrow measure of money ($M1$), and that in a static and deterministic economy, it would make no difference which alternative is chosen. Indeed, provided the targets were chosen consistently, they could be enforced simultaneously. However, under conditions of uncertainty, due to instability of behavior or of the financial structure and to imperfect knowledge of economic relations, the central bank's choice of alternative monetary aggregate targets would lead to different results with respect to the stochastic stability of nominal income and its dynamic adjustment to policy actions. In other words, the "velocity" relations between nominal income and alternative monetary or credit aggregates are not equally stable and, consequently, the central bank needs to be concerned with the optimal form of nominal income control.

In this subsection we provide some illustrations of the way behavioral and institutional factors interact with the stochastic environment to determine the relative effectiveness of two aggregates in minimizing the variances of aggregate output and the price level, in the presence of various disturbances. The two aggregates considered are the conventional narrow measure of money ($M1$) and a broad monetary aggregate ($M2$), which in our model is equivalent to the total quantity of credit extended by the consolidated banking system.

This analysis will be based on a log-linear version of the second model of the financial sector outlined in Subsection 4.2 and an appropriate linear specification of the determinants of equilibrium in the real sector. The behavioral equations contain additive stochastic terms which, in general, are assumed proportional to the long-run equilibrium levels of the variables they affect, and serially uncorrelated and independently distributed (except where dependence is induced through the budget constraints).

We consider first the limiting case when firms do not borrow directly from households but only through intermediaries, that is $\phi = 1$ in equation (113), and the spread between the rate of return on bonds and bank loans is constant, implying that the share of loans in banks' earning assets is constant, that is $\psi(i_L - i_G) = \psi$. In this case, we may express the behavioral equations of the system in terms of a single nominal and real rate, labelled i and r, respectively, which corresponds to the (after-tax) rate on time deposits. The complete log-linear stochastic model is then given by the following equations:

$$\text{IS:} \quad Y = C + I + G , \tag{120}$$

$$C = \bar{C} + c(\hat{Y}^D - \bar{Y}^D) + u_C \bar{C} , \quad c > 0 , \tag{120a}$$

$$I = \delta \bar{K} + v(q - \bar{q})K_{-1} + u_I \delta \bar{K} , \quad v > 0 , \qquad G = \bar{G} + u_G \bar{G} , \tag{120b}$$

$$\hat{Y}^D = \hat{Y} - G - \delta' K_{-1} , \quad \delta' > 0 , \tag{120c}$$

$$q = \bar{q} + a_1(r - \bar{r}) + a_2(\hat{\pi}_{+1} - \bar{\pi}) + u_q , \quad a_1 < 0, a_2 < 0 , \tag{120d}$$

$$\text{PC:} \quad (p - p_{-1}) = \alpha(y - \bar{y}) + (\hat{p} - p_{-1}) + u_p , \quad \alpha > 0 , \tag{121}$$

$$\text{AS:} \quad y = \bar{y} + \alpha^{-1}(p - \hat{p}) + \varepsilon_s , \quad \varepsilon_s = -u_p/\alpha , \tag{121'}$$

$$\text{LM1:} \quad m1 = \overline{m1} + (p - \bar{p}) + k_1(i - \bar{i}) + b_1(y - \bar{y}) + u_{M1} ,$$
$$k_1 \leq 0, b_1 > 0 , \tag{122}$$

$$\text{LM2:} \quad m2 = \overline{m2} + (p - \bar{p}) + k_2(i - \bar{i}) + b_2(y - \bar{y}) + u_{M2} ,$$
$$k_2 \gtrless 0, b_2 > 0 , \tag{123}$$

$$\text{LB:} \quad lb = \overline{lb} + (p - \bar{p}) + h(y - \bar{y}) + (1 - h)(I - \delta \bar{K})/\bar{K} + u_{LB} ,$$

$$\bar{h} = \bar{H}_p / \overline{LB} = 1 - l\overline{PK}/(1 - z)\psi \overline{LB} > 0 , \tag{124}$$

$$u_{LB} = \bar{h}u_{M0} + (1 - \bar{h})u_L .$$

The first five equations define the determinants of equilibrium in the market for final goods expressed in terms of the levels of the components of aggregate demand. The aggregate demand for consumption and investment is approximated linearly around the long-run equilibrium path, with a bar above a variable denoting its equilibrium value. Investment demand depends upon the real market value of a unit of capital relative to its steady-state value $(q - \bar{q})$, which is a function of the real interest rate and expected inflation.[43] Anticipated disposable income, $\hat{Y}^D$, can be expressed through (120c) by conveniently assuming that the government maintains its budget balanced in real terms and households anticipate "rationally" the current level of income and government expenditures but expect no real capital gains on their assets.

Substituting (120a)–(120d) into (120), letting $K_{-1} = \bar{K}$ and $\hat{Y} = Y$, subtracting the resulting expression from the corresponding steady-state equilibrium condition and employing the approximation $y - \bar{y} \equiv \log Y - \log \bar{Y} \cong Y/\bar{Y} - 1$, we derive the following condition for equilibrium in the goods market:

$$y = \bar{y} + a(r - \bar{r}) + a'(\hat{\pi}_{+1} - \bar{\pi}) + u , \tag{125}$$

where

$$a = m_x v a_1(\delta \bar{K}/\bar{Y}) < 0 , \qquad a' = (a_2/a_1)a < 0 , \qquad m_x = (1 - c)^{-1} , \tag{125a}$$

and

$$u = m_x[s_C u_C + s_I(u_I + v u_q)] + s_G u_G , \tag{125b}$$

The above equation corresponds to the Hicksian *IS* curve, expressed in the same log-linear format as in Section 2 (Table 10.1). It clearly exhibits the different sources of potential instability of aggregate demand which may be relevant to the choice of the monetary target. It is apparent that u represents a weighted average of the random components of consumption (u_C), government expenditures (u_G) and investment, which in turn reflects two types of shocks: those associated with the real investment decisions of firms, u_I, and those originating in the stock market, u_q. The weights are the respective shares in total output.

Aggregate price dynamics are summarized by the expectations-adjusted Phillips-curve specification (121) which, at this aggregate level of abstraction, is formally equivalent to a Lucas-type aggregate supply specification, as shown by (121'). It is assumed that expectations are formed "rationally", which means that they are consistent with the model in which they are imbedded. The hypothesis of "rational" expectations and equation (121) imply that the price level can adjust freely within each period, independently of the history of inflation, but the parameter α captures the speed at which the price level responds to the deviations of aggregate output from the long-run equilibrium

---

[43]Both parameters a_1 and a_2 in (120d) are functions of tax parameters and the debt–capital ratio. In particular, anticipated inflation may affect investment due to the effects of tax provisions in the presence of leverage. The parameter δ' in (120c) depends upon the rate of capital depreciation δ and the real costs of adjusting the stock of capital.

within each period, including the limiting cases of perfect price flexibility and Keynesian rigidity.

The remaining three equations, (122)–(124), state the equilibrium conditions in the money markets ($M1$ and $M2$) and in the market for bank loans. The specifications of money market equilibrium are derived by adding the relevant equations (115)–(117), employing (118) and then obtaining a log-linear approximation around the steady state. The interest semi-elasticities, k_1 and k_2, incorporate the parameters in (118).[44] Finally, the equilibrium condition in the market for bank loans, L_b, is obtained for the case when the central bank controls the total quantity of bank credit $LB = L_b + B_{gb} + B_c = M2$. In this case, the banks' supply of loans can be expressed as $L_b^s = \psi(1 - z)(\overline{LB} - H_p^d)$, where z is the (presumably) uniform required reserve ratio on all bank assets, $\overline{LB}$ is the fixed quantity of total bank credit, and H_p^d is the currency held by the public.[45]

We can examine now the effects of monetary policies which aim at enforcing some predeterminate and preannounced path of a monetary aggregate MJ ($J = 1, 2$). To derive the (implied) corresponding paths of aggregate output and the price level, it is useful to first obtain an intermediate relation, the so-called aggregate demand schedule, which defines the relation between output demanded, the price level and anticipated inflation, consistent with joint equilibrium in the goods and financial markets given the quantity of $M1$ (or $M2$). The aggregate demand schedules under the two monetary targets ($M1$ and $M2$), obtained by eliminating r from (125) using (122) or (123), respectively, and employing the Fisher hypothesis $i = r + (\hat{p}_{+1} - p)$, are:

$$y^d - \bar{y} = d_{1j}[(mj - \bar{m}j) - (p - \bar{p})] + d_{2j}(\hat{p}_{+1} - p) + \varepsilon_d(mj), \quad j = 1, 2,$$

$$(126)$$

where

$$\varepsilon_d(mj) = \beta_j(k_j u - au_{Mj}), \qquad u = (u_I - u_S + vu_q)/\eta_s + s_G u_G,$$

$$d_{1j} = a\beta_j > 0,$$

$$d_{2j} = -k_j d_{ij}(1 - a_2/a_1) \simeq -k_j d_{ij} > 0,$$

$$a = va_1/\eta_s < 0,$$

$$\beta_j = (ab_j + k_j)^{-1} < 0, \quad j = 1, 2.$$

---

[44] The parameters k_1, k_2 in this subsection differ from the parameters (k_1, k_2) and (k_1', k_2') in Subsection 3.6 which correspond to different hypotheses concerning the determination of bank deposit rates.

[45] Equation (124) is derived by equating L_b^s to the demand for bank loans $L_b^d = lPK$, assuming that $H_p^d = b_0 PY$, solving for LB and employing the approximation $\ln(x/\bar{x}) \cong (X/\bar{X}) - 1$. The stochastic term in (124) is a weighted average of the random component of the demand for currency, weighted by the share of currency in $M2$, and the stochastic component in the loan market u_L, which reflects disturbances affecting both the demand and supply side, that is random variations in ψ and ϕ in (113).

η_s is the elasticity of saving with respect to income, at equilibrium, and u_S is the stochastic term component of aggregate saving.

Solving (126) and (121) simultaneously and employing the hypothesis of "rational" expectations, we obtain the anticipated price level and output in terms of the relevant monetary aggregates:

$$\hat{p} = (1 - k_j)^{-1}[\hat{m}j - k_j\hat{p}_{+1} - (\overline{mj} - \bar{p})], \quad j = 1, 2, \tag{127a}$$

$$\hat{y} = \bar{y}. \tag{127b}$$

The difference equation, (127a), solved in the forward direction, implies that the anticipated price level depends on the anticipated path of the stock of money in all future periods:

$$\hat{p} = (1 - k_j)^{-1} \sum_{i=0}^{\infty} [-k_j/(1 - k_j)]^i \hat{m}j_{+i} - (\overline{mj} - \bar{p}), \quad j = 1, 2, \tag{128}$$

provided that $\lim_{i \to \infty} [-k_j/(1 - k_j)]^i \hat{p}_{+i} = 0$. The critical parameters determining the effects of alternative monetary strategies on the anticipated (and actual) path of the price level are the interest (semi)elasticities of the demands for $M1$ and $M2$. Since, these elasticities are clearly different, with $k_2 > k_1$, the monetary authority, through its choice of the monetary target, will affect the dynamic behavior of the price level. In particular, if the financial structure is such that the share of time deposits in $M2$ is large, k_2 may be zero or even positive and thus the coefficient $(-k_2/(1 - k_2))$ in (128) will be zero or negative. Thus, when $0 > k_2 > k_1$ under "rational", forward-looking expectations, future changes in the broad money aggregate will be characterized by weaker "announcement effects" on the current price level than changes in narrow money.[46]

Unanticipated fluctuations of the price level and output can be induced either by the various disturbances affecting the real and financial markets or by unanticipated fluctuations in the stock of money due to unforeseen shifts in policies (policy surprises) or to random fluctuations in the "money multipliers", relating the stocks of the chosen monetary targets to the policy instruments. If the monetary policy pursued by the central bank is pre-announced, fully anticipated and successfully enforced, the variances of aggregate output and the price level under the two monetary aggregates are given

---

[46]There also exists a potential for instability in the sense that the anticipated and actual price levels can become unbounded functions of the anticipated path of the broad monetary aggregate, if the interest elasticity of the demand for $M2$ is positive and sufficiently large.

by:

$$V(y \mid mj) = (1 + \alpha\gamma_j)^{-2}[V(\varepsilon_d \mid mj) + \alpha^2\gamma_j^2 V(\varepsilon_s)] ,$$

$$V(p \mid mj) = \alpha^2(1 + \alpha\gamma_j)^{-2}[V(\varepsilon_d \mid mj) + V(\varepsilon_s)] , \quad j = 1, 2 ,$$

(129)

where

$$V(\varepsilon_d \mid mj) = \beta_j^2[k_j^2 V(u) + a^2 V(u_{Mj})] , \qquad V(\varepsilon_s) = V(u_p)/\alpha^2 ,$$

$$\gamma_j = d_{1j} + d_{2j} = a(1 - k_j)\beta_j , \qquad \beta_j = (ab_j + k_j)^{-1} .$$

The parameters β_j and γ_j ($j = 1, 2$) reflect aggregate demand parameters such as the interest and income elasticities of the demand for $M1$ and $M2$, and depend on the monetary target chosen. The slopes in the $p-y$ plane of the aggregate demand schedules given by (126) in the Mj regime are equal to $-(1/\gamma_j)$, $j = 1, 2$. As already noted, the interest (semi)elasticity of $M2$ is algebraically larger than that of $M1$. If the income elasticity of $M2$ is at least as high as that of $M1$, that is $b_2 > b_1$, then the aggregate demand schedule under an $M2$ target will be less steep than under an $M1$ target, as shown in Figure 10.2.

When the central bank targets total bank credit, the variances of output and the price level can be expressed in terms of characteristics of the financial

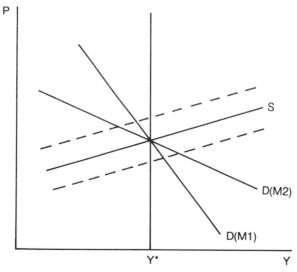

Figure 10.2. Price and output effects of supply shocks under an $M1$ and an $M2$ target.

structure of corporate firms and banks. Employing (121), (124) and (125), the hypothesis of "rational" expectations, and assuming the bank credit target is fully anticipated and successfully enforced, we obtain:

$$V(y \mid lb) = (1 + \alpha\gamma_L)^{-2}[V(\varepsilon_d \mid lb) + \alpha^2\gamma_L^2 V(\varepsilon_s)],$$

$$V(p \mid lb) = \alpha^2(1 + \alpha\gamma_L)^{-2}[V(\varepsilon_d \mid lb) + V(\varepsilon_s)],$$

where   (130)

$$V(\varepsilon_d \mid lb) = \omega^2[V(u_s) + V(u_L)/\delta^2]/\eta_s^2 + (1 - \omega)^2 V(u_{M0}),$$

$$\gamma_L = [b_0 + ls/(1 - z)\psi]^{-1}(\overline{LB}/\overline{PY}),$$

$$\omega = [1 + b_0(1 - z)\psi/ls]^{-1}.$$

The variance of the aggregate demand disturbance, ε_d, has been expressed as a weighted average of the sum of the variances of aggregate saving and the excess demand for bank credit, and the variance of currency demand. The weights depend on the proportion of investment financed through bank loans (the debt–capital ratio, l), the proportion of bank assets employed in financing investment, $(1 - z)\psi$, and the currency–income ratio, b_0.

The conditions which determine the relative superiority of the various monetary and credit aggregates as intermediate targets can now be inferred from (129) and (130). To analyze them it is useful to consider a number of limiting cases. If the dominant disturbance in the economy is due to supply shocks (in productivity, terms of trade, etc.), it can be readily verified from (129) and (130) that, since we can expect $\gamma_2 > \gamma_1$, an $M2$ target should result in a smaller variance of the price level than an $M1$ target, but at the cost of a larger variance in output. This result follows from the fact that with $\gamma_2 > \gamma_1$, $D(M1)$ is steeper than $D(M2)$ as illustrated in Figure 10.2. Clearly, under these conditions, neither target dominates the other, and the choice between them would have to be based on an assessment of the relative welfare costs associated with output and price instability.

The implications of stochastic disturbances affecting only aggregate demand can be examined by considering first the limiting case of a very elastic short-run supply schedule $(\alpha = 0)$, which corresponds to the Keynesian case of price rigidity, and implies that $V(p \mid mj) = 0$ and $V(y \mid mj) = V(\varepsilon_d \mid mj)$, $j = 1, 2$. From (129) and (130) one can deduce that $M2$ or LB will dominate $M1$ in terms of output variance if

$$\omega_2^2 V(u_s) + \omega^2 V(u_L)/\delta^2 < \omega_1^2[V(u_l) + v^2 V(u_q)]$$

$$+ [(1 - \omega_1)^2 V(u_{M1})/b_1^2 - (1 - \omega)^2 V(u_{M0})]\eta_s^2,$$ (131)

where

$$\omega_2^2 = \omega^2 - \omega_1^2, \qquad \omega = [1 + b_0 \psi (1 - z)/ls]^{-1},$$
$$\omega_1 = k_1 \beta_1 = [1 + va_1 b_1/\eta_s k_1]^{-1}.$$

The above inequality implies that bank credit, or $M2$, is a preferable target if the variability in saving behavior, $V(u_s)$, and in the borrowing–lending policies of firms and banks, $V(u_L)$, is small relative to an average of the variability in the stock market, $V(u_q)$, in the investment behavior of firms, $V(u_1)$, and in the demand for money, $V(u_{M1})$, other than currency $V(u_{M0})$. Given the variances of the stochastic terms, the relative performance for $M1$ and $M2$ in terms of output depends on the characteristics of the financial structure, such as l and ψ, and on behavioral parameters. In particular, if saving and lending–borrowing behavior is very stable (relative to the demand for currency), then the greater the proportion of debt or "intermediated" financing, l, the greater the advantage of $M2$. If, however, the demand for money ($M1$) is totally insensitive to interest rate fluctuations ($k_1 = 0$ and thus $\omega_1 = 0$) and if it is very stable (relative to the demand for saving and credit), then an $M1$ target is always superior to an $M2$ target. In short, $M2$ can be characterized as a better target in what may be called a "Keynesian economy" of stable saving, "animal spirits", and volatility in financial markets, and in which firms are highly levered and, correspondingly, a large share of investment financing is inter-mediated.

If we drop the assumption of price rigidity and with expectations formed "rationally", it is found that the effects of demand disturbances are transmitted partly to output and partly to the price level, depending upon the slope of the stochastic short-run Phillips curve. As to the relative effectiveness of $M1$ and $M2$ targets, two general conclusions emerge from (129) and (130). First, in contrast to what happens with supply shocks, there is no trade-off between output and price variability which can be achieved by shifting between $M1$ and $M2$. In the case of demand shocks, if one target results in smaller output variability it will also give rise to smaller price variability. Second, price flexibility is favorable to an $M2$ target in the following sense: as α rises, both the variances of output and of the price level under an $M2$ target decline relative to the corresponding variances under an $M1$ target. These two results imply that, in the circumstances reviewed in the previous paragraph, in which $M2$ dominates $M1$ under price rigidity, it will dominate it a fortiori as α grows larger; on the other hand, if $M2$ does not dominate $M1$ under price rigidity, it may (though it need not) dominate it for a sufficiently large value of α.

The effectiveness of alternative intermediate targets in the presence of demand shocks is examined next allowing for the possibility of "disintermedia-tion", i.e. of firms borrowing directly from the public or through a non-bank financial intermediary. The existence of substitutes for bank loans, on the part of borrowers, and for bank deposits, on the part of lenders, could affect in a crucial way the effectiveness of alternative targets; indeed, one might conjecture that a bank credit target would become ineffective, if not infeasible, with the availability of close substitutes.

A formal analysis of this issue requires modification of the linear stochastic model described by equations (120)–(124) in two respects: first, equations (120d), (122) and (123) should be expressed as functions of two interest rates, the rate on bank loans and that on directly marketable corporate bonds, or alternatively, as functions of a weighted average of these two rates ($r = \bar{\phi} r_L + (1 - \bar{\phi}) r_B$) and the spread $s_B = r_L - r_B$. Second, equation (124) must be replaced by a log-linearization of the more general specification (113) for equilibrium in the market for bank loans.

The central bank's choice of a financial target affects the condition for equilibrium in the bank credit market, including its stochastic component, by influencing the supply side. Under an $M1$ target, the left-hand side of (113) becomes $\psi(s_B)[(1 - z_D)(1 - h_1)\overline{M1} + T]$, while under a bank credit, or $M2$ target, the supply of bank loans is given by $\psi(s_B)(1 - z)[\overline{LB} - h_1 M1]$, where h_1 is the share of currency held by the public in $M1$. Under "rational" expectations, the unanticipated fluctuations of output under the jth monetary target can be shown to take the form:

$$(y - \hat{y}) = [(mj - \widehat{mj}) - k_{js}(s_B - \hat{s}_B) + \eta_j]/D_j , \quad j = 1, 2 , \tag{132}$$

where

$$D_j = b_j + k_{jr}/a + (1 - k_{jr})\alpha , \tag{132a}$$

$$\eta_j = (k_{jr}/a)u - u_{Mj} + (1 - k_{jr})\alpha\varepsilon_s . \tag{132b}$$

The parameters k_{jr} and k_{js} are the (derived) semi-elasticities of the demand for the jth monetary aggregate with respect to the average borrowing rate and the interest rate spread, defined above. Note that the disturbance term η_j depends on the random components of the IS, the demand for the jth monetary aggregate and the aggregate supply function (u, u_{Mj}, ε_s). But $(y - \hat{y})$ also depends on the unanticipated variations of the spread and the stock of the jth aggregate.

The spread between the bank loan rate and the market rate in (132) cannot be determined directly only from the appropriate version of (113), since that equation depends on y as well as on the average level of interest rates. Employing the relevant equilibrium conditions in the money, loan and goods markets, the unexpected variations in the spread under a broad money target can be expressed as:

$$(s_B - \hat{s}_B) = [(m2 - \widehat{m2}) - \phi_2(y - \hat{y}) + \zeta_2]/(1 - h_1)\phi^* , \tag{133}$$

where

$$\phi_2 = c_{2r}/a + h_1 b_1 + (1 - h_1 k_{1r})\alpha \,, \tag{133a}$$

$$c_{2r} = h_1(k_{1r} + k_{1s}) + (1 - h_1)\delta\theta_r \,, \tag{133b}$$

$$\zeta_2 = (c_{2r}/a)u - v_{L|M2} + (1 - h_1 k_{1r})\alpha\varepsilon_s \,, \tag{133c}$$

$$v_{L|M2} = (1 - h_1)(u_I + \nu u_q)\delta + h_1 u_{M1} + (1 - h_1)u_{L|M2} \,. \tag{133d}$$

In (133), $\phi^* = (d\phi/ds_B)(s_B/\phi)$ is the elasticity of substitution of bank loans for market credit and in (133b) θ_r is the total interest elasticity of the market value of capital. Note that the elasticity of substitution, ϕ^*, affects the spread only through the denominator of (133). The stochastic term, ζ_2, depends on the *IS* and aggregate supply shocks (u, ε_s) and on the total disturbance $v_{L|M2}$ in the loan market under an *M2* target defined by (133d), where $u_{L|M2}$ represents the random component of the net demand for bank loans, due to random fluctuations in ϕ and ψ. The effects of disturbances on aggregate real and nominal income under a broad money or credit target can now be obtained by solving simultaneously (121), (132), with $j = 2$, and (133) for $(y - \hat{y})$ recalling that with "rational" expectations, $\hat{y} = \bar{y}$.

We can now examine the implications of additional channels of financing outside the banking system. A first conclusion is that real and nominal income can be controlled effectively by employing a broad money or bank credit target even if, for firms, the substitution between bank and non-bank forms of credit is perfect. This rejects the contrary conjecture stated earlier. In fact, a second interesting result is that, when the substitution is perfect, a bank credit target may be expected to be more effective than a narrow money target in stabilizing both output and the price level with respect to the traditional, Keynesian-type, demand shocks. However, a bank credit target may be superior to an *M1* target even for smaller rates of substitution. With high substitution, the same *M2*-credit target is also superior to a narrow money target in containing the effects of disturbances in the demand for financial assets, with the exception of shocks affecting the public's choice between time deposits and market instruments (bonds).

The main reason for these results is that perfect substitution between the two sources of borrowing by firms implies that the spread between the bank lending rate and the market rate must be constant and independent of the overall level of interest rates, aggregate income, as well as the various disturbances affecting the goods and financial markets. As can be inferred from (133) for the case of a broad money target, as the elasticity of substitution, ϕ^*, of bank loans for market credit approaches infinity, $(s_B - \hat{s}_B)$ goes to zero. Consequently, in this case the stochastic behavior of output can be derived directly from (132) for $j = 1, 2$. Its variance as well as that of the price level [obtained from (121) and (132)] can be expected to be smaller under a bank credit *M2* target than under an *M1* target with respect to real and most financial demand shocks. This is primarily because the total interest elasticity of $M2$ should be much smaller than that of $M1$, that is $|k_{1r}| > |k_{2r}|$. The interest inelasticity of the demand for broad money reflects the fact that $M2$ includes interest-bearing time and savings deposits, with deposit rates adjusting to changes in market rates. On the other hand, a movement of all interest rates can be expected to have a greater impact on the demand for $M1$, which typically pays no interest or a low interest which is not adjusted frequently to changes in market rates. In the limiting case, when the financial structure and public preferences are such that $k_{2r} = 0$, a broad money or bank credit target insures that demand disturbances have no effect at all on real and nominal income, as can be seen from (132b). To see the mechanism involved, suppose there is an unanticipated increase in investment demand, causing a rise in interest rates. If the control variable were $M1$, the rise in interest rates, while partially containing the aggregate demand shock, would also reduce the demand for $M1$, making it possible for income to rise above equilibrium. But if the target variable were $M2$, the demand for it, in the case of perfect substitution, would be unaffected both by the rise in the level of interest rates and by the spread, which is constant; hence, aggregate income cannot change and interest rates must rise sufficiently so as to offset fully the impact of demand disturbances.

With respect to supply shocks, a bank credit target is less effective in reducing the variability of real output than a narrow money target, but it is more effective in stabilizing the price level. This result is, to a large extent, also a consequence of the relatively low interest rate sensitivity of the demand for total bank liabilities. For instance, if there is an unfavorable supply shock, the new equilibrium will require a higher level of prices and a lower output: the question is how much of the burden will be borne by each? The rise in prices will create excess demand for money, at the received level of income, thereby raising interest rates. If the demand for money were relatively elastic, as would presumably be the case for narrow money, then the needed reduction in money demand could be satisfied by a relatively small rise in interest rates and hence a small reduction in income. But with an $M2$ target, and an inelastic demand for it, interest rates would have to rise more and income would have to fall more. In the limiting case of zero interest elasticity of the demand for the targeted aggregate, the whole adjustment must be borne by a fall in output. The response of the price level to the shock will be the opposite to that of income since, for a given supply shock, the smaller the output adjustment, the larger the adjustment of prices.

The implications of imperfect substitution between bank and non-bank credit for the effectiveness of the two targets are examined more fully in Modigliani and Papademos (1987) partly on the basis of illustrative values of behavioral parameters and stylized facts about the financial structure of the U.S. economy. The main conclusions of this analysis are the following. As the degree of substitution increases, the bank credit ($M2$) target becomes relatively more effective in reducing both output and price fluctuations in the presence of all demand shocks, except for some financial shocks. When the degree of substitution is low, the bank credit target is especially inferior if the dominant source of instability originates in the market for bank loans. On the other hand, with respect to supply shocks, as the substitution rises, the effectiveness of bank credit in stabilizing output decreases, although its effectiveness in stabilizing the price level is enhanced. Another interesting conclusion is that the degree of substitution between bank and market credit by firms has negligible effects on the stochastic behavior of output and the price level under the narrow money target. Thus, the Hicksian analysis, which relies on the properties of money demand without reference to the characteristics of the demand for other financial assets and liabilities, is generally applicable under the conventional $M1$ target being largely unaffected of the extent of substitution between bank and market forms of credit.

5. Summary and conclusions

In this chapter we have examined various aspects of the relation between the supply of money and nominal income and their implications for the conduct of monetary policy. Section 2 focused on traditional versions of the monetary mechanism – the mechanism through which the monetary authority endeavors to control nominal income. In these versions the monetary aggregate controlled by the central bank is money as traditionally defined to consist of all the means of payment ($M1$), and the control is assumed to be complete. We have examined the nature and stability of the income velocity of the narrow measure of money implied by four basic macroeconomic models: (i) the classical model of the quantity theory of money; (ii) a model combining the classical assumptions of perfect price flexibility and instantaneous market clearing with the Keynesian hypothesis of liquidity preference and Fisher's law on the relationship between the nominal and real interest rates and expected inflation; (iii) the Keynesian model of liquidity preference, complete wage rigidity and static expectations; and (iv) a general macroeconomic model incorporating an expectations-augmented Phillips curve or a Lucas aggregate supply specification. All models have been expressed in comparable specifications and incorporate additive stochastic terms. For each model we have derived the implied relation between the money supply and nominal income – or its two components, output and the price level; and we have shown the implications of alternative assumptions concerning behavior, the mechanism of market clearing and the nature of expectations – in particular, adaptive and "rational" expectations – for the nature of the income velocity of money, and its stochastic and dynamic stability.

Section 3 dealt with the process of creation of money, recognizing that it is neither created directly nor rigidly controlled by the central bank. The section deals with five related topics. The first is the money multiplier approach, stressed in "textbook" formulations, which assumes fixed proportions between holdings of reserves and currency and bank deposits and leads to the conclusion that the supplies of the narrow and broad measures of money can be expressed as fixed multiples of the (non-borrowed) monetary base, considered precisely controllable by the central bank. The multiplier approach has then been generalized to allow for the effects of interest rates and income on the ratios describing portfolio preferences, on the basis of plausible but ad hoc behavioral assumptions. However, these extended monetary base multipliers are semi-reduced forms (endogenous quantities) which are not invariant to the actions of the monetary authorities, e.g. to a change in the monetary base.

An alternative approach relies on explicit structural models in which the interaction of the public's demand for assets, banks' profit maximization, and central bank's actions determine the stock of money and interest rates simultaneously. Subsection 3.4 presents one such structural model, emphasizing the role of bank asset management under uncertainty. The last two parts of section 3 have dealt with the process of money creation in a deregulated environment in which the role of banks' behavior in the money supply mechanism becomes more crucial. Subsection 3.5 has surveyed recent theoretical analyses of the behavior of the banking firm, especially with respect to liability management, concentrating on the implications for the money supply process. It has been shown how liability management and the structure of bank liabilities can be affected by three essential factors: by the degree of market power enjoyed by banks, operating or "real resource" costs associated with the provision of deposit and transactions services, and default losses on bank loans. A fairly general model has been presented which allows for the joint determination of the structure of bank liabilities and the scale of the banking firm. Finally, Subsection 3.6 contains a simple stochastic aggregative model of money stock determination which incorporates stylized relations consistent with the above microeconomic analysis.

Section 4 examined the more general issue of the feasibility and desirability of endeavoring to control nominal income through financial aggregates other than the money supply as conventionally defined. This is an important issue, especially after the recent fundamental structural changes and innovations in financial markets, which have affected the stability of the relations between nominal income and various financial aggregates, and in light of empirical evidence which suggests that $M1$ may not be the most effective means of controlling nominal income. The study of this issue requires a broader theoretical framework which takes explicitly into account the role of the structure of financial markets in the monetary mechanism. In Subsection 4.2 we have presented two macroeconomic models which serve this purpose. Both models include a banking sector and specify the determinants of equilibrium in the credit markets. But the first model relies on the simplifying assumption of a single type of credit, namely bank loans, and confines the analysis to the Keynesian short run. The second formulation allows for both bank and non-bank credit and models explicitly the corporate sector's investment and financial decisions, taking into account the effects of inflation, the fiscal structure and their interaction.

It has been shown that monetary authorities can control real and nominal income by controlling the supply of alternative monetary and credit aggregates other than the money supply ($M1$), and that in a static and deterministic economy it would make no difference which alternative was chosen. However, when the central bank controls a broad monetary or bank credit aggregate, the monetary mechanism involves a different adjustment process than the conventional one, and it is best understood in terms of a paradigm which focuses on the interaction of the credit and goods markets.

Under conditions of uncertainty, the choice of a financial aggregate affects the stochastic properties, and in particular the variances, of real and nominal income. It has been shown that the relative effectiveness of a narrow money target and a broad money or credit target depends upon (1) the origin and relative significance of shocks, (2) behavioral factors such as the interest elasticity of the demand for money and non-monetary assets, and the degree of substitution between bank and market debt, (3) elements of the financial structure such as the share of investment financed by borrowing, (4) the degree of flexibility of prices, and (5) in the presence of certain shocks, on the policy-makers' assessment of the relative welfare costs associated with output and price instability.

Our analysis of the monetary mechanism highlights areas calling for further research, including four main topics. The first is the accuracy with which the monetary authority can achieve the desired path of the chosen aggregate, employing the instruments under its direct control. This issue can be examined by combining the analyses of Subsections 3.5 and 4.3. A related question is under what conditions the central bank can control nominal income and the path of alternative financial aggregates more effectively by employing as an instrument $M0$ or interest rates. Although use of the interest rate as a policy instrument, in the presence of price flexibility, may result in the indeterminacy of nominal income, the central bank, nonetheless, can use interest rates as instruments to effectively control the path of a financial aggregate and thus indirectly as instruments of nominal income control [e.g. McCallum (1981)].

A second issue is the extension of the analysis to an open economy. An important question is the way the "degree of openness" of an economy shapes the effectiveness of alternative monetary and credit aggregates and of the exchange rate as a means of controlling nominal income [e.g. Artis and Currie (1981), Bhandari (1985), Papademos and Rozwadowski (1983)].

Another, general, issue relates to the so-called "Goodhart's Law". According to this proposition a central bank's attempt to tightly control the path of a chosen monetary aggregate may result in destabilizing the relation of that aggregate to nominal income, thus impairing its usefulness as an intermediate target. It has been argued that the validity of this proposition rests on the endogenous responses of market participants who, motivated by their own profit-maximizing behavior, attempt to offset the imposed monetary controls. The stochastic analysis of the last section suggests a different explanation for the Goodhart effect, pointing instead to the role of the stochastic properties of the error component of the corresponding velocity. It is bound to be different when a given aggregate is chosen as the target and hence becomes exogenous and when some other aggregate is controlled and hence the given aggregate is endogenous. Furthermore, at least under certain conditions, one would expect the variance of the error component of the velocity to be larger when the aggregate is exogenous than when endogenous, which is consistent with Goodhart's Law. The framework in Subsection 4.3 can be utilized to examine the existence and likely magnitude of this effect.

A final issue which deserves further analysis is whether the targeting and control of monetary aggregates is the most efficient means of formulating and implementing monetary policy. B. Friedman (1975, 1977) has shown that in general the conduct of monetary policy in terms of intermediate targets may not be the most efficient. Nevertheless, since the early 1970s monetary aggregates have been employed in many countries as intermediate targets, partly as a consequence of the difficulties encountered in employing interest rates as intermediate targets in an inflationary environment, and partly as a result of the considerable time lags in obtaining reasonably accurate information concerning the behavior of nominal income and the effects of changes in policy instruments on the final policy objectives. Thus, the practical problem faced by many monetary authorities has been, to a large extent, that of choosing the most effective monetary target rather than that of deciding whether to use any. Central banks have adopted a variety of financial aggregates as targets or policy indicators; but most have not pursued them rigidly, often employing more than one aggregate or using them jointly with other financial variables as indicators or control devices. Our analysis has shed some light on the reasons behind central banks' preferences and practices. A general conclusion which emerges is that, to achieve a nominal income objective, monetary policy should be conducted flexibly, without relying exclusively on a single approach or on a single monetary aggregate, including the money supply.

References

Akhtar, M.A. (1983) 'Financial innovations and their implications for monetary policy: An international perspective', *Economic Papers*, no. 9. Basle: Bank for International Settlements.

Allais, M. (1947) *Economie & intérêt: Présentation nouvelle des problèmes fondamentaux relatifs au rôle économique du taut de l'intérêt et de leurs solutions*, 2 vols. Paris: Librairie des Publications Officielles.

Andersen, L.C. and A.E. Burger (1969) 'Asset management and commercial bank portfolio behavior: Theory and practice', *Journal of Finance*, 24: 207–222.

Ando, A. (1974) 'Some aspects of stabilization policies, the monetarist controversy and the MPS model', *International Economic Review*, 15: 541–571.

Ando A. and F. Modigliani (1963) 'The "lifecycle" hypothesis of saving: Aggregate implications and tests', *American Economic Review*, 53: 55–84.

Ando, A. and F. Modigliani (1975) 'Some reflections on describing structures of financial sectors (Appendix with K. Shell), in: G. Fromm and L.R. Klein, eds., *The Brookings model: Perspective and recent developments*. Amsterdam: North-Holland, pp. 524–563.

Argy, V. (1985) 'Money supply theory and the money multiplier', *Australian Economic Papers*, 4: 27–36.

Artis, M.J. and D.A. Currie (1981) 'Monetary targets and the exchange rate: A case for conditional targets', *Oxford Economic Papers*, 33, Supplement: 176–203.

Baily, M.N. and J. Tobin (1977) 'Macroeconomic effects of selective public employment and wage subsidies', *Brookings Papers on Economic Activity*, 2: 511–541.

Baltensperger, E. (1972a) 'Economies of scale, firm size, and concentration in banking', *Journal of Money, Credit and Banking*, 4: 467–488.

Baltensperger, E. (1972b) 'Cost of banking activities – interactions between risk and operating costs', *Journal of Money, Credit and Banking*, 4: 595–611.

Baltensperger, E. (1980) 'Alternative approaches to the theory of the banking firm', *Journal of Monetary Economics*, 6: 1–37.

Baumol, W.J. (1952) 'The transactions demand for cash: An inventory theoretic approach', *Quarterly Journal of Economics*, 66: 545–556.

Becker, W.E. Jr. (1975) 'Determinants of the United States currency–demand deposit ratio', *Journal of Finance*, 30: 57–74.

Benston, G.J. (1972) 'Economies of scale in financial institutions', *Journal of Money, Credit, and Banking*, 4: 312–341.

Berkman, N.G. (1980) 'Abandoning monetary aggregates', in: *Controlling monetary aggregates*, Vol. III. Boston: Federal Reserve Bank of Boston, pp. 76–100.

Bhandari, J.S., ed., (1985) *Exchange rate management under uncertainty*. Cambridge, Mass.: MIT Press.

Brainard, W.C. (1967) 'Financial intermediaries and a theory of monetary control', in: D.D. Hester and J. Tobin, eds., *Financial markets and economic activity*, Cowles Foundation monograph 11. New York: Wiley.

Brennan, M.J. (1971) 'Capital market equilibrium with divergent borrowing and lending rates', *Journal of Financial and Quantitative Analysis*, 6: 1197–1205.

Brunner, K. (1961) 'A schema for the supply theory of money', *International Economic Review*, 11: 79–109.

Brunner, K. and A.H. Meltzer (1964) 'Some further investigations of demand and supply functions for money', *Journal of Finance*, 19: 240–283.

Brunner, K. and A.H. Meltzer (1968) 'Liquidity traps for money, bank credit and interest rates', *Journal of Political Economy*, 76: 1–37.

Brunner, K. and A.H. Meltzer (1972) 'Money, debt and economic activity', *Journal of Political Economy*, 80: 951–977.

Brunner, K. and A.H. Meltzer (1976) 'An aggregative theory for a closed economy', in: J.L. Stein, ed., *Monetarism*. Amsterdam: North-Holland, pp. 69–103.

Burger, A.E. (1971) *The money supply process*. Belmont, California: Wadsworth.

Burns, A. (1973) 'The role of the money supply in the conduct of monetary policy', *Federal Reserve Bank of Richmond Monthly Review*, December: 2–8.

Cagan, P. (1956) 'The monetary dynamics of hyperinflation', in: M. Friedman, ed., *Studies in the quantity theory of money*. Chicago: University of Chicago Press.

Cagan, P. (1958) 'Demand for currency relative to the total money supply', *Journal of Political Economy*, 66: 303–328.

Cagan, P. (1965) *Determinants and effects of changes in the stock of money* 1875–1960. New York: Columbia University Press.

Cagan, P. (1979) 'Financial developments and the erosion of monetary controls', in: *Contemporary economic problems*, Washington: American Enterprise Institute, pp. 117–151.

Cagan, P. (1982) 'The choice among monetary aggregates as targets and guides for monetary policy', *Journal of Money, Credit and Banking*, 14: 661–686.

Davis, R.G. (1981) 'Recent evolution in US financial markets – implications for monetary policy', *Greek Economic Review*, 3: 259–309.

De Leeuw, F. (1965) 'A model of financial behavior' in: J. Duesenberry et al., eds., *The Brookings quarterly econometric model of the United States*. Chicago: Rand-McNally, pp. 465–530.

De Leeuw, F. and E. Gramlich (1969) 'The channels of monetary policy: A further report on the Federal Reserve–MIT model', *Journal of Finance*, 24: 265–290.

Dewald, W. (1963) 'Free reserves, total reserves and monetary control', *Journal of Political Economy*, 71: 141–153.

Dornbusch, R. and S. Fischer (1987) *Macroeconomics*, 4th edn. New York: McGraw-Hill.

Duesenberry, J.S. (1949) *Income, saving and the theory of consumer behavior*. Cambridge, Mass.: Harvard University Press.

Edgeworth, F.Y. (1888) 'The mathematical theory of banking', *Journal of the Royal Statistical Society*, 51: 113–127.

Eisner, R. (1962) 'Investment plans and realizations', *American Economic Review*, 52: 190–203.

Eisner, R. (1978) *Factors in business investment*. Cambridge, Mass.: Ballinger.

Fama, E.F. (1980) 'Banking in the theory of finance', *Journal of Monetary Economics*, 6: 39–57.

Fand, D.I. (1967) 'Some implications of money supply analysis', *The American Economic Review*, 57: 380–400.

Fand, D.I. (1970) 'Some issues in monetary economics: Can the Federal Reserve control the money stock', *Federal Reserve Bank of St. Louis Review*, 52: 10–27.

Fischer, S. (1977) 'Long-term contracts, rational expectations, and the optimal money supply rule', *Journal of Political Economy*, 85: 191–206.

Fischer, S. (1983) 'A framework for monetary and banking analysis', *Economic Journal*, 93, Supplement: 1–16.

Fisher, I. (1911) *The purchasing power of money*, rev. edn. 1920. New York: Macmillan.

Flannery, M.J. (1981) 'Market interest rates and commercial bank profitability: An empirical investigation', *Journal of Finance*, 36: 1085–1101.

Flannery, M.J. (1982) 'Retail bank deposits as quasi-fixed factors of production', *American Economic Review*, 72: 527–536.

Friedman, B.M. (1975) 'Targets, instruments and indicators of monetary policy', *Journal of Monetary Economics*, 1: 443–474.

Friedman, B.M. (1977) 'The inefficiency of short-run monetary aggregates for monetary policy', *Brookings Papers on Economic Activity*, 2: 293–335.

Friedman, B.M. (1980) 'The relative stability of money and credit "velocities" in the United States', Working Paper, Harvard University.

Friedman, B.M. (1983) 'Monetary policy with a credit aggregate target', *Carnegie-Rochester Conference Series on Public Policy*, 18: 117–147.

Friedman, B.M. (1986) 'Money, credit, and interest rates in the business cycle', in: R.J. Gordon, ed., *The American business cycle: Continuity and change*. Chicago: University of Chicago Press.

Friedman, B.M. (1988) 'Lessons on monetary policy from the 1980s', *Journal of Economic Perspectives*, 2: 51–72.

Friedman, M. (1956) 'The quantity theory of money: A restatement', in: M. Friedman, ed., *Studies in the quantity theory of money*. Chicago: University of Chicago Press.

Friedman, M. (1957) *A theory of the consumption function*, National Bureau of Economic Research, General Series no. 63. Princeton: Princeton University Press.

Friedman, M. (1959) 'The demand for money: Some theoretical and empirical results', *Journal of Political Economy*, 67: 327–351.

Friedman, M. (1968) 'The role of monetary policy', *American Economic Review*, 58: 1–17.

Friedman, M. and A. Schwartz (1963) *A monetary history of the United States 1867–1960*. Princeton: Princeton University Press.

Frost, P.A. (1971) 'Banks' demand for excess reserves', *Journal of Political Economy*, 79: 805–825.

Goldfeld, S.M. (1966) *Commercial bank behavior and economic activity*. Amsterdam: North-Holland.

Goldfeld, S.M. (1976) 'The case of the missing money', *Brookings Papers on Economic Activity*, 1976-3: 683–730.

Goldfeld, S.M. and E. Kane (1966) 'The determinants of member-bank borrowing', *Journal of Finance*, 21: 499–514.

Goodhart, C.A.E. (1982) 'Structural changes in the banking system and the determination of the stock of money', paper presented to the Conference on Western European Priorities at the Center for European Policy Studies, Brussels.

Greenbaum, S.I. (1967) 'A study of bank cost', *National Banking Review*, 4: 415–437.

Gurley, J.G. and E.S. Shaw (1960) *Money in a theory of finance*, with a mathematical appendix by A.C. Enthoven. Washington: The Brookings Institution.

Hart, A.G. (1981) 'Regaining Control over an Open-ended Money Supply,' in: Joint Economic Committee, *Stagflation: The causes, effects and solutions, Vol. 4 of Special Study on Economic Change*. Washington: GPO.

Hart, O.D. and D.M. Jaffee (1974) 'On the application of portfolio theory of depository financial intermediaries', *Review of Economic Studies*, 41: 129–147.

Havrilesky, T.M. and J.T. Boorman (1978) *Monetary macroeconomics*. Arlington Heights: AHM Publishing Corporation.

Hendershott, P.H. and F. De Leeuw (1970) 'Free reserves, interest rates and deposits: A synthesis', *Journal of Finance*, 25: 599–613.

Hess, A.C. (1971) 'An explanation of short-run fluctuations in the ratio of currency to demand deposits', *Journal of Money, Credit and Banking*, 3: 666–679.

Hester, D. and J. Pierce (1968) 'Cross-section analysis and bank dynamics', *Journal of Political Economy*, 76, part II: 755–776.

Hester, D.D. and J. Tobin, eds. (1967) *Financial markets and economic activity*, Cowles Foundation monograph 21. New York: Wiley.

Hicks, J.R. (1935) 'A suggestion for simplifying the theory of money', *Economica*, 2: 1–19; reprinted in *Readings in monetary theory*, American Economic Association. 13–32, Homewood: Irwin, 1951, pp. 13–32.

Hicks, J.R. (1937) 'Mr. Keynes and the "Classics": A suggested interpretation', *Econometrica*, 5: 147–159.

Hosek, W.R. (1970) 'Determinants of the money multiplier', *Quarterly Review of Economics and Business*, Summer: 37–46.

Johnson, H.G. (1962) 'Monetary theory and policy', *American Economic Review*, 52: 335–384.

Jorgenson, D.W. (1963) 'Capital theory and investment behavior', *American Economic Review*, 53: 247–259.

Jorgenson, D.W. (1971) 'Econometric studies of investment behavior: A survey', *Journal of Economic Literature*, 9: 1111–1147.

Judd, J.P. and J.L. Scadding (1982) 'The search for a stable money demand functions', *Journal of Economic Literautre*, 20: 993–1023.

Kahane, Y. (1977) 'Capital adequacy and the regulation of financial intermediaries', *Journal of Banking and Finance*, 1: 207–218.

Kareken, J.H. (1967) 'Commerical banks and the supply of money: A market-determined demand deposit rate', *Federal Reserve Bulletin*, October: 1699–1712.

Kaufman, G.G. (1966) 'The demand for currency', *Staff economic studies*. Washington, D.C.: Board of Governors of the Federal Reserve System.

Kaufman, H. (1979) 'A new target for monetary policy', Statement presented to a seminar at the Board of Governors of the Federal Reserve System, Washington, D.C.

Kaufman, H.M. and R.E. Lombra (1980) 'The demand for excess reserves, liability management, and the money supply process', *Economic Inquiry*, 18: 555–566.

Keynes, J.M. (1930) *A treatise on money*, 2 vols. London: Macmillan.

Keynes, J.M. (1936) *The general theory of employment, interest and money*. London: Macmillan.

Klein, M.A. (1971) 'A theory of the banking firm', *Journal of Money, Credit and Banking*, 3: 205–218.

Koehn, M. and A.M. Santomero (1980) 'Regulation of bank capital and portfolio risk', *Journal of Finance*, 35: 1235–1244.

Kopcke, R.W. (1983) 'Must the ideal "money stock" be controllable?', *New England Economic Review*, March/April: 10–23.

Lange, O. (1938) 'The rate of interest and the optimum propensity to consume', *Economica*, 5: 12–32.

Le Roy, S. (1979) 'Monetary control under lagged reserve accounting', *Southern Economic Journal*, 46: 460–470.

Le Roy, S. and D. Lindsey (1978) 'Determining the monetary instrument: A diagrammatic exposition', *American Economic Review*, 68: 929–934.

Lipsey, R.G. (1960) 'The relation between unemployment and the rate of change of money wage rates in the United Kingdom, 1862–1957: A further analysis', *Economica*, 27: 1–31.

Lombra, R.E. and H.M. Kaufman (1984) 'The money supply process: Identification, stability, and estimation', *Southern Economic Journal*, 50: 1147–1159.

Longbrake, W.A. and J.A. Haslem (1975) 'Productive efficiency in commercial banking: The effects of size and legal form of organization on the cost of producing demand deposit services', *Journal of Money, Credit, and Banking*, 7: 317–330.

Lucas, R.E., Jr. (1972a) 'Expectations and the neutrality of money', *Journal of Economic Theory*, 4: 103–124.

Lucas, R.E., Jr. (1972b) 'Econometric testing of the natural rate hypothesis', in: O. Eckstein, ed., *The econometrics of price determination*. Washington, D.C.: Board of Governors of the Federal Reserve System.

Marshall, A. (1923) *Money, credit and commerce*. London: Macmillan.

McCallum, B.T. (1981) 'Price level determinacy with an interest rate rule and rational expectations', *Journal of Monetary Economics*, 8: 319–329.

Meade, J.E. (1934) 'The amount of money and the banking system', *Economic Journal*, 44: 77–83.

Meigs, A.J. (1962) *Free reserves and the money supply*. Chicago: University of Chicago Press.

Merton, R.C. (1977) 'An analytic derivation of the cost of deposit insurance and loan guarantees: An application of modern option pricing theory', *Journal of Banking and Finance*, 1: 3–11.

Miller, S.M. (1975) 'A theory of the banking firm: Comment', *Journal of Monetary Economics*, 1: 123–128.

Modigliani, F. (1944) 'Liquidity preference and the theory of interest and money', *Econometrica*, 12: 45–88.

Modigliani, F. (1963) 'The monetary mechanism and its interaction with real phenomena', *Review of Economics and Statistics*, 45: 79–107.

Modigliani, F. (1968) 'Liquidity preference', in: *International encyclopedia of the social sciences*, Vol 9. London: Macmillan and Free Press, pp. 394–409.

Modigliani, F. (1972) 'The Dynamics of Portfolio Adjustment and the Flow of Savings Through Financial Intermediaries,' in: E.N. Gramlich and D.M. Jaffee, eds., *Savings deposits, mortgages, and housing: Studies for the Federal Reserve–MIT–Penn econometric model*. Lexington, Mass: Lexington Books, pp. 63–102.

Modigliani, F. (1982) 'Debt, dividend policy, taxes, inflation and market valuation', *The Journal of Finance*, 37: 255–273.

Modigliani, F. and R. Brumberg (1954) 'Utility analysis and the consumption function: Interpretation of cross-section data', in: K. Kurihara, ed., *Post-Keynesian economics*. New Brunswick, N.J.: Rutgers University Press.

Modigliani, F. and M.H. Miller (1958) 'The cost of capital, corporation finance and the theory of investment', *American Economic Review*, 48: 261–297.

Modigliani, F. and L. Papademos (1975) 'Targets for monetary policy in the coming year', *Brookings Papers on Economic Activity*, 1: 141–163.

Modigliani, F. and L. Papademos (1978) 'Optimal demand policies against stagflation', *Weltwirtschaftliches Archiv*, 114: 736–782.

Modigliani, F. and L. Papademos (1980) 'The structure of financial markets and the monetary mechanism', in: *Controlling monetary aggregates*, Vol. III. Boston: Federal Reserve Bank of Boston, pp. 111–155.

Modigliani, F. and L. Papademos (1987) 'Money, credit, and the monetary mechanism', in: M. deCecco and J.P. Fitoussi, eds., *Monetary theory and economic institutions*. London: Macmillan, pp. 121–160.

Modigliani, F., R. Rasche and J.P. Cooper (1970) 'Central bank policy, the money supply, and the short-term rate of interest', *Journal of Money, Credit and Banking*, 2: 166–218.

Monti, M. (1972) 'Deposit, credit, and interest rate determination under alternative bank objective functions', in: G.P. Szego and K. Snell, eds., *Mathematical methods in investment and finance*. Amsterdam: North-Holland, pp. 430–454.

Moosa, S.A. (1977) 'Dynamic portfolio-balance behavior of time deposits and "money"', *Journal of Finance*, 32: 709–717.

Mundell, R.A. (1964) 'Inflation, saving, and the real rate of interest', *Journal of Political Economy*, 71: 280–283.

Niehans, J. (1978) *The theory of money*. Baltimore: The Johns Hopkins University Press.

Orgler, Y.E. and R.A. Taggart, Jr. (1983) 'Implications of corporate capital structure theory for banking institutions', *Journal of Money, Credit, and Banking*, 15: 212–221.

Orr, D. and W.G. Mellon (1961) 'Stochastic reserve losses and bank credit', *American Economic Review*, 51: 614–623.

Offenbacher, E. and R. Porter (1982) 'Update and extensions on econometric properties of selected monetary aggregates', Board of Governors of the Federal Reserve System.

Papademos, L. (1987) 'Aggregate nominal income dynamics and monetary policy', Research paper. Bank of Greece.

Papademos, L. and F. Modigliani (1983) 'Inflation, financial and fiscal structure, and the monetary mechanism', *European Economic Review*, 21: 203–250.

Papademos, L. and F. Rozwadowski (1983) 'Monetary and credit targets in an open economy', in: D. Hodgman, ed., *The political economy of monetary policy: National and international aspects*. Boston: Federal Reserve Bank of Boston, pp. 275–306.

Patinkin, D. (1956) *Money, interest, and prices* (second edition, 1965). New York: Harper and Row.

Patinkin, D. (1961) 'Financial intermediaries and the logical structure of monetary theory', *American Economic Review*, 51: 95–116.

Perry, G.L. (1966) *Unemployment, money wage rates, and inflation*. Cambridge, Mass.: MIT Press.

Pesek, B. (1970) 'Bank's supply function and the equilibrium quantity of money', *Canadian Journal of Economics*, 3: 357–385.

Phelps, E.S. (1968) 'Money-wage dynamics and labor-market equilibrium', *Journal of Political Economy*, 76: 678–711.

Phelps, E.S. et al. (1970) *Microeconomic foundations of employment and inflation theory*. New York: W.W. Norton.

Phelps, E.S. and J.B. Taylor (1977) 'Stabilizing powers of monetary policy under rational expectations', *Journal of Political Economy*, 85: 163–190.

Phillips, A.W. (1958) 'The relation between unemployment and the rate of change of money wage rates in the United Kingdom, 1861–1957', *Economica*, 25: 283–299.

Phillips, C.A. (1920) *Bank credit*. New York: Macmillan.

Pierce, J. and T. Thomson (1972) 'Some issues in controlling the stock of money', in: *Controlling monetary aggregates*, Vol. II: *The implementation*. Boston: Federal Reserve Bank of Boston, pp. 115–136.

Pigou, A.C. (1917) 'The value of money', *Quarterly Journal of Economics*, 32: 38–65,; reprinted in *Readings in monetary theory*, American Economic Association. Homewood: Irwin, 1951, pp. 162–183.

Poole, W. (1968) 'Commercial bank reserve management in a stochastic model: Implications for monetary policy', *Journal of Finance*, 23: 769–791.

Poole, W. (1970) 'Optimal choice of monetary policy instruments in a simple stochastic macro model', *Quarterly Journal of Economics*, 84: 197–216.

Porter, R.C. (1961) 'A model of bank portfolio selection', *Yale Economic Essays*, 1: 323–359.

Pringle, J.J. (1974) 'The capital decision in commercial banks', *Journal of Finance*, 29: 779–795.

Pyle, D.H. (1971) 'On the theory of financial intermediation', *Journal of Finance*, 26: 737–747.

Rasche, R.H. (1972) 'A review of empirical studies of the money supply mechanism', *Federal Reserve Bank of St. Louis Review*, 54, 7: 11–19.

Rasche, R.H. and J.M. Johannes (1987) *Controlling the growth of monetary aggregates*. Boston: Kluwer Academic Publishers.

Ratti, R.A. (1979) 'Stochastic reserve losses and bank credit expansion', *Journal of Monetary Economics*, 5: 283–294.

Roper, D.E. and J.J. Turnovsky (1980) 'The optimum monetary aggregate for stabilization policy', *Quarterly Journal of Economics*, 95: 333–355.

Samuelson, P.A. and R.M. Solow (1960) 'Analytical aspects of anti-inflation policy', *American Economic Review*, 50: 177–194.

Santomero, A.M. (1984) 'Modeling the banking firm: A survey', *Journal of Money, Credit and Banking*, 16: 576–602.

Santomero, A.M. and J.J. Siegel (1981) 'Bank regulation and macro-economic stability', *American Economic Review*, 71: 39–53.

Sargent, T.J. (1976) 'A classical macroeconomic model for the United States', *Journal of Political Economy*, 84: 207–237.

Sargent, T.J. and N. Wallace (1975) 'Rational expectations, the optimal monetary instrument, and the optimal money supply rule', *Journal of Political Economy*, 83: 241–254.

Saving, T.R. (1977) ' A theory of money supply with competitive banking', *Journal of Monetary Economics*, 3: 289–303.

Saving, T.R. (1979) 'Money supply theory with competitively determined deposit rates and activity charges', *Journal of Money, Credit and Banking*, 11: 22–31.

Sealey, C.W., Jr. and J.T. Lindley (1977) 'Inputs, outputs, and a theory of production and cost at depository financial institutions', *Journal of Finance*, 32: 1251–1266.

Sharpe, W.F. (1978) 'Bank capital adequacy, deposit insurance, and security values', *Journal of Financial and Quantitative Analysis*, 13: 701–718.

Stillson, R.T. (1974) 'An analysis of information and transaction services in financial institutions', *Journal of Money, Credit and Banking*, 6: 517–535.

Taylor, J.B. (1980) 'Aggregate dynamics and staggered contracts', *Journal of Political Economy*, 88: 1–23.

Teigen, R. (1964) 'Demand and supply functions of money in the U.S.: Some structural estimates', *Econometrica*, 32: 476–509.

Teigen, R. (1969) 'An aggregated quarterly model of the U.S. monetary sector', in: K. Brunner, ed., *Targets and indicators of monetary policy*. San Francisco: Chandler, pp. 175–214.

Tobin, J. (1956) 'The interest-elasticity of the transactions demand for cash', *Review of Economics and Statistics*, 38: 241–247.

Tobin, J. (1958) 'Liquidity preference as behavior towards risk', *Review of Economic Studies*, 25: 65–86.

Tobin, J. (1963) 'Commercial banks as creators of "Money" ', in: D. Carson, ed., *Banking and monetary studies*. Homewood: R.D. Irwin, pp. 408–419.

Tobin, J. (1965) 'Money and economic growth', *Econometrica*, 33: 671–684.

Tobin, J. (1969) 'A general equilibrium approach to monetary theory', *Journal of Money, Credit and Banking*, 1: 15–29.

Tobin, J. and W.C. Brainard (1963) 'Financial intermediaries and the effectiveness of monetary controls', *American Economic Review, Papers and Proceedings*, 53: 383–400.

Towey, R.W. (1974) 'Money creation and the theory of the banking firm', *Journal of Finance*, 27: 57–72.

Wilson, J.S.G., (1986) *Banking policy and structure: A comparative analysis*. London: Croom Helm.

PART 5

PRICING NON-MONEY ASSETS

Chapter 11

CAPITAL MARKET THEORY AND THE PRICING OF FINANCIAL SECURITIES

ROBERT MERTON*

Harvard University Graduate School of Business Administration

Contents

* This chapter is a revised and expanded version of Merton (1982a). I thank A.M. Eikeboom for technical assistance and D.A. Hannon for editorial assistance.

Handbook of Monetary Economics, Volume I, Edited by B.M. Friedman and F.H. Hahn
© *Elsevier Science Publishers B.V., 1990*

1. Introduction

The core of financial economic theory is the study of individual behavior of households in the intertemporal allocation of their resources in an environment of uncertainty and of the role of economic organizations in facilitating these allocations. The intersection between this specialized branch of micro-economics and macroeconomic monetary theory is most apparent in the theory of capital markets [cf. Fischer and Merton (1984)]. It is therefore appropriate on this occasion to focus on the theories of portfolio selection, capital asset pricing, and the roles that financial markets and intermediaries can play in improving allocational efficiency.

The complexity of the interaction of time and uncertainty provides intrinsic excitement to study of the subject, and as we shall see, the mathematics of capital market theory contains some of the most interesting applications of probability and optimization theory. As exemplified by option pricing and modern portfolio theory, the research with all its seemingly abstruse mathematics has nevertheless had a direct and significant influence on practice. This conjoining of intrinsic intellectual interest with extrinsic application is, indeed, a prevailing theme of theoretical research in financial economics.

The tradition in economic theory is to take the existence of households, their tastes, and endowments as exogenous to the theory. This tradition does not, however, extend to economic organizations and institutions. They are regarded as existing primarily because of the functions they serve instead of functioning primarily because they exist. Economic organizations are endogenous to the theory. To derive the functions of financial instruments, markets, and inter-mediaries, a natural starting point is, therefore, to analyze the investment behavior of individual households.

It is convenient to view the investment decision by households as having two parts: (1) the "consumption–saving" choice where the individual decides how much income and wealth to allocate to current consumption and how much to save for future consumption including bequests; and (2) the "portfolio selec-tion" choice where the investor decides how to allocate savings among the available investment opportunities. In general, the two decisions cannot be made independently. However, many of the important findings in portfolio theory can be more easily derived in a one-period environment where the consumption–savings allocation has little substantive impact on the results. Thus, we begin in Section 2 with the formulation and solution of the basic portfolio selection problem in a static framework taking as given the individ-ual's consumption decision.

Using the analysis of Section 2, we derive necessary conditions for static financial equilibrium that are used to determine restrictions on equilibrium security prices and returns in Sections 3 and 4. In Sections 4 and 5 these restrictions are used to derive spanning or mutual fund theorems that provide a basis for an elementary risk-pooling theory of financial intermediation.

In Section 6 the combined consumption–portfolio selection problem is formulated in a more realistic and more complex dynamic setting. As shown in Section 7, dynamic models in which agents can revise and act on their decisions continuously in time produce significantly sharper results than their discrete-time counterparts and do so without sacrificing the richness of behavior found in an intertemporal decision-making environment.

The continuous-trading model is used in Section 8 to derive a theory of option, corporate-liability, and general derivative-security pricing. In Section 9 the dynamic portfolio strategies used to derive these prices are shown to provide a theory of production for the creation of risk-sharing instruments by financial intermediaries. The closing section of the chapter examines inter-temporal-equilibrium pricing of securities and analyzes the conditions under which allocations in the continuous-trading model are Pareto efficient.

As is evident from this brief overview of content, the chapter does not cover a number of important topics in capital market theory. For example, there is no attempt to make explicit how individuals and institutions acquire the information needed to make their decisions, and in particular how they modify their behavior in environments where there are significant differences in the information available to various participants. Thus, we do not cover either the informational efficiency of capital markets or the principal–agent problem and theory of auctions as applied to financial contracting, intermediation, and markets.[1] Although the analysis is not institutionally based, the context is one of a domestic economy. Adler and Dumas (1983) provide an excellent survey article on applications of the theory in an international context.

2. One-period portfolio selection

The basic investment-choice problem for an individual is to determine the optimal allocation of his or her wealth among the available investment opportunities. The solution to the general problem of choosing the best

---

[1] On the informational efficiency of the stock market, see Fama (1965, 1970a), Samuelson (1965), Hirshleifer (1973), Grossman (1976), Grossman and Stiglitz (1980), Black (1986), and Merton (1987a, 1987b). On financial markets and incomplete information generally, see the excellent survey paper by Bhattacharya (1989). On financial markets and auction theory, see Hansen (1985), Parsons and Raviv (1985), and Rock (1986). On the role of behavioral theory in finance, see Hogarth and Reder (1986).

investment mix is called *portfolio selection theory*. The study of portfolio selection theory begins with its classic one-period or static formulation.

There are n different investment opportunities called *securities* and the random variable one-period return per dollar on security j is denoted by $Z_j (j = 1, \ldots, n)$, where a "dollar" is the "unit of account". Any linear combination of these securities which has a positive market value is called a *portfolio*. It is assumed that the investor chooses at the beginning of a period that feasible portfolio allocation which maximizes the expected value of a von Neumann–Morgenstern utility function[2] for end-of-period wealth. Denote this utility function by $U(W)$, where W is the end-of-period value of the investor's wealth measured in dollars. It is further assumed that U is an increasing strictly concave function on the range of feasible values for W and that U is twice-continuously differentiable.[3] Because the criterion function for choice depends only on the distribution of end-of-period wealth, the only information about the securities that is relevant to the investor's decision is his subjective joint probability distribution for $(Z_1, \ldots, Z_n)$.

In addition, it is assumed that:

Assumption 1. "Frictionless markets". There are no transactions costs or taxes, and all securities are perfectly divisible.

Assumption 2. "Price taker". The investor believes that his actions cannot affect the probability distribution of returns on the available securities. Hence, if w_j is the fraction of the investor's initial wealth W_0, allocated to security j, then $\{w_1, \ldots, w_n\}$ uniquely determines the probability distribution of his terminal wealth.

A *riskless security* is defined to be a security or feasible portfolio of securities whose return per dollar over the period is known with certainty.

Assumption 3. "No-Arbitrage opportunities". All riskless securities must have the same return per dollar. This common return will be denoted by R.

---

[2]von Neumann and Morgenstern (1947). For an axiomatic description, see Herstein and Milnor (1953) and Machina (1982). Although the original axioms require that U be bounded, the continuity axiom can be extended to allow for unbounded functions. See Samuelson (1977) for a discussion of this and the St. Petersburg Paradox.

[3]The strict concavity assumption implies that investors are everywhere risk-averse. Although strictly convex or linear utility functions on the entire range imply behavior that is grossly at variance with observed behavior, the strict concavity assumption also rules out Friedman–Savage type utility functions whose behavioral implications are reasonable. The strict concavity also implies $U'(W) > 0$, which rules out investor satiation.

Assumption 4. "No-Institutional restrictions". Short sales of all securities, with full use of proceeds, is allowed without restriction. If there exists a riskless security, then the borrowing rate equals the lending rate.[4]

Hence, the only restriction on the choice for the $\{w_j\}$ is the budget constraint that $\sum_1^n w_j = 1$.

Given these assumptions, the portfolio-selection problem can be formally stated as:

$$\max_{\{w_1, \ldots, w_n\}} \mathrm{E}\left\{ U\left(\sum_1^n w_j Z_j W_0 \right) \right\}, \tag{2.1}$$

subject to $\sum_1^n w_j = 1$, where E is the expectation operator for the subjective joint probability distribution. If $(w_1^*, \ldots, w_n^*)$ is a solution to (2.1), then it will satisfy the first-order conditions:

$$\mathrm{E}\{U'(Z^* W_0) Z_j\} = \lambda / W_0, \quad j = 1, 2, \ldots, n, \tag{2.2}$$

where the prime denotes derivative; $Z^* \equiv \sum_1^n w_j^* Z_j$ is the random variable return per dollar on the optimal portfolio; and λ is the Lagrange multiplier for the budget constraint. Together with the concavity assumptions on U, if the $n \times n$ variance–covariance matrix of the returns $(Z_1, \ldots, Z_n)$ is non-singular and an interior solution exists, then the solution is unique.[5] This non-singularity condition on the returns distribution eliminates "redundant" securities (i.e. securities whose returns can be expressed as exact linear combinations of the returns on other available securities).[6] It also rules out that any one of the securities is a riskless security.

If a riskless security is added to the menu of available securities [call it the $(n + 1)$st security], then it is the convention to express (2.1) as the following

---

[4]Borrowings and short sales are demand loans collateralized by the investor's total portfolio. The "borrowing rate" is the rate on riskless-in-terms-of-default loans. Although virtually every individual loan involves some chance of default, the empirical "spread" in the rate on actual margin loans to investors suggests that this assumption is not a "bad approximation" for portfolio selection analysis. However, an explicit analysis of risky loan evaluation and bankruptcy is provided in Sections 8 and 9.

[5]The existence of an interior solution is assumed throughout the analyses in the chapter. For a complete discussion of necessary and sufficient conditions for the existence of an interior solution, see Leland (1972) and Bertsekas (1974).

[6]For a trivial example, shares of IBM with odd serial numbers are distinguishable from ones with even serial numbers and are, therefore, technically different securities. However, because their returns are identical, they are perfect substitutes from the point of view of investors. In portfolio theory, securities are operationally defined by their return distributions, and therefore two securities with identical returns are indistinguishable.

unconstrained maximization problem:

$$\max_{\{w_1, \ldots, w_n\}} \mathrm{E}\left\{ U\left[\left(\sum_1^n w_j(Z_j - R) + R \right) W_0 \right] \right\}, \tag{2.3}$$

where the portfolio allocations to the risky securities are unconstrained because the fraction allocated to the riskless security can always be chosen to satisfy the budget constraint (i.e. $w^*_{n+1} = 1 - \sum_1^n w^*_j$). The first-order conditions can be written as:

$$\mathrm{E}\{U'(Z^*W_0)(Z_j - R)\} = 0, \quad j = 1, 2, \ldots, n, \tag{2.4}$$

where Z^* can be rewritten as $\sum_1^n w^*_j(Z_j - R) + R$. Again, if it is assumed that the variance–covariance matrix of the returns on the risky securities is non-singular and an interior solution exists, then the solution is unique.

As formulated, neither (2.1) nor (2.3) reflects the physical constraint that end-of-period wealth cannot be negative. Moreover, although Assumption 4 permits short sales and borrowing, no explicit description was given to the treatment of personal bankruptcy. A proper specification of the portfolio problem thus requires the additional constraint that $Z^* \geq 0$ with probability one.[7]

This non-negativity constraint does not by itself address the institutional rules for bankruptcy, because the probability assessments on the $\{Z_j\}$ are subjective. A set of rules that does is to forbid borrowing and short selling in conjunction with limited-liability securities where, by law, $Z_j \geq 0$. These rules can be formalized as restrictions on the permissible set of $\{w_j\}$, such that $w_j \geq 0, j = 1, 2, \ldots, n + 1$, and (2.1) or (2.3) can be solved using the methods of Kuhn and Tucker (1951) for inequality constraints. However, imposition of these specific restrictions generally leads to unnecessary and significant losses in the allocational efficiency of the capital markets. Moreover, they do not reflect real-world institutional constraints.

In Sections 4 and 5, using alternative rules, we introduce personal bankruptcy into the static model and analyze the portfolio-selection problem with the non-negativity constraint on wealth. In Sections 7–9 we formally analyze intertemporal portfolio behavior and the pricing of securities when investors, firms, and their creditors all recognize the prospect of default. Those analyses shall show that the important results derived for the classical, unconstrained version of the model are robust with respect to these restrictions. Thus, until

---

[7] If U is such that $U'(0) = \infty$, and by extension, $U'(W) = \infty$, $W < 0$, then from (2.2) or (2.4) it is easy to show that the probability of $Z^* \leq 0$ is a set of measure zero. Mason (1981) and Karatzas, Lehoczky, Sethi and Shreve (1986) study the effects of various bankruptcy rules on portfolio behavior.

those sections, the non-negativity constraint on wealth and the treatment of bankruptcy are ignored.

The optimal demand functions for risky securities, $\{w_j^* W_0\}$, and the resulting probability distribution for the optimal portfolio will, of course, depend on the risk preferences of the investor, his initial wealth, and the joint distribution for the securities' returns. It is well known that the von Neumann–Morgenstern utility function can only be determined up to a positive affine transformation. Hence, the preference orderings of all choices available to the investor are completely specified by the Pratt–Arrow[8] *absolute risk-aversion function*, which can be written as:

$$A(W) \equiv \frac{-U''(W)}{U'(W)} \, , \tag{2.5}$$

and the change in absolute risk-aversion with respect to a change in wealth is, therefore, given by:

$$\frac{\mathrm{d}A}{\mathrm{d}W} = A'(W) = A(W)\left[A(W) + \frac{U'''(W)}{U''(W)} \right]. \tag{2.6}$$

By the assumption that $U(W)$ is increasing and strictly concave, $A(W)$ is positive, and such investors are called *risk-averse*. An alternative, but related, measure of risk-aversion is the *relative risk-aversion function*, defined to be:

$$\underline{R}(W) \equiv -\frac{U''(W)W}{U'(W)} = A(W)W \, , \tag{2.7}$$

and its change with respect to a change in wealth is given by:

$$\underline{R}'(W) = A'(W)W + A(W) \, . \tag{2.8}$$

The *certainty-equivalent end-of-period wealth*, W_c, associated with a given portfolio for end-of-period wealth whose random variable value is denoted by W, is defined to be that value such that

$$U(W_c) = E\{U(W)\} \, , \tag{2.9}$$

i.e. W_c is the amount of money such that the investor is indifferent between having this amount of money for certain or the portfolio with random variable outcome W. The term "risk-averse" as applied to investors with strictly

---

[8]The behavior associated with the utility function $V(W) \equiv aU(W) + b$, $a > 0$, is identical to that associated with $U(W)$. Note: $A(W)$ is invariant to any positive affine transformation of $U(W)$. See Pratt (1964).

concave utility functions is descriptive in the sense that the certainty-equivalent end-of-period wealth is always less than the expected value of the associated portfolio, $E\{W\}$, for all such investors. The proof follows directly by Jensen's Inequality: if U is strictly concave, then

$$U(W_c) = E\{U(W)\} < U(E\{W\}) ,$$

whenever W has positive dispersion, and because U is an increasing function of W, $W_c < E\{W\}$.

The certainty-equivalent can be used to compare the risk-aversions of two investors. An investor is said to be *more risk-averse* than a second investor if, for every portfolio, the certainty-equivalent end-of-period wealth for the first investor is less than or equal to the certainty-equivalent end-of-period wealth associated with the same portfolio for the second investor with strict inequality holding for at least one portfolio.

While the certainty-equivalent provides a natural definition for comparing risk-aversions across investors, Rothschild and Stiglitz[9] have in a corresponding fashion attempted to define the meaning of "increasing risk" for a security so that the "riskiness" of two securities or portfolios can be compared. In comparing two portfolios with the same expected values, the first portfolio with random variable outcome denoted by W_1 is said to be *less risky* than the second portfolio with random variable outcome denoted by W_2 if

$$E\{U(W_1)\} \geq E\{U(W_2)\} , \tag{2.10}$$

for all concave U with strict inequality holding for some concave U. They bolster their argument for this definition by showing its equivalence to the following two other definitions:

> There exists a random variable Z such that W_2 has the
> same distribution as $W_1 + Z$, where the conditional
> expectation of Z given the outcome of W_1 is zero   (2.11)
> (i.e. W_2 is equal in distribution to W_1 plus some
> "noise").

> If the points of F and G, the distribution functions of
> W_1 and W_2, are confined to the closed interval
> $[a, b]$, and $T(y) \equiv \int_a^y [G(x) - F(x)] \, dx$, then   (2.12)
> $T(y) \geq 0$ and $T(b) = 0$ (i.e. W_2 has more "weight in
> its tails" than W_1).

[9]Rothschild and Stiglitz (1970, 1971). There is an extensive literature, not discussed here, that uses this type of risk measure to determine when one portfolio "stochastically dominates" another. Cf. Hadar and Russell (1969, 1971), Hanoch and Levy (1969), and Bawa (1975).

A feasible portfolio with returns per dollar Z will be called an *efficient portfolio* if there exists an increasing, strictly concave function V such that $E\{V'(Z)(Z_j - R)\} = 0$, $j = 1, 2, \ldots, n$. Using the Rothschild–Stiglitz definition of "less risky", a feasible portfolio will be an efficient portfolio only if there does not exist another feasible portfolio which is less risky than it is. All portfolios that are not efficient are called *inefficient portfolios*.

From the definition of an efficient portfolio, it follows that no two portfolios in the efficient set can be ordered with respect to one another. From (2.10) it follows immediately that every efficient portfolio is a possible optimal portfolio, i.e. for each efficient portfolio there exists an increasing, concave U and an initial wealth W_0 such that the efficient portfolio is a solution to (2.1) or (2.3). Furthermore, from (2.10), all risk-averse investors will be indifferent between selecting their optimal portfolios from the set of all feasible portfolios or from the set of all efficient portfolios. Hence, without loss of generality, assume that all optimal portfolios are efficient portfolios.

With these general definitions established, we now turn to the analysis of the optimal demand functions for risky assets and their implications for the distributional characteristics of the underlying securities. A note on notation: the symbol "Z_e" will be used to denote the random variable return per dollar on an efficient portfolio, and a bar over a random variable (e.g. $\bar{Z}$) will denote the expected value of that random variable.

Theorem 2.1. *If Z denotes the random variable return per dollar on any feasible portfolio and if $(Z_e - \bar{Z}_e)$ is riskier than $(Z - \bar{Z})$ in the Rothschild and Stiglitz sense, then $\bar{Z}_e > \bar{Z}$.*

Proof. By hypothesis, $E\{U([Z - \bar{Z}]W_0)\} > E\{U([Z_e - \bar{Z}_e]W_0)\}$. If $\bar{Z} \geq \bar{Z}_e$, then trivially, $E\{U(ZW_0)\} > E\{U(Z_e W_0)\}$. But Z is a feasible portfolio and Z_e is an efficient portfolio. Hence, by contradiction, $\bar{Z}_e > \bar{Z}$.

Corollary 2.1a. *If there exists a riskless security with return R, then $\bar{Z}_e \geq R$, with equality holding only if Z_e is a riskless security.*

Proof. The riskless security is a feasible portfolio with expected return R. If Z_e is riskless, then by Assumption 3, $\bar{Z}_e = R$. If Z_e is not riskless, then $(Z_e - \bar{Z}_e)$ is riskier than $(R - R)$. Therefore, by Theorem 2.1, $\bar{Z}_e > R$.

Theorem 2.2. *The optimal portfolio for a non-satiated, risk-averse investor will be the riskless security (i.e. $w_{n+1}^* = 1$, $w_j^* = 0$, $j = 1, 2, \ldots, n$) if and only if $\bar{Z}_j = R$ for $j = 1, 2, \ldots, n$.*

Proof. From (2.4), $\{w_1^*, \ldots, w_n^*\}$ will satisfy $E\{U'(Z^* W_0)(Z_j - R)\} = 0$. If $\bar{Z}_j = R$, $j = 1, 2, \ldots, n$, then $Z^* = R$ will satisfy these first-order conditions. By the strict concavity of U and the non-singularity of the variance–covariance matrix of returns, this solution is unique. This proves the "if" part. If $Z^* = R$ is an optimal solution, then we can rewrite (2.4) as $U'(RW_0)\mathrm{E}(Z_j - R) = 0$. By the non-satiation assumption, $U'(RW_0) > 0$. Therefore, for $Z^* = R$ to be an optimal solution, $\bar{Z}_j = R$, $j = 1, 2, \ldots, n$. This proves the "only if" part.

Hence, from Corollary 2.1a and Theorem 2.2, if a risk-averse investor chooses a risky portfolio, then the expected return on that portfolio exceeds the riskless rate, and a risk-averse investor will choose a risky portfolio if, at least, one available security has an expected return different from the riskless rate.

Define the notation $\mathrm{E}(Y \mid X_1, \ldots, X_q)$ to mean the *conditional expectation of the random variable* Y, conditional on knowing the realizations for the random variables $(X_1, \ldots, X_q)$.

Theorem 2.3. *Let Z_p denote the return on any portfolio p that does not contain security s. If there exists a portfolio p such that for security s, $Z_s = Z_p + \varepsilon_s$, where $\mathrm{E}(\varepsilon_s) = \mathrm{E}(\varepsilon_s \mid Z_j, \ j = 1, \ldots, n, \ j \neq s) = 0$, then the fraction of every efficient portfolio allocated to security s is the same and equal to zero.*

Proof. The proof follows by contradiction. Suppose Z_e is the return on an efficient portfolio with fraction $\delta_s \neq 0$ allocated to security s. Let Z be the return on a portfolio with the same fractional holdings as Z_e except instead of security s, it holds the fraction δ_s in feasible portfolio Z_p. Hence, $Z_e = Z + \delta_s(Z_s - Z_p)$ or $Z_e = Z + \delta_s \varepsilon_s$. By hypothesis, $\bar{Z}_e = \bar{Z}$, and because portfolio Z does not contain security s, by construction, $\mathrm{E}(\varepsilon_s \mid Z) = 0$. Therefore, for $\delta_s \neq 0$, Z_e is riskier than Z in the Rothschild–Stiglitz sense. But this contradicts the hypothesis that Z_e is an efficient portfolio. Hence, $\delta_s = 0$ for every efficient portfolio.

Corollary 2.3a. *Let ψ denote the set of n securities with returns $(Z_1, \ldots, Z_{s-1}, Z_s, Z_{s+1}, \ldots, Z_n)$ and ψ' denote the same set of securities, except Z_s is replaced with $Z_{s'}$. If $Z_{s'} = Z_s + \varepsilon_s$ and $\mathrm{E}(\varepsilon_s) = \mathrm{E}(\varepsilon_s \mid Z_1, \ldots, Z_{s-1}, Z_s, Z_{s+1}, \ldots, Z_n) = 0$, then all risk-averse investors would prefer to choose their optimal portfolios from ψ rather than ψ'.*

The proof is essentially the same as the proof of Theorem 2.3, with Z_s replacing Z_p. Unless the holdings of Z_s in every efficient portfolio are zero, ψ will be strictly preferred to ψ'.

Theorem 2.3 and its corollary demonstrate that all risk-averse investors would prefer any "unnecessary" uncertainty or "noise" to be eliminated. In particular, by this theorem, the existence of lotteries is shown to be inconsistent with strict risk-aversion on the part of all investors.[10] While the inconsistency of strict risk-aversion with observed behavior such as betting on the numbers can be "explained" by treating lotteries as consumption goods, it is difficult to use this argument to explain other implicit lotteries such as callable, sinking-fund bonds where the bonds to be redeemed are selected at random.

As illustrated by the partitioning of the feasible portfolio set into its efficient and inefficient parts and the derived theorems, the Rothschild–Stiglitz definition of increasing risk is quite useful for studying the properties of optimal portfolios. However, it is important to emphasize that these theorems apply only to efficient portfolios and not to individual securities or inefficient portfolios. For example, if $(Z_j - Z_j)$ is riskier than $(Z - Z)$ in the Rothschild–Stiglitz sense and if security j is held in positive amounts in an efficient or optimal portfolio (i.e. $w_j^* > 0$), then it *does not* follow that $\bar{Z}_j$ must equal or exceed $\bar{Z}$. In particular, if $w_j^* > 0$, it does not follow that $\bar{Z}_j$ must equal or exceed R. Hence, to know that one security is riskier than a second security using the Rothschild–Stiglitz definition of increasing risk provides no normative restrictions on holdings of either security in an efficient portfolio. And because this definition of riskier imposes no restrictions on the optimal demands, it cannot be used to derive properties of individual securities' return distributions from observing their relative holdings in an efficient portfolio. To derive these properties, a second definition of risk is required. Development of this measure is the topic of Section 3.

3. Risk measures for securities and portfolios in the one-period model

In the previous section it was suggested that the Rothschild–Stiglitz measure is not a natural definition of risk for a security. In this section a second definition of increasing risk is introduced, and it is argued that this second measure is a more appropriate definition for the risk of a security. Although this second measure will not in general provide the same orderings as the Rothschild–Stiglitz measure, it is further argued that the two measures are not in conflict, and indeed, are complementary.

If Z_e^K is the random variable return per dollar on an efficient portfolio K, then let $V_K(Z_e^K)$ denote an increasing, strictly concave function such that, for $V_K' \equiv dV_K / dZ_e^K$,

$$E\{V_K'(Z_j - R)\} = 0, \quad j = 1, 2, \ldots, n,$$

i.e. V_K is a concave utility function such that an investor with initial wealth

---

[10]I believe that Christian von Weizsäcker proved a similar theorem in unpublished notes some years ago. However, I do not have a reference.

$W_0 = 1$ and these preferences would select this efficient portfolio as his optimal portfolio. While such a function V_K will always exist, it will not be unique. If $\text{cov}[x_1, x_2]$ is the functional notation for the covariance between the random variables x_1 and x_2, then define the random variable, Y_K, by:

$$Y_K \equiv \frac{V'_K - E\{V'_K\}}{\text{cov}[V'_K, Z^K_e]} . \tag{3.1}$$

Y_K is well defined as long as Z^K_e has positive dispersion because $\text{cov}[V'_K, Z^K_e] < 0$.[11] It is understood that in the following discussion "efficient portfolio" will mean "efficient portfolio with positive dispersion". Let Z_p denote the random variable return per dollar on any feasible portfolio p.

Definition. The measure of risk of portfolio p relative to efficient portfolio K with random variable return Z^K_e, b^K_p, is defined by:

$$b^K_p \equiv \text{cov}[Y_K, Z_p] ,$$

and portfolio p is said to be *riskier than portfolio p' relative to efficient portfolio K* if $b^K_p > b^K_{p'}$.

Theorem 3.1. *If Z_p is the return on a feasible portfolio p and Z^K_e is the return on efficient portfolio K, then $\bar{Z}_p - R = b^K_p(\bar{Z}^K_e - R)$.*

Proof. From the definition of V_K, $E\{V'_K(Z_j - R)\} = 0$, $j = 1, 2, \ldots, n$. Let δ_j be the fraction of portfolio p allocated to security j. Then, $Z_p = \sum^n_1 \delta_j(Z_j - R) + R$, and $\sum^n_1 \delta_j E\{V'_K(Z_j - R)\} = E\{V'_K(Z_p - R)\} = 0$. By a similar argument, $E\{V'_K(Z^K_e - R)\} = 0$. Hence, $\text{cov}[V'_K, Z^K_e] = (R - \bar{Z}^K_e)E\{V'_K\}$ and $\text{cov}[V'_K, Z_p] = (R - \bar{Z}_p)E\{V'_K\}$. By Corollary 2.1a, $\bar{Z}^K_e > R$. Therefore, $\text{cov}[Y_K, Z_p] = (R - \bar{Z}_p)/(R - \bar{Z}^K_e)$.

Hence, the expected excess return on portfolio p, $\bar{Z}_p - R$, is in direct proportion to its risk, and because $\bar{Z}^K_e > R$, the larger is its risk, the larger is its expected return. Thus, Theorem 3.1 provides the first argument why b^K_p is a natural measure of risk for individual securities.

A second argument goes as follows. Consider an investor with utility function U and initial wealth W_0 who solves the portfolio selection problem:

$$\max_w E\{U([wZ_j + (1 - w)Z]W_0)\} ,$$

[11]For a proof, see Theorem 236 in Hardy, Littlewood and Pölya (1959).

where Z is the return on a portfolio of securities and Z_j is the return on security j. The optimal mix, w^*, will satisfy the first-order condition:

$$E\{U'([w^*Z_j + (1 - w^*)Z]W_0)(Z_j - Z)\} = 0. \tag{3.2}$$

If the original portfolio of securities chosen was this investor's optimal portfolio (i.e. $Z = Z^*$), then the solution to (3.2) is $w^* = 0$. However, an optimal portfolio is an efficient portfolio. Therefore, by Theorem 3.1, $\bar{Z}_j - R = b_j^*(\bar{Z}^* - R)$. Hence, the "risk–return tradeoff" provided in Theorem 3.1 is a condition for personal portfolio equilibrium. Indeed, because security j may be contained in the optimal portfolio, $w^* W_0$ is similar to an excess demand function. b_j^* measures the contribution of security j to the Rothschild–Stiglitz risk of the optimal portfolio in the sense that the investor is just indifferent to a marginal change in the holdings of security j provided that $\bar{Z}_j - R = b_j^*(\bar{Z}^* - R)$. Moreover, by the Implicit Function Theorem, we have from (3.2) that

$$\frac{\partial w^*}{\partial \bar{Z}_j} = \frac{w^* W_0 E\{U''(Z - Z_j)\} - E\{U'\}}{W_0 E\{U''(Z - Z_j)^2\}} > 0, \quad \text{at } w^* = 0. \tag{3.3}$$

Therefore, if $\bar{Z}_j$ lies above the "risk–return" line in the $(\bar{Z}, b^*)$ plane, then the investor would prefer to increase his holdings in security j, and if $\bar{Z}_j$ lies below the line, then he would prefer to reduce his holdings. If the risk of a security increases, then the risk-averse investor must be "compensated" by a corresponding increase in that security's expected return if his current holdings are to remain unchanged.

A third argument for why b_p^K is a natural measure of risk for individual securities is that the ordering of securities by their systematic risk relative to a given efficient portfolio will be identical to their ordering relative to any other efficient portfolio. That is, given the set of available securities, there is an unambiguous meaning to the statement "security j is riskier than security i". To show this equivalence along with other properties of the b_p^K measure, we first prove a lemma.

Lemma 3.1. (a) $E[Z_p | V_K'] = E[Z_p | Z_e^K]$ for efficient portfolio K. (b) If $E[Z_p | Z_e^K] = \bar{Z}_p$, then $\text{cov}[Z_p, V_K'] = 0$. (c) $\text{cov}[Z_p, V_K'] = 0$ for efficient portfolio K if and only if $\text{cov}[Z_p, V_L'] = 0$ for every efficient portfolio L.

Proof. (a) V_K' is a continuous, monotonic function of Z_e^K and hence, V_K' and Z_e^K are in one-to-one correspondence. (b) $\text{cov}[Z_p, V_K'] = E[V_K'(Z_p - \bar{Z}_p)] = E\{V_K' E[Z_p - \bar{Z}_p | Z_e^K]\} = 0$. (c) By definition, $b_p^K = 0$ if and only if $\text{cov}[Z_p, V_K'] = 0$. From Theorem 3.1, if $b_p^K = 0$, then $\bar{Z}_p = R$. From Corollary

2.1a, $\bar{Z}_e^L > R$ for every efficient portfolio L. Thus, from Theorem 3.1, $b_p^L = 0$ if and only if $\bar{Z}_p = R$.

Properties of the b_p^K measure of risk are:

Property 1. If L and K are efficient portfolios, then for any portfolio p, $b_p^K = b_L^K b_p^L$.

From Corollary 2.1a, $\bar{Z}_e^K > R$ and $\bar{Z}_e^L > R$. From Theorem 3.1, $b_L^K = (\bar{Z}_e^L - R)/(\bar{Z}_e^K - R)$, $b_p^K = (\bar{Z}_p - R)/(\bar{Z}_e^K - R)$, and $b_p^L = (\bar{Z}_p - R)/(\bar{Z}_e^L - R)$. Hence, the b_p^K measure satisfies a type of "chain rule" with respect to different efficient portfolios.

Property 2. If L and K are efficient portfolios, then $b_K^K = 1$ and $b_K^L > 0$.

Property 2 follows from Theorem 3.1 and Corollary 2.1a. Hence, all efficient portfolios have positive systematic risk, relative to any efficient portfolio.

Property 3. $\bar{Z}_p = R$ if and only if $b_p^K = 0$ for every efficient portfolio K.

Property 3 follows from Theorem 3.1 and Properties 1 and 2.

Property 4. Let p and q denote any two feasible portfolios and let K and L denote any two efficient portfolios. $b_p^K \gtreqqless b_q^K$ if and only if $b_p^L \gtreqqless b_q^L$.

Property 4 follows from Property 3 if $b_p^L = b_q^L = 0$. Suppose $b_p^L \neq 0$. Then Property 4 follows from Properties 1 and 2 because $(b_q^L/b_p^L) = (b_K^L b_q^K)/(b_K^L b_p^K) = (b_q^K/b_p^K)$. Thus, the b_p^K measure provides the same orderings of risk for any reference efficient portfolio.

Property 5. For each efficient portfolio K and any feasible portfolio p, $Z_p = R + b_p^K(Z_e^K - R) + \varepsilon_p$, where $E(\varepsilon_p) = 0$ and $E[\varepsilon_p V_L'(Z_e^L)] = 0$ for every efficient portfolio L.

From Theorem 3.1, $E(\varepsilon_p) = 0$. If portfolio q is constructed by holding \$1 in portfolio p, \$$b_p^K$ in the riskless security, and short selling \$$b_p^K$ of efficient portfolio K, then $Z_q = R + \varepsilon_p$. From Property 3, $\bar{Z}_q = R$ implies that $b_q^L = 0$ for every efficient portfolio L. But $b_q^L = 0$ implies $0 = \text{cov}[Z_q, V_L'] = E[\varepsilon_p V_L']$ for every efficient portfolio L.

Property 6. If a feasible portfolio p has portfolio weights $(\delta_1, \ldots, \delta_n)$, then $b_p^K = \sum_1^n \delta_j b_j^K$.

Property 6 follows directly from the linearity of the covariance operator with respect to either of its arguments. Hence, the systematic risk of a portfolio is the weighted sum of the systematic risks of its component securities.

The Rothschild–Stiglitz measure of risk is clearly different from the b_j^K measure here. The Rothschild–Stiglitz measure provides only for a partial ordering, while the b_j^K measure provides a complete ordering. Moreover, they can give different rankings. For example, suppose the return on security j is independent of the return on efficient portfolio K, then $b_j^K = 0$ and $\bar{Z}_j = R$. Trivially, $b_R^K = 0$ for the riskless security. Therefore, by the b_j^K measure, security j and the riskless security have equal risk. However, if security j has positive variance, then by the Rothschild–Stiglitz measure, security j is more risky than the riskless security. Despite this, the two measures are not in conflict and, indeed, are complementary. The Rothschild–Stiglitz definition measures the "total risk" of a security in the sense that it compares the expected utility from holding a security *alone* with the expected utility from holding another security *alone*. Hence, it is the appropriate definition for identifying optimal portfolios and determining the efficient portfolio set. However, it is not useful for defining the risk of securities generally because it does not take into account that investors can mix securities together to form portfolios. The b_j^K measure does take this into account because it measures the only part of an individual security's risk which is relevant to an investor: namely, the part that contributes to the total risk of his optimal portfolio. In contrast to the Rothschild–Stiglitz measure of total risk, the b_j^K measures the "systematic risk" of a security (relative to efficient portfolio K). Of course, to determine the b_j^K, the efficient portfolio set must be determined. Because the Rothschild–Stiglitz measure does just that, the two measures are complementary.

Although the expected return of a security provides an equivalent ranking to its b_p^K measure, the b_p^K measure is not vacuous. There exist non-trivial information sets which allow b_p^K to be determined without knowledge of $\bar{Z}_p$. For example, consider a model in which all investors agree on the joint distribution of the returns on securities. Suppose we know the utility function U for some investor and the probability distribution of his optimal portfolio, Z^*W_0. From (3.2) we therefore know the distribution of $Y(Z^*)$. For security j, define the random variable $\varepsilon_j \equiv Z_j - \bar{Z}_j$. Suppose, furthermore, that we have enough information about the joint distribution of $Y(Z^*)$ and ε_j to compute $\text{cov}[Y(Z^*), \varepsilon_j] = \text{cov}[Y(Z^*), Z_j] = b_j^*$, but do not know $\bar{Z}_j$.[12] However, Theorem 3.1 is a necessary condition for equilibrium in the securities market.

---

[12]A sufficient amount of information would be the joint distribution of Z^* and ε_j. What is necessary will depend on the functional form of U'. However, in no case will knowledge of $\bar{Z}_j$ be a necessary condition.

Hence, we can deduce the equilibrium expected return on security j from $\bar{Z}_j = R + b_j^*(\bar{Z}^* - R)$. Analysis of the necessary information sets required to deduce the equilibrium structure of security returns is an important topic in portfolio theory and one that will be explored further in succeeding sections.

The manifest behavioral characteristic shared by all risk-averse utility maximizers is to diversify (i.e. to spread one's wealth among many investments). The benefits of diversification in reducing risk depend upon the degree of statistical interdependence among returns on the available investments. The greatest benefits in risk reduction come from adding a security to the portfolio whose realized return tends to be higher when the return on the rest of the portfolio is lower. Next to such "counter-cyclical" investments in terms of benefit are the non-cyclic securities whose returns are orthogonal to the return on the portfolio. Least beneficial are the pro-cyclical investments whose returns tend to be higher when the return on the portfolio is higher and lower when the return on the portfolio is lower. A natural summary statistic for this characteristic of a security's return distribution is its conditional expected-return function, conditional on the realized return of the portfolio. Because the risk of a security is measured by its marginal contribution to the risk of an optimal portfolio, it is perhaps not surprising that there is a direct relation between the risk measure of portfolio p, b_p, and the behavior of the conditional expected-return function, $G_p(Z_e) \equiv E[Z_p | Z_e]$, where Z_e is the realized return on an efficient portfolio.

Theorem 3.2. *If Z_p and Z_q denote the returns on portfolios p and q, respectively, and if for each possible value of Z_e, $dG_p(Z_e)/dZ_e \geq dG_q(Z_e)/dZ_e$ with strict inequality holding over some finite probability measure of Z_e, then portfolio p is riskier than portfolio q and $\bar{Z}_p > \bar{Z}_q$.*

Proof. From (3.1) and the linearity of the covariance operator, $b_p - b_q = \text{cov}[Y(Z_e), Z_p - Z_q] = E[Y(Z_e)(Z_p - Z_q)]$ because $E[Y(Z_e)] = 0$. By the property of conditional expectations, $E[Y(Z_e)(Z_p - Z_q)] = E(Y(Z_e)[G_p(Z_e) - G_q(Z_e)]) = \text{cov}[Y(Z_e), G_p(Z_e) - G_q(Z_e)]$. Thus, $b_p - b_q = \text{cov}[Y(Z_e), G_p(Z_e) - G_q(Z_e)]$. From (3.1), $Y(Z_e)$ is a strictly increasing function of Z_e and, by hypothesis, $G_p(Z_e) - G_q(Z_e)$ is a non-decreasing function of Z_e for all Z_e and a strictly increasing function of Z_e over some finite probability measure of Z_e. From Theorem 236 in Hardy, Littlewood and Pólya (1959), it follows that $\text{cov}[Y(Z_e), G_p(Z_e) - G_q(Z_e)] > 0$, and therefore, $b_p > b_q$. From Theorem 3.1, it follows that $\bar{Z}_p > \bar{Z}_q$.

Theorem 3.3. *If Z_p and Z_q denote the returns on portfolios p and q, respectively, and if, for each possible value of Z_e, $dG_p(Z_e)/dZ_e - dG_q(Z_e)/dZ_e = a_{pq}$, a constant, then $b_p = b_q + a_{pq}$ and $\bar{Z}_p = \bar{Z}_q + a_{pq}(\bar{Z}_e - R)$.*

Proof. By hypothesis, $G_p(Z_e) - G_q(Z_e) = a_{pq} Z_e + h$, where h does not depend on Z_e. As in the proof of Theorem 3.2, $b_p - b_q = \text{cov}[Y(Z_e), G_p(Z_e) - G_q(Z_e)] = \text{cov}[Y(Z_e), a_{pq} Z_e + h]$. Thus, $b_p - b_q = a_{pq}$ because $\text{cov}[Y(Z_e), Z_e] = 1$ and $\text{cov}[Y(Z_e), h] = 0$. From Theorem 3.1, $\bar{Z}_p = R + b_q(\bar{Z}_e - R) + a_{pq}(\bar{Z}_e - R) = \bar{Z}_q + a_{pq}(\bar{Z}_e - R)$.

Theorem 3.4. *If, for all possible values of Z_e,*
  (i) $dG_p(Z_e)/dZ_e > 1$, *then* $\bar{Z}_p > \bar{Z}_e$,
  (ii) $0 < dG_p(Z_e)/dZ_e < 1$, *then* $R < \bar{Z}_p < \bar{Z}_e$;
  (iii) $dG_p(Z_e)/dZ_e < 0$, *then* $\bar{Z}_p < R$;
  (iv) $dG_p(Z_e)/dZ_e = a_p$, *a constant, then* $\bar{Z}_p = R + a_p(\bar{Z}_e - R)$.

The proof follows directly from Theorems 3.2 and 3.3 by substituting either Z_e or R for Z_q and noting that $dG_q(Z_e)/dZ_e = 1$ for $Z_q = Z_e$ and $dG_q(Z_e)/dZ_e = 0$ for $Z_q = R$.

As Theorems 3.2–3.4 demonstrate, the conditional expected-return function provides considerable information about a security's risk and equilibrium expected return. It is, moreover, common practice for security analysts to provide conditioned forecasts of individual security returns, conditioned on the realized return of a broad-based stock portfolio such as the Standard & Poor's 500. As is evident from these theorems, the conditional expected-return function does not in general provide sufficient information to determine the exact risk of a security. As follows from Theorems 3.3 and 3.4(iv), the exception is the case where this function is linear in Z_e. Although surely a special case, it is a rather important one as will be shown in Section 4.

4. Spanning theorems, mutual fund theorems, and bankruptcy constraints

Definition. A set of M feasible portfolios with random variable returns $(X_1, \ldots, X_M)$ is said to *span* the space of portfolios contained in the set Ψ if and only if for any portfolio in Ψ with return denoted by Z_p, there exist numbers $(\delta_1, \ldots, \delta_M)$, $\sum_1^M \delta_j = 1$, such that $Z_p = \sum_1^M \delta_j X_j$.

If N is the number of securities available to generate the portfolios in Ψ and if M^* denotes the smallest number of feasible portfolios that span the space of portfolios contained in Ψ, then $M^* \le N$.

Fischer (1972) and Merton (1982a, pp. 611–614) use comparative statics analysis to show that little can be derived about the structure of optimal portfolio demand functions unless further restrictions are imposed on the class of investors' utility functions or the class of probability distributions for securities' returns. A particularly fruitful set of such restrictions is the one that provides for a non-trivial (i.e. $M^* < N$) spanning of either the feasible or efficient portfolio sets. Indeed, the spanning property leads to a collection of "mutual fund" or "separation" theorems that are fundamental to modern financial theory.

A *mutual fund* is a financial intermediary that holds as its assets a portfolio of securities and issues as liabilities shares against this collection of assets. Unlike the optimal portfolio of an individual investor, the portfolio of securities held by a mutual fund need not be an efficient portfolio. The connection between mutual funds and the spanning property can be seen in the following theorem:

Theorem 4.1.   *If there exist M mutual funds whose portfolios span the portfolio set Ψ, then all investors will be indifferent between selecting their optimal portfolios from Ψ or from portfolio combinations of just the M mutual funds.*

The proof of the theorem follows directly from the definition of spanning. If Z^* denotes the return on an optimal portfolio selected from Ψ and if X_j denotes the return on the jth mutual fund's portfolio, then there exist portfolio weights $(\delta_1^*, \ldots, \delta_M^*)$ such that $Z^* = \sum_1^M \delta_j^* X_j$. Hence, any investor would be indifferent between the portfolio with return Z^* and the $(\delta_1^*, \ldots, \delta_M^*)$ combination of the mutual fund shares.

Although the theorem states "indifference", if there are information-gathering or other transactions costs and if there are economies of scale, then investors would prefer the mutual funds whenever $M < N$. By a similar argument, one would expect that investors would prefer to have the smallest number of funds necessary to span Ψ. Therefore, the smallest number of such funds, M^*, is a particularly important spanning set. Hence, the spanning property can be used to derive an endogenous theory for the existence of financial intermediaries with the functional characteristics of a mutual fund. Moreover, from these functional characteristics a theory for their optimal management can be derived.

For the mutual fund theorems to have serious empirical content, the minimum number of funds required for spanning M^* must be significantly smaller than the number of available securities N. When such spanning obtains, the investor's portfolio-selection problem can be separated into two steps: first, individual securities are mixed together to form the M^* mutual funds; second, the investor allocates his wealth among the M^* funds' shares. If the investor knows that the funds span the space of optimal portfolios, then he need only know the joint probability distribution of $(X_1, \ldots, X_{M^*})$ to determine his optimal portfolio. It is for this reason that the mutual fund theorems are also called "separation" theorems. However, if the M^* funds can be constructed only if the fund managers know the preferences, endowments, and probability beliefs of each investor, then the formal separation property will have little operational significance.

In addition to providing an endogenous theory for mutual funds, the existence of a non-trivial spanning set can be used to deduce equilibrium properties of individual securities' returns and to derive optimal rules for business firms making production and capital budgeting decisions. Moreover, in virtually every model of portfolio selection in which empirical implications beyond those presented in Sections 2 and 3 are derived, some non-trivial form of the spanning property obtains.

While the determination of conditions under which non-trivial spanning will obtain is, in a broad sense, a subset of the traditional economic theory of aggregation, the first rigorous contributions in portfolio theory were made by Arrow (1953, 1964), Markowitz (1959), and Tobin (1958). In each of these papers, and most subsequent papers, the spanning property is derived as an implication of the specific model examined, and therefore such derivations provide only sufficient conditions. In two notable exceptions, Cass and Stiglitz (1970) and Ross (1978) "reverse" the process by deriving necessary conditions for non-trivial spanning to obtain. In this section necessary and sufficient conditions for spanning are developed along the lines of Cass and Stiglitz and Ross, leaving until Section 5 discussion of the specific models of Arrow, Markowitz and Tobin.

Let Ψ^f denote the set of all feasible portfolios that can be constructed from a riskless security with return R and n risky securities with a given joint probability distribution for their random variable returns $(Z_1, \ldots, Z_n)$. Let Ω denote the $n \times n$ variance–covariance matrix of the returns on the n risky assets.

Theorem 4.2. *Necessary conditions for the M feasible portfolios with returns $(X_1, \ldots, X_M)$ to span the portfolio set Ψ^f are (i) that the rank of $\Omega \leq M$ and (ii) that there exist numbers $(\delta_1, \ldots, \delta_M)$, $\sum_1^M \delta_j = 1$, such that the random variable $\sum_1^M \delta_j X_j$ has zero variance.*

Proof. (i) The set of portfolios Ψ^f defines a $(n + 1)$ dimensional vector space. By definition, if $(X_1, \ldots, X_M)$ spans Ψ^f, then each risky security's return can be represented as a linear combination of $(X_1, \ldots, X_M)$. Clearly, this is only possible if the rank of $\Omega \leq M$. (ii) The riskless security is contained in Ψ^f. Therefore, if $(X_1, \ldots, X_M)$ spans Ψ^f, then there must exist a portfolio combination of $(X_1, \ldots, X_M)$ which is riskless.

Proposition 4.1. *If $Z_p = \sum_1^n a_j Z_j + b$ is the return on some security or portfolio and if there are no "arbitrage opportunities" (Assumption 3), then (1) $b = [1 - \sum_1^n a_j]R$ and (2) $Z_p = R + \sum_1^n a_j(Z_j - R)$.*

Proof. Let Z^+ be the return on a portfolio with fraction δ_j^+ allocated to security j, $j = 1, \ldots, n$; δ_p allocated to the security with return Z_p; $(1 - \delta_p - \sum_1^n \delta_j^+)$ allocated to the riskless security with return R. If δ_j^+ is chosen such that $\delta_j^+ = -\delta_p a_j$, then $Z^+ = R + \delta_p(b - R[1 - \sum_1^n a_j])$. Z^+ is a riskless security, and therefore, by Assumption 3, $Z^+ = R$. But δ_p can be chosen arbitrarily. Therefore, $b = [1 - \sum_1^n a_j]R$. Substituting for b, it follows directly that $Z_p = R + \sum_1^n a_j(Z_j - R)$.

As long as there are no arbitrage opportunities, from Theorem 4.2 and Proposition 4.1 it can be assumed without loss of generality that one of the portfolios in any candidate spanning set is the riskless security. If, by convention, $X_M = R$, then in all subsequent analyses the notation $(X_1, \ldots, X_m, R)$ will be used to denote an M-portfolio spanning set where $m \equiv M - 1$ is the number of risky portfolios (together with the riskless security) that span Ψ^f.

Theorem 4.3. *A necessary and sufficient condition for $(X_1, \ldots, X_m, R)$ to span Ψ^f is that there exist numbers (a_{ij}) such that $Z_j = R + \sum_1^m a_{ij}(X_i - R)$, $j = 1, 2, \ldots, n$.*

Proof. If $(X_1, \ldots, X_m, R)$ span Ψ^f, then there exist portfolio weights $(\delta_{1j}, \ldots, \delta_{Mj})$, $\sum_1^M \delta_{ij} = 1$, such as $Z_j = \sum_1^M \delta_{ij} X_i$. Noting that $X_M = R$ and substituting $\delta_{Mj} = 1 - \sum_1^m \delta_{ij}$, we have that $Z_j = R + \sum_1^m \delta_{ij}(X_i - R)$. This proves necessity. If there exist numbers (a_{ij}) such that $Z_j = R + \sum_1^m a_{ij}(X_i - R)$, then pick the portfolio weights $\delta_{ij} = a_{ij}$ for $i = 1, \ldots, m$, and $\delta_{Mj} = 1 - \sum_1^m \delta_{ij}$, from which it follows that $Z_j = \sum_1^M \delta_{ij} X_i$. But every portfolio in Ψ^f can be written as a portfolio combination of $(Z_1, \ldots, Z_n)$ and R. Hence, $(X_1, \ldots, X_m, R)$ spans Ψ^f and this proves sufficiency.

Let Ω_X denote the $m \times m$ variance–covariance matrix of the returns on the m portfolios with returns $(X_1, \ldots, X_m)$.

Corollary 4.3a. *A necessary and sufficient condition for $(X_1, \ldots, X_m, R)$ to be the smallest number of feasible portfolios that span (i.e. $M^* = m + 1$) is that the rank of Ω equals the rank of $\Omega_X = m$.*

Proof. If $(X_1, \ldots, X_m, R)$ span Ψ^f and m is the smallest number of risky portfolios that does, then $(X_1, \ldots, X_m)$ must be linearly independent, and therefore rank $\Omega_X = m$. Hence, $(X_1, \ldots, X_m)$ form a basis for the vector space of security returns $(Z_1, \ldots, Z_n)$. Therefore, the rank of Ω must equal the rank of Ω_X. This proves necessity. If the rank of $\Omega_X = m$, then $(X_1, \ldots, X_m)$ are linearly independent. Moreover, $(X_1, \ldots, X_m) \in \Psi^f$. Hence, if the rank of $\Omega = m$, then there exist numbers (a_{ij}) such that $Z_j - \bar{Z}_j = \sum_1^m a_{ij}(X_i - \bar{X}_i)$ for

$j = 1, 2, \ldots, n$. Therefore, $Z_j = b_j + \sum_1^m a_{ij} X_i$, where $b_j \equiv \bar{Z}_j - \sum_1^m a_{ij} \bar{X}_i$. By the same argument as that used to prove Proposition 4.1, $b_j = [1 - \sum_1^m a_{ij}] R$. Therefore, $Z_j = R + \sum_1^m a_{ij}(X_i - R)$. By Theorem 4.3, $(X_1, \ldots, X_m, R)$ span Ψ^f.

It follows from Corollary 4.3a that a necessary and sufficient condition for non-trivial spanning of Ψ^f is that some of the risky securities are redundant securities. Note, however, that this condition is sufficient only if securities are priced such that there are no arbitrage opportunities.

In all these derived theorems the only restriction on investors' preferences was that they prefer more to less. In particular, it was not assumed that investors are necessarily risk-averse. Although Ψ^f was defined in terms of a known joint probability distribution for $(Z_1, \ldots, Z_n)$, which implies homogeneous beliefs among investors, inspection of the proof of Theorem 4.3 shows that this condition can be weakened. If investors agree on a set of portfolios $(X_1, \ldots, X_m, R)$ such that $Z_j = R + \sum_1^m a_{ij}(X_i - R)$, $j = 1, 2, \ldots, n$, and if they agree on the numbers (a_{ij}), then by Theorem 4.3, $(X_1, \ldots, X_m, R)$ span Ψ^f even if investors *do not* agree on the joint distribution of $(X_1, \ldots, X_m)$. These appear to be the weakest restrictions on preferences and probability beliefs that can produce non-trivial spanning and the corresponding mutual fund theorem. Hence, to derive additional theorems it is now further assumed that all investors are risk-averse and that investors have homogeneous probability beliefs.

Define Ψ^e to be the set of all efficient portfolios contained in Ψ^f.

Proposition 4.2. *If Z_e is the return on a portfolio contained in Ψ^e, then any portfolio that combines positive amounts of Z_e with the riskless security is also contained in Ψ^e.*

Proof. Let $Z = \delta(Z_e - R) + R$ be the return on a portfolio with positive fraction δ allocated to Z_e and fraction $(1 - \delta)$ allocated to the riskless security. Because Z_e is an efficient portfolio, there exists a strictly concave, increasing function V such that $E\{V'(Z_e)(Z_j - R)\} = 0$, $j = 1, 2, \ldots, n$. Define $U(W) \equiv V(aW + b)$, where $a \equiv 1/\delta > 0$ and $b \equiv (\delta - 1)R/\delta$. Because $a > 0$, U is a strictly concave and increasing function. Moreover, $U'(Z) = aV'(Z_e)$. Hence, $E\{U'(Z)(Z_j - R)\} = 0$, $j = 1, 2, \ldots, n$. Therefore, there exists a utility function such that Z is an optimal portfolio, and thus Z is an efficient portfolio.

It follows immediately from Proposition 4.2 that for every number $\bar{Z}$ such that $\bar{Z} \geq R$, there exists at least one efficient portfolio with expected return equal to $\bar{Z}$. Moreover, we also have that if $(X_1, \ldots, X_M)$ are the returns on M candidate portfolios to span the space of efficient portfolios Ψ^e, then without loss of generality it can be assumed that one of the portfolios is the riskless security.

Theorem 4.4. *Let* $(X_1, \ldots, X_m)$ *denote the returns on m feasible portfolios. If for security j there exist numbers* (a_{ij}) *such that* $Z_j = \bar{Z}_j + \sum_1^m a_{ij}(X_i - \bar{X}_i) + \varepsilon_j$, *where* $E[\varepsilon_j V_K'(Z_e^K)] = 0$ *for some efficient portfolio* K, *then* $\bar{Z}_j = R + \sum_1^m a_{ij}(\bar{X}_i - R)$.

Proof. Let Z_p be the return on a portfolio with fraction δ allocated to security j; fraction $\delta_i = -\delta a_{ij}$ allocated to portfolio X_i, $i = 1, \ldots, m$; and $1 - \delta - \sum_1^m \delta_i$ allocated to the riskless security. By hypothesis, Z_p can be written as $Z_p = R + \delta[\bar{Z}_j - R - \sum_1^m a_{ij}(\bar{X}_i - R)] + \delta\varepsilon_j$, where $E[\delta\varepsilon_j V_K'] = \delta E[\varepsilon_j V_K'] = 0$. By construction, $E(\varepsilon_j) = 0$, and hence, $\text{cov}[Z_p, V_K'] = 0$. Therefore, the systematic risk of portfolio p, $b_p^K = 0$. From Theorem 3.1, $\bar{Z}_p = R$. But δ can be chosen arbitrarily. Therefore, $\bar{Z}_j = R + \sum_1^m a_{ij}(\bar{X}_i - R)$.

Hence, if the return on a security can be written in this linear form relative to the portfolios $(X_1, \ldots, X_m)$, then its expected excess return, $\bar{Z}_j - R$, is completely determined by the expected excess returns on these portfolios and the weights (a_{ij}).

Theorem 4.5. *If, for every security j, there exist numbers* (a_{ij}) *such that* $Z_j = R + \sum_1^m a_{ij}(X_i - R) + \varepsilon_j$, *where* $E[\varepsilon_j | X_1, \ldots, X_m] = 0$, *then* $(X_1, \ldots, X_m, R)$ *span the set of efficient portfolios* Ψ^e.

Proof. Let w_j^K denote the fraction of efficient portfolio K allocated to security j, $j = 1, \ldots, n$. By hypothesis, we can write $Z_e^K = R + \sum_1^m \delta_i^K(X_i - R) + \varepsilon^K$, where $\delta_i^K \equiv \sum_1^n w_j^K a_{ij}$, and $\varepsilon^K \equiv \sum_1^n w_j^K \varepsilon_j$, where $E[\varepsilon^K | X_1, \ldots, X_m] = \sum_1^n w_j^K E[\varepsilon_j | X_1, \ldots, X_m] = 0$. Construct the portfolio with return Z by allocating fraction δ_i^K to portfolio X_i, $i = 1, \ldots, m$, and fraction $1 - \sum_1^m \delta_i^K$ to the riskless security. By construction, $Z_e^K = Z + \varepsilon^K$, where $E[\varepsilon^K | Z] = E[\varepsilon^K | \sum_1^m \delta_i^K X_i] = 0$ because $E[\varepsilon^K | X_1, \ldots, X_m] = 0$. Hence, for $\varepsilon^K \neq 0$, Z_e^K is riskier than Z in the Rothschild–Stiglitz sense, which contradicts that Z_e^K is an efficient portfolio. Thus, $\varepsilon^K \equiv 0$ for every efficient portfolio K, and all efficient portfolios can be generated by a portfolio combination of $(X_1, \ldots, X_m, R)$.

Therefore, if we can find a set of portfolios $(X_1, \ldots, X_m)$ such that every security's return can be expressed as a linear combination of the returns $(X_1, \ldots, X_m, R)$, plus noise relative to these portfolios, then we have a set of portfolios that span Ψ^e. The following theorem, first proved by Ross (1978), shows that security returns can always be written in a linear form relative to a set of spanning portfolios.

Theorem 4.6. *Let* w_j^K *denote the fraction of efficient portfolio* K *allocated to security j*, $j = 1, \ldots, n$. $(X_1, \ldots, X_m, R)$ *span* Ψ^e *if and only if there exist* *numbers (a_{ij}) for every security j such that $Z_j = R + \sum_1^m a_{ij}(X_i - R) + \varepsilon_j$, where $E[\varepsilon_j | \sum_1^m \delta_i^K X_i] = 0$, $\delta_i^K \equiv \sum_1^n w_j^K a_{ij}$, for every efficient portfolio K.*

Proof. The "if" part follows directly from the proof of Theorem 4.5. In that proof, we only needed that $E[\varepsilon^K | \sum_1^m \delta_i^K X_i] = 0$ for every efficient portfolio K to show that $(X_1, \ldots, X_m, R)$ span Ψ^e. The proof of the "only if" part is long and requires the proof of four specialized lemmas [see Ross (1978), appendix)]. It is, therefore, not presented here.

Corollary 4.6. *(X, R) span Ψ^e if and only if there exists a number a_j for each security j, $j = 1, \ldots, n$, such that $Z_j = R + a_j(X - R) + \varepsilon_j$, where $E(\varepsilon_j | X) = 0$.*

Proof. The "if" part follows directly from Theorem 4.5. The "only if" part is as follows. By hypothesis, $Z_e^K = \delta^K(X - R) + R$ for every efficient portfolio K. If $\bar{X} = R$, then from Corollary 2.1a, $\delta^K = 0$ for every efficient portfolio K and R spans Ψ^e. Otherwise, from Theorem 2.2, $\delta^K \neq 0$ for every efficient portfolio. By Theorem 4.6, $E[\varepsilon_j | \delta^K X] = 0$, for $j = 1, \ldots, n$ and every efficient portfolio K. But, for $\delta^K \neq 0$, $E[\varepsilon_j | \delta^K X] = 0$ if and only if $E[\varepsilon_j | X] = 0$.

In addition to Ross (1978), there have been a number of studies of the properties of efficient portfolios [cf. Chen and Ingersoll (1983), Dybvig and Ross (1982), and Nielsen (1986)]. However, there is still much to be determined. For example, from Theorem 4.6, a necessary condition for $(X_1, \ldots, X_m, R)$ to span Ψ^e is that $E[\varepsilon_j | Z_e^K] = 0$, for $j = 1, \ldots, n$ and every efficient portfolio K. For $m > 1$, this condition is not sufficient to ensure that $(X_1, \ldots, X_m, R)$ span Ψ^e. The condition that $E[\varepsilon_j | \sum_1^m \lambda_i X_i] = 0$ for all numbers λ_i implies that $E[\varepsilon_j | X_1, \ldots, X_m] = 0$. If, however, the $\{\lambda_i\}$ are restricted to the class of optimal portfolio weights $\{\delta_i^K\}$ as in Theorem 4.6 and $m > 1$, it does not follow that $E[\varepsilon_j | X_1, \ldots, X_m] = 0$. Thus, $E[\varepsilon_j | X_1, \ldots, X_m] = 0$ is sufficient, but not necessary, for $(X_1, \ldots, X_m, R)$ to span Ψ^e. It is not known whether any material cases of spanning are ruled out by imposing this stronger condition. Empirical application of the spanning conditions generally assumes that the condition $E[\varepsilon_j | X_1, \ldots, X_m] = 0$ obtains.

Since Ψ^e is contained in Ψ^f, any properties proved for portfolios that span Ψ^e must be properties of portfolios that span Ψ^f. From Theorems 4.3, 4.5, and 4.6, the essential difference is that to span the efficient portfolio set it is not necessary that linear combinations of the spanning portfolios exactly replicate the return on each available security. Hence, it is not necessary that there exist redundant securities for non-trivial spanning of Ψ^e to obtain. Of course, all three theorems are empty of any empirical content if the size of the smallest spanning set M^* is equal to $(n + 1)$.

As discussed in the introduction to this section, all the important models of portfolio selection exhibit the non-trivial spanning property for the efficient portfolio set. Therefore, for all such models that do not restrict the class of admissible utility functions beyond that of risk-aversion, the distribution of individual security returns must be such that $Z_j = R + \sum_1^m a_{ij}(X_i - R) + \varepsilon_j$, where ε_j satisfies the conditions of Theorem 4.6 for $j = 1, \ldots, n$. Moreover, given some knowledge of the joint distribution of a set of portfolios that span Ψ^e with $(Z_j - \bar{Z}_j)$, there exists a method for determining the (a_{ij}) and $\bar{Z}_j$.

Proposition 4.3. *If, for every security j, $E(\varepsilon_j | X_1, \ldots, X_m) = 0$ with $(X_1, \ldots, X_m)$ linearly independent with finite variances and if the return on security j, Z_j, has a finite variance, then the (a_{ij}), $i = 1, 2, \ldots, m$, in Theorems 4.5 and 4.6 are given by:*

$$a_{ij} = \sum_1^m v_{ik} \, \mathrm{cov}[X_k, Z_j] \, ,$$

where v_{ik} is the i-kth element of Ω_X^{-1}.

The proof of Proposition 4.3 follows directly from the condition that $E(\varepsilon_j | X_k) = 0$, which implies that $\mathrm{cov}[\varepsilon_j, X_k] = 0$, $k = 1, \ldots, m$. The condition that $(X_1, \ldots, X_m)$ be linearly independent is trivial in the sense that knowing the joint distribution of a spanning set one can always choose a linearly independent subset. The only properties of the joint distributions required to compute the (a_{ij}) are the variances and covariances of $X_1, \ldots, X_m$ and the covariances between Z_j and $X_1, \ldots, X_m$. In particular, knowledge of $\bar{Z}_j$ is not required because $\mathrm{cov}[X_k, Z_j] = \mathrm{cov}[X_k, Z_j - \bar{Z}_j]$. Hence, for $m < n$ (and especially so for $m \ll n$), there exists a non-trivial information set which allows the (a_{ij}) to be determined without knowledge of $\bar{Z}_j$. If $\bar{X}_1, \ldots, \bar{X}_m$ are known, then $\bar{Z}_j$ can be computed by the formula in Theorem 4.4. By comparison with the example in Section 3, the information set required there to determine $\bar{Z}_j$ was a utility function and the joint distribution of its associated optimal portfolio with $(Z_j - \bar{Z}_j)$. Here, we must know a complete set of portfolios that span Ψ^e. However, here only the second-moment properties of the joint distribution need be known, and no utility function information other than risk-aversion is required.

A special case of no little interest is when a single risky portfolio and the riskless security span the space of efficient portfolios and Corollary 4.6 applies. Indeed, the classic mean–variance model of Markowitz and Tobin, which is discussed in Section 5, exhibits this strong form of separation. Moreover, most macroeconomic models have highly aggregated financial sectors where investors' portfolio choices are limited to simple combinations of two securities: "bonds" and "stocks". The rigorous microeconomic foundation for such aggregation is precisely that Ψ^e is spanned by a single risky portfolio and the riskless security.

If X denotes the random variable return on a risky portfolio such that (X, R) spans Ψ^e, then the return on any efficient portfolio, Z_e, can be written as if it had been chosen by combining the risky portfolio with return X with the riskless security. Namely, $Z_e = \delta(X - R) + R$, where δ is the fraction allocated to the risky portfolio and $(1 - \delta)$ is the fraction allocated to the riskless security. By Corollary 2.1a, the sign of δ will be the same for every efficient portfolio, and therefore all efficient portfolios will be perfectly positively correlated. If $\bar{X} > R$, then by Proposition 4.2, X will be an efficient portfolio and $\delta > 0$ for every efficient portfolio.

Proposition 4.4. *If $(Z_1, \ldots, Z_n)$ contain no redundant securities, δ_j denotes the fraction of portfolio X allocated to security j, and w_j^* denotes the fraction of any risk-averse investor's optimal portfolio allocated to security j, $j = 1, \ldots, n$, then for every such risk-averse investor:*

$$w_j^* / w_k^* = \delta_j / \delta_k , \quad j, k = 1, 2, \ldots, n .$$

The proof follows immediately because every optimal portfolio is an efficient portfolio, and the holdings of risky securities in every efficient portfolio are proportional to the holdings in X. Hence, the relative holdings of risky securities will be the same for all risk-averse investors. Whenever Proposition 4.4 holds and if there exist numbers (δ_j^*), where $\delta_j^* / \delta_k^* = \delta_j / \delta_k$, $j, k = 1, \ldots, n$, and $\sum_1^n \delta_j^* = 1$, then the portfolio with proportions $(\delta_1^*, \ldots, \delta_n^*)$ is called the *Optimal Combination of Risky Assets*. If such a portfolio exists, then without loss of generality it can always be assumed that $X = \sum_1^n \delta_j^* Z_j$.

Proposition 4.5. *If (X, R) spans Ψ^e, then Ψ^e is a convex set.*

Proof. Let Z_e^1 and Z_e^2 denote the returns on two distinct efficient portfolios. Because (X, R) spans Ψ^e, $Z_e^1 = \delta_1(X - R) + R$ and $Z_e^2 = \delta_2(X - R) + R$. Because they are distinct, $\delta_1 \neq \delta_2$, and so assume $\delta_1 \neq 0$. Let $Z \equiv \lambda Z_e^1 + (1 - \lambda) Z_e^2$ denote the return on a portfolio which allocates fraction λ to Z_e^1 and $(1 - \lambda)$ to Z_e^2, where $0 \leq \lambda \leq 1$. By substitution, the expression for Z can be rewritten as $Z = \delta(Z_e^1 - R) + R$, where $\delta \equiv [\lambda + (\delta_2/\delta_1)(1 - \lambda)]$. Because Z_e^1 and Z_e^2 are efficient portfolios, the sign of δ_1 is the same as the sign of δ_2. Hence, $\delta \geq 0$. Therefore, by Proposition 4.2, Z is an efficient portfolio. It follows by induction that for any integer k and numbers λ_i such that $0 \leq \lambda_i \leq 1$, $i = 1, \ldots, k$, and $\sum_1^k \lambda_i = 1$, $Z^k \equiv \sum_1^k \lambda_i Z_e^i$ is the return on an efficient portfolio. Hence, Ψ^e is a convex set.

Definition.   A *market portfolio* is defined as a portfolio that holds all available securities in proportion to their market values. To avoid the problems of "double counting" caused by financial intermediaries and inter-investor issues of securities, the equilibrium market value of a security for this purpose is defined to be the equilibrium value of the aggregate demand by individuals for the security. In models where all physical assets are held by business firms and business firms hold no financial assets, an equivalent definition is that the market value of a security equals the equilibrium value of the aggregate amount of that security issued by business firms. If V_j denotes the market value of security j and V_R denotes the value of the riskless security, then

$$\delta_j^M = \frac{V_j}{\sum_1^n V_j + V_R} , \quad j = 1, 2, \ldots, n ,$$

where δ_j^M is the fraction of security j held in a market portfolio.

Theorem 4.7.   *If Ψ^e is a convex set, and if the securities' market is in equilibrium, then a market portfolio is an efficient portfolio.*

Proof.   Let there be K risk-averse investors in the economy with the initial wealth of investor k denoted by W_0^k. Define $Z^k \equiv R + \sum_1^n w_j^k(Z_j - R)$ to be the return per dollar on investor k's optimal portfolio, where w_j^k is the fraction allocated to security j. In equilibrium, $\sum_1^K w_j^k W_0^k = V_j$, $j = 1, 2, \ldots, n$, and $\sum_1^K W_0^k \equiv W_0 = \sum_1^n V_j + V_R$. Define $\lambda_k \equiv W_0^k / W_0$, $k = 1, \ldots, K$. Clearly, $0 \le \lambda_k \le 1$ and $\sum_1^K \lambda_k = 1$. By definition of a market portfolio, $\sum_1^K w_j^k \lambda_k = \delta_j^M$, $j = 1, 2, \ldots, n$. Multiplying by $(Z_j - R)$ and summing over j, it follows that $\sum_1^K \lambda_k \sum_1^n w_j^k(Z_j - R) = \sum_1^K \lambda_k(Z^k - R) = \sum_1^n \delta_j^M(Z_j - R) = Z_M - R$, where Z_M is defined to be the return per dollar on the market portfolio. Because $\sum_1^K \lambda_k = 1$, $Z_M = \sum_1^K \lambda_k Z^k$. But every optimal portfolio is an efficient portfolio. Hence, Z_M is a convex combination of the returns on K efficient portfolios. Therefore, if Ψ^e is convex, then the market portfolio is contained in Ψ^e.

Because a market portfolio can be constructed without the knowledge of preferences, the distribution of wealth, or the joint probability distribution for the outstanding securities, models in which the market portfolio can be shown to be efficient are more likely to produce testable hypotheses. In addition, the efficiency of the market portfolio provides a rigorous microeconomic justification for the use of a "representative man" to derive equilibrium prices in aggregated economic models, i.e. the market portfolio is efficient if and only if there exists a concave utility function such that maximization of its expected value with initial wealth equal to national wealth would lead to the market portfolio as the optimal portfolio. Indeed, it is currently fashionable in the real world to advise "passive" investment strategies that simply mix the market portfolio with the riskless security. Provided that the market portfolio is efficient, by Proposition 4.2 no investor following such strategies could ever be convicted of "inefficiency". Moreover, the market portfolio will be efficient if markets are "complete" in the sense of Arrow (1953, 1964) and Debreu (1959) and investors have homogeneous beliefs. Unfortunately, general necessary and sufficient conditions for the market portfolio to be efficient have not as yet been derived.

However, even if the market portfolio were not efficient, it does have the following important property:

Proposition 4.6. *In all portfolio models with homogeneous beliefs and risk-averse investors, the equilibrium expected return on the market portfolio exceeds the return on the riskless security.*

The proof follows directly from the proof of Theorem 4.7 and Corollary 2.1a. Clearly, $\bar{Z}_M - R = \sum_1^K \lambda_k (\bar{Z}^k - R)$. By Corollary 2.1a, $\bar{Z}^k \geq R$ for $k = 1, \ldots, K$, with strict inequality holding if Z^k is risky. But, $\lambda_k > 0$. Hence, $\bar{Z}_M > R$ if any risky securities are held by any investor. Note that using no information other than market prices and quantities of securities outstanding, the market portfolio (and combinations of the market portfolio and the riskless security) is the only risky portfolio where the sign of its equilibrium expected excess return can always be predicted.

Returning to the special case where Ψ^e is spanned by a single risky portfolio and the riskless security, it follows immediately from Proposition 4.5 and Theorem 4.7 that the market portfolio is efficient. Because all efficient portfolios are perfectly positively correlated, it follows that the risky spanning portfolio can always be chosen to be the market portfolio (i.e. $X = Z_M$). Therefore, every efficient portfolio (and hence, every optimal portfolio) can be represented as a simple portfolio combination of the market portfolio and the riskless security with a positive fraction allocated to the market portfolio. If all investors want to hold risky securities in the same relative proportions, then the only way in which this is possible is if these relative proportions are identical to those in the market portfolio. Indeed, if there were one best investment strategy, and if this "best" strategy were widely known, then whatever the original statement of the strategy, it must lead to simply this imperative: "hold the market portfolio".

Because for every security $\delta_j^M \geq 0$, it follows from Proposition 4.4 that in equilibrium, every investor will hold non-negative quantities of risky securities, and therefore it is never optimal to short sell risky securities. Hence, in models where $m = 1$, the introduction of restrictions against short sales will not affect the equilibrium.

Theorem 4.8. *If (Z_M, R) span Ψ^e, then the equilibrium expected return on security j can be written as*:

$$\bar{Z}_j = R + \beta_j(\bar{Z}_M - R),$$

where

$$\beta_j \equiv \frac{\text{cov}[Z_j, Z_M]}{\text{var}(Z_M)}.$$

The proof follows directly from Corollary 4.6 and Proposition 4.3. This relation, called the *Security Market Line*, was first derived by Sharpe (1964) as a necessary condition for equilibrium in the mean–variance model of Markowitz and Tobin when investors have homogeneous beliefs. This relation has been central to most empirical studies of securities' returns published during the last two decades. Indeed, the switch in notation from a_{ij} to β_j in this special case reflects the almost universal adoption of the term, "the 'beta' of a security", to mean the covariance of that security's return with the market portfolio divided by the variance of the return on the market portfolio.

In the special case of Theorem 4.8, β_j measures the systematic risk of security j relative to the efficient portfolio Z_M (i.e. $\beta_j = b_j^M$ as defined in Section 3), and therefore beta provides a complete ordering of the risk of individual securities. As is often the case in research, useful concepts are derived in a special model first. The term "systematic risk" was first coined by Sharpe and was measured by beta. The definition in Section 3 is a natural generalization. Moreover, unlike the general risk measure of Section 3, β_j can be computed from a simple covariance between Z_j and Z_M. Securities whose returns are positively correlated with the market are pro-cyclical, and will be priced to have positive equilibrium expected excess returns. Securities whose returns are negatively correlated are counter-cyclical, and will have negative equilibrium expected excess returns.

In general, the sign of b_j^k cannot be determined by the sign of the correlation coefficient between Z_j and Z_e^k. However, as shown in Theorems 3.2–3.4, because $\partial Y(Z_e^k)/\partial Z_e^k > 0$ for each realization of Z_e^k, $b_j^k > 0$ does imply a generalized positive "association" between the return on Z_j and Z_e^k. Similarly, $b_j^k < 0$ implies a negative "association".

Let $\Psi_{\min}$ denote the set of portfolios contained in Ψ^f such that there exists no other portfolio in Ψ^f with the same expected return and a smaller variance.

Let $Z(\mu)$ denote the return on a portfolio contained in $\Psi_{\min}$ such that $\bar{Z}(\mu) = \mu$, and let δ_j^{μ} denote the fraction of this portfolio allocated to security j, $j = 1, \ldots, n$.

Theorem 4.9. *If $(Z_1, \ldots, Z_n)$ contain no redundant securities, then* (a) *for each value μ, δ_j^{μ}, $j = 1, \ldots, n$, are unique;* (b) *there exists a portfolio contained in $\Psi_{\min}$ with return X such that (X, R) span $\Psi_{\min}$; and* (c) $\bar{Z}_j - R = a_j(\bar{X} - R)$, *where $a_j \equiv \mathrm{cov}(Z_j, X)/\mathrm{var}(X)$, $j = 1, 2, \ldots, n$.*

Proof. Let σ_{ij} denote the i-jth element of Ω and because $(Z_1, \ldots, Z_n)$ contain no redundant securities, Ω is non-singular. Hence, let v_{ij} denote the i-jth element of Ω^{-1}. All portfolios in $\Psi_{\min}$ with expected return μ must have portfolio weights that are solutions to the problem: $\min \sum_1^n \sum_1^n \delta_i \delta_j \sigma_{ij}$ subject to the constraint $\bar{Z}(\mu) = \mu$. Trivially, if $\mu = R$, then $Z(R) = R$ and $\delta_j^R = 0$, $j = 1, 2, \ldots, n$. Consider the case where $\mu \neq R$. The n first-order conditions are:

$$0 = \sum_1^n \delta_j^{\mu} \sigma_{ij} - \lambda_{\mu}(\bar{Z}_i - R), \quad i = 1, 2, \ldots, n,$$

where λ_{μ} is the Lagrange multiplier for the constraint. Multiplying by δ_i^{μ} and summing, we have that $\lambda_{\mu} = \mathrm{var}[Z(\mu)]/(\mu - R)$. By definition of $\Psi_{\min}$, λ_{μ} must be the same for all $\bar{Z}(\mu)$. Because Ω is non-singular, the set of linear equations has the unique solution:

$$\delta_j^{\mu} = \lambda_{\mu} \sum_1^n v_{ij}(\bar{Z}_i - R), \quad j = 1, 2, \ldots, n.$$

This proves (a). From this solution, $\delta_j^{\mu}/\delta_k^{\mu}$, $j, k = 1, 2, \ldots, n$, are the same for every value of μ. Hence, all portfolios in $\Psi_{\min}$ with $\mu \neq R$ are perfectly correlated. Hence, pick any portfolio in $\Psi_{\min}$ with $\mu \neq R$ and call its return X. Then every $Z(\mu)$ can be written in the form $Z(\mu) = \delta_{\mu}(X - R) + R$. Hence, (X, R) span $\Psi_{\min}$ which proves (b), and from Corollary 4.6 and Proposition 4.3, (c) follows directly.

From Theorem 4.9, a_k will be equivalent to b_k^K as a measure of a security's systematic risk provided that the $Z(\mu)$ chosen for X is such that $\mu > R$. Like β_k, the only information required to compute a_k is the joint second moments of Z_k and X. Which of the two equivalent measures will be more useful obviously depends upon the information set that is available. However, as the following theorem demonstrates, the a_k measure is the natural choice in the case when there exists a spanning set for Ψ^e with $m = 1$.

Theorem 4.10. *If (X, R) span Ψ^{e} and if X has a finite variance, then Ψ^{e} is contained in $\Psi_{\min}$.*

Proof. Let Z_{e} be the return on any efficient portfolio. By hypothesis, Z_{e} can be written as $Z_{\mathrm{e}} = R + a_{\mathrm{e}}(X - R)$. Let Z_p be the return on any portfolio in Ψ^{f} such that $\bar{Z}_{\mathrm{e}} = \bar{Z}_p$. By Corollary 4.6, Z_p can be written as $Z_p = R + a_p(X - R) + \varepsilon_p$, where $E(\varepsilon_p) = E(\varepsilon_p | X) = 0$. Therefore, $a_p = a_{\mathrm{e}}$ if $\bar{Z}_p = \bar{Z}_{\mathrm{e}}$; $\mathrm{var}(Z_p) = a_p^2 \, \mathrm{var}(X) + \mathrm{var}(\varepsilon_p) \geq a_p^2 \, \mathrm{var}(X) = \mathrm{var}(Z_{\mathrm{e}})$. Hence, Z_{e} is contained in $\Psi_{\min}$. Moreover, Ψ^{e} will be the set of all portfolios in $\Psi_{\min}$ such that $\mu \geq R$.

Thus, whenever there exists a spanning set for Ψ^{e} with $m = 1$, the means, variances, and covariances of $(Z_1, \ldots, Z_n)$ are sufficient statistics to completely determine all efficient portfolios. Such a strong set of conclusions suggests that the class of joint probability distributions for $(Z_1, \ldots, Z_n)$ which admit a two-fund separation theorem will be highly specialized. However, as the following theorems demonstrate, the class is not empty.

Theorem 4.11. *If $(Z_1, \ldots, Z_n)$ have a joint normal probability distribution, then there exists a portfolio with return X such that (X, R) span Ψ^{e}.*

Proof. Using the procedure applied in the proof of Theorem 4.9, construct a risky portfolio contained in $\Psi_{\min}$, and call its return X. Define the random variables, $\varepsilon_k \equiv Z_k - R - a_k(X - R)$, $k = 1, \ldots, n$. By part (c) of that theorem, $E(\varepsilon_k) = 0$, and by construction, $\mathrm{cov}[\varepsilon_k, X] = 0$. Because $Z_1, \ldots, Z_n$ are normally distributed, X will be normally distributed. Hence, ε_k is normally distributed, and because $\mathrm{cov}[\varepsilon_k, X] = 0$, ε_k and X are independent. Therefore, $E(\varepsilon_k) = E(\varepsilon_k | X) = 0$. From Corollary 4.6, it follows that (X, R) span Ψ^{e}.

It is straightforward to prove that if $(Z_1, \ldots, Z_n)$ can have *arbitrary* means, variances, and covariances, and can be mutually independent, then a necessary condition for there to exist a portfolio with return X such that (X, R) span Ψ^{e} is that $(Z_1, \ldots, Z_n)$ be joint normally distributed. However, it is important to emphasize both the word "arbitrary" and the prospect for independence. For example, consider a joint distribution for $(Z_1, \ldots, Z_n)$ such that the joint probability density function, $p(Z_1, \ldots, Z_n)$, is a symmetric function. That is, for each set of admissible outcomes for $(Z_1, \ldots, Z_n)$, $p(Z_1, \ldots, Z_n)$ remains unchanged when any two arguments of p are interchanged. An obvious special case is when $(Z_1, \ldots, Z_n)$ are independently and identically distributed and $p(Z_1, \ldots, Z_n) = p(Z_1)p(Z_2) \cdots p(Z_n)$.

Theorem 4.12. *If $p(Z_1, \ldots, Z_n)$ is a symmetric function with respect to all its arguments, then there exists a portfolio with return X such that (X, R) spans Ψ^{e}.*

Proof. By hypothesis, $p(Z_1, \ldots, Z_i, \ldots, Z_n) = p(Z_i, \ldots, Z_1, \ldots, Z_n)$ for each set of given values $(Z_1, \ldots, Z_n)$. Therefore, from the first-order conditions for portfolio selection, (2.4), every risk-averse investor will choose $\delta_1^* = \delta_i^*$. But, this is true for $i = 1, \ldots, n$. Hence, all investors will hold all risky securities in the same relative proportions. Therefore, if X is the return on a portfolio with an equal dollar investment in each risky security, then (X, R) will span Ψ^e.

Samuelson (1967) was the first to examine this class of symmetric density functions in a portfolio context. Chamberlain (1983) has shown that the class of elliptical distributions characterize the distributions that imply mean–variance utility functions for all risk-averse expected utility maximizers. However, for distributions other than Gaussian to obtain, the security returns cannot be independently distributed.

The Arbitrage Pricing Theory (APT) model developed by Ross (1976a) provides an important class of linear-factor models that generate (at least approximate) spanning without assuming joint normal probability distributions. Suppose the returns on securities are generated by:

$$Z_j = \bar{Z}_j + \sum_1^m a_{ij} Y_i + \varepsilon_j, \quad j = 1, \ldots, n, \tag{4.1}$$

where $\mathrm{E}(\varepsilon_j) = \mathrm{E}(\varepsilon_j \mid Y_1, \ldots, Y_m) = 0$ and without loss of generality, $\mathrm{E}(Y_i) = 0$ and $\mathrm{cov}[Y_i, Y_j] = 0$, $i \neq j$. The random variables $\{Y_i\}$ represent common factors that are likely to affect the returns on a significant number of securities. If it is possible to construct a set of m portfolios with returns $(X_1, \ldots, X_m)$ such that X_i and Y_i are perfectly correlated, $i = 1, 2, \ldots, m$, then the conditions of Theorem 4.5 will be satisfied and $(X_1, \ldots, X_m, R)$ will span Ψ^e.

Although in general it will not be possible to construct such a set, by imposing some mild additional restrictions on $\{\varepsilon_j\}$, Ross (1976a) derives an asymptotic spanning theorem as the number of available securities, n, becomes large. While the rigorous derivation is rather tedious, a rough description goes as follows. Let Z_p be the return on a portfolio with fraction δ_j allocated to security j, $j = 1, 2, \ldots, n$. From (4.1), Z_p can be written as:

$$Z_p = \bar{Z}_p + \sum_1^m a_{ip} Y_i + \varepsilon_p, \tag{4.2}$$

where $\bar{Z}_p = R + \sum_1^n \delta_j(\bar{Z}_j - R)$; $a_{ip} \equiv \sum_1^n \delta_j a_{ij}$; $\varepsilon_p \equiv \sum_1^n \delta_j \varepsilon_j$. Consider the set of portfolios (called *well-diversified portfolios*) that have the property $\delta_j \equiv \mu_j/n$, where $|\mu_j| \leq M_j < \infty$ and M_j is independent of n, $j = 1, \ldots, n$. Virtually by the definition of a common factor, it is reasonable to assume that for every $n \gg m$, a significantly positive fraction of all securities, λ_i, have $a_{ij} \neq 0$, and this will be true for each common factor i, $i = 1, \ldots, m$. Similarly, because the $\{\varepsilon_j\}$ denote the variations in securities' returns not explained by common factors, it is also reasonable to assume for large n that for each j, ε_j is uncorrelated with virtually all other securities' returns. Hence, if the number of common factors, m, is fixed, then for all $n \geqslant m$, it should be possible to construct a set of well-diversified portfolios $\{X_k\}$ such that for X_k, $a_{ik} = 0$, $i = 1, \ldots, m$, $i \neq k$, and $a_{kk} \neq 0$. It follows from (4.2) that X_k can be written as:

$$X_k = \bar{X}_k + a_{kk} Y_k + \frac{1}{n} \sum_1^n \mu_j^k \varepsilon_j, \quad k = 1, \ldots, m .$$

But $|\mu_j^k|$ is bounded, independently of n, and virtually all the $\{\varepsilon_j\}$ are uncorrelated. Therefore, by the Law of Large Numbers, as $n \to \infty$, $X_k \to \bar{X}_k + a_{kk} Y_k$ with probability one. So, as n becomes very large, X_k and Y_k become perfectly correlated, and by Theorem 4.5, asymptotically $(X_1, \ldots, X_m, R)$ will span Ψ^e. In particular, if $m = 1$, then asymptotically two-fund separation will obtain independent of any other distributional characteristics of Y_1 or the $\{\varepsilon_j\}$.

As can be seen from Theorem 2.3 and its corollary, all efficient portfolios in the APT model are well-diversified portfolios. Unlike in the mean–variance model, returns on all efficient portfolios need not, however, be perfectly correlated. The model is also attractive because, at least in principle, the equilibrium structure of expected returns and risks of securities can be derived without explicit knowledge of investors' preferences or endowments. Indeed, whenever non-trivial spanning of Ψ^e obtains and the set of risky spanning portfolios can be identified, much of the structure of individual securities returns can be empirically estimated. For example, if we know of a set of portfolios $\{X_i\}$ such that $E(\varepsilon_j | X_1, \ldots, X_m) = 0$, $j = 1, \ldots, n$, then by Theorem 4.5, $(X_1, \ldots, X_m, R)$ span Ψ^e. By Proposition 4.3, ordinary-least-squares (OLS) regression of the realized excess returns on security j, $Z_j - R$, on the realized excess returns of the spanning portfolios, $(X_1 - R, \ldots, X_m - R)$, will always give unbiased estimates of the $\{a_{ij}\}$. Of course, to apply time-series estimation, it must be assumed that the spanning portfolios $(X_1, \ldots, X_m)$ and $\{a_{ij}\}$ are intertemporally stable. For these estimators to be efficient, further restrictions on the $\{\varepsilon_j\}$ are required to satisfy the Gauss–Markov Theorem.

Early empirical studies of stock market securities' returns rarely found more than two or three statistically significant common factors.[13] Given that there are

---

[13]Cf. King (1966), Livingston (1977), Farrar (1962), Feeney and Hester (1967), and Farrell (1974). Unlike standard "factor analysis", the number of common factors here does not depend upon the fraction of total variation in an individual security's return that can be "explained". Rather, what is important is the number of factors necessary to "explain" the *covariation* between pairs of individual securities.

tens of thousands of different corporate liabilities traded in U.S. securities markets, there appears to be empirical foundation for the assumptions of the APT model. More-recent studies have, however, concluded that the number of common factors may be considerably larger, and some have raised serious questions about the prospect for identifying the factors by using stock-return data alone.[14]

Although the analyses derived here have been expressed in terms of restrictions on the joint distribution of security returns without explicitly mentioning security prices, it is obvious that these derived restrictions impose restrictions on prices through the identity that $Z_j \equiv V_j/V_{j0}$, where V_j is the random variable, end-of-period aggregate value of security j and V_{j0} is its initial value. Hence, given the characteristics of any two of these variables, the characteristics of the third are uniquely determined. For the study of equilibrium pricing, the usual format is to determine equilibrium V_{j0} given the distribution of V_j.

Theorem 4.13. *If $(X_1, \ldots, X_m)$ denote a set of linearly independent portfolios that satisfy the hypothesis of Theorem 4.5, and all securities have finite variances, then a necessary condition for equilibrium in the securities' market is that*

$$
V_{j0} = \frac{\bar{V}_j - \sum_1^m \sum_1^m v_{ik} \, \text{cov}[X_k, V_j](\bar{X}_i - R)}{R}, \quad j = 1, \ldots, n, \tag{4.3}
$$

where v_{ik} is the i-kth element of Ω_X^{-1}.

Proof. By linear independence, Ω_X is non-singular. From the identity $V_j \equiv Z_j V_{j0}$ and Theorem 4.5, $V_j = V_{j0}[R + \sum_1^m a_{ij}(X_i - R) + \varepsilon_j]$, where $E(\varepsilon_j \mid X_1, \ldots, X_m) = E(\varepsilon_j) = 0$. Taking expectations, we have that $\bar{V}_j = V_{j0}[R + \sum_1^m a_{ij}(\bar{X}_i - R)]$. Noting that $\text{cov}[X_k, V_j] = V_{j0} \, \text{cov}[X_k, Z_j]$, we have from Proposition 4.3 that $V_{j0} a_{ij} = \sum_1^m v_{ik} \, \text{cov}[X_k, V_j]$. By substituting for a_{ij} in the $\bar{V}_j$ expression and rearranging terms, the theorem is proved.

Hence, from Theorem 4.13, a sufficient set of information to determine the equilibrium value of security j is the first and second moments for the joint distribution of $(X_1, \ldots, X_m, V_j)$. Moreover, the valuation formula has the following important "linearity" properties:

Corollary 4.13a. *If the hypothesized conditions of Theorem 4.13 hold and if the end-of-period value of a security is given by $V = \sum_1^n \lambda_j V_j$, then in*

---

[14]There is considerable controversy on this issue. See Chamberlain and Rothschild (1983), Dhrymes, Friend and Gultekin (1984, 1985), Roll and Ross (1980), Rothschild (1986), Shanken (1982), and Trzcinka (1986).

equilibrium:

$$V_0 = \sum_1^n \lambda_j V_{j0} \, .$$

The proof of the corollary follows by substitution for V in formula (4.3). This property of formula (4.3) is called "value-additivity".

Corollary 4.13b. *If the hypothesized conditions of Theorem* 4.13 *hold and if the end-of-period value of a security is given by* $V = qV_j + u$, *where* $E(u) = E(u \mid X_1, \ldots, X_m) = \bar{u}$ *and* $E(q) = E(q \mid X_1, \ldots, X_m, V_j) = \bar{q}$, *then in equilibrium*:

$$V_0 = \bar{q} V_{j0} + \bar{u}/R \, .$$

The proof follows by substitution for V in formula (4.3) and by applying the hypothesized conditional-expectation conditions to show that $\text{cov}[X_k, V] = \bar{q} \, \text{cov}[X_k, V_j]$. Hence, to value two securities whose end-of-period values differ only by multiplicative or additive "noise", we can simply substitute the expected values of the noise terms.

As discussed in Merton (1982a, pp. 642–651), Theorem 4.13 and its corollaries are central to the theory of optimal investment decisions by business firms. To finance new investments, the firm can use internally available funds, issue common stock or issue other types of financial claims (e.g. debt, preferred stock, and convertible bonds). The selection from the menu of these financial instruments is called the firm's financing decision. Although the optimal investment and financing decisions by a firm generally require simultaneous determination, under certain conditions the optimal investment decision can be made independently of the method of financing.

Consider firm j with random variable end-of-period value V^j and q different financial claims. The kth such financial claim is defined by the function $f_k(V^j)$, which describes how the holders of this security will share in the end-of-period value of the firm. The production technology and choice of investment intensity, $V_j(I_j; \theta_j)$ and I_j, are taken as given where θ_j is a random variable. If it is assumed that the end-of-period value of the firm is independent of its choice of financial liabilities,[15] then $V^j = V_j(I_j; \theta_j)$, and $\sum_1^q f_k \equiv V_j(I_j; \theta_j)$ for every outcome θ_j.

---

[15]This assumption formally rules out financial securities that alter the tax liabilities of the firm (e.g. interest deductions) or ones that can induce "outside" costs (e.g. bankruptcy costs). However, by redefining $V_j(I_j; \theta_j)$ as the pre-tax-and-bankruptcy value of the firm and letting one of the f_k represent the government's tax claim and another the lawyers' bankruptcy-cost claim, the analysis in the text will be valid for these extended securities as well [cf. Merton (1990, ch. 13)].

Suppose that if firm j were all equity-financed, there exists an equilibrium such that the initial value of firm j is given by $V_{j0}(I_j)$.

Theorem 4.14. *If firm j is financed by q different claims defined by the functions $f_k(V^j)$, $k = 1, \ldots, q$, and if there exists an equilibrium such that the return distribution of the efficient portfolio set remains unchanged from the equilibrium in which firm j was all equity-financed, then*

$$\sum_1^q f_{k0} = V_{j0}(I_j),$$

where f_{k0} is the equilibrium initial value of financial claim k.

Proof. In the equilibrium in which firm j is all equity-financed, the end-of-period random variable value of firm j is $V_j(I_j; \theta_j)$ and the initial value, $V_{j0}(I_j)$, is given by formula (4.3), where $(X_1, \ldots, X_m, R)$ span the efficient set. Consider now that firm j is financed by the q different claims. The random variable end-of-period value of firm j, $\sum_1^q f_k$, is still given by $V_j(I_j; \theta_j)$. By hypothesis, there exists an equilibrium such that the distribution of the efficient portfolio set remains unchanged, and therefore the distribution of $(X_1, \ldots, X_m, R)$ remains unchanged. By inspection of formula (4.3), the initial value of firm j will remain unchanged, and therefore $\sum_1^q f_{k0} = V_{j0}(I_j)$.

Hence, for a given investment policy, the way in which the firm finances its investment will not affect the market value of the firm unless the choice of financial instruments changes the return distributions of the efficient portfolio set. Theorem 4.14 is representative of a class of theorems that describe the impact of financing policy on the market value of a firm when the investment decision is held fixed, and this class is generally referred to as the *Modigliani–Miller Hypothesis*, after the pioneering work in this direction by Modigliani and Miller.[16]

Clearly, a sufficient condition for Theorem 4.14 to obtain is that each of the financial claims issued by the firm are "redundant securities" whose payoffs can be replicated by combining already-existing securities. This condition is satisfied by the subclass of corporate liabilities that provide for *linear* sharing rules (i.e. $f_k(V) = a_k V + b_k$, where $\sum_1^q a_k = 1$ and $\sum_1^q b_k = 0$). Unfortunately, as will be shown in Section 8, most common types of financial instruments issued by corporations have non-linear payoff structures. As Stiglitz (1969, 1974) has shown for the Arrow–Debreu and Capital Asset Pricing Models,

---

[16]Modigliani and Miller (1958). See also Stiglitz (1969, 1974), Fama (1978), and Miller (1977). The "MM" concept has also been applied in other parts of monetary economics as in Wallace (1981).

linearity of the sharing rules is not a necessary condition for Theorem 4.14 to obtain. Nevertheless, the existence of non-linear payoff structures among wide classes of securities makes the establishment of conditions under which the hypothesis of Theorem 4.14 is valid no small matter.

Beyond the issue of whether firms can optimally separate their investment and financing decisions, the fact that many securities have non-linear sharing rules raises serious questions about the robustness of spanning models. As already discussed, the APT model, for example, has attracted much interest because it makes no explicit assumptions about preferences and places seemingly few restrictions on the joint probability distribution of security returns. In the APT model, $(X_1, \ldots, X_m, R)$ span the set of optimal portfolios and there exist m numbers $(a_{1k}, \ldots, a_{mk})$ for each security k, $k = 1, \ldots, n$, such that $Z_k = \sum_1^m a_{ik}(X_i - R) + R + \varepsilon_k$, where $E(\varepsilon_k) = E(\varepsilon_k | X_1, \ldots, X_m) = 0$.

Suppose that security k satisfies this condition and security q has a payoff structure that is given by $Z_q = f(Z_k)$, where f is a non-linear function. If security q is to satisfy this condition, then there must exist numbers $(a_{1q}, \ldots, a_{mq})$ so that for all possible values of $(X_1, \ldots, X_m)$, $E[f(\sum_1^m a_{ik}(X_i - R) + R + \varepsilon_k) | X_1, \ldots, X_m] = \sum_1^m a_{iq}(X_i - R) + R$. However, unless $\varepsilon_k \equiv 0$ and $\varepsilon_q \equiv 0$, such a set of numbers cannot be found for a general non-linear function f.

Since the APT model only has practical relevance if for most securities, $\mathrm{var}(\varepsilon_k) > 0$, it appears that the reconciliation of non-trivial spanning models with the widespread existence of securities with non-linear payoff structures requires further restrictions on either the probability distributions of securities returns or investor preferences. How restrictive these conditions are cannot be answered in the abstract. First, the introduction of general-equilibrium pricing conditions on securities will impose some restrictions on the joint distribution of returns. Second, the discussed benefits to individuals from having a set of spanning mutual funds may induce the creation of financial intermediaries or additional financial securities, that together with pre-existing securities will satisfy the conditions of Theorem 4.6. Although the intertemporal models of Sections 7–10 will explore these possibilities in detail, we examine here one important area of non-linear risk-sharing: namely, personal bankruptcy.

With limited liability on the n risky assets $(Z_j \geq 0, j = 1, \ldots, n)$, an unconstrained portfolio return, $Z = \sum_1^n w_j(Z_j - R) + R$, can take on negative values only if there is short selling (i.e. $w_j < 0$ for some j) or borrowing (i.e. $\sum_1^n w_j > 1$). In the formulation of the portfolio-selection problem, the investor's portfolio is placed in escrow as collateral for all loans. However, because the portfolio represents the investor's entire wealth, the value of the portfolio is the only recourse for the investor's creditors to be paid. Hence, if an investor's optimal unconstrained portfolio has the possibility that $Z^* < 0$, then the lenders of securities or cash may receive less than their promised payments.

Suppose, for example, that the investor's portfolio has $w_j^* \geq 0$ and $\sum_1^n w_j^* > 1$, so that he borrows. Under our assumptions that neglect personal bankruptcy, the investor borrows $(\sum_1^n w_j^* - 1)W_0$ and pays $R(\sum_1^n w_j^* - 1)W_0$ at the end of the period. If, however, we take account of personal bankruptcy, then the payment actually received by the investor's creditor is $R(\sum_1^n w_j^* - 1)W_0$ if $Z^* \geq 0$ and $[R(\sum_1^n w_j^* - 1) + Z^*]W_0 = (\sum_1^n w_j^* Z_j)W_0$ if $Z^* < 0$. Thus, the actual sharing rule between the investor and his creditor is that the investor receives $W_0 \max[0, Z^*]$ and the creditor receives $W_0 \min[(\sum_1^n w_j^* - 1)R, \sum_1^n w_j^* Z_j] = W_0[(\sum_1^n w_j^* - 1)R - \max(0, -Z^*)]$. Therefore, personal bankruptcy creates, de facto, a set of securities with payoffs that are non-linear functions of the returns on the n underlying risky assets.

Under the terms for borrowing and short selling in the unconstrained case, the investor's end-of-period wealth is given by $Z^* W_0$. Under the same terms, but with bankruptcy, the investor receives $W_0 \max[0, Z^*]$. In effect, the bankruptcy provision guarantees that the value of the investor's portfolio is never negative, and the provider of that guarantee is the investor's creditor. That is, the payoff pattern to the investor is as if he held the unconstrained portfolio, $Z^* W_0$, together with a "portfolio-value" guarantee with payoff $W_0 \max[0, -Z^*]$. But, of course, the lenders of securities and cash recognize that they are implicitly supplying this guarantee to the investor and realize that if $Z^* < 0$, they will receive less than their promised payments. They will therefore charge for the guarantee.

Let $F(w_1, \ldots, w_n)$ denote the price charged by creditors for a guarantee security with payoff function $\max(0, -\sum_1^n w_j(Z_j - R) - R)$. As will be discussed in Section 8, this payoff function is identical to the one for a put option (on the portfolio) with a zero exercise price. $F \geq 0$, and we assume that the price schedule is a twice-continuously-differentiable function. $F = 0$ only if creditors believe that $\text{prob}\{\sum_1^n w_j(Z_j - R) + R < 0\} = 0$, and $F_j(w_1, \ldots, w_n) \equiv \partial F(w_1, \ldots, w_n)/\partial w_j = 0$, $j = 1, \ldots, n$, if $\text{prob}\{\sum_1^n w_j(Z_j - R) + R > 0\} = 1$.

To capture the effect of personal bankruptcy and ensure the non-negativity of end-of-period wealth, we require that the investor must always purchase a guarantee security on his underlying risky-asset portfolio. The payoff function to one "unit" is $\sum_1^n w_j(Z_j - R) + R + \max(0, -\sum_1^n w_j(Z_j - R) - R) = \max(0, \sum_1^n w_j(Z_j - R) + R)$ and the price per unit is $1 + F(w_1, \ldots, w_n)$. The return per dollar invested in each unit is thus $\max(0, \sum_1^n w_j(Z_j - R) + R)/[1 + F(w_1, \ldots, w_n)]$. The portfolio-selection problem taking account of personal bankruptcy is formulated as:

$$\max_{\{w_1, \ldots, w_n\}} \text{E}\left\{ U\left[\max\left(0, \sum_1^n w_j(Z_j - R) + R\right) W_0/[1 + F(w_1, \ldots, w_n)] \right] \right\}.$$

$$(4.4)$$

If the price schedule $\{F\}$ is such that an interior maximum exists, then the first-order conditions for the optimal portfolio, $(Z^* = \sum_1^n w_j^*(Z_j - R) + R)$, are given by

$$E^+\left\{U'[Z^*W_0/(1 + F^*)]\left[Z_j - R - \frac{F_j^* Z^*}{(1 + F^*)}\right]\right\} = 0, \quad j = 1, \dots, n,$$

$$(4.5)$$

where E^+ is the partial-expectation operator over the portion of the joint distribution of $Z_1, \dots, Z_n$ such that $Z^* \geq 0$; $F^* = F(w_1^*, \dots, w_n^*)$, and $F_j^* = F_j(w_1^*, \dots, w_n^*)$, $j = 1, \dots, n$.

With homogeneous probability beliefs among investors and creditors, if prob$\{Z^* > 0\} = 1$, then $E^+ = E$, $F^* = 0$, and $F_j^* = 0$, $j = 1, \dots, n$. Hence, for all such optimal portfolios, we have from (4.5) that $E\{U'[Z^*W_0](Z_j - R)\} = 0$, $j = 1, \dots, n$, which is identical to (2.4). Therefore, the optimal portfolios selected by these investors will be the same with or without explicit recognition of the personal-bankruptcy constraint.

By inspection, the solution for Z^* in (4.5) depends on the price schedule $\{F\}$ and therefore, without further specification, little can be said about the relation between such portfolios and the portfolios contained in the unconstrained efficient portfolio set, Ψ^e. Consider, however, an institutional environment in which there is a default-free intermediary that will buy and sell put options on any security or portfolio of securities. $F(w_1, \dots, w_n)$ must, therefore, equal the price of a put option with zero exercise price on a portfolio with return $\sum_1^n w_j(Z_j - R) + R$. Because the put options are traded, personal-portfolio equilibrium in an unconstrained environment requires that the returns on these put options satisfy (2.4) in the same way that any Z_j does. Hence, for any $Z_e \in \Psi^e$ and any $(w_1, \dots, w_n)$, we have that

$$E\left\{V'(Z_e)\left[\frac{\max\left(0, \sum_1^n w_j(Z_j - R) + R\right)}{[1 + F(w_1, \dots, w_n)]} - R\right]\right\} = 0,$$

$$(4.6)$$

where V is the strictly risk-averse utility function such that Z_e is the associated optimal portfolio. We can rewrite (4.6) as:

$$1 + F(w_1, \dots, w_n) = E\left\{G(Z_e)\max\left(0, \sum_1^n w_j(Z_j - R) + R\right)\right\}\Big/ R$$

$$= E^+\left\{G(Z_e)\left(\sum_1^n w_j(Z_j - R) + R\right)\right\}\Big/ R,$$

$$(4.7)$$

where $G \equiv V'(Z_e)/E\{V'(Z_e)\}$ and, as in (4.5), E^+ is the partial-expectation operator over the region $\sum_1^n w_j(Z_j - R) + R \geq 0$. By differentiating (4.7), we have that

$$F_j(w_1, \ldots, w_n) = E^+\{G(Z_e)(Z_j - R)\}/R, \quad j = 1, \ldots, n. \tag{4.8}$$

An economic interpretation of pricing formula (4.7) is as follows. Let $dP(Z_1, \ldots, Z_n)$ denote the joint probability density function for $Z_1, \ldots, Z_n$. Define $dQ(Z_1, \ldots, Z_n) \equiv G(Z_e)\, dP(Z_1, \ldots, Z_n)$. By definition, $G > 0$ and $E\{G\} = 1$. Hence, dQ is a well-defined probability density function with the property that $dQ = 0$ if and only if $dP = 0$. From (4.7), the pricing function can be expressed as:

$$1 + F(w_1, \ldots, w_n) = E_Q\left\{\max\left(0, \sum_1^n w_j(Z_j - R) + R\right)\right\}/R \tag{4.9}$$

$$= E_Q^+\left\{\left(\sum_1^n w_j(Z_j - R) + R\right)\right\}/R,$$

where E_Q and E_Q^+ are the corresponding expectation operators over dQ. By inspection, (4.9) is the classic present value formula with discounting at the riskless interest rate. Because (4.9) applies for any choice of $(w_1, \ldots, w_n)$, it follows that the expected return (as measured over the dQ distribution) on every traded security is the same and equal to R. Hence, dQ is a "risk-adjusted" distribution for all traded securities. In the development of their utility-based pricing theory for warrants and options, Samuelson and Merton (1969) call dQ the "util-prob" distribution for security returns. Although all investors have the same dP, dQ will, in general, be different for each investor.

Under the pricing assumption of (4.7) and (4.8), we have the following connection between the set of optimal underlying risky-asset portfolios with personal bankruptcy and the unconstrained efficient portfolio set, Ψ^e.

Theorem 4.15. *If, for every $Z_e(\equiv \sum_1^n w_j^e(Z_j - R) + R) \in \Psi^e$, the portfolio-guarantee price schedule in (4.5) satisfies (4.7) and (4.8) for $w_j = w_j^e$, $j = 1, \ldots, n$, then for any strictly concave and increasing U, there exists a solution $(w_1^*, \ldots, w_n^*)$ to (4.5) such that $Z^* \in \Psi^e$.*

Proof. Consider any strictly concave and increasing U. Let Z^{**} denote the return on the associated optimal unconstrained portfolio, $(w_1^{**}, \ldots, w_n^{**})$, for initial wealth W_0^+. From (2.4), $E\{U'[Z^{**}W_0^+](Z_j - R)\} = 0$, $j = 1, \ldots, n$, and hence, $Z^{**} \in \Psi^e$. Therefore, by hypothesis, (4.7) and (4.8) apply for $G = U'[Z^{**}W_0^+]/E\{U'[Z^{**}W_0^+]\}$ and $w_j = w_j^{**}$, $j = 1, \ldots, n$. From (4.7) and

(4.8), it follows that $F_j(w_1^{**}, \ldots, w_n^{**})/[1 + F(w_1^{**}, \ldots, w_n^{**})] = E^+\{U'[Z^{**}W_0^+](Z_j - R)\}/E^+\{U'[Z^{**}W_0^+]Z^{**}\}$, $j = 1, \ldots, n$. By rearranging terms, $E^+\{U'[Z^{**}W_0^+][Z_j - R - F_j(w_1^{**}, \ldots, w_n^{**})Z^{**}/[1 + F(w_1^{**}, \ldots, w_n^{**})]]\} = 0$, $j = 1, \ldots, n$. Therefore, by inspection, for $w_j^* = w_j^{**}$, $j = 1, \ldots, n$, and $W_0^* = W_0/(1 + F^*)$, $Z^* = Z^{**}$, will satisfy (4.5). Hence, there exists a solution to (4.5) such that $Z^* \in \Psi^e$.

Provided that the solution to (4.5) is unique, under the hypothesized conditions of Theorem 4.15, any set of portfolios, $(X_1, \ldots, X_m, R)$, that spans Ψ^e will also span the set of optimal underlying risky-asset portfolios $\{Z^*\}$, which take account of the personal bankruptcy constraint.

To motivate the pricing schedule given in (4.7) and (4.8), we posited the existence of a default-free intermediary that buys or sells put options on any security or portfolio. This assumption implies a very rich set of available risk-sharing financial instruments for investors. Although sufficient, such a set is not required for the hypothesized conditions of Theorem 4.15 to obtain. Suppose, for example, that no put options are traded, and the intermediary issues only portfolio guarantees as part of a unit containing the underlying risky-asset portfolio and restricts each investor to the purchase of only one type of unit. If borrowing and short selling are permitted, this is no more than an institutional representation for the lenders of securities and cash, and there is, otherwise, no expansion in the set of risk-sharing opportunities for investors. Nevertheless, provided that prices charged for the guarantees satisfy (4.7) and (4.8), Theorem 4.15 still obtains. Moreover, (4.7) and (4.8) are consistent with competitive-equilibrium pricing provided that the intermediary is default free.

Theorem 4.15 will not apply for portfolios in Ψ^e such that there is no feasible investment strategy for the intermediary to ensure no default if it charges a finite price for the portfolio guarantee. Two models in which such feasible strategies always exist and Theorem 4.15 applies are the Arrow–Debreu complete-markets model and the continuous-time, intertemporal model. Indeed, Theorem 4.15 was first proved by Cox and Huang (1989) in the context of the continuous-time model. However, the effects of the non-linearities induced by personal bankruptcy on the spanning theorems for the static model of this section are not as yet fully worked out.

An alternative approach to the development of non-trivial spanning theorems is to derive a class of utility functions for investors such that even with arbitrary joint probability distributions for the available securities, investors within the class can generate their optimal portfolios from the spanning portfolios. Let Ψ^u denote the set of optimal portfolios selected from Ψ^f by investors with strictly concave von Neumann–Morgenstern utility functions $\{U_i\}$. Cass and Stiglitz (1970) have proved the following theorem.

Theorem 4.16. *There exists a portfolio with return X such that (X, R) span Ψ^u if and only if $A_i(W) = 1/(a_i + bW) > 0$, where A_i is the absolute risk-aversion function for investor i in Ψ^u.*[17]

The family of utility functions whose absolute risk-aversion functions can be written as $1/(a + bW) > 0$ is called the "HARA" (hyperbolic absolute risk aversion) family.[18] By appropriate choices for a and b, various members of the family will exhibit increasing, decreasing, or constant absolute and relative risk-aversion. Hence, if each investor's utility function could be approximated by some member of the HARA family, then it might appear that this alternative approach would be fruitful. However, it should be emphasized that the b in the statement of Theorem 4.16 does not have a subscript i, and therefore, for separation to obtain, all investors in Ψ^u must have virtually the same utility function.[19] Moreover, they must agree on the joint probability distribution for $(Z_1, \ldots, Z_n)$. Hence, the only significant way in which investors can differ is in their endowments of initial wealth.

Cass and Stiglitz (1970) also examine the possibilities for more-general non-trivial spanning (i.e. $1 \le m < n$) by restricting the class of utility functions and conclude, ". . . it is the requirement that there be *any* mutual funds, and not the limitation on the *number* of mutual funds, which is the restrictive feature of the property of separability" (p. 144). Hence, the Cass and Stiglitz analysis is essentially a negative report on this approach to developing spanning theorems.

In closing this section, two further points should be made. First, although virtually all the spanning theorems require the generally implausible assumption that all investors agree upon the joint probability distribution for securities, it is not so unreasonable when applied to the theory of financial intermediation and mutual fund management. In a world where the economic concepts of "division of labor" and "comparative advantage" have content, then it is quite reasonable to expect that an efficient allocation of resources would lead to some individuals (the "fund managers") gathering data and actively estimating the joint probability distributions and the rest either buying this information directly or delegating their investment decisions by "agreeing to agree" with the fund managers' estimates. If the distribution of returns is

---

[17] For this family of utility functions, the probability distribution for securities cannot be completely arbitrary without violating the von Neumann–Morgenstern axioms. For example, it is required that for every realization of W, $W > -a/b$ for $b > 0$ and $W < -a/b$ for $b < 0$. The latter condition is especially restrictive.

[18] A number of authors have studied the properties of this family. See Merton (1971, p. 389) for references.

[19] As discussed in footnote 17, the range of values for a_i cannot be arbitrary for a given b. Moreover, the sign of b uniquely determines the sign of $A'(W)$.

such that non-trivial spanning of Ψ^e does not obtain, then there are no gains to financial intermediation over the direct sale of the distribution estimates. However, if non-trivial spanning does obtain and the number of risky spanning portfolios, m, is small, then a significant reduction in redundant information processing and transactions can be produced by the introduction of mutual funds. If a significant coalition of individuals can agree upon a common source for the estimates and if they know that, based on this source, a group of mutual funds offered spans Ψ^e, then they need only be provided with the joint distribution for these mutual funds to form their optimal portfolios. On the supply side, if the characteristics of a set of spanning portfolios can be identified, then the mutual fund managers will know how to structure the portfolios of the funds they offer. We explore this point further in Section 9.

The second point concerns the riskless security. It has been assumed throughout that there exists a riskless security. Although some of the specifications will change slightly, virtually all the derived theorems can be shown to be valid in the absence of a riskless security.[20] However, the existence of a riskless security vastly simplifies many of the proofs.

5. Two special models of one-period portfolio selection

The two most cited models in the literature of portfolio selection are the *time–state preference model* of Arrow (1953, 1964) and Debreu (1959) and the *mean–variance model* of Markowitz (1959) and Tobin (1958). Because these models have been central to the development of the microeconomic theory of investment, there are already many review and survey articles devoted just to each of these models.[21] Hence, only a focused description of each model is presented here, with specific emphasis on how each model fits within the framework of the analyses presented in the other sections. In particular, we show that these models are special cases of the spanning models of the preceding section. We also use the Arrow–Debreu model to re-examine the portfolio-selection problem with the non-negativity constraint on wealth. Under appropriate conditions, both the Arrow–Debreu and Markowitz–Tobin models can be interpreted as multi-period, intertemporal portfolio-selection models. However, such an interpretation is postponed until later sections.

The structure of the Arrow–Debreu model is described as follows. Consider an economy where all possible configurations for the economy at the end of the period can be described in terms of M possible states of nature. The states are

---

[20]Cf. Ross (1978) for spanning proofs in the absence of a riskless security. Black (1972) and Merton (1972) derive the two-fund theorem for the mean–variance model with no riskless security.

[21]For the Arrow–Debreu model, see Hirshleifer (1965, 1966, 1970), Myers (1968), and Radner (1972). For the mean–variance model, see Jensen (1972a, 1972b), and Sharpe (1970).

mutually exclusive and exhaustive. It is assumed that there are N risk-averse individuals with initial wealth W_0^k and a von Neumann–Morgenstern utility function $U^k(W)$ for investor k, $k = 1, \ldots, N$. Each individual acts on the basis of subjective probabilities for the states of nature denoted by $P_k(\theta)$, $\theta = 1, \ldots, M$. While these subjective probabilities can differ across investors, it is assumed for each investor that $0 < P_k(\theta) < 1$, $\theta = 1, \ldots, M$. As was assumed in Section 2, there are n risky securities with returns per dollar Z_j and initial market value, V_{j0}, $j = 1, \ldots, n$, and the "perfect market" assumptions of that section, Assumptions 1–4, are assumed here as well. Moreover, if state θ obtains, then the return on security j will be $Z_j(\theta)$, and all investors agree on the functions $\{Z_j(\theta)\}$. Because the set of states is exhaustive, $[Z_j(1), \ldots, Z_j(M)]$ describe all the possible outcomes for the returns on security j. In addition, there are available M "*pure*" securities with the properties that, $i = 1, \ldots, M$, one unit (share) of pure security i will be worth \$1 at the end of the period if state i obtains and will be worthless if state i does not obtain. If Π_i denotes the price per share of pure security i and if X_i denotes its return per dollar, then for $i = 1, \ldots, M$, X_i as a function of the states of nature can be written as $X_i(\theta) = 1/\Pi_i$ if $\theta = i$ and $X_i(\theta) = 0$ if $\theta \neq i$. All investors agree on the functions $\{X_i(\theta)\}$, $i, \theta = 1, \ldots, M$.

Let $Z = Z(N_1, \ldots, N_M)$ denote the return per dollar on a portfolio of pure securities that holds N_j shares of pure security j, $j = 1, \ldots, M$. If $V_0(N_1, \ldots, N_M) \equiv \Sigma_1^M N_j \Pi_j$ denotes the initial value of this portfolio, then the return per dollar on the portfolio, as a function of the states of nature, can be written as $Z(\theta) = N_\theta/V_0$, $\theta = 1, \ldots, M$.

Proposition 5.1. *There exists a riskless security, and its return per dollar R equals $1/(\Sigma_1^M \Pi_j)$.*

Proof. Consider the pure-security portfolio that holds one share of each pure security $(N_j = 1, j = 1, \ldots, M)$. The return per dollar Z is the same in every state of nature and equals $1/V_0(1, \ldots, 1)$. Hence, there exists a riskless security and, by Assumption 3, its return R is given by $1/(\Sigma_1^M \Pi_j)$.

Proposition 5.2. *For each security j with return Z_j, there exists a portfolio of pure securities, whose return per dollar exactly replicates Z_j.*

Proof. Let $Z^j \equiv Z(Z_j(1), \ldots, Z_j(M))$ denote the return on a portfolio of pure securities with $N_\theta = Z_j(\theta)$, $\theta = 1, \ldots, M$. It follows that $V_0(Z_j(1), \ldots, Z_j(M)) = \Sigma_1^M \Pi_i Z_j(i)$ and $Z^j(\theta) = Z_j(\theta)/V_0$, $\theta = 1, \ldots, M$. Consider a three-security portfolio with return Z_p where fraction V_0 is invested in Z^j; fraction -1 is invested in Z_j; and fraction $1 - V_0 - (-1) = (2 - V_0)$ is invested in the riskless security. The return per dollar on this portfolio as a function of the states of nature can be written as:

$$Z_p(\theta) = (2 - V_0)R + V_0 Z^j(\theta) - Z_j(\theta) = (2 - V_0)R ,$$

which is the same for all states. Hence, Z_p is a riskless security, and by Assumption 3, $Z_p(\theta) = R$. Therefore, $V_0 = 1$, and $Z^j(\theta) = Z_j(\theta)$, $\theta = 1, \ldots, M$.

Proposition 5.3. *The set of pure securities with returns $(X_1, \ldots, X_M)$ span the set of all feasible portfolios that can be constructed from the M pure securities and the n other securities.*

The proof follows immediately from Propositions 5.1 and 5.2. Hence, whenever a complete set of pure securities exists or can be constructed from the available securities, then every feasible portfolio can be replicated by a portfolio of pure securities. Models in which such a set of pure securities exists are called *complete-markets models* in the sense that any additional securities or markets would be redundant. Necessary and sufficient conditions for such a set to be constructed from the available n risky securities alone and therefore, for markets to be complete, are that $n \geq M$; a riskless asset can be created and Assumption 3 holds; and the rank of the variance–covariance matrix of returns, Ω, equals $M - 1$.

The connection between the pure securities of the Arrow–Debreu model and the mutual fund theorems of Section 4 is immediate. To put this model in comparable form, we can choose the alternative spanning set $(X_1, \ldots, X_m, R)$, where $m \equiv M - 1$. From Theorem 4.3, the returns on the risky securities can be written as:

$$Z_j = R + \sum_1^m a_{ij}(X_i - R) , \quad j = 1, \ldots, n , \tag{5.1}$$

where the numbers (a_{ij}) are given by Proposition 4.3.

Note that nowhere in the derivation were the subjective probability assessments of the individual investors required. Hence, individual investors need not agree on the joint distribution for $(X_1, \ldots, X_m)$. However, by Theorem 4.3, investors cannot have arbitrary beliefs in the sense that they must agree on the (a_{ij}) in (5.1).

Proposition 5.4. *If $V_j(\theta)$ denotes the end-of-period value of security j, if state θ obtains, then a necessary condition for equilibrium in the securities market is that*

$$V_{j0} = \sum_1^M \Pi_k V_j(k) , \quad j = 1, \ldots, n .$$

The proof follows immediately from the proof of Proposition 5.2. It was shown there that $V_0 = \sum_1^M \Pi_k Z_j(k) = 1$. Multiplying both sides by V_{j0} and noting the identity $V_j(k) \equiv V_{j0} Z_j(k)$, it follows that $V_{j0} = \sum_1^M \Pi_k V_j(k)$.

However, by Theorem 4.13 and Proposition 5.3, it follows that the $\{V_{j0}\}$ can also be written as:

$$V_{j0} = \frac{\bar{V}_j - \sum_1^m \sum_1^m v_{ik} \operatorname{cov}[X_k, V_j](\bar{X}_i - R)}{R} , \quad j = 1, \ldots, n , \qquad (5.2)$$

where v_{ik} is the i-kth element of Ω_X^{-1}. Hence, from (5.2) and Proposition 5.4, it follows that the (a_{ij}) in (5.1) can be written as:

$$a_{ij} = [Z_j(i) - R]/[1/\Pi_i - R] , \quad i = 1, \ldots, m; \quad j = 1, \ldots, n . \qquad (5.3)$$

From (5.3), given the prices of the securities $\{\Pi_i\}$ and $\{V_{i0}\}$, the $\{a_{ij}\}$ will be agreed upon by all investors if and only if they agree upon the $\{V_j(i)\}$ functions.

While it is commonly believed that the Arrow–Debreu model is completely general with respect to assumptions about investors' beliefs, the assumption that all investors agree on the $\{V_j(i)\}$ functions can impose non-trivial restrictions on these beliefs. In particular, when there is production, it will in general be inappropriate to define the states, tautologically, by the end-of-period values of the securities, and therefore investors will at least have to agree on the technologies specified for each firm.[22] However, as discussed in Section 4, it is unlikely that a model without some degree of homogeneity in beliefs (other than agreement on currently observed variables) can produce testable restrictions. Among models that do produce such testable restrictions, the assumptions about investors' beliefs in the Arrow–Debreu model are among the most general.

To perhaps provide further intuition about the solution of the portfolio-

---

[22]If the states are defined in terms of end-of-period values of the firm in addition to "environmental" factors, then the firms' production decisions will, in general, alter the state–space description which violates the assumptions of the model. Moreover, I see no obvious reason why individuals are any more likely to agree upon the $\{V_j(i)\}$ functions than upon the probability distributions for the environmental factors. If sufficient information is available to partition the states into fine enough categories to produce agreement on the $\{V_j(i)\}$ functions, then, given this information, it is difficult to imagine how rational individuals would have heterogeneous beliefs about the probability distributions for these states. As with the standard certainty model, agreement on the technologies is necessary for Pareto optimality in this model. However, as Peter Diamond has pointed out to me, it is not sufficient. Sufficiency demands the stronger requirement that everyone be "right" in their assessment of the technologies. See Varian (1985) and Black (1986, footnote 5) on whether differences of opinion among investors can be supported in this model.

selection problem with the non-negativity constraint on wealth as analyzed in Section 4, we reformulate that problem in the context of the Arrow–Debreu model as follows: the investor selects a portfolio of pure securities so as to maximize his expected utility of end-of-period wealth, subject to his budget constraint and the feasibility requirement that wealth cannot be negative. Without loss of generality, we can restrict the choices to just the pure securities, because from Proposition 5.3 these securities span the set of all feasible portfolios.

If N_j denotes the number of shares of pure security j held, $j = 1, \ldots, M$, then the budget constraint requires that $W_0 = \sum_1^M N_j \Pi_j$. If $W(\theta)$ denotes end-of-period wealth in state θ, then from the payoff structure for pure securities, $W(\theta) = N_\theta$, and the non-negativity-of-wealth constraint implies that $N_\theta \geq 0$, $\theta = 1, \ldots, M$. The constrained optimization problem can thus be expressed as:

$$\max_{\{N_j\}} \left\{ \sum_1^M P(j)U(N_j) + \lambda \left[W_0 - \sum_1^M \Pi_j N_j \right] + \sum_1^M \gamma_j N_j \right\}, \tag{5.4}$$

where $P(\theta)$ is the investor's subjective probability for state θ and λ and $\gamma_1, \ldots, \gamma_M$ are Kuhn–Tucker multipliers.

From (5.4), the first-order conditions for the optimal portfolio $\{N_j^*\}$ can be written as:

$$0 = P(j)U'(N_j^*) - \lambda^* \Pi_j + \gamma_j^*, \quad j = 1, \ldots, M, \tag{5.5a}$$

$$0 = W_0 - \sum_1^M \Pi_j N_j^*, \tag{5.5b}$$

$$0 = \gamma_j^* N_j^*, \quad j = 1, \ldots, M. \tag{5.5c}$$

Because $U' > 0$ and $U'' < 0$, we have from (5.5a) and (5.5c) that

$$\gamma_j^* = \max[0, \lambda^* \Pi_j - P(j)U'(0)], \quad j = 1, \ldots, M. \tag{5.6}$$

As noted in footnote 7, we have by inspection of (5.6) that $\gamma_j^* = 0$, $j = 1, \ldots, M$, if $U'(0) = \infty$, and therefore, for such utility functions, the non-negativity constraint on wealth is never binding.

Because U' is monotonic and strictly decreasing, it is globally invertible. Define $G(y) \equiv (U')^{-1}(y)$. From (5.5a) and (5.5c) we have that

$$N_j^* = \max[0, G(\lambda^* \Pi_j / P(j))], \quad j = 1, \ldots, M. \tag{5.7}$$

Thus, from (5.7), only the multiplier λ^* need be found to complete the solution for the optimal portfolio. Substituting for N_j^* from (5.7) into (5.5b) we have that

$$0 = W_0 - \sum_1^M \Pi_j \max[0, G(\lambda^* \Pi_j / P(j))] . \tag{5.8}$$

Because $dG/dy < 0$ and $\Pi_j \geq 0$, λ^* can be determined as the unique solution to the algebraic transcendental equation (5.8).

To compare the solution to the portfolio problem here with the solutions of the preceding sections that do not take explicit account of the non-negativity constraint on wealth, note that the unconstrained formulation of (5.4) simply imposes $\gamma_j \equiv 0$, $j = 1, \ldots, M$. If $\{N_j^{**}\}$ denotes the optimal unconstrained solution, then from (5.5a) with $\gamma_j^* = 0$, we have that

$$N_j^{**} = G(\lambda^{**} \Pi_j / P(j)) , \quad j = 1, \ldots, M , \tag{5.9}$$

where λ^{**} is the multiplier associated with the budget constraint (5.5b). As in (5.8), λ^{**} is determined as the solution to:

$$0 = W_0 - \sum_1^M \Pi_j G(\lambda^{**} \Pi_j / P(j)) . \tag{5.10}$$

Noting that $\max[0, G(\lambda^* \Pi_j / P(j))] = G(\lambda^* \Pi_j / P(j)) + \max[0, -G(\lambda^* \Pi_j / P(j))]$, we can rearrange terms and rewrite (5.8) as:

$$W_0^+ = \sum_1^M \Pi_j G(\lambda^* \Pi_j / P(j)) , \tag{5.11}$$

where $W_0^+ \equiv W_0 - \sum_1^M \Pi_j \max[0, -G(\lambda^* \Pi_j / P(j))]$. If the non-negativity constraint in (5.4) is binding, so that the constrained and unconstrained solutions are not identical, then for at least one state j, $G(\lambda^* \Pi_j / P(j)) < 0$. It follows from the definition of W_0^+ that $W_0^+ < W_0$. By inspection of (5.10) and (5.11), we see that the formal structure of the constrained solution is the same as for the unconstrained solution, except that the value of the initial endowment in the latter case, W_0^+, is smaller.

From (5.9) and (5.10), the optimal unconstrained portfolio allocation depends on initial wealth, W_0 [i.e. $N_j^{**} = N_j^{**}(W_0)$]. The end-of-period value of the optimal portfolio in state j is given by $W^{**}(j) = N_j^{**}(W_0)$, $j = 1, \ldots, M$. The payoff structure to a security that makes up the "shortfall" between the payoffs to this unconstrained portfolio and zero is given by $\max[0, -W^{**}(j)]$ in state j, $j = 1, \ldots, M$. As discussed in Section 4, this security can be interpreted as a portfolio-value or loan guarantee that pays the difference between the promised payments to the investor's creditors and the value of the portfolio. From Proposition 5.4, the equilibrium initial price of such a guarantee, $F[W_0]$, is given by:

$$F[W_0] = \sum_1^M \Pi_j \max[0, -W^{**}(j)]$$

$$= \sum_1^M \Pi_j \max[0, -N_j^{**}(W_0)]. \tag{5.12}$$

As in Section 4, we have a rather intuitive economic interpretation of the optimal constrained portfolio strategy: the investor solves for his optimal unconstrained portfolio as a function of initial wealth, $\{N_j^{**}(W_0)\}$. If $N_j^{**}(W_0) < 0$ for some state j, then to implement the strategy, the investor must borrow cash or short sell securities. However, the creditors making these loans recognize that the collateral (i.e. the portfolio) may have insufficient value to meet the promised payments. They therefore require that the investor purchase a loan guarantee either from them or from a third-party guarantor. Either way the investor pays for the guarantee and therefore he only has W_0^+ to allocate to the pure securities in his "unconstrained" portfolio, where W_0^+ is the solution to $0 = W_0^+ + F[W_0^+] - W_0$. Thus, his feasible unconstrained solution is $\{N_j^{**}(W_0^+)\}$. Although $N_j^{**}(W_0^+)$ may be negative in some states, the payoffs to the entire portfolio including the guarantee, $N_j^{**}(W_0^+) + \max[0, -N_j^{**}(W_0^+)]$, is always non-negative. From (5.9), (5.11), and (5.12) it is straightforward to show that $N_j^*(W_0) = N_j^{**}(W_0^+) + \max[0, -N_j^{**}(W_0^+)]$, $j = 1, \ldots, M$. If, of course, $N_j^{**}(W_0) \geq 0$ for $j = 1, \ldots, M$, then $F[W_0] = 0$ and $W_0^+ = W_0$.

As noted in Section 4, Cox and Huang (1989) were the first to recognize this relation between the unconstrained and constrained solutions, and although they did so in the framework of a continuous-time dynamic model, their derivation is more like the one here than the development in Section 4. In Sections 7–9 we analyze the non-negativity constraint and bankruptcy issue in the context of the continuous-time model. This completes our examination of the Arrow–Debreu model, and we turn now to the Markowitz–Tobin model.

The most elementary type of portfolio selection model in which all securities are not perfect substitutes is one where the attributes of every optimal portfolio can be characterized by two numbers: its "risk" and its "return". The mean–variance portfolio selection model of Markowitz (1959) and Tobin (1958) is such a model. In this model, each investor chooses his optimal portfolio so as to maximize a utility function of the form $H[E(W), \mathrm{var}(W)]$, subject to his budget constraint, where W is his random variable end-of-period wealth. The investor is said to be "risk-averse in a mean–variance sense" if $H_1 > 0$, $H_2 < 0$, $H_{11} < 0$, $H_{22} < 0$, and $H_{11}H_{22} - H_{12}^2 > 0$, where subscripts denote partial derivatives.

In an analogous fashion to the general definition of an efficient portfolio in Section 2, a feasible portfolio will be called a *mean–variance efficient portfolio* if there exists a risk-averse mean–variance utility function such that this feasible portfolio would be preferred to all other feasible portfolios. Let Ψ_{mv}^e denote the set of mean–variance efficient portfolios. As defined in Section 4, Ψ_{min} is the set of feasible portfolios such that there exists no other portfolio with the same expected return and a smaller variance. For a given initial wealth W_0, every risk-averse investor would prefer the portfolio with the smallest variance among those portfolios with the same expected return. Hence, Ψ_{mv}^e is contained in Ψ_{min}.

Proposition 5.5. *If $(Z_1, \ldots, Z_n)$ are the returns on the available risky securities, then there exists a portfolio contained in Ψ_{mv}^e with return X such that (X, R) span Ψ_{mv}^e and $\bar{Z}_j - R = a_j(\bar{X} - R)$, where $a_j \equiv \mathrm{cov}(Z_j, X)/\mathrm{var}(X)$, $j = 1, 2, \ldots, n$.*

The proof follows immediately from Theorem 4.9.[23] Hence, all the properties derived in the special case of two-fund spanning ($m = 1$) in Section 4 apply to the mean–variance model. Indeed, because all such investors would prefer a higher expected return for the same variance of return, Ψ_{mv}^e is the set of all portfolios contained in Ψ_{min}, such that their expected returns are equal to or exceed R. Hence, as with the complete-markets model, the mean–variance model is also a special case of the spanning models developed in Section 4.

If investors have homogeneous beliefs, then the equilibrium version of the mean–variance model is called the *Capital Asset Pricing Model*.[24] It follows from Proposition 4.5 and Theorem 4.7 that, in equilibrium, the market portfolio can be chosen as the risky spanning portfolio. From Theorem 4.8, the equilibrium structure of expected returns must satisfy the Security Market Line.

Because of the mean–variance model's attractive simplicity and its strong empirical implications, a number of authors[25] have studied the conditions

---

[23]In particular, the optimal portfolio demand functions are of the form derived in the proof of Theorem 4.9. For a complete analytic derivation, see Merton (1972).

[24]Sharpe (1964), Lintner (1965), and Mossin (1966) are generally credited with independent derivations of the model. Black (1972) extended the model to include the case of no riskless security.

[25]Cf. Borch (1969), Feldstein (1969), Tobin (1969), Samuelson (1967), and Chamberlain (1983).

under which such a criterion function is consistent with the expected utility maxim. Like the studies of general spanning properties cited in Section 4, these studies examined the question in two parts. (i) What is the class of probability distributions such that the expected value of an arbitrary concave utility function can be written solely as a function of mean and variance? (ii) What is the class of strictly concave von Neumann–Morgenstern utility functions whose expected value can be written solely as a function of mean and variance for arbitrary distributions? Since the class of distributions in (i) was shown in Section 4 to be equivalent to the class of finite-variance distributions that admit two-fund spanning of the efficient set, the analysis will not be repeated here. To answer (ii), it is straightforward to show that a necessary condition is that U have the form $W - bW^2$, with $b > 0$. This member of the HARA family is called the *quadratic* and will satisfy the von Neumann axioms only if $W \le 1/2b$ for all possible outcomes for W. Even if U is defined to be $\max[W - bW^2, 1/4b]$, so that U satisfies the axioms for all W, its expected value for general distributions can be written as a function of just $E(W)$ and $\text{var}(W)$ only if the maximum possible outcome for W is less than $1/2b$.

Although both the Arrow–Debreu and Markowitz–Tobin models were shown to be special cases of the spanning models in Section 4, they deserve special attention because they are unquestionably the genesis of these general models.

6. Intertemporal consumption and portfolio selection theory

As in the preceding analyses the majority of papers on investment theory under uncertainty have assumed that individuals act so as to maximize the expected utility of end-of-period wealth and that intraperiod revisions are not feasible. Therefore, all events which take place after next period are irrelevant to their decisions. Of course, investors do care about events beyond "next period", and they can review and change their allocations periodically. Hence, the one-period, static analyses will only be robust under those conditions such that an intertemporally-maximizing individual acts, each period, as if he were a one-period, expected utility-of-wealth maximizer. In this section the lifetime consumption–portfolio selection problem is solved, and conditions are derived under which the one-period static portfolio problem is an appropriate "surrogate" for the dynamic, multi-period portfolio problem.

As in the early contributions by Hakansson (1970), Samuelson (1969), and Merton (1969), the problem of choosing optimal portfolio and consumption rules for an individual who lives T years is formulated as follows. The individual investor chooses his consumption and portfolio allocation for each period so as to maximize[26]

$$E_0\left\{\sum_0^{T-1} U[C(t), t] + B[W(T), T]\right\},\tag{6.1}$$

where $C(t)$ is consumption chosen at age t; $W(t)$ is wealth at age t; E_t is the conditional expectation operator conditional on knowing all relevant information available as of time t; the utility function (during life) U is assumed to be strictly concave in C; and the "bequest" function B is also assumed to be concave in W.

It is assumed that there are n risky securities with random variable returns between time t and $t+1$ denoted by $Z_1(t+1), \ldots, Z_n(t+1)$, and there is a riskless security whose return between t and $t+1$, $R(t)$, will be known with certainty as of time t.[27] When the investor "arrives" at date t, we will know the value of his portfolio, $W(t)$. He chooses how much to consume, $C(t)$, and then reallocates the balance of his wealth, $W(t) - C(t)$, among the available securities. Hence, the accumulation equation between t and $t+1$ can be written as:[28]

$$W(t+1) = \left[\sum_1^n w_j(t)[Z_j(t+1) - R(t)] + R(t)\right][W(t) - C(t)],\tag{6.2}$$

where $w_j(t)$ is the fraction of his portfolio allocated to security j at date t, $j = 1, \ldots, n$. Because the fraction allocated to the riskless security can always be chosen to equal $1 - \sum_1^n w_j(t)$, the choices for $w_1(t), \ldots, w_n(t)$ are unconstrained.

It is assumed that there exist m state variables, $\{S_k(t)\}$, such that the

[26]The additive independence of the utility function and the single-consumption good assumptions are made for analytic simplicity and because the focus of the chapter is on capital market theory and not the theory of consumer choice. Fama (1970b) in discrete time and Meyer (1970) and Huang and Kreps (1985) in continuous time, analyze the problem for non-additive and temporally-dependent utilities. Although T is treated as known in the text, the analysis is essentially the same for an uncertain lifetime with T a random variable [cf. Richard (1975) and Merton (1971)]. The analysis is also little affected by making the direct-utility function "state-dependent" (i.e. having U depend on other variables in addition to consumption and time). See Merton (1990, ch. 6) for a summary of these various generalizations on preferences.

[27]This definition of a riskless security is purely technical and without normative significance. For example, investing solely in the riskless security will not allow for a certain consumption stream because $R(t)$ will vary stochastically over time. On the other hand, a T-period, riskless-in-terms-of-default coupon bond, which allows for a certain consumption stream, is not a riskless security because its one-period return is uncertain. For further discussion, see Merton (1970, 1973b).

[28]It is assumed that all income comes from investment in securities. The analysis would be the same with wage income provided that investors can sell shares against future income. However, because institutionally this cannot be done, the "non-marketability" of wage income will cause systematic effects on the portfolio and consumption decisions.

stochastic processes for $\{Z_1(t+1), \ldots, Z_n(t+1), R(t+1), S_1(t+1), \ldots, S_m(t+1)\}$ are Markov with respect to $S_1(t), \ldots, S_m(t)$, and $S(t)$ denotes the m-vector of state-variable values at time t.[29]

The method of stochastic dynamic programming is used to derive the optimal consumption and portfolio rules. Define the function $J[W(t), S(t), t]$ by:

$$J[W(t), S(t), t] \equiv \max \mathrm{E}_t \left\{ \sum_t^{T-1} U[C(\tau), \tau] + B[W(T), T] \right\}. \tag{6.3}$$

J, therefore, is the (utility) value of the balance of the investor's optimal consumption–investment program from date t forward and, in this context, is called the "derived" utility of wealth function. By the Principle of Optimality, (6.3) can be rewritten as:

$$J[W(t), S(t), t] = \max\{U[C(t), t] + \mathrm{E}_t(J[W(t+1), S(t+1), t+1])\}, \tag{6.4}$$

where "max" is over the current decision variables $[C(t), w_1(t), \ldots, w_n(t)]$. Substituting for $W(t+1)$ in (6.4) from (6.2) and differentiating with respect to each of the decision variables, we can write the $n+1$ first-order conditions for a regular interior maximum as:[30]

$$0 = U_C[C^*(t), t] - \mathrm{E}_t \left\{ J_W[W(t+1), S(t+1), t+1] \left(\sum_1^n w_j^*(Z_j - R) + R \right) \right\} \tag{6.5}$$

and

$$0 = \mathrm{E}_t\{J_W[W(t+1), S(t+1), t+1](Z_j - R)\}, \quad j = 1, 2, \ldots, n, \tag{6.6}$$

where $U_C \equiv \partial U / \partial C$, $J_W \equiv \partial J / \partial W$, and (C^*, w_j^*) are the optimal values for the decision variables. As in the static analysis of Section 2, we do not explicitly impose the feasibility conditions that $C^* \geq 0$ and $W \geq 0$. Henceforth, except where needed for clarity, the time indices will be dropped. Using (6.6), (6.5)

---

[29]Many non-Markov stochastic processes can be transformed to fit the Markov format by expanding the number of state variables [cf. Cox and Miller (1968, pp. 16–18)]. To avoid including "surplus" state variables, it is assumed that $\{S(t)\}$ represent the minimum number of variables necessary to make $\{Z_j(t+1)\}$ Markov.

[30]Cf. Dreyfus (1965) for the dynamic programming technique. Sufficient conditions for existence are described in Bertsekas (1974). Uniqueness of the solutions is guaranteed by: (1) strict concavity of U and B; (2) no redundant securities; and (3) no arbitrage opportunities. See Cox, Ingersoll and Ross (1985a) for corresponding conditions in the continuous-time version of the model.

can be written as:

$$0 = U_c[C^*, t] - RE_t\{J_W[W(t+1), S(t+1), t+1]\} . \tag{6.7}$$

To solve for the complete optimal program, one first solves (6.6) and (6.7) for C^* and w^* as functions of $W(t)$ and $S(t)$ when $t = T - 1$. This can be done because $J[W(T), S(T), T] = B[W(T), T]$, a known function. Substituting the solutions for $C^*(T-1)$ and $w^*(T-1)$ in the right-hand side of (6.4), (6.4) becomes an equation and, therefore, one has $J[W(T-1), S(T-1), T-1]$. Using (6.6), (6.7), and (6.4) one can proceed to solve for the optimal rules in earlier periods in the usual "backwards" recursive fashion of dynamic programming. Having done so, one has a complete schedule of optimal consumption and portfolio rules for each date expressed as functions of the (then) known state variables $W(t)$, $S(t)$, and t. Moreover, as Samuelson (1969) has shown, the optimal consumption rules will satisfy the "envelope condition" expressed as:

$$J_W[W(t), S(t), t] = U_c[C^*(t), t] , \tag{6.8}$$

i.e. at the optimum, the marginal utility of wealth (future consumption) will just equal the marginal utility of (current) consumption. Moreover, from (6.8), it is straightforward to show that $J_{WW} < 0$ because $U_{CC} < 0$. Hence, J is a strictly concave function of wealth.

A comparison of the first-order conditions for the static portfolio-selection problem, (2.4) in Section 2, with the corresponding conditions (6.6) for the dynamic problem will show that they are formally quite similar. Of course, they do differ in that, for the former case, the utility function of wealth is taken to be exogenous while, in the latter, it is derived. However, the more fundamental difference in terms of portfolio-selection behavior is that J is not only a function of W, but also a function of S. The analogous condition in the static case would be that the end-of-period utility function of wealth is also state dependent.

To see that this difference is not trivial, consider the Rothschild–Stiglitz definition of "riskier" that was used in the one-period analysis to partition the feasible portfolio set into its efficient and inefficient parts. Let W_1 and W_2 be the random variable, end-of-period values of two portfolios with identical expected values. If W_2 is equal in distribution to $W_1 + Z$, where $E(Z | W_1) = 0$, then from (2.10) and (2.11), W_2 is riskier than W_1 and every risk-averse maximizer of the expected utility of end-of-period wealth would prefer W_1 to W_2. However, consider an intertemporal maximizer with a strictly concave, derived utility function J. It will not, in general, be true that $E_t\{J[W_1, S(t+1), t+1]\} > E_t\{J[W_2, S(t+1), t+1]\}$. Therefore, although the intertemporal maximizer selects his portfolio for only one period at a time, the optimal portfolio selected may be one that would never be chosen by any risk-averse, one-period maximizer. Hence, the portfolio-selection behavior of an inter-temporal maximizer is, in general, operationally distinguishable from the behavior of a static maximizer.

To adapt the Rothschild–Stiglitz definition to the intertemporal case, a stronger condition is required: namely if W_2 is equal in distribution to $W_1 + Z$, where $E[Z|W_1, S(t+1)] = 0$, then every risk-averse intertemporal maximizer would prefer to hold W_1 rather than W_2 in the period t to $t+1$. The proof follows immediately from the concavity of J and Jensen's Inequality. Namely, $E_t\{J[W_2, S(t+1), t+1]\} = E_t\{E(J[W_2, S(t+1), t+1]|W_1, S(t+1))\}$. By Jensen's Inequality, $E(J[W_2, S(t+1), t+1]|W_1, S(t+1)) < J[E(W_2|W_1, S(t+1)), S(t+1), t+1] = J[W_1, S(t+1), t+1]$, and therefore $E_t\{J[W_2, S(t+1), t+1]\} < E_t\{J[W_1, S(t+1), t+1]\}$. Hence, "noise" as denoted by Z must not only be noise relative to W_1, but noise relative to the state variables $S_1(t+1), \ldots, S_m(t+1)$. All the analyses of the preceding sections can be formally adapted to the intertemporal framework by simply requiring that the "noise" terms there, ε, have the additional property that $E_t(\varepsilon|S(t+1)) = E_t(\varepsilon) = 0$. Hence, in the absence of further restrictions on the distributions, the resulting efficient portfolio set for intertemporal maximizers will be larger than in the static case.

However, under certain conditions,[31] the portfolio selection behavior of intertemporal maximizers will be "as if" they were one-period maximizers. For example, if $E_t[Z_j(t+1)] \equiv \bar{Z}_j(t+1) = E_t[Z_j(t+1)|S(t+1)]$, $j = 1, 2, \ldots, n$, then the additional requirement that $E_t(\varepsilon|S(t+1)) = 0$ will automatically be satisfied for any feasible portfolio, and the original Rothschild–Stiglitz "static" definition will be a valid. Indeed, in the cited papers by Hakansson, Samuel-son, and Merton, it is assumed that the security returns $\{Z_1(t), \ldots, Z_n(t)\}$ are serially independent and identically distributed in time which clearly satisfies this condition.

Define the *investment opportunity set at time t* to be the joint distribution for $\{Z_1(t+1), \ldots, Z_n(t+1)\}$ and the return on the riskless security, $R(t)$. The Hakansson et al. papers assume that the investment opportunity set is constant through time. The condition $\bar{Z}_j(t+1) = E_t[Z_j(t+1)|S(t+1)]$, $j = 1, \ldots, n$, will also be satisfied if changes in the investment opportunity set are either completely random or time dependent in a non-stochastic fashion. Moreover, with the possible exception of a few special cases, these are the only conditions on the investment opportunity set under which $\bar{Z}_j(t+1) = E_t[Z_j(t+1)|S(t+1)]$, $j = 1, \ldots, n$. Hence, for arbitrary concave utility functions, the one-period analysis will be a valid surrogate for the intertemporal analysis only if changes in the investment opportunity set satisfy these conditions.

---

[31] See Fama (1970b) for a general discussion of these conditions.

Of course, by inspection of (6.6), if J were of the form $V[W(t), t] + H[S(t), t]$ so that $J_W = V_W$ is only a function of wealth and time, then for arbitrary investment opportunity sets such an intertemporal investor will act "as if" he is a one-period maximizer. Unfortunately, the only concave utility function that will produce such a J function and satisfy the additivity specification in (6.1) is $U[C, t] = a(t) \log[C]$ and $B[W, T] = b(T) \log[W]$, where either $a = 0$ and $b > 0$ or $a > 0$ and $b \geq 0$. While some have argued that this utility function is of special normative significance,[32] any model whose results depend singularly upon all individuals having the same utility function and where, in addition, the utility function must have a specific form, can only be viewed as an example, and not the basis for a general theory.

Hence, in general, the one-period static analysis will not be rich enough to describe the investor behavior in an intertemporal framework. Indeed, without additional assumptions, the only derived restrictions on optimal demand functions and equilibrium security returns are the ones that rule out arbitrage. Hence, to deduce additional properties, further assumptions about the dynamics of the investment opportunity set are needed.

7. Consumption and portfolio selection theory in the continuous-time model

There are three time intervals or horizons involved in the consumption–portfolio problem.[33] First, there is the *trading horizon*, which is the *minimum* length of time between which successive transactions by economic agents can be made in the market. In a sequence-of-markets analysis, it is the length of time between successive market openings, and is therefore part of the specification of the structure of markets in the economy. While this structure will depend upon the tradeoff between the costs of operating the market and its benefits, this time scale is not determined by the individual investor, and is the same for all investors in the economy. Second, there is the *decision horizon*, which is the length of time between which the investor makes successive decisions, and it is the minimum time between which he would take any action. For example, an investor with a fixed decision interval of one month, who makes a consumption decision and portfolio allocation today, will under no conditions make any new decisions or take any action prior to one month from

---

[32]See Latane (1959), Markowitz (1976), and Rubinstein (1976) for arguments in favor of this view, and Samuelson (1971), Goldman (1974), and Merton and Samuelson (1974) for arguments in opposition to this view.

[33]These introductory paragraphs are adapted from Merton (1975, pp. 662–663). See the books by Duffie (1988), Ingersoll (1987), and Merton (1990) for development of the continuous-time model and extensive bibliographies.

now. This time scale is determined by the costs to the individual of processing information and making decisions, and is chosen by the individual. Third, there is the *planning horizon*, which is the maximum length of time for which the investor gives any weight in his utility function. Typically, this time scale would correspond to the balance of his lifetime and is denoted by T in the formulation (6.1).

The static approach to portfolio selection implicitly assumes that the individual's decision and planning horizons are the same: "one period". While the intertemporal approach distinguishes between the two, when individual demands are aggregated to determine market equilibrium relations, it is implicitly assumed in both approaches that the decision interval is the same for all investors, and therefore corresponds to the trading interval.

If h denotes the length of time in the trading interval, then every solution derived has, as an implicit argument, h. Clearly, if h changes, then the derived behavior of investors would change, as indeed would any deduced equilibrium relations.[34] I might mention, somewhat parenthetically, that empirical researchers often neglect to recognize that h is part of a model's specification. For example, in Theorem 4.6 the returns on securities were shown to have a linear relation to the returns on a set of spanning portfolios. However, because the n-period return on a security is the *product* (and not the sum) of the one-period returns, this linear relation can only obtain for the single time interval, h. If we define a fourth time interval, the *observation horizon*, to be the length of time between successive observations of the data by the researcher, then the usual empirical practice is to implicitly assume that the decision and trading intervals are equal to the observation interval. This is done whether the observation interval is daily, weekly, monthly, or annually!

If the frictionless-markets assumption (Assumption 1) is extended to include no costs of information processing or operating the markets, then it follows that all investors would prefer to have h as small as physically possible. Indeed, the aforementioned general assumption that all investors have the same decision interval will, in general, only be valid if all such costs are zero. This said, it is natural to examine the limiting case when h tends to zero and trading takes place continuously in time.

Consider an economy where the trading interval, h, is sufficiently small that the state description of the economy can change only "locally" during the interval $(t, t + h)$. Formally, the Markov stochastic processes for the state variables, $S(t)$, are assumed to satisfy the property that one-step transitions are permitted only to the nearest neighboring states. The analogous condition in

---

[34]If investor behavior were invariant to h, then investors would choose the same portfolio if they were "frozen" into their investments for ten years as they would if they could revise their portfolios every day.

the limiting case of continuous time is that the sample paths for $S(t)$ are continuous functions of time, i.e. for every realization of $S(t + h)$, except possibly on a set of measure zero, $\lim_{h \to 0}[S_k(t + h) - S_k(t)] = 0$, $k = 1, \ldots, m$. If, however, in the continuous limit the uncertainty of "end-of-period" returns is to be preserved, then an additional requirement is that $\lim_{h \to 0}[S_k(t + h) - S_k(t)]/h$ exists almost nowhere, i.e. even though the sample paths are continuous, the increments to the states are not, and therefore, in particular, "end-of-period" rates of return will not be "predictable" even in the continuous-time limit. The class of stochastic processes that satisfy these conditions are called *diffusion processes*.[35]

Although such processes are almost nowhere differentiable in the usual sense, under some mild regularity conditions there is a generalized theory of stochastic differential equations which allows their instantaneous dynamics to be expressed as the solution to the system of equations:[36]

$$dS_i(t) = G_i(S, t) \, dt + H_i(S, t) \, dq_i(t) \, , \quad i = 1, \ldots, m \, , \tag{7.1}$$

where $G_i(S, t)$ is the instantaneous expected change in $S_i(t)$ per unit time at time t; H_i^2 is the instantaneous variance of the change in $S_i(t)$, where it is understood that these statistics are conditional on $S(t) = S$. The $dq_i(t)$ are Wiener processes with the instantaneous correlation coefficient per unit of time between $dq_i(t)$ and $dq_j(t)$ given by the function $\eta_{ij}(S, t)$, $i, j = 1, \ldots, m$.[37] Moreover, specifying the functions $\{G_i, H_i, \eta_{ij}\}$, $i, j = 1, \ldots, m$, is sufficient to completely determine the transition probabilities for $S(t)$ between any two dates.[38]

Under the assumption that the returns on securities can be described by diffusion processes, Merton (1969, 1971) has solved the continuous-time analog to the discrete-time formulation in (6.1), namely:

$$\max \mathrm{E}_0 \left\{ \int_0^T U[C(t), t] \, dt + B[W(T), T] \right\} . \tag{7.2}$$

Neither negative consumption nor negative wealth is physically possible.

---

[35] See Feller (1966), Itô and McKean (1964), and Cox and Miller (1968).

[36] (7.1) is a short-hand expression for the stochastic integral:

$$S_i(t) = S_i(0) + \int_0^t G_i(S, \tau) \, d\tau + \int_0^t H_i(S, \tau) \, dq_i(\tau) \, ,$$

where $S_i(t)$ is the solution to (7.1) with probability one. For a general discussion and proofs, see Itô and McKean (1964), McKean (1969), McShane (1974), and Harrison (1985).

[37] $\int_0^t dq_i = q_i(t) - q_i(0)$ is normally distributed with a zero mean and variance equal to t.

[38] See Feller (1966, pp. 320–321) and Cox and Miller (1968, p. 215). The transition probabilities will satisfy the Kolmogorov or Fokker–Planck partial differential equations.

Hence, a feasible consumption–investment strategy for (7.2) must satisfy $C(t) \geq 0$ and $W(t) \geq 0$ for $t \in [0, T]$. Because explicit recognition of these constraints does little to complicate the analysis, we do so along the lines of Karatzas, Lehoczky, Sethi and Shreve (1986) and Cox and Huang (1989).[39] The constraint on consumption is captured by the usual Kuhn–Tucker method. The constraint on wealth is imposed by making zero wealth an "absorbing state" so that if $W(t) = 0$, then $W(\tau) = 0$ and $C(\tau) = 0$ for $\tau \in [t, T]$.

Adapting the notation in Merton (1971),[40] the rate of return dynamics on security j can be written as:

$$dP_j/P_j = \alpha_j(S, t)\, dt + \sigma_j(S, t)\, dZ_j, \quad j = 1, \ldots, n, \tag{7.3}$$

where α_j is the instantaneous conditional expected rate of return per unit time; σ_j^2 is its instantaneous conditional variance per unit time; and dZ_j are Wiener processes, with the instantaneous correlation coefficient per unit time between $dZ_j(t)$ and $dZ_k(t)$ given by the function $\rho_{jk}(S, t)$, $j, k = 1, \ldots, n$. In addition to the n risky securities, there is a riskless security whose instantaneous rate of return per unit time is the interest rate $r(t)$.[41] To complete the model's dynamics description, define the functions $\mu_{ij}(S, t)$ to be the instantaneous correlation coefficients per unit time between $dq_i(t)$ and $dZ_j(t)$, $i = 1, \ldots, m$; $j = 1, \ldots, n$.[42]

As in the discrete-time case, define J by:

$$J[W(t), S(t), t] \equiv \max E_t \left\{ \int_t^T U[C(\tau), \tau]\, d\tau + B[W(T), T] \right\}, \tag{7.4}$$

subject to $J[0, S(t), t] = \int_t^T U[0, \tau]\, d\tau + B[0, T]$, which reflects the requirement that $W(t) = 0$ is an absorbing state.

---

[39] Karatzas et al. use the dynamic programming technique. Cox and Huang use an alternative method based on a martingale representation technology. As discussed in Merton (1990, ch. 6), this method is especially powerful for solving optimization problems of this sort.

[40] Merton (1971, p. 377). dP_j/P_j in continuous time corresponds to $Z_j(t + 1) - 1$ in the discrete-time analysis.

[41] $r(t)$ corresponds to $R(t) - 1$ in the discrete-time analysis, and is the "force-of-interest" continuous rate. While the rate earned between t and $t + dt$, $r(t)$, is known with certainty as of time t, $r(t)$ can vary stochastically over time.

[42] Unlike in the Arrow–Debreu model, for example, it is not assumed here that the returns are necessarily completely described by the changes in the state variables, dS_i, $i = 1, \ldots, m$, i.e., the dZ_j need not be instantaneously perfectly correlated with some linear combination of $dq_1, \ldots, dq_m$. Rather, it is only assumed that $(dP_1/P_1, \ldots, dP_n/P_n, dS_1, \ldots, dS_m)$ is Markov in $S(t)$.

The continuous-time analog to (6.4) can be written as:[43]

$$0 = \max\left\{U[C, t] + \lambda C + J_t + J_W\left[\left(\sum_1^n w_j(\alpha_j - r) + r\right)W - C\right] + \sum_1^m J_i G_i\right.$$

$$+ \tfrac{1}{2}J_{WW}\sum_1^n\sum_1^n w_i w_j \sigma_{ij} W^2 + \tfrac{1}{2}\sum_1^m\sum_1^m J_{ij}H_i H_j \eta_{ij}$$

$$\left. + \sum_1^m\sum_1^n J_{iW} w_j \sigma_j H_i \mu_{ij} W\right\}, \tag{7.5}$$

where λ is the Kuhn–Tucker multiplier reflecting the non-negativity constraint on consumption. The subscripts t, W, and i on J denote partial derivatives with respect to the arguments, t, W, and S_i ($i = 1, \ldots, m$) of J, respectively, and $\sigma_{ij} \equiv \sigma_i \sigma_j \rho_{ij}$ is the instantaneous covariance of the returns of security i with security j, i, $j = 1, \ldots, n$. As was the case in (6.4), the "max" in (7.5) is over the current decision variables $[C(t), w_1(t), \ldots, w_n(t)]$. If C^* and w^* are the optimal rules, then the $(n + 1)$ first-order conditions for (7.5) can be written as:

$$0 = U_C[C^*, t] + \lambda^* - J_W[W, S, t] \tag{7.6}$$

and

$$0 = J_W(\alpha_j - r) + J_{WW}\sum_1^n w_i^* \sigma_{ij} W + \sum_1^m J_{iW}\sigma_j H_i \mu_{ij}, \quad j = 1, \ldots, n. \tag{7.7}$$

The Kuhn–Tucker condition, $\lambda^* C^* = 0$, implies that $\lambda^* = \max[0, J_W[W, S, t] - U_C[0, t]]$. Hence, for regions in which $C^* > 0$, equation (7.6) is identical to the "envelope condition", (6.8), in the unconstrained discrete-time analysis. However, unlike (6.6) in the discrete-time case, (7.7) is a system of equations which is *linear* in the optimal demands for risky securities. Hence, if none of the risky securities is redundant, then (7.7) can be solved explicitly for the optimal demand functions using standard matrix inversion, i.e.

$$w_j^*(t)W(t) = K\sum_1^n v_{kj}(\alpha_k - r) + \sum_1^m B_i \zeta_{ij}, \quad j = 1, \ldots, n, \tag{7.8}$$

where v_{kj} is the k-jth element of the inverse of the instantaneous variance–

[43]See Merton (1971, p. 381) and Kushner (1967, ch. IV, theorem 7).

covariance matrix of returns $[\sigma_{ij}]$;

$$\zeta_{ij} \equiv \sum_1^n v_{kj}\sigma_k H_i \mu_{ik} , \qquad K \equiv -J_W/J_{WW} \quad \text{and} \quad B_i \equiv -J_{iW}/J_{WW} ,$$

$$i = 1, \ldots , m \quad \text{and} \quad j = 1, \ldots , n.$$

As an immediate consequence of (7.8), we have the following mutual fund theorem:

Theorem 7.1. *If the returns dynamics are described by (7.1) and (7.3), then there exist $(m + 2)$ mutual funds constructed from linear combinations of the available securities such that, independent of preferences, wealth distribution, or planning horizon, investors will be indifferent between choosing from linear combinations of just these $(m + 2)$ funds or linear combinations of all n risky securities and the riskless security.*

Proof. Let mutual fund #1 be the riskless security; let mutual fund #2 hold fraction $\delta_j = \sum_1^n v_{kj}(\alpha_k - r)$ in security j, $j = 1, \ldots , n$, and the balance $(1 - \sum_1^n \delta_j)$ in the riskless security; let mutual fund #$(2 + i)$ hold fraction $\delta_j^i \equiv \zeta_{ij}$ in security j, $j = 1, \ldots , n$, and the balance $(1 - \sum_1^n \delta_j^i)$ in the riskless security for $i = 1, \ldots , m$. Consider a portfolio of these mutual funds which allocates $d_2(t) = K$ dollars to fund #2; $d_{2+i}(t) = B_i$ dollars to fund #$(2 + i)$, $i = 1, \ldots , m$; and $d_1(t) = W(t) - \sum_2^{2+m} d_i(t)$ dollars to fund #1. By inspection of (7.8), this portfolio of funds exactly replicates the optimal portfolio holdings chosen from among the original n risky securities and the riskless security. However, the fractional holdings of these securities by the $(m + 2)$ funds do not depend upon the preferences, wealth, or planning horizon of the individuals investing in the funds. Hence, every investor can replicate his optimal portfolio by investing in the $(m + 2)$ funds.

Of course, as with the mutual fund theorems of Section 4, Theorem 7.1 is vacuous if $m \geq n + 1$. However, for $m \ll n$, the $(m + 2)$ portfolios provide for a non-trivial spanning of the efficient portfolio set, and it is straightforward to show that the instantaneous returns on individual securities will satisfy the same linear specification relative to these spanning portfolios as was derived in Theorem 4.6 for the one-period analysis.

It was shown in the discrete-time analysis of Section 6 that if $E_t[Z_j(t + 1)|S(t)] = \bar{Z}_j(t + 1)$, $j = 1, \ldots , n$, then the intertemporal maximizer's demand behavior is "as if" he were a static maximizer of the expected utility of end-of-period wealth. The corresponding condition in the continuous-time case is that the instantaneous rates of return on all available securities are uncorrelated with the unanticipated changes in all state variables $S(t)$ (i.e. $\mu_{ij} = 0$,

$i = 1, \ldots, m$, and $j = 1, \ldots, n$). Under this condition, the optimal demand functions in (7.8) can be rewritten as:

$$w_j^*(t)W(t) = K \sum_1^n v_{kj}(\alpha_k - r), \quad j = 1, \ldots, n .$$ (7.9)

A special case of this condition occurs when the investment opportunity set is non-stochastic [i.e. either $H_i = 0$, $i = 1, \ldots, m$, or $(\alpha_i, \sigma_{ij}, r)$ are, at most, deterministic functions of time, $i, j = 1, \ldots, n$]. Optimal demands will also satisfy (7.9) if preferences are such that the marginal utility of wealth of the derived-utility function does not depend on $S(t)$ (i.e. $B_i = 0$, $i = 1, \ldots, m$). By inspection of (7.6) this condition will obtain if the optimal consumption function C^* does not depend on $S(t)$. In direct correspondence to the discrete-time finding in Section 6, the only time-additive and independent utility function to satisfy this condition is $U[C, t] = a(t) \log[C(t)]$, a preference function which also has the property that $C^*(t) > 0$ and $\lambda^* = 0$.

By inspection of (7.9) the relative holdings of risky securities, $w_j^*(t)/w_i^*(t)$, are the same for all investors, and thus, under these conditions, the efficient portfolio set will be spanned by just two funds: a single risky fund and a riskless fund. Moreover, by the procedure used to prove Theorem 4.9 and Theorem 4.10 in the static analysis, the efficient portfolio set here can be shown to be generated by the set of portfolios with minimum (instantaneous) variance for a given expected rate of return. Hence, under these conditions the continuous-time intertemporal maximizer will act "as if" he were a static, Markowitz–Tobin mean–variance maximizer. Although the demand functions are formally identical to those derived from the mean–variance model, the analysis here assumes neither quadratic preferences nor elliptic or normally distributed security returns. Indeed, if for example the investment opportunity set $\{\alpha_j, r, \sigma_{ij}; i, j = 1, 2, \ldots, n\}$ is constant through time, then from (7.3) the return on each risky security will be log-normally distributed, which implies that all securities have limited liability.[44]

In the general case described in Theorem 7.1, the qualitative behavioral differences between an intertemporal maximizer and a static maximizer can be clarified further by analyzing the characteristics of the derived spanning portfolios.

As already shown, fund #1 and fund #2 are the "usual" portfolios that would be mixed to provide an optimal portfolio for a static maximizer. Hence, the intertemporal behavioral differences are characterized by funds #$(2 + i)$, $i = 1, \ldots, m$. At the level of demand functions, the "differential demand" for

---

[44]See Merton (1971, pp. 384–388). It is also shown there that the returns will be lognormal on the risky fund which, together with the riskless security, spans the efficient portfolio set. Joint lognormal distributions are not elliptical distributions.

risky security j, ΔD_j^*, is defined to be the difference between the demand for that security by an intertemporal maximizer at time t and the demand for that security by a static maximizer of the expected utility of "end-of-period" wealth where the absolute risk-aversion and current wealth of the two maximizers are the same. Noting that $K \equiv -J_W/J_{WW}$ is the reciprocal of the absolute risk-aversion of the derived utility of wealth function, from (7.8) we have that

$$\Delta D_j^* = \sum_1^m B_i \zeta_{ij}, \quad j = 1, \ldots, n. \tag{7.10}$$

Lemma 7.1. *Define:*

$$dY_i \equiv dS_i - \left(\sum_1^n \delta_j^\dagger \left(\frac{dP_j}{P_j} - r\,dt \right) + r\,dt \right).$$

The set of portfolio weights $\{\delta_j^\dagger\}$ that minimize the (instantaneous) variance of dY_i are given by $\delta_j^\dagger = \zeta_{ij}$, $j = 1, \ldots, n$ and $i = 1, \ldots, m$.

Proof. The instantaneous variance of dY_i is equal to $[H_i^2 - 2\sum_1^n \delta_j^\dagger H_i \sigma_j \mu_{ij} + \sum_1^n \sum_1^n \delta_j^\dagger \delta_k^\dagger \sigma_{jk}]$. Hence, the minimizing set of $\{\delta_j^\dagger\}$ will satisfy $0 = -H_i \sigma_j \mu_{ij} + \sum_1^n \delta_k^\dagger \sigma_{jk}$, $j = 1, \ldots, n$. By matrix inversion, $\delta_j^\dagger = \zeta_{ij}$.

The instantaneous rate of return on fund #$(2 + i)$ is exactly $[r\,dt + \sum_1^n \zeta_{ij}(dP_j/P_j - r\,dt)]$. Hence, fund #$(2 + i)$ can be described as that feasible portfolio whose rate of return most closely replicates the stochastic part of the instantaneous change in state variable $S_i(t)$, and this is true for $i = 1, \ldots, m$.

Consider the special case where there exist securities that are instantaneously perfectly correlated with changes in each of the state variables. Without loss of generality, assume that the first m securities are the securities such that dP_i/P_i is perfectly positively correlated with dS_i, $i = 1, \ldots, m$. In this case,[45] the demand function (7.8) can be rewritten in the form:

$$w_i^*(t)W(t) = K \sum_1^n v_{ik}(\alpha_k - r) + B_i H_i/\sigma_i, \quad i = 1, \ldots, m,$$

$$= K \sum_1^n v_{ik}(\alpha_k - r), \quad\quad\quad i = m + 1, \ldots, n. \tag{7.11}$$

[45]As will be shown in Section 10, this case is similar in spirit to the Arrow–Debreu complete-markets model.

Hence, the relative holdings of securities $m + 1$ through n will be the same for all investors, and the differential demand functions can be rewritten as:

$$\Delta D_i^* = B_i H_i / \sigma_i , \quad i = 1, \ldots, m ,$$
$$= 0 , \quad\quad\quad i = m + 1, \ldots, n . \tag{7.12}$$

The composition of fund #$(2 + i)$ reduces to a simple combination of security i and the riskless security.

The behavior implied by the demand functions in (7.8) can be more easily interpreted if they are rewritten in terms of the direct-utility and optimal-consumption functions. The optimal-consumption function has the form $C^*(t) = C^*(W, S, t)$, and from (7.6) it follows immediately that, for $C^*(t) > 0$:

$$K = -U_C[C^*, t] / (U_{CC}[C^*, t] \partial C^* / \partial W) , \tag{7.13}$$
$$B_i = -(\partial C^* / \partial S_i) / (\partial C^* / \partial W) , \quad i = 1, \ldots, m . \tag{7.14}$$

Because $\partial C^* / \partial W > 0$, it follows that the sign of B_i equals the sign of $(-\partial C^* / \partial S_i)$. An unanticipated change in a state variable is said to be *unfavorable* if, ceteris paribus, such a change would reduce current optimal consumption, e.g. an unanticipated increase in S_i would be unfavorable if $\partial C^* / \partial S_i < 0$. Inspection of (7.12), for example, shows that for such an individual the differential demand for security i (which is perfectly positively correlated with changes in S_i) will be positive. If there is an unanticipated increase in S_i, then, ceteris paribus, there will be an unanticipated increase in his wealth. Because $\partial C^* / \partial W > 0$, this increase in wealth will tend to offset the negative impact on C^* caused by the increase in S_i, and therefore the unanticipated variation in C^* will be reduced. In effect, by holding more of this security, the investor expects to be "compensated" by larger wealth in the event that S_i changes in the unfavorable direction. Of course, if $\partial C^* / \partial S_i > 0$, then the investor takes a differentially short position. However, in all cases investors will allocate their wealth to the funds #$(2 + i)$, $i = 1, \ldots, m$, so as to "hedge" against unfavorable changes in the state variables $S(t)$.[46]

Analysis of the usual static model does not produce such hedging behavior because the utility function is posited to depend only on end-of-period wealth and therefore implicitly assumes that $\partial C^* / \partial S_i = 0$, $i = 1, \ldots, m$. Thus, in addition to their manifest function of providing an "efficient" risk–return tradeoff for end-of-period wealth, securities in the intertemporal model have a

---

[46]This behavior obtains even when the return on fund #$(2 + i)$ is not instantaneously perfectly correlated with dS_i. See Merton (1990, ch. 15).

latent function of allowing consumers to hedge against other uncertainties.[47] The effect on equilibrium security prices from these "hedging demands" is examined in Section 10.

As a consequence of the richer role played by securities in the intertemporal model, the number of securities required to span the set of optimal portfolios will, in general, be larger than in the corresponding one-period model. It is therefore somewhat surprising that non-trivial spanning can obtain in the continuous-trading model. In the one-period analysis of Section 4, it was shown that for general preferences a necessary and sufficient condition for a set of portfolios to span the efficient portfolio set is that the returns on every security can be written as a linear function of the returns on the spanning portfolios plus noise. As discussed in Section 4, in the absence of complete markets in the Arrow–Debreu sense, the widespread existence of corporate liability and other securities with non-linear payoff structures appears to virtually rule out non-trivial spanning unless further restrictions are imposed on either preferences or the probability distributions of security returns. The hypothesized conditions of Theorem 7.1 require only that investors be risk-averse with smooth preferences. Thus, it follows that the key to the spanning result is the combination of continuous trading and diffusion processes for the dynamics of security returns. As will be shown in the sections to follow, diffusion processes are "closed" under non-linear transformations. That is, the dynamics of a reasonably well-behaved function of diffusion-driven random variables will also be described by a diffusion process. Thus, unlike in the static and discrete-time dynamic models, the creation of securities whose payoff structures are non-linear functions of existing security prices will not, in general, cause the size of the portfolio spanning set to increase.

8. Options, contingent claims analysis, and the Modigliani–Miller Theorem

Futures contracts, options, loan guarantees, mortgage-backed securities, and virtually all corporate liabilities are among the many types of securities with the feature that their payoffs are contractually linked to the prices of other traded securities at some future date. Contingent claims analysis (CCA) is a technique for determining the price of such "derivative" securities. As indicated in Sections 4 and 7, the fact that these contractual arrangements often involve

---

[47]For further discussion of this analysis, descriptions of specific sources of uncertainty, and extensions to discrete-time examples, see Merton (1970, 1973b, 1975, 1977a). Breeden (1979) and Merton (1990, ch. 6) show that similar behavior obtains in the case of multiple consumption goods with uncertain relative prices. However, C^* is a vector and J_W is the "shadow" price of the "composite" consumption bundle. Hence, the corresponding derived "hedging" behavior is to minimize the unanticipated variations in J_W.

non-linear sharing rules has important implications for both corporate finance and the structure of equilibrium asset prices. For this reason and because derivative securities represent a significant and growing fraction of the out-standing stock of financial instruments, CCA is a mainstream topic in financial economic theory.

Although closely connected with the continuous-time portfolio models ana-lyzed in the previous section, the origins of CCA are definitely rooted in the pioneering work of Black and Scholes (1973) on the theory of option pricing. Thus, we begin the study of derivative-security pricing with an analysis of option securities.

A "European-type call (put) option" is a security that gives its owner the right to buy (sell) a specified quantity of a financial or real asset at a specified price, the "exercise price", on a specified date, the "expiration date". An American-type option allows its owner to exercise the option on or before the expiration date. If the owner chooses not to exercise the option on or before the expiration date, then it expires and becomes worthless.

If $V(t)$ denotes the price of the underlying asset at time t and E denotes the exercise price, then from the contract terms, the price of the call option at the expiration date T is given by $\max[0, V(T) - E]$ and the price of the put option is $\max[0, E - V(T)]$. If there is positive probability that $V(T) > E$, and positive probability that $V(T) < E$, then these options provide examples of securities with contractually derived non-linear sharing rules with respect to the underly-ing asset.

Although academic study of option pricing can be traced back to at least the turn of the century, the "watershed" in this research is the Black and Scholes (1973) model, which uses arbitrage arguments to derive option prices.[48] It was, of course, well known before 1973 that if a portfolio of securities can be constructed to exactly match the payoffs to some security, then that security is redundant, and to rule out arbitrage, its price is uniquely determined by the prices of securities in the replicating portfolio. It was also recognized that because the price of an option at its expiration date is perfectly functionally related to the price of its underlying asset, the risk of an option position could be reduced by taking an offsetting position in the underlying asset. However, because portfolios involve linear combinations of securities and because the option has a non-linear payoff structure, there is no static (i.e. "buy-and-hold") portfolio strategy in the underlying asset that can exactly replicate the payoff to the option. Thus, it would seem that an option cannot be priced by arbitrage conditions alone. Black and Scholes had the fundamental insight that a *dynamic* portfolio strategy in the underlying asset and the riskless security can be used to hedge the risk of an option position. With the idea in mind that

---

[48]Black (1987) gives a brief history on how he and Scholes came to discover their model.

the precision of the hedge can be improved by increasing the frequency of portfolio revisions, they focused on the limiting case of continuous trading. By assuming that the price dynamics of the underlying asset are described by a geometric Brownian motion and that the interest rate is constant, Black and Scholes derive a trading strategy that perfectly hedges the option position. They are, thus, able to determine the option price from the equilibrium condition that the return on a perfectly hedged portfolio must equal the interest rate.

Under the assumption that the dynamics for the underlying asset price are described by a diffusion process with a continuous sample path, Merton (1970, 1973a, 1977b) uses the mathematics of Itô stochastic integrals to prove that with continuous trading, the Black–Scholes dynamic portfolio strategy will exactly replicate the payoff to an option held until exercise or expiration. Therefore, under these conditions the Black–Scholes option price is a necessary condition to rule out arbitrage. Using a simplified version of the arbitrage proof in Merton (1977b), we derive the Black–Scholes price for a European call option.

Following the notation in Section 7, we assume that the dynamics of the underlying asset price are described by a diffusion process given by:

$$dV = \alpha V \, dt + \sigma V \, dZ , \tag{8.1}$$

where σ is, at most, a function of V and t. No cash payments or other distributions will be made to the owners of this asset prior to the expiration date of the option.

Let $F(V, t)$ be the solution to the partial differential equation:

$$\tfrac{1}{2}\sigma^2 V^2 F_{11} + rVF_1 - rF + F_2 = 0 \tag{8.2}$$

subject to the boundary conditions:

(a) $F(0, t) = 0$,
(b) F/V bounded, $\tag{8.3}$
(c) $F(V, T) = \max[0, V - E]$,

where subscripts denote partial derivatives with respect to the arguments of F. A solution to (8.2)–(8.3) exists and is unique.[49]

Consider a continuous-time portfolio strategy where the investor allocates the fraction $w(t)$ to the underlying asset and $[1 - w(t)]$ to the riskless security.

---

[49](8.2) is a classic linear partial-differential equation of the parabolic type. If σ^2 is a continuous function, then there exists a unique solution that satisfies boundary conditions (8.3). The usual method for solving this equation is Fourier transforms.

If $w(t)$ is a right-continuous function and $P(t)$ denotes the value of the portfolio at time t, then, from Section 7, the dynamics for P can be written as:

$$dP = [w(\alpha - r) + r]P \, dt + w\sigma P \, dZ . \tag{8.4}$$

Suppose the investor selects the particular portfolio strategy $w(t) = F_1(V, t)V(t)/P(t)$. Note that the strategy rule $w(t)$ for each t depends on the partial derivative of the known function F, the current price of the underlying asset, and the current value of the portfolio. By substitution into (8.4), we have that

$$dP = [F_1V(\alpha - r) + rP] \, dt + F_1 V\sigma \, dZ . \tag{8.5}$$

Since F is twice-continuously differentiable, Itô's Lemma[50] can be applied to express the stochastic process for $F(V(t), t)$ as:

$$dF = [\tfrac{1}{2}\sigma^2 V^2 F_{11} + \alpha V F_1 + F_2] \, dt + F_1 V\sigma \, dZ . \tag{8.6}$$

But F satisfies (8.2) and therefore (8.6) can be rewritten as:

$$dF = [F_1V(\alpha - r) + rF] \, dt + F_1 V\sigma \, dZ . \tag{8.7}$$

From (8.5) and (8.7), $dP - dF = [P - F]r \, dt$, an ordinary differential equation with the well-known solution:

$$P(t) - F(V(t), t) = [P(0) - F(V(0), 0)] e^{rt} . \tag{8.8}$$

If the initial investment in the portfolio is chosen so that $P(0) = F(V(0), 0)$, then from (8.8), $P(t) = F(V(t), t)$ for $0 \leq t \leq T$. From (8.3) we have that $P(t) = 0$ if $V(t) = 0$ and $P(T) = \max[0, V(T) - E]$. Thus, we have constructed a feasible portfolio strategy in the underlying asset and the riskless security that exactly replicates the payoff structure to an European call option with exercise price E and expiration date T. By the standard no-arbitrage condition, two securities with identical payoff structures must have the same price. Thus, the equilibrium call option price at time t is given by $F(V(t), t)$, the Black–Scholes price.

The derivation did not *assume* that the equilibrium option price depends only on the price of the underlying asset and the riskless interest rate. Thus, if the option price is to depend on other prices or stochastic variables, then, by

---

[50] Itô's Lemma is for stochastic differentiation, the analog to the Fundamental Theorem of the calculus for deterministic differentiation. For a statement of the Lemma and applications in economics, see Merton (1971, 1973a, 1982b, 1990). For its rigorous proof, see McKean (1969, p. 44).

inspection of (8.2), it must be because either σ^2 or r is a function of these prices. Similarly, the findings that the option price is a twice continuously-differentiable function of the underlying asset price and that its dynamics follow a diffusion process are derived results and not assumptions.

Because Black and Scholes derived (8.2)–(8.3) for the case where σ^2 is a constant (i.e. geometric Brownian motion), they were able to obtain a closed-form solution, given by:

$$F(V, t) = V\Phi(x_1) - E\,e^{-r(T-t)}\Phi(x_2),$$ (8.9)

where $x_1 \equiv [\log(V/E) + (r + \sigma^2/2)(T - t)]/\sigma\sqrt{T - t}$; $x_2 \equiv x_1 - \sigma\sqrt{T - t}$; and $\Phi(\cdot)$ is the cumulative Gaussian density function. From (8.9) it follows that the portfolio–construction rule is given by $w(t) = F_1 V/F = \Phi(x_1)V/F(V, t)$.

By inspection of (8.2) or (8.9), a striking feature of the Black–Scholes analysis is that the determination of the option price and the replicating portfolio strategy does not require knowledge of either the expected return on the underlying asset α or investor risk preferences and endowments. Indeed, the only variable or parameter required that is not directly observable is the variance-rate function, σ^2. This feature, together with the relatively robust nature of an arbitrage derivation, gives the Black–Scholes model an important practical significance, and it has been widely adopted in the practicing financial community.

In the derivation of the equilibrium call-option price, the only place that the explicit features of the call option enter is in the specification of the boundary conditions (8.3). Hence, by appropriately adjusting the boundary conditions, the same methodology can be used to derive the equilibrium prices of other derivative securities with payoff structures contingent on the price of the underlying asset. For example, to derive the price of a European put option, one need only change (8.3) so that F satisfies $F(0, t) = E\exp[-r(T - t)]$; $F(V, t)$ bounded; and $F(V, T) = \max[0, E - V]$.

Although options are rather specialized financial instruments, the Black–Scholes option pricing methodology can be applied to a much broader class of securities.

A prototypal example analyzed in Black and Scholes (1973) and Merton (1970, 1974) is the pricing of debt and equity of a corporation. Consider the case of a firm financed by equity and a single homogeneous zero-coupon debt issue. The contractual obligation of the firm is to pay B dollars to the debtholders on the maturity date T, and in the event that the firm does not pay (i.e. defaults), then ownership of the firm is transferred to the debtholders. The firm is prohibited from making payments or transferring assets to the equityholders prior to the debt being retired. Let $V(t)$ denote the market value of the firm at time t. If at the maturity date of the debt, $V(T) \geq B$, then the debtholders will receive their promised payment B and the equityholders will have the "residual" value, $V(T) - B$. If, however, $V(T) < B$, then there are inadequate assets within the firm to pay the debtholders their promised amount. By the limited-liability provision of corporate equity, the equity-holders cannot be assessed to make up the shortfall, and it is clearly not in their interests to do so voluntarily. Hence, if $V(T) < B$, then default occurs and the value of the debt is $V(T)$ and the equity is worthless. Thus, the contractually derived payoff function for the debt at time T, f_1, can be written as:

$$f_1(V, T) = \min[V(T), B],$$ \hfill (8.10)

and the corresponding payoff function for equity, f_2, can be written as:

$$f_2(V, T) = \max[0, V(T) - B].$$ \hfill (8.11)

Provided that default is possible but not certain, we have from (8.10) and (8.11) that the sharing rule between debtholders and equityholders is a non-linear function of the value of the firm. Moreover, the payoff structure to equity is isomorphic to a European call option where the underlying asset is the firm, the exercise price is the promised debt payment, and the expiration date is the maturity date. Because $\min[V(T), B] = V(T) - \max[0, V(T) - B]$, the debtholders' position is functionally equivalent to buying the firm outright from the equityholders at the time of issue and simultaneously giving them an option to buy back the firm at time T for B. Hence, provided that the conditions of continuous-trading opportunities and a diffusion-process representation for the dynamics of the firm's value are satisfied, the Black–Scholes option pricing theory can be applied directly to the pricing of levered equity and corporate debt with default risk.

The same methodology can be applied quite generally to the pricing of derivative securities by adjusting the boundary conditions in (8.3) to match the contractually derived payoff structure. Cox, Ingersoll and Ross (1985b) use this technique to price default-free bonds in their widely used model of the term structure of interest rates. The survey articles by Smith (1976) and Mason and Merton (1985) and the books by Cox and Rubinstein (1985) and Merton (1990) provide applications of CCA in a broad range of areas, including the pricing of general corporate liabilities, project evaluation and financing, pension fund and deposit insurance, and employment contracts such as guaranteed wage floors and tenure. CCA can also take account of differential tax rates on different types of assets as demonstrated by Scholes (1976) and Constantinides and Scholes (1980). Although, in most applications, (8.2)–(8.3) will not yield closed-form solutions, powerful computational methods have been developed to provide high-speed numerical solutions for both the security price and its first derivative.

As shown in Section 4, the linear generating process for security returns which is required for non-trivial spanning in Theorem 4.6 is generally not satisfied by securities with non-linear sharing rules. However, if the underlying asset-price dynamics are diffusions, we have shown that the dynamics of equilibrium derivative-security prices will also follow diffusion processes. The existence of such securities is, therefore, consistent with the hypothesized conditions of Theorem 7.1. Hence, the creation of securities with non-linear sharing rules will not adversely affect the spanning results derived for the continuous-time portfolio selection model of Section 7. Using a replication argument similar to the one presented here, Merton (1974, 1977b) proves that Theorem 4.14, the Modigliani–Miller Theorem, obtains under the conditions of continuous trading and a diffusion representation for the dynamics of the market value of the firm.

9. Bankruptcy, transactions costs, and financial intermediation in the continuous-time model[51]

In Sections 4 and 5 we analyzed the static portfolio-selection problem, taking account of the non-negativity constraint on wealth and the prospect of personal bankruptcy. Much the same analysis could be applied to the discrete-time dynamic portfolio model of Section 6. Although, *given* the distribution of security returns in these models, we can describe an algorithm for computing the constrained optimal-portfolio demands from the unconstrained ones, the non-linear sharing rules induced by explicit recognition of bankruptcy add considerable complexity to the determination of conditions under which non-trivial spanning of the efficient portfolio set obtains. This is especially so in models where spanning occurs because of a specific assumption about the joint probability distribution for returns as, for example, in the Markowitz–Tobin mean–variance model.

In contrast, the continuous-time model of Section 7 is easily adapted to include the effects of bankruptcy on portfolio choice and on the return distributions of both investor and creditor portfolios. From the perspective of investor behavior, we have, by inspection of (7.8), that the structure of optimal-portfolio demands is not materially changed by including the non-negativity constraints on wealth and consumption. Just as CCA was used in Section 8 to determine the price and return characteristics of corporate debt

---

[51]This section is adapted from Merton (1989) and Merton (1990, ch. 14).

with default possibilities, so from the perspective of creditor behavior it can be used to evaluate price and return characteristics of cash or security loans made to an investor whose portfolio provides the sole collateral for these loans. As we have seen, the introduction of non-linear sharing rules (in this case, between an investor and his creditors) does not by itself violate the diffusion assumption of security and portfolio returns. Therefore, the non-linearities induced by taking account of personal bankruptcy do not alter the set of spanning portfolios, and hence do not affect the conclusions of Theorem 7.1.

Theorem 7.1 can be used for product identification and implementation in the continuous-time theory of financial intermediation. That is, if individual securities are "pre-packaged" into a specified group of portfolios, then investors can achieve the same optimal allocations by selecting from just this group as they could by choosing from the entire universe of available securities. Theorem 7.1 thus serves to identify a class of risk-pooling investment products for which there is a natural demand. Moreover, by specifying the dynamic trading rules for creating these portfolios, the theorem also provides the "blueprints" or production technologies for intermediaries to manufacture these products.

As we have seen, contingent claims analysis can be used to price derivative securities, including ones issued by intermediaries. The contribution of CCA to the theory of intermediation is, however, deeper than just the pricing of financial products. It also contributes to the theory of product implementation by providing the production technologies to create risk-sharing products. The portfolio-replication process used to derive the derivative-security price in Section 8 applies whether or not the security actually exists. Thus, the specified dynamic portfolio strategy used to create an arbitrage position against a traded derivative security is also a prescription for synthesizing an otherwise non-existent security. The investment required to fund the replicating portfolio $F(V(0), 0)$ in (8.8) becomes, in this context, the production cost to the intermediary that creates the security. The blueprint for the dynamic production process is given by the rules: hold $F_1(V(t), t)V(t)$ in the underlying risky asset and $F(V(t), t) - F_1(V(t), t)V(t)$ in the riskless security at each time t for $t = 0$ until $t = T$. The "raw materials" for the manufacturing process are the underlying risky asset and the riskless security. The "output" produced is a set of cash flows that are identical to the prescribed payoffs of the financial product issued.

In Theorem 7.1, as in the mutual fund theorems of Section 4, investors are shown to be indifferent between selecting their portfolios either from the $m + 2$ portfolios that span the efficient set or from all $n + 1$ available securities. Similarly, investors are indifferent as to whether or not derivative securities are available because they can use portfolio rules (8.2)–(8.3) to replicate the payoffs to these securities. It would, thus, seem that the rich menu of financial intermediaries and financial instruments observed in the real world has no important risk-pooling or risk-sharing function in the environment posited in Section 7.

Such indifference is indeed the case if, as assumed, *all* investors can gather information and transact without cost. Hence, some type of transaction-cost structure in which financial intermediaries and market makers have a comparative advantage over individual investors and general business firms is required to provide a raison d'être for financial intermediation and markets for derivative securities.

Grossman and Laroque (1987) have shown that including transaction costs in consumption goods alone does not affect the basic structure of optimal portfolio demands in the continuous-trading model. However, from the work of Leland (1985), Constantinides (1986), and Sun (1987), incorporation of such costs for asset trading in the continuous-time model leads to considerable technical difficulties.[52] Moreover, development of a satisfactory equilibrium theory of allocations and prices in the presence of transactions costs in assets promises still more complexity because it requires a simultaneous endogenous determination of prices, allocations, *and* the least-cost form of financial intermediation and market structure.

To circumvent all this complexity and also preserve a role for intermediation, Merton (1989, 1990, ch. 14) introduces a continuous-time model in which many agents cannot trade costlessly, but the lowest-cost transactors (by definition, financial intermediaries) can.[53] In this model, the dynamic portfolio analysis of Section 7 and CCA of Section 8 can be applied to determine the production costs for financial products issued by intermediaries. However, unlike in the standard zero-transaction-cost model, these risk-pooling and risk-sharing products can significantly improve economic efficiency. That is, as customers of intermediaries, high-transaction-cost agents can achieve investment allocations that are not otherwise possible by direct asset-market transactions.

If, in addition, agents and intermediaries are price-takers in the traded-securities markets and if there is a sufficient number of potential producers

---

[52] With diffusion processes and proportional transactions costs, investors cannot trade continuously. The reason is that with continuous trading, transactions costs at each trade will be proportional to $|dZ|$, where dZ is a Brownian motion. However, for any non-infinitesimal T, $\int_0^T |dZ| = \infty$ almost certainly and hence, with continuous trading, the total transactions cost is unbounded with probability one.

[53] This model also appears in Merton (1978) where the cost of surveillance by the deposit insurer is, in equilibrium, borne by the depositors in the form of a lower yield on their deposits. If all investors can transact without cost, then none would hold deposits and instead would invest directly in higher-yielding UST bills. Thus, to justify this form of intermediation, it is necessary to assume that at least some investors face positive transactions cost for such direct investments in the market.

who can trade continuously at zero marginal cost, then the equilibrium prices of financial products equal the production costs of the lowest-cost producers. In this competitive version of the model, equilibrium prices for derivative-security products are given by the solution to (8.2) with the appropriate boundary conditions. Merton (1990, ch. 14) shows that in this environment a set of feasible contracts between customers and intermediaries exists that allows all agents to achieve optimal consumption–bequest allocations as if they could trade continuously without cost. Thus, in this limiting case of fully-efficient and competitive intermediation, equilibrium asset prices and allocations are the same as in the zero-transactions-cost version of the model. However, mutual funds and derivative securities provide important economic benefits to investors and corporate issuers, even though these securities are priced in equilibrium as if they were redundant. With these remarks on the robustness of the model as background, we turn now to the issues of general-equilibrium pricing and the efficiency of allocations for the continuous-trading model of Section 7.

10. Intertemporal capital asset pricing

Using the continuous-time model of portfolio selection described in Section 7, Merton (1973b) and Breeden (1979) aggregate individual investor demand functions and impose market-clearing conditions to derive an intertemporal model of equilibrium asset prices. Solnik (1974) and Stulz (1981) use the model to derive equilibrium prices in an international context. By assuming constant-returns-to-scale production technologies with stochastic outputs and technical progress described by diffusion processes, Cox, Ingersoll and Ross (1985a) develop a general-equilibrium version of the model which explicitly integrates the real and financial sectors of the economy. Huang (1985a, 1985b, 1987) further strengthens the foundation for these models by showing that if information in an economy with continuous-trading opportunities evolves according to diffusion processes, then intertemporal-equilibrium security prices will also evolve according to diffusion processes.

In Proposition 5.5 it was shown that if X denotes the return on any mean–variance efficient portfolio (with positive dispersion), then the expected returns on each of the n risky assets used to construct this portfolio will satisfy $\bar{Z}_j - R = a_j(\bar{X} - R)$, where $a_j \equiv \operatorname{cov}(Z_j, X)/\operatorname{var}(X)$, $j = 1, \ldots, n$. Because the returns on all mean–variance efficient portfolios are perfectly positively correlated, this relation will apply with respect to any such portfolio. Moreover, because Proposition 5.5 is purely a mathematical result, it follows immediately for the model of Section 7 that at time t:

$$\alpha_j(t) - r(t) = a_j^*(t)[\alpha^*(t) - r(t)], \quad j = 1, \ldots, n, \tag{10.1}$$

where α^* is the expected return on an (instantaneously) mean–variance efficient portfolio and a_j^* equals the instantaneous covariance of the return on security j with this portfolio divided by the instantaneous variance of the portfolio's return. Thus, knowledge of the expected return and variance of a mean–variance efficient portfolio together with the covariance of that portfolio's return with the return on asset j is sufficient information to determine the risk and expected return on asset j. It is, however, generally difficult to identify an ex ante mean–variance efficient portfolio by statistical estimation alone and hence, the practical application of (10.1) is limited.

As shown in Sections 4 and 5, the Sharpe–Lintner–Mossin Capital Asset Pricing Model provides an example where identification without estimation is possible. Because all investors in that model hold the same relative proportions of risky assets, market-clearing conditions for equilibrium imply that the market portfolio is mean–variance efficient. The mathematical identity (10.1) is thus transformed into the Security Market Line (Theorem 4.8) which has economic content. The market portfolio can, in principle, be identified without knowledge of the joint distribution of security returns.

From (7.8) the relative holdings of risky assets will not in general be the same for all investors in the continuous-trading model. Thus, the market portfolio need not be mean–variance efficient as a condition for equilibrium, and therefore the Security Market Line will not obtain in general. However, Merton (1973b, p. 881, 1977a, p. 149, 1990, p. 510) and Breeden (1979, p. 273) show that equilibrium expected returns will satisfy:

$$\alpha_j(t) - r(t) = \sum_1^{m+1} B_{ij}(t)[\alpha^i(t) - r(t)] , \quad j = 1, \ldots, n , \tag{10.2}$$

where α^1 is the expected return on the market portfolio; α^i is the expected return on a portfolio with the maximum feasible correlation of its return with the change in state variable S_{i-1}, $i = 2, \ldots, m + 1$; and the $\{B_{ij}\}$ correspond to the theoretical multiple-regression coefficients from regressing the (instantaneous) returns of security j on the returns of these $m + 1$ portfolios. (10.2) is a natural generalization of the Security Market Line and is therefore aptly called the *Security Market Hyperplane*.

Let dX^i/X^i, $i = 1, \ldots, m + 1$, denote the instantaneous rate of return on the ith portfolio whose expected return is represented on the right-hand side of (10.2). It follows immediately from the definition of the $\{B_{ij}\}$ that the return dynamics on asset j can be written as:

$$dP_j/P_j = r(t) \, dt + \sum_1^{m+1} B_{ij}(t)(dX^i/X^i - r(t) \, dt) + d\varepsilon_j , \tag{10.3}$$

where $d\varepsilon_j$ is a diffusion process such that $E_t(d\varepsilon_j) = E_t(d\varepsilon_j | dX^1/X^1, \ldots, dX^{m+1}/X^{m+1}) = 0$. (10.3) is the continuous-trading dynamic analog to the result derived for static models of spanning in Theorem 4.6. If the $\{B_{ij}(t)\}$ are sufficiently slowly varying functions of time relative to the intervals over which successive returns are observed, then from (10.3) these risk-measure coefficients can, in principle, be estimated using time-series regressions of individual security returns on the spanning portfolios' returns.

From Lemma 7.1 we have that $dX^{i+1}/X^{i+1} = dS_i - dY_i$, $i = 1, \ldots, m$, where dY_i is uncorrelated with all securities' returns and therefore is uncorrelated with dX^k/X^k, and $d\varepsilon_j$, $k = 1, \ldots, m+1$, and $j = 1, \ldots, n$. It follows from (10.3) that

$$dP_j/P_j = A_j(t) \, dt + B_{1j}(t)[dX^1/X^1 - r(t) \, dt] + \sum_2^{m+1} B_{ij}(t) \, dS_{i-1} + d\varepsilon'_j \, ,$$

$$(10.4)$$

where $A_j(t)$ is a locally non-stochastic drift term and $d\varepsilon'_j \equiv d\varepsilon_j - \sum_2^{m+1} B_{ij}(t)[dY_{i-1} - E_t(dY_{i-1})]$. Although $E_t(d\varepsilon'_j) = 0$ and $E_t(d\varepsilon_j | dX^1/X^1, dS_1, \ldots, dS_m) = 0$, it is *not* the case that $E_t(d\varepsilon'_j | dX^1/X^1, dS_1, \ldots, dS_m) = 0$ (unless $dY_i \equiv 0$, $i = 1, \ldots, m$). Hence, unlike (10.3), (10.4) is not a properly specified regression equation because dS_i and dY_k are not uncorrelated for every $i, k = 1, \ldots, m$. Thus, it is not in general valid to regress speculative-price returns on the change in non-speculative-price state variables to obtain estimates of the $\{B_{ij}(t)\}$.

By Itô's Lemma, in the region where $C_q > 0$, the unanticipated change in investor q's optimal consumption rate can be written as:

$$dC_q - E_t(dC_q) = (\partial C_q/\partial W_q) \sum_1^n w_j^* W_q \sigma_j \, dZ_j + \sum_1^m (\partial C_q/\partial S_i) H_i \, dq_i \, ,$$

$$(10.5)$$

where $\{w_j^*\}$ is his optimal holding of security j as given in (7.8). Let dX^*/X^* denote the return on the mean–variance efficient portfolio, which allocates fraction $\sum_1^n v_{ij}(\alpha_i - r)$ to security j, $j = 1, \ldots, n$, and the balance to the riskless security. By substitution for $w_j^* W_q$ from (7.8) and rearranging terms, we can rewrite (10.5) as:

$$dC_q - E_t(dC_q) = V_q(dX^*/X^* - \alpha^* \, dt) - \sum_1^m (\partial C_q/\partial S_i)[dY_i - E_t(dY_i)] \, ,$$

$$(10.6)$$

where $V_q \equiv [\partial C_q/\partial W_q] K_q$ and dY_i is as defined in Lemma 7.1. From Lemma 7.1, dP_j/P_j and dY_i are uncorrelated for $j = 1, \ldots, n$ and $i = 1, \ldots, m$. It follows, therefore, that $\text{cov}[dC_q, dP_j/P_j] = V_q \text{cov}[dX^*/X^*, dP_j/P_j]$. If $\bar{C} \equiv \Sigma_q C_q$ denotes aggregate consumption, then by the linearity of the covariance operator, we have that

$$\text{cov}[d\bar{C}, dP_j/P_j] = V \text{cov}[dX^*/X^*, dP_j/P_j], \quad j = 1, \ldots, n, \tag{10.7}$$

where $V \equiv \Sigma_q V_q$. But, from (10.1), $(\alpha_j - r) = \text{cov}[dX^*/X^*, dP_j/P_j](\alpha^* - r)/\text{var}[dX^*/X^*]$. Hence, from (10.1) and (10.7), we have that

$$\alpha_k - r = \beta_{kC}(\alpha_j - r)/\beta_{jC}, \quad k, j = 1, \ldots, n, \tag{10.8}$$

where $\beta_{kC} \equiv \text{cov}[d\bar{C}, dP_k/P_k]/\text{var}[d\bar{C}]$. Thus, from (10.8) a security's risk can be measured by a single composite statistic: namely, the covariance between its return and the change in aggregate consumption. Breeden (1979, pp. 274–276) was the first to derive this relation which combines the generality of (10.2)–(10.4) with the simplicity of the classic Security Market Line.[54]

If in the model of Section 7 the menu of available securities is sufficiently rich that investors can perfectly hedge against unanticipated changes in each of the state variables $S_1, \ldots, S_m$, then from Lemma 7.1 $\text{var}(dY_i) = 0$ for $i = 1, \ldots, m$. From (10.6), unanticipated changes in each investor's optimal consumption rate are instantaneously perfectly correlated with the returns on a mean–variance efficient portfolio and therefore, are instantaneously perfectly correlated with unanticipated changes in aggregate consumption. This special case analyzed in (7.11) and (7.12) takes on added significance because Breeden (1979) among others has shown that intertemporal equilibrium allocations will be Pareto efficient if such perfect hedging opportunities are available.

This efficiency finding for general preferences and endowments is perhaps surprising, because it is well known that a competitive equilibrium does not in general produce Pareto-optimal allocations without complete Arrow–Debreu markets. Because the dynamics of the model in Section 7 are described by diffusion processes, there is a continuum of possible states over any finite interval of time. Therefore, complete markets in this model would seem to require an uncountable number of pure Arrow–Debreu securities. However, as we know from the work of Arrow (1953) and Radner (1972), an Arrow–Debreu equilibrium allocation can be achieved without a full set of pure time–state contingent securities if the menu of available securities is sufficient for agents to use dynamic-trading strategies to replicate the payoff structures of the pure securities. Along the lines of the contingent-claims analysis of Section

[54]Although equilibrium condition (10.2) will apply in the cases of either state-dependent direct utility, $U(C, S, t)$, utilities which depend on the path of past consumption, or models with transactions costs for the consumption good, (10.8) will no longer obtain under these conditions [cf. Grossman and Laroque (forthcoming) and Merton (1990, ch. 15)].

8, we now show that if perfect hedging of the state variables is feasible, then the Radner conditions are satisfied by the continuous-trading model of Section 7.

By hypothesis, it is possible to construct portfolios whose returns are instantaneously perfectly correlated with changes in each of the state variables, $[dS_1(t), \ldots, dS_m(t)]$, as described by (7.1). For notational simplicity and without loss of generality, assume that the first m available risky securities are these portfolios so that $dZ_i = dq_i$, $i = 1, \ldots, m$.

With subscripts denoting partial derivatives of Π, with respect to $(S_1, \ldots, S_m, t)$, let $\Pi(S, t; \bar{S}, T)$ satisfy the linear partial differential equation:

$$0 = \tfrac{1}{2} \sum_1^m \sum_1^m H_i H_j \eta_{ij} \Pi_{ij} + \sum_1^m [G_j - H_j(\alpha_j - r)/\sigma_j]\Pi_j + \Pi_{m+1} - r\Pi \qquad (10.9)$$

subject to the boundary conditions: $\Pi(S, t; \bar{S}, T) \geq 0$ and $\int_{\bar{S}} \Pi(S, t; \bar{S}, T) \, d\bar{S}_1 \ldots d\bar{S}_m \leq 1$ for all S and $t < T$; for a given $\varepsilon > 0$, $\Pi(S, T; \bar{S}, T) = 1/\varepsilon$ if $\bar{S}_k - \varepsilon/2 \leq S_k \leq \bar{S}_k + \varepsilon/2$ for each $k = 1, 2, \ldots, m$ and $\Pi(S, T; \bar{S}, T) = 0$ otherwise.[55]

Consider the continuous-trading portfolio strategy that allocates the fraction $\delta_j(t) = \Pi_j H_j/[\sigma_j V(t)]$ to security j, $j = 1, \ldots, m$, and the balance to the riskless asset, where $V(t)$ denotes the value of the portfolio at time t. From (7.3) the dynamics of the portfolio value can be written as:

$$dV = V\left\{\left[\sum_1^m \delta_j(\alpha_j - r) + r\right] dt + \sum_1^m \delta_j \sigma_j \, dZ_j\right\}$$

$$= \left[\sum_1^m \Pi_j H_j(\alpha_j - r)/\sigma_j + rV\right] dt + \sum_1^m \Pi_j H_j \, dq_j, \qquad (10.10)$$

because $dZ_j = dq_j$, $j = 1, \ldots, m$.

Because Π is twice-continuously differentiable, we can use Itô's Lemma to write the dynamics of $\Pi(S(t), t)$ as:

$$d\Pi = \left(\tfrac{1}{2} \sum_1^m \sum_1^m H_i H_j \eta_{ij} \Pi_{ij} + \sum_1^m [G_j \Pi_j] + \Pi_{m+1}\right) dt + \sum_1^m \Pi_j H_j \, dq_j. \qquad (10.11)$$

But, $\Pi(S, t)$ satisfies (10.9) and hence (10.11) can be rewritten as:

$$d\Pi = \left[\sum_1^m \Pi_j H_j(\alpha_j - r)/\sigma_j + r\Pi\right] dt + \sum_1^m \Pi_j H_j \, dq_j. \qquad (10.12)$$

---

[55] Under mild regularity conditions on the functions H, η, G, α, σ, and r, a solution exists and is unique.

From (10.10) and (10.12), $d\Pi - dV = r(\Pi - V)\,dt$. Therefore, if the initial investment in the portfolio is chosen so that $V(0) = \Pi(S(0), 0)$, then $V(t) = \Pi(S(t), t)$ for $0 \le t \le T$.

Thus, by using $(m + 1)$ available securities, a dynamic portfolio strategy has been constructed with a payoff structure that matches the boundary conditions of (10.9). By taking the appropriate limit as $\varepsilon \to 0$, the solution of (10.9) provides the portfolio prescription to exactly replicate the payoff to a pure Arrow–Debreu security, which pays \$1 at time T if $S_k(T) = \bar{S}_k$, $k = 1, \ldots, m$, and pays 0 otherwise.[56] by changing the parameters $\bar{S}$ and T, one can generate the portfolio rules to replicate all of the uncountable number of Arrow–Debreu securities using just $m + 1$ securities.[57]

As in the similar analysis of derivative-security pricing in Section 8, we have here that $\Pi(S, t)$ will also be the equilibrium price for the corresponding Arrow–Debreu security. Note, however, that unlike the analysis in Section 8, the solution to (10.9) requires knowledge of the expected returns $(\alpha_1, \ldots, \alpha_m)$. The reason is that the state variables of the system are not speculative prices. If they were, then to avoid arbitrage, G_j, H_j, α_j, σ_j, and r would have to satisfy the condition $[G_j - rS_j]/H_j = (\alpha_j - r)/\sigma_j$, $j = 1, \ldots, m$. In that case, the coefficient of Π_j in (10.9) can be rewritten as rS_j, $j = 1, \ldots, m$, and the solution of (10.9) does not require explicit knowledge of either G_j or α_j.

As we saw in Section 8, options are a fundamental security in the theory of derivative-security pricing. As demonstrated in a discrete-time context by Ross (1976b), options can also be used in an important way to complete markets and thereby, to improve allocational efficiency.

The close connection between pure state securities and options in the continuous-time model is perhaps best exemplified by the work of Breeden and Litzenberger (1978). They analyze the pricing of state-contingent claims in the scalar case where a single variable is sufficient to describe the state of the economy. A "butterfly-spread" option strategy holds a long position in two call options, one with exercise price $E - \Delta$ and the other with exercise price $E + \Delta$,

---

[56] Of course, with a continuum of states, the price of any one Arrow–Debreu security, like the probability of a state, is infinitesimal. The solution to (10.9) is analogous to a probability density and therefore, the actual Arrow–Debreu price is $\Pi(S, t)\,d\bar{S}_1 \ldots d\bar{S}_m$. The limiting boundary condition for $t = T$ in (10.9) is a vector, generalized Dirac delta function.

[57] The derivation can be generalized to the case in Section 7, where $dZ_{m+1}, \ldots, dZ_n$ are not perfectly correlated with the state variables by adding the mean–variance efficient portfolio to the $m + 1$ portfolios used here. As shown in Merton (1990, chs. 14 and 16), such a portfolio must generally be included as part of the state-space description if these path-independent pure securities are to span the entire optimal consumption–bequest allocation set. Cox, Ingersoll and Ross (1985a) present a more general version of partial differential equation (10.9), which describes general-equilibrium pricing for all assets and securities in the economy. See Duffie (1986, 1988) for discussion of existence of equilibrium in these general models.

and a short position in two call options with exercise price E, where the expiration dates of the options are the same. If options are available on a security whose price $V(t)$ is in one-to-one correspondence with the state variable, then the payoff to a state-contingent claim which pays $1 at time T if $V(T) = E$ and $0 otherwise, can be approximated by $1/\Delta$ units of a butterfly spread. This approximation becomes exact in the limit as $\Delta \to dE$, the infinitesimal differential. Breeden and Litzenberger thus show that the pure state security price is given by $(\partial^2 F/\partial E^2)\, dE$, where F is the call-option pricing function derived in Section 8. Under the specialized conditions for which the Black–Scholes formula (8.9) applies, the solution for the pure state security price has a closed-form given by $\exp[-r(T-t)]\Phi'(x_2)\, dE/(\sigma E\sqrt{T-t})$.

In the intertemporal version of the Arrow–Debreu complete-markets model, there is a security for every possible state of the economy, but markets need only be open "once" because agents will have no need for further trade. In the model of this section, there are many fewer securities, but agents trade continuously. Nevertheless, both models have many of the same properties. It appears, therefore, that a good substitute for having a large number of markets and securities is to have the existing markets open more frequently for trade.

In addressing this point as well as the robustness of the continuous-time model, Duffie and Huang (1985) derive necessary and sufficient conditions for continuous-trading portfolio strategies with a finite number of securities to effectively complete markets in a Radner economy. As discussed in Section 5, the Arrow–Debreu model permits some degree of heterogeneity in beliefs among agents. Just so, Duffie and Huang show that the spanning results derived here for continuous trading are robust with respect to heterogeneous probability assessments among agents provided that their subjective probability measures are uniformly absolutely continuous. In later work [Duffie and Huang (1986)] they derive conditions where these results obtain in the more general framework of differential information among agents.[58]

Although continuous trading is, of course, only a theoretical proposition, the continuous-trading solutions will be an asymptotically valid approximation to the discrete-time solutions as the trading interval becomes small.[59] An in-depth discussion of the mathematical and economic assumptions required for the valid application of the continuous-time analysis is beyond the scope of this chapter.[60] However, actual securities markets are open virtually all the time,

---

[58]Other research in this area includes Williams (1977), Hellwig (1982), Gennotte (1986), and Dothan and Feldman (1986).

[59]See Samuelson (1970) and Merton and Samuelson (1974). Merton (1975, p. 663) discusses special cases in which the limiting discrete-time solutions do not approach the continuous-time solutions.

[60]Merton (1982b, 1990) discusses in detail the economic assumptions required for the continuous-time methodology. Moreover, most of the mathematical tools for manipulation of these models are derived using only elementary probability theory and the calculus.

and hence the required assumptions are rather reasonable when applied in that context.

In summary, we have seen that all the interesting models of portfolio selection and capital market theory share in common, the property of non-trivial spanning. If, however, a model is to be broadly applicable, then it should also satisfy the further conditions that: (i) the number of securities required for spanning be considerably smaller than both the number of agents and the number of possible states for the economy; and (ii) the creation of securities with non-linear sharing rules by an individual investor or firm should not, in general, alter the size of the spanning set. As we have also seen, the continuous-trading model with vector diffusions for the underlying state variables meets these criteria. Motivated in part by the important work of Harrison and Kreps (1979), Duffie and Huang (1985) use martingale representation theorems to show that with continuous trading these conditions can also obtain for a class of non-Markov, path-dependent processes, some of which do not have continuous sample paths.[61] It remains, however, an open and important research question as to whether in the absence of continuous trading these criteria can be satisfied in interesting models with general preferences and endowments.

[61] If the underlying dynamics of the system include Poisson-driven processes with discontinuous sample paths, then the resulting equilibrium prices will satisfy a mixed partial difference-differential equation. In the case of non-Markov path-dependent processes, the valuation conditions cannot be represented as a partial differential equation.

References

Adler, M. and B. Dumas (1983) 'International portfolio choice and corporation finance: A synthesis', *Journal of Finance*, 38: 925–984.

Arrow, K.J. (1953) 'Le rôle des valeurs boursières pour la répartition la meilleure des risques', *Econometrie*, Colloques Internationaux du Centre National de la Recherche Scientifique, Vol. XI, Paris, pp. 41–47.

Arrow, K.J. (1964) 'The role of securities in the optimal allocation of risk bearing,' *Review of Economic Studies*, 31: 91–96.

Bawa, V.S. (1975) 'Optimal rules for ordering uncertain prospects', *Journal of Financial Economics*, 2: 95–121.

Bertsekas, D.P. (1974) 'Necessary and sufficient conditions for existence of an optimal portfolio', *Journal of Economic Theory*, 8: 235–247.

Bhattacharya, S. (1989) 'Financial markets and incomplete information: A review of some recent developments', in: S. Bhattacharya and G.M. Constantinides, eds., *Frontiers of modern financial theory: Financial markets and incomplete information*. Totowa: Rowman and Littlefield.

Black, F. (1972) 'Capital market equilibrium with restricted borrowing', *Journal of Business*, 45: 444–455.

Black, F. (1986) 'Noise', *Journal of Finance*, 41: 529–543.

Black, F. (1987) 'The week's citation classic', *Current Contents/Social and Behavioral Science*, 33: 17 August. Philadelphia: Institute for Scientific Information, p. 16.

Black, F. and M. Scholes (1973) 'The pricing of options and corporate liabilities', *Journal of Political Economy*, 81: 637–654.

Borch, K. (1969) 'A note on uncertainty and indifference curves', *Review of Economic Studies*, 36: 1–4.

Breeden, D.T. (1979) 'An intertemporal asset pricing model with stochastic consumption and investment opportunities', *Journal of Financial Economics*, 7: 265–296.

Breeden, D.T. and R. Litzenberger (1978) 'Prices of state-contingent claims implicit in option prices', *Journal of Business*, 51: 621–651.

Cass, D. and J.E. Stiglitz (1970) 'The structure of investor preferences and asset returns, and separability in portfolio allocation: A contribution to the pure theory of mutual funds', *Journal of Economic Theory*, 2: 122–160.

Chamberlain, G. (1983) 'A characterization of the distributions that imply mean–variance utility functions', *Journal of Economic Theory*, 29: 185–201.

Chamberlain, G. and M. Rothschild (1983) 'Arbitrage and mean–variance analysis on large asset markets', *Econometrica*, 51: 1281–1301.

Chen, N. and J.E. Ingersoll (1983) 'Exact pricing in linear factor models with finitely-many assets: A note', *Journal of Finance*, 38: 985–988.

Constantinides, G. (1986) 'Capital market equilibrium with transactions costs', *Journal of Political Economy*, 94: 842–862.

Constantinides, G. and M. Scholes (1980) 'Optimal liquidation of assets in the presence of personal taxes: Implications for asset pricing', *Journal of Finance*, 35: 439–443.

Cox, D.A. and H.D. Miller (1968) *The theory of stochastic processes*. New York: John Wiley.

Cox, J.C. and C. Huang (1989) 'Optimum consumption and portfolio policies when asset prices follow a diffusion process', *Journal of Economic Theory*, 49: 33–83.

Cox, J.C. and C. Huang (forthcoming) 'A variational problem arising in financial economics with an application to a portfolio turnpike theorem', *Journal of Mathematical Economics*.

Cox, J.C. and M. Rubinstein (1985) *Options markets*. Englewood Cliffs: Prentice-Hall.

Cox, J.C., J.E. Ingersoll and S.A. Ross (1985a) 'An intertemporal general equilibrium model of asset prices', *Econometrica*, 53: 363–384.

Cox, J.C., J.E. Ingersoll and S.A. Ross (1985b) 'A theory of the term structure of interest rates', *Econometrica*, 53: 385–408.

Debreu, G. (1959) *Theory of value*. New York: John Wiley.

Dhrymes, P., I. Friend and N. Gultekin (1984) 'A critical examination of the empirical evidence on the arbitrage pricing theory', *Journal of Finance*, 39: 323–347.

Dhrymes, P., I. Friend and N. Gultekin (1985) 'New tests of the APT and their implications', *Journal of Finance*, 40: 659–674.

Dothan, M.U. and D. Feldman (1986) 'Equilibrium interest rates and multiperiod bonds in a partially observable economy', *Journal of Finance*, 41: 369–382.

Dreyfus, S.E. (1965) *Dynamic programming and the calculus of variations*. New York: Academic Press.

Duffie, D. (1986) 'Stochastic equilibria: Existence, spanning number, and the "no expected financial gain from trade" hypothesis', *Econometrica* 54: 1161–1184.

Duffie, D. (1988) *Security markets: Stochastic models*. New York: Academic Press.

Duffie, D. and C. Huang (1985) 'Implementing Arrow–Debreu equilibria by continuous trading of few long-lived securities', *Econometrica*, 53: 1337–1356.

Duffie, D. and C. Huang (1986) 'Multiperiod securities markets with differential information: Martingales and resolution times', *Journal of Mathematical Economics*, 15: 283–303.

Dybvig, P. and S.A. Ross (1982) 'Portfolio efficient sets', *Econometrica*, 50: 1525–1546.

Fama, E. (1965) 'The behavior of stock market prices', *Journal of Business*, 38: 34–105.

Fama, E. (1970a) 'Efficient capital markets: A review of theory and empirical work', *Journal of Finance*, 25: 383–417.

Fama, E. (1970b) 'Multiperiod consumption–investment decisions', *American Economic Review*, 60: 163–174.

Fama, E. (1978) 'The effects of a firm's investment and financing decisions on the welfare of its securityholders', *American Economic Review*, 68: 272–284.

Farrar, D.E. (1962) *The investment decision under uncertainty*. Englewood Cliffs: Prentice-Hall.

Farrell, J.L. (1974) 'Analyzing covariation of returns to determine homogeneous stock groupings', *Journal of Business*, 47: 186–207.

Feeney, G.J. and D. Hester (1967) 'Stock market indices: A principal components analysis', in: D. Hester and J. Tobin, eds., *Risk aversion and portfolio choice*. New York: John Wiley.

Feldstein, M.S. (1969) 'Mean–variance analysis in the theory of liquidity preference and portfolio selection', *Review of Economic Studies*, 36: 5–12.

Feller, W. (1966) *An introduction to probability theory and its applications*, Vol. 2. New York: John Wiley.

Fischer, S. (1972) 'Assets, contingent commodities, and the Slutsky equations', *Econometrica*, 40: 371–385.

Fischer, S. and R.C. Merton (1984) 'Macroeconomics and finance: The role of the stock market', in: K. Brunner and A.H. Melzer, eds., *Essays on macroeconomic implications of financial and labor markets and political processes*, Vol. 21. Amsterdam: North-Holland.

Friend, I. and J. Bicksler, eds. (1977) *Studies in risk and return*, Vols. I & II. Cambridge, Mass.: Ballinger.

Gennotte, G. (1986) 'Optimal portfolio choice under incomplete information', *Journal of Finance*, 41: 733–746.

Goldman, M.B. (1974) 'A Negative report on the "near-optimality" of the max-expected-log policy as applied to bounded utilities for long-lived programs', *Journal of Financial Economics*, 1: 97–103.

Grossman, S. (1976) 'On the efficiency of competitive stock markets where traders have diverse information', *Journal of Finance*, 31: 573–585.

Grossman, S. and G. Laroque (forthcoming) 'Asset pricing and optimal portfolio choice in the presence of illiquid durable consumption goods', *Econometrica*.

Grossman, S. and J.E. Stiglitz (1980) 'On the impossibility of informationally efficient markets', *American Economic Review*, 70: 393–408.

Hadar, J. and W.R. Russell (1969) 'Rules for ordering uncertain prospects', *American Economic Review*, 59: 25–34.

Hadar, J. and W.R. Russell (1971) 'Stochastic dominance and diversification', *Journal of Economic Theory*, 3: 288–305.

Hakansson, N. (1970) 'Optimal investment and consumption strategies under risk for a class of utility functions', *Econometrica*, 38: 587–607.

Hanoch, G. and H. Levy (1969) 'The efficiency analysis of choices involving risk', *Review of Economic Studies*, 36: 335–346.

Hansen, L. (1985) 'Auctions with contingent payments', *American Economic Review*, 75: 862–865.

Hardy, G.H., J.E. Littlewood and G. Pólya (1959) *Inequalities*. Cambridge: Cambridge University Press.

Harrison, J.M. (1985) *Brownian motion and stochastic flow systems*. New York: John Wiley.

Harrison, J.M. and D. Kreps (1979) 'Martingales and arbitrage in multiperiod securities markets', *Journal of Economic Theory*, 20: 381–408.

Hellwig, M.F. (1982) 'Rational expectations equilibrium with conditioning on past prices', *Journal of Economic Theory*, 26: 279–312.

Herstein, I. and J. Milnor (1953) 'An axiomatic approach to measurable utility', *Econometrica*, 21: 291–297.

Hirshleifer, J. (1965) 'Investment decision under uncertainty: Choice-theoretic approaches', *Quarterly Journal of Economics*, 79: 509–536.

Hirshleifer, J. (1966) 'Investment decision under uncertainty: Applications of the state-preference approach', *Quarterly Journal of Economics*, 80: 252–277.

Hirshleifer, J. (1970) *Investment, interest and capital*. Englewood Cliffs: Prentice-Hall.

Hirshleifer, J. (1973) 'Where are we in the theory of information?', *American Economic Review*, 63: 31–39.

Hogarth, R.M. and M.W. Reder, eds. (1986) 'The behavioral foundations of economic theory', *Journal of Business* No. 4, Part 2, 59: S181–S505.

Huang, C. (1985a) 'Information structure and equilibrium asset prices', *Journal of Economic Theory*, 34: 33–71.

Huang, C. (1985b) 'Information structures and viable price systems', *Journal of Mathematical Economics*, 14: 215–240.

Huang, C. (1987) 'An intertemporal general equilibrium asset pricing model: The case of diffusion information', *Econometrica*, 55: 117–142.

Huang, C. and K. Kreps (1985) 'Intertemporal preferences with a continuous time dimension: An exploratory study', Massachusetts Institute of Technology, Mimeo.

Ingersoll, Jr., J.E. (1987) *Theory of financial decision making*. Totowa: Rowman and Littlefield.

Itô, K. and H.P. McKean, Jr. (1964) *Diffusion processes and their sample paths*. New York: Academic Press.

Jensen, M.C., ed. (1972a) *Studies in the theory of capital markets*. New York: Praeger.

Jensen, M.C. (1972b) 'Capital markets: Theory and evidence', *Bell Journal of Economics and Management Science*, 3: 357–398.

Karatzas, I., J. Lehoczky, S. Sethi and S. Shreve (1986) 'Explicit solutions of a general consumption/investment problem', *Mathematics of Operations Research*, 11: 261–294.

King, B.R. (1966) 'Market and industry factors in stock price behavior', *Journal of Business*, 39, Supplement: 139–190.

Kuhn, H.W. and A.W. Tucker (1951) 'Nonlinear programming', in: J. Neyman, ed., *Proceedings of the Second Berkeley Symposium of Mathematical Statistics and Probability*. Berkeley: University of California Press.

Kushner, H.J. (1967) *Stochastic stability and control*. New York: Academic Press.

Latane, H. (1959) 'Criteria for choice among risky ventures', *Journal of Political Economy*, 67: 144–155.

Leland, H. (1972) 'On the existence of optimal policies under uncertainty', *Journal of Economic Theory*, 4: 35–44.

Leland, H. (1985) 'Option pricing and replication with transactions costs', *Journal of Finance*, 40: 1283–1301.

Lintner, J. (1965) 'The valuation of risk assets and the selection of risky investments in stock portfolios and capital budgets', *Review of Economics and Statistics*, 47: 13–37.

Livingston, M. (1977) 'Industry movements of common stocks', *Journal of Finance*, 32: 861–874.

Machina, M. (1982) ' "Expected utility" analysis without the independence axiom', *Econometrica*, 50: 277–323.

Markowitz, H. (1959) *Portfolio selection: Efficient diversification of investment*. New York: John Wiley.

Markowitz, H. (1976) 'Investment for the long run: New evidence for an old rule', *Journal of Finance*, 31: 1273–1286.

Mason, S. (1981) 'Consumption and investment incentives associated with welfare programs', Working Paper 79-34, Harvard Business School.

Mason, S. and R.C. Merton (1985) 'The role of contingent claims analysis in corporate finance,' in: E. Altman and M. Subrahmanyan, eds., *Recent advances in corporate finance*. Homewood: Richard D. Irwin.

McKean, Jr., H.P. (1969) *Stochastic integrals*. New York: Academic Press.

McShane, E.J. (1974) *Stochastic calculus and stochastic models*. New York: Academic Press.

Merton, R.C. (1969) 'Lifetime portfolio selection under uncertainty: The continuous-time case', *Review of Economics and Statistics*, 51: 247–257.

Merton, R.C. (1970) 'A dynamic general equilibrium model of the asset market and its application to the pricing of the capital structure of the firm', Working Paper 494-70, MIT Sloan School of Management.

Merton, R.C. (1971) 'Optimum consumption and portfolio rules in a continuous-time model', *Journal of Economic Theory*, 3: 373–413.

Merton, R.C. (1972) 'An analytic derivation of the efficient portfolio frontier', *Journal of Financial and Quantitative Analysis*, 7: 1851–1872.

Merton, R.C. (1973a) 'Theory of rational option pricing', *Bell Journal of Economics and Management Science*, 4: 141–183.

Merton, R.C. (1973b) 'An intertemporal capital asset pricing model', *Econometrica*, 41: 867–887.

Merton, R.C. (1974) 'On the pricing of corporate debt: The risk structure of interest rates', *Journal of Finance*, 29: 449–470.

Merton, R.C. (1975) 'Theory of finance from the perspective of continuous time', *Journal of Financial and Quantitative Analysis*, 10: 659–674.

Merton, R.C. (1977a) 'A re-examination of the capital asset pricing model', in: I. Friend and J. Bicksler, eds., *Studies in risk and return*, Vols. I & II. Cambridge, Mass.: Ballinger.

Merton, R.C. (1977b) 'On the pricing of contingent claims and the Modigliani–Miller theorem', *Journal of Financial Economics*, 5: 241–249.

Merton, R.C. (1978) 'On the cost of deposit insurance when there are surveillance costs', *Journal of Business*, 51: 439–452.

Merton, R.C. (1982a) 'On the microeconomic theory of investment under uncertainty', in: K.J. Arrow and M. Intriligator, eds., *Handbook of mathematical economics*, Vol. II. Amsterdam: North-Holland.

Merton, R.C. (1982b) 'On the mathematics and economics assumptions of continuous-time financial models', in: W.F. Sharpe and C.M. Cootner, eds., *Financial economics*: *Essays in honor of Paul Cootner*. Englewood Cliffs: Prentice-Hall.

Merton, R.C. (1987a) 'On the current state of the stock market rationality hypothesis', in: S. Fischer, R. Dornbusch and J. Bossons, eds., *Macroeconomics and finance*: *Essays in honor of Franco Modigliani*. Cambridge, Mass.: MIT Press.

Merton, R.C. (1987b) 'A simple model of capital market equilibrium with incomplete information', *Journal of Finance*, 42: 483–510.

Merton, R.C. (1989) 'On the application of the continuous-time theory of finance to financial intermediation and insurance', Twelfth Annual Lecture of the Geneva Association, *The Geneva Papers on Risk and Insurance*, 14: 225–262.

Merton, R.C. (1990) *Continuous-time finance*. Oxford: Basil Blackwell.

Merton, R.C. and P.A. Samuelson (1974) 'Fallacy of the log-normal approximation to optimal portfolio decision making over many periods', *Journal of Financial Economics*, 1: 67–94.

Meyer, R.F. (1970) 'On the relationship among the utility of assets, the utility of consumption, and investment strategy in an uncertain, but time-invariant world', in: J. Lawrence, ed., *OR69: Proceedings of the Fifth International Congress on Operational Research*. Tavistock Publications.

Miller, M.H. (1977) 'Debt and taxes', *Journal of Finance*, 32: 261–276.

Modigliani, R. and M.H. Miller (1958) 'The cost of capital, corporation finance, and the theory of investment', *American Economic Review*, 48: 261–297.

Mossin, J. (1966) 'Equilibrium in a capital asset market', *Econometrica*, 35: 768–783.

Myers, S.C. (1968) 'A time–state–preference model of security valuation', *Journal of Financial and Quantitative Analysis*, 3: 1–33.

Nielsen, L.T. (1986) 'Mutual fund separation: Factor structure and robustness', Working Paper 86/87-2-3, Graduate School of Business, University of Texas at Austin.

Parsons, J. and A. Raviv (1985) 'Underpricing of seasoned issues', *Journal of Financial Economics*, 14: 377–397.

Pratt, J.W. (1964) 'Risk aversion in the small and in the large', *Econometrica*, 32: 122–136.

Radner, R. (1972) 'Existence of plans, prices, and price expectations in a sequence of markets', *Econometrica*, 40: 289–303.

Richard, S. (1975) 'Optimal consumption, portfolio, and life insurance rules for an uncertain lived individual in a continuous-time model', *Journal of Financial Economics*, 2: 187–204.

Rock, K. (1986) 'Why new issues are underpriced', *Journal of Financial Economics*, 15: 187–212.

Roll, R. and S.A. Ross (1980) 'An empirical investigation of the arbitrage pricing theory', *Journal of Finance*, 35: 1073–1103.

Ross, S.A. (1976a) 'Arbitrage theory of capital asset pricing', *Journal of Economic Theory*, 13: 341–360.

Ross, S.A. (1976b) 'Options and efficiency', *Quarterly Journal of Economics*, 90: 75–89.

Ross, S.A. (1978) 'Mutual fund separation in financial theory: The separating distributions', *Journal of Economic Theory*, 17: 254–286.

Rothschild, M. (1986) 'Asset pricing theories', in: W.P. Heller, R.M. Starr and D.A. Starrett, eds., *Uncertainty, information and communication*: *Essays in honor of Kenneth J. Arrow*, Vol. III. Cambridge: Cambridge University Press.

Rothschild, M. and J.E. Stiglitz (1970) 'Increasing risk I: A definition', *Journal of Economic Theory*, 2: 225–243.

Rothschild, M. and J.E. Stiglitz (1971) 'Increasing risk II: Its economic consequences', *Journal of Economic Theory*, 3: 66–84.

Rubinstein, M. (1976) 'The strong case for the generalized logarithmic utility model as the premier model of financial markets', *Journal of Finance*, 31: 551–572.

Samuelson, P.A. (1965) 'Proof that properly anticipated prices fluctuate randomly', *Industrial Management Review*, 6: 41–49. Reprinted in Samuelson (1972).

Samuelson, P.A. (1967) 'General proof that diversification pays', *Journal of Financial and Quantitative Analysis*, 2: 1–13. Reprinted in Samuelson (1972).

Samuelson, P.A. (1969) 'Lifetime portfolio selection by dynamic stochastic programming', *Review of Economics and Statistics*, 51: 239–246. Reprinted in Samuelson (1972).

Samuelson, P.A. (1970) 'The fundamental approximation theory of portfolio analysis in terms of means, variances, and higher moments', *Review of Economic Studies*, 37: 537–542. Reprinted in Samuelson (1972).

Samuelson, P.A. (1971) 'The "Fallacy" of maximizing the geometric mean in long sequences of investing or gambling', *Proceedings of the National Academy of Sciences*, 68: 2493–2496. Reprinted in Samuelson (1972).

Samuelson, P.A. (1972) in: R.C. Merton, ed., *The collected scientific papers of Paul A. Samuelson*, Vol. III. Cambridge, Mass.: MIT Press.

Samuelson, P.A. (1977) 'St. Petersburg paradoxes: Defanged, dissected, and historically described', *Journal of Economic Literature*, 15: 24–55.

Samuelson, P.A. and R.C. Merton (1969) 'A complete model of warrant pricing that maximizes utility', *Industrial Management Review*, 10 (Winter): 17–46. Reprinted in Samuelson (1972).

Scholes, M. (1976) 'Taxes and the pricing of options', *Journal of Finance*, 31: 319–332.

Shanken, J. (1982) 'The arbitrage pricing theory: Is it testable?', *Journal of Finance*, 37: 1129–1140.

Sharpe, W. (1964) 'Capital asset prices: A theory of market equilibrium under conditions of risk', *Journal of Finance*, 19: 425–442.

Sharpe, W. (1970) *Portfolio theory and capital markets*. New York: McGraw-Hill.

Smith, Jr., C.W. (1976) 'Option pricing: A review', *Journal of Financial Economics*, 3: 3–52.

Solnik, B.H. (1974) 'An equilibrium model of the international capital market', *Journal of Economic Theory*, 8: 500–524.

Stiglitz, J.E. (1969) 'A re-examination of the Modigliani–Miller theorem', *American Economic Review*, 59: 78–93.

Stiglitz, J.E. (1974) 'On the irrelevance of corporate financial policy', *American Economic Review*, 64: 851–886.

Stulz, R.M. (1981) 'A model of international asset pricing', *Journal of Financial Economics*, 9: 383–406.

Sun, T. (1987) 'Transactions costs and intervals in a discrete-continuous time setting for consumption and portfolio choice', in: *Connections between discrete-time and continuous-time financial models*, Ph.D. Dissertation, Graduate School of Business, Stanford University, ch. 1.

Tobin, J. (1958) 'Liquidity preference as behavior towards risk', *Review of Economic Studies*, 25: 68–85.

Tobin, J. (1969) 'Comment on Borch and Feldstein', *Review of Economic Studies*, 36: 13–14.

Trzcinka, C. (1986) 'On the number of factors in the arbitrage pricing model', *Journal of Finance*, 41: 347–368.

Varian, H. (1985) 'Divergence of opinion in complete markets: A note', *Journal of Finance*, 40: 309–318.

von Neumann, J. and O. Morgenstern (1947) *Theory of games and economic behavior*, 2nd edn. Princeton: Princeton University Press.

Wallace, N. (1981) 'A Modigliani–Miller theorem for open-market operations', *American Economic Review*, 71: 267–274.

Williams, J.T. (1977) 'Capital asset prices with heterogeneous beliefs', *Journal of Financial Economics*, 5: 219–239.

Chapter 12

SPECIFICATION AND ESTIMATION OF INTERTEMPORAL ASSET PRICING MODELS

KENNETH J. SINGLETON*

Stanford University and NBER

Contents

*I have benefited from helpful comments by Ben Friedman and Rick Green. This research was supported by the National Science Foundation.

Handbook of Monetary Economics, Volume I, Edited by B.M. Friedman and F.H. Hahn

1. Introduction

This chapter attempts to synthesize, augment, and critique recent econometric work on dynamic, equilibrium asset pricing models. Ross (1978), Harrison and Kreps (1979), Chamberlain and Rothschild (1983), and Hansen and Richard (1987), among others, have shown that (under certain "no arbitrage" conditions) asset prices can be represented as a linear functional on a space of random payoffs. In order to deduce testable restrictions from these pricing relations, the "benchmark" payoff that represents the pricing functional must be identified with an estimable economic construct. Sufficient structure must be imposed on the economic environment, including the specifications of preferences, technology, the distributions of the underlying sources of uncertainty in the economy, and the set of feasible trades in security markets, to obtain econometrically identified asset pricing relations. This chapter reviews previous specifications of econometric models of asset price determination, and explores the properties of several extensions of these models. Particular attention is given to the tradeoffs involved in achieving econometric identification, both in terms of the economic and statistical assumptions that must be made and the limitations of the requisite data that are used in implementing alternative models.

The increased interest in the econometric implications of intertemporal asset pricing relations can be traced to several important developments in economic theory and econometric method. In the latter half of the 1970s, Rubinstein (1974, 1976), Cox, Ingersoll and Ross (1985), Lucas (1978), and Breeden (1979) deduced general equilibrium relations between consumption decisions, asset prices, and production decisions in the context of dynamic models under uncertainty. These relations were derived under the assumptions that agents had common information sets, consumers had access to a complete set of contingent claims markets, and consumers had identical preferences and equal access to all production technologies. These assumptions facilitated proofs of existence and characterizations of equilibrium asset prices. Moreover, these models served to significantly expand our understanding of the nature of hedging demands induced by aggregate uncertainty in dynamic models.

The asset pricing relations implied by these models were typically highly non-linear and not easily analyzed with existing econometric techniques. Not surprisingly, then, the initial studies explored the properties of several very special cases of these models. Hall (1978), Sargent (1978), and Flavin (1981), as well as many others subsequently, investigated versions of the permanent income–life cycle model of consumption. Preferences were assumed to be quadratic and constraints were assumed to be linear. These assumptions implied that interest rates on discount bonds were constants and consumption followed a random walk. Virtually all of the empirical studies of the permanent income model have focused on the random walk implication, which has not been supported by the data. The implication of constant real interest rates is also inconsistent with historical evidence.

Grossman and Shiller (1981) were the first to study the relation between consumption and asset returns implied by the representative agent models of Rubinstein (1970), Lucas (1978), and Breeden (1979). They studied the co-movements of consumption and returns in the context of a model in which consumers were risk averse and had perfect foresight about the future. Subsequently, Hansen and Singleton (1982, 1983) developed methods for estimating the parameters of asset pricing relations implied by stochastic dynamic models that incorporate fairly general specifications of concave preference functions. These methods have been applied to study asset pricing relations implied by a wide variety of specifications of preferences, including the HARA class and certain CES-type functions.

The theoretical underpinnings of all of these econometric studies are essentially those of the pioneering studies by Rubinstein (1976) and Lucas (1978). Though extended versions of these models have incorporated non-time-separable utility and multiple goods, the market structures and homogeneity conditions are the same. By proceeding in this manner, the probability models estimated have retained easily interpretable links to the formal theory. Consequently, recent econometric studies have provided useful feedback on the strengths and weaknesses of these theories for explaining intertemporal consumption and investment decisions.

A primary objective of this chapter is to summarize the large body of empirical evidence on the goodness-of-fit of intertemporal asset pricing models. In Section 2 I briefly describe the representation of asset prices in terms of a linear functional on a space of random payoffs. When agents can trade a "complete" set of contingent claims to goods in the future the benchmark payoff that defines this functional can be identified with the intertemporal marginal rate of substitution of a numeraire good. Most of the recent empirical studies of dynamic asset pricing models have examined special cases of this linear functional with the marginal rate of substitution specified parametrically using a member of the family of S-branch utility functions. Therefore, a representation of this family of utility functions along with some of its properties are also described in Section 2.

Section 3 discusses the literature on linear asset pricing models. No attempt is made to present a comprehensive survey of this voluminous literature. Instead, attention is focused primarily on the following two related issues. First, the conditions under which linear asset pricing models can be deduced as special cases of dynamic equilibrium models are explored. In particular, versions of the simple present-value model for stocks and the expectations theory of the term structure of interest rates are interpreted as general equilibrium models. Then, drawing upon this discussion, empirical tests of traditional linear models are re-interpreted as tests of the validity of certain intertemporal equilibrium models. Some of the empirical evidence presented in the literature to support or refute these models is re-assessed, and some new evidence is presented.

Several non-linear asset pricing models in which agents have preferences defined over a single consumption good ("non-durable goods") are discussed in Section 4. Common features of these models are that preferences are specified parametrically, markets for contingent claims to goods are complete, and there are no taste shocks. The limitations of these models in representing the historical co-movements of consumption and real returns on stocks and bonds are explored in depth. Among the issues addressed are the autocorrelation properties of the disturbances, the sensitivity of the results to the length of the holding period of the investments, and the relation between the average growth in consumption, the average real returns, and the estimated parameters for the post-war period. The findings from this analysis strongly suggest that the single-good, representative agent model of asset prices is incapable of explaining several important features of the data.

One possible explanation for the poor performance of models with consumption defined over non-durable goods is that utility is not separable across non-durable goods and durable goods or leisure. This explanation is explored in Section 5, where multi-good models of asset pricing are discussed. Most of this discussion focuses on the properties of models in which utility is defined over the service flows from goods that are durable in character, though models incorporating leisure are also discussed briefly. The implications of these models for the relative volatility of asset returns and the decision variables of agents, as well as the behavior of the implied risk premia, are reviewed. In addition, the extent to which these models overcome some of the empirical failings of the single-good models is assessed.

Finally, in Section 6 some remarks about directions for future research on intertemporal asset pricing models suggested by previous studies and the additional evidence in this chapter are presented.

2. The economic environment

Suppose that there is a complete set of markets for contingent claims to future quantities of a finite number of goods in the economy; and there are no taxes, short-sale restrictions, or transactions costs. Also, suppose agents have a common information set I_t at date t and that utility is concave. Let Q_{t+1}^c denote the closed subspace of square integrable payoffs from securities that are elements of I_{t+1} (i.e. I_{t+1} measurable) and are denominated in terms of the numeraire good. Then the price at date t of the payoff of $q_{t+1} \in Q^c_{t+1}$, denoted by $\pi_t(q_{t+1})$, can be expressed as a conditional inner product of q_{t+1} with the marginal rate of substitution of the numeraire good at date t for the numeraire good at date $t+1$ (m^1_{t+1}):[1]

$$\pi_t(q_{t+1}) = E[m^1_{t+1}q_{t+1} \mid I_t], \quad q_{t+1} \in Q^c_{t+1}. \tag{1}$$

In principle, (1) holds for each individual consumer. For the purpose of empirical work with time series data, however, it is often convenient to work with aggregate data on consumption and leisure decisions. Accordingly, one must either ignore distributional effects or impose sufficient structure on the problem to allow for aggregation up to a representative "stand-in" consumer.

Under the assumptions of complete markets and additively separable, concave, state independent utility for individual agents, there exists a utility function in the same class defined over aggregate consumption which prices securities in Q^c_{t+1} [Constantinides (1982)]. That is, if m^1_{t+1} in (1) is set equal to the marginal rate of substitution associated with this utility function of aggregate consumption, then (1) yields the same prices as those obtained with the individual agents' m^1_{t+1}. In general, the functional form of the utility function defined over aggregate consumption will not be the same as any of the individual agents' utility functions. Also, the demands of the stand-in consumer must agree with the aggregate demands only at the equilibrium price. Thus, many interesting economic issues, including the consequences of many interventions by policy authorities, cannot be addressed using this framework.

Most of the utility functions that have been studied empirically admit a stronger, exact form of demand aggregation. Rubinstein (1974) has shown that there is exact demand aggregation for single-good models in which agents preferences reside in the HARA class and markets are complete. More recently, Eichenbaum, Hansen and Richard (1985) have shown that aggregation extends to certain multi-good models in which goods are durable in character and the service flows from goods are produced according to linear technologies. Consistent with most of the recent literature, economic environments that imply exact demand aggregation will be explored in this chapter.

To be concrete, consider the following version of the S-branch utility function discussed by Eichenbaum, Hansen and Richard (1985). Let s_{jt} denote an m-dimensional vector of services from consumption goods for consumer j at

---

[1]See, for example, Lucas (1978) and Hansen and Richard (1987). Hansen and Richard (1987) explore the representation of asset pricing functions in much more general setups then the one considered here.

date t, and suppose the jth consumer ranks alternative streams of consumption services using the utility function:

$$[1/(\delta\sigma)]E\left[\sum_{t=1}^{\infty} \beta'\{U(s_{jt})^{\sigma} - 1\}|I_0\right], \tag{2}$$

where $\delta = (1 - \sigma)$ and U is given by

$$U(s_{jt}) = \left\{\sum_{i=1}^{m} \theta_i\{\delta[s_{jt}^i]\}^{\alpha}\right\}^{1/\alpha}.$$

The parameter β is a subjective discount factor between zero and one and the θ_i satisfy $0 < \theta_i < 1$ and $\sum \theta_i = 1$. There are two branches to this utility function corresponding to whether σ is less than or greater than one. Special cases of (2) and (3) include period utility functions that have the Cobb–Douglas form ($\sigma < 1$, $\alpha = 0$), and quadratic utility ($\sigma = 2$, $\alpha = 1$). These cases are discussed in more detail in Sections 4 and 5.

I shall assume that the dimension (m) of the vector of service flows s_{jt} is the same as the number of consumption goods in the economy.[2] Additionally, the service flows are assumed to be generated by the linear technology:

$$s_{jt} = A(L)e_{jt}, \tag{4}$$

where e_{jt} is the m-dimensional vector of endowments of the m goods for consumer j at date t and $A(L)$ is a polynomial in the lag operator given by

$$A(L) = \sum_{\tau=0}^{\infty} a_{\tau}L^{\tau}. \tag{5}$$

A positive value of the $i\ell$th entry of a_{τ}, $\tau > 0$, implies that acquisition of the ℓth good in period $t - \tau$ contributes to the production of services from the ith good in period t, while a negative entry implies that the ℓth good contributes disservices to the service flow from good i. Examples of both positive and negative a_{τ} are discussed subsequently.

Eichenbaum, Hansen and Richard (1985) show that if there is a complete set of contingent claims to services from goods and agents have identical utility functions given by (2)–(5), then equilibrium prices for securities in a representative consumer economy are identical to those of the underlying multi-consumer economy. Furthermore, if the polynomial $A(L)$ has a one-sided inverse and certain other regularity conditions are satisfied, then the existence

---

[2] Eichenbaum, Hansen and Richard (1985) also discuss the case where the dimension of the endowment vector does not equal the dimension of s_{jt}.

of complete markets in claims to future services implies complete markets in claims to future goods and vice versa. Thus, for the purposes of empirical work, one can proceed with the use of aggregate per-capita data even though consumers are heterogeneous with regard to their endowments (e.g. "rich" and "poor").

Throughout Sections 3 through 5 of this chapter, agents are assumed to have utility functions that are special cases of (2)–(5). These special cases include the time-separable linear risk tolerance and risk neutral specifications adopted in many econometric studies of intertemporal asset pricing models. They also include members of this class of preference functions that accommodate much richer patterns of intertemporal substitution. Recent studies of asset prices using the parameterization (2)–(5) with non-trivial $A(L)$ in (5) have been motivated in part by the limitations of time-separable specifications in explaining asset return behavior.

Even with the flexibility and generality of (2)–(5), the models to be examined in subsequent sections remain very restrictive in several potentially important respects. First, strong homogeneity assumptions are imposed – agents have common utility functions and a common information set. Second, unobserved (by the econometrician) taste shocks are excluded. The economic environment is also one where all agents are interior with regard to their consumption and labor supply decisions, so the "frictions" that would preclude such equilibria are assumed to be absent.

In particular, exchange via fiat money is a key feature of economic activity in modern industrial economies, and most securities have payoffs denominated in terms of domestic currencies. There is no role for fiat money in the economic environment set forth above. Strictly speaking, then, there are no securities with nominal payoffs in terms of money; all payoffs are in terms of a numeraire good. Exact counterparts to the latter securities are not traded in the United States. Therefore, it has become common practice to substitute real returns on claims to the dividend streams of common stocks or real holding period returns on government and corporate bonds for the purposes of econometric analyses of relation (1). In principle, this substitution may not be innocuous, since the pricing relations implied by models which formally incorporate the frictions underlying the desire for monetary exchange may lead to quite different pricing relations. Examples of these differences are presented in the studies of monetary models with cash-in-advance constraints by Lucas (1984) and Townsend (1984).

A counterpart of (1) formally holds in monetary economies for closed subspaces Q_t^m of square-integrable nominal payoffs in I_t. More precisely, under certain regularity conditions, Hansen and Richard (1987) have shown that there exists an element p_t^* in Q_t^m such that the price of a typical payoff $q_t^m \in Q_t^m$ is given by $E[p_{t+1}^* q_{t+1}^m \mid I_t]$. The nature of the benchmark payoff p_t^*

depends on the monetary model being investigated. There has been relatively little empirical work on intertemporal pricing relations implied by monetary models. Singleton (1985) estimated a model with preferences given by a special case of (2)–(5) and a cash-in-advance constraint that was assumed to always be binding. The results suggest that the introduction of this constraint do not markedly affect the qualitative conclusions from the analysis of the corresponding version of (1). However, more extensive analyses of different monetary models may well reveal a significant role for the frictions underlying monetary exchange. In any case, most of the remainder of this chapter abstracts from these considerations associated with money in order to review the large literature which has studied (1) using real returns on traded securities in the United States.

Another consequence of the homogeneity and complete markets assumptions typically made in deducing (1) is that the determination of quantities demanded and supplied in asset markets is simplified. The representative agent prices assets correctly and holds all the fixed outstanding supply of capital assets. When agents receive different endowments, they will in general actively trade claims to future dividends and borrow and lend among themselves in these environments. However, it might be argued that these models exclude many additional and potentially important motives for trade in security markets. This possibility is discussed further in the concluding section of this chapter.

3. Linear asset pricing models

Linear or log-linear asset pricing models have received most of the attention in the empirical literature on asset pricing. Reasons for this attention include: (i) their simplicity, (ii) they have the feature of being testable without the use of non-asset market data, and perhaps most importantly (iii) historically much of the empirical evidence has not been unfavorable to these models. This section explores the properties of several important special cases of the pricing relation (1) that lead to relations which are linear or log-linear in prices or returns, and which do not involve consumption directly.

3.1. Linear expectations models of asset returns under risk neutrality

As is well known, the assumption that agents are risk neutral has strong implications for the stochastic properties of returns on traded securities. To see the nature of these implications in the context of the economic environment underlying (1), suppose that consumers are risk neutral in the sense that they have linear period utility functions for the numeraire service flow. Then the period utility function of the representative consumer can be expressed as

$$U(s_t^1, s_t^2, \ldots, s_t^m) = as_t^1 + f(s_t^2, \ldots, s_2^m),$$ (6)

where s^1 is the numeraire service flow. Equation (1) becomes:

$$\pi_t(q_{t+1}) = \beta E[q_{y+1} \mid I_t],$$ (7)

with the prices and payoffs of the securities denominated in terms of the service flow s_1. Equation (7) can be rewritten equivalently as:

$$E[r_{t+1} \mid I_t] = 1/\beta,$$ (8)

where $r_{t+1} \equiv q_{t+1}/\pi_t(q_{t+1})$. Note that setting $\sigma = 1$ and $\alpha = 1$ in (2) and (3) results in a special case of (6) that is linear in all service flows, and hence also leads to (7) and (8).

An immediate implication of (8) is that expected real returns on all risky securities must be equal. This implication is clearly inconsistent with the point estimates of mean returns for most sample periods. However, standard errors of these estimates are often sufficiently large for the null hypothesis of equal mean returns across securities not to be rejected at conventional significance levels. See, for example, Merton (1980) for a discussion of estimation of the expected return on equities. Nevertheless, sufficient evidence has accumulated for there to be general agreement that this implication of risk neutrality is not satisfied by the data on equity returns.

Much more attention has been focused on a different implication of (7). Specifically, if q_{t+1} denotes the sum of the price of a share of common stock at date $t+1$ plus the divident payment at date $t+1$ (d_{t+1}) and speculative bubbles [see, for example, Tirole (1982)] are ruled out, then (7) can be solved recursively forward to obtain the familiar present value relation:

$$\pi_t(p_{t+1} + d_{t+1}) = \sum_{j=1}^{\infty} \beta^j E[d_{t+j} \mid I_t].$$ (9)

Shiller (1981) and LeRoy and Porter (1980) have shown that, in the context of the model (9), the variance of the price of the stock must be less than or equal to the variance of the dividend process. Furthermore, when both the price and dividend processes are stationary stochastic processes about a geometric trend path,

$$\text{var}[\pi_t^*] \equiv \text{var}\left[\sum_{j=1}^{\infty} \beta^j d_{t+j}^\tau\right] \geq \text{var}[\pi_t(p_{t+1}^\tau + d_{t+1}^\tau)],$$ (10)

where the superscript τ indicates detrended variables. In fact, prices are much more volatile than the "ex post rational" price π_t^* both for individual and portfolios of stocks.

Formal tests of the null hypotheses that (9) and (10) hold also generally support the conclusion that prices are too volatile, though this conclusion must be qualified by the observations in Flavin (1983) and Kleidon (1985). Flavin (1983) found that variance bound tests of expectations theories of the term structure were biased in small samples toward rejection of the model. Similar results may apply to tests of (10) using stock market data. Kleidon (1985) studied the properties of $\text{var}[\pi_t]$ and $\text{var}[\pi_t^*]$ under the assumption that dividends follow a geometric random walk. In several Monte Carlo experiments Kleidon found that, for this representation of dividends, the inequality (10) was typically violated by the sample variances for over 90 percent of the trials, even though (10) held by construction in the population. Moreover, the failure of (10) was exacerbated by removing the geometric trend. Thus, if dividends follow a geometric random walk, as the empirical evidence suggests is approximately the case, then (10) does not lead to a valid test of the model (9).

Valid asymptotic tests of (9) under the assumption that there is a unit root in the dividend process have been discussed by Shiller (1981), Kleidon (1985), Scott (1985), Campbell and Shiller (1986), and Mattey and Meese (1986), among others. Overall, the evidence from these studies also seems to cast considerable doubt on the validity of (9) though disagreement about the strength of the evidence remains.

Of course, under risk neutrality the relation (9) must be satisfied for all securities with admissible payoffs. This observation is especially problematical for proponents of (8) when attention is focused on bonds. According to (8), the real returns on all bonds over the same holding period must be equal, which is a strong version of the expectations theory of the term structure of interest rates. Fama (1984b) found that differences between nominal holding period returns were typically significant at the short end of the yield curve. (Differences in mean holding period returns on long-term bonds were also quite large, but these estimates were also imprecise.) With linear utility, real returns on riskless (i.e. certain payoff) discount bonds are also constants. Consequently, the term structure of interest rates for real riskless bonds has a constant shape over the business cycle.

3.2. Linear expectations models of asset returns with risk averse agents

Asset pricing models that are linear in the logarithms of the variables have also been studied extensively in the literature. Such time series representations can be deduced from models in which agents are risk averse by imposing a distributional assumption on the variables in the model. In this respect the log-linear models illustrate the tradeoffs one often faces between flexibility in specifying preferences and the structure that must be imposed on the sources of uncertainty to obtain "closed-form" expressions for asset returns.

Let m_{t+n}^n denote the marginal rate of substitution between consumption at date t and consumption at date $t + n$ and let r_{t+n}^ℓ, $\ell = 1, \ldots, L$, denote L n-period holding period returns on feasible investment strategies.[3] Also, let $x_t' = (\log m_{t+n}^n, \log r_{t+n}^1, \ldots, \log r_{t+n}^L)$, suppose that $(x_t: -\infty < t < \infty)$ is a normally distributed, stationary stochastic process, and let ψ_t denote the information generated by $\{x_s: s \le t\}$. The expectation of the n-period version of (1) conditioned on ψ_t is:

$$E[m_{t+n}^n r_{t+n}^\ell \mid \psi_t] = 1 \tag{11}$$

which, under the distributional assumption, can be expressed equivalently as:

$$E[m_{t+n}^n r_{t+n}^\ell \mid \psi_t] = \exp\{E[\log(m_{t+n}^n r_{t+n}^\ell) \mid \psi_t] + \tfrac{1}{2}\mathrm{var}[\log(m_{t+n}^n r_{t+n}^\ell) \mid \psi_t]\}, \tag{12}$$

$\ell = 1, \ldots, L$. Taking logarithms of (12), and using the restriction that [from (11)] the resulting expression is zero, gives:

$$E[\log r_{t+n}^\ell \mid \psi_t] = -E[\log m_{t+n}^n \mid \psi_t] - \tfrac{1}{2}\mathrm{var}[\log(m_{t+n}^n r_{t+n}^\ell) \mid \psi_t]. \tag{13}$$

Under log-normality, the conditional means are linear and the conditional variance is constant in (13). Thus, (13) implies restrictions on the linear time series representation of $\log m_{t+n}^n$ and the logarithms of the returns.

There are many economic environments which are consistent with the distributional assumptions underlying (13). For instance, suppose agents have constant relative risk averse preferences defined over a single, non-durable consumption good. This utility function is obtained as a special case of the S-branch utility function as follows. Let $m = 1$ (single good) and suppose that the consumption good is non-durable so that acquisitions at date t are consumed at date t $[A(L) = 1]$. Also, suppose that $\alpha = 0$ and $\sigma < 1$. Then the period utility function simplifies to

$$U(c_t) = (1/\sigma)(c_t)^\sigma, \tag{14}$$

---

[3]Examples of investment strategies are: buy and hold an n'-period security for n periods ($n' > n$), or roll over a sequence of short-term securities for n periods.

where c_t is the level of consumption of the non-durable good. The marginal rate of substitution for the jth agent, m_{jt+n}^n, is $\beta^n(c_{jt+n}/c_{jt})^{\sigma-1}$.

Next, consider an endowment economy in which agents have preferences of the form (14) and the endowment of the jth consumer follows the process:

$$y_{jt} = y_{jt-1}\varepsilon_t \, , \tag{15}$$

where ε_t is an i.i.d. endowment shock. In this economy, prices are set such that m_{jt+n}^n can be replaced in (1) by the marginal rate of substitution expressed in terms of aggregate consumption, m_{t+n}^n. Furthermore, $\Sigma\, c_{jt} = \Sigma\, y_{jt}$. Now the price of a claim to the aggregate endowment flow from period t forward is proportional to $\Sigma_j\, y_{jt}$, and the price of an n-period pure discount bond is $E_t[m_{t+n}^n]$.[4] Therefore, if the aggregate endowment follows a log-normal process, then the returns on this stock-like claim to future endowments and the returns on pure discount bonds that pay off units of the aggregate endowment will be jointly log-normally distributed with aggregate consumption.

An alternative log-linear model is obtained by combining the assumptions of exponential utility, normally distributed endowments, and log-normal returns [Ferson (1983)]. The exponential utility function is also a special case of utility functions (2)–(5). Clearly, these justifications for log-linear models are very restrictive. In particular, both models have the property that the relative prices of securities are constants, which certainly is not true for the available empirical counterparts to the prices of the securities described above.

A more appealing justification for the assumption is simply that it is a primitive assumption of the model. That is, consumption growth rates and returns are taken to be log-normally distributed and it is understood that this assumption implicitly imposes restrictions on the underlying sources of uncertainty in the model. Pursuing the example of an endowment economy, suppose that $(L + 1)$ agents have different endowment streams and that the L equities being priced are claims to future values of L of these endowments (the future "dividends"). Furthermore, suppose the distribution of endowments is such that the L endowments associated with the returns r_{t+n}^ℓ are jointly log-normal with aggregate consumption $(=\Sigma_{\ell=1}^{L+1} y_{\ell t})$. Then if preferences are given by (17), a log-linear model like (13) applies to the returns on these L equity claims. [Of course, the $(L + 1)$st claim does not satisfy (13).]

Hansen and Singleton (1983) conducted two different tests of the model with preferences (14) and log-normal consumption. First, substituting (14) into (13)

---

[4]The equilibrium price for this economy can be derived using arguments similar to those in Brock's (1980) discussion of a production economy with log utility.

gives:

$$E[\log r^{\ell}_{t+n} \mid \psi_t] = -n \log \beta - \alpha E\left[\log\left(\frac{c_{t+n}}{c_t}\right)\Big|\psi_t\right]$$

$$-\tfrac{1}{2}\alpha^2 \operatorname{var}\left\{\log\left(\frac{c_{t+n}}{c_t}\right)r^{\ell}_{t+n} \mid \psi_t\right\}. \tag{16}$$

Equation (16) imposes restrictions on the autoregressive representations of $\log(c_{t+n}/c_t)$ and the logarithms of asset returns. These restrictions were tested for various combinations of returns and the results provide substantial evidence against this model using monthly data on real returns for aggregate and industry-average stock portfolios and Treasury bills. Ferson (1983) also provides evidence against this model using quarterly data. The tests of (16) are premised on accurate measurement of consumption.

The second test considered by Hansen and Singleton was based on a weaker implication of (16). Taking the difference between the versions of (16) for two different securities leads to the result that $E[\log r^{\ell}_{t+n} - \log r^{k}_{t+n} \mid \psi_t]$ equals a constant. Consequently the difference between the logarithms of the nominal returns on the two securities must be serially uncorrelated. Substantial evidence against this hypothesis was obtained using an aggregate stock return and the one-month Treasury bill return. Notice that this implication of the model can be tested without having to measure consumption or the price deflator accurately.

Moreover, tests based on the difference between the logarithms of returns accommodate certain types of unobserved shocks to preferences. (Recall that all of the tests discussed up to this point require that unobserved taste shocks be absent.) Let preferences be given by

$$U(c_t) = (1/\sigma)(c_t \varepsilon_t)^{\sigma}, \tag{17}$$

where ε_t is a taste shock that may be serially correlated. For this model, $m^{n}_{t+n} = \beta^{n}[(c_{t+n}\varepsilon_{t+n})/(c_t\varepsilon_t)]^{\alpha}$ is a non-linear function of the unobserved taste shocks. However, under the assumption of log-normal shocks, $\log m^{n}_{t+n}$ cancels from the difference $E[\log r^{l}_{t+n} - \log r^{k}_{t+n} \mid \psi_t]$. Therefore, the conclusions reached by Hansen and Singleton (1983) also apply to this model.

Using arguments like those in Hansen and Singleton (1983) and Breeden (1986), a log-linear version of the expectations theory of the term structure of interest rates can also be derived [see also Dunn and Singleton (1986)]. Taking the difference between the version of (13) for any two securities ℓ and

k gives:

$$E[\log r^{\ell}_{t+n} \mid \psi_t] = E[\log r^k_{t+n} \mid \psi_t] + \phi^{\ell k}_n , \tag{18}$$

where ϕ^{ℓ}_n is given by

$$\tfrac{1}{2} \text{var}[\log r^l_{t+n} + \log m^n_{t+n} \mid \psi_t] - \tfrac{1}{2} \text{var}[\log r^k_{t+n} + \log m^n_{t+n} \mid \psi_t] . \tag{19}$$

Since $\{x_t\}$ is a normally distributed stochastic process, the conditional expectations are linear functions. Furthermore, the conditional variances are constants and, hence, $\phi^{\ell k}_n$ is a constant.

Next, choose r^{ℓ}_{t+n} to be the return from buying and holding until maturity an n-period, pure discount bond and choose $r^k_{t+n} = \prod_{s=t}^{t+n-1} r_{s+1}$, which is the return from a strategy of rolling over a sequence of n one-period, pure discount bonds. Then (18) becomes a log-linear expectations model of the real term structure of interest rates with a constant intercept $\phi^{\ell k}_n$:

$$E[\log r^{\ell}_{t+n} \mid \psi_t] = \sum_{s=t}^{t+n-1} E[\log r_{s+1} \mid \psi_t] + \phi^{\ell k}_n . \tag{20}$$

Notice that the expected inflation rates implicit in the real returns in (20) cancel from the relation, leaving an expectations relation that can be expressed in terms of nominal returns. Accordingly, (20) can be tested using return data alone.

To my knowledge, this relation has not been tested explicitly in the empirical literature on the term structure. However, since the logarithm of the total return is approximately equal to the rate of return, the large body of literature that has tested the rate-of-return version of the linear expectations model with constant intercept can be interpreted approximately as a test of (20). Recent evidence suggests that the model is not consistent with the data. See, for example, Fama (1976, 1984a), Shiller (1979), Singleton (1980), Hansen and Sargent (1981), Shiller, Campbell and Schoenholtz (1983), and Mankiw and Summers (1984). A more thorough review of the literature on the expectations theory of the term structure is presented in Chapter 13 by Shiller and McCulloch, in this Handbook.

3.3. Implications for autocorrelations of returns

One of the most widely studied properties of the distribution of stock returns is the shape of the autocorrelation function, with particular attention having been given to the question of whether stock returns are serially uncorrelated. The degree of autocorrelation in stock returns depends on the specification of the economic environment. The optimal use of public information by traders ("informational efficiency") does not, by itself, imply serially uncorrelated returns. Indeed, intertemporal asset pricing models based on variants of the neoclassical stochastic growth model or life-cycle theories of consumer behavior typically yield serially correlated returns under the assumption of "rational" expectations.

Several special circumstances in which intertemporal models imply serially uncorrelated returns were discussed in Subsections 3.2 and 3.3. Specifically, an implication of risk neutrality is that real returns on all securities with payoffs denominated in the numeraire service are serially uncorrelated [see (8)]. Risk neutrality also implies that expected returns are equal across securities. Alternatively, if $E[\log m_{t+n}^n \mid \psi_t]$ is constant in the log-linear relation (13) and the conditional variance is constant, then the logarithms of real returns are serially uncorrelated in the presence risk aversion. The mean $E[\log m_{t+n}^n \mid \psi_t]$ is constant, for instance, in an economy with constant relative risk averse preferences and constant conditionally expected consumption growth [see Rubinstein (1976) and equation (16)]. In contrast to the model with risk neutral consumers, expected returns may differ across securities in this model if the covariances of $\log m_{t+n}^n$ and the $\log r_{t+n}^\ell$ differ.

Notice that these relations do *not* imply that nominal returns are serially uncorrelated. Deducing the restriction of serially uncorrelated nominal returns in general equilibrium amounts to finding conditions which guarantee that the benchmark payoff for pricing nominal payoffs, p_{t+1}^*, is constant over time for the relevant set of monetary payoffs. For the monetary models examined to date, a simple condition like risk neutrality is evidently not sufficient for a constant p_{t+1}^* [for example, Frenkel and Razin (1983)].

Also, the restrictions that $E[r_{t+n}^\ell \mid I_t]$ or $E[\log r_{t+n}^\ell \mid \psi_t]$ are constants cannot be tested using market return data alone. Both payoffs and prices are denominated in terms of the numeraire service flow. This observation leads to two difficulties with interpreting many previous tests as tests of general equilibrium models. First, "real" prices and payoffs are obtained by deflating nominal magnitudes by some price index. Second, the calculation of real returns requires non-market data on the price deflator for the numeraire service flow. The problem of constructing the appropriate deflator is simplified substantially by using as the numeraire service the service from a non-durable good. That is, one can choose s_t^1 such that s_t^1 equals the acquisitions of the good c_t^1 and then use the implicit price deflator for this good to construct real returns. Clearly, this practice does not avoid entirely measurement problems associated with consumption data.

Perhaps in part for these reasons, Fama (1965), and many others subsequently, have tested the hypothesis of serially uncorrelated returns for individual stocks and portfolios of common stocks using data on nominal returns. Stock returns do exhibit some serial dependence, especially for returns on portfolios of common stocks. Table 12.1 displays the F-statistics from the regressions of the real returns on four industry portfolio returns on information available at the beginning of the month over which returns are calculated.[5] The four industries (Retail Trade, Durable Goods, Finance, and Business Equipment) were selected at random from the seventeen industrial categories used by Fama and French (1986b). Each return was regressed on six lagged values of itself (DV), the current and six lagged values of the first difference of the nominal one month Treasury bill return, and the contemporary difference between the three- and six-month Treasury bill returns ($DTB1$ and $TB6-TB1$, respectively), and the Decile 10 (large firms) portfolio calculated by Fama and French (1986b). Nominal instead of real bill returns were used, because the current values of the bill returns are known at the beginning of the period and the corresponding real returns are unknown to investors until the maturity date of the bills.

The F-statistics for the null hypothesis that the coefficients on the own lagged values of the returns provide only weak evidence against the null

Table 12.1
F-tests from time series regressions for industry portfolio returns,
January 1959–December 1983[a]

	Dependent variable			
	Retail	Durables	Finance	Business equipment
DV[b]	1.5169	1.0629	2.6673	1.1759
(1–6 lags)	(0.1728)	(0.3853)	(0.0157)	(0.3195)
$TB6-TB3$	1.2981	1.3414	1.3001	1.0997
(0–6 lags)	(0.2514)	(0.2310)	(0.2505)	(0.3636)
$DTB1$	1.4719	1.6038	1.7374	1.5887
(0–6 lags)	(0.1775)	(0.1344)	(0.1005)	(0.1389)
Decile 10	1.6164	1.6738	3.3364	1.2204
(1–6 lags)	(0.1428)	(0.1276)	(0.0035)	(0.2961)
$F(26, 266)$[c]	2.2631	1.9432	2.1889	1.7692
	(0.0007)	(0.0050)	(0.0010)	(0.0141)
R^2	0.1840	0.1622	0.1790	0.1498
SEE	0.0580	0.0636	0.0576	0.0624

[a]Probability values of the test statistics are displayed in parentheses.
[b]DV = dependent variable.
[c]F-statistic for testing the null hypothesis that the coefficients on all twenty-six regressors are zero.

[5]Real returns were calculated by dividing the nominal return by one plus the inflation rate as measured by the implicit consumption deflator for "non-durable goods plus services" from the National Income and Product Accounts.

hypothesis of zero coefficients, except for the Finance industry. This pattern is consistent with the results from previous tests for serial correlation using the past histories of stock returns alone. Such tests have typically provided little evidence against (8). However, for all of the industries there is evidence of predictability of stock returns using other publicly available information (based on the overall *F*-statistic).

The corresponding results for four decile portfolio returns (1 = smallest, 10 = largest) are displayed in Table 12.2. Again all of the portfolio returns exhibit significant autocorrelations. Another feature of these results is that the coefficients of determination decline as the firm size is increased, suggesting that predictability of portfolio turns is dependent on firm size. Campbell (1986) has undertaken a more systematic study of the predictability of stock returns using information in the term structure of government bonds. He finds coefficients of determination as high as 0.296 for the period 1959 through 1983. Together these findings call into question the validity of (8), even approximately, as a pricing relation that describes stock return data.

A different approach to assessing whether stock returns are serially uncorrelated has recently been proposed by Fama and French (1986a, 1986b). The basic idea of their approach is as follows. Let x_t denote the logarithm of the total payoff per share of an equity at date t (price plus any dividends). Then the null hypothesis that an equity return is serially uncorrelated can be stated as $E[x_t - x_{t-1} \mid I_{t-1}] = \mu$, where μ is the constant unconditional mean of

Table 12.2
F-tests from time series regressions for decile portfolios,
January 1959–December 1983[a]

	Dependent variable			
	Decile 1	Decile 4	Decile 7	Decile 10
DV^b	1.7610	1.9807	0.9512	0.5482
(1–6 lags)	(0.1074)	(0.0688)	(0.4589)	(0.7712)
TB6–TB3	1.7613	1.2521	1.3946	1.4599
(0–6 lags)	(0.0954)	(0.2747)	(0.2078)	(0.1818)
DTB1	2.7938	1.6583	1.3948	1.3396
(0–6 lags)	(0.0081)	(0.1196)	(02076)	(0.2317)
Decile 10	3.5885	2.2157	1.0018	
(1–6 lags)	(0.0020)	(0.0420)	(0.4246)	
$F(26, 2666)^c$	2.8481	2.0962	1.8102	1.8920*d
	(0.1 × 10⁻⁴)	(0.0029)	(0.0112)	(0.0132)
R^2	0.2210	0.1727	0.1528	0.1241
SEE	0.0719	0.0562	0.0508	0.0421

[a]Probability values of the test statistics are displayed in parentheses.
[b]*DV* = dependent variable.
[c]*F*-statistic for testing the null hypothesis that the coefficient on all twenty-six regressors are zero.
[d]This statistic is distributed as $F(20, 272)$.

$(x_t - x_{t-1})$. An additional implication of this hypothesis is that

$$E[x_{t+q} - x_t \mid I_t] = q\mu , \quad q = 1, 2, \dots . \tag{21}$$

Fama and French (1986a) investigate (21) for various integer values of $q \geq 1$ by calculating sample estimates of $E[(x_{t+q} - x_t - q\mu)(x_t - x_{t-q} - q\mu)]$, which equals zero under (21). They find that with monthly data and q equal to 36 and 60 that the estimated autocorrelations are typically non-zero and range between -0.3 and -0.5.

Lo and MacKinlay (1986) have suggested an alternative test of (21) based on the observation that

$$\mathrm{var}(x_{t+q} - x_t) = q \, \mathrm{var}(x_{t+1} - x_t) \tag{22}$$

if (21) is satisfied. More explicitly, let $\{y_t\}$ be a martingale difference sequence relative to the sequence of information sets $\{I_t\}$ (i.e. $E[y_t \mid I_{t-1}] = 0$); and let $\hat{\sigma}_q^2$ denote the sample variance of the process $\{y_{qt}\}$ with $y_{qt} \equiv \sum_{j=0}^{q-1} y_{t-j}$. Then using arguments similar to those in Lo and MacKinlay it can be shown that

$$\sqrt{N}\tau(q) \equiv \sqrt{N}\left[\frac{\hat{\sigma}_q^2/q}{\hat{\sigma}_1^2} - 1\right] \Rightarrow N(0, \delta^2) , \tag{23}$$

where

$$\delta^2 = \sum_{j=1}^{q-1} \left(\frac{2(q-j)}{q}\right)^2 \frac{E[y_t^2 y_{t-j}^2]}{E[y_t^2]^2} , \tag{24}$$

N is sample size and $\Rightarrow$ denotes convergence in distribution. Lo and MacKinlay implemented this test for small values of q with $(x_t - x_{t-1})$ equal to the one week return on various stock portfolios and $y_t = (x_t - x_{t-1} - \mu)$, $\mu = E(x_t - x_{t-1})$. They found that the portfolio returns examined exhibited positive serial correlation and that $\tau(q)$ was often significantly different from zero at conventional significance levels.

Table 12.3 displays the τ statistics calculated using the same y_t as in Lo and MacKinlay (1986) except with t indexing months [i.e. $(x_t - x_{t-1})$ denotes the monthly portfolio return]. Below each τ statistic in square brackets is the sample estimate of the corresponding $\mathrm{corr}[y_{qt}, y_{qt-q}]$, where q indicates the length of the holding period in months. Consistent with the findings of Fama and French (1986a), the sample autocorrelation of $\{y_{60,t}\}$ is negative and quite large in absolute value for the sample period 1926–1985. However, the τ statistics do not lead to rejection at conventional significance levels of the null

Table 12.3
Tests of the random walk hypothesis based on the variances of multi-period returns[a]

Decile	$q = 3$	$q = 6$	$q = 12$	$q = 36$	$q = 60$
		January 1926–December 1985			
1	1.870	1.026	0.877	0.371	0.194
	[−0.047]	[0.028]	[0.049]	[−0.121]	[−0.174]
4	1.830	0.816	0.712	−0.001	−0.394
	[−0.072]	[0.029]	[−0.032]	[−0.336]	[−0.527]
7	1.615	0.856	0.797	−0.270	−0.771
	[−0.036]	[0.041]	[−0.096]	[−0.432]	[−0.474]
10	1.097	0.235	0.428	−0.421	−0.867
	[−0.072]	[0.067]	[−0.099]	[−0.410]	[−0.291]
		January 1936–December 1985			
1	0.469	−0.454	−0.021	−0.169	−0.061
	[0.028]	[−0.057]	[0.004]	[0.012]	[−0.179]
4	0.930	1.100	0.422	−0.616	−0.758
	[0.074]	[−0.053]	[−0.139]	[−0.177]	[−0.418]
7	0.572	0.914	0.260	−1.014	−1.095
	[0.083]	[−0.064]	[−0.220]	[−0.169]	[−0.240]
10	−0.287	0.255	−0.085	−1.348	−1.275
	[0.062]	[−0.044]	[−0.245]	[−0.059]	[0.036]

[a]Test statistics are distributed as $N(0, 1)$ under the null hypothesis. The numbers in square brackets are sample estimates of $\text{corr}[y_{qt}, y_{qt-q}]$.

hypothesis of no autocorrelation in returns. On the other hand, the estimates of $\text{corr}[y_{3t}, y_{3t-3}]$ are relatively small and yet the significance levels of the τ statistics are less than 6 percent for deciles 1, 4, and 7.

The sample period 1936–1985 omits the Great Depression from the analysis. Interestingly, this omission results in much less evidence of serial correlation in the Fama–French data. In particular, the estimates of $|\text{corr}[y_{60,t}, y_{60,t-60}]|$ are uniformly smaller than the corresponding estimates for the sample period 1926–1985. Also, the τ statistics provide much less evidence against the null hypothesis of serially uncorrelated returns when $q = 3$.

Although Fama and French (1986a, 1986b) and Lo and MacKinlay (1986) focused on the autocorrelation of individual returns, (21) is a much stronger restriction on the distribution of returns. The conditional mean restriction (21) implies that $y_t \equiv (x_t - x_{t-1} - \mu)z_{t-1}$ satisfies $E[y_t \mid I_t] = 0$, and hence is serially uncorrelated, for any variable z_{t-1} in agents' information set at date $t - 1$. This restriction on the joint distribution of returns $(x_t - x_{t-1})$ and other variables known at date $t - 1$ (z_{t-1}) can also be examined using the τ statistic. Table 12.4 displays the τ statistics obtained with $z_{t-1} = DTB1_t$ (the first difference of the nominal one month U.S. Treasury bill return) and $z_{t-1} = 1$ for the sample period January 1959–December 1985. Since the payoff at maturity of a Treasury bill is known at the date of issue, $DTB1_t$ is in agents' information set

Table 12.4

Tests of the random walk hypothesis based on the variances of
stock return – Treasury bill return products,[a]
January 1959–December 1985

Decile	$q = 2$	$q = 3$	$q = 6$	$q = 12$
		$z_{t-1} = DTB1_t$		
1	0.843	1.314	1.650	1.992
	[0.165]	[0.136]	[0.109]	[0.025]
4	1.115	1.621	1.791	2.074
	[0.261]	[0.184]	[0.114]	[−0.078]
7	1.118	1.376	1.624	1.837
	[0.183]	[0.165]	[0.101]	[−0.150]
10	0.895	0.932	1.324	1.467
	[0.127]	[0.163]	[0.069]	[−0.177]
		$z_{t-1} = 1$		
1	1.365	1.037	0.443	−0.489
	[−0.001]	[−0.029]	[−0.177]	[−0.098]
4	2.462	1.854	1.471	0.628
	[0.020]	[0.049]	[−0.059]	[−0.077]
7	2.394	1.868	1.612	0.674
	[0.039]	[0.073]	[−0.067]	[−0.211]
10	0.107	−0.196	0.230	−0.155
	[−0.034]	[0.067]	[−0.070]	[−0.318]

[a]Test statistics are distributed as $N(0, 1)$ under the null hypothesis. The numbers in square brackets are sample estimates of corr$[y_{qt}, y_{qt-q}]$.

at date $t - 1$. With $z_{t-1} = DTB1_t$ there is a tendency for the value of the τ statistics to increase as q increases from 2 to 12, and the random walk hypothesis is rejected at the 5 percent level for deciles 1, 4, and 7. In contrast, there is more evidence against the null hypothesis (21) with $z_t = 1$ when q is small. Another difference between the results is that returns are more negatively autocorrelated than the products of returns and $DTB1_t$ for large values of q.

Finally, tests for industrial production-stock return products are displayed in Table 12.5. Letting o_t denote the logarithm of industrial production, the τ statistics were calculated with $y_{1t} = (x_t - x_{t-1} - \mu)(o_{t-1} - o_{t-p-1})$ for various values of p. For instance, with $(q = 6, p = 6)$, the one-month stock return was multiplied by the six-month growth rate in industrial production ($p = 6$) lagged one month and then this product was averaged over six periods ($q = 6$). With $q = 36$, the test statistics exceed 2 for the decile portfolios 4 and 7. Even stronger evidence of persistence in stock returns emerges from an analysis of the Retail and Durable Goods Industry portfolios. Once again, the autocorrelations of y_{qt} and y_{qt-q} are negative especially for $q = 36$.

Table 12.5

Tests of the random walk hypothesis based on the variances of stock return–industrial production growth products,[a] January 1959–December 1985

Decile	$q = 3$ $p = 3$	$q = 6$ $p = 6$	$q = 12$ $p = 12$	$q = 36$ $p = 12$
1	−0.679	0.099	0.079	0.750
	[−0.068]	[−0.012]	[−0.105	[−0.263]
4	−0.085	1.561	1.235	2.701
	[−0.033]	[−0.069]	[0.021]	[−0.267]
7	0.688	0.655	1.294	2.609
	[0.028]	[−0.081]	[−0.115]	[−0.275]
10	0.420	2.181	0.061	0.657
	[−0.007]	[−0.137]	[−0.196]	[−0.338]

Industry	$q = 3$ $p = 3$	$q = 6$ $p = 6$	$q = 12$ $p = 12$	$q = 36$ $p = 12$
Retail	0.354	1.661	2.505	5.010
	[0.021]	[−0.066]	[0.018]	[−0.231]
Durables	0.171	2.185	1.634	3.169
	[0.021]	[−0.029]	[−0.046]	[−0.200]
Finance	−0.902	−0.394	0.028	0.972
	[−0.140]	[−0.095]	[0.029]	[−0.245]
Business	0.585	2.518	1.116	1.804
equipment	[0.047]	[−0.013]	[−0.096]	[−0.330]

[a] $y_t = (x_t - x_{t-1} - \mu)(o_{t-1} - o_{t-p-1})$, where o_t = industrial production at date t.

$$y_{qt} = \sum_{j=0}^{q-1} y_{t-j} = \sum_{j=0}^{q-1} (x_t - x_{t-1} - \mu)(o_{t-1} - o_{t-p-1}).$$

The number in square brackets is the sample estimate of corr(y_{qt}, y_{qt-q}).

3.4. Discussion

In order for an asset pricing model to capture the time series properties of stock and bond returns it must be capable of explaining the following features of the data. First, the model must imply that asset returns are serially correlated. Second, it must accommodate considerable diversity in the correlations of asset returns – short-term debt instruments and aggregate portfolios of common stocks exhibit moderate serial correlation, and long-term bonds and individual stocks are somewhat less correlated over time. Third, the variance tests reported in Lo and MacKinlay and in Tables 12.3–12.5 suggest that stock returns are autocorrelated over both short (several weeks) and long (several years) holding periods. Furthermore, the autocorrelation over short holding periods tends to be positive, while it is negative over long holding periods.

There is also evidence from the analysis of the joint distribution of stock and bill returns that the autocorrelation in stock returns is related to aggregate fluctuations. Most notably, the persistence of stock returns seems to be related to movements in industrial production. This finding is consistent with the implications of stochastic growth models and the view that movements in intermediate and long-term stock returns are related to consumption and investment decisions. In addition, the persistence in the products of returns and industrial production may be a reflection of non-linear relations between stock returns and economic fundamentals.

Finally, the model must explain the apparently large variances in asset returns relative to the variability of the underlying determinants of asset returns. The linear models discussed in this section seem to perform poorly along all of these dimensions.

Now, in principle, allowing agents to be risk averse can lead to a model with all of these features. From (16) it is seen that the conditional means of the (logarithm of) returns will inherit the autocorrelation properties of the logarithm of the intertemporal marginal rate of substitution of consumption, which in turn are correlated with output growth. Furthermore, as Michener (1982) has illustrated, risk aversion can potentially explain the volatility in stock prices relative to the volatility of dividends without having to resort to a non-stationary dividend process. The model underlying (16) is not consistent with one important feature of the data, however. Equation (16) also implies that all returns must have the same autocorrelation properties, which is not the case.

Partially in response to the limitations of these linear and log-linear models, several authors have examined the empirical properties of asset pricing models with risk averse agents and in which the distributional assumptions underlying (16) are not imposed. The potential for this extension to capture the time series behavior of asset returns is discussed in the next section. In addition, some have emphasized the potential importance of multiple goods. Models with multiple decision variables are examined in Section 5.

4. Non-linear asset pricing models: The single-good case

Instead of attempting to deduce linear asset pricing models under strong restrictions on preferences and the underlying sources of uncertainty in the economy, one can proceed to study the stochastic Euler equation (2) directly. While this approach permits substantial flexibility in specifying preferences, it is instructive at the outset to examine in depth the simple case of a single-good economy in which the consumption good is non-durable. This environment is sufficiently rich to gain substantial insight into the degree to which representative agent models of intertemporal consumption and investment decisions are consistent with the historical time paths of aggregate consumption and real returns.

Hansen and Singleton (1982), Dunn and Singleton (1983), and Brown and Gibbons (1985) investigated single-good economies in which agents have constant relative in risk averse preferences as in (14). Therefore, for illustrative purposes, much of my discussion will also focus on this model. The stochastic Euler equation underlying these studies is obtained by substituting (14) into (1):

$$E[\beta^n(c_{t+n}/c_t)^{\sigma-1} r_{t+n} \mid I_t] = 1 , \tag{25}$$

where $r_{t+n} = (q_{t+n}/\pi_t(q_{t+n}))$. Interpreting the variable

$$u_{t+n} = \beta^n(c_{t+n}/c_t)^{\sigma-1} r_{t+n} - 1 \tag{26}$$

as the disturbance for an econometric analysis, Hansen and Singleton (1982) show how to use the fact that $E[u_{t+n} \mid I_t] = 0$ to construct instrumental variables estimators of the unknown paramaters (β, σ) and to test overidentifying restrictions implied by (25).

Briefly, the conditional mean restriction (25) implies that $E[u_{t+n} z_t] = 0$, for all $z_t \in I_t$, and therefore elements of agents' information set at date t can be used as instrumental variables for the disturbance u_{t+n}. After selecting s instruments to be used in estimating q parameters $(s \geq q)$, the parameter estimates are chosen by minimizing a quadratic form in the sample means of $u_{t+n} z_{jt}$, $j = 1, \ldots, s$. In this manner, these sample means are made close to their population value of zero under the null hypothesis according to the distance measure defined by the quadratic form. This approach amounts to setting q linear combinations of the s sample orthogonality conditions to zero. If $s > q$, then there are $s - q$ independent linear combinations of the s orthogonality conditions that are not set to zero in estimation, but that should be close to zero if the model is true. These overidentifying restrictions can be tested using a chi square goodness-of-fit statistic [see Hansen (1982) and Hansen and Singleton (1982)].

These tests of (25) accommodate heterogeneity across consumers in the sense that agents may have different endowment processes (see Section 2). These analyses are also robust to certain econometric difficulties. In particular, the model accommodates geometric growth in real per-capita consumption over time, since only the ratio (c_{t+n}/c_t) appears in (25). Also, the disturbance u_{t+n} may be conditionally heteroskedastic; that is, $\text{var}[u_{t+n} \mid I_t]$ may be an essentially arbitrary function of the elements of agents' information set I_t. Thus, the model allows for the possibility that the volatility of stock and bond returns varies across different stages of the business cycle. More generally, this model does not assume that the returns or consumption be drawn from any particular family of distributions, in contrast to the log-linear expectations models of asset prices.

In spite of the significant weakening of the assumptions underlying the linear expectations models, Hansen and Singleton (1982, 1984) found that relation (25) is generally not supported by the data on aggregate stock and Treasury bill returns for the period January 1959 through December 1978. When consumption was measured as National Income and Product Accounts (NIPA) "non-durables plus services" and the monthly return ($n = 1$) was the value-weighted return on the NYSE, the probability values of the test statistics ranged from 0.57 to 0.30. However, for one choice of instruments the estimate of the parameter σ was outside the concave region of the parameter space (i.e. $\hat{\sigma} > 1$). Replacing the value-weighted with the equally-weighted aggregate stock return resulted in probability values ranging between 0.24 and 0.02. Moreover, three of the four sets of instruments considered lead to estimates of σ exceeding unity. When combinations of returns were examined (several stock returns or stock and bill returns), $\hat{\sigma}$ was again greater than unity *and* the probability values of the test statistics were typically less than 0.01. Similar findings are reported in Dunn and Singleton (1986) for real returns on several investment strategies using Treasury bills. The principal difference is that they also find substantial evidence against the model for individual returns on bills, as well as combinations of returns. Finally, using a different approach, Mehra and Prescott (1985) calculate the equity premiums implied by their equilibrium model for a range of plausible values for the risk-free rate and with the second moments of consumption fixed at the values of the sample second moments for the period 1889–1978. They conclude that their model is not consistent with the average excess return of an equity-type security that pays off the aggregate endowment stream over the risk-free return.

There are, of course, many possible explanations of these findings, including the misspecification of the agents' objective function and constraint set, mismeasurement of consumption, misspecification of the decision interval and associated problems with temporal aggregation, and the omission of taxes. Some insight into the plausibility of these explanations can be gained from further exploration of the empirical evidence. Consider first the problem of mismeasurement of aggregate consumption. Although much of the variation in aggregate consumption of non-durable goods is due to changes in retail sales, which is collected monthly, various interpolations and extrapolations are used to construct the monthly and quarterly data. These approximations may distort both the autocorrelation function of non-durable goods and the correlations between consumptions and returns. This in turn may explain why sample versions of the orthogonality conditions $E[u_{t+n} z_t] = 0$, $z_t \in I_t$, cannot be made close to zero for values of (β, σ) in the admissible region of the parameter space.

If the mismeasurement of consumption distorts the low order autocorrelations more than higher order autocorrelations, then this problem may be alleviated somewhat by working with monthly data point-sampled at long intervals. That is, instead of using monthly returns one would use longer term securities so that $m_{t+n}^{n} = \beta^{n}(c_{t+n}/c_{t})^{\sigma-1}$ involves monthly consumptions sampled at widely separated points in time. Table 12.6 displays the results from estimating the parameters of the model studied by Hansen and Singleton (1982, 1984) using monthly data on real returns with one; six; and twelve-month maturities. In the case of stocks, the investment strategy involves rolling over the value-weighted portfolio of stocks on the NYSE for the stated number of months (i.e. *VWRn* is the *n*-month rollover strategy); similarly, *TBILLn* denotes the return on an *n*-month Treasury bill. The time period of analysis is August 1963 through December 1978. Earlier months were omitted because trading of twelve-month Treasury bills was initiated in 1963.[6] For the Treasury

Table 12.6
Parameter estimates and test statistics for single-good models and
individual returns for various maturities,
August 1963–December 1978[a]

Return	$\hat{\beta}$	$\hat{\sigma}$	χ^2	DF
*TBILL*1	1.0003	0.7254	19.54	3
	(0.0003)	(0.0867)	(0.0002)	
*TBILL*6	1.0002	0.7816	16.27	3
	(0.0006)	(0.2467)	(0.0010)	
*TBILL*12	1.0007	0.3931	6.603	3
	(0.0007)	(0.2922)	(0.0857)	
*VWR*1	0.9963	1.646[b]	1.010	3
	(0.0056)	(2.091)	(0.7990)	
*VWR*6	0.9926	3.955[b]	0.2086	3
	(0.0103)	(4.261)	(0.9762)	
*VWR*12	1.0003	−0.3143	6.027	3
	(0.0047)	(1.972)	(0.1103)	
*TBILL*12 &	1.0019	0.0036	1.451	4
*VWR*12	(0.0010)	(0.4814)	(0.8350)	
*TBILL*12 &	0.998	1.366[b]	50.718	5
*VWR*12	(0.043)	(0.0000)		

[a]Standard errors of the parameter estimates and probability values of the test statistics are indicated in parentheses.
[b]The estimated value of σ is outside the concave region of the parameter space.

[6]The instruments were the constant unity, (c_t/c_{t-1}), (c_{t-1}/c_{t-2}), r_{t-n} and r_{t-n-1}, where $n = 1, 6$, or 12. Thus, five orthogonality conditions were used to estimate two parameters, leaving three overidentifying restrictions that are tested.

bill returns, there is a pronounced tendency for the fit of the model to improve as the maturity is lengthened. Not only do the test statistics decline, but the coefficient of relative risk aversion increases to a value closer to logarithmic utility ($\sigma = 0$). However, in spite of this improvement in fit, the test statistic remains quite large for *TBILL*12.

The pattern of results for the stock returns is altogether different. For the one- and six-month returns, $\hat{\sigma}$ is well outside the concave region of the parameter space. Correspondingly, the chi square statistics are very small relative to their degrees of freedom. In contrast, for *VWR*12, $\hat{\sigma}$ is within the concave region of the parameter space. Also, the test statistic is substantially larger, although there is not strong evidence against the model. Overall there is no systematic improvement in fit as n increases across stock and bill returns, which suggests that mismeasurement that distorts primarily the low order autocorrelations of consumption growth is not the explanation for previous findings.

Nevertheless, for a given type of security the length of the holding period does affect the results. Also, there are systematic differences in the fit of the model across securities. Further insight into these results is obtained by examining the autocorrelation properties of the variables comprising this single-good model. An immediate implication of (25) is that the disturbance (26) follows a moving average process of order $(n-1)$ [see Hansen and Singleton (1982)]. This is an implication of the fact that u_{t+n} is in agents' information set at date $t + n$ and $E[u_{t+n} \mid I_t] = 0$. It follows that if the model is correct, then the autocorrelation properties of $\beta^n(c_{t+n}/c_t)^{\sigma-1}$ and $r_{t,n}$ must interact in a manner that leads to an MA$(n-1)$ representation for their product.

The moving average representations of (c_{t+6}/c_t), *TBILL*6, *VWR*6, and the corresponding versions of the disturbance (26) (u_{t+6}^{T6} and u_{t+6}^{V6}, for *TBILL*6 and *VWR*6, respectively) are displayed in Table 12.7. The coefficients in the MA representation for u_{t+6}^{T6} are significantly different from zero at the 2 percent level out to lag seven.[7] Thus, the implication of the theory that this disturbance follows an MA(5) process is not satisfied. Moreover, disturbance u_{t+6}^{T6} seems to be inheriting the autocorrelation properties of *TBILL*6; compare the coefficients in the third and fourth columns of Table 12.7 with each other and with those for the consumption ratio in the second column. Next, consider the results for *VWR*6. Again, u_{t+6}^{V6} seems to be inheriting the autocorrelation properties of the return (in this case *VWR*6) and not that of the consumption

---

[7]The standard errors displayed in Table 12.7 should be interpeted with caution for at least two reasons. First, the disturbances u_{t+6}^{T6} and u_{t+6}^{V6} involve estimated parameters and the standard errors have not been adjusted for the randomness in the first stage estimates. Second, the shocks underlying the MA representation may be conditionally heteroskedastic.

Table 12.7
Moving average representations of variables in the single-good models,
August 1963–December 1978[a]

			Dependent variable[b]			
Lag	(c_{t+6}/c_t)	*TBILL6*	u_{t+6}^{T6}	*VWR6*	u_{t+6}^{V6}	u_{t+12}^{T12}
1	0.7883*	1.023*	1.005*	1.020*	1.086*	1.015*
	(0.085)	(0.081)	(0.079)	(0.079)	(0.080)	(0.083)
2	0.7823*	1.015*	0.966*	0.911*	1.124*	0.948*
	(0.101)	(0.114)	(0.111)	(0.115)	(0.119)	(0.118)
3	1.118*	1.114*	1.062*	0.209	0.430*	1.052*
	(0.129)	(0.137)	(0.131)	(0.137)	(0.150)	(0.141)
4	1.030*	0.974*	0.944*	0.160	0.279	0.952*
	(0.127)	(0.146)	(0.140)	(0.136)	(0.153)	(0.164)
5	1.072*	0.932*	0.891*	0.265	0.319	0.919*
	(0.131)	(0.146)	(0.140)	(0.138)	(0.153)	(0.179)
6	0.143	0.451*	0.458*	0.049	0.129	0.734*
	(0.122)	(0.137)	(0.132)	(0.137)	(0.151)	(0.180)
7	0.336*	0.284**	0.279**	−0.284	0.131	0.534*
	(0.103)	(0.115)	(0.111)	(0.115)	(0.120)	(0.190)
8	0.252*	0.067	0.087	−0.199**	−0.167	0.446**
	(0.085)	(0.081)	(0.079)	(0.080)	(0.082)	(0.179)
9						0.277
						(0.164)
10						0.244
						(0.141)
11						0.187
						(0.117)
12						0.013
						(0.082)
Constant	1.021	1.003	0.0015	1.003	0.0009	−0.0013
	(0.0017)	(0.0018)	(0.0016)	(0.012)	(0.016)	(0.0042)
R^2	0.724	0.847	0.851	0.678	0.732	0.877

[a]Standard errors are displayed in parentheses. A *(**) denotes a coefficient that is significantly different from zero at time 1% (2%) level based on a two-sided test and the standard normal distribution.
[b]The variables u_{t+6}^{T6}, u_{t+6}^{V6}, and u_{t+12}^{T12} are the versions of the disturbance (26) for the returns *TBILL6*, *VWR6*, and *TBILL12*, respectively.

ratio. Though, in contrast to the results for *TBILL6*, the return *VWR6* and u_{t+6}^{V6} exhibit only low order serial correlation, much less correlation than in is implied by an MA(5) process.

The findings that the disturbances are inheriting the autocorrelation properties of the returns may well explain why the probability value of the test statistic for *TBILL6* is much larger than the test statistic for *VWR6* – the disturbance u_{t+6}^{T6} exhibits too much autocorrelation, while the disturbance u_{t+6}^{V6} exhibits less autocorrelation than might be expected from the theory. Additional evidence consistent with this interpretation is displayed in the last column of Table 12.7. The MA representation for the disturbance u_{t+12}^{T12} associated with *TBILL12* indicates that there is no significant autocorrelation beyond lag eight, whereas the theory accommodates correlation out to lag eleven. At the same time, the probability value of the chi square statistic for $TBILL12$ is relatively small. In sum, it is the autocorrelation properties of the returns that largely explain the differences in test statistics both across maturity, holding fixed the type of security, and across types of securities.

There are also striking differences in the point estimates of (β, σ) across bills and stocks. Notice that, whenever $\hat{\beta}$ exceeds unity, $\hat{\sigma}$ is less than unity and vice versa. The results in the previous studies of this model display a similar pattern. Heuristically, this finding can be interpreted as follows. Taking the unconditional expectation of (25) gives:

$$E[\beta^n(c_{t+n}/c_t)^{\sigma-1}r_{t+n}] = 1 . \tag{27}$$

The estimation algorithm selects estimates of β and σ so as to make sample versions of the moment conditions, including (27), as close to zero as possible. For the sample period August 1963 through December 1978, (c_{t+6}/c_t) shows little tendency to deviate from its average value. Suppose then that estimates of β and σ are chosen as if (c_{t+n}/c_t) is fixed at its mean value, say μ_{cn}. Then, in order to satisfy (27), β and σ should be chosen such that $\delta_n = \beta^n(\mu_{cn})^{\sigma-1}E[r_{t+n}]$ approximately equals unity. For this sample period, $\mu_{c6} = 1.0133$. The mean of $TBILL6$ is 1.0035 and the estimated value of β^6 from Table 12.6 is 1.0012. Thus, a value of $\hat{\sigma}$ less than unity is required to make δ_n close to unity. Similarly, the mean of $VWR6$ is 1.0047 and the estimated value of β^6 is 0.9564, which is consistent with a value of $\hat{\sigma}$ that is much larger than unity.

Of course, these observations do not explain why there is a pattern of $\hat{\beta}$ being less than unity for the value-weighted return on the NYSE and $\hat{\beta}$ being greater than unity for returns on Treasury bills. An explanation of this pattern requires a more thorough analysis of the covariance properties of the returns and consumption data and of the products of the instruments and the disturbance (26).

These observations do suggest, however, that the growth rate of consumption during the sample period was on average too large relative to real returns on both stocks and Treasury bills for this model to yield plausible parameter estimates. Since β is approximately unity, (26) implies that $E[(c_{t+n}/c_t)^{\sigma-1}r_{t+n}]$ approximatley equals unity. Suppose that $\sigma = 0$ (log utility). Then for this condition to be satisfied in the sample, periods during which consumption growth rates far exceed real rates of return must be offset by periods during which the real return far exceeds the growth rate of consumption. In fact, for the sample period 1959 through 1978, consumption growth was positive a large majority of the months while there were long periods during which the real rates of return on stocks were negative.

An obvious question at this juncture is whether the omission of taxes from these studies might explain the findings. This omission works in favor of, not against, the model. If r_{t+n} is replaced by an after-tax real return, then the average value of this return will be lower on average than the unadjusted return. This in turn means that, for a given mean μ_{cn}, β will have to exceed unity by an even wider margin for the condition (27) to be satisfied in the sample. In the context of a model with leisure (see Subsection 5.2), Eichenbaum, Hansen and Singleton (1988) estimated the parameters of the corresponding Euler questions using before- and after-tax real returns on Treasury bills. Consistent with this discussion, they found that in both cases $\hat{\beta}$ exceeded unity and $\hat{\beta}$ was much larger when after-tax real returns were used.

It can also be shown that there are not two (approximately equal) local minima to the critierion functions used in estimation, one with $(\beta < 1, \sigma > 1)$ and one with $(\beta > 1, \alpha < 1)$. For example, the results from estimating the one-good model for $TBILL12$ and $VWR12$ simultaneously are displayed in the seventh row of Table 12.6.[8] Interestingly, for this run $\hat{\sigma}$ is well inside the concave region of the parameter space, although $\hat{\beta}$ is slightly larger than unity. Furthermore, the chi square statistic is small relative to the degrees of freedom. Nevertheless, the apparent good fit of this model is deceiving. When β is restricted to be 0.998, corresponding to an annualized real rate of interest of approximately 2.5 percent, $\hat{\sigma}$ is greater than unity, and the probability value of the chi square statistic is essentially zero (row 8, Table 12.6). This sensitivity of the results to the choice of β highlights the important influence of the average values of the returns and the consumption growth rate on the values of the parameter estimates.

For comparability with earlier studies, the statistics displayed in Tables 12.6 and 12.7 were calculated for a sample period ending in December 1978. The corresponding estimates for the value-weighted return over the sample period January 1959 through December 1985 are displayed in Table 12.8. While the test statistics do not provide much evidence against the model, estimates of σ are again outside the concave region of the parameter space in two out of three cases. Evidently, the qualitative nature of the results is not sensitive to extending the sample period through 1985.

From the result in Tables 12.6–12.8, it seems that mismeasurement alone is not sufficient to explain such a poor fit of the single-good model. Another explanation is that temporal aggregation, perhaps combined with mismeasurement, underlie the results. Christiano (1984) has shown in the context of the log-linear model (13) that aggregation over time may distort both the parameter estimates and the magnitudes of the test statistics. One approach to

---

[8]The instruments were unity, (c_t/c_{t-1}), and r_{t-n}^j for the jth disturbance, $j = 1, 2$. This gives six orthogonality conditions for use in estimating two parameters.

Table 12.8
Parameter estimates and test statistics for single-good models
and stock returns for various maturities,
January 1959–December 1985[a]

Returns	$\hat{\beta}$	$\hat{\sigma}$	χ^2	DF
VWR1	0.9945	1.730[b]	2.077	3
	(0.0040)	(1.980)	(0.5565)	
VWR6	0.9995	0.3769	2.414	3
	(0.0070)	(3.532)	(0.4910)	
VWR12	0.9840	6.006[b]	4.610	3
	(0.0047)	(2.336)	(0.2027)	

[a]Standard errors of the parameter estimates and probability values of the test statistics are indicated in parentheses.
[b]The estimated value of σ is outside the concave region of the parameter space.

circumventing these difficulties is suggested by the analysis in Rubinstein (1976). If agents have logarithmic utility, then for certain production and exchange economies the intertemporal marginal rate of substitution of consumption is proportional to the inverse of the total return on the aggregate wealth portfolio. It follows that

$$E[r_{t+n}/r^w_{t+n} \mid I_t] = k_n , \qquad (28)$$

where r^w_{t+n} is the n-period return on the wealth portfolio and k_n is a constant that depends on n. The assumption of logarithmic utility can be replaced by the more general assumption of constant relative risk averse utility, but at the expense of assuming independently and identically distributed growth rates in consumption over time.

Hansen, Richard and Singleton (1981) and Brown and Gibbons (1985) have studied relation (28) empirically using the value-weighted return on the NYSE ($VWRn$) as a measure of r^w_{t+n}. Brown and Gibbons did not test overidentifying restrictions implied by (28). The implication of (28) that the ratios of returns r_{t+n}/r^w_{t+n} are serially uncorrelated was tested using returns on individual stocks by Hansen, Richard and Singleton, however. For an economy in which there is a single non-durable good and $VWRn$ is an accurate measure of the return r^w_{t+n}, this test avoids the problems of temporal aggregation and measurement of consumption or the deflator [(r_{t+n}/r^w_{t+n}) can be formed as the ratio of two nominal returns]. The findings suggest that the model underlying (28) is not consistent with the data.

In sum, and without denying that some mismeasurement is surely present, I believe that the more important factors underlying previous findings are likely to be misspecification of preferences or violation of the conditions for aggregation across consumers. For instance, omitting relevant decision variables from the analysis may be an important source of misspecification in all of the models discussed in this section. This particular type of misspecification of the objective function is explored in the next section of this chapter.

5. Multi-good models of asset prices

There are several dimensions along which the structure of preferences in the single-good models examined in Section 4 may be misspecified. First, it may be the case that the assumption that preferences are separable across non-durable goods and all other decision variables is correct, but that the wrong functional forms for utility have been considered. Since a variety of functional forms have been studied, including quadratic, power, and exponential, the choice of functional form may not be the primary explanation for the poor fit. Second, the assumption that utility is separable across the decision variables of agents may be incorrect. For instance, utility may be a non-separable function of consumption of non-durable goods and consumption of leisure. Third, no distinction has been made between the acquisitions of goods, which are what the National Income and Product Accounts (NIPA) measure, and the consumption of goods. If levels of purchases and consumptions do not coincide, as they surely will not in the case of durable goods, then the implicit specifications of the technologies for transforming acquisitions of goods into services from these goods may be incorrect. This section explores the properties of asset pricing models that attempt to address the second source of misspecification.

5.1. Models with durable goods

If goods are durable in character, then acquisitions of goods will not coincide with the consumption of these goods. The misclassification of goods as being non-durable on a monthly basis is a potentially important source of misspecification, because it may distort both the autocorrelation properties of consumption growth, as well as the mean and variance of consumption. In the NIPA, goods are classified as non-durable if they have a typical lifetime of less than three years. Clearly, many of the goods called non-durable should be considered durable for the purpose of analyses of models with monthly or quarterly decision intervals.

The possibility that preferences for services from NIPA non-durable goods are not separable from preferences for services from NIPA durable goods is another potentially important source of misspecification. There are notable co-movements in durable goods purchases and the levels of interest rates. Accordingly, by introducing the services from durable goods into the model explicitly, and assuming that utility from the services of NIPA non-durable and durable goods are not separable, the model may better represent the "consumption risk" inherent in asset returns.

This possibility was pursued empirically by Dunn and Singleton (1986) and Eichenbaum and Hansen (1985), who considered the following extensions of the model in Hansen and Singleton (1982).[9] The function $U(s_{jt})$ was chosen to be the special case of (3) with $\sigma < 1$ and $\alpha = 0$:

$$U(s_{jt}) = (s_{jt}^1)^\delta (s_{jt}^2)^{(1-\delta)} . \tag{29}$$

Additionally, the service technologies were given by:

$$\begin{vmatrix} s_{jt}^1 \\ s_{jt}^2 \end{vmatrix} = \begin{vmatrix} 1 + \alpha L & 0 \\ 0 & \theta(1 - \theta L)^{-1} \end{vmatrix} \begin{vmatrix} e_{jt}^1 \\ e_{jt}^2 \end{vmatrix} , \tag{30}$$

where e_{jt}^1 and e_{jt}^2 are the endowments of NIPA "non-durable goods plus services" and "durable goods", respectively. In this model, NIPA non-durable goods provide services for two periods (months), while durable goods provide a perpetual flow of services that decline geometrically in magnitude over time.

Substituting (30) into (29) gives an indirect period utility function defined over acquisitions of goods. Let MU_{1t} and MU_{2t} denote the partial derivatives of $\sum_{t=0}^\infty \beta^t U(s_{jt})$ with respect to e_{jt}^1 and e_{jt}^2, respectively; and p_t denote the relative price of durables in terms of non-durables. The Euler equations that have typically been studied for this model are:

$$E_t MU_{1t} - E_t[MU_{1,t+1} r_{t+1}] = 0 \tag{31}$$

and

$$p_t E_t MU_{1t} - E_t MU_{2t} = 0 . \tag{32}$$

The expectations appear in (31) and (32) because acquisitions of goods at date t provide utility for more than one period. See Dunn and Singleton (1986) for details.

Upon estimating the model for the period January 1959 through December 1978, Dunn and Singleton (1986) and Eichenbaum and Hansen (1985) found that the overidentifying restrictions were typically not rejected at conventional significance levels for individual returns. The returns considered were the three-month real holding period returns on U.S. Treasury bills for buy-and-

---

[9]Dunn and Singleton (1983) also examined a model in which NIPA non-durable goods provided services over time. Their findings are discussed in Subsection 5.2.

hold and rollover investment strategies (Dunn and Singleton) and one-month holding period returns on one-month bills and an aggregate stock portfolio (Eichenbaum and Hansen). The lack of evidence against this model, especially using Treasury bill returns, stands in sharp contrast to the results for the single-good model with preferences given by (14). On the other hand, when the Euler equations for two different returns were examined simultaneously, there was substantial evidence agains the overidentifying restrictions. In this respect, the results are similar to the earlier findings for the model (25).

Eichenbaum and Hansen (1985) also investigated a quadratic version of the S-branch utility function with the linear technology (30). Specifically, the function $U(s_{jt})$ was chosen to be the special case of (3) with $\sigma = 2$ and $\alpha = 2$:

$$U(s_{jt}) = -\left\{\left[s_{jt}^j - \frac{\alpha_1}{2}(s_{jt}^1)^2\right] + \left[\alpha_2 s_{jt}^2 - \frac{\alpha_3}{2}(s_{jt}^2)^2\right] + \alpha_4 s_{jt}^1 s_{jt}^2\right\}, \tag{33}$$

α_1, α_2, $\alpha_3 > 0$. A potentially important difference between the specifications (29) and (33) is that the quadratic model does not restrict the substitution elasticity between the service flows from "non-durable" and "durable" goods to unity. Eichenbaum and Hansen report substantial evidence against the null hypothesis that utility is separable across the two consumption services [$\alpha_4 = 0$ in (33)]. However, in spite of its more flexible substitution possibilities, chi square statistics with probability values of 0.004 and 0.006 are obtained using $TBILL1$ [Eichenbaum and Hansen (1985)] and $VWR1$ [Singleton (1985)].

Three patterns of results emerge from these empirical studies of asset pricing models with multiple goods. First, for power utility, the introduction of durable goods seems to improve the fit of the models when individual returns are examined, perhaps with the exception of the one-month Treasury bill. For quadratic utility, the p-values remain small for both $TBILL1$ and $VWR1$. Second, the fit of the consumption-based models is typically better for aggregate stock indexes and long-term bonds than for real Treasury bill returns. Third, there is substantial evidence against the overidentifying restrictions in models with and without durable goods, and for power and quadratic utility, when two or more returns are studied simultaneously.

The improvement in fit from introducing durable goods into the single-good model (25) is documented in Table 12.9. The first six rows are taken from tables 1 and 2 in Dunn and Singleton (1986). The probability values of the test statistics in rows 4 through 6 are substantially larger than the corresponding values in rows 1 through 3. There are two differences between the models with preferences given by (14) and (29)–(30) that might explain these results: services from NIPA durable goods enter (29) in a non-separable way and NIPA non-durable goods provide services for two periods according to the technology (30). To determine whether allowing "non-durable" goods to provide services

Table 12.9
Parameter estimates for one- and two-good models of Treasury bill returns,[a]
January 1959–December 1978

Returns	$\hat{\beta}$	$\hat{\sigma}$	$\hat{\delta}$	$(1-\hat{\theta})$	$\hat{\alpha}$	χ^2	DF
	Unrestricted one-good model – Dunn and Singleton						
TBILL1		0.7843	*	*	*	18.37	3
		(0.0796)				(0.001)	
TBILL3		1.0095	*	*	*	11.113	3
		(0.1029)				(0.011)	
TB6H3		0.8260	*	*	*	9.97	3
		(0.0953)				(0.019)	
	Unrestricted two-good model – Dunn and Singleton						
TBILL1	1.0025	−0.2194	0.8963	0.9908	0.2669	13.83	5
	(0.0013)	(0.5557)	(0.0415)	(0.0094)	(0.0465)	(0.017)	
TBILL3	1.0036	−0.9139	0.9228	0.9961	0.5460	6.05	5
	(0.0030)	(1.212)	(0.1552)	(0.0188)	(0.2241)	(0.301)	
TB6H3	1.0028	−0.6124	0.9322	0.9975	0.5577	6.38	5
	(0.0023)	(0.9110)	(0.1133)	(0.0116)	(0.2131)	(0.271)	
	Restricted two-good model: $\sigma = 0$						
TBILL3	1.0016	0.0000	0.8981	0.9933	0.6494	16.65	6
	(0.0003)		(0.0688)	(0.0121)	(0.3732)	(0.011)	
TB6H3	1.0140	0.0000	0.8863	0.9914	0.5420	12.06	6
	(0.0003)		(0.0340)	(0.0081)	(0.2649)	(0.061)	
	Restricted two-good model: $\beta = 0.996$						
TBILL3	0.996	0.9999	0.8860	0.9988	−0.7387	248.9	6
			(0.1175)	(0.0153)	(0.1183)	(0.000)	
TB6H3	0.996	0.9999	0.8294	1.0057	−0.8413	714.31	6
			(0.0602)	(0.0073)	(0.0129)	(0.000)	

[a]Standard errors of the coefficients and probability values of the test statistics are indicated in parentheses.

over time is sufficient to improve the fit of the model, Dunn and Singleton also estimated a single-good model with preferences given by

$$U(s_{jt}) = (s_{1t})^{\sigma}/\sigma , \qquad s_{1t} = e_{1t} + \alpha e_{1t-1} . \tag{34}$$

The probability value of the chi square statistic for this model was 0.001, so the introduction of durable goods seems to be an important factor in the improvement of fit.

More direct evidence on this question is displayed in the seventh and eighth rows in Table 12.9. The two-good model (29)–(30) was re-estimated with power utility and σ constrained to equal 0. With $\sigma = 0$, preferences are of the logarithmic form:

$$U(s_{jt}) = \xi \log s_{jt}^1 + (1 - \xi) \log s_{jt}^2 , \quad 0 < \xi < 1 , \tag{35}$$

which is separable across the decision variables s_{jt}^1 and s_{jt}^2. Although $\sigma = 0$ is well within a one standard deviation confidence interval for the runs with *TBILL3* and *TB6H3* (rows 5 and 6), restricting σ to equal zero leads to a substantial increase in the chi square statistic for the models (rows 7 and 8).[10] These results corroborate those of Eichenbaum and Hansen for quadratic utility and *TBILL1*, which also support non-separable specifications of preferences.

Comparable results for *VWR1* are presented in Table 12.10. Unlike the findings for Treasury bills, there is little evidence agains either the one- or two-good models for the instruments chosen. Moreover, restricting σ to equal zero (logarithmic utility) in the two-good model leads to a comparable test statistic and more plausible point estimates of the share parameter δ and the decay parameter θ. It turns out that the hypothesis $\alpha_4 = 0$ cannot be rejected at conventional significance levels for the quadratic specification (33) [Singleton (1985)]. Thus, there is not much evidence against the separable specification of utility (across service flows) when returns on common stocks are studied.

A plausible explanation for the results in Tables 12.9 and 12.10 lies in the differences in the properties of the second moments of returns on stocks and Treasury bills. The aggregate stock return is much more volatile than Treasury

Table 12.10

Parameter estimates for one- and two-good models of the value-weighted return on the NYSE (*VWR1*),[a] January 1959–December 1978

$\hat{\beta}$	$\hat{\sigma}$	$\hat{\delta}$	$(1-\hat{\theta})$	$\hat{\alpha}$	χ^2	DF
		One-good model – Hansen and Singleton				
0.9982	−2.035	*	*	*	1.07	1
(0.0045)	(1.876)				(0.301)	
		Unrestricted two-good model				
1.0083	−4.1809	0.9734	1.0029	0.3735	5.68	5
(0.0257)	(4.8345)	(0.5583)	(0.0319)	(0.0747)	(0.338)	
		Restricted two-good model: $\sigma = 0$				
0.9985	0.0000	0.8452	0.9752	0.6279	5.96	6
(0.0024)		(0.0104)	(0.0092)	(0.4889)	(0.427)	
		Restricted two-good model: $\sigma = 0.996$				
0.996	0.9999	0.9936	1.0053	−0.7651	5.56	6
	(0.2337)	(0.0116)	(0.4200)	(0.474)		

[a]Standard errors of the coefficients and probability values of the test statistics are indicated in parentheses.

[10]The discrepancy between the test of $\sigma = 0$ using the large sample *t*-ratio and the difference between the minimized objective functions as test statistics suggests that the large sample distribution is not an accurate approximation to the small sample distribution of one or both of these statistics.

bill returns. Also, bill returns exhibit large and significant autocorrelations at much longer lags than the aggregate stock return (Table 12.7). Accordingly, the introduction of the smooth series "services from durable goods", which is highly autocorrelated and correlated with bill rates, may well improve the fit of the model. On the other hand, because of their high volatility and low autocorrelation, stock returns continue to dominate the behavior of the disturbance from the Euler equation (31), so the introduction of "services from durable goods" does not affect the fit of the model.

Additional support for this interpretation is provided by the analysis in Dunn and Singleton (1983). They estimated the one-service model with preference function (34), using monthly returns on long-term bonds and $VWR1$ for the period 1972 through 1978. For all of the runs considered, the estimated value of $(\sigma - 1)$ was small and insignificantly different from zero. Additionally, there was little evidence against the model from the chi square statistics. Now the long-term bond return is also much more volatile than the bill returns and, in contrast to bills, exhibits very little autocorrelation. It is perhaps not surprising then that the results from bond returns are similar to those from stock returns. This conclusion should be viewed as tentative, since Dunn and Singleton (1983) considered a much shorter sample period than the other studies discussed above. Nevertheless, there is some evidence that stocks and long-term bonds behave qualitatively in similar ways in the context of these intertemporal asset pricing models. This possibility warrants further investigation.

In Section 4 it was shown that the autocorrelation of the disturbance was not the only factor in the poor fit of the model. There was the additional consideration of the average values of the growth rate of consumption and the asset returns. The last two rows of Table 12.9 display the results from estimating the two-good model with β restricted to equal 0.996 and σ restricted to be less than unity (utility to be concave).[11] The deterioration in the fit of the model with the imposition of these restrictions is even more striking when durable goods are included in the analysis. The chi square statistic is now enormous. Also, the estimated value of σ is essentially on the boundary of the parameter space, which is why a standard error is not reported for $\hat{\sigma}$. Finally, the estimated value of α indicates that past acquisitions of NIPA non-durable goods provide *disservices* in the current period.

For comparison, the restricted two-good model was re-estimated using $VWR1$ as the return and the results are displayed in the last row of Table 12.10. Once again σ is on the boundary of the parameter space and α is negative. However, in contrast to the results for Treasury bills, the chi square statistic has changed little from the value for the unrestricted model. This

---

[11]Comparable results were obtained with $\beta = 0.998$.

seems to be yet another piece of evidence supporting the view that, with the high variability and low autocorrelation of $VWR1$, little information can be extracted about the structure of preferences of agents from aggregate stock return and consumption data alone over the holding periods considered here.

Would a smaller value of σ improve the fit of the model? Certainly more risk aversion will induce more volatility in the intertemporal marginal rate of substitution of consumption. Nevertheless, it turns out that decreasing σ leads to a *deterioration* in the fit of the model. This deterioration can be documented in two complementary ways. First, for the single-good utility function (14) with $\sigma < 0$, a smaller value of σ increases $|\sigma - 1|$ and, hence, $\mu_{cn}^{\sigma-1}$ falls, where $\mu_{cn}(>1)$ is the average value of (c_{t+n}/c_t). Consequently, for the orthogonality condition (27) to be satisfied using Treasury bill returns, $\hat{\beta}$ would have to exceed unity by more than it does in Table 12.6. In particular, the data do not support a smaller value of σ and a value of β less than unity.

Second, Dunn and Singleton (1986) investigated the implications of changing σ for the "unconditional" risk premiums implied by the utility functions (29)–(30). An implication of the Euler equations (1) for any two n-period returns is that

$$E[r_{t+n}^1] - E[r_{t+n}^2] = -\text{cov}[r_{t+n}^1 - r_{t+n}^2, MU_c^*(t+n)]/E[MU_c^*(t+n)],$$

$$\tag{36}$$

where $MU_c^*(t)$ is the marginal utility with respect to c_t scaled by $[(s_t^1)^{\delta\gamma-1}(s_t^2)^{(1-\delta)\gamma}]$ (in order to allow for real growth in acquisitions of goods). Letting $n = 3$ and choosing r_{t+3}^1 and r_{t+3}^2 to be the returns $TBILL3$ and the three-month real return on a six-month bill ($TB6H3$), Dunn and Singleton found that the sample estimate of $(E[r_{t+3}^1] - E[r_{t+3}^2])$ was -0.0012, while the estimate of the right-hand side of (36) (calculated at the point estimate $\hat{\sigma} = -1.66$) was 1.37×10^{-7}. The estimated risk premium is much too small and has the wrong sign. Moreover, decreasing $\hat{\sigma}$, holding all of the other parameters fixed at their estimated values, leads to a larger positive value of the sample unconditional premiums. Thus, as risk aversion is increased the difference between the sample excess return and the premium (which according to the theory should be equal to the excess return) increases.

5.2. Introducing leisure into asset pricing models

The intertemporal asset pricing models discussed up to this point have all assumed implicitly or explicitly that preferences are separable across consumption and leisure choices. Two recent studies have replaced this assumption with the assumption that utility can be represented as a non-separable function of non-durable goods and leisure plus a separable function of the services from durable goods.[12]

Mankiw, Rotemberg and Summers (1985) examined models in which the period utility function was given by

$$U(c_t, l_t) = \frac{1}{1-\gamma} \left[\frac{c_t^{1-\alpha} - 1}{1-\alpha} + d \, \frac{l_t^{1-\beta} - 1}{1-\beta} \right]^{1-\gamma},\tag{37}$$

where c_t and l_t denote consumptions of non-durable goods and leisure at date t, respectively. When $\alpha = \beta$, (37) becomes the CES form of the utility function. This particular utility function is not a special case of the S-branch function introduced in Section 2. Thus, empirical studies using this function should be interpreted as studies of a "representative stand-in consumer", and not of a representative agent obtained from aggregating the decisions of a large number of individual consumers with possibly different endowments. In addition, the model implies the following deterministic relation between consumption, leisure, and the real wage rate:

$$\frac{w_t \partial U / \partial c_t}{\partial U / \partial l_t} - 1 = 0.\tag{38}$$

Relation (38) is not satisfied by the data and, therefore, if (38) is required to hold, then the model is trivially inconsistent with the data. To circumvent this difficulty, Mankiw, Rotemberg and Summers assume that, because of measurement problems or the presence of contracts, (38) holds only up to an additive error term.

Upon estimating the model using the three-month Treasury bill as the asset in their version of (1), the authors found substantial evidence against the model. In several cases the concavity parameter $\hat{\sigma}$ was outside the concave region of the parameter space. Also, the chi square goodness-of-fit statistics were often in the 1 percent critical region. Complementary evidence against similar models of consumption and leisure choice is presented in Clark and Summers (1982). However, the utility specification (37), when combined with the econometric procedures used by Mankiw, Rotemberg and Summers, does not accommodate growth in per capita consumption or the real wage. Also, implicit in (37) is the assumption that leisure provides services only in the current period. Thus, (37) does not permit the rich intertemporal substitution

---

[12] There is an enormous literature on the linkages between consumption and leisure choices, but most of this literature does not consider explicitly the linkages between these choices and asset price behavior.

possibilities for leisure that Kydland and Prescott (1982) have shown emerge from allowing leisure to provide services over time.[13]

The model of consumption and leisure choice studied by Eichenbaum, Hansen and Singleton (1988) circumvented these limitations of the utility function (37). They considered a version of the utility function (29)–(30) with s_t^1 denoting services from NIPA "non-durables plus services" and s_t^2 denoting leisure services (durable goods were excluded from the analysis). The technology linking the service flow s_t^1 to acquisitions of "non-durable" goods was given by the first row of (30). Two versions of the technology for producing leisure services were examined: the first was given by $[1 + bL/(1 - \eta L)]l_t$, where l_t denotes consumption of leisure at date t; and the second was given by $(l_t + bl_{t-1})$. The first specification is identical to the leisure service specification proposed by Kydland and Prescott (1982).

Eichenbaum, Hansen and Singleton estimated this model using *TBILL*1 as the return and several measures of hours worked for the period 1959 through 1978. Interestingly, the estimates of the parameter b in the leisure service technologies were always less than zero when the counterpart to the intertemporal relation (38) was included in the econometric analysis. In other words, the findings are consistent with current leisure providing *disservices* in future periods, which is not consistent with intertemporal substitution of leisure.[14]

Another interesting feature of their results is that $\hat{\sigma}$ was always less than unity (concave utility) and $\hat{\beta}$ always exceeded unity. Furthermore, for most of the specifications considered, $(\hat{\beta} - 1)$ was more than five standard deviations from zero. The probability value of the chi square goodness-of-fit statistics ranged between 0.0001 and 0.02, so even with β unconstrained there was evidence against the model. It seems likely that restricting β to be less than unity would lead to a further deterioration in the fit of the model.

These observations suggest that many of the limitations of models with single or multiple consumption goods carry over to models that incorporate leisure in a non-separable way. This is perhaps not surprising in light of the fact that per capita hours of leisure time have not grown over this period and the variation in l_t is small relative to asset returns. Consequently, the estimate of β is still largely determined by the relative values of the growth rate of consumption and the average real interest rate. Introducing leisure does not help in

---

[13] Mankiw, Rotemberg and Summers (1985) also did not allow "non-durable" consumption goods to provide services over time, which is another potentially important source of misspecification.

[14] Deaton (1985) provides complementary evidence against the representative agent model of consumption and leisure choice by comparing the co-movements of consumption and hours worked over the postwar period.

explaining the co-movements of aggregate consumption and interest rates observed historically.

6. Concluding remarks

The research summarized in this chapter is best viewed as an early step toward providing a better understanding of the relations between movements in consumption, production, and asset prices. The results indicate that co-movements in consumptions and various asset returns are not well described by a wide variety of representative agent models of asset price determination. There are several dimensions along which the models fit poorly. First, the average consumption growth rates were too large relative to average real asset returns during the postwar period in the United States to be consistent with these theories. In addition, the serial correlations of the disturbances do not match those implied by the models. Because of the relatively small volatility of aggregate consumptions, the disturbances inherit the autocorrelation properties of the returns in the econometric equations. Finally, the volatility of monthly stock markets returns is so large that precise statements about the values of the parameters characterizing preferences and the covariances of stock returns and consumptions are not possible. The fit of the models with stock returns did improve some when the holding period was extended to one year, however, and the results on the autocorrelations of stock returns and industrial produ-tion over longer holding periods suggests that further analyses of these links over holding periods is warranted.

There are several directions in which this research is currently proceeding. The paper by Scheinkman and Weiss (1986) illustrated the potential import-tance of incomplete insurance for consumption behavior. More recently, Townsend (1986) has explored the properties of consumption and savings in dynamic models in which incomplete insurances arises endogenously due to private information. This work is at an early state and has not yet addressed return–consumption linkages. Similarly, Rogerson (1986) has explored some implications of fixed costs and the associated non-convexities for optimal labor supply decisions by households. All of these studies provide models which may imply substantial differences between the time series properties of aggregate and individual household consumption, leisure, and savings.

At the individual security market level, work is also proceeding on the incorporation of heterogeneous beliefs into models of asset price determina-tion. Hellwig (1980), Diamond and Verrechia (1981), Kyle (1984), and Altug (1986), among others, have deduced the properties of asset prices in a one-period model in which traders are heterogeneously informed and learn about the information of other traders from the equilibrium price. In Singleton

(1987), a repeated version of these models is solved in order to study the autocorrelation properties of asset prices in a multi-period model. It is clear from these studies that noise introduced at the individual market level [see also Black (1986)] can lead to substantial volatility of prices on a week-to-week basis that obscures the influence of underlying fundamentals on asset prices. The empirical results presented in Section 3 suggest that there are systematic links between stock returns and aggregate output over long holding periods. An interesting area for future research is the integration of these considerations into a model with multi-period consumption and leisure choice.

Third, and related to the first issue, progress is being made on modeling explicitly the motives for transacting in fiat money and the pricing of assets in monetary economies. Lucas (1984) and Townsend (1984) deduced asset pricing formulas in cash-in-advance economies and contrasted these relations to the counterparts in non-monetary economies. These and related models offer economic environments in which the negative correlation between stock returns and inflation can be explored.

References

Altug, S. (1986) 'The effect of insider trading by a dominant trader in a simple securities model', manuscript, University of Minnesota.

Black, F. (1986) 'Noise', *Journal of Finance*, 41: 529–543.

Breeden, D. (1979) 'An intertemporal asset pricing model with stochastic consumption and investment opportunities', *Journal of Financial Economics*, 7: 265–269.

Breeden, D.T. (1986) 'Consumption production, and interest rates: A synthesis', *Journal of Financial Economics*, 16: 3–39.

Breeden, D. and R. Litzenberger (1978) 'Prices of state contingent claims implicit in option prices', *Journal of Business*, 51: 621–651.

Brock, W.A. (1980) 'Asset prices in a production economy', in: J.J. McCall, ed., *The economics of uncertainty*. Chicago: University of Chicago Press.

Brown, D.P. and M.R. Gibbons (1985) 'A simple econometric approach for utility-based asset pricing models', *Journal of Finance*, 40: 359–381.

Campbell, J.Y. (1987) 'Stock returns and the term structure', *Journal of Financial Economics*, 18: 373–399.

Cambell, J.Y. and R.J. Shiller (1986) 'Cointegration and tests of the present values models', NBER Working Paper 1885.

Chamberlain, G. and M. Rothschild (1983) 'Arbitrage, factor structure, and mean–variance analysis in large asset markets', *Econometrica*, 51: 1281–1304.

Christiano, L. (1984) 'The effects of temporal aggregation over time on tests of the representative agent model of consumption', manuscipt, Carnegie-Mellon University.

Clark, K.B. and L.H. Summers (1982) 'Labor force participation: Timing and persistence', *Review of Economic Studies*, 49: 825–894.

Constantinides, G. (1982) 'Intertemporal asset pricing with heterogeneous consumers and without demand aggregation', *Journal of Business*, 55: 253–267.

Cox, J., J. Ingersoll and S. Ross (1985) 'A theory of the term structure of interest rates', *Econometrica*, 53: 385–408.

Deaton, A. (1985) 'Life-cycle models of consumption: Is the evidence consistent with the theory?', manuscript, Princeton University.

Diamond, D.W. and R.E. Verrecchia (1981) 'Information aggregation in a noisy rational expectation economy', *Journal of Financial Economics*, 9: 221–235.

Dunn, K.D. and K.J. Singleton (1983) 'An empirical analysis of the pricing of mortgage backed securities', *Journal of Finance*, 36: 769–799.

Dunn, K. and K.J. Singleton (1986) 'Modeling the term structure of interest rates under nonseparable utility and durability of goods', *Journal of Financial Economics*.

Eichenbaum, M. and L.P. Hansen (1985) 'Estimating models with intertemporal substitution using aggregate time series data', manuscript, Carnegie-Mellon University.

Eichenbaum, M., L.P. Hansen and S.F. Richard (1985) 'The dynamic equilibrium pricing of durable consumption goods', manuscript, Carnegie-Mellon University.

Eichenbaum, M., L.P. Hansen and K.J. Singleton (1988) 'A time series analysis of a representative agent model of consumption and leisure choice under uncertainty,' *Quarterly Journal of Economics*: 51–78.

Fama, E.F. (1965) 'The behavior of stock market prices', *Journal of Business*, 38: 34–105.

Fama, E.F. (1976) 'Forward rates as predictors of future spot rates', *Journal of Financial Economics*, 3: 361–377.

Fama, E.F. (1984a) 'Term premium in bond returns', *Journal of Financial Economics*, 13: 529–546.

Fama, E.F. (1984b) 'The information in the term structure', *Journal of Financial Economics*, 13: 509–528.

Fama, E.F. and K. French (1986a) 'Permanent and temporary components of stock prices', Working Paper, Center for Research in Security Prices, University of Chicago.

Fama, E.F. and K. French (1986b) 'Common factors in the serial correlation of stock returns', Working Paper, Center for Research in Security Prices, University of Chicago.

Ferson, W. (1983) 'Expectations of real interest rates and aggregate consumption: Empirical tests', *Journal of Financial and Quantitative Analysis*, 18: 477–497.

Flavin, M.A. (1981) 'The adjustment of consumption to changing expectations about future income', *Journal of Political Economy*, 89: 974–1009.

Flavin, M.A. (1983) 'Excess volatility in financial markets: A reassessment of the empirical evidence', *Journal of Political Economy*, 91: 929–956.

Frenkel, J. and A. Razin (1980) 'Stochastic prices tests of the efficiency of foreign exchange markets', *Economics Letters*, 6: 165–170.

Grossman, S.J. and R.J. Shiller (1981) 'The determinants of the variability of stock market prices', *American Economic Review*, 71: 222–227.

Hall, R.E. (1978) Stochastic implications of the life-cycle-permanent income hypothesis: Theory and evidence', *Journal of Political Economy*, 86: 971–987.

Hansen, L.P. (1982) 'Large sample properties of generalized method of moment estimators', *Econometrica*, 50: 1029–1054.

Hansen, L.P. and R.J. Hodrick (1980) 'Forward exchange rates as optimal predictors of future spot rates: An econometric analysis', *Journal of Political Economy*, 88: 829–863.

Hansen, L.P. and S.F. Richard (1987) 'The role of conditioning information in deducing testable restrictions implied by dynamic asset pricing models', *Econometrica*, 55.

Hansen, L.P. and T.J. Sargent (1980) 'Formulating and estimating dynamic linear rational expectations models', *Journal of Economic Dynamics and Control*, 2: 7–46.

Hansen, L.P. and T.J. Sargent (1981) 'Exact linear rational expectations models: Specification and estimation', Federal Reserve Bank of Minneapolis, Staff Report No. 71.

Hansen, L.P. and T.J. Sargent (1982) 'Instrumental variables procedures for estimating linear rational expectations models', *Journal of Monetary Economics*.

Hansen, L.P. and K.J. Singleton (1982) 'Generalized instrumental variables estimation of nonlinear rational expectations models', *Econometrica*, 50: 1269–1286.

Hansen, L.P. and K.J. Singleton (1983) 'Stochastic consumption, risk aversion and the temporal behavior of asset returns', *Journal of Political Economy*, 91: 249–265.

Hansen, L.P. and K.J. Singleton (1984) 'Addendum', *Econometrica*, 52.

Hansen, L.P., S. Richard and K.J. Singleton (1981) 'Econometric implications of the intertemporal asset pricing model', manuscript, Carnegie-Mellon University.

Harrison, J. and D. Kreps (1979) 'Martingales and arbitrage in multiperiod securities markets', *Journal of Economic Theory*, 20: 381–408.

Hellwig, M.F. (1980) 'On the aggregation of information in competitive stock markets', *Journal of Economic Theory*, 22: 477–498.

Ibbotson, R.G. and R.A. Sinquefield (1982) *Stocks, bonds, bills, and inflation: The past and the future*. Chicago: The Financial Analysis Research Foundation.

Kleidon A. (1985) 'Variance bounds tests and stock price valuation models', manuscript, Stanford University.

Kydland, F. and E. Prescott (1982) 'Time to build and aggregate fluctuations', *Econometrica*, 50: 1345–1370.

Kyle, P. (1984) 'Equilibrium in a speculator market with strategically informed trading', manuscript, Princeton University.

LeRoy, S. and R. Porter (1980) 'The present-value relation: Tests based on implied variance bounds', *Econometrica*, 49: 555–574.

Lo, A.W. and A.C. MacKinlay (1986) 'Stock market prices do not follow random walks: Evidence from a simple specification test', NBER Working Paper 2168.

Lucas, R.E., Jr. (1978) 'Asset prices in an exchange economy', *Econometrica*, 46: 1429–1446.

Lucas, R.E., Jr. (1984) 'Money in a theory of finance', in: K. Brunner and A. Meltzer, eds., *Carnegie-Rochester Conference on Public Policy*, Vol. 21. Amsterdam: North-Holland.

Mankiw, N.G. and L.H. Summers (1984) 'Do long-term interest rates overreact to short-term interest rates?', *Brookings Papers on Economic Activity*: 223–248.

Mankiw, G., J. Rotemberg and L. Summers (1985) 'Intertemporal substitution in macroeconomics', *Quarterly Journal of Economics*.

Marsh, T.A., 'Capital asset pricing models in a term structure context', manuscript, M.I.T.

Marsh, T.A. and R.C. Merton (1984) 'Dividend variability and variance bounds tests for the rationality of stock market prices', manuscript, M.I.T.

Mattey, J. and R. Meese (1986) 'Empirical assessment of present value relations', *Econometric Review*.

Mehra, R. and E. Prescott (1985) 'The equity puzzle', *Journal of Monetary Economics*, 15: 145–161.

Merton, R.C. (1980) 'On estimating the expected return on the market', *Journal of Financial Economics*, 8: 323–361.

Michener, R.W. (1982) 'Variance bounds in a simple model of asset pricing', *Journal of Political Economy*, 90: 166–175.

Rogerson, R. (1986) 'Nonconvexities and the aggregate labor market', manuscript, University of Rochester.

Ross, S.A. (1978) 'A simple approach to the valuation of risky streams', *Journal of Business*, 3: 453–476.

Rubinstein, M. (1974) 'An aggregation theorem for security markets', *Journal of Financial Economics*, 1: 225–234.

Rubinstein, M. (1976) 'The valuation of uncertain income streams and the pricing of options', *Bell Journal Economics and Management Science*, 7: 407–425.

Sargent, T.J. (1978) 'Rational expectations, econometric exogeneity, and consumption', *Journal of Political Economy*, 86: 673–700.

Scheinkman, J. and L. Weiss (1986) 'Borrowing constraints an aggregate economic activity,' *Econometrica*, 54: 23–46.

Scott, L.O. (1985) 'The present value model of stock prices: Regression tests and Monte Carlo results', *Review of Economics and Statistics*: 599–605.

Shiller, R.J. (1979) 'The volatility of long-term interest rates and expectations models of the term structure', *Journal of Political Economy*, 87: 1190–1219.

Shiller, R.J. (1981) 'The use of volatility measures in assessing market efficiency', *Journal of Finance*, 36: 291–304.

Shiller, R.J. (1981) 'Do stock prices move too much to be justified by subsequent changes in dividends?', *American Economic Review*, 71: 321–436.

Shiller, R.J. (1982) 'Consumption, asset markets, and macroeconomic fluctuations', *Carnegie-Rochester Conference Volume*. Amsterdam: North-Holland.

Shiller, R.J. (1984) 'Stock prices and social dynamics', Cowles Foundation Discussion Paper 719.

Shiller, R.J., J.Y. Campbell and K.L. Schoenholtz (1983) 'Forward rates and future policy: Interpreting the term structures of interest rates', *Brookings Papers on Economic Activity*, 1983: 173–217.

Singleton, K.J. (1980) 'Expectations models of the term structure and implied variance bounds', *Journal of Political Economy*, 88: 1159–1176.

Singleton, K.J. (1985) 'Testing specifications of economic agents' intertemporal optimum problems against non-nested alternatives', *Journal of Econometrics*.

Singleton, K.J. (1987) 'Asset prices in a time series model with disparately informed, competitive traders', in: W. Barnett and K. Singleton, eds., *Austin symposium in economics*. Cambridge: Cambridge University Press.

Sundaresen, S. (1984) 'Consumption and equilibrium interest rates in stochastic production economies', *Journal of Finance*, 39: 77–92.

Tirole, J. (1982) 'On the possibility of speculation under rational expectations', *Econometrica*, 50: 1163–1182.

Townsend, R.M. (1984) 'Asset prices in a monetary economy', Carnegie-Mellon University, manuscript.

Townsend, R.M. (1986) 'Private information and limited insurance: Explaining consumption anamolies', University of Chicago, manuscript.

Chapter 13

THE TERM STRUCTURE OF INTEREST RATES

ROBERT J. SHILLER*

Yale University

with an Appendix by

J. HUSTON McCULLOCH

Ohio State University

Contents

*The author is indebted to John Campbell, Benjamin Friedman, Jonathan Ingersoll, Edward Kane, Stephen LeRoy, Jeffrey Miron, and J. Huston McCulloch for helpful comments and discussions, and to Jeeman Jung, Sejin Kim, Plutarchos Sakellaris, and James Robinson for research assistance. Research was supported by the National Science Foundation.

The research reported here is part of the NBER's research program in Financial Markets and Monetary Economics. Any opinions expressed are those of the authors and not those of the National Bureau of Economic Research.

Handbook of Monetary Economics, Volume I, Edited by *B.M. Friedman and F.H. Hahn*
© *Elsevier Science Publishers B.V., 1990*

1. Introduction

The term of a debt instrument with a fixed maturity date is the time until the maturity date. The term structure of interest rates at any time is the function relating interest rate to term. Figure 13.1 shows the U.S. term structure of nominal interest rates according to one definition for each year since 1948. Usually the term structure is upward sloping; long-term interest rates are higher than short-term interest rates and the interest rate rises with term. Sometimes the term structure is downward sloping. Sometimes it is hump shaped, with intermediate terms having highest interest rates.

The study of the term structure inquires what market forces are responsible for the varying shapes of the term structure. In its purest form, this study considers only bonds for which we can disregard default risk (that interest or principal will not be paid by the issuer of the bond), convertibility provisions (an option to convert the bond to another financial instrument), call provisions (an option of the issuer to pay off the debt before the maturity date), floating rate provisions (provisions that change the interest payments according to some rule) or other special features.[1] Thus, the study of the term structure may be regarded as the study of the market price of time, over various intervals, itself.

What follows is an effort to consolidate and interpret the literature on the term structure as it stands today. The notation adopted is a little more complicated than usual, to allow diverse studies to be treated in a uniform notation. Definitions of rates of return, forward rates and holding returns for all time intervals are treated here in a uniform manner and their interrelations, exact or approximate, delineated. The concept of duration is used throughout to simplify mathematical expressions. Continuous compounding is used where possible to avoid arbitrary distinctions based on compounding assumptions. The relations described here can be applied approximately to conventionally defined interest rates or exactly to the continuously compounded McCulloch data in Appendix B. The McCulloch data, published here for the first time, are the cleanest interest rate data available in that they are based on a broad spectrum of government bond prices and are corrected for coupon and special tax effects.

Section 2 is a brief introduction to some key concepts in the simplest case, namely that of pure discount bonds. Section 3 sets forth the full definitions and concepts and their interrelations. Section 4 sets forth theories of the term

---

[1]The U.S. government bonds used to produce Figure 13.1 are in some dimensions good approximations to such bonds: default risk must be considered very low, the bonds are not convertible, and there are no floating rate provisions. However, many long-term U.S. bonds are callable five years before maturity, and some bonds are given special treatment in estate tax law.

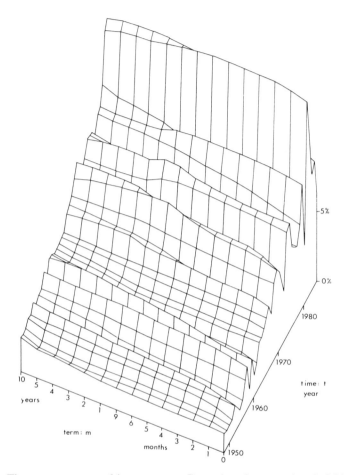

Figure 13.1. The term structure of interest rates. Data plotted are par bond yields to maturity, $r_p(t, t + m)$, against time t and term m, annual data, end of June 1948–85. Curves on the surface parallel to the m-axis show the term structure for various years. Curves on the surface parallel to the t-axis show the path through time of interest rates of various maturities. Maturities shown are 0, 1, 2, 3, 4, 5, 6, and 9 months and 1, 2, 3, 4, 5, and 10 years. Note that longer maturities are at the left, the reverse of the usual plot of term structures, so an "upward sloping" term structure slopes up to the left. Source of data: Table 13.A.3 of Appendix B.

structure, and Section 5 the empirical work on the term structure. Section 6 is an overview and interpretation of the literature.

2. Simple analytics of the term structure: Discount bonds

A discount bond is a promise by the issuer of the bond of a single fixed payment (the "principal") to the holder of the bond at a given date (the "maturity"). There are no intervening interest payments; thus the bond sells for less than the principal before the maturity date, i.e. it is expected to sell at a discount. The issuer of the bond has no other obligation than to pay the principal on the maturity date. An investment in a discount bond is not illiquid because the holder can sell it at any time to another investor. Let us denote by $p_d(t, T)$ the market price at time t of a discount bond whose principal is one dollar and whose maturity date is T, $t \leq T$. The subscript d denotes discount bond, to contrast this price from the par bond price to be defined below. The "term" of the bond (which will be represented here by the letter m) is the time to maturity, $m = T - t$. Thus, the term of any given bond steadily shrinks through time: a three-month bond becoming a two-month bond after one month and a one-month bond after two months.

All discount bonds maturing at date T for which there is no risk of default by the issuer ought to be perfectly interchangeable, and to sell at time t for $p_d(t, T)$ times the principal. The price $p_d(t, T)$ is thus determined by the economy-wide supply and demand at time t for credit to be repaid at time T. The determination of $p_d(t, T)$ is thus macroeconomic in nature, and is not at the discretion of any individual issuer or investor.

The price $p_d(t, T)$ of a discount bond may be generally expected to increase gradually with time t until the maturity date T, when it reaches its maximum, equal to one dollar. The increase in price for any holder of the bond over the period of time that he or she holds it is the return to holding it. The actual increase in price, since it is determined by market forces, may not be steady and may vary from time to time. It is useful to have some measure of the prospective increase in price that is implicit in the price $p_d(t, T)$. The yield to maturity (or interest rate) $r_d(t, T)$ at time t on the discount bond maturing at time T can be defined, given $p_d(t, T)$, as the *steady* rate at which the price should increase if the bond is to be worth one dollar at time T. If the growth of price is to be steady, then the price at time t', $t \leq t' \leq T$, should be given by $p_d(t, T) e^{(t' - t) r_d(t, T)}$. Setting this price equal to one dollar where $t' = T$, and solving for $r_d(t, T)$, we find that the yield to maturity is given by

$$r_d(t, T) = -\log_n(p_d(t, T))/(T - t).$$

The term structure of interest rates, for discount bonds, is the function relating $r_d(t, t + m)$ to m. We may also refer to $r_d(t, t + m)$ as the "m-period rate"; if m is very small as the "short rate" and if m is very large as the "long rate".

Note that the term structure at any given date is determined exclusively by bond prices quoted on that day; there is a term structure in every daily newspaper. Those making plans on any day might well consult the term structure on that day. We can all lend (that is, invest) at the rates shown in the paper, and while we cannot all borrow (that is, issue bonds) at these rates, the rates shown are likely to be indicative of the rates at which we can borrow. If the one-year interest rate is high and the two-year interest rate is low (i.e. if there is a descending term structure in this range), then individual firms, or governments, who plan to borrow for one year may be rather discouraged, and inclined to defer their borrowing plans for another year. Those who plan to lend this year rather than next would be encouraged. The reverse would happen if the term structure were ascending. Most individuals, of course, do not pay close attention to the term structure, but many do, and firms and governments do as well. The term structure on any day is determined by those who enter their preferences in the market on that day. A descending term structure on that day means that if the term structure had been flat there would be an excess supply of one-year bonds or an excess demand for two-year bonds. The descending term structure arises, of course, to choke off this excess supply or demand.

In making plans using the term structure it is helpful to realize that the term structure on any given date has in it implicit future interest rates, called forward rates. In the above example, where the term structure is descending between one and two years, it is implicit in the term structure that the one-year interest rate can be guaranteed to be lower next year than it is this year. To guarantee the forward rate one must be able both to buy and to issue bonds at quoted prices. One achieves this by trading in bonds of different maturities available today. One buys a discount bond at time t maturing at time T at price $p_d(t, T)$ and issues an amount of discount bonds maturing at t' at price $p_d(t, t')$, where $t < t' < T$. If the number of bonds issued equals $p_d(t, T)/p_d(t, t')$, then one will have broken even, at time t. That is, one will not have acquired or lost any cash today in the transaction. However, at time t' one must pay the principal on the bonds issued, equal to $p_d(t, T)/p_d(t, t')$. At time T one will receive the principal on the $(T - t)$-period bond, equal to 1. Thus, the outcome of the transaction is in effect that one is committing oneself at time t to buy a discount bond at time t' maturing at time T with price $p_d(t, T)/p_d(t, t')$. The forward rate $f_d(t, t', T)$ at time t applying to the time interval t' to T is the yield to maturity on this contract:

$$f_d(t, t', T) = -\log_n(p_d(t, T)/p_d(t, t'))/(T - t'), \quad t < t' < T.$$

This may also be called the $t' - t$ period ahead forward rate of term $T - t'$. One can also guarantee that one can borrow at the forward rate $f_d(t, t', T)$ by buying discount bonds maturing at t' and issuing bonds maturing at T.

One might thus consider, in deciding whether or not to defer borrowing or lending plans, a comparison of the spot rate $r_d(t, T)$ with the forward rate of corresponding maturity k periods in the future, $f_d(t, t + k, T + k)$. There is also another margin to consider. One might hold one's borrowing or lending plans fixed, deciding, let us say, to invest at time $t + k$, but to consider whether to tie down the interest rate today at $f_d(t, t + k, T + k)$ or to wait and take one's chances with regard to the future spot rate $r_d(t + k, T + k)$.

The subject of the literature surveyed here is how people who are making decisions at the various margins interact to determine the term structure. Before embarking on this, it is important to broaden our definitions and concepts.

3. Fundamental concepts

3.1. Bonds: Their definition

The term "bond" will be used here for any debt instrument, whether technically bond, bill, note, commercial paper, etc. and whether or not payments are defined in nominal (money) terms or in real terms (that is, tied to a commodity price index).

A bond represents a claim on a prespecified sequence of payments. A bond which is issued at time I and matures at time T is defined by a w-element vector of payment dates $(t_1, t_2, \ldots, t_{w-1}, T)$, where $I < t_i \leq T$ for all i, and by a w-element vector of corresponding positive payments $(s_1, s_2, s_3, \ldots, s_w)$. In theoretical treatments of the term structure, payments may be assumed to be made continually in time, so that the payment stream is represented by a positive function of time $s(t)$, $I < t \leq T$.

Two kinds of payment sequences are common. For the discount bond referred to above the vector of payment dates contains a single element T and the vector of payments contains the single element called the principal. A coupon bond, in contrast, promises a payment at regular intervals of an amount c called the coupon and a payment of the last coupon and principal (the latter normalized here at 1) at the maturity date. Thus, for example, a coupon bond that will mature in an integer number of periods and whose coupons are paid at integer intervals has vector of payment dates $(I + 1, I + 2, \ldots, I + w - 1, I + w)$, and vector of payments $(c, c, \ldots, c, c + 1)$. A perpetuity or consol is a special case of a coupon bond for which T, the maturity date, is infinity.

The purchaser at time t of a bond maturing at time T pays price $p(t, T)$ and is entitled to receive those payments corresponding to the t_i that are greater than t, so long as the purchaser continues to hold the bond.[2] A coupon bond is

---

[2]In the United States coupon bonds are typically traded "and accrued interest" (rather than "flat") which means that the price $p(t, T)$ actually paid for a coupon bond between coupon dates is equal to its quoted price plus accrued interest which is a fraction of the next coupon. The fraction is the time elapsed since the last coupon payment divided by the time interval between coupons.

said to be selling at par at time t if $p(t, T)$ is equal to the value of the principal, by our convention equal to 1.00.

A coupon bond may be regarded as a portfolio of discount bonds. If coupons are paid once per time period, for example, then the portfolio consists of an amount c of discount bonds maturing at time $I + 1$, an amount c discount bonds maturing at time $I + 2$, etc. and an amount $c + 1$ of discount bonds maturing at time T. Should all such discount bonds be traded, we would expect, by the law of one price, that (disregarding discrepancies allowed by taxes, transactions costs and other market imperfections) the price of the portfolio of discount bonds should be the same as the price of the coupon bond.[3]

There is thus (abstracting from market imperfections) a redundancy in bond prices, and if both discount and coupon bonds existed for all maturities, we could arbitrarily confine our attention to discount bonds only or coupon bonds only. In practice, we do not generally have prices on both kinds of bonds for the same maturities. In the United States, for example, discount bonds were until recently available only for time to maturity of one year or less. There is also redundancy among coupon bonds, in that one can find coupon bonds of differing coupon for the same maturity date.

3.2. Interest rates: Their definition

The *yield to maturity* (or, loosely, interest rate) at time t of a bond maturing at time T is defined implicitly as the rate $r(t, T)$ that discounts its vector of payments s to the price $p(t, T)$:

$$p(t, T) = \sum_{t_i > t} s_i \, e^{-(t_i - t)r(t, T)} . \tag{1}$$

The right-hand side of this expression is just the present value, discounted at rate $r(t, T)$, of the remaining payments accruing to bond holders. For discount bonds, this expression reduces to the expression given in Section 2 above. The yield to maturity may also be given an interpretation as above. Given the price $p(t, T)$, $r(t, T)$ is that steady rate of appreciation of price between payment dates so that if the price falls by the amount s_i at each t_i before T, the price equals S_T at time T. In theoretical treatments of the term structure in which the

---

[3]Conversely, a discount bond may be considered a portfolio of coupon bonds, though in this case the portfolio involves negative quantities. For example, a two-period discount bond may be regarded as a portfolio of one- and two-period coupon bonds whose coupons are c_1 and c_2, respectively. The portfolio would consist of $-(c_2)/[(c_1 + 1)(c_2 + 1)]$ of the one-period coupon bonds and $1/(c_2 + 1)$ of the two-period coupon bonds.

payments are assumed to be made continually in time, the summation in (1) is replaced by an integral.

The expression (1) gives the continuously compounded yield to maturity $r(t, T)$. One can define a yield to maturity with any compounding interval h: $r(t, T, h) = (e^{hr(t,T)} - 1)/h$. In the United States, where coupons are traditionally paid semiannually, it is customary to express yields to maturity at annual rates with semiannual compounding.[4] Continuous compounding will be assumed here for consistency, as we do not wish to allow such things as the interval between coupon dates to dictate the compounding interval.[5]

For coupon bonds it is customary to define the *current yield* as the total coupons paid per year divided by the price. Current yield is not used to represent the interest rate and should not be confused with the yield to maturity.

If coupon payments are made once per period, then equation (1) is a $(T - t)$-order polynomial equation in $e^{-r(t,T)}$ which therefore has $T - t$ roots. However, given that $s_i \geq 0$ for all i, there is only one real positive root, and this is taken for the purpose of computing the yield to maturity $r(t, T)$.

Roots of polynomials of order n can be given an explicit formula in terms of the coefficients of the polynomial only if n is less than five. Thus, yields to maturity for $T - t$ greater than or equal to five can be determined from price only by iterative or other approximation procedures, or with the use of bond tables.

The term structure of interest rates at time t is the function relating yield to maturity $r(t, t + m)$ to term m. A plot of $r(t, t + m)$ against m is also known as a yield curve at time t. There is a term structure for discount bonds and a term structure for coupon bonds. If we assume the law of one price as described in the preceding section, then, given the coupons, there is a relation between the different term structures.

3.3. Par bonds

Consider a bond that pays coupons continuously at rate c per period until the maturity date T when a lump-sum payment of 1 is made. If we disregard taxes and other market imperfections, the law of one price implies that the price of

---

[4] Thus, computing yield by solving (1) and converting to semiannual compounding (using $h = 0.5$) gives us exactly the yields in bond value tables, as in Financial Publishing Company (1970), so long as the term m is an integer multiple of $h = 0.5$. Whether or not m is an integer multiple of h, this also gives exactly yields to maturity as presented in Stigum (1981, p. 111) if $p(t, T)$ is represented as price plus accrued interest.

[5] Continuously compounded yield to maturity has also been referred to as "instantaneous compound interest", "force of interest", or "nominal rate convertible instantaneously". See, for example, Skinner (1913).

this bond in terms of $p_d(t, T)$ is given by

$$p_p(t, T) = \int_t^T cp_d(t, s)\, ds + p_d(t, T)\,. \tag{2}$$

The yield $r_p(t, T)$ of a par bond is found from $p_p(t, T)$ by setting the left-hand side of this expression to 1 and solving for c:[6]

$$r_p(t, T) = \frac{1 - p_d(t, T)}{\int_t^T p_d(t, s)\, ds}\,. \tag{3}$$

3.4. Instantaneous and perpetuity rates

The interest rate of term zero is $r_p(t, t)$, defined as the limit of $r_p(t, T)$ as $T \to t$, or as $r_d(t, t)$ defined as the limit of $r_d(t, T)$ as T approaches t. It is the instantaneous interest rate, which is of course not directly observed in any market. Since $r_p(t, t) = r_d(t, t)$ we can adopt the simpler notation r_t to refer to this instantaneous rate of interest. At the other extreme is $r_p(t, \infty)$, the limit of $r_p(t, T)$ as T approaches ∞. This is the consol or perpetuity yield, which is just the inverse of the integral of $p_d(t, s)$ from $s = t$ to $s = \infty$[7].

3.5. Estimates of the term structure

At any point of time t there will be an array of outstanding bonds differing by term, $m = T - t$, and by payment streams. Of course, not all possible times to maturity will be observed on available bonds at any given time t, and for some terms there will be more than one bond available. There has long been interest in estimates of rates of interest on standard bonds in terms of a standard list of times to maturity, interpolated from the rates of interest on bonds of those maturities that are actively traded.

[6]Note that for a par bond the yield to maturity equals the coupon. Note also that in the presence of taxes the law of one price need not imply (2) or (3). McCulloch's (1975b) formula for $r_p(t, T)$ collapses to (3) if the income tax rate is zero.
[7]Corresponding to the consol yield, we may also define the yield of a discount bond of infinite term, $r_d(t, \text{infinity})$, defined as the limit of $r_d(t, T)$ as T goes to infinity. Dybvig, Ingersoll and Ross (1986) have a curious result concerning $r_d(t, \text{infinity})$ in the context of a state price density model. They show that if $r_d(t, \text{infinity})$ exists for all t, then $r_d(t, \text{infinity}) \le r_d(s, \text{infinity})$ with probability one when $t < s$. Otherwise, arbitrage profits would obtain. Thus, the long-term interest rate so defined can never fall. Intuitively, this seemingly strange result follows from the fact that for large enough T the price $p_d(t, T)$ is virtually zero and hence cannot decline, but will rise dramatically if there is any decline in $r_d(t, T)$.

The U.S. Treasury reports constant maturity yields for its own securities, that appear regularly in the *Federal Reserve Bulletin*. Salomon Brothers (1983) provides yield curve data for government bonds of a wide range of maturities. Durand (1942, and updated) provides yield curve data for corporate bonds. These data are interpolated judgmentally.[8]

McCulloch (1971, 1975b) used a spline interpolation method that deals statistically with the redundancy of bonds and deals systematically with some differences among bonds, such as tax provisions pertaining to them. His method produced an estimate of an after-tax discount function and from that the price $p_d(t, T)$ of a taxable discount bond as a continuous function of T. Expression (1) was then used to convert this estimated function into a function $r_d(t, T)$. Values of his estimated continuous function for various values of t and T appear in Table 13.A.1. His method allows for the fact that, in the U.S. personal income tax law, capital gains are not taxable until the bond is sold and that, until the 1986 Tax Act, capital gains on bonds originally issued at par were taxed at a rate which was lower than the income tax rate. He describes his function in Appendix B. Other functional forms for estimation of the term structure have been discussed by Chambers, Carlton and Waldman (1984), Jordan (1984), Nelson and Siegel (1985), Schaefer (1981), Shea (1984, 1985), and Vasicek and Fong (1982).

McCulloch used his estimated $p_d(t, T)$ to produce an estimate of the term structure of par bond yields, using an equation differing from (3) above only for tax effects.

3.6. Duration

The term $m = T - t$ of a bond is the time to the last payment, and is unrelated to the times or magnitudes of intervening payments $s_1, s_2, \ldots, s_{w-1}$. Since bonds can be regarded as portfolios of discount bonds, it may be more useful to describe bonds by a weighted average of the terms of the constituent bonds rather than by the term of the longest bond in the portfolio. The duration of a bond, as defined by Macaulay (1938), is such a weighted average of the terms of the constituent discount bonds, where the weights correspond to the amount of the payments times a corresponding discount factor.[9] The use of the discount factor in the definition implies that terms of very long-term constituent bonds

---

[8]Other important sources of historical data may be noted. Homer (1963) and Macaulay (1938) provide long historical time series. Amsler (1984) has provided a series of high quality preferred stock yields that might proxy for a perpetuity yield in the United States, a series which is much longer than that supplied by Salomon Brothers (1983).

[9]Hicks (1946) independently defined "average period", which is equivalent to Macaulay's first definition of duration.

will tend to have relatively little weight in the duration formula. Thus, 30-year coupon bonds and 40-year coupon bonds have similar durations; indeed, they are similar instruments since the payments beyond 30 years into the future are heavily discounted and not important today relative to the coupons that come much sooner.

Macaulay actually gave two different definitions of duration that differed in the specification of the discount factor. The first definition of the duration of a bond of term m at time t uses the yield to maturity of the bond:[10]

$$D(m, t) = \frac{\sum_{t_i > t} (t_i - t) s_i\, e^{-(t_i - t)r(t, t + m)}}{\sum_{t_i > t} s_i\, e^{-(t_i - t)r(t, t + m)}}. \tag{4}$$

The second definition of duration of a bond of term m at time t uses prices of discount bonds as discount factors:

$$D'(m, t) = \frac{\sum_{t_i > t} (t_i - t) s_i p_d(t, t_i)}{\sum_{t_i > t} s_i p_d(t, t_i)}. \tag{4'}$$

By either definition of duration, if the bond is a discount bond, then the duration equals the term m, that is, we shall write $D_d(m, t) = m$. Otherwise, (since payments s_i are positive) the duration is less than the time to maturity.

If a bond is selling at par and coupons are paid continually, then duration using (4) is:

$$D_p(m, t) = \frac{1 - e^{-m r_p(t, t + m)}}{r_p(t, t + m)}. \tag{5}$$

Thus, the duration of a perpetuity, whose term is infinite, is $1/r_p(t, \infty)$.

The duration using yields to maturity to discount $D(m, t)$ is the derivative of the log of $p(t, T)$, using (1), with respect to the yield to maturity $r(t, T)$.[11] Thus, duration may be used as an index of the "risk" of a bond. The concept of duration has thus played a role in the literature on "immunization" from interest rate risk of portfolios of financial intermediaries. A portfolio is fully immunized if there is complete cash-flow matching, that is, if the payments

---

[10]The second argument, t, of duration will be dropped below in contexts where the interest rate $r(t, t + m)$ is replaced by a constant.

[11]This fact was used by Hicks and was rediscovered by Samuelson (1945), Fisher (1966), Hopewell and Kaufman (1973), and others.

received on assets exactly equal payments paid on liabilities. When such cash-flow matching is infeasible, portfolio managers may instead try to match the overall duration of their assets with the duration of their liabilities. As long as the term structure makes only parallel shifts, the yields on bonds of all terms being increased or decreased by the same amount, then duration matching will perfectly immunize the portfolio and there is no uncertainty about net worth. However, the term structure rarely makes a parallel shift, long-term interest rates being more stable than short-term interest rates, and so duration tends to overstate the relative riskiness of long-term bonds. Other methods of immunization have been proposed that take this into account [see Ingersoll, Skelton and Weil (1978)].

3.7. Forward rates[12]

The time t discount bond forward rate applying to the interval from t' to T, $f_d(t, t', T)$, alluded to in Section 2 above, is defined in terms of yields to maturity and duration in Table 13.1, expression (a). Using (1) one verifies that this expression is the same as the expression given in Section 2 above. The forward rate compounded once per h periods is $f_d(t, t', T, h) = (\exp(hf_d(t, t', T)) - 1)/h$.

The limit of expression (a) of Table 13.1 as t' approaches T, denoted $f_d(t, T, T)$ or just $f(t, T)$ is the instantaneous forward rate:[13]

$$f(t, T) = r_d(t, T) + (T - t)\,dr_d(t, T)/dT \tag{6}$$

---

[12]The earliest use of the term "forward rate", and the first indication that it can be thought of as a rate on a forward contract that can be computed from the term structure, appears to be in Hicks (1946) [first published (1939)]. Kaldor (1939) speaks of forward rates and their interpretation as rates in forward contracts, but attributes the idea to Hicks. Macaulay (1938) speaks of computing "implicit interest rates" without making an analogy to forward contracts (p. 30). Of course, the notion that long rates are averages of future short rates has a longer history; the earlier authors appear not to have written of computing forward rates from the long rates, or of showing an analogy of such rates to rates in forward contracts.

I wrote to Sir John Hicks asking if he had coined the term forward rate in the term structure. He replied that he only remembers being influenced by a 1930 paper in Swedish by Lindahl, later published in English (1939), which is couched, Hicks writes, "in terms of expected rates rather than forward rates; it is likely that the change from one to the other is my own contribution".

[13]McCulloch, who was concerned with the effects of taxation, writes (1975b, p. 823) what appears to be a different expression for the instantaneous forward rate. If we adopt some of the notation of this paper this is:

$$f(t, T) = -\{\partial\delta(t, T)/\partial T)/\{(1 - z)\delta(t, T)\}\,,$$

where $\delta(t, T)$ is the price at time t of an *after-tax* dollar at time T, and z is the marginal tax rate. However, since $\delta(t, T) = \exp(-(1 - z)(T - t)r_d(t, T))$, his formula is identical to the one shown here, i.e. the tax rate drops out of the formula expressed in terms of $r_d(t, T)$. The tax rate *should* drop out because both the interest rate $r_d(t, T)$ and the forward rate are taxable.

Table 13.1
Formulas for computation of forward rates and holding rates

I. Time t forward rate applying to interval from t' to T, $t \le t' \le T$:

(a) $f_i(t, t', T) = \dfrac{D_i(T - t)r_i(t, T) - D_i(t' - t)r_i(t, t')}{D_i(T - t) - D_i(t' - t)}$.

II. Holding period rate or return from t to t' on bond maturing at time T, $t \le t' \le T$:

(b) $h_i(t, t', T) = \dfrac{D_i(T - t)r_i(t, T) - [D_i(T - t) - D_i(t' - t)]r_i(t', T)}{D_i(t' - t)}$.

III. Holding period rate of return from t to t' rolling over bonds of term $m = T - t$, $t \le T \le t'$:

(c) $h_i(t, t', T) = \left\{ \displaystyle\sum_{k=0}^{s-1} (D_i(km + m) - D_i(km))r_i(t + km, t + km + m) \right.$

$\left. + [D_i(t' - t) - D_i(sm)]h_i(t + sm, t', t + sm + m) \right\} \Big/ D_i(t' - t)$,

where s = largest integer $\le (t' - t)/m$.

Note: In the above formulas, substitute $i =$ d for discount bonds, $i =$ p for par bonds. Par bond formulas give linear approximation to true rates. Duration (from which the second argument, t, has been dropped here) is given by $D_d(m) = m$, $D_p(m) = (1 - e^{-R_t m})/R_t$, where R_t is the point of linearization, which might be taken as $r_p(t, T)$. These formulas may be applied to data in Tables 13.A.1 and 13.A.3.

or

$$f(t, t + m) = r_d(t, t + m) + m \, dr_d(t, t + m)/dm . \qquad (7)$$

It follows that the instantaneous forward rate follows the same relation to the spot rate as does marginal cost to average cost. To see this relation, think of m as output produced and $r_d(t, t + m)$ as price of a unit of output. As with the familiar cost curves, the instantaneous forward rate (marginal) equals the instantaneous spot rate (average) when m equals zero, that is, $f(t, t) = r_t$. The forward rate is less than the spot rate where the slope of the term structure is negative, and is greater than the spot rate where the slope of the term structure is positive. An example showing a term structure and forward rate curve is shown in Figure 13.2.[14]

Solving the differential equation (7) we can show:

$$f_d(t, t', T) = (T - t')^{-1} \int_{t'}^{T} f(t, s) \, ds . \qquad (8)$$

[14] Instantaneous forward rates computed using McCulloch's data for large $T - t$ seem to be very erratic. Vasicek and Fong (1982) have suggested that the problem would be eliminated if McCulloch had used exponential splines instead of the ordinary splines of his procedure; however, McCulloch (1984) has disputed whether this would solve the problem.

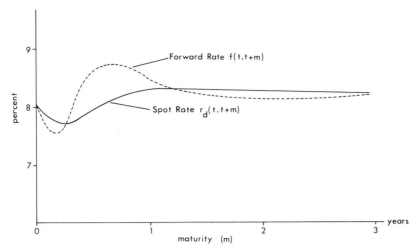

Figure 13.2. The term structure of interest rates $r_d(t, t+n)$ (solid line) and the instantaneous forward rate $f(t, t+n, t+n)$ (dashed line) for the end of August 1978. Source of data: Tables 13.A.1 and 13.A.2 in Appendix B.

Thus, the forward rate $f_d(t, t', T)$ is a simple average of the instantaneous forward rates between t' and T (see Figure 13.3).

Par bond forward rates can also be computed. These are especially useful if one wishes to make comparisons with spot interest rates as commonly quoted, since longer-term bonds usually trade near par. At time t one can guarantee for oneself a par bond issued at time t' and maturing at time T ($t \leq t' \leq T$) by buying at time t one discount bond maturing at time T, buying discount bonds maturing continually between t' and T whose principal accrues at rate c, and selling a discount bond maturing at date t' such that the proceeds of the sale exactly equal the total purchases made. If one then chooses c such that the number of bonds maturing at time t' sold is 1, one will have guaranteed for oneself, in effect, the rate of interest on a par bond at time t' maturing at T. The par forward rate $F_p(t, t', T)$ equals c or:[15]

$$F_p(t, t', T) = \frac{p_d(t, t') - p_d(t, T)}{\displaystyle\int_{t'}^{T} p_d(t, s)\, ds} .$$

(9)

[15]This formula for the forward rate differs slightly from that in McCulloch (1975b, p. 825). His formula replaces $p_d(x, y)$ with $\delta(x, y) = p_d(x, y)^{1-z}$ and divides by $(1-z)$, where z is the marginal tax rate. His formula is *not* quite identical to the one shown here if $z > 0$. However, the Volterra–Taylor linearization (like that which follows immediately in the text) of his expression in terms of instantaneous forward rates *is* identical to equation (10) below, and the tax rate drops out of that.

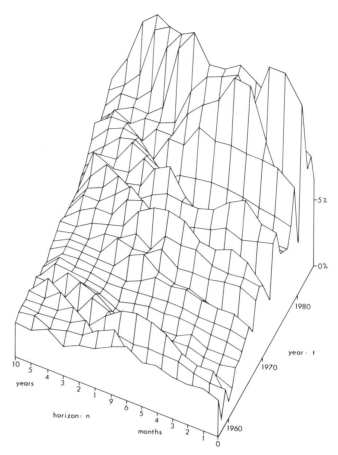

Figure 13.3. Instantaneous forward rates. Data plotted are $f(t - n, t, t)$ against time t and horizon n. The annual data series $f(t, t, t) = r_t$ seen at the far right of the surface is the instantaneous interest rate for the end of June of each year, 1957 to 1985. Curves on the surface parallel to the n axis show the path through time of the "forecast" implicit in the term structure of the instantaneous forward rate applying to the date shown on the t axis. If there were perfect foresight, we would expect these curves to be horizontal straight lines. In the expectations theory of the term structure with zero risk premium, they should be random walks. Curves on the surface parallel to the t-axis show the path through time of a forward rate of fixed forecast horizon. Data plotted here are from Table 13.A.2 of Appendix B.

Note the similarity between this expression and expression (3) for the par spot rate, above.

The limit of expression (9) as t' approaches T is the same as the values given by expressions (6) or (7) above for the instantaneous discount forward rate, hence the omission in those expressions of the d or p subscript.

It can be shown that the par bond forward rate is a *weighted* average of instantaneous forward rates, where the weights are proportional to the prices of the discount bond maturing at the date to which the instantaneous forward rate applies:[16]

$$
F_p(t, t', T) = \frac{\int_{t'}^{T} p_d(t, s) f(t, s)\, ds}{\int_{t'}^{T} p_d(t, s)\, ds} .
\tag{9'}
$$

This expression may be compared with the corresponding expression for discount bonds, expression (8) above. This expression gives more weight to instantaneous forward rates in the near future, rather than equal weight to all forward rates as in expression (8).

Using (8) for $t = t'$ and substituting for $p_d(t, s)$ in the above expression makes $F_d(t, t', T)$ a functional of $f(t, s)$ considered as a function of s. Following Campbell (1984, 1986b), this functional can be linearized around $f(t, s) = R$ using a Volterra–Taylor expansion [Volterra (1959)]. We will refer to the linear approximation to the forward rate $F_p(t, t', T)$ as $f_p(t, t', T)$. This is:[17]

$$
f_p(t, t', T) = \frac{R}{e^{-(t'-t)R} - e^{-(T-t)R}} \int_{t'}^{T} e^{-R(s-t)} f(t, s)\, ds .
\tag{10}
$$

Using expression (10) and that $f_p(t, t, T) = r_p(t, T)$ gives us again expression (a) in Table 13.1 for this forward rate in terms of par interest rates only.[18] The expression for forward rates on par bonds is the same as that on discount bonds except that duration on par bonds, $D_p(s - t)$, replaces the duration on discount bonds, $D_d(s - t) = s - t$, where $s = t', T$. It might also be noted that expression (a) in Table 13.1 gives the true par forward rate $F_p(t, t', T)$ exactly if a slightly different but less convenient, definition of duration is used.[19]

---

[16]See McCulloch (1977).

[17]The lower case f here denotes a linear approximation to the upper case F above. In contrast, for discount bonds the linear approximation is no different from the true forward rate, so lower case f is used for both. A discrete time version of (10) appears in Shiller (1979).

[18]The quality of this approximation to $F_p(t, t', T)$ is discussed in Shiller, Campbell and Schoenholtz (1983). The approximation is good except when both $t' - t$ and $T - t'$ are large.

[19]If we use Macaulay's definition of duration using prices of discount bonds as discount factors, (4'), and compute duration at time t of a bond whose continuous coupon is not constant through time but at time $t + i$ always equals $f(t, t + i)$, then one finds that duration is given by:

$$
D'(m) = \int_{t}^{t+m} p_d(t, s)\, ds .
$$

Using expression (9) [and the fact that $F_p(t, t, T) = r_p(t, T)$] one finds that $F_p(t, t', T)$ equals the right-hand side of expression (a) in Table 13.1, where the above $D'(m)$ replaces $D_p(m)$.

3.8. Holding period rates

A holding period rate is a rate of return to buying a bond (or sequence of bonds) and selling at a later date. The simple discount bond holding period rate, $h_d(t, t', T)$, where $t \leq t' \leq T$, is the rate of return from buying at time t a discount bond maturing at date T and selling it at date t'; see Table 13.1, expression (b). The rollover discount bond holding period rate, $h_d(t, t', T)$, where $t < T < t'$, is the rate of return from buying at time t a discount bond of term $m = T - t$, reinvesting ("rolling over") the proceeds in another m-period discount bond at time $t + m$, and continuing until time t' when the last m-period discount bond is sold [Table 13.1, expression (c)].

The par bond holding period rate, $H_p(t, t', T)$, where $t \leq t' \leq T$, is the yield to maturity on the stream of payments accruing to someone who buys at time t a par bond maturing at T, receives the stream of coupons between t' and T, and sells the bond at time T. This holding period rate can be defined as an implicit function of the coupon on the bond $r_p(t, T)$ and the selling price, which in turn is a function of $r_p(t', T)$ as well as the coupon $r_p(t, T)$. This implicit function may be linearized around $H_p(t, t', T) = r_p(t, T) = r_p(t', T) = R$ to yield the approximate $h_p(t, t', T)$ shown in Table 13.1, expression (b).[20] The rollover par bond holding period rate, $H_p(t, t', T)$, $t < T < t'$, is the yield to maturity on the stream of payments accruing to someone who buys at time t a par bond maturing at time $T = t + m$, reinvests proceeds in a par bond maturing at time $t + 2m$, and continues until time t' when the last par bond is sold. The linear approximation $h_p(t, t', T)$ appears in Table 13.1, expression (c).

4. Theories of the term structure

4.1. Expectations theories of the term structure

The expectations hypothesis, in the broadest terms, asserts that the slope of the term structure has something to do with expectations about future interest rates. The hypothesis is certainly very old, although it apparently did not receive an academic discussion until Fisher (1896).[21] Other important early

---

[20] The quality of this linear approximation to $H_p(t, t', T)$ is generally quite good; see Shiller, Campbell and Schoenholtz (1983) and Campbell (1986b).

[21] Fisher (1896) appears to say that the market has perfect foresight (p. 91). I have been unable to find any earlier discussion of the expectations theory of the term structure. Bohm-Bawerk (1891) discussed how expectations of future short rates affect today's long rate, but appears to conclude that the term structure is always flat (p. 280). Perhaps there is a hint of the expectations theory in Clark (1895, p. 395). Malkiel (1966) claims (p. 17) that "one can find anticipations of the expectations theory" in Sidgwick (1887) and Say (1853). In reading any of these works, one is led to conclude that the hint of the expectations theory is very slight.

discussions were in Fisher (1930), Williams (1938), Lutz (1940), and Hicks (1946). The expectations hypothesis probably derives from observing the way people commonly discuss choices between long and short debt as investments. They commonly speak of the outlook for future interest rates in deciding whether to purchase a long-term bond rather than a short-term bond as an investment. If interest rates are expected to decline, people may advise "locking in" the high long-term interest rate by buying a long-term bond. If everyone behaves this way, it is plausible that the market yield on long-term interest rates would be depressed in times when the short rate is expected to decline until the high demand for long-term interest rates is eliminated. Thus, relatively downward-sloping term structures are indicative of expectations of a decline in interest rates, and relatively upward-sloping term structures of a rise.

Early term structure theorists apparently could not think of any formal representation of the expectations hypothesis other than that forward rates equalled actual future spot rates (plus possibly a constant).[22] Early empirical work finding fault with the expectations hypothesis for the inaccuracy of the forecasts [Macaulay (1938), Hickman (1942), and Culbertson (1957)] were later dismissed by subsequent writers who thought that the issue should instead be whether the forward rates are in accord with a model of expectations [Meiselman (1962), Kessel (1965)]. Since the efficient markets revolution in finance in the 1960s, such a model has generally involved the assumption of rational expectations.

4.2. Risk preferences and the expectations hypothesis

Suppose economic agents can be characterized by a representative individual whose utility function has the simple form:

$$U = \sum_{t=0}^{\infty} u(C_t)/(1 + \mu)^t, \tag{11}$$

where C_t is consumption at time t, μ is the subjective rate of time preference, and $u(C_t)$ is momentary utility or "felicity". Calling v_t the real value (value in terms of the consumption good rather than money) of any asset or portfolio of assets including reinvested coupons or dividends, a first-order condition for maximization of expected utility is that

$$u'(C_t)v(t) = E_t\{(1 + \mu)^{t-t'}u'(C_{t'})v(t')\}, \quad t < t' < T. \tag{12}$$

[22]Conard (1959) wrote: "I assume not only that expectations concerning future rates are held with confidence by all investors, but also that these expectations are realized. Only by adding this last assumption is it possible to build a theory whose predictions can be meaningfully tested empirically" (p. 290).

If there is risk neutrality, then $u(C_t)$ is linear in C_t and $u(C_t) = a + bC_t$. It follows from (12) that

$$\frac{E_t v(t')}{v(t)} = (1 + \mu)^{t'-t} . \tag{13}$$

If the asset is a discount index bond maturing at time T, then $v(t') = p_d(t', T)$ and the left-hand side of this expression is one plus the expected holding return compounded every $t' - t$ periods, i.e. it is one plus $E_t(e^{xh_d(t,t',T)} - 1)/x$, where x equals $t' - t$. This means that under risk neutrality expected holding period returns as computed in the left-hand side of (13) will be equalized, i.e. will not depend on T. This in turn suggests that a particular formal expectations theory of the term structure follows from risk neutrality. Of course, risk neutrality may not seem a very attractive assumption, but approximate risk neutrality might be invoked to justify the intuitive expectations hypothesis described in the preceding section. Invoking risk neutrality to justify an expectations theory of the term structure was done by Meiselman (1962), Bierwag and Grove (1967), Malkiel (1966), Richard (1978), and others.

There are, however, fundamental problems with the expectations hypothesis as derived from risk neutrality. It is not possible for all expected holding period returns as defined in the left-hand side of (13) to be equalized if future interest rates are uncertain. This point was emphasized by Stiglitz (1970), who also attributed it to C.C. von Weizsacker. If one-period expected holding period returns are equalized for a one-period compounding interval, then $1/p_d(0, 1) = E_0 p_d(1, 2)/p_d(0, 2)$. If two-period expected holding period returns are equalized for a two-period compounding interval, then $1/p_d(0, 2) = E_0(1/p_d(1, 2))/p_d(0, 1)$. It follows that $E_0 p_d(1, 2) = 1/E_0(1/(p_d(1, 2)))$. This is a contradiction, since Jensen's inequality states that for any random variable x that is always greater than zero, unless x is nonstochastic, $E(x) > 1/E(1/x)$).

For index bonds, equation (13) implies that interest rates are *not* random, and that therefore Jensen's inequality does not come into play [Cox, Ingersoll and Ross (1981), LeRoy (1982a)]. This can be easily seen by substituting $p_d(t, t')$ for $v(t)$ in (13). Since t' is the maturity date, and the real value of the index bond at maturity is specified as $v(t') = 1$, it follows that $v(t')$ is not random. Clearly, (13) then implies that $p_d(t, t')$ is not random either. It will be known with certainty at any date before t. Thus, while risk neutrality gives us an expectations hypothesis, it gives us a perfect foresight version that is extreme and uninteresting. It would be possible to alter the utility function (11) to allow the subjective rate of time preference μ to vary through time, and that would give us a time varying yield curve. Still, we would have a perfect foresight model and a model in which preferences alone determine interest rates.[23]

Risk neutrality is of course not a terribly attractive assumption, given various evidence on human behavior. The theoretical literature does not appear to contain any argument for appealing simple restrictions on preferences or technology that singles out for us an attractive version of the expectations hypothesis; see LeRoy (1982a) for a discussion. Cox, Ingersoll and Ross (1981) offered two sets of assumptions other than risk neutrality that can produce an expectations hypothesis for the term structure: one involving locally certain consumption changes, the other involving state-independent logarithmic utility. But by offering such special cases they are not giving any reason to suspect that the expectations hypothesis should be taken seriously in applied work.

Applied workers, actually, have rarely taken seriously the risk neutrality expectations hypothesis as it has been defined in the theoretical literature, and so the theoretical discussion of this expectations hypothesis may be something of a red herring. The applied literature has defined the expectations hypothesis to represent constancy through time of differences in expected holding returns, or constancy through time of the difference between forward rates and expected spot rates, and not that these constants are zero. We shall see in the next subsection that these theories can be described as assuming constancy of the "term premia". Campbell (1986b) has stressed that some of the important conclusions of this theoretical literature do not carry over to the definitions of the expectations hypothesis in the empirical literature.[24]

4.3. Definitions of term premia[25]

There is little agreement in the empirical literature on definitions of term premia, and often term premia are defined only for certain special cases. Here,

---

[23]Cox, Ingersoll and Ross (1981) emphasize that risk neutrality itself does not necessarily imply that interest rates are nonstochastic. Utility is not concave, and investors could be at a corner solution to their maximization problem in which (13) does not hold. However, they argued that in this case the expectations hypothesis will not generally be valid.

LeRoy (1983) showed [correcting errors in his own papers (1982a, 1982b)] a sense in which when there is "near risk neutrality", that is, when utility functions are nearly linear, the expectations hypothesis is approximately satisfied.

[24]Cox, Ingersoll and Ross (1981) showed that if there are fewer relevant state variables in an economy than there are bond maturities outstanding and if bond prices follow Itô processes, then only one version of the rational expectations hypothesis, what they called the "local expectations hypothesis", can obtain in a rational expectations equilibrium. Campbell showed that this conclusion hinges on the assumption of a zero, not just constant, risk premium. He also showed a sense in which the other versions of the expectations hypothesis (which they claimed to reject as inconsistent with rational expectations equilibrium) may not be importantly different from their local expectations hypothesis.

[25]Much of this subsection follows Campbell and Shiller (1984) and Campbell (1986b).

some definitions will be adopted which are clarifications and generalizations of definitions already commonplace. As suggested in the discussion in the preceding subsection, economic theory does not give us guidance as to how to define term premia, and so choices will be made here to retain essential linearity, which will simplify discussion.

The forward term premium, $\Phi_{f,i}(t, t', T)$, $i = \mathrm{p}, \mathrm{d}$, will be defined as the difference between the forward rate and the expectation of the corresponding future spot rate. Unless otherwise noted, this expectation will be defined as a rational expectation, i.e. E_t is the mathematical expectation conditional on information available at time t. Thus we have:

$$\Phi_{f,i}(t, t', T) = f_i(t, t', T) - E_t r_i(t', T), \quad t < t' < T, \quad i = \mathrm{p}, \mathrm{d}. \tag{14}$$

The holding period term premium, $\Phi_{h,i}(t, t', T)$, for $t < t' < T$, will be defined as the difference between the conditional expected holding period yield and the corresponding spot rate:

$$\Phi_{h,i}(t, t', T) = E_t h_i(t, t', T) - r_i(t, t'), \quad t < t' < T, \quad i = \mathrm{p}, \mathrm{d}. \tag{15}$$

The rollover term premium, $\Phi_{r,i}(t, t', m)$, for $t < t + m < t'$, will be defined as the difference between the yield on a bond maturing at time t' and the conditional expected holding period return from rolling over a sequence of m-period bonds:[26]

$$\Phi_{r,i}(t, t', m) = r_i(t, t') - E_t h_i(t, t', t + m), \quad t < t + m < t', \quad i = \mathrm{p}, \mathrm{d}. \tag{16}$$

Although earlier authors did not always clearly intend rational expectations and often used different conventions about compounding, we can loosely identify the above definitions with definitions given by earlier authors. Hicks (1946), who is commonly credited with first defining these in the term structure literature, referred to both $\Phi_f(t, t', T)$ and $\Phi_r(t, t', m)$ as the "risk premium".[27] Because of a subsequent liquidity theory of interest by Lutz (1940), and analogy with the Keynes' (1936) liquidity preference theory, the risk premium has also become known as the "liquidity premium". In this survey, the phrase "term premium" will be used throughout as synonymous with risk premium and liquidity premium; it is preferred to these because the phrase does not

---

[26] Note that this risk premium has the form interest rate minus expected holding yield, in contrast to expected holding period yield minus interest rate in the preceding expression. This way of defining risk premia seems to be conventional; the rate on the longer asset comes first with a positive sign.

[27] See Hicks (1946, p. 147).

have an association with a specific theory of the term structure. The holding period term premium $\Phi_{h,i}(t, t', T)$ is referred to as the expected "excess return" in finance textbooks.

From the definitions in Table 13.1, there are simple proportional relations between holding period term premia and forward rate term premia:

$$\Phi_{h,i}(t, t', T) = \{D_i(T - t)/D_i(t' - t) - 1\}\Phi_{f,i}(t, t', T), \quad t < t' < T.$$

(17)

We also have the following relations for the rollover term premium, where $t < t + m < t'$, $t' - t = sm$, s integer:

$$\Phi_{r,i}(t, t', m) = (1/D_i(t' - t)) \sum_{k=0}^{s-1} [D_i(km + m)$$
$$- D_i(km)]\Phi_{f,i}(t, t + km, t + km + m),$$

(18)

$$\Phi_{r,i}(t, t', m) = (1/D_i(t' - t)) \sum_{k=0}^{s-1} [D_i(km + m)$$
$$- D_i(km)]E_t\Phi_{h,i}(t + km, t + km + m, t + sm),$$

(19)

4.4. Early presumptions pertaining to the sign of the term premium

Hicks (1946) thought that there was a tendency for term premia to be positive. In this context he referred to the forward rate term premium, $\Phi_{f,i}(t, t', T)$, but if this term premium is always positive, then by (17) above so must the holding period term premium $\Phi_{h,i}(t, t', T)$ and, by (18), the rollover term premium $\Phi_{r,i}(t, t', m)$.

Hicks' reasons to expect that term premia should be positive had their motivation in the theory of "normal backwardation" in commodity forward markets of Keynes (1930). Hicks wrote:[28]

> ... the forward market for loans (like the forward market for commodities) may be expected to have a constitutional weakness on one side, a weakness which offers an opportunity for speculation. If no extra return is offered for long lending, most people (and institutions) would prefer to lend short, at least in the sense that they would prefer to hold their money on deposit in some way or other. But this situation would leave a large excess demand to borrow long which would not be met. Borrowers would thus tend to offer better terms in order to persuade lenders to switch over into the long market.

[28] Hicks (1946, p. 146).

He offered no evidence (other than that on average risk premia themselves) that would support such a "constitutional weakness" on one side of the forward market.

Lutz (1940) offered a "liquidity theory of interest" that also predicted positive term premia:

> . . . The most liquid asset, money, does not bear interest. Securities, being less liquid than money, bear an interest rate which is higher the longer the maturity, since the danger of capital loss due to a change in the interest rate in the market is supposed to be the greater (and therefore liquidity the smaller) the longer the security has to run.[29]

His theory appears to ascribe term premia to own-variance, contrary to received wisdom in finance theory today.

Such theories were disputed by Modigliani and Sutch (1966) by merely pointing out that it is not clearly rational for individuals to prefer to lend short or to be concerned with short-term capital losses. If one is saving for a child's college education 10 years ahead, it is least risky to put one's savings in the form of a (real) 10-year bond rather than roll over short bonds. They proposed as an alternative to Hicks' theory the "preferred habitat theory". A trader's habitat is the investment horizon he or she is most concerned about, and that person will prefer to borrow or lend at that term. There is a separate supply and demand for loanable funds in each habitat, which could give rise to any pattern of term premia. Traders may be "tempted out of their natural habitat by the lure of higher expected returns"[30] but because of risk aversion this will not completely level term premia. The idea that individuals have a single habitat must be described as heuristic.[31] The intertemporal capital asset pricing model typically assumes maximization of an intertemporal utility function that involves the entire future consumption stream, with exponentially declining weights, and thus no single "habitat". However, the Modigliani–Sutch conclusion that term premia might as well, on theoretical grounds, be positive as negative seems now to be generally accepted.[32]

---

[29]Lutz (1940, p. 62).

[30]Modigliani and Sutch (1966, p. 184).

[31]Cox, Ingersoll and Ross (1981) consider an economy in which all investors desire to consume at one fixed date. They find that the risk premium, defined as the expected instantaneous return minus the instantaneous interest rate, may not be lowest for bonds maturing at this date. Still, they argue that a preferred habitat theory holds if the habitat is defined in terms of a "stronger or weaker tendency to hedge against changes in the interest rate" (p. 786).

[32]LeRoy (1982b) has argued that the risk premia are likely to be positive on theoretical grounds in a model without production, but had no results on the sign of the risk premium when production is introduced.

4.5. Risk preferences and term premia

If the representative agent maximizes the utility function (11), and therefore satisfies the first-order condition (12), then it follows that:[33]

$$e^{-(\tau_2-\tau_1)r_d(\tau_1,\tau_2)} = E_{\tau_1} S(\tau_1, \tau_2) \,, \tag{20}$$

where $S(\tau_1, \tau_2)$ is the marginal rate of substitution between time τ_1 and τ_2.[34] For equation (20), the precise definition of $S(\tau_1, \tau_2)$ will depend on whether we are dealing with index bonds or bonds whose principal is defined in nominal terms, that is, on whether $r_d(\tau_1, \tau_2)$ is a real or nominal rate. With index bonds, $S(\tau_1, \tau_2)$ is defined as $u'(C(\tau_2))/(u'(C(\tau_1))(1+\mu)^{(\tau_2-\tau_1)})$. With bonds whose principal is defined in nominal terms, $S(\tau_1, \tau_2)$ is defined as $u'(C(\tau_2))/u'(C(\tau_1)) \times (\pi(\tau_1)/\pi(\tau_2))/(1+\mu)^{(\tau_2-\tau_1)}$. Here $\pi(\tau)$ is a commodity price index at time τ, that is, the price of the consumption good in terms of the unit of currency. Thus, $S(\tau_1, \tau_2)$ is the marginal rate of substitution between consumption at time τ_1 and consumption at time τ_2 if the bond is an index bond, and between a nominal dollar at time τ_1 and a nominal dollar at time τ_2 if the bond is a conventional nominal bond.[35]

It follows from equation (20) for $t < t' < T$ [setting (τ_1, τ_2) in (20) as (t, t'), (t, T) and (t', T)] that:

$$e^{-(T-t)r_d(t,T)} = e^{-(t'-t)r_d(t,t')} E_t\, e^{-(T-t')r_d(t',T)}$$
$$+ \text{cov}_t(S(t, t'), S(t', T)) \,. \tag{21}$$

In order to put this in terms of the above definitions of term premia, we use the linearization $e^x \approx (1 + x)$ for small x to derive from the above:

$$\Phi_{f,d}(t, t', T) \approx -\text{cov}_t(S(t, t'), S(t', T))/(T - t') \,. \tag{22}$$

The term premium $\Phi_{f,d}(t, t', T)$ depends on the covariance between the marginal rate of substitution between t and t' and the marginal rate of substitution between t' and T.[36] If this covariance is negative, then forward

---

[33] To show this, use $v(t') = v(\tau_2) = 1$ and $v(t) = v(\tau_1) = p_d(\tau_1, \tau_2) = \exp(-(\tau_2 - \tau_1)\, r_d(\tau_1, \tau_2))$ in (12) where $\tau_1 < \tau_2$ so that $r_d(\tau_1, \tau_2)$ as well as $v(\tau_1)$ is known at time τ_1.

[34] It follows that increasing the uncertainty at time τ_1 about consumption at τ_2 will, if there is diminishing marginal utility, lower $r_d(r_1, \tau_2)$). This point was made by Fisher (1907, p. 214).

[35] Benninga and Protopapadakis (1983) describe the relation of risk premia on nominal bonds to risk premia on index bonds.

[36] LeRoy (1984) gives an expression for the term premium defined as the expected real j-period return on an i-period nominal bond minus the return to maturity of a j-period real bond.

rates tend to be above expected spot rates, as Hicks originally hypothesized, and the risk premium is positive.[37] In the case of index bonds, a negative covariance means that if real consumption should increase faster than usual between t and t', it tends to increase less fast than usual between t' and T. In the case of nominal bonds, the interpretation of the sign of the term premium is less straightforward. But consider the utility function $u(C_t) = \log(C_t)$. Then for nominal bonds $S(t, t')$ equals nominal consumption at time t divided by nominal consumption at time $t + 1$. Then, the nominal term premium $\Phi_{f,d}(t, t', T)$ would tend to be positive if it happens that when nominal consumption increases faster than usual between t and t' it tends to increase less fast than usual between t' and T.

One can also derive [taking unconditional expectations of (20)] an expression like (21) for unconditional expectations:

$$\mathrm{E}\,e^{-(T-t)r_d(t,T)} = \mathrm{E}\,e^{-(t'-t)r_d(t,t')}\,\mathrm{E}\,e^{-(T-t')r_d(t',T)}$$

$$+ \mathrm{cov}(S(t, t'), S(t', T)) . \tag{23}$$

From which, by a linearization, we have:

$$\mathrm{E}(\Phi_{f,d}(t, t', T)) \approx -\mathrm{cov}(S(t, t'), S(t', T))/(T - t') . \tag{24}$$

Thus, the mean term premium $\Phi_{f,d}(t, t', T)$ is positive if the unconditional covariance between $S(t, t')$ and $S(t', T)$ is negative. Such a negative covariance might be interpreted as saying that marginal utility is "unsmooth" between $\tau = t$ and $\tau = T$. This means that when detrended marginal utility increases between $\tau = t$ and $\tau = t'$ it tends to decrease between t' and T. A positive covariance, and hence a negative term premium, would tend to occur if marginal utility is "smooth" between $\tau = t$ and $\tau = T$.

If the values of bonds of all maturities are assumed to be deterministic functions of a small number of state variables that are continuous diffusion processes, then theoretical restrictions on risk premia beyond those defined here can also be derived [e.g. Brennan and Schwartz (1980), Cox, Ingersoll and Ross (1981), Dothan (1978), Langetieg (1980), Marsh (1980), Richard (1978) and Vasicek (1978)]. When bond values are such deterministic functions of diffusion processes, if the restrictions did not hold there would be riskless

---

[37] Woodward (1983) discusses term premia in terms of the serial correlation of marginal utility of consumption rather than the serial correlation of marginal rates of substitution. Her principal result is that in a case where the correlation conditional on information at t between $u'(c_{t'})$ and $u'(c_T)$ is negative, then the sign of the term premium may be sensitive to the definition of the premium. She defines as an alternative definition of the term premium, the "solidity premium", based on forward and actual discounts. The negative correlation she defines is an unlikely special case. Actual aggregate consumption in the United States roughly resembles a random walk [Hall (1978)] for which the correlation she defines is positive.

arbitrage opportunities. The assumption of such a state variable representation has been convenient for theoretical models. It has even led to a complete general equilibrium model of the term structure in a macro economy [Cox, Ingersoll and Ross (1985a, 1985b)], a model subjected to empirical testing by Brown and Dybvig (1986).

5. Empirical studies of the term structure

5.1. Empirical expectations hypotheses for the term structure

One need not assume rational expectations to proceed with studying an expectations theory of the term structure if one has data on expectations or can infer expectations from other data. The first study of the term structure using an expectations model was performed by Meiselman (1962). Meiselman proposed the "error learning hypothesis" that economic agents revise their expectations in proportion to the error just discovered in their last period expectation for today's one-period rate. This hypothesis then implies that $f_i(t, t+n, t+n+1) - f_i(t-1, t+n, t+n+1) = a_n + b_n(r_i(t, t+1) - f_i(t-1, t, t+1))$. He estimated a_n and b_n by regression analysis using U.S. Durand's annual data 1901–54 for $n = 1, 2, \ldots, 8$. He took as encouraging for the model that the signs of the estimated b_n were all positive and declined with n. However, Buse (1967) criticized his conclusion, saying that ". . . such results are implied by any set of smoothed yield curves in which the short-term interest rates have shown a greater variability than long-term interest rates".

It was pointed out later by Diller (1969) and Nelson (1970a) that the error learning principle is a property of optimal linear forecasts. They found that the coefficients b_n that Meiselman estimated compared rather favorably with the coefficients implied by an estimated linear forecasting equation. However, the univariate form of the error learning principle proposed by Meiselman applies only to univariate optimal linear forecasts [Shiller (1978)], and thus the Meiselman theory is unfortunately restrictive.

Other authors have used survey expectations data for market expectations of future interest rates. Survey methods seem particularly attractive since surveys can be focused on the institutional investors who hold most government and corporate bonds, and who are probably not well described in terms of the expected utility of consumption models described in the preceding section.[38]

Friedman (1979) used data 1969–78 from a quarterly survey of financial market participants by the *Goldsmith–Nagan Bond and Money Market Letter*.

---

[38]See Board of Governors (1985, pp. 20 and 54). Of course, individuals ultimately have claims on the assets of these institutions; still there is an institutional layer between them and the bonds held on their behalf.

He found that the term premium on U.S. Treasury bills, $\Phi_d(t, t+1, t+2)$ and $\Phi_d(t, t+2, t+3)$ (where time is measured in months), was positive on average and depended positively on the level of interest rates. He showed [Friedman (1980c)] that his model differed substantially from a rational expectations model, in that the survey expectations could be improved upon easily. Kane and Malkiel (1967) conducted their own survey of banks, life insurance companies and nonfinancial corporations to learn about the relation of expectations to the term structure of interest rates. They learned that many investors seemed not to formulate specific interest rate expectations (especially for the distant future) and those that did, did not have uniform expectations. Kane (1983) found using additional Kane–Malkiel survey data 1969–72 that term premia appear positively related to the level of interest rates.

5.2. The rational expectations hypothesis in empirical work

Although the rational expectations hypothesis regarding the term structure has had many forms, it has its simplest form used in empirical work in terms of the continuously compounded yields discussed here. Often, the other forms of the hypothesis do not differ importantly from that discussed here [see Shiller, Campbell and Schoenholtz (1983) and Campbell (1986b)]. In the definition to be used here, the rational expectations hypothesis is that all term premia, $\Phi_{h,i}(t, t+n, t+m+n)$, $0<m$, $0<n$, $\Phi_{f,i}(t, t+n, t+m+n)$, $0<m$, $0<n$, and $\Phi_{r,i}(t, t+n, m)$, $0<m<n$, do not depend on time t.[39] This means that all term premia depend only on maturity and not time, and the changing slope of the term structure can only be interpreted in terms of the changing expectations for future interest rates.[40]

The literature testing forms of the rational expectations hypothesis like that defined here is enormous.[41] It is difficult to summarize what we know about the expectations hypothesis from this literature. We are studying a two-dimensional array of term premia; term premia depend on m (the maturity of the

[39]When dealing with par bonds, the expectations model defined here relates to the linearized model. The assumption here is that the point of linearization R does not depend on the level of interest rates, otherwise the model will not be linear in interest rates.

[40]Note that in this expectations hypothesis, stated in terms of continuously compounded yields, it is possible for all risk premia to be zero. We do not encounter the Jensen's inequality problem alluded to above in connection with risk neutrality. The problem alluded to by von Weizsaecker and Stiglitz was essentially one of compounding, and is eliminated when we couch the model in terms of continuously compounded interest rates.

[41]The literature has to do almost entirely with nominal interest rates, as a term structure of index bonds is observed only for brief periods in certain countries. Campbell and Shiller (1988) in effect looked at the real term structure in the postwar U.S. corporate stock price data by correcting the dividend price ratio for predictable changes in real dividends, leaving a long-term real consol component of the dividend price ratio. The expectations hypothesis was not supported by the evidence.

forward instrument) and n (the time into the future that the forward instrument begins). Term premia may be approximately constant for some m and n and not for others; certain functions of term premia may be approximately constant and not others. Term premia may be approximately constant for some time periods and not others, or in some countries and not others.

Testing for the constancy of term premia ultimately means trying to predict the right-hand side of the equations defining term premia [equations (14), (15) or (16) above] from which the conditional expectations operator E_t is deleted, in terms of information at time t. This means predicting either excess holding period returns or the difference between forward rates and corresponding spot rates in terms of information at time t. Because of the relations between the definitions of term premia [equations (17), (18), or (19) above] it does not matter whether the regression has excess holding yields or the difference between forward rates and corresponding spot rates as the variable explained; the difference has to do only with a multiplicative constant for the dependent variable. Of course, most studies do not use the exact definitions of term premia defined here, in terms of continuously compounded rates or, in the case of par bonds, linearized holding yields, but the differences in definition are generally not important.

Some studies may report some tests of the rational expectations hypothesis that have the appearance of something very different; for example, Roll (1970) tested (and rejected using 1–13 week U.S. Treasury bill data 1949–64) the martingale property of forward rates by testing whether changes in forward rates $f_d(t, t', T) - f_d(t - 1, t', T)$ are serially correlated through time t. But in fact testing the hypothesis that there is no such serial correlation is no different from testing the hypothesis that *changes* in the difference between forward rates and corresponding spot rates cannot be predicted based on information consisting of past changes in forward rates. For another example, some researchers have noted that for large m and small n the holding return $h_i(t, t + n, t + m)$ is approximately equal to $r_i(t, t + m) - r_i(t + n, t + n + m)$, the change in the long rate, divided by $D_i(n)$. If n is very small, $1/D_i(n)$ is a very large number, and the excess holding return is heavily influenced by the change in the long rate. The rational expectations hypothesis thus suggests that $r_i(t, t + m) - r_i(t + n, t + n + m)$ is approximately unforecastable, and hence that long rates are in this sense approximately random walks. The random walk property for long-term interest rates was tested by Phillips and Pippenger (1976, 1979), Pesando (1981, 1983), and Mishkin (1978).[42]

---

[42] The random walk property is an approximation useful only under certain assumptions [see Mishkin (1980) and Begg (1984)]. Phillips and Pippenger (1976, 1979) used the random walk approximation to assert that the Modigliani and Sutch (1966) and Modigliani and Shiller (1973) distributed lag regressions explaining the long rate must be spurious. Looking at the out-of-sample fit of the equation does not suggest that term-structure equations like that in Modigliani–Shiller are completely spurious: see Ando and Kennickell (1983).

Of all the studies of the rational expectations hypothesis for the term structure, of greatest interest are the results in which the explanatory variable is approximately (or approximately proportional to) the spread between a forward rate $f_i(t, m, n)$ and the spot rate of the same maturity as the forward rate, $r_i(t, t + m)$. This spread forecasts the change in $r_i(t, t + m)$ over the next n periods. Regressions in the literature that can be interpreted at least approximately as regressions of the actual change in spot rates $r_i(t + n, t + m + n) - r_i(t, t + m)$ on the predicted change $f_i(t, m, n) - r_i(t, t + m)$ and a constant are shown in Table 13.2.

What is clear from Table 13.2 is that the slope coefficient is quite far below one – and often negative – for low forecast horizon n, regardless of the maturi-

Table 13.2

Regressions of changes in m-period interest rates on changes predicted by the term structure: $r_i(t + n, t + m + n) - r_i(t, t + m)$ on $f_i(t, t + n, t + m + n) - r_i(t, t + m)$ and constant

Study	Country	Sample	m (years)	n (years)	Slope coef.	Std. error	R^2
Shiller	U.S.	1966–77	>20.0	0.25	−5.56	1.67	0.201
(1979)[a]	U.S.	1919–58	>20.0	1.00	−0.44	0.75	0.01
	U.K.	1956–77	∞	0.25	−5.88	2.09	0.09
Shiller,	U.S.	1959–74	0.25	0.25	0.27	0.18	0.03
Campbell and	U.S.	1959–73	30.0	0.50	−1.46	(1.79)	0.02
Schoenholtz							
(1983)[b]							
Mankiw	Canada	1961–84	0.25	0.25	0.10	(0.07)	0.02
(1986)[c]	W. Germany	1961–84	0.25	0.25	0.14	(0.07)	0.03
Fama	U.S.	1959–82	1/12	1/12	0.46	(0.07)	0.13
(1984a)[d]			1/12	2/12	0.25	(0.10)	0.02
			1/12	3/12	0.26	(0.12)	0.02
			1/12	4/12	0.17	(0.10)	0.01
			1/12	5/12	0.11	(0.10)	0.00
Fama and Bliss	U.S.	1964–84	1.00	1.00	0.09	(0.28)	0.00
(1987)[e]			1.00	2.00	0.69	(0.26)	0.08
			1.00	3.00	1.30	(0.10)	0.24
			1.00	4.00	1.61	(0.34)	0.48
Shiller (1986)[f]	U.S.	1953–86	0.25	rollover*	0.61	(0.17)	0.090

Note: Expectations theory of the term structure asserts that the slope coefficient should be 1.00. Not all regressions summarized here were in exactly the form shown here; in some cases a linearization was assumed to transform results to the form shown here. Significance level refers to a test of hypothesis that the coefficient is 1.00.

*Dependent variable is approximately $S^*(m, n)$ and the independent variable is $S(m, n)$ as defined in expression (26) in text.

[a] Page 1210, table 3, rows 1, 4 and 5. Column 2 coefficient was converted using duration implicit in γ_n given in Table 13.1 rows 1, 4 and 5 column 1.

[b] Page 192, table 3, rows 4 and 10, columns 5 and 6.

[c] Page 81, table 9, rows 2 and 4, columns 3 and 4.

[d] Page 517, table 4, rows 6–10, columns 1–2.

[e] Page 686, table 3, rows 1–4, columns 3–4.

[f] Page 103.

ty m of the forward interest rate, but rises closer to one for higher n. This result may at first seem counterintuitive. One might have thought that forecasts into the near future would be more accurate than forecasts into the more distant future; the reverse seems to be true.

When both n and m are small, both less than a year or so, the slope coefficients are positive (the right sign) but substantially lower than one. Thus, for example, when two-month interest rates exceed one-month rates by more than the average term premium, $\Phi_{r,i}(t, 2, 1)$, the one-month rate does tend to increase as predicted, but by substantially less than the predicted amount.[43]

The results in Table 13.2 look especially bad for the rational expectations hypothesis when the forecast horizon n is small (a year or less in the table) and the maturity of the forward rate m is large (20 or more years in the table). Here, the spread between the forward rate and spot rate predicts the wrong direction of change of interest rates. One might consider it the "essence" of the rational expectations hypothesis that an unusually high spread between the forward rate and current spot rate portends increases in interest rates, not the decreases as observed.

It is helpful in interpreting this result to consider a caricature, the case of a perpetuity (for which $m = \infty$) paying coupon c once per period, and where, for simplicity, the term premium is zero. Then the price of the perpetuity $p_p(t, \infty)$ equals coupon over yield $c/r_p(t, \infty, 1)$, and the spread between the one-period-ahead forward consol yield and the one-period spot rate is proportional to the spread between the consol yield and the one-period rate. When the consol yield is above the one-period interest rate, $r(t, t + 1, 1)$, then its current yield $c/p_p(t, \infty)$ is greater than the one-period rate $r(t, t + 1, 1)$. This would suggest that consols are then a better investment for the short run than is short debt. Since the rational expectations hypothesis with zero term premium would deny this, it follows that the consol yield $r_p(t, \infty, 1)$ should be expected to increase over the next period, producing a decline in price, a capital loss that offsets the high current yield. But, in fact when the consol yield is high relative to the short rate the consol yields tends to fall subsequently and not rise.[44] The capital gain tends to augment rather than offset the high current yield. The naive rule that long bonds are a better investment (in an expected value sense) whenever long rates are above short rates is thus confirmed.

---

[43]Regressions for large n and small m are not in Table 13.2. Since such forward rates are very sensitive to rounding error or small noise in the long-term interest rates, we cannot accurately measure such forward rates.

Some more favorable results for the expectations theory with small n were reported in Shiller (1981a); however, these results were later found to be related to a couple of anomalous observations [Shiller, Campbell and Schoenholtz (1983)].

[44]That long rates tend to move opposite the direction indicated by the expectations theory was first noted by Macaulay (1938, p. 33): "the yields of bonds of the highest grade should *fall* during a period when short rates are higher than the yields of bonds and *rise* during a period in which short rates are the lower. Now experience is more nearly the opposite."

Froot (1987) attempted a decomposition of the departure from 1.00 of the coefficient in Table 13.2 here into two parts: a part due to expectation error and a part due to time-varying term premium. He used survey data published in the investor newsletter *Reporting on Governments* (continuing the Goldsmith–Nagan data series) to represent expectations. He found that for three-month-ahead forecasts of three-month rates, the departure from 1.00 is due primarily to time-varying term premium. But for forecasts of changes in 30-year mortgage rates, the expectations error bears most of the blame for the departure of the coefficient from 1.00.[45]

5.3. The volatility of long-term interest rates

According to the rational expectations theory of the term structure, n-period interest rates are a weighted moving average of one-period interest rates plus a constant term premium; that is, from (16) and Table 13.1:[46]

$$r_i(t, t + m) = D_i(m)^{-1} \sum_{k=0}^{m-1} (D_i(k + 1) - D_i(k))$$

$$\times E_t r_i(t + k, t + k + 1) + \Phi_m, \quad i = p, d, \tag{25}$$

where $\Phi_m = \Phi_{r,i}(t, t + m, 1)$ is constant through time. Since long moving averages tend to smooth the series averaged, one might expect to see that long rates are a very smooth series. Are long-term rates too "choppy" through time to accord with the expectations theory? It is natural to inquire whether this is so and, if so, whenever it is possibly related to the poor results for the expectations hypothesis that were obtained in the Table 13.2 regressions.

Because of the choppiness of long-term interest rates, short-term holding returns on long-term bonds, which are related to the short-term change in long-term interest rates, are quite variable. Culbertson (1957), in his well-known critique of expectations models of interest rates, thought the volatility of holding yields was evidence against the model. He showed a time-series plot of holding yields on long bonds and, noting their great variability, remarked "what sort of expectations, one might ask, could possibly have produced this result?".[47]

It is possible, using the expectations hypothesis, to put limits on the variability of both long-term interest rates themselves and on short-term

---

[45] See Froot (1987, table 3). Note that his regressions are run in a slightly different form than in Table 13.2 here, but that our Table 13.2 coefficients can be inferrred from his.

[46] For par bonds, it is necessary to evaluate $D_p(k)$ with (5) using a fixed point of linearization r, so that (25) will be linear in interest rates.

[47] Culbertson (1957, p. 508).

holding returns on long-term debt. The expectations hypothesis implies that $r_i(t, t + m) = E_t r_i^*(t, t + m) + \Phi_m$, where $r_i^*(t, t + m)$ is the "perfect foresight" or "ex post rational" long-term interest rate defined as:

$$r_i^*(t, t + m) = D_i(m)^{-1} \sum_{k=0}^{m-1} (D_i(k + 1) - D_i(k))$$

$$\times E_t r_i(t + k, t + k + 1), \quad i = p, d. \tag{26}$$

It follows that $r_i^*(t, t + m) = r_i(t, t + m) + \Phi_m + u_{mt}$, where u_{mt} is a forecast error made at time t and observed at time $t + m$. Since u_{mt} is a forecast error, if forecasts are rational, u_{mt} cannot be correlated with anything known at time t; otherwise the forecast could be improved. Hence, u_{mt} must be uncorrelated with $r_i(t, t + m)$. Since the variance of the sum of two independent variables is the sum of their variances it follows that $\text{var}(r_i^*(t, t + m)) = \text{var}(r_i(t, t + m)) + \text{var}(u_{mt})$, and since $\text{var}(u_{mt})$ cannot be negative, the rational expectations model implies [Shiller (1979)]:[48]

$$\text{var}(r_i(t, t + m)) \leq \text{var}(r_i^*(t, t + m)), \quad i = p, d, \tag{27}$$

so there is an upper bound to the variance of m-period rates given by the variance of $r_i^*(t, t + m)$. One can also put an upper bound to the variance of the holding period return in terms of the one-period rate [Shiller (1981a)]:

$$\text{var}(h_i(t, t + 1, t + m)) \leq (D(m)/D(1)) \text{var}(r_i(t, t + 1)), \quad i = p, d, \tag{28}$$

where in the case $i = p$ of par bonds, $D(m)$ and $D(1)$ are computed from equation (5) above with interest rate $2r$, where r is the point of linearization.

Both of the above inequalities were found to be violated using U.S. data and m of 2 or more years [Shiller (1979, 1981a, 1986) and Singleton (1980b)]. Their rejection could have either of two interpretations: the rational expectations hypothesis could be wrong, in such a way as to make long rates much more volatile than they should be, or the measures of the upper bound in the inequalities could be faulty: the measures of $\text{var}(r_i^*(t, t + m))$ or $\text{var}(r_i(t, t + 1))$ could understate the true variance.

The latter view of the violation of the inequalities was argued by Flavin (1983) who showed with Monte Carlo experiments that if the one-period interest rate $r_i(t, t + 1)$ is a first-order autoregressive process with the auto-regressive parameter close to one (see the next subsection), the inequalities are likely to be violated in small samples even if the rational expectations model is true. Such a process shows a great deal of persistence, and $r_i(t, t + 1)$ may thus

---

[48]LeRoy and Porter (1981) also noted this inequality in a different context.

stay on one side of the true mean throughout the sample. Thus, the sample variance around the sample mean of $r_i(t, t+1)$ or of $r_i^*(t, t+m)$ may be a strikingly downward biased measure of their true variance.

Flavin's is apparently a variable interpretation of the excess volatility results. The volatility tests do not allow us to tell whether there is too much variability in long rates or just nonstationarity in short rates. They *do* allow us to reject the idea that movements in long rates can be interpreted in terms of rational expectations of movements in short rates within the range historically observed.

5.4. Encouraging results for the rational expectations hypothesis

It does not follow from the Table 13.2 results with small n that the spread between very long-term interest rates and short-term interest rates is totally wrong from the standpoint of the expectations hypothesis. One way of summarizing the relatively good results [Shiller (1986)] for this spread for larger n is to compute both actual and perfect foresight spreads between very long-term interest rates and short-term interest rates. Defining the spread $S_{ti}(m) = r_i(t, t+m) - r_i(t, t+1)$ (m integer > 1), then the rational expectations hypothesis implies:

$$S_{ti}(m) = E_t S_{ti}^*(m) + \Phi_m, \quad i = p, d, \tag{29}$$

$$S_{ti}^*(m) = r_i^*(t, t+m) - r_i(t, t+1). \tag{30}$$

From the definition (26) of $r_i^*(t, t+m)$, it can be shown that $S_{ti}^*(m)$ is the duration weighted average of expected changes in the n-period rate. Equation (29) thus asserts that when long rates are high relative to short rates the weighted average of increases in short rates should tend to be high. The values of $S_{td}(m)$ and $S_{td}^*(m)$ are plotted for $m = 10$ in Figure 13.4 for those years for which data are available in Appendix B. The correspondence between $S_{td}^*(m)$ and $S_{td}(m)$ is apparent. This might be viewed as a striking confirmation of some element of truth in the expectations hypothesis. Moreover, a variance inequality analogous to (28) above is that $\mathrm{var}(S_{ti}(m)) \le \mathrm{var}(S_{ti}^*(m))$. This variance inequality is satisfied by the data. This result does not by itself establish whether or not Flavin's view of the variance inequality violation described in the preceding section is correct.[49]

---

[49]Indeed, even if $S_{ti}(m)$ and $S_{ti}^*(m)$ look good by this criterion, there could be some small noise contaminating $S_{ti}(m)$ which, if the noise is not highly serially uncorrelated, could cause holding period yields to be much more volatile than would be implied by the expectations model. Moreover, the appearance of $S_{ti}(m)$ and $S_{ti}^*(m)$ may also be relatively little affected by a gross overstatement of the variability of $r_i(t, t+m)$, so long as it is substantially less variable than the short rate [see Shiller (1986)].

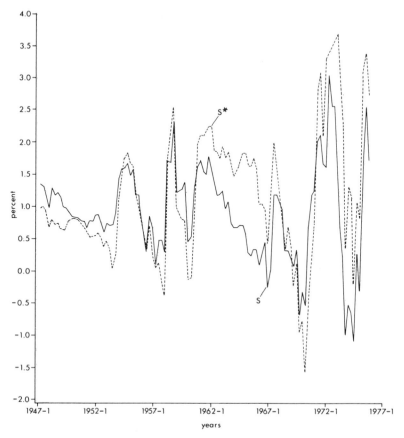

Figure 13.4. The long–short spread $S_{td}(n) = r_d(t, t + n) - r_d(t, t + 1)$, solid line, and the perfect-foresight spread $S^*_{td}(n) = r^*_d(t, t + n) - r_d(t, t + 1)$, dashed line, where $r^*_d(t, t + n)$ is the perfect foresight n-period rate defined by expression (26), $n = 40$ quarters. Thus, $r^*_d(t, t + n) = (\Sigma (\tau = t, t + 39)r(\tau, \tau + 1))/40$. Data plotted are quarterly series for the end of the first month of each quarter using McCulloch's three-month and ten-year discount bond yield series, Table 13.A.1, Appendix B. $S_{td}(n)$ is plotted for 1947 first quarter to 1975 third quarter at annual rates.

One must consider, though, whether this apparent confirmation of the expectations theory for large m could also be described in a less inspiring way: as reflecting largely just that the long rate is much smoother than the short rate. In fact, the correspondence in postwar U.S. data between $S^*_{td}(10, 1)$ and $S_{td}(10, 1)$ would still be apparent if the long rate $r(t, t + 10)$ had been a simple trend through the path of short rates. Short-term interest rates have shown an apparent tendency to revert to trend; thus, a duration weighted average of future changes in the short rate is approximately minus the detrended short rate.

It was shown by Modigliani and Shiller (1973) and Shiller (1972) [following

Sutch (1968)] that a regression of a long rate on a distributed lag of short rates produces distributed lag coefficients that crudely resembled the "optimal" distributed lag coefficients implied by an autoregression in first differences for the short rate. Similarly, a regression of the long rate on a distributed lag of short rates and a distributed lag of inflation rates is consistent with a vector autoregression in first differences using the short rate and the inflation rate.[50] The basic principle of these analyses can be illustrated by assuming for simplicity here (as in Flavin) that the short rate $r_p(t, t+1)$ follows a first-order autoregressive (AR-1) process around a mean μ: $r_p(t+1, t+2) - \mu = \lambda(r_p(t, t+1) - \mu) + \varepsilon_t$, $0 < \lambda < 1$, where ε_t is a realization of a random variable with zero mean independent of ε_{t-k}, $k \neq 0$. The optimal forecast at time t of $r_p(t+k, t+k+1)$ is:

$$E_t r_p(t+k, t+k+1) = \mu + \lambda^k(r_p(t, t+1) - \mu) . \tag{31}$$

From (25) and (5) for $m = \infty$ and $i = p$ the consol yield is given by:

$$r_p(t, t+\infty) = (1 - \gamma) \sum_{k=0}^{\infty} \gamma^k E_t r_p(t+k, t+k+1) + \Phi , \tag{32}$$

where $\gamma = e^{-r}$ and r is the point of linearization. Thus, the consol yield is a sort of present value of expected future one period rates. Together, (31) and (32) imply:

$$r_p(t, t+\infty) = \frac{(1 - \gamma)}{(1 - \gamma\lambda)} r_p(t, t+1) + \Phi . \tag{33}$$

One can therefore evaluate the rational expectations model by first regressing $r_p(t+1, t+2)$ on $r_p(t, t+1)$ and a constant [i.e. estimating λ in (31)], and computing the theoretical coefficient of $r(t)$ using (33). This theoretical coefficient can be compared with the slope coefficient in a regression of $r_p(t, t+\infty)$ onto $r_p(t, t+1)$ and a constant. Now, in fact, our assumption that $r_p(t, t+1)$ was forecast by the market according to (31) would imply that (33) should hold without error. However, it can be shown that whether or not $r_p(t, t+1)$ is an AR-1 process if $E_t r_p(t+k, t+k+1)$ is the optimal forecast of $r_p(t+k, t+k+1)$ conditional on an information set that includes $r_p(t, t+1)$, then a theoretical regression of $r_p(t, t+\infty)$ on $r_p(t, t+1)$ and a constant should produce the coefficient $(1 - \gamma)/(1 - \gamma\lambda)$, where λ is the slope coefficient in a theoretical regression of $r_p(t+1, t+2)$ on $r_p(t, t+1)$, [Shiller (1972)]. With

---

[50] Distributed lag regressions explaining the term structure have had different functional forms: see, for example, Bierwag and Grove (1967), Cargill and Meyer (1972) or Malkiel (1966). A comparison of eight different distributed lag models of the term structure is in Dobson, Sutch and Vanderford (1976).

this assumption there is an error term in (33) reflecting information held by market participants beyond $r(t, t + 1)$. Comparing such estimated coefficients using more complicated autoregressive models was the method used in the aforementioned papers.

Note that if γ and λ are both near one, then $(1 - \gamma)/(1 - \gamma\lambda)$ may be very sensitive to λ. When data are limited, we cannot tell with much accuracy what λ is, and hence cannot pin down what the value of $(1 - \gamma)/(1 - \gamma\lambda)$ is. Thus, we cannot say with much assurance whether the consol yield in fact is or is not too volatile.

Such simple comparisons of estimated coefficients are not formal tests of the rational expectations model. Rather, they are indications of the "fit" of the model. If we are given data on a consol yield $r_p(t, \infty)$ and the one-period rate $r_p(t, 1)$, then a likelihood ratio test of all restrictions of the model [except for a restriction implied by the stationarity of $r_p(t, \infty)$] amounts to nothing more than a regression of the excess return $h_p(t, t + 1, \infty) - r_p(t, t + 1) = (r_p(t, \infty) - \gamma r_p(t + 1, \infty))/(1 - \gamma) - r_p(t, t + 1)$ on information at time t. [Shiller (1981a), Campbell and Shiller (1987)].

Note that such tests may not have much power to determine whether long rates are too volatile to accord with market efficiency. Suppose, for example, that the short rate $r_p(t, t + 1)$ is a first-order autoregressive process as above, and suppose that the long rate overreacts to the short rate, $r_p(t, \infty) = (\mu + \Phi) + b(r_p(t, 1) - \mu)$, where $b > (1 - \gamma)/(1 - \gamma\lambda)$. Then the excess holding return $h_p(t, t + 1, \infty) - r_p(t, t + 1)$, defined as $(r_p(t, \infty) - \gamma r_p(t + 1, \infty))/(1 - \gamma) - r_p(t, t + 1)$, is equal (up to a constant) to $(c - 1)r_p(t, t + 1) - \gamma c r_p(t + 1, t + 2)$, where $c = b/(1 - \gamma)$. If γ is close to one and c large, then this excess return is approximately proportional to b, and changing b would do little more than scale it up or down. If the excess return is not very forecastable for one b, it is likely also to be not very forecastable for another b. Then, a regression of excess holding returns on the short rate may have little power to detect even major departures of b from $(1 - \gamma)/(1 - \gamma\lambda)$.

Tests of the rational expectations model are not so straightforward when using data on a single long rate that is not a consol yield and a short rate. Sargent (1979) showed how, using a companion-form vector autoregression, it is readily possible to test the restrictions implied by the rational expectations model even with such data. He was unable to reject these restrictions on the vector autoregression of long and short rates using a likelihood ratio test. However, it was later discovered that Sargent's paper did not test all restrictions, and when the additional restrictions were incorporated into the analysis, the hypothesis was rejected [Hansen and Sargent (1981), Shiller (1981a)]. These rejections, however, do not deny the *similarity* between actual and optimal distributed lag coefficients. Campbell and Shiller (1987) used a cointegrated vector autoregressive framework, where the vector contained two elements, the long rate and the short rate, and confirmed both that the rational expectations model is rejected with a Wald test and that the model is of some value in describing how long rates respond to short rates and their own lagged values.

There is also some evidence that the relation of long rates to lagged interest rates changes approximately appropriately when the stochastic properties of interest rates change. It was shown by Shiller (1987) that such a correspondence between the distribution lag coefficients holds up crudely speaking even when one uses nineteenth-century U.S. data, or nineteenth- or twentieth-century British data. In the nineteenth century in Britain, for example, short rates appeared to be sharply mean reverting, so that long rates should have been nearly constant: indeed the distributed lag regressions of the British consol yield on the short rates showed sharply reduced coefficients relative to the twentieth-century coefficients in a distributed lag regression of long rates on short rates. Mankiw, Miron and Weil (1987) found an abrupt, and they interpreted appropriate, given the rational expectations model, change in the distributed lag coefficients, at the time of the founding of the Federal Reserve.

How is it then that the forward-spot spread $f(t, t + m, t + m + n) - r_p(t, t + m)$ seems to predict well only for large n and not small n? Fama and Bliss (1987) interpreted this finding as reflecting the fact that interest rates are not very forecastable into the near future, but better forecastable into the more distant future. He gave as an example the story of AR-1 Model described in connection with equations (31)–(33) above. The expectation as of time t or the change $r(t + n, t + n + 1) - r(t, t + 1)$ is $(\gamma^n - 1)(r(t, t + 1) - \mu)$. For γ close to, but below, one, the variance of the expected change is quite small for small n, and grows with n. Thus, for small n any noise in the term premium might swamp out the component in the forward-spot spread $F(t, t + n, t + m + n) - r(t, t + m)$ that is due to predictable change in interest rates.

5.5. Interpreting departures from the expectations theory

Of course, as a matter of tautology, the fact that the coefficients in Table 13.2 do not all equal one has something to do with time-varying term premia. But the nature of the time varying term premia has not been given an ample description for all n and m.

One story for the negative coefficients in Table 13.2 for large m (≥ 20 years) and small n ($\leq$ one year) is that there might be noise in term premia on long-term interest rates unrelated to short-term interest rates. The noise might be due to exogenous shift to investor demand, or even to changing fashions and fads in investing. Suppose, for example, that this "noise" is serially uncorrelated, as though it were due to an error in measuring long-term interest

rates.[51]   Consider   for   simplicity   consols, $m = \infty$,   for   which
$f_p(t, t + n, \infty) - r_p(t, \infty) = (D_p(n)/(D_p(\infty) - D_p(n))(r_p(t, \infty) - r_p(t, n))$.   If   one
regresses $r_p(t + n, \infty) - r_p(t, \infty)$ on this, then one has $r_p(t, \infty)$ on both sides of
the equation with opposite signs. Thus, any "noise" in $r_p(t, \infty)$ might give a
negative slope coefficient in the regression.

This simple story about extraneous noise like measurement error in long
rates, while suggestive, is not completely adequate in explaining the wrong
signs in the Table 13.2 regressions for large m and small n. If the problem were
just exogenous noise in long rates then an instrumental variables approach to
the estimation of the above regressions with economic variables as instruments
would correct the wrong sign; yet it does not [Mankiw (1986)].

A different story for the wrong sign in the regression is that long rates do not
react properly to short rates. The distributed lag regressions noted above of
long rates on short rates, while similar to the distributed lag implied by an
autoregressive forecasting regression for short rates, are not quite the same. In
fact, the distributed lag coefficients of long rates on short rates tend to show
too simple a pattern, like a simple exponential decay pattern instead of a
relatively choppy pattern seen in the optimal responses of long rates to short
rates implied by the forecasting equation [Shiller (1987)]. This result might
come about because people who price long bonds tend to blur the past
somewhat in their memories, or because people use a simple "conventional"
pricing rule for long bonds.[52]

5.6. Seasonality and interest rates

The above discussion suggests that the expectations hypothesis works best
when interest rate movements are well forecastable. With many economic
variables seasonal movements are forecastable far into the future. If there is
any seasonality in interest rates, one would expect to see a seasonal pattern to
the term structure. We would not expect that long rates and short rates should
show the same seasonal pattern, that is, reach their highest point in the same
month. Instead, the expectations theory would predict a phase shift between

---

[51] Just as well, the wrong signs in some regressions could be due to measurement error in interest
rates, a point considered and rejected as the main explanation for the wrong signs by Shiller (1979)
and Mankiw (1986). However, measurement error is taken more seriously by Brown and Dybvig
(1986). They needed measurement error to study the one-factor version of the Cox–Ingersoll–
Ross model because without it there would be a perfect dependence among the interest rates of
different maturity.

[52] Keynes (1936) said that the long rate is "highly conventional . . . its actual value is largely
governed by the prevailing view as to what its value is expected to be". The idea here is apparently
that a simple rule of thumb used to price long-term bonds may become validated when market
prices appear to follow the rule.

long and short rates. Macaulay (1938) investigated whether this occurred using data on call money and time rates 1890 to 1913, and concluded that there was "evidence of definite and relatively successful forecasting",[53] for seasonal movements, though not for movements other than seasonals.

Sargent (1971) noted that the maturity on the call rates was not well defined, and in fact the actual maturities of the call loans are likely to have had a seasonality themselves. He thus sought to reproduce Macaulay's work using more recent data for which maturity can be defined more precisely. Sargent showed that in a perfect foresight model the simple expectations theory for discount bonds implies that the m-period rate $r_d(t, t+m)$ should lead the one-period rate $r_d(t, t+1)$ by $(m-1)/2$ periods across all frequencies. He used U.S. Treasury Bill rates on one to thirteen week bills for 1953 to 1960. He found that long rates did tend to lead short rates at the seasonal frequencies, but by much less than the theoretical $(m-1)/2$.

The post World War II data set that Sargent used, however, contained a much milder seasonal than was evident in the prewar data that Macaulay had used. The Federal Reserve was founded in 1913 to "provide an elastic currency" and this clearly meant that one of their missions was to eliminate seasonals, which they then largely did [see Shiller (1980) and Miron (1984, 1986)].[54] Mankiw and Miron (1986), using a time series on pre-1913 U.S. interest rates of three and six months maturity, found more encouraging results for the expectations theory.

5.7. The sign of term premia

Kim (1986) investigated whether the observed term premium between nominal three- and six-month treasury bills in the United States 1959–86 could be reconciled with the covariance between $S(t, t+3)$ and $S(t+3, t+6)$ as described by equation (22) or (24) as the theory prescribes. He used a co-integrated vector autoregressive model for the two log interest rates, log consumption and a log price index, and a lognormality assumption for the error term. He transformed the vector with the co-integrating vector so that the transformed vector has as elements the spread between the two log interest rates, the change in one of the interest rates, the change in log real consumption and the change in the log price index. For the model, the covariance in equation (22) is constant through time. He tested the restrictions across the

---

[53]Macaulay (1938, p. 36).
[54]Clark (1986) questioned whether the decline in seasonality was due to the founding of the Fed. He noted that seasonals disappeared in the United States and other countries at about the same time, and that seasonals disappeared approximately three years before the seasonals in currency and high powered money changed.

mean vector, coefficient vector, and variance matrix of residuals using a Wald test. The test rejected the restrictions; on the other hand, the sign of the term premium is as predicted by the sign of the covariance.

Other studies of consumption and the term structure of interest rates looked at short-term real returns on long and short bonds and their correlation with real consumption changes to see if the difference in mean real returns between long and short bonds could be reconciled with the covariance of real returns with real marginal rates of substitution. Grossman, Melino and Shiller (1987) found that the excess real one-period returns between long-term debt and short-term debt had negligible correlation with real per capita consumption changes with annual U.S. data 1890–1981 and with U.S. quarterly data 1953–83. They rejected at high significance levels the covariance restrictions using a vector autoregression model including real returns on long-term debt, short-term debt, and corporate stocks.[55]

5.8. Modelling time-varying term premia

Since the rational expectations hypothesis can be rejected, as discussed above, it follows that the term premium is time varying. Although the term premium is not observed itself without error, we can study its projection onto any information set by regressing the variables represented on the right-hand sides of the expressions defining term premia, i.e. (14), (15), and (16) above, from which the expectations operators have been deleted, onto information available at time t. The above discussion of the projection onto the forward-spot spread concerns only one possible such regression. There is no theory of the term structure well-developed enough to allow us to predict what variables to use, so the empirical literature here often looks like a "fishing expedition".

Kessel (1965) regressed the forward-spot spread $f_d(t, t+1, t+2) - r_d(t+1, t+2)$ on $r_d(t, t+1)$, where the time unit is four weeks, to test whether term premia are related to the level of interest rates. He found, using monthly U.S. Treasury Bill data 1949–61, that there was a positive coefficient on $r_d(t, t+1)$. However, Nelson (1972b), using analogous methodology, found the opposite sign for the coefficient of the interest rate. Both Kessel and Nelson gave theories why risk considerations should imply the sign they got. Shiller (1979) in effect regressed $f_p(t, t+1, t+m+1) - r_p(t+1, t+m+1)$ on $r_p(t, t+m)$ for m very large with quarterly, monthly, and annual time periods for U.S. and U.K. history and found a consistently positive coefficient, which was interpreted as a sign of possible excess volatility of long rates. Campbell and Shiller

---

[55]Mankiw (1986) inquired whether the time variation in the covariance could be reconciled with time variation in the spread between long and short rates in the United States, Canada, the United Kingdom, and Germany 1961–84. He concluded that it could not.

(1984) in effect found a negative slope coefficient in a regression (in effect) of $f_d(t, t+1, t+241) - r_d(t+1, t+241)$ on $r_d(t, t+1)$, where time is measured in months, and interpreted this result as reflecting a possible underreaction of long rates to short rates. It is difficult to produce a useful summary of these conflicting results.

Other researchers have used some indicators of time-varying risk premia in such regressions. Modigliani and Shiller (1973) and Shiller, Campbell and Schoenholtz (1983) used a moving standard deviation of interest rates. Fama (1976), Mishkin (1982), and Jones and Roley (1983) used other measures of the variability in interest rates. Such measures were often statistically signifi-cant. Engle, Lilien and Robins (1987) used an ARCH model to model time-varying variance of interest rates, and concluded that the risk premium so modelled helps to explain the failures of the expectations theory.

Still other variables have been used to explain time-varying term premia. Nelson (1972b) used an index of business confidence. Shiller, Campbell and Schoenholtz (1983) used a measure of the volume of trade in bonds. Keim and Stambaugh (1986) used a low-grade yield spread variable (the difference between yields on long-term under-BAA-rated corporate bonds and short-term Treasury bills), and a small-firm variable (the log of the share price, averaged equally across the quintile of smallest market value on the New York Stock Exchange). Campbell (1987) used a latent variable model of the returns on bills, bonds and common stocks to infer time-varying risk premia in all three markets.

5.9. Flow of funds models

Clearly, term premia do vary and are correlated with observable economic variables. But what kind of structural model might clarify why they vary? One might expect that when the federal government issues a large amount of long-term debt, the supply of long-term debt should rise and, other things equal, term premia should rise. One might also expect that in time when funds flow into life insurance companies, major purchasers of long-term bonds, then the demand for long-term debt should rise and, other things equal, term premia should decline. Thus, the term structure might be related to such flows of funds.[56]

---

[56]Conversely, when the government attempts to peg the term structure, there should be consequential flows of demand across maturities. Walker (1954) noted that when the Federal Reserve attempted to peg an upward-sloping term structure there was a great shift out of short-term securities into long-term securities by the holders of government debt. Such a shift is implied by the expectations hypothesis.

There was a flurry of research on the effects of government debt policy on the term structure following the policy, brought in by the Kennedy Administration in the United States in 1961, known as "Operation Twist". Operation Twist consisted of Federal Reserve open market operations and Treasury debt management operations directed toward shortening the average term to maturity of outstanding public debt, with the intention of "twisting" the term structure.[57] Okun (1963) and Scott (1965) correlated the term structure with federal debt measures without accounting for expectations. Modigliani and Sutch (1966, 1967) added dummy or debt composition variables to their distributed lag regressions of long rates on short rates, but found evidence of only a "weak" effect of national debt on the term structure. Indeed, the simple distributed lag on short rates explained long rates so well that there was little room for much improvement of fit using debt policy variables.[58] The Modigliani–Sutch conclusions were criticized by Wallace (1967) for the assumption that government debt policy is exogenous over the sample period.

There is a substantial literature on models that relate interest rates to such flows of funds; see, for example, Ando and Modigliani (1975), Brainard and Tobin (1968), De Leeuw (1965), Friedman (1977a, 1980a), Hendershott (1971), or Backus, Brainard, Smith and Tobin (1980). But much of this literature makes no explicit use of expectations of future interest rates that ought to play a pivotal role in the term structure of interest rates. Many of the models are not complete, e.g. providing estimates of some demands for funds, and not providing a general equilibrium that might give a theory of the term structure.

Friedman and Roley (1979) and Roley (1982) estimated a flow of funds model [along the lines of Friedman (1977a, 1980b), and Roley (1977)] but incorporating as determinants of the demand functions not yields to maturity but rational expectations of short-run returns.

Flow of funds modelling has offered the promise of estimating consistently general equilibrium models of the determination of interest rates, but such modelling has to date been hampered by the same problems that have prevented any consensus on other macroeconometric models. A lot of subjective judgment goes into specifying the identifying restrictions, exogeneity specifications and other assumptions that lie behind a complicated simultaneous equation model. Hence, there is a lot of uncertainty about the validity of particular models.

---

[57] Operation Twist also involved relaxing some interest rate ceilings. The federal debt structure during the early 1960s in fact went in exactly the opposite direction to what was implied by Operation Twist, as the Treasury's debt policy was contradicting the Fed's. See Friedman (1981).

[58] Friedman (1977a, 1981) did find a significant coefficient in a term structure equation for a variable which was the ratio of outstanding federal long-term securities to outstanding federal short-term securities.

6. Some concluding observations

There has been a lot of progress in our understanding of the term structure in the last twenty years. We now have formal heuristic theoretical models of the term structure in terms of the ultimate objectives of economic agents and the stochastic properties of forcing variables. These models are beginnings that have changed our way of thinking about the term structure. We now have an extensive empirical literature describing in great detail how the term structure is correlated with other economic variables. But we could hope for still more progress.

It is of course very difficult to say where the actual opportunities for productive research lie, but it is possible to say where there are problems to be solved.

Theoretical work on the term structure, while it has offered many insights, still does not allow us to say much about the term structure we observe. Most theorists are currently using a representative individual utility of consumption model, while most corporate and government bonds in the United States are held by institutions. Even if institutions were somehow behaving as if they were representative consumers, we must face the fact that the expected present value of utility of consumption model has not held up well in tests of the returns on assets other than bonds. Probably, the theoretical model is just not a good descriptor of human behavior.

Most of the theoretical work on the expectations hypothesis has worked on the term structure of index bonds, but freely tradable true index bonds of varying maturity are virtually nonexistent. The theoretical literature has tried to find justifications for a zero term premia model, while the assumption of zero term premia has never been an issue for empirical researchers. That term premia are not zero and change through time has not suggested any well-posed problems for theoretical researchers working in the current paradigm that would produce any idea as to how to expect them to change.

Empirical work on the term structure has produced consensus on little more than that the rational expectations model, while perhaps containing an element of truth, can be rejected. There is no consensus on why term premia vary. There does not seem even to be agreement on how to describe the correlation of the term premia with other variables. A lot more research could be done leading to consensus on, for example, the senses in which long rates may be influenced by government fiscal policy, term premia are related to some measures of risk, interest rates overreact or underreact to short rates, or be influenced by or depend on rules of thumb or "satisficing" behavior. Flow of funds models have some interest, but seem to have been largely dropped by researchers in the wake of the rational expectations revolution, just when they should have been integrated with it.

Appendix A: Mathematical symbols

$D_i(m, t) =$ Duration of an m-period bond at time t. Second argument will sometimes be omitted, $i =$ d: discount bond, $i =$ p: par bond.

$f_d(t, t', T) =$ The forward discount interest rate at time t applying to the interval from t' to T, $t \leq t' \leq T$. The term of the forward instrument is $m = T - t'$.

$F_p(t, t', T) =$ The forward par interest rate at time t applying to the interval from t' to T, $t \leq t' \leq T$. The term of the forward instrument is $m = T - t'$.

$f_p(t, t', T) =$ Linear approximation to $F_p(t, t', T)$.

$h_d(t, t', T) =$ The discount holding period return. If $t \leq t' \leq T$ it is the return from buying a discount bond at time t that matures at time T and selling it at time t'. If $t \leq T \leq t'$, it is the rate of return from rolling over discount bonds of maturity $m = T - t$, until time t'.

$H_p(t, t', T) =$ The par holding period return. If $t \leq t' \leq T$, it is the return from buying a par bond at time t that matures at time T, receiving coupons between t and t' and selling it at time t'. If $t \leq T \leq t'$, it is the rate of return from rolling over par bonds of maturity $m = T - t$ until time t'.

$h_p(t, t', T) =$ Linear approximation to $H_p(t, t', T)$.

$m =$ the term of a bond, equal to the time to maturity $T - t$.

$p(t, T) =$ The price at time t of a bond that matures at time T, whose principal is 1.

$p_i(t, T) =$ The price at time t of a bond that matures at time T, whose principal is 1, $i =$ d: discount bond, $i =$ p: par bond.

$r(t, T) =$ The interest rate (yield to maturity) at date t on a bond that matures at date T, continuous compounding.

$r(t, T, h) =$ The interest rate (yield to maturity), compounded every h periods, at date t on a bond that matures at date T.

$r_d(t, T) =$ The interest rate (yield to maturity) at date t on a discount bond that matures at date T, continuous compounding.

$r_p(t, T) =$ The interest rate (yield to maturity) at date t on a par bond that matures at date T, continuous compounding.

$s_i =$ The amount of the ith payment made on a bond, made at date t_i on a coupon bond $s_i = c$, $i < T$, $s_T = 1 + c$.

$t_i =$ The date of the ith payment on a bond.

$T =$ The date on which a bond matures.

$\Phi_{f,i}(t, t', T) =$ Forward term premium, equal to $f_i(t, t', T) - E_t r_i(t', T)$, $t < t' < T$, $i =$ p, d.

$\Phi_{h,i}(t, t', T) =$ Holding period term premium, equal to $E_t h_i(t, t', T) - r_i(t, t')$, $t < t' < T$, $i =$ p, d.

$\Phi_{r,i}(t, t', m) =$ Rollover term premium, equal to $r_i(t, t') - E_t h_i(t, t', t + m)$, $t < t + m < t'$, $i = \text{p, d}$.

$w =$ The number of payments promised by a bond when it was issued.

Appendix B: U.S. term structure data, 1946–87[59] (by J. Huston McCulloch)

The three tables that follow summarize the term structure of interest rates on U.S. Treasury securities from December 1946 to February 1987.

Table 13.A.1 shows the zero-coupon yield curve on an annual percentage, continuously compounded basis. This yield curve is inferred from the prices of whole securities, rather than being based on the recently developed (but much less liquid) market for stripped Treasury securities. In Shiller's notation, this is $100 r_d(t, t + m)$, as used in his (1).

Table 13.A.2 shows the instantaneous forward rate curve on the same annual percentage, continuous compounding basis. This curve shows the marginal return to lengthening an investment in m-year zeroes by one instant. The zero coupon yield for maturity m is the unweighted average of these forward rates between 0 and m. In Shiller's notation, these forward rates are $100 f(t, t + m)$, as used in his (7).

Table 13.A.3 shows the par bond yield curve, again on an annual percentage, continuously compounded basis. This is defined as the (unique) coupon rate that would make a bond of maturity m be quoted at par, and gives a precise meaning to the ambiguous conventional concept of a "yield curve" for coupon bonds. The par bond yield for maturity m is a weighted average, with declining weights, of the forward rates between 0 and m. The tabulated values are essentially $100 r_p(t, t + m)$, as used in Shiller's (3).

These values were computed by fitting the discount function that gives the present value of a future dollar to Treasury security prices. This discount function [$p_d(t, T)$ in Shiller's nomenclature] was curve fit with a cubic spline, as described in McCulloch (1975b), and as modified at NBER-West during 1977–78.[60]

Briefly, the data sets include most of the marketable U.S. government bills, notes and bonds. Closing bid and asked quotations for the last working day of

---

[59] Written by J. Huston McCulloch while he was Visiting Professor at l'Ecole Superieure des Sciences Economiques et Commerciales (ESSEC), Cergy, France, on professional leave from the Ohio State University Economics Department.

[60] This NBER version fits the actual "flat" price to the sum of the values of the individual payments. This is slightly more accurate than the version I developed at the Treasury in 1973 and described in McCulloch (1975b), which fit the "and interest" price to an idealized continuous coupon flow. McCulloch (1971) contains further background information on this procedure.

In only one instance prior to March 1986, namely the zero-maturity rates for May 1958, did the cubic spline indicate a negative interest rate, of -0.11 percent. This value was not significantly negative, however (its estimated standard error was 0.54 percent), and so it was replaced with a zero in the tables. The zero at $m = 0$ for May 1947 is the actually estimated value. Since March 1986 forward rates in the range 27 to 29 years have often been negative, but these maturities are beyond the range of the tables.

the month indicated, as reported in dealer quote sheets or the next day's *Wall Street Journal*, were averaged. These observations were given weights inversely proportional to the bid-asked spread. Callable bonds were treated as if maturing on their call dates, if currently selling above par, and as if running to final maturity, if currently selling below par. "Flower bonds" (redeemable at par in payment of estate taxes if owned by the decedent at the time of death) could not all be eliminated, as they constituted the bulk of the observations for many maturities during the earlier part of the period. Accordingly, they were selectively eliminated during these years if the estate feature appeared to be active. For further details see McCulloch (1981, pp. 229–230). Since August 1985, callables are not used.

During the early 1970s, a legislative ceiling on the interest rates the Treasury could pay on long-term debt effectively prevented the issue of new bonds. As existing bonds approached maturity, the longest available maturity therefore fell to under 15 years, so that values over 10 years are occasionally missing during this period. The longest available maturity sometimes also fluctuates by five years from month to month if the longest securities are callable and hovering near par. Since the cubic spline does not lend itself to extrapolation, this methodology cannot be used to infer longer term interest rates than those shown.[61]

The curve-fitting procedure was adjusted for tax effects, as described in McCulloch (1975b). The capital gains advantage on deep discount bonds could not be ignored during the earlier part of the period, when most of the long-term bonds were heavily discounted. The importance of this adjustment greatly diminished after 1969, however, when the tax laws were changed so that commercial banks were required to treat capital gains and losses symetrically. After this date, the best fitting apparent marginal tax rate generally was much lower than before, and was often less than 10 percent.[62]

The par bond yields in Table 13.A.3 are based on hypothetical continuous-coupon bonds, and therefore are on a continuous-compounding basis directly comparable to the rates in Tables 13.A.1 and 13.A.2. "Bond yields" quoted in the press and elsewhere are instead on a semiannual compounding basis. Following Shiller's terminology (Section 2), each continuously compounded value, $r_p(t, t + m)$, in Table 13.A.3 may be converted to its semiannually compounded equivalent value, $r_p(t, t + m, 0.5)$, by means of

$$r_p(t, t + m, 0.5) = 2(e^{0.5 r_p(t, t+m)} - 1).$$

This adjustment would make the rates several basis points higher than in the tables.

---

[61] The exponential spline approach proposed by Vasicek and Fong (1982) has the considerable virtue of making such as extrapolation meaningful. Chen (1986) has implemented the VF approach along with a modification proposed by the present author, with mixed preliminary results; the forward curves are better behaved at the long end, but often the restrictions implicit in the VF model and in the modified model can be formally rejected with a likelihood ratio test.

[62] It should be noted that the identity (9′) holds for the values in Table 13.A.3, but only using the discount function that applies to *after-tax* payments. Cf. Shiller's footnote 12.

Table 13.A.1

McCulloch zero coupon yield curve series, continuous compounding, end of month data, 12/46–2/87

Year	Mo	0 mo	1 mo	2 mo	3 mo	4 mo	5 mo	6 mo	9 mo	1 yr	2 yr	3 yr	4 yr	5 yr	10 yr	15 yr	20 yr	25 yr
1946	12	0.18	0.32	0.42	0.48	0.52	0.55	0.58	0.65	0.72	0.95	1.15	1.30	1.41	1.82	2.16	2.32	
1947	1	0.16	0.32	0.43	0.49	0.52	0.56	0.58	0.65	0.72	0.94	1.12	1.27	1.39	1.82	2.16	2.33	
	2	0.19	0.33	0.42	0.47	0.51	0.54	0.57	0.65	0.71	0.95	1.14	1.29	1.41	1.82	2.14	2.32	
	3	0.13	0.32	0.44	0.51	0.55	0.58	0.61	0.68	0.74	0.94	1.10	1.25	1.36	1.80	2.13	2.31	
	4	0.08	0.30	0.44	0.52	0.57	0.61	0.64	0.71	0.78	1.00	1.17	1.31	1.42	1.81	2.14	2.32	
	5	0.00	0.29	0.47	0.57	0.63	0.67	0.70	0.77	0.83	1.02	1.17	1.30	1.40	1.81	2.14	2.31	
	6	0.08	0.33	0.49	0.57	0.62	0.65	0.68	0.76	0.82	1.02	1.19	1.32	1.43	1.85	2.19	2.34	
	7	0.06	0.38	0.58	0.67	0.73	0.77	0.80	0.86	0.93	1.10	1.23	1.34	1.43	1.83	2.21	2.33	
	8	0.16	0.53	0.75	0.86	0.92	0.95	0.98	1.02	1.05	1.12	1.19	1.26	1.35	1.81	2.19	2.30	
	9	0.52	0.74	0.88	0.95	0.99	1.01	1.02	1.06	1.08	1.15	1.22	1.31	1.40	1.85	2.21	2.32	
	10	0.45	0.73	0.91	1.00	1.05	1.08	1.10	1.15	1.20	1.28	1.37	1.45	1.54	1.95	2.30	2.37	
	11	0.60	0.81	0.95	1.02	1.06	1.09	1.11	1.16	1.20	1.32	1.43	1.53	1.63	2.06	2.36	2.43	
	12	0.93	0.90	0.90	0.91	0.93	0.95	0.98	1.04	1.11	1.34	1.52	1.66	1.78	2.18	2.41		
1948	1	1.04	0.96	0.92	0.91	0.92	0.94	0.96	1.02	1.08	1.32	1.52	1.66	1.78	2.19	2.41		
	2	1.02	0.97	0.94	0.95	0.96	0.97	0.99	1.05	1.11	1.33	1.51	1.64	1.76	2.17	2.41		
	3	1.00	0.98	0.97	0.98	1.00	1.01	1.03	1.08	1.14	1.33	1.50	1.63	1.74	2.17	2.43		
	4	0.98	0.98	0.99	1.01	1.02	1.04	1.05	1.10	1.15	1.33	1.48	1.60	1.72	2.16	2.45		
	5	0.97	0.99	1.00	1.02	1.03	1.04	1.05	1.09	1.12	1.25	1.37	1.48	1.60	2.08	2.40		
	6	0.95	0.98	1.00	1.02	1.03	1.05	1.06	1.11	1.15	1.32	1.46	1.58	1.70	2.18	2.45		
	7	1.02	0.99	0.98	0.99	1.01	1.02	1.04	1.10	1.16	1.37	1.53	1.65	1.77	2.19	2.43		
	8	1.13	1.06	1.03	1.03	1.05	1.07	1.09	1.15	1.21	1.43	1.59	1.71	1.81	2.20	2.43		
	9	1.09	1.08	1.08	1.10	1.12	1.14	1.16	1.22	1.28	1.48	1.62	1.73	1.82	2.19	2.43		
	10	1.11	1.08	1.08	1.09	1.11	1.13	1.16	1.23	1.29	1.51	1.65	1.77	1.86	2.22	2.46		
	11	1.10	1.10	1.11	1.12	1.14	1.15	1.17	1.23	1.28	1.46	1.59	1.70	1.80	2.20	2.46		
	12	1.06	1.11	1.14	1.16	1.18	1.19	1.21	1.24	1.28	1.40	1.52	1.63	1.74	2.18	2.44		
1949	1	1.09	1.13	1.15	1.17	1.18	1.19	1.20	1.22	1.25	1.35	1.46	1.57	1.68	2.14	2.43		
	2	1.16	1.14	1.13	1.14	1.14	1.15	1.16	1.19	1.23	1.36	1.48	1.59	1.69	2.13	2.40		
	3	1.03	1.11	1.16	1.19	1.20	1.21	1.22	1.24	1.26	1.34	1.43	1.53	1.64	2.10	2.41		
	4	1.00	1.12	1.14	1.15	1.16	1.17	1.18	1.20	1.23	1.33	1.43	1.54	1.64	2.10	2.42		
	5	1.00	1.09	1.15	1.18	1.19	1.20	1.21	1.21	1.24	1.31	1.40	1.50	1.60	2.09	2.42		
	6	0.81	1.02	1.13	1.18	1.19	1.20	1.20	1.19	1.18	1.17	1.24	1.34	1.46	2.00	2.35		
	7	0.80	0.96	1.05	1.08	1.10	1.10	1.10	1.10	1.09	1.10	1.19	1.31	1.43	1.98	2.30		

	0 mo	1 mo	2 mo	3 mo	4 mo	5 mo	6 mo	9 mo	1 yr	2 yr	3 yr	4 yr	5 yr	10 yr	15 yr	20 yr	25 yr
8	0.86	0.98	1.05	1.08	1.09	1.09	1.10	1.10	1.10	1.12	1.20	1.30	1.40	1.91	2.26		
9	0.88	1.01	1.08	1.10	1.11	1.11	1.11	1.10	1.09	1.10	1.18	1.29	1.40	1.92	2.23		
10	0.82	0.99	1.07	1.10	1.11	1.11	1.11	1.11	1.11	1.12	1.20	1.31	1.42	1.92	2.23		
11	0.82	1.01	1.12	1.16	1.17	1.18	1.17	1.16	1.15	1.14	1.21	1.31	1.42	1.91	2.23		
12	0.93	1.03	1.09	1.11	1.12	1.12	1.12	1.12	1.12	1.14	1.22	1.31	1.40	1.87	2.19		

1950

	0 mo	1 mo	2 mo	3 mo	4 mo	5 mo	6 mo	9 mo	1 yr	2 yr	3 yr	4 yr	5 yr	10 yr	15 yr	20 yr	25 yr
1	0.97	1.07	1.13	1.15	1.16	1.16	1.16	1.15	1.15	1.16	1.25	1.36	1.47	1.96	2.25		
2	1.00	1.10	1.16	1.18	1.19	1.19	1.19	1.18	1.17	1.17	1.25	1.36	1.48	1.99	2.28		
3	0.89	1.08	1.19	1.23	1.24	1.24	1.24	1.23	1.21	1.20	1.28	1.39	1.51	2.02	2.31		
4	0.92	1.11	1.22	1.26	1.27	1.27	1.27	1.26	1.27	1.24	1.34	1.43	1.55	2.05	2.34		
5	0.93	1.14	1.25	1.29	1.31	1.31	1.30	1.28	1.29	1.30	1.32	1.49	1.60	2.07	2.36		
6	0.90	1.13	1.25	1.29	1.30	1.31	1.31	1.33	1.29	1.25	1.39	1.44	1.56	2.10	2.36		
7	0.86	1.16	1.31	1.36	1.37	1.37	1.36	1.39	1.36	1.34	1.33	1.51	1.56	2.11	2.39		
8	1.00	1.25	1.37	1.41	1.43	1.42	1.42	1.44	1.43	1.44	1.41	1.61	1.62	2.12	2.42		
9	1.10	1.29	1.40	1.43	1.44	1.45	1.45	1.44	1.52	1.56	1.52	1.72	1.70	2.15	2.42		
10	0.83	1.18	1.37	1.43	1.48	1.49	1.50	1.52	1.36	1.52	1.64	1.70	1.80	2.19	2.43		
11	1.07	1.31	1.43	1.48	1.49	1.50	1.50	1.49	1.49	1.52	1.60	1.70	1.80	2.22	2.43		
12	0.79	1.25	1.49	1.57	1.60	1.61	1.61	1.58	1.55	1.52	1.59	1.68	1.78	2.23	2.45		

1951

	0 mo	1 mo	2 mo	3 mo	4 mo	5 mo	6 mo	9 mo	1 yr	2 yr	3 yr	4 yr	5 yr	10 yr	15 yr	20 yr	25 yr
1	0.80	1.21	1.44	1.54	1.57	1.59	1.60	1.59	1.57	1.57	1.63	1.70	1.77	2.18	2.44		
2	0.78	1.21	1.45	1.55	1.58	1.59	1.59	1.57	1.55	1.55	1.62	1.71	1.81	2.25	2.46		
3	1.24	1.44	1.56	1.61	1.64	1.66	1.68	1.73	1.76	1.87	1.96	2.03	2.08	2.31	2.48	2.58	
4	0.93	1.33	1.55	1.63	1.68	1.70	1.72	1.75	1.77	1.85	1.92	2.00	2.07	2.40	2.61	2.70	
5	0.96	1.34	1.56	1.65	1.69	1.72	1.74	1.78	1.81	1.89	1.97	2.06	2.16	2.56	2.76	2.71	
6	0.90	1.38	1.64	1.73	1.77	1.79	1.81	1.81	1.81	1.84	1.93	2.02	2.11	2.51	2.72	2.70	
7	1.29	1.49	1.61	1.65	1.67	1.68	1.69	1.70	1.70	1.77	1.85	1.94	2.02	2.40	2.64	2.68	
8	1.32	1.54	1.65	1.68	1.69	1.70	1.70	1.69	1.68	1.73	1.81	1.90	1.99	2.35	2.53	2.60	
9	1.49	1.60	1.66	1.65	1.71	1.73	1.76	1.78	1.82	1.92	2.00	2.07	2.14	2.43	2.70	2.65	
10	0.81	1.26	1.53	1.66	1.71	1.74	1.73	1.80	1.78	1.91	2.01	2.09	2.17	2.51	2.72	2.68	
11	1.05	1.39	1.58	1.66	1.70	1.72	1.76	1.76	2.09	1.88	1.98	2.07	2.16	2.53	2.70	2.73	
12	1.55	1.70	1.79	1.84	1.86	1.88	1.89	1.92	2.04	2.02	2.09	2.17	2.24	2.54	2.70	2.75	

1952

	0 mo	1 mo	2 mo	3 mo	4 mo	5 mo	6 mo	9 mo	1 yr	2 yr	3 yr	4 yr	5 yr	10 yr	15 yr	20 yr	25 yr
1	0.94	1.33	1.54	1.62	1.66	1.69	1.72	1.76	1.79	1.88	1.97	2.06	2.14	2.49	2.70	2.74	
2	0.90	1.34	1.56	1.65	1.70	1.73	1.75	1.81	1.85	1.97	2.08	2.18	2.28	2.64	2.79	2.78	
3	1.10	1.37	1.52	1.59	1.63	1.66	1.68	1.73	1.77	1.90	2.01	2.10	2.18	2.52	2.74	2.79	
4	1.39	1.58	1.68	1.72	1.75	1.76	1.77	1.80	1.81	1.87	1.94	2.06	2.10	2.44	2.61	2.63	
5	1.43	1.64	1.75	1.79	1.82	1.83	1.84	1.87	1.89	1.95	2.00	2.06	2.12	2.39	2.58	2.65	
6	1.65	1.80	1.80	1.83	1.85	1.87	1.88	1.92	1.95	2.05	2.13	2.19	2.24	2.42	2.61	2.68	
7	1.72	1.75	1.86	1.89	1.91	1.92	1.94	1.98	2.01	2.13	2.22	2.28	2.32	2.47	2.61	2.68	
8	1.46	1.71	1.85	1.91	1.95	1.98	2.00	2.05	2.09	2.21	2.30	2.36	2.41	2.56	2.69	2.74	
9	1.06	1.46	1.70	1.81	1.87	1.91	1.94	2.00	2.04	2.17	2.27	2.35	2.43	2.70	2.83	2.83	

Table 13.A.1 (cont.)

		0 mo	1 mo	2 mo	3 mo	4 mo	5 mo	6 mo	9 mo	1 yr	2 yr	3 yr	4 yr	5 yr	10 yr	15 yr	20 yr	25 yr
1952	10	1.32	1.59	1.75	1.82	1.86	1.89	1.92	1.97	2.01	2.13	2.22	2.28	2.34	2.54	2.69	2.75	
	11	1.55	1.78	1.92	1.99	2.00	2.05	2.07	2.11	2.13	2.21	2.27	2.31	2.35	2.52	2.69	2.77	
	12	1.82	1.94	2.02	2.06	2.08	2.09	2.11	2.14	2.16	2.24	2.30	2.34	2.38	2.56	2.76		
1953	1	1.63	1.82	1.93	1.97	2.00	2.02	2.03	2.06	2.09	2.18	2.26	2.33	2.40	2.66	2.80		
	2	1.86	2.02	2.11	2.15	2.16	2.18	2.19	2.20	2.22	2.26	2.31	2.37	2.44	2.73	2.90		
	3	1.95	1.99	2.01	2.03	2.05	2.06	2.07	2.10	2.13	2.24	2.33	2.41	2.48	2.76	2.92		
	4	1.78	2.06	2.23	2.35	2.34	2.47	2.50	2.58	2.63	2.79	2.91	3.01	3.09	3.31	3.10	3.14	3.19
	5	1.43	1.94	1.89	2.03	2.11	2.17	2.20	2.28	2.33	2.48	2.59	2.69	2.76	3.01	3.29	3.22	3.19
	6	1.18	1.61	2.06	2.12	2.16	2.19	2.21	2.26	2.31	2.45	2.57	2.66	2.74	3.00	3.06	3.06	3.12
	7	1.72	1.94	1.89	2.12	2.16	2.03	2.06	2.14	2.21	2.45	2.64	2.74	2.86	3.05	3.05	3.11	
	8	1.62	1.79	2.06	1.95	1.99	2.03	2.06	2.14	2.21	2.45	2.57	2.66	2.74	3.09	3.13	3.15	
	9	0.86	1.22	1.46	1.59	1.67	1.72	1.77	1.87	1.95	2.18	2.34	2.43	2.49	2.65	2.80	2.98	
	10	0.65	0.98	1.19	1.31	1.39	1.44	1.49	1.69	1.70	1.99	2.16	2.34	2.44	2.71	2.88	2.99	
	11	1.36	1.44	1.49	1.53	1.56	1.59	1.62	1.69	1.76	1.98	2.16	2.30	2.40	2.75	2.95	3.04	
	12	1.09	1.25	1.35	1.42	1.46	1.49	1.52	1.60	1.66	1.88	2.03	2.13	2.21	2.48	2.71	2.88	
1954	1	1.05	0.96	0.92	0.93	0.95	0.97	1.00	1.10	1.19	1.53	1.78	1.95	2.09	2.49	2.69	2.82	
	2	0.84	0.89	0.92	0.94	0.97	0.99	1.01	1.06	1.12	1.34	1.56	1.78	1.98	2.47	2.53	2.61	
	3	0.99	0.99	0.99	1.00	1.01	1.02	1.04	1.09	1.14	1.34	1.55	1.75	1.93	2.42	2.54	2.63	
	4	0.62	0.67	0.71	0.75	0.78	0.81	0.83	0.91	0.99	1.23	1.42	1.60	1.77	2.34	2.51	2.60	
	5	0.51	0.60	0.66	0.69	0.73	0.76	0.79	0.87	0.96	1.28	1.58	1.84	2.03	2.51	2.61	2.67	
	6	0.67	0.62	0.60	0.62	0.63	0.66	0.69	0.77	0.85	1.15	1.41	1.65	1.85	2.43	2.51	2.56	
	7	0.64	0.68	0.71	0.73	0.75	0.77	0.79	0.84	0.90	1.16	1.44	1.69	1.89	2.39	2.48	2.53	
	8	1.30	1.11	1.00	0.96	0.95	0.95	0.96	0.99	1.04	1.25	1.49	1.71	1.91	2.46	2.51	2.54	
	9	0.90	0.90	0.93	0.94	0.97	1.00	1.03	1.12	1.20	1.45	1.64	1.81	1.98	2.46	2.50	2.55	
	10	0.72	0.85	0.93	0.98	1.02	1.06	1.06	1.18	1.26	1.55	1.79	1.98	2.12	2.44	2.52	2.59	
	11	0.86	0.93	0.98	1.02	1.05	1.08	1.10	1.18	1.25	1.53	1.79	1.99	2.14	2.49	2.63	2.68	
	12	0.92	0.95	0.98	1.01	1.04	1.07	1.10	1.20	1.29	1.61	1.88	2.08	2.21	2.51	2.64	2.69	
1955	1	1.19	1.10	1.07	1.09	1.13	1.17	1.22	1.35	1.47	1.85	2.05	2.19	2.29	2.65	2.79	2.82	2.82
	2	0.91	1.14	1.29	1.38	1.45	1.51	1.56	1.70	1.82	2.16	2.32	2.40	2.47	2.71	2.83	2.88	2.90
	3	1.33	1.33	1.35	1.39	1.43	1.48	1.52	1.65	1.78	2.13	2.30	2.40	2.47	2.70	2.80	2.84	2.85
	4	1.44	1.50	1.55	1.60	1.65	1.69	1.73	1.85	1.95	2.25	2.38	2.46	2.53	2.76	2.86	2.86	2.85
	5	0.91	1.15	1.32	1.43	1.51	1.57	1.62	1.76	1.87	2.19	2.35	2.46	2.53	2.73	2.80	2.82	2.83
	6	1.04	1.27	1.43	1.53	1.60	1.66	1.71	1.85	1.96	2.29	2.47	2.58	2.66	2.86	2.90	2.88	2.85

	25 yr	20 yr	15 yr	10 yr	5 yr	4 yr	3 yr	2 yr	1 yr	9 mo	6 mo	5 mo	4 mo	3 mo	2 mo	1 mo	0 mo
7	2.93	2.97	3.01	2.99	2.83	2.76	2.66	2.49	2.19	2.08	1.96	1.92	1.87	1.82	1.75	1.67	1.56
8	2.94	2.94	2.96	2.96	2.90	2.85	2.78	2.66	2.41	2.33	2.23	2.19	2.15	2.10	2.04	1.95	1.83
9	2.93	2.92	2.91	2.89	2.79	2.72	2.62	2.46	2.28	2.23	2.17	2.17	2.16	2.15	2.14	2.20	2.13
10	2.88	2.86	2.85	2.81	2.70	2.66	2.60	2.50	2.31	2.25	2.18	2.15	2.13	2.10	2.07	2.05	2.03
11	2.95	2.93	2.92	2.89	2.85	2.84	2.83	2.81	2.69	2.63	2.55	2.51	2.47	2.41	2.31	2.11	1.80
12	2.89	2.90	2.92	2.92	2.88	2.87	2.86	2.84	2.73	2.68	2.61	2.59	2.56	2.53	2.49	2.42	2.34

1956

	25 yr	20 yr	15 yr	10 yr	5 yr	4 yr	3 yr	2 yr	1 yr	9 mo	6 mo	5 mo	4 mo	3 mo	2 mo	1 mo	0 mo
1	2.86	2.85	2.84	2.81	2.73	2.69	2.64	2.56	2.45	2.41	2.38	2.36	2.35	2.33	2.31	2.28	2.24
2	2.88	2.88	2.87	2.84	2.77	2.74	2.71	2.66	2.55	2.49	2.41	2.38	2.38	2.32	2.19	1.97	1.60
3	2.95	2.99	3.04	3.07	3.06	3.05	3.04	2.98	2.73	2.62	2.48	2.43	2.38	2.32	2.26	2.20	2.13
4	3.06	3.05	3.04	3.06	3.13	3.16	3.21	3.23	3.04	2.94	2.83	2.78	2.74	2.70	2.66	2.63	2.61
5	2.97	2.93	2.90	2.89	2.94	2.95	2.96	2.95	2.86	2.81	2.74	2.71	2.67	2.62	2.53	2.37	2.13
6	2.93	2.93	2.94	2.97	2.97	2.96	2.92	2.85	2.69	2.63	2.55	2.52	2.48	2.45	2.40	2.33	2.24
7	3.04	3.06	3.11	3.19	3.27	3.28	3.27	3.20	2.94	2.79	2.60	2.53	2.44	2.35	2.24	2.08	1.88
8	3.17	3.22	3.29	3.40	3.54	3.55	3.54	3.48	3.24	3.10	2.93	2.86	2.78	2.69	2.58	2.40	2.50
9	3.07	3.14	3.24	3.34	3.42	3.50	3.48	3.51	3.34	3.23	3.11	3.05	3.00	2.93	2.84	2.70	2.27
10	3.21	3.22	3.33	3.47	3.51	3.50	3.48	3.46	3.34	3.24	3.11	3.05	2.98	2.89	2.76	2.56	2.53
11	3.28	3.31	3.39	3.49	3.63	3.66	3.70	3.74	3.69	3.62	3.44	3.36	3.27	3.15	3.01	2.81	3.10
12	3.42	3.52	3.63	3.71	3.71	3.71	3.72	3.77	3.80	3.76	3.63	3.54	3.43	3.29	3.15	3.08	2.06

1957

	25 yr	20 yr	15 yr	10 yr	5 yr	4 yr	3 yr	2 yr	1 yr	9 mo	6 mo	5 mo	4 mo	3 mo	2 mo	1 mo	0 mo
1	3.23	3.12	3.14	3.21	3.25	3.24	3.24	3.26	3.27	3.26	3.23	3.21	3.18	3.14	3.10	3.06	3.05
2	3.23	3.06	3.06	3.06	3.39	3.40	3.42	3.45	3.47	3.46	3.42	3.39	3.35	3.29	3.19	2.97	2.39
3	3.25	3.19	3.25	3.37	3.42	3.43	3.44	3.45	3.36	3.28	3.16	3.11	3.07	3.01	2.95	2.89	2.81
4	3.39	3.30	3.38	3.53	3.57	3.56	3.56	3.54	3.43	3.34	3.21	3.17	3.12	3.07	3.03	3.02	3.05
5	3.24	3.17	3.49	3.68	3.68	3.64	3.60	3.56	3.54	3.44	3.38	3.36	3.33	3.30	3.26	3.21	3.14
6	3.49	3.42	3.63	3.90	3.83	3.77	3.74	3.75	3.71	3.65	3.54	3.49	3.44	3.36	3.26	3.08	2.81
7	3.54	3.41	3.59	3.88	3.92	3.87	3.84	3.84	3.80	3.74	3.63	3.57	3.51	3.42	3.40	3.06	2.66
8	3.59	3.44	3.57	3.80	3.82	3.80	3.84	3.99	4.19	4.06	3.90	3.82	3.71	3.58	3.53	3.23	2.50
9	3.44	3.59	3.80	4.01	4.00	4.02	4.10	4.21	4.01	4.10	3.95	3.89	3.81	3.70	3.54	3.36	2.78
10	3.58	3.67	3.79	3.91	3.95	3.97	4.01	4.05	4.01	3.94	3.83	3.78	3.72	3.65	3.54	2.64	3.10
11	3.64	3.72	3.57	3.34	3.42	3.45	3.48	3.48	3.34	3.34	3.37	3.34	3.28	3.19	3.01	2.71	2.06
12	3.45	3.28	3.20	3.06	2.01	2.81	2.70	2.77	2.77	2.70	2.70	2.70	2.70	2.70	2.77	2.70	2.00

1958

	25 yr	20 yr	15 yr	10 yr	5 yr	4 yr	3 yr	2 yr	1 yr	9 mo	6 mo	5 mo	4 mo	3 mo	2 mo	1 mo	0 mo
1	3.35	3.30	3.27	3.17	2.89	2.80	2.70	2.54	2.14	1.95	1.72	1.64	1.56	1.49	1.44	1.46	1.53
2	3.30	3.26	3.21	3.06	2.65	2.52	2.36	2.15	1.81	1.66	1.48	1.41	1.34	1.27	1.20	1.14	1.10
3	3.37	3.28	3.13	2.92	2.58	2.47	2.32	2.10	1.66	1.49	1.31	1.25	1.18	1.11	1.05	0.99	0.94
4	3.24	3.17	3.05	2.84	2.41	2.26	2.00	1.80	1.46	1.37	1.27	1.24	1.21	1.18	1.16	1.15	1.18
5	3.17	3.16	3.12	2.92	2.34	2.18	2.00	1.77	1.32	1.14	0.92	0.83	0.74	0.63	0.49	0.25	0.00
6	3.30	3.28	3.21	3.02	2.55	2.41	2.23	1.90	1.30	1.11	0.92	0.85	0.79	0.74	0.72	0.75	0.84
7	3.66	3.57	3.40	3.19	2.91	2.74	2.45	2.02	1.47	1.31	1.13	1.07	1.00	0.92	0.83	0.70	0.54

Table 13.A.1 (cont.)

Year	mo	0 mo	1 mo	2 mo	3 mo	4 mo	5 mo	6 mo	9 mo	1 yr	2 yr	3 yr	4 yr	5 yr	10 yr	15 yr	20 yr	25 yr
1958	8	1.35	1.87	2.20	2.38	2.49	2.58	2.65	2.82	2.96	3.36	3.55	3.65	3.70	3.76	3.74	3.73	3.72
	9	1.00	1.95	2.57	2.89	3.04	3.14	3.20	3.31	3.36	3.50	3.62	3.71	3.75	3.75	3.72	3.72	3.76
	10	1.08	1.82	2.30	2.53	2.67	2.76	2.83	2.98	3.09	3.38	3.54	3.64	3.68	3.71	3.69	3.68	3.71
	11	0.83	1.90	2.58	2.91	3.07	3.16	3.23	3.33	3.38	3.48	3.55	3.60	3.63	3.64	3.65	3.68	3.71
	12	2.13	2.42	2.62	2.74	2.84	2.91	2.97	3.10	3.19	3.46	3.64	3.75	3.82	3.90	3.85	3.78	3.77
1959	1	2.32	2.47	2.61	2.76	2.90	3.01	3.09	3.27	3.40	3.74	3.90	3.97	4.00	3.99	4.00	4.02	4.02
	2	2.04	2.38	2.64	2.83	2.97	3.07	3.15	3.29	3.38	3.60	3.72	3.77	3.79	3.80	3.90	4.02	4.07
	3	2.44	2.57	2.72	2.89	3.06	3.19	3.29	3.48	3.59	3.83	3.92	3.97	3.98	3.97	3.97	3.98	3.99
	4	2.78	2.74	2.80	2.94	3.10	3.23	3.32	3.49	3.61	3.88	4.04	4.13	4.18	4.20	4.12	4.02	3.97
	5	2.80	2.75	2.82	3.03	3.27	3.47	3.60	3.79	3.86	3.98	4.10	4.18	4.21	4.18	4.11	4.05	4.02
	6	2.70	2.77	2.93	3.16	3.42	3.62	3.75	3.91	3.97	4.14	4.33	4.41	4.41	4.41	4.14	4.10	4.07
	7	1.97	2.40	2.75	3.04	3.31	3.56	3.79	4.26	4.41	4.34	4.40	4.53	4.58	4.49	4.20	4.05	4.07
	8	3.14	3.48	3.74	3.95	4.13	4.27	4.39	4.55	4.56	4.44	4.52	4.63	4.67	4.47	4.25	4.07	3.98
	9	3.43	3.64	3.90	4.22	4.53	4.77	4.90	4.99	4.93	4.69	4.70	4.71	4.69	4.47	4.26	4.09	4.00
	10	2.14	3.17	3.79	4.06	4.20	4.32	4.42	4.56	4.55	4.36	4.44	4.61	4.69	4.52	4.23	4.06	3.98
	11	2.31	3.53	4.23	4.52	4.68	4.77	4.84	4.93	4.95	4.87	4.81	4.77	4.73	4.52	4.31	4.14	4.06
	12	4.02	4.08	4.28	4.56	4.77	4.88	4.94	5.01	5.02	4.95	4.88	4.83	4.81	4.70	4.51	4.30	4.20
1960	1	3.28	3.54	3.82	4.11	4.33	4.47	4.56	4.68	4.71	4.69	4.72	4.74	4.76	4.63	4.36	4.34	4.16
	2	3.58	3.81	4.05	4.25	4.35	4.38	4.38	4.38	4.40	4.49	4.57	4.61	4.60	4.40	4.25	4.16	4.03
	3	2.40	2.68	2.91	3.10	3.23	3.34	3.41	3.55	3.63	3.79	3.91	3.99	4.03	4.07	4.06	4.05	3.99
	4	2.89	2.97	3.02	3.07	3.18	3.34	3.53	3.98	4.16	4.25	4.36	4.46	4.49	4.34	4.27	4.25	4.23
	5	1.82	2.60	3.02	3.16	3.24	3.34	3.45	3.76	3.93	4.14	4.25	4.31	4.31	4.15	4.16	4.20	4.18
	6	1.25	1.65	1.97	2.20	2.38	2.52	2.65	2.95	3.18	3.70	3.89	3.94	3.99	4.20	4.10	3.93	3.84
	7	1.65	1.83	2.02	2.21	2.38	2.50	2.60	2.79	2.91	3.17	3.28	3.37	3.47	3.82	3.83	3.75	3.70
	8	1.45	1.97	2.36	2.61	2.77	2.85	2.87	2.85	2.88	3.14	3.30	3.45	3.56	3.87	3.88	3.86	3.81
	9	2.69	2.34	2.31	2.53	2.75	2.86	2.89	2.83	2.80	3.05	3.30	3.48	3.59	3.81	3.86	3.91	3.86
	10	1.22	1.61	1.93	2.19	2.38	2.52	2.61	2.76	2.85	3.14	3.36	3.54	3.66	3.90	3.93	3.98	3.88
	11	1.24	1.79	2.19	2.44	2.59	2.69	2.77	2.91	3.01	3.31	3.53	3.70	3.81	4.00	4.02	3.98	3.94
	12	1.87	2.03	2.16	2.27	2.36	2.41	2.44	2.51	2.58	2.87	3.12	3.30	3.44	3.75	3.83	3.85	3.85
1961	1	1.88	2.04	2.18	2.30	2.40	2.47	2.52	2.64	2.76	3.15	3.40	3.55	3.65	3.85	3.91	3.93	3.93
	2	2.47	2.48	2.54	2.62	2.69	2.75	2.80	2.90	2.97	3.19	3.34	3.46	3.53	3.73	3.80	3.83	3.84
	3	2.02	2.19	2.32	2.42	2.50	2.57	2.64	2.78	2.86	3.05	3.25	3.43	3.56	3.82	3.87	3.85	3.82
	4	1.42	1.93	2.20	2.27	2.30	2.38	2.48	2.73	2.85	3.04	3.20	3.35	3.47	3.76	3.82	3.80	3.77

1962

Month	0 mo	1 mo	2 mo	3 mo	4 mo	5 mo	6 mo	9 mo	1 yr	2 yr	3 yr	4 yr	5 yr	10 yr	15 yr	20 yr	25 yr
5	2.10	2.24	2.34	2.40	2.46	2.53	2.60	2.79	2.92	3.20	3.37	3.50	3.59	3.83	3.85	3.80	3.74
6	1.80	2.08	2.24	2.31	2.37	2.45	2.54	2.75	2.90	3.28	3.50	3.64	3.73	3.90	3.94	3.93	3.90
7	1.12	1.74	2.10	2.24	2.32	2.41	2.50	2.73	2.88	3.26	3.56	3.76	3.87	4.00	3.99	3.95	3.91
8	1.89	1.99	2.24	2.36	2.48	2.62	2.71	2.93	3.00	3.37	3.61	3.77	3.87	4.00	4.01	3.98	4.02
9	1.74	1.96	2.15	2.34	2.50	2.58	2.70	2.88	3.05	3.32	3.53	3.66	3.74	3.87	3.93	3.98	4.06
10	1.74	1.96	2.15	2.32	2.47	2.58	2.67	2.85	2.96	3.24	3.46	3.61	3.71	3.90	3.92	3.93	4.00
11	2.28	2.28	2.47	2.60	2.68	2.75	2.80	2.93	3.03	3.33	3.53	3.68	3.80	4.04	4.01	4.00	4.00
12	2.32	2.48	2.63	2.75	2.84	2.90	2.94	3.06	3.15	3.42	3.59	3.73	3.84	4.09	4.07	4.01	4.04

1963

Month	0 mo	1 mo	2 mo	3 mo	4 mo	5 mo	6 mo	9 mo	1 yr	2 yr	3 yr	4 yr	5 yr	10 yr	15 yr	20 yr	25 yr
1	2.95	2.93	2.94	2.98	3.02	3.02	3.01	2.98	2.99	3.15	3.33	3.50	3.63	3.92	3.95	3.94	4.00
2	2.82	2.84	2.88	2.94	2.97	2.97	2.95	2.92	2.94	3.16	3.38	3.55	3.69	3.99	4.04	4.03	4.01
3	1.83	2.20	2.55	2.85	3.04	3.12	3.12	3.03	2.99	3.15	3.38	3.56	3.70	4.02	4.06	4.04	3.99
4	2.85	2.85	2.89	2.94	2.99	3.12	3.12	3.05	3.08	3.28	3.46	3.60	3.71	4.02	4.08	4.09	4.03
5	2.91	2.95	3.00	3.06	3.10	3.12	3.12	3.10	3.13	3.31	3.51	3.65	3.76	4.00	4.06	4.06	4.06
6	2.99	2.98	3.19	3.29	3.36	3.40	3.42	3.11	3.15	3.33	3.53	3.69	3.81	4.02	4.06	4.06	4.05
7	2.88	3.05	3.38	3.44	3.48	3.50	3.53	3.44	3.46	3.58	3.70	3.83	3.88	4.04	4.03	4.02	4.01
8	3.08	3.26	3.42	3.47	3.52	3.56	3.57	3.58	3.60	3.63	3.71	3.86	3.92	4.04	4.04	4.02	4.01
9	3.53	3.44	3.46	3.54	3.60	3.64	3.65	3.59	3.59	3.65	3.75	3.94	3.94	4.10	4.10	4.06	4.07
10	3.25	3.36	3.46	3.57	3.64	3.67	3.70	3.66	3.67	3.75	3.85	3.92	4.01	4.10	4.16	4.11	4.09
11	3.01	3.27	3.51	3.59	3.64	3.69	3.72	3.72	3.74	3.79	3.97	4.03	3.98	4.13	4.14	4.13	4.13
12	3.52	3.51	3.53	3.65	3.68	3.73	3.76	3.78	3.81	3.91	3.97	4.03	4.07	4.18	4.20	4.19	4.18

1964

Month	0 mo	1 mo	2 mo	3 mo	4 mo	5 mo	6 mo	9 mo	1 yr	2 yr	3 yr	4 yr	5 yr	10 yr	15 yr	20 yr	25 yr
1	3.35	3.42	3.49	3.55	3.60	3.64	3.67	3.73	3.78	3.88	3.94	4.00	4.05	4.21	4.21	4.17	4.14
2	3.51	3.53	3.58	3.65	3.72	3.77	3.80	3.86	3.90	3.98	4.03	4.07	4.11	4.24	4.22	4.18	4.14
3	3.57	3.51	3.52	3.60	3.68	3.73	3.77	3.85	3.91	4.07	4.14	4.18	4.20	4.26	4.25	4.22	4.19
4	3.18	3.32	3.43	3.51	3.57	3.62	3.66	3.75	3.81	3.97	4.06	4.13	4.17	4.21	4.21	4.21	4.20
5	3.00	3.29	3.46	3.52	3.55	3.60	3.64	3.76	3.82	3.92	3.98	4.03	4.07	4.20	4.19	4.15	4.13

Table 13.A.1 (cont.)

	0 mo	1 mo	2 mo	3 mo	4 mo	5 mo	6 mo	9 mo	1 yr	2 yr	3 yr	4 yr	5 yr	10 yr	15 yr	20 yr	25 yr
1964																	
6	3.28	3.46	3.54	3.55	3.55	3.59	3.63	3.72	3.75	3.83	3.92	4.00	4.06	4.16	4.16	4.14	4.13
7	3.02	3.32	3.46	3.51	3.54	3.60	3.65	3.73	3.74	3.75	3.88	4.00	4.08	4.21	4.21	4.19	4.18
8	3.21	3.40	3.51	3.56	3.60	3.65	3.69	3.77	3.79	3.84	3.93	4.02	4.08	4.23	4.23	4.21	4.18
9	3.50	3.53	3.57	3.63	3.69	3.74	3.78	3.85	3.87	3.89	3.95	4.01	4.06	4.19	4.21	4.20	4.18
10	3.39	3.45	3.53	3.62	3.70	3.75	3.79	3.85	3.88	3.92	3.97	4.02	4.06	4.17	4.19	4.17	4.16
11	3.63	3.63	3.81	3.90	3.97	4.03	4.08	4.14	4.13	4.13	4.13	4.14	4.15	4.19	4.20	4.20	4.18
12	3.13	3.56	3.80	3.89	3.94	3.98	4.00	4.02	4.00	3.99	4.04	4.08	4.12	4.22	4.23	4.22	4.19
1965																	
1	3.81	3.85	3.89	3.93	3.97	4.02	4.06	4.06	4.03	3.98	4.02	4.06	4.10	4.19	4.21	4.20	4.19
2	3.61	3.87	4.00	4.04	4.07	4.11	4.13	4.15	4.14	4.09	4.08	4.10	4.13	4.23	4.23	4.20	4.18
3	3.60	3.82	3.94	3.98	4.01	4.05	4.07	4.10	4.09	4.07	4.09	4.12	4.14	4.20	4.21	4.20	4.19
4	3.82	3.89	3.94	3.99	4.02	4.00	4.07	4.08	4.07	4.07	4.10	4.11	4.14	4.23	4.23	4.21	4.19
5	3.74	3.86	3.93	3.95	3.98	3.92	4.03	4.06	4.07	4.07	4.08	4.07	4.11	4.20	4.22	4.21	4.19
6	3.71	3.79	3.84	3.89	3.89	3.96	3.93	3.94	3.93	3.95	4.02	4.07	4.17	4.20	4.23	4.22	4.21
7	3.81	3.81	3.88	3.93	3.93	4.04	3.98	3.99	4.00	4.06	4.11	4.15	4.17	4.28	4.27	4.25	4.24
8	3.70	3.81	3.88	3.98	3.98	4.04	4.09	4.12	4.10	4.13	4.17	4.20	4.23	4.41	4.37	4.31	4.28
9	3.93	3.95	4.01	4.11	4.19	4.24	4.28	4.33	4.35	4.34	4.33	4.34	4.36	4.41	4.40	4.33	4.29
10	3.85	3.92	4.02	4.13	4.22	4.26	4.29	4.33	4.35	4.38	4.40	4.43	4.44	4.46	4.49	4.44	4.37
11	3.67	3.93	4.09	4.18	4.25	4.32	4.37	4.42	4.44	4.50	4.54	4.55	4.56	4.54	4.54	4.44	4.37
12	4.31	4.44	4.52	4.57	4.66	4.75	4.82	4.92	4.96	5.08	5.10	5.04	4.97	4.70	4.59	4.51	4.45
1966																	
1	4.50	4.52	4.61	4.72	4.79	4.82	4.84	4.87	4.90	5.04	5.10	5.08	5.02	4.79	4.64	4.54	4.50
2	4.24	4.50	4.65	4.74	4.82	4.90	4.97	5.08	5.13	5.18	5.21	5.25	5.28	5.20	4.94	4.72	4.66
3	4.19	4.40	4.53	4.61	4.70	4.79	4.85	4.94	4.97	5.02	5.01	4.99	4.96	4.82	4.70	4.61	4.57
4	4.44	4.63	4.69	4.70	4.74	4.82	4.87	4.93	4.95	5.04	5.04	5.02	5.02	4.95	4.81	4.67	4.60
5	4.21	4.49	4.65	4.69	4.75	4.86	4.95	5.02	5.06	5.25	5.26	5.18	5.11	4.94	4.82	4.73	4.68
6	4.22	4.49	4.60	4.62	4.69	4.80	4.87	4.95	5.02	5.36	5.39	5.31	5.26	5.11	4.97	4.83	4.73
7	4.09	4.58	4.78	4.81	4.90	5.01	5.09	5.17	5.21	5.40	5.48	5.48	5.46	5.26	5.01	4.80	4.71
8	4.21	4.79	5.06	5.12	5.28	5.12	5.76	5.89	5.94	6.30	6.28	6.14	6.01	5.57	5.29	5.08	4.77
9	5.00	5.20	5.35	5.48	5.61	5.74	5.83	5.92	5.91	5.79	5.68	5.56	5.42	5.07	4.96	4.89	4.65
10	4.24	4.85	5.19	5.36	5.50	5.62	5.70	5.74	5.72	5.61	5.53	5.46	5.38	5.08	4.86	4.71	4.76
11	3.66	4.62	5.15	5.28	5.32	5.32	5.41	5.43	5.48	5.68	5.55	5.41	5.37	5.27	5.05	4.86	4.59
12	4.60	4.70	4.82	4.94	5.02	5.07	5.08	5.05	5.03	5.02	4.98	4.93	4.87	4.72	4.67	4.63	4.59
1967																	
1	4.37	4.54	4.61	4.61	4.61	4.63	4.64	4.63	4.63	4.68	4.70	4.70	4.69	4.62	4.56	4.51	4.48
2	3.77	4.37	4.59	4.60	4.61	4.64	4.66	4.64	4.68	4.91	4.86	4.79	4.80	4.87	4.83	4.75	4.68
3	3.91	4.01	4.10	4.16	4.18	4.17	4.16	4.14	4.14	4.24	4.30	4.35	4.42	4.60	4.64	4.63	4.60

1968 (rows are maturities, columns are months of the year)

Maturity	4	5	6	7	8	9	10	11	12
25 yr	4.80	4.88	5.06	5.08	5.19	5.22	5.49	5.58	
20 yr	4.90	4.92	5.06	5.13	5.18	5.27	5.50	5.72	5.78
15 yr	4.96	4.97	5.25	5.29	5.39	5.60	5.77	5.81	
10 yr	4.94	4.96	5.35	5.42	5.52	5.71	5.82	5.77	
5 yr	4.72	4.71	5.20	5.44	5.51	5.68	5.78	5.79	
4 yr	4.63	4.62	5.11	5.40	5.45	5.64	5.73	5.84	
3 yr	4.57	4.64	5.25	5.08	5.38	5.40	5.63	5.67	5.89
2 yr	4.44	4.53	5.14	5.39	5.39	5.61	5.62	5.88	
1 yr	4.06	4.04	4.93	5.16	5.31	5.40	5.50	5.75	5.90
9 mo	3.99	3.95	4.93	5.06	5.21	5.36	5.44	5.81	5.90
6 mo	3.93	3.84	4.54	4.78	4.95	5.16	5.22	5.60	5.72
5 mo	3.89	3.74	4.35	4.60	4.82	5.02	5.04	5.43	5.59
4 mo	3.82	3.61	4.17	4.38	4.67	4.83	4.82	5.23	5.40
3 mo	3.77	3.49	4.18	4.49	4.59	4.63	5.04	5.16	
2 mo	3.74	3.43	3.96	4.04	4.26	4.35	4.45	4.76	4.85
1 mo	3.54	3.35	3.75	3.79	3.93	4.19	4.27	4.43	
0 mo	3.01	3.20	3.32	3.29	3.49	3.80	3.57	3.90	

1969

Maturity	1	2	3	4	5	6	7	8	9	10	11	12
25 yr	5.41	5.56	5.49	5.44	5.35	5.33	5.45	5.61	5.64			
20 yr	5.56	5.63	5.94	5.68	5.72	5.55	5.43	5.41	5.62	5.83	6.02	6.41
15 yr	5.68	5.69	6.02	5.81	5.89	5.66	5.49	5.50	5.68	5.87	6.08	6.47
10 yr	5.73	5.44	5.97	5.93	5.98	5.75	5.53	5.56	5.65	5.79	5.95	6.42
5 yr	5.68	5.70	5.90	6.03	5.94	5.82	5.52	5.51	5.53	5.65	5.74	6.43
4 yr	5.63	5.72	5.91	6.06	5.93	5.83	5.51	5.49	5.63	5.70	6.48	
3 yr	5.59	5.71	5.92	6.03	6.06	5.86	5.51	5.47	5.61	5.66	6.55	
2 yr	5.58	5.65	5.86	6.02	6.17	5.94	5.50	5.37	5.46	5.63	5.65	6.59
1 yr	5.45	5.51	5.69	5.94	6.17	5.94	5.46	5.41	5.41	5.70	5.86	6.62
9 mo	5.33	5.45	5.60	5.90	6.15	5.87	5.46	5.43	5.44	5.70	5.87	6.63
6 mo	5.17	5.34	5.47	5.80	6.08	5.69	5.44	5.45	5.45	5.67	5.78	6.56
5 mo	5.11	5.28	5.41	5.75	6.01	5.60	5.38	5.36	5.40	5.66	5.73	6.49
4 mo	5.04	5.21	5.34	5.68	5.92	5.51	5.30	5.29	5.33	5.64	5.67	6.39
3 mo	4.95	5.12	5.28	5.61	5.84	5.42	5.23	5.26	5.28	5.59	5.60	6.31
2 mo	4.84	5.01	5.18	5.51	5.76	5.34	5.19	5.24	5.46	5.47	6.24	
1 mo	4.74	4.79	4.94	5.34	5.57	5.29	5.10	5.05	5.20	5.34	5.07	6.14
0 mo	4.64	4.37	4.52	5.06	5.20	5.27	4.92	4.60	5.13	5.25	4.32	5.98

1970

Maturity	1	2	3	4	5
25 yr	6.17	6.10			
20 yr	6.43	6.22		6.83	
15 yr	6.77	6.44	6.80	7.35	
10 yr	7.44	6.81	6.84	7.71	7.70
5 yr	7.92	7.13	7.11	7.83	7.59
4 yr	7.95	7.17	7.09	7.82	7.64
3 yr	7.96	7.18	7.00	7.79	7.73
2 yr	7.97	7.07	6.85	7.71	7.73
1 yr	7.96	6.89	6.65	7.53	7.45
9 mo	7.99	6.90	6.61	7.44	7.32
6 mo	8.06	6.98	6.59	7.33	7.21
5 mo	8.07	7.01	6.59	7.28	7.19
4 mo	8.05	7.02	6.57	7.20	7.16
3 mo	8.01	7.01	6.48	7.03	7.04
2 mo	7.93	6.94	6.39	6.78	6.82
1 mo	7.62	6.68	6.43	6.52	6.56
0 mo	6.95	6.10	6.64	6.29	6.28

Table 13.A.1 (cont.)

	0 mo	1 mo	2 mo	3 mo	4 mo	5 mo	6 mo	9 mo	1 yr	2 yr	3 yr	4 yr	5 yr	10 yr	15 yr	20 yr	25 yr
1970																	
6	5.46	6.12	6.45	6.52	6.58	6.68	6.80	7.06	7.22	7.52	7.61	7.63	7.63	7.50			
7	4.32	5.92	6.50	6.43	6.38	6.50	6.66	6.86	6.89	7.29	7.45	7.46	7.48	7.60			
8	6.07	6.24	6.33	6.38	6.45	6.56	6.67	6.79	6.78	7.15	7.31	7.32	7.35	7.57			
9	5.61	5.56	5.71	6.03	6.32	6.48	6.54	6.59	6.60	6.68	6.82	6.97	7.08	7.30			
10	5.05	5.45	5.76	5.96	6.09	6.17	6.23	6.30	6.34	6.52	6.71	6.86	6.97	7.20			
11	5.40	4.75	4.97	5.07	5.08	5.06	5.05	5.10	5.16	5.39	5.62	5.88	6.49	6.49	6.52	6.32	
12	3.98	4.57	4.84	4.90	4.92	4.93	4.91	4.89	4.99	5.47	5.74	5.89	6.00	6.34	6.51	6.39	
1971																	
1	3.99	4.11	4.15	4.17	4.22	4.25	4.25	4.19	4.24	4.73	5.23	5.62	5.87	6.17	6.04	5.98	
2	3.13	3.25	3.35	3.43	3.50	3.56	3.61	3.69	3.75	4.23	4.78	5.20	5.49	6.12	6.32	6.32	
3	3.46	3.46	3.54	3.64	3.69	3.69	3.69	3.74	3.81	4.15	4.52	4.86	5.15	5.72	5.85	5.91	
4	3.49	3.81	3.97	4.04	4.14	4.24	4.33	4.51	4.64	5.20	5.63	5.90	6.05	6.15			
5	3.92	4.20	4.35	4.38	4.40	4.44	4.51	4.75	4.97	5.49	5.78	5.97	6.12	6.53			
6	4.52	4.95	5.13	5.12	5.15	5.29	5.47	5.83	6.06	6.49	6.77	6.74	6.80	6.83			
7	4.78	5.21	5.33	5.31	5.42	5.64	5.82	6.02	6.06	6.50	6.66	6.86	6.91	6.95			
8	4.49	4.46	4.42	4.40	4.47	4.64	4.82	5.12	5.27	5.55	5.70	5.82	5.93	6.30			
9	4.55	4.47	4.52	4.65	4.78	4.89	4.99	5.17	5.27	5.51	5.70	5.87	5.95	5.97	6.12		
10	3.56	4.06	4.29	4.37	4.44	4.47	4.48	5.19	4.60	5.06	5.19	5.49	5.76	5.96			
11	3.67	4.06	4.28	4.35	4.39	4.45	4.50	4.63	4.75	5.07	5.27	5.60	5.84	5.85			
12	3.24	3.33	3.51	3.70	3.87	3.99	4.03	4.11	4.29	4.84	5.04	5.29	5.49	5.97			
1972																	
1	2.41	3.02	3.28	3.38	3.53	3.68	3.78	3.99	4.18	4.84	5.29	5.56	5.76	6.40			
2	3.36	3.25	3.29	3.44	3.60	3.72	3.82	4.05	4.24	4.83	5.23	5.49	5.68	6.26			
3	3.32	3.42	3.64	3.93	4.16	4.33	4.47	4.78	5.00	5.52	5.78	5.94	6.04	6.22			
4	3.30	3.28	3.44	3.67	3.86	4.01	4.12	4.34	4.50	5.15	5.55	5.72	5.83	6.21			
5	3.31	3.50	3.67	3.81	3.95	4.09	4.21	4.43	4.56	5.00	5.34	5.56	5.73	6.14			
6	3.39	3.68	3.91	4.11	4.31	4.51	4.69	5.02	5.17	5.48	5.68	5.83	5.94	6.24			
7	3.41	3.56	3.70	3.86	4.04	4.25	4.43	4.74	4.88	5.36	5.72	5.86	5.97	6.40			
8	4.27	4.35	4.42	4.51	4.65	4.85	5.02	5.28	5.37	5.67	5.89	6.02	6.09	6.51			
9	4.65	4.48	4.52	4.74	4.98	5.17	5.31	5.53	5.63	5.86	5.97	6.01	6.10	6.62			
10	4.49	4.54	4.65	4.82	4.97	5.10	5.19	5.36	5.48	5.81	5.98	6.04	5.99	6.45			
11	4.82	4.79	4.83	4.92	5.04	5.16	5.26	5.36	5.36	5.67	5.88	5.93	5.84	6.34			
12	4.77	4.93	5.08	5.22	5.34	5.43	5.48	5.56	5.59	5.90	6.04	6.07	6.12	6.41			
1973																	
1	5.22	5.44	5.62	5.77	5.87	5.93	5.97	6.02	6.06	6.26	6.35	6.34	6.34	6.45	6.65	6.94	
2	5.49	5.59	5.73	5.90	6.03	6.11	6.16	6.29	6.39	6.61	6.66	6.64	6.62	6.55	6.60		
3	5.77	6.08	6.34	6.53	6.70	6.82	6.91	6.99	6.96	6.79	6.71	6.68	6.65	6.58	6.60		

4	5.95	6.01	6.17	6.39	6.55	6.64	6.68	6.73	6.72	6.65	6.62	6.61	6.61	6.57	6.61		
5	6.00	6.53	6.86	7.01	7.07	7.10	7.10	7.09	7.05	6.80	6.64	6.63	6.66	6.78	6.86	6.94	
6	7.30	7.45	7.56	7.62	7.69	7.76	7.81	7.79	7.59	7.04	6.87	6.79	6.76	6.79	6.91	7.04	
7	7.96	8.29	8.39	8.36	8.39	8.52	8.65	8.77	8.66	8.17	7.88	7.70	7.59	7.34	7.25	7.32	
8	8.41	8.64	8.71	8.68	8.67	8.70	8.74	8.67	8.47	7.71	7.30	7.13	7.06	7.04	7.13	7.22	
9	7.59	7.13	7.04	7.25	7.49	7.67	7.78	7.77	7.58	6.93	6.69	6.62	6.62	6.76	6.91	7.01	
10	6.74	7.15	7.36	7.41	7.48	7.63	7.69	7.35	6.98	6.82	6.93	6.91	6.84	6.89	7.21	7.41	
11	7.85	7.49	7.43	7.62	7.85	8.02	8.07	7.80	7.43	6.73	6.72	6.70	6.67	6.79	7.06	7.25	
12	7.13	7.29	7.45	7.57	7.64	7.63	7.59	7.34	7.11	6.72	6.70	6.67	6.63	6.79	7.19	7.49	

1974	0 mo	1 mo	2 mo	3 mo	4 mo	5 mo	6 mo	9 mo	1 yr	2 yr	3 yr	4 yr	5 yr	10 yr	15 yr	20 yr	25 yr
1	7.36	7.52	7.62	7.66	7.63	7.55	7.47	7.23	7.02	6.73	6.75	6.76	6.77	7.00	7.32	7.53	
2	7.18	7.58	7.65	7.59	7.56	7.54	7.48	7.19	6.99	6.76	6.80	6.83	6.85	7.09	7.41	7.62	
3	8.01	8.51	8.65	8.64	8.61	8.58	8.56	8.45	8.29	7.82	7.69	7.61	7.55	7.49	7.58	7.74	
4	8.52	8.73	8.90	9.01	9.01	8.98	8.99	9.06	8.94	8.28	8.16	8.09	8.03	7.89	7.86	7.94	
5	7.55	7.66	7.95	8.29	8.46	8.47	8.51	8.75	8.73	8.02	7.98	7.95	7.89	7.83	7.91	8.02	
6	7.65	7.65	7.69	7.76	7.88	8.04	8.21	8.62	8.68	8.19	8.27	8.22	8.11	7.84	7.80	7.86	
7	7.04	7.55	7.74	7.74	7.86	8.07	8.26	8.61	8.65	8.42	8.45	8.39	8.28	8.01	7.91	7.97	
8	9.17	9.20	9.23	9.30	9.43	9.59	9.73	9.92	9.74	8.76	8.51	8.44	8.40	8.27	8.11	8.16	
9	6.26	6.06	6.07	6.32	6.79	7.31	7.70	8.24	8.29	7.95	8.01	7.97	7.90	7.89	8.11	8.43	
10	6.37	7.12	7.70	8.09	8.17	8.09	8.02	7.94	7.86	7.72	7.85	7.85	7.80	7.75	7.85	8.05	
11	7.44	7.45	7.52	7.63	7.73	7.81	7.83	7.69	7.51	7.26	7.41	7.49	7.52	7.70	7.89	7.97	
12	6.51	6.77	7.00	7.18	7.26	7.26	7.23	7.16	7.13	7.18	7.23	7.21	7.17	7.43	7.90	8.10	

1975	0 mo	1 mo	2 mo	3 mo	4 mo	5 mo	6 mo	9 mo	1 yr	2 yr	3 yr	4 yr	5 yr	10 yr	15 yr	20 yr	25 yr
1	5.47	5.53	5.67	5.84	5.94	6.00	6.02	6.05	6.15	6.71	6.98	7.13	7.24	7.48	7.58	7.71	8.11
2	4.48	4.98	5.33	5.55	5.67	5.73	5.77	5.85	5.92	6.26	6.59	6.85	7.06	7.49	7.59	7.68	
3	5.06	5.27	5.48	5.66	5.76	5.82	5.86	6.01	6.16	6.70	7.00	7.22	7.40	7.93	8.21	8.31	
4	4.77	5.15	5.41	5.60	5.80	6.01	6.20	6.58	6.86	7.59	7.79	7.89	7.97	8.13	8.16	8.25	
5	4.66	4.94	5.14	5.28	5.40	5.50	5.60	5.85	6.07	6.84	7.20	7.41	7.56	7.97	8.15	8.18	8.03
6	5.59	5.67	5.83	6.04	6.18	6.26	6.32	6.62	6.85	7.21	7.48	7.63	7.70	7.87	7.96	8.04	
7	5.97	6.00	6.13	6.34	6.56	6.75	6.90	7.13	7.26	7.65	7.83	7.91	7.94	8.03	8.12	8.18	8.24
8	5.73	5.98	6.24	6.50	6.74	6.93	7.08	7.34	7.46	7.70	7.89	8.00	8.02	8.09	8.23	8.36	8.44
9	6.24	6.31	6.47	6.69	6.91	7.09	7.23	7.46	7.62	8.03	8.19	8.26	8.28	8.37	8.49	8.56	8.59
10	5.25	5.36	5.49	5.63	5.73	5.81	5.86	6.07	6.29	6.96	7.24	7.41	7.55	7.93	8.10	8.18	
11	4.67	5.13	5.46	5.68	5.86	6.02	6.15	6.38	6.57	7.23	7.49	7.66	7.82	8.22	8.32	8.32	8.32
12	4.98	5.06	5.16	5.29	5.42	5.53	5.63	5.89	6.10	6.68	7.04	7.27	7.42	7.80	7.98	8.08	

1976	0 mo	1 mo	2 mo	3 mo	4 mo	5 mo	6 mo	9 mo	1 yr	2 yr	3 yr	4 yr	5 yr	10 yr	15 yr	20 yr	25 yr
1	4.52	4.52	4.63	4.79	4.92	5.02	5.11	5.33	5.56	6.39	6.90	7.23	7.45	7.89	7.97	7.98	
2	4.46	4.67	4.89	5.10	5.29	5.47	5.61	5.90	6.11	6.76	7.09	7.29	7.43	7.80	7.96	8.04	
3	4.77	4.78	4.89	5.05	5.22	5.37	5.50	5.80	6.04	6.65	6.98	7.18	7.33	7.69	7.82	7.89	
4	4.86	4.70	4.80	4.99	5.17	5.31	5.43	5.74	6.01	6.58	6.88	7.11	7.28	7.69	7.87	7.95	
5	4.86	5.24	5.48	5.61	5.78	5.96	6.11	6.40	6.66	7.25	7.46	7.60	7.68	7.89	8.04	8.13	

Table 13.A.1 (cont.)

Year	Mo	0 mo	1 mo	2 mo	3 mo	4 mo	5 mo	6 mo	9 mo	1 yr	2 yr	3 yr	4 yr	5 yr	10 yr	15 yr	20 yr	25 yr
1976	6	5.26	5.30	5.36	5.48	5.63	5.80	5.93	6.15	6.36	6.91	7.17	7.36	7.49	7.81	7.94	8.02	
	7	5.09	5.10	5.16	5.27	5.41	5.55	5.65	5.85	6.08	6.69	6.97	7.20	7.39	7.85	7.97	8.02	
	8	4.80	4.98	5.09	5.17	5.28	5.41	5.50	5.65	5.83	6.43	6.67	6.90	7.11	7.66	7.82	7.88	
	9	5.13	5.07	5.09	5.18	5.28	5.38	5.47	5.59	5.73	6.27	6.54	6.80	7.01	7.56	7.74	7.82	
	10	4.69	4.74	4.85	4.98	5.08	5.15	5.20	5.30	5.46	6.02	6.27	6.50	6.73	7.46	7.72	7.82	
	11	4.37	4.41	4.46	4.51	4.56	4.63	4.68	4.77	4.88	5.39	5.66	5.79	6.01	7.09	7.64	7.80	
	12	4.22	4.26	4.34	4.45	4.53	4.59	4.63	4.72	4.84	5.35	5.66	5.90	6.11	6.83	7.15	7.32	
1977	1	4.58	4.57	4.66	4.81	4.95	5.06	5.15	5.34	5.55	6.17	6.46	6.72	6.91	7.38	7.62	7.73	7.94
	2	4.41	4.52	4.65	4.78	4.90	4.99	5.07	5.30	5.52	6.11	6.46	6.76	6.98	7.44	7.69	7.86	7.85
	3	4.54	4.51	4.55	4.65	4.75	4.83	4.91	5.17	5.41	5.97	6.38	6.69	6.91	7.42	7.68	7.82	7.79
	4	4.33	4.44	4.58	4.72	4.85	4.95	5.05	5.30	5.51	6.07	6.40	6.70	6.92	7.45	7.67	7.77	7.76
	5	4.80	4.90	5.00	5.11	5.21	5.30	5.37	5.55	5.70	6.13	6.38	6.64	6.84	7.39	7.64	7.76	
	6	4.98	4.96	5.01	5.12	5.23	5.32	5.39	5.52	5.64	6.06	6.29	6.53	6.73	7.27	7.45	7.56	7.69
	7	5.16	5.25	5.36	5.48	5.60	5.72	5.81	5.97	6.09	6.41	6.63	6.84	6.99	7.38	7.55	7.63	
	8	5.35	5.38	5.49	5.65	5.82	5.94	6.03	6.18	6.26	6.47	6.65	6.78	6.80	7.25	7.47	7.61	
	9	5.75	5.74	5.85	6.04	6.19	6.28	6.34	6.47	6.57	6.75	6.85	6.97	7.06	7.33	7.53	7.66	7.73
	10	6.27	6.11	6.16	6.37	6.55	6.65	6.71	6.88	7.01	7.20	7.29	7.38	7.42	7.55	7.72	7.86	7.90
	11	5.31	5.67	5.97	6.19	6.36	6.48	6.58	6.76	6.87	7.07	7.18	7.24	7.28	7.51	7.71	7.84	7.87
	12	5.38	5.82	6.13	6.32	6.46	6.55	6.63	6.81	6.92	7.10	7.25	7.37	7.45	7.68	7.86	7.98	8.03
1978	1	5.69	6.07	6.35	6.53	6.67	6.77	6.86	7.02	7.12	7.28	7.42	7.53	7.61	7.81	8.01	8.16	8.20
	2	5.98	6.23	6.41	6.56	6.68	6.81	6.92	7.08	7.16	7.44	7.58	7.69	7.76	7.92	8.09	8.22	8.27
	3	6.84	6.56	6.51	6.62	6.76	6.87	6.97	7.18	7.32	7.58	7.69	7.78	7.85	8.02	8.19	8.29	8.29
	4	5.86	6.03	6.25	6.51	6.74	6.93	7.09	7.37	7.52	7.78	7.83	7.88	7.93	8.10	8.27	8.36	8.32
	5	6.33	6.44	6.60	6.81	7.02	7.21	7.36	7.64	7.78	7.96	8.01	8.08	8.13	8.27	8.44	8.50	8.30
	6	6.24	6.61	6.95	7.01	7.48	7.63	7.75	8.00	8.20	8.29	8.34	8.32	8.31	8.39	8.56	8.53	8.40
	7	6.40	6.55	6.76	7.00	7.24	7.44	7.62	8.00	8.20	8.26	8.29	8.28	8.29	8.39	8.47	8.46	8.36
	8	8.05	7.88	7.76	7.70	7.73	7.84	7.95	8.00	8.30	8.26	8.23	8.21	8.20	8.43	8.51	8.46	8.31
	9	8.35	8.00	8.15	8.32	8.48	8.59	8.66	8.68	8.66	8.45	8.30	8.27	8.29	8.20	8.23	8.29	8.38
	10	8.95	8.65	8.84	8.94	9.09	9.31	9.50	9.74	9.66	9.25	9.07	8.93	8.63	8.66	8.65	8.69	8.67
	11	8.99	8.99	9.06	9.17	9.31	9.45	9.58	9.79	9.76	9.25	8.86	8.68	8.63	8.62	8.60	8.51	8.41
	12	7.63	8.63	9.25	9.55	9.70	9.77	9.86	10.22	10.33	9.79	9.33	9.09	9.01	8.86	8.75	8.65	8.53
1979	1	9.64	9.51	9.49	9.56	9.63	9.68	9.73	9.86	9.80	9.34	8.87	8.68	8.67	8.72	8.67	8.63	8.55
	2	9.58	9.63	9.65	9.67	9.73	9.82	9.90	10.00	9.97	9.58	9.20	9.02	8.98	8.97	8.90	8.78	8.65

1980

mo	25 yr	20 yr	15 yr	10 yr	5 yr	4 yr	3 yr	2 yr	1 yr	9 mo	6 mo	5 mo	4 mo	3 mo	2 mo	1 mo	0 mo
3	8.68	8.79	8.86	8.90	8.89	8.93	9.12	9.49	9.77	9.86	9.83	9.80	9.76	9.71	9.65	9.59	9.54
4	8.83	8.95	9.06	9.12	9.08	9.08	9.24	9.63	9.91	9.99	9.93	9.90	9.86	9.78	9.67	9.58	9.54
5	8.80	8.90	8.91	8.87	8.76	8.77	8.91	9.27	9.61	9.72	9.78	9.79	9.80	9.80	9.78	9.78	9.80
6	8.54	8.67	8.70	8.63	8.50	8.50	8.57	8.71	8.71	9.23	9.25	9.24	9.23	9.40	9.13	8.98	8.73
7	8.63	8.76	8.82	8.74	8.74	8.74	8.82	9.02	9.48	9.64	9.63	9.59	9.53	9.40	9.22	9.14	9.22
8	8.68	8.80	8.89	8.99	9.10	9.16	9.28	9.56	10.21	10.30	10.19	10.10	10.02	10.02	10.10	10.11	9.98
9	8.63	8.88	9.11	9.16	9.22	9.30	9.45	9.78	10.48	10.57	10.52	10.48	10.44	10.39	10.34	10.22	9.99
10	9.43	9.74	9.28	10.31	10.77	10.96	11.23	11.59	11.73	12.68	12.43	12.72	12.67	12.49	12.15	11.66	11.24
11	9.50	9.69	9.86	10.11	10.21	10.24	10.34	10.80	11.33	11.72	12.03	11.95	11.83	11.77	11.69	11.23	10.27
12	9.51	9.79	9.96	10.02	10.03	10.12	10.39	10.86	11.41	11.82	12.30	12.35	12.35	12.28	11.88	12.90	10.88

1981

mo	0 mo	1 mo	2 mo	3 mo	4 mo	5 mo	6 mo	9 mo	1 yr	2 yr	3 yr	4 yr	5 yr	10 yr	15 yr	20 yr	25 yr
1	13.97	14.72	15.06	15.02	14.86	14.69	14.54	14.10	13.65	12.80	12.49	12.40	12.36	12.19	12.17	11.74	10.96
2	13.60	14.20	14.56	14.70	14.68	14.62	14.56	14.31	14.00	13.52	13.46	13.38	12.91	12.78	12.22	11.93	11.43
3	13.10	13.03	12.94	12.82	12.72	12.66	12.65	12.74	12.86	12.81	12.93	13.00	13.01	12.69	12.65	12.16	11.14
4	12.57	14.11	14.99	15.20	15.10	15.00	14.96	14.87	14.69	14.30	13.82	14.00	13.90	12.89	13.39	12.31	11.65
5	16.27	16.21	16.01	15.67	15.31	15.06	14.95	14.86	14.42	14.15	13.93	13.54	13.31	13.11	12.80	12.60	11.41
6	14.03	14.41	14.61	14.65	14.52	14.67	14.66	14.56	14.56	14.19	13.74	13.87	13.74	13.29	13.11	12.93	11.57
7	14.50	14.98	15.27	15.41	15.52	15.67	15.80	15.88	15.75	15.33	15.60	14.66	14.66	13.89	13.67	13.96	11.62
8	15.40	15.64	15.84	16.00	16.15	16.33	16.51	16.63	16.35	16.15	15.60	15.60	15.46	14.61	14.39	13.96	12.61
9	12.64	13.68	14.38	14.76	15.04	15.35	15.65	16.02	15.91	16.11	15.82	15.85	15.70	15.06	15.14	14.41	12.43
10	12.75	12.97	13.09	13.13	13.21	13.42	13.69	14.12	14.10	14.16	14.35	14.35	14.36	14.21	14.21	13.61	12.21
11	10.17	10.24	10.37	10.57	10.78	10.94	11.06	11.31	11.56	12.23	12.53	12.59	12.72	12.95	12.79	12.59	11.86
12	8.26	9.71	10.79	11.51	11.97	12.30	12.55	13.05	13.33	13.51	13.58	13.72	13.77	13.67	13.70	13.27	11.88

1982

mo	0 mo	1 mo	2 mo	3 mo	4 mo	5 mo	6 mo	9 mo	1 yr	2 yr	3 yr	4 yr	5 yr	10 yr	15 yr	20 yr	25 yr
1	11.73	12.14	12.51	12.84	13.11	13.29	13.41	13.64	13.81	13.85	13.91	13.94	13.90	13.80	13.87	13.26	12.10
2	11.85	11.98	12.27	12.72	13.19	13.47	13.56	13.55	13.75	13.88	13.82	13.80	13.71	13.58	13.85	13.42	12.35
3	14.57	13.96	13.66	13.66	13.77	13.84	13.86	13.88	13.95	14.11	14.06	13.98	13.94	13.64	13.51	13.19	12.00
4	12.31	12.32	12.46	12.71	12.94	13.09	13.16	13.29	13.46	13.64	13.61	13.48	13.46	13.31	13.04	12.76	12.16

Table 13.A.1 (cont.)

		0 mo	1 mo	2 mo	3 mo	4 mo	5 mo	6 mo	9 mo	1 yr	2 yr	3 yr	4 yr	5 yr	10 yr	15 yr	20 yr	25 yr
1982	5	11.56	11.62	11.72	11.85	12.01	12.14	12.24	12.55	12.87	13.23	13.37	13.45	13.49	13.30	13.22	12.96	12.15
	6	10.65	11.74	12.57	13.12	13.46	13.68	13.81	14.03	14.21	14.32	14.43	14.35	14.27	13.84	13.65	13.25	12.07
	7	8.49	9.15	9.82	10.50	11.08	11.50	11.77	12.26	12.65	12.93	13.31	13.34	13.35	13.28	13.27	13.05	12.18
	8	7.54	7.51	7.78	8.33	8.96	9.48	9.84	10.56	11.17	11.89	12.26	12.34	12.47	12.44	12.23	12.25	11.79
	9	6.88	6.94	7.24	7.77	8.39	8.90	9.23	9.82	10.37	11.21	11.56	11.61	11.65	11.74	11.59	11.40	11.11
	10	7.81	7.72	7.83	8.11	8.41	8.63	8.73	8.97	9.45	10.01	10.52	10.60	10.75	10.87	10.82	10.95	10.41
	11	7.67	7.87	8.11	8.39	8.65	8.81	8.87	8.95	9.32	9.84	10.33	10.52	10.71	10.97	10.96	11.19	10.65
	12	8.05	8.07	8.11	8.17	8.25	8.31	8.34	8.45	8.79	9.45	9.92	10.17	10.33	10.59	10.67	10.79	10.37
1983	1	8.01	8.07	8.15	8.26	8.38	8.46	8.52	8.67	8.96	9.60	10.09	10.32	10.55	11.04	11.18	11.52	11.13
	2	7.90	7.91	7.96	8.06	8.17	8.23	8.24	8.28	8.61	9.20	9.70	9.78	9.86	10.36	10.63	11.08	10.35
	3	8.36	8.56	8.72	8.86	8.95	9.01	9.02	9.06	9.25	9.73	10.01	10.18	10.31	10.64	10.83	11.00	10.45
	4	8.01	8.10	8.19	8.28	8.35	8.39	8.41	8.49	8.72	9.23	9.63	9.81	9.97	10.32	10.52	10.69	10.15
	5	8.38	8.56	8.71	8.83	8.93	9.00	9.05	9.16	9.32	9.89	10.36	10.36	10.52	10.86	11.11	11.22	10.85
	6	8.25	8.57	8.81	8.98	9.09	9.18	9.24	9.39	9.58	10.13	10.40	10.57	10.69	11.53	11.21	11.82	10.72
	7	8.63	8.95	9.22	9.43	9.60	9.72	9.81	10.04	10.35	10.98	11.15	11.35	11.53	11.78	11.84	12.08	11.59
	8	8.74	9.01	9.46	9.46	9.65	9.80	9.91	10.13	10.36	11.01	11.35	11.56	11.69	11.79	11.89	11.53	11.44
	9	8.77	8.77	8.83	8.92	9.04	9.15	9.24	9.48	9.70	10.36	10.66	10.92	11.13	11.38	11.43	11.81	10.94
	10	8.46	8.49	8.58	8.72	8.87	9.01	9.12	9.38	9.62	10.38	10.83	11.10	11.29	11.64	11.77	11.53	11.37
	11	8.17	8.58	8.88	9.07	9.19	9.28	9.37	9.58	9.71	10.44	10.69	11.09	11.26	11.47	11.55	11.62	11.14
	12	8.18	8.63	8.97	9.20	9.33	9.42	9.50	9.71	9.89	10.63	10.93	11.25	11.43	11.66	11.74	11.85	11.36
1984	1	8.87	8.94	9.02	9.10	9.18	9.25	9.32	9.49	9.63	10.39	10.69	11.03	11.20	11.53	11.58	11.69	11.45
	2	8.45	8.86	9.17	9.37	9.51	9.60	9.68	9.85	9.98	10.77	11.05	11.43	11.61	11.85	11.91	12.06	11.85
	3	9.22	9.50	9.76	9.97	10.12	10.22	10.27	10.39	10.61	11.30	11.58	11.91	12.07	12.31	12.21	12.29	12.16
	4	9.26	9.49	9.73	9.96	10.15	10.27	10.34	10.53	10.81	11.56	11.89	12.17	12.34	12.60	12.52	12.64	12.44
	5	9.65	9.56	9.69	10.04	10.46	10.79	11.01	11.43	11.93	12.69	13.29	13.31	13.40	13.62	13.43	13.26	13.25
	6	9.84	9.39	9.84	10.18	10.47	10.73	10.98	11.60	11.99	12.85	13.09	13.31	13.51	13.51	13.26	13.23	13.31
	7	9.67	10.03	10.33	10.57	10.76	10.91	11.03	11.32	11.63	12.29	12.34	12.44	12.52	12.65	12.56	12.59	12.24
	8	10.78	10.74	10.76	10.82	10.92	11.02	11.13	11.41	11.67	12.21	12.28	12.41	12.49	12.47	12.35	12.14	12.29
	9	10.52	10.44	10.44	10.50	10.60	10.69	10.76	10.83	11.16	11.77	11.93	12.14	12.15	12.15	12.00	11.88	11.74
	10	8.07	8.57	8.96	9.25	9.44	9.57	9.65	9.83	10.15	10.89	11.13	11.28	11.39	11.55	11.48	11.41	11.21
	11	7.47	8.00	8.38	8.62	8.77	8.88	8.99	9.29	9.53	10.31	10.69	10.96	11.23	11.43	11.49	11.60	11.20
	12	6.30	7.23	7.84	8.13	8.19	8.25	8.37	8.81	9.13	9.93	10.44	10.76	11.11	11.46	11.55	11.59	11.20
1985	1	7.29	7.73	8.03	8.19	8.27	8.35	8.44	8.73	8.98	9.76	10.22	10.53	10.78	11.12	11.31	11.18	10.93
	2	6.77	7.67	8.32	8.71	8.91	9.04	9.13	9.36	9.65	10.46	10.93	11.24	11.50	11.86	12.03	11.96	11.87

	0 mo	1 mo	2 mo	3 mo	4 mo	5 mo	6 mo	9 mo	1 yr	2 yr	3 yr	4 yr	5 yr	10 yr	15 yr	20 yr	25 yr
3	7.67	8.04	8.32	8.51	8.66	8.77	8.87	9.14	9.42	10.30	10.68	11.03	11.28	11.59	11.73	11.84	11.39
4	7.24	7.52	7.76	7.98	8.16	8.30	8.39	8.62	8.94	9.79	10.28	10.60	10.90	11.40	11.61	11.71	11.46
5	6.69	7.00	7.20	7.32	7.39	7.43	7.48	7.67	8.01	8.84	9.31	9.58	9.86	10.33	10.82	10.80	10.62
6	6.49	6.72	6.90	7.03	7.13	7.20	7.25	7.45	7.75	8.64	9.16	9.56	9.85	10.29	10.65	10.91	10.35
7	6.82	7.06	7.25	7.40	7.51	7.60	7.66	7.84	8.09	8.98	9.51	9.91	10.17	10.65	10.99	11.11	10.67
8	6.35	7.24	7.22	7.27	7.36	7.46	7.55	7.76	7.93	8.80	9.33	9.58	9.80	10.33	10.90	10.82	10.07
9	7.02	7.11	7.19	7.26	7.31	7.38	7.44	7.70	7.81	8.74	9.00	9.54	9.85	10.46	11.02	10.98	10.38
10	6.95	7.16	7.30	7.35	7.39	7.44	7.51	7.68	7.81	8.58	9.00	9.22	9.53	10.08	10.73	10.47	9.57
11	5.66	6.59	7.16	7.38	7.40	7.41	7.46	7.65	7.75	8.32	8.65	8.97	9.24	9.59	10.12	10.31	9.79
12	5.19	6.24	6.90	7.17	7.23	7.26	7.30	7.42	7.50	7.88	8.22	8.39	8.56	9.02	9.60	9.82	9.35
1986																	
1	6.38	6.81	7.06	7.16	7.19	7.22	7.27	7.40	7.48	7.92	8.19	8.46	8.66	9.28	9.78	9.56	8.90
2	6.51	6.89	7.12	7.20	7.20	7.20	7.29	7.29	7.33	7.65	7.76	7.90	8.02	8.12	8.47	8.53	8.27
3	6.73	6.58	6.49	6.46	6.47	6.47	6.47	6.56	6.72	6.92	7.06	7.24	7.32	7.43	7.61	7.88	7.90
4	5.82	5.98	6.10	6.18	6.23	6.27	6.30	6.39	6.49	6.91	7.07	7.22	7.31	7.48	7.73	8.11	8.11
5	5.96	6.23	6.34	6.43	6.50	6.55	6.60	6.71	6.87	7.39	7.76	7.98	8.02	8.21	8.49	9.03	8.95
6	5.08	6.01	6.06	6.11	6.15	6.17	6.17	6.23	6.41	6.86	7.15	7.30	7.37	7.49	7.90	8.67	8.63
7	4.37	5.50	5.77	5.88	5.92	5.93	5.94	6.03	6.18	6.61	6.89	7.10	7.22	7.64	8.22	8.69	8.34
8	5.14	4.86	5.15	5.24	5.23	5.23	5.26	5.40	5.48	5.99	6.25	6.51	6.65	7.35	7.79	8.11	7.88
9	4.65	5.14	5.26	5.32	5.38	5.45	5.53	5.70	5.82	6.44	6.79	7.07	7.24	7.86	8.38	8.73	8.47
10	5.06	5.03	5.24	5.30	5.32	5.36	5.41	5.57	5.69	6.20	6.51	6.76	6.93	7.64	8.23	8.33	7.84
11	4.07	5.24	5.37	5.46	5.51	5.54	5.56	5.61	5.70	6.13	6.40	6.60	6.74	7.28	8.01	8.53	8.16
12		5.00	5.57	5.80	5.81	5.78	5.77	5.82	5.95	6.37	6.70	6.70	6.81	7.33	8.03	8.62	8.32
1987																	
1	5.23	5.51	5.67	5.70	5.70	5.71	5.74	5.84	5.88	6.25	6.46	6.63	6.78	7.35	7.94	8.33	8.04
2	5.44	5.49	5.53	5.55	5.58	5.61	5.65	5.77	5.89	6.29	6.48	6.64	6.76	7.27	7.82	8.20	7.98

Table 13.A.2.

McCulloch instantaneous forward rate data, continuous compounding, end of month data, 12/46–2/87

1946

	0 mo	1 mo	2 mo	3 mo	4 mo	5 mo	6 mo	9 mo	1 yr	2 yr	3 yr	4 yr	5 yr	10 yr	15 yr	20 yr	25 yr
12	0.18	0.45	0.57	0.61	0.65	0.70	0.74	0.87	0.98	1.38	1.66	1.83	1.94	2.53	3.05	2.26	

1947

	0 mo	1 mo	2 mo	3 mo	4 mo	5 mo	6 mo	9 mo	1 yr	2 yr	3 yr	4 yr	5 yr	10 yr	15 yr	20 yr	25 yr
1	0.16	0.45	0.58	0.62	0.66	0.70	0.74	0.86	0.96	1.34	1.61	1.79	1.93	2.57	3.01	2.49	
2	0.19	0.44	0.56	0.60	0.65	0.69	0.74	0.86	0.98	1.37	1.65	1.81	1.93	2.52	3.00	2.49	
3	0.13	0.47	0.62	0.66	0.69	0.73	0.76	0.87	0.96	1.30	1.57	1.76	1.91	2.55	2.93	2.60	
4	0.08	0.49	0.65	0.69	0.73	0.77	0.81	0.92	1.03	1.39	1.64	1.78	1.88	2.52	2.98	2.49	
5	0.00	0.52	0.74	0.78	0.81	0.84	0.87	0.96	1.05	1.35	1.58	1.75	1.94	2.59	3.00	2.45	
6	0.00	0.53	0.71	0.75	0.78	0.82	0.85	0.96	1.05	1.39	1.64	1.80	1.87	2.59	3.07	2.15	
7	0.06	0.64	0.85	0.88	0.91	0.94	0.97	1.05	1.13	1.40	1.59	1.73	1.81	2.60	3.17	1.80	
8	0.16	0.82	1.07	1.08	1.09	1.09	1.10	1.11	1.14	1.25	1.40	1.60	1.86	2.68	3.09	1.79	
9	0.52	0.92	1.08	1.09	1.09	1.10	1.13	1.13	1.16	1.29	1.45	1.66	1.97	2.69	3.01	2.03	
10	0.45	0.96	1.17	1.18	1.19	1.21	1.22	1.26	1.30	1.46	1.63	1.80	2.10	2.73	3.08	1.70	
11	0.60	0.99	1.15	1.17	1.19	1.21	1.23	1.28	1.33	1.54	1.74	1.93	2.31	2.81	2.99	2.06	
12	0.93	0.89	0.91	0.96	1.01	1.06	1.11	1.24	1.36	1.76	2.00	2.16		2.80	2.85		

1948

	0 mo	1 mo	2 mo	3 mo	4 mo	5 mo	6 mo	9 mo	1 yr	2 yr	3 yr	4 yr	5 yr	10 yr	15 yr	20 yr	25 yr
1	1.04	0.90	0.88	0.93	0.98	1.02	1.07	1.21	1.34	1.76	2.02	2.18	2.32	2.80	2.86		
2	1.02	0.93	0.93	0.97	1.02	1.06	1.10	1.23	1.34	1.73	1.98	2.14	2.29	2.82	2.88		
3	1.00	0.96	0.98	1.02	1.06	1.10	1.14	1.24	1.35	1.69	1.93	2.11	2.27	2.86	2.94		
4	0.98	0.99	1.01	1.05	1.09	1.12	1.15	1.26	1.35	1.66	1.88	2.07	2.25	2.91	2.97		
5	0.97	1.01	1.03	1.06	1.08	1.10	1.16	1.19	1.25	1.49	1.72	1.94	2.14	2.95	3.01		
6	0.95	1.00	1.04	1.07	1.10	1.13	1.16	1.24	1.33	1.62	1.85	2.07	2.27	2.85	2.93		
7	1.02	0.97	0.98	1.03	1.07	1.12	1.21	1.28	1.39	1.73	1.94	2.13	2.29	2.81	2.85		
8	1.13	1.02	1.01	1.06	1.11	1.16	1.26	1.34	1.46	1.80	1.99	2.15	2.30	2.81	2.84		
9	1.09	1.08	1.11	1.15	1.20	1.24	1.28	1.40	1.51	1.81	1.98	2.13	2.28	2.78	2.86		
10	1.11	1.07	1.09	1.14	1.19	1.24	1.29	1.43	1.54	1.86	2.03	2.18	2.31	2.81	2.81		
11	1.10	1.10	1.13	1.17	1.21	1.25	1.28	1.39	1.48	1.76	1.94	2.12	2.28	2.88	2.88		
12	1.06	1.15	1.19	1.22	1.24	1.26	1.28	1.35	1.41	1.65	1.87	2.07	2.25	2.90			

1949

	0 mo	1 mo	2 mo	3 mo	4 mo	5 mo	6 mo	9 mo	1 yr	2 yr	3 yr	4 yr	5 yr	10 yr	15 yr	20 yr	25 yr
1	1.09	1.16	1.19	1.21	1.22	1.24	1.25	1.30	1.35	1.57	1.80	2.01	2.21	2.92	2.89		
2	1.16	1.12	1.13	1.15	1.18	1.20	1.23	1.30	1.37	1.61	1.82	2.01	2.19	2.86	2.87		
3	1.03	1.18	1.23	1.24	1.25	1.26	1.27	1.30	1.33	1.51	1.73	1.94	2.14	2.92	2.90		
4	1.10	1.14	1.17	1.18	1.20	1.21	1.23	1.28	1.33	1.53	1.75	1.95	2.14	2.93	2.92		
5	1.00	1.17	1.23	1.24	1.24	1.25	1.25	1.27	1.30	1.47	1.69	1.92	2.13	2.95	2.94		
6	0.81	1.18	1.27	1.25	1.23	1.21	1.20	1.16	1.14	1.23	1.52	1.79	2.04	2.95	2.87		
7	0.80	1.09	1.16	1.14	1.13	1.11	1.10	1.08	1.07	1.21	1.51	1.79	2.04	2.89	2.81		

1950

	0 mo	1 mo	2 mo	3 mo	4 mo	5 mo	6 mo	9 mo	1 yr	2 yr	3 yr	4 yr	5 yr	10 yr	15 yr	20 yr	25 yr
8	0.86	1.07	1.14	1.13	1.12	1.11	1.10	1.09	1.10	1.22	1.47	1.71	1.93	2.83	2.84		
9	0.88	1.11	1.16	1.14	1.13	1.11	1.10	1.07	1.06	1.20	1.48	1.74	1.98	2.79	2.80		
10	0.82	1.11	1.17	1.15	1.14	1.13	1.16	1.09	1.09	1.23	1.50	1.74	1.97	2.77	2.80		
11	0.82	1.16	1.25	1.22	1.20	1.18	1.13	1.13	1.10	1.22	1.48	1.73	1.96	2.76	2.77		
12	0.93	1.12	1.15	1.15	1.14	1.13	1.12	1.11	1.12	1.24	1.48	1.69	1.90	2.70	2.77		

1951

	0 mo	1 mo	2 mo	3 mo	4 mo	5 mo	6 mo	9 mo	1 yr	2 yr	3 yr	4 yr	5 yr	10 yr	15 yr	20 yr	25 yr
1	0.97	1.15	1.20	1.19	1.17	1.16	1.15	1.13	1.13	1.28	1.55	1.80	2.03	2.77	2.73	2.76	
2	1.00	1.18	1.24	1.22	1.20	1.19	1.17	1.14	1.13	1.27	1.56	1.82	2.06	2.82	2.70	2.81	
3	0.89	1.24	1.32	1.29	1.27	1.24	1.22	1.18	1.15	1.30	1.58	1.85	2.09	2.86	2.71	2.08	
4	0.92	1.30	1.34	1.32	1.30	1.28	1.27	1.23	1.22	1.37	1.63	1.88	2.10	2.91	2.67	2.26	
5	0.93	1.30	1.39	1.36	1.33	1.30	1.28	1.22	1.19	1.33	1.62	1.89	2.13	2.91	2.62	2.29	
6	0.90	1.39	1.48	1.36	1.34	1.32	1.30	1.27	1.25	1.42	1.69	1.94	2.16	3.01	2.60	2.82	
7	0.86	1.43	1.52	1.48	1.39	1.34	1.37	1.22	1.17	1.33	1.64	1.92	2.17	2.98	2.54	2.24	
8	1.00	1.44	1.52	1.49	1.44	1.40	1.44	1.31	1.27	1.43	1.69	1.93	2.15	2.97	2.58	2.16	
9	1.10	1.49	1.60	1.55	1.47	1.45	1.44	1.40	1.39	1.56	1.78	1.98	2.18	2.92	2.51	2.39	
10	0.81	1.46	1.57	1.71	1.57	1.56	1.50	1.53	1.54	1.69	1.88	2.05	2.21	2.92	2.46	2.72	
11	1.05	1.65	1.82	1.81	1.53	1.51	1.84	1.47	1.47	1.66	1.88	2.09	2.28	3.11	3.02		
12	0.79	1.82	1.92	1.93	1.66	1.61	1.96	1.48	1.44	1.61	1.84	2.06	2.26	3.00	3.02		

1952

	0 mo	1 mo	2 mo	3 mo	4 mo	5 mo	6 mo	9 mo	1 yr	2 yr	3 yr	4 yr	5 yr	10 yr	15 yr	20 yr	25 yr
1	0.94	1.63	1.78	1.79	1.80	1.81	1.83	1.86	1.90	2.06	2.23	2.40	2.55	3.07	3.10	2.42	
2	0.90	1.67	1.81	1.83	1.85	1.87	1.89	1.94	1.99	2.20	2.39	2.57	2.73	3.16	2.96	2.50	
3	1.10	1.58	1.71	1.73	1.76	1.78	1.80	1.86	1.92	2.14	2.31	2.45	2.58	3.08	3.21	2.44	
4	1.39	1.73	1.81	1.81	1.82	1.82	1.85	1.85	1.88	2.00	2.16	2.30	2.49	2.95	3.04	2.41	
5	1.43	1.80	1.87	1.88	1.89	1.90	1.90	1.93	1.95	2.06	2.18	2.31	2.42	2.86	2.89	2.66	
6	1.65	1.82	1.88	1.90	1.92	1.94	1.96	2.02	2.07	2.23	2.34	2.39	2.44	2.82	3.05	2.53	
7	1.72	1.87	1.94	1.96	1.98	2.00	2.02	2.09	2.15	2.33	2.44	2.48	2.52	2.74	2.95	2.72	
8	1.46	1.90	2.02	2.05	2.07	2.09	2.11	2.18	2.23	2.42	2.53	2.57	2.61	2.83	3.05	2.55	
9	1.06	1.78	2.02	2.04	2.06	2.07	2.09	2.15	2.20	2.39	2.54	2.67	2.78	3.11	2.98	2.71	

Table 13.A.2 (cont.)

1952

	0 mo	1 mo	2 mo	3 mo	4 mo	5 mo	6 mo	9 mo	1 yr	2 yr	3 yr	4 yr	5 yr	10 yr	15 yr	20 yr	25 yr
10	1.32	1.80	1.96	1.98	2.00	2.02	2.04	2.10	2.15	2.33	2.45	2.52	2.59	2.88	3.02	2.81	
11	1.55	1.97	2.11	2.13	2.14	2.15	2.16	2.20	2.23	2.35	2.42	2.47	2.53	2.88	3.11	2.81	
12	1.82	2.04	2.12	2.14	2.15	2.17	2.18	2.22	2.26	2.38	2.45	2.49	2.55	2.97	3.28		

1953

	0 mo	1 mo	2 mo	3 mo	4 mo	5 mo	6 mo	9 mo	1 yr	2 yr	3 yr	4 yr	5 yr	10 yr	15 yr	20 yr	25 yr
1	1.63	1.97	2.06	2.07	2.08	2.10	2.11	2.15	2.19	2.35	2.48	2.61	2.72	3.05	3.11		
2	1.86	2.15	2.22	2.22	2.22	2.23	2.23	2.24	2.26	2.35	2.48	2.64	2.77	3.18	3.23		
3	1.95	2.02	2.06	2.08	2.10	2.12	2.14	2.19	2.25	2.44	2.59	2.71	2.82	3.19	3.28	3.29	3.53
4	1.78	2.29	2.44	2.45	2.47	2.48	2.49	2.53	2.57	2.71	2.84	2.97	3.07	3.48	3.26	2.95	3.33
5	1.43	2.33	2.59	2.62	2.64	2.67	2.69	2.76	2.83	3.06	3.24	3.35	3.44	3.27	3.07	3.14	3.76
6	1.18	1.96	2.31	2.34	2.36	2.38	2.40	2.47	2.52	2.73	2.90	3.02	3.12	3.26	3.05	3.34	
7	1.72	2.11	2.23	2.26	2.28	2.31	2.33	2.40	2.47	2.71	2.89	3.01	3.11	3.31	3.15	3.52	
8	1.62	1.93	2.04	2.09	2.14	2.19	2.19	2.36	2.49	2.88	3.11	3.01	3.26	2.92	3.17	3.77	
9	0.86	1.52	1.82	1.88	1.92	1.97	2.01	2.13	2.23	2.56	2.72	2.79	2.73	3.31	3.29	3.33	
10	0.65	1.25	1.52	1.58	1.64	1.69	1.75	1.90	2.05	2.49	2.72	2.79	2.84	2.92	3.31	3.20	
11	1.36	1.50	1.59	1.64	1.68	1.73	1.77	1.89	2.01	2.39	2.64	2.77	2.89	3.26	3.37	3.41	
12	1.09	1.38	1.52	1.56	1.61	1.65	1.69	1.81	1.91	2.24	2.40	2.47	2.55	2.97	3.30		

1954

	0 mo	1 mo	2 mo	3 mo	4 mo	5 mo	6 mo	9 mo	1 yr	2 yr	3 yr	4 yr	5 yr	10 yr	15 yr	20 yr	25 yr
1	1.05	0.89	0.90	0.97	1.05	1.12	1.19	1.39	1.57	2.12	2.40	2.55	2.68	3.03	3.17	3.24	
2	0.84	0.92	0.98	1.01	1.05	1.09	1.23	1.23	1.34	1.78	2.23	2.62	2.89	2.77	2.64	3.13	
3	0.99	0.98	1.00	1.03	1.06	1.10	1.13	1.23	1.34	1.75	2.17	2.53	2.79	2.82	2.77	3.08	
4	0.62	0.72	0.78	0.80	0.89	0.95	1.00	1.14	1.27	1.64	1.96	2.30	2.62	2.90	2.78	3.01	
5	0.51	0.67	0.74	0.67	0.85	0.91	0.96	1.13	1.29	1.92	2.42	2.73	2.90	2.84	2.57	2.99	
6	0.67	0.59	0.61	0.79	0.73	0.79	0.84	1.01	1.17	1.71	2.15	2.59	2.83	2.77	2.60	2.94	
7	0.64	0.72	0.76	0.90	0.82	0.86	0.89	1.01	1.13	1.73	2.15	2.59	2.78	2.79	2.52	2.83	
8	1.30	0.96	0.87	1.03	0.94	0.97	1.01	1.12	1.23	1.72	2.17	2.57	2.88	2.73	2.53	2.87	
9	0.90	0.91	0.96	1.12	1.09	1.15	1.20	1.36	1.50	1.87	2.15	2.50	2.83	2.70	2.70	2.96	
10	0.72	0.95	1.06	1.12	1.17	1.23	1.23	1.43	1.58	2.07	2.43	2.63	2.73	2.91	2.87	2.93	
11	0.86	0.99	1.07	1.10	1.17	1.21	1.26	1.40	1.54	2.08	2.49	2.68	2.75	2.86	2.91	2.80	
12	0.92	0.98	1.04			1.23	1.29	1.47	1.64	2.22	2.59	2.72	2.74			2.69	

1955

	0 mo	1 mo	2 mo	3 mo	4 mo	5 mo	6 mo	9 mo	1 yr	2 yr	3 yr	4 yr	5 yr	10 yr	15 yr	20 yr	25 yr
1	1.19	1.04	1.08	1.19	1.29	1.39	1.48	1.73	1.95	2.38	2.53	2.66	2.79	3.14	2.98	2.82	2.83
2	0.91	1.33	1.51	1.60	1.70	1.78	1.87	2.09	2.27	2.63	2.63	2.70	2.79	3.07	3.04	2.98	2.98
3	1.33	1.34	1.41	1.51	1.61	1.71	1.80	2.04	2.24	2.61	2.66	2.73	2.80	3.02	2.97	2.91	2.94
4	1.44	1.55	1.65	1.74	1.82	1.90	1.98	2.18	2.35	2.64	2.67	2.74	2.84	3.09	2.95	2.81	2.81
5	0.91	1.36	1.60	1.69	1.77	1.85	1.92	2.13	2.29	2.62	2.74	2.81	2.85	2.97	2.90	2.86	2.90
6	1.04	1.47	1.68	1.77	1.85	1.93	2.01	2.22	2.39	2.75	2.89	2.96	3.00	3.06	2.89	2.76	2.77

Maturity	7	8	9	10	11	12
25 yr	2.78	2.94	2.99	2.99	3.01	2.85
20 yr	2.80	2.90	2.94	2.93	2.98	2.82
15 yr	2.94	2.92	2.94	2.94	2.97	2.88
10 yr	3.13	2.99	2.96	2.93	2.97	2.97
5 yr	3.12	3.05	3.03	2.86	2.89	2.93
4 yr	3.10	3.06	3.05	2.86	2.87	2.91
3 yr	3.04	3.06	3.02	2.83	2.86	2.90
2 yr	2.92	3.00	2.81	2.76	2.91	2.93
1 yr	2.59	2.74	2.46	2.56	2.90	2.92
9 mo	2.43	2.60	2.37	2.45	2.83	2.85
6 mo	2.22	2.45	2.27	2.32	2.74	2.76
5 mo	2.15	2.39	2.24	2.28	2.71	2.72
4 mo	2.07	2.32	2.21	2.23	2.67	2.68
3 mo	1.99	2.26	2.18	2.12	2.63	2.63
2 mo	1.90	2.19	2.14	2.12	2.59	2.59
1 mo	1.77	2.05	2.13	2.07	2.36	2.50
0 mo	1.56	1.83	2.16	2.03	1.80	2.34

1956

Maturity	1	2	3	4	5	6	7	8	9	10	11	12
25 yr	2.94	2.95	2.81	3.12	3.16	2.95	2.99	2.99	3.57	3.25	2.94	
20 yr	2.88	2.90	2.80	3.08	3.09	2.91	2.97	2.78	2.95	3.09	3.08	
15 yr	2.88	2.91	3.03	3.03	2.97	2.90	2.93	3.03	3.01	2.91	3.12	3.33
10 yr	2.91	2.93	3.05	2.99	2.84	2.91	3.01	3.13	3.23	3.23	3.26	3.60
5 yr	2.88	2.87	3.10	3.00	2.88	3.02	3.23	3.45	3.30	3.55	3.46	3.75
4 yr	2.86	2.85	3.10	3.01	2.91	3.05	3.29	3.54	3.31	3.55	3.51	3.70
3 yr	2.83	2.82	3.11	3.06	2.95	3.07	3.35	3.63	3.37	3.53	3.57	3.62
2 yr	2.74	2.80	3.30	3.01	3.04	3.43	3.69	3.57	3.55	3.69	3.64	
1 yr	2.58	2.74	2.56	3.39	3.03	2.93	3.45	3.70	3.62	3.90	3.88	
9 mo	2.52	2.68	2.99	3.26	2.99	2.84	3.29	3.56	3.57	3.58	3.96	3.97
6 mo	2.45	2.60	2.77	3.07	2.91	2.72	3.02	3.33	3.40	3.44	3.90	4.07
5 mo	2.43	2.57	2.69	3.00	2.88	2.67	2.91	3.22	3.36	3.36	3.81	4.05
4 mo	2.41	2.53	2.59	2.91	2.85	2.62	2.79	3.11	3.24	3.28	3.69	3.93
3 mo	2.38	2.49	2.82	2.82	2.81	2.65	2.99	3.16	3.19	3.53	3.71	
2 mo	2.36	2.45	2.39	2.73	2.77	2.51	2.51	2.85	3.06	3.09	3.34	3.40
1 mo	2.31	2.26	2.27	2.65	2.58	2.41	2.26	2.62	2.87	2.81	3.04	3.10
0 mo	2.24	1.60	2.81	2.61	2.13	2.24	1.88	2.12	2.50	2.27	2.53	3.10

1957

Maturity	1	2	3	4	5	6	7	8	9	10	11	12
25 yr	4.28	3.23	4.03	4.48	4.35	5.44	5.44	5.40	4.31	3.87	0.74	
20 yr	3.25	3.10	2.80	3.08	3.09	2.99	3.17	3.36	3.03	2.95	3.63	3.24
15 yr	2.95	3.14	3.17	2.99	2.92	2.78	2.77	2.95	3.03	3.03	3.37	3.49
10 yr	3.06	3.25	3.17	3.27	3.38	3.51	3.37	3.40	3.80	3.74	3.56	3.43
5 yr	3.27	3.36	3.40	3.60	3.84	4.13	4.16	3.98	3.97	3.90	3.23	3.06
4 yr	3.26	3.36	3.40	3.59	3.79	3.98	4.06	3.81	3.82	3.86	3.32	2.96
3 yr	3.23	3.35	3.40	3.57	3.71	3.77	3.88	3.54	3.78	3.86	3.43	2.86
2 yr	3.21	3.38	3.47	3.61	3.65	3.72	3.84	3.64	4.02	3.99	3.49	2.79
1 yr	3.28	3.48	3.61	3.71	3.64	3.87	3.95	4.16	4.22	4.22	3.53	2.74
9 mo	3.31	3.52	3.57	3.66	3.61	3.90	3.99	4.44	4.20	4.20	3.54	2.75
6 mo	3.34	3.56	3.49	3.49	3.53	3.82	3.92	4.35	4.12	4.10	3.55	2.77
5 mo	3.34	3.56	3.35	3.41	3.49	3.76	3.87	4.28	4.05	4.05	3.55	2.79
4 mo	3.32	3.55	3.27	3.31	3.45	3.69	3.80	4.18	4.17	3.98	3.56	2.80
3 mo	3.27	3.52	3.35	3.21	3.40	3.72	4.00	4.09	3.91	3.56	2.81	
2 mo	3.19	3.47	3.17	3.09	3.35	3.52	3.63	3.86	3.98	3.82	3.55	2.82
1 mo	3.09	3.33	2.96	3.01	3.27	3.31	3.38	3.52	3.60	3.58	3.11	2.78
0 mo	3.05	2.39	2.81	3.05	3.14	2.81	2.66	2.50	2.78	3.10	2.06	2.66

1958

Maturity	1	2	3	4	5	6	7
25 yr	3.71	3.53	3.61	3.50	3.21	3.35	3.76
20 yr	3.41	3.42	3.76	3.55	3.20	3.43	4.13
15 yr	3.39	3.45	3.68	3.51	3.38	3.54	4.00
10 yr	3.54	3.57	3.43	3.41	3.66	3.65	3.58
5 yr	3.28	3.24	3.06	3.06	3.12	3.19	3.54
4 yr	3.17	3.09	2.97	2.95	2.86	3.03	3.64
3 yr	3.06	2.91	2.85	2.74	2.59	2.92	3.52
2 yr	2.98	2.65	2.68	2.39	2.34	2.82	3.00
1 yr	2.83	2.31	2.27	1.84	1.98	2.03	2.10
9 mo	2.59	2.15	2.01	1.66	1.74	1.70	1.81
6 mo	2.20	1.87	1.70	1.46	1.41	1.31	1.50
5 mo	2.05	1.76	1.58	1.40	1.28	1.17	1.39
4 mo	1.87	1.63	1.45	1.33	1.14	1.02	1.28
3 mo	1.68	1.49	1.31	1.26	1.00	0.87	1.17
2 mo	1.48	1.34	1.17	1.18	0.84	0.71	1.05
1 mo	1.41	1.19	1.04	1.14	0.55	0.69	0.85
0 mo	1.53	1.10	0.94	1.18	0.00	0.84	0.54

Table 13.A.2 (cont.)

		0 mo	1 mo	2 mo	3 mo	4 mo	5 mo	6 mo	9 mo	1 yr	2 yr	3 yr	4 yr	5 yr	10 yr	15 yr	20 yr	25 yr
1958	8	1.35	2.30	2.68	2.78	2.87	2.96	3.05	3.28	3.48	3.92	3.95	3.94	3.90	3.75	3.68	3.67	3.79
	9	1.00	2.73	3.48	3.52	3.52	3.51	3.52	3.35	3.55	3.76	3.96	3.96	3.88	3.66	3.66	3.79	4.16
	10	1.08	2.43	2.98	3.04	3.10	3.15	3.20	3.35	3.48	3.80	3.91	3.91	3.85	3.66	3.63	3.71	4.04
	11	0.83	2.78	3.55	3.56	3.55	3.54	3.54	3.53	3.53	3.64	3.75	3.74	3.71	3.65	3.70	3.80	3.96
	12	2.13	2.66	2.93	3.06	3.16	3.24	3.29	3.41	3.53	3.89	4.07	4.11	4.08	3.87	3.64	3.58	3.93
1959	1	2.32	2.61	2.92	3.19	3.38	3.48	3.55	3.72	3.87	4.21	4.22	4.16	4.09	3.94	4.07	4.08	3.88
	2	2.04	2.68	3.09	3.32	3.45	3.49	3.53	3.62	3.70	3.91	3.97	3.90	3.83	3.90	4.27	4.42	4.09
	3	2.44	2.70	3.04	3.43	3.67	3.77	3.80	3.90	3.98	4.10	4.12	4.08	4.02	3.95	3.99	4.02	4.06
	4	2.78	2.76	3.02	3.43	3.68	3.76	3.80	3.90	3.99	4.27	4.40	4.40	4.35	4.09	3.81	3.68	3.92
	5	2.80	2.89	3.10	3.76	4.20	4.28	4.23	4.11	4.05	4.24	4.43	4.38	4.30	4.03	3.91	3.85	4.02
	6	2.70	2.79	3.32	3.96	4.37	4.43	4.34	4.16	4.10	4.57	4.75	4.53	4.32	3.91	3.98	3.97	3.96
	7	1.97	2.79	3.39	3.85	4.34	4.79	5.10	5.07	4.68	4.17	4.82	4.90	4.68	3.97	3.66	3.59	3.90
	8	3.14	3.78	4.21	4.53	4.77	4.92	4.97	4.73	4.50	4.36	4.89	4.93	4.73	4.01	3.62	3.52	3.99
	9	3.43	3.87	4.48	5.22	5.67	5.68	5.46	4.92	4.55	4.60	4.79	4.68	4.55	3.88	3.67	3.53	3.87
	10	2.14	3.99	4.62	5.12	4.70	4.92	4.95	4.66	4.39	4.19	4.98	5.15	4.86	4.08	3.60	3.53	3.91
	11	2.31	4.49	5.10	5.12	5.15	5.18	5.17	5.05	4.94	4.70	4.69	4.63	4.53	4.08	3.73	3.59	3.93
	12	4.02	4.21	4.80	5.36	5.38	5.27	5.21	5.11	5.02	4.78	4.70	4.69	4.70	4.39	3.85	3.61	4.11
1960	1	3.28	3.81	4.42	4.91	5.04	5.03	4.99	4.85	4.75	4.70	4.81	4.84	4.81	4.07	3.77	5.18	4.40
	2	3.58	4.04	4.53	4.72	4.56	4.40	4.36	4.42	4.47	4.68	4.77	4.64	4.48	4.03	3.91	3.95	3.96
	3	2.40	2.94	3.32	3.57	3.71	3.78	3.82	3.84	3.86	4.07	4.23	4.22	4.18	4.07	4.02	3.97	4.05
	4	2.89	3.04	3.11	3.29	3.72	4.27	4.66	4.84	4.57	4.36	4.74	4.71	4.49	4.10	4.18	4.18	3.71
	5	1.82	3.20	3.52	3.41	3.56	3.89	4.16	4.47	4.40	4.39	4.53	4.41	4.29	4.01	4.31	4.31	3.81
	6	1.25	2.02	2.51	2.79	3.02	3.20	3.36	3.74	3.96	4.36	4.14	4.12	3.95	4.26	3.59	3.32	3.73
	7	1.65	2.02	2.40	2.76	2.96	3.04	3.10	3.23	3.32	3.50	3.55	3.72	4.06	4.11	3.62	3.42	3.73
	8	1.45	2.42	2.99	3.23	3.44	3.18	2.90	2.86	3.07	3.61	3.77	3.92	4.05	4.09	3.73	3.62	4.00
	9	2.69	2.15	2.58	3.27	3.04	3.06	2.92	2.61	2.85	3.64	3.94	4.05	4.15	4.00	3.91	3.85	3.90
	10	1.22	1.96	2.51	2.86	3.04	3.06	3.05	3.09	3.20	3.63	3.96	4.13	4.23	4.09	3.91	3.78	3.77
	11	1.24	2.27	2.84	3.01	3.09	3.11	3.14	3.24	3.38	3.83	4.11	4.23	3.99	4.14	3.96	3.80	3.74
	12	1.87	2.17	2.41	2.57	2.63	2.61	2.61	2.72	2.88	3.41	3.77	3.93		4.06	3.95	3.85	3.81
1961	1	1.88	2.19	2.44	2.64	2.74	2.77	2.80	3.00	3.22	3.78	3.97	4.03	4.05	4.06	4.01	3.96	3.93
	2	2.47	2.52	2.69	2.87	2.97	3.01	3.05	3.15	3.24	3.55	3.75	3.83	3.87	3.95	3.94	3.90	3.83
	3	2.02	2.35	2.54	2.67	2.81	2.94	3.03	3.07	3.11	3.42	3.85	4.04	4.07	4.05	3.89	3.72	3.62
	4	1.42	2.32	2.49	2.35	2.52	2.87	3.11	3.21	3.19	3.35	3.70	3.88	3.97	4.02	3.85	3.68	3.56

(continuation — previous year, months 5–12)

mo	25 yr	20 yr	15 yr	10 yr	5 yr	4 yr	3 yr	2 yr	1 yr	9 mo	6 mo	5 mo	4 mo	3 mo	2 mo	1 mo	0 mo
5	3.45	3.54	3.76	4.01	4.01	3.93	3.80	3.62	3.33	3.24	3.04	2.90	2.72	2.57	2.49	2.35	2.10
6	3.77	3.84	3.95	4.05	4.09	4.07	4.00	3.85	3.43	3.28	3.06	2.89	2.66	2.47	2.45	2.30	1.80
7	3.72	3.77	3.90	4.05	4.27	4.36	4.34	3.91	3.39	3.27	3.05	2.88	2.65	2.51	2.56	2.23	1.12
8	4.36	3.99	3.96	4.07	4.22	4.26	4.24	3.91	3.40	3.40	3.31	3.18	2.96	2.72	2.52	2.30	1.89
9	4.36	4.22	4.09	4.02	4.02	4.05	4.05	3.83	3.42	3.30	3.16	3.11	3.07	2.89	2.51	2.12	1.74
10	4.50	4.04	3.91	4.02	4.12	4.09	4.02	3.73	3.34	3.25	3.14	3.08	2.98	2.80	2.52	2.16	1.74
11	4.68	3.87	3.83	4.12	4.29	4.20	4.06	3.81	3.40	3.27	3.11	3.05	2.98	2.89	2.78	2.51	2.00
12	4.65	3.87	3.88	4.20	4.34	4.21	4.04	3.84	3.49	3.36	3.20	3.15	3.12	3.06	2.90	2.64	2.32

1962

mo	25 yr	20 yr	15 yr	10 yr	5 yr	4 yr	3 yr	2 yr	1 yr	9 mo	6 mo	5 mo	4 mo	3 mo	2 mo	1 mo	0 mo
1	4.39	3.87	3.92	4.22	4.38	4.31	4.19	3.99	3.63	3.48	3.30	3.22	3.10	2.97	2.89	2.72	2.20
2	4.51	4.00	4.05	4.36	4.38	4.19	3.94	3.66	3.34	3.24	3.15	3.12	3.09	3.03	2.92	2.69	2.24
3	3.95	4.00	4.06	4.19	4.12	4.04	3.89	3.63	3.11	2.91	2.70	2.78	3.04	3.16	2.94	2.66	2.65
4	3.85	3.86	3.99	4.18	4.12	3.97	3.82	3.68	3.28	3.12	3.00	2.98	2.97	2.91	2.81	2.72	2.67
5	3.85	3.83	3.96	4.16	4.24	4.20	3.96	3.48	3.15	3.10	2.96	2.89	2.81	3.05	2.91	2.73	2.91
6	3.90	3.88	4.00	4.16	4.22	4.20	4.06	3.76	3.23	3.06	2.99	3.02	3.06	3.14	2.95	2.90	2.98
7	4.92	4.22	4.07	4.20	4.31	4.28	4.11	3.75	3.47	3.44	3.36	3.30	3.23	3.10	3.02	2.82	2.53
8	4.23	3.98	4.03	4.21	4.29	4.23	3.98	3.41	3.13	3.20	3.25	3.22	3.17	3.10	2.96	2.78	2.88
9	4.08	3.93	4.00	4.18	4.30	4.27	4.02	3.51	3.01	2.92	2.88	2.98	3.11	2.98	2.91	2.72	2.68
10	4.10	3.80	3.90	4.20	4.26	4.14	3.92	3.59	3.03	2.86	2.88	2.94	3.00	3.04	2.87	2.67	2.38
11	4.35	3.81	3.86	4.22	4.18	3.99	3.76	3.50	3.14	3.04	2.99	2.99	2.99	3.04	3.12	2.93	2.35
12	4.66	3.84	3.80	4.20	4.05	3.79	3.65	3.58	3.17	2.99	2.96	3.01	3.08	3.07	2.97	2.92	2.98

1963

mo	25 yr	20 yr	15 yr	10 yr	5 yr	4 yr	3 yr	2 yr	1 yr	9 mo	6 mo	5 mo	4 mo	3 mo	2 mo	1 mo	0 mo
1	4.53	3.99	3.93	4.12	4.19	4.10	3.87	3.52	3.08	2.96	2.94	3.00	3.09	3.11	3.01	2.93	2.95
2	4.07	3.95	4.06	4.23	4.26	4.18	3.97	3.62	3.09	2.92	2.85	2.92	3.02	3.07	2.99	2.88	2.82
3	3.95	3.94	4.04	4.26	4.31	4.22	4.00	3.62	2.96	2.77	3.05	3.28	3.57	3.60	3.21	2.56	1.83
4	4.09	4.09	4.17	4.28	4.20	4.10	3.94	3.69	3.23	3.11	3.10	3.12	3.15	3.21	2.99	2.88	2.83
5	4.09	4.04	4.00	4.22	4.22	4.16	4.01	3.75	3.10	3.08	3.11	3.15	3.22	3.21	3.11	3.00	2.91
6	4.05	4.03	4.12	4.19	4.28	4.25	4.08	3.77	3.25	3.10	3.11	3.16	3.22	3.54	3.09	2.98	2.99
7	3.97	3.97	4.09	4.11	4.18	4.16	4.05	3.83	3.56	3.49	3.50	3.54	3.58	3.57	3.43	3.21	2.88
8	4.02	3.93	4.03	4.09	4.26	4.26	4.06	3.72	3.62	3.68	3.64	3.63	3.60	3.64	3.55	3.41	3.08
9	4.28	3.98	3.99	4.18	4.31	4.28	4.08	3.81	3.73	3.60	3.71	3.68	3.70	3.76	3.46	3.38	3.53
10	4.24	3.93	4.00	4.25	4.36	4.28	4.13	3.93	3.79	3.68	3.79	3.76	3.79	3.82	3.64	3.47	3.25
11	4.24	4.07	4.11	4.23	4.25	4.18	4.06	3.90	3.82	3.77	3.79	3.81	3.84	3.82	3.75	3.50	3.01
12	4.14	4.15	4.21	4.27	4.25	4.21	4.15	4.06	3.94	3.91	3.88	3.87	3.85	3.77	3.61	3.52	3.52

1964

mo	25 yr	20 yr	15 yr	10 yr	5 yr	4 yr	3 yr	2 yr	1 yr	9 mo	6 mo	5 mo	4 mo	3 mo	2 mo	1 mo	0 mo
1	4.09	4.01	4.12	4.31	4.30	4.21	4.11	4.03	3.92	3.89	3.84	3.81	3.78	3.71	3.61	3.49	3.35
2	4.09	3.99	4.10	4.30	4.32	4.24	4.16	4.10	4.02	3.99	3.96	3.96	3.95	3.88	3.71	3.56	3.51
3	4.07	4.08	4.17	4.29	4.31	4.28	4.27	4.29	4.14	4.05	3.96	3.95	3.95	3.85	3.62	3.49	3.57
4	4.13	4.17	4.21	4.23	4.30	4.34	4.31	4.20	4.02	3.97	3.90	3.85	3.79	3.71	3.61	3.44	3.18
5		4.01	4.10	4.27	4.29	4.22	4.13	4.05	4.01	4.01	3.94	3.83	3.69	3.63	3.68	3.52	3.00

Table 13.A.2 (cont.)

	0 mo	1 mo	2 mo	3 mo	4 mo	5 mo	6 mo	9 mo	1 yr	2 yr	3 yr	4 yr	5 yr	10 yr	15 yr	20 yr	25 yr
1964																	
6	3.28	3.59	3.60	3.54	3.63	3.78	3.87	3.88	3.86	3.99	4.19	4.28	4.28	4.21	4.11	4.07	4.16
7	3.02	3.54	3.61	3.60	3.73	3.86	3.93	3.82	3.73	3.94	4.29	4.41	4.39	4.28	4.17	4.11	4.16
8	3.21	3.55	3.65	3.68	3.77	3.89	3.95	3.89	3.84	4.00	4.22	4.32	4.36	4.31	4.18	4.09	4.11
9	3.50	3.56	3.68	3.81	3.91	3.98	4.00	3.95	3.90	3.99	4.12	4.22	4.29	4.30	4.20	4.13	4.15
10	3.39	3.52	3.70	3.88	3.97	3.99	4.00	3.96	3.90	4.02	4.12	4.20	4.26	4.26	4.17	4.10	4.12
11	3.85	3.85	4.07	4.13	4.22	4.30	4.31	4.21	4.14	4.12	4.14	4.17	4.20	4.23	4.21	4.16	4.10
12	3.13	3.90	4.08	4.07	4.12	4.14	4.11	3.99	3.93	4.07	4.19	4.25	4.29	4.30	4.22	4.13	4.07
1965																	
1	3.81	3.89	3.95	4.05	4.19	4.25	4.20	3.97	3.87	4.02	4.15	4.22	4.27	4.28	4.21	4.14	4.10
2	3.61	4.06	4.14	4.13	4.22	4.27	4.25	4.14	4.07	4.03	4.09	4.20	4.29	4.29	4.18	4.10	4.13
3	3.60	3.99	4.08	4.06	4.14	4.21	4.21	4.09	4.04	4.10	4.18	4.22	4.25	4.25	4.20	4.13	4.15
4	3.82	3.94	4.04	4.11	4.15	4.16	4.14	4.06	4.02	4.12	4.19	4.22	4.23	4.24	4.21	4.17	4.14
5	3.74	3.96	4.00	4.01	4.08	4.13	4.14	4.11	4.09	4.08	4.14	4.23	4.31	4.29	4.18	4.11	4.15
6	3.71	3.85	3.91	3.94	3.99	4.03	4.01	3.90	3.88	4.08	4.20	4.25	4.29	4.27	4.20	4.14	4.13
7	3.81	3.83	3.92	4.03	4.07	4.07	4.06	4.01	4.03	4.18	4.26	4.27	4.28	4.26	4.21	4.17	4.16
8	3.70	3.90	4.00	4.08	4.22	4.31	4.28	4.10	4.07	4.21	4.29	4.32	4.34	4.29	4.21	4.18	4.24
9	3.93	3.99	4.19	4.37	4.45	4.44	4.47	4.42	4.39	4.30	4.33	4.42	4.48	4.37	4.20	4.13	4.25
10	3.85	4.00	4.26	4.44	4.46	4.44	4.43	4.41	4.41	4.42	4.47	4.51	4.53	4.37	4.18	4.09	4.20
11	3.67	4.14	4.33	4.40	4.54	4.62	4.59	4.49	4.51	4.60	4.61	4.59	4.58	4.47	4.33	4.19	4.09
12	4.31	4.55	4.62	4.77	5.06	5.20	5.16	5.08	5.13	5.21	5.00	4.76	4.58	4.39	4.30	4.23	4.22
1966																	
1	4.50	4.58	4.85	4.99	4.98	4.95	4.93	4.94	5.04	5.27	5.11	4.90	4.74	4.44	4.26	4.23	4.51
2	4.24	4.70	4.86	4.98	5.16	5.27	5.29	5.31	5.28	5.22	5.32	5.40	5.41	4.75	4.16	4.09	5.01
3	4.19	4.57	4.71	4.85	5.07	5.18	5.15	5.09	5.08	5.03	4.96	4.89	4.82	4.57	4.37	4.33	4.59
4	4.44	4.75	4.71	4.76	5.02	5.16	5.12	5.00	5.14	5.14	4.98	4.97	5.01	4.70	4.37	4.23	4.47
5	4.22	4.72	4.82	4.79	5.14	5.40	5.31	5.10	5.23	5.49	5.04	4.88	4.84	4.67	4.51	4.43	4.54
6	4.09	4.68	4.65	4.72	5.11	5.28	5.17	5.10	5.39	5.76	5.16	5.05	5.06	4.83	4.54	4.33	4.34
7	4.21	4.92	4.91	4.94	5.36	5.53	5.43	5.28	5.41	5.68	5.55	5.44	5.34	4.77	4.29	4.14	4.66
8	5.00	5.22	5.29	5.34	6.31	5.87	6.55	5.96	6.31	6.65	5.91	5.56	5.38	4.92	4.56	4.42	4.71
9	5.24	5.29	5.61	5.87	6.16	6.31	6.23	5.98	5.85	5.54	5.34	5.03	4.77	4.75	4.73	4.53	4.08
10	4.24	5.37	5.63	5.77	6.06	6.14	5.99	5.48	5.62	5.43	5.32	5.15	4.98	4.60	4.31	4.21	4.62
11	3.66	5.32	5.75	5.42	5.50	6.14	5.56	5.48	5.74	5.71	5.00	5.07	5.33	4.89	4.40	4.21	4.64
12	4.60	4.81	5.07	5.25	5.27	5.21	5.09	4.96	4.99	4.98	4.85	4.70	4.60	4.57	4.53	4.48	4.43
1967																	
1	4.37	4.65	4.65	4.60	4.67	4.69	4.65	4.62	4.67	4.75	4.72	4.66	4.61	4.49	4.39	4.35	4.44
2	3.77	4.78	4.70	4.56	4.74	4.78	4.67	4.64	4.94	5.05	4.56	4.69	4.96	4.85	4.64	4.44	4.34
3	3.91	4.11	4.26	4.28	4.18	4.12	4.10	4.11	4.20	4.41	4.44	4.61	4.77	4.76	4.67	4.54	4.36

1968

mo	0 mo	1 mo	2 mo	3 mo	4 mo	5 mo	6 mo	9 mo	1 yr	2 yr	3 yr	4 yr	5 yr	10 yr	15 yr	20 yr	25 yr
4	3.01	3.91	3.87	3.86	4.08	4.17	4.12	4.14	4.41	4.98	4.74	4.92	5.20	5.09	4.86	4.57	4.24
5	3.20	3.46	3.54	3.74	4.17	4.35	4.26	4.16	4.50	5.22	4.55	4.76	5.27	5.10	4.87	4.71	4.77
6	3.32	4.07	4.19	4.33	4.79	5.31	5.63	5.64	5.48	5.29	5.40	5.73	5.81	5.10	4.57	4.61	5.78
7	3.49	4.16	4.34	4.65	5.28	5.53	5.67	5.68	5.37	4.95	5.27	5.58	5.69	5.27	4.88	4.73	5.15
8	3.80	4.31	4.81	5.09	5.33	5.82	5.84	5.63	5.60	5.37	5.37	5.37	5.61	5.19	4.88	4.91	5.67
9	4.34	4.25	4.72	5.37	5.73	6.13	6.12	5.70	5.45	5.38	5.51	5.70	5.71	5.32	4.98	4.88	5.33
10	4.80	4.51	4.87	5.24	5.64	6.39	6.53	5.85	5.67	5.72	5.63	5.77	5.89	5.56	5.24	5.20	5.89
11	4.32	4.87	5.51	5.68	5.99	6.38	6.40	6.04	5.40	5.66	5.88	5.94	5.94	5.78	5.60	5.58	
12	5.98	4.90	5.58	5.99	6.25	6.38	6.40	6.04	5.81	5.92	5.83	5.61	5.61	5.86	5.86	5.37	4.07

1969

mo	0 mo	1 mo	2 mo	3 mo	4 mo	5 mo	6 mo	9 mo	1 yr	2 yr	3 yr	4 yr	5 yr	10 yr	15 yr	20 yr	25 yr
1	4.64	4.84	5.06	5.26	5.36	5.42	5.51	5.77	5.85	5.61	5.65	5.83	5.85	5.70	5.42	5.02	4.55
2	4.37	5.11	5.30	5.39	5.54	5.63	5.64	5.67	5.71	5.84	5.82	5.65	5.63	5.70	5.62	5.28	
3	4.52	5.27	5.48	5.49	5.59	5.72	5.81	5.91	5.98	6.06	5.97	5.86	5.90	6.13	6.03	5.16	
4	5.06	5.56	5.77	5.85	5.95	6.05	6.10	6.07	6.04	6.16	6.13	5.97	5.91	5.71	5.44	4.90	4.99
5	5.20	5.85	5.98	6.04	6.30	6.44	6.39	6.23	6.22	6.01	5.57	5.82	6.08	5.90	5.48	5.10	4.25
6	5.27	5.33	5.47	5.67	5.88	6.83	6.21	6.20	6.13	5.78	5.51	5.76	5.77	5.59	5.35	5.13	4.94
7	4.92	5.24	5.29	5.37	5.64	5.75	5.65	6.44	5.49	5.53	5.60	5.55	5.58	5.49	5.34	5.05	4.88
8	4.60	5.37	5.38	5.26	5.56	5.71	5.61	5.38	5.33	5.38	5.62	5.66	5.68	5.50	5.27	5.36	4.92
9	5.13	5.26	5.31	5.40	5.61	5.71	5.59	5.32	5.39	5.54	5.81	5.71	5.71	5.79	5.65	5.23	4.24
10	5.25	5.44	5.75	5.86	5.75	5.71	5.75	5.75	5.65	5.48	6.36	5.87	5.79	6.03	5.96	5.85	3.93
11	4.32	5.64	5.92	5.85	5.92	6.01	6.05	5.98	5.68	5.56		6.20	5.94	6.33	6.25		2.77
12	5.98	6.27	6.40	6.51	6.77	6.95	6.91	6.65	6.54	6.56			6.23	6.54	6.52		

1970

mo	0 mo	1 mo	2 mo	3 mo	4 mo	5 mo	6 mo	9 mo	1 yr	2 yr	3 yr	4 yr	5 yr	10 yr	15 yr	20 yr	25 yr
1	6.95	8.11	8.22	8.15	8.17	8.09	7.95	7.82	7.93	7.95	7.93	7.89	7.70	6.14	4.97	6.62	3.92
2	6.10	7.10	7.19	7.11	7.00	6.88	6.79	6.76	6.98	7.42	7.29	7.02	6.86	6.08	5.41	6.09	5.28
3	4.66	6.30	6.49	6.87	6.78	6.60	6.58	6.73	6.85	7.21	7.36	7.36	7.08	6.22	8.02	4.64	
4	6.29	6.77	7.32	7.60	7.66	7.57	7.59	7.73	7.82	7.95	7.94	7.30	7.85	7.23	5.96		
5	6.28	6.83	7.31	7.57	7.43	7.26	7.33	7.73	7.95	7.96	7.49	7.33	7.49	7.97			

Table 13.A.2 (cont.)

Year		0 mo	1 mo	2 mo	3 mo	4 mo	5 mo	6 mo	9 mo	1 yr	2 yr	3 yr	4 yr	5 yr	10 yr	15 yr	20 yr	25 yr
1970	6	5.46	6.61	6.77	6.64	6.91	7.26	7.48	7.64	7.73	7.87	7.72	7.63	7.59	7.06			
	7	4.32	7.01	6.69	6.07	6.61	7.28	7.52	7.00	7.99	7.99	7.56	7.46	7.67	7.20			
	8	6.07	6.37	6.44	6.53	6.81	7.17	7.27	6.80	6.82	7.86	7.43	7.35	7.58	7.54			
	9	5.61	5.60	6.23	7.03	7.23	6.95	6.77	6.66	6.63	6.91	7.28	7.49	7.55	7.27			
	10	5.05	5.81	6.26	6.44	6.51	6.51	6.48	6.44	6.49	6.90	7.24	7.40	7.42	7.37			
	11	4.40	5.04	5.28	5.21	5.02	4.95	5.06	5.30	5.42	5.81	6.41	6.85	6.90	6.83	6.26	5.09	
	12	3.98	5.00	5.08	4.99	4.99	4.90	4.80	5.03	5.54	6.18	6.34	6.36	6.46	6.85	6.68	5.14	
1971	1	3.99	4.19	4.18	4.27	4.41	4.31	4.14	4.17	4.57	5.80	6.58	6.91	6.83	6.09	5.55	6.50	
	2	3.13	3.36	3.51	3.66	3.78	3.83	3.84	3.86	4.00	5.40	6.26	6.62	6.68	6.79	6.59	6.01	
	3	3.46	3.50	3.76	3.88	3.76	3.69	3.74	3.92	4.11	4.88	6.60	6.15	6.36	6.20	6.06	6.24	
	4	3.49	4.05	4.15	4.28	4.55	4.75	4.83	4.90	5.16	6.25	6.66	6.71	6.60	5.82			
	5	3.92	4.42	4.49	4.42	4.53	4.73	4.95	5.48	5.74	6.23	6.44	6.65	6.84	6.55			
	6	4.52	5.26	5.22	5.09	5.50	6.15	6.43	6.67	6.32	7.00	6.99	7.02	7.05	6.36			
	7	4.78	5.48	5.31	5.38	6.19	6.72	6.71	6.19	5.74	7.34	7.19	7.10	7.13	6.59			
	8	4.49	4.42	4.35	4.44	5.01	5.59	5.74	5.72	5.74	5.91	6.10	6.28	6.44	6.66	7.81		
	9	4.55	4.46	4.73	5.05	5.28	5.42	5.48	5.57	5.22	5.89	6.29	6.38	6.20	6.07			
	10	3.56	4.42	4.54	4.57	4.65	4.58	4.48	4.65	5.21	5.36	5.83	6.79	6.75	5.82			
	11	3.67	4.37	4.53	4.45	4.60	4.76	4.81	4.99	5.11	5.43	6.13	6.86	6.61	5.63			
	12	3.24	3.47	3.91	4.27	4.47	4.38	4.19	4.53	5.11	5.33	5.73	6.24	6.34	6.53			
1972	1	2.41	3.46	3.52	3.72	4.20	4.31	4.30	4.57	4.94	5.96	6.32	6.44	6.68	7.07			
	2	2.36	3.22	3.51	3.94	4.15	4.27	4.37	4.66	4.95	5.82	6.15	6.36	6.56	6.86			
	3	3.32	3.58	4.20	4.74	4.96	5.07	5.20	5.56	5.79	6.22	6.38	6.43	6.43	6.32			
	4	3.30	3.36	3.89	4.33	4.53	4.64	4.70	4.90	5.13	6.29	6.28	6.21	6.35	6.64			
	5	3.31	3.68	3.97	4.23	4.52	4.75	4.85	4.90	5.02	5.81	6.15	6.32	6.42	6.55			
	6	3.39	3.94	4.33	4.69	5.13	5.48	5.67	5.64	5.64	5.94	6.19	6.36	6.46	6.43			
	7	3.41	3.70	4.00	4.37	4.84	5.25	5.42	5.29	5.33	6.32	6.36	6.29	6.52	6.80			
	8	4.27	4.42	4.56	4.85	5.37	5.81	5.92	5.69	5.65	6.25	6.35	6.47	6.68	6.76			
	9	4.65	4.42	4.81	5.49	5.86	5.98	6.01	5.94	5.94	6.22	6.10	6.22	6.60	7.22			
	10	4.49	4.62	4.94	5.32	5.53	5.62	5.67	5.77	5.89	6.33	6.23	6.26	6.49	6.76			
	11	4.82	4.80	4.96	5.21	5.55	5.75	5.73	5.41	5.40	6.39	6.14	6.10	6.35	6.66			
	12	4.77	5.08	5.38	5.61	5.75	5.79	5.76	5.67	5.76	6.47	6.17	6.20	6.44	6.57			
1973	1	5.22	5.64	5.96	6.14	6.18	6.15	6.14	6.14	6.21	6.63	6.39	6.29	6.35	6.77	7.36	8.39	
	2	5.49	5.71	6.06	6.37	6.44	6.41	6.43	6.63	6.77	6.82	6.67	6.55	6.52	6.50	7.05		
	3	5.77	6.37	6.78	7.07	7.27	7.37	7.32	6.99	6.76	6.55	6.57	6.58	6.56	6.48	6.92		

1974

mo	0 mo	1 mo	2 mo	3 mo	4 mo	5 mo	6 mo	9 mo	1 yr	2 yr	3 yr	4 yr	5 yr	10 yr	15 yr	20 yr	25 yr
4	5.95	6.13	6.59	6.98	7.03	6.95	6.89	6.75	6.65	6.56	6.58	6.60	6.58	6.53	6.98	7.41	
5	6.00	6.96	7.32	7.29	7.23	7.17	7.11	6.99	6.86	6.31	6.44	6.72	6.83	6.96	7.06	7.61	
6	7.30	7.59	7.71	7.80	7.97	8.09	8.07	7.34	6.74	6.49	6.55	6.60	6.66	6.99	7.29	8.18	
7	7.96	8.50	8.38	9.18	8.74	9.26	9.37	8.64	7.58	7.42	7.42	7.14	7.11	7.05	7.16	7.51	
8	8.41	8.78	8.70	8.60	8.73	8.91	8.88	8.16	8.09	8.12	6.54	6.71	6.83	7.18	7.43	7.26	
9	7.59	6.85	7.24	8.02	8.38	8.36	8.20	7.33	6.69	7.09	6.30	6.54	6.71	7.08	7.30	7.67	
10	6.74	7.46	7.59	7.51	8.01	8.26	7.62	5.98	6.04	6.97	7.03	6.67	6.52	7.45	8.11		
11	7.85	7.28	7.64	8.32	8.70	8.59	8.00	6.65	6.04	6.50	6.71	6.57	6.55	7.29	7.86	7.48	
12	7.13	7.45	7.75	7.86	7.74	7.50	7.19	6.57	6.32	6.58	6.64	6.50	6.49	7.48	8.39	8.01	

1975

mo	0 mo	1 mo	2 mo	3 mo	4 mo	5 mo	6 mo	9 mo	1 yr	2 yr	3 yr	4 yr	5 yr	10 yr	15 yr	20 yr	25 yr
1	5.47	5.64	6.02	6.26	6.24	6.17	6.10	6.20	6.72	7.46	7.56	7.63	7.68	7.74	8.22	7.83	11.49
2	4.48	5.40	5.89	6.05	5.99	5.94	5.96	6.06	6.23	6.96	6.92	7.79	7.95	7.84	8.31	7.97	
3	5.06	5.48	5.90	6.08	6.05	6.06	6.14	6.46	6.81	7.46	7.75	8.02	8.22	8.67	7.96	7.96	
4	4.77	5.47	5.81	6.16	6.66	7.05	7.20	7.50	7.92	8.32	8.15	8.23	8.29	8.26	7.85	8.60	
5	4.66	5.18	5.47	5.65	5.83	6.01	6.16	6.52	6.98	7.88	8.11	8.10	7.99	8.09	8.21	8.77	6.87
6	5.59	5.79	6.24	6.59	6.59	6.57	6.81	7.49	7.50	7.82	8.18	8.04	8.03	8.23	7.80	8.52	
7	5.97	6.08	6.49	7.01	7.38	7.60	7.66	7.59	7.74	8.18	8.50	8.08	8.05	8.35	7.77	8.49	
8	5.73	6.24	6.87	7.27	7.60	7.80	7.86	7.83	7.83	8.12	8.36	8.23	8.34	8.41	7.74	8.88	8.71
9	6.24	6.42	6.87	7.39	7.72	7.87	7.92	7.99	8.20	8.51	8.06	8.41	8.15	8.63	7.93	9.52	8.77
10	5.25	5.48	5.76	6.01	6.08	6.16	6.21	6.73	7.18	7.77	8.35	8.02	8.53	8.61	8.27	9.86	8.80
11	4.67	5.52	6.00	6.26	6.54	6.76	6.82	6.94	7.35	8.02	8.06	8.31	8.04	8.11	8.34	9.18	
12	4.98	5.15	5.41	5.67	5.89	6.07	6.22	6.59	6.86	7.56	7.92	8.00	8.04	8.29	9.16	7.61	8.62

1976

mo	0 mo	1 mo	2 mo	3 mo	4 mo	5 mo	6 mo	9 mo	1 yr	2 yr	3 yr	4 yr	5 yr	10 yr	15 yr	20 yr	25 yr
1	4.52	4.58	4.94	5.24	5.38	5.47	5.58	5.99	6.51	7.67	8.12	8.28	8.36	8.24	8.05	8.02	
2	4.46	4.89	5.31	5.71	6.03	6.26	6.38	6.60	6.92	7.66	7.83	7.95	8.04	8.24	8.31	8.24	
3	4.77	4.84	5.19	5.55	5.86	6.07	6.22	6.46	6.89	7.52	7.70	7.87	7.98	8.09	8.07	8.08	
4	4.86	4.67	5.17	5.58	5.78	5.95	6.11	6.61	7.03	7.22	7.70	7.90	7.98	8.18	8.24	8.14	
5	4.86	5.55	5.81	6.02	6.52	6.84	6.88	7.14	7.72	7.74	7.99	8.02	7.99	8.25	8.40	8.36	

Table 13.A.2 (cont.)

	0 mo	1 mo	2 mo	3 mo	4 mo	5 mo	6 mo	9 mo	1 yr	2 yr	3 yr	4 yr	5 yr	10 yr	15 yr	20 yr	25 yr
1976																	
6	5.26	5.35	5.54	5.88	6.34	6.58	6.55	6.70	7.26	7.49	7.85	7.99	8.03	8.19	8.22	8.28	
7	5.09	5.14	5.33	5.64	6.00	6.18	6.17	6.44	7.00	7.37	7.73	8.02	8.23	8.28	8.15	8.24	
8	4.80	5.13	5.25	5.43	5.79	5.99	5.96	6.06	6.65	7.02	7.39	7.80	8.00	8.21	8.08	8.04	
9	5.13	5.05	5.23	5.48	5.70	5.86	5.86	5.92	6.39	6.91	7.35	7.75	7.96	8.13	8.09	8.06	
10	4.69	4.82	5.11	5.34	5.42	5.44	5.44	5.65	6.19	6.66	6.94	7.43	7.89	8.24	8.19	8.03	
11	4.37	4.45	4.55	4.66	4.82	4.94	4.94	5.03	5.40	6.19	6.09	6.48	7.28	8.57	8.76	7.49	
12	4.22	4.33	4.54	4.75	4.82	4.80	4.82	5.02	5.40	6.14	6.42	6.78	7.19	7.71	7.85	7.77	
1977																	
1	4.58	4.61	4.94	5.28	5.44	5.53	5.60	5.91	6.43	6.85	7.31	7.64	7.68	8.01	8.15	7.85	8.10
2	4.41	4.65	4.92	5.17	5.31	5.40	5.54	5.98	6.32	6.91	7.43	7.84	7.86	8.05	8.30	8.35	
3	4.54	4.51	4.73	4.97	5.10	5.22	5.40	5.95	6.22	6.90	7.45	7.74	7.81	8.09	8.27	8.16	7.66
4	4.33	4.56	4.86	5.13	5.31	5.46	5.60	5.95	6.29	6.82	7.36	7.75	7.84	8.08	8.13	7.99	7.76
5	4.80	5.00	5.21	5.42	5.58	5.71	5.81	6.02	6.27	6.68	7.17	7.58	7.72	8.08	8.16	7.99	7.58
6	4.98	4.97	5.20	5.46	5.63	5.73	5.75	5.84	6.18	6.53	7.04	7.42	7.61	7.84	7.80	7.87	
7	5.16	5.35	5.60	5.86	6.09	6.24	6.30	6.33	6.53	6.82	7.30	7.56	7.65	7.85	7.88	8.01	8.07
8	5.35	5.45	5.77	6.18	6.39	6.45	6.48	6.50	6.53	6.88	7.11	7.25	7.38	7.79	8.01	8.08	
9	5.75	5.79	6.19	6.57	6.66	6.63	6.65	6.81	6.89	6.94	7.22	7.37	7.43	7.78	8.03	8.08	7.83
10	6.27	6.06	6.48	6.99	7.10	7.04	7.06	7.18	7.42	7.36	7.59	7.64	7.56	7.88	8.21	8.26	7.76
11	5.31	6.00	6.49	6.78	6.94	7.00	7.06	7.18	7.21	7.38	7.40	7.41	7.52	7.94	8.21	8.19	7.65
12	5.38	6.20	6.61	6.80	6.91	6.98	7.06	7.25	7.23	7.41	7.68	7.78	7.80	8.07	8.32	8.32	8.09
1978																	
1	5.69	6.40	6.80	7.00	7.14	7.24	7.31	7.39	7.39	7.56	7.82	7.91	7.92	8.21	8.56	8.55	8.07
2	5.98	6.44	6.74	6.94	7.19	7.42	7.49	7.36	7.46	7.79	7.97	8.06	8.03	8.24	8.58	8.60	8.21
3	6.84	6.40	6.62	7.03	7.27	7.40	7.50	7.70	7.79	7.86	8.01	8.09	8.10	8.36	8.62	8.51	8.09
4	5.86	6.22	6.75	7.26	7.60	7.80	7.91	7.96	8.02	7.94	7.99	8.08	8.13	8.47	8.69	8.46	7.90
5	6.33	6.58	6.98	7.47	7.83	8.05	8.18	8.20	8.19	8.06	8.21	8.33	8.33	8.59	8.87	8.32	6.47
6	6.24	6.96	7.60	8.05	8.24	8.28	8.60	8.85	8.67	8.45	8.32	8.24	8.36	8.76	8.69	8.12	7.87
7	6.40	6.74	7.23	7.73	8.11	8.39	8.61	8.72	8.68	8.34	8.29	8.27	8.34	8.61	8.60	8.17	7.94
8	8.05	7.73	7.57	7.65	8.05	8.43	8.93	8.60	8.46	8.14	8.18	8.17	8.18	8.21	8.41	8.48	8.29
9	7.89	8.13	8.50	8.83	9.02	9.05	—	9.87	8.58	7.98	8.07	8.31	8.42	8.54	8.60	8.17	7.85
10	8.35	8.90	9.07	9.28	9.89	10.16	10.48	10.03	8.98	8.88	8.59	8.43	8.44	8.63	8.74	8.82	8.20
11	8.95	9.05	9.25	9.54	9.89	10.16	10.26	10.03	9.31	8.44	7.94	8.32	8.53	8.64	8.44	8.04	8.17
12	7.63	9.44	10.11	10.19	10.09	10.10	10.49	11.11	10.07	8.92	8.16	8.56	8.74	—	8.45	8.18	8.07
1979																	
1	9.64	9.43	9.57	9.80	9.87	9.91	10.05	9.99	9.27	8.53	7.75	8.43	8.78	8.68	8.56	8.39	8.08
2	9.58	9.66	9.69	9.77	10.05	10.30	10.32	10.06	9.69	8.77	8.30	8.68	8.93	8.89	8.63	8.23	8.25

	0 mo	1 mo	2 mo	3 mo	4 mo	5 mo	6 mo	9 mo	1 yr	2 yr	3 yr	4 yr	5 yr	10 yr	15 yr	20 yr	25 yr
3	9.54	9.64	9.77	9.88	9.94	9.97	9.99	9.77	9.29	9.04	8.08	8.58	8.88	8.87	8.71	8.39	8.23
4	9.54	9.65	9.90	10.08	10.06	10.06	10.13	9.98	9.40	9.11	8.29	8.87	9.18	9.08	8.81	8.41	8.45
5	9.80	9.77	9.81	9.83	9.78	9.72	9.70	9.48	9.10	8.64	8.12	8.55	8.85	9.02	8.98	8.68	8.10
6	9.22	9.18	9.32	9.33	9.31	9.29	9.29	9.04	8.46	8.46	8.21	8.40	8.62	8.87	8.79	8.28	7.94
7	9.98	9.14	9.55	9.91	9.88	9.82	9.80	9.42	8.66	8.66	8.36	8.63	8.88	8.89	8.75	8.37	7.91
8	9.99	10.17	9.96	9.87	10.24	10.56	10.61	10.32	9.57	8.71	8.77	8.84	8.88	8.81	8.63	8.33	8.18
9	9.99	10.39	10.48	11.16	10.62	10.73	10.73	10.52	9.87	8.75	8.77	8.88	8.94	9.17	8.71	7.70	8.06
10	11.24	12.19	12.94	13.28	13.07	12.82	12.74	12.29	11.08	10.91	10.25	10.09	9.96	9.69	9.23	8.50	8.04
11	10.27	11.94	12.10	11.88	12.21	12.52	12.25	10.21	10.48	9.14	9.79	10.02	10.13	9.69	9.23?	9.02	8.39
12	7.12	12.66	13.55	12.73	12.43	12.25	11.74	10.27	10.25	9.99	9.15	9.50	9.82	9.99	9.66	8.82	8.07

1980

	0 mo	1 mo	2 mo	3 mo	4 mo	5 mo	6 mo	9 mo	1 yr	2 yr	3 yr	4 yr	5 yr	10 yr	15 yr	20 yr	25 yr
1	11.03	12.50	12.67	12.44	12.53	12.58	12.17	10.71	11.06	10.16	10.09	10.46	10.80	11.07	10.68	9.91	9.56
2	13.29	14.41	14.63	14.38	14.78	15.54	15.77	14.90	14.95	12.36	11.89	11.79	11.73	11.56	10.78	9.32	8.62
3	13.89	15.85	15.37	14.61	15.82	17.71	17.71	14.10	13.56	11.82	11.18	11.07	11.11	12.33	11.95	8.45	8.06
4	10.28	10.51	10.82	11.13	11.38	11.51	11.44	10.86	10.43	9.95	10.32	10.53	10.69	11.17	10.91	9.72	8.61
5	12.57	7.62	7.89	8.13	8.79	8.91	8.93	8.85	9.65	8.47	10.32	10.53	10.56	10.89	10.27	9.65	8.82
6	8.22	8.60	9.19	9.16	7.99	8.40	8.64	8.54	8.97	9.25	9.58	9.92	10.19	10.86	10.46	9.52	8.72
7	4.09	8.89	9.41	11.16	9.04	9.06	9.10	9.28	9.80	9.80	10.29	10.65	10.44	11.61	11.32	9.23	7.66
8	6.47	9.99	10.90	11.16	11.24	11.14	11.09	11.63	11.08	11.01	11.23	11.90	11.40	11.99	12.02	9.37	8.19
9	8.27	11.43	11.85	12.19	12.33	12.27	12.16	11.79	11.68	11.47	11.41	11.48	11.82	12.00	12.29	9.65	8.89
10	10.23	12.83	13.90	13.69	13.51	13.51	13.53	12.91	12.39	12.32	12.05	12.06	11.69	11.86	12.34	8.94	7.63
11	13.63	14.98	15.26	14.64	14.47	14.98	15.47	14.02	12.45	12.53	12.18	11.92	11.85	11.91	11.34	8.32	8.03
12	10.88	14.56	16.07	15.34	14.22	13.67	13.37	11.90	10.97	11.96	11.78	11.87	11.85	11.91	11.34	8.32	8.03

1981

	0 mo	1 mo	2 mo	3 mo	4 mo	5 mo	6 mo	9 mo	1 yr	2 yr	3 yr	4 yr	5 yr	10 yr	15 yr	20 yr	25 yr
1	13.97	15.26	15.32	14.62	14.14	13.91	13.70	12.68	12.07	11.82	12.00	12.22	12.18	12.11	11.76	8.87	7.78
2	13.60	14.68	15.06	14.79	14.48	14.30	14.16	13.39	12.83	13.31	13.27	13.01	12.84	12.54	12.07	8.82	9.18
3	13.10	12.95	12.73	12.46	12.39	12.52	12.68	13.14	13.20	12.88	13.27	13.15	12.90	12.35	12.40	8.34	7.34
4	12.57	15.33	16.06	15.15	14.58	14.66	14.83	14.35	13.92	13.87	13.69	13.58	13.42	13.15	12.64	8.07	9.40
5	16.27	16.08	15.47	14.53	14.05	14.19	14.56	14.48	13.92	13.40	12.91	12.50	12.39	12.64	12.25	8.95	8.03
6	14.03	14.70	15.65	14.82	14.63	14.71	14.68	14.04	14.04	14.11	13.72	13.47	13.32	12.78	12.50	8.85	7.97
7	14.50	15.37	16.20	16.44	16.04	17.28	16.48	15.56	15.30	14.28	14.67	14.13	13.26	13.58	12.79	7.71	7.17
8	15.40	15.86	16.20	16.44	16.81	17.28	17.47	15.93	15.46	14.61	15.31	15.40	14.43	13.26	14.19	9.68	5.77
9	15.64	14.55	15.42	15.66	16.19	16.95	17.31	15.90	15.66	14.30	15.78	15.62	14.62	13.83	14.06	7.26	8.37
10	12.75	13.14	13.22	13.26	13.77	15.30	15.30	14.38	15.66	14.30	14.62	14.54	14.24	14.06	12.68	10.53	8.37
11	10.17	10.34	10.71	11.22	11.54	11.62	11.64	12.09	12.52	13.21	12.83	12.95	13.52	12.38	13.88	10.53	7.72
12	8.26	14.56	12.59	13.18	13.51	13.72	13.88	14.15	14.11	13.54	14.00	14.10	13.84	13.45	13.88	8.43	7.72

1982

	0 mo	1 mo	2 mo	3 mo	4 mo	5 mo	6 mo	9 mo	1 yr	2 yr	3 yr	4 yr	5 yr	10 yr	15 yr	20 yr	25 yr
1	11.73	12.53	13.22	13.75	14.01	14.00	13.70	14.26	14.26	13.94	14.09	13.91	13.61	14.03	13.49	8.54	9.42
2	11.85	12.19	13.01	14.23	14.78	14.30	13.66	13.92	12.83	13.68	13.76	13.59	13.12	14.27	13.97	8.56	8.81
3	14.57	13.51	13.39	13.93	14.17	14.06	13.92	14.02	14.22	14.15	13.81	13.71	13.78	12.83	13.59	9.41	7.71
4	12.31	12.39	12.89	13.49	13.71	13.57	13.46	13.79	14.06	13.74	13.25	13.13	13.55	12.39	12.63	10.60	10.40

Table 13.A.2 (cont.)

1982

	0 mo	1 mo	2 mo	3 mo	4 mo	5 mo	6 mo	9 mo	1 yr	2 yr	3 yr	4 yr	5 yr	10 yr	15 yr	20 yr	25 yr
5	11.56	11.70	11.96	12.31	12.58	12.73	12.85	13.52	14.02	13.48	13.72	13.67	13.61	12.65	13.31	9.99	10.38
6	10.65	12.70	13.94	14.40	14.56	14.52	14.44	14.59	14.84	13.48	14.45	13.89	14.01	12.68	13.71	8.69	9.82
7	8.49	9.81	11.19	12.44	13.11	13.17	13.09	13.54	13.92	13.66	13.81	13.21	13.65	12.51	13.81	9.60	11.17
8	7.54	7.63	8.61	10.26	11.33	11.62	11.66	12.54	13.27	12.70	12.79	12.63	13.34	11.04	12.62	11.01	10.26
9	6.88	7.12	8.08	9.65	10.71	10.95	10.83	11.46	12.40	12.07	12.07	11.61	12.05	11.20	11.34	10.03	10.88
10	7.81	7.73	8.24	9.07	9.48	9.36	9.18	9.65	11.39	11.04	11.42	10.80	11.87	9.68	11.69	10.06	6.60
11	7.67	8.09	8.64	9.24	9.51	9.36	9.01	9.65	10.99	10.41	11.42	11.00	12.05	9.74	12.13	10.45	6.96
12	8.05	8.10	8.22	8.40	8.53	8.52	8.46	9.16	10.26	10.20	11.10	10.84	11.15	10.25	11.41	10.21	7.21

1983

	0 mo	1 mo	2 mo	3 mo	4 mo	5 mo	6 mo	9 mo	1 yr	2 yr	3 yr	4 yr	5 yr	10 yr	15 yr	20 yr	25 yr
1	8.01	8.14	8.35	8.63	8.79	8.80	8.78	9.35	10.15	10.61	11.13	11.07	11.98	10.40	12.56	11.55	7.54
2	7.90	7.94	8.12	8.52	8.52	8.41	8.22	8.84	10.14	9.88	10.73	9.69	10.98	9.39	12.86	10.04	5.94
3	8.36	8.74	9.02	9.20	9.25	9.17	9.06	9.40	10.10	10.27	10.72	10.68	11.13	10.38	11.96	10.04	7.10
4	8.01	8.19	8.37	8.53	8.59	8.52	8.47	9.02	9.69	10.01	10.52	10.34	10.96	9.97	11.74	9.65	6.98
5	8.38	8.85	8.98	9.16	9.26	9.29	9.29	9.54	10.45	10.69	11.06	10.98	11.34	11.29	12.21	10.06	7.85
6	8.25	8.85	9.23	9.38	9.47	9.52	9.56	9.88	10.45	10.73	11.06	11.12	11.25	11.82	11.83	10.06	7.86
7	8.63	9.25	9.70	9.99	10.17	10.23	10.27	10.83	11.64	11.41	11.68	12.15	12.26	11.09	11.98	11.42	9.76
8	8.74	9.26	9.70	10.07	10.33	10.45	10.47	10.76	11.34	11.79	12.17	12.20	12.30	11.82	12.98	11.06	7.84
9	8.77	8.80	8.98	9.27	9.51	9.65	9.76	10.15	10.57	11.14	11.49	11.88	12.01	11.09	12.16	10.48	7.80
10	8.46	8.55	8.81	9.19	9.48	9.63	9.71	10.10	10.59	11.50	11.89	11.98	12.11	11.64	12.34	10.89	8.11
11	8.17	8.93	9.37	9.51	9.61	9.74	9.88	10.02	10.64	11.27	11.82	12.07	11.87	11.33	12.19	10.64	8.93
12	8.18	9.03	9.54	9.69	9.75	9.85	9.97	10.28	10.64	11.44	11.95	12.26	12.05	11.40	12.52	10.94	9.08

1984

	0 mo	1 mo	2 mo	3 mo	4 mo	5 mo	6 mo	9 mo	1 yr	2 yr	3 yr	4 yr	5 yr	10 yr	15 yr	20 yr	25 yr
1	8.87	9.02	9.18	9.34	9.49	9.61	9.70	9.92	10.29	11.15	11.80	12.02	11.84	11.35	12.13	11.40	10.14
2	8.45	9.22	9.68	9.85	9.95	10.04	10.12	10.24	10.61	11.36	12.31	12.49	12.23	11.62	12.54	11.91	10.66
3	9.22	9.77	10.22	10.53	10.63	10.54	10.49	10.91	11.61	11.91	12.65	12.87	13.06	11.74	12.46	12.23	11.41
4	9.26	9.73	10.21	10.77	10.77	10.70	10.69	11.29	11.80	12.36	12.85	13.03	13.60	11.96	12.94	12.51	11.39
5	9.65	9.58	10.18	11.31	12.02	12.16	12.03	12.82	13.80	14.16	13.83	13.47	14.27	13.15	12.94	12.79	11.72
6	8.83	9.89	10.63	11.10	11.45	12.03	11.67	12.43	13.28	12.61	13.82	13.95	13.60	12.44	12.71	12.12	13.03
7	9.67	10.36	10.86	11.21	11.55	11.57	11.67	12.23	13.07	12.81	12.57	12.84	12.81	12.36	12.96	12.12	13.03
8	10.78	10.73	10.84	11.09	11.34	11.55	11.72	12.21	12.67	12.61	12.55	12.91	12.73	12.44	12.71	12.57	12.57
9	10.52	10.40	10.50	10.79	11.00	11.09	11.14	12.07	12.07	12.31	12.66	12.91	12.39	12.36	11.71	11.88	11.74
10	8.07	9.02	9.64	9.95	10.08	11.00	11.02	11.54	12.07	11.57	11.66	11.79	11.89	11.48	11.68	11.23	11.70
11	7.47	8.46	9.01	9.15	9.26	9.42	9.63	10.09	10.43	11.44	11.55	12.03	12.44	11.35	11.36	10.78	9.97
12	6.30	8.00	8.74	8.52	8.35	8.68	9.22	10.00	10.18	11.23	11.52	12.08	12.84	11.47	11.99	10.76	9.80

1985

	0 mo	1 mo	2 mo	3 mo	4 mo	5 mo	6 mo	9 mo	1 yr	2 yr	3 yr	4 yr	5 yr	10 yr	15 yr	20 yr	25 yr
1	7.29	8.10	8.50	8.51	8.55	8.75	9.02	9.56	9.91	10.94	11.30	11.65	11.83	11.58	11.46	10.08	10.55
2	6.77	8.45	9.35	9.53	9.55	9.57	9.60	10.12	10.89	11.55	12.05	12.32	12.73	12.23	12.20	11.52	10.76

	0 mo	1 mo	2 mo	3 mo	4 mo	5 mo	6 mo	9 mo	1 yr	2 yr	3 yr	4 yr	5 yr	10 yr	15 yr	20 yr	25 yr
3	7.67	8.36	8.79	9.01	9.17	9.29	9.42	9.96	10.55	11.36	11.76	12.26	12.31	11.80	12.37	11.30	8.07
4	7.24	7.78	8.23	8.58	8.79	8.85	8.87	9.44	10.31	10.95	11.40	11.79	12.37	11.84	12.16	11.59	8.87
5	6.69	7.25	7.53	7.56	7.60	7.66	7.76	8.47	9.52	9.79	10.39	10.56	11.34	11.17	11.74	10.12	9.23
6	6.49	6.92	7.20	7.38	7.47	7.49	7.56	8.24	8.97	9.89	10.53	10.89	11.14	10.50	12.06	10.29	6.56
7	6.82	7.27	7.59	7.79	7.92	7.96	7.99	8.50	9.16	10.27	10.90	11.20	11.25	11.26	11.90	10.56	7.12
8	7.35	7.18	7.24	7.52	7.76	7.92	8.04	8.28	8.73	9.69	10.86	10.10	11.32	11.22	12.22	8.58	6.55
9	7.02	7.20	7.34	7.44	7.55	7.69	7.87	8.58	9.29	9.89	10.29	10.72	11.32	11.74	11.91	9.49	6.90
10	6.95	7.34	7.48	7.46	7.55	7.75	7.95	8.00	8.62	9.07	10.23	9.95	11.51	11.10	12.07	7.11	6.49
11	5.66	7.34	7.95	7.60	7.40	7.54	7.84	8.02	8.19	8.82	9.87	10.01	10.61	11.25	11.73	9.51	6.22
12	5.19	7.09	7.82	7.53	7.34	7.43	7.57	7.68	7.83	8.31	9.30	8.71	9.80	9.90	11.27	9.25	5.68

1986

	0 mo	1 mo	2 mo	3 mo	4 mo	5 mo	6 mo	9 mo	1 yr	2 yr	3 yr	4 yr	5 yr	10 yr	15 yr	20 yr	25 yr
1	6.38	7.15	7.42	7.29	7.26	7.43	7.61	7.65	7.86	8.39	9.09	9.39	9.51	10.50	10.51	7.14	6.57
2	6.51	7.19	7.43	7.28	7.18	7.24	7.37	7.43	7.49	8.18	7.92	8.60	8.27	8.72	9.34	7.93	6.74
3	6.73	6.46	6.38	6.45	6.49	6.48	6.51	7.02	7.31	7.13	7.58	7.86	7.36	7.80	8.25	8.85	6.25
4	5.82	6.12	6.29	6.37	6.42	6.44	6.48	6.68	6.91	7.64	7.31	7.91	7.38	7.96	8.66	9.48	5.41
5	6.11	6.35	6.53	6.66	6.75	6.79	6.82	7.14	7.52	8.08	8.89	8.30	8.18	8.60	9.73	10.97	4.22
6	5.96	6.06	6.16	6.26	6.28	5.98	6.19	6.65	7.14	7.43	7.92	7.59	7.83	7.84	9.79	11.57	2.16
7	5.08	5.84	6.15	6.06	5.99	6.21	6.04	6.43	6.77	7.28	7.59	7.79	7.55	8.75	9.96	9.63	2.81
8	4.37	5.25	5.53	5.29	5.17	5.31	5.52	5.70	5.88	6.35	7.29	7.20	7.29	8.47	8.94	8.79	3.96
9	5.14	5.27	5.38	5.50	5.65	5.82	5.96	6.06	6.36	7.08	7.88	7.90	7.99	8.97	9.80	9.33	4.58
10	4.65	5.33	5.48	5.38	5.42	5.60	5.76	5.96	6.21	6.91	7.34	7.62	7.58	9.06	9.43	7.50	4.20
11	5.06	5.39	5.59	5.65	5.67	5.67	5.66	5.81	6.14	6.37	7.51	6.88	7.98	8.33	10.32	9.29	3.03
12	4.07	5.75	6.38	6.03	5.69	5.65	5.76	6.14	6.44	7.40	7.06	6.61	8.03	8.33	10.37	9.79	3.15

1987

	0 mo	1 mo	2 mo	3 mo	4 mo	5 mo	6 mo	9 mo	1 yr	2 yr	3 yr	4 yr	5 yr	10 yr	15 yr	20 yr	25 yr
1	5.23	5.73	5.85	5.71	5.69	5.81	5.96	6.02	6.06	6.77	7.02	7.28	7.49	8.52	9.62	8.91	4.00
2	5.44	5.53	5.59	5.62	5.68	5.78	5.90	6.13	6.35	6.53	7.23	7.03	7.48	8.31	9.39	8.88	4.50

Table 13.A.3

McCulloch par bond yield curve series, continuous compounding, end of month data, 12/46–2/87

Year	Mo	0 mo	1 mo	2 mo	3 mo	4 mo	5 mo	6 mo	9 mo	1 yr	2 yr	3 yr	4 yr	5 yr	10 yr	15 yr	20 yr	25 yr
1946	12	0.18	0.32	0.42	0.48	0.52	0.55	0.58	0.65	0.72	0.95	1.14	1.29	1.41	1.80	2.10	2.25	
1947	1	0.16	0.32	0.43	0.48	0.52	0.56	0.58	0.65	0.72	0.94	1.12	1.26	1.38	1.80	2.10	2.26	
	2	0.19	0.33	0.42	0.47	0.51	0.54	0.57	0.65	0.71	0.95	1.14	1.28	1.40	1.79	2.09	2.25	
	3	0.13	0.32	0.44	0.51	0.55	0.58	0.61	0.68	0.74	0.94	1.10	1.24	1.36	1.78	2.07	2.23	
	4	0.08	0.30	0.45	0.52	0.57	0.61	0.64	0.71	0.78	1.00	1.17	1.29	1.39	1.78	2.08	2.24	
	5	0.00	0.29	0.47	0.57	0.63	0.67	0.70	0.77	0.83	1.02	1.19	1.32	1.43	1.82	2.13	2.27	
	6	0.08	0.33	0.49	0.57	0.62	0.65	0.68	0.76	0.82	1.02	1.23	1.34	1.43	1.80	2.13	2.26	
	7	0.06	0.38	0.58	0.67	0.73	0.77	0.80	0.87	0.92	1.10	1.18	1.26	1.35	1.78	2.14	2.23	
	8	0.16	0.53	0.76	0.86	0.92	0.95	0.97	1.02	1.05	1.12	1.22	1.30	1.39	1.82	2.13	2.25	
	9	0.52	0.74	0.88	0.95	0.98	1.01	1.02	1.06	1.08	1.15	1.36	1.45	1.53	1.92	2.24	2.31	
	10	0.45	0.73	0.91	1.00	1.05	1.08	1.10	1.14	1.18	1.28	1.42	1.52	1.62	2.03	2.30	2.37	
	11	0.59	0.81	0.95	1.02	1.06	1.09	1.11	1.16	1.20	1.32	1.52	1.66	1.77	2.17	2.40		
	12	0.93	0.90	0.90	0.91	0.93	0.95	0.97	1.04	1.11	1.34							
1948	1	1.04	0.96	0.92	0.91	0.92	0.94	0.96	1.02	1.08	1.32	1.51	1.66	1.78	2.18	2.40		
	2	1.02	0.97	0.94	0.95	0.96	0.97	0.99	1.05	1.11	1.33	1.50	1.64	1.76	2.16	2.40		
	3	1.00	0.98	0.97	0.98	1.00	1.01	1.03	1.08	1.14	1.33	1.49	1.60	1.73	2.14	2.38		
	4	0.98	0.98	0.99	1.00	1.02	1.04	1.05	1.10	1.12	1.25	1.37	1.48	1.71	2.13	2.39		
	5	0.97	0.99	1.00	1.02	1.03	1.04	1.06	1.09	1.16	1.31	1.45	1.58	1.59	2.05	2.34		
	6	0.95	0.99	0.98	0.99	1.01	1.02	1.04	1.10	1.16	1.37	1.53	1.65	1.69	2.14	2.39		
	7	1.02	1.06	1.03	1.04	1.05	1.07	1.09	1.15	1.21	1.43	1.58	1.71	1.76	2.18	2.41		
	8	1.13	1.08	1.09	1.10	1.12	1.14	1.16	1.22	1.28	1.48	1.61	1.72	1.81	2.19	2.41		
	9	1.09	1.08	1.08	1.09	1.11	1.13	1.16	1.22	1.29	1.51	1.65	1.76	1.82	2.21	2.41		
	10	1.11	1.10	1.11	1.12	1.14	1.16	1.17	1.23	1.28	1.46	1.59	1.69	1.86	2.17	2.40		
	11	1.06	1.11	1.14	1.16	1.18	1.19	1.21	1.24	1.28	1.40	1.52	1.63	1.79	2.15	2.38		
	12													1.73				
1949	1	1.09	1.13	1.15	1.17	1.18	1.19	1.20	1.22	1.25	1.35	1.46	1.57	1.67	2.11	2.37		
	2	1.16	1.14	1.13	1.13	1.14	1.15	1.16	1.20	1.23	1.36	1.48	1.58	1.68	2.10	2.34		
	3	1.03	1.11	1.16	1.19	1.20	1.21	1.24	1.24	1.26	1.33	1.43	1.53	1.63	2.07	2.35		
	4	1.10	1.12	1.14	1.15	1.16	1.17	1.18	1.20	1.23	1.33	1.43	1.50	1.63	2.07	2.35		
	5	1.00	1.09	1.15	1.18	1.19	1.20	1.21	1.23	1.24	1.31	1.40	1.48	1.60	2.06	2.35		
	6	0.81	1.02	1.13	1.18	1.19	1.20	1.20	1.19	1.18	1.17	1.24	1.34	1.45	1.97	2.28		
	7	0.79	0.96	1.05	1.08	1.10	1.10	1.10	1.10	1.09	1.10	1.19	1.30	1.42	1.94	2.24		

(continuation — months 8–12)

	0 mo	1 mo	2 mo	3 mo	4 mo	5 mo	6 mo	9 mo	1 yr	2 yr	3 yr	4 yr	5 yr	10 yr	15 yr	20 yr	25 yr
8	0.86	0.98	1.05	1.08	1.09	1.09	1.10	1.10	1.10	1.12	1.19	1.29	1.40	1.88	2.20		
9	0.88	1.01	1.08	1.10	1.11	1.11	1.11	1.10	1.09	1.10	1.18	1.28	1.40	1.89	2.18		
10	0.82	0.98	1.07	1.16	1.17	1.17	1.17	1.16	1.11	1.12	1.20	1.31	1.41	1.89	2.18		
11	0.82	1.01	1.12	1.16	1.17	1.17	1.17	1.16	1.15	1.14	1.21	1.31	1.41	1.88	2.17		
12	0.93	1.03	1.09	1.11	1.12	1.12	1.12	1.12	1.12	1.14	1.21	1.30	1.40	1.84	2.14		

1950

	0 mo	1 mo	2 mo	3 mo	4 mo	5 mo	6 mo	9 mo	1 yr	2 yr	3 yr	4 yr	5 yr	10 yr	15 yr	20 yr	25 yr
1	0.97	1.07	1.13	1.15	1.16	1.16	1.15	1.15	1.15	1.16	1.25	1.35	1.46	1.93	2.19		
2	1.00	1.10	1.16	1.18	1.19	1.19	1.18	1.18	1.17	1.17	1.25	1.36	1.47	1.96	2.22		
3	0.89	1.08	1.19	1.23	1.24	1.24	1.24	1.23	1.21	1.20	1.28	1.39	1.50	1.99	2.25		
4	0.92	1.11	1.22	1.25	1.27	1.27	1.27	1.26	1.25	1.26	1.34	1.44	1.55	2.02	2.28		
5	0.93	1.13	1.25	1.29	1.30	1.31	1.30	1.28	1.26	1.25	1.32	1.43	1.54	2.04	2.30		
6	0.90	1.16	1.25	1.24	1.30	1.31	1.31	1.30	1.29	1.30	1.38	1.49	1.60	2.07	2.33		
7	0.86	1.25	1.31	1.36	1.37	1.37	1.36	1.33	1.29	1.25	1.33	1.44	1.56	2.08	2.33		
8	1.00	1.29	1.37	1.41	1.42	1.42	1.42	1.39	1.36	1.34	1.41	1.51	1.61	2.08	2.33		
9	1.10	1.54	1.40	1.44	1.44	1.45	1.45	1.44	1.41	1.44	1.52	1.61	1.70	2.12	2.37		
10	0.83	1.18	1.37	1.44	1.48	1.49	1.50	1.52	1.52	1.56	1.64	1.72	1.80	2.18	2.37		
11	1.07	1.31	1.43	1.47	1.49	1.50	1.50	1.49	1.49	1.52	1.60	1.70	1.79	2.20	2.39		
12	0.79	1.25	1.49	1.57	1.60	1.61	1.61	1.58	1.55	1.52	1.59	1.68	1.77	2.19	2.40		

1951

	0 mo	1 mo	2 mo	3 mo	4 mo	5 mo	6 mo	9 mo	1 yr	2 yr	3 yr	4 yr	5 yr	10 yr	15 yr	20 yr	25 yr
1	0.80	1.21	1.44	1.54	1.57	1.59	1.60	1.59	1.57	1.57	1.63	1.70	1.77	2.16	2.39	2.53	
2	0.78	1.21	1.45	1.55	1.58	1.59	1.59	1.57	1.54	1.55	1.62	1.71	1.80	2.21	2.41	2.64	
3	1.24	1.44	1.55	1.61	1.64	1.66	1.68	1.73	1.76	1.87	1.96	2.00	2.08	2.29	2.45	2.69	
4	0.93	1.33	1.55	1.63	1.68	1.70	1.72	1.75	1.77	1.84	1.92	2.06	2.07	2.37	2.56	2.69	
5	0.96	1.34	1.56	1.64	1.69	1.72	1.74	1.78	1.81	1.89	1.97	2.02	2.15	2.53	2.72	2.66	
6	0.90	1.38	1.64	1.73	1.77	1.79	1.80	1.81	1.81	1.84	1.85	2.01	2.10	2.48	2.67	2.64	
7	1.29	1.49	1.61	1.65	1.67	1.68	1.69	1.70	1.70	1.77	1.81	1.93	2.01	2.37	2.59	2.57	
8	1.32	1.54	1.66	1.69	1.69	1.73	1.70	1.69	1.68	1.72	1.92	1.90	1.98	2.33	2.49	2.62	
9	1.49	1.60	1.66	1.68	1.71	1.74	1.76	1.78	1.82	1.92	1.99	2.07	2.13	2.41	2.59	2.67	
10	0.81	1.26	1.53	1.65	1.71	1.73	1.73	1.80	1.82	1.91	2.00	2.09	2.17	2.49	2.67	2.70	
11	1.05	1.39	1.58	1.66	1.70	1.72	1.73	1.76	1.78	1.88	1.97	2.07	2.16	2.51	2.68	2.71	
12	1.55	1.70	1.79	1.84	1.86	1.88	1.89	1.92	1.94	2.02	2.09	2.16	2.23	2.51	2.66		

1952

	0 mo	1 mo	2 mo	3 mo	4 mo	5 mo	6 mo	9 mo	1 yr	2 yr	3 yr	4 yr	5 yr	10 yr	15 yr	20 yr	25 yr
1	0.94	1.33	1.54	1.62	1.66	1.69	1.71	1.76	1.79	1.88	1.97	2.05	2.13	2.46	2.65	2.69	
2	0.91	1.34	1.56	1.65	1.70	1.73	1.75	1.81	1.85	1.97	2.08	2.18	2.27	2.62	2.76	2.76	
3	1.10	1.37	1.52	1.59	1.63	1.66	1.68	1.73	1.77	1.90	2.01	2.10	2.18	2.51	2.72	2.76	
4	1.39	1.58	1.68	1.72	1.75	1.76	1.77	1.79	1.81	1.87	1.94	2.01	2.09	2.42	2.59	2.61	
5	1.43	1.64	1.75	1.79	1.82	1.83	1.84	1.87	1.89	1.95	2.00	2.06	2.12	2.38	2.56	2.63	
6	1.65	1.75	1.86	1.83	1.85	1.87	1.88	1.92	1.95	2.05	2.13	2.19	2.23	2.42	2.59	2.66	
7	1.72	1.80	1.89	1.89	1.91	1.92	1.94	1.98	2.01	2.13	2.21	2.28	2.32	2.47	2.59	2.65	
8	1.46	1.71	1.85	1.91	1.95	1.97	2.00	2.05	2.09	2.21	2.30	2.36	2.41	2.55	2.68	2.72	
9	1.06	1.46	1.70	1.81	1.87	1.91	1.94	2.00	2.04	2.17	2.27	2.35	2.42	2.68	2.80	2.81	

Table 13.A.3 (cont.)

		0 mo	1 mo	2 mo	3 mo	4 mo	5 mo	6 mo	9 mo	1 yr	2 yr	3 yr	4 yr	5 yr	10 yr	15 yr	20 yr	25 yr
1952	10	1.32	1.59	1.75	1.82	1.86	1.89	1.92	1.97	2.00	2.12	2.21	2.28	2.33	2.53	2.66	2.72	
	11	1.55	1.78	1.92	1.99	2.02	2.05	2.07	2.11	2.13	2.21	2.27	2.31	2.35	2.51	2.66	2.74	
	12	1.82	1.94	2.02	2.05	2.08	2.09	2.11	2.14	2.16	2.24	2.30	2.34	2.38	2.55	2.73		
1953	1	1.63	1.82	1.92	1.97	2.00	2.02	2.03	2.07	2.09	2.18	2.26	2.33	2.39	2.64	2.77		
	2	1.86	2.02	2.11	2.14	2.16	2.18	2.18	2.20	2.12	2.26	2.31	2.37	2.44	2.71	2.86		
	3	1.95	1.99	2.01	2.13	2.05	2.06	2.07	2.10	2.13	2.24	2.33	2.41	2.48	2.74	2.88		
	4	1.78	2.06	2.23	2.30	2.34	2.37	2.39	2.43	2.46	2.55	2.62	2.69	2.75	2.99	3.08	3.11	3.16
	5	1.43	1.93	2.22	2.35	2.42	2.47	2.50	2.58	2.63	2.79	2.91	3.00	3.08	3.29	3.28	3.22	3.20
	6	1.18	1.61	1.89	2.03	2.11	2.17	2.20	2.28	2.33	2.48	2.59	2.68	2.75	2.99	3.03	3.04	3.09
	7	1.72	1.94	2.06	2.12	2.16	2.19	2.21	2.26	2.31	2.45	2.57	2.66	2.74	2.97	3.03	3.09	
	8	1.62	1.79	1.89	1.95	1.99	2.03	2.06	2.14	2.21	2.42	2.63	2.76	2.85	3.07	3.12	3.14	
	9	0.86	1.22	1.46	1.59	1.67	1.72	1.77	1.87	1.94	2.18	2.33	2.42	2.48	2.64	2.77	2.93	
	10	0.65	0.97	1.19	1.31	1.39	1.44	1.49	1.60	1.69	1.99	2.20	2.34	2.43	2.69	2.86	2.96	
	11	1.36	1.44	1.49	1.53	1.56	1.59	1.62	1.69	1.75	1.98	2.16	2.29	2.40	2.92	2.92	3.01	
	12	1.09	1.25	1.35	1.42	1.46	1.49	1.52	1.60	1.66	1.88	2.03	2.13	2.20	2.47	2.68	2.83	
1954	1	1.05	0.96	0.92	0.92	0.95	0.97	1.00	1.10	1.19	1.53	1.78	1.95	2.08	2.48	2.68	2.80	
	2	0.84	0.89	0.92	0.94	0.97	0.99	1.01	1.06	1.12	1.34	1.56	1.78	1.97	2.45	2.52	2.59	
	3	0.99	0.99	0.99	1.00	1.01	1.02	1.04	1.09	1.14	1.34	1.54	1.75	1.93	2.41	2.52	2.61	
	4	0.62	0.67	0.71	0.75	0.78	0.81	0.83	0.91	0.99	1.23	1.42	1.59	1.77	2.33	2.49	2.58	
	5	0.51	0.60	0.66	0.69	0.73	0.76	0.79	0.87	0.96	1.28	1.58	1.83	2.03	2.50	2.60	2.66	
	6	0.67	0.62	0.60	0.61	0.63	0.66	0.68	0.77	0.85	1.15	1.41	1.64	1.85	2.42	2.49	2.54	
	7	0.64	0.68	0.71	0.73	0.75	0.77	0.79	0.84	0.90	1.16	1.44	1.69	1.89	2.38	2.47	2.51	
	8	1.30	1.11	1.00	0.96	0.95	0.95	0.96	0.99	1.04	1.25	1.48	1.71	1.91	2.44	2.50	2.53	
	9	0.90	0.90	0.92	0.94	0.97	1.00	1.03	1.12	1.20	1.45	1.64	1.80	1.98	2.45	2.49	2.53	
	10	0.72	0.85	0.93	0.98	1.02	1.06	1.09	1.18	1.26	1.55	1.78	1.97	2.11	2.43	2.51	2.58	
	11	0.86	0.93	0.98	1.02	1.05	1.08	1.10	1.18	1.25	1.53	1.79	1.99	2.13	2.48	2.62	2.67	
	12	0.92	0.95	0.98	1.01	1.04	1.07	1.10	1.20	1.29	1.61	1.88	2.08	2.20	2.49	2.62	2.67	
1955	1	1.19	1.10	1.07	1.09	1.13	1.17	1.22	1.35	1.47	1.84	2.05	2.18	2.29	2.63	2.77	2.80	2.80
	2	0.91	1.14	1.29	1.38	1.45	1.51	1.56	1.70	1.82	2.16	2.31	2.40	2.46	2.70	2.81	2.85	2.87
	3	1.33	1.33	1.35	1.39	1.43	1.47	1.52	1.65	1.78	2.13	2.29	2.39	2.46	2.69	2.78	2.81	2.83
	4	1.44	1.50	1.55	1.60	1.65	1.69	1.73	1.85	1.95	2.25	2.38	2.46	2.52	2.75	2.84	2.84	2.84
	5	0.91	1.15	1.32	1.43	1.50	1.57	1.62	1.75	1.87	2.18	2.35	2.45	2.52	2.72	2.79	2.81	2.82
	6	1.04	1.27	1.43	1.53	1.60	1.66	1.71	1.84	1.96	2.28	2.46	2.58	2.65	2.84	2.88	2.87	2.85

(continued from preceding page)

mo	25 yr	20 yr	15 yr	10 yr	5 yr	4 yr	3 yr	2 yr	1 yr	9 mo	6 mo	5 mo	4 mo	3 mo	2 mo	1 mo	0 mo
7	2.94	2.97	2.99	2.97	2.82	2.75	2.65	2.49	2.19	2.08	1.96	1.92	1.87	1.82	1.75	1.67	1.55
8	2.94	2.94	2.95	2.95	2.89	2.85	2.78	2.66	2.41	2.33	2.23	2.19	2.15	2.10	2.04	1.95	1.83
9	2.92	2.91	2.90	2.88	2.78	2.72	2.61	2.46	2.28	2.23	2.19	2.17	2.16	2.15	2.14	2.15	2.16
10	2.87	2.85	2.83	2.80	2.70	2.64	2.59	2.50	2.31	2.25	2.18	2.15	2.13	2.10	2.07	2.05	2.03
11	2.94	2.93	2.91	2.89	2.85	2.84	2.83	2.81	2.69	2.63	2.55	2.51	2.47	2.41	2.31	2.11	1.80
12	2.89	2.90	2.92	2.92	2.88	2.87	2.86	2.84	2.73	2.68	2.61	2.59	2.56	2.53	2.49	2.42	2.34

1956

mo	25 yr	20 yr	15 yr	10 yr	5 yr	4 yr	3 yr	2 yr	1 yr	9 mo	6 mo	5 mo	4 mo	3 mo	2 mo	1 mo	0 mo
1	2.85	2.84	2.83	2.81	2.72	2.68	2.63	2.55	2.45	2.41	2.37	2.36	2.35	2.33	2.31	2.28	2.24
2	2.88	2.87	2.86	2.83	2.76	2.74	2.71	2.66	2.54	2.49	2.41	2.38	2.34	2.28	2.18	1.97	1.60
3	2.97	3.05	3.04	3.07	3.06	3.05	3.03	2.98	2.73	2.62	2.48	2.43	2.38	2.32	2.26	2.20	2.81
4	3.06	3.05	3.05	3.06	3.13	3.16	3.21	3.22	3.04	2.94	2.82	2.78	2.74	2.70	2.66	2.63	2.61
5	2.96	2.92	2.90	2.90	2.94	2.95	2.96	2.95	2.86	2.81	2.74	2.71	2.67	2.62	2.53	2.37	2.13
6	2.93	2.94	2.95	2.97	2.97	2.95	2.92	2.85	2.69	2.63	2.55	2.52	2.48	2.45	2.40	2.33	2.24
7	3.06	3.08	3.13	3.19	3.27	3.27	3.26	3.20	2.93	2.79	2.60	2.52	2.44	2.35	2.24	2.08	1.88
8	3.21	3.25	3.32	3.41	3.54	3.54	3.53	3.47	3.23	3.10	2.93	2.86	2.78	2.69	2.58	2.40	2.12
9	3.11	3.17	3.26	3.34	3.42	3.50	3.49	3.50	3.33	3.23	3.11	3.05	3.00	2.93	2.84	2.70	2.50
10	3.25	3.26	3.35	3.47	3.51	3.50	3.48	3.46	3.33	3.24	3.10	3.05	2.98	2.89	2.76	2.56	2.78
11	3.32	3.35	3.41	3.50	3.63	3.66	3.70	3.74	3.69	3.61	3.44	3.36	3.26	3.15	3.01	2.81	2.53
12	3.47	3.56	3.64	3.71	3.71	3.71	3.72	3.77	3.80	3.76	3.63	3.54	3.42	3.29	3.15	3.08	3.10

1957

mo	25 yr	20 yr	15 yr	10 yr	5 yr	4 yr	3 yr	2 yr	1 yr	9 mo	6 mo	5 mo	4 mo	3 mo	2 mo	1 mo	0 mo
1	3.21	3.13	3.15	3.22	3.25	3.24	3.24	3.26	3.27	3.26	3.23	3.21	3.18	3.14	3.10	3.06	3.05
2	3.25	3.27	3.31	3.36	3.39	3.40	3.42	3.45	3.47	3.46	3.42	3.39	3.35	3.29	3.18	2.94	2.39
3	3.32	3.34	3.21	3.37	3.37	3.46	3.44	3.45	3.36	3.27	3.16	3.11	3.07	3.01	3.11	2.89	2.81
4	3.40	3.41	3.41	3.53	3.57	3.56	3.56	3.54	3.42	3.33	3.21	3.17	3.12	3.07	3.07	3.02	3.05
5	3.43	3.50	3.52	3.68	3.67	3.64	3.60	3.56	3.49	3.44	3.38	3.36	3.33	3.30	3.26	3.21	3.14
6	3.54	3.49	3.67	3.89	3.82	3.77	3.74	3.74	3.71	3.65	3.54	3.49	3.43	3.36	3.36	3.08	2.81
7	3.57	3.51	3.65	3.89	3.92	3.87	3.84	3.84	3.80	3.74	3.62	3.57	3.51	3.42	3.30	3.06	2.66
8	3.60	3.66	3.62	4.01	3.82	3.80	3.85	3.99	4.11	4.06	3.90	3.82	3.71	3.58	3.40	3.07	2.50
9	3.64	3.72	3.81	3.92	4.00	3.97	4.10	4.05	4.18	4.10	3.95	3.89	3.72	3.70	3.53	3.36	2.78
10	3.69	3.67	3.55	3.90	3.95	4.03	4.01	4.05	4.01	3.94	3.83	3.78	3.72	3.65	3.54	3.23	3.10
11	3.47	3.22	3.17	3.35	3.42	3.45	3.48	3.48	3.45	3.43	3.37	3.34	3.28	3.19	3.01	2.63	2.06
12	3.58	3.22	3.36	3.05	2.85	2.81	2.78	2.77	2.77	2.78	2.79	2.79	2.79	2.78	2.77	2.73	2.66

1958

mo	25 yr	20 yr	15 yr	10 yr	5 yr	4 yr	3 yr	2 yr	1 yr	9 mo	6 mo	5 mo	4 mo	3 mo	2 mo	1 mo	0 mo
1	3.32	3.28	3.25	3.15	2.88	2.79	2.69	2.54	2.14	1.95	1.72	1.64	1.56	1.49	1.44	1.46	1.53
2	3.27	3.24	3.18	3.04	2.64	2.52	2.36	2.14	1.80	1.66	1.48	1.41	1.34	1.27	1.20	1.14	1.10
3	3.32	3.12	3.10	2.90	2.57	2.46	2.32	2.09	1.66	1.49	1.31	1.25	1.18	1.11	1.05	0.99	0.94
4	3.19	3.13	3.01	2.81	2.40	2.25	2.05	1.79	1.46	1.37	1.27	1.24	1.21	1.18	1.16	1.16	1.18
5	3.14	3.23	3.09	2.98	2.33	2.17	1.99	1.76	1.32	1.14	0.91	0.83	0.79	0.63	0.49	0.25	0.00
6	3.25	3.51	3.16	2.98	2.54	2.40	2.22	1.90	1.30	1.11	1.13	0.85	1.00	0.74	0.72	0.75	0.84
7	3.58	3.51	3.36	3.17	2.89	2.72	2.44	2.02	1.47	1.30	1.13	1.07	1.00	0.92	0.83	0.70	0.54

Table 13.A.3 (cont.)

Year		0 mo	1 mo	2 mo	3 mo	4 mo	5 mo	6 mo	9 mo	1 yr	2 yr	3 yr	4 yr	5 yr	10 yr	15 yr	20 yr	25 yr
1958	8	1.35	1.87	2.20	2.38	2.49	2.58	2.65	2.82	2.96	3.35	3.54	3.64	3.69	3.75	3.74	3.73	3.72
	9	1.00	1.95	2.57	2.88	3.04	3.14	3.20	3.30	3.36	3.50	3.62	3.70	3.74	3.74	3.72	3.72	3.75
	10	1.08	1.82	2.30	2.53	2.67	2.76	2.83	2.98	3.09	3.37	3.53	3.62	3.67	3.70	3.68	3.68	3.70
	11	0.83	1.90	2.58	2.91	3.07	3.16	3.23	3.33	3.38	3.47	3.55	3.60	3.62	3.64	3.65	3.67	3.70
	12	2.13	2.42	2.62	2.75	2.84	2.91	2.97	3.09	3.19	3.45	3.63	3.74	3.80	3.88	3.85	3.80	3.79
1959	1	2.32	2.47	2.61	2.76	2.89	3.00	3.09	3.27	3.40	3.73	3.89	3.96	3.99	3.99	3.99	4.01	4.01
	2	2.04	2.38	2.64	2.83	2.97	3.07	3.14	3.29	3.38	3.60	3.71	3.76	3.78	3.79	3.87	3.96	4.01
	3	2.44	2.57	2.72	2.89	3.06	3.19	3.29	3.48	3.59	3.82	3.92	3.96	3.98	3.97	3.97	3.98	3.99
	4	2.78	2.74	2.80	2.94	3.10	3.22	3.32	3.49	3.61	3.87	4.03	4.12	4.16	4.19	4.12	4.08	4.01
	5	2.80	2.75	2.82	3.03	3.27	3.47	3.60	3.79	3.86	3.97	4.10	4.17	4.20	4.18	4.17	4.05	4.05
	6	2.70	2.77	2.93	3.16	3.42	3.62	3.75	3.91	3.96	4.13	4.31	4.39	4.40	4.24	4.24	4.14	4.11
	7	1.97	2.40	2.75	3.04	3.30	3.56	3.79	4.25	4.40	4.45	4.39	4.52	4.57	4.42	4.32	4.12	4.06
	8	3.14	3.48	3.74	3.95	4.13	4.27	4.38	4.54	4.56	4.34	4.51	4.62	4.66	4.51	4.32	4.17	4.11
	9	3.43	3.64	3.90	4.21	4.53	4.76	4.90	4.99	4.92	4.69	4.70	4.71	4.70	4.50	4.29	4.19	4.12
	10	2.14	3.17	3.79	4.06	4.20	4.32	4.42	4.55	4.55	4.36	4.44	4.60	4.67	4.50	4.29	4.15	4.08
	11	2.31	3.53	4.23	4.52	4.67	4.77	4.84	4.93	4.94	4.87	4.81	4.78	4.74	4.55	4.37	4.23	4.16
	12	4.02	4.08	4.27	4.56	4.77	4.88	4.94	5.01	5.02	4.95	4.88	4.84	4.81	4.72	4.56	4.41	4.33
1960	1	3.28	3.54	3.82	4.11	4.33	4.47	4.56	4.68	4.71	4.69	4.71	4.74	4.76	4.65	4.43	4.39	4.21
	2	3.58	3.81	4.05	4.25	4.35	4.37	4.37	4.38	4.40	4.48	4.57	4.60	4.59	4.42	4.30	4.23	4.01
	3	2.40	2.68	2.91	3.09	3.23	3.33	3.41	3.55	3.62	3.78	3.90	3.98	4.02	4.06	4.06	4.05	4.04
	4	2.89	2.97	3.02	3.08	3.18	3.34	3.45	3.97	4.15	4.24	4.35	4.45	4.48	4.35	4.29	4.27	4.25
	5	1.82	2.60	3.02	3.16	3.24	3.52	3.53	3.76	3.92	4.13	4.24	4.30	4.30	4.16	4.16	4.20	4.18
	6	1.25	1.66	1.97	2.21	2.37	2.50	2.60	2.95	3.18	3.69	3.88	3.93	3.98	4.10	4.10	3.97	3.90
	7	1.65	1.83	2.02	2.61	2.77	2.85	2.87	2.79	2.91	3.16	3.28	3.36	3.45	3.79	3.81	3.75	3.71
	8	1.45	1.97	2.36	2.53	2.75	2.86	2.89	2.85	2.88	3.13	3.31	3.44	3.57	3.84	3.86	3.81	3.81
	9	2.68	2.34	2.31	2.18	2.38	2.51	2.60	2.83	2.80	3.04	3.29	3.52	3.64	3.79	3.83	3.84	3.84
	10	1.22	1.61	1.93	2.44	2.59	2.69	2.77	2.76	2.85	3.13	3.35	3.68	3.78	3.87	3.91	3.89	3.88
	11	1.24	1.79	2.19	2.27	2.36	2.41	2.44	2.90	3.00	3.30	3.52	3.68	3.78	3.97	3.99	3.97	3.94
	12	1.87	2.03	2.16	2.27	2.36	2.41	2.44	2.51	2.58	2.87	3.11	3.29	3.41	3.71	3.79	3.81	3.82
1961	1	1.88	2.04	2.18	2.30	2.40	2.47	2.52	2.64	2.76	3.14	3.38	3.53	3.63	3.82	3.88	3.90	3.91
	2	2.47	2.48	2.54	2.62	2.69	2.75	2.80	2.90	2.97	3.18	3.34	3.45	3.52	3.71	3.77	3.80	3.81
	3	2.02	2.19	2.32	2.42	2.50	2.57	2.64	2.78	2.86	3.05	3.24	3.42	3.54	3.79	3.84	3.83	3.81
	4	1.42	1.93	2.20	2.27	2.30	2.38	2.48	2.72	2.84	3.03	3.20	3.34	3.45	3.72	3.78	3.78	3.76

Month	0 mo	1 mo	2 mo	3 mo	4 mo	5 mo	6 mo	9 mo	1 yr	2 yr	3 yr	4 yr	5 yr	10 yr	15 yr	20 yr	25 yr
5	2.10	2.24	2.34	2.40	2.46	2.53	2.60	2.79	2.91	3.20	3.37	3.49	3.58	3.80	3.83	3.79	3.75
6	1.80	2.08	2.24	2.31	2.37	2.45	2.54	2.75	2.90	3.28	3.49	3.62	3.71	3.88	3.91	3.91	3.89
7	1.12	1.74	2.10	2.24	2.32	2.41	2.50	2.73	2.88	3.25	3.54	3.74	3.85	3.98	3.98	3.95	3.92
8	1.89	2.05	2.24	2.36	2.48	2.60	2.71	2.92	3.05	3.36	3.60	3.75	3.84	3.98	3.99	3.98	4.00
9	1.74	1.99	2.15	2.34	2.50	2.62	2.70	2.88	3.00	3.31	3.52	3.65	3.72	3.85	3.90	3.94	4.00
10	1.74	1.96	2.15	2.32	2.47	2.58	2.67	2.84	2.96	3.24	3.45	3.59	3.69	3.87	3.89	3.90	3.95
11	2.00	2.28	2.47	2.60	2.68	2.75	2.80	2.93	3.03	3.32	3.52	3.67	3.78	4.00	3.96	3.96	3.99
12	2.32	2.48	2.63	2.75	2.83	2.89	2.94	3.05	3.14	3.41	3.58	3.71	3.82	4.06	4.05	4.01	4.03

1962

Month	0 mo	1 mo	2 mo	3 mo	4 mo	5 mo	6 mo	9 mo	1 yr	2 yr	3 yr	4 yr	5 yr	10 yr	15 yr	20 yr	25 yr
1	2.20	2.48	2.66	2.75	2.82	2.88	2.95	3.09	3.21	3.52	3.70	3.83	3.93	4.12	4.11	4.06	4.06
2	2.24	2.49	2.65	2.76	2.84	2.89	2.93	3.02	3.09	3.29	3.46	3.60	3.73	4.07	4.11	4.08	4.10
3	2.64	2.63	2.71	2.83	2.90	2.90	2.87	2.85	2.89	3.14	3.34	3.54	3.60	3.87	3.96	3.97	3.97
4	2.67	2.69	2.73	2.78	2.82	2.85	2.87	2.93	3.00	3.25	3.42	3.53	3.63	3.91	3.95	3.95	3.93
5	2.91	2.45	2.66	2.72	2.74	2.76	2.79	2.87	2.94	3.27	3.31	3.50	3.64	3.91	3.95	3.94	3.92
6	2.98	2.93	2.92	2.95	2.98	2.99	2.99	3.00	3.03	3.42	3.48	3.64	3.75	3.96	3.99	3.98	3.97
7	2.53	2.68	2.81	2.90	2.97	3.03	3.08	3.19	3.26	3.26	3.59	3.74	3.84	4.04	4.07	4.07	4.13
8	2.52	2.69	2.77	2.85	2.92	2.98	3.02	3.09	3.11	3.11	3.34	3.53	3.66	3.95	3.99	3.99	4.00
9	2.68	2.53	2.74	2.83	2.90	2.93	2.93	2.92	2.93	3.08	3.31	3.51	3.63	3.94	3.98	3.97	3.97
10	2.38	2.53	2.65	2.75	2.81	2.84	2.85	2.85	2.88	3.10	3.32	3.49	3.63	3.94	3.97	3.94	3.93
11	2.35	2.67	2.86	2.93	2.95	2.96	2.97	2.98	3.01	3.17	3.32	3.45	3.57	3.92	3.95	3.92	3.93
12	2.98	2.94	2.94	2.97	3.00	3.00	3.00	2.99	3.01	3.21	3.34	3.43	3.52	3.88	3.91	3.88	3.92

1963

Month	0 mo	1 mo	2 mo	3 mo	4 mo	5 mo	6 mo	9 mo	1 yr	2 yr	3 yr	4 yr	5 yr	10 yr	15 yr	20 yr	25 yr
1	2.95	2.93	2.94	2.98	3.02	3.02	3.01	2.98	2.99	3.15	3.33	3.49	3.62	3.89	3.93	3.93	3.97
2	2.82	2.84	2.88	2.94	2.97	2.97	2.95	2.92	2.94	3.15	3.37	3.54	3.67	3.96	4.01	4.01	4.00
3	1.83	2.20	2.55	2.85	3.04	3.12	3.12	3.03	2.99	3.15	3.37	3.55	3.69	3.99	4.03	4.02	4.02
4	2.83	2.85	2.89	2.94	2.99	3.02	3.03	3.05	3.08	3.27	3.45	3.59	3.70	3.97	4.04	4.06	4.06
5	2.91	2.95	3.00	3.06	3.10	3.12	3.12	3.10	3.11	3.31	3.50	3.64	3.74	3.98	4.04	4.04	4.04
6	2.99	2.98	3.00	3.05	3.10	3.12	3.12	3.11	3.12	3.32	3.52	3.68	3.79	3.99	4.04	4.04	4.04
7	3.08	3.05	3.19	3.29	3.36	3.40	3.42	3.44	3.46	3.58	3.70	3.80	3.87	4.00	4.03	4.02	4.01
8	3.53	3.26	3.38	3.44	3.47	3.50	3.53	3.57	3.60	3.63	3.71	3.85	3.91	4.00	4.03	4.01	4.01
9	3.26	3.44	3.42	3.47	3.52	3.56	3.57	3.59	3.59	3.65	3.74	3.93	3.93	4.09	4.08	4.06	4.07
10	3.25	3.36	3.46	3.54	3.60	3.64	3.65	3.66	3.67	3.75	3.84	3.92	4.00	4.17	4.15	4.11	4.10
11	3.01	3.27	3.53	3.57	3.64	3.67	3.69	3.72	3.74	3.79	3.85	4.02	3.97	4.11	4.11	4.12	4.12
12	3.52	3.51	3.69	3.58	3.64	3.69	3.72	3.78	3.81	3.91	3.97	4.02	4.06	4.16	4.19	4.19	4.18

1964

Month	0 mo	1 mo	2 mo	3 mo	4 mo	5 mo	6 mo	9 mo	1 yr	2 yr	3 yr	4 yr	5 yr	10 yr	15 yr	20 yr	25 yr
1	3.35	3.42	3.49	3.55	3.60	3.64	3.67	3.73	3.78	3.88	3.94	3.99	4.04	4.19	4.20	4.17	4.15
2	3.51	3.53	3.58	3.65	3.72	3.77	3.80	3.86	3.89	3.98	4.02	4.07	4.11	4.22	4.22	4.18	4.16
3	3.57	3.51	3.52	3.60	3.67	3.73	3.77	3.85	3.91	4.07	4.14	4.17	4.19	4.26	4.25	4.23	4.20
4	3.18	3.32	3.43	3.50	3.57	3.62	3.66	3.75	3.81	3.96	4.06	4.13	4.16	4.20	4.21	4.20	4.20
5	3.00	3.29	3.46	3.52	3.55	3.60	3.64	3.76	3.82	3.92	3.98	4.02	4.07	4.18	4.18	4.16	4.14

Table 13.A.3 (cont.)

Year	Mo	0 mo	1 mo	2 mo	3 mo	4 mo	5 mo	6 mo	9 mo	1 yr	2 yr	3 yr	4 yr	5 yr	10 yr	15 yr	20 yr	25 yr
1964	6	3.28	3.46	3.54	3.54	3.55	3.58	3.62	3.71	3.75	3.83	3.91	3.99	4.05	4.14	4.15	4.14	4.13
	7	3.02	3.32	3.46	3.51	3.54	3.60	3.65	3.73	3.74	3.75	3.87	3.99	4.07	4.20	4.20	4.19	4.18
	8	3.21	3.40	3.51	3.56	3.60	3.64	3.69	3.77	3.79	3.83	3.93	4.01	4.08	4.21	4.22	4.20	4.18
	9	3.50	3.53	3.57	3.63	3.69	3.74	3.78	3.85	3.87	3.89	3.95	4.00	4.05	4.18	4.20	4.19	4.18
	10	3.39	3.45	3.53	3.62	3.70	3.75	3.79	3.85	3.88	3.92	3.97	4.02	4.06	4.16	4.18	4.17	4.16
	11	3.37	3.63	3.81	3.90	3.97	4.03	4.08	4.14	4.15	4.13	4.13	4.14	4.15	4.18	4.19	4.19	4.18
	12	3.13	3.56	3.80	3.89	3.94	3.98	4.00	4.02	4.00	3.99	4.04	4.08	4.12	4.21	4.22	4.21	4.20
1965	1	3.81	3.85	3.89	3.92	3.97	4.02	4.06	4.06	4.03	3.98	4.02	4.06	4.09	4.18	4.20	4.20	4.19
	2	3.61	3.87	4.00	4.04	4.07	4.11	4.13	4.15	4.14	4.09	4.08	4.10	4.12	4.22	4.22	4.20	4.19
	3	3.60	3.82	3.94	3.98	4.01	4.04	4.07	4.10	4.08	4.07	4.09	4.12	4.14	4.21	4.21	4.20	4.19
	4	3.82	3.88	3.94	3.99	4.02	4.05	4.07	4.08	4.07	4.07	4.10	4.11	4.14	4.19	4.20	4.21	4.20
	5	3.74	3.86	3.93	3.95	3.98	4.00	4.03	4.06	4.07	4.07	4.08	4.07	4.10	4.23	4.23	4.21	4.20
	6	3.71	3.79	3.84	3.87	3.89	3.92	3.93	3.94	3.93	3.95	4.01	4.07	4.17	4.19	4.21	4.22	4.19
	7	3.81	3.81	3.88	3.89	3.93	3.96	3.97	3.99	4.00	4.05	4.07	4.15	4.23	4.22	4.22	4.22	4.21
	8	3.70	3.81	3.88	3.93	3.98	4.04	4.09	4.12	4.10	4.13	4.17	4.20	4.30	4.27	4.27	4.25	4.24
	9	3.93	3.95	4.01	4.11	4.18	4.24	4.28	4.33	4.35	4.34	4.33	4.34	4.36	4.40	4.37	4.33	4.31
	10	3.85	3.92	4.02	4.13	4.22	4.26	4.29	4.33	4.35	4.38	4.40	4.42	4.44	4.45	4.40	4.35	4.32
	11	3.67	3.92	4.09	4.18	4.25	4.32	4.37	4.42	4.44	4.50	4.54	4.55	4.56	4.54	4.50	4.45	4.41
	12	4.31	4.44	4.52	4.57	4.66	4.75	4.82	4.92	4.96	5.07	5.09	5.04	4.97	4.73	4.62	4.55	4.50
1966	1	4.50	4.52	4.61	4.72	4.79	4.82	4.84	4.87	4.90	5.04	5.09	5.07	5.03	4.82	4.68	4.60	4.56
	2	4.24	4.50	4.65	4.74	4.82	4.90	4.96	5.08	5.13	5.18	5.21	5.24	5.27	5.21	4.99	4.81	4.76
	3	4.19	4.40	4.53	4.61	4.70	4.78	4.85	4.94	4.97	5.01	5.01	4.99	4.96	4.84	4.73	4.66	4.62
	4	4.44	4.63	4.69	4.70	4.74	4.82	4.87	4.93	4.95	5.04	5.04	5.02	5.02	4.96	4.83	4.73	4.67
	5	4.21	4.50	4.65	4.69	4.75	4.86	4.87	5.02	5.05	5.25	5.38	5.18	5.12	5.13	4.85	4.78	4.73
	6	4.22	4.50	4.60	4.62	4.69	4.79	4.87	4.94	5.02	5.35	5.47	5.31	5.26	5.28	5.00	4.90	4.81
	7	4.08	4.58	4.78	4.81	4.90	5.01	5.09	5.17	5.21	5.40	5.47	5.48	5.46	5.28	5.07	4.90	4.82
	8	4.44	4.79	5.06	5.12	5.28	5.56	5.75	5.88	5.94	6.29	6.28	6.14	6.02	5.62	5.37	5.20	5.10
	9	5.00	5.20	5.35	5.48	5.61	5.74	5.83	5.92	5.91	5.80	5.68	5.57	5.44	5.11	5.01	4.95	4.86
	10	4.24	4.85	5.19	5.35	5.49	5.62	5.69	5.73	5.71	5.61	5.54	5.47	5.39	5.11	4.93	4.79	4.74
	11	3.66	4.62	5.15	5.28	5.32	5.37	5.41	5.43	5.48	5.68	5.56	5.42	5.38	5.28	5.11	4.95	4.86
	12	4.60	4.70	4.82	4.94	5.02	5.07	5.08	5.05	5.03	5.02	4.99	4.94	4.88	4.74	4.69	4.65	4.62
1967	1	4.37	4.54	4.61	4.61	4.62	4.63	4.63	4.63	4.63	4.68	4.70	4.70	4.68	4.62	4.57	4.53	4.51
	2	3.77	4.37	4.59	4.59	4.61	4.64	4.66	4.64	4.68	4.91	4.86	4.79	4.80	4.86	4.83	4.77	4.72
	3	3.91	4.01	4.10	4.16	4.18	4.17	4.16	4.14	4.14	4.24	4.29	4.35	4.41	4.58	4.62	4.62	4.60

1968

Maturity	4	5	6	7	8	9	10	11	12
25 yr	4.83	4.89	5.12	5.13	5.22	5.28	5.53		5.66
20 yr	4.90	4.92	5.13	5.23	5.32	5.55	5.74		5.78
15 yr	4.94	4.95	5.27	5.31	5.41	5.63	5.78		5.80
10 yr	4.92	4.94	5.44	5.33	5.42	5.51	5.71	5.81	5.77
5 yr	4.70	4.70	5.41	5.20	5.44	5.50	5.67	5.77	5.80
4 yr	4.62	4.62	5.32	5.11	5.40	5.45	5.64	5.73	5.84
3 yr	4.56	4.63	5.25	5.08	5.37	5.40	5.62	5.67	5.88
2 yr	4.43	4.52	5.21	5.13	5.39	5.38	5.60	5.62	5.88
1 yr	4.06	4.04	5.08	5.15	5.31	5.40	5.49	5.75	5.89
9 mo	3.99	3.95	4.92	5.05	5.20	5.35	5.44	5.80	5.89
6 mo	3.93	3.84	4.54	4.77	4.95	5.16	5.43	5.60	5.72
5 mo	3.88	3.74	4.35	4.38	4.82	5.02	5.03	5.42	5.58
4 mo	3.82	3.61	4.17	4.38	4.67	4.83	4.81	5.23	5.40
3 mo	3.77	3.49	4.05	4.18	4.49	4.59	4.63	5.04	5.16
2 mo	3.74	3.43	3.96	4.04	4.26	4.34	4.45	4.76	4.84
1 mo	3.54	3.34	3.75	3.93	4.25	4.18	4.27	4.43	
0 mo	3.01	3.21	3.32	3.49	4.34	3.80	3.57	3.90	

1969

Maturity	1	2	3	4	5	6	7	8	9	10	11	12
25 yr	5.49				5.65	5.63	5.52	5.39	5.38	5.50	5.67	5.76
20 yr	5.60	5.65	5.95	5.74	5.78	5.60	5.45	5.44	5.62	5.82	6.01	6.42
15 yr	5.68	5.69	6.00	5.84	5.91	5.68	5.50	5.51	5.66	5.85	6.04	6.46
10 yr	5.72	5.69	5.96	5.94	5.99	5.53	5.55	5.55	5.78	5.93		6.42
5 yr	5.67	5.70	5.90	6.03	5.95	5.82	5.52	5.50	5.65	5.74		6.44
4 yr	5.63	5.71	5.91	6.06	5.94	5.83	5.51	5.46	5.63	5.70		6.49
3 yr	5.59	5.71	5.91	6.06	6.03	5.87	5.50	5.41	5.47	5.61	5.66	6.56
2 yr	5.58	5.64	5.86	6.01	6.17	5.94	5.50	5.37	5.45	5.63	5.65	6.59
1 yr	5.45	5.51	5.68	5.94	6.17	5.94	5.46	5.41	5.41	5.70	5.86	6.62
9 mo	5.33	5.44	5.60	5.90	6.15	5.87	5.46	5.43	5.44	5.70	5.87	6.63
6 mo	5.17	5.34	5.47	5.80	6.08	5.69	5.43	5.41	5.67	5.78		6.56
5 mo	5.11	5.28	5.41	5.75	6.01	5.38	5.36	5.40	5.66	5.73		6.48
4 mo	5.04	5.21	5.34	5.68	5.92	5.51	5.30	5.29	5.33	5.64	5.67	6.39
3 mo	4.95	5.12	5.30	5.61	5.84	5.42	5.23	5.26	5.28	5.59	5.60	6.31
2 mo	4.84	5.01	5.18	5.51	5.76	5.34	5.19	5.24	5.28	5.46	5.47	6.24
1 mo	4.74	4.79	4.94	5.33	5.57	5.29	5.10	5.05	5.20	5.34	5.07	6.14
0 mo	4.64	4.37	4.52	5.07	5.20	5.27	4.92	4.59	5.25		4.32	5.98

1970

Maturity	1	2	3	4	5
25 yr	6.29	6.17			
20 yr	6.82	6.44			7.18
15 yr	7.07	6.60	6.83	7.50	
10 yr	7.55	6.87	6.88	7.74	7.68
5 yr	7.93	7.12	7.09	7.82	7.60
4 yr	7.95	7.16	7.07	7.81	7.64
3 yr	7.96	7.17	6.78	7.78	7.72
2 yr	7.97	7.07	6.84	7.70	7.72
1 yr	7.96	6.89	6.65	7.52	7.44
9 mo	7.99	6.90	6.61	7.44	7.31
6 mo	8.06	6.98	6.27	7.32	7.20
5 mo	8.07	7.00	6.59	7.27	7.19
4 mo	8.05	7.02	6.57	7.19	7.16
3 mo	8.01	7.01	6.48	7.03	7.03
2 mo	7.93	6.94	6.39	6.78	6.82
1 mo	7.62	6.68	6.43	6.52	6.56
0 mo	6.95	6.10	6.64	6.29	6.28

Table 13.A.3 (cont.)

	0 mo	1 mo	2 mo	3 mo	4 mo	5 mo	6 mo	9 mo	1 yr	2 yr	3 yr	4 yr	5 yr	10 yr	15 yr	20 yr	25 yr
1970																	
6	5.46	6.12	6.44	6.52	6.57	6.68	6.79	7.05	7.21	7.51	7.60	7.61	7.61	7.52			
7	4.32	5.92	6.50	6.43	6.38	6.50	6.66	6.86	6.89	7.27	7.43	7.44	7.46	7.57			
8	6.07	6.24	6.33	6.38	6.44	6.56	6.67	6.79	6.78	7.13	7.29	7.30	7.33	7.52			
9	5.62	5.56	5.71	6.03	6.32	6.47	6.53	6.59	6.60	6.67	6.81	6.94	7.04	7.24			
10	5.05	5.45	5.76	5.96	6.09	6.17	6.22	6.30	6.34	6.51	6.69	6.83	6.93	7.13			
11	4.40	4.75	4.97	5.07	5.08	5.06	5.05	5.09	5.16	5.38	5.60	5.84	6.02	6.39	6.44	6.34	
12	3.98	4.57	4.84	4.90	4.92	4.93	4.91	4.89	4.99	5.46	5.72	5.86	5.96	6.26	6.39	6.35	
1971																	
1	3.99	4.11	4.15	4.17	4.22	4.25	4.25	4.19	4.24	4.72	5.19	5.56	5.79	6.09	6.01	5.98	
2	3.12	3.25	3.34	3.42	3.50	3.56	3.61	3.69	3.74	4.21	4.74	5.14	5.41	5.97	6.15	6.17	
3	3.46	3.46	3.54	3.64	3.69	3.69	3.69	3.74	3.81	4.15	4.50	4.83	5.09	5.62	5.74	5.80	
4	3.49	3.81	3.97	4.04	4.13	4.24	4.33	4.50	4.63	5.18	5.48	5.85	6.00	6.11			
5	3.92	4.20	4.35	4.38	4.40	4.44	4.51	4.75	4.96	5.47	5.75	5.93	6.07	6.43			
6	4.52	4.95	5.12	5.12	5.15	5.29	5.46	5.82	6.05	6.47	6.64	6.72	6.77	6.81			
7	4.79	5.21	5.33	5.31	5.42	5.63	5.82	6.01	6.06	6.48	6.74	6.83	6.88	6.93			
8	4.49	4.46	4.42	4.65	4.47	4.64	4.82	5.11	5.26	5.54	5.69	5.80	5.90	6.22	6.03		
9	4.55	4.47	4.52	4.65	4.78	4.89	4.99	5.16	5.27	5.50	5.68	5.84	5.92	5.95			
10	3.56	4.06	4.29	4.37	4.43	4.47	4.48	4.49	4.75	5.04	5.17	5.56	5.71	5.91			
11	3.67	4.06	4.28	4.35	4.39	4.45	4.50	4.63	4.75	5.06	5.26	5.56	5.78	5.82			
12	3.24	3.33	3.50	3.70	3.87	3.98	4.03	4.11	4.29	4.82	5.02	5.25	5.44	5.87			
1972																	
1	2.41	3.02	3.28	3.38	3.53	3.68	3.78	3.99	4.18	4.83	5.26	5.52	5.70	6.28			
2	3.36	3.25	3.29	3.44	3.60	3.72	3.82	4.05	4.23	4.82	5.20	5.45	5.63	6.15			
3	3.32	3.42	3.64	3.92	4.16	4.33	4.46	4.77	5.00	5.50	5.76	5.91	6.00	6.17			
4	3.30	3.28	3.44	3.67	3.86	4.01	4.12	4.33	4.49	5.12	5.52	5.68	5.79	6.13			
5	3.32	3.50	3.67	3.81	3.95	4.09	4.21	4.43	4.56	4.98	5.31	5.53	5.68	6.06			
6	3.39	3.67	3.91	4.11	4.31	4.51	4.69	5.01	5.16	5.47	5.66	5.83	5.91	6.19			
7	3.41	3.56	3.70	3.86	4.04	4.25	4.43	4.73	4.87	5.35	5.69	5.83	5.93	6.32			
8	4.27	4.35	4.42	4.51	4.65	4.84	5.02	5.27	5.36	5.66	5.87	6.00	6.10	6.44			
9	4.64	4.48	4.52	4.74	4.98	5.17	5.31	5.53	5.63	5.85	5.96	6.00	6.07	6.53			
10	4.49	4.54	4.65	4.82	4.97	5.09	5.18	5.36	5.47	5.80	5.96	6.02	6.08	6.38			
11	4.82	4.79	4.83	4.92	5.04	5.16	5.26	5.36	5.36	5.65	5.86	5.91	5.97	6.27			
12	4.77	4.93	5.08	5.22	5.34	5.42	5.48	5.55	5.59	5.89	6.03	6.06	6.10	6.36			
1973																	
1	5.22	5.44	5.62	5.77	5.87	5.93	5.96	6.02	6.06	6.26	6.34	6.34	6.33	6.42	6.57	6.75	
2	5.49	5.59	5.73	5.90	6.03	6.11	6.16	6.28	6.39	6.60	6.65	6.64	6.62	6.56	6.59		
3	5.77	6.08	6.33	6.53	6.69	6.82	6.91	6.99	6.96	6.79	6.72	6.69	6.67	6.60	6.60		

1974

Maturity	4	5	6	7	8	9	10	11	12
25 yr									
20 yr				6.87	6.96	7.17	6.92	7.09	7.21
15 yr	6.60	6.82	6.88	7.33	7.12	6.86	7.14	6.97	7.03
10 yr	6.58	6.76	6.80	7.41	7.07	6.75	6.88	6.77	6.76
5 yr	6.61	6.67	6.78	7.64	7.11	6.85	6.77	6.80	6.65
4 yr	6.62	6.64	6.82	7.75	7.19	6.65	6.91	6.71	6.68
3 yr	6.62	6.66	6.89	7.91	7.35	6.71	6.93	6.74	6.72
2 yr	6.65	6.81	7.06	8.19	7.74	6.96	6.83	6.75	6.74
1 yr	6.72	7.05	7.60	8.66	8.47	7.58	6.99	7.44	7.12
9 mo	6.72	7.09	7.79	8.77	8.67	7.77	7.35	7.80	7.34
6 mo	6.68	7.10	7.81	8.74	8.74	7.77	7.69	8.06	7.59
5 mo	6.63	7.10	7.75	8.51	8.70	7.67	7.63	8.02	7.63
4 mo	6.55	7.07	7.68	8.38	8.67	7.49	7.48	7.85	7.63
3 mo	6.39	7.01	7.62	8.36	8.68	7.25	7.41	7.62	7.57
2 mo	6.17	6.86	7.56	8.39	8.70	7.04	7.36	7.43	7.45
1 mo	6.01	6.53	7.45	8.64	8.13	7.15	7.36	7.49	7.29
0 mo	5.95	6.00	7.30	7.96	8.41	7.59	6.74	7.85	7.13

1975

Maturity	1	2	3	4	5	6	7	8	9	10	11	12
25 yr	7.77			8.00			8.14	8.29	8.49		8.25	
20 yr	7.59	7.56	8.13	8.16	8.05	7.96	8.11	8.24	8.47	8.04	8.24	7.94
15 yr	7.50	7.49	8.05	8.11	8.02	7.90	8.07	8.16	8.42	7.98	8.23	7.87
10 yr	7.42	7.39	7.82	8.08	7.86	7.82	8.00	8.06	8.34	7.84	8.13	7.71
5 yr	7.20	6.85	7.35	7.92	7.50	7.67	7.91	8.00	8.25	7.50	7.77	7.37
4 yr	7.10	6.81	7.18	7.85	7.36	7.60	7.88	7.97	8.23	7.37	7.63	7.23
3 yr	6.95	6.56	6.97	7.76	7.16	7.45	7.81	7.87	8.17	7.21	7.46	7.01
2 yr	6.69	6.25	6.68	7.55	6.82	7.20	7.64	7.69	8.01	6.94	7.21	6.66
1 yr	6.15	5.92	6.16	6.85	6.06	6.84	7.25	7.45	7.61	6.29	6.56	6.09
9 mo	6.05	5.89	6.00	6.57	5.84	6.62	7.13	7.33	7.46	6.06	6.38	5.89
6 mo	6.02	5.61	5.86	6.20	5.60	6.32	6.89	7.08	7.22	5.86	6.15	5.63
5 mo	6.00	5.73	5.82	6.01	5.50	6.25	6.74	6.93	7.09	5.80	6.02	5.53
4 mo	5.94	5.67	5.76	5.79	5.40	6.18	6.56	6.74	6.91	5.73	5.86	5.41
3 mo	5.84	5.55	5.66	5.59	5.28	6.03	6.34	6.50	6.69	5.63	5.68	5.29
2 mo	5.67	5.33	5.48	5.41	5.14	5.83	6.13	6.24	6.47	5.49	5.46	5.16
1 mo	5.53	4.98	5.27	5.15	4.94	5.67	6.00	5.98	6.31	5.36	5.12	5.06
0 mo	5.47	4.48	5.06	4.77	4.66	5.59	5.73	5.97	6.25	5.25	4.67	4.99

1976

Maturity	1	2	3	4	5
25 yr					
20 yr	7.91	7.94	7.79	7.83	8.02
15 yr	7.89	7.87	7.74	7.76	7.95
10 yr	7.80	7.73	7.62	7.61	7.84
5 yr	7.39	7.39	7.28	7.23	7.64
4 yr	7.18	7.26	7.14	7.08	7.57
3 yr	6.86	7.06	6.95	6.85	7.43
2 yr	6.37	6.74	6.63	6.56	7.23
1 yr	5.55	6.10	6.03	6.01	6.65
9 mo	5.33	5.89	5.80	5.73	6.39
6 mo	5.10	5.61	5.50	5.42	6.11
5 mo	5.02	5.46	5.37	5.30	5.96
4 mo	4.92	5.29	5.22	5.17	5.77
3 mo	4.79	5.09	5.05	4.99	5.61
2 mo	4.63	4.88	4.89	4.79	5.48
1 mo	4.52	4.67	4.78	4.70	5.24
0 mo	4.52	4.46	4.77	4.86	4.86

Table 13.A.3 (cont.)

Year	Month	0 mo	1 mo	2 mo	3 mo	4 mo	5 mo	6 mo	9 mo	1 yr	2 yr	3 yr	4 yr	5 yr	10 yr	15 yr	20 yr	25 yr
1976	6	5.26	5.30	5.36	5.47	5.63	5.80	5.93	6.14	6.35	6.90	7.14	7.32	7.44	7.73	7.84	7.90	
	7	5.09	5.10	5.16	5.27	5.41	5.55	5.65	5.85	6.07	6.67	6.94	7.16	7.33	7.75	7.86	7.90	
	8	4.80	4.98	5.09	5.17	5.28	5.40	5.50	5.59	5.82	6.41	6.65	6.77	7.06	7.56	7.70	7.76	
	9	5.13	5.07	5.09	5.18	5.28	5.38	5.46	5.59	5.73	6.25	6.52	6.77	6.96	7.46	7.62	7.69	
	10	4.69	4.75	4.85	4.98	5.08	5.15	5.20	5.30	5.45	6.01	6.25	6.47	6.69	7.34	7.56	7.65	
	11	4.37	4.41	4.46	4.50	4.56	4.63	4.77	4.87	4.88	5.38	5.63	5.96	5.96	6.85	7.25	7.38	
	12	4.22	4.26	4.34	4.45	4.53	4.59	4.63	4.72	4.84	5.34	5.64	5.87	6.07	6.72	7.00	7.14	
1977	1	4.58	4.57	4.66	4.81	4.95	5.06	5.14	5.34	5.54	6.15	6.43	6.68	6.85	7.27	7.46	7.55	7.72
	2	4.41	4.52	4.65	4.79	4.90	4.99	5.07	5.30	5.51	6.09	6.42	6.71	6.92	7.34	7.54	7.66	7.66
	3	4.54	4.51	4.55	4.65	4.75	4.83	4.91	5.17	5.40	5.95	6.35	6.64	6.84	7.31	7.52	7.63	7.63
	4	4.33	4.58	4.58	4.72	4.84	4.95	4.91	5.30	5.50	6.05	6.37	6.65	6.86	7.33	7.52	7.60	7.60
	5	4.80	4.90	5.00	5.11	5.21	5.29	5.37	5.55	5.70	6.12	6.36	6.60	6.79	7.28	7.49	7.58	
	6	4.98	4.96	5.01	5.12	5.23	5.32	5.39	5.52	5.63	6.04	6.27	6.50	6.69	7.17	7.33	7.42	7.55
	7	5.16	5.25	5.36	5.48	5.60	5.72	5.81	5.97	6.08	6.40	6.61	6.80	6.95	7.30	7.44	7.51	
	8	5.35	5.38	5.49	5.65	5.82	5.94	6.02	6.18	6.26	6.46	6.63	6.76	6.86	7.17	7.35	7.45	
	9	5.75	5.74	5.85	6.03	6.18	6.28	6.33	6.47	6.56	6.74	6.84	6.95	7.03	7.27	7.43	7.53	7.57
	10	6.28	6.11	6.16	6.37	6.54	6.65	6.71	6.87	7.00	7.20	7.28	7.36	7.40	7.47	7.64	7.74	7.77
	11	5.30	5.67	5.97	6.19	6.36	6.48	6.57	6.75	6.86	7.06	7.17	7.22	7.27	7.51	7.62	7.72	7.75
	12	5.38	5.82	6.13	6.32	6.45	6.55	6.63	6.80	6.91	7.08	7.23	7.35	7.42	7.62	7.75	7.83	7.87
1978	1	5.69	6.07	6.35	6.53	6.67	6.77	6.85	7.02	7.11	7.27	7.40	7.51	7.58	7.75	7.89	7.98	8.01
	2	5.98	6.22	6.41	6.55	6.68	6.81	6.91	7.08	7.15	7.42	7.56	7.67	7.73	7.87	7.99	8.07	8.10
	3	6.84	6.56	6.51	6.62	6.75	6.87	6.96	7.18	7.32	7.56	7.68	7.76	7.82	7.97	8.09	8.15	8.17
	4	5.86	6.03	6.25	6.50	6.74	6.93	7.08	7.36	7.51	7.77	7.82	7.87	7.91	8.05	8.17	8.22	8.22
	5	6.33	6.44	6.60	6.81	7.02	7.20	7.35	7.63	7.77	7.95	7.99	8.06	8.10	8.22	8.33	8.38	8.32
	6	6.24	6.61	6.94	7.24	7.47	7.63	7.74	8.01	8.19	8.28	8.33	8.31	8.31	8.41	8.49	8.48	8.44
	7	6.40	6.55	6.76	7.00	7.23	7.43	7.61	7.98	8.18	8.25	8.28	8.28	8.28	8.36	8.42	8.42	8.39
	8	8.04	7.87	7.76	7.70	7.73	7.84	7.95	8.19	8.29	8.26	8.23	8.29	8.21	8.20	8.22	8.25	8.26
	9	7.89	8.00	8.15	8.32	8.47	8.59	8.65	8.68	8.66	8.46	8.32	8.29	8.30	8.41	8.46	8.46	8.42
	10	8.34	8.65	8.84	8.94	9.09	9.30	9.49	9.73	9.65	9.26	9.10	8.96	8.87	8.72	8.70	8.71	8.70
	11	8.95	8.99	9.06	9.17	9.30	9.45	9.58	9.78	9.75	9.27	8.91	8.74	8.69	8.66	8.64	8.59	8.55
	12	7.63	8.63	9.24	9.55	9.70	9.77	9.85	10.21	10.31	9.82	9.39	9.16	9.08	8.94	8.86	8.80	8.74
1979	1	9.64	9.51	9.49	9.56	9.63	9.68	9.73	9.85	9.80	9.36	8.93	8.75	8.73	8.74	8.71	8.69	8.65
	2	9.58	9.63	9.65	9.67	9.73	9.82	9.90	10.00	9.97	9.60	9.25	9.08	9.04	9.00	8.95	8.89	8.84

1980

mo	0 mo	1 mo	2 mo	3 mo	4 mo	5 mo	6 mo	9 mo	1 yr	2 yr	3 yr	4 yr	5 yr	10 yr	15 yr	20 yr	25 yr
3	9.54	9.59	9.65	9.71	9.76	9.80	9.83	9.86	9.78	9.50	9.16	8.98	8.94	8.93	8.90	8.84	8.82
4	9.54	9.58	9.67	9.78	9.86	9.90	9.93	9.99	9.91	9.64	9.29	9.14	9.12	9.14	9.10	9.05	8.99
5	9.80	9.78	9.78	9.79	9.80	9.79	9.78	9.72	9.62	9.29	8.96	8.82	8.80	8.87	8.90	8.90	8.86
6	8.73	8.98	9.13	9.19	9.23	9.24	9.25	9.23	9.11	8.73	8.85	8.53	8.52	8.82	8.66	8.65	8.61
7	9.22	9.14	9.22	9.40	9.53	9.59	9.62	9.63	9.49	9.04	9.33	8.77	8.77	8.82	8.82	8.79	8.74
8	9.98	10.11	10.10	10.03	10.03	10.08	10.19	10.29	10.21	9.59	9.51	9.21	9.15	9.04	8.97	8.92	8.86
9	9.99	10.22	10.34	10.39	10.43	10.48	10.52	10.57	10.48	9.82	9.74	9.37	9.36	9.51	9.17	9.07	8.96
10	11.24	11.73	12.15	12.48	12.66	12.72	12.72	12.68	12.45	11.64	11.30	11.06	10.89	10.50	10.30	10.15	10.02
11	10.27	11.23	11.69	11.77	11.83	11.94	12.02	11.73	11.35	10.84	10.41	10.31	10.27	10.18	10.02	9.93	9.84
12	7.12	10.27	11.87	12.27	12.34	12.34	12.29	11.84	11.44	10.90	10.46	10.21	10.12	10.08	10.03	9.96	9.85

1981

mo	0 mo	1 mo	2 mo	3 mo	4 mo	5 mo	6 mo	9 mo	1 yr	2 yr	3 yr	4 yr	5 yr	10 yr	15 yr	20 yr	25 yr
1	13.97	14.72	15.05	15.02	14.86	14.69	14.55	14.12	13.69	12.87	12.57	12.48	12.43	12.29	12.26	12.10	11.86
2	13.60	14.20	14.56	14.69	14.68	14.62	14.56	14.32	14.02	13.56	13.50	13.42	13.34	13.06	12.97	12.75	12.49
3	13.10	13.03	12.94	12.82	12.72	12.65	12.65	12.74	12.86	12.81	12.91	12.98	12.99	12.77	12.74	12.56	12.24
4	12.57	14.11	14.98	15.20	15.10	15.00	14.96	14.87	14.69	14.33	13.89	14.06	13.98	13.67	13.59	13.35	13.04
5	16.27	16.21	16.01	15.68	15.32	15.08	14.97	14.87	14.43	14.20	13.97	13.65	13.45	13.09	13.02	12.83	12.55
6	14.03	14.41	14.94	14.65	14.64	14.64	14.66	14.57	14.57	14.21	13.97	13.92	13.81	13.46	13.34	13.15	12.82
7	14.50	14.98	15.84	15.40	15.52	15.66	15.79	15.87	15.75	15.36	15.10	14.98	14.57	14.19	14.04	13.77	13.36
8	15.39	15.64	16.11	16.00	16.16	16.32	16.50	16.62	16.35	16.17	15.68	15.67	15.56	14.95	14.79	14.64	14.29
9	12.63	13.68	14.27	14.75	15.03	15.33	15.63	15.63	15.90	16.09	15.85	15.86	15.75	15.30	15.29	15.10	14.60
10	12.75	12.97	13.09	13.12	13.21	13.41	13.68	14.10	14.08	14.14	14.32	14.31	14.32	14.24	14.23	14.07	13.72
11	10.17	10.24	10.37	10.57	10.77	10.94	11.05	11.30	11.55	12.19	12.47	12.53	12.65	12.87	12.79	12.72	12.48
12	8.26	9.71	10.79	11.50	11.96	12.28	12.53	13.02	13.29	13.48	13.55	13.67	13.71	13.67	13.68	13.56	13.19

1982

mo	0 mo	1 mo	2 mo	3 mo	4 mo	5 mo	6 mo	9 mo	1 yr	2 yr	3 yr	4 yr	5 yr	10 yr	15 yr	20 yr	25 yr
1	11.73	12.14	12.51	12.84	13.17	13.28	13.40	13.63	13.79	13.83	13.90	13.92	13.90	13.82	13.85	13.67	13.34
2	11.85	11.98	12.27	12.71	13.10	13.46	13.54	13.73	13.73	13.87	13.86	13.80	13.73	13.61	13.74	13.62	13.35
3	14.57	13.96	13.67	13.66	13.77	13.84	13.86	13.88	13.94	14.10	14.06	13.99	13.96	13.75	13.66	13.55	13.21
4	12.31	12.32	12.46	12.71	12.94	13.08	13.15	13.28	13.44	13.62	13.60	13.50	13.48	13.38	13.23	13.12	12.93

Table 13.A.3 (cont.)

Year	mo	0 mo	1 mo	2 mo	3 mo	4 mo	5 mo	6 mo	9 mo	1 yr	2 yr	3 yr	4 yr	5 yr	10 yr	15 yr	20 yr	25 yr
1982	5	11.56	11.62	11.72	11.85	12.00	12.13	12.24	12.53	12.84	13.20	13.34	13.41	13.45	13.34	13.28	13.19	12.95
	6	10.65	11.74	12.56	13.11	13.45	13.67	13.80	14.01	14.19	14.30	14.40	14.35	14.28	14.00	13.87	13.72	13.36
	7	8.49	9.15	9.82	10.49	11.07	11.48	11.75	12.23	12.61	12.90	13.25	13.28	13.30	13.29	13.27	13.21	12.94
	8	7.54	7.51	7.78	8.33	8.96	9.46	9.82	10.53	11.12	11.84	12.18	12.27	12.39	12.44	12.30	12.31	12.16
	9	6.88	6.94	7.24	7.77	8.39	8.88	9.21	9.80	10.34	11.16	11.50	11.55	11.60	11.70	11.62	11.53	11.41
	10	7.80	7.72	7.83	8.11	8.41	8.62	8.73	8.96	9.44	9.99	10.47	10.56	10.85	10.85	10.91	10.90	10.64
	11	7.67	7.87	8.11	8.39	8.64	8.81	8.87	8.95	9.31	9.82	10.28	10.46	10.64	10.93	10.91	11.05	10.82
	12	8.05	8.07	8.11	8.17	8.25	8.31	8.33	8.45	8.78	9.42	9.87	10.11	10.25	10.51	10.58	10.66	10.49
1983	1	8.01	8.07	8.15	8.26	8.38	8.46	8.51	8.67	8.95	9.57	10.04	10.26	10.47	10.93	11.03	11.23	11.10
	2	7.90	7.91	7.96	8.06	8.17	8.23	8.24	8.28	8.60	9.18	9.65	9.74	9.81	10.28	10.71	10.79	10.45
	3	8.36	8.56	8.72	8.86	8.95	9.00	9.02	9.06	9.24	9.71	9.98	10.13	10.25	10.56	10.68	10.79	10.60
	4	8.01	8.10	8.19	8.28	8.35	8.39	8.41	8.49	8.71	9.21	9.59	9.76	9.91	10.24	10.38	10.49	10.29
	5	8.38	8.56	8.71	8.83	8.93	9.00	9.05	9.16	9.31	9.87	10.14	10.31	10.45	10.76	10.93	11.04	10.90
	6	8.25	8.57	8.81	8.98	9.09	9.17	9.24	9.38	9.57	10.11	10.36	10.52	10.63	10.90	11.05	11.08	10.91
	7	8.63	8.95	9.22	9.43	9.60	9.72	9.80	10.03	10.33	10.95	11.12	11.29	11.45	11.68	11.73	11.73	11.67
	8	8.74	9.01	9.25	9.46	9.65	9.80	9.91	10.12	10.35	10.97	11.29	11.48	11.61	11.73	11.78	11.88	11.71
	9	8.77	8.78	8.83	8.92	9.04	9.15	9.24	9.47	9.69	10.32	10.60	10.85	11.03	11.27	11.32	11.38	11.20
	10	8.46	8.49	8.58	8.72	8.87	9.01	9.12	9.37	9.61	10.34	10.76	11.01	11.18	11.50	11.59	11.63	11.51
	11	8.17	8.58	8.87	9.07	9.19	9.28	9.37	9.57	9.70	10.40	10.70	10.99	11.15	11.36	11.42	11.46	11.33
	12	8.18	8.63	8.97	9.19	9.32	9.42	9.50	9.70	9.88	10.58	10.87	11.16	11.31	11.54	11.59	11.66	11.54
1984	1	8.87	8.94	9.02	9.10	9.18	9.25	9.32	9.48	9.62	10.35	10.63	10.94	11.09	11.39	11.44	11.50	11.44
	2	8.45	8.86	9.17	9.37	9.50	9.60	9.68	9.84	9.98	10.73	10.98	11.32	11.48	11.72	11.77	11.84	11.80
	3	9.22	9.50	9.75	9.96	10.12	10.21	10.26	10.38	10.60	11.25	11.52	11.80	11.94	12.18	12.14	12.18	12.15
	4	9.25	9.49	9.73	9.96	10.15	10.26	10.33	10.52	10.79	11.51	11.82	12.06	12.21	12.46	12.44	12.49	12.45
	5	9.65	9.56	9.83	10.18	10.46	10.72	10.99	11.57	11.89	12.63	13.18	13.22	13.32	13.52	13.44	13.39	13.38
	6	9.83	9.39	9.69	10.04	10.45	10.78	10.96	11.41	11.95	12.78	13.00	13.20	13.29	13.41	13.31	13.29	13.31
	7	9.67	10.03	10.32	10.56	10.76	10.91	11.02	11.39	11.61	12.24	12.30	12.36	12.43	12.58	12.39	12.32	12.34
	8	10.78	10.74	10.76	10.82	10.92	11.02	11.12	11.41	11.65	12.17	12.25	12.39	12.46	12.58	12.45	12.32	12.34
	9	10.52	10.44	10.44	10.50	10.56	10.63	10.76	10.96	11.15	11.73	11.91	12.07	12.14	12.13	12.06	12.01	11.97
	10	8.07	8.00	8.96	9.24	9.45	9.57	9.64	9.94	10.13	10.85	11.08	11.21	11.31	11.47	11.42	11.42	11.32
	11	7.47	8.00	8.38	8.62	8.76	8.88	8.98	9.28	9.51	10.26	10.62	10.87	11.10	11.32	11.37	11.43	11.37
	12	6.30	7.23	7.84	8.12	8.19	8.25	8.36	8.80	9.11	9.88	10.36	10.65	10.95	11.30	11.38	11.41	11.31
1985	1	7.29	7.72	8.03	8.19	8.27	8.34	8.43	8.72	8.97	9.72	10.15	10.43	10.65	10.96	11.10	11.07	11.00
	2	6.77	7.67	8.32	8.70	8.91	9.04	9.13	9.35	9.63	10.41	10.86	11.13	11.36	11.70	11.82	11.81	11.80

Year	Mo	0 MO	1 MO	2 MO	3 MO	4 MO	5 MO	6 MO	9 MO	1 YR	2 YR	3 YR	4 YR	5 YR	10YR	15YR	20YR	25YR
	3	7.67	8.04	8.32	8.51	8.65	8.77	8.86	9.13	9.40	10.25	10.61	10.92	11.14	11.43	11.54	11.60	11.49
	4	7.24	7.52	7.76	7.98	8.16	8.29	8.38	8.61	8.93	9.74	10.20	10.49	10.76	11.20	11.35	11.42	11.37
	5	6.69	7.00	7.20	7.32	7.38	7.43	7.48	7.67	8.00	8.80	9.25	9.50	9.75	10.17	10.49	10.52	10.48
	6	6.50	6.72	6.90	7.03	7.13	7.20	7.25	7.44	7.74	8.60	9.09	9.45	9.71	10.11	10.34	10.49	10.35
	7	6.82	7.06	7.25	7.40	7.51	7.60	7.66	7.83	8.08	8.93	9.44	9.80	10.04	10.46	10.69	10.78	10.66
	8	7.35	7.24	7.22	7.27	7.36	7.46	7.54	7.75	7.92	8.76	9.25	9.49	9.68	10.15	10.49	10.51	10.30
	9	7.02	7.11	7.19	7.25	7.31	7.37	7.44	7.69	8.00	8.70	9.19	9.45	9.72	10.23	10.59	10.62	10.47
	10	6.95	7.16	7.30	7.35	7.39	7.44	7.51	7.67	7.81	8.54	8.93	9.14	9.41	9.89	10.27	10.23	9.97
	11	5.66	6.59	7.16	7.38	7.40	7.41	7.46	7.64	7.74	8.29	8.60	8.89	9.12	9.45	9.75	9.87	9.76
	12	5.19	6.24	6.89	7.16	7.23	7.25	7.29	7.41	7.49	7.86	8.17	8.33	8.48	8.87	9.22	9.36	9.25
1986	1	6.38	6.80	7.06	7.16	7.19	7.21	7.27	7.40	7.48	7.89	8.15	8.39	8.57	9.07	9.38	9.35	9.15
	2	6.51	6.89	7.11	7.20	7.20	7.20	7.22	7.29	7.33	7.63	7.74	7.87	7.97	8.07	8.29	8.34	8.26
	3	6.73	6.58	6.49	6.46	6.47	6.47	6.47	6.56	6.72	6.91	7.04	7.21	7.28	7.38	7.51	7.65	7.68
	4	5.82	5.98	6.10	6.18	6.23	6.27	6.30	6.39	6.49	6.89	7.05	7.19	7.27	7.41	7.58	7.78	7.81
	5	6.11	6.23	6.34	6.43	6.50	6.55	6.59	6.71	6.86	7.37	7.73	7.94	7.98	8.16	8.36	8.69	8.70
	6	5.96	6.01	6.06	6.11	6.15	6.17	6.17	6.23	6.40	6.84	7.11	7.25	7.33	7.44	7.70	8.07	8.12
	7	5.08	5.50	5.76	5.88	5.92	5.93	5.94	6.03	6.17	6.60	6.86	7.05	7.16	7.51	7.88	8.14	8.07
	8	4.37	4.86	5.15	5.24	5.23	5.45	5.26	5.39	5.48	5.97	6.22	6.46	6.59	7.17	7.48	7.67	7.63
	9	5.14	5.20	5.26	5.32	5.38	5.36	5.53	5.69	5.81	6.42	6.76	7.03	7.19	7.74	8.15	8.40	8.31
	10	4.65	5.03	5.24	5.30	5.32	5.32	5.41	5.57	5.69	6.18	6.47	6.70	6.86	7.44	7.84	7.94	7.80
	11	5.07	5.24	5.37	5.45	5.51	5.54	5.56	5.61	5.70	6.12	6.37	6.55	6.68	7.16	7.62	7.91	7.84
	12	4.08	5.00	5.57	5.80	5.81	5.78	5.76	5.82	5.94	6.35	6.66	6.68	6.77	7.22	7.67	7.98	7.94
1987	1	5.23	5.51	5.66	5.70	5.70	5.71	5.74	5.84	5.88	6.24	6.44	6.60	6.73	7.20	7.60	7.82	7.77
	2	5.44	5.49	5.53	5.55	5.58	5.61	5.64	5.77	5.88	6.27	6.45	6.61	6.71	7.14	7.51	7.73	7.69

References

Amsler, C. (1984), 'A "pure" long-term interest rate and the demand for money', *Journal of Economics and Business*, 36: 359–370.

Ando, A. and A. Kennickell (1983) 'A reappraisal of the Phillips curve and the term structure of interest rates', University of Pennsylvania.

Ando, A. and F. Modigliani (1975) 'Some reflections on describing structures in financial sectors', in: G. Fromm and L. Klein, eds., *The Brookings model: Perspectives and recent developments*. Amsterdam: North-Holland.

Backus, D., W.C. Brainard, G. Smith and J. Tobin (1980) 'A model of U.S. financial and nonfinancial economic behavior', *Journal of Money, Credit and Banking*, 12: 259–293.

Begg, D.K.H. (1984) 'Rational expectations and bond pricing: Modelling the term structure with and without certainty equivalence', *Economic Journal*, 94: 45–58.

Benninga, S. and A. Protopapadakis (1983) 'Real and nominal interest rates under uncertainty: The Fisher theorem and the term structure', *Journal of Political Economy* 91: 856–867.

Bierwag, G.O. and M.A. Grove (1967) 'A model of the term structure of interest rates', *Review of Economics and Statistics*, 49: 50–62.

Bohm-Bawerk, E.V. (1891) *The positive theory of capital*. G.E. Stechert & Co.

Board of Governors of the Federal Reserve System (1985) *Flow of funds accounts financial assets and liabilities year-end, 1961–84*. Washington.

Bodie, Z., A. Kane and R. McDonald (1984) 'Why haven't nominal rates declined?', *Financial Analysts Journal*, 40: 16–27.

Brainard, W.C. and J. Tobin (1968) 'Pitfalls in financial model building', *American Economic Review Papers and Proceedings*, 58: 99–122.

Brealey, R. and S. Schaefer (1977) 'Term structure with uncertain inflation', *Journal of Finance*, 32: 277–289.

Brennan, M.J. and E.S. Schwartz (1980) 'Conditional predictions of bond prices and returns', *Journal of Finance*, 35: 405–417.

Brown, S. and P. Dybvig (1986) 'The empirical implications of the Cox, Ingersoll, Ross theory of the term structure of interest rates', *Journal of Finance*, 41: 616–630.

Buse, A. (1967) 'Interest rates, the Meiselman model and random numbers', *Journal of Political Economy*, 75: 49–62.

Campbell, J.Y. (1984) 'Asset duration and time-varying risk premia', unpublished Ph.D. dissertation, Yale University.

Campbell, J.Y. (1986a) 'Bond and stock returns in a simple exchange model', *Quarterly Journal of Economics*, 101: 786–803.

Campbell, J.Y. (1986b) 'A defense of traditional hypotheses about the term structure of interest rates', *Journal of Finance*, 41: 183–193.

Campbell, J.Y. (1987) 'Stock returns and the term structure', *Journal of Financial Economics*, 18: 373–399.

Campbell, J.Y. and R.J. Shiller (1984) 'A simple account of the behavior of long-term interest rates', *American Economic Review Papers and Proceedings*, 74: 44–48.

Campbell, J.Y. and R.J. Shiller (1987) 'Cointegration and tests of present value models', *Journal of Political Economy*, 95: 1062–1088.

Campbell, J.Y. and R.J. Shiller (1988) 'The dividend price ratio and expectations of future dividends and discount factors', *Review of Financial Studies*, 1: 195–228.

Cargill, T.F. and R.A. Meyer (1972) 'A spectral approach to estimating the distributed lag relationship between long-term and short-term interest rates', *International Economic Review*, 13: 223–238.

Chambers, D.R., W.T. Carlton and D.W. Waldman (1984) 'A new approach to the estimation of the term structure of interest rates', *Journal of Financial and Quantitative Analysis*, 19: 233–252.

Chen, E.T. (1986) 'Estimation of the term structure of interest rates via cubic exponential spline functions', unpublished doctoral dissertation draft, The Ohio State University.

Clark, J.B. (1895) 'The gold standard of currency in light of recent theory', *Political Science Quarterly*, 10: 389–403.

Clark, T.A. (1986) 'Interest rate seasonals and the Federal Reserve', *Journal of Political Economy*, 94: 76–125.

Conard, J.W. (1959) *An introduction to the theory of interest*. Berkeley and Los Angeles: University of California Press.

Cox, J.C., J.E. Ingersoll, Jr. and S.A. Ross (1981) 'A reexamination of traditional hypotheses about the term structure of interest rates', *Journal of Finance*, 36: 769–799.

Cox, J.C., J.E. Ingersoll, Jr. and S.A. Ross (1985a) 'An intertemporal general equilibrium model of asset prices', *Econometrica*, 53: 363–384.

Cox, J.C., J.E. Ingersoll, Jr. and S.A. Ross (1985b) 'A theory of the term structure of interest rates', *Econometrica*, 53: 385–408.

Culbertson, J.M. (1957) 'The term structure of interest rates', *Quarterly Journal of Economics*, 71: 485–517.

De Leeuw, F. (1965) 'A Model of Financial Behavior', in: J. Duesenberry et al., eds., *The Brookings quarterly economic model of the United States*. Chicago: Rand McNally, pp. 465–530.

Diller, S. (1969) 'Expectations and the term structure of interest rates', in: J. Mincer, ed., *Economic forecasts and expectations*. New York: National Bureau of Economic Research.

Dobson, S.W. (1978) 'Estimating term structure equations with individual bond data', *Journal of Finance*, 33: 75–92.

Dobson, S.W., R.C. Sutch and D.E. Vanderford (1976) 'An evaluation of alternative empirical models of the term structure of interest rates', *Journal of Finance*, 31: 1035–1065.

Dothan, L.U. (1978) 'On the term structure of interest rates', *Journal of Financial Economics*, 6: 59–69.

Durand, D. (1942) *Basic yields of corporate bonds, 1900–1942*, Technical Paper No. 3, NBER.

Dybvig, P.H., J.E. Ingersoll Jr. and S.A. Ross (1986) 'Long forward rates can never fall', Unpublished paper, Yale University.

Dunn, K.B. and K.J. Singleton (1984) 'Modelling the term structure of interest rates under nonseparable utility and durability of goods', NBER Working Paper 1415.

Echols, M.E. and J.W. Elliott (1976) 'A quantitative yield curve model for estimating the term structure of interest rates', *Journal of Financial and Quantitative Analysis*, 11: 87–114.

Engle, R.F., D.M. Lilien and R.P. Robins (1987) 'Estimating time varying risk premia in the term structure: The ARCH-M model', *Econometrica*, 55: 391–407.

Fama, E.F. (1976) 'Inflation uncertainty and expected return on Treasury bills', *Journal of Political Economy*, 84: 427–448.

Fama, E.F. (1984a) 'The information in the term structure', *Journal of Financial Economics*, 13: 509–528.

Fama, E.F. (1984b) 'Term premiums in bond returns', *Journal of Financial Economics*, 13: 529–546.

Fama, E.F. (1986) 'Term premiums and default premiums in money markets', *Journal of Financial Economics*, 17: 175–196.

Fama, E.F. and R.R. Bliss (1987) 'The information in long-maturity forward rates', *American Economic Review*, 77: 680–692.

Financial Publishing Company (1970) *Expanded bond values tables*. London: Routledge & Kegan Paul, Ltd.

Fisher, I. (1896) 'Appreciation and interest', Publications of the American Economic Association, pp. 23–29 and 88–92.

Fisher, I. (1907) *The rate of interest, its nature, determination and relation to economic phenomena*. New York: Macmillan.

Fisher, I. (1930) *Theory of interest*. New York: Macmillan.

Fisher, L. (1966) 'An algorithm for finding exact rates of return', *Journal of Business*, 39: 111–118.

Flavin, M. (1983) 'Excess volatility in the financial markets: A reassessment of the empirical evidence', *Journal of Political Economy*, 91: 929–956.

Flavin, M. (1984a) 'Excess sensitivity of consumption to current income: Liquidity constraints or myopia?', NBER Working Paper 1341.

Flavin, M. (1984b) 'Time series evidence on the expectations hypothesis of the term structure', *Carnegie-Rochester Conference Series on Public Policy*, 20: 211–238.

Friedman, B.M. (1977a) 'Financial flow variables and the short-run determination of long-run interest rates', *Journal of Political Economy*, 85: 661–689.

Friedman, B.M. (1977b) 'The inefficiency of short-run monetary targets for monetary policy', *Brookings Papers on Economic Activity*, 2: 293–335.

Friedman, B.M. (1979) 'Interest rate expectations versus forward rates: Evidence from an expectations survey', *Journal of Finance*, 34: 965–973.

Friedman, B.M. (1980a) 'The determination of long-term interest rates: Implications for fiscal and monetary policies', *Journal of Money, Credit and Banking*, 12(Part 2): 331–352.

Friedman, B.M. (1980b) 'The effect of shifting wealth ownership on the term structure of interest rates: The case of pensions', *Quarterly Journal of Economics*, 94: 567–590.

Friedman, B.M. (1980c) 'Survey evidence on the rationality of interest rate expectations', *Journal of Monetary Economics*, 6: 453–465.

Friedman, B.M. (1981) 'Debt management policy, interest rates and economic activity', NBER Working Paper.

Friedman, B.M. and V.V. Roley (1979) 'Investors portfolio behavior under alternative models of long-term interest rate expectations: Unitary, rational or autoregressive', *Econometrica*, 47: 1475–1497.

Froot, K.A. (1987) 'New hope for the expectations hypothesis of the term structure of interest rates', Sloan School of Management.

Grossman, S.J., A. Melino and R.J. Shiller (1987) 'Estimating the continuous time consumption based asset pricing model', *Journal of Business and Economic Statistics*, 5: 315–327.

Hall, R.E. (1978) 'Stochastic implications of the life cycle-permanent income hypothesis', *Journal of Political Economy*, 6: 971–988.

Hamburger, M.J. and E.N. Platt (1975) 'The expectations hypothesis and the efficiency of the Treasury bill market', *Review of Economics and Statistics*, 57: 190–199.

Hansen, L.P. and T.J. Sargent (1981) 'Exact linear rational expectations models: Specification and estimation', Staff Report, Federal Reserve Bank of Minneapolis.

Hansen, L.P. and K.J. Singleton (1983) 'Stochastic consumption, risk aversion, and the temporal behavior of asset returns', *Journal of Political Economy*, 91: 249–265.

Hendershott, P.H. (1971) 'A flow of funds model estimated for the non-bank finance sector', *Journal of Money, Credit and Banking*, 3: 815–832.

Hickman, W.B. (1942) 'The term structure of interest rates: An exploratory analysis', NBER. Results shown in Kessel (1965, Appendix A, pp. 103–105).

Hicks, J.R. (1946) *Value and capital*, 2nd edn. Oxford: Oxford University Press.

Homer, S. (1963) *A history of interest rates*. New Brunswick: Rutgers University Press.

Hopewell, M. and G. Kaufman (1973) 'Bond price volatility and term to maturity: A generalized respecification', *American Economic Review*, 63: 749–753.

Huizinga, J. and F.S. Mishkin (1984) 'The measurement of ex-ante real interest rates on assets with different risk characteristics', unpublished paper, Graduate School of Business, University of Chicago.

Ingersoll, J.E., Jr., J. Skelton and R.L. Weil (1978) 'Duration forty years later', *Journal of Financial and Quantitative Analysis*, 13: 627–650.

Jarrow, R.A. (1981) 'Liquidity premiums and the expectations hypothesis', *Journal of Banking and Finance*, 5: 539–546.

Jones, D.S. and V.V. Roley (1983) 'Rational expectations and the expectations model of the term structure: A test using weekly data', *Journal of Monetary Economics*, 12: 453–465.

Jordan, J.V. (1984) 'Tax effects in term structure estimation', *Journal of Finance*, 39: 393–406.

Kaldor, N. (1939) 'Speculation and instability', *Review of Economic Studies*, 7: 1–27.

Kane, E.J. (1970) 'The term structure of interest rates: An attempt to reconcile teaching with practice', *The Journal of Finance*, 25: 361–374.

Kane, E.J. (1980) 'Market incompleteness and divergences between forward and future interest rates', *Journal of Finance*, 35: 221–234.

Kane, E.J. (1983) 'Nested tests of alternative term structure theories', *Review of Economics and Statistics*, 65: 115–123.

Kane, E.J. and B.G. Malkiel (1967) 'The term structure of interest rates: An analysis of a survey of interest rate expectations', *Review of Economics and Statistics*, 49: 343–355.

Keim, D.B. and R.F. Stambaugh (1986) 'Predicting returns in the stock and bond markets', *Journal of Financial Economics*, 17: 357–390.

Kessel, R.A. (1965) *The cyclical behavior of the term structure of interest rates*. New York: NBER.

Keynes, J.M. (1930) *Treatise on money*. New York: Macmillan.

Keynes, J.M. (1936) *The general theory of employment, interest and money*. London: Macmillan & Co. Ltd.

Kim, S.-J. (1986) 'Explaining the risk premium: Nominal interest rates, inflation and consumption', Yale University.

Langetieg, T.C. (1980) 'A multivariate model of the term structure', *Journal of Finance*, 35: 71–97.

LeRoy, S.F. (1982a) 'Expectations models of asset prices: A survey of theory', *Journal of Finance*, 37: 185–217.

LeRoy, S.F. (1982b) 'Risk aversion and the term structure of real interest rates', *Economics Letters*, 10: 355–361.

LeRoy, S.F. (1983) 'Risk aversion and the term structure of real interest rates: A correction', *Economics Letters*, 12: 339–340.

LeRoy, S.F. (1984) 'Nominal prices and interest rates in general equilibrium: Endowment shocks', *Journal of Business*, 57: 197–213.

LeRoy, S.F. and R.D. Porter (1981) 'The present value relation: Tests based on implied variance bounds', *Econometrica*, 49: 555–574.

Lindahl, E. (1939) *Studies in the theory of money and capital*. New York: Rinehart and Company.

Long, J.B. (1974) 'Stock prices, inflation and the term structure of interest rates', *Journal of Financial Economics*, 1: 131–170.

Lutz, F.A. (1940) 'The structure of interest rates', *Quarterly Journal of Economics*, 55: 36–63.

Macaulay, F.R. (1938) *Some theoretical problems suggested by the movements of interest rates, bond yields, and stock prices in the Unites States since 1856*. New York: NBER.

Malkiel, B.G. (1966) *The term structure of interest rates: Expectations and behavior patterns*. Princeton: Princeton University Press.

Mankiw, N.G. (1986) 'The term structure of interest rates revisited', *Brookings Papers on Economic Activity*, 1986, 1: 61–96.

Mankiw, N.G. and J.A. Miron (1986) 'The changing behavior of the term structure of interest rates', *Quarterly Journal of Economics*, 101: 211–228.

Mankiw, N.G and L.H. Summers (1984) 'Do long-term interest rates overreact to short-term interest rates?', *Brookings Papers on Economic Activity*, 00: 223–242.

Mankiw, N.G., J.A. Miron and D.N. Weil (1987) 'The adjustment of expectations of a change in regime: A study of the founding of the Federal Reserve, *American Economic Review*, 77: 358–374.

Marsh, T.A. (1980) 'Equilibrium term structure models: Test methodology', *Journal of Finance*, 35: 421–435.

Marsh, T.A. and E.R. Rosenfeld (1983) 'Stochastic processes for interest rates and equilibrium bond prices', *Journal of Finance*, 38: 635–646.

McCallum, J.S. (1975) 'The expected holding period return, uncertainty and the term structure of interest rates', *Journal of Finance*, 30: 307–323.

McCulloch, J.H. (1971) 'Measuring the term structure of interest rates', *Journal of Business*, 44: 19–31.

McCulloch, J.H. (1975a) 'An estimate of the liquidity premium', *Journal of Political Economy*, 83: 95–119.

McCulloch, J.H. (1975b) 'The tax adjusted yield curve', *Journal of Finance*, 30: 811–830.

McCulloch, J.H. (1977) 'Cumulative unanticipated changes in interest rates', NBER Working Paper 222.

McCulloch, J.H. (1981) 'Interest rate risk and capital adequacy for traditional banks and financial intermediaries', in: S.J. Maisel, ed., *Risk and capital adequacy in commercial banks*. Chicago: University of Chicago Press and NBER, pp. 223–248.

McCulloch, J.H. (1984) 'Term structure modeling using constrained exponential splines', Ohio State University.

Meiselman, D. (1962) *The term structure of interest rates*. Englewood Cliffs: Prentice-Hall.

Melino, A. (1983) 'Estimation of a rational expectations model of the term structure', in: *Essays on estimation and inference in linear rational expectations models*, unpublished Ph.D. Dissertation, Harvard University.

Melino, A. (1986) 'The term structure of interest rates: Evidence and theory', NBER Working Paper 1828.

Michaelsen, J.B. (1965) 'The term structure of interest rates and holding period yields on government securities', *Journal of Finance*, 20: 444–463.

Miron, J.A. (1984) 'The economics of seasonal time series', Ph.D. dissertation, M.I.T.

Miron, J.A. (1986) 'Financial panics, the seasonality of the nominal interest rate, and the founding of the fed', *American Economic Review*, 76: 125–140.

Mishkin, F.S. (1978) 'Efficient markets theory: Implications for monetary policy', *Brookings Papers on Economic Activity*, 1978, 2: 707–752.

Mishkin, F.S. (1980) 'Is the preferred habitat model of the term structure inconsistent with financial market efficiency?', *Journal of Political Economy*, 88: 406–411.

Mishkin, F.S. (1982) 'Monetary policy and short-term interest rates: An efficient markets–rational expectations approach', *Journal of Monetary Economics*, 37: 63–72.

Modigliani, F. and R.J. Shiller (1973) 'Inflation, rational expectations and the term structure of interest rates', *Economica*, 40: 12–43.

Modigliani, F.R. and R. Sutch (1966) 'Innovations in interest rate policy', *American Economic Review*, 56: 178–197.

Modigliani, F. and R. Sutch (1967) 'Debt management and the term structure of interest rates: An analysis of recent experience', *Journal of Political Economy*, 75: 569–589.

Nelson, C.R. (1970a) 'A critique of some recent empirical research in the explanation of the term structure of interest rates', *Journal of Political Economy*, 78: 764–767.

Nelson, C.R. (1970b) 'Testing a model of the term structure of interest rates by simulation of market forecasts', *Journal of the American Statistical Association*, 65: 1163–1190.

Nelson, C.R. (1972a) 'Estimation of term premiums from average yield differentials in the term structure of interest rates', *Econometrica*, 40: 277–287.

Nelson, C.R. (1972b) *The term structure of interest rates*. New York: Basic Books.

Nelson, C.R. and A.F. Siegel (1985) 'Parsimonious modelling of yield curves for U.S. Treasury bills', NBER Working Paper 1594.

Okun, A.M. (1963) 'Monetary policy, debt management, and interest rates: A quantitative appraisal', in: Commission on Money and Credit, *Stabilization Policies*. Englewood Cliffs: Prentice-Hall, pp. 331–380.

Pesando, J.E. (1975) 'Determinants of term premiums in the market for United States Treasury bills', *Journal of Finance*, 30: 1317–1327.

Pesando, J.E. (1978) 'On the efficiency of the bond market: Some Canadian evidence', *Journal of Political Economy*, 86: 1057–1076.

Pesando, J.E. (1981) 'On forecasting interest rates: An efficient markets perspective', *Journal of Monetary Economics*, 8: 305–318.

Pesando, J.E. (1983) 'On expectations, term premiums and the volatility of long-term interest rates', *Journal of Monetary Economics*, 12: 467–474.

Phillips, L. and J. Pippenger (1976) "Preferred habitat vs. efficient market: A test of alternative hypotheses', *Federal Reserve Bank of St. Louis Review*, 58: 151–164.

Phillips, L. and J. Pippenger (1979) 'The term structure of interest rates in the MPS model: Reality or illusion?', *Journal of Money, Credit and Banking*, 11: 151–164.

Richard, S.F. (1978) 'An arbitrage model of the term structure of interest rates', *Journal of Financial Economics*, 6: 33–57.

Roley, V.V. (1977) 'A structural model of the U.S. government securities market', unpublished Ph.D. dissertation, Harvard University.

Roley, V.V. (1981) 'The determinants of the Treasury security yield curve', *Journal of Finance*, 36: 1103–1126.

Roley, V.V. (1982) 'The effect of federal debt management policy on corporate bond and equity yields', *Quarterly Journal of Economics*, 97: 645–668.

Roll, R. (1970) *The behavior of interest rates*. New York: Basic Books.

Roll, R. (1971) 'Investment diversification and bond maturity', *Journal of Finance*, 26: 51–66.
Salomon Brothers, Inc. (1983) *An analytical record of yields and yield spreads: From 1945*. New York.
Samuelson, P.A. (1945) 'The effect of interest rate increases on the banking system', *American Economic Review*, 35: 16–27.
Sargent, T.J. (1971) 'Expectations at the short end of the yield curve: An application of Macaulay's test', in: J.M. Guttentag, ed., *Essays on interest rates*, Vol. II. New York: NBER, pp. 391–412.
Sargent, T.J. (1979) 'A note on the estimation of the rational expectations model of the term structure', *Journal of Monetary Economics*, 5: 133–143.
Say, J.B. (1853) *A treatise on political economy*. Philadelphia: Lippincott Grambo & Co.
Schaefer, S.M. (1981) 'Measuring a tax-specific term structure of interest rates in the market for British Government securities', *Economic Journal*, 91: 415–438.
Scott, R.H. (1965) 'Liquidity and the term structure of interest rates', *Quarterly Journal of Economics*, 79: 135–145.
Shea, G.S. (1984) 'Pitfalls in smoothing interest rate term structure data: Equilibrium models and spline approximations', *Journal of Financial and Quantitative Analysis*, 19: 253–269.
Shea, G.S. (1985) 'Interest rate term structure equations with exponential splines: A note', *Journal of Finance*, 40: 319–325.
Shiller, R.J. (1972) 'Rational expectations and the structure of interest rates', unpublished Ph.D. dissertation, M.I.T.
Shiller, R.J. (1978) 'Rational expectations and the dynamic structure of macroeconomic models: A critical review', *Journal of Monetary Economics*, 4: 1–44.
Shiller, R.J. (1979) 'The volatility of long-term interest rates and expectations models of the term structure', *Journal of Political Economy*, 87: 1190–1219.
Shiller, R.J. (1980) 'Can the federal reserve control real interest rates?', in: S. Fischer, ed., *Rational expectations and economic policy*, Chicago: NBER and University of Chicago Press.
Shiller, R.J. (1981a) 'Alternative tests of rational expectations Models: The case of the term structure', *Journal of Econometrics*, 16: 71–87.
Shiller, R.J. (1981b) 'Do stock prices move too much to be justified by subsequent changes in dividends?', *American Economic Review*, 71: 421–436.
Shiller, R.J. (1986) 'Comments and discussion', *Brookings Papers on Economic Activity*, 1986, 1: 100–107.
Shiller, R.J. (1987) 'Conventional valuation and the term structure of interest rates', in: R. Dornbusch, S. Fischer and J. Bossons, eds., *Macroeconomics and finance: Essays in honour of Franco Modigliani*. Cambridge, Mass.: MIT Press.
Shiller, R.J., J.Y. Campbell and K.L. Schoenholtz (1983) 'Forward rates and future policy: Interpreting the term structure of interest rates', *Brookings Papers on Economic Activity*, 1983, 1: 173–217.
Sidgwick, H. (1887) *The principles of political economy*. London: Macmillan.
Singleton, K.J. (1980a) 'A latent time series model of the cyclical behavior of interest rates', *International Economic Review*, 21: 559–575.
Singleton, K.J. (1980b) 'Expectations models of the term structure and implied variance bounds', *Journal of Political Economy*, 88: 1159–1176.
Singleton, K.J. (1980c) 'Maturity-specific disturbances and the term structure of interest rates', *Journal of Money, Credit and Banking*, 12 (Part I): 603–614.
Skinner, E.B. (1913) *The mathematical theory of investment*. Boston: Ginn and Co.
Startz, R. (1982) 'Do forecast errors or term premia really make the difference between long and short rates?', *Journal of Financial Economics*, 10: 323–329.
Stiglitz, J. (1970) 'A consumption-oriented theory of the demand for financial assets and the term structure of interest rates', *Review of Economic Studies*, 37: 321–351.
Stigum, M. (1978) *The money market: Myth, reality and practice*. Homewood: Dow Jones–Irwin.
Stigum, M. (1981) *Money market calculations: Yields, break-evens and arbitrage*. Homewood: Dow Jones–Irwin.
Summers, L.H. (1982) 'Do we really know that markets are efficient?', NBER Working Paper.

Sutch, R. (1968) 'Expectations, risk and the term structure of interest rates,' unpublished Ph.D. dissertation, M.I.T.

Telser, L.G. (1967) 'A critique of some recent empirical research on the explanation of the term structure of interest rates', *Journal of Political Economy*, 75: 546–561.

Vasicek, O.A. (1978) 'An equilibrium characterization of the term structure', *Journal of Financial Economics*, 6: 33–57.

Vasicek, O.A. and H. G. Fong (1982) 'Term structure modelling using exponential splines', *Journal of Finance*, 37: 339–348.

Volterra, V. (1959) *Theory of functionals and of integral and integrodifferential equations*. New York: Dover.

Walker, C.E. (1954) 'Federal reserve policy and the structure of interest rates in government securities', *Quarterly Journal of Economics*, 68: 19–42.

Wallace, N. (1967) 'Comment', *Journal of Political Economy*, 75: 590–592.

Walsh, C.E. (1985) 'A rational expectations model of term premia with some implications for empirical asset demand functions', *Journal of Finance*, 40: 63–83.

Williams, J.B. (1938) *The theory of investment value*. Cambridge, Mass.: Harvard University Press.

Wood, J.H. (1963) 'Expectations, errors and the term structure of interest rates', *Journal of Political Economy*, 71: 160–171.

Woodward, S. (1983) 'The liquidity premium and the solidity premium', *American Economic Review*, 73: 348–361.

INDEX